CCH® Study MATE™

Your Personal Online Tax "Tutor" 24/7!

If you find taxes difficult, you're not alone! Now you have CCH® Study MATE™, a personal online "tutor." With Study MATE you can plug into online learning any time of day or night. Study MATE walks you through the most important concepts covered in your textbook using individual learning sessions designed to make learning as easy as possible.

CCH® Study MATE™
Mentor for Accounting and Tax Education

Home | Log In | Register

HOME >

Technical Support
866 798-5897 • support@learning.net

Welcome to Study MATE.
Study MATE provides a new and exciting way to expand your knowledge of taxes, auditing, and accounting. The courses provide examples, observations, and study questions to help you further develop your knowledge in these areas. Think of Study MATE as your own personal study partner.

Already enrolled?
Member Login
User Name:
Password:
Forget Password? Login

New Users:

If you have an *access code* (provided with your CCH textbook)...
1. Whether you are a professor or student, register for an account by clicking on the appropriate sign up box.
2. Click on a library title or course name to enroll in a library and use your access code as payment.
3. Complete the courses in the library.

» Students — Sign up here if you are a student
» Professors — Sign up here if you are a professor

If you want to *purchase* a topic or entire library...
1. Whether you are a professor, student, or practitioner, register for an account by clicking on the appropriate sign up box.
2. Click on a library title to view the courses available, and then click on a library title or course name to enroll and pay by credit card.
3. Complete the courses you purchased.

» Students — Sign up here if you are a student
» Professors — Sign up here if you are a professor
» Practitioners — Other members may sign up here.

Study MATE is easy to use, and since you've bought our book, you have free access to our Fundamental Tax Topics Library for a full year! Study MATE courses are designed with web learning in mind, so you can navigate your way through them independently. They are relatively short, but each course covers a substantial amount of material—including the top concepts covered in your textbook. These are student-centered courses with presentations that are different than those found in the text, so they give you another voice—another opportunity for concepts to sink in.

How Many Courses Do I Take?

Your instructor may want you to access all the courses in the fundamental series, you may be asked to take selective courses on certain topics, or your instructor may leave it up to you to use Study MATE as you choose.

So, How Do I Get In?

Getting started is easy.

1. Go to www.cchstudymate.com and follow the instructions for new users with an access code to sign up for a free account. Fill in the information on the registration page including a user ID and password of your choice.
2. Once you have registered, click on the Fundamental Tax Topics library title to view the list of courses. Click to enroll in the entire Fundamental Tax Topics library. At the payment screen, use your access code as payment. Now you are ready to start your first course.
3. Click on the course title to begin. Use your access code now and begin using Study MATE today!

ACCESS CODE:

CCHSM_CCH_1_9565

Technical Support: 866-798-5897 • support@learning.net

Over for course features ▶▶▶

Access CCH Study MATE at www.cchstudymate.com
For your records, print your User ID and Password below:

User ID: ______________________

Password: ______________________

CCH, a Wolters Kluwer business • 4025 West Peterson Ave. • Chicago, IL 60646-6085

CCH® StudyMATE™

Features of each course:

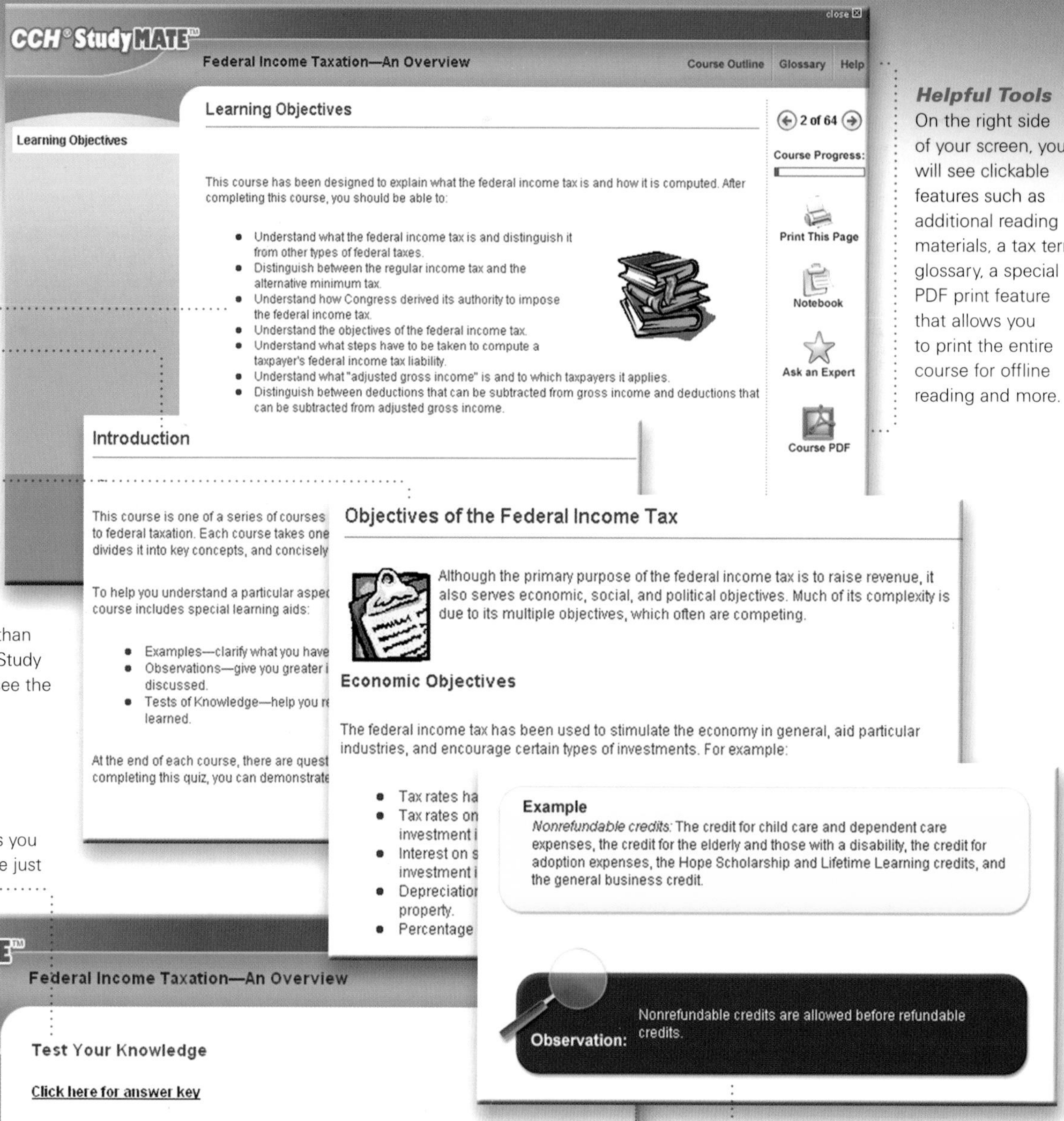

CCH® StudyMATE™

Federal Income Taxation—An Overview

Course Outline | Glossary | Help

Learning Objectives

Learning Objectives

2 of 64

Course Progress:

This course has been designed to explain what the federal income tax is and how it is computed. After completing this course, you should be able to:

- Understand what the federal income tax is and distinguish it from other types of federal taxes.
- Distinguish between the regular income tax and the alternative minimum tax.
- Understand how Congress derived its authority to impose the federal income tax.
- Understand the objectives of the federal income tax.
- Understand what steps have to be taken to compute a taxpayer's federal income tax liability.
- Understand what "adjusted gross income" is and to which taxpayers it applies.
- Distinguish between deductions that can be subtracted from gross income and deductions that can be subtracted from adjusted gross income.

Print This Page

Notebook

Ask an Expert

Course PDF

Learning Objectives
A list of what you will learn in the course.

Introduction
A brief introduction to the course.

Helpful Tools
On the right side of your screen, you will see clickable features such as additional reading materials, a tax term glossary, a special PDF print feature that allows you to print the entire course for offline reading and more.

Introduction

This course is one of a series of courses to federal taxation. Each course takes one divides it into key concepts, and concisely

To help you understand a particular aspec course includes special learning aids:

- Examples—clarify what you have
- Observations—give you greater i discussed.
- Tests of Knowledge—help you r learned.

At the end of each course, there are quest completing this quiz, you can demonstrate

Objectives of the Federal Income Tax

Although the primary purpose of the federal income tax is to raise revenue, it also serves economic, social, and political objectives. Much of its complexity is due to its multiple objectives, which often are competing.

Economic Objectives

The federal income tax has been used to stimulate the economy in general, aid particular industries, and encourage certain types of investments. For example:

- Tax rates ha
- Tax rates on investment i
- Interest on s investment i
- Depreciatior property.
- Percentage

Example
Nonrefundable credits: The credit for child care and dependent care expenses, the credit for the elderly and those with a disability, the credit for adoption expenses, the Hope Scholarship and Lifetime Learning credits, and the general business credit.

Observation: Nonrefundable credits are allowed before refundable credits.

Discussions and Illustrations of the Concepts
Each course is designed to cover only the most important concepts. Your teacher may expect you to understand more than the concepts covered in Study MATE, but here you will see the core concepts.

Paced Learning
After some concepts are presented, the "Test Your Knowledge" feature helps you think back on what you've just read so you retain it.

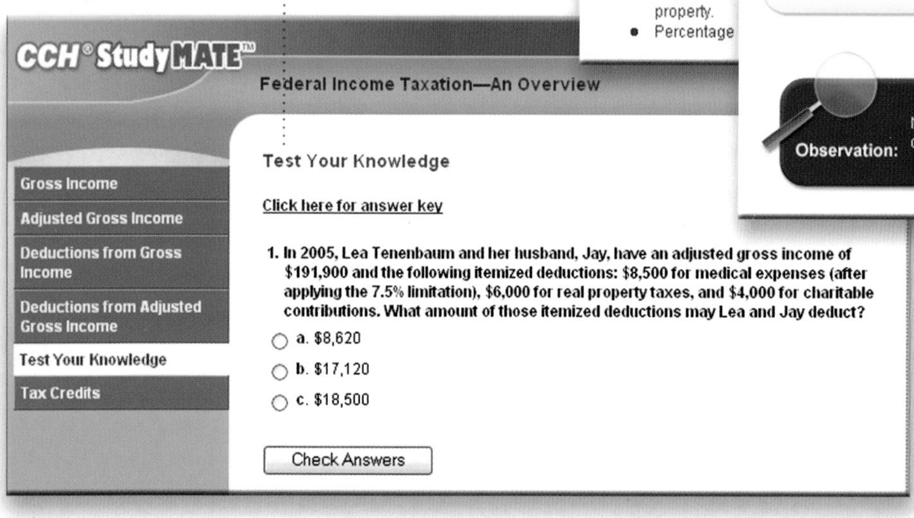

CCH® StudyMATE™

Federal Income Taxation—An Overview

Gross Income
Adjusted Gross Income
Deductions from Gross Income
Deductions from Adjusted Gross Income
Test Your Knowledge
Tax Credits

Test Your Knowledge

Click here for answer key

1. In 2005, Lea Tenenbaum and her husband, Jay, have an adjusted gross income of $191,900 and the following itemized deductions: $8,500 for medical expenses (after applying the 7.5% limitation), $6,000 for real property taxes, and $4,000 for charitable contributions. What amount of those itemized deductions may Lea and Jay deduct?

a. $8,620
b. $17,120
c. $18,500

Check Answers

Examples and Observations
Presented to illustrate ideas and principles using colors and graphics to make your experience more memorable.

Testing—One, Two, Three

At the end of each course, a 15-question quiz is presented. The quiz questions are not easily answered—they really test whether you understand the concepts! You can take the quiz up to three times if you like and after successfully completing the quiz, you can print a certificate for your records and e-mail the certificate to your instructor to show you've successfully completed the course.

Get started! ▸▸▸

a Wolters Kluwer business

ESSENTIALS OF FEDERAL INCOME TAXATION FOR INDIVIDUALS AND BUSINESS

2007 EDITION

LINDA M. JOHNSON
HERBERT C. SIEG

Editorial Staff
Editor: Lawrence M. Norris, M. S.

ISBN 13: 978-0-8080-1583-3
ISBN 10: 0-8080-1583-4

4025 W. Peterson Ave.
Chicago, IL 60646-6085
1 800 248 3248
www.CCHGroup.com

This book was previously published by Prentice-Hall, Inc.

Printed in the United States of America

List of acronyms used:

AAA—Accumulated Adjustments Account
ACRS—Accelerated Cost Recovery System
ACV—Amortized Carrying Value
ADS—Alternate Depreciation System
AE&P—Accumulated Earnings and Profits
AFR—Applicable Federal Rate
AGI—Adjusted Gross Income
AMT—Alternative Minimum Tax
AMTI—Alternative Minimum Tax Income
APR—Annual Percentage Rate
CD—Certificate of Deposit
CDE—Community Development Entity
CE&P—Current Earnings and Profits
CPA— Certified Public Accountant
CPI—Consumer Price Index
CTC—Child Tax Credit
DB—Declining Balance
DRD—Dividend Received Deduction
DRIP—Dividend Reinvestment Plan
E&P—Earnings and Profits
EIC—Earned Income Credit
EFT—Electronic Funds Transfer
EIN—Employer Identification Number
FEMA—Federal Emergency Management Agency
FICA—Federal Insurance Contributions Act
FMV—Fair Market Value
FUTA—Federal Unemployment Tax Act
HDHP—High-Deductible Health Plan
HI—Health Insurance
HMO—Health Maintenance Organization
HOH—Head of Household
HSA—Health Savings Account
IRA—Individual Retirement Arrangement
IRS—Internal Revenue Service
LLC—Limited Liability Company
LLP—Limited Liability Partnership
MACRS—Modified Accelerated Cost Recovery System
MFJ—Married Filing Jointly
MFS—Married Filing Separately
NOL—Net Operating Loss
OASDI—Old Age, Survivors, and Disability Insurance
OID—Original Issue Discount
PSC—Personal Service Corporation
SBA—Small Business Administration
SEP—Simplified Employee Pension
SIMPLE—Savings Incentive Match Plan for Employees
SL—Straight-line
SSN—Social Security Number
TI—Taxable Income
TIN—Taxpayer Identification Number

Contents

Tax Forms

Preface

WHY STUDY FEDERAL INCOME TAXATION?

Essentials of Federal Income Taxation for Individuals and Business, 2007 Edition, covers the taxation of individuals for the 2006 tax year. It provides complete coverage in an easy-to-read and easy-to-understand format for your first course in taxation. This practical text helps you understand tax laws and improve the reporting quality of your tax returns. The coverage does not assume that you have had an introductory accounting course. If you are interested in learning how to prepare tax returns, including your own, studying this text and mastering its content will help you solve actual tax problems and succeed in business. At press time, the 2007 Edition contains the latest information and tax forms available for the 2006 tax year. It also contains the latest information for the 2007 tax planning process.

FULL OF OUTSTANDING FEATURES

Many outstanding features make the new 2007 Edition the main reference for completing 2006 federal income tax returns. Before you start reading *Essentials of Federal Income Taxation for Individuals and Business, 2007 Edition,* you are encouraged to spend a little time looking over the next few pages. The 2007 Edition benefits from the helpful comments and suggestions contributed by instructors and students who have taught and learned federal income taxation from previous editions.

BUSINESS ENTITY OPTION

While this text focuses on the income taxation of individuals, it is also makes available an optional course of study that examines the taxation of income earned by corporations and partnerships, as well as sole proprietorships. This option is included in response to the growing number of instructors who believe that an introductory tax course should compare and contrast the tax challenges facing the different forms of business organizations.

Those who choose to place more attention on the taxation of business entities are encouraged to study the chapters in the following sequence: 1, 2, 14, 15, 3, 4, 5, 6, 7, 8, 9, 10, 11, 12, and 13. Chapters 1 and 2 cover the basic tax structure for individuals. Chapters 14 and 15 introduce the students to the taxation of income earned by corporations and partnerships. All subsequent chapters (3–13) include at least one special business entity problem. These problems require students to relate material covered in the chapter to the different forms of business.

The business entity problems are located near the end of each chapter's "Questions and Problems." Their solutions generally require information from Chapters 14 and 15. Conse-

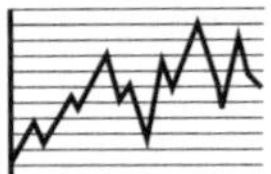

quently, students will be reviewing these chapters on a regular basis throughout the course. The business entity problems are indicated by the icon.

OTHER SPECIAL FEATURES

- Highlighted tax tips, observations, and facts designed to enrich the learning experience are included in every chapter. These highlights are indicated by the icon.

- Indicates homework problems suitable for completion using 1040 software.

- The temporary tax rules from the Katrina Emergency Tax Relief Act of 2005 and the Gulf Opportunity Zone Act of 2005 have been incorporated into the chapters and are highlighted by the icon.

- Information for filled-in tax forms is included.

Feature: Each filled-in tax form is supported by information given by the taxpayer.
Benefit: This concise presentation makes it easier for you to relate tax data to the form. The format presents required information supplied by the taxpayer and entered by the taxpayer or tax preparer. You can then follow along and see how this information is used to complete the form.

9-10 *CHAPTER 9 Rental Activities*

REPORTING RENTAL ACTIVITIES ON SCHEDULE E

Taxpayers use Schedule E (Form 1040), Supplemental Income and Loss, to report income and expenses from rental activities. In Part I (line 1), taxpayers describe the rental realty and provide its location. In Part I (line 2), taxpayers answer a question that determines whether the property qualifies as a residence. Taxpayers also report in Part I rental income (line 3) and expenses (lines 5 through 20) in computing their overall income or loss from the rental activity (line 22). For taxpayers who answer "Yes" to the question in Part I (line 2), total expenses (line 21) cannot exceed rental income (line 3). For taxpayers who answer "No" to this question, the vacation home rules do not apply and there is no limit on the total expenses. However, the expenses may be limited under either the *at-risk* or *passive loss* rules (discussed later in the chapter).

Information for Figure 9-1: Filled-In Schedule E

During 2006, Kurt F. and Heather M. Reding received rents of **$38,168** from an eight-unit apartment complex. The Redings paid $375,000 for the apartment building in 1996, which includes $100,000 for the land. They depreciate the building using MACRS (straight-line over 27.5 years). Expenses related to the building include **$250** advertising, **$2,500** cleaning and maintenance, **$1,227** insurance, **$300** legal fees, **$14,329** mortgage interest, **$3,262** supplies, **$4,290** real estate taxes, and **$1,800** utilities.

The Redings also own a condominium in Naples, Florida, that they used for 30 days in 2006. The Redings rented the condo for 90 days and received fair rentals totaling **$12,000.** None of the tenants were members of the Redings' family. The Redings paid $220,000 for the condo in 1995 and depreciate it using MACRS (straight-line over 27.5 years). The expenses related to the condo include $9,200 home mortgage interest, $3,400 real estate taxes, $1,000 utilities, $300 insurance, and $100 cleaning and maintenance.

Other Information

1A: Description: 8-unit apartment building, 505 West Street, Verona, WI
1B: Description: Condominium, 1500 Vanderbelt Beach Road, Naples, FL
2A: **No.** Personal use did not exceed the *greater of* (i) 14 days or (ii) 10% of the days rented at fair rental.
2B: **Yes.** The Redings's 30 days of personal use exceeds the *greater of* (i) 14 days or (ii) 9 days (10% of the 90 days rented at fair rental). Therefore, total rental expenses cannot exceed rental income.
7B: Cleaning and maintenance, **$75.00** (90 rental days/120 total days used × $100)
9B: Insurance, **$225.00** (90/120 × $300)
12B: Mortgage interest, **$6,900.00** (90/120 × $9,200)
16B: Taxes, **$2,550.00** (90/120 × $3,400)
17B: Utilities, **$750.00** (90/120 × $1,000)
20A: Depreciation expense, **$10,000.00** ($275,000/27.5)
20B: Depreciation expense, **$1,500.00** ($220,000/27.5 × 90/120 = $6,000; however, total rental expenses cannot exceed rental income of $12,000. Expenses other than depreciation total $10,500 [line 19B]; therefore depreciation is limited to $1,500).

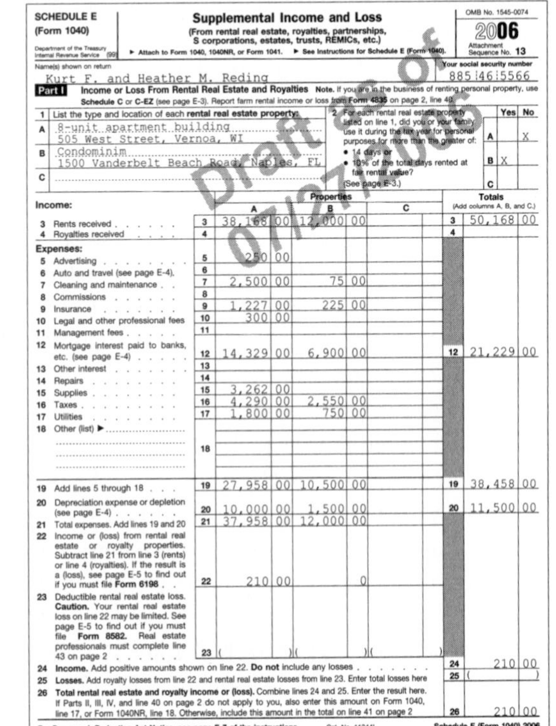

FIGURE 9-1 Filled-In Schedule E, Page 1

SCHEDULE E (Form 1040) — **Supplemental Income and Loss** (From rental real estate, royalties, partnerships, S corporations, estates, trusts, REMICs, etc.) — OMB No. 1545-0074 — 2006
Department of the Treasury Internal Revenue Service (99) ► Attach to Form 1040, 1040NR, or Form 1041. ► See Instructions for Schedule E (Form 1040). Attachment Sequence No. 13

Name(s) shown on return: Kurt F. and Heather M. Reding — Your social security number: 885 46 5566

Part I Income or Loss From Rental Real Estate and Royalties **Note.** If you are in the business of renting personal property, use **Schedule C** or **C-EZ** (see page E-3). Report farm rental income or loss from **Form 4835** on page 2, line 40.

1 List the type and location of each **rental real estate property:**
A 8-unit apartment building, 505 West Street, Vernoa, WI
B Condominim, 1500 Vanderbelt Beach Road, Naples, FL
C

2 For each rental real estate property listed on line 1, did you or your family use it during the tax year for personal purposes for more than the greater of:
• 14 days or
• 10% of the total days rented at fair rental value?
(See page E-3.)

	Yes	No
A		X
B	X	
C		

		Properties A	Properties B	Properties C	Totals (Add columns A, B, and C.)
Income:					
3 Rents received	3	38,168 00	12,000 00		3 50,168 00
4 Royalties received	4				4
Expenses:					
5 Advertising	5	250 00			
6 Auto and travel (see page E-4)	6				
7 Cleaning and maintenance	7	2,500 00	75 00		
8 Commissions	8				
9 Insurance	9	1,227 00	225 00		
10 Legal and other professional fees	10	300 00			
11 Management fees	11				
12 Mortgage interest paid to banks, etc. (see page E-4)	12	14,329 00	6,900 00		12 21,229 00
13 Other interest	13				
14 Repairs	14				
15 Supplies	15	3,262 00			
16 Taxes	16	4,290 00	2,550 00		
17 Utilities	17	1,800 00	750 00		
18 Other (list) ►	18				
19 Add lines 5 through 18	19	27,958 00	10,500 00		19 38,458 00
20 Depreciation expense or depletion (see page E-4)	20	10,000 00	1,500 00		20 11,500 00
21 Total expenses. Add lines 19 and 20	21	37,958 00	12,000 00		
22 Income or (loss) from rental real estate or royalty properties. Subtract line 21 from line 3 (rents) or line 4 (royalties). If the result is a (loss), see page E-5 to find out if you must file **Form 6198**	22	210 00	0		
23 Deductible rental real estate loss. **Caution.** Your rental real estate loss on line 22 may be limited. See page E-5 to find out if you must file **Form 8582.** Real estate professionals must complete line 43 on page 2	23	( )	( )	( )	
24 **Income.** Add positive amounts shown on line 22. **Do not** include any losses					24 210 00
25 **Losses.** Add royalty losses from line 22 and rental real estate losses from line 23. Enter total losses here					25 ( )
26 **Total rental real estate and royalty income or (loss).** Combine lines 24 and 25. Enter the result here. If Parts II, III, IV, and line 40 on page 2 do not apply to you, also enter this amount on Form 1040, line 17, or Form 1040NR, line 18. Otherwise, include this amount in the total on line 41 on page 2					26 210 00

For Paperwork Reduction Act Notice, see page E-7 of the instructions. Cat. No. 11344L **Schedule E (Form 1040) 2006**

- Comprehensive problems are included in most chapters.

  Feature: These problems incorporate many concepts introduced in the chapter. Many of these involve completing a tax return or portions of a tax return. **Benefit:** This learning application integrates and summarizes the concepts covered in the chapter. Completing the comprehensive problems will help you see how the concepts from the chapter are reported on the tax return.

COMPREHENSIVE PROBLEM

21. On January 2, 1995, Janis R. Jetson (SSN 344-46-5768), a cash basis taxpayer, purchased a two-unit apartment building at 1626 Flat Street, Detroit, Michigan 48270-8224. The costs of the land and building were $10,000 and $41,250, respectively. Jetson depreciates the building using the straight-line method over 27.5 years. Both apartments are the same size, with one on the ground floor and the other upstairs. Jetson has lived in the upstairs apartment since she acquired the building. The tenant in the ground-floor apartment at the time the building was purchased has continued to rent from Jetson. The tenant pays $350 a month in rent. On June 30 the tenant moved out. The apartment was vacant until August 1, even though Jetson advertised and attempted to rent it. On August 1, a new tenant moved in, paying rent of $400 per month. Rent is due on the first day of the month. Information on the apartment follows:

Revenue	
Rent from the first tenant (6 months @ $350)	$2,100
Rent from the second tenant (5 months @ $400)	2,000
Total revenue	$4,100
Expenses	
Entire house:	
Real estate taxes	$1,700
Janitor and yard work	160
Electricity and water	440
Repairs	300
Heat (gas)	800
Interest on mortgage	1,100
Insurance	376
Expenses other than depreciation	$4,876
Ground-floor apartment:	
Advertising	100
Painting and papering	420
Repairs	70
	$ 590
Upstairs apartment:	
Repairs	$ 90
Cleaning and maintenance	480
	$ 570

In addition to the rental property, Jetson works as an administrative assistant and earned $17,600 in wages. From this amount, $1,080 of federal income tax was withheld. Jetson also earned $147 in interest from Bank of America. Jetson is single and has no dependents. She does not want to contribute $3 to the presidential campaign fund.

Prepare Form 1040 and Schedule E, Supplemental Income and Loss, on the pages that follow. She claims the standard credit for federal telephone excise tax paid.

- Nine cumulative problems are included.

  Feature: The first two cumulative problems tie together concepts from Chapters 1 and 2. The next two cumulative problems tie together the concepts from Chapters 1-4. The fifth cumulative problem ties together the concepts from Chapters 1-6. The sixth cumulative problem ties together the concepts from Chapters 8-10. The seventh cumulative problem ties together the concepts from Chapters 8-12, and the eighth cumulative problem ties together the concepts from the first 12 chapters of the book. The last cumulative problem ties together concepts from Chapters 14 and 15.
  Benefit: These learning applications integrate and summarize concepts of several chapters to test your understanding and help you step back and see the big picture.

CUMULATIVE PROBLEM (CHAPTERS 1–6)

Frank A. (SSN 811-26-3717) and Sandra K. (SSN 820-47-9231) Anderson (ages 48 and 51, respectively) reside at 2121 Century Avenue, Middleton, CA 92657, with their three children whom they fully support: Martha A. (age 9), Charles R. (age 11), and Carol T. (age 14). The children's social security numbers are Martha 998-21-5246, Charles 998-21-5247, and Carol 998-21-1827.

The Andersons file a joint return, and neither elects to have money go to the presidential election campaign fund. Frank is employed by Maintaineers, Inc., as a customer representative. Sandra is employed by Mission Instruments as a computer operator. Details of their salaries and withholdings, are as follows:

	Gross Wages	*State Income Tax Withheld*	*Federal Income Tax Withheld*	*Social Security Tax Withheld*	*Medicare Insurance Tax Withheld*
Frank	$52,500	$3,623	$2,100	$3,255	$761
Sandra	24,000	1,656	980	1,488	348

In addition to his salary, Frank received a business travel expense reimbursement of $6,600 from Maintaineers, Inc., which was not included on his Form W-2. By agreement with his employer, none of the allowance was for meals and entertainment expenses. Frank must make an adequate accounting of his expenses to his employer and return any excess reimbursements. His daily business journal disclosed that from January 2 (the date of purchase) through December 31, he drove his own automobile 29,151 miles, of which 16,735 were business related. Frank's average roundtrip commuting distance is six miles, and his commuting miles total 1,440 for the year. Since Frank dislikes keeping records, he uses the standard mileage rate to determine his automobile tax deduction. His substantiated paid business expenses are as follows:

Travel expenses	$2,168*
Parking fees	210
Meals and entertainment	560
Miscellaneous expenses	91

*Excludes meals, entertainment, and auto expenses

Sandra belongs to a car pool and drives to work every fourth week. In addition, her car is used on vacations.

In August, Sandra received $400 of interest when she cashed in a CD from State Bank. The Middleton Farmers Bank credited $300 of interest to the Andersons' joint savings account during the year. The Andersons itemized deductions in 2005 and overpaid their state income tax by $142, all of which provided a tax benefit. They received a refund of this amount in March, 2006. Since they both work outside the home, they are unable to be there when their children return from school. This year the Andersons paid a neighbor, Gloria Dryden (SSN 992-31-4270), $4,100 to care for their children in her home after school hours and during the summer vacation period while the Andersons were at work. Gloria Dryden's address is 2132 Century Avenue, Middleton, CA 92657.

During January, Sandra received unemployment compensation of $1,000, covering two months between jobs. During 2006, Frank paid $6,000 in alimony to his ex-wife (SSN 329-68-4180). Frank is covered by a qualified pension plan at work; Sandra is not. The Andersons are interested in contributing to their respective traditional IRAs the maximum that they can deduct on their 2006 tax return. Both contributions take place before April 15, 2007.

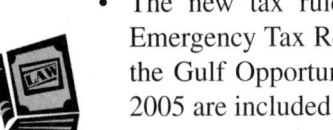

- Tax questions and problems requiring use of the IRS website are included in each chapter.

  Feature: The answers to these questions and problems are found in the information contained in IRS forms and/or publications.
  Benefit: You will learn how to find answers to tax questions from IRS publications available on the internet. You will also learn how to find needed tax forms, fill them out while on the internet, and print out copies of the completed forms. These learning applications provide you the opportunity to obtain knowledge about tax law using information outside of the textbook.

6-38 *CHAPTER 6 Other Itemized Deductions*

20. Internet Problem: Researching Publication 463.

The Alpha-Beta Company rents a 12-seat luxury skybox at a football stadium for the entire season. The season consists of eight home games. Alpha-Beta uses the skybox exclusively for entertaining clients. The cost of renting the skybox for the season is $20,000. In contrast, nonluxury box seats sell for $50 for each game.

How much can Alpha-Beta deduct for its luxury skybox?

Go to the IRS Web site. Locate Publication 463, and find an answer to the above question involving luxury skyboxes. Print out a copy of the page where you found your answer. Underline or highlight the pertinent information.

See Appendix A for instructions on use of the IRS Web site.

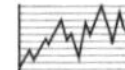

21. Business Entity Problem: This problem is designed for those using the "business entity" approach. The solution may require information from Chapters 14 and 15.

For each statement, check true or false.	*True*	*False*
a. Self-employed taxpayers use Form 2106 to report their deductible travel expenses.	_____	_____
b. A self-employed taxpayer may claim the federal per diem for meals instead of deducting the actual meal costs.	_____	_____
c. Employers that reimburse their employees using an "accountable reimbursement plan" are able to deduct the entire cost of meal reimbursements paid to their employees.	_____	_____
d. When a self-employed taxpayer incurs deductible education expenses, the expenses are deductible as a miscellaneous itemized deduction subject to the 2% rule.	_____	_____
e. When a taxpayer owns an S corporation that breeds and races horses, the pass-through losses from the corporation may be treated as hobby losses if the corporation has never shown a profit in its ten years of operation.	_____	_____

- The new tax rules from the Katrina Emergency Tax Relief Act of 2005 and the Gulf Opportunity Zone Tax Act of 2005 are included in the 2007 Edition.

  Feature: New tax rules contain many provisions designed to provide temporary tax relief to persons living in and around the various areas that were greatly affected by Hurricanes Katrina, Rita, or Wilma. The new tax laws that affect topics covered in the 2007 Edition have been incorporated into the chapters.
  Benefit: These rules affect the preparation of 2006 tax returns. By including these tax rules in the 2007 Edition, you are up to date with all of the rules needed to complete a 2006 individual tax return.

5-18 *CHAPTER 5 Personal Itemized Deductions*

EXAMPLE 24

Jack Reese donates $1,000 to his alma mater. His gift allows him to buy season tickets to the university's football and basketball games. The Code treats $800 of the gift ($1,000 x 80%) as a charitable contribution. The rest ($200) is treated as a nondeductible payment for the right to purchase athletic tickets.

Charitable contributions account for about 14% of the total itemized deductions claimed by taxpayers.

Noncash Gifts, Schedule A (Line 16)

Among other items, taxpayers may deduct car expenses and donations of property. For car expenses, taxpayers may use either the standard mileage rate of $.14 per mile or actual expenses. Limits on deductions of property contributed to a charity follow the same rules that apply to cash contributions. The type of property contributed, the recipient, and the property's use determine the amount of the deduction. Property contributions fall into two categories: (1) ordinary income property (includes short-term capital gain property) and (2) capital gain property held over 12 months. Contributions in both categories may include real estate, tangible personal property, or intangible personal property.

Generally, the deduction for noncash gifts is equal to the FMV of the property at the time of donation. This holds true when the FMV is less than the taxpayer's basis (investment) in the property. However, when the FMV is greater than the basis, the amount of the deduction depends on whether the item takes the form of (1) ordinary income property or long-term capital gain property and (2) how the charity uses the property. When the deduction exceeds $500, the donor shows the details of the donation on Form 8283. For any noncash donation, a letter from the qualifying organization must specify how the organization uses the property.

The Katrina Emergency Tax Relief Act of 2005 allows taxpayers who use their automobile for charitable purposes related to Hurricane Katrina to deduct a (higher) mileage rate equal to 70% of the standard business mileage rate, rounded to the next highest cent. Thus, special mileage rate for 2006 is $.32 per mile ($.445 × 70%, rounded up). The higher mileage rate remains in effect through 2006.

Tangible personal property consists of most property that a taxpayer owns except assets used for trade or business and real estate. The usual items contributed under this category include clothing, toys, furniture, appliances, and books. Normally, the FMV of these items is less than the taxpayer's basis. The FMV of household goods and clothing is their thrift shop or garage sale value. "Blue books" are the common source of values for most types of vehicles.

The intangible assets most commonly donated include stocks, bonds, and mutual funds. For the most part, these assets are widely traded and their FMV is easy to determine.

Taxpayers who donate vehicles to charities can only deduct what the charity obtains from selling it. The charity, under threat of penalties, must report the sales price to both the donor and the IRS.

Helpful information included in the 2007 Edition!!

- Highlights of 2006 and 2007 tax changes are listed and described in the Preface.

  Feature: A summary of 2006 and 2007 tax law changes appears on pages x–xii.
  Benefit: This summary brings you up to date quickly with major tax law changes since the last edition.

- Frequently used tax facts are given.

  Feature: Frequently used tax facts appear on the inside front cover.
  Benefit: This helpful page provides a quick and easy reference source for frequently used tax facts.

- Numerous examples are provided. Over 75% more examples have been included in the 2007 edition than in prior editions.

  Feature: Every chapter includes numerous easy-to-follow examples.
  Benefit: These examples illustrate the application of tax laws and relate tax laws to true-life situations.

- Information on how to access IRS forms and publications from the IRS website is given.

  Feature: Information on how to obtain forms and publications from the IRS through the internet appears in Appendix A after the Tax Tables and EIC Tables.
  Benefit: This information will help you access the most up-to-date forms, instructions to forms, and IRS publications referenced in the text.

Features New for *Essentials of Federal Income Taxation for Individuals and Businesses, 2007 Edition*

- The business entity chapter (formerly Chapter 14) has been expanded to Chapters 14 (C Corporations) and 15 (Partnerships and S Corporations). Tax return problems for each of these entities have been incorporated into the chapters to keep the coverage consistent with the other chapters in the textbook.
- Over 75% new examples have been added to the 2007 edition to provide real world examples to the concepts discussed in the textbook.
- Over one-third new homework problems have been added to the 2007 edition to give students a greater variety of homework problems to solve.
- The 2007 edition contains more than double the number of comprehensive problems and cumulative problems than in prior editions. These new problems give students more opportunity to work real world problems that pull together multiple concepts either within the chapter or across chapters.
- A discussion of the new tax credits is included in the textbook. The Alternative Vehicles Credit and the Residential Energy Credit are discussion in Chapter 2. The New Markets Credit is discussed in Chapter 12.
- The discussion of fringe benefits in Chapter 4 has been expanded.
- The rules governing the new designated Roth contributions to 401(k) plans are discussed in Chapter 4.
- The standard credit for Federal telephone excise tax paid available only on 2006 tax returns has been incorporated into each of the tax return problems.

Other Successful Features of *Essentials of Federal Income Taxation for Individuals and Business, 2007 Edition*

- Comprehensive coverage of self-employed taxpayers (Chapter 7)
- Index of tax forms, schedules, and worksheets following the table of contents
- Detailed outline at beginning of each chapter
- Line numbers set off in parentheses to show location of tax facts on forms
- Tax tips throughout book for tax planning and tax reduction
- Problems at end of chapters designated for tax software solution
- Assignments that provide actual application and check understanding
- Acronym list on copyright page that provides actual words

Highlights of 2006 and 2007 Tax Changes

Inside Front Cover

- 2006 Tax Rate Schedules
- 2006 and 2007 Standard Deduction amounts
- 2006 and 2007 Personal and Dependency Exemption amounts
- 2006 and 2007 FICA Tax Rates and Base amounts
- 2006 Standard Mileage Rates

Chapter 1

- The personal and dependency exemption for 2006 increased to $3,300.
- Inflation adjustments increased the basic standard deduction amounts for taxpayers in 2006.
- The basic standard deduction for dependents in 2006 is the *lesser of* (i) $850 or (ii) earned income + $300. This amount is up from the *lesser of* (i) $800 or (ii) earned income + $250 in 2005.
- The deduction for personal and dependency exemptions is phased down 2% for each $2,500 step of AGI over the 2006 thresholds ($1,250 for MFS). This is down from a 3% phase-down in 2005.
- An additional $500 exemption is allowed in 2006 to certain taxpayers providing rent-free housing to a "displaced Katrina individual."

Chapter 2

- The phase-out for education credits starts at $90,000 (up from $87,000 in 2005) for marrieds filing jointly. It increased to $45,000 for single taxpayers (up from $43,000).
- Disqualified income for purposes of the earned income credit has increased to $2,800 (up from $2,700 in 2005).
- In 2006 the child tax credit is refundable up to 15% of earned income in excess of $11,300 (up from $11,000 in 2005).
- In 2006, the adoption credit is $10,960 (up from $10,630 in 2005). The phase-out starts at $164,410 (up from $159,450 in 2005).

- The maximum HOPE education credit increased to $1,650 in 2006 (up from $1,500 in 2005). For students attending schools located in the Gulf Opportunity Zone, the maximum HOPE credit doubles to $3,300 and the percentage used in computing the lifetime learning credit doubles to 40%.
- The Retirement Savers Contribution Credit is now a permanent tax credit.
- Two new credits: The Alternative Motor Vehicles Credit (more commonly called the hybrid car tax credit) and the Residential Energy Tax Credit are discussed.
- The refundable credit for Federal telephone excise tax paid is discussed.
- Automatic extensions of time to file a federal income tax return have been extended to six months starting in 2006.

Chapter 3

- Taxpayers taking a "qualified hurricane distribution" from their IRAs may spread the taxable portion of the distribution over three years.
- The "kiddie tax" rules now apply to children under the age of 18 (up from age 14 in 2005). Unearned income in excess of $1,700 is taxed at the parents' tax rate (up from $1,600 in 2005).

Chapter 4

- The exclusion for foreign income increased to $82,400 in 2006 (up from $80,000 in 2005). This amount will continue to be indexed annually for inflation.
- The exclusion for interest income from Series EE and I government bonds when the proceeds are used to pay for qualified education is phased out when AGI exceeds $63,100 for unmarried taxpayers ($94,700 for couples that file MFJ).
- The maximum contribution to both traditional and Roth IRAs remains at $4,000 in 2006. Persons age 50 and older can contribute an additional $1,000 in 2006 (up from $500 in 2005). The AGI phase-out ranges are presented in the chapter.
- The rules governing designated contributions to the new Roth 401(k) are presented in the chapter.
- The IRS will not assess the 10% penalty on the first $100,000 of "qualified hurricane distributions."
- Employees can exclude up to $205 each month for employer-provided qualified parking (up from $200 a month in 2005). The exclusion for employer-provided qualified transportation remains at $105.
- In 2006, taxpayers can exclude from gross income up to $10,960 of child adoption costs paid or reimbursed by the employer (up from $10,630 in 2005).
- The mileage rate for moving increased to $.18 per mile in 2006 (up from $.15 per mile in 2005).
- The educator's expense deduction and the deduction for tuition and fees expired at the end of 2005 and were not renewed by Congress at the time the book went to press.

Chapter 5

- The AGI phase-out threshold for itemized deductions increased from $145,950 to $150,500 (half of these amounts for MFS). The phase down is equal to the *lesser of* (i) 2% of the taxpayer's excess AGI or (ii) 53 1/3% of deductions subject to the phase-out. This represents two-thirds of the percentages applicable to 2005 tax returns (which were 3% and 80%, respectively).

- The mileage rate for medical increased to $.18 per mile in 2006 (up from $.15 per mile in 2005).
- The mileage rate for charitable contributions remains at $.14 for 2006. However, the mileage rate for charitable contribution work related to Hurricane Katrina is $.32 in 2006 (70% of the $.445 standard federal rate, rounded up).
- The itemized deduction for state and local sales taxes expired at the end of 2005 and was not renewed by Congress at the time this book went to press.

Chapter 7

- The standard mileage rate is $.445 per mile for business miles driven in 2006.
- In 2006, the 15.3% self-employment tax rate applies to the first $94,200 of net earnings from self-employment. The 2.9% tax rate applies to net earnings from self-employment in excess of $94,200.
- The annual limit for contributions to 401(k) retirement plans increased to $15,000 (up from $14,000 in 2005). Employees age 50 and older can contribute an additional $5,000 in 2006 (up from $4,000 in 2005).
- The annual limit for contributions to a SIMPLE retirement plan remains at $10,000 for 2006. Workers age 50 and older can contribute an additional $2,500 in 2006 (up from $2,000 in 2005).
- The maximum contribution to defined benefit plans (including SEP plans) increased to $44,000 in 2006 (up from $42,000 in 2005).
- The maximum contribution that can be made to any 401(k) plan (including the new Roth 401(k)) is $15,000 in 2006 (up from $14,000 in 2005). Taxpayers age 50 and older can contribution an additional $5,000 (up from $4,000 in 2005).

Chapter 8

- A provision in the Gulf Opportunity Zone Act of 2005 allows businesses (including sole proprietorships) affected by Hurricanes Katrina, Rita and Wilma to take a 50% bonus first year depreciation on qualifying property placed in service in the Gulf Opportunity Zone (Go Zone) between the date of the hurricane and December 31, 2007. Bonus depreciation also applies to certain residential rental property placed in service before December 31, 2008.
- The dollar limit for purposes of the immediate expensing of Section 179 property increased to $108,000 in 2006 (up from $105,000 in 2005). The phase-out of this amount begins when more than $430,000 of Section 179 property is placed in service during 2006 (up from $420,000 in 2005).
- Depreciation deduction limits for most automobiles placed in service in 2006 are limited to $2,960 in the first year, $4,800 in the second year, $2,850 in the third year, and $1,775 in each subsequent year. These amounts are based on 100% business use.
- The indexed inclusion amounts for leased vehicles valued between $35,000 and $40,000 are included in the chapter.

Chapter 10

- Taxpayers with business or investment property located in the Hurricane Katrina disaster area may have an additional three years to replace their property and avoid being taxed on any realized gains.

Chapter 12

- The AMT exemption for couples filing a joint return increased to $62,550 in 2006 (up from $58,000 for 2005). The exemption for couples who file separately increased to $31,275 (up from $29,000 in 2005). For unmarried taxpayers, the 2006 AMT exemption increased to $42,500 (up from $40,250 in 2005).
- The work opportunity credit expired at the end of 2005. However, Congress is expected to extend it, as it has done several times in the past. Congress expanded the list of eligible workers to include Hurricane Katrina employees hired before August 27, 2007. The rules for who qualifies as a Hurricane Katrina employee are discussed in the chapter.
- The welfare-to-work credit expired at the end of 2005. However, Congress is expected to extend it, as it has done several times in the past.
- The New Markets Credit (part of the General Business Credit) is discussed in the chapter.

Chapter 13

- In 2006, large depositors of payroll taxes, withheld income taxes, and corporate income taxes must use the electronic funds transfer system (EFTS) to make their deposits. For 2006, large depositors are those who had deposits in excess of $200,000 in 2004. For 2007, businesses with more than $200,000 of deposits in 2005 must use the EFTS to make their deposits.
- For 2006, employers withhold 6.2% of their employees' wages, up to wages of $94,200 for each employee (up from $90,000 in 2005), for social security taxes. They also withhold 1.45% of employees' wages for Medicare taxes (no limit).
- Household employees (maids, babysitters, nannies, etc.) are subject to FICA withholding if they are paid $1,500 or more during 2006 (up from $1,400 in 2005).

SPECIAL NOTE REGARDING FINAL TAX FORMS AND SCHEDULES FOR THE 2006 TAX YEAR

Normally, the IRS would have released the final version of the 2006 tax forms and schedules by the time this book went to press. This textbook contains the most recent version of each tax form and schedule available at the time the book went to press – including the use of draft forms when the final version was not yet available. Final versions of any tax form or schedule can be obtained from the IRS website using the instructions on the inside back cover of this textbook. If you are using final forms and schedules to complete homework problems, please note that line number references used in this book reflect the line numbers on the forms and schedules used and illustrated throughout the textbook. Although the final version of a tax form often is identical to the draft version, slight differences between the draft and final versions of any tax form are possible, and changes to the line numbers may occur.

CURRENT DEVELOPMENTS

The 2007 Edition contains all of the current tax law as of the time the book went to press. In the event that Congress passes legislation before the next edition that affects the course material, students can find a summary of the tax bill at: http://tax.CCHGroup.com/taxleg/.

ACKNOWLEDGMENTS

We express our appreciation to the many instructors and students who have contributed suggestions to make this textbook more interesting, understandable, and practical to those who study federal income taxation. As a result of their very helpful recommendations, the 2007 Edition will better satisfy the learning needs of students and the teaching needs of instructors. Our goal is to continue to make improvements with each edition. In this regard, we welcome and appreciate any comments, criticisms or suggestions you may have about the book.

Linda M. Johnson
Herbert C. Seig

1

Overview of the Tax Structure

CHAPTER CONTENTS

CHAPTER OVERVIEW

The Sixteenth Amendment to the Constitution empowers Congress to levy and collect income taxes. After its ratification, Congress enacted the Revenue Act of 1913. For individual taxpayers, the Act taxed income at a 1% rate. At $20,000, the Act imposed an additional 1% surtax. This surtax gradually increased to 6% for taxable income above $500,000.

The government continues to use a progressive tax rate structure. This means that as income rises, the tax rate increases. In 2006, tax rates range from 10% to 35%. The current rate schedules appear on the inside front cover of this book.

Our current tax system, like the original one, requires taxpayers to determine their own taxes. It also requires each taxpayer to file a tax return and pay any tax due the government by certain deadlines. Taxpayers who fail to meet these requirements face possible fines, penalties, and imprisonment. In addition, the Internal Revenue Service (IRS) charges interest on unpaid taxes. Many taxpayers seek help from tax professionals, who prepare about half of filed tax returns.

Although many taxpayers use paid professionals, every taxpayer should have a basic understanding of the tax laws. This understanding will help them prepare their returns or identify facts needed by a preparer. It also will help them review a professionally-prepared return before filing it. Understanding the tax laws can help in recognizing potential problems before financial events take place. Through proper planning, taxpayers can reduce the tax bite. The first part of this chapter provides an overview of our current income tax system. The latter part presents basic tax planning principles.

Since 1913, the Internal Revenue Code has grown to well over 2,000 pages in length.

INCOME TAX OBJECTIVES

The federal income tax system raises money to cover part of the government's annual operating costs. However, to better understand certain tax rules, people must realize that Congress also uses tax laws to achieve various economic, political, and social goals. These include redistributing the country's wealth, as well as encouraging economic growth, full employment, and certain behaviors. For example, if the goal is to increase employment, Congress can lower taxes, which gives taxpayers more money to spend. This, in turn, creates more demand for products and services. The result is a need for an increased number of workers to make the products and provide the services.

An example of Congress's use of the tax laws to encourage certain behavior involves tax breaks to those that buy hybrid cars. Hybrid cars are more fuel efficient and emit fewer pollutants than standard cars. However, they cost several thousand dollars more than their non-hybrid counterparts. Even with higher gas prices, the higher price of hybrid cars has kept many consumers from buying them. The tax breaks given to those that buy hybrid cars was increased in 2006 to encourage consumers to buy them over standard models. If these tax breaks work, the desired result will be a decrease in U.S. demand for gasoline and an overall improvement in air quality.

BASIC TAX FORMULA

Governments levy taxes by assessing a tax rate to a tax base. In the income tax system, the tax base is taxable income. Simply put, taxable income is the difference between the amount of income the government decides to tax and deductions it allows against this income. Anything that causes wealth to increase generally is regarded as income. However, not all items that increase one's wealth are taxed. Income that the government taxes is called "gross income." Most deductions involve expenses that the government allows to reduce gross income. However, some deductions are not tied to expenditures. Gross income is the subject of Chapters 3 and 4. Tax deductions are discussed later in the chapter and are also the focus of Chapters 5 and 6.

TAXABLE INCOME FORMULA

Income from all sources
– Exempt income
= Gross income
– Deductions
= Taxable income

For purposes of this textbook a "taxpayer" is any person or entity required to file an income tax return with the Internal Revenue Service (IRS). Although this term suggests that taxes are being paid, not all taxpayers pay income taxes. Flow-through entities report their gross income and tax deductions to the IRS. However, it is the owners of these entities that pay taxes on their respective shares of the entity's taxable income. Partnerships and S corporations are examples of flow-through entities. They are the focus of Chapter 15.

Regular corporations ("C corporations") are business entities that pay tax each year on their taxable income. In this regard, they are similar to individual taxpayers. Although the focus of this textbook begins with the individual taxpayer, the taxation of businesses is presented in the book as well. Many of the tax laws described in this textbook apply equally to all types of taxpayers. However, sometimes special rules apply only to one group of taxpayers. For example, the basic formula for computing taxable income presented above is the same for both corporations and individuals. However, individuals are entitled to more types of deductions and thus use an expanded taxable income formula. For purposes of this textbook, unless from the discussion it is clear that use of the term "taxpayer" refers to a particular type of taxpayer (for example, an individual or a corporation), when the term "taxpayer" is used when discussing a tax law, such law applies to all types of taxpayers, including corporations, individuals, and flow-through entities. If a tax law is unique to one type of taxpayer, then the title of the section or the discussion itself will state the type of taxpayer to which the law applies.

After C corporations and individuals compute income tax on their taxable income, they compute their tax liability using the tax rates set by Congress. Although different tax rates may apply, the federal income tax rates are progressive, which means that as taxable income increases, so too does the tax rate. These taxpayers may owe other taxes in addition to the income taxes. Individuals may owe self-employment taxes, penalties for early distributions from retirement accounts, or alternative minimum tax (AMT). Corporations also may be subject to AMT. These taxpayers may also be entitled to subtract tax credits from these taxes to arrive at their taxes owed (or refund due) at the end of the year. Tax credits can be business-related or personal in nature. The former applies to all types of businesses. The latter applies only to individual taxpayers.

CALCULATION OF TAXES OWED (TO BE REFUNDED)

Taxable income
× Tax rate
= Income tax liability
+ Additional taxes
– Tax credits
= Final tax due (refund)

DEDUCTIONS VERSUS CREDITS

The distinction between a deduction and a credit is important. Tax credits reduce tax liability. Tax deductions reduce taxable income. Tax credits reduce the taxpayer's taxes by the amount of the tax credit. Deductions reduce the taxpayer's taxes by the amount of the deduction times the taxpayer's tax rate. For example, a $100 deduction saves the taxpayer $15 if the tax rate is 15% ($100 x 15%), but saves him $35 if the tax rate is 35% ($100 x 35%). A $100 tax credit, on the other hand, reduces taxes by $100 regardless of the tax rate.

INDIVIDUAL TAXPAYERS

Although there are a variety of types of income, the concept of gross income is the same for all taxpayers. That is, there is some income that the government taxes, while other types of income are not subject to income tax. The tax laws also allow a variety of deductions in the calculation of taxable income. Individual taxpayers can reduce their taxable income by a mix of business and personal deductions. Accordingly, the tax laws separate the deductions available to individuals into two categories: deductions for adjusted gross income (AGI) and deductions from AGI. The latter are deductions that are more personal in nature. They are the focus of Chapters 5 and 6.

BASIC TAX FORMULA FOR INDIVIDUALS

	Income from all sources
–	Exempt income
=	Gross income
–	Deductions for AGI (adjusted gross income)
=	AGI
–	Deductions from AGI
	Itemized deductions or standard deduction
	Exemptions (personal and dependency)
=	Taxable income
×	Tax rate
=	Income tax liability
+	Additional taxes
–	Tax credits
=	Final tax due (refund)

The tax rate that individual taxpayers apply to taxable income depends on their filing status. A person's filing status depends on whether he or she is married on the last day of the tax year, along with other factors. More about the rules for each filing status will be presented later in the chapter. There are five filing statuses:

1. Married filing jointly (MFJ)
2. Married filing separately (MFS)
3. Head of household (HOH)
4. Single
5. Surviving spouse (SS)

Individuals who are required to file an income tax return file one of the following tax returns:

1. Form 1040EZ, Income Tax Return for Single and Joint Filers with No Dependents
2. Form 1040A, U.S. Individual Income Tax Return
3. Form 1040, U.S. Individual Income Tax Return

Form 1040EZ is the easiest of the tax forms to complete (hence its title). However, only certain taxpayers can use Form 1040EZ, as will be explained in Chapter 2. Form 1040A is introduced in Chapters 2 and 4. Although many individual taxpayers can use either Form 1040EZ or 1040A, many must file Form 1040.

GROSS INCOME

Taxpayers must be able to determine their gross income. The Internal Revenue Code's (Code) definition of gross income includes all wealth that flows to a taxpayer from whatever source derived. It then exempts some income from taxation. The Code lists the following different gross income sources (and implies that others exist):

1. Compensation for services, including fees, commissions, fringe benefits, etc.
2. Gross income from business
3. Gains from the disposal of property
4. Interest
5. Rents
6. Royalties
7. Dividends
8. Alimony and separate maintenance payments
9. Annuities
10. Income from life insurance proceeds
11. Pensions
12. Income from forgiven debt
13. Share of distributive partnership income and prorata share of S Corporation income
14. Income in respect of a decedent
15. Income from an interest in an estate or trust

To determine gross income, taxpayers generally examine their various sources of income and sort out taxable income from exempt income. Regardless of the form or name of an income item, proper authority must exist to exclude the item from gross income. Taxpayers may find such authority in the tax statutes, the Code, Treasury Regulations, IRS rulings, or case law. From gross income, taxpayers subtract allowed deductions to arrive at taxable income.

Importance of Gross Income

It is important that taxpayers correctly compute their gross income. When gross income exceeds a certain amount, taxpayers must file an income tax return. Failure to file a proper return on time can result in tax penalties. Also, when a taxpayer accidentally understates gross income by more than 25%, the law extends the time the IRS has to conduct an audit. Finally, individuals may be allowed or denied a dependency exemption deduction depending on the person's gross income.

DEDUCTIONS AVAILABLE TO INDIVIDUAL TAXPAYERS

Individual taxpayers have two broad groups of deductions. They subtract one group from gross income to arrive at AGI. They subtract the other group from AGI to arrive at taxable income. Some call them *for* or *from* deductions. Others call them *above-* or *below-the-line* deductions. Taxpayers subtract **above-the-line** deductions from gross income to arrive at AGI. They subtract **below-the-line** deductions from AGI to arrive at taxable income.

There are two types of below-the-line deductions. One is the *greater of* a taxpayer's itemized deductions or standard deduction. The other includes exemptions (personal and dependency). The Code limits the amount of exemptions and itemized deductions that a taxpayer may claim. AGI generally serves as a basis for determining these limitations. Corporations, partnerships, estates, and trusts do not compute AGI.

Deductions for AGI

The Code defines an individual's AGI as gross income less certain deductions. Some of the major deductions include:

1. Trade and business deductions for business owners
2. Losses on the disposal of business or investment property (subject to limitations)
3. Deductions related to rent and royalty income
4. Certain contributions to retirement plans of self-employed individuals
5. Certain contributions to traditional Individual Retirement Accounts
6. Penalties for early withdrawals from certificates of deposits
7. Alimony
8. Qualified moving expenses
9. One-half of self-employment tax
10. Health insurance premiums paid by self-employed persons
11. Individual contributions to a medical savings or health savings account
12. Interest paid on student loans

Deductions from AGI

After computing AGI, individuals reduce AGI by either itemized deductions or a standard deduction. They also reduce it by personal and dependency exemptions. The next few sections present the standard deduction and exemptions. Itemized deductions fall into seven groups.

1. Medical
2. Taxes
3. Interest
4. Charitable contributions
5. Casualty and theft losses
6. Job expenses and some miscellaneous deductions
7. Other miscellaneous deductions

STANDARD DEDUCTION

The standard deduction is a deduction from AGI that only applies to individual taxpayers. It consists of two amounts: the basic standard deduction and the additional standard deduction. Both amounts are subject to inflation adjustments each year. Taxpayers normally use the standard deduction when it exceeds their total itemized deductions. Taxpayers filing Form 1040EZ or Form 1040A must use the standard deduction. Also, when spouses file separate returns, both spouses must either itemize deductions or take the standard deduction. Thus, if one spouse itemizes, the other spouse's standard deduction is "zero." This forces the other spouse to itemize as well.

EXAMPLE 1

Joe and Tina Reyes are married, but will file separate tax returns in the current year. Joe's itemized deductions exceed the standard deduction for MFS. He subtracts his itemized deductions from his AGI in computing taxable income on his tax return. Because of this, Tina can deduct the *greater of* her itemized deductions or a $0 standard deduction from AGI in computing her taxable income.

Although taxpayers may deduct certain personal expenses as itemized deductions, about 70% use the standard deduction. For most taxpayers this constitutes one of the two major deductions on the tax return. The other is the exemption amount. An employed person who does not pay alimony or make payments to a qualified retirement program usually has little, if anything, else to deduct against gross income. This makes computing taxable income fairly easy for most Americans. They simply add up their gross income from various sources and deduct the standard deduction and the exemption amounts to arrive at taxable income.

Basic Standard Deduction

There are four basic standard deduction amounts. Filing status usually determines which amount applies. Although most individuals can deduct the basic standard deduction amount, some cannot. A special rule applies to persons who are claimed as a dependent of another taxpayer, as will be explained later (Standard Deduction for Dependents).

BASIC STANDARD DEDUCTION FOR 2006

Filing Status	Amount
Married filing jointly, or surviving spouse	$10,300
Head of household	7,550
Single	5,150
Married filing separately	5,150

Additional Standard Deduction

In addition to the basic standard deduction, blind and elderly taxpayers claim extra deductions. Taxpayers become elderly when they reach age 65. This additional deduction is available only for the taxpayer, which includes both spouses when a joint return is filed. A taxpayer cannot claim an additional standard deduction for a dependent who is elderly or blind. The additional standard deduction increases only the basic standard deduction; it never increases the taxpayer's itemized deductions. There are two additional standard deduction amounts. The taxpayer's filing status determines which one is used.

ADDITIONAL STANDARD DEDUCTION FOR 2006

MFJ, MFS and surviving spouse	$1,000
Single and head of household	1,250

Each incidence of age and blindness carries with it an additional deduction. In the case of married taxpayers, each spouse is eligible for both deductions. Thus, if both spouses are age 65, the total additional standard deduction is $2,000 (2 × $1,000). If both spouses are age 65 and one is blind, the extra deduction is $3,000 (3 × $1,000). For a single person, age 65 and blind, the extra deduction is $2,500 (2 × $1,250).

For a taxpayer to get an additional standard deduction, his or her status as elderly or blind must exist at the end of the tax year (or at death). For tax purposes, individuals age the day before their calendar birthday. Thus, a taxpayer who turns 65 on January 1 is 65 for tax purposes as of December 31 of the preceding year.

A taxpayer may claim the additional deduction for blindness either by failing a visual ability or field of vision test. For the visual ability test, sight in either eye cannot exceed 20/200 with a corrective lens. For the field of vision test, the person's field of vision cannot exceed 20 degrees.

The taxpayer supports a blindness claim with a certified statement from an eye doctor. The statement verifies that the taxpayer is totally blind or fails either the visual ability or field of vision test. The statement is attached to the taxpayer's tax return. If the blindness is irreversible, the taxpayer simply refers to this statement on future returns.

EXAMPLE 2

Joe and Tina Reyes are married, but will file separate tax returns in 2006. Joe's itemized deductions total $7,000; Tina's total $400. Joe's $7,000 of itemized deductions exceeds the $5,150 standard deduction allowed for MFS. He subtracts the $7,000 from his AGI in computing taxable income. As a result, Tina can deduct $400 from AGI (the *greater of* her $400 itemized deductions or $0 standard deduction).

EXAMPLE 3

Don and Nancy Miner are married and file a joint return in 2006. As of December 31, 2006, Don is 67 and Nancy is 64. Neither have any problems with their vision. The Miners add to their $10,300 basic standard deduction $1,000 for Don's age. Their total standard deduction for 2006 equals $11,300. If the Miners' itemized deductions exceed this amount, they will itemize. Otherwise they will subtract $11,300 from their AGI when computing their taxable income for 2006.

EXAMPLE 4

Pam Starkey is 70 and blind. Her filing status is single. Starkey's 2006 total standard deduction equals $7,650 ($5,150 + ($1,250 x 2)).

Standard Deduction for Dependents

A person (e.g., child) who qualifies as a dependent of another taxpayer (e.g., parent) computes the basic standard deduction as the *greater of* two amounts: (i) $850 or (ii) earned income plus $300. The deduction cannot exceed the basic standard deduction for the dependent's filing status. However, any additional standard deduction for which the dependent qualifies is added to the basic standard deduction.

When married taxpayers are claimed as dependents and file separate returns, the following rules apply. If one or both spouses are dependents of other taxpayers, and both spouses use the standard deduction, the basic standard deduction is limited to the *greater of* (i) $850, or (ii) earned income plus $300. However, if one spouse itemizes deductions, the standard deduction for the other spouse is zero.

EXAMPLE 5

Same as in Example 4, except that in 2006, Pam is claimed as a dependent on her son's tax return. Her 2006 basic standard deduction is limited to $850 (the *greater of* (i) $850 or (ii) $0 earned income + $300). She adds to this amount a $2,500 additional standard deduction and deducts $3,350 ($850 + $2,500) from AGI when computing her 2006 taxable income

A dependent usually completes a worksheet similar to Figure 1-1, which helps in computing the standard deduction.

Information for Figure 1-1: Filled-In Standard Deduction Worksheet for Dependents

This figure presents a filled-in Standard Deduction Worksheet for 16-year-old Gloria Moore. Gloria's parents claim her as a dependent. Gloria has perfect vision. She earned $1,400 at a weekend office job. Her standard deduction equals $1,700, the *greater of* (i) $850 or (ii) her earned income plus $300. This amount does not exceed the basic standard deduction for a single individual ($5,150).

FIGURE 1-1: Filled-In Standard Deduction Worksheet for Dependents

1.	Enter your earned income (defined below) plus $300.	1.	1,700
2.	Minimum amount.	2.	850
3.	Enter the larger of line 1 or line 2.	3.	1,700
4.	Enter $5,150 if single ($5,150 if married filing separately; $10,300 if married filing jointly, or qualifying widow(er); $7,550 if head of household).	4.	5,150
5.	Standard deduction:		
	a. Enter the smaller of line 3 or line 4. If under 65 and not blind, this is the standard deduction. Otherwise go to line 5b.	5a.	1,700
	b. If 65 or older or blind, multiply $1,250 ($1,000 if married filing jointly or separately, or qualifying widow[er]) by the number of incidences of age and blindness.	5b.	0
	c. Add lines 5a and 5b to determine standard deduction.	5c.	1,700

Earned income includes salaries, tips, professional fees, and other compensation received for personal services performed. It also includes taxable scholarships and net profit from self-employment activit)ies.

EXEMPTIONS

Exemptions, like the standard deduction, reduce AGI. For 2006, this reduction is $3,300 for each exemption claimed. Generally, the taxpayer may claim an exemption for one's self and each person who qualifies as a dependent. If a married couple files a joint tax return, each spouse can claim a personal exemption. Exemptions provide many taxpayers with their biggest tax deductions. For example, a married taxpayer with two dependent children reduces AGI by $13,200 (4 × $3,300). This far exceeds the couple's $10,300 standard deduction.

Phase-Down of Exemptions

When AGI reaches a certain level, the taxpayer phases down (reduces) the dollar amount of the exemptions. In 2006, for every $2,500 ($1,250 for MFS) of AGI (or fraction thereof) over a base amount, the exemption deduction goes down by two-thirds of 2 percentage points. When the excess exceeds $122,500 ($61,250 for MFS), the taxpayer's deduction equals $1,100 times the total number of exemptions claimed.

BASE AMOUNTS—EXEMPTION PHASE-DOWN FOR 2006

Filing Status	Start When AGI Over	Stop When AGI Over
Married filing jointly	$225,750	$348,250
Surviving spouse	225,750	348,250
Head of household	188,150	310,650
Single	150,500	273,000
Married filing separately	112,875	174,125

Information for Figure 1-2: Filled-In Personal Exemption Worksheet

This figure shows the phase-down worksheet for Jack and Laura Johnson. The Johnsons use the worksheet to compute their deduction for four exemptions. They file jointly and have $249,310 of AGI.

FIGURE 1-2: Filled-In Personal Exemption Worksheet

Is the amount of AGI more than the amount shown on line 3 below for your filing status?
NO. Stop. Multiply $3,300 by the total number of exemptions claimed. This is your exemption deduction.
YES. Complete the worksheet below to figure your deduction for exemptions.

1. Multiply $3,300 by the total number of exemptions claimed. — 1. 13,200
2. Enter the amount of AGI. — 2. 249,310
3. Enter the amount shown below for your filing status:
   a. Married filing separately, enter $112,875.
   b. Single, enter $150,500.
   c. Head of household, enter $188,150.
   d. Married filing jointly, or qualifying widow(er), enter $225,750. — 3. 225,750

4. Subtract line 3 from line 2. If zero or less, stop here; the amount from line 1 above is the exemption deduction. — 4. 23,560

   Note: If line 4 is more than $122,500 (more than $61,250 if MFS), stop here; your exemption deduction is $1,100 times the number of exemptions claimed.
5. Divide line 4 by $2,500 ($1,250 if married, filing separately). If the result is not a whole number, round it up to the next higher whole number (for example, round 0.0004 to 1). — 5. 10
6. Multiply line 5 by 2% (.02) and enter the result as a decimal amount. — 6. .20
7. Multiply line 1 by line 6. — 7. 2,640
8. Multiply line 7 by 66.67%. — 8. 1,760
9. Deduction for exemptions. Subtract line 8 from line 1. — 9. 11,440

EXAMPLE 6

Jack Emerald's AGI for 2006 is $142,302. He is married at the end of 2006, but files separately from his wife. He claims one personal exemption for himself. Because his AGI exceeds the $112,875 threshold for MFS, Emerald's personal exemption is $2,244.

Initial exemption		$3,300
AGI	$142,302	
AGI threshold for MFS	(112,875)	
Excess AGI	$ 29,427	
	÷ $1,250	
	23.54	
Rounded to nearest whole number	24	
	× .02	
	.48	
	× 3,300	
	$ 1,584	
	× 66.67%	(1,056)
Personal exemption		$2,244

This reduction in the personal and dependency exemption deduction for high-income taxpayers was enacted as part of the Tax Reform Act of 1986. The original tax law reduced total exemptions by 2% for each $2,500 increment ($1,250 for MFS) of AGI in excess of a threshold amount that varied by filing status. The Economic Growth and Tax Relief Reconciliation Act of 2001 repealed this limit over a four year period. In 2006 and 2007, reduction will equal two-thirds of 2%. In 2008 and 2009, the reduction will be one-third of 2%. After 2009, higher income taxpayers will no longer be required to reduce their exemption amounts. However, all changes made by the 2001 Tax Act, including this one, are set to expire after 2010. If that happens, then starting in 2011, the tax law will revert back to the original law requiring a full 2% phase down.

Personal Exemptions

Normally, a taxpayer deducts a personal exemption for him or herself. However, a person who qualifies as the dependent of another taxpayer cannot take a personal exemption. This rule applies even if the other taxpayer does not actually claim an exemption for the qualifying dependent.

The death of a taxpayer does not affect the amount of the personal exemption. The full exemption is deducted on a decedent's final return. No proration or reduction is necessary.

Exemptions for Spouse

Spouses are covered by special rules. A taxpayer may claim an exemption for the spouse (spousal exemption) on a joint return. When filing separately, a taxpayer may claim a spousal exemption only if the spouse:

1. Has no gross income, and
2. Does not qualify as a dependent of another taxpayer.

A spousal exemption is available for a spouse when spouses are separated by a temporary (pending) divorce decree. However, if the divorce is finalized by the end of the year, the taxpayer may not claim a spousal exemption.

The taxpayer takes a full exemption for a spouse who dies during the year. If the taxpayer remarries during that year, the Code denies a spousal exemption for the deceased.

Exemptions for Dependents

The taxpayer also claims an exemption for each person who qualifies as a "dependent." While minor children and elderly parents generally make up the taxpayer's list of dependents, others may qualify. Dependents fall into one of three groups: (1) qualifying relatives, (2) qualifying nonrelatives, or (3) qualifying children. Several requirements must be met if the taxpayer is to claim a dependency exemption for a person in one of these groups. If a person fails to meet any requirement, no dependency exemption may be taken for that individual. Also, the tax laws require that each dependent's social security number be shown on the tax return in order to claim the exemption.

An additional $500 exemption is allowed during 2005 and 2006 to taxpayers who provide rent-free housing to a "Hurricane Katrina displaced individual" for at least 60 consecutive days. **Hurricane Katrina displaced individuals** are persons whose principal place of abode on August 28, 2005 was in the Hurricane Katrina disaster area (as specified by the federal government) and (1) whose homes were located in the core disaster area (as specified by the federal government) and who were displaced from their homes, or (2) whose homes were located outside the core disaster area and who were displaced from their homes because their homes were damaged or because they were evacuated from their homes. Only one $500 additional exemption is allowed for each qualified displaced person. The exemption is taken in the year in which the 60 consecutive day period ends. Taxpayers can deduct up to $2,000 in total additional exemptions over the 2005 and 2006 tax years (the equivalent for providing housing to four qualified displaced persons). For example, a taxpayer who provides rent-free housing to a family of five from October 1, 2005 until May 1, 2006, would take an additional $2,000 exemption on their 2005 tax return (the 60 consecutive day period ends on November 30, 2005). To claim an additional exemption, taxpayers would be required to provide on their tax returns the SSN of the displaced person(s) for whom they are taking the additional exemption. This special exemption is not subject to the phase-down that applies to personal and dependency exemptions.

DEPENDENCY EXEMPTION REQUIREMENTS

The following sections examine the rules for each group of dependents. A dependent must meet all requirements listed for the applicable group. The taxpayer may claim an exemption for a qualified dependent, even if the dependent files a tax return. That dependent, however, cannot claim a personal exemption on his or her own return.

The taxpayer may also claim a full exemption for a dependent who either was born or died during the year. An exemption cannot be claimed for a stillborn child.

QUALIFYING RELATIVES

One group of persons who can be claimed as a dependent are qualifying relatives of the taxpayer. A qualifying relative is anyone who meets the following five tests but does not meet the definition of a "qualifying child" (defined later in the chapter).

1. Relationship test
2. Citizenship test
3. Support test
4. Gross income test
5. Joint return test

Relationship Test

For income tax purposes, the Code specifies the persons who qualify as a taxpayer's relatives. A relative does not have to live with the taxpayer to qualify as a dependent.

RELATIVES OF A TAXPAYER

- Brother, sister, half-brother, half-sister, stepbrother, or stepsister
- Child, grandchild or other descendant of the taxpayer, including a legally adopted child
- Father-in-law, mother-in-law, son-in-law, daughter-in-law, brother-in-law, or sister-in-law
- Nephew or niece (but only if related by blood, not by marriage)
- Parent, grandparent, or other direct ancestor (but not a foster parent, foster grandparent, etc.)
- Stepchild of the taxpayer, but not the stepchild's descendants
- Stepparent
- Uncle or aunt (but only if related by blood, not by marriage)

At the time of a couple's marriage, the law sets up permanent legal relationships with the in-laws. These relationships continue after divorce or death. Thus, a husband may claim an exemption for his mother-in-law after his wife's death. The mother-in-law, a permanent relative, does not have to live with her son-in-law. Aunts, uncles, nieces, and nephews are relatives only if their relationship to the taxpayer is established by blood (not through marriage). On a joint return, relatives of either spouse may qualify as dependents. Thus, even though the aunt of one's spouse does not qualify as one's relative, on a joint return the aunt is a relative of the spouse and may qualify as the couple's dependent.

EXAMPLE 7

Kay's mother has two sisters, Kay's Aunt Jane and her Aunt Reva. Jane's husband is Kay's Uncle Gene. Jane and Gene have a son, Joseph, who is Kay's cousin. For tax purposes, Kay's aunts qualify as her relatives since they are related to her by blood. Her Uncle Gene is not a relative since his relationship to Kay is established by his marriage to her Aunt Jane. Cousins are not included in the definition of a relative; thus, the Code does not count Joseph as Kay's relative.

EXAMPLE 8

Margaret and Ken Simms adopted Rachel in 1980 shortly after her birth. Rachel and her lineal descendents (children, grandchildren, etc.) are forever relatives of both Margaret and Ken.

EXAMPLE 9

Dan and April were married in 1998. At the time of their marriage, April's parents forever became Dan's mother-in-law and a father-in-law, respectively. Thus, they will qualify as Dan's relatives, even if he and April divorce or should April die.

Citizenship Test

A dependent usually must be a citizen of the United States. However, a resident of the United States, Canada, or Mexico can also qualify as a dependent. A foreign-born relative living in another country normally will not qualify.

Support Test

A taxpayer claiming a dependency exemption usually must provide more than 50% of the dependent's total support during the tax year. On a joint return, the support coming from either spouse counts. Support includes the taxpayer's payments for a variety of items, including food, clothing, education, medical and dental care, entertainment, transportation, and lodging.

When a taxpayer furnishes a dependent's lodging, the IRS treats its fair rental value as support. Fair rental value means the rent a taxpayer could expect to receive from a stranger for the same lodging. Fair rental value covers the use of one room or a proportionate share of a house. Capital items such as automobiles and furniture qualify as support if given to (or purchased for) a dependent. Also, support includes wedding costs paid for a dependent.

Support does not include scholarships received at educational institutions. For example, a relative receives a $4,500 college scholarship in a year in which the taxpayer provides $3,800 for the relative's support. If no other sources of support exist, the taxpayer meets the support requirements to claim a dependency exemption. Here, the law treats the taxpayer as providing 100% of the relative's support.

Usually the status and source of support funds make no difference. Social security income, student loans and welfare payments qualify if the dependent uses them to buy support items. However, the definition of support excludes amounts a state pays for training and educating a handicapped or mentally ill child. In addition, payments for life insurance and funeral expenses are not support expenditures.

To determine if a taxpayer provides over 50% of a dependent's support, the taxpayer calculates the dependent's total support, which consists of three amounts:

1. Fair rental value of lodging
2. Proper share of expenses incurred or paid directly to or for the dependent
3. Share of household expenses (such as food but not lodging) unrelated to specific household members

EXAMPLE 10

Martha Friedman's elderly parents have lived with Friedman for the entire year. They share the home with Friedman, her husband, and their dependent child. Friedman's parents do not pay any rent. The fair rental value of the lodging the parents use equals $3,800 ($1,900 for each parent). Friedman's father receives nontaxable social security income of $3,250, which he spends equally on support items for himself and for his wife. Dental expenses for Friedman's mother total $2,200. Friedman pays $700 of these expenses, and Friedman's brother pays $1,500. Friedman's parents eat their meals with Friedman's family. The cost of all meals consumed in the home equals $4,670. Each parent's share comes to $934 (1/5 of $4,670). The separate and combined support for Friedman's parents for the year are as follows:

	Mother	Father	Total
Lodging (fair rental value provided by Friedman)	$1,900	$1,900	3,800
Direct expenses:			
Social security spent by parents	1,625	1,625	3,250
Dental expense paid by Friedman	700	0	700
Dental expense paid by Friedman's brother	1,500	0	1,500
Share of food provided by Friedman	934	934	1,868
Total	$6,659	$4,459	$11,118

Friedman provided support of $3,534 ($1,900 + $700 + $934) to her mother and $2,834 ($1,900 + $934) to her father. Because this constitutes over 50% of the support for each parent, she may qualify to claim an exemption for each of them.

Multiple Support Agreement

Sometimes, a group of people (e.g., children) together provide for a dependent's (e.g., parent) support, but no one person (including the dependent) provides over 50% of the support. A special rule allows one member of the group to claim the exemption. The group member claiming the exemption may change from year to year. To qualify for the exemption, the group member must pass the following tests:

1. Provide more than 10% of the dependent's support,
2. Provide, with the other group members, more than 50% of the dependent's support, and
3. Meet the other four dependency tests

In addition, the group must agree as to the member receiving the exemption. It is not uncommon to rotate the dependency exemption among members from year to year. Once the group reaches this agreement:

1. Group members who do not claim the exemption need to complete and give to the claiming member a signed statement waiving their right to claim the exemption. The statement must include: (a) the applicable year, (b) the name of person being

supported, and (c) the name, address, and social security number of person waiving the exemption.

2. The claiming member holds on to this statement to support the claimed exemption. It is not filed with the tax return.
3. The claiming member completes and files Form 2120, Multiple Support Declaration, with the tax return. This form lists those eligible persons waiving their right to claim an exemption for the dependent in question.

EXAMPLE 11

Elaine lives with Logan for the entire year. Logan, Marty, Nancy, Michael, and Linda provide 100% of Elaine's support. Each person's relationship to Elaine, plus the amounts of support they provided are as follows.

	Amounts	**%**
Logan (Elaine's son)	$ 1,000	10
Marty (Elaine's son-in-law)	2,500	25
Nancy (Elaine's stepdaughter)	2,500	25
Michael (Elaine's brother)	2,500	25
Linda (Elaine's friend)	1,500	15
Total	$10,000	100%

Qualifying group members include Marty, Nancy, and Michael. Logan and Linda do not qualify as group members. Logan does not provide more than 10% of Elaine's support. Since Elaine is not one of Linda's relatives, for Elaine to pass the relationship test, she would have to live with Linda the entire year. Elaine qualifies as a relative to Marty, Nancy, and Michael. Thus, each pass the relationship test. Marty, Nancy, and Michael must decide which of them will claim the dependency exemption.

Information for Figure 1-3: Filled-In Form 2120

Using Form 2120, Helen B. Jones, acknowledges that she will claim the dependency exemption for Joseph R. Brown, her father. She lists her brother, Robert A. Brown, as an eligible person who is waiving his right to claim the father as a dependent.

Gross Income Test

For 2006, a dependent's gross income usually must be less than the $3,300 personal exemption amount. In addition to wages, dividends, and taxable interest, gross income includes gross receipts from rental property before expenses are deducted. To compute the gross income of a business, cost of goods sold are subtracted from net sales and any miscellaneous income is added to the difference. The definition of gross income excludes a dependent's tax-exempt municipal bond interest, many social security benefits, and all Medicare benefits.

Joint Return Test

To qualify as the dependent of another taxpayer, a married dependent cannot file a joint return. However, an exception applies when the IRS treats a married couple's joint return as strictly a means for claiming a refund of all prepaid taxes during the year. Generally, a joint return is a refund claim when it meets the following conditions:

FIGURE 1-3: Filled-In Form 2120

Form **2120**
(Rev. October 2005)
Department of the Treasury
Internal Revenue Service

Multiple Support Declaration

▶ **Attach to Form 1040 or Form 1040A.**

OMB No. 1545-0074

Attachment Sequence No. **114**

Name(s) shown on return: Helen B. Jones

Your social security number: 134 62 8736

During the calendar year 2006, the eligible persons listed below each paid over 10% of the support of:

Joseph R. Brown
Name of your qualifying relative

I have a signed statement from each eligible person waiving his or her right to claim this person as a dependent for any tax year that began in the above calendar year.

Robert A. Brown — 132 48 9866
Eligible person's name — Social security number

321 Valley Road, Cincinnati, OH 45209-2402
Address (number, street, apt. no., city, state, and ZIP code)

Eligible person's name — Social security number

Address (number, street, apt. no., city, state, and ZIP code)

Eligible person's name — Social security number

Address (number, street, apt. no., city, state, and ZIP code)

Eligible person's name — Social security number

Address (number, street, apt. no., city, state, and ZIP code)

1. Neither spouse is required to file a tax return.
2. A separate return filed by either spouse would not create a tax liability.
3. The only reason for filing a return is to get a refund of all federal taxes withheld.

EXAMPLE 12

Amy Adams provides 75% of her parent's support. Her father earns $3,100 at a part-time job. Her mother receives $4,000 of interest from tax-exempt bonds. To get a refund of withheld income taxes, the father and mother file a joint return. Because their combined gross income is only $3,100, the law does not require them to file a tax return. In addition, the father would have a zero tax liability on a separate return. Consequently, Adams can claim both the mother and father as dependents.

QUALIFYING NONRELATIVES

An unrelated person may qualify as the taxpayer's dependent. To qualify, a nonrelative must meet the following dependency tests that apply to relatives.

1. Citizenship test
2. Support test
3. Gross income test
4. Joint return test

In addition, an unrelated person must live with the taxpayer the entire year. However, if the relationship between the person and the taxpayer is violation of local law, no dependency exemption is allowed.

The death or birth of these persons will shorten the "entire year" requirement to that period during which they were alive. Another exception exists for temporary absences, such as attendance at school, vacations, and indefinite nursing home and hospital stays.

EXAMPLE 13

For the past two years, Nancy Sharp lived with her younger cousin Mary Blunt. In January, Sharp moved to a nursing home. The doctor informed Blunt that Sharp will stay in the nursing home indefinitely. For tax purposes, Sharp still lives with Blunt. Thus, if the other dependency tests are met, Blunt can claim a dependency exemption for Sharp.

QUALIFYING CHILDREN

A third group of persons who may qualify as a dependent are those who meet the rules of a qualifying child. **Qualifying children** must meet each of the six tests listed below.

1. **Relationship.** Qualifying children fall into one of these categories:
   a. Taxpayer's natural children, step-children, adopted children, eligible foster children, or descendants of any of these children. An eligible foster child is a child placed with the taxpayer by an authorized agency or by a court order.
   b. Taxpayer's brothers and sisters, half-brothers and half-sisters, step-brothers and step-sisters, or descendants of these siblings.
2. **Age.** Qualifying children must be under the age of 19, or under the age of 24 and full-time students. The age test does not apply to children who are permanently and totally disabled. Students need to meet the educational institution's full-time enrollment standard and attend classes during some part of each of five calendar months of the year. The institution must have a full-time faculty and course offerings plus a regular body of attending students. The qualifying child does not have to be attending school at the end of the year. If a qualifying child graduates, a taxpayer may claim an exemption if the other dependency requirements are met. A qualifying child who has a full-time day job and attends night school cannot be a full-time student. Enrollment in correspondence or employment training courses will not qualify a person as a full-time student.
3. **Principal Residence.** Qualifying children must have the same principal residence as the taxpayer for more than half of the year. Temporary absences, such as those due to illness, education, business, or vacations, are ignored.
4. **Support**. Qualifying children must not provide over half of their own support.
5. **Joint Return**. As with relatives, qualifying children may not file a joint return in situations where a tax return is required.
6. **Citizenship**. Qualifying children must be citizens of the United States, or residents of Canada or Mexico. However, an exception exists for foreign born children adopted by U.S. citizens living abroad. These children qualify as dependents if they live with the taxpayer the entire year.

Qualifying children are not subject to the "gross income" and "support" tests that apply to qualifying relatives. Also, children who are not "qualifying children" because they do not meet the requirements, may still qualify as dependents under the "qualifying relative" rules.

EXAMPLE 14

Mary's household includes her son, her son's daughter (Mary's granddaughter), her sister, her sister's son (Mary's nephew), her step-brother, and her step-brother's daughter (her niece). All of these individuals satisfy the relationship test with respect to Mary. Thus, if the other five tests are met, these persons may qualify as Mary's dependent under the dependency rules for qualifying children.

Dependency Exemption for Child of Divorced or Separated Parents

Another situation arises when the parents of a child (son or daughter) are divorced or separated. One parent can claim an exemption for the child if together the parents have custody of the child more than half of the year. The law gives the exemption to the parent with the longer actual custody (**custodial parent**). However, the custodial parent may give the exemption to the noncustodial parent. Here, the custodial parent completes Form 8332 (Figure 1-4) and gives it to the noncustodial parent. In place of Form 8332, the custodial parent may provide the noncustodial parent with a signed and dated release document stating that the custodial parent (signing parent) will not claim the exemption. The release may cover either one or several years. For each year affected, the noncustodial parent must attach the release statement to Form 1040 of Form 1040A.

In situations where multiple taxpayers qualify to claim a qualifying child as a dependent, the child can only be claimed by one person. The Code provides the following "tie break" rules.

- When only one of the child's parents is among the group of persons who qualifies to claim the child as a dependent, the dependency exemption goes to the parent.
- When both parents qualify to claim the child as a dependent, the exemption goes to the custodial parent.
- When both parents of the child qualify to claim the child as a dependent and the child spends equal amounts of time with each parent (no custodial parent), the exemption goes to the parent with the highest AGI.
- When neither parent qualifies to claim the child as a dependent, the dependency exemption goes to the (non-parent) taxpayer with the highest AGI who can claim the child as a dependent.

EXAMPLE 15

Hanna and her son, Jeffrey, live with Hanna's father. Hanna's AGI is $20,000; her father's AGI is $60,000. Jeffrey is a qualifying child to both Hanna and her father. As Jeffrey's mother, Hanna is entitled to claim the dependency exemption. AGI is irrelevant in this situation.

EXAMPLE 16

Roy and Karen Oswald divorced in 2004. Their 6-year-old son, Adam, spends half of his time with each parent. Roy's AGI is $32,000; Karen's is $34,000. Since there is no custodial parent, the dependency exemption goes to the parent (Karen) with the higher AGI.

The "qualifying child" requirements were first introduced in 2005. Taxpayers also use these rules to determine their eligibility for:

1. Head of household filing status
2. Earned income credit
3. Child tax credit
4. Child and dependent care credit

Information for Figure 1-4: Filled-In Form 8332

Using Form 8332, Anthony B. Black, the custodial parent, agrees not to claim an exemption for his daughter, Janet A. Black. The exemption belongs to Joyce C. Redding (Janet's mother), who files her tax return and Form 8332 with the IRS.

The custodial parent prepares Form 8332. The form contains two parts. The top part covers the current year, and the bottom part covers future years.

FIGURE 1-4: Filled-In Form 8332

Form **8332**
(Rev. January 2006)
Department of the Treasury
Internal Revenue Service

Release of Claim to Exemption for Child of Divorced or Separated Parents

► **Attach to noncustodial parent's return each year exemption is claimed.**

OMB No. 1545-0074

Attachment Sequence No. **115**

Name of noncustodial parent claiming exemption: Joyce C. Redding

Noncustodial parent's social security number (SSN) ► 693 : 24 : 6802

Part I **Release of Claim to Exemption for Current Year**

I agree not to claim an exemption for Janet A. Black
Name(s) of child (or children)

for the tax year 20 06.

Anthony B. Black — Signature of custodial parent releasing claim to exemption

280 : 64 : 2396 — Custodial parent's SSN

2-5-06 — Date

Note. If you choose not to claim an exemption for this child (or children) for future tax years, also complete Part II.

Part II **Release of Claim to Exemption for Future Years** (If completed, see **Noncustodial parent** on page 2.)

I agree not to claim an exemption for ______
Name(s) of child (or children)

for the tax year(s) ______.
(Specify. See instructions.)

Signature of custodial parent releasing claim to exemption | Custodial parent's SSN | Date

TAX BASE FORMULA—ANOTHER VIEW

Figure 1-5 provides another view of the tax base formula. It should enhance the meaning of new tax terms and concepts.

FIGURE 1-5: Computation of 2006 Taxable Income

Income from all sources:		
Rent from apartment, $2,400; Salary, $16,200; Dividends on common stock, $720; Interest on savings, $80; Municipal bond interest, $30		$19,430
Gross income exclusions:		
Municipal bond interest, $30		(30)
Gross income		$19,400
Deductions for AGI:		
Expenses of apartment (rental property)		(1,400)
AGI		$18,000
Deductions from AGI:		
Standard deduction (single person)	$5,150	
Exemptions (one personal exemption)	3,300	(8,450)
Taxable Income		$ 9,550

FILING STATUS

As previously stated, any taxpayer who files a return falls into one of five filing status groups. In some cases, filing status determines which tax return the taxpayer must file. The filing status also determines the standard deduction amount used in computing taxable income and the tax rate schedule or tax table used in calculating the tax liability.

Married couples generally have two filing options: married filing jointly or married filing separately. However, head of household status is available to married taxpayers in certain cases. The filing statuses available to unmarried persons include surviving spouse, head of household, and single. Both married filing jointly and surviving spouse share the most favorable tax rates, followed by head of household and then single. The least favorable of the tax rates apply to taxpayers who file married filing separately. Whenever possible, taxpayers would like to qualify for the most favorable tax rate possible for their marital status.

Married Filing a Joint Return

For tax purposes, a taxpayer's marital status is determined on the last day of the tax year. Thus, an individual who is married on the last day of the tax year may file a joint return with his or her spouse. Likewise, an individual who receives a legal divorce or separation before the end of the year may not file a joint return. However, when the divorce or separation has not been finalized at year-end, the couple may file a joint return.

A husband and wife can file a joint return even if only one has income. A husband and wife must both sign a jointly filed tax return. Usually, each spouse is liable for the entire tax liability. Thus, the law may enforce the collection of any tax liability against either spouse. This liability continues after a divorce.

When an asset is jointly owned, it can be seized to settle the debt of either owner.

Year of Death

Marital status is also determined at the date of death in the event that one spouse dies. The tax law generally requires a final income tax return for a decedent. The final return and any other return(s) still due would be filed by the executor, administrator, legal representative, or survivor. A widow(er) may file a joint return with the decedent. When the widow(er) files a joint return, two personal exemptions are allowed in the year of death.

Special reporting rules apply if the spouse dies in 2006 or dies in 2007 before the 2006 return is filed. The survivor should enter the word *deceased,* the name of the deceased spouse, and the date of death across the top of the return. In the signature space, the survivor should enter *filing as surviving spouse.* When someone other than the widow(er) is the personal representative of the deceased, that person's signature should appear in the deceased's signature line with the words *personal representative.*

If a widowed person remarries before the end of the year, the widow(er) may file a joint return with the new spouse. A remarried widow(er) cannot file a joint return with the deceased spouse even if the survivor's new spouse files separately.

Technical assistance should be obtained when affairs of a decedent are complex. Assistance is especially helpful when the problems relate to the determination of income and expenses properly reported on the decedent's final return. These items must be separated from those properly recognized after the date of death and are not included on the final return. For example, a cash-basis taxpayer includes in income only those amounts actually or constructively received as of the date of death. Income received after death is attributable to the beneficiary of the decedent's property.

Married Filing a Separate Return

When a husband and a wife have separate incomes, they may pay less taxes as a couple by filing separate returns. Taxpayers should compute their tax liabilities using both the joint and separate return statuses to see which one yields the least tax liability.

On rare occasion, a taxpayer may list a spouse as an exemption on a separate return. For the taxpayer to do so, the spouse cannot have any gross income or qualify as a dependent of another taxpayer. Also, the spouse cannot file a separate return. The taxpayer reports the full name and social security number of the spouse on the return.

Several factors may work against filing separate returns. Several tax credits, like the child and dependent care credit and the earned income credit, are not available to taxpayers who file married filing separately. If spouses live together at any time in the tax year and file separately, neither may claim an elderly or disabled person credit.

Filling Separate Returns in Community Property States

The laws of the state of the taxpayer's residence control whether property is considered community property or separate property. Classification of expenses as community or separate usually follows the classification of the income that caused their creation. If a taxpayer and spouse live in the same community property state and itemize deductions, they usually divide equally expenses paid from joint funds.

Election to File Joint or Separate Return

An election to file a joint or separate return for one year does not carry over to future years. Each year stands alone. After a couple files a joint return, they cannot change to separate returns after the due date of the tax return. However, spouses who file separately may change to a joint return even after the due date passes. This change must be made within three years of the due date of the tax return.

Surviving Spouse

For two tax years following the year of a spouse's death, special status as a "surviving spouse" may apply. Persons filing as a surviving spouse use the "married filing jointly" tax rates to compute their tax liability. They also use the married filing jointly basic and additional standard deduction amounts. For phasing down exemptions, surviving spouse status uses the "married filing jointly" threshold. It is important to note that even though surviving spouses use the joint return tax rates and other amounts they do not file a "joint return." Surviving spouse status is not available to a spouse who remarries. A widow(er) who remarries files a joint or separate return with his or her new spouse.

The Code classifies a **surviving spouse** as a qualifying widow(er) with a dependent son or daughter. Frequently, taxpayers confuse the special surviving spouse status with the common definition of surviving spouse (the spouse whose life continues after the other spouse dies). A surviving spouse under the common definition may or may not qualify for the special status. To qualify for the surviving spouse status for tax purposes, a widow(er) must:

1. Not remarry before the end of the year,
2. Qualify to file a joint return with the deceased spouse in the year of death, and
3. Furnish over 50% of the household maintenance costs where the widow(er) and a dependent son or daughter live for the entire year. This child may be the taxpayer's qualifying foster, adopted, natural, or stepchild.

Temporary absences from the household do not affect the ability to file as a surviving spouse. Thus, a son or daughter who attends a boarding school and returns home for vacation periods remains a member of the surviving spouse's household. Hospital stays receive the same treatment.

EXAMPLE 17

Ron Gentry maintains a household where he and his 12-year-old dependent daughter live. Ron's wife died in 2006. Ron files a joint return in 2006. Assuming Ron does not remarry and continues to claim his daughter as a dependent, he will file surviving spouse in 2007 and 2008.

Head of Household (HOH)

Tax rates for taxpayers filing as HOH are higher than for those who file married filing jointly. However, HOH rates fall below those for single persons. Head of household status usually applies to unmarried persons.

To qualify for HOH status, the taxpayer must furnish over half the cost of maintaining a household for a "qualifying child" (see definition presented earlier) or other person they claim as a dependent. With the exception of a dependent parent, these other dependents must live with the taxpayer for more than half of the year. In addition:

1. A "qualifying child" who is married must meet the dependency tests for a relative (see dependency tests for relatives presented earlier).
2. Other children who do not meet the definition of a "qualifying child" must also meet the dependency tests for a relative.
3. When a dependent child is used to obtain HOH status, custodial parents do not lose this status when they waive their right to claim a child's dependency exemption for their son or daughter.
4. A dependent parent need not live with the taxpayer. However, the taxpayer must provide over 50% of the parent's household costs for the year.
5. HOH status is not available if the dependency exemption is obtained through a multiple support agreement.
6. The taxpayer cannot qualify to file as a surviving spouse.

Maintaining a household means that the taxpayer pays more than 50% of the household costs for the year, which usually cover payments for the mutual benefit of household occupants. These costs include amounts paid for food, telephone, water, fuel, electricity, and repairs. They do not include the value of services supplied by the taxpayer or household members.

EXAMPLE 18

Candy Owen is single and maintains a household where she and her 25-year-old unmarried son live. Candy provides virtually all of her son's support during the year. The son is a full-time student and has no gross income. Because of his age, the son does not meet the definition of a qualifying child. He does, however, meet the dependency tests for a relative. Thus, Candy claims her son as a dependent and files as head of household.

EXAMPLE 19

Same as in Example 18, except that the son's gross income for the year is $4,000. Candy cannot claim her son as a dependent. The dependency tests for qualifying relatives require that the person's gross income not exceed the exemption amount ($3,300 in 2006). Candy's filing status is single.

EXAMPLE 20

Tom and Drew Perry divorced in 2004. Together they share custody of their 9-year-old son, Mark, for more than six months of the year and provide over half of his support. Tom has custody of Mark, but as part of the divorce, he waived his right to claim Mark as a dependent. Even though Drew is entitled to the dependency exemption for Mark, for purposes of filing as head of household, Mark is a qualifying child for Tom, but not for Drew. Thus, Tom files as head of household. Drew's filing status is single.

EXAMPLE 21

Pat Dorman's husband died in 2005. Pat maintains a household where she lives with her married son and his wife. The son and daughter-in-law each have gross income that exceeds the exemption amount. Thus, neither qualifies as Pat's dependent. Pat also pays over half of the costs to maintain a household for her aging mother, who qualifies as Pat's dependent. Pat files as head of household because she maintains a household for her dependent mother. A dependent parent is the only person who can qualify Pat for head of household filing status without having to live with her.

EXAMPLE 22

Same as in Example 21, except that Pat lives with her unmarried son, who is 18 and a full-time student. The son's gross income exceeds the exemption amount. The son is a qualifying child to Pat, and accordingly, she is entitled to claim him as a dependent. Pat files as surviving spouse in 2006 and 2007, the two tax years that follow her husband's death. In 2008, Pat will qualify to file as head of household, provided she continues to maintain a household where she lives with a qualifying child or other dependent for over half of the year.

Abandoned Spouses (Married Persons Who Live Apart)

Married persons who do not live with their spouses during the last six months of the year may qualify as abandoned spouses. For tax purposes, abandoned spouses are treated as not married and thus can qualify for head of household (HOH) filing status. To qualify for abandoned spouse treatment, the taxpayer and spouse need to meet the following tests.

1. The taxpayer does not file a joint return.
2. For more than six months of the year, the taxpayer lives with a son or daughter who is a natural, step-, adopted, or qualifying foster child.
3. The taxpayer pays more than 50% of the home's maintenance cost for the tax year.
4. At least one son or daughter qualifies as a dependent of the taxpayer. This rule does not apply if the taxpayer passes the tests to claim the exemption but, by written agreement, gives the exemption to the noncustodial parent.
5. The taxpayer did not live with his or her spouse at any time during the last six months of the tax year.

EXAMPLE 23

Jim and Danielle Nova are legally separated. They have not lived together since March, 2006. Although the Novas' two children live with Danielle, as part of the separation agreement, Jim is entitled to claim them as dependents. As of the end of 2006, the Novas' divorce had not been finalized. Even though Danielle cannot claim the children as dependents, she nonetheless meets the rules for an abandoned spouse. Her filing status for 2006 is head of household. Jim will claim the two children as his dependents, but his filing status is married filing separately.

Single Taxpayer

An unmarried person who does not qualify to file as surviving spouse or as head of household must file as a single taxpayer. A person separated by a final divorce decree or separate maintenance agreement files as a single taxpayer unless head of household filing status applies. Likewise, a widow(er) files as a single taxpayer unless the rules for filing as a surviving spouse or as head of household are met.

FILING REQUIREMENTS FOR INDIVIDUALS

Under our self-reporting tax system, persons who meet certain conditions must file an income tax return. Current filing requirements depend primarily on:

1. Net earnings from self-employment, or
2. Gross income and filing status.

The filing requirements apply to all minors and adults, single and married, U.S. citizens and resident aliens. These requirements can apply to nonresident aliens married to U.S. citizens. In addition, the filing requirements apply to resident aliens who subject their worldwide incomes to U.S. taxes by filing joint returns. Nonresident aliens who earn income in the U.S. must file income tax returns.

Self-Employment Income Test

A self-employed person files a tax return when net earnings from the self-employment is at least $400. Note that net earnings, not gross income, determines when a self-employed person must file a return. Generally, net earnings from self-employment is 92.35% of profits reported on Schedule C, Profit (or Loss) from Business (see Chapter 7).

Gross Income Test

When gross income reaches a certain level, a person must file a tax return. For non-self-employed individuals, the gross income filing thresholds are a combination of the exemption amount and the standard deduction available for the taxpayer (and the spouse if filing jointly). Filing requirements normally include the additional standard deduction available for attaining age 65. They do not take blindness into consideration. Nor do they consider dependency exemptions. Thus, for marrieds filing jointly, where one spouse is 65 and the other is blind, the filing requirement is $17,900. This represents a combination of the exemption amount, $6,600 (2 × $3,300); the basic standard deduction, $10,300; and the additional standard deduction for age 65, $1,000. Blindness is not a factor.

FIGURE 1-6: Who Must File a 2006 Return

U.S. citizens and resident aliens must file 2006 tax returns if their gross income amounts equal or exceed the following:

1.	Single	$ 8,450
	65 or over	9,700
2.	Married filing jointly	16,900
	One 65 or over	17,900
	Both 65 or over	18,900
3.	Married filing separately	3,300
4.	Head of household	10,850
	65 or over	12,100
5.	Surviving spouse	13,600
	65 or over	14,600

Single dependents must file a return when gross income exceeds *greater of* (i) $850 or (ii) earned income (up to $4,850) plus $300. Any "additional standard deductions" for age and blindness that apply increase the threshold. When there is unearned income, single dependents must file when unearned income exceeds $850 plus any additional standard deductions.

Married dependents must file a return when unearned income exceeds $850. They also must file when gross income exceeds the *greater of* (i) $850 or (ii) earned income (up to $4,850 plus $300. In both situations, the gross income filing threshold rises for the additional standard deductions for both age and blindness. A married dependent whose spouse files separately and itemizes deductions must file when gross income is $5 or more.

Note that in determining whether a dependent must file a tax return, the additional standard deduction for both age and blindness increase the gross income threshold. For example, the threshold for a blind, 65-year-old, single person claimed as a dependent on another's return is $3,350 in 2006 if the dependent has no earned income. This amount includes the basic standard deduction of $850 and a $2,500 additional standard deduction ($1,250 for age + $1,250 for blindness). Because the personal exemption for a dependent is zero, it does not affect a dependent's gross income threshold.

The following persons must file a return regardless of gross income:

1. A person with $400 of net earnings from self-employment,
2. A person receiving advanced earned income credit payments from his or her employer, and
3. A person receiving tips from which social security tax was not withheld.

EXAMPLE 24

John Jones works part time as a waiter at a local restaurant. Jones receives tips from customers that he does not report to his employer for income tax withholding purposes. Because Jones owes social security and Medicare taxes on these tips, he files a return and pays the tax.

TAX YEAR

Although most individuals use the calendar year for tax reporting, a few use a fiscal year. Some corporations and partnerships use a fiscal year. A **fiscal year** consists of any twelve-month period that ends on the last day of a calendar month other than December. Unless otherwise stated, this book assumes that all taxpayers use the calendar year.

Tax returns for individuals are due on or before the 15th day of the fourth month following the close of the tax year. For calendar year taxpayers, this is would be April 15 of the following year (corporate returns are due one month earlier). However, if this date falls on Saturday, Sunday, or a legal holiday, the due date is the next business day. A taxpayer files a timely return when the return is postmarked on or before the due date and it is properly addressed with the correct amount of postage.

TAXPAYER RESPONSIBILITIES

Under our self-reporting tax system, the law requires taxpayers to compute their tax liabilities, file proper returns on time, and pay the taxes when due. Taxpayers who do not meet these responsibilities face possible fines, penalties, and imprisonment. In addition, the IRS charges them interest on unpaid taxes. The IRS wants taxpayers to file their returns with the proper regional service centers.

Packaged filing materials sent to taxpayers at return time usually contain special mailing envelopes. The IRS encourages the use of these envelopes for mailing of completed returns. If the envelopes bear special codes, their use may speed return processing and reduce related costs. Taxpayers who expect to receive refunds should use the mailing envelopes when they are marked with special codes.

Taxpayers should develop and maintain organized tax record systems. In addition, they should carefully review their returns and correct any preparation errors before mailing their returns to the IRS.

Maintain Records

The taxpayer needs to keep adequate records to support all return items. The retention period usually ends six years after a return's due date (or filing date if later). However, the taxpayer should keep records showing the cost of property (home) longer. A photocopy of the return and tax calculations should also be retained. Last year's return and calculations can serve as a checklist for next year's return.

RECORD KEEPING—HOW LONG?

Keep records for general tax items for seven years.

- The normal closing date for a tax year is three years after the later of the return's due date or the filing date. If a taxpayer files a return for the year 20x0 before its due date (April 15, 20x1), tax year 20x0 closes on April 15, 20x4.
- The closing date for inadvertent omission of more than 25% of gross income reported on a return is six years after the later of the return's due date or the filing date. If a taxpayer files a return for the year 20x0 before its due date (April 15, 20x1), and the inadvertent omission rule for gross income applies, tax year 20x0 closes with April 15, 20x7.

- Keep general tax records for seven years after the year for which tax return is filed as support for IRS audit queries.

Keep records on *all* property for as long as it is owned plus seven years.

- Investment in depreciable property decreases yearly until property is fully depreciated. Property disposals may take place after property is fully depreciated. Taxpayers must report gain (and sometimes loss) on disposal of *all* property items. Keep *all* property records for the later of the last open tax year or the year of property disposal, plus seven years, as support for IRS audit queries.

Minimize Errors

Honesty and care in preparing returns will help reduce the chances of controversy. Taxpayers should follow these suggestions:

1. Get appropriate forms, schedules, and instructions. The IRS normally mails packages of forms, schedules, and instructions to last year's tax filers. A taxpayer who does not receive these items should get the materials from the local IRS office, the proper IRS regional service center, or from the IRS web page. The instructions contain tollfree telephone ordering numbers.
2. Study the instructions and assemble data before preparing the return.
3. Enter data on a tax organizer (if available).
4. Review the IRS identification label for correct facts. Supply all data. Check all calculations. Look for minor omissions due to carelessness or hasty processing.

STATUTORY LIMIT FOR ASSESSING ADDITIONAL TAXES

Normal Limit
Three years after the *later of* the return's due date or the filing date

Income Omissions
Six years after the *later of* the return's due date or the filing date for taxpayer's inadvertent omission of more than 25% of gross income reported on return

Fraudulent Return
Tax year never closes

PROPERTY DISPOSALS

Earlier, this chapter stated that gross income includes gains from disposing of property. It also stated that losses from disposing of business or investment property can qualify as deductions for AGI. The following overview shows how these transactions mesh with previously presented concepts and with the tax calculation process. Chapters 10 and 11 provide a more detailed discussion of property transactions.

Uses of Property

Taxpayers hold property for personal-use, for investment (income-producing), and for business purposes. The Code taxes most gains from property disposals. However, some disposals fall under the nontaxable sale or exchange rules (Chapter 10).

A taxpayer who disposes of personal-use property (e.g., automobile, personal residence, snowblower) at a loss cannot deduct it. An exception exists for stolen porperty or property destroyed by a casualty (Chapter 5). A sale of business or investment property at a loss generally creates a tax deduction for the seller. If the property is sold to a related party, however, the taxpayer cannot deduct the loss.

Capital Assets

Most property items owned by individuals fall under the broad grouping known as capital assets. Basically, the Code defines capital assets as all property except:

1. Property held for resale (inventory),
2. Real and depreciable property used in a trade or business,
3. Accounts receivable acquired in normal business operations, and
4. Most artistic works created by the taxpayer.

Thus, with few exceptions, capital assets include all property not listed above. These assets are generally investment property and property an individual's personal belongings.

Rate of Tax on Capital Gains

Ordinary income (e.g., salary and wages) may be taxed at 10%, 15%, 25%, 28%, 33%, or 35% depending on the amount of the taxpayer's taxable income. However, on sales of capital assets, a maximum tax rate of 15% (5% for persons in the 10% or 15% tax bracket) may apply. Generally, individuals must hold capital assets for more than one year to receive the special 15% (5%) tax rate. The sale of capital assets held for one year or less produces short-term capital gain or loss. Usually, the holding period for property starts the day after a taxpayer gets it. Thus, the purchase date belongs to the seller.

When the taxpayer's long-term capital gains exceed the long-term capital losses for the year, the excess is a net long-term capital gain. When long-term capital losses exceed long-term capital gains, the excess is a net long-term capital loss. A short-term capital loss results when short-term capital losses exceed short-term capital gains. When short-term capital gains exceed short-term capital losses, the excess is a net short-term capital gain. For the lower tax rates to apply, an individual must have "net capital gain," which is defined as the excess of net long-term capital gain over net short-term capital loss. If a taxpayer has both a net long-term and a net short-term capital gain, then net capital gain equals the amount of net long-term capital gain (since there is no net short-term capital loss). If the taxpayer has a net long-term capital loss, net capital gain is $0 (since there is no net long-term capital gain).

If losses exceed gains, an individual taxpayer can deduct up to $3,000 as a deduction "for AGI." Any remaining loss is deductible in future years. Chapter 11 provides in-depth coverage of capital gains and losses.

EXAMPLE 25

Mary Martin sold stock held for investment. The result was a $500 short-term capital loss. She also had a $2,000 gain from the sale of stock held for two years. Thus, she had a net capital gain of $1,500. A maximum tax rate of 15% applies to this gain.

EXAMPLE 26

Frank Wanto sells stock that results in a short-term capital loss of $6,000. He also sells stock held long-term at a gain of $2,000. The net result is a loss of $4,000. He deducts $3,000 as a deduction for AGI and the other $1,000 is available as a deduction next year.

REDUCING THE TAX BITE

A taxpayer has the right to use all legal means to avoid or postpone a tax. Through proper tax planning, the taxpayer may reduce the tax bite. As a basic goal, taxpayers should try to reduce current and future taxes. In addition, it is generally a good idea to defer taxes to future years if possible. Although personal aims can alter these goals, taxpayers should follow acceptable, proven principles when setting up tax plans.

TAX PLANNING PRINCIPLES

1. Acquire working knowledge of tax laws.
2. Plan transactions in advance to reduce taxes.
3. Maximize unrealized income.
4. Keep good records.

Acquire Working Knowledge of Tax Laws

The tax laws contain an overwhelming number of provisions covering a multitude of personal, business, and investment situations. The average taxpayer should not expect to develop even a general familiarity with all aspects of these laws. However, the "game of life" necessarily involves taxation, and it is difficult to play the game without a working knowledge of the basic rules. Taxpayers should focus on those laws that impact their particular personal and business environments. Developing a working knowledge of these rules is most beneficial in reducing current and future taxes. It will improve tax problem recognition skills. It will also lead to improved record keeping and reduced time for tax return preparation. For taxpayers who use computer tax software, knowledge of the tax laws will provide some assurance that the software produces proper results.

Although taxpayers may hire tax advisers to prepare their returns, knowledge of the tax laws should help minimize the adviser's fee. Most advisers base their fees on a return's complexity and the preparation time. For a knowledgeable taxpayer, the adviser will not have to charge for explaining simple transactions. Although advisers can prepare tax plans, they charge fees for their time. If the taxpayer wastes the adviser's time with general conversation, the taxpayer should expect a bill for this time. To the tax adviser, time is money.

Plan Transactions in Advance to Reduce Taxes

The way the law taxes a completed event or transaction is fairly clear. Consequently, it is important for taxpayers to plan their transactions in advance. Once an action is taken, the tax consequences are usually locked in. Proper planning of the action, however, can produce desirable tax results.

To facilitate planning, taxpayers should become familiar with methods that will:

1. Accelerate or postpone the recognition of revenue.
2. Accelerate or postpone the recognition of expenses.

Taxpayers also need to be aware of those available deductions and tax credits that will benefit their particular situations.

Taxpayers whose total itemized deductions are about the same as their standard deduction amount can use the bunching process, which results in a slowdown or a speedup of itemized deduction payments. By using the bunching process, the taxpayer influences the year in which an itemized deduction falls. Taxpayers who use this process itemize their deductions in one year and take the standard deduction in the next. Most taxpayers who use bunching find charitable contributions, medical expenses, property taxes, and state income taxes easiest to control.

Usually, taxpayers do not bunch their personal and dependency exemptions. However, taxpayers with dependents under the multiple support rules can use the bunching process. Also, couples might arrange their marriage dates (December versus January) to reduce the tax bite. By controlling the amount they pay to support other taxpayers, they can control the numbers of dependency exemptions they can claim. Finally, to some degree, taxpayers can control their tax credits. Usually, they should claim their credits as early as possible to generate cash (tax) savings sooner rather than later.

EXAMPLE 27

Bob Bruno files as a single taxpayer. Bruno's total itemized deductions are usually around $5,000, which includes $1,500 of charitable contributions he annually makes to his church each December. For 2006, the greater of Bruno's standard deduction or itemized deductions would be the $5,150 standard deduction for single taxpayers. If Bruno were to delay making the $1,500 charitable contribution for 2006 until early 2007, then he would still deduct $5,150 in 2006. However, his 2007 itemized deductions of $6,500 ($5,000 + $1,500) would exceed his standard deduction. By using this bunching strategy, Bruno would get a greater deduction from AGI in 2007.

Although tax planning is advantageous for everyone, the law restricts the advantages for the average employed person. Because the great majority of such people use the standard deduction, tax planning has its limits. Most tax benefits, unfortunately, favor business owners. People who have their own businesses stand to gain the most through tax planning. Those who are not business owners lose out. However, current trends show an increasing number of people starting their own businesses. Consequently, a greater number of taxpayers will benefit from comprehensive tax planning.

For business owners, greater deduction possibilities exist. They can convert many itemized deductions and nondeductible items into deductions from gross income. Knowledge of these situations is highly beneficial.

Timing the recognition of revenues and expenses is more easily done in a business setting. For example, taxpayers in service businesses who use the cash method of accounting can control end-of-year income. They might increase income by accelerating service billings or postpone it by delaying them. Other taxpayers who use the cash method of accounting (most persons) can control end-of-year gains and losses by advancing or delaying the closing dates in property transactions. Taxpayers who control transaction timing can adjust their income and deductions to take full advantage of the tax laws.

As indicated previously, taxpayers can reduce their taxes by careful planning. Some tax plans cover a short-term period, while others cover a long-term period. A short-term plan tries to reduce taxes over the next few years; a long-term plan tries to reduce them over a longer time span. Long-term plans usually involve complex techniques beyond the scope of this book. They include selecting retirement plans and developing estate, gift, and trust strategies. A taxpayer with stable income, deductions, exemptions, and credits usually uses a one-to-three-year tax plan. When uncertainty exists, the taxpayer should consider liberal, conservative, and middle-of-the-road assumptions. In all cases, the plan should be updated annually.

Maximize Unrealized Income

Some taxpayers want more after-tax dollars so they can spend it on consumable items. Others prefer to accumulate wealth. For those who want to accumulate wealth, the principle of maximizing unrealized income is important. Taxpayers can generally accumulate more wealth by investing in assets that produce income that is not currently taxable. Such income can then compound without being taxed each year.

The tax laws operate under the realization principle, where gains from property are not taxed until realized (the property is disposed of). Thus, taxpayer that invest in property that appreciates in value (e.g. stocks or real estate) can defer (delay) the tax on the unrealized gain (i.e., the appreciation).

Keep Good Records

To do a good job of tax planning, taxpayers need a good record-keeping system, which allows easy access to the nature, purposes, and amounts of old transactions. The underlying files should contain invoices, canceled notes or checks, payment receipts, property titles, and copies of old tax returns. An orderly indexing system helps taxpayers find stored documents. Finally, a good record-keeping system helps prevent taxpayers from overlooking deductions at tax return time.

WATCH FOR TAX OPPORTUNITIES

As taxpayers learn more about the tax laws, they can spot planning opportunities more quickly. Remember the basic goal: reduce current and future taxes. As you study each chapter, keep this goal in mind and watch for tax-reducing suggestions.

Name ______________________

Section ______________ Date ____________

QUESTIONS AND PROBLEMS

1. **Tax Laws.** Which amendment to the Constitution gave Congress the power to levy and collect income taxes? What was the origination date of our current income tax system?

2. **Tax Laws.** Susan Klammer engages a local tax professional to prepare her tax return each year. She sees no reason to learn more about the tax laws. At tax return time every year, all she wants to know is the fastest route to her tax preparer's office. After she files her return each year, she just wants to forget the whole thing. Explain why it would be to Klammer's advantage to know about the tax laws.

3. **Income Tax Objectives.** The primary objective of the U.S. income tax system is to raise revenues to cover government spending. Name some of the other objectives of our income tax system.

4. **Taxable Income Formula.** Is the basic taxable income formula the same for most taxpayers? What is the difference between the basic formula and the expanded formula used by individuals?

5. **Gross Income.** The Code lists a number of different gross income sources. When a taxpayer receives something that is not one of the listed items, is it exempt from tax? Explain your answer.

6. **Itemized Deductions.** Itemized deductions fall into one of seven groups. Two of the groups are (1) job expenses and most other miscellaneous itemized deductions and (2) other miscellaneous deductions. What are the other five groups?

7. **Standard Deduction.** Under what circumstances is an individual's standard deduction is $0?

8. **Itemized Deductions.** Clarence Archer is eligible to claim itemized deductions. Explain how itemized deductions relate to the determination of taxable income.

9. **Standard Deduction.** Who qualifies for the additional standard deduction? What additional amount is available?

10. **Standard Deduction.** Compute each taxpayer's 2006 total standard deduction.

    a. Bryce, age 20, is a full-time student. His parents claim him as a dependent. Bryce has interest income of $320 and wages from a part-time job of $3,800.

    b. Same as in Part a., except that Bryce's wages are $5,500.

    c. Heather, age 66, is married and files a separate return. Her husband also uses the standard deduction on his return.

    d. Juliet, age 19, is blind and claimed as a dependent by her parents. Her only income is $5,200 of interest.

11. Exemptions. Henry and Margaret were married on December 28. Henry, age 22 and a full-time student, had no gross income during the year. He lived with his parents and was supported by them prior to his marriage. Margaret's gross salary for the year was $35,000.

a. Under what circumstances is Margaret entitled to claim an exemption for Henry?

b. Under what circumstances are Henry's parents entitled to claim an exemption for him?

12. Exemptions. How many exemptions can be claimed on a joint income tax return by an employed taxpayer who is married and has two unmarried children? One child, a daughter age 17, has no income. The other child, a son age 22, is a part-time college student. The son earned $3,400 during the year. The taxpayer provides over half of each child's support. The taxpayer's spouse is not employed.

13. Exemptions. Kevin Kirby, age 67 and blind, is married to Susan Kirby, age 56 with good vision. They have a divorced daughter, age 37, who, along with her 18-year-old son, is living with them. The Kirbys provided more than half the support of their daughter and her son. The daughter has earned wages of $4,800, and her son, who is a part-time college student, has earned wages of $3,600. How many exemptions can the Kirbys claim on their 2006 tax return? Explain.

14. Exemptions. Vera and Billy Cohen were divorced during the year. Vera was awarded custody of the children, George, age 6, and Jean, age 9. There was no agreement about who would receive the dependency exemptions for the children. All support for the children is provided by Billy.

a. Who is to receive the dependency exemptions?

b. Might the other parent receive the exemptions under certain conditions? Explain.

15. Exemptions.

a. If Shirley Brown has a child born at 10 P.M. on December 31 of the taxable year, can she claim a full exemption for this child for the year or must she prorate her exemption?

b. If a qualifying dependent of a taxpayer dies on January 4 of the taxable year, may the taxpayer claim a full exemption for the dependent for the year or must the taxpayer prorate the exemption?

c. If Mark Freeze's divorce decree is finalized before the end of the taxable year, can he claim a full exemption for his spouse for the part of the year during which he was married? Explain.

16. Exemptions.

a. What is the amount of each exemption in 2006?

b. How does adjusted gross income affect the amount allowed for exemptions?

17. Exemptions. Jenna Wren claims one personal exemption and three dependency exemptions on her 2006 tax return. Her filing status is head of household. Compute Jenna's personal and dependency exemption deduction if her AGI is:

a. $184,500.

b. $218,300.

c. $318,600.

18. Exemptions. Andy Noble claims one personal and one dependency exemption. His filing status is single. Compute Andy's personal and dependency exemption deduction if his AGI is:

a. $164,000.

b. $196,300.

c. $218,600.

19. **Exemptions.** Isabel Retsma is married, but files separately from her husband in 2006. Isabel claims one personal exemption and no dependents. Compute Isabel's personal and dependency exemption deduction if her AGI is:

a. $114,200.

b. $168,600.

c. $189,100.

20. **Exemptions.** John and Jamie Kerr do not claim any dependents on their joint tax return. Compute their personal exemption deduction if the Kerrs' AGI is:

a. $214,600.

b. $268,000.

c. $289,900

21. Dependents. Indicate by inserting an *X* in the proper column which of the following persons are qualifying children or relatives of the taxpayer. Assume the listed person is not a member of the taxpayer's household.

	Qualifying Child?	*Relative?*
a. Taxpayer's cousin	______	______
b. Taxpayer's father	______	______
c. Taxpayer's foster mother	______	______
d. Taxpayer's stepsister	______	______
e. Taxpayer's brother-in-law	______	______
f. Taxpayer's grandchild	______	______
g. Taxpayer's half brother	______	______
h. Taxpayer's nephew by blood	______	______
i. Father of taxpayer's former spouse	______	______
j. Taxpayer's uncle (of deceased spouse)	______	______
k. Taxpayer's son-in-law	______	______
l. Taxpayer's grandfather	______	______
m. Taxpayer's mother-in-law (taxpayer's spouse deceased)	______	______

22. Filing Status. Using the following data, indicate each taxpayer's proper filing status for the current year.

a. Unmarried; divorced last year; no dependents __________________

b. Married; spouse has been properly claimed as a dependent on another taxpayer's return __________________

c. Married on December 31, no dependents __________________

d. Widower; spouse died last year; has a dependent 6-year-old child; has not remarried __________________

e. Married; separated from spouse by a separate maintenance decree; has no dependents __________________

f. Married; maintains a household for more than six months of the year for self and an adopted 4-year-old child who qualifies as a dependent; spouse left home on February 15 of current year and has not been seen since __________________

g. Unmarried; maintains a principal residence for entire year for self and an 8-year-old grandchild who is a dependent of the taxpayer __________________

h. Married; has $15,000 of gross income; spouse has filed a separate return __________________

i. Widower; spouse died January 16 last year; has not remarried; has a parent who lives alone; maintained parent's home for the entire year; parent qualifies as a dependent __________________

23. Filing Status. Graciela Autry provides 52% of the household costs for her widowed mother during the year and claims her as a dependent. Can Autry she file a return as a HOH if her mother lives alone? Explain the reason behind your answer.

24. Filing Requirements.

a. Andy Fryer, age 15, is claimed as a dependent on his parents' tax return. He earned $600 from his paper route and other after-school jobs. Fryer deposited most of his earnings in a savings account at the local bank. The bank notified him that his interest income was $400. Must Fryer file an income tax return for 2006? Provide a full explanation for your answer, including how his gross income threshold is calculated.

b. Marla Tierney, age 25, is claimed as a dependent on her parents' tax return. She is one of several full-time students at Milton College who received a $5,000 tax-free academic scholarship. Also, her bank informed her that she has interest income of $125. Tierney also earned $525 from her work as a self-employed, independent living consultant. Her expenses in connection with this work were $75. Must Tierney file an income tax return for 2006? Provide a full explanation for your answer, including how her threshold filing requirement is calculated.

c. Joe Blystone, age 20 and single, graduated from college last year. He has not been able to find a full-time job. For the current year, Blystone had gross income from a part-time job of $5,000. He had no other income sources. Although he used some of his earned income for support items, the majority of his support came from his parents. Blystone is not required to file a return for the current year. Should he file a return? Why or why not?

25. Fiscal Year. Most individual taxpayers use the calendar year for reporting their taxable income. However, a few use the fiscal year. What is a fiscal year?

26. Tax Years. The date a tax year closes is an important date from a taxpayer's point of view because it stops the IRS from assessing a tax deficiency on a closed tax year. It is an important date from the government's point of view because it stops a taxpayer from making a refund claim on a closed tax year.

a. If a taxpayer files her tax return for 2006 on April 1, 2007, when does her 2006 tax year close under the normal closing rule? In your answer, provide a specific closing date and time.

b. If a taxpayer inadvertently omits too much gross income from his or her income tax return, the normal closing of a tax year is extended by three years. What percentage of the taxpayer's gross income must be omitted from his or her income tax return in order for the closing year to be extended? As part of your answer, indicate exactly how this percentage is applied.

27. Standard Deduction and Filing Requirements. For each of the following sets of individuals determine (1) the amount of their total standard deduction and (2) the maximum amount of gross income each can have before having to file an income tax return for 2006.

a. Steve Odem is 36 years old. His filing status is single and his vision is 20/20.

b. Maggie Reed is a 70 years old widow. She is claimed as a dependent on her son's tax return. Maggie lost her vision three years ago and is permanently blind. Reed's gross income includes investment income, but no earned income.

c. Same as in Part b., except that Reed does not have any investment income.

d. Same as in Part b., except that Reed is not claimed as a dependent on her son's return.

e. Jeannie and Tom Ellis file a joint tax return. Jennie will turn 65 on January 1, 2007; Tom will turn 69 on March 8, 2007. Neither have any vision problems.

f. Sally James files a separate tax return from her husband. James is 40 years old and blind.

g. Joe Rawkin's wife died in 2006. Joe is 70 years old and has good eyesight. At the time of her death, Joe's wife was 60 and had good eyesight.

28. Capital Assets.

a. In the tax laws, a capital asset is defined in terms of what it is not. What broad groups of assets are not capital assets?

b. Explain the general holding period rules for capital assets, and indicate the time an asset must be held to receive a maximum tax rate of 15% (5%).

29. Capital Gains.

a. Jerry Long sold some stock certificates held for investment during the year. Describe how the following sales would be treated.

Stock	*Purchase Date*	*Sale Date*	*Cost*	*Selling Price*
ABC	1-5-06	11-5-06	$10,000	$ 8,000
XYZ	8-9-00	9-8-06	6,000	10,500

b. If the selling price of the stock Long sold on 11-5-06 were $5,000 (instead of $8,000), how would this affect his tax return?

30. Tax Planning.

a. Define the concept of tax planning and distinguish between short-term and long-term tax planning.

b. What is the primary reason for tax planning?

c. Identify three tax-planning principles that will help a taxpayer achieve a tax-planning objective.

d. Under what circumstances should a taxpayer plan to control the timing of payments that are deductible as itemized deductions?

31. Internet Problem: Downloading and Completing Form 2120.

Go to the IRS Web site, download Form 2120, and complete the form using the following information.

Helen Baker (SSN 123-45-6789) has acknowledged in writing that Jim Moon (SSN 987-65-4321), her brother, will take the dependency exemption in 2006 for their mother, Mary C. Moon.

Jim's address: 420 Dogwood Lane, Marlborough, NH 03455.

Helen's address: 5283 West Main Street, Keene, NH 03431.

See Appendix A for instructions on use of the IRS Web site.

2

Tax Determination, Payments, and Reporting Procedures

CHAPTER CONTENTS

CHAPTER OVERVIEW

Chapter 1 presented the tax structure and the process for determining taxable income. Chapter 2 shows how individual taxpayers compute the amount of their tax liability. It reviews the role of tax payments and personal tax credits in determining the final amount due to or from the government. The chapter illustrates Form W-2, Form 1040EZ, Form 1040A, and Form 4868, Application for Automatic Extension of Time to File U.S. Individual Tax Return.

INDIVIDUAL INCOME TAX RATES

The Code dictates the tax rates for individual taxpayers. It currently specifies the use of a progressive rate structure—the higher the income, the higher the tax rate that applies. The rates currently in use are 10%, 15%, 25%, 28%, 33%, and 35%. The IRS presents these rates to taxpayers as **Tax Rate Schedules** and a **Tax Table.** Understanding their structure helps in understanding the tax calculation process.

To determine their tax, taxpayers need to know their taxable income and filing status. Taxpayers with $100,000 or more of taxable income must use the Tax Rate Schedules. Those with less than $100,000 must use the Tax Table. All Form 1040EZ and Form 1040A filers must find their tax from the Tax Table. They cannot use the Tax Rate Schedules. The Tax Rate Schedules are found on the inside front cover of this book. The Tax Tables are in the back of the book.

TAXPAYER FILING STATUS BY RANK—LOWEST TO HIGHEST TAX FOR THE SAME AMOUNT OF INCOME

1. Married filing jointly (also, surviving spouse)
2. Head of household
3. Single
4. Married filing separately

Tax Rate Schedules

Four Tax Rate Schedules apply, one for each filing status. (Married filing jointly and surviving spouse use the same tax rates). The rate schedules are harder to use than the Tax Table. Taxpayers using a rate schedule must actually compute their tax. The Tax Table requires no tax calculations. Those using the Tax Rate Schedule to compute their tax follow these steps:

1. Choose the correct rate schedule (based on filing status).
2. Locate the proper income bracket and note the tax applicable to the lowest income in that bracket.
3. Subtract the lowest income in that bracket from taxable income.
4. Multiply this difference by the listed tax rate.
5. Add this result to the tax in Step 2 to arrive at the tax on taxable income.

Example 1 illustrates an application of the Tax Rate Schedules.

EXAMPLE 1

Four taxpayers each have $100,000 of taxable income. The following list shows their filing status and income tax for 2006 as determined from the Tax Rate Schedules found on the inside front cover of the book.

Filing Status	Tax
Married filing jointly	$18,115
Head of household	20,358
Single	22,332
Married filing separately	22,991

The following schedule illustrates the tax calculation for married couples that file jointly.

	Computations	Tax
Taxable income (TI)	$100,000	
Less	– 61,300*	$ 8,440
TI taxed at 25% rate	$ 38,700	
Multiply by rate	× 25%	9,675
Tax on TI of $100,000		$18,115

*Note that the 10% rate and the 15% rate combined produce a tax of $8,440 on $61,300 of TI (($15,100 × 10%) + ($46,200 × 15%)). Also note that the 25% rate applies only to the next $38,700 of TI. Then note that the total tax on $100,000 of TI equals the sum of the taxes for each income level, rounded to the nearest dollar.

TAX TABLE CANNOT BE USED BY

1. A person filing for a short period (less than 12 months) because of a change in accounting period
2. A person claiming the foreign earned income exclusion
3. A person filing Form 1040 with taxable income of $100,000 or more
4. An estate or trust

Tax Table

The tax law generally requires that taxpayers with less than $100,000 of taxable income use the Tax Table to determine their tax. Consequently, the great majority of people use the Tax Table. It is easier to use than the Tax Rate Schedules. Taxpayers simply locate their tax on a table listing taxes according to taxable income and filing status.

The Tax Table contains separate columns for each filing status. A surviving spouse uses the same column as married filing jointly. This book excludes the tables that go with Form 1040EZ and Form 1040A since they contain the same data. Thus, Form 1040EZ and Form 1040A filers can use the Tax Table in this book to find their tax.

If line 43 (taxable income) is—		And you are—			
At least	But less than	Single	Married filing jointly *	Married filing sepa-rately	Head of a house-hold
		Your tax is—			
23,000					
23,000	**23,050**	3,076	2,699	3,076	2,916
23,050	**23,100**	3,084	2,706	3,084	2,924
23,100	**23,150**	3,091	2,714	3,091	2,931
23,150	**23,200**	3,099	2,721	3,099	2,939
23,200	**23,250**	3,106	2,729	3,106	2,946
23,250	**23,300**	3,114	2,736	3,114	2,954
23,300	**23,350**	3,121	2,744	3,121	2,961
23,350	**23,400**	3,129	2,751	3,129	2,969

To determine the Tax Table amounts, the IRS uses the Tax Rate Schedules to compute the tax on the midpoint of each income range. For a single taxpayer with $23,000 of taxable income, the Tax Table shows a tax of $3,076. This amount represents the tax on $23,025 – the midpoint of $23,000 and $23,050. The table shows this amount on the line that includes taxable income of $23,000. Since the taxpayer is single, the proper tax appears at the intersection of the income line and the "Single" column.

INDEXING

Congress legislated inflation adjustments for the standard deduction, additional standard deduction, personal and dependency exemptions, tax rate schedules, and the Tax Table. It also legislated inflation adjustments for the AGI threshold where individuals begin to lose some of their deductions for personal and dependency exemptions and itemized deductions. The IRS adjusts these items each year using Consumer Price Index (CDI) data.

PAYING THE TAX LIABILITY

When it comes to paying the tax liability, taxpayers generally pay their taxes through the tax withholding system imposed on employers. They also may make estimated payments. Other factors that can reduce the tax liability include tax credits, prior year overpayments, excess social security taxes withheld, and payments mailed with their requests to extend the filing deadline of their tax returns. Taxpayers subtract these items from their tax liability to determine the net amount due to or from the government.

Federal Taxes Withheld

The law requires employers to withhold income, social security, and Medicare taxes from most wages they pay their employees. To help employers determine correct tax withholdings, the IRS publishes tax withholding tables. Employers use these tables in conjunction with personal data provided by their employees on Form W-4, Employee's Withholding Allowance Certificate (Chapter 13). By cross referencing the information on the two documents, employers can determine the proper amount of tax withholding.

Employers deposit withheld taxes with an authorized depository. Deposit frequency usually depends on the amount withheld for a specific base pay period. Employers file withholding and deposit reports with the government throughout the year and after the year ends.

Before February 1 of each year, employers inform employees of their previous year's earnings and tax withholdings. They use Form W-2, Wage and Tax Statement, to communicate this information to employees. When preparing their tax returns, employees enter their income tax withholdings in the "Payments" section.

Estimated Tax Payments

The tax withholding system only applies to certain types of income. In addition to wages, payers of interest, dividends and pensions are able to withhold taxes on the payee's behalf if the payee requests it. The taxes associated with all other types of income must be paid to the IRS through quarterly estimated tax payments. Thus, corporations and self-employed individuals usually must make estimated tax payments to cover the taxes owed on their business income. When self-employed persons also work as employees, they can have their employers withhold extra taxes from their pay to cover the taxes on their self-employment income.

Credits against the Tax

Tax credits reduce the tax liability dollar for dollar. Some are refundable, but most are nonrefundable. **Refundable credits** offset the taxpayer's tax liability, but they also entitle the taxpayer to a payment from the government when the amount of the credits exceeds the tax liability. **Nonrefundable credits,** in contrast, can only offset the taxpayer's tax liability. When such credits exceed the tax liability, taxpayers receive no payments for the excess.

CALCULATION OF TAXES OWED (TO BE REFUNDED)

Taxable income
× Tax rate
= Tax liability
– Nonrefundable tax credits
\+ Additions to tax
= Remaining tax liability (never less than $0)
– Refundable tax credits
= Final tax due (refund)

The only tax credits allowed on Form 1040EZ are the refundable credits for prepayment of income taxes and the earned income credit. Many of the personal tax credits can be claimed on Form 1040A; however, some require taxpayers to file Form 1040.

TAX CREDITS ALLOWED ON FORM 1040A

[Form 1040 filers can claim these and other business credits (Chapter 12).]

Nonrefundable

1. Child and dependent care credit
2. Elderly or disabled credit
3. Education credits
4. Retirement savings contributions credit
5. Child tax credit

Refundable

1. Earned income credit (EIC)
2. Additional child tax credit
3. Federal tax witholdings other prepayments
4. Excess OASDI withholdings
5. Credit for Federal telephone excise tax paid

Excess OASDI Witholding

In addition to withholding income taxes, employers also withhold FICA taxes as provided by the FICA Act. FICA taxes consist of two elements: (1) social security or OASDI taxes (old age, survivors, and disability insurance) and (2) Medicare or HI (hospital insurance) taxes. Taxpayers can determine their maximum OASDI tax for 2006 ($5,840.40) by multiplying $94,200 by 6.2%. They can determine their HI tax by multiplying their total wages, tips, and other compensation by 1.45%. No upper wage limit exists for the Medicare tax.

Sometimes employees have too much in OASDI taxes withheld from their wages. This can occur when a person works for two or more employers. Here, each employer withholds OASDI taxes on the first $94,200 of wages and HI taxes on all wages. When a taxpayer's Forms W-2, Wage and Tax Statement, show excess OASDI withholdings via multiple employers, they treat the excess as a tax payment which may result in a refund.

Form 1040A filers report excess OASDI withholdings as part of their total payments. To the left of the reporting line, they should write "excess OASDI" and the correct amount. Form 1040 filers also show excess OASDI withholdings on their return but on the line designated, "Excess social security and tier 1 RRTA tax withheld." Taxpayers cannot use Form 1040EZ to recover excess OASDI withholding. When one employer withholds too much in OASDI taxes, the taxpayer should ask that employer for a refund. Taxpayers cannot recover excess withholding by one employer on their tax returns.

On a joint return, a taxpayer and spouse determine their withheld OASDI taxes separately. Then, each determines if too much withholding took place by subtracting the tax from the proper maximum.

EXAMPLE 2

The Forms W-2 for Elaine and Morton Levy contain OASDI information shown below. Because Elaine works for only one employer, her withheld OASDI tax is limited to $5,840.40. Morton can claim a credit for excess OASDI withholdings of $1,599.60 ($7,440.00 – $5,840.40).

Employer	Total Social Security Wages Paid in 2006	OASDI Tax Withheld
Elaine Levy:		
Melville Dye Co.	$100,000	$5,840.40
Morton Levy:		
Step Mfg. Co.	$80,000	$4,960.00
United Corp.	40,000	2,480.00
	$120,000	$7,440.00

FORM W-2, WAGE AND TAX STATEMENT

Employers use Form W-2, Wage and Tax Statement, to report to the employee and the government the amount of the employee's earnings and taxes withheld. Form W-2 must be sent to the employee before February 1, and to the government before March 1.

Information for Figure 2-1: Filled-In Form W-2

Figure 2-1 shows a filled-in Form W-2 for Elaine Levy who works for Melville Dye Co.

Other Information

1: Levy's 2006 wages, **$120,000.00**
2: Federal income tax withheld, **$19,250.00**
3: Social security wages, **$94,200.00**
4: Social security tax withheld, **$5,840.40 ($94,200 × 6.2%)**
5: Medicare wages and tips, **$120,000.00**

6: Medicare tax withheld, **$1,740.00 ($120,000 × 1.45%)**
15: **WI** (Wisconsin)
16: State wages, tips, etc., **$120,000.00**
17: State income tax withheld, **$3,000.00**

FIGURE 2-1 Filled-In Form W-2

a Control number	22222	Void ☐	For Official Use Only ▶ OMB No. 1545-0008

b Employer identification number (EIN)	88-6045185	1 Wages, tips, other compensation	120000.00
		2 Federal income tax withheld	19250.00
c Employer's name, address, and ZIP code	Melville Dye Co. 2722 Grandview Blvd. Green Bay, WI 54307	3 Social security wages	94200.00
		4 Social security tax withheld	5840.40
		5 Medicare wages and tips	120000.00
		6 Medicare tax withheld	1740.00
		7 Social security tips	
		8 Allocated tips	
d Employee's social security number	259-42-8041	9 Advance EIC payment	
		10 Dependent care benefits	
e Employee's first name and initial	Elaine A.	11 Nonqualified plans	
Last name	Levy	12a See instructions for box 12	
Suff.		12b	
f Employee's address and ZIP code	104 Bayside Drive Green Bay, WI 54307	13 Statutory employee ☐ Retirement plan ☐ Third-party sick pay ☐	
		12c	
		14 Other	
		12d	

15 State	Employer's state ID number	16 State wages, tips, etc.	17 State income tax	18 Local wages, tips, etc.	19 Local income tax	20 Locality name
WI		100000.00	3000.00			

Form **W-2** **Wage and Tax Statement** **2006**

Department of the Treasury—Internal Revenue Service

For Privacy Act and Paperwork Reduction Act Notice, see back of Copy D.

Copy A For Social Security Administration — Send this entire page with Form W-3 to the Social Security Administration; photocopies are **not** acceptable.

Cat. No. 10134D

Do Not Cut, Fold, or Staple Forms on This Page — Do Not Cut, Fold, or Staple Forms on This Page

PERSONAL TAX CREDITS

Some tax credits are personal in nature. Others relate to business activities. This chapter covers personal tax credits. Chapter 12 covers the business tax credits.

Congress created several personal tax credits for individual taxpayers in an attempt to encourage specific desired behaviors and to provide tax relief to certain deserving taxpayer groups.

Child and Dependent Care Credit

A nonrefundable child and dependent care credit is available to individual taxpayers who pay someone to care for a qualifying person while they work. The credit equals a percentage of the qualified expenses incurred for the care of one or more qualifying persons. The percentage used in computing the credit ranges from 20% to 35%, depending on the taxpayer's AGI. Taxpayers with AGI up to $15,000 compute their credit by multiplying their qualified expenses by 35%. For each $2,000 range of AGI over $15,000, this percentage decreases by 1% until it reaches 20% for taxpayers with AGI in excess of $43,000. Figure 2-2 shows the percentages that apply for each level of AGI.

FIGURE 2-2 Child and Dependent Care Credit

Amount of AGI	Applicable Percentage	Amount of AGI	Applicable Percentage
Up to $15,000	35%	$29,001–31,000	27%
$15,001–17,000	34%	31,001–33,000	26%
17,001–19,000	33%	33,001–35,000	25%
19,001–21,000	32%	35,001–37,000	24%
21,001–23,000	31%	37,001–39,000	23%
23,001–25,000	30%	39,001–41,000	22%
25,001–27,000	29%	41,001–43,000	21%
27,001–29,000	28%	43,001 and over	20%

Qualifying Person

To claim the child and dependent care credit, one of the following persons must live with the taxpayer for more than half of the year:

1. A "qualifying child" (defined in Chapter 1) under age 13 whom the taxpayer may claim as a dependent
2. A dependent physically or mentally unable to provide self-care
3. A spouse physically or mentally unable to provide self-care

The taxpayer is not required to provide over half the cost of maintaining the household. For divorced or separated couples, only the custodial parent can claim the child as a qualifying person. Even when the custodial parent allows the noncustodial parent to claim the dependency exemption (by signing Form 8332; see Chapter 1), the noncustodial parent cannot claim the child as a qualifying person. When both parents share custody of a child, the parent having custody for the longer period during the year can claim the child as a qualifying person.

Qualified Expenses

For purposes of the child and dependent care credit, **qualified expenses** are the amounts taxpayers spend for child and dependent care so that they can work, look for work, or go to school. The costs can include payments for household services such as cooking and housekeeping. However, the main function for the cost must be to provide protection and care for a qualifying person.

The qualified expenses can be for services provided in the taxpayer's home or for out-of-home care. Payments to a relative count towards for the credit unless the taxpayer can claim the relative as a dependent. However, payments to the taxpayer's child under age 19 or the taxpayer's spouse never count as qualified expenses.

EXAMPLE 3

While Jerry Herron works, he pays his 22-year-old daughter, Frances, to watch his 4-year-old son, Adam. Herron claims Adam, but not Frances, as a dependent. Payments to Frances for Adam's care are qualified expenses. Had Frances been 18 years old or younger, or had Herron been able to claim Frances as a dependent, the payments would not have been qualified expenses.

Qualified expenses must be reduced by reimbursements the taxpayer receives from an employer's dependent care plan when the reimbursements are excluded from the taxpayer's gross income. Reimbursements that are included in the taxpayer's gross income do not affect the child and dependent care credit calculation. Chapter 4 describes an employer's dependent care plans in greater detail.

EXAMPLE 4

During the year, Al and Lisa Sherman paid a child care provider $6,000 to look after their sons (ages 4 and 6) while they worked. Al was reimbursed $2,500 from his employer's dependent care plan. The $2,500 was not included in Al's gross income. The Shermans' qualified expenses equal $3,500 ($6,000 – $2,500).

Limitations on Qualified Expenses

The Code initially limits the amount of qualified expenses to (i) $3,000 for one qualifying person and (ii) $6,000 for two or more qualifying persons. These dollar amounts are also reduced by nontaxable reimbursements that the taxpayer receives from an employer's dependent care plan. The Code further limits these amounts to the taxpayer's earned income. If the taxpayer is married, the maximum qualified expenses are limited to the earned income of the spouse with the lower income. Thus, the **maximum qualified expenses** are the *lesser of* (i) the taxpayer's qualified expenses reduced by nontaxable reimbursements from a dependent care plan, (ii) the dollar limits ($3,000/$6,000) reduced by the nontaxable reimbursements, or (iii) the taxpayer's earned income.

EXAMPLE 5

Marlin Jones paid $2,100 in qualified expenses for the care of his 7-year-old son. Jones's earned income equals $15,500. Jones's maximum qualified expenses are $2,100 [the *lesser of* (i) qualified expenses of $2,100, (ii) $3,000 limit for one qualifying person, or (iii) earned income of $15,500].

EXAMPLE 6

Assume the same facts as in Example 5, except that Jones's employer has a dependent care plan, from which Jones received $1,500 during the year. The $1,500 reimbursement was excluded from Jones's gross income. Jones's maximum qualified expenses are $600 [the *lesser of* (i) $600 of qualified expenses ($2,100 – $1,500), (ii) $1,500 limit for one qualifying person ($3,000 – $1,500), or (iii) earned income of $15,500].

Usually a taxpayer's spouse must be gainfully employed to be eligible for the child and dependent care credit. However, a special rule applies to spouses who are either disabled or full-time students. This rule assumes the spouse has some earned income for purposes of the earned income limitation. The amount deemed earned is $250 per month when the taxpayer has one qualifying person and $500 when the taxpayer has two or more qualifying persons. The amount is "deemed" earned only for those months that the spouse is a full-time student or incapable of self-care.

EXAMPLE 7

Paul and Kim Foxx have two children, ages 3 and 5. During the year Paul worked full time. Kim did not work, but she attended college full time 10 months out of the year. The Foxxes paid $6,600 in qualified child care expenses. Since the Foxxes' child care expenses of $6,600 exceed the $6,000 limit for two or more qualifying persons, the Foxxes' qualified expenses are initially limited to $6,000. Even though Kim does not work, she is "deemed" to be employed for 10 months of the year with earnings of $5,000 ($500 × 10 months). Since Kim's "deemed" earnings of $5,000 are less than $6,000, the Foxxes' maximum qualified expenses for purposes of computing the child and dependent care credit are $5,000.

Giving a full-time student spouse who does not work "deemed" earned income allows the couple to claim the child care credit. Without this special rule, the *lesser of* qualified expenses, the dollar limits, and earned income would be zero in situations where the full-time student spouse did not work. However, these "deemed" earnings are not income to the spouse and are not included in the calculation of the couples' taxable income.

To compute the child and dependent care credit, taxpayers multiply their maximum qualified expenses by the applicable percentage (from Figure 2-2).

EXAMPLE 8

Assume that in Example 7, the Foxxes' only source of gross income is Paul's wages of $29,500. Taxpayers with AGI between $29,001 and $31,000 multiply their maximum qualified expenses by 27% (Figure 2-2). Thus, their nonrefundable child and dependent care credit would equal $1,350 ($5,000 x 27%). Although Kim's "deemed" wages of $5,000 were used in determining the couple's maximum qualified expenses, they are not real wages. Accordingly, they are not used in computing the couple's AGI.

Claiming the Credit

To claim the child and dependent care credit, married taxpayers must file a joint return. An exception exists for abandoned spouses. Taxpayers filing Form 1040 claim this credit on Form 2441, Child and Dependent Care Expenses. Taxpayers filing Form 1040A claim the credit on Schedule 2 (Form 1040A), Child and Dependent Care Expenses. Because Schedule 2 (Form 1040A) and Form 2441 are similar, only Form 2441 is illustrated in Figure 2-3.

Information for Figure 2-3: Filled-In Form 2441

Patricia E. and Clyde R. Smith live and work in Chicago. Patricia works full time during 2006 and earns $30,000. Clyde works part time during the year and earns $10,500. The Smiths have no other sources of income and have no deductions for AGI. The Smiths' 6-year-old twins live with them and qualify as their dependents. For the year, the Smiths paid Lucy Burke $6,200 to care for their children after school until the Smiths got home from work.

Other Information

2(c): Qualified expenses paid during the year for the qualifying person listed in column (a), **$3,100.00** (one-half of $6,200) This amount is listed for both Michael and Mary.

7: AGI, **$40,500.00** ($30,000 + $10,500)

8: Decimal amount from table, **.22** (based on AGI of $40,500)

10: Form 1040, line 46, minus Form 1040, line 47, **$1,799.00.**

FIGURE 2-3 Filled-In Form 2441, Page 1

Form **2441** Department of the Treasury Internal Revenue Service (99)

Child and Dependent Care Expenses

▶ Attach to Form 1040 or Form 1040NR.

▶ See separate instructions.

OMB No. 1545-0074 **2006** Attachment Sequence No. **21**

Name(s) shown on Form 1040: Patricia E. and Clyde R. Smith

Your social security number: 376 78 7371

Before you begin: You need to understand the following terms. See **Definitions** on page 1 of the instructions.

- **Dependent Care Benefits**
- **Qualifying Person(s)**
- **Qualified Expenses**

Part I Persons or Organizations Who Provided the Care—You **must** complete this part. (If you need more space, use the bottom of page 2.)

1 (a) Care provider's name	(b) Address (number, street, apt. no., city, state, and ZIP code)	(c) Identifying number (SSN or EIN)	(d) Amount paid (see instructions)
Lucy Burke	1606 N. Elm Street Chicago, IL 60631-1314	677-33-6605	6,200 00

Did you receive dependent care benefits? No ▶ Complete only Part II below. Yes ▶ Complete Part III on the back next.

Caution. If the care was provided in your home, you may owe employment taxes. See the instructions for Form 1040, line 62, or Form 1040NR, line 57.

Part II Credit for Child and Dependent Care Expenses

2 Information about your **qualifying person(s).** If you have more than two qualifying persons, see the instructions.

(a) Qualifying person's name — First	Last	(b) Qualifying person's social security number	(c) **Qualified expenses** you incurred and paid in 2006 for the person listed in column (a)
Michael	Smith	559 47 8493	3,100 00
Mary	Smith	559 47 8403	3,100 00

		Line	Amount
3	Add the amounts in column (c) of line 2. **Do not** enter more than $3,000 for one qualifying person or $6,000 for two or more persons. If you completed Part III, enter the amount from line 33	3	6,000 00
4	Enter your **earned income.** See instructions	4	30,000 00
5	If married filing jointly, enter your spouse's earned income (if your spouse was a student or was disabled, see the instructions); **all others,** enter the amount from line 4	5	10,500 00
6	Enter the **smallest** of line 3, 4, or 5	6	6,000 00
7	Enter the amount from Form 1040, line 38, or Form 1040NR, line 36 — 7: 40,500 00		
8	Enter on line 8 the decimal amount shown below that applies to the amount on line 7	8	X .22

If line 7 is:

Over — But not over	Decimal amount is	Over — But not over	Decimal amount is
$0—15,000	.35	$29,000—31,000	.27
15,000—17,000	.34	31,000—33,000	.26
17,000—19,000	.33	33,000—35,000	.25
19,000—21,000	.32	35,000—37,000	.24
21,000—23,000	.31	37,000—39,000	.23
23,000—25,000	.30	39,000—41,000	.22
25,000—27,000	.29	41,000—43,000	.21
27,000—29,000	.28	43,000—No limit	.20

		Line	Amount
9	Multiply line 6 by the decimal amount on line 8. If you paid 2005 expenses in 2006, see the instructions	9	1,320 00
10	Enter the amount from Form 1040, line 46, minus any amount on Form 1040, line 47, or Form 1040NR, line 43, minus any amount on Form 1040NR, line 44	10	1,799 00
11	**Credit for child and dependent care expenses.** Enter the **smaller** of line 9 or line 10 here and on Form 1040, line 48, or Form 1040NR, line 45	11	1,320 00

For Paperwork Reduction Act Notice, see page 4 of the instructions. Cat. No. 11862M Form **2441** (2006)

Child Tax Credit (CTC)

In 2006, taxpayers may be able to claim a $1,000 tax credit for each "qualifying child" (defined in Chapter 1). However, the child must be under the age of 17 as of the end of the tax year and claimed as a dependent on the taxpayer's tax return. For divorced or separated parents, the CTC is available only to the parent that claims the child as a dependent.

The full CTC is available to unmarried taxpayers whose AGI does not exceed $75,000. For married couples that file jointly, the full CTC is available as long as AGI does not exceed $110,000. It cannot exceed $55,000 if they file separate returns. (A married toaxpayer that files head of household under the abandoned spouse rules is considered unmarried.) The taxpayer loses $50 of the credit for each $1,000 (or portion thereof) that AGI exceeds these thresholds. For purposes of the CTC, AGI is computed by adding back excluded foreign income (discussed in Chapter 4).

EXAMPLE 9

In 2006, Tom and Carol Normand file a joint tax return. They claim their two children, ages 8 and 9, as dependents. The Normands' AGI is $116,400. Because AGI exceeds $110,000, the Normands are not entitled to the full $2,000 CTC ($1,000 × 2). Their $1,650 CTC is determined as follows.

Initial CTC ($1,000 × 2 qualifying children)		$2,000
AGI	$116,400	
Less: AGI threshold for MFJ	(110,000)	
Excess AGI	6,400	
	÷ $1,000	
	6.4	
Number of $1,000 intervals (or portion thereof)	7	
	× $50	(350)
CTC for 2006		$1,650

EXAMPLE 10

In 2006, John Myers files as head of household and claims his 10-year-old nephew as a dependent. Myers's 2006 AGI is $77,430. Since a nephew is a qualifying child, Myers computes the $850 CTC as follows.

Initial CTC ($1,000 × 1 qualifying child)		$1,000
AGI	$77,430	
Less: AGI threshold for unmarried taxpayers	(75,000)	
Excess AGI	2,430	
	÷ $1,000	
	2.43	
Number of $1,000 intervals (or portion thereof)	3	
	× $50	(150)
CTC for 2006		$850

The phase out of the CTC is $50 per $1,000 of excess AGI (or portion thereof). Thus, the amount of AGI which causes the CTC to be completely phased out depends not only on the taxpayer's filing status, but also on the number of qualifying children.

While the CTC is generally nonrefundable, it may be a refundable credit for certain taxpayers. However, before computing the refundable portion of the CTC, taxpayers first compute the amount of the CTC that is nonrefundable. They do this by subtracting from their total tax liability all nonrefundable personal credits, other than the CTC. These include the child and dependent care credit, the education credits, the adoption credit, the retirement savings contributions credit, and the foreign tax credit. The *lesser of* (i) the remaining tax liability or (ii) the taxpayer's CTC represents the nonrefundable portion of the credit. Taxpayers report their nonrefundable CTC on Form 1040 (line 53) or Form 1040A (line 33).

EXAMPLE 11

In 2006, Kate and Matthew Stewart file a joint return. They claim their three children (all under age 17) as dependents. The Stewarts' AGI is $55,970 and their total tax liability is $3,621. They are only entitled to one tax credit—the CTC. Since the Stewarts' AGI is less than $110,000, they do not lose any of their $3,000 CTC ($1,000 × 3 qualifying children) due to excess AGI. The Stewarts report the entire $3,000 CTC as a nonrefundable credit on Form 1040 (line 53).

Calculation of Refundable Child Tax Credit

The amount of the taxpayer's CTC that cannot be taken as a nonrefundable credit is refundable up to 15% of the taxpayer's earned income in excess of $11,300. Taxpayers compute the refundable portion of the CTC on Form 8812, Additional Child Tax Credit, and report this amount on Form 1040 (line 68) or Form 1040A (line 41).

EXAMPLE 12

In 2006, Joel and Ruth Floyd file a joint return. They claim their two children, ages 8 and 10, as dependents. The Floyds' AGI is $41,700, which includes Joel and Ruth's wages of $40,200. The Floyds' tax liability before credits is $1,979, and they are entitled to a $1,130 child and dependent care credit. After subtracting this credit from their taxes, the Floyds' remaining tax liability is $849 ($1,979 – $1,130). Since their AGI is less than $110,000, the $2,000 CTC ($1,000 × 2) is not reduced due to excess AGI. Therefore, they report $849 as their nonrefundable CTC on Form 1040 (line 53). They then complete Form 8812, Additional Child Tax Credit, to determine the refundable portion of their CTC.

Because of the rest of the CTC of $1,151 ($2,000 – $849) does not exceed 15% of the Floyds' earned income in excess $11,300 (15% × ($40,200 – $11,300) = $4,335), the Floyds report a $1,151 refundable CTC on Form 1040 (line 68).

Information for Figure 2-4: Filled-In Form 8812

Figure 2-4 shows a completed Form 8812, Additional Child Tax Credit, for the Floyds in Example 12.

Other Information

1: CTC to be claimed ($1,000 × 2 children), **$2,000**

2: Nonrefundable CTC, **$849**

4: Taxable earned income, **$40,200**

5: Taxable earned income in excess of $11,300, **$28,900**

FIGURE 2-4 Filled-In Form 8812

Form **8812**

Department of the Treasury
Internal Revenue Service (99)

Additional Child Tax Credit

1040 / 1040A / 1040NR → 8812

Complete and attach to Form 1040, Form 1040A, or Form 1040NR.

OMB No. 1545-0074

2006

Attachment Sequence No. **47**

Name(s) shown on return: Joel and Ruth Floyd

Your social security number: 861 22 9418

Part I All Filers

1	Enter the amount from line 1 of your Child Tax Credit Worksheet on page 42 of the Form 1040 instructions, page 39 of the Form 1040A instructions, or page 20 of the Form 1040NR instructions. If you used Pub. 972, enter the amount from line 8 of the worksheet on page 4 of the publication		2,000 00
2	Enter the amount from Form 1040, line 53, Form 1040A, line 33, or Form 1040NR, line 48		849 00
3	Subtract line 2 from line 1. If zero, **stop**; you cannot take this credit		1,151 00
4a	Enter your total earned income (see instructions on back)	40,200 00	
b	Nontaxable combat pay (see instructions on back) [4b]		
5	Is the amount on line 4a more than $11,300? ☐ **No.** Leave line 5 blank and enter -0- on line 6. ☐ **Yes.** Subtract $11,300 from the amount on line 4a. Enter the result	28,900 00	
6	Multiply the amount on line 5 by 15% (.15) and enter the result		4,335 00
	Next. Do you have three or more qualifying children? ☐ **No.** If line 6 is zero, stop; you cannot take this credit. Otherwise, skip Part II and enter the **smaller** of line 3 or line 6 on line 13. ☒ **Yes.** If line 6 is equal to or more than line 3, skip Part II and enter the amount from line 3 on line 13. Otherwise, go to line 7.		

Part II Certain Filers Who Have Three or More Qualifying Children

7	Withheld social security and Medicare taxes from Form(s) W-2, boxes 4 and 6. If married filing jointly, include your spouse's amounts with yours. If you worked for a railroad, see instructions on back		
8	**1040 filers:** Enter the total of the amounts from Form 1040, lines 27 and 59, plus any uncollected social security and Medicare or tier 1 RRTA taxes included on line 63. **1040A filers:** Enter -0-. **1040NR filers:** Enter the total of the amounts from Form 1040NR, line 54, plus any uncollected social security and Medicare or tier 1 RRTA taxes included on line 58.		
9	Add lines 7 and 8		
10	**1040 filers:** Enter the total of the amounts from Form 1040, lines 66a and 67. **1040A filers:** Enter the total of the amount from Form 1040A, line 40a, plus any excess social security and tier 1 RRTA taxes withheld that you entered to the left of line 43 (see instructions on back). **1040NR filers:** Enter the amount from Form 1040NR, line 61.		
11	Subtract line 10 from line 9. If zero or less, enter -0-		
12	Enter the **larger** of line 6 or line 11		
	Next, enter the **smaller** of line 3 or line 12 on line 13.		

Part III Additional Child Tax Credit

13	**This is your additional child tax credit**	1,151 00

Enter this amount on Form 1040, line 68, Form 1040A, line 41, or Form 1040NR, line 62.

1040 / 1040A / 1040NR

For Paperwork Reduction Act Notice, see back of form. Cat. No. 10644E Form **8812** (2006)

For most taxpayers, the refundable credit does not exceed 15% of the taxpayer's earned income in excess of $11,300. However, in situations where the refundable credit is limited, a special rule for calculating the refundable CTC exists for taxpayers with three or more qualifying children. This special rule is complex and beyond the scope of this textbook. Those interested in learning more about the calculation of the refundable CTC for taxpayers in this special situation should refer to Publication 972.

Higher Education Credits

Two nonrefundable education credits are available for individual taxpayers who pay tuition and fees during the year on behalf of eligible students. The first credit is the HOPE scholarship credit. The second is the lifetime learning credit. Taxpayers cannot claim both credits for the same student. However, they can claim both credits in the same year, but for different students. These credits are not available once a taxpayer's AGI exceeds a certain level. Married persons that file separately are not eligible for the education credits.

HOPE Scholarship Credit

The HOPE scholarship credit provides for a maximum $1,650 tax credit for *each* eligible student. *Eligible students* for purposes of the HOPE tax credit are students enrolled in their first two years of post-secondary education. The student must also be enrolled at least half-time during one semester or quarter during the year. To qualify for the HOPE credit, the tuition normally must be paid in the same year as the year in which the semester or quarter begins. However, tuition paid in one year for a course that starts within three months of the next year, qualifies for the credit in the year it is paid. Thus, tuition paid in 2006 for classes that begin before April 1, 2007, counts towards the 2006 education credit.

To compute the amount of HOPE credit, taxpayers add 100% of the first $1,100 of tuition and fees to 50% of the *lesser of* (i) $1,100 or (ii) the tuition and fees in excess of $1,100. The maximum HOPE tax credit is $1,650 [(100% × $1,100) + (50% × $1,100)].

EXAMPLE 13

On December 22, 2005, Brad Waltham paid $800 for his son's tuition for the Spring 2006 semester. The son is a freshman during the Spring semester. On August 15, 2006, Waltham paid $840 for his son's Fall 2006 tuition. Waltham's HOPE credit for 2006 equals $840. The $800 paid in 2005 qualified for the HOPE credit in 2005.

EXAMPLE 14

On January 5, 2006, Edgar Putnam paid $1,800 for tuition to attend classes full time at a local college during the Spring semester. On August 3, 2006 he paid $2,000 for tuition for the Fall semester. Putnam is a sophomore during all of 2006. Putnam's HOPE credit for 2006 equals $1,650 ($1,100 + (50% x $1,100)).

A provision in the Gulf Opportunity Zone Act of 2005 doubles the amounts used in computing the HOPE credit for eligible students who attend education institutions located in the Hurricane Katrina disaster area (as specified by the federal government). Thus, the HOPE credit for these students will be 100% of the first $2,200 of their qualified expenses plus 50% of their next $2,200. The maximum HOPE credit for each eligible student is $3,300. The tax law only requires that the student be enrolled and pay tuition at an eligible institution. There is no requirement that the student be a resident of the disaster area. Also, the Act permits certain room and board expenses to be included in computing the amount of the HOPE credit.

Lifetime Learning Credit

The lifetime learning credit provides for a maximum $2,000 tax credit *per year.* This differs from the HOPE credit where the maximum credit is $1,650 *per eligible student.* Other differences between the two credits are as follows.

1. A student need not attend at least half-time to qualify for the lifetime learning credit.
2. Tuition paid for education that extends beyond the first two years of college qualifies for the lifetime learning credit.

To compute the lifetime learning credit, taxpayers multiply 20% by the *lesser of* (i) $10,000 or (ii) qualified tuition costs for the year. As with the HOPE tax credit, tuition paid in 2006 for classes beginning before April 1, 2007, qualify for the lifetime learning credit in 2006.

EXAMPLE 15

On August 10, 2006, Becky Brown paid $3,000 to cover her tuition for the Fall semester. Brown is a graduate student in the nursing program at State University. Brown's lifetime learning credit for 2006 equals $600 ($3,000 × 20%).

EXAMPLE 16

On December 16, 2006, Joe and Ann Johnson paid $6,000 for their daughter's and $7,000 for their son's Spring 2007 tuition. The spring semester began on January 16, 2007. Both children are seniors in college. The Johnson's lifetime learning credit for 2006 equals $2,000 [(*lesser of* $10,000 or $13,000) × 20%]. The maximum lifetime learning credit is $2,000 *per taxpayer* each year.

The eligibility requirements for the HOPE tax credit are more stringent than for those for the lifetime learning credit. However; the maximum credit for the HOPE tax credit is $1,650 for each eligible student. The maximum credit for the lifetime learning credit is $2,000 per tax return.

EXAMPLE 17

On January 5, 2006, Angie Edwin paid tuition of $3,800 to attend college full time during the Spring semèster. On June 25, 2006, she paid $1,600 for tuition for summer classes. On August 13, 2006 she paid $3,300 for tuition for the Fall semester. Edwin is a junior during all of 2006. Her 2006 lifetime learning credit equals $1,740 (20% x ($3,800 + $1,600 + $3,300).

Earned Income Credit

The earned income credit (EIC) is a special tax credit that provides some tax relief to lower-paid workers. This refundable credit really works like a "negative income tax." Taxpayers showing a small amount of AGI may actually receive a government subsidy by claiming the EIC. Taxpayers receive this money when the EIC exceeds their tax liability.

Congress also designed this credit to encourage people to become contributing, working members of society. Within limits, as a person's earned income (wages) goes up, the amount of this credit increases. This is intended to encourage people to seek employment.

Taxpayers Qualifying for Credit

To qualify for the EIC, taxpayers must either

1. Be over age 24, but not over 64, as of the end of the tax year and not be claimed as a dependent by another person, or
2. Have a "qualifying child."

Taxpayers claiming the EIC for a qualifying child must provide the child's name, age and social security number (SSN). If any of these are not provided, the EIC will be denied with respect to that child. In Chapter 1 "qualifying children" were defined as those persons that pass four tests: relationship, residency, age and citizenship. In addition, they cannot provide over half of their own support. For purposes of the EIC, qualifying children must only meet the four tests. The rule that they not provide over half of their own support does not apply.

While unmarried children do not have to be the taxpayer's dependents, married children must qualify as dependents of the taxpayer. However, the custodial parent receives the EIC when the dependency exemption for a married child has been given to the noncustodial parent.

Married couples must file a joint return to claim the EIC. If the parents are divorced or separated and the child is a qualifying child for both parents, the child is treated as a qualifying child of the custodial parent. If there is no custodial parent, then the parent with the highest AGI gets to claim the EIC for the child. In other situations where the child may be a qualifying child for more than one taxpayer, the credit goes to the child's parent. If neither person is the child's parent, then the taxpayer with the highest AGI gets to claim the EIC for the child. These tie-break rules are the same as those used in determining which person can claim the dependency exemption for a qualifying child (from Chapter 1).

EXAMPLE 19

Jake, age 26, and his son, age 5, live with Jake's father Frank for the whole year. Jake's AGI is $15,000, and Frank's AGI is $20,000. The son is a qualifying child to both Jake and Frank. Since Jake is the parent, he claims the EIC.

Taxpayers with disqualified income in excess of $2,800 cannot take the EIC. Disqualified income includes dividends, interest (including tax-exempt interest), net rental income, and net capital gain.

Credit Rates and Dollars

Generally, as taxable earned income increases, the EIC increases. However, the credit is phased out when income exceeds a certain level. This phase-down is based on the higher of earned income or AGI. Taxpayers use the Earned Income Credit Worksheet to compute the proper EIC using the Earned Income Credit tables (found after the tax tables at the back of the textbook). Taxpayers retain this worksheet for their records. However, those with qualifying children must also complete and file Schedule EIC.

For purposes of the EIC, earned income does not include nontaxable employee compensation such as: salary deferrals under retirement plans, salary reductions under cafeteria plans, dependent care and adoptions benefits, and educational assistance benefits.

Advance Payment of EIC

Employees with a qualifying child may have the right to an advance payment of the EIC. Taxpayers without a qualifying child cannot receive an advance payment of EIC. Eligible employees wanting to receive advance EIC payments must file with their employer Form W-5, Earned Income Credit Advance Payment Certificate. Employees who do not want to receive advance EIC payments can claim the credit when they file their returns and do not file a Form W-5.

Taxpayers who receive an advance EIC payment must file Form 1040 or 1040A. They must file a return even if they do not meet the general tax return filing requirements. The employer reports the amount of advance EIC payments to employees and to the IRS on Form W-2, Wages and Tax Statement (box 9). When advance credit payments exceed a taxpayer's allowable EIC, the taxpayer must return the excess to the government.

Information for Figure 2-6: Filled-In Schedule EIC Worksheet

James Williams earned $9,665 in wages in 2006. His employer did not withhold income taxes. James filed a Form W-5 and received $630 in EIC advance payments. Sarah Williams earned $6,100 in wages. Her employer withheld $384 for federal income taxes. The Williamses also earned $1,150 of interest on their joint savings account.

The Williamses file a joint tax return and claim dependency exemptions for their three children. Figure 2-7 shows the Williamses' filled-in Schedule EIC. They claim a $4,512 EIC on Form 1040 (line 66a) and attach Schedule EIC (Form 1040A or 1040) to their tax return. The Williamses report their $630 advance EIC payment on Form 1040 (line 61). The $630 advance reduces the amount of the Williamses' refund they get for 2006 from claiming the EIC.

FIGURE 2-6 Filled-In Schedule EIC Worksheet

1. Enter your earned income. ($9,665 + $6,100) — 1. 15,765
2. Look up the EIC on the amount on line 1 above in the EIC Table. Enter the credit here. — 2. 4,536
3. Enter your AGI. ($15,765 + $1,150) — 3. 16,915
4. Are the amounts on lines 1 and 3 the same?
   Yes. Skip line 5; enter the amount from line 2 on line 6
   No. Go to line 5.
5. If you have:
   a. No qualifying children, is the amount on line 3 less than $6,750 ($8,750 if married filed jointly)?
   b. 1 or more qualifying children, is the amount on line 3 less than $14,850 ($16,850 if married filed jointly)?

   Yes. Leave line 5 blank; enter the amount from line 2 on line 6

   No. Look up the EIC on the amount on line 3 above in the EIC Table. Enter the credit here. — 5. 4,512
6. **Your earned income credit** (the smaller of line 2 or line 5). — 6. 4,512

FIGURE 2-7 Filled-In Schedule EIC

SCHEDULE EIC
(Form 1040A or 1040)

Department of the Treasury
Internal Revenue Service (99)

Earned Income Credit

Qualifying Child Information

Complete and attach to Form 1040A or 1040 only if you have a qualifying child.

1040A 1040 EIC

OMB No. 1545-0074

2006

Attachment Sequence No. **43**

Name(s) shown on return: James R. and Sarah O. Williams

Your social security number: 282 56 9320

Before you begin: See the instructions for Form 1040A, lines 40a and 40b, or Form 1040, lines 66a and 66b, to make sure that **(a)** you can take the EIC, and **(b)** you have a qualifying child.

CAUTION

- If you take the EIC even though you are not eligible, you may not be allowed to take the credit for up to 10 years. See back of schedule for details.
- It will take us longer to process your return and issue your refund if you do not fill in all lines that apply for each qualifying child.
- Be sure the child's name on line 1 and social security number (SSN) on line 2 agree with the child's social security card. Otherwise, at the time we process your return, we may reduce or disallow your EIC. If the name or SSN on the child's social security card is not correct, call the Social Security Administration at 1-800-772-1213.

Qualifying Child Information	Child 1	Child 2
1 Child's name If you have more than two qualifying children, you only have to list two to get the maximum credit.	First name / Last name: Martha A. Williams	First name / Last name: Karl B. Williams
2 Child's SSN The child must have an SSN as defined on page 44 of the Form 1040A instructions or page 48 of the Form 1040 instructions unless the child was born and died in 2006. If your child was born and died in 2006 and did not have an SSN, enter "Died" on this line and attach a copy of the child's birth certificate.	826 34 3710	850 21 5263
3 Child's year of birth	Year 1 9 9 2 *If born after 1987, skip lines 4a and 4b; go to line 5.*	Year 1 9 9 5 *If born after 1987, skip lines 4a and 4b; go to line 5.*
4 If the child was born before 1988— **a** Was the child under age 24 at the end of 2006 and a student?	☐ **Yes.** *Go to line 5.* ☐ **No.** *Continue.*	☐ **Yes.** *Go to line 5.* ☐ **No.** *Continue.*
b Was the child permanently and totally disabled during any part of 2006?	☐ **Yes.** *Continue.* ☐ **No.** The child is not a qualifying child.	☐ **Yes.** *Continue.* ☐ **No.** The child is not a qualifying child.
5 Child's relationship to you (for example, son, daughter, grandchild, niece, nephew, foster child, etc.)	daughter	son
6 Number of months child lived with you in the United States during 2006 • If the child lived with you for more than half of 2006 but less than 7 months, enter "7." • If the child was born or died in 2006 and your home was the child's home for the entire time he or she was alive during 2006, enter "12."	12 months *Do not enter more than 12 months.*	12 months *Do not enter more than 12 months.*

TIP

You may also be able to take the additional child tax credit if your child **(a)** was under age 17 at the end of 2006, **and (b)** is a U.S. citizen or resident alien. For more details, see the instructions for line 41 of Form 1040A or line 68 of Form 1040.

For Paperwork Reduction Act Notice, see Form 1040A or 1040 instructions. Cat. No. 13339M **Schedule EIC (Form 1040A or 1040) 2006**

Adoption Credit

Taxpayers can take a nonrefundable tax credit for qualified adoption expenses. For adoptions of U.S. citizens or residents, the credit is taken in the year the expenses are paid only if the adoption is finalized in that year or was finalized in a prior year. Otherwise the credit is taken in the year after the year in which the expenses are paid. This is often called the one-year delay rule. When the adoption expenses are spread over more than one year, the limits on the amount of the credit for the tax year in which the adoption occurs are used. The adoption credit can be taken even if the adoption is never finalized. For adoptions of a foreign child, the adoption credit can only be taken in the year the adoption is finalized. The limitations in effect in the year the adoption is finalized are used in computing the credit.

For 2006, the amount of the adoption credit is limited to the first $10,960 of qualified adoption expenses. The amount of the credit is cumulative. Thus, if expenses are paid over 2005 and 2006 for an adoption finalized in 2006, the $10,960 limit would apply. The amount of the adoption credit is further limited for taxpayers with AGI in excess of $164,410 in 2006. Those with AGI in excess of this amount reduce their credit by:

(the *lesser of* $10,960 or adoption expenses) ×
(AGI in excess of $164,410 ÷ $40,000)

EXAMPLE 20

In 2005, Lester and Amy Holden paid $12,000 in qualified adoption expenses. The adoption was finalized in 2006. The Holdens' AGI in 2005 was $169,450. It was $179,450 in 2006. Since the adoption was not finalized in 2005, the Holdens will take a $6,839 adoption credit in 2006.

Lesser of (i) $10,960 or (ii) $12,000 of qualified adoption expenses	$10,960
Less phase-out of credit [$10,960 × (($179,450 – $164,410) ÷ $40,000)]	(4,121)
Adoption credit	$6,839

Qualified adoption expenses include the expenses directly related to the legal adoption of a child who is under the age of 18 at the time of the adoption or is physically and mentally incapable of self-care. Such costs include adoption fees (provided they are reasonable and necessary), court costs, and attorney's fees. Both the qualified adoption expenses and the $10,960 limit must be reduced by nontaxable reimbursements that the taxpayer receives from an employer's adoption assistance plan (discussed in Chapter 4).

EXAMPLE 21

Assume the same facts as in Example 20, except that the Holdens receive $2,000 from an employer adoption assistance plan. The Holdens' credit would be $5,591.

Initial credit, *lesser of* ($10,960 – $2,000) or ($12,000 – $2,000)	$8,960
Less phase-out of credit [$8,960 × (($179,450 – $164,410) ÷ $40,000)]	(3,369)
Adoption credit	$5,591

The full $10,960 credit is allowed for the adoption of a special needs child regardless of the amount actually paid for qualified adoption expenses.

Form to Use

Taxpayers claiming the adoption credit complete Form 8839, Qualified Adoption Expenses. The adoption credit is nonrefundable. However, any portion of the credit not allowed because the taxpayer does not have enough tax liability can be carried over for five years. Taxpayers claiming the adoption credit enter the amount of the credit on Form 1040 (line 54).

Retirement Savings Contributions Credit

Certain taxpayers may take a nonrefundable tax credit for contributions (including amounts withheld from their paychecks) to retirement savings plans. The credit is in addition to any deduction or exclusion relating to the retirement plan contribution. The credit applies to traditional and Roth IRAs and other qualified retirement plans such as 401(k) plans, 403(b) annuities, 457 plans, SIMPLE and SEP plans.

The amount of the credit is based on filing status and AGI. The credit is determined by multiplying the contribution (not to exceed $2,000 per person) by a percentage taken from the following table which is based on AGI levels. The contribution eligible for the credit must be reduced by any distributions received from qualified retirement plans.

Joint Return		Head of Household		All Other Cases		Applicable %
Over	**Not Over**	**Over**	**Not Over**	**Over**	**Not Over**	
$ 0	$30,000	$ 0	$22,500	$ 0	$15,000	50%
30,000	32,500	22,500	24,375	15,000	16,250	20
32,500	50,000	24,375	37,500	16,250	25,000	10
50,000	—	37,500	—	25,000	—	0

Joint filers with AGI in excess of $50,000 receive no credit. For heads of households the amount is $37,500, and for all others it is $25,000. No credit is available for dependents and full-time students. Also, taxpayers must be at least 18 years old to qualify for the credit.

EXAMPLE 22

Dave Ogg reports $31,000 of AGI on his joint return. During the year Ogg contributed $4,000 to his Roth IRA. Ogg reports a tax credit of $400 ($2,000 × 20%) for his Roth IRA contribution on Form 1040 (line 51) or Form 1040A (line 32).

Foreign Tax Credit

The foreign tax credit applies to both individuals and corporations. This credit reduces the U.S. income tax by the taxes paid to foreign countries. The credit results in more equitable tax treatment, because it prevents foreign income from being taxed twice—once by the foreign country and again by the United States. As an alternative, individuals can use foreign taxes paid as an itemized deduction. When taxpayers use foreign taxes as a credit, the credit cannot exceed the U.S. income tax that applies to the foreign income. Form 1116, Foreign Tax Credit, is available from the IRS and should be used to compute the amount of foreign tax credit.

Alternative Motor Vehicle Credit

The alternative motor vehicle credit is a nonrefundable tax credit that consists of four tax credits for new vehicles purchased and placed in service after 2005. One of these credits is the qualified hybrid motor vehicle credit. This credit is available starting in 2006 to individuals and businesses that buy a new hybrid car or truck. The amount of the credit ranges from $400 to $3,400 based on car's fuel economy. The IRS certifies which vehicles qualify for the credit. The formula used to compute the amount of the credit is complex. However, the IRS announces the amount of credit available for each eligible model.

The hybrid vehicle tax credit is available for new vehicles purchased after 2005. Vehicles purchased for resale do not qualify for the credit. The amount of the credit will be reduced once 60,000 qualifying vehicles for the model have been sold. Thus, tax credits for the more popular models will be phased out sooner than for less popular models.

Residential Energy Credits

Various residential energy tax credits are available to individuals for purchases made during 2006 and 2007. These nonrefundable tax credits include a 10% credit for buying qualified home energy efficiency improvements and a 30% alternative energy credit. The intent of these credits is to encourage taxpayers to make purchases during 2006 and 2007 to make their homes more energy efficient.

The 10% credit applies to eligible home energy improvements. This includes adding insulation, replacing windows, and installing high efficiency heating and cooling equipment. It also includes buying and installing skylights, metal roofs and storm doors. The credit is also allowed for costs related to residential energy property expenses. These include $50 for each advanced main air circulating fan, $150 for each qualified natural gas, propane, or oil furnace or hot water heater, and $300 for each item of qualified energy efficient property. The maximum credit that can be taken during 2006 and 2007 combined is $500, with the credit for windows being capped at $200.

The alternative energy credit is available to individuals that buy and install qualified solar water heating, solar electricity equipment, and fuel cell property during 2006 and 2007. The costs for fuel cell property qualify only if purchased for the taxpayer's principal residence. The limit is $500 for each half kilowatt of capacity of fuel cell property installed each year. There is no maximum dollar limit for the purchase of fuel cell property. Solar equipment qualifies for the credit if purchased for any residence owned used by the taxpayer. This would include second residences and vacation homes. The annual credit for each type of solar equipment purchased is 30% of the costs, with an annual limit of $2,000. Thus, a taxpayer can claim up to a $4,000 credit in 2006 – $2,000 for solar water heating system and $2,000 for solar electricity equipment. The 30% alternative energy credit is separate from and in addition to the 10% credit for energy efficiency improvements.

EXAMPLE 23

During 2006, Tim Elwood pays $2,500 to have storm doors installed on his residence and pays $6,000 to have new energy efficient windows installed. He also purchases a solar water heating system and solar electricity equipment for his home. The systems cost $8,000 and $6,200, respectively. Elwood's nonrefundable residential energy credit equals $4,310. The credit includes a $450 credit for home energy improvements ((10% x $2,500) + ($6,000 x 10%, but not to exceed $200 for new windows)) plus a $3,860 alternative energy credit ((30% x $8,000, not to exceed $2,000 for the solar water heating system) + (30% x $6,200 for the solar electricity equipment)). In 2007, Elwood is entitled to take up to a $50 credit ($500 maximum in 2006 and 2007 less $450 claimed in 2006) for purchases of qualified home energy improvements (other than windows, for which he took the maximum credit for in 2006).

Other Personal Tax Credits

Elderly or Disabled Credit

Taxpayers age 65 or older, and taxpayers under 65 who retire with a permanent and total disability, may receive a special nonrefundable credit. Primarily, this credit benefits elderly, low-income taxpayers who receive little or no social security income. When both spouses are 65 or older, the maximum credit available under this provision is $1,125. It decreases as AGI and social security payments increase.

Form 1040A filers use Schedule 3 (Form 1040A) to compute their credit for the elderly or the disabled. Form 1040 filers use Schedule R to determine their credit. The credit is not available to Form 1040EZ filers.

Credit for Federal Telephone Excise Tax

The Code imposes an excise tax on long-distance telephone usage. The Federal government decided in May 2006 to stop this tax. It is allowing taxpayers to claim a refund for taxes paid from March 1, 2003 until July 31, 2006. They do this by taking a refundable tax credit for the amount of excise taxes paid on their 2006 income tax returns. Instead of using actual taxes paid, individuals with one exemption can claim a credit of $30. Those with two exemptions can claim a credit of $40. Taxpayers filing a tax return claiming three exemptions can get a $50 credit. Those with four or more exemptions can claim a credit of $60. This refundable credit can be taken on Form 1040EZ, Form 1040A or Form 1040.

FORM 1040EZ

Preparers of Form 1040EZ, Income Tax Return for Single and Joint Filers with No Dependents, will find it easy to use. It is a one-page form that is fairly simple to complete. Taxpayers using this form may report only certain types of income: wages, salaries, tips, taxable scholarships/fellowships, unemployment compensation, interest totaling $1,500 or less, and Alaska Permanent Fund dividends. They have only two possible deductions: the standard deduction and exemptions. Taxpayers who are dependents, however, receive no exemption, and their standard deduction may require an adjustment.

Also available on Form 1040EZ is the earned income credit (EIC). Taxpayers who do not have a "qualifying child" in their household may use Form 1040EZ to claim the EIC. The presence of a "qualifying child" requires Form 1040A or Form 1040. Other tax credits also require use of these forms.

FORM 1040EZ TESTS—USERS MUST

1. Be single or joint filer, under age 65 and not blind
2. Claim the standard deduction
3. Not claim any dependency exemptions
4. Have gross income only from wages, salaries, tips, taxable scholarship or fellowship grants, interest, unemployment compensation, qualified state tuition program earnings, and Alaska Permanent Fund dividends
5. Have taxable interest income of $1,500 or less
6. Have taxable income of less than $100,000
7. Have no dividend income
8. Earn less than $20 in monthly tips from one employer that are omitted from Form W-2
9. Not receive any advance earned income credit (EIC) payments

---

Taxpayer Identification

On all tax returns, taxpayers must clearly identify themselves. They must place their name, address, and social security number at the top of the form. Those receiving a preaddressed taxpayer identification label should examine the label carefully, correct errors in ink, and paste the corrected label in the space provided. When unclear data appears on this label, taxpayers should not use it. They should insert their own identification data at the top of the return.

Presidential Election Campaign Fund

Taxpayers can instruct the IRS whether or not to transfer $3 of their tax payments to the presidential election campaign fund. They simply place an *X* in the proper box located under the name and address data. This election does not affect the amount of taxes owed or refunded.

Reporting Taxable Income

Form 1040EZ tax filers use lines 1 through 4 to report and summarize their income. These filers then subtract out their standard deduction and any exemptions that may apply (line 5). The remainder is taxable income.

All taxpayers receive a standard deduction. However, persons who are dependents may not claim an exemption for themselves. **Nondependents** deduct $8,450 ($5,150 + $3,300) if single and $16,900 ($10,300 + $3,300 + $3,300) if married. **Dependents** use a worksheet to determine their standard deduction, which is the *greater of* (i) $850 or (ii) earned income plus $300. It cannot exceed $5,150 if single or $10,300 if married.

Figuring the Tax, Refund, or Amount Due

After figuring taxable income, 1040EZ filers list all their tax payments. An item that acts as a tax payment is the earned income credit (EIC) (line 8a). Taxpayers then use taxable income (line 6) to determine their tax from the Tax Tables. They enter it on the form (line 11) and subtract the total payments (line 10) to compute the refund (line 12a) or the amount owed (line 13).

Taxpayers receiving a refund may choose to receive it in the form of a check or a direct deposit. They may also apply the refund to next year's tax liability. Direct deposit refunds are faster, more secure, and more convenient for the taxpayer than refunds by check. They are also less expensive for the government to issue. To receive a direct deposit refund, taxpayers must include two numbers in the spaces provided on the tax return: (1) the bank's routing number, and (2) the taxpayer's bank account number. This information is found on the taxpayer's check, but one should verify these figures with the financial institution to make sure the correct numbers are used.

All tax filers must attach Copy B of Form W-2 to their tax return. If an amount is owed, the taxpayer should also enclose a check for the balance due. Taxpayers may incur a penalty for not paying enough tax during the year. Those in this situation who file Form 1040EZ let the IRS compute the penalty and send them a bill. If they choose to compute the penalty themselves, they cannot use Form 1040EZ. Instead, they must use either Form 1040A or Form 1040.

DO NOT MAKE A PAYMENT TO *IRS*

Due to the loss of some taxpayer payments (checks or money orders being altered or stolen), make all payments to the *United States Treasury.* Never leave a payee line blank. Also, include the following taxpayer data and form identification on each payment:

1. Name
2. Address
3. Social security number (SSN)
4. Daytime phone number
5. Year and form name (2006 Form 1040EZ, 2006 Form 1040A, or 2006 Form 1040)

Signature and Certification

Taxpayers sign Form 1040EZ at the bottom of the page. They also enter their occupation and the current date. Taxpayers should normally file their return no later than April 15, the due date for calendar year filers. If this date falls on Saturday, Sunday, or a legal holiday, the law extends the filing deadline to the end of the next business day.

After attaching Copy B of Form W-2 to the return, the return is ready for mailing. Taxpayers should keep evidence of their timely mailing by getting a "Proof of Mailing" from the post office when they mail their returns. Taxpayers keep this receipt with copies of their completed tax returns.

Information for Figure 2-8: Filled-In Form 1040EZ

Amelia Z. Sanchez works as a sales clerk. In addition to her wages, Sanchez received interest earned on her savings account. Sanchez has no other sources of income. Also, no other taxpayer can claim her as a dependent. Figure 2-7 shows Sanchez's Form 1040EZ.

Other Information

1: Total wages, salaries, and tips, **$22,920.00** (source: Form W-2)

2: Taxable interest income, **$395.00** (source: Form 1099-INT)

7: Federal income tax withheld, **$2,002.00** (source: Form W-2)

9: Credit for federal excise tax paid, **$30** (one exemption)

FORM 1040A

Form 1040A, U.S. Individual Income Tax Return, is a two-page return. It is more challenging than Form 1040EZ, but much less complex than Form 1040. It allows for more types of income than Form 1040EZ. It also allows more types of deductions and personal tax credits.

Page 1 lists the taxpayer's various incomes. It also allows four deductions to arrive at adjusted gross income. Page 2 provides for the standard deduction and allowable exemptions to produce taxable income. After identifying the amount of the tax, the form allows for tax reductions: tax credits, withheld taxes, and other payments. The taxpayer then computes the refund or the amount due. Finally, taxpayers report any estimated tax penalty and add it to the amount due.

Form 1040A has four supporting schedules. Taxpayers use Schedule 1 to report their taxable interest and dividend income, Schedule 2 to compute their child and dependent care credit, and Schedule 3 to compute their elderly or disabled credit. They may also use Schedule EIC (Form 1040A or 1040). The next paragraph contains a brief discussion of Form 1040A. Chapter 4 contains more on this form.

Who May Use Form 1040A

Only taxpayers with taxable incomes of less than $100,000 can use Form 1040A. The income of Form 1040A filers can include only wages, salaries, interest, dividends, tips, annuities, pensions, social security benefits, distributions from individual retirement arrangements (IRAs), unemployment compensation, taxable scholarships and fellowships, Alaska Permanent Fund dividends, and certain capital gain distributions. Form 1040A permits only four deductions for AGI: penalty on early withdrawal of savings, qualifying IRA contributions, certain interest on student loans, and jury duty pay given to your employer. Also, this form allows taxpayers to reduce AGI only by the standard deduction and allowable exemptions.

FIGURE 2-8 Filled-In Form 1040EZ

Form **1040EZ**	Department of the Treasury—Internal Revenue Service **Income Tax Return for Single and Joint Filers With No Dependents** (99) **2006**		OMB No. 1545-0074
Label (See page 11.) **Use the IRS label.** Otherwise, please print or type. LABEL HERE	Your first name and initial: Amelia Z.	Last name: Sanchez	**Your social security number** 295 24 1408
	If a joint return, spouse's first name and initial	Last name	**Spouse's social security number**
	Home address (number and street). If you have a P.O. box, see page 11.: 8290 Edgewater Drive	Apt. no.	You **must** enter your SSN(s) above.
	City, town or post office, state, and ZIP code. If you have a foreign address, see page 11.: Chula Vista, CA 91911		Checking a box below will not change your tax or refund.
Presidential Election Campaign (page 12)	Check here if you, or your spouse if a joint return, want $3 to go to this fund?		[X] **You** [ ] **Spouse**

Income Attach Form(s) W-2 here. Enclose, but do not attach, any payment.	1	Wages, salaries, and tips. This should be shown in box 1 of your Form(s) W-2. Attach your Form(s) W-2.	1	22,920 00
	2	Taxable interest. If the total is over $1,500, you cannot use Form 1040EZ.	2	395 00
	3	Unemployment compensation and Alaska Permanent Fund dividends (see page 13).	3	
	4	Add lines 1, 2, and 3. This is your **adjusted gross income.**	4	23,315 00
	5	If someone can claim you (or your spouse if a joint return) as a dependent, check the applicable box(es) below and enter the amount from the worksheet on back. [X] **You** [ ] **Spouse** If no one can claim you (or your spouse if a joint return), enter $8,450 if **single;** $16,900 if **married filing jointly.** See back for explanation.	5	8,450 00
	6	Subtract line 5 from line 4. If line 5 is larger than line 4, enter -0-. This is your **taxable income.** ▶	6	14,865 00
Payments and tax	7	Federal income tax withheld from box 2 of your Form(s) W-2.	7	2,002 00
	8a	**Earned income credit (EIC).**	8a	
	b	Nontaxable combat pay election. 8b		
	9	Credit for federal telephone excise tax paid. Attach Form 8913 if required.	9	30 00
	10	Add lines 7, 8a, and 9. These are your **total payments.** ▶	10	2,032 00
	11	**Tax.** Use the amount on **line 6 above** to find your tax in the tax table on pages 24–32 of the booklet. Then, enter the tax from the table on this line.	11	1,854 00
Refund Have it directly deposited! See page 18 and fill in 12b, 12c, and 12d or Form 8888.	12a	If line 10 is larger than line 11, subtract line 11 from line 10. This is your **refund.** If Form 8888 is attached, check here ▶ [ ]	12a	178 00
	▶ b	Routing number ▶ c Type: [ ] Checking [ ] Savings		
	▶ d	Account number		
Amount you owe	13	If line 11 is larger than line 10, subtract line 10 from line 11. This is the **amount you owe.** For details on how to pay, see page 19. ▶	13	

Third party designee Do you want to allow another person to discuss this return with the IRS (see page 19)? [ ] **Yes.** Complete the following. [ ] **No**

Designee's name ▶ Phone no. ▶ ( ) Personal identification number (PIN) ▶

Sign here Under penalties of perjury, I declare that I have examined this return, and to the best of my knowledge and belief, it is true, correct, and accurately lists all amounts and sources of income I received during the tax year. Declaration of preparer (other than the taxpayer) is based on all information of which the preparer has any knowledge.

Joint return? See page 11. Keep a copy for your records.

Your signature	Date	Your occupation	Daytime phone number
Amelia Z. Sanchez	4/5/07	Sales Clerk	( )
Spouse's signature. If a joint return, **both** must sign.	Date	Spouse's occupation	

Paid preparer's use only

Preparer's signature ▶	Date	Check if self-employed [ ]	Preparer's SSN or PTIN
Firm's name (or yours if self-employed), address, and ZIP code ▶		EIN	
		Phone no. ( )	

For Disclosure, Privacy Act, and Paperwork Reduction Act Notice, see page 23. Cat. No. 11329W Form **1040EZ** (2006)

Information for Figure 2-9: Filled-In Form 1040A

Sarah and James Wilson's filled-in Form 1040A is shown in Figure 2-9. The Wilsons have three dependent children, two of whom are under age 17.

Other Information

7: Wages, **$31,765** ($19,665 + $12,100) (source: Form W-2)

8: Taxable interest, **$150** (source: Form 1099-INT)

33: Child tax credit to be claimed, **$2,000** (two qualifying children × $1,000.00). Reported as follows: child tax credit (line 33): **$513** (source: Form 8812) additional child tax credit (line 41): **$1,487** (source: Form 8812).

38: Tax withheld, **$0** (source: Form W-2)

40a: Earned income credit, **$1,353** (source: Schedule EIC Worksheet)

42: Credit for federal excise tax paid, **$60** (four or more exemptions)

Since the Wilsons have no tax liability, they cannot give money to the presidential election campaign.

FORM 1040

Form 1040, U.S. Individual Income Tax Return, is the most common tax return. Form 1040, a two-page return, has a similar format to Form 1040A. Page 1 focuses on the computation of AGI. Page 2 calculates taxable income, tax liability, and the amount of refund due or taxes owed. Form 1040 may involve numerous supporting schedules.

Taxpayers must use Form 1040 when they do not qualify to use either Form 1040EZ or Form 1040A. They may also elect Form 1040 over one of these other forms to save taxes (more deductions and credits are available). This form is the taxpayer's most comprehensive reporting device. It provides for all types of income, deductions, credits, and other taxes that might be owed. Basically Form 1040 has no limits on the amounts and the items that can be reported. Chapter 4 illustrates Form 1040.

Form 1040PC

Another version of Form 1040 is Form 1040PC. As the ownership of personal computers increases, more and more people prepare their tax return using approved computer software. The IRS can process this return (Form 1040PC) faster and more accurately than the regular Form 1040.

ELECTRONIC FILING

The IRS encourages electronic filing of tax returns. The IRS Restructuring and Reform Act of 1998 requires the IRS to have 80% of all tax returns filed electronically by 2007. Over half of all 2005 tax returns were filed electronically.

FIGURE 2-9 Filled-In Form 1040A, Page 1

Form **1040A** Department of the Treasury—Internal Revenue Service
U.S. Individual Income Tax Return (99) **2006** IRS Use Only—Do not write or staple in this space.

OMB No. 1545-0074

Label (See page 18.) LABEL HERE
Use the IRS label. Otherwise, please print or type.

Your first name and initial	Last name	Your social security number
Sarah R.	Wilson	282 56 9320
If a joint return, spouse's first name and initial	Last name	Spouse's social security number
James E.	Wilson	271 04 7926
Home address (number and street). If you have a P.O. box, see page 18.	Apt. no.	▲ You **must** enter your SSN(s) above. ▲
1624 West Third Street		
City, town or post office, state, and ZIP code. If you have a foreign address, see page 18.		Checking a box below will not change your tax or refund.
Muskegon, MU 49441		

Presidential Election Campaign ▶ Check here if you, or your spouse if filing jointly, want $3 to go to this fund (see page 18) ▶ ☐ You ☐ Spouse

Filing status Check only one box.

1 ☐ Single
2 ☒ Married filing jointly (even if only one had income)
3 ☐ Married filing separately. Enter spouse's SSN above and full name here. ▶
4 ☐ Head of household (with qualifying person). (See page 19.) If the qualifying person is a child but not your dependent, enter this child's name here. ▶
5 ☐ Qualifying widow(er) with dependent child (see page 19)

Exemptions

6a ☒ **Yourself.** If someone can claim you as a dependent, **do not** check box 6a.
b ☒ **Spouse**
c **Dependents:**

Boxes checked on 6a and 6b: 2

If more than six dependents, see page 21.

(1) First name	Last name	(2) Dependent's social security number	(3) Dependent's relationship to you	(4) ✓ if qualifying child for child tax credit (see page 21)
Martha A.	Wilson	826 45 3710	daughter	☐
Karl B.	Wilson	850 21 5263	son	☒
Susan K.	Wilson	860 40 5721	daughter	☒
				☐
				☐
				☐

No. of children on 6c who:
• **lived with you** 3
• **did not live with you due to divorce or separation (see page 22)**
Dependents on 6c not entered above

d Total number of exemptions claimed. **Add numbers on lines above** ▶ 5

Income

Attach Form(s) W-2 here. Also attach Form(s) 1099-R if tax was withheld.

If you did not get a W-2, see page 24.

Enclose, but do not attach, any payment.

7	Wages, salaries, tips, etc. Attach Form(s) W-2.	7	31,765 00
8a	**Taxable** interest. Attach Schedule 1 if required.	8a	150 00
b	**Tax-exempt** interest. **Do not** include on line 8a.	8b	
9a	Ordinary dividends. Attach Schedule 1 if required.	9a	
b	Qualified dividends (see page 25).	9b	
10	Capital gain distributions (see page 25).	10	
11a	IRA distributions. 11a — **11b** Taxable amount (see page 25).	11b	
12a	Pensions and annuities. 12a — **12b** Taxable amount (see page 26).	12b	
13	Unemployment compensation, Alaska Permanent Fund dividends, and jury duty fees.	13	
14a	Social security benefits. 14a — **14b** Taxable amount (see page 28).	14b	
15	Add lines 7 through 14b (far right column). This is your **total income.** ▶	15	31,915 00

Adjusted gross income

16	Penalty on early withdrawal of savings (see page XX).	16	
17	IRA deduction (see page 28).	17	
18	Student loan interest deduction (see page 31).	18	
19	Jury duty pay you gave your employer (see page XX).	19	
20	Add lines 16 through 19. These are your **total adjustments.**	20	
21	Subtract line 20 from line 15. This is your **adjusted gross income.** ▶	21	31,915 00

For Disclosure, Privacy Act, and Paperwork Reduction Act Notice, see page 58. Cat. No. 11327A Form **1040A** (2006)

FIGURE 2-9 Filled-In Form 1040A, Page 2

Form 1040A (2006) Page **2**

Tax, credits, and payments

22	Enter the amount from line 21 (adjusted gross income).	22	31,915 00
23a	Check if: ☐ **You** were born before January 2, 1942, ☐ Blind; ☐ **Spouse** was born before January 2, 1942, ☐ Blind. **Total boxes checked** ▶	23a	
b	If you are married filing separately and your spouse itemizes deductions, see page 32 and check here ▶ ☐	23b	
24	Enter your **standard deduction** (see left margin).	24	10,300 00
25	Subtract line 24 from line 22. If line 24 is more than line 22, enter -0-.	25	21,615 00
26	If line 22 is over $112,875, or you provided housing to a person displaced by Hurricane Katrina, see page 33. Otherwise, multiply $3,300 by the total number of exemptions claimed on line 6d.	26	16,500 00
27	Subtract line 26 from line 25. If line 26 is more than line 25, enter -0-. This is your **taxable income.** ▶	27	5,115 00
28	**Tax,** including any alternative minimum tax (see page 34).	28	513 00
29	Credit for child and dependent care expenses. Attach Schedule 2.	29	
30	Credit for the elderly or the disabled. Attach Schedule 3.	30	
31	Education credits. Attach Form 8863.	31	
32	Retirement savings contributions credit. Attach Form 8880.	32	
33	Child tax credit (see page 38). Attach Form 8901 if required.	33	513 00
34	Add lines 29 through 33. These are your **total credits.**	34	513 00
35	Subtract line 34 from line 28. If line 34 is more than line 28, enter -0-.	35	0
36	Advance earned income credit payments from Form(s) W-2, box 9.	36	
37	Add lines 35 and 36. This is your **total tax.** ▶	37	0
38	Federal income tax withheld from Forms W-2 and 1099.	38	0
39	2006 estimated tax payments and amount applied from 2005 return.	39	
40a	**Earned income credit (EIC).**	40a	1,353 00
b	Nontaxable combat pay election.	40b	
41	Additional child tax credit. Attach Form 8812.	41	1,487 00
42	Credit for federal telephone excise tax paid. Attach Form 8913 if required.	42	60 00
43	Add lines 38, 39, 40a, 41, and 42. These are your **total payments.** ▶	43	2,900 00

Standard Deduction for—
- People who checked any box on line 23a or 23b **or** who can be claimed as a dependent, see page 32.
- All others:

Single or Married filing separately, $5,150

Married filing jointly or Qualifying widow(er), $10,300

Head of household, $7,550

If you have a qualifying child, attach Schedule EIC.

Refund

44	If line 43 is more than line 37, subtract line 37 from line 43. This is the amount you **overpaid.**	44	2,900 00
45a	Amount of line 44 you want **refunded to you.** If Form 8888 is attached, check here ▶ ☐	45a	2,900 00
▶ b	Routing number ▶ c Type: ☐ Checking ☐ Savings		
▶ d	Account number		
46	Amount of line 44 you want **applied to your 2007 estimated tax.**	46	

Direct deposit? See page 53 and fill in 45b, 45c, and 45d or Form 8888.

Amount you owe

47	**Amount you owe.** Subtract line 43 from line 37. For details on how to pay, see page 54. ▶	47	
48	Estimated tax penalty (see page 54).	48	

Third party designee

Do you want to allow another person to discuss this return with the IRS (see page 55)? ☐ **Yes.** Complete the following. ☐ **No**

Designee's name ▶ Phone no. ▶ ( ) Personal identification number (PIN) ▶

Sign here

Joint return? See page 18. Keep a copy for your records.

Under penalties of perjury, I declare that I have examined this return and accompanying schedules and statements, and to the best of my knowledge and belief, they are true, correct, and accurately list all amounts and sources of income I received during the tax year. Declaration of preparer (other than the taxpayer) is based on all information of which the preparer has any knowledge.

Your signature	Date	Your occupation	Daytime phone number
Sarah R. Wilson	2-26-07	Cook	( )
Spouse's signature. If a joint return, **both** must sign.	Date	Spouse's occupation	
James E. Wilsion	2-26-07	Janitor	

Paid preparer's use only

Preparer's signature ▶ Date Check if self-employed ☐ Preparer's SSN or PTIN

Firm's name (or yours if self-employed), address, and ZIP code ▶ EIN Phone no. ( )

Printed on recycled paper Form **1040A** (2006)

IRS HOME PAGE

The IRS provides much useful information through its Internet home page (http://www.irs.gov). This is a good source of forms, publications, and other material that may be downloaded. (See the inside back cover and Appendix A).

EXTENSIONS OF TIME TO FILE

Individuals and other tax entities may obtain an automatic six month extension of time to file their income tax returns. This provides them with more time to file their tax returns but *does not* give them more time to pay their taxes. Taxpayers must pay their taxes by original due date for their returns even when they file an extension. Interest is charged on any unpaid amounts and penalties may be assessed as well.

Type of Taxpayer	*Form Number for Extension*
Individual (Form 1040, Form 1040A, or Form 1040EZ)	Form 4868
Partnership (Form 1065)	Form 8736
S Corporation (Form 1120S)	Form 7004
C Corporation (Form 1120 or Form 1120A)	Form 7004

Information for Figure 2-10: Filled-In Form 4868

Figure 2-10 shows a filled-in Form 4868, Application for Automatic Extension of Time to File U.S. Individual Income Tax Return, for Carla Kramer. She expects her total tax liability to be $4,580, and she had $4,400 withheld from her wages. Kramer sends a check for $180 payable to the United States Treasury with the extension.

FIGURE 2-10 Filled-In Form 4868

Form **4868**
Department of the Treasury
Internal Revenue Service

Application for Automatic Extension of Time To File U.S. Individual Income Tax Return
For calendar year 2006, or other tax year beginning , 2006, ending , 200 .

OMB No. 1545-0074
2006

Part I Identification

1 Your name(s) (see instructions)
Carla A. Kramer

Address (see instructions)
6820 W. 59th Street

City, town, or post office: Memphis
State: TN
ZIP code: 38105-1960

2 Your social security number: 652 19 9990
3 Spouse's social security number:

Part II Individual Income Tax

4	Estimate of total tax liability for 2006	$ 4,580.00
5	Total 2006 payments	4,400.00
6	**Balance due.** Subtract line 5 from line 4 (see instructions)	180.00
7	Amount you are paying (see instructions) ▶	180.00
8	Check here if you are "out of the country" and a U.S. citizen or resident (see instructions) ▶	☐
9	Check here if you file Form 1040NR and did not receive wages as an employee subject to U.S. income tax withholding ▶	☐

For Privacy Act and Paperwork Reduction Act Notice, see page 4. Cat. No. 13141W Form **4868** (2006)

Name ______________________________

Section ______________ Date ___________

QUESTIONS AND PROBLEMS

1. **Using the Tax Rate Schedules.** The IRS publishes Tax Rate Schedules and a Tax Table. When must taxpayers use the Rate Schedules instead of the Tax Table to compute their income tax liability?

2. **Comparison of Tax Table and Rate Schedule.** Mark Long, a single person, files his tax return as a HOH. He has taxable income of $49,750.

   a. Compute Long's tax liability from the Tax Table in the space provided.

   b. Compute Long's tax liability using the Tax Rate Schedule that applies. Is there a difference in the two tax figures? Why?

3. **Tax Computation.** Barbara Landerson, age 25, files as a single taxpayer. She is employed at a monthly salary of $2,050. She claims no dependents. Her employer withheld $2,200 from her wages for income taxes for 12 months' of work. Compute of Landerson's income tax due to or from the IRS. Landerson claims the standard credit for federal telephone excise tax paid by taxpayers claiming one exemption.

4. **Tax Computations.** Compute the taxable income and income tax liability (before refunds and credits) for each of the following taxpayers. Each taxpayer uses the standard deduction.

a. An unmarried taxpayer, age 30, claims one dependency exemption. She files as surviving spouse. Her AGI is $45,900.

b. An unmarried taxpayer, age 74, is unmarried and claims no dependents. His AGI is $19,290.

c. A taxpayer, age 40, is married but files a separate return from his spouse. The taxpayer is the noncustodial parent of his 8-year-old child. His wife has signed Form 8832 giving him the right to claim their daughter as a dependent. AGI is $130,580.

d. An unmarried taxpayer, age 72, is claimed as a dependent on her son's return. Her AGI consists of $3,000 of taxable interest.

e. A married couple, ages 67 and 66, file a joint return. They claim one dependent and their AGI is $160,855.

5. **Tax Credits vs. Tax Deductions.** What is the difference between a tax credit and a tax deduction? If a taxpayer with a marginal tax rate of 15% has a $1,000 deduction, how much tax will she save? How much tax will she save with a $1,000 tax credit?

6. **Excess OASDI Withholding.** Maria and Chad Harmon each worked full-time during 2006. Maria worked for the same employer. Chad worked for two employers. The amounts each had withheld from their pay for OASDI and Medicare taxes are shown below. Compute the Harmons' OASDI tax credit that they will claim on their 2006 tax return. Is this credit a refundable or nonrefundable credit, and how should they go about claiming this credit on their 2006 tax return?

Employee	Total Social Security Wages Paid	OASDI Tax Witheld	Medicare Tax Witheld
Maria	$66,000	$4,030	$ 957
Chad: Employer #1	70,000	4,340	1,015
Chad: Employer #2	42,000	2,604	609

7. **Child and Dependent Care Credit.** Bud and Katie Milner file a joint return. During 2006, they paid $11,000 to their nanny to look after their three children, ages 2, 9, and 11. Bud and Katie both work and earned $24,000 and $31,000, respectively. The wages are the Milners' only source of income, and they have no deductions for AGI.

   a. Compute the Milners' child and dependent care credit.

   b. Compute the Milners' child and dependent care credit assuming Katie received a $3,000 reimbursement from her employer's dependent care plan.

8. **Child and Dependent Care Credit.** During 2006, Todd and Jo Mendin pay their 17-year-old daughter, Erin, $5,000 to look after their 10-year-old son, TJ. The Mendins file a joint return in 2006 and claim Erin and TJ as their dependents. The Mendlins' AGI is $84,000.

   a. Compute the Mendlins' 2006 child and dependent care credit.

   b. Would your answer change if Erin were 22-years-old, but still claimed as a dependent on her parents' return?

   c. Would your answer change if the Mendins paid Todd's mother $5,000 to look after TJ?

9. **Child and Dependent Care Credit.** Denise and Marcus Anders claim their two children, ages 7 and 11, as dependents. During the year, Denise worked full time and earned $23,200. Marcus was a full-time student at the local college for 9 months during the year. The Anders paid $5,500 in qualified child care expenses to allow Denise to work and Marcus to attend college.

   a. Compute the Anders's 2006 child and dependent care credit.

   b. Would your answer change if Marcus attended college full time for five months in the Spring semester, but only took classes part-time during the Fall semester?

10. Child Tax Credit. Compute the 2006 child tax credit for each of the following taxpayers.

a. Jack Bennett is married but does not file a joint return with his spouse. Bennett claims his 6-year-old son as a dependent and files as head of household under the abandoned spouse rules. Bennett's AGI is $84,440.

b. Margaret Eren is divorced. She and her ex-husband share custody of their four children, ages 2-8. The children live with Eren and she is the custodial parent. Eren has not signed away her right to claim the children as her dependents. Her AGI is $95,694.

c. Michelle Dorrin is 43-years old and a single parent. She claims dependency exemptions for her three children, ages 9, 14 and 17. Her AGI is $123,639.

d. Randy and Tammy O'Brien file a joint return. Tammy's 16-year-old sister lives with them the entire year. They claim the sister and their 2-year-old daughter as dependents. The O'Briens' AGI is $145,800.

11. Child Tax Credit. Compute the 2006 child tax credit for each of the following taxpayers.

a. Jay and Marie Stockton file a joint return and claim their three children, all under age 17, as dependents. The Stocktons' AGI is $121,400.

b. Tom Stevenson files as head of household. He claims his twin sons, age 4, as dependents. Stevenson's AGI is $80,340.

c. Jennifer Thompson files as head of household. She claims her 12-year-old daughter as a dependent. Thompson's AGI is $78,450.

12. **Refundable Child Tax Credit.** Pat and Diedra Dobson file a joint tax return for 2006. The Dobsons' 2006 AGI equals $28,900, of which $27,300 is Pat and Diedra's taxable wages. The Dobsons take the standard deduction and claim dependency exemptions for their two teenage children, ages 13 and 15. Other than the child tax credit, the Dobsons do not claim any nonrefundable personal tax credits. Compute the Dobsons' nonrefundable and refundable child tax credit for 2006.

13. **Education Tax Credit.** In 2006, Jean Loptien (single) paid $3,000 for her son's tuition. Rob is a full-time student and a freshman this year at Northwest University. Loptien's AGI in 2006 is $32,000.

    a. Compute Loptein's 2006 education tax credit.

    b. Same as in Part a., except that Loptien's AGI is $49,000.

14. Education Tax Credit. Curt and Kathy Norton paid $3,200 of tuition for their son, a senior in college. Of this amount, $1,500 was paid on December 28, 2005, for the Spring 2006 semester, and $1,700 was paid on August 4, 2006, for the Fall 2006 semester. The Nortons' 2006 AGI is $70,000.

a. Compute the Norton's 2006 education tax credit.

b. Same as in Part a., except that the Norton's AGI is $102,816.

15. Education Tax Credit. In 2006, Paul and Karen Mitchell pay $2,000 for their daughter's tuition for the Spring and Fall 2006 semesters. Their daughter is a full-time graduate student. The Mitchells also paid $3,500 for their son's tuition for the Spring and Fall semesters. In Fall 2006, their son began his sophomore year of college. The Mitchells' AGI is $44,200.

a. Compute the Mitchells' education tax credit for 2006.

b. Same as in Part a., except that the Mitchells' AGI is $97,842.

c. How would your answers to Parts a. and b. change if the Mitchells' children attended college at Tulane University (located in the Hurricane Katrina disaster area)?

16. **Earned Income Credit.** For each of the following cases, compute the taxpayer's earned income credit for 2006.

a. Pat and Ron Barnett file a joint return, claiming their two sons, ages 3 and 5, as dependents. The Barnetts' AGI is $14,400, which consists entirely of Ron's wages.

b. Joseph Williams is a 25-year-old graduate student. His gross income consists of $5,000 of wages, and $80 in interest from a savings account. Williams files as single and claims no dependents.

c. Suzanne and Vernon Zimmerman file a joint return, claiming their 6-year-old daughter as a dependent. The Zimmermans' AGI consists of Vernon's $16,375 in wages, and $400 in dividend income.

d. Sarah Sprinter files as head of household, claiming her 2-year-old son as a dependent. Sprinter's AGI consists of $18,000 in wages and $3,200 in interest income.

17. **Earned Income Credit.** For each of the following situations, determine who is entitled to claim the qualifying child for purpose of the earned income credit.

a. Kate (age 30) and her son, Jimmy (age 3) live with Kate's father, Fred, during all of 2006. Jimmy is a qualifying child to both Kate and Fred. Kate's AGI is $20,000; Fred's AGI is $64,000.

b. Ned and Terry Reston are divorced. They share custody of their twin sons, age 13. The boys live with Ned half of the year and with Tammy the other half of the year. Tammy lives with her parents. The twins are qualifying children to Ned, Terry and Terry's parents. Ned's AGI is $45,000. Terry's AGI is $20,200, and her parent's AGI is $36,900.

c. Same as in Part b., except that the boys spend more days with Terry during the year than with Ned.

d. Same as in Part b., except that the boys spend more days with Ned during the year than with Terry.

e. Mary's parents are both deceased. Mary is 15 and is being raised by her aunt. Her grandparents also participate in her upbringing and support. Mary is a qualifying child for both her aunt and her grandparents. The aunt's AGI is $21,500. The grandparents' AGI is $45,300.

18. **Advanced Earned Income Credit.** A taxpayer files with his employer Form W-5, Earned Income Credit Advance Payment Certificate. During 2006, the taxpayer receives an advance on his EIC equal to $1,648. On his 2006 tax return, the taxpayer computes his EIC to be $2,200. Discuss how this advance is treated when the taxpayer files his 2006 tax return.

19. Adoption Credit. In 2005, a couple paid $6,000 in qualified adoption expenses to adopt a child that is a U.S. citizen. In 2006, they paid an additional $4,200 in qualified adoption expenses. The adoption was finalized in 2006. The couples' AGI is $115,000 in both 2005 and 2006.

a. Compute the couples' adoption credit. In what year(s) is it taken?

b. How would your answer to Part a. change in the couples' AGI was $185,000 in both 2005 and 2006?

c. How would your answer to Part a. change if the couple adopted a child with special needs?

d. How would your answer to Part a. change if the adoption fell through?

20. Adoption Credit. In 2005, a couple paid $12,000 in qualified adoption expenses to adopt a child that is a U.S. citizen. The adoption was finalized in 2006. The couples' AGI is $175,670.

a. Compute the couples' adoption credit. In what year(s) is it taken?

b. How would your answer to Part a. change if the couple adopted a foreign child?

c. How would your answer to Part b. change if the adoption fell through?

21. **Adoption Credit.** In 2006, John and Mary Hoppe paid $14,000 in qualified adoption expenses of a healthy child for an adoption that was finalized in 2006. The Hoppes' AGI for 2006 is $177,060. In addition, the Hoppes received $3,000 from an employer adoption assistance plan. What is the Hoppes' adoption credit?

22. **Retirement Savings Contributions Credit.** Tom Wherry's joint tax return shows $45,000 of AGI. During the year, Wherry contributed $1,500 to his Roth IRA and $1,500 to his wife's Roth IRA. What credit is available for these contributions?

23. **Residential Energy Credit.** During 2006, Maureen Conner purchases a solar water heating system and solar electricity equipment for her. The systems cost $5,000 and $7,400, respectively. Compute Conner's residential energy credit.

24. **Residential Energy Credit.** During 2006, Manny O'Neill pays $4,100 to have a high efficiency heating and cooling system installed in his principal residence. During 2007, he has insulation installed at a cost of $1,600. Compute O'Neill's residential energy credit for 2006 and 2007.

25. **1040EZ Requirements.** The taxpayers described in Parts a. through g. want to file Form 1040EZ. For each taxpayer, state whether he or she can file Form 1040EZ. If a taxpayer cannot file Form 1040EZ, state the reason(s) for your answer.

    a. A single taxpayer has tax-exempt interest income of $1,400 and taxable income of $99,900 from wages.

b. A married taxpayer filing a separate return has taxable income of $47,290, including interest income of $100.

c. A single taxpayer has taxable income of $35,683, including $1,700 of interest income. The taxpayer also has $200 of tax-exempt interest.

d. A HOH taxpayer has taxable income of $30,400, including interest income of $250. The taxpayer has two dependents.

e. A single taxpayer has taxable income of $47,800, including dividend income of $300.

f. A single taxpayer has taxable income of $31,654, including tip income of $4,500 included as wages on Form W-2 and interest income of $75.

g. A married taxpayer filing jointly has taxable income of $47,290, including interest income of $100. Both the taxpayer and spouse are elderly and blind. They cannot claim another person as a dependency exemption.

26. Form 1040EZ. Jeanne M. Searson (SSN 369-48-5783), a 27-year-old unmarried clerk, lives at 4502 Lakeside Drive, Echo, CA 92040-1234. Her Forms W-2, Wage and Tax Statements, contain the following information:

	Gross Wages	*Income Tax Withheld*	*FICA Wages*	*FICA Taxes Withheld*
Interlake Co.	$ 5,240	$169	$ 5,240	$401
Data-Mate Co. (present employer)	6,280	206	6,280	480
Totals	$11,520	$375	$11,520	$881

In addition to her wages, Searson received $25 in interest on her passbook account at the Echo Savings and Loan Bank. She wants $3 of her tax money to go to the presidential election campaign fund. Using the Form 1040EZ provided, prepare her tax return for 2006. Searson claims the standard credit for federal telephone excise tax paid for one exemption. She signs the return on February 6, 2007.

(Use for Problem 26.)

Form **1040EZ**

Department of the Treasury—Internal Revenue Service

Income Tax Return for Single and Joint Filers With No Dependents (99) **2006**

OMB No. 1545-0074

Label
(See page 11.)
Use the IRS label.
Otherwise, please print or type.

LABEL HERE

Your first name and initial | Last name | **Your social security number**

If a joint return, spouse's first name and initial | Last name | **Spouse's social security number**

Home address (number and street). If you have a P.O. box, see page 11. | Apt. no.

▲ You **must** enter your SSN(s) above. ▲

City, town or post office, state, and ZIP code. If you have a foreign address, see page 11.

Checking a box below will not change your tax or refund.

Presidential Election Campaign (page 12) ▶ Check here if you, or your spouse if a joint return, want $3 to go to this fund? . . . ▶ ☐ **You** ☐ **Spouse**

Income **Attach Form(s) W-2 here.** Enclose, but do not attach, any payment.	1	Wages, salaries, and tips. This should be shown in box 1 of your Form(s) W-2. Attach your Form(s) W-2.	1
	2	Taxable interest. If the total is over $1,500, you cannot use Form 1040EZ.	2
	3	Unemployment compensation and Alaska Permanent Fund dividends (see page 13).	3
	4	Add lines 1, 2, and 3. This is your **adjusted gross income.**	4
	5	If someone can claim you (or your spouse if a joint return) as a dependent, check the applicable box(es) below and enter the amount from the worksheet on back. ☐ **You** ☐ **Spouse** If no one can claim you (or your spouse if a joint return), enter $8,450 if **single;** $16,900 if **married filing jointly.** See back for explanation.	5
	6	Subtract line 5 from line 4. If line 5 is larger than line 4, enter -0-. This is your **taxable income.** ▶	6
Payments and tax	7	Federal income tax withheld from box 2 of your Form(s) W-2.	7
	8a	**Earned income credit (EIC).**	8a
	b	Nontaxable combat pay election. 8b	
	9	Credit for federal telephone excise tax paid. Attach Form 8913 if required.	9
	10	Add lines 7, 8a, and 9. These are your **total payments.** ▶	10
	11	**Tax.** Use the amount on **line 6 above** to find your tax in the tax table on pages 24–32 of the booklet. Then, enter the tax from the table on this line.	11
Refund Have it directly deposited! See page 18 and fill in 12b, 12c, and 12d or Form 8888.	12a	If line 10 is larger than line 11, subtract line 11 from line 10. This is your **refund.** If Form 8888 is attached, check here ▶ ☐	12a
	▶ b	Routing number ☐☐☐☐☐☐☐☐☐ ▶ c Type: ☐ Checking ☐ Savings	
	▶ d	Account number ☐☐☐☐☐☐☐☐☐☐☐☐☐☐☐☐☐	
Amount you owe	13	If line 11 is larger than line 10, subtract line 10 from line 11. This is the **amount you owe.** For details on how to pay, see page 19. ▶	13

Third party designee — Do you want to allow another person to discuss this return with the IRS (see page 19)? ☐ **Yes.** Complete the following. ☐ **No**

Designee's name ▶ | Phone no. ▶ ( ) | Personal identification number (PIN) ▶ ☐☐☐☐☐

Sign here
Joint return? See page 11.
Keep a copy for your records.

Under penalties of perjury, I declare that I have examined this return, and to the best of my knowledge and belief, it is true, correct, and accurately lists all amounts and sources of income I received during the tax year. Declaration of preparer (other than the taxpayer) is based on all information of which the preparer has any knowledge.

Your signature | Date | Your occupation | Daytime phone number ( )

Spouse's signature. If a joint return, **both** must sign. | Date | Spouse's occupation

Paid preparer's use only

Preparer's signature ▶ | Date | Check if self-employed ☐ | Preparer's SSN or PTIN

Firm's name (or yours if self-employed), address, and ZIP code ▶ | EIN | Phone no. ( )

For Disclosure, Privacy Act, and Paperwork Reduction Act Notice, see page 23. Cat. No. 11329W Form **1040EZ** (2006)

27. Tax Planning. Marilyn Doming and Charles Smith, unmarried individuals, are both 29 years of age. For 2006 Doming and Smith will earn wages of $60,000 and $35,000 respectively, their only source of income. They are thinking about getting married in either December or January. Before setting a wedding date, they want to know how much they will save in federal income taxes if they get married in December and file a joint return. They ask you to compare their combined federal income taxes as single individuals with their taxes as a married couple filing jointly. Neither taxpayer has any dependents. Also, no other taxpayer can claim Doming or Smith as a dependent. Regardless of their marital status, they will claim the standard deduction(s).

28. Form 1040EZ. Cele P. (SSN 248-40-8455) and Marvin K. (SSN 248-40-7834) Goldman, ages 36 and 38, received interest income of $390 on their savings account at the Portage Bank in 2005. Cele and Marvin are both employed by Portage Hardware, 13 W. Main Street, Portage, MO 49067. Cele is a cashier at the hardware store, and Marvin is a sales representative. Their home address is 248 Maple Street in Portage. Cele and Marvin had no other sources of income. Since they have no itemized deductions, they claim the standard deduction. Neither Cele nor Marvin is blind, disabled, or a dependent. They decide to take advantage of the opportunity for joint filers to use Form 1040EZ. Both want $3 to go to the presidential election campaign fund. The Goldmans claim the standard credit for federal excise tax paid by taxpayers claiming two exemptions. Using the following Form W-2 data, prepare the Goldmans' Form 1040EZ for 2006. They sign and file their Form 1040EZ on January 20, 2007.

	Gross Wages	*Income Tax Withheld*	*OASDI Wages*	*OASDI Tax Withheld*	*Medicare Wages*	*Medicare Tax Withheld*	*State Income Tax Withheld*
Cele	$13,400	$ 957	$13,400	$ 830	$13,400	$194	$ 402
Marvin	21,900	1,228	21,900	1,358	21,900	318	657
Totals	$35,300	$2,185	$35,300	$2,188	$35,300	$512	$1,059

(Use for Problem 28.)

Form **1040EZ**

Department of the Treasury—Internal Revenue Service

Income Tax Return for Single and Joint Filers With No Dependents (99) **2006**

OMB No. 1545-0074

Label

(See page 11.)

Use the IRS label. Otherwise, please print or type.

LABEL HERE

Your first name and initial | Last name | **Your social security number**

If a joint return, spouse's first name and initial | Last name | **Spouse's social security number**

Home address (number and street). If you have a P.O. box, see page 11. | Apt. no.

You **must** enter your SSN(s) above.

City, town or post office, state, and ZIP code. If you have a foreign address, see page 11.

Checking a box below will not change your tax or refund.

Presidential Election Campaign (page 12) ▶ Check here if you, or your spouse if a joint return, want $3 to go to this fund? . . . ▶ ☐ **You** ☐ **Spouse**

Income

Attach Form(s) W-2 here.

Enclose, but do not attach, any payment.

1	Wages, salaries, and tips. This should be shown in box 1 of your Form(s) W-2. Attach your Form(s) W-2.	1
2	Taxable interest. If the total is over $1,500, you cannot use Form 1040EZ.	2
3	Unemployment compensation and Alaska Permanent Fund dividends (see page 13).	3
4	Add lines 1, 2, and 3. This is your **adjusted gross income.**	4
5	If someone can claim you (or your spouse if a joint return) as a dependent, check the applicable box(es) below and enter the amount from the worksheet on back. ☐ **You** ☐ **Spouse** If no one can claim you (or your spouse if a joint return), enter $8,450 if **single;** $16,900 if **married filing jointly.** See back for explanation.	5
6	Subtract line 5 from line 4. If line 5 is larger than line 4, enter -0-. This is your **taxable income.** ▶	6

Payments and tax

7	Federal income tax withheld from box 2 of your Form(s) W-2.	7
8a	**Earned income credit (EIC).**	8a
b	Nontaxable combat pay election. 8b	
9	Credit for federal telephone excise tax paid. Attach Form 8913 if required.	9
10	Add lines 7, 8a, and 9. These are your **total payments.** ▶	10
11	**Tax.** Use the amount on **line 6 above** to find your tax in the tax table on pages 24–32 of the booklet. Then, enter the tax from the table on this line.	11

Refund

Have it directly deposited! See page 18 and fill in 12b, 12c, and 12d or Form 8888.

12a	If line 10 is larger than line 11, subtract line 11 from line 10. This is your **refund.** If Form 8888 is attached, check here ▶ ☐	12a
▶ b	Routing number ☐☐☐☐☐☐☐☐☐ ▶ **c** Type: ☐ Checking ☐ Savings	
▶ d	Account number ☐☐☐☐☐☐☐☐☐☐☐☐☐☐☐☐☐	

Amount you owe

13	If line 11 is larger than line 10, subtract line 10 from line 11. This is the **amount you owe.** For details on how to pay, see page 19. ▶	13

Third party designee

Do you want to allow another person to discuss this return with the IRS (see page 19)? ☐ **Yes.** Complete the following. ☐ **No**

Designee's name ▶ Phone no. ▶ ( ) Personal identification number (PIN) ▶ ☐☐☐☐☐

Sign here

Joint return? See page 11. Keep a copy for your records.

Under penalties of perjury, I declare that I have examined this return, and to the best of my knowledge and belief, it is true, correct, and accurately lists all amounts and sources of income I received during the tax year. Declaration of preparer (other than the taxpayer) is based on all information of which the preparer has any knowledge.

Your signature	Date	Your occupation	Daytime phone number ( )
Spouse's signature. If a joint return, **both** must sign.	Date	Spouse's occupation	

Paid preparer's use only

Preparer's signature ▶	Date	Check if self-employed ☐	Preparer's SSN or PTIN
Firm's name (or yours if self-employed), address, and ZIP code ▶		EIN	
		Phone no. ( )	

For Disclosure, Privacy Act, and Paperwork Reduction Act Notice, see page 23. Cat. No. 11329W Form **1040EZ** (2006)

29. Form 1040A. John J. (SSN 291-27-4631) and Mary A. (SSN 293-41-7032) Jackson, ages 66 and 65 respectively, have good vision. John is a retired electrician. Mary is a homemaker. The Jacksons live at 4622 Beaver Lake Road, Blooming Grove, MN 55164. They have no dependents. They decide to file a joint return on Form 1040A. From their traditional IRAs, they received $3,517, all of which is taxable. John received a pension of $20,000 from the Huellett Company, of which $16,800 is taxable. The Jacksons also receive $3,100 in nontaxable social security benefits. From time to time their five children, who are all farmers, help them with gifts of food. Prepare the Jacksons' Form 1040A tax return. The Jacksons claim the standard credit for federal telephone excise tax paid by taxpayers claiming two exemptions. They sign and file their return on February 7, 2007.

30. Internet Problem: Filling out Form 4868.

Cheryl Bier chooses to obtain an extension of time to file her tax return. Bier expects her total tax liability to be $16,500. She had $15,800 withheld from her wages. Bier (SSN 678-59-1234) lives at 829 North Broadway, Garden Grove, CA 92842.

Go to the IRS Web site and locate Form 4868. Using the computer, fill in the form for Bier and print out a completed copy.

See Appendix A for instructions on use of the IRS Web site.

(Use for Problem 29.)

Form **1040A** Department of the Treasury—Internal Revenue Service
U.S. Individual Income Tax Return (99) **2006** IRS Use Only—Do not write or staple in this space.

OMB No. 1545-0074

Label (See page 18.)
LABEL HERE
Use the IRS label. Otherwise, please print or type.

Your first name and initial	Last name	**Your social security number**
If a joint return, spouse's first name and initial	Last name	**Spouse's social security number**
Home address (number and street). If you have a P.O. box, see page 18.	Apt. no.	▲ You **must** enter your SSN(s) above. ▲
City, town or post office, state, and ZIP code. If you have a foreign address, see page 18.		Checking a box below will not change your tax or refund.

Presidential Election Campaign ▶ Check here if you, or your spouse if filing jointly, want $3 to go to this fund (see page 18) ▶ ☐ **You** ☐ **Spouse**

Filing status Check only one box.
1 ☐ Single
2 ☐ Married filing jointly (even if only one had income)
3 ☐ Married filing separately. Enter spouse's SSN above and full name here. ▶
4 ☐ Head of household (with qualifying person). (See page 19.) If the qualifying person is a child but not your dependent, enter this child's name here. ▶
5 ☐ Qualifying widow(er) with dependent child (see page 19)

Exemptions
6a ☐ **Yourself.** If someone can claim you as a dependent, **do not** check box 6a.
b ☐ **Spouse**

Boxes checked on 6a and 6b ____

c **Dependents:**

If more than six dependents, see page 21.

(1) First name Last name	(2) Dependent's social security number	(3) Dependent's relationship to you	(4) ✓ if qualifying child for child tax credit (see page 21)
			☐
			☐
			☐
			☐
			☐
			☐

No. of children on 6c who:
- **lived with you** ____
- **did not live with you due to divorce or separation (see page 22)** ____

Dependents on 6c not entered above ____

d Total number of exemptions claimed. **Add numbers on lines above** ▶ ☐

Income

Attach Form(s) W-2 here. Also attach Form(s) 1099-R if tax was withheld.

If you did not get a W-2, see page 24.

Enclose, but do not attach, any payment.

7 Wages, salaries, tips, etc. Attach Form(s) W-2. 7
8a **Taxable** interest. Attach Schedule 1 if required. 8a
b **Tax-exempt** interest. **Do not** include on line 8a. 8b
9a Ordinary dividends. Attach Schedule 1 if required. 9a
b Qualified dividends (see page 25). 9b
10 Capital gain distributions (see page 25). 10
11a IRA distributions. 11a | 11b Taxable amount (see page 25). 11b
12a Pensions and annuities. 12a | 12b Taxable amount (see page 26). 12b
13 Unemployment compensation, Alaska Permanent Fund dividends, and jury duty fees. 13
14a Social security benefits. 14a | 14b Taxable amount (see page 28). 14b
15 Add lines 7 through 14b (far right column). This is your **total income.** ▶ 15

Adjusted gross income

16 Penalty on early withdrawal of savings (see page XX). 16
17 IRA deduction (see page 28). 17
18 Student loan interest deduction (see page 31). 18
19 Jury duty pay you gave your employer (see page XX). 19
20 Add lines 16 through 19. These are your **total adjustments.** 20
21 Subtract line 20 from line 15. This is your **adjusted gross income.** ▶ 21

For Disclosure, Privacy Act, and Paperwork Reduction Act Notice, see page 58. Cat. No. 11327A Form **1040A** (2006)

(Use for Problem 29.)

Form 1040A (2006) Page **2**

Tax, credits, and payments

22 Enter the amount from line 21 (adjusted gross income). 22

23a Check if: ☐ **You** were born before January 2, 1942, ☐ Blind; ☐ **Spouse** was born before January 2, 1942, ☐ Blind } **Total boxes checked** ▶ 23a ☐

b If you are married filing separately and your spouse itemizes deductions, see page 32 and check here ▶ 23b ☐

Standard Deduction for—
- People who checked any box on line 23a or 23b **or** who can be claimed as a dependent, see page 32.
- All others:

Single or Married filing separately, $5,150

Married filing jointly or Qualifying widow(er), $10,300

Head of household, $7,550

24 Enter your **standard deduction** (see left margin). 24

25 Subtract line 24 from line 22. If line 24 is more than line 22, enter -0-. 25

26 If line 22 is over $112,875, or you provided housing to a person displaced by Hurricane Katrina, see page 33. Otherwise, multiply $3,300 by the total number of exemptions claimed on line 6d. 26

27 Subtract line 26 from line 25. If line 26 is more than line 25, enter -0-. This is your **taxable income.** ▶ 27

28 **Tax,** including any alternative minimum tax (see page 34). 28

29 Credit for child and dependent care expenses. Attach Schedule 2. 29

30 Credit for the elderly or the disabled. Attach Schedule 3. 30

31 Education credits. Attach Form 8863. 31

32 Retirement savings contributions credit. Attach Form 8880. 32

33 Child tax credit (see page 38). Attach Form 8901 if required. 33

34 Add lines 29 through 33. These are your **total credits.** 34

35 Subtract line 34 from line 28. If line 34 is more than line 28, enter -0-. 35

36 Advance earned income credit payments from Form(s) W-2, box 9. 36

37 Add lines 35 and 36. This is your **total tax.** ▶ 37

38 Federal income tax withheld from Forms W-2 and 1099. 38

39 2006 estimated tax payments and amount applied from 2005 return. 39

If you have a qualifying child, attach Schedule EIC.

40a **Earned income credit (EIC).** 40a

b Nontaxable combat pay election. 40b

41 Additional child tax credit. Attach Form 8812. 41

42 Credit for federal telephone excise tax paid. Attach Form 8913 if required. 42

43 Add lines 38, 39, 40a, 41, and 42. These are your **total payments.** ▶ 43

Refund

44 If line 43 is more than line 37, subtract line 37 from line 43. This is the amount you **overpaid.** 44

Direct deposit? See page 53 and fill in 45b, 45c, and 45d or Form 8888.

45a Amount of line 44 you want **refunded to you.** If Form 8888 is attached, check here ▶ ☐ 45a

▶ b Routing number ▶ c Type: ☐ Checking ☐ Savings

▶ d Account number

46 Amount of line 44 you want **applied to your 2007 estimated tax.** 46

Amount you owe

47 **Amount you owe.** Subtract line 43 from line 37. For details on how to pay, see page 54. ▶ 47

48 Estimated tax penalty (see page 54). 48

Third party designee

Do you want to allow another person to discuss this return with the IRS (see page 55)? ☐ **Yes.** Complete the following. ☐ **No**

Designee's name ▶ Phone no. ▶ ( ) Personal identification number (PIN) ▶

Sign here

Joint return? See page 18. Keep a copy for your records.

Under penalties of perjury, I declare that I have examined this return and accompanying schedules and statements, and to the best of my knowledge and belief, they are true, correct, and accurately list all amounts and sources of income I received during the tax year. Declaration of preparer (other than the taxpayer) is based on all information of which the preparer has any knowledge.

Your signature	Date	Your occupation	Daytime phone number ( )
Spouse's signature. If a joint return, **both** must sign.	Date	Spouse's occupation	

Paid preparer's use only

Preparer's signature	Date	Check if self-employed ☐	Preparer's SSN or PTIN
Firm's name (or yours if self-employed), address, and ZIP code		EIN	
		Phone no. ( )	

Printed on recycled paper

Form **1040A** (2006)

COMPREHENSIVE PROBLEM

31. Tonya Tornan is a single parent. During 2006 she earned wages $26,000. Her employer withheld $560 in federal income taxes and she received advanced EIC payments of $1,200 during the year. Tornan claims her two dependent children, age 5 and 8, as dependents. The wages are Tornan's only source of gross income. Compute Tornan's taxable income and her taxes due to (or from) the government when she files her 2006 tax return. She claims the standard credit for federal telephone excise tax paid by taxpayers claiming three exemptions.

CUMULATIVE PROBLEM 1 (CHAPTERS 1-2)

The solutions to the following Cumulative Problems require use of information provided in Chapters 1 and 2.

Jack Bennett is married but does not file a joint return with his spouse. He is 36 years of age and has excellent vision. Bennett and his ex-wife share custody of their 10-year-old son. They have lived in separate households since May, 2006. Bennett is not the custodial parent, but his wife has signed Form 8332 giving him the dependency exemption. Bennett's AGI is $63,440 and he uses the standard deduction. His employer withheld $8,800 for federal income taxes during the year. Compute Bennett's 2006 taxable income and taxes owed (to be refunded). He claims the standard credit for federal telephone excise tax paid by taxpayers claiming two exemptions.

CUMULATIVE PROBLEM 2 (CHAPTERS 1-2)

Emily and David Chen claim their three children, ages 5-10, as dependents. During 2006, Emily worked full time and earned $36,800. Her employer withheld $1,500 for federal income taxes. David attended college full-time for the entire year. Other than Emily's wages, the couple's only other source of earned income is $800 of taxable interest. The Chens paid $2,500 in qualified child care expenses to allow Emily to work and David to attend college. Compute the couple's taxable income and taxes owed (to be refunded) on their 2006 joint tax return. The couple uses the standard deduction. They are both under age 65 and have no problems with their vision. They claim the standard credit for federal telephone excise tax paid.

Gross Income Inclusions

CHAPTER CONTENTS

CHAPTER OVERVIEW

Chapters 1 and 2 presented an overview of the basic tax and reporting structure. They illustrated several tax forms, schedules, and worksheets, including the two simplest tax returns, Form 1040EZ and Form 1040A. The next few chapters will focus on particular segments of the taxable income formula, starting with gross income.

The amount of gross income helps determine whether an individual must file a tax return or whether a person qualifies as a dependent. Strangely, however, none of the tax forms includes a line for reporting gross income; it does not appear on any of the tax returns. This chapter identifies many income items that taxpayers must include in gross income. Chapter 4 examines income sources the tax law excludes from gross income.

GENERAL GUIDELINES

Gross income is all income from every source, except those sources specifically excluded by tax law. Thus, taxpayers face two problems:

1. Recognizing potential income items
2. Identifying those income items specifically excluded by law

This situation raises the question, "What is income?" Although the Code does not define income, it is generally considered to be any increase in wealth (assets minus liabilities). Taxpayers generally report income only in the year it is realized as determined by their accounting method (cash or accrual). Cash basis taxpayers report income in the year money, property, or services are actually or constructively received in an income producing event. **Constructive receipt** takes place when assets are credited or made available to the taxpayer without restriction (e.g., interest on a bank deposit credited to the taxpayer's account.) Taxpayers report property and services received at their fair market value (FMV).

Accrual basis taxpayers normally report income in the year they earn it, regardless of when they receive the cash. They report service revenue in income in the year they perform the services. They report interest in income in the year the interest accrues. They report the revenues from the sale of goods in the year the sale occurs.

Although appreciation in property values may cause an increase in wealth, the tax law does not recognize mere appreciation of assets as income. Instead, taxpayers must convert the property into cash or other property before realizing a gain. Furthermore, only the excess of the amount realized over the taxpayer's investment in the property (known as "basis") is taxable.

Exceptions

Cash basis taxpayer usually report income in the year when it is actually or constructively received. Sometimes income is imputed, as is the case when taxpayers buy taxable bonds at a discount (see Example 16) or when they make below market loans (discussed later in the chapter).

Accrual basis taxpayers normally report income in the year they earn it. However, certain advanced payments are taxed in the year received. This includes payments for interest income and for warranty services offered by third parties. It also can include prepaid rent. The Code taxes most other types of advanced payments over two tax years. Income earned in the year the payment is received is reported in income in that year. The rest is reported as income in the next year. This rule holds even if the payment is for goods and services that extend into the third year or beyond.

EXAMPLE 1

On November 5, 20x1, Jenny Murray buys an appliance from ASE, a local retailer. She pays ASE $900 for a warranty that will cover all repair costs for the first two years. ASE uses a calendar tax year and the accrual method. Since the warranty was offered by the seller (and not a third party), ASE prorates the income over two years. In 20x1, it reports income of $75 ($900/24 x 2 months). It reports the rest ($900 - $75 = $825) in 20x2. Even though the warranty extends into 20x3, ASE cannot defer (delay) the income beyond the second tax year.

EXAMPLE 2

Same as in Example 1, except that Murray purchases the warranty from a third party. The third party must include the $900 in income in 20x1. The rule that allows the deferral of income to the next tax year does not apply to warranties offered by third parties..

EXAMPLE 3

On August 1, 20x1, Jan's Dance Studio received $1,800 for 36 dance lessons. Eight lessons are given in 20x1. On its 20x1 tax return, Jan's reports $400 ($1,800/36 x 8). It reports the rest ($1,800 – $400 = $1,400) in 20x2.

EXAMPLE 4

Same as in Example 3, except that Jan's received $2,400 for 48 dance lessons under a two-year contract. Ten lessons are given in 20x1, 20 were given in 20x2, and 15 were given in 20x3. The customer forfeited the last three lessons. On its 20x1 tax return, Jan's reports income of $500 ($2,400/48 x 10). It reports the rest ($2,400 – $500 = $1,900) in 20x2. The fact that some of the services were provided in 20x3 (or never provided at all) does not affect the timing of when the $2,400 is reported in gross income.

PROFIT FROM BUSINESS OR PROFESSION

The Code taxes a person's income from a business or profession. Also, it usually allows a taxpayer to deduct losses from such activities. Taxpayers report their business or professional profits or losses on Form 1040. They report supporting details on Schedule C (Chapter 7).

For a taxpayer involved with passive income activities, loss limitations can apply. A passive activity is one in which a taxpayer does not spend a regular, continuous, and substantial amount of time (Chapter 9).

COMPENSATION

Employees may report bonuses, commissions, salaries, tips, and wages on Form 1040EZ, Form 1040A, or Form 1040. Students who receive taxable scholarships treat them like additional compensation, and therefore, may report them on any of these forms. To use Form 1040EZ or Form 1040A, a taxpayer must have taxable income under $100,000. Also, when total compensation from more than one employer exceeds $94,200, the taxpayer cannot use Form 1040EZ. Independent contractors who receive fees for their services report them as business income on Schedule C.

Fees, Bonuses, Commissions, Salaries, and Wages

Compensation is something received for services rendered, and most compensation is taxable under the Code regardless of the form it takes. When a person receives compensation in the form of property, the Code taxes its fair market value (FMV). For example, when a person speaks at a conference being held on a cruise ship and is paid by being given a free cruise, the speaker includes the FMV of the cruise in gross income.

FAIR MARKET VALUE (FMV)

FMV is the price that a willing buyer wants to pay and a willing seller wants to accept. FMV assumes that neither buyer nor seller must buy or sell. FMV also assumes that buyer and seller have reasonable knowledge of all necessary facts. In the absence of an actual sale or exchange, FMV can be determined by expert appraisal or other supporting evidence.

Compensation includes fees charged by accountants, doctors, lawyers, and engineers for professional services. It also includes fees for baby-sitting, lawncare, snow shoveling, and newspaper delivery. Unless an exception applies, any taxpayer providing services for another taxpayer and receiving something of value in return receives taxable compensation. Taxpayers include as compensation amounts withheld from their pay for social security, Medicare, and income taxes. Compensation also includes amounts withheld for life insurance premiums, health insurance premiums, union dues, work clothes, and so on. Unless specifically exempt by statute, U.S. Constitution, or IRS de minimis rule, compensation includes all employee fringe benefits. Although some exceptions exist, compensation includes military service pay.

Tips

The Code taxes tips as other compensation. This includes cash tips and credit card tips received from customers or other employees. The IRS requires taxpayers who receive tips to follow special reporting rules.

Reporting to Employer

The IRS expects employees to file tip reports with their employers by the 10th of the month following the month in which they receive tips. An employer may require more frequent reporting. Employees who receive tips in December 20x1 and report the tips to their employers in January 20x2 include the tips in 20x2 gross income. When employees fail to turn in tip reports they include their tips in gross income in the year of receipt.

Tips of Less than $20

An employee who receives less than $20 in monthly tips while working for one employer need not tell the employer about the tips. In addition, the employee does not pay social security or Medicare taxes on these tips, but must add them to their wages on either Form 1040EZ, Form 1040A, or Form 1040.

EXAMPLE 5

Randy Sutton works for a hotel. Sometimes hotel patrons give him tips. However, his total tips are always less than $20 a month. Sutton's tips for 20x1 total $165. He adds this amount to his taxable wages when he files his 20x1 tax return. He does not pay social security or Medicare taxes on this income.

Tips of $20 or More

An employee who receives $20 or more in monthly tips while working for one employer must report them to the employer. The IRS provides Form 4070, Employee's Report of Tips to Employer, for this purpose. Employees do not have to use Form 4070 if they must supply their employer with the same information.

Taxpayers who have monthly tips of $20 or more, but fail to report them to their employers, add the unreported tips to their other wages on Form 1040. They then compute related social security and Medicare taxes on Form 4137, Social Security and Medicare Tax on Unreported Tip Income, and enter the total tax on Form 1040. In addition, they complete Schedule U (Form 1040), U.S. Schedule of Unreported Tip Income. Taxpayers attach the form and schedule to their tax returns. The social security office uses Schedule U to determine the employee's retirement benefits. Employees reporting all their tips to their employers do not use Form 4137.

Employees who do not report tips to their employers when required to do so may be assessed penalties equal to 50% of the related social security and Medicare taxes.

Information for Figure 3-1: Filled-In Form 4070

Susan K. Maples works Friday and Saturday evenings as a waitress. Most of Maples's customers enter her tips on their credit charge slips. However, some leave cash tips. At the end of the evening, the restaurant bookkeeper informs Maples of her total charges in tips and pays her cash for these tips. Maples pays out some money to the head chef and one of the bus persons. At month's end, Maples prepares Form 4070 and gives it to her employer. Figure 3-1 shows Maples's Form 4070.

FIGURE 3-1 Filled In Form 4070

Form **4070** (Rev. August 2005) Department of the Treasury Internal Revenue Service	**Employee's Report of Tips to Employer**	OMB No. 1545-0074
Employee's name and address Susan K. Maples 2232 Marshall Street, Tampa, FL 33603		**Social security number** 820 : 26 : 3292
Employer's name and address (include establishment name, if different) Firesides Restaurant 22 South Shore Drive Tampa, FL 33614		**1** Cash tips received 304.00 **2** Credit and debit card tips received 790.00 **3** Tips paid out 245.00
Month or shorter period in which tips were received from May 1 , 2006 , to May 31 , 2006		**4** Net tips (lines **1** + **2** - **3**) 849.00
Signature *Susan K. Maples*		Date June 2, 2006
For Paperwork Reduction Act Notice, see the instructions on the back of this form.	Cat. No. 41320P	Form **4070** (Rev. 8-2005)

Maples's employer will include the $849 of net tips in her taxable wages that will be reported to her at the end of the year on her W-2. Her employer will withhold income taxes, social security and Medicare taxes on these extra wages.

Information for Figure 3-2: Filled-In Form 4137 and Schedule U

Robert R. Cooper works part time as a waiter. Cooper lost his record of tips for November 1. In February, he found his tally sheet for November 1 and discovered that he understated his reported tips for the previous November by $95.

Cooper fills in Form 4137 and Schedule U. He attaches a statement explaining why he did not report the $95 to his employer. On his tax return, he adds the $95 to his other "Wages, salaries, tips, etc." on Form 1040. He also enters $7.27 on Form 1040 for social security and Medicare taxes. Figure 3-2 shows Cooper's filled-in Form 4137 and Schedule U.

Allocating Tips to Employees

The government generally assumes that food and beverage servers earn tips equal to at least 8% of gross sales. Consequently, when employees of certain large restaurants and cocktail lounges report less than this amount to their employers, the employers must report the difference as additional income on the employees' Form W-2. These "allocated tips" appear on Form W-2 (box 8) as a separate item. Employers do not report them with wages and reported tips. However, employees add their allocated tips to their taxable wages on Form 1040.

Sometimes an IRS district director will approve a threshold percentage below 8%. However, a director cannot approve a percentage below 2%. When a percentage below 8% applies, employers allocate tips using this percentage.

When customers of a business tip less than 8%, the employer or a majority of employees should petition the IRS for an allocation rate of less than 8%.

Only employees who get tips directly from customers receive allocated tips. Also, only employees reporting tips below the threshold percentage participate in the allocation. Cooks and service bartenders do not receive allocated tips.

FIGURE 3-2 Filled-In Form 4137 and Schedule U

Form **4137** Department of the Treasury Internal Revenue Service (99)

Social Security and Medicare Tax on Unreported Tip Income

▶ See instructions on back.
▶ Attach to Form 1040.

OMB No. 1545-0074 **2006** Attachment Sequence No. **24**

Name of person who received tips (as shown on Form 1040). If married, complete a separate Form 4137 for each spouse with unreported tips.: Robert R. Cooper

Social security number: 394-99-1132

Name(s) of employer(s) to whom you were required to, but did not, report your tips: Pig & Poke Restaurant

1	Total cash and charge tips you **received** in 2006 (see instructions)	1	5,095 00
2	Total cash and charge tips you **reported** to your employer in 2006	2	5,000 00
3	Subtract line 2 from line 1. This amount is income you **must** include in the total on Form 1040, line 7	3	95 00
4	Cash and charge tips you received but did not report to your employer because the total was less than $20 in a calendar month (see instructions)	4	
5	Unreported tips subject to Medicare tax. Subtract line 4 from line 3. Enter here and on line 2 of Schedule U below	5	95 00
6	Maximum amount of wages (including tips) subject to social security tax — 6: 94,200 00		
7	Total social security wages and social security tips (total of boxes 3 and 7 on Form(s) W-2) or railroad retirement (tier 1) compensation — 7: 16,200 00		
8	Subtract line 7 from line 6. If line 7 is more than line 6, enter -0- here and on line 9 and go to line 11	8	78,000 00
9	Unreported tips subject to social security tax. Enter the **smaller** of line 5 or line 8 here and on line 1 of Schedule U below. If you received tips as a federal, state, or local government employee, see instructions	9	95 00
10	Multiply line 9 by .062	10	5 89
11	Multiply line 5 by .0145	11	1 38
12	Add lines 10 and 11. Enter the result here and on Form 1040, line 59 ▶	12	7 27

For Paperwork Reduction Act Notice, see instructions on back. Form **4137** (2006)

Do Not Detach

SCHEDULE U (Form 1040) Department of the Treasury Internal Revenue Service

U.S. Schedule of Unreported Tip Income

For crediting to your social security record

2006

Note: *The amounts you report below are for your social security record. This record is used to figure any benefits, based on your earnings, payable to you and your dependents or your survivors. Fill in each item accurately and completely.*

Print or type name of person who received tip income (as shown on Form 1040): Robert R. Cooper

Social security number: 349-99-1132

Address (number, street, and apt. no., or P.O. box if mail is not delivered to your home): 748 Grand Road

Occupation: Waiter

City, town or post office, state, and ZIP code: Denison, OH 44621

1	Unreported tips subject to social security tax. Enter the amount from line 9 (Form 4137) above ▶	1	95 00
2	Unreported tips subject to Medicare tax. Enter the amount from line 5 (Form 4137) above ▶	2	95 00

To ensure that employees report and employers allocate properly, the IRS requires affected business owners or managers to keep supporting records. It also requires them to report annually gross sales and employee tips to the IRS. To report, businesses use Form 8027, Employer's Annual Information Return of Tip Income and Allocated Tips.

The allocation and reporting requirement usually applies to a business employing more than ten persons on a typical business day. Only businesses that serve food or beverages on the premises and have regular tipping customers file Form 8027. Cafeterias, fast-food outlets, and businesses outside the U.S. do not file Form 8027. Also, businesses that add service charges of 10% or more to 95% of their food or beverage bills do not file Form 8027.

Employers do not withhold income, social security, or Medicare taxes from allocated tips. Thus, employees receiving allocated tips must file Form 4137 with Form 1040 and pay the social security and Medicare taxes on the allocated tips.

DIVORCE AND SEPARATION AGREEMENTS

When a married couple gets a divorce or becomes legally separated, three money issues arise:

1. Division of property acquired during the marriage (property settlement)
2. Spousal support (alimony)
3. Support of the children (child support)

Property Settlement

A property settlement involves the transfer of cash and other property between spouses or former spouses during the process of splitting up marital assets. Neither party reports income or deductions on such a settlement. The transferee's investment ("tax basis") in the property received is the same as that of the transferor.

EXAMPLE 6

Tim and Cher Hudsen's divorce was finalized in 2006. As part of the divorce decree, Tim transfers to Cher title to the couple's vacation home. At the time of the transfer the home is worth $250,000. Tim bought the home prior to their marriage. He paid $110,000 for the home. Cher does not report gross income on the transfer. Her tax basis in the home is $110,000. This amount is used to determine Cher's taxable gain should she later sell the home.

Alimony

Property settlements are neither taxable to the recipient nor deductible by the payer. Spousal support (alimony), on the other hand, is both. A person receiving spousal support reports it as "Alimony received" on Form 1040. The payer deducts the same amount for AGI and provides the IRS with the recipient's social security number (SSN). The IRS charges the taxpayer $50 for failure to report the recipient's SSN. Taxpayers cannot use Form 1040EZ or Form 1040A to report either the receipt or payment of alimony.

For separations and divorces that occur after 1984, payments to a spouse must meet several conditions in order to qualify as alimony:

1. The payment must be made in cash.
2. The payment cannot be for child support.
3. The payment must be required under a legal divorce decree or a separate maintenance or divorce instrument.
4. The governing decree or instrument must not label payments as something other than alimony.
5. The payer must not be required to make payments after the recipient's death.
6. The parties may not live in the same household at the time of payment.

Usually, the Code does not classify payments between legally separated or divorced persons as alimony when they live together. Even when taxpayers separate themselves within a household, the rule still applies. However, when within a month after a payment date, the Code treats the payment as alimony.

A different set of rules applies to divorces and separations occurring before 1985. These rules may be found in IRS Publication 504.

Alimony Recapture

Special rules apply when alimony payments in the second or third postseparation year decrease by more than $15,000 from the payments made in the previous year. Because property settlement generally takes place soon after the divorce or separation agreement, these rules act as a safeguard against taxpayers disguising property settlements as alimony. When the change in payments exceeds the statutory limits, the law requires a "recapture" of the excessive alimony payments. The payer must include the excessive payments in gross income, and the payee may deduct them for AGI. These recapture rules apply only in the third year. In that year, the couple computes excessive payments for both year one and year two and includes them on the tax return accordingly. These rules generally keep couples from using alimony as a method of converting property settlements into deductible alimony payments.

Because the alimony recapture rules do not apply after the third postseparation year, the payor of alimony could arrange for payments declining by more than $15,000 to start after the third postseparation year. This will avoid the recapture rules. Also, the recapture rules do not affect level payments and payments increasing during the three-year period.

Child Support

The Code excludes child support payments from income. The exclusion applies to payments clearly labeled as child support as well as those that can be implied as child support. For example, if payments to a former spouse decline when the child reaches age 18, the law treats the amount of the reduction as child support. When the total alimony and child support payments are less than the required amount, payments will first apply toward child support. For a divorce or separation before 1985, child support must be clearly labeled in the agreement. Otherwise, the payments are treated as alimony.

EXAMPLE 7

Buddy and Suzie Hollands divorced in 2003. As part of the divorce decree, Buddy is to pay Suzie $1,600 each month. The agreement states that $700 represents support for their 8-year-old son. During 2006, Buddy pays Suzie $19,200 ($1,600 x 12). Suzie reports in gross income the $10,800 she received that represents alimony ($1,600 - $700 = $900 x 12). Buddy deducts this same amount for AGI on his tax return and gives the IRS Suzie's SSN.

EXAMPLE 8

Same as in Example 7, except that the divorce decree states that the entire $1,600 payment represents alimony. However, Buddy's payments drop to $900 once the son turns 18. The tax laws treat the $700 reduction as child support. Since $8,400 of the total payments ($700 x 12) is considered nontaxable child support, Suzie reports $10,800 ($19,200 - $8,400) in gross income as alimony. Buddy deducts this same $10,800 for AGI.

EXAMPLE 9

Same as in Example 7, except that Buddy fails to make two of his required payments in 2006. Suzie receives $16,000 ($1,600 x 10) during the year. Of this amount, $8,400 is considered to be child support ($700 x 12). Suzie reports $7,600 ($16,000 - $8,400) in gross income as alimony. Buddy deducts this same $7,600 for AGI.

DIVIDEND INCOME

Corporations frequently distribute cash, property, rights to purchase stock, and other accommodations to shareholders. Each year, they report the value of these distributions to shareholders on information return Form 1099-DIV, Dividends and Distributions.

Ordinary Dividends

The Code taxes distributions from a corporation's earnings and profits (E&P) as ordinary dividends. Both cash and accrual basis shareholders include dividends in gross income in the year received. When a corporation distributes noncash property to its shareholders from its E&P, shareholders increase gross income by the property's market value. Unless a corporation identifies a distribution for special tax treatment, the Code taxes it as an ordinary dividend.

Most ordinary dividends received by individuals are taxed at a rate of 15%. A 5% rate applies to taxpayers in the 15% and 10% tax brackets. These are the same rates that apply to net capital gains. Some dividends are ineligible for these reduced rates. Examples of nonqualified dividends include those paid by credit unions, mutual insurance companies, farmer's cooperatives, and mutual savings banks. These items are really interest.

EXAMPLE 10

James Arbogast, single, has taxable income of $49,000, including qualified dividends of $5,000. This level of taxable income places Arbogast in the 25% tax bracket and gives him a 15% tax rate on qualified dividends. Thus, he determines his tax on $44,000 ($49,000 – $5,000) from the Tax Table—$7,564. To this amount he adds his tax on the dividends—$750 ($5,000 × 15%). His total tax is $8,314 ($7,564 + $750).

Nominee Dividends

Sometimes, taxpayers receive ordinary dividends as nominees (middlemen who forward the payment to the actual owners) for other taxpayers. For example, parents sometimes can receive dividends for their children. If the paying corporation shows the nominee's SSN on Form 1099-DIV, the nominee prepares another Form 1099-DIV. The nominee sends the original of the newly prepared Form 1099-DIV to the IRS, gives a copy to the actual shareholder, and keeps a copy for his or her files.

Dividend Reinvestment Plans (DRIPs)

Some corporations offer shareholders dividend reinvestment plans. In these plans, a trustee receives the dividends and usually purchases additional stock in the paying corporation for participating shareholders. Although, the shareholders never actually receive the dividends, they include them in gross income as ordinary dividends.

Return of Capital Distributions

When corporations with no E&P distribute cash or property to their shareholders, the amounts distributed are treated a return of the shareholders' investment in the stock. These "return-of-capital" distributions are not taxed, but instead reduce a shareholders' tax basis in the stock until it reaches zero. Once the stock's basis reaches zero, the Code taxes any additional distribution as a capital gain. The gain is long-term or short-term, depending on how long the taxpayer has owned the stock.

Distributions from Mutual Funds

Mutual funds make five types of distributions: (1) ordinary dividends, (2) return-of-capital distributions, (3) capital gain distributions, (4) exempt interest distributions, and (5) foreign investment dividends. The rules governing ordinary dividends and return-of-capital distributions are the same as those covered in the previous sections. The following sections cover the remaining types of distributions.

Capital Gain Distributions

A capital gain distribution from a mutual fund represents its net long-term capital gain for the year. Distributing companies report capital gain distributions to shareholders on Form 1099-DIV. Shareholders report them as long-term capital gains on Schedule D, Capital Gains and Losses, rather than as dividends on Schedule B, Interest and Ordinary Dividends. Some mutual funds hold on to the long-term capital gains and pay capital gains tax. Mutual funds pay a 35% tax rate on undistributed capital gains. This tax is then passed on to shareholders, who claim it as a tax payment on Form 1040. The shareholder increases his or her basis in the mutual fund shares by the long-term capital gains net of tax. Mutual funds report the gain and related tax to shareholders on Form 2439, Notice to Shareholder of Undistributed Long-Term Capital Gains. Shareholders attach this form to their tax returns.

EXAMPLE 11

At the end of the year, Medical Investors (MI), a mutual fund, had 5,650,200 shares of issued and outstanding stock. For the year, it elected to retain net long-term capital gains of $833,726 and pay the related tax of $291,804 ($833,726 × 35%). As a result, shareholders of MI will include $0.1475569 per share in gross income as undistributed net long-term capital gains. They will also claim a tax credit of $0.0516448 per share for their share of tax paid on the gains.

During the year, Margaret Smith owned 2,000 shares of MI. She reports the $295 of undistributed long-term capital gain from Form 2439 (2,000 × $0.1475569) on Schedule D, Capital Gains and Losses. She claims a credit of $103 (2,000 × $0.0516448) under "Other payments" on Form 1040 for her share of the taxes paid by MI. Smith increases her basis in MI by $192 ($295 - $103)

Exempt Bond Interest Distributions

Under certain conditions, the Code does not tax an exempt interest distribution from a mutual fund. For tax-free treatment, the fund must hold 50% or more of its investments in tax-exempt municipal bonds at the end of each calendar quarter. Also, it must pay out 90% or more of this interest to shareholders annually.

Foreign Investment Dividends

Some mutual funds invest in foreign corporations. Dividends from these companies are subject to foreign income taxation. When a fund receives dividends from a foreign corporation, it will pay income tax to the foreign country. The fund may forward some or all of the dividends to the shareholders who must then pay U.S. income taxes on the distribution. At the end of the year, the mutual fund will inform shareholders about their shares of foreign income taxes paid the foreign-source dividends that were distributed to them. The shareholders deduct these taxes as itemized deductions or claim them as foreign tax credits on Form 1116, Foreign Tax Credit (Individual, Estate, or Trust).

"Dividends" Paid on Insurance Premiums

"Dividends" paid from life insurance companies are actually a return of premiums paid during the year. These amounts are not taxable.

Reporting Dividend Income

Taxpayers cannot use Form 1040EZ to report dividend income or capital gains. However, they may report exempt bond interest from mutual funds on Form 1040EZ. They do this by entering the letters *TEI* (tax-exempt interest) and the amount in the blank space following the request for "Taxable interest."

Taxpayers may use Form 1040A to report dividend income. The IRS wants taxpayers to report all dividends received. Any dividends not taxed to them (e.g., nominee dividends and return of capital distributions) are then shown as a subtraction from the reported dividends. This technique is shown in Figure 3-3, which illustrates the use of Schedule 1 (Form 1040A) to report dividends. Individuals may also report dividend income on Form 1040. Dividends totaling over $1,500 requires the filing of either Schedule 1 or Schedule B. Schedule B (Form

1040) is similar to Schedule 1 (Form 1040A). Taxpayers report capital gain distributions directly on Schedule D, Capital Gains and Losses. Also, when taxpayers are required to use Schedule D, the tax on dividends is computed on that schedule. When Schedule D is not required, taxpayers compute their tax on qualified dividends using a special worksheet.

Information for Figure 3-3: Filled-In Schedule 1 (Form 1040A), Part II

Jackie C. Hirsch uses Schedule 1 (Form 1040A), Part II to report the ordinary dividends she receives. Hirsch receives dividends from Blue Publishing Company and Native Son Corporation as a nominee for her 10-year-old son. Hirsch owns stock in Bay Weaving Company and Pike Moving Company. Hirsch reports the nominee dividends separately on Schedule 1 and includes them in her total. She then backs out the nominee dividends to arrive at her taxable dividends.

FIGURE 3-3 FILLED-IN SCHEDULE 1 (FORM 1040A), PART II

Part II

Ordinary dividends

(See back of schedule and the instructions for Form 1040A, line 9a.)

Note. If you received a Form 1099-DIV or substitute statement from a brokerage firm, enter the firm's name and the ordinary dividends shown on that form.

	List name of payer.		Amount	
5	Blue Publishing Company	5	210	00
	Native Son Corporation		75	00
	Nominee Distribution		285	00
	Bay Weaving Company		530	00
	Pike Moving Company		1,340	00
	Total		2,155	00
	Less: Nominee Distribution		(285	00)
6	Add the amounts on line 5. Enter the total here and on Form 1040A, line 9a.	6	1,870	00

For Paperwork Reduction Act Notice, see Form 1040A instructions. Cat. No. 12075R **Schedule 1 (Form 1040A) 2006**

FARM INCOME OR LOSS

Taxpayers report net income (or loss) from farming on Form 1040. They report the details of income and expenses on Schedule F. Special income and expense rules apply to farming because of the unique activities associated with growing crops, raising animals, and maintaining land and other resources. IRS Publication 225 provides information on farming activities.

GAINS AND LOSSES

When taxpayers sell or exchange property, a gain or loss results. As a general rule, taxpayers report on their tax returns all gains, but they report losses only from sales or exchanges of investment or business property. Chapter 10 explains how gains and losses are computed.

Taxpayers report gains and losses from the sale or exchange of business property on Form 4797, Sale of Business Property. For individual taxpayers, the sum of these gains and losses appears on Form 1040. Individuals report gains from sales or exchanges of personal-use property, as well as gains and losses from investment property on Schedule D, Capital Gains and Losses. The total gain or loss from these sales eventually appears on Form 1040. Chapter 11 describes Form 4797 and Schedule D in detail.

INTEREST INCOME

Interest represents a charge for the use of money. Gross income includes interest on bank deposits, notes, mortgages (including seller-financed mortgages), corporate bonds, and U.S. savings bonds. Gross income also includes interest on income tax refunds. Unless an exception applies, all interest is included in gross income. In some cases, the IRS requires taxpayers to impute interest income on low interest or no interest loans.

Interest Reported as Dividends

Some organizations pay interest but call it something else. The IRS classifies as interest some dividend distributions. These distributions include earnings on deposits and share accounts in (1) cooperative banks, (2) credit unions, (3) domestic building and loan associations, (4) savings and loan associations, and (5) mutual savings banks. Taxpayers who own money market and savings certificates report income from these investments as interest. Taxpayers who receive distributions of exempt (tax-free) interest from mutual funds report them as interest on Schedule B (Form 1040). However, they then subtract them from the total, thereby excluding them from gross income.

Savings Accounts and Certificates

Gross income includes interest from banks, savings bonds, and seller-financed mortgages. When a financial institution credits a depositor's account with interest, the depositor includes the interest in gross income under the constructive receipt rule. Once the interest has been credited to the taxpayer's account, it belongs to the taxpayer and is taxable at that time.

Gross income includes interest on certificates of deposit. For interest deferred more than one year, the Code requires taxpayers to recognize the accrued interest as income under the original issue discount (OID) rules. (See OID, later in the chapter.)

Merchandise Premiums

Some financial institutions (banks, savings and loan associations, and credit unions) offer merchandise incentives to attract deposits. Such merchandise represents prepaid interest. The Code taxes the FMV of this property as interest when a taxpayer receives it.

U.S. Savings Bonds

The federal government issues U.S. savings bonds. Investors can buy Series EE savings bonds by paying a fraction of their face value (amount paid at maturity). They then redeem the bonds for full face value at maturity. The difference between the bond's cost and its face value represents interest (the amount paid to investors for the use of their money). Investors can also buy Series I savings bonds from the government. These bonds are purchased at face value. Interest on Series I bonds accrues every three months. The accrued interest is added to the redemption value of the bond.

The tax laws allow cash-basis investors two options for reporting the interest on U.S. savings bonds. First, they can wait until they redeem the bonds to report all accrued interest. The difference between the redemption amount (which includes accrued interest) and the amount paid for the bonds would be included in gross income. Under the second option, investors can elect to report the interest in gross income as it accrues each year. The accrued interest is the difference between in the bond's redemption value at end and the start of the year.

U.S. Treasury Bills, Notes, and Bonds

In addition to savings bonds, the U.S. government also issues Treasury bills, Treasury notes and Treasury bonds. Treasury bills are short-term and mature in 4-, 13-, or 26-weeks. They are issued at a discount (for less than face value) in multiples of $1,000. The difference between the discounted price investors pay and the face value is interest income. Investors report the interest in gross income in the year the Treasury bill matures.

Treasury notes have maturity periods ranging from one to 10 years. Treasury bonds have maturity periods of more than 10 years. Both Treasury notes and bonds are issued in denominations of $1,000. Both pay interest every six months (semiannually). Cash basis investors report interest in gross income in the year it is paid. When the notes or bonds mature, investors redeem them for face value.

Sometimes Treasury notes and bonds are issued at a discount (less than face value). The difference between issue price and face value is called **original issue discount**. This amount represents additional interest income the investor earns over the life of the bond. Unless the discount is *de minimis* (small in amount), the investor reports the OID in gross income as it accrues over the life of the bond (see discussion on OID bonds later in the chapter). The OID reported in income is then added to the investor's basis (investment) in the bond. When the bond mature, the investor will have reported all OID in gross income and the investor's basis in the bond will equal its face value.

An important tax-planning feature comes with the purchase of U.S. Treasury bills, notes, and bonds, as the owners of these instruments do not pay state and local income taxes on related interest.

Accrued Interest

When a taxpayer purchases a bond between interest dates, the interest up to the purchase date belongs to the seller. The buyer pays this interest to the seller at the time of purchase and deducts it from the first interest payment he or she receives. The buyer then includes all future interest on the bond in gross income.

EXAMPLE 12

On October 1, 20x3, a cash basis investor pays $10,133.33 for bonds. The bonds were originally issued on December 1, 20x1 at their $10,000 face value. The bonds pay $200 interest on June 1 and December 1. Included in the purchase price is $133.33 of interest that had accrued from June 1, 20x3 – October 1, 20x3 ($200/6 x 4 months). On December 1, 20x3 the corporation pays the investor $200. The investor reports $66.67 ($200 - $133.33) in gross income on his 20x3 tax return.

Original Issue Discount (OID) Bonds

Taxpayers that use the cash method include interest on bonds in gross income when they receive it. However, when an investor purchases a bond issued at a discount, another situation arises. Because bondholders receive the full maturity value at redemption time, they must recognize the discount (maturity value minus issue price) as income. But, does the taxpayer recognize it all at redemption time, or should a portion of it be recognized each year over the life of the bond? Basically, the answer depends on the size of the discount and the life of the bond. Another issue is whether to treat the income as ordinary interest or as capital gain.

To answer these questions, the taxpayer must first determine the original issue discount (OID). The Code defines OID as the difference between a bond's face value and its issue price.

EXAMPLE 13

A corporation issues a 20-year, $100,000 zero-coupon bond (no coupons attached) for $12,861. Thus, an investor pays the corporation $12,861 for the right to receive $100,000 20 years from today. The OID equals $87,139 ($100,000 – $12,861).

The Code treats the OID as $0 when the amount of OID is de minimis (a small amount). The Code defines **de minimis OID** as less than one-fourth of 1% (0.0025) of the face value times the number of full years to maturity. When the de minimis rule applies, the holder includes the discount in income when the bond is sold or redeemed. If the bond is a capital asset in the holder's hands, the Code treats the income as a capital gain.

EXAMPLE 14

A corporation issues a 10-year, $100,000 bond for $98,000. Although the real OID equals $2,000, the Code treats it as $0. The $2,000 discount falls below the OID threshold of $2,500 [(.0025 × $100,000 face value of bond) × 10 full years to maturity]. The investor's tax basis (investment) in the bond stays at $98,000. If the investor holds the bond to maturity, at that time the $2,000 will be reported as capital gain ($100,000 face value - $98,000 basis in the bond).

When the discount exceeds the de minimis amount, the taxpayer recognizes the OID as income over the life of the bond by including a portion in gross income each year. For OID instruments issued after April 3, 1993, taxpayers use the effective interest rate method to determine the interest earned. In making this computation, a taxpayer multiplies his investment (basis) in the bond by a the interest rate—the rate needed to produce the desired yield.

The interest must be compounded semiannually. The taxpayer reports the difference between the resulting product and the interest actually paid on the bond as ordinary income. This amount reduces the remaining OID and increases the taxpayer's basis in the bonds. Note that this is an exception to the cash basis method of accounting because the bondholder must recognize income long before receiving the cash.

EXAMPLE 15

On October 1, 20x1, a corporation issues a 30-year, $1,000,000 zero-coupon bond for $169,700. The annual yield to maturity equals 6% compounded semiannually. The bond's original issue discount equals $830,300 ($1,000,000 – $169,700). Earned interest for 20x1 and 20x2 follows:

Interest Income for 20x1:	
October 1, 20x1 through December 31, 20x1	
([6% × $169,700] × 3/12)	$ 2,545.50
Interest Income for 20x2:	
January 1, 20x2 through March 31, 20x2 ([6% × $169,700] × 3/12)	$ 2,545.50
April 1, 20x2 through September 30, 20x2	
([6% × ($169,700 + $2,545.50)] × 6/12)	5,243.73
October 1, 20x2 through December 31, 20x2	
([6% × ($169,700 + $2,545.50 + $5,243.73)] × 3/12)	2,700.52
	$10,489.75

Over the 30 years, the investor writes off the discount and recognizes interest income of $830,300. At the end of the 30 years, the carrying value of the bond equal its $1,000,000 face value ($169,700 + $830,300).

Issuers of OID bonds compute for investors the amount of discount to be included in income. They report this amount on Form 1099-OID, Statement for Recipients of Original Issue Discount. This reporting requirement applies when the calendar year OID equals $10 or more and the term of the bond exceeds one year. For original purchasers of OID debt instruments, the write-off amounts on Form 1099-OID represent interest income. They report these amounts on their tax returns with other interest income. In Example 15, the corporation issues to the investor of the $1,000,000 bond a Form 1099-OID for 20x1. On this form, the investor is told of the $2,545.50 of OID. This amount is reported as interest income on the investor's 20x1 tax return. Likewise, the corporation issues a Form 1099-OID to the investor for 20x2 reporting the $10,489.75 of OID. This amount is reported on the investor's 20x2 tax return.

For OID instruments issued before April 4, 1993, different write-off rules apply. Also, original issue discount rules do not apply to U.S. Savings Bonds or short-term debt instruments with maturity dates of one year or less from their issue dates.

Market Discount Bonds

A market discount arises when an investor purchases a bond from a bondholder (rather than the issuing company) for less than its amortized carrying value. **Amortized carrying value (ACV)** equals a bond's issue price plus all previous OID included in gross income. Taxpayers purchasing a bond with a market discount may elect to include a share of the market discount each year as interest income or wait until the bond is sold and recognize it as interest income at that time. The amount of market discount must be recognized as ordinary interest income either at the time of sale (redemption) or annually over the life of the bond. It never results in capital gain.

Some bondholders must deal with both OID and market discount. Note that an investor must accrue the OID income over the life of the bond using the effective interest rate method. Bondholders with market discount who elect to amortize the interest may choose either the effective rate method or the straight-line method of accruing interest.

EXAMPLE 16

On January 1, 2006, Ron Nealy pays $9,320 for corporate bonds. The bonds were originally issued on January 1, 1990 for $9,200 and have a $10,000 face value. They mature on January 1, 2020. At the time the bonds were issued, the OID was $800 ($10,000 - $9,200). This amount exceeds the $750 threshold for de minimis OID ($10,000 x .0025 x 30 full years to maturity). Thus, the prior owner(s) included some of the OID in gross income each year. The amortized OID was added it to the bond's ACV. As of January 1, 2006 the ACV of the bond is $9,410.

Nealy purchased the bonds at a $90 market discount ($9,320 - $9,410 ACV). He can elect to include a share of this amount in gross income each year from 2006-2019. The amount would be taxed as interest income and would increase his basis in the bonds. His other choice is to wait until he sells the bonds or until they mature to report the $90 as interest income. As of January 1, 2006, the bond had remaining OID of $590 ($10,000 - $9,410). Each year, the corporation will issue Nealy a Form 1099-OID to let him know how much of this OID he must include in gross income. Nealy will increase his tax basis in the bonds by the amount of OID he includes in gross income.

Bond Premiums on Taxable Bonds

Taxpayers who purchase taxable bonds at a premium (an amount in excess of face value) can choose to offset interest income by a portion of the bond's premium. They decrease the basis of the bond by the premium written off. Taxpayers may also choose not to write off bond premiums and report more interest income each year; thus, they have a higher basis in the bonds at sale or redemption. A higher basis translates into less gain or more loss to recognize at disposition. This choice applies to all bonds a taxpayer owns, not just a specific bond.

EXAMPLE 17

Donna Hansen pays $102,000 for bonds that have a face value of $100,000. Hansen has two options for dealing with the $2,000 premium on these bonds. She can amortize the premium over the life of the bonds and reduce the amount of interest income she reports in gross income each year. If she does this, she will decrease her basis in the bonds by the amortized amount. At maturity, her basis would then equal the face value of the bonds. Her second option is to not reduce the amount of interest she reports in gross income and keep her basis in the bonds at $102,000. If she holds the bonds to maturity she will report a long-term capital loss when the bonds are redeemed. If she sells the bonds prior to maturity, the difference between the amount realized from the sale and $102,000 will result in a gain or loss.

Imputed Interest on Below-Market Loans

For a loan made at a low or no stated interest rate, the IRS may impute interest. This means the lender must recognize interest income equal to the imputed interest, and the borrower has an implied interest payment to the lender. To impute the interest, the IRS uses the AFR (applicable federal rate), compounded semiannually. The difference between the interest using the AFR and the interest actually being charged on the loan is the imputed interest.

Published Applicable Federal Rates

Each month the IRS publishes AFRs for short-term, mid-term, and long-term maturities. Taxpayers use the short-term rates for demand loans and loans maturing in three years or less. They use the mid-term rates for debts with four- to nine-year maturities and long-term rates for loans maturing in more than nine years.

POTENTIAL BELOW-MARKET LOAN SITUATIONS

1. Tax-avoidance loans
2. Gift loans (for example, a loan from a parent to a child)
3. Loans between a corporation and a shareholder
4. Compensation-related loans between employer and employee

Gift Loans

Loans to family members (gift loans) fall under the imputed interest rules. Unless an exception applies, the IRS imputes interest on a gift loan where the interest is less than the AFR rate. The lender includes the interest in gross income. Under certain conditions, the borrower may deduct the interest payment (see Chapter 5). In addition, since as the lender never actually has possession of this interest income, the tax laws assume that the lender makes annual gifts to the borrower equal to the imputed interest. Depending on the amount of the gifts, the lender may have to a file a gift tax return.

GIFT LOAN EXCEPTIONS AND LIMITATIONS

1. No interest is imputed on loans of $10,000 or less, unless the loan proceeds are used to purchase income-producing property.
2. No interest is imputed on a loan of $100,000 or less if the borrower's net investment income for the year does not exceed $1,000.
3. Imputed interest cannot exceed the borrower's net investment income for the year on a loan of $100,000 or less between individuals.
4. The above limitations on imputed interest do not apply if tax avoidance is the reason for a loan.

EXAMPLE 18

John and Sandra Grady want to save money to buy a house. Sandra's parents offer to lend John and Sandra $10,000 without interest, provided John and Sandra sign a ten-year note for the funds. John and Sandra agree to these terms and sign the note. If John and Sandra use the loan proceeds to make the down payment, and not to buy income-producing property, the IRS will not impute interest.

EXAMPLE 19

Marilyn and Bob Lange are having trouble saving enough for a down payment on a home. Marilyn's parents offer to loan them $10,000. No interest would be charged on the loan. The $10,000 would be due after 10 years. The Langes intend to use the proceeds to invest in stock and bonds. They plan is to let the balance grow until the have enough for a down payment. Normally, gift loans of $10,000 or less are not subject to the imputed interest rules. However, since the proceeds were used to buy income-producing property, this de minimis exception does not apply. The amount of the gift loan does not exceed $100,000. Thus, no imputed interest will be charged as long as the Lange's net investment income (NII) does not exceed $1,000. If their NII exceeds $1,000, then the imputed interest is limited to the amount of the Lange's NII. NII includes taxable interest, dividends and capital gains from investments minus any deductible investment-related expenses.

For example, if the Lange's NII for the year is $900, then no imputed interest would be charged. If the Lange's NII were $1,100, then the amount of imputed interest could not exceed $1,100. Imputed interest would be the interest charged using the long-term AFR (for loans longer than nine years) less the $0 of interest they pay the parents. Should the imputed interest rules apply, the IRS treats the Langes as having paid Marilyn's parents this amount as interest. The parents report the imputed interest in gross income. Because the proceeds were used to purchase investments, the Langes may be able to deduct this amount as investment interest expense (an itemized deduction). The parents are then deemed to make a gift to the Langes for this same amount.

EXAMPLE 20

Same as in Example 19, except that the Langes do not buy income producing property with the $10,000. Since the amount of the loan does not exceed $10,000, the exception for de minimis gift loans applies. No interest would be imputed.

EXAMPLE 21

Same as in Example 20, except that the parents loan the Langes $10,001. The exception for de minimis gift loans does not apply. The same reasoning as in given in Example 19 holds. Thus, as long as the Lange's NII does not exceed $1,000, no interest will be imputed. If NII exceeds $1,000, the amount of imputed interest cannot exceed their NII since the loan amount does not exceed $100,000.

Compensation-Related Loans

When an employer makes a loan to one of its employees and charges no or inadequate interest, the IRS may impute interest. The imputed interest rules apply to all loans made for tax avoidance purposes. They also apply to compensation-related loans in excess of $10,000.

The amount of imputed interest is the difference between the amount of interest using the AFR and the actual interest paid. In a compensation-related loan, the employee is deemed to pay the imputed interest to the employer. The employer is then deemed to pay the employee compensation this same amount. The employer reports the interest in gross income. The employee may or may not deduct the interest expense depending on the use of the proceeds. For example, if the proceeds from the loan were used for personal reasons, the interest would not be deductible. However, if the proceeds were used to purchase an investment, the interest may be deductible as an itemized deduction. The compensation deemed paid to the employee would be included as wage income on the employee's tax return. The employer would deduct this same amount as wage expense on its tax return.

EXAMPLE 22

Backe & Co. loans its employee, Mark Ross, $20,000. The terms of the note require no interest to be paid and for the $20,000 to be repaid at the end of five years. At the time the loan was made, the current annual AFR mid-term rate (for loans between three and nine years) was 9% (4.5% semiannually). Since no interest is being paid, at the end of the year Ross is deemed to have paid $1,840.50 of interest to Backe & Co. [($20,000 × 4.5%) + ($20,900 × 4.5%)]. Backe & Co. includes the $1,840.50 of interest in gross income. Whether Ross will be able to deduct the $1,840.50 depends on how he used the loan proceeds. Backe & Co. is then deemed to pay wages to Ross for $1,840.50 and deducts the $1,840.50 on its tax return. Ross includes the wages in gross income.

Corporation-Shareholder Loan

When an employer makes a loan to one of its shareholders and charges interest below the AFR, the IRS may impute interest. The imputed interest rules apply to all loans made for tax avoidance purposes. They also apply to corporation-shareholder loans that exceed $10,000. When the imputed interest rules apply, the shareholder is deemed to pay the imputed interest to the corporation. The corporation, in turn, is deemed to pay a dividend to the shareholder for the same amount. The corporation includes the interest in gross income. The shareholder may or may not deduct the interest expense depending on the facts surrounding the loan. The deemed dividends paid to the shareholder would be reported as dividend income on the shareholder's tax return. There is no deduction for dividends paid by the corporation.

EXAMPLE 23

Same as in Example 22, except that Mark Ross is a shareholder, instead of an employee, of Backe & Co. At the end of the year, Ross is deemed to have paid $1,840.50 of interest to Backe & Co., which it includes in gross income. In turn, Backe & Co. is deemed to pay a $1,840.50 dividend to Ross, which he includes in gross income.

EXAMPLE 24

Same as in Example 23, except that the terms of the loan required Ross to pay 4% simple interest annually. Ross now pays $800 interest to Backe & Co. annually ($20,000 x 4%). At the end of the year, Ross is deemed to have paid additional interest to Backe & Co. of $1,040.50 ($1,840.50 using the AFR compounded semiannually minus $800 interest paid). The imputed interest is taxed as interest income to Backe & Co. and as dividend income to Ross.

SUMMARY OF BELOW MARKET LOANS

Type of Loan	*Tax Consequences to the Lender*	*Tax Consequences to the Borrower*
Gift loan	Interest income Gift tax (perhaps)	Interest expense (perhaps)
Employer-employee loan	Interest income Wage expense	Interest expense (perhaps) Wage income
Corporation-shareholder loan	Interest income	Interest expense (perhaps) Dividend income

Reporting Interest Income

Taxpayers may report taxable interest income on Form 1040EZ, Form 1040A, or Form 1040. The IRS also wants to see the amount of tax-exempt interest on these forms.

Normally, a taxpayer receiving interest income of $10 or more receives a Form 1099-INT from the payer. This form identifies taxable interest and any state or federal tax withholding that might have taken place. Copies of Form 1099-INT go to the payee and the IRS. Payees normally do not file this form with their returns, but they should keep copies with their tax records.

Information for Figure 3-4: Filled-In Form 1099-INT

Figure 3-4 illustrates a filled-in Form 1099-INT for Katrina Hansen who earned $195.28 in interest on her savings account.

Form 1040EZ

Form 1040EZ can only be used to report taxable interest income of $1,500 or less. If taxable interest exceeds $1,500, the taxpayer must use Form 1040A or 1040. Tax-exempt can be reported on all three tax returns, regardless of the amount. A Form 1040EZ files report tax-exempt interest income in the blank space after the "Taxable interest" request. They enter first the letters *TEI,* then the amount of tax-exempt interest. However, taxpayers who exclude Educational Savings Bond interest from gross income cannot use Form 1040EZ (see Chapter 4).

A taxpayer who withdraws certificate of deposit funds before the certificate's due date usually pays a penalty. This penalty may be deducted on Form 1040 as a deduction for AGI. It cannot be deducted on Form 1040EZ or Form 1040A.

FIGURE 3-4 FILLED-IN FORM 1099-INT

9292 ☐ VOID ☐ CORRECTED

PAYER'S name, street address, city, state, ZIP code, and telephone no.		Payer's RTN (optional)	OMB No. 1545-0112	
Champaign Savings and Loan 1501 North Main Street La Salle, IL 61301		1 Interest income $ 2 Early withdrawal penalty $	2006 Form **1099-INT**	**Interest Income**
PAYER'S federal identification number 77-5054162	RECIPIENT'S identification number 272-96-5023	3 Interest on U.S. Savings Bonds and Treas. obligations $ 195.28		**Copy A**
RECIPIENT'S name Katrina Hansen		4 Federal income tax withheld $	5 Investment expenses $	**For Internal Revenue Service Center** **File with Form 1096.**
Street address (including apt. no.) 410 E. Locust Street		6 Foreign tax paid $	7 Foreign country or U.S. possession	For Privacy Act and Paperwork Reduction Act Notice, see the **2006 General Instructions for Forms 1099, 1098, 5498, and W-2G.**
City, state, and ZIP code LaSalle, IL 61301		8 Tax-exempt interest $	9 Specified private activity bond interest $	
Account number (see instructions)	2nd TIN not. ☐			

Form **1099-INT** Cat. No. 14410K Department of the Treasury - Internal Revenue Service

Do Not Cut or Separate Forms on This Page — Do Not Cut or Separate Forms on This Page

Most all taxable interest can be reported on Form 1040A. However, Form 1040 must be used to report the following types of taxable interest.

1. When the taxpayer includes in gross income OID other than the amount reported on Form 1099-OID.
2. When the taxpayer has accrued interest on bonds bought between interest dates.
3. When the taxpayer elects to reduce interest income by writing off a bond premium.

Form 1040A

Form 1040A files with taxable interest income of $1,500 or less reports it on the "Taxable interest" line and do not prepare a separate reporting schedule. If they have taxable interest income of more than $1,500, they complete Schedule 1, Part I. Figure 3-5 shows the filled-in Schedule 1 interest income section for a Form 1040A filer. On this schedule, interest amounts from different payers are listed separately. The listing should include all tax-exempt interest. It also should include interest the taxpayer received as a nominee and Educational Savings Bond interest excluded from gross income.

The taxpayer adds these amounts together and enters the total of all interest received. He or she then lists again tax-exempt and nominee interest, determines a subtotal for these items, and deducts it from the total of all interest received. Note that Form 1040A does not have special lines for the total and subtotals. Next to the subtotal for tax-exempt interest, the recipient writes *Tax-Exempt Interest.* Next to the subtotal for nominee interest, the taxpayer writes *Nominee Distribution.* The taxpayer also enters the total tax-exempt interest income on the face of Form 1040A.

Schedule 1 handles excludable Educational Savings Bond interest on a separate line. This interest comes from Form 8815, Exclusion of Interest From Series EE and I U.S. Savings Bonds Issued After 1989 (Chapter 4). The amount reduces the listed interest income to get taxable interest. The taxpayer transfers this final amount to the "Taxable interest" line on Form 1040A, page 1.

Information for Figure 3-5: Filled-In Schedule 1 (Form 1040A), Part I

Ruth Baker uses Schedule 1 (Form 1040A), Part I to report her interest income. Baker receives interest from Erie Lake Distributing Company and Buckeye Lake Brewing Company as a nominee for her 7-year-old daughter. The remaining interest belongs to Baker who has tax-exempt interest of $60 from city of Madison bonds.

FIGURE 3-5 Filled-In Schedule 1 (Form 1040A), Part I

Schedule 1 (Form 1040A) Department of the Treasury—Internal Revenue Service
Interest and Ordinary Dividends for Form 1040A Filers (99) **2006** OMB No. 1545-0074

Name(s) shown on Form 1040A: Ruth O. Baker | **Your social security number**: 727 : 69 : 3205

Part I Interest (See back of schedule and the instructions for Form 1040A, line 8a.)

Note. If you received a Form 1099-INT, Form 1099-OID, or substitute statement from a brokerage firm, enter the firm's name and the total interest shown on that form.

			Amount
1	List name of payer. If any interest is from a seller-financed mortgage and the buyer used the property as a personal residence, see back of schedule and list this interest first. Also, show that buyer's social security number and address.		
	Erie Lake Distributing Company	1	700 00
	Buckeye Lake Brewing Company		250 00
	Nominee Distribution		950 00
	City of Madison Bond Interest		60 00
	Franklin Lake Winery, Inc.		1,175 00
	Nym Lake Distilled Water Company		580 00
	Second Federal National Bank		700 00
	Total Interest		3,465 00
	Less: Nominee Distribution 950		
	Tax-exempt Interest 60		(1,010 00)
2	Add the amounts on line 1.	2	2,455 00
3	Excludable interest on series EE and I U.S. savings bonds issued after 1989. Attach Form 8815.	3	
4	Subtract line 3 from line 2. Enter the result here and on Form 1040A, line 8a.	4	2,455 00

Form 1040

Unless specific exemptions apply, taxpayers include all interest income in gross income. There are no restrictions on the amount or type of interest income that a person may report on Form 1040. When taxable interest income exceeds $1,500, the taxpayer lists each interest item separately on Schedule B, Part I. Schedule B is not illustrated because it is very similar to Form 1040A, Schedule 1.

CHILDREN WITH UNEARNED INCOME (KIDDIE TAX)

Children under age 18 with unearned income may find that the Code taxes some of their unearned income at their parents' highest tax rate. Unearned income is basically investment income from sources such as dividends, interest, capital gains, rents, royalties, and annuities. This tax law reduces the potential tax savings arising when parents transfer investments to their children, who normally pay taxes at lower rates.

The parent's highest (marginal) tax rate applies only to the child's net unearned income. The child's tax rate (from the Tax Tables) determines the tax on the remaining income.

Total unearned income
Less: $850
Less: The
greater of (i) $850 of the standard deduction or
(ii) Itemized deductions directly related
to the production of the unearned income

Equals: Net Unearned Income (NUI)

Computation of the child's total tax for the year requires the following steps:

NUI × parent's highest tax rate
Plus: Remaining taxable income × child's tax rate

Equals: Child's total tax

In 2006, the kiddie tax applies only to a child under age 18 who has unearned income of more than $1,700 and at least one living parent or step-parent. Taxpayers use Form 8615 to calculate the tax. Figure 3-6 illustrates the use of this form.

Prior to 2006, the kiddie tax only applied to children under age 14. Recent tax laws changes increased the age to 18.

Information for Figure 3-6: Filled-In Form 8615

Helen Wong, age 16, receives $3,000 of interest from her investments. Helen has no other income and no itemized deductions. Consequently, her taxable income is $2,150 ($3,000 – standard deduction of $850). Helen has no brothers or sisters. Her parents file a joint return. They have taxable income of $70,200 before including Helen's investment income. Helen's final tax of **$411** is computed on Form 8615 using the following information.

Other Information

9: Tax on parents' taxable income of $70,200 plus Helen's net unearned income of $1,300 ($3,000 – $1,700), **$10,996**
10: Tax on parents' taxable income of $70,200, **$10,671**
15: Tax on amount taxed at child's rate ($850), **$86**
17: Tax on Helen's taxable income of $2,150, **$216**

FIGURE 3-6 Filled-In Form 8615

Form **8615** | **Tax for Children Under Age 18 With Investment Income of More Than $1,700** | OMB No. 1545-0074 | **2006**

Department of the Treasury
Internal Revenue Service (99)

▶ Attach only to the child's Form 1040, Form 1040A, or Form 1040NR.
▶ See separate instructions.

Attachment Sequence No. 33

Child's name shown on return	Child's social security number
Helen I. Wong	344 72 0156

Before you begin: If the child, the parent, or any of the parent's other children under age 18 must use the Schedule D Tax Worksheet or has income from farming or fishing, see **Pub. 929,** Tax Rules for Children and Dependents. It explains how to figure the child's tax using the **Schedule D Tax Worksheet** or **Schedule J** (Form 1040).

A Parent's name (first, initial, and last). **Caution:** *See instructions before completing.*	B Parent's social security number
Kenneth A. Wong	324 51 9234

C Parent's filing status (check one):
☐ Single ☒ Married filing jointly ☐ Married filing separately ☐ Head of household ☐ Qualifying widow(er)

Part I Child's Net Investment Income

		Line	Amount
1	Enter the child's investment income (see instructions)	1	3,000 00
2	If the child **did not** itemize deductions on **Schedule A** (Form 1040 or Form 1040NR), enter $1,700. Otherwise, see instructions	2	1,700 00
3	Subtract line 2 from line 1. If zero or less, **stop;** do not complete the rest of this form but **do** attach it to the child's return	3	1,300 00
4	Enter the child's **taxable income** from Form 1040, line 43; Form 1040A, line 27; or Form 1040NR, line 40	4	2,150 00
5	Enter the **smaller** of line 3 or line 4. If zero, **stop;** do not complete the rest of this form but **do** attach it to the child's return	5	1,300 00

Part II Tentative Tax Based on the Tax Rate of the Parent

		Line	Amount
6	Enter the parent's **taxable income** from Form 1040, line 43; Form 1040A, line 27; Form 1040EZ, line 6; Form 1040NR, line 40; or Form 1040NR-EZ, line 14. If zero or less, enter -0-	6	70,200 00
7	Enter the total, if any, from Forms 8615, line 5, of **all other** children of the parent named above. **Do not** include the amount from line 5 above	7	0
8	Add lines 5, 6, and 7 (see instructions)	8	71,500 00
9	Enter the tax on the amount on line 8 based on the **parent's** filing status above (see instructions). If the Qualified Dividends and Capital Gain Tax Worksheet, Schedule D Tax Worksheet, or Schedule J (Form 1040) is used to figure the tax, check here ▶ ☐	9	10,996 00
10	Enter the parent's tax from Form 1040, line 44; Form 1040A, line 28, minus any alternative minimum tax; Form 1040EZ, line 11; Form 1040NR, line 41; or Form 1040NR-EZ, line 15. **Do not** include any tax from **Form 4972** or **8814.** If the Qualified Dividends and Capital Gain Tax Worksheet, Schedule D Tax Worksheet, or Schedule J (Form 1040) was used to figure the tax, check here ▶ ☐	10	10,671 00
11	Subtract line 10 from line 9 and enter the result. If line 7 is blank, also enter this amount on line 13 and go to **Part III**	11	325 00
12a	Add lines 5 and 7 — 12a: 1,300 00		
b	Divide line 5 by line 12a. Enter the result as a decimal (rounded to at least three places)	12b	×1. 00
13	Multiply line 11 by line 12b	13	325 00

Part III Child's Tax—If lines 4 and 5 above are the same, enter -0- on line 15 and go to line 16.

		Line	Amount
14	Subtract line 5 from line 4 — 14: 850 00		
15	Enter the tax on the amount on line 14 based on the **child's** filing status (see instructions). If the Qualified Dividends and Capital Gain Tax Worksheet, Schedule D Tax Worksheet, or Schedule J (Form 1040) is used to figure the tax, check here ▶ ☐	15	86 00
16	Add lines 13 and 15	16	411 00
17	Enter the tax on the amount on line 4 based on the **child's** filing status (see instructions). If the Qualified Dividends and Capital Gain Tax Worksheet, Schedule D Tax Worksheet, or Schedule J (Form 1040) is used to figure the tax, check here ▶ ☐	17	216 00
18	Enter the **larger** of line 16 or line 17 here and on the **child's** Form 1040, line 44; Form 1040A, line 28; or Form 1040NR, line 41	18	411 00

For Paperwork Reduction Act Notice, see the instructions. Cat. No. 64113U Form **8615** (2006)

Printed on recycled paper

Child's Income on Parent's Return

Under certain conditions, parents can choose to report their child's income on their Form 1040. For this reporting, parents cannot use Form 1040EZ or Form 1040A. When parents choose this reporting option, the child does not file a return. For the family to make the choice, the child's income must consist only of interest and dividends over $850 and under $8,500. Also, the child cannot have income taxes withheld or pay estimated income taxes. Parents use Form 8814, Parents' Election to Report Child's Interest and Dividends, to compute the tax due on the child's interest and dividends.

Taxpayers can minimize the family's tax liability by making gifts of income-producing property to lower-bracket family members. Children can receive $850 of income each year without paying taxes. The next $850 is taxed at the child's 10% tax rate. Shifting more than $1,700 of investment income to a child produces no benefit, as the excess is taxed at the parents' tax rate.

TRADITIONAL IRA DISTRIBUTIONS

An individual retirement account (IRA) is a type of retirement fund. There are two types of IRAs: traditional IRAs and Roth IRAs. The attractive feature of IRAs is that earnings from these accounts are not taxed when earned. Instead, these amounts are either taxed when taken out (for traditional IRAs) or never taxed at all (for Roth IRAs). To get this special treatment, there are rules on how long the amounts must stay in the IRA. Roth IRAs are discussed in Chapter 4. The discussion that follows pertains to traditional IRAs.

Persons with earned income (wages or self-employment earnings) can contribute to a traditional IRA. Some people can deduct the amounts they contribute to their IRAs. Those who cannot take the deduction may still contribute to traditional IRAs. These are called "nondeductible contributions." The rules regarding the deductibility of contributions to IRAs are discussed in Chapter 4.

In addition to the earnings in IRA accounts, amounts in IRAs made with deductible contributions have not been taxed. For instance, assume a person who earns $10,000 contributes $2,000 to an IRA. If the $2,000 is deducted for AGI, the person's AGI only increases by $8,000 ($10,000 - $2,000). Thus, only $8,000 of the $10,000 has been taxed. In contrast, the person's AGI would include $10,000 if the $2,000 was not deductible. Hence, nondeductible contributions are made with what is called "after-tax" dollars. This means that the amounts contributed have been taxed.

Deductible IRA contributions are made with what is called "pre-tax" dollars. These amounts have not been taxed. When persons take amounts out of their traditional IRAs, they must include in gross income all amounts that have not been taxed. This includes the portion that represents earnings and deductible contributions. When a person takes amounts out early from an IRA, a 10% penalty on the taxable amount is added to the income taxes due. The Code does not tax a rollover from one IRA directly into another IRA. It also does not tax amounts an employee rolls over from an employer's qualified pension plan into an IRA.

Each year, those that receive IRA distributions are sent Form 1099-R, Distributions from Pensions, Annuities, Retirement or Profit-Sharing Plans, IRAs, Insurance Contracts, etc. This form gives the total distributions received during the year. Sometimes it also reports the taxable amount. Form 1040EZ cannot be used to report IRA distributions. Anyone owing a 10% penalty on early withdrawals from an IRA must use Form 1040. Otherwise, Form

1040A or Form 1040 may be used to report IRA distributions. Taxpayers report on the tax return both their total distributions and the taxable amount. If no nondeductible contributions were made to the IRA, all amounts withdrawn are taxed. However, if any of the amounts in the IRA come from nondeductible contributions, the following formula is used to determine the nontaxable portion of the distribution.

$$\frac{\text{Total nondeductible contributions}}{\text{Total value of IRA (including contributions and earnings)}} \times \text{Distribution} = \text{Nontaxable distribution}$$

EXAMPLE 25

Over the years, Peter Voltar has made nondeductible contributions to his traditional IRA totaling $40,000. The total value of the IRA is $150,000. During the current year, Voltar withdraws $30,000 from the IRA. He is not subject to the 10% penalty. The nontaxable portion of his distribution is $8,000 ($40,000/$150,000 x $30,000). He reports both the $30,000 total and the $22,000 taxable ($30,000 - $8,000) amounts on his tax return. Only the taxable portion ($22,000) is included in his gross income.

EXAMPLE 26

Same as in Example 25, except that all of Voltar's contributions were deductible. Voltar reports the $30,000 as his total and taxable distribution on his tax return. The $30,000 is included in his gross income.

Taxpayers who take a "qualified hurricane distribution" from their IRAs spread the taxable portion of the distribution over three tax years. Starting in the year they receive the distribution, they will include in gross income one-third of the taxable portion of the distribution. They also have the option to elect to include the entire taxable amount in gross income in the year they receive the distribution. A **qualified hurricane distribution** is any distribution made after August 24, 2005 (for Katrina), September 23, 2005 (for Rita), or October 23, 2005 (for Wilma) and before January 1, 2007 by an individual whose principal place of abode on that date was located in a hurricane disaster area (as specified by the federal government) and who sustained an economic loss as a result of the hurricane.

PENSIONS

Retired workers receive a pension if they participated in their employer's pension plan during their working years. Persons receiving a pension get a series of cash payments (benefits) that last for the rest of their lives. Many pensions pay benefits for the lives of the retiree's spouse as well. Often contributions to the employee's pension plan were made either by the employer or by the employee with pre-tax contributions. The pension benefits from these plans have never been taxed and are 100% taxable when paid to the retiree. However, if the employee's contributions were made with after-tax dollars, a formula similar to that used to compute the nontaxable portion of IRA withdrawals must be used to determine the nontaxable pension benefits. Each year, employers send retirees a Form 1099-R. This form gives the total benefits paid during the year. Often the employer is able to provide the retiree with both the taxable and nontaxable portions of those benefits.

Persons who started receiving their pensions from a qualified retirement plan after November 18, 1996 use the following formula to compute the nontaxable portion of their monthly pension benefits.

$$\frac{\text{After-tax contributions}}{\text{Number of monthly payments}} = \text{Nontaxable amount}$$

The number of anticipated monthly payments is determined from the following table:

Age as of Starting Date	*Number ofPayments*
55 and under	360
56–60	310
61–65	260
66–70	210
71 and over	160

When benefits are paid over the lives of both the retiree and the retiree's spouse, the number of anticipated monthly payments is determined by the couple's combined ages using the following table.

Combined age as of Starting Date	*Number of Payments*
110 and under	410
111–120	360
121–130	310
131–140	260
141 and over	210

When the payments are not made on a monthly basis, the number of payments requires adjustment. For example, if the payments are quarterly, the taxpayer divides the number of payments by four. If the number of payments is fixed, the number of payments becomes the denominator.

These procedures apply only to qualified pension plans where some or all of the taxpayer's contributions have already been taxed. It does not apply to IRAs. If no taxes have been paid on any of the contributions into the plan, all payments are taxed.

Because the formula for determining the nontaxable pension payments uses life expectancy tables, it is possible that the payments will continue beyond the expected number of payments. Likewise, they could stop before the full amount of the after-tax contributions has been recovered. For pensions starting after November 18, 1996, any payments received beyond the number of payments used in the formula are fully taxable. If payments stop before the last of the number of payments used in the formula, any unrecovered amounts are taken as an itemized deduction on the final income tax return of the deceased.

EXAMPLE 27

Jason Smart, age 65, retired from his job in 20x1. On July 1, 20x1 he started receiving $4,000 a month from his employer's qualified retirement plan. Over the years, Smart had contributed $124,800 to the plan with after-tax dollars. Each month, the nontaxable portion of Smart's payment is $480 ($124,800/260 payments). Thus, for 20x1 his total benefits are $24,000 ($4,000 x 6). His taxable amount is $21,120 ($24,000 – ($480 x 6)). He includes the $21,120 in gross income. For 20x2, his total benefits are $48,000 ($4,000 x 12). His taxable amount is $42,240 ($48,000 – ($480 x 12)). He includes this amount in his gross income for 20x2.

EXAMPLE 28

Same as in Example 27, except that Smart dies on March 9, 20x9. At the time of his death, Smith had received 94 of the 260 payments he was expected to receive over his lifetime. In 20x9 Smart's final income tax return shows total pension benefits of $12,000 ($4,000 x 3) and taxable benefits of is $10,560 ($12,000 – ($480 x 3)). The $10,560 is included in gross income. The unrecovered contributions of $79,680 ($124,800 – ($480 x 94)) are taken as an itemized deduction on Smart's 20x9 final tax return.

EXAMPLE 29

Same as in Example 27, except that Smart is married and his wife is age 62 at the time he begins receiving his pension payments. The pension benefits will continue for both Jason and his wife's lives. Each month, the nontaxable portion of the Smarts' payment is $402.58 ($124,800/310). Thus, for 20x1 taxable amount of their pension benefits is $21,584. 52 ($24,000 – ($402.58 x 6)). For 20x2, the taxable amount is $43,169 ($48,000 – ($402.58 x 12)).

ANNUITIES

Recipients of annuity payments pay for the right to receive cash payments for the rest of their lives (life annuity) or for a set period of time (term annuity). The amount paid for this right is generally made with after-tax dollars. The portion of each annuity payment that comes from these previously taxed amounts is not taxed. These amounts are a return of the recipient's previously taxed investment in the annuity. The formula used to determine the nontaxable portion of the annuity payments is as follows:

$$\frac{\text{Amount paid for the annuity}}{\text{Total expected return}} \times \text{Amount received} = \text{Nontaxable proceeds}$$

When computing the total expected return for a life annuity, life expectancy tables are used to estimate how long the recipient is expected to live (and how long the payments will last). For a term annuity, the term of the annuity is used to compute the expected return. Once determined, the ratio in the formula does not change. For annuities starting after 1986, it is used each year until the recipient has recovered the entire investment in the annuity. After that, all payments are subject to tax. If the payments are based on the recipient's life expectancy, and the recipient dies before recovering his or her entire investment, the tax laws allow the unrecovered amounts to be deducted as loss on the deceased's final tax return. Prior to 1987, the formula was used until the payments stopped. No loss was allowed for any unrecovered amounts.

EXAMPLE 30

Sally Smith purchased a life annuity for $72,000. It pays equal annual installments of $8,000 beginning January 1, 2006. Her life expectancy is 12 years. She computes the taxable portion of each payment as follows:

Investment in contract	$72,000
Expected return ($8,000 × 12 years)	$96,000
Income exclusion percentage ($72,000 ÷ 96,000)	75%
Amount received during a year	$ 8,000
Recovery exclusion ($8,000 × 75%)	(6,000)
Taxable portion	$ 2,000

For the first 12 years, Smith includes $2,000 in gross income from the annuity. After the 12th year, she includes all $8,000 in gross income each year.

RENTS AND ROYALTIES

Taxpayers usually report rent or royalty income on Form 1040 as "Rental real estate, royalties, etc." However, business-related rent or royalty income is reported as "Business income or (loss)." Taxpayers cannot use Form 1040EZ or Form 1040A to report rent or royalty income. Gross income includes the gross rent or royalty income a taxpayer receives. The tax law then treats ordinary, necessary, and reasonable rental expenses as deductions for AGI. When allowable deductions exceed related income, limits on the deductions may apply (see Chapter 9).

UNEMPLOYMENT COMPENSATION

Under federal or state law, workers unemployed for short periods receive unemployment compensation. Recipients of this compensation report it on Form 1040A or Form 1040 as "Unemployment compensation." Payers of $10 or more of this compensation report it annually to the IRS and the recipient on Form 1099-G, Statement for Recipients of Certain Government Payments.

SOCIAL SECURITY BENEFITS

Many retirees are not taxed on the social security benefits they recieve. Some, however, pay taxes on a portion of their monthly social security benefits. The tax law limits the amount subject to tax to either 50% or 85% of the benefits, depending on the taxpayer's level of income. For higher-income taxpayers, a larger portion of social security payments is subject to tax. Taxpayers report both gross and taxable social security benefits on either Form 1040A or Form 1040. Instructions to these forms contain similar worksheets for calculating taxable benefits. Example 31 shows the formula for determining taxable social security benefits.

EXAMPLE 31

Jim Smith, a married taxpayer filing jointly, has adjusted gross income (AGI) of $75,000 before $13,500 of social security (OASDI) and $5,000 of tax-exempt interest.

1. AGI before social security	$75,000
2. Add 50% of social security income	6,750
3. Total	$81,750
4. Add tax-exempt income	5,000
5. Revised AGI	$86,750
6. Less base amount ($0, $25,000, or $32,000)*	(32,000)
7. Net	$54,750
8. Multiplied by	× 50%
9. Base for comparison	$27,375
10. Taxable OASDI = the *lesser* of line 9 or line 2	$ 6,750

*$32,000, married filing jointly; $0, married filing separately and living with his or her spouse part of year; $25,000, all others

If the amount on line 5 does not exceed $44,000 for a married taxpayer filing jointly ($0 for a married taxpayer filing separately who lived with his or her spouse part of year; $34,000 for other filers), the amount on line 10 equals the taxable amount of OASDI benefits.

If the amount on line 5 exceeds $44,000, $0, or $34,000, respectively, more computations are needed as follows.

11. If married filing jointly, enter the smaller of $6,000 ($0 for a married taxpayer filing separately who lived with his or her spouse part of year; $4,500 for other taxpayers) or the amount on line 10	$ 6,000
12. For a married taxpayer filing jointly, subtract $44,000 ($0 for a married taxpayer filing separately who lived with his or her spouse part of year; $34,000 for other taxpayers) from the amount on line 5, and multiply the difference by 85%	36,338
13. Add lines 11 and 12	$42,338
14. 85% of social security	$11,475
15. Taxable OASDI = the *lesser of* line 13 or line 14	$11,475

TAX BENEFIT RULE

When taxpayers get back amounts they deducted in a prior tax year, the amounts they are refunded may be subject to tax. The **tax benefit rule** gets its name because the amounts refunded are included in gross income if the taxpayer benefited from deducting these amounts in a prior tax year. A "benefit" results if the deduction reduced the taxpayer's taxes in that year. In years in which taxpayers report negative taxable income, no tax benefit generally results. When the deduction involves an itemized deduction, the amount recovered is not taxable if the taxpayer took the standard deduction in the prior year. Even when the taxpayer itemized, the recovered amounts are taxable only to the extent that they resulted in less taxes paid.

In the year a taxpayer receives a refund for an amount deducted as an itemized deduction in a prior year, the amount included in gross income is the *lesser of* (i) the amount refunded or (ii) the taxpayer's excess itemized deductions. Taxpayers' excess itemized deductions are their total itemized deductions minus the standard deduction amount they could have instead taken to reduce AGI. This calculation is shown in Example 32 below.

EXAMPLE 32

In 2005 Karen Black, age 35 and single, deducted $3,260 on her federal income tax return for real estate taxes. As a result of a billing error in the county assessor's office, Black overpaid her 2005 real estate taxes. In 2006, she received a real estate tax refund of $700. Including the $3,260 of real estate taxes that she paid in 2005, her total deducted itemized deductions for that year equaled $5,200. The standard deduction for a single taxpayer like Black was $5,000 in 2005. To determine her gross income from the tax refund, she first determines her excess itemized deductions for 2005. Her excess itemized deductions are $200 ($5,200 – $5,000). She includes $200 in gross income (the *lesser of* $700 or $200).

State and Local Income Tax Refunds

A common example of the tax benefit rule is a refund of state and local income taxes. Taxpayers can deduct as an itemized deduction any amounts they pay during the year for state or local income taxes. This includes amounts employers withhold from their pay, as well as any estimated payments they make during the year. Amounts withheld from employees' paychecks in 20x1 to cover their state and local income taxes owed for the 20x1 tax year are deducted as itemized deductions on their 20x1 federal income tax return.

Like the federal income tax return, taxpayers file their state and local tax returns in the next tax year. Thus, a taxpayer's 20x1 state income tax return is not due until 20x2. As a result, taxpayers that overpay their 20x1 income taxes do not receive their refunds until the next tax year. The tax benefit rule requires that a refund of state or local income taxes be included in gross income in the year received if the taxpayer "benefited" from taking a deduction for the amount in a prior tax year. In the year a taxpayer receives a state or local income tax refund, the amount included in gross income is the *lesser of* (i) the amount refunded or (ii) the taxpayer's excess itemized deductions.

EXAMPLE 33

In 2005 Foster Green, age 46 and single, deducted $4,260 on his federal income tax return for state income taxes. Green has excellent vision. In 2006, Green received a state income tax refund of $700. On his 2005 tax return, Green deducted itemized deductions of $8,863. The 2005 standard deduction for a single taxpayer like Green was $5,000. For 2005 Green's excess itemized deductions equaled $3,863 ($8,863 – $5,000). Thus, he includes in gross income the *lesser* (i) the refunded amount, or (ii) his excess itemized deductions ($3,863). Green includes $700 in gross income in 2006.

ILLEGAL INCOME

Income from illegal activities is included in gross income. Taxpayers may deduct the ordinary and necessary business expenses (rents, wages, utilities, etc.) required to produce this income. However, illegal payments (bribes to police and judges) are not deductible. In the case of illegal drug trafficking, the cost of goods sold reduces gross receipts to yield gross income, but no other expenses are deductible.

OTHER INCOME

Income from various other sources is also included in gross income. These sources include awards and prizes, and hobby income. Other income also includes gambling winnings. Taxpayers may claim itemized deductions for gambling losses up to the amounts of their winnings. Persons in the trade or business of gambling deduct losses for AGI.

Gross income includes amounts taxpayers receive from sales contests, raffles, and radio and television contest programs. It also includes the value of door prizes and prizes and awards from employers. A limited exclusion (up to $400) exists for employees receive for length of service and safety achievement. These awards must be in the form of personal property (not cash). Unless de minimis rules apply (hams and turkeys for special holidays), gross income includes all other awards or prizes from employers. Taxpayers include property prizes and awards in gross income at their FMV. Gross income can include awards in recognition of past religious, charitable, scientific, educational, artistic, literary, or civic accomplishments. Such awards include Pulitzer and Nobel Prizes. An exception applies if the recipient of such an award immediately assigns it to a qualified governmental unit or tax-exempt charity.

Name ______________________________

Section ______________ Date ___________

QUESTIONS AND PROBLEMS

1. **Compensation.** Mark Wellaby, M.D., practices medicine. During the current year he received the following items in payment for his services: cash of $48,000; farm produce worth $1,000; common stock with a total par value of $500; and a $485, 90-day noninterest-bearing note dated December 1. The stock at the time of receipt had a fair market value of $1,000. At December 31, the fair market value of the stock had dropped to $900. Compute Dr. Wellaby's gross income.

2. **Receipt of advanced payments.** On May 1, 20x1, an insurance company sells a three-year insurance policy to one of its customers. The cost of the premiums is $1,200. The insurance company uses the accrual basis and a calendar year.

   a. What amount of the $1,200 must the company include in its gross income over the term of the policy (20x1 – 20x4)?

   b. Would your answer change if the company used the cash basis?

3. **Tips.** The following questions involve tip income. Answer each question by inserting an X in the proper column.

	True	*False*
a. Employees receiving less than $20 in monthly tips while working for one employer need not report them to the employer.	_____	_____
b. Employees receiving less than $20 in monthly tips do not have to pay social security and Medicare taxes on their tips.	_____	_____
c. Employees receiving less than $20 in monthly tips do not have to pay income taxes on their tips.	_____	_____
d. The IRS normally assumes that food and beverage servers make at least 10% of gross sales in tips.	_____	_____
e. When tips reported to employers are less than the IRS's assumed tipping rate, some employers must report the difference as additional income on the employee's Form W-2.	_____	_____
f. "Allocated tips" are subject to withholding for income, social security, and Medicare taxes.	_____	_____

4. **Tips.** Marge Connor is a hostess at a local diner. As a hostess, Conner normally does not receive tips. However, on occasion she will help out with an order and the waitress will give Connor part of her tips. During the current year, Conner's total tips were $200.

   a. Discuss the tax consequences of the tip income if Conner did not receive more than $20 in tips in any one month during the year.

   b. How would your answer to Part a. differ if she received more than $20 in tips during the month of May?

5. **Alimony.** For a divorce or legal separation after 1984, alimony payments are deductible by the payer and includable in the payee's gross income. However, to be considered alimony, the payments must meet six conditions. What are these conditions?

6. **Property Settlements, Alimony, and Child Support.** Distinguish between the three types of payments former spouses may make to one another and discuss the tax treatment to both the paying spouse and the recipient spouse of each type of payment.

7. **Alimony and Child Support.** Under the terms of their divorce, Henry is to pay Winona $1,000 a month. The terms of the agreement specify that $550 of each payment is to be for child support.

   a. If Henry makes all of his required payments during the current year, how much must Winona include in gross income? What amount can Henry deduct?

   b. Would your answer to Part a. change if the agreement were silent as to how much of each payment constituted child support? If so, how?

   c. Would your answer to Part a. change if Henry only makes 8 of the 12 required pay ments during the year? If so, how?

8. **Property Settlements, Alimony, and Child Support.** Under the terms of a divorce agreement, Gary is to pay $200 per month as child support to Judy who has custody of their 12-year-old child. Judy is also to receive $1,200 per month for 12 years, but this payment will change to $1,000 per month when the child reaches age 18. Gary is also to transfer stock to Judy. The stock cost $20,000 and has a market value of $50,000. The divorce is finalized on May 1. In the first year under the agreement, Judy receives the stock and eight months of cash payments.

   a. How do these transfers affect Judy's gross income and Gary's AGI?

   b. How would your answer to Part a. change if during the first year Gary only made six of the eight required cash payments? If so, how?

9. **Alimony Recapture.** The terms of a couple's divorce decree call for the husband to make monthly payments of $4,000 to his ex-wife for three years. All of the payments count as alimony. After the third year, the monthly payments are reduced to $1,000. Will this reduction in alimony be subject to the alimony recapture rules? Explain.

10. Dividends. What are dividends and how are they taxed?

11. Tax on Dividends. Tiffany and Randy Crowder file a joint return. They have taxable income of $79,000, including qualified dividends of $3,000. Compute their tax liability.

12. Dividend Distributions.

a. Name five types of distributions that a taxpayer might receive from a mutual fund.

b. For Form 1040A filers with more than $1,500 of gross dividends, what kinds of dividend distributions can be reported on Schedule 1?

13. Mutual Fund Distributions. Susan Rhiner owns shares of stock in a mutual investment fund. In January 2006, the fund sent her a distribution notice showing that she received the following distributions from the fund in 2006.

Ordinary cash dividend	$526
Capital gains distributed	150
Capital gains undistributed	370

Rhiner verifies the reported data from her records. The mutual fund also sent her a Form 2439 showing that her share of the income tax paid by the fund in 2006 on its undistributed capital gains was $129.50. Rhiner has no other investments. She paid $10,100 for her mutual fund shares on January 16, 2006.

a. What amount of the distribution of the mutual fund is reported on Rhiner's Form 1040, and how is it reported?

b. Compute Rhiner's basis in the mutual fund shares at the end of the year.

14. Acquiring Series EE Bonds. Norma Demar, age 30 and single, who has never owned U.S. Savings Bonds, wants to invest $2,000 in Series EE bonds. What options does Demar have in reporting the interest income from these bonds?

15. Interest on Series EE Bonds. Following are the issue price, original face (maturity) value, and selected redemption values of Series EE bonds purchased by Richard Grady in 2006.

		Redemption Value	
Issue Price	*Face Maturity Value*	*End of 2006*	*End of 2007*
$ 600	$1,200	$ 638.00	$ 673.20
200	400	232.56	260.72
1,000	2,000	1,025.60	1,051.60
50	100	53.60	57.64
150	300	156.08	162.24

In 2006, Grady elects to report the increase in redemption value each year on Series EE bonds. At the election date he owned no other U.S. bonds. What amount does Grady include in gross income from these bonds in 2006? In 2007? Assume there are no redemptions or additional purchases.

16. Accrued Interest on Bonds. On September 30, 2006, Ramona Zwick purchased a $40,000 par value bond of the DPQ Corporation. She paid the seller $40,800 ($40,000 par value + $800 accrued interest). The 8% bond pays interest semiannually on December 31 and June 30. Zwick received the first semiannual interest payment of $1,600 on December 31, 2006. From the DPQ bonds, how much interest income does Zwick have in 2006? Explain.

17. Original Issue Discount. On July 1, 2006, Gerald Johnson a cash basis taxpayer paid $32,870 for a 25-year, zero-coupon bond with a maturity value of $100,000. The annual yield to maturity is 4.5%.

a. What is the OID on the bond?

b. What portion of the OID would be included in taxable interest income for 2006?

c. What portion of the OID would be included in taxable interest income for 2007?

d. When is a Form 1099-OID prepared? Who prepares it? To whom are copies sent? What information does it contain?

18. Original Issue Discount. A 30-year bond with a face value of $100,000 is issued at a discount. How large can the discount be and still be treated as de minimis OID? Discuss how the tax laws treat OID.

19. Market Discount. On January 1, 2006, Dolly Patton pays $9,380 for corporate bonds. The bonds were originally issued on January 1, 2001 for $9,330 and have a $10,000 face value. They mature on January 1, 2026. The bond's amortized carrying value (ACV) on January 1, 2006 was $9,450. What portion of the $620 difference between the $9,380 Patton paid for the bonds and their $10,000 face value is OID? What portion is market discount? Discuss how Patton treats these amounts on her tax returns.

20. Bond Premium. Dean Barker pays $104,700 for bonds with a face value of $100,000. Describe the tax consequences to Barker of buying bonds at a premium.

21. Below Market Loans. Under what circumstances do the below market loan rules apply? Describe the tax consequences of making a below market loan. Be sure to discuss the consequences to both the borrower and the lender.

22. Imputed Interest.

a. What are AFRs? What purpose do they serve?

b. How is the imputed interest on a below market loan computed?

23. Gift Loans. Janet Bowman's parents lend Janet and her husband $125,000 to buy a new home. The loan is for ten years with no interest.

a. Must interest be imputed on the loan? If so, how would the amount of imputed interest be determined?

b. If the loan to in Part a. were $100,000, would interest have to be imputed? If so, how would the amount of imputed interest be determined?

c. If the loan in Part a. were $10,000, would interest have to be imputed?

24. Compensation-Related Loans. A company loans its employee, Liz Kittner, $50,000. The terms of the note require that Kittner pay interest annually based on a 1.5% annual rate of interest. In addition, Kittner is to repay the $50,000 at the end of three years. At the time the loan was made, the current annual AFR short-term, mid-term and long-term rates were 4%, 5% and 6%, respectively. Determine the tax consequences of this loan to both the company and to Kittner.

25. **Corporation-Shareholder Loans.** A corporation loans its shareholder, Lynda Matsen, $120,000. The terms of the loan require that Matsen pay interest annually based on a 2.5% annual rate of interest. In addition, Matsen is to repay the $120,000 at the end of six years. At the time the loan was made, the current annual AFR short-term, mid-term and long-term rates were 4.5%, 5.5% and 6.5%, respectively. Determine the tax consequences of this loan to both the corporation and to Matsen.

26. **Kiddie Tax.** Dee deCastro, age 10, received taxable interest of $4,200 during the year. She has no other income, and her total itemized deductions are $150. She has no brothers or sisters. DeCastro is a dependent of her parents, who report taxable income of $75,000. If deCastro's parents do not elect to report her income on their return, what is the amount of deCastro's income that will be taxed at her parents' tax rate?

27. **Pension Benefits.** On August 10, 2006, Don Wilson turned 65 and received his first pension. Over the years, he had contributed $68,900 to his employer's qualified retirement plan. Taxes were paid on $24,700 of this amount. The remaining $44,200 was contributed after the law was changed to permit pre-tax contributions to the plan. Wilson is to receive monthly annuity payments of $425 on the same day every month for the remainder of his life.

    a. From the annuity payments Wilson receives in 2006, what amount is part of his gross income?

    b. If Wilson receives 12 annuity payments in 2007, what is his gross income from these payments?

    c. If Wilson lives longer than his expected 260 payments, how much of each month's $425 payment will be included in his gross income?

d. How would your answer to Parts a. - c. change if Don were married and his pension benefits were to continue for both his and his wife's lives? Don's wife is 61 as on August 10, 2006.

28. Annuity Income. Fifteen years ago, Cal Greguska purchased an annuity contract for $92,400. The contract stated that he would receive $550 a month for life, starting on January 1, 1996. On this date, Greguska's remaining life expectancy was 20 years. For 2006, how much of the annuity payments can Greguska exclude from his gross income?

29. Taxable Social Security Benefits. Taxpayers A through D have reported the following social security (SS) information. Fill in blank lines e. through h. on the table for each taxpayer. On line h., show how to compute the amount of the taxable SS benefits included in income for each taxpayer. Assume C did not live with his spouse during the tax year.

Item	*A*	*B*	*C*	*D*
Taxpayer status	Single	MFJ	MFS	MFJ
a. SS benefits	$7,800	$9,400	$6,200	$11,000
b. AGI before SS benefits	$25,000	$32,300	$12,000	$24,000
c. 50% SS benefits received	3,900	4,700	3,100	5,500
d. Tax-exempt interest	500	0	0	400
e. Revised AGI	$________	$________	$________	$________
f. Less base exemption	(________)	(________)	(________)	(________)
g. Net amount	$________	$________	$________	$________
h. Taxable SS benefits (*lesser of* line c. or 1/2 of g.)	$________	$________	$________	$________

30. Taxable Social Security Benefits. Taxpayers E through G have reported the following social security (SS) information for the year. Assume the taxpayers married and filing separately lived together part of the tax year. Fill in the blank lines d. through r. on the table for each taxpayer. On line r. show how to compute the amount of taxable SS benefits included in income for each taxpayer.

	A	*B*	*C*
	Single	*MFJ*	*MFS*
Social Security benefits received	$ 7,800	$ 12,900	$ 11,000
First-Tier Formula			
a. AGI before SS	$ 50,000	$ 48,000	$ 5,000
b. 50% SS benefits received	3,900	6,450	5,500
c. Tax-exempt interest	500	400	400
d. Revised AGI	$______	$______	$______
e. Less base for first-tier benefits ($0, $25,000, or $32,000)	(______)	(______)	(______)
f. Net	$______	$______	$______
g. 50% of line f.	______	______	______
h. 50% of SS (line b.)	______	______	______
i. Taxable first-tier benefits (*lesser of* line g. or h.)	______	______	______
Second-Tier Formula			
j. Revised AGI (line d. above)	$______	$______	$______
k. Less base for second-tier benefits ($0, $34,000, or $44,000)	(______)	(______)	(______)
l. Net	$______	$______	$______
m. Multiplied by 85%	× 85%	× 85%	× 85%
n. Line l. × line m.	$______	$______	$______
o. *Lesser of* line i. or w.	______	______	______
p. Line n. + line o.	$______	$______	$______
q. SS × 85%	______	______	______
r. Taxable benefits (*lesser of* line p. or q.)	$______	$______	$______
s. Base amount for second-tier benefits	$ 34,000	$ 44,000	$ 0
t. Less base amount for first-tier benefits	(25,000)	(32,000)	(0)
u. Line s. minus line t.	$ 9,000	$ 12,000	$ 0
v. Multiplied by 50%	× 50%	× 50%	× 50%
w. Line u. × line v.	$ 4,500	$ 6,000	$ 0

31. Tax Benefit Rule.

a. Explain the tax benefit rule as it applies to refunds of state and local income taxes.

b. Explain the tax benefit rule as it applies to refunds of federal income taxes.

32. Tax Benefit Rule. In 2005 Lou Sharp, age 35 and single, deducted $5,325 on his federal income tax return for California income taxes. Sharp has excellent vision. In 2006, Sharp received a state income tax refund of $875. For 2005, Sharp deducted $11,154 in itemized deductions. After these deductions, Sharp's taxable income equaled $100,000. The 2005 standard deduction for a single taxpayer like Sharp equaled $5,000. How much must Sharp include in his 2006 gross income from the California income tax refund?

33. Internet Problem: Filling out Form 4137.

Hannah Homerding (SSN 234-56-7891) works as a waitress at the Texas Steakhouse Restaurant. As she prepared her tax return for 2006, she discovered that she forgot to report tips of $1,250 to her employer for the month of June. She had properly reported the rest of her tips ($28,750) to the restaurant during the year. Homerding lives at 19 Cabintown Road, Fort Worth, TX 76101. Her Form W-2 for the year lists her total social security wages and tips at $35,750.

Go to the IRS Web site and locate Form 4137. Using the computer, fill in Form 4137 and Schedule U for Homerding and print out a completed copy.

See Appendix A for instructions on use of the IRS Web site.

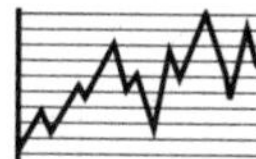

34. Business Entity Problem: This problem is designed for those using the "business entity" approach. The solution may require information from Chapters 14 and 15.

Please answer the following true and false questions in the space provided.

	True	*False*
a. Corporations owning less than 80% of another corporation are generally taxed on at least a portion of the dividends they receive from that company.	______	______
b. Corporations receiving dividends from another corporation are taxed on 70% of the dividend income if they own 10% of the other company.	______	______
c. S corporations receiving a dividend from another corporation do not pay taxes on the dividend.	______	______
d. Partnerships receiving dividends from a corporation must include the dividends in the calculation of "ordinary income."	______	______
e. A shareholder receiving a property distribution from a corporation must recognize the property distribution at its market value at distribution date.	______	______
f. A partner receiving a property distribution from the partnership must recognize the property distribution at its market value at distribution date.	______	______

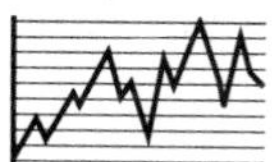

35. Business Entity Problem: This problem is designed for those using the "business entity" approach. The solution may require information from Chapter 14.

Jason Lang owns a corporation. At December 31, the end of the corporation's tax year, the company has earnings and profits of $20,000 before consideration of any distribution to the owner. On December 31, the company distributes property with a market value of $50,000 to Lang. The basis of the property is $30,000.

a. If the corporation is in the 25% tax bracket, what are the tax implications to the corporation?

b. What are the tax implications to Lang?

COMPREHENSIVE PROBLEM

36. Neale D. (SSN 394-57-7584) and Judith L. (SSN 746-38-4457) Hamilton file a joint Form 1040. The Hamiltons have no foreign accounts or trusts. During the year, they received the interest and dividends shown below.

From the following information, prepare Schedule B (Form 1040), Interest and Ordinary Dividends, for the Hamiltons using the Schedule B reproduced in this problem. Assume they received information returns from all payers.

Interest Received in Cash	*Amount*
U.S. Treasury bond	$ 600.00
State of Michigan general obligation bond	75.00
City of Meadowood utility bond	160.00
Mortgage of Mr. and Mrs. K. J. Roe (purchased from E. Johnson)	732.50
Ace Manufacturing Company note	50.00
K. R. Smith, personal note	115.00
American Telephone and Telegraph debenture note	60.00

Dividends Received in Cash	*Amount*
BXL Mutual Fund return-of-capital dividend	$ 450.00
Red Corporation dividend on preferred stock	280.00
Credit union dividend (interest)	90.00
L.M.O. Mutual Fund capital gain distribution	15.00
USX Corporation dividend on common stock	1,341.20
Dow Chemical Company dividend on common stock reinvested in common stock through company dividend reinvestment plan	185.00

4

Gross Income Exclusions and Deductions for AGI

CHAPTER CONTENTS

CHAPTER OVERVIEW

Chapter 3 discussed gross income inclusions. This chapter examines gross income exclusions and adjustments to income (deductions from gross income to arrive at AGI). Figures 4-6 and 4-7 show how taxpayers report income and deductions for AGI on Form 1040A and Form 1040.

EXCLUSIONS FROM GROSS INCOME

Income includes all wealth that flows to a taxpayer. Gross income is all income that the government taxes. Exclusions are items of income not subject to tax. This section discusses several fully or partially items of income that are exempt from gross income.

Gifts and Inheritances

The recipient of a gift or inheritance excludes from gross income the value of the gifted or inherited property. The donor of gifted property may be subject to gift tax. A decedent's estate may be subject to estate tax. However, the recipient is not subject to income tax on these transfers. Once the property is transferred, any subsequent income the property earns is subject to income tax under the normal tax laws described in this textbook.

Foreign-Earned Income Exclusion

For 2006, taxpayers may elect to exclude up to $82,400 of "earned income" from foreign countries. To qualify for this exclusion, the taxpayer must either reside in a foreign country for the entire year or be physically present in a foreign country for 330 full days during a 12-month period.

When the taxpayer resides in a foreign country only part of the year, the exclusion must be prorated. For example, if a taxpayer resides in France for the last 210 days in 2006 and the first 300 days in 2007, the taxpayer meets the 330-day/12-month requirement for each year. However, assuming the maximum exclusion in both years is $82,400, the maximum exclusion must be prorated in both years:

	Maximum Exclusion
2006: (210/365) × $82,400 =	$47,408
2007: (300/365) × $82,400 =	$67,726

As an alternative to the exclusion, a taxpayer may elect to include the foreign income in gross income and take a tax credit for the income taxes paid to foreign countries. The foreign tax credit is discussed in Chapter 12. Persons claiming the foreign-earned income exclusion report it as an adjustment to total income on Form 1040. They write-in the amount on Form 1040 (line 36).

EXAMPLE 1

On June 4, 2006, Jane Cates's employer sends her to work in the Paris office. She is there until October 27, 2007. Cates's annual pay is $90,000. Her earnings while working in France were $52,500 in 2006 and $75,000 in 2007. Cates was not present in France for the entire year in 2006 or 2007, but lived there 330 days during a 12-month period. Assuming the maximum exclusion in both years is $82,400, she can reduce her AGI by $47,408 in 2006 and $67,726 in 2007 (see calculations above). Her other option is to include the $90,000 in AGI and use the rules from Chapter 12 to take a foreign tax credit for the income taxes she pays to the French government.

EXAMPLE 2

Same as in Example 1, except that Cates works in France until February 15, 2008. Assuming the maximum exclusion stays at $82,400 through 2008, her foreign earned income exclusion for 2007 is $82,400. She does not prorate the $82,400 because she lived in France during all of 2007. In 2008, she can reduce her AGI by up to $10,385 (46 days/365 x $82,400).

The purpose of the foreign-earned income exclusion and foreign tax credit is to give tax relief to U.S. citizens and residents who might end up paying income taxes to both the U.S. and the foreign country where they work. The maximum exclusion is adjusted each year to reflect changes in the cost of living.

Fringe Benefits

A fringe benefit is a type of pay employees receive. It is often in the form of services provided to them by their employers. When an employer provides fringe benefits, the employee avoids paying the costs for these services themselves. Thus, fringe benefits are a source of wealth to employees, and as such are income. A fringe benefit is taxable unless the tax laws exclude it gross income. Many tax laws exist that exclude fringe benefits. In the sections that follow, some of the more common fringe benefits will be discussed.

Most fringe benefits rules tax the value of benefits provided to key employees and highly paid employees if the plan favors these employees. This rule does not affect employees who are not "key employees" or "highly paid employees." Any plan maintained under a collective bargaining agreement is not considered to favor key or highly paid employees. For 2006, a key employee is (1) an officer of the company whose annual pay exceeds $140,000; (2) an employee who owns at least 5% of the company; or (3) an employee who owns at least one percent of the company and whose pay exceeds $150,000. Highly paid employees are employees, their spouses and dependents who (1) are an officer of the company; (2) own more than 5% of the voting stock in the company; or (3) are highly paid. The tax laws for defining what is considered "highly paid" vary depending on the type of fringe benefit. These rules are beyond the scope of this discussion and can be found in IRS Publication 15-B, Employer's Guide to Fringe Benefits.

The discrimination rules (where the exclusion is disallowed to key and highly paid employees if the plan favors them) apply to most fringe benefits. As the various fringe benefits are discussed, unless otherwise stated that the discrimination rules do not apply, you should assume that they do.

The Code denies an exclusion to both key and highly paid employees when the benefit plan favors them. However, it continues to allow all other employees to exclude the benefits from gross income. This rule is intended to encourage employers to provide benefits to all of their employees, not just those who are officers, shareholders, or highly paid. As a result, most employers structure their benefit plans avoid having them favor key or highly paid employees.

FRINGE BENEFITS EMPLOYERS MAY OFFER

- Accident and health insurance
- Adoption assistance
- Athletic facilities
- Dependent care assistance
- De minimis benefits
- Educational assistance
- Group-term life insurance
- Meals and lodging provided on the employer's premises
- Moving expense reimbursement
- No-additional-cost services
- Retirement planning services
- Transportation benefits
- Tuition reduction
- Working condition fringe benefits

The major advantage of fringe benefits is that employees do not pay taxes on the value of the services being provided.

Accident and Health Insurance

Many employers offer their employees health insurance coverage. Employees exclude from gross income the premiums employers pay on their behalf. Employees also exclude any insurance reimbursements they receive for medical care. These exclusions do not apply to key and highly paid employees if the employer's plan favors them.

EXAMPLE 3

Santex, Inc. provides its employees with health insurance coverage. During the year, it pays $8,000 of insurance premiums for each of its employees. As long as Santex's plan does not favor key or highly paid employees, none of the employees are taxed on the $8,000 of insurance premiums. However, if the plan discriminates in favor of these employees, then the employer adds $8,000 to the taxable wages of its key and highly paid employees.

Dependent Care Assistance

An employee can exclude from gross income up to $5,000 of amounts employers pay to provide dependent care for their employees under a dependent care assistance program. Only an employee's children and dependents can receive such care. Also, the care must be provided to allow the employee to work. Instead of making care payments to outsiders, an employer can provide care at the work site.

The exclusion cannot exceed the *lesser of* two amounts: (i) $5,000 or (ii) the earned income of the spouse with the lesser earnings. For married persons filing separately, the dollar limit is $2,500. When calculating the earned income limits, if the taxpayer or spouse is a full-time student or is incapacitated, the Code assumes that this person earns $250 a month. When two qualifying persons are receiving care, the assumed $250 a month rises to $500 a month. Those who use the exclusion must reduce their child and dependent care payments by the excluded amount when computing child and dependent care credit. A taxpayer who claims the exclusion must report the name, address, and social security number of the care provider on the tax return.

Instead of providing dependent care for their employees, employers can set up plans that allow employees to be reimbursed for their dependent care costs from accounts that employees fund with their own wages. These accounts are commonly known as dependent care flexible spending accounts (FSAs). A dependent care FSA allows employees to set aside each year up to $5,000 of their wages from which they can pay qualified dependent care costs. Employers withhold these amounts from employees' pay. Amounts withheld are excluded from employees' taxable wages. Like deductible IRAs, contributions to FSAs are made with pre-tax dollars. As employees pay for qualified dependent care costs, they submit receipts to their plan provider for reimbursement from their FSA accounts.

EXAMPLE 4

Janet Holbring's employer offers a dependent care FSA. For the current year, Holbring elects to contribute $5,000 of her $45,000 wages to her FSA. As Holbring pays for dependent care, she will submit her receipts to the plan provider for reimbursement. Holbring's W-2 will report taxable wages of $40,000. The $5,000 she uses to fund her FSA is excluded from gross income. The FSA allows taxpayers to pay dependent care costs with pre-tax dollars. Hence, Holbring's total dependent care costs are actually less than the $5,000 she paid to the child care provider.

One draw back of FSAs is the "use it or lose it" feature. If the amount set aside is not spent on qualified expenses during the year, the employee forfeits what is left in the account. Employers also may provide medical FSAs to their employees to allow them to contribute pre-tax wages to an account to pay for medical costs not covered by insurance. When an employer provides both medical and dependent care FSAs, employees have the option of contributing up to $5,000 each year to each FSA. However, only qualified medical costs can be reimbursed from a medical FSA. Only qualified dependent care costs can be paid from a dependent care FSA.

Adoption Assistance

Under an adoption assistance program, employers pay or reimburse employees for qualified adoption costs. For 2006, employees exclude from gross income up to $10,960 of such costs. This amount is phased-out when the employee's AGI falls between $164,410 and $194,410. These amounts are the same as those used in computing the adoption credit (Chapter 2). Amounts excluded from gross income reduce the amount eligible for the credit.

EXAMPLE 5

Jim Anders' employer offers an adoption assistance program. During 2006, Anders is reimbursed $8,000 for adoption costs incurred during the year. Anders' AGI in 2006 is $120,000. Since this amount is less than the $164,410 threshold, the entire $8,000 is excluded from his gross income.

Educational Assistance

Under an educational assistance plan, employers pay or reimburse employees for qualified education costs. Each year, employees can exclude up to $5,250. The exclusion covers amounts paid for tuition, fees, books and supplies. Both graduate and undergraduate courses are included.

EXAMPLE 6

Randell Lyon's employer offers an educational assistance program. During 2006, Lyons is reimbursed $4,000 for tuition, books and fees for courses he took at the local college. Since this amount is less than the $5,250 maximum exclusion, the $4,000 is excluded from Lyon's gross income.

Tuition Reduction

Colleges and universities can exclude from its employees' wages the value of a qualified tuition reduction they give employees. A tuition reduction for graduate education qualifies for the exclusion if it is for the education of a graduate student who performs teaching or research activities for the institution. For undergraduate courses, the exclusion is allowed if the education is for of one of the following persons.

1. A current employee.
2. A former employee who retired or left on disability.
3. A widow(er) of a person who died while working as an employee.
4. A widow(er) of a former employee who retired or left on disability.
5. A dependent child or spouse of any person listed above.

Group-Term Life Insurance

Sometimes an employer buys life insurance for employees under a group-term plan, where the employees name their beneficiaries. For each employee, the employer can purchase up to $50,000 of plan insurance without increasing the employee's gross income. When the coverage exceeds $50,000, the employee adds to gross income the cost of the excess insurance. To determine this cost, the employer uses a table of uniform premiums (Figure 4-1) found in the income tax regulations.

FIGURE 4-1 Uniform Premium Table

Age*	Taxable Amount Each Month for $1,000 of Excess Coverage
Under 30	$ .08
30–34	.09
35–39	.11
40–44	.17
45–49	.29
50–54	.48
55–59	.75
60–64	1.17
65–69	2.10
70 and over	3.76

* Applicable bracket depends on the employee's age at the end of the year

When using the table, the employer determines the excess coverage under the plan for employees whose coverage exceeds $50,000. Next, the employer divides the excess coverage by $1,000. The table of uniform premiums lists the insurance rates by age. The employer determines each employee's age on the last day of the business year and looks up the monthly rate for each employee's age. The employer then multiplies the monthly rate by the excess coverage stated in $1,000 units. Finally, the employer multiplies the product by the number of months of insurance coverage. The formula used is as follows:

Taxable Amount = Monthly Rate from Figure 4-1 × Number of $1,000 Increments of Excess Coverage × Number of Months of Coverage

When the employee pays part of the premiums, the employer subtracts *all* of the employee's payments from the cost of the excess insurance. When the cost exceeds an employee's payments, the excess is included in the employee's gross income as additional taxable wages. When an employee's payments exceed the cost of the excess insurance, the employee does not have any additional gross income. The employer includes the taxable portion of purchased life insurance as wages on the employee's Form W-2, Wage and Tax Statement.

When an employee has group-term life insurance coverage in excess of $50,000, the taxable amount is computed using the table in Figure 4-1. This amount may differ from the actual amount the employer paid for the coverage. However, the tax law requires that employers use the monthly amounts in Figure 4-1 to compute the amounts to include in employees' gross income.

EXAMPLE 7

Bow Company pays an annual premium for $90,000 of life insurance for Harry R. Socket, age 56. Bow shares the cost with Socket, who pays Bow $22.50 a month through the payroll deduction plan. With these payments, Socket gets 12 months of group-term life insurance protection. If Socket dies before the coverage period ends, his wife collects $90,000. For Socket's age, the table in Figure 4-1 shows a monthly cost of $0.75. Bow adds $90 to Socket's taxable wages, as computed below.

Group-term life insurance coverage	$90,000
Less exempt coverage	(50,000)
Taxable coverage	$40,000
Cost subject to gross income inclusion	
[$40,000/$1,000 = 40; 40 × $0.75 × 12 (Figure 4-1)]	$ 360
Less payments by Socket ($22.50 × 12)	(270)
Gross income	$ 90

Employers whose plan favors key employees must include in their key employees' gross income the full cost of group-term life insurance provided to them. The taxable amount is the *greater of* (i) the actual premiums paid, or (ii) the amount using the table in Figure 4-1.

EXAMPLE 8

Jeffrey Toms is 45 years old and a key employee at his firm. The employer provides Toms with $200,000 of group life insurance coverage. The employer's actual cost for this coverage is $800; Toms pays nothing. If the plan favors key employees, Toms must include $800 in gross income. This amount is the *greater of* (i) the employer's $800 actual cost, or (ii) $696, as determined using the monthly amounts in Figure 4-1 ($.29 x 200 x 12). The employer would add $800 to Toms's taxable wages on Form W-2. If the plan does not favor key employees, the employer adds $522 ($150,000 excess coverage ÷ $1,000 = 150 x $.29 x 12) to Toms's taxable wages.

Other Fringe Benefits

Employers may also offer a number of other fringe benefits. These include (1) athletic facilities, (2) employee discounts, (3) no-additional-cost services, (4) meals and lodging provided on the employer's premises, (5) moving reimbursements, (6) parking and transportation, (7) working fringe benefits, (8) retirement plan services, and (9) *de minimis* fringe benefits.

1. **Athletic facilities.** Employees exclude from gross income the value of the use of athletic facilities provided on the employer's property. These services include tennis courts, swimming pools, weight rooms, etc. To qualify for the exclusion, substantially all of the facility's use must be by employees, their spouses and their dependent children.

2. **Qualified employee discounts.** Employees may exclude from gross income discounts from their employers on goods and services. To qualify for the exclusion, the employee must work in the segment of the employer's business giving the discount. For example, airline employees cannot exclude discounts they receive at a hotel owned by the airline. For services, the amount of the discount cannot exceed 20% of the item's retail value. For goods, the discount cannot exceed the employer's average markup for the property line.
3. **No-additional-cost services.** Employees exclude from gross income the value of services that do not cause large added costs or lost revenues to the employer. To get the exclusion, the employee must work in the line of business providing the services. Examples of no-additional-cost services are the use of hotel rooms, travel on airlines, buses and trains.
4. **Meals and lodging.** Employees exclude the value of meals and lodging provided by their employer when they are provided on the employer's premises for the convenience of the employer. For example, nurses and doctors may be allowed to eat in the hospital cafeteria free-of-charge so that they can be reached, if needed in an emergency. Likewise, resident advisors of college dorms may exclude the value of the room and board provided to them rent-free if the college requires them to live in the dorm as a condition of their employment. When tax-free lodging is provided to an employee, the value of meals and lodging furnished to the employee's spouse and dependents is also excluded from gross income.
5. **Moving reimbursements.** Employees can exclude from gross income amounts their employers pay or reimburse to them for qualified moving expenses. To qualify for the exclusion, the costs covered by the employer must be those that the employee would have been able to deduct for AGI. The rules for the deduction of moving expenses are covered later in this chapter.
6. **Parking and transportation.** In 2006, employees exclude from gross income up to $205 for qualified parking their employers provide. They also can exclude up to $105 for employer-provided qualified transportation. **Qualified parking** includes parking provided near the employer's business or near the place where the employee commutes to work using mass transit or carpools. **Qualified transportation** includes transit passes and transportation to the employer's workplace in a commuter vehicle. Unlike many of the other fringe benefits employers provide, the discrimination rules do not apply. Thus, key employees and highly paid employees can exclude the value of parking and transportation, even when these benefits favor them.
7. **Working condition fringe benefits.** Usually employees deduct their job-related expenses as itemized deductions (see Chapter 6). When an employer pays for these costs, employees exclude their value from gross income. This includes amounts that qualify as deductible education costs that exceed the $5,250 fringe benefit under an employer's educational assistance plan. The discrimination rules do not apply to these fringe benefits. Thus, key employees and highly paid employees can exclude the value of working condition fringe benefits, even when these benefits favor them.
8. **Qualified retirement plan services.** Employees exclude from gross income the value of any qualified retirement plan services provided to them or their spouses by their employer.
9. ***De minimis* fringe benefits.** Employees exclude from gross income benefits of a small value that they receive from employers. Examples include occasional personal use of copy machines and office supplies. They also may include occasional tickets to entertainment and sporting events and office parties. Employees also exclude small holiday gifts, such as turkeys and hams. The discrimination rules do not apply to de minimis fringe benefits.

After using the above formula to determine the potential excludable bond interest, taxpayers must determine if the phase-out applies. First, they determine a modified AGI amount (AGI without the Educational Savings Bond interest and the foreign earned income exclusions). Second, they compare this figure with a $63,100 threshold ($94,700 for a joint return). If modified AGI exceeds the threshold, the phase-out applies. The interest exclusion phases out proportionately over a range of $15,000 ($30,000 for joint filers).

PHASE-DOWN OF EXCLUDABLE EDUCATIONAL SAVINGS BONDS INTEREST

$$\text{Excludable Bond Interest} \times \frac{\text{Modified AGI} - \$63{,}100^{*}}{\$15{,}000^{**}} = \text{Reduction in Excludable Interest}$$

* $94,700 for a joint return

** $30,000 for a joint return

Information for Figure 4-2: Filled-In Form 8815

Figure 4-2 shows the use of Form 8815 to compute excludable Educational Savings Bond interest for Frederick and Ida Smith who file a joint return. Fred and Ida have a dependent child, Inez. During the year, the Smiths paid $5,000 for Inez's tuition at Kent State University, where she attends full-time. Inez received a $1,000 nontaxable scholarship.

In September, the Smiths redeemed $10,000 of Series EE bonds. Of the cash received, $1,500 is interest and $8,500 is principal. The Smith's modified AGI is $99,350.

After reporting all $1,500 as interest, the Smiths enter the $507 on Form 1040, Schedule B, as "Excludable interest on series EE and I U.S. savings bonds."

Scholarships and Fellowships

A student excludes from gross income the portion of scholarships and fellowship grants used to pay tuition and course-required fees, books, supplies, and equipment. Only degree candidates get this exclusion. Degree candidates include undergraduate and graduate students who pursue studies aimed at getting academic or professional degrees. Postdoctoral fellowship students do not get this exclusion. Graduate students who teach or do research at their degree-granting institutions can exclude tuition waivers they receive.

Students with taxable scholarships report this amount as additional wages on their tax returns. Taxable scholarships can be reported on Form 1040EZ, Form 1040A or Form 1040. The student writes in the words "SCH =" and the taxable amount in the space to the left of where taxable wages are reported. Thus, these amounts count as earned income for purposes of computing the standard deduction for those claimed as a dependent on another's return.

The exclusion for scholarships does not apply to compensation for services rendered even if all candidates for the degree are required to perform the services.

FIGURE 4-2 Filled-In Form 8815

Form **8815**
Department of the Treasury
Internal Revenue Service (99)

Exclusion of Interest From Series EE and I U.S. Savings Bonds Issued After 1989
(For Filers With Qualified Higher Education Expenses)
► **Attach to Form 1040 or Form 1040A.**

OMB No. 1545-0074
2006
Attachment Sequence No. **57**

Name(s) shown on return	Your social security number
Frederick B. and Ida A. Smith	382 60 1057

1 (a) Name of person (you, your spouse, or your dependent) who was enrolled at or attended an eligible educational institution	(b) Name and address of eligible educational institution
Inez I. Smith	Kent State University West Lake Road, Ashtabula, OH 44004

If you need more space, attach a statement.

2	Enter the total qualified higher education expenses you paid in 2006 for the person(s) listed in column (a) of line 1. See the instructions to find out which expenses qualify			2	5,000 00
3	Enter the total of any nontaxable educational benefits (such as nontaxable scholarship or fellowship grants) received for 2006 for the person(s) listed in column (a) of line 1 (see instructions)			3	1,000 00
4	Subtract line 3 from line 2. If zero or less, **stop.** You **cannot** take the exclusion			4	4,000 00
5	Enter the total proceeds (principal and interest) from all series EE and I U.S. savings bonds **issued after 1989** that you **cashed during 2006**			5	10,000 00
6	Enter the interest included on line 5 (see instructions)			6	1,500 00
7	If line 4 is equal to or more than line 5, enter "1.000." If line 4 is less than line 5, divide line 4 by line 5. Enter the result as a decimal (rounded to at least three places)			7	× .40
8	Multiply line 6 by line 7			8	600 00
9	Enter your modified adjusted gross income (see instructions) **Note:** *If line 9 is $78,100 or more if single or head of household, or $124,700 or more if married filing jointly or qualifying widow(er),* ***stop.*** *You* ***cannot*** *take the exclusion.*	9	99,350 00		
10	Enter: $63,100 if single or head of household; $94,700 if married filing jointly or qualifying widow(er)	10	94,700 00		
11	Subtract line 10 from line 9. If zero or less, skip line 12, enter -0- on line 13, and go to line 14	11	4,650 00		
12	Divide line 11 by: $15,000 if single or head of household; $30,000 if married filing jointly or qualifying widow(er). Enter the result as a decimal (rounded to at least three places)			12	× .155
13	Multiply line 8 by line 12			13	93 00
14	**Excludable savings bond interest.** Subtract line 13 from line 8. Enter the result here and on Schedule B (Form 1040), line 3, or Schedule 1 (Form 1040A), line 3, whichever applies ►			14	507 00

EXAMPLE 14

Mandy Krais is awarded a $10,000 scholarship to attend State College. Krais is claimed as a dependent on her parent's return. Krais's tuition and course-required books and fees for the year are $6,000. The rest of the scholarship is used to cover her room and board. Krais excludes $6,000 of the scholarship from gross income. On her tax return she writes in "SCH = $4,000" and adds the $4,000 to her taxable wages. This amount is also used in computing her limited standard deduction (the *lesser of* (i) $850 or (ii) earned income + $300).

Compensation for Physical Injury and Sickness

A taxpayer who receives workers' compensation for a physical injury or illness excludes it from gross income. Any payments received from accident and health insurance plans purchased by the taxpayer are also excluded. However, when a taxpayer's employer purchases the insurance, only medical expense reimbursements are excluded.

Generally, any compensation a person receives for physical injury or sickness is excludable from gross income. However, punitive damages received out of a physical injury case are generally taxable. All damages received for nonphysical injuries (e.g., employment discrimination, injury to reputation, and emotional distress) are taxable.

Roth IRAs

Another source of tax-free income is the earnings from Roth IRAs. Taxpayers make nondeductible contributions to Roth IRAs and in return, the earnings grow tax-free. Taxpayers make withdrawals tax- and penalty-free if the distribution is made after the Roth IRA has been open for five tax years and any one of the following conditions is met.

1. The distribution is made after the taxpayer attains age 59½.
2. The distribution is made to a beneficiary as a result of the taxpayer's death.
3. The distribution is made on account of the taxpayer's disability.
4. The distribution is used to pay first-time homebuyer expenses (subject to a $10,000 lifetime limit).

When distributions do not meet at least one of the above criteria, amounts received in excess of the taxpayer's contributions are included in gross income. A 10% early withdrawal penalty also applies to the amount taxed. Please note, however, that taxpayers can withdraw their contributions at any time and for any reason without tax or penalty. Since contributions to a Roth IRA are not deductible, there is never any tax when only contributions are taken from a Roth IRA. However, once the taxpayer has withdrawn amounts from the Roth IRA they can not be returned to the IRA to grow tax-free.

EXAMPLE 15

After making contributions of $4,500 over a three-year period, Arlo Brown (age 35) withdraws the $5,400 balance in his Roth IRA to buy a new car. Of this amount, $4,500 is a tax-free withdrawal of his contribution. Brown must pay income tax on the earnings of $900. He also pays a nondeductible early withdrawal penalty of $90 (10% × $900).

The maximum annual contribution to a Roth IRA is the *lesser of* (i) $4,000 or (ii) 100% of the taxpayer's earned income. Taxpayers at least 50 years old may make "catch-up" contributions to their Roth IRAs. This is an opportunity to make up for retirement contributions missed earlier in life. The extra amount for 2006 is $1,000 before applying the phase-out limits. The maximum contribution limit phases out proportionately between the following AGI levels:

1. Unmarried: $95,000–$110,000
2. Married—Joint filers: $150,000–$160,000; Married—Separate filers: $0–$10,000

Taxpayers round their contribution limit up to the nearest $10. If their reduced contribution limit is more than $0, but less than $200, they increase the limit to $200.

EXAMPLE 16

Grace Matteo is single and 43 years old. She wants to contribute the most she can to a Roth IRA. Her AGI is $97,160. For 2006, Matteo may contribute $3,430. She computes her maximum contribution as follows:

Reduction factor:

[($97,160 – $95,000) / $15,000 phase-out range] × $4,000 = $576

Contribution limit:

$4,000 – $576 = $3,424, rounded up to nearest $10: $3,430

EXAMPLE 17

Kathy and Adam Keck are both age 60. Their 2006 AGI is $158,482, most of which comes from taxable wages. Kathy and Adam each compute the maximum contribution they can make to their respective Roth IRAs as follows:

Reduction factor:

[($158,482 - $150,000)/$10,000 phase-out range] x $5,000 = $4,241

Contribution limit:

$5,000 - $4,241 = $759, rounded up to nearest $10: $760

Taxpayers filing jointly with over $160,000 of AGI ($110,000 for singles) cannot contribute to a Roth IRA. They may, however, make contributions to a traditional IRA. The contribution would be deductible unless one or both spouses are covered under an employer plan.

Taxpayers may take the funds from one Roth IRA and deposit them into another Roth IRA tax-free. Some taxpayers may also convert a traditional IRA into a Roth IRA. Such a conversion produces taxable income to the extent of any earnings or deductible contributions converted into the Roth IRA. However, amounts converted to a Roth IRA are not subject to the 10% penalty on early withdrawal.

Roth 401(k) Plans

Beginning in 2006, an employer's 401(k) plan may let employees make designated Roth 401(k) contributions. **Designated Roth contributions** are made with post-tax wages. This means that that amounts designated as Roth contributions do not reduce the employee's taxable wages. However, as with Roth IRAs, qualified distributions from Roth 401(k) plans are tax-free once the account has been around for five years. Like with Roth IRAs, the part of a nonqualified distribution that is earnings are included in gross income and subject to a 10% penalty tax. Although Roth contributions are similar to Roth IRA contributions, the two differ in several ways.

1. There is no income limit on who can made designated Roth contributions. [Contributions allowed to a Roth IRA are phased out once unmarried taxpayer's AGI exceeds $95,000 ($150,000 for MFJ taxpayers)].
2. In 2006, employees can contribution up to $15,000 of their wages (plus $5,000 for catch-up contributions if age 50 or older). [The 2006 limits for Roth IRAs are $4,000 and $5,000, respectively].
3. Qualified distributions are the same as those used for Roth IRAs. However, withdrawing amounts for first-time home purchases is not a qualified distribution from a Roth 401(k).

Coverdell Education Savings Accounts

Taxpayers may contribute up to $2,000 per child (beneficiary) per year to an education savings account. The contribution is nondeductible. Distributions from these accounts are excluded from gross income of the beneficiary if they are later used to pay qualified education expenses before the child reaches age 30. However, the exclusion is not available in a year in which either the HOPE credit or the lifetime learning credit is claimed.

Qualified expenses include the following postsecondary education expenses: tuition, fees, books, supplies, equipment, and room and board. For room and board to qualify, the student must attend school on at least a half-time basis in a program leading to a recognized educational credential. When distributions during the year exceed the qualified higher education expenses, the law treats some of the excess as a distribution of earnings and taxes it.

Contributions must be for a child under the age of 18. The annual contribution limit of $2,000 is phased out proportionately between these AGI levels:

1. Unmarried: $95,000–$110,000
2. Married—Joint filers: $190,000–$220,000; Married—Separate filers: $0–$10,000

Because the maximum annual contribution to a child's education savings account is $2,000, the combined contributions from all donors (e.g., parents and grandparents) cannot exceed $2,000 *per child*. A 6% penalty applies to excess contributions.

When the beneficiary reaches age 30, any unused amount in the account must be distributed to the beneficiary. Any earnings included in the distribution will be added to the beneficiary's gross income and taxed. A 10% penalty on the earnings will also be assessed. To avoid this situation, the unused amount may be rolled over into an education savings account of a sibling or child of the beneficiary tax and penalty free.

529 Plans

Many states, colleges and brokerage firms have set up qualified tuition programs from which individuals can later pay college expenses for their children, or perhaps their grandchildren. The more common name for these accounts are **529 plans**. Contributions to 529 plans are not deductible, but amounts grow in these accounts tax free if the funds are later used to pay qualified education expenses for the child. Qualified expenses include tuition, fees, books, and supplies, as well as room and board. However, these amounts must be reduced by any tax-free assistance the student uses to pay for these costs. For example, if the student receives a nontaxable scholarship, qualified expenses are computed net of the scholarship. Likewise, if the parent is reimbursed amounts from an employer's educational assistance plan, qualified expenses are computed net of the reimbursement. If the child ends up not going to college, the plan will refund the amounts in the account to the contributor. Any portion returned that is earnings is taxed to the contributor as interest income.

EXAMPLE 18

Starting in 2002, Paul West has contributed $5,000 each year to a 529 plan for his daughter, Susan. At the end of 2006, the balance in the plan is $30,000. Early in 2007, $6,000 is withdrawn from the account to pay for Susan's tuition and fees at Northwest College. None of the $6,000 is taxable. The $24,000 left in the account can be used in the future to pay more of Susan's qualified education expenses.

EXAMPLE 19

Same as in Example 18, except that Susan received a $4,000 scholarship to cover her tuition. Qualified expenses would be $2,000 ($6,000 - $4,000). If $1,000 of the $6,000 is earnings, then two-thirds of the $1,000 ($4,000 nonqualified distribution ÷ $6,000 distributed = 2/3), or $666.67, would be included in Susan's gross income.

When amounts are withdrawn from a 529 plan that are not used for qualified education expenses, the taxable amounts are included in the student's gross income. However, when the child does not attend college, the funds revert back to the contributor and the taxable amounts are included in the contributor's gross income.

DEDUCTIONS FOR AGI

The IRS classifies certain deductions from gross income (to arrive at AGI) as **adjustments to income.** Other deductions from gross income appear on supporting forms and schedules (e.g., Schedule C), with the net result shown in the income section of Form 1040. A taxpayer using Form 1040EZ has no adjustments to income. A Form 1040A filer has only four adjustments to income. These include IRA deductions, student loan interest, jury duty pay remitted to the employer, and penalty on early withdrawal of savings. A Form 1040 filer can deduct a number of adjustments to income. Figure 4-3 lists deductions for which there are separate lines on the form. The taxpayer can also write in more adjustments on the dotted portion of line 36 before entering the total deductions.

FIGURE 4-3 Deductions Listed on Form 1040

1. Archer Medical Savings Account (MSA) deduction
2. Certain business expenses of reservists, performing artists, and fee-basis government officials
3. Health savings account deduction
4. Moving expenses
5. One-half of self-employment tax
6. Self-employed SEP, SIMPLE, and qualified plans
7. Self-employed health insurance deduction
8. Penalty on early withdrawal of savings
9. Alimony paid
10. IRA deduction
11. Student loan interest deduction
12. Jury pay given to an employer
13. Domestic production activities deduction

WRITE-IN ADJUSTMENTS TO INCOME ON FORM 1040 (LINE 36)

1. Foreign housing deduction
2. Write-off of forestation or reforestation costs
3. Some supplemental unemployment benefit repayments

DEDUCTIONS FROM GROSS INCOME NOT LISTED SEPARATELY ON FORM 1040 (PAGE 1)

1. Trade or business deductions, Schedule C (Chapter 7)
2. Losses from property sales, Schedule D (Chapter 11)
3. Rent and royalty expenses, Schedule E (Chapter 9)

Certain Business Expenses of Reservists, Performing Artists, and Fee-Basis Government Officials

Members of a reserve component of the Armed Forces who travel more than 100 miles away from home to perform services as a member of the reserves can deduct their travel expenses as a deduction for AGI. The deduction is limited to the amount the federal government pays its employees for travel expenses. Expenses of travel that do not take reservists more than 100 miles form home are deducted as a miscellaneous itemized deduction. Reservists initially report their travel expenses on Form 2106, Employee Business Expenses. Chapter 6 describes the use of Form 2106.

Certain performing artists may qualify to deduct their employee business expenses as deduction for AGI rather than as a miscellaneous itemized deduction. To qualify, all of the following requirements must be met.

1. Performing artist must be employed by at least two employers in the performing arts.
2. Performing artist must receive at least $200 from each of two of these employers.
3. Performing-arts business expenses must exceed 10% of gross income from the performing arts.
4. AGI cannot exceed $16,000 before deducting these business expenses.

Taxpayers who do not meet all of the above requirements deduct their business expenses as a miscellaneous itemized deduction. The business expenses are initially reported on Form 2106. To claim a deduction for AGI, married taxpayers must file jointly unless they have lived apart at all times during the year.

State and local government officials who are paid on a fee basis may also deduct their related employee business expenses as a deduction for AGI. They too initially report their expenses on Form 2106.

Individual Retirement Arrangements (IRAs)

To provide greater savings for retirement, working taxpayers can contribute to a traditional Individual Retirement Arrangement (IRA). Like the Roth IRA, this savings program allows the earnings to accumulate tax-free. However, unlike Roth IRAs, the earnings are taxed when withdrawn. Certain taxpayers can also deduct their IRA contributions from gross income. For these people, the contributions and the earnings are tax-free until funds are withdrawn from the account. When withdrawn, both the earnings and the deductible contributions are taxed.

IRA Contribution Limits

Contributions to an IRA must come from earned income. For IRA purposes, the tax law treats alimony as earned income. However, interest, dividends, and other types of investment income are not earned income.

The maximum annual contribution to an IRA is the *lesser of* (i) $4,000 or (ii) 100% of the taxpayer's earned income. The amount is $8,000 for a married couple, as long as the couple has at least $8,000 of combined earnings. Each spouse must establish a separate IRA, and the maximum annual contribution to any one person's IRA cannot exceed $4,000 a year. Otherwise, the contribution may be split between the accounts as the spouses see fit.

Taxpayers age 50 and older can contribution an extra $1,000 to their IRAs during 2006. If both spouses are at least 50 years old, they can contributed a total of $10,000 ($5,000 to each IRA) to their IRAs during 2006. A married couple need not file a joint return to contribute to an IRA.

In the year a taxpayer reaches age 70½, usually no further contributions are allowed. The deadline for making both traditional and Roth IRA contributions for the current year is April 15 of the next year.

EXAMPLE 20

Jim and Jeanette Beckman (both age 45) file a joint return. During 2006, Jim earns $50,000 at his job. Jeanette does not work. Jim and Jeanette can each contribute up to $4,000 to their respective IRAs. They have until April 15, 2007 to make their contributions.

EXAMPLE 21

Same as in Example 20, except that Jim is age 50. Jim can contribute up to $5,000 to his IRA. He can contribution up to $4,000 to Susan's IRA.

IRA contributions made between January 1 and April 15 could be considered contributions for either the current or previous tax year. Generally IRA trustees will assume the contribution made in this time frame is for the current year. If the taxpayer wants the contribution to count towards the prior year, then the taxpayer needs to instruct the IRA trustee of this in writing at the time the payment is made.

Excess Contributions to an IRA

When traditional and Roth IRA contributions exceed the allowed limit, the IRS assesses a 6% excise tax on the excess. This "excise" tax is not assessed if the taxpayer withdraws the excess (plus any related earnings) before the due date of the taxpayer's tax return. Taxpayers who must pay the excise tax use Form 5329, Return For Additional Taxes Attributable to Qualifying Retirement Plans (including IRAs), Annuities, and Modified Endowment Contracts.

Limitation on IRA Deductions

Taxpayers who are not active participants in an employer-sponsored retirement plan can deduct up to $4,000 ($5,000 if 50 or older) for contributions made to a traditional IRA for 2006. Anyone participating in an employer-sponsored retirement plan may face a deduction phase-out if "net AGI" exceeds a certain amount. However, the spouse of a participant in an employer plan can still receive a full IRA deduction as long as the couple's "net AGI" does not exceed $150,000.

For participants in an employer-sponsored retirement plan, the phase-out takes place when "net AGI" falls within these ranges:

Unmarried (single and head of household)	$50,000–$60,000
Married filing jointly	$75,000–$85,000
Married filing separately and not living with spouse any part of the year	$50,000–$60,000
Married filing separately and living with spouse part of the year	$0–$10,000
Nonparticipating spouse who files married filing jointly with participating spouse	$150,000–$160,000

When "net AGI" exceeds these ranges, no deduction is allowed. However, a retirement plan participant with "net AGI" less than these amounts can deduct up to $4,000 ($5,000 if 50 or older) of the IRA contributions for 2006. The taxpayer determines **net AGI** before the IRA deduction, the interest exclusion for series EE and I educational savings bonds and the foreign earned income exclusion.

A participant in a qualified plan whose AGI is within the phase-out range must compute a reduced IRA deduction. The maximum deduction is reduced proportionately for each dollar of AGI that falls within the $10,000 phase out range. As with the Roth IRA, taxpayers round their reduced contributions limit up to the nearest $10. If their deduction limit is more than $0, but less than $200, they increase the deduction to $200.

EXAMPLE 22

Stan Decker, age 52, is married and files a joint return with his wife, Dorothy, age 48. They both want to make the largest possible deductible contributions to their IRAs. Their net AGI is $79,000. Stan is an active participant in his employer's retirement plan. Dorothy does not have a retirement plan at work. Because the Deckers' net AGI is within the phase-out range and Stan is in a retirement plan at work, his maximum deductible contribution is $3,000 [$5,000 – ($4,000/$10,000 × $5,000)]. In contrast, Dorothy is not in an employer-sponsored retirement plan, and because net AGI does not exceed $150,000, she can contribute and deduct $4,000 to her traditional IRA.

EXAMPLE 23

Same as Example 22, except that Deckers' net AGI was $157,000. Stan may contribute up to $5,000 but cannot deduct any contribution he makes to his IRA because net AGI exceeds the $85,000 ceiling of the MFJ phase-out range. Dorothy can deduct up to $1,200 of her contributions [$4,000 – ($7,000/$10,000 × $4,000)]. If she contributes the maximum $4,000, she will only be able to deduct $1,200.

EXAMPLE 24

Laura Inkster, age 38, is single and has net AGI of $52,433. Included in this amount is $50,000 of wage income. Inkster can contribute up to $4,000 to an IRA for 2006. However, the maximum that she can deduct is $3,030. If Inkster contributes more than $3,030 (but less than $4,000) to her IRA for 2006, the excess over $3,030 will be a nondeductible contribution to her IRA.

Reduction factor:

[($52,433 - $50,000)/$10,000] x $4,000 = $973

Contribution limit:

$4,000 - $973 = $3,027, rounded up to nearest $10: $3,030

EXAMPLE 25

Same as in Example 24, except that Inkster's net AGI is $59,820. She can still contribute up to $4,000 to an IRA for 2006, but will only be able to deduct $200.

Reduction factor:

[($59,820- $50,000)/$10,000] x $4,000 = $3,928

Contribution limit:

$4,000 - $3,928 = $72, rounded up to $200

Employer Plans

Employer plans include qualifying pension plans, profit-sharing plans, stock bonus plans, qualifying annuity plans, 401(k) plans, and simplified employee pension plans. Keoghs and other retirement plans of self-employed taxpayers also count as employer plans. Finally, employers' retirement plans include tax-sheltered annuities and pension plans under Sections 403(b) and 457.

Nondeductible Contributions

While some taxpayers do not qualify to deduct their contributions to a traditional IRA, they can still make nondeductible contributions of up to $4,000 ($5,000 if 50 or older) to their IRAs for 2006. When they withdraw amounts from these IRAs, the previously taxed (nondeductible) contributions are not taxed. For people who cannot deduct the full $4,000 ($5,000 if 50 or older) contribution to a traditional IRA, the tax law encourages the use of a Roth IRA. Taxpayers can deposit the nondeductible portion of their IRA contribution into a Roth IRA instead of a traditional IRA. When amounts are withdrawn from their Roth IRA after retirement, neither the contributions nor the earnings are taxed. However, income limits apply to Roth IRAs (see discussion earlier in the chapter.)

Taxpayers who make both deductible and nondeductible contributions to the same IRA should keep good records. They must be able to show the amount of their nondeductible contributions, which are tax-free when withdrawn. To help with this task, the IRS provides Form 8606. Taxpayers who make nondeductible IRA contributions should file Form 8606, even if they do not file a tax return.

The maximum contribution taxpayers under age 50 can make to all IRAs during the year (includes both Roth and traditional) is the *lesser of* $4,000 or the taxpayer's earned income. Thus, qualifying taxpayers cannot contribute $4,000 to a traditional IRA and another $4,000 to a Roth IRA. Doing this will result in a 6% excise tax on the excess $4,000 contribution.

Distributions from an IRA

When taxpayers begin receiving IRA distributions, they must determine what part represents nondeductible contributions. The Code taxes the distribution of deductible contributions and earnings withdrawn as ordinary income. The part relating to nondeductible contributions is not taxed. Taxpayers use the IRA distribution formula from Chapter 3 to compute the nontaxable portion of the amounts withdrawn from a traditional IRA.

If a taxpayer receives an IRA distribution before reaching age 59½, the IRS can assess a 10% penalty on the taxable amount withdrawn. However, the IRS does not assess the penalty when the distribution is:

1. Due to death or disability,
2. Used to pay medical expenses in excess of 7.5% of AGI,
3. Used by an unemployed person to buy health insurance,
4. Used to pay qualified higher education expenses, or
5. Used to pay expenses of a qualified first-time homebuyer ($10,000 lifetime limit).

The IRS will not assess the 10% penalty on the first $100,000 of distributions made by taxpayers who suffered an economic loss due to hurricanes Katrina, Rita and Wilma. To be eligible for this special rule, the distribution must occur after the date of the hurricane (August 24, 2005 for Katrina; September 24, 2005 for Rita; October 23, 2005 for Wilma) and before January 1, 2007. In addition, the taxpayer's main place of abode on those dates must have been in a hurricane disaster area, as specified by the federal government. Although the 10% penalty does not apply to these distributions, taxpayers making withdrawals must pay income tax on the taxable portion of these distributions. However, the tax laws allow the income to be spread over three tax years. Taxpayers have 3 years from the time of the withdrawal to redeposit the funds back into the IRA so that they can resume earning tax deferred growth on those amounts.

A taxpayer does not have to start withdrawing IRA funds until April 1 of the calendar year after turning 70½. Thus, a taxpayer who reaches age 70½ in 20x1 does not have to start withdrawing IRA funds until April 1, 20x2. The taxpayer may choose to withdraw the entire balance or receive periodic distributions. Failure to make a timely withdrawing will result in penalties.

Student Loan Interest

Taxpayers may deduct up to $2,500 each year for AGI for interest they paid on money borrowed to pay qualified higher education expenses for themselves, their spouses, and dependents. There is no deduction for any person paying student loan interest who is claimed as a dependent on another person's tax return.

Qualified education expenses include tuition, books, supplies, and room and board. These expenses must be those of a student enrolled at least half-time in a program leading to a recognized credential at a qualified institution of higher education.

Several limitations on the deduction exist. First, the interest deduction is phased out evenly as "modified AGI" increases from $50,000 to $65,000 ($105,000 to $135,000 on joint returns). "Modified AGI" is AGI plus any foreign-earned income or housing exclusion and without the deductions for student loan interest and domestic production activities deduction. Second, taxpayers may not use this interest deduction if the interest is deductible under another section of the Code (e.g., home equity loan). Third, married taxpayers must file jointly to claim the deduction.

EXAMPLE 26

During 2006, Dan Reeves paid $800 interest on a qualified student loan. Dan files a joint return with his wife. Their modified AGI is $130,000. Their deduction for student loan interest is reduced by $667. They deduct $133 for AGI on their joint tax return.

Reduction amount:

[(Modified AGI – AGI threshold)/phase out range] x interest paid

[($130,000 - $105,000)/$30,000] x $800 = $667

Student loan interest deduction:

$800 - $667 = $133

EXAMPLE 27

During 2006, Lee Avery paid interest of $1,620 on a qualified student loan. Avery is single. His modified AGI is $61,400. His deduction for student loan interest is reduced by $1,231. He deducts $389 for AGI on his 2006 tax return.

Reduction amount:

[($61,400 - $50,000)/$15,000] x $1,620 = $1,231

Student loan interest deduction:

$1,620 - $1,231 = $389

Health Savings Account Deduction

Workers deduct their contributions to **health savings accounts** (HSAs) for AGI. HSAs are high-deductible health care plans. They allow taxpayers to save money to pay for medical expenses. In 2006, the maximum that can be contributed to an HSA is the *lesser of* (i) 100% of the taxpayer's annual deductible, or (ii) $2,700 for individual/$5,450 for family coverage. Taxpayers 55 and older can contribute an additional $700 in 2006. All contributions for the current year must be made by April 15 of the next tax year. Once a taxpayer retires, contributions to an HSA must stop. Amounts contributed to HSAs in excess of the allowed amounts are subject to a 10% penalty tax.

For 2006, a **high-deductible health plan** is one that has at least a $1,050 deductible for individual coverage and a $2,100 deductible for family coverage. Eligible taxpayers cannot also be covered under a health care plan offering the same coverage that does not qualify as a high-deductible plan.

Amounts withdrawn from an HSA to pay for medical expenses are excluded from gross income. Any balance in an HSA at the end of the year stays in the account to pay medical expenses in future tax years. Amounts withdrawn and not used to pay medical expenses are included in gross income and subject to a 10% penalty tax. However, when withdrawn after the taxpayer retires, the amounts are included in gross income but avoid the penalty tax. Since the earnings on amounts put in an HSA are not taxed until withdrawn (if ever), health workers and their families can accumulate a sizeable sum in their HSAs over the years.

EXAMPLE 28

During 2006, Kelly Hope contributes the maximum $5,450 to his employer's HSA plan at work. The deductible for his family plan is $2,500, which counts as a high-deductible plan. During 2006, Hope withdraws $600 from the HSA to pay for unreimbursed medical costs for his family. At the end of the year, the balance in the account is $5,100 ($5,450 contributed - $600 withdrawn + $250 earnings). Hope is not taxed on either the $600 withdrawn or the $250 of earnings. The $5,100 balance carries forward to 2007 where it can be used to pay medical costs in that year or continue to earn income.

Moving Expenses

A taxpayer may deduct certain unreimbursed moving expenses as a deduction for AGI. These expenses arise when a change in principal residence occurs as a result of a change in job location. Moving expenses include payments to move a taxpayer and the taxpayer's family and property to the new location so the taxpayer can start work. Self-employed persons and employees who pay their own (or part of their own) qualified moving expenses can deduct the expenses paid as a deduction for AGI. To get the deduction, the mileage and employment tests must be met. Any reimbursements an employee receives from an employer are excludable fringe benefits.

Timing the Move

Usually, a taxpayer moves to a new job location near the time employment starts. However, circumstances may delay the moving of some family members. The delay may result from children being in school or the family waiting to sell the old residence. Moving expenses qualify for the deduction if they are incurred within one year of the taxpayer's start-of-work date. If moving expenses are incurred later than one year after the start-of-work date, the taxpayer may still get a deduction. Here, the taxpayer must prove that something prevented an earlier move (for example, waiting for a child to graduate from high school). However, the IRS does not consider failure to sell one's previous home an acceptable reason for delay.

Definition of Principal Residence

To qualify for the deduction, the taxpayer must live in the old and new residences, treating both as a principal residence. Here, *home* may be a house, a condominium, or an apartment. A second residence, such as a beach house or seasonal home, does not qualify as a principal home. The need for a principal residence can create problems for a new college graduate starting a first job. Persons starting work for the first time can deduct moving expenses as long as they move from a former principal residence to a new one. Usually, a college student's residence hall living quarters do not qualify as a principal residence.

Fully Deductible Moving Expenses

Moving expenses include the reasonable costs of transportation and lodging for the taxpayer and members of the household (including expenses on the arrival day). Although only one trip is deductible, all household members need not travel together or at the same time. Moving expenses also include the costs of packing, crating, in-transit storage, and moving of household goods and personal effects. In addition, they include expenses for special handling of pets. In one case, a taxpayer deducted the cost of moving a sailboat because the boat was used regularly for recreation. However, moving expenses usually exclude the cost of moving a nurse or a personal attendant. In addition, no deduction exists for meals eaten along the way.

EXAMPLE 29

A taxpayer pays $4,200 in moving costs so that he could start work at his new job in another state. This included the cost of a moving van, $3,500; transportation, $550; and meals $150. The taxpayer can deduct $4,050 ($3,500 + $550). The meals are not deductible.

A taxpayer using a personal automobile for moving can deduct out-of-pocket expenses like gasoline, oil, minor repairs, etc. To deduct those expenses, the taxpayer must maintain an adequate expense record. However, a taxpayer can use the optional $.18 per mile standard mileage method. Here, the taxpayer needs only to verify the mileage. Parking fees and tolls are added to the expenses under either method.

EXAMPLE 30

John Samms took a new job in Atlanta, Georgia. His new job is 650 miles away. Samms pays a moving company $2,800 to move his personal belongings. While driving himself and his family to their new home, Samms pays $90 in gas, $220 in lodging and $60 for meals. He also paid $9 in tolls. Because Samms's new home was not ready when he arrived in Atlanta, he paid $1,200 in temporary living expenses and $300 to store his personal belongs. Samms's employer reimbursed him $1,500 for his qualified moving costs. Samms's qualified moving expenses total $3,146. This includes the $2,800 for moving his personal effects, $117 for mileage ($650 x $.18), $9 for tolls and $220 for lodging. The cost for meals and post-transit storage are not qualified moving expenses. Samms reduces this amount by the $1,500 reimbursement he receives from his employer and deducts the rest ($1,646) as a deduction for AGI on Form 1040. Samms takes the deduction for his mileage (at $.18 per mile) because this amount exceeds his actual costs for gasoline during the move.

For 2006, the standard mileage rate used to compute the moving expense deduction is only $.18 per mile, while the standard rate for business mileage is $.445 cents per mile. Both, however, require a business purpose.

Nondeductible Expenses

Nondeductible moving expenses include such items as mortgage prepayment penalties, costs of refitting carpets and draperies, losses arising from the disposal of property, and similar items. These nondeductible expenses also include a commission paid to sell a former residence or acquire a new one or to break a lease or get a new one. House-hunting expenses and temporary living expenses are also not deductible.

Mileage and Employment Tests

Taxpayers can deduct moving expenses only if they meet the mileage and employment tests. These tests help ensure that the deduction is allowed for work-related moves, and not for those made for personal reasons.

Mileage Test. A taxpayer can deduct moving expenses only if the new job site is 50 or more miles farther from the former residence than was the old job site. If an old job location does not exist, the distance between the new place of work and the former residence must equal or exceed 50 miles.

EXAMPLE 31

The distance between a taxpayer's old residence and former workplace was 12 miles. This was the taxpayer's former commute to work. To qualify as a deductible move, the location of the new workplace must be at least 62 miles from the old residence (50 miles + 12 miles).

Employment Test. An employee who deducts moving expenses must be employed full-time in the area of the new job site for 39 weeks during the 12 months right after the move. This test does not apply if the employee fails this test due to disability, death, discharge not due to willful misconduct, or transfer for the employer's benefit. The employee can deduct moving expenses in the year of payment even though the 39-week employment test has not been met by the due date of the tax return. However, the employee must have a reasonable expectation of meeting this test in the future.

EXAMPLE 32

A taxpayer moved to a new job on September 1, 20x1, and expects to work indefinitely at the new job site. Deductible moving expenses are $3,450. On the 20x1 tax return, the taxpayer deducts these expenses even though the employment test will not be met until June of 20x2.

A taxpayer may deduct moving expenses in the year of payment. However, if at a later date the taxpayer fails to meet the employment test, two choices exist. The taxpayer can include the deducted expenses in gross income of the year the test is failed. Or, the taxpayer can file an amended return for the deduction year and remove the deduction.

Self-Employed Persons

Self-employed persons can deduct the same types of moving costs as employees if they meet the mileage test and a stricter employment test. During the 24-month period right after the move, a self-employed person must provide services on a full-time basis (as either a self-employed person or an employee) for 78 weeks. Thirty-nine of those weeks must fall within the 12-month period right after the move. Like an employee, a self-employed person can take the moving expense deduction even though the 78-week employment test has not been met by the due date of the tax return. A self-employed taxpayer who fails the employment test has the same choices as an employee—include the deducted amounts in gross income in the year the test is failed, or file an amended return for the year the deduction was taken.

Reimbursements

Employees exclude from gross income reimbursements they receive from their employers for qualified moving costs. They also exclude amounts employers pay directly to third parties for qualified moving costs. Amounts an employer pays for moving costs that do not qualify for the moving expense deduction are taxable to the employee as additional wages. Employees deduct their out-of-pocket qualified moving expenses for AGI.

Employers must provide a breakdown of the amounts they reimburse their employees for company-related moves. They do this by completing Form 4782 and giving it to the employee. This form is for the employee's records and is not attached to the tax return. Taxpayers (both employees and self-employed persons) report their deductible moving expenses on Form 3903. They then attach Form 3903 to their tax returns. Figure 4-4 shows Form 4792. Figure 4-5 shows Form 3903.

Information for Figure 4-4: Filled-In Form 4782

The Lew Company employs Lois Clarke as an accountant. Clarke's recent promotion to senior accountant in April required a move from Chicago, Illinois, to Atlanta, Georgia, a distance of 629 miles. Lew pays a maximum of $2,000 for its employees' moves. Figure 4-4 shows that Lew paid Clarke **$2,000** for moving expenses (**$1,900** for moving household goods and personal effects and **$100** for travel and lodging).

FIGURE 4-4 Filled-In Form 4782

Form **4782** (Rev. July 1997) Department of the Treasury Internal Revenue Service	**Employee Moving Expense Information** Payments made during the calendar year ▸ 2006 ▸ **Instructions for employers are on the back.**		OMB No. 1545-0182 **Do not file. Keep for your records.**
Name of employee: Lois A. Clarke			Social security number: 296 : 26 : 6254
Moving Expense Payments	**(a)** Amount paid to employee	**(b)** Amount paid to a third party for employee's benefit and value of services furnished in kind	**(c)** Total (Add columns **(a)** and **(b)**.)
1 Transportation and storage of household goods and personal effects 1	1,900 00		1,900 00
2 Travel and lodging payments for expenses of moving from old to new home. **Do not** include meals 2	100 00		100 00
3 All other payments (list type and amount). **Note:** *These amounts must be included in the employee's income and are subject to withholding* ▸ 3			
4 Total. Add the amounts in column (c) of lines 1 through 3 . . . . ▸ 4			2,000 00

Information for Figure 4-5: Filled-In Form 3903

Lois Clarke (see Figure 4-4) uses Form 3903 to report deductible moving expenses.

Other Information

1: Cost of moving personal effects, **$2,675**

2: Travel and lodging, **$198** ($85 for lodging + 629 x $.18 for travel)

4: Employer reimbursement, **$2,000** (source: Form W-2, box 12)

Clarke uses the optional mileage method (instead of actual costs) for her travel expense. She enters her deductible moving expenses ($873) on Form 1040 as "Moving expenses."

FIGURE 4-5 Filled-In Form 3903

Form **3903** — Department of the Treasury, Internal Revenue Service

Moving Expenses

▶ Attach to Form 1040 or Form 1040NR.

OMB No. 1545-0074 — **2006** — Attachment Sequence No. **62**

Name(s) shown on return: Lois A. Clarke — **Your social security number**: 296 26 6254

Before you begin: √ See the **Distance Test** and **Time Test** in the instructions to find out if you can deduct your moving expenses.

√ See **Members of the Armed Forces** on the back, if applicable.

		Line	Amount
1	Transportation and storage of household goods and personal effects (see instructions)	1	2,675 00
2	Travel (including lodging) from your old home to your new home (see instructions). **Do not** include the cost of meals	2	198 00
3	Add lines 1 and 2	3	2,873 00
4	Enter the total amount your employer paid you for the expenses listed on lines 1 and 2 that is **not** included in box 1 of your Form W-2 (wages). This amount should be shown in box 12 of your Form W-2 with code **P**	4	2,000 00
5	Is line 3 **more than** line 4? ☐ **No.** You **cannot** deduct your moving expenses. If line 3 is less than line 4, subtract line 3 from line 4 and include the result on Form 1040, line 7, or Form 1040NR, line 8. ☒ **Yes.** Subtract line 4 from line 3. Enter the result here and on Form 1040, line 26, or Form 1040NR, line 26. This is your **moving expense deduction**	5	873 00

Self-Employment Tax

People who are self-employed in 2006 pay a self-employment tax of 15.3% on the first $94,200 of net earnings from self-employment and 2.9% on earnings over that amount. They deduct one-half of this tax for AGI on Form 1040. Chapter 7 provides more on the self-employment tax.

Self-Employed Health Insurance Deduction

Self-employed taxpayers deduct their health insurance premiums for AGI. The deduction equals the *lesser of* (i)100% of the health insurance premiums paid for the taxpayer, spouse, and dependents or (ii) net profit from the taxpayer's business reduced by any retirement plan contributions. The taxpayer treats any nondeductible premiums for health insurance as a medical expense (Chapter 5).

Self-employed persons cannot take this deduction for any month in which they are eligible to participate in an employer's health plan (or in the plan of a spouse's employer). Also, a self-employed taxpayer with employees cannot take the deduction when the plan favors the taxpayer.

EXAMPLE 33

Pete Douglas is self-employed. His wife, Emma, works full-time for five months during the year. During those months, she is eligible for health insurance coverage through her employer. However, due to Emma's unsteady full-time employment, the Douglases have chosen to pay for their own health insurance coverage through Pete's business. During the current year, they paid $1,200 a month for family coverage ($14,400 for the year). Since Emma was eligible for health insurance coverage through her employer for five months during the year, the Douglases can only deduct $8,400 in the current year ($1,200 x 7 months). They deduct this amount for AGI on Form 1040, page 1.

Keogh, SIMPLE, and SEP Plans

Keogh, SIMPLE, and simplified employee pension (SEP) plans allow self-employed persons to make deductible contributions to retirement plans for themselves. A taxpayer deducts the contributions as a deduction for AGI on Form 1040, page 1. Chapter 7 describes the rules for contributing to these plans.

Penalty on Early Withdrawal of Savings

Money invested in certificates of deposit (CDs) usually earn higher interest rates than normal savings accounts. Banks offer the higher rates for funds that remain on deposit until maturity. CDs can have maturities ranging anywhere from 1-month to 10-years. Usually, the longer the term, the higher the interest rate. In return for these higher rates, banks impose a large penalty if the investor cashes in the CD early. A taxpayer who cashes in the CD early includes the full interest income in gross income on Form 1040 ("Taxable interest") and deducts the lost interest as a deduction for AGI ("Penalty on early withdrawal of savings").

EXAMPLE 34

In 2003, Marty Andrews invested $50,000 in a 5-year CD. In return, the bank promised to pay her an annual interest rate of 4.0% on her $50,000 investment. In 2006, Andrews decides to cash in her CD. She receives a check from the bank for $53,606, even through at the time of the withdrawal, the balance in her account was $55,231.The difference between these two amounts was the penalty for early withdrawal. At the end of the year, the bank will issue Andrews a Form 1099-INT reporting interest paid to her in the amount of $5,231 ($55,231 - $50,000) and a $1,625 early withdrawal penalty ($55,231 - $53,606). Andrews will report the full amount of interest income on Schedule B. She will then deduct the penalty as a deduction for AGI on Form 1040, page 1. Thus, only the net of these two amounts ($55,231 - $1,625 = $53,606) will increase her AGI.

Alimony

As discussed in Chapter 3, a person who pays alimony deducts it for AGI. The recipient includes the same amount in gross income. When the tax law requires the person who pays alimony to recapture some of it as income, the recipient gets a deduction for the same amount.

Domestic Production Activity Deduction

Taxpayers have available an above-the-line deduction equal to the *lesser of* (i) 3% of their qualified production activity income or (ii) taxable income. This deduction is available to anyone who manufactures, grows, or extracts products in the United States. The amount deductible cannot exceed 50% of the W-2 wages paid during the year for these activities. Thus, to increase their W-2 wages, companies may want to hire more employees instead of independent contractors.

Qualified production activity income is basically "net income" computed on receipts from the sale of products produced in the U.S. This amount is compared with the company's taxable income, and the lower of the two amounts is used in calculating the deduction. However, for individual taxpayers, AGI is substituted for taxable income.

REPORTING EXHIBITS

Figure 4-6 shows how taxpayers use Form 1040A to determine AGI, taxable income, the tax, and a tax refund. Figure 4-7 shows how taxpayers determine AGI using Form 1040 (page 1) and Schedule B.

Information for Figure 4-6: Filled-In Form 1040A

Karl and Jill Cook file a joint Form 1040A for 2006. They have a 7-year-old dependent daughter. The payroll data for Karl and Jill from their Forms W-2 are as follows:

Employer	*Wages*	*Federal Income Tax Withheld*	*FICA Taxes Withheld*	*Other Deductions*	*Net*
Pike Corp.:					
Karl E. Cook	$26,200	$192	$2,004	$1,500 IRA	
				60 Ins.	$22,444
First Bank:					
Jill R. Cook	5,950	24	455		5,471
Totals	$32,150	$216	$2,459	$1,560	$27,915

Karl's employer carries a $10,000 group-term insurance policy on his life. He shares the cost of this policy with his employer through payroll deductions. The total withheld from Karl's pay for insurance premiums equals $60. Although the Cooks received net wages of $27,915, they pay tax on their gross wages of $32,150 ($26,200 + $5,950).

Karl has a traditional IRA account. During the past two years he made contributions of $125 a month ($1,500 each year) by payroll deduction.

Other Information

8a: Taxable interest, **$640** from Citizens Bank (source: Form 1099-INT)
17: IRA deduction, **$1,500** (source: payroll deduction, W-2)
29: Credit for child care, **$389** (source: Schedule 2, Form 1040A)
32: Retirement savings contribution credit, **$300** (source: Form 8880)
33: Child tax credit, **$419** ($1,108 – ($389 + $300))
40a: Earned income credit (EIC), **$292** (source: EIC worksheet)
41: Additional child tax credit, **$581** ($1,000 – $419)
42: Credit for federal telephone excise tax paid, **$50** (for three exemptions)

FIGURE 4-6 Filled-In Form 1040A, Page 1

Form **1040A** Department of the Treasury—Internal Revenue Service
U.S. Individual Income Tax Return (99) **2006** IRS Use Only—Do not write or staple in this space.
OMB No. 1545-0074

Label (See page 18.)
LABEL HERE
Use the IRS label. Otherwise, please print or type.

Your first name and initial	Last name	Your social security number
Karl E.	Cook	269-09-9092
If a joint return, spouse's first name and initial	Last name	Spouse's social security number
Jill R.	Cook	390-16-2222
Home address (number and street). If you have a P.O. box, see page 18.	Apt. no.	▲ You **must** enter your SSN(s) above. ▲
400 South Elm Street		
City, town or post office, state, and ZIP code. If you have a foreign address, see page 18.		Checking a box below will not change your tax or refund.
Chicago, IL 60631-1314		

Presidential Election Campaign ▶ Check here if you, or your spouse if filing jointly, want $3 to go to this fund (see page 18) ▶ ☒ **You** ☒ **Spouse**

Filing status Check only one box.
1 ☐ Single
2 ☒ Married filing jointly (even if only one had income)
3 ☐ Married filing separately. Enter spouse's SSN above and full name here. ▶
4 ☐ Head of household (with qualifying person). (See page 19.) If the qualifying person is a child but not your dependent, enter this child's name here. ▶
5 ☐ Qualifying widow(er) with dependent child (see page 19)

Exemptions
6a ☒ **Yourself.** If someone can claim you as a dependent, **do not** check box 6a.
b ☒ **Spouse**
Boxes checked on 6a and 6b: 2

c **Dependents:**

If more than six dependents, see page 21.

(1) First name	Last name	(2) Dependent's social security number	(3) Dependent's relationship to you	(4) ✓ if qualifying child for child tax credit (see page 21)
Nan C.	Wilson	624-18-1111	daughter	☒
				☐
				☐
				☐
				☐
				☐

No. of children on 6c who:
• lived with you: 1
• did not live with you due to divorce or separation (see page 22): ____
Dependents on 6c not entered above: ____

d Total number of exemptions claimed. Add numbers on lines above ▶ 3

Income

Attach Form(s) W-2 here. Also attach Form(s) 1099-R if tax was withheld.

If you did not get a W-2, see page 24.

Enclose, but do not attach, any payment.

7	Wages, salaries, tips, etc. Attach Form(s) W-2.	7	32,150 00
8a	**Taxable** interest. Attach Schedule 1 if required.	8a	640 00
b	**Tax-exempt** interest. **Do not** include on line 8a. 8b		
9a	Ordinary dividends. Attach Schedule 1 if required.	9a	
b	Qualified dividends (see page 25). 9b		
10	Capital gain distributions (see page 25).	10	
11a	IRA distributions. 11a — **11b** Taxable amount (see page 25).	11b	
12a	Pensions and annuities. 12a — **12b** Taxable amount (see page 26).	12b	
13	Unemployment compensation, Alaska Permanent Fund dividends, and jury duty fees.	13	
14a	Social security benefits. 14a — **14b** Taxable amount (see page 28).	14b	
15	Add lines 7 through 14b (far right column). This is your **total income.** ▶	15	32,790 00

Adjusted gross income

Line	Description		Amount		Total
16	Penalty on early withdrawal of savings (see page XX).	16			
17	IRA deduction (see page 28).	17	1,500 00		
18	Student loan interest deduction (see page 31).	18			
19	Jury duty pay you gave your employer (see page XX).	19			
20	Add lines 16 through 19. These are your **total adjustments.**			20	1,500 00
21	Subtract line 20 from line 15. This is your **adjusted gross income.** ▶			21	31,290 00

For Disclosure, Privacy Act, and Paperwork Reduction Act Notice, see page 58. Cat. No. 11327A Form **1040A** (2006)

FIGURE 4-6 Filled-In Form 1040A, Page 2

Form 1040A (2006) Page **2**

Tax, credits, and payments

Line	Description	Sub-line	Sub-amount	Line	Amount
22	Enter the amount from line 21 (adjusted gross income).			22	31,290 00
23a	Check if: ☐ **You** were born before January 2, 1942, ☐ Blind; ☐ **Spouse** was born before January 2, 1942, ☐ Blind — **Total boxes checked** ▶ 23a ☐				
b	If you are married filing separately and your spouse itemizes deductions, see page 32 and check here ▶ 23b ☐				
24	Enter your **standard deduction** (see left margin).			24	10,300 00
25	Subtract line 24 from line 22. If line 24 is more than line 22, enter -0-.			25	20,990 00
26	If line 22 is over $112,875, or you provided housing to a person displaced by Hurricane Katrina, see page 33. Otherwise, multiply $3,300 by the total number of exemptions claimed on line 6d.			26	9,900 00
27	Subtract line 26 from line 25. If line 26 is more than line 25, enter -0-. This is your **taxable income.** ▶			27	11,090 00
28	**Tax,** including any alternative minimum tax (see page 34).			28	1,108 00
29	Credit for child and dependent care expenses. Attach Schedule 2.	29	389 00		
30	Credit for the elderly or the disabled. Attach Schedule 3.	30			
31	Education credits. Attach Form 8863.	31			
32	Retirement savings contributions credit. Attach Form 8880.	32	300 00		
33	Child tax credit (see page 38). Attach Form 8901 if required.	33	419 00		
34	Add lines 29 through 33. These are your **total credits.**			34	1,108 00
35	Subtract line 34 from line 28. If line 34 is more than line 28, enter -0-.			35	0
36	Advance earned income credit payments from Form(s) W-2, box 9.			36	
37	Add lines 35 and 36. This is your **total tax.** ▶			37	0
38	Federal income tax withheld from Forms W-2 and 1099.	38	216 00		
39	2006 estimated tax payments and amount applied from 2005 return.	39			
40a	**Earned income credit (EIC).**	40a	292 00		
b	Nontaxable combat pay election. 40b				
41	Additional child tax credit. Attach Form 8812.	41	581 00		
42	Credit for federal telephone excise tax paid. Attach Form 8913 if required.	42	50 00		
43	Add lines 38, 39, 40a, 41, and 42. These are your **total payments.** ▶			43	1,139 00

Standard Deduction for—
- People who checked any box on line 23a or 23b **or** who can be claimed as a dependent, see page 32.
- All others:

Single or Married filing separately, $5,150

Married filing jointly or Qualifying widow(er), $10,300

Head of household, $7,550

If you have a qualifying child, attach Schedule EIC.

Refund

Line	Description	Sub-line	Sub-amount	Line	Amount
44	If line 43 is more than line 37, subtract line 37 from line 43. This is the amount you **overpaid.**			44	1,139 00
45a	Amount of line 44 you want **refunded to you.** If Form 8888 is attached, check here ▶ ☐			45a	1,139 00
▶ b	Routing number ☐☐☐☐☐☐☐☐☐ ▶ c Type: ☐ Checking ☐ Savings				
▶ d	Account number ☐☐☐☐☐☐☐☐☐☐☐☐☐☐☐☐☐				
46	Amount of line 44 you want **applied to your 2007 estimated tax.**	46			

Direct deposit? See page 53 and fill in 45b, 45c, and 45d or Form 8888.

Amount you owe

Line	Description	Sub-line	Sub-amount	Line	Amount
47	**Amount you owe.** Subtract line 43 from line 37. For details on how to pay, see page 54. ▶			47	
48	Estimated tax penalty (see page 54).	48			

Third party designee

Do you want to allow another person to discuss this return with the IRS (see page 55)? ☐ **Yes.** Complete the following. ☐ **No**

Designee's name ▶ Phone no. ▶ ( ) Personal identification number (PIN) ▶ ☐☐☐☐☐

Sign here

Joint return? See page 18. Keep a copy for your records.

Under penalties of perjury, I declare that I have examined this return and accompanying schedules and statements, and to the best of my knowledge and belief, they are true, correct, and accurately list all amounts and sources of income I received during the tax year. Declaration of preparer (other than the taxpayer) is based on all information of which the preparer has any knowledge.

Your signature	Date	Your occupation	Daytime phone number
Karl E. Cook	2-16-07	Clerk	( )
Spouse's signature. If a joint return, **both** must sign.	Date	Spouse's occupation	
Jill R. Cook	2-16-07	Teller	

Paid preparer's use only

Preparer's signature ▶	Date	Check if self-employed ☐	Preparer's SSN or PTIN
Firm's name (or yours if self-employed), address, and ZIP code ▶		EIN	
		Phone no.	( )

Printed on recycled paper

Form **1040A** (2006)

Karl uses the Tax Table to find the couple's tax ($1,108) on taxable income. After subtracting the various refundable and nonrefundable credits, the Cooks choose to receive the excess as a refund.

Because the interest income does not exceed $1,500, the Cooks do not report it on Schedule 1.

Information for Figure 4-7: Filled-In Form 1040, Page 1 and Schedule B (Form 1040)

Neal and Jane Cole file a joint return using Form 1040. They have no dependents.

Other Information (Form 1040)

7: Wages, **$45,000** ($17,600 + $27,400) (source: Form W-2)
8a: Interest, **$1,600** (source: Schedule B, line 4)
32: IRA deduction: **$1,380** (source: taxpayer, $880, and spouse, $500)

Because the Coles have over $1,500 in interest income, they prepare Schedule B (Form 1040), Parts I and III. They have no interest in any foreign accounts or trusts.

Other Information (Schedule B)

1: **Hearthland Bank, $1,600** (source: Form 1099-INT)

FIGURE 4-7 Filled-In Form 1040, Page 1

Form **1040** Department of the Treasury—Internal Revenue Service **U.S. Individual Income Tax Return** **2006** (99) IRS Use Only—Do not write or staple in this space.

For the year Jan. 1–Dec. 31, 2006, or other tax year beginning , 2006, ending , 20 OMB No. 1545-0074

Label (See instructions on page 16.) **Use the IRS label.** Otherwise, please print or type.

Your first name and initial	Last name	Your social security number
Neal R.	Cole	678 42 1720
If a joint return, spouse's first name and initial	Last name	Spouse's social security number
Jane B.	Cole	701 62 3714
Home address (number and street). If you have a P.O. box, see page 16.	Apt. no.	▲ You **must** enter your SSN(s) above. ▲
1002 Lakeview Lane		
City, town or post office, state, and ZIP code. If you have a foreign address, see page 16.		Checking a box below will not change your tax or refund.
Dallas, TX 75211-3674		

Presidential Election Campaign ▶ Check here if you, or your spouse if filing jointly, want $3 to go to this fund (see page 16) ▶ ☒ **You** ☒ **Spouse**

Filing Status Check only one box.

1 ☐ Single
2 ☒ Married filing jointly (even if only one had income)
3 ☐ Married filing separately. Enter spouse's SSN above and full name here. ▶
4 ☐ Head of household (with qualifying person). (See page 17.) If the qualifying person is a child but not your dependent, enter this child's name here. ▶
5 ☐ Qualifying widow(er) with dependent child (see page 17)

Exemptions

6a ☒ **Yourself.** If someone can claim you as a dependent, **do not** check box 6a
b ☒ **Spouse**
Boxes checked on 6a and 6b: 2

c **Dependents:**

(1) First name Last name	(2) Dependent's social security number	(3) Dependent's relationship to you	(4) ✓ if qualifying child for child tax credit (see page 19)
			☐
			☐
			☐
			☐

If more than four dependents, see page 19.

No. of children on 6c who:
• lived with you ____
• did not live with you due to divorce or separation (see page 20) ____
Dependents on 6c not entered above ____

d Total number of exemptions claimed — Add numbers on lines above ▶ 2

Income

Attach Form(s) W-2 here. Also attach Forms W-2G and 1099-R if tax was withheld.

If you did not get a W-2, see page 22.

Enclose, but do not attach, any payment. Also, please use **Form 1040-V.**

7	Wages, salaries, tips, etc. Attach Form(s) W-2	7	45,000 00
8a	**Taxable** interest. Attach Schedule B if required	8a	1,600 00
b	**Tax-exempt** interest. **Do not** include on line 8a — 8b		
9a	Ordinary dividends. Attach Schedule B if required	9a	
b	Qualified dividends (see page 23) — 9b		
10	Taxable refunds, credits, or offsets of state and local income taxes (see page 23)	10	
11	Alimony received	11	
12	Business income or (loss). Attach Schedule C or C-EZ	12	
13	Capital gain or (loss). Attach Schedule D if required. If not required, check here ▶ ☐	13	
14	Other gains or (losses). Attach Form 4797	14	
15a	IRA distributions — 15a; b Taxable amount (see page 25)	15b	
16a	Pensions and annuities — 16a; b Taxable amount (see page 25)	16b	
17	Rental real estate, royalties, partnerships, S corporations, trusts, etc. Attach Schedule E	17	
18	Farm income or (loss). Attach Schedule F	18	
19	Unemployment compensation	19	
20a	Social security benefits — 20a; b Taxable amount (see page 27)	20b	
21	Other income. List type and amount (see page 29)	21	
22	Add the amounts in the far right column for lines 7 through 21. This is your **total income** ▶	22	46,600 00

Adjusted Gross Income

23	Archer MSA deduction. Attach Form 8853	23	
24	Certain business expenses of reservists, performing artists, and fee-basis government officials. Attach Form 2106 or 2106-EZ	24	
25	Health savings account deduction. Attach Form 8889	25	
26	Moving expenses. Attach Form 3903	26	
27	One-half of self-employment tax. Attach Schedule SE	27	
28	Self-employed SEP, SIMPLE, and qualified plans	28	
29	Self-employed health insurance deduction (see page 30)	29	
30	Penalty on early withdrawal of savings	30	
31a	Alimony paid b Recipient's SSN ▶	31a	
32	IRA deduction (see page 31)	32	1,380 00
33	Student loan interest deduction (see page 33)	33	
34	Jury duty pay you gave to your employer	34	
35	Domestic production activities deduction. Attach Form 8903	35	
36	Add lines 23 through 31a and 32 through 35	36	1,380 00
37	Subtract line 36 from line 22. This is your **adjusted gross income** ▶	37	45,220 00

For Disclosure, Privacy Act, and Paperwork Reduction Act Notice, see page 78. Cat. No. 11320B Form **1040** (2006)

FIGURE 4-7 Filled-In Parts I and III, Schedule B (Form 1040)

Schedules A&B (Form 1040) 2006 OMB No. 1545-0074 Page **2**

Name(s) shown on Form 1040. Do not enter name and social security number if shown on other side.
Neal R. and Jane B. Cole

Your social security number 678 42 1720

Schedule B—Interest and Ordinary Dividends

Attachment Sequence No. **08**

Part I Interest

(See page B-1 and the instructions for Form 1040, line 8a.)

Note. If you received a Form 1099-INT, Form 1099-OID, or substitute statement from a brokerage firm, list the firm's name as the payer and enter the total interest shown on that form.

			Amount
1	List name of payer. If any interest is from a seller-financed mortgage and the buyer used the property as a personal residence, see page B-1 and list this interest first. Also, show that buyer's social security number and address ▶ Hearthland Bank	1	1,600 00
2	Add the amounts on line 1	2	1,600 00
3	Excludable interest on series EE and I U.S. savings bonds issued after 1989. Attach Form 8815	3	
4	Subtract line 3 from line 2. Enter the result here and on Form 1040, line 8a ▶	4	1,600 00

Note. If line 4 is over $1,500, you must complete Part III.

Part II Ordinary Dividends

(See page B-1 and the instructions for Form 1040, line 9a.)

Note. If you received a Form 1099-DIV or substitute statement from a brokerage firm, list the firm's name as the payer and enter the ordinary dividends shown on that form.

			Amount
5	List name of payer ▶	5	
6	Add the amounts on line 5. Enter the total here and on Form 1040, line 9a . ▶	6	

Note. If line 6 is over $1,500, you must complete Part III.

Part III Foreign Accounts and Trusts

(See page B-2.)

	You must complete this part if you **(a)** had over $1,500 of taxable interest or ordinary dividends; or **(b)** had a foreign account; or **(c)** received a distribution from, or were a grantor of, or a transferor to, a foreign trust.	**Yes**	**No**
7a	At any time during 2006, did you have an interest in or a signature or other authority over a financial account in a foreign country, such as a bank account, securities account, or other financial account? See page B-2 for exceptions and filing requirements for Form TD F 90-22.1.	☐	☒
b	If "Yes," enter the name of the foreign country ▶		
8	During 2006, did you receive a distribution from, or were you the grantor of, or transferor to, a foreign trust? If "Yes," you may have to file Form 3520. See page B-2	☐	☒

For Paperwork Reduction Act Notice, see Form 1040 instructions. **Schedule B (Form 1040) 2006**

Printed on recycled paper

Name ______________________________

Section _______________ Date ___________

QUESTIONS AND PROBLEMS

1. **Foreign Earned Income Exclusion.** From March 8, 2006 until August 17, 2007 Eva Saints is sent to London on a temporary work assignment. Saint's salary during 2006 is $100,000, of which $82,000 is earned while working in London. Her salary during 2007 is $125,000, of which $77,000 is earned while working in London.

   a. How much of Saints's salary is taxed in 2006-2007? Assume the maximum foreign earned income exclusion for 2007 remains at $82,400.

   b. How is the foreign earned income exclusion reported on Saints's tax return?

   c. Besides taking the exclusion for foreign earned income, what other options are available to Saints?

2. **Foreign Earned Income Exclusion.** From October 5, 2006 until September 7, 2007, Jack Roche was sent to work at his employer's office in Rome, Italy. Roche's salary during 2006 was $72,000. Of this amount, $18,000 was earned while working in Rome.

   a. How much of Roche's salary can be excluded from gross income in 2006?

   b. How, if at all, would your answer to Part a. differ if Roche's assignment lasted until August 7, 2007?

3. **Fringe Benefits.** Most fringe benefits may not discriminate in favor of key or highly-paid employees, whereas other fringe benefits may favor these employees.
   a. For each category of fringe benefits given, state whether the discrimination rules apply, and give two examples of specific fringe benefits in that category.

Fringe Benefit Category	*Discrimination Rules Apply (Yes or No)*	*Examples of Specific Benefits in Each Category*
De minimis fringe benefits	____________	____________
Qualified employee discounts	____________	____________
Working condition fringe benefits	____________	____________
No-additional-cost services	____________	____________
On-premise athletic facilities	____________	____________

   b. What are the tax consequences of violating the discrimination rules?

4. **Group-Term Life Insurance.** Paines Distributing pays an annual premium for $90,000 of nondiscriminatory group-term life insurance coverage on its president, Fred J. Noble. Noble is 44 years of age. His wife, Melanie, is the policy's beneficiary. For this group-term life insurance, Noble pays the company $0.80 per year for each $1,000 of coverage. His share of the insurance premium is deducted from his gross salary under the Paines payroll deduction plan. What portion of the group-term life insurance cost must Noble include in his gross income?

5. **Group-Term Life Insurance.** Remix, Inc. provides group-term life insurance coverage for each of its employees. The amount of coverage is equal to one year's salary. Remix pays 100% of the cost for the premiums. Tony Wright and Ruth Udah are employees of Remix. Wright is 46 years old; his salary for the year is $85,000. Udah is 52 years old; her salary for the year is $120,000. Udah is a key employee of Remix; Wright is not.

   a. Discuss the consequences to Wright and Udah if Remix's plan does not favor key and highly paid employees.

   b. Discuss the consequences to Wright and Udah if Remix's plan favors key and highly paid employees.

6. **Employer-Provided Health Insurance.** Monix Enterprises provides its employees with health insurance coverage. During the year, it pays $7,500 of insurance premiums for each of its employees. Randy Eckles is a highly paid employee of Monix. Jonathon Hill is not one of Monix's highly paid employees.

   a. Discuss the consequences to Eckles and Hill if Monix's plan favors highly paid employees.

   b. Discuss the consequences to Eckles and Hill if the plan does not favor highly paid employees.

7. **Fringe Benefits.** A retailer gives a 20% discount to its full-time employees; key employees are entitled to a 30% discount. During the year, two full-time employees, Fritz Barkin and Tad Trapper, each buy goods that sell for $2,000. Barkin is a key employee; Trapper is not. Discuss the tax consequences to Barkin and Trapper of the discounts they each respectively received during the year.

8. **Bond Interest.** Marilyn Sippola is a single taxpayer who owns five different bonds listed below. During the current year she received the interest amounts shown. In the space provided for each bond, state the amount of interest to be included in or excluded from gross income. If excluded, state why.

Bond	*Issue*	*Date Purchase Bonds Owned*	*Interest Received*
A	Racer Tannery	12–10–95	$ 276
B	Village of Austinburg	7–1–97	800
C	U.S. Treasury	2–1–99	600
D	Matured Series EE U.S. Savings	11–1–98	1,000
E	Kingsville School District	7–10–96	500

Bond	*Interest Includable*	*Interest Excludable and Why*
A	______________________	______________________
B	______________________	______________________
C	______________________	______________________
D	______________________	______________________
E	______________________	______________________

9. **Form 8815.** Michael J. Dugan (SSN 372-90-6729) receives $15,000 ($12,000 principal and $3,000 interest) from the redemption of a Series EE U.S. Savings Bond. He uses the proceeds to pay university tuition and fees totaling $8,250 for his two dependent children, Colleen R. and Patrick T. Dugan. Colleen is 21 years of age, and Patrick is 20. With the exception of temporary absences from home to attend the University of Michigan in Ann Arbor (48104) as full-time students, they live with their parents. During the year, Colleen and Patrick each receive a tax-exempt university scholarship of $2,250.

   Michael and Rachel Dugan live at 2790 Lakeview Road, Muskegon, MI 49441. Michael's salary is $106,000. They file a joint return. Rachel has no gross income. Prepare Form 8815 on the following page for the Dugans.

10. **Exclusion for Series EE and I U.S. Savings Bonds.** Irina Devloe cashes in Series I Savings Bonds during 2006. She receives $18,755, of which $15,000 was principal and the rest interest. Devloe uses the proceeds to pay out-of-state tuition and fees totaling $16,500 for her son, who is a full-time student during 2006. She uses the rest of the proceeds to pay for her son's room and board. Devloe's filing status is head of household for 2006. Devloe's only other source of income is her $62,000 salary. Compute Devloe's exclusion for Series EE and I interest and her AGI for 2006.

11. **Scholarships.** On August 1, 2006, Robert Dunnbar was granted a $5,400 scholarship for each of four academic years (nine months each year) to earn a degree from Birdhaven University. The scholarship grant includes $3,600 for tuition, fees, and books and $1,800 for room and board. Payment is one-ninth each month, starting September 10, 2006, and is made on the tenth of each month thereafter.

    a. How much of the scholarship payments can Dunnbar exclude from gross income in 2006? Why?

    b. If Dunnbar is not a degree candidate, is there any limitation to the amount of his exclusion? Explain.

(Use for Problem 9.)

Form **8815**

Department of the Treasury
Internal Revenue Service (99)

Exclusion of Interest From Series EE and I U.S. Savings Bonds Issued After 1989

(For Filers With Qualified Higher Education Expenses)

▶ Attach to Form 1040 or Form 1040A.

OMB No. 1545-0074

2006

Attachment Sequence No. 57

Name(s) shown on return	Your social security number

1 (a) Name of person (you, your spouse, or your dependent) who was enrolled at or attended an eligible educational institution	(b) Name and address of eligible educational institution

If you need more space, attach a statement.

2	Enter the total qualified higher education expenses you paid in 2006 for the person(s) listed in column (a) of line 1. See the instructions to find out which expenses qualify	2	
3	Enter the total of any nontaxable educational benefits (such as nontaxable scholarship or fellowship grants) received for 2006 for the person(s) listed in column (a) of line 1 (see instructions)	3	
4	Subtract line 3 from line 2. If zero or less, **stop.** You **cannot** take the exclusion	4	
5	Enter the total proceeds (principal and interest) from all series EE and I U.S. savings bonds **issued after 1989** that you **cashed during 2006**	5	
6	Enter the interest included on line 5 (see instructions)	6	
7	If line 4 is equal to or more than line 5, enter "1.000." If line 4 is less than line 5, divide line 4 by line 5. Enter the result as a decimal (rounded to at least three places)	7	× .
8	Multiply line 6 by line 7	8	
9	Enter your modified adjusted gross income (see instructions) **Note:** *If line 9 is $78,100 or more if single or head of household, or $124,700 or more if married filing jointly or qualifying widow(er),* ***stop.*** *You* ***cannot*** *take the exclusion.*	9	
10	Enter: $63,100 if single or head of household; $94,700 if married filing jointly or qualifying widow(er)	10	
11	Subtract line 10 from line 9. If zero or less, skip line 12, enter -0- on line 13, and go to line 14	11	
12	Divide line 11 by: $15,000 if single or head of household; $30,000 if married filing jointly or qualifying widow(er). Enter the result as a decimal (rounded to at least three places)	12	× .
13	Multiply line 8 by line 12	13	
14	**Excludable savings bond interest.** Subtract line 13 from line 8. Enter the result here and on Schedule B (Form 1040), line 3, or Schedule 1 (Form 1040A), line 3, whichever applies ▶	14	

For Paperwork Reduction Act Notice, see back of form. Cat. No. 10822S Form **8815** (2006)

12. Gross Income Exclusions. Indicate, by placing an *X* in the proper column, the includable or excludable status of the following income items received relative to gross income.

	Item	*Includable*	*Excludable*
a.	"Dividend" on life insurance policy	_____	_____
b.	Dividends from employees' credit union	_____	_____
c.	Embezzlement proceeds	_____	_____
d.	FMV of automobile won on television giveaway program	_____	_____
e.	Free parking in employer's lot (value = $100/month)	_____	_____
f.	Gambling winnings (no losses)	_____	_____
g.	Gold necklace found in ocean	_____	_____
h.	Health resort fee paid for taxpayer by employer	_____	_____
i.	Life insurance proceeds paid because of insured's death	_____	_____
j.	Workers' compensation	_____	_____

13. Physical Injury and Sickness Payments. For each of the following taxpayers, discuss how much (if any) of the payments they receive during the year are included in their gross income.

a. Anne LaMont sued her employer for discrimination and was awarded $50,000.

b. Todd Reymier was physically injured on the job. He is reimbursed $16,400 for medical expenses he paid as a result of his injuries. Todd's employer paid 100% of the premiums on his health insurance policy.

c. Maggie Carter was physically injured on the job. She received $12,000 of workers' compensation during the year.

d. Sandra O'Connell had an adverse reaction to the drug her doctor prescribed. She sues the drug company and is awarded $12 million. Of this amount, $11.5 million is for punitive damages.

14. **Roth IRAs.** Kenya and Carl Reed are ages 48 and 50, respectively. Their AGI for 2006 is $152,520, most of which stems from taxable wages. Compute the maximum amount the Reeds can contribute to their respective Roth IRAs for 2006.

15. **Roth IRA.** Kathy Craig, age 40, is single and wants to contribute to a Roth IRA in 2006. Her AGI is $97,500. Compute the maximum contribution that she may make to her Roth IRA. Where does she deduct this amount on her tax return?

16. **IRA Contributions.** Joyce and Barry Bright are both employed and 56 years of age. In 2006 Barry has earned wages of $1,500, and Joyce has earned wages of $77,530. Joyce is an active participant in her employer-maintained qualified annuity pension plan. For 2006, the Brights plan to file a joint tax return. Their net AGI is $81,340.

    a. What is the latest date by which an IRA payment must be made in order for it to be claimed on the Brights' 2006 return?

    b. Can the payments be claimed on Form 1040EZ? On Form 1040A?

    c. What is the maximum amount Joyce and Barry can each contribute to an IRA and be able to deduct for 2006?

    d. Are the earnings on the IRA payments made in 2006 subject to federal income taxes in 2006? Explain.

17. **IRA Deduction.** Fred and Diane Workingman file a joint return. Neither taxpayer is covered by a retirement plan at work. Fred's gross income from wages is $37,900. Diane's gross income from wages is $31,500. Diane also received taxable interest income of $600. Since establishing their IRAs, Diane and Fred have contributed the following amounts to them:

Diane:	April 6, 2006	$ 750
	July 1, 2006	750
	October 3, 2006	750
	January 4, 2007	750
Fred:	June 16, 2006	$1,500
	February 3, 2007	1,500

Earnings credited to their IRAs during 2006 were $890 for Diane and $340 for Fred. Calculate the Workingmans' maximum allowable 2006 IRA deductions and their AGI.

18. **Traditional IRA Characteristics.** For each statement, check true or false.

	True	*False*
a. Contributions to a nonworking spouse's IRA must be equal to the IRA contributions of the working spouse.	_____	_____
b. Contributions to a traditional IRA are deductible in the determination of AGI for a single employee whose only income is wages of $25,000.	_____	_____
c. Distributions from a traditional IRA must begin no later than April 1 of the calendar year after the IRA depositor reaches age 70½.	_____	_____
d. The earnings of a traditional IRA are taxed to the employee in the year earned.	_____	_____
e. The income earned on nondeductible traditional IRA contributions is not taxable until it is withdrawn.	_____	_____
f. The maximum deductible amount for contributions to an IRA in 2006 is $4,000 by a married couple of which only one spouse works and earns $25,000.	_____	_____

19. **Nondeductible IRA Contributions.** Mike and Mary Sweeney, both age 42, each want to set aside $4,000 for their retirement using a retirement account. They prefer to make deductible contributions. Mike and Mary have $60,000 and $45,000 of earned income, respectively. Their net AGI is $102,000. Mary is covered by an employer-maintained retirement plan. Mike has no such plan.

a. What tax consequences do they face if they use traditional IRAs for their savings plans?

b. Can you suggest a better plan? If so, what would it be?

c. How would your responses change if Mary's earned income was $100,000 and Mike's was $85,000?

20. Student Loan Interest. During 2006, Larry Matthews paid $580 interest on a qualified student loan. Matthews files his tax return as a single taxpayer. His modified AGI is $54,810. Compute Matthews's deduction for AGI for the interest on his student loan.

21. Deductions for AGI. For each statement, check true or false.

		True	*False*
a.	Reservists who travel less than 100 miles from home to perform services as a member of the reserves deduct their travel expenses as a miscellaneous itemized deduction.	_____	_____
b.	Qualified performing artists may deduct their business expenses from gross income to arrive at adjusted gross income.	_____	_____
c.	To receive the tax benefits of a "performing artist," the individual's adjusted gross income cannot exceed $14,000 before deducting business expenses.	_____	_____
d.	State and local government officials paid on a fee basis report their business expenses on Form 2106.	_____	_____
e.	To maximize their deduction benefits, "performing artists" who are married must file jointly unless they have lived apart at all times during the year.	_____	_____
f.	Taxpayers 55-years-old may contribute an additional $1,000 to their health savings accounts.	_____	_____
g.	Retired taxpayers may continue to make deductible contributions to a health savings account.	_____	_____
h.	Withdrawals from a health savings account that are not used for medical expenses may be subject to a 15% penalty tax.	_____	_____

22. Health Savings Accounts. Sandy German's employer offers an HSA plan. Discuss the tax consequences to German if she participates in the plan. German is 44-years-old, unmarried, and does not claim any dependents on her tax return.

23. Moving Expenses. Trey Wilson accepted a new job in Baltimore, Maryland, which is 1,025 miles from his old job. In April he flew out to Baltimore to start his new job. His wife, Veronica remained at their old home so that the children could finish out the school year. In June, the Wilsons paid a moving company $6,200 to move their personal effects to Baltimore. Veronica then drove the family out to their new home. Trey's airfare to Baltimore was $450. Veronica paid $114 for gas, $260 for lodging and $110 for meals while en route to Baltimore. Trey's employer reimbursed him $5,000 for the cost of the moving company.

a. Compute the Wilsons' moving expense deduction.

b. Where do they report this amount on their tax return?

24. Moving Expenses. Jim Beam incurs the following moving expenses as a result of a change in job location:

Expenses of moving household goods	$ 4,500
Travel and lodging for family in moving to new residence	345
Meals en route	72
Pre-move house-hunting trips	925
Temporary living expenses in new location	700
Real estate commission on sale of old residence	12,000
Total moving expenses	$18,542

If Beam qualifies for a moving expense deduction, what amount may he deduct?

25. Self-Employed Health Insurance Deduction. Ashley Evans is self-employed as a free lance artist. During 2006, Evans paid $650 a month for health insurance coverage through her business. From August 1 through October 31, Evans worked 30 hours a week for an ad agency. During that period, she was eligible for her employer's health insurance, but opted not to enroll in it.

a. How much, if any, of the $7,800 in health insurance premiums can Evans deduct?

b. Where on her tax return does she take this deduction?

26. Self-Employed Health Insurance Deduction.

a. What is the maximum self-employed health insurance deduction that can be claimed as a deduction for AGI?

b. Under what conditions would a taxpayer not be eligible for the self-employed health insurance deduction?

27. Miscellaneous Questions. For each statement, check true or false.

	True	*False*
a. Withdrawals from a Roth IRA may be subject to a 6% early withdrawal penalty.	_____	_____
b. Regardless of the number of children, a taxpayer may contribute only $2,000 each year to a Coverdell Education Savings Account.	_____	_____
c. Contributions to a Coverdell Education Savings Account are deductible for AGI.	_____	_____
d. Contributions to a Coverdell Education Savings Account must be for a person under age 18.	_____	_____
e. The student loan interest deduction is available only for the first 60 months of interest payments.	_____	_____
f. In 2006, employees may exclude up to $225 per month for parking provided by the employer, even if the parking privilege is discriminatory.	_____	_____
g. Under a qualified tuition program (529 plan), if the child does not go to college, a refund is made to the child who must pay taxes on the interest income included in the refund.	_____	_____
h. Some employers provide meals to their employees. For the value of the meals to be tax-free, the meals must be served on the premises of the employer for the convenience of the employer.	_____	_____

28. Miscellaneous Questions.

a. Explain the deduction for the penalty on early withdrawal of savings.

b. What are the tax consequences of purchasing a new truck with funds from a Roth IRA when the taxpayer is age 50?

c. What are the tax consequences of purchasing a new truck with funds from a traditional IRA when the taxpayer is age 50?

29. Internet Problem: Filling out Form 3903.

In April, Charles Randall (SSN 567-89-1234), who works for Evergreen Productions, received a promotion and was required to move from Cleveland, Ohio, to Kansas City, Missouri, a move of 825 miles. Randall paid the following moving expenses:

House-hunting trip expenses	$1,600
Moving van	3,300
Cost of meals enroute	85
Lodging enroute	120

Randall also drove his personal automobile 825 miles to the new residence. Evergreen Productions reimbursed Randall for only 75% of his "qualified moving expenses."

Go to the IRS Web site and locate Form 3903. Using the computer, fill in the form for Randall and print out a completed copy.

See Appendix A for instructions on use of the IRS Web site.

30. Business Entity Problem: This problem is designed for those using the "business entity" approach. The solution may require information from Chapters 14 and 15.

For each statement, check true or false.

	True	*False*
a. Self-employed persons may deduct 50% of their self-employment tax from AGI.	______	______
b. Companies reimbursing their employees for house-hunting expenses and temporary quarters do not report these reimbursements as income on the employee's Form W-2.	______	______
c. When a company provides "free meals" as part of the employee's compensation package, the company includes the value of the meals as taxable income on the employee's Form W-2.	______	______
d. In 2006, a company pays $250 per month to provide its CEO with a parking space. The company must include $540 on the CEO's Form W-2 as taxable wages.	______	______
e. When a company reimburses an employee for nondeductible moving expenses, it must report the reimbursement on the employee's Form W-2.	______	______
f. Employers may annually provide up to $5,250 of tax-free educational assistance to their employees to pursue a Master's Degree.	______	______
g. When a company provides over $50,000 of group-term life insurance to an employee, it must report the taxable portion of the premiums as wages on the employee's Form W-2.	______	______
h. A self-employed person who provides health insurance for himself, but not his three employees, may deduct the premium for AGI.	______	______
i. Taxpayers may claim a tax credit equal to 3% of their qualified production activity income or taxable income, whichever is lower.	______	______
j. The domestic production activities deduction cannot exceed 100% of the W-2 wages paid during the year.	______	______

COMPREHENSIVE PROBLEM

31. Using the following information for an unmarried taxpayer (age 52 with no dependents), compute 2006 taxable income. Prepare an analysis showing each item and amount under the appropriate headings of (1) income; (2) gross income exclusions; (3) gross income inclusions; (4) deductions for AGI; (5) AGI; (6) deductions from AGI, including both the standard deduction and exemptions; and (7) taxable income.

Cash Received

Interest on savings account	$ 1,728
Gift of money from parent	1,000
Rent from farmland owned	30,000
Proceeds of life insurance policy received upon parent's death	40,000
Nondegree candidate fellowship, granted 8/20/06, of $450 per month for four months	1,800
Gross salary of $33,000 less $8,100 state and federal income taxes, $2,046 social security taxes, and $479 health insurance premiums. Net pay received	22,375
Employer's share of health insurance premiums, $1,437	0
De minimis employee fringe benefits valued at $25	0
Company provided parking costing employer $300 per month for 12 months	0
Total cash received	$96,903

Cash Payments

Expenses of farmland rental (real estate taxes)	$ 1,750
Personal living expenses	26,600
Total cash payments	$28,350

CUMULATIVE PROBLEM 1 (CHAPTERS 1–4)

This problem is suitable for manual preparation or computer software application.

Using the following information, prepare a tax return for Erica Hansen. Use Form 1040A with supporting Schedule 1, Schedule EIC, Form 8812, and Form 8863.

Erica L. Hansen (SSN 376-38-4930), age 42, is a single parent with three children. She resides at 19 Sunset Road, Normal, Illinois 61761. She chooses to support the presidential campaign fund.

Her household includes Randall L. Hansen, her 19-year-old son (SSN 369-62-3418), Tiffany A. Hansen, her 12-year-old daughter (SSN 396-30-6439), and Donna M. Hansen, her 14-year-old daughter (SSN 653-29-8177). Erica provides over half of the support of each child. Donna has no income of her own, but Randall earns $4,200 during the year delivering papers and mowing lawns. All children lived in the household for 12 months.

Erica works as an office manager for Universal Development Corporation. Her Form W-2 information follows:

Gross wages	$33,500
Social security tax withheld	2,077
Medicare tax withheld	486
Federal income tax withheld	300
State income tax withheld	1,005

Erica had other income consisting of the following:

Interest received:	
First Federal Savings Bank	$775
Olympic Savings—certificate of deposit cashed in	175
State of Maryland bonds	300
Dividends received:	
Dividend on life insurance policy with Country Farm Insurance Company	$ 20

Randall, a freshman, is a full-time student at Heartland College in Normal, Illinois. To Erica pays qualified education expenses paid during the year of $6,000.

Erica is a participant in an employer-sponsored retirement plan. However, she wants to make the largest possible *deductible* contribution to her traditional IRA. She also wants to take advantage of the HOPE scholarship credit.

If Erica has overpaid her taxes, she prefers to receive a refund. She signs and dates her return on April 5, 2007. She claims the standard credit for federal telephone excise tax paid.

EIC Calculation:

Look up the amount in the EIC Tables for both earned income (Form 1040A, line 7) and AGI (Form 1040A, line 22). The smaller of these two amounts is the EIC reported on Form 1040A, line 40a.

Additional Child Tax Credit:

Enter on Form 8812 (line 1) $1,000 for each qualifying child.

CUMULATIVE PROBLEM 2 (CHAPTERS 1–4)

This problem is suitable for manual preparation or computer software application.

Using the following information, prepare a tax return for John Bryan. Use Form 1040, Schedule B, Form 8815 and Form 3903.

John Bryan (SSN 573-99-5878) works as a manager for an oil company. In 2006, he was relocated by his employer him from Houston, Texas to Wichita Falls, Kansas. His moving costs include $230 for an airline ticket and $5,300 that he paid to a local moving company. His employer reimbursed him $3,000 for the move. This amount was not included in his W-2 wages. His taxable salary for 2006 was $121,300, from which his employer withheld $11,450 and $1,900, respectively for federal and state income taxes.

During 2006, Bryan cashed in Series I Savings Bonds and received $28,457. He paid $25,000 for the bonds several years ago. Bryan used most of the proceeds to pay tuition and fees totaling $22,800 for his dependent twin daughters, April (SSN 549-43-5584) and Amber (SSN 549-43-5589) Bryan. Both attend Rice University in Houston full-time, but live with Bryan when not in school. They both are juniors in 2006. Bryan used the rest of the proceeds to pay personal expenses.

Bryan is divorced. During 2006, he paid alimony totaling $50,000 to his ex-wife, Anne Bryan (SSN 558-99-5377). Bryan's only other income includes $1,400 of interest from a Texas Commerce Bank certificate of deposit and $1,840 of interest from State of Iowa government bonds. He does not have an interest in any foreign accounts or trusts. Bryan's address is 1143 W. Adams Ave., Wichita Falls, KS 76300. Bryan uses the standard deduction, is under age 64, and has good eyesight. He signs and dates his return on April 10, 2007. He claims the standard credit for federal telephone excise tax paid.

Additional Information:

The amount on line 9 (Form 8815) is Bryan's "modified AGI," which is Bryan's AGI calculated without regard to the exclusion for interest from the Series I bonds. To compute "modified AGI" on line 9 (Form 8815), calculate Bryan's AGI (including his deductions for AGI) including interest income from Schedule B (line 2).

(Use for Cumulative Problem 1.)

Form **1040A** Department of the Treasury—Internal Revenue Service
U.S. Individual Income Tax Return (99) **2006** IRS Use Only—Do not write or staple in this space.
OMB No. 1545-0074

Label (See page 18.)
LABEL HERE
Use the IRS label. Otherwise, please print or type.

Your first name and initial	Last name	Your social security number
If a joint return, spouse's first name and initial	Last name	Spouse's social security number
Home address (number and street). If you have a P.O. box, see page 18.	Apt. no.	▲ You **must** enter your SSN(s) above. ▲
City, town or post office, state, and ZIP code. If you have a foreign address, see page 18.		Checking a box below will not change your tax or refund.

Presidential Election Campaign ▶ Check here if you, or your spouse if filing jointly, want $3 to go to this fund (see page 18) ▶ ☐ **You** ☐ **Spouse**

Filing status
Check only one box.

1 ☐ Single
2 ☐ Married filing jointly (even if only one had income)
3 ☐ Married filing separately. Enter spouse's SSN above and full name here. ▶
4 ☐ Head of household (with qualifying person). (See page 19.) If the qualifying person is a child but not your dependent, enter this child's name here. ▶
5 ☐ Qualifying widow(er) with dependent child (see page 19)

Exemptions

6a ☐ **Yourself.** If someone can claim you as a dependent, **do not** check box 6a.
b ☐ **Spouse**
} **Boxes checked on 6a and 6b** ____

c **Dependents:**

If more than six dependents, see page 21.

(1) First name Last name	(2) Dependent's social security number	(3) Dependent's relationship to you	(4) √ if qualifying child for child tax credit (see page 21)
			☐
			☐
			☐
			☐
			☐
			☐

No. of children on 6c who:
• **lived with you** ____
• **did not live with you due to divorce or separation (see page 22)** ____
Dependents on 6c not entered above ____

d Total number of exemptions claimed.
Add numbers on lines above ▶ ☐

Income

Attach Form(s) W-2 here. Also attach Form(s) 1099-R if tax was withheld.

If you did not get a W-2, see page 24.

Enclose, but do not attach, any payment.

7	Wages, salaries, tips, etc. Attach Form(s) W-2.		7
8a	**Taxable** interest. Attach Schedule 1 if required.		8a
b	**Tax-exempt** interest. **Do not** include on line 8a.	8b	
9a	Ordinary dividends. Attach Schedule 1 if required.		9a
b	Qualified dividends (see page 25).	9b	
10	Capital gain distributions (see page 25).		10
11a	IRA distributions. 11a	**11b** Taxable amount (see page 25).	11b
12a	Pensions and annuities. 12a	**12b** Taxable amount (see page 26).	12b
13	Unemployment compensation, Alaska Permanent Fund dividends, and jury duty fees.		13
14a	Social security benefits. 14a	**14b** Taxable amount (see page 28).	14b
15	Add lines 7 through 14b (far right column). This is your **total income.** ▶		15

Adjusted gross income

16	Penalty on early withdrawal of savings (see page XX).	16	
17	IRA deduction (see page 28).	17	
18	Student loan interest deduction (see page 31).	18	
19	Jury duty pay you gave your employer (see page XX).	19	
20	Add lines 16 through 19. These are your **total adjustments.**		20
21	Subtract line 20 from line 15. This is your **adjusted gross income.** ▶		21

For Disclosure, Privacy Act, and Paperwork Reduction Act Notice, see page 58. Cat. No. 11327A Form **1040A** (2006)

(Use for Cumulative Problem 1.)

Form 1040A (2006) Page **2**

Tax, credits, and payments

22 Enter the amount from line 21 (adjusted gross income). 22

23a Check if: { ☐ **You** were born before January 2, 1942, ☐ Blind ; ☐ **Spouse** was born before January 2, 1942, ☐ Blind } **Total boxes checked** ▶ 23a ☐

b If you are married filing separately and your spouse itemizes deductions, see page 32 and check here ▶ 23b ☐

Standard Deduction for—
- People who checked any box on line 23a or 23b **or** who can be claimed as a dependent, see page 32.
- All others:

Single or Married filing separately, $5,150

Married filing jointly or Qualifying widow(er), $10,300

Head of household, $7,550

24 Enter your **standard deduction** (see left margin). 24

25 Subtract line 24 from line 22. If line 24 is more than line 22, enter -0-. 25

26 If line 22 is over $112,875, or you provided housing to a person displaced by Hurricane Katrina, see page 33. Otherwise, multiply $3,300 by the total number of exemptions claimed on line 6d. 26

27 Subtract line 26 from line 25. If line 26 is more than line 25, enter -0-. This is your **taxable income.** ▶ 27

28 **Tax,** including any alternative minimum tax (see page 34). 28

29 Credit for child and dependent care expenses. Attach Schedule 2. 29

30 Credit for the elderly or the disabled. Attach Schedule 3. 30

31 Education credits. Attach Form 8863. 31

32 Retirement savings contributions credit. Attach Form 8880. 32

33 Child tax credit (see page 38). Attach Form 8901 if required. 33

34 Add lines 29 through 33. These are your **total credits.** 34

35 Subtract line 34 from line 28. If line 34 is more than line 28, enter -0-. 35

36 Advance earned income credit payments from Form(s) W-2, box 9. 36

37 Add lines 35 and 36. This is your **total tax.** ▶ 37

38 Federal income tax withheld from Forms W-2 and 1099. 38

39 2006 estimated tax payments and amount applied from 2005 return. 39

If you have a qualifying child, attach Schedule EIC.

40a **Earned income credit (EIC).** 40a

b Nontaxable combat pay election. 40b

41 Additional child tax credit. Attach Form 8812. 41

42 Credit for federal telephone excise tax paid. Attach Form 8913 if required. 42

43 Add lines 38, 39, 40a, 41, and 42. These are your **total payments.** ▶ 43

Refund

44 If line 43 is more than line 37, subtract line 37 from line 43. This is the amount you **overpaid.** 44

Direct deposit? See page 53 and fill in 45b, 45c, and 45d or Form 8888.

45a Amount of line 44 you want **refunded to you.** If Form 8888 is attached, check here ▶ ☐ 45a

▶ b Routing number ☐☐☐☐☐☐☐☐☐ ▶ c Type: ☐ Checking ☐ Savings

▶ d Account number ☐☐☐☐☐☐☐☐☐☐☐☐☐☐☐☐☐

46 Amount of line 44 you want **applied to your 2007 estimated tax.** 46

Amount you owe

47 **Amount you owe.** Subtract line 43 from line 37. For details on how to pay, see page 54. ▶ 47

48 Estimated tax penalty (see page 54). 48

Third party designee

Do you want to allow another person to discuss this return with the IRS (see page 55)? ☐ **Yes.** Complete the following. ☐ **No**

Designee's name ▶ Phone no. ▶ ( ) Personal identification number (PIN) ▶ ☐☐☐☐☐

Sign here

Joint return? See page 18. Keep a copy for your records.

Under penalties of perjury, I declare that I have examined this return and accompanying schedules and statements, and to the best of my knowledge and belief, they are true, correct, and accurately list all amounts and sources of income I received during the tax year. Declaration of preparer (other than the taxpayer) is based on all information of which the preparer has any knowledge.

Your signature	Date	Your occupation	Daytime phone number ( )
Spouse's signature. If a joint return, **both** must sign.	Date	Spouse's occupation	

Paid preparer's use only

Preparer's signature ▶	Date	Check if self-employed ☐	Preparer's SSN or PTIN
Firm's name (or yours if self-employed), address, and ZIP code ▶		EIN	
		Phone no. ( )	

Printed on recycled paper

Form **1040A** (2006)

(Use for Cumulative Problem 1.)

Schedule 1 (Form 1040A)

Department of the Treasury—Internal Revenue Service

Interest and Ordinary Dividends for Form 1040A Filers (99) **2006** OMB No. 1545-0074

Name(s) shown on Form 1040A | **Your social security number**

Part I

Interest

(See back of schedule and the instructions for Form 1040A, line 8a.)

Note. If you received a Form 1099-INT, Form 1099-OID, or substitute statement from a brokerage firm, enter the firm's name and the total interest shown on that form.

			Amount
1	List name of payer. If any interest is from a seller-financed mortgage and the buyer used the property as a personal residence, see back of schedule and list this interest first. Also, show that buyer's social security number and address.	1	
2	Add the amounts on line 1.	2	
3	Excludable interest on series EE and I U.S. savings bonds issued after 1989. Attach Form 8815.	3	
4	Subtract line 3 from line 2. Enter the result here and on Form 1040A, line 8a.	4	

Part II

Ordinary dividends

(See back of schedule and the instructions for Form 1040A, line 9a.)

Note. If you received a Form 1099-DIV or substitute statement from a brokerage firm, enter the firm's name and the ordinary dividends shown on that form.

			Amount
5	List name of payer.	5	
6	Add the amounts on line 5. Enter the total here and on Form 1040A, line 9a.	6	

For Paperwork Reduction Act Notice, see Form 1040A instructions. Cat. No. 12075R **Schedule 1 (Form 1040A) 2006**

(Use for Cumulative Problem 1.)

SCHEDULE EIC
(Form 1040A or 1040)

Department of the Treasury
Internal Revenue Service (99)

Earned Income Credit

Qualifying Child Information

1040A
1040
EIC

Complete and attach to Form 1040A or 1040 only if you have a qualifying child.

OMB No. 1545-0074

2006

Attachment Sequence No. **43**

Name(s) shown on return

Your social security number

Before you begin: See the instructions for Form 1040A, lines 40a and 40b, or Form 1040, lines 66a and 66b, to make sure that **(a)** you can take the EIC, and **(b)** you have a qualifying child.

CAUTION

- If you take the EIC even though you are not eligible, you may not be allowed to take the credit for up to 10 years. See back of schedule for details.
- It will take us longer to process your return and issue your refund if you do not fill in all lines that apply for each qualifying child.
- Be sure the child's name on line 1 and social security number (SSN) on line 2 agree with the child's social security card. Otherwise, at the time we process your return, we may reduce or disallow your EIC. If the name or SSN on the child's social security card is not correct, call the Social Security Administration at 1-800-772-1213.

Qualifying Child Information	**Child 1**		**Child 2**	
1 Child's name If you have more than two qualifying children, you only have to list two to get the maximum credit.	First name	Last name	First name	Last name
2 Child's SSN The child must have an SSN as defined on page 44 of the Form 1040A instructions or page 48 of the Form 1040 instructions unless the child was born and died in 2006. If your child was born and died in 2006 and did not have an SSN, enter "Died" on this line and attach a copy of the child's birth certificate.				
3 Child's year of birth	Year ___ ___ ___ ___ *If born after 1987, skip lines 4a and 4b; go to line 5.*		Year ___ ___ ___ ___ *If born after 1987, skip lines 4a and 4b; go to line 5.*	
4 If the child was born before 1988— **a** Was the child under age 24 at the end of 2006 and a student?	☐ **Yes.** *Go to line 5.*	☐ **No.** *Continue.*	☐ **Yes.** *Go to line 5.*	☐ **No.** *Continue.*
b Was the child permanently and totally disabled during any part of 2006?	☐ **Yes.** *Continue.*	☐ **No.** The child is not a qualifying child.	☐ **Yes.** *Continue.*	☐ **No.** The child is not a qualifying child.
5 Child's relationship to you (for example, son, daughter, grandchild, niece, nephew, foster child, etc.)				
6 Number of months child lived with you in the United States during 2006 • If the child lived with you for more than half of 2006 but less than 7 months, enter "7." • If the child was born or died in 2006 and your home was the child's home for the entire time he or she was alive during 2006, enter "12."	______ months *Do not enter more than 12 months.*		______ months *Do not enter more than 12 months.*	

TIP You may also be able to take the additional child tax credit if your child **(a)** was under age 17 at the end of 2006, **and (b)** is a U.S. citizen or resident alien. For more details, see the instructions for line 41 of Form 1040A or line 68 of Form 1040.

For Paperwork Reduction Act Notice, see Form 1040A or 1040 instructions. Cat. No. 13339M **Schedule EIC (Form 1040A or 1040) 2006**

(Use for Cumulative Problem 1.)

Form **8812**

Department of the Treasury
Internal Revenue Service (99)

Additional Child Tax Credit

Complete and attach to Form 1040, Form 1040A, or Form 1040NR.

1040 / 1040A / 1040NR / 8812

OMB No. 1545-0074

2006

Attachment Sequence No. **47**

Name(s) shown on return | **Your social security number**

Part I **All Filers**

1 Enter the amount from line 1 of your Child Tax Credit Worksheet on page 42 of the Form 1040 instructions, page 39 of the Form 1040A instructions, or page 20 of the Form 1040NR instructions. If you used Pub. 972, enter the amount from line 8 of the worksheet on page 4 of the publication **1**

2 Enter the amount from Form 1040, line 53, Form 1040A, line 33, or Form 1040NR, line 48 . . . . **2**

3 Subtract line 2 from line 1. If zero, **stop;** you cannot take this credit **3**

4a Enter your total earned income (see instructions on back) **4a**

b Nontaxable combat pay (see instructions on back) **4b**

5 Is the amount on line 4a more than $11,300?

☐ **No.** Leave line 5 blank and enter -0- on line 6.

☐ **Yes.** Subtract $11,300 from the amount on line 4a. Enter the result . **5**

6 Multiply the amount on line 5 by 15% (.15) and enter the result **6**

Next. Do you have three or more qualifying children?

☐ **No.** If line 6 is zero, stop; you cannot take this credit. Otherwise, skip Part II and enter the **smaller** of line 3 or line 6 on line 13.

☐ **Yes.** If line 6 is equal to or more than line 3, skip Part II and enter the amount from line 3 on line 13. Otherwise, go to line 7.

Part II **Certain Filers Who Have Three or More Qualifying Children**

7 Withheld social security and Medicare taxes from Form(s) W-2, boxes 4 and 6. If married filing jointly, include your spouse's amounts with yours. If you worked for a railroad, see instructions on back **7**

8 **1040 filers:** Enter the total of the amounts from Form 1040, lines 27 and 59, plus any uncollected social security and Medicare or tier 1 RRTA taxes included on line 63.

1040A filers: Enter -0-.

1040NR filers: Enter the total of the amounts from Form 1040NR, line 54, plus any uncollected social security and Medicare or tier 1 RRTA taxes included on line 58. **8**

9 Add lines 7 and 8 . . . . **9**

10 **1040 filers:** Enter the total of the amounts from Form 1040, lines 66a and 67.

1040A filers: Enter the total of the amount from Form 1040A, line 40a, plus any excess social security and tier 1 RRTA taxes withheld that you entered to the left of line 43 (see instructions on back).

1040NR filers: Enter the amount from Form 1040NR, line 61. **10**

11 Subtract line 10 from line 9. If zero or less, enter -0- **11**

12 Enter the **larger** of line 6 or line 11 . . . . **12**

Next, enter the **smaller** of line 3 or line 12 on line 13.

Part III **Additional Child Tax Credit**

13 **This is your additional child tax credit** **13**

1040 / 1040A / 1040NR

Enter this amount on Form 1040, line 68, Form 1040A, line 41, or Form 1040NR, line 62.

For Paperwork Reduction Act Notice, see back of form. Cat. No. 10644E Form **8812** (2006)

(Use for Cumulative Problem 1.)

Form **8863**

Department of the Treasury
Internal Revenue Service (99)

Education Credits (Hope and Lifetime Learning Credits)

▶ See instructions.
▶ Attach to Form 1040 or Form 1040A.

OMB No. 1545-0074

2006

Attachment Sequence No. **50**

Name(s) shown on return | Your social security number

Caution: *You **cannot** take the Hope credit and the lifetime learning credit for the **same student** in the same year.*

Part I Hope Credit. Caution: *You **cannot** take the Hope credit for more than **2** tax years for the **same student.***

1	(a) Student's name (as shown on page 1 of your tax return) First name / Last name	(b) Student's social security number (as shown on page 1 of your tax return)	(c) Qualified expenses (see instructions). **Do not** enter more than $2,200* for each student.	(d) Enter the **smaller** of the amount in column (c) or $1,100**	(e) Add column (c) and column (d)	(f) Enter one-half of the amount in column (e)

* For each student who attended an eligible educational institution in the Gulf Opportunity Zone, **do not** enter more than $4,400.
** For each student who attended an eligible educational institution in the Gulf Opportunity Zone, enter the **smaller** of the amount in column (c) or $2,200.

2 Tentative Hope credit. Add the amounts on line 1, column (f). If you are taking the lifetime learning credit for another student, go to Part II; otherwise, go to Part III . . . . ▶ **2**

Part II Lifetime Learning Credit

3	(a) Student's name (as shown on page 1 of your tax return) First name / Last name	(b) Student's social security number (as shown on page 1 of your tax return)	(c) Qualified expenses (see instructions)

4	Add the amounts on line 3, column (c), and enter the total	4	
5a	Enter the **smaller** of line 4 or $10,000	5a	
b	For students who attended an eligible educational institution in the Gulf Opportunity Zone, enter the smaller of $10,000 or their qualified expenses included on line 4 (see special rules on page 3)	5b	
c	Subtract line 5b from line 5a	5c	
6a	Multiply line 5b by 40% (.40)	6a	
b	Multiply line 5c by 20% (.20)	6b	
c	**Tentative lifetime learning credit.** Add lines 6a and 6b and go to Part III	6c	

Part III Allowable Education Credits

7	Tentative education credits. Add lines 2 and 6c			7	
8	Enter: $110,000 if married filing jointly; $55,000 if single, head of household, or qualifying widow(er)	8			
9	Enter the amount from Form 1040, line 38*, or Form 1040A, line 22	9			
10	Subtract line 9 from line 8. If zero or less, **stop;** you cannot take any education credits	10			
11	Enter: $20,000 if married filing jointly; $10,000 if single, head of household, or qualifying widow(er)	11			
12	If line 10 is equal to or more than line 11, enter the amount from line 7 on line 13 and go to line 14. If line 10 is less than line 11, divide line 10 by line 11. Enter the result as a decimal (rounded to at least three places)			12	× .
13	Multiply line 7 by line 12 ▶			13	
14	Enter the amount from Form 1040, line 46, or Form 1040A, line 28			14	
15	Enter the total, if any, of your credits from Form 1040, lines 47 through 49, or Form 1040A, lines 29 and 30	15			
16	Subtract line 15 from line 14. If zero or less, **stop;** you cannot take any education credits	16			
17	**Education credits.** Enter the **smaller** of line 13 or line 16 here and on Form 1040, line 50, or Form 1040A, line 31			17	

* If you are filing Form 2555, 2555-EZ, or 4563, or you are excluding income from Puerto Rico, see Pub. 970 for the amount to enter.

For Paperwork Reduction Act Notice, see page 4. Cat. No. 25379M Form **8863** (2006)

(Use for Cumulative Problem 2.)

Form **1040** Department of the Treasury—Internal Revenue Service
U.S. Individual Income Tax Return 2006 (99) IRS Use Only—Do not write or staple in this space.

For the year Jan. 1–Dec. 31, 2006, or other tax year beginning , 2006, ending , 20 OMB No. 1545-0074

Label (See instructions on page 16.) **Use the IRS label.** Otherwise, please print or type. LABEL HERE

Your first name and initial | Last name | **Your social security number**

If a joint return, spouse's first name and initial | Last name | **Spouse's social security number**

Home address (number and street). If you have a P.O. box, see page 16. | Apt. no. | ▲ You **must** enter your SSN(s) above. ▲

City, town or post office, state, and ZIP code. If you have a foreign address, see page 16. | Checking a box below will not change your tax or refund.

Presidential Election Campaign ▶ Check here if you, or your spouse if filing jointly, want $3 to go to this fund (see page 16) ▶ ☐ **You** ☐ **Spouse**

Filing Status

Check only one box.

1 ☐ Single
2 ☐ Married filing jointly (even if only one had income)
3 ☐ Married filing separately. Enter spouse's SSN above and full name here. ▶
4 ☐ Head of household (with qualifying person). (See page 17.) If the qualifying person is a child but not your dependent, enter this child's name here. ▶
5 ☐ Qualifying widow(er) with dependent child (see page 17)

Exemptions

6a ☐ **Yourself.** If someone can claim you as a dependent, **do not** check box 6a
b ☐ **Spouse**

Boxes checked on 6a and 6b ____

c **Dependents:**

(1) First name Last name	(2) Dependent's social security number	(3) Dependent's relationship to you	(4) ✓ if qualifying child for child tax credit (see page 19)
			☐
			☐
			☐
			☐

If more than four dependents, see page 19.

No. of children on 6c who:
• lived with you ____
• did not live with you due to divorce or separation (see page 20) ____
Dependents on 6c not entered above ____

d Total number of exemptions claimed

Add numbers on lines above ▶ ☐

Income

Attach Form(s) W-2 here. Also attach Forms W-2G and 1099-R if tax was withheld.

If you did not get a W-2, see page 22.

Enclose, but do not attach, any payment. Also, please use **Form 1040-V.**

7	Wages, salaries, tips, etc. Attach Form(s) W-2		7
8a	**Taxable** interest. Attach Schedule B if required		8a
b	**Tax-exempt** interest. **Do not** include on line 8a	8b	
9a	Ordinary dividends. Attach Schedule B if required		9a
b	Qualified dividends (see page 23)	9b	
10	Taxable refunds, credits, or offsets of state and local income taxes (see page 23)		10
11	Alimony received		11
12	Business income or (loss). Attach Schedule C or C-EZ		12
13	Capital gain or (loss). Attach Schedule D if required. If not required, check here ▶ ☐		13
14	Other gains or (losses). Attach Form 4797		14
15a	IRA distributions 15a	b Taxable amount (see page 25)	15b
16a	Pensions and annuities 16a	b Taxable amount (see page 25)	16b
17	Rental real estate, royalties, partnerships, S corporations, trusts, etc. Attach Schedule E		17
18	Farm income or (loss). Attach Schedule F		18
19	Unemployment compensation		19
20a	Social security benefits 20a	b Taxable amount (see page 27)	20b
21	Other income. List type and amount (see page 29)		21
22	Add the amounts in the far right column for lines 7 through 21. This is your **total income** ▶		22

Adjusted Gross Income

23	Archer MSA deduction. Attach Form 8853	23	
24	Certain business expenses of reservists, performing artists, and fee-basis government officials. Attach Form 2106 or 2106-EZ	24	
25	Health savings account deduction. Attach Form 8889	25	
26	Moving expenses. Attach Form 3903	26	
27	One-half of self-employment tax. Attach Schedule SE	27	
28	Self-employed SEP, SIMPLE, and qualified plans	28	
29	Self-employed health insurance deduction (see page 30)	29	
30	Penalty on early withdrawal of savings	30	
31a	Alimony paid b Recipient's SSN ▶	31a	
32	IRA deduction (see page 31)	32	
33	Student loan interest deduction (see page 33)	33	
34	Jury duty pay you gave to your employer	34	
35	Domestic production activities deduction. Attach Form 8903	35	
36	Add lines 23 through 31a and 32 through 35		36
37	Subtract line 36 from line 22. This is your **adjusted gross income** ▶		37

For Disclosure, Privacy Act, and Paperwork Reduction Act Notice, see page 78. Cat. No. 11320B Form **1040** (2006)

(Use for Cumulative Problem 2.)

Form 1040 (2006) Page **2**

Tax and Credits

Standard Deduction for—
- People who checked any box on line 39a or 39b **or** who can be claimed as a dependent, see page 36.
- All others:

Single or Married filing separately, $5,150

Married filing jointly or Qualifying widow(er), $10,300

Head of household, $7,550

Line	Description		Line	Amount
38	Amount from line 37 (adjusted gross income)		38	
39a	Check if: ☐ **You** were born before January 2, 1942, ☐ Blind. ☐ **Spouse** was born before January 2, 1942, ☐ Blind. **Total boxes checked ▶ 39a**			
b	If your spouse itemizes on a separate return or you were a dual-status alien, see page 35 and check here ▶39b ☐			
40	**Itemized deductions** (from Schedule A) **or** your **standard deduction** (see left margin)		40	
41	Subtract line 40 from line 38		41	
42	If line 38 is over $112,875, or you provided housing to a person displaced by Hurricane Katrina, see page 37. Otherwise, multiply $3,300 by the total number of exemptions claimed on line 6d		42	
43	**Taxable income.** Subtract line 42 from line 41. If line 42 is more than line 41, enter -0-		43	
44	**Tax** (see page 37). Check if any tax is from: **a** ☐ Form(s) 8814 **b** ☐ Form 4972		44	
45	**Alternative minimum tax** (see page 39). Attach Form 6251		45	
46	Add lines 44 and 45 ▶		46	
47	Foreign tax credit. Attach Form 1116 if required	47		
48	Credit for child and dependent care expenses. Attach Form 2441	48		
49	Credit for the elderly or the disabled. Attach Schedule R	49		
50	Education credits. Attach Form 8863	50		
51	Retirement savings contributions credit. Attach Form 8880	51		
52	Residential energy credits. Attach Form 5695	52		
53	Child tax credit (see page XX). Attach Form 8901 if required	53		
54	Credits from: **a** ☐ Form 8396 **b** ☐ Form 8839 **c** ☐ Form 8859	54		
55	Other credits: **a** ☐ Form 3800 **b** ☐ Form 8801 **c** ☐ Form_____	55		
56	Add lines 47 through 55. These are your **total credits**		56	
57	Subtract line 56 from line 46. If line 56 is more than line 46, enter -0- ▶		57	

Other Taxes

Line	Description		Line	Amount
58	Self-employment tax. Attach Schedule SE		58	
59	Social security and Medicare tax on tip income not reported to employer. Attach Form 4137		59	
60	Additional tax on IRAs, other qualified retirement plans, etc. Attach Form 5329 if required		60	
61	Advance earned income credit payments from Form(s) W-2, box 9		61	
62	Household employment taxes. Attach Schedule H		62	
63	Add lines 57 through 62. This is your **total tax** ▶		63	

Payments

If you have a qualifying child, attach Schedule EIC.

Line	Description		Line	Amount
64	Federal income tax withheld from Forms W-2 and 1099	64		
65	2006 estimated tax payments and amount applied from 2005 return	65		
66a	**Earned income credit (EIC)**	66a		
b	Nontaxable combat pay election ▶ 66b			
67	Excess social security and tier 1 RRTA tax withheld (see page 59)	67		
68	Additional child tax credit. Attach Form 8812	68		
69	Amount paid with request for extension to file (see page 59)	69		
70	Payments from: **a** ☐ Form 2439 **b** ☐ Form 4136 **c** ☐ Form 8885	70		
71	Credit for federal telephone excise tax paid. Attach Form 8913 if required	71		
72	Add lines 64, 65, 66a, and 67 through 71. These are your **total payments** ▶		72	

Refund

Direct deposit? See page 59 and fill in 74b, 74c, and 74d, or Form 8888.

Line	Description		Line	Amount
73	If line 72 is more than line 63, subtract line 63 from line 72. This is the amount you **overpaid**		73	
74a	Amount of line 73 you want **refunded to you.** If Form 8888 is attached, check here ▶ ☐		74a	
▶ b	Routing number ▶ **c** Type: ☐ Checking ☐ Savings			
▶ d	Account number			
75	Amount of line 73 you want **applied to your 2007 estimated tax** ▶	75		

Amount You Owe

Line	Description		Line	Amount
76	**Amount you owe.** Subtract line 72 from line 63. For details on how to pay, see page 60 ▶		76	
77	Estimated tax penalty (see page 60)	77		

Third Party Designee

Do you want to allow another person to discuss this return with the IRS (see page 61)? ☐ **Yes.** Complete the following. ☐ **No**

Designee's name ▶ Phone no. ▶ ( ) Personal identification number (PIN) ▶

Sign Here

Joint return? See page 17. Keep a copy for your records.

Under penalties of perjury, I declare that I have examined this return and accompanying schedules and statements, and to the best of my knowledge and belief, they are true, correct, and complete. Declaration of preparer (other than taxpayer) is based on all information of which preparer has any knowledge.

Your signature	Date	Your occupation	Daytime phone number ( )
Spouse's signature. If a joint return, **both** must sign.	Date	Spouse's occupation	

Paid Preparer's Use Only

Preparer's signature	Date	Check if self-employed ☐	Preparer's SSN or PTIN
Firm's name (or yours if self-employed), address, and ZIP code		EIN	
		Phone no.	( )

Form **1040** (2006)

Printed on recycled paper

(Use for Cumulative Problem 2.)

Schedules A&B (Form 1040) 2006 OMB No. 1545-0074 Page **2**

Name(s) shown on Form 1040. Do not enter name and social security number if shown on other side. **Your social security number**

Schedule B—Interest and Ordinary Dividends

Attachment Sequence No. **08**

Part I Interest

(See page B-1 and the instructions for Form 1040, line 8a.)

Note. If you received a Form 1099-INT, Form 1099-OID, or substitute statement from a brokerage firm, list the firm's name as the payer and enter the total interest shown on that form.

			Amount
1	List name of payer. If any interest is from a seller-financed mortgage and the buyer used the property as a personal residence, see page B-1 and list this interest first. Also, show that buyer's social security number and address ▶	1	
2	Add the amounts on line 1	2	
3	Excludable interest on series EE and I U.S. savings bonds issued after 1989. Attach Form 8815	3	
4	Subtract line 3 from line 2. Enter the result here and on Form 1040, line 8a ▶	4	

Note. If line 4 is over $1,500, you must complete Part III.

Part II Ordinary Dividends

(See page B-1 and the instructions for Form 1040, line 9a.)

Note. If you received a Form 1099-DIV or substitute statement from a brokerage firm, list the firm's name as the payer and enter the ordinary dividends shown on that form.

			Amount
5	List name of payer ▶	5	
6	Add the amounts on line 5. Enter the total here and on Form 1040, line 9a ▶	6	

Note. If line 6 is over $1,500, you must complete Part III.

Part III Foreign Accounts and Trusts

(See page B-2.)

	You must complete this part if you **(a)** had over $1,500 of taxable interest or ordinary dividends; or **(b)** had a foreign account; or **(c)** received a distribution from, or were a grantor of, or a transferor to, a foreign trust.	**Yes**	**No**
7a	At any time during 2006, did you have an interest in or a signature or other authority over a financial account in a foreign country, such as a bank account, securities account, or other financial account? See page B-2 for exceptions and filing requirements for Form TD F 90-22.1	☐	☐
b	If "Yes," enter the name of the foreign country ▶		
8	During 2006, did you receive a distribution from, or were you the grantor of, or transferor to, a foreign trust? If "Yes," you may have to file Form 3520. See page B-2	☐	☐

For Paperwork Reduction Act Notice, see Form 1040 instructions. **Schedule B (Form 1040) 2006**

Printed on recycled paper

(Use for Cumulative Problem 2.)

Form **8815**
Department of the Treasury
Internal Revenue Service (99)

Exclusion of Interest From Series EE and I U.S. Savings Bonds Issued After 1989

(For Filers With Qualified Higher Education Expenses)

▶ Attach to Form 1040 or Form 1040A.

OMB No. 1545-0074
2006
Attachment Sequence No. **57**

Name(s) shown on return | **Your social security number**

1 (a) Name of person (you, your spouse, or your dependent) who was enrolled at or attended an eligible educational institution	(b) Name and address of eligible educational institution

If you need more space, attach a statement.

2	Enter the total qualified higher education expenses you paid in 2006 for the person(s) listed in column (a) of line 1. See the instructions to find out which expenses qualify	2	
3	Enter the total of any nontaxable educational benefits (such as nontaxable scholarship or fellowship grants) received for 2006 for the person(s) listed in column (a) of line 1 (see instructions)	3	
4	Subtract line 3 from line 2. If zero or less, **stop.** You **cannot** take the exclusion	4	
5	Enter the total proceeds (principal and interest) from all series EE and I U.S. savings bonds **issued after 1989** that you **cashed during 2006**	5	
6	Enter the interest included on line 5 (see instructions)	6	
7	If line 4 is equal to or more than line 5, enter "1.000." If line 4 is less than line 5, divide line 4 by line 5. Enter the result as a decimal (rounded to at least three places)	7	× .
8	Multiply line 6 by line 7	8	
9	Enter your modified adjusted gross income (see instructions) — 9 ______ **Note:** *If line 9 is $78,100 or more if single or head of household, or $124,700 or more if married filing jointly or qualifying widow(er),* ***stop.*** *You* ***cannot*** *take the exclusion.*		
10	Enter: $63,100 if single or head of household; $94,700 if married filing jointly or qualifying widow(er) — 10 ______		
11	Subtract line 10 from line 9. If zero or less, skip line 12, enter -0- on line 13, and go to line 14 — 11 ______		
12	Divide line 11 by: $15,000 if single or head of household; $30,000 if married filing jointly or qualifying widow(er). Enter the result as a decimal (rounded to at least three places)	12	× .
13	Multiply line 8 by line 12	13	
14	**Excludable savings bond interest.** Subtract line 13 from line 8. Enter the result here and on Schedule B (Form 1040), line 3, or Schedule 1 (Form 1040A), line 3, whichever applies ▶	14	

For Paperwork Reduction Act Notice, see back of form. Cat. No. 10822S Form **8815** (2006)

(Use for Cumulative Problem 2.)

Form **3903**
Department of the Treasury
Internal Revenue Service

Moving Expenses

▶ **Attach to Form 1040 or Form 1040NR.**

OMB No. 1545-0074
2006
Attachment Sequence No. **62**

Name(s) shown on return | **Your social security number**

Before you begin: √ See the **Distance Test** and **Time Test** in the instructions to find out if you can deduct your moving expenses.
√ See **Members of the Armed Forces** on the back, if applicable.

1	Transportation and storage of household goods and personal effects (see instructions) . .	**1**	
2	Travel (including lodging) from your old home to your new home (see instructions). **Do not** include the cost of meals	**2**	
3	Add lines 1 and 2	**3**	
4	Enter the total amount your employer paid you for the expenses listed on lines 1 and 2 that is **not** included in box 1 of your Form W-2 (wages). This amount should be shown in box 12 of your Form W-2 with code **P**	**4**	
5	Is line 3 **more than** line 4? ☐ **No.** You **cannot** deduct your moving expenses. If line 3 is less than line 4, subtract line 3 from line 4 and include the result on Form 1040, line 7, or Form 1040NR, line 8. ☐ **Yes.** Subtract line 4 from line 3. Enter the result here and on Form 1040, line 26, or Form 1040NR, line 26. This is your **moving expense deduction**	**5**	

General Instructions

What's New

For 2006, the standard mileage rate for using your vehicle to move to a new home is 18 cents a mile.

Purpose of Form

Use Form 3903 to figure your moving expense deduction for a move related to the start of work at a new principal place of work (workplace). If the new workplace is outside the United States or its possessions, you must be a U.S. citizen or resident alien to deduct your expenses.

If you qualify to deduct expenses for more than one move, use a separate Form 3903 for each move.

For more details, see Pub. 521, Moving Expenses.

Moving Expenses You Can Deduct

You can deduct the reasonable expenses of moving your household goods and personal effects and of traveling from your old home to your new home. Reasonable expenses can include the cost of lodging (but not meals) while traveling to your new home. You cannot deduct the cost of sightseeing trips.

Who Can Deduct Moving Expenses

If you move to a new home because of a new principal workplace, you may be able to deduct your moving expenses whether you are self-employed or an employee. But you must meet both the distance test and time test that follow.

TIP *Members of the Armed Forces may not have to meet the distance test and time test. See instructions on the back.*

Distance Test

Your new principal workplace must be at least 50 miles farther from your old home than your old workplace was. For example, if your old workplace was 3 miles from your old home, your new workplace must be at least 53 miles from that home. If you did not have an old workplace, your new workplace must be at least 50 miles from your old home. The distance between the two points is the shortest of the more commonly traveled routes between them.

TIP *To see if you meet the distance test, you can use the worksheet below.*

Distance Test Worksheet

Keep a Copy for Your Records

1. Number of miles from your **old home** to your **new workplace** . . . . **1.** ______ miles

2. Number of miles from your **old home** to your **old workplace** . . . . **2.** ______ miles

3. Subtract line 2 from line 1. If zero or less, enter -0-. **3.** ______ miles

Is line 3 at least 50 miles?

☐ **Yes.** You meet this test.

☐ **No.** You do not meet this test. You **cannot** deduct your moving expenses. **Do not** complete Form 3903.

For Paperwork Reduction Act Notice, see back of form. Cat. No. 12490K Form **3903** (2006)

5

Personal Itemized Deductions

CHAPTER CONTENTS

CHAPTER OVERVIEW

Generally, the tax law does not allow individuals to deduct personal expenses on their tax returns. There are exceptions, however. Several types of personal expenses can be deducted as itemized deductions. As an alternative to itemizing, taxpayers may choose to take the standard deduction if that amount is greater.

Individuals have two basic types of expense deductions. One type reduces gross income to yield adjusted gross income (AGI). Expenses incurred in a trade or business are examples of this type of deduction. The other type of expense (which includes itemized deductions) reduces AGI.

The most desirable deduction is one for AGI. One reason for this is that the tax law uses AGI as a base to limit some deductions from AGI. As examples, medical expenses are deductible only to the extent they exceed 7.5% of AGI. Employment-related expenses and investment expenses are deductible to the extent they exceed 2% of AGI. Thus, the lower the amount of AGI, the better the chance of deducting more itemized deductions. Another reason deductions for AGI are preferred is that 70–75% of taxpayers use the standard deduction in lieu of itemizing deductions. These taxpayers lose the benefit of any possible itemized deductions.

As a result of these situations, taxpayers should look for ways to maximize their deductions for AGI. For example, many self-employed people are able to shift what normally would be either itemized deductions or nondeductible expenditures into deductions for AGI. Examples include home office expenses and costs of travel, transportation, entertainment, and business gifts. These are topics covered in Chapter 7.

This chapter and Chapter 6 present the most common itemized deductions, which appear on Schedule A. These two chapters explain when and how these deductions can be taken. Chapter 5 describes the most common personal deductions available on Schedule A, such as medical expenses, taxes, interest, charitable contributions, and casualty or theft losses. It explains the limits related to each type of deduction and describes the overall limit on itemized deductions for taxpayers with higher incomes. Chapter 6 expands the details of the miscellaneous and job-related deductions, which this chapter covers briefly.

Currently, the standard deduction exceeds most taxpayers' total itemized deductions, and the IRS annually indexes and increases its benefits. For those who do itemize, it should be noted that, generally, taxpayers may itemize deductions only for their own expenses, when paid from their own funds. Only in limited cases is it possible to take deductions for expenses of other people when paid by the taxpayer. These exceptions are pointed out in the chapter.

REPORTING ITEMIZED DEDUCTIONS (SCHEDULE A)

Generally, a taxpayer deducts the larger of either the standard deduction or the total amount of itemized deductions. However, when spouses file separately and one itemizes deductions, the other spouse must also itemize.

Taxpayers deciding to use Schedule A work through the computations and complete related forms where appropriate. These include forms such as Form 4952 (Investment Interest), Form 8283 (Noncash Charitable Contributions), Form 4684 (Casualty and Theft Losses), and Form 2106 (Employee Business Expenses). After applying any necessary limits, taxpayers report the total of each itemized deduction on Schedule A and compute the overall total. Certain high-income individuals then face another limit on the total amount of itemized deductions that the law will allow. Any remaining deduction carries from Schedule A to Form 1040, page 2, where it reduces AGI.

ITEMIZED DEDUCTIONS REPORTED ON SCHEDULE A

Medical and Dental Expenses (line 4)
Taxes You Paid (line 9)
Interest You Paid (line 14)
Gifts to Charity (line 18)
Casualty and Theft Losses (line 19)
Job Expenses and Most Miscellaneous Deductions (line 26)
Other Miscellaneous Deductions (line 27)
Total Itemized Deductions (line 28)

STANDARD DEDUCTIONS FOR 2006

Filing Status	**Basic Amount**		**Elderly OR Blind**		**Elderly AND Blind**
Single	$5,150	add	$1,250	or	$2,500
Married filing jointly, and surviving spouse	10,300	add	1,000*	or	2,000*
Married filing separately	5,150	add	1,000	or	2,000
Head of household	7,550	add	1,250	or	2,500

*Applies to each taxpayer.

FILLED-IN SCHEDULE A

Figure 5-1 shows a filled-in Schedule A for Steven T. and Laurie R. Neal. This Schedule A illustrates the reporting of the itemized deductions discussed in this chapter.

Information for Figure 5-1: Filled-In Schedule A

Steven and Laurie Neal file a joint return. They have $143,750 of AGI. Shown in Figure 5-1 is a copy of the filled-in Schedule A, which they received from their accountant. The amount of each deduction is described throughout the chapter.

FIGURE 5-1 Filled-In Schedule A

SCHEDULES A&B (Form 1040) — Department of the Treasury, Internal Revenue Service (99)

Schedule A—Itemized Deductions

(Schedule B is on back)

▶ Attach to Form 1040. ▶ See Instructions for Schedules A&B (Form 1040).

OMB No. 1545-0074 — 2006 — Attachment Sequence No. 07

Name(s) shown on Form 1040: Steven T. and Laurie R. Neal — Your social security number: 304 66 4201

Section	Line	Description	Line ref	Amount	Line ref	Total
Medical and Dental Expenses		**Caution.** Do not include expenses reimbursed or paid by others.				
	1	Medical and dental expenses (see page A-2)	1	12,000 00		
	2	Enter amount from Form 1040, line 38 [2] 143,750 00				
	3	Multiply line 2 by 7.5% (.075)	3	10,781 00		
	4	Subtract line 3 from line 1. If line 3 is more than line 1, enter -0-			4	1,219 00
Taxes You Paid (See page A-2.)	5	State and local income taxes	5	2,050 00		
	6	Real estate taxes (see page A-5)	6	1,000 00		
	7	Personal property taxes	7	250 00		
	8	Other taxes. List type and amount ▶	8			
	9	Add lines 5 through 8			9	3,300 00
Interest You Paid (See page A-5.)	10	Home mortgage interest and points reported to you on Form 1098	10	2,500 00		
	11	Home mortgage interest not reported to you on Form 1098. If paid to the person from whom you bought the home, see page A-6 and show that person's name, identifying no., and address ▶	11			
Note. Personal interest is not deductible.	12	Points not reported to you on Form 1098. See page A-6 for special rules	12			
	13	Investment interest. Attach Form 4952 if required. (See page A-6.)	13	1,866 00		
	14	Add lines 10 through 13			14	4,366 00
Gifts to Charity	15	Gifts by cash or check. If you made any gift of $250 or more, see page A-7	15	3,725 00		
If you made a gift and got a benefit for it, see page A-7.	16	Other than by cash or check. If any gift of $250 or more, see page A-7. You **must** attach Form 8283 if over $500	16	43,250 00		
	17	Carryover from prior year	17			
	18	Add lines 15 through 17			18	46,975 00
Casualty and Theft Losses	19	Casualty or theft loss(es). Attach Form 4684. (See page A-8.)			19	-0-
Job Expenses and Certain Miscellaneous Deductions (See page A-8.)	20	Unreimbursed employee expenses—job travel, union dues, job education, etc. Attach Form 2106 or 2106-EZ if required. (See page A-8.) ▶	20			
	21	Tax preparation fees	21			
	22	Other expenses—investment, safe deposit box, etc. List type and amount ▶ Investment expense	22	3,009 00		
	23	Add lines 20 through 22	23	3,009 00		
	24	Enter amount from Form 1040, line 38 [24] 143,750 00				
	25	Multiply line 24 by 2% (.02)	25	2,875 00		
	26	Subtract line 25 from line 23. If line 25 is more than line 23, enter -0-			26	134 00
Other Miscellaneous Deductions	27	Other—from list on page A-9. List type and amount ▶			27	-0-
Total Itemized Deductions	28	Is Form 1040, line 38, over $150,500 (over $75,250 if married filing separately)? ☒ **No.** Your deduction is not limited. Add the amounts in the far right column for lines 4 through 27. Also, enter this amount on Form 1040, line 40. ☐ **Yes.** Your deduction may be limited. See page A-9 for the amount to enter. ▶			28	55,994 00
	29	If you elect to itemize deductions even though they are less than your standard deduction, check here ▶ ☐				

For Paperwork Reduction Act Notice, see Form 1040 instructions. — Cat. No. 11330X — Schedule A (Form 1040) 2006

MEDICAL AND DENTAL EXPENSES, SCHEDULE A (LINE 4)

Most taxpayers cannot take advantage of the medical and dental deduction. To be deductible, unreimbursed medical expenses must exceed 7.5% of the taxpayer's AGI. Taxpayers with health insurance seldom exceed this limit. Generally, taxpayers deduct only their own expenses. Couples that file a joint return can deduct expenses of either spouse. However, for the medical deduction, taxpayers can deduct the costs of medical and dental care for others. Qualifying individuals typically include children or a parent. The IRS defines qualifying individuals for the medical deduction as those people who meet the following three dependency tests from Chapter 1: (1) citizenship, (2) support, and (3) relationship. "Qualifying children" do not have to meet the "Support test."

The other two tests, (4) gross income and (5) joint return, do not affect the medical expense deduction. For example, a taxpayer may deduct $750 spent on medicine for her father who is not a dependent because his gross income exceeds $3,300.

Two major areas of tax planning apply to medical costs:

1. When one spouse receives extensive medical care, the couple should consider filing separate returns. The 7.5% reduction of medical expenses applies to a lower AGI when only one spouse's income is reported on the return.
2. A group of family members sharing the costs of medical care for a relative can allow one member of the group to deduct the medical expenses. The selected family member deducts only those expenses he or she paid. All members of the group sign statements releasing the dependency exemption to the selected family member (see Chapter 1). The IRS permits group members to rotate the family member using the dependency exemptions.

Only about 5% of the taxpayers claim a medical expense deduction.

THREE GROUPS OF MEDICAL EXPENSES

1. Prescription drugs and insulin
2. All medical and dental insurance premiums paid by the taxpayer
3. Other medical expenses

Prescription Drugs and Insulin

Only prescriptions drugs count as deductible medical expenses. Even when prescribed, the purchase of over-the-counter medicine and vitamins does not qualify as a deductible medical expense. Some commonly used over-the-counter nondeductible drugs include iron and calcium supplements, low-sodium foods, birth control devices, cold medicines, aspirin, allergy medications, and antacid tablets.

EXAMPLE 1

For Steven Neal's cold and fever, a doctor prescribed an antibiotic, and an over-the-counter cold remedy. Neal's co-pay for the antibiotic was $25. The insurance company paid the rest. The cold remedy cost $5. Only the $25 paid for the antibiotic may be deducted.

Medical and Dental Insurance Premiums

Medical expenses include the full amounts of insurance premiums covering medical and dental care. Self-employed taxpayers can deduct the family's total insurance premiums for AGI. However, the deduction for AGI is only allowed for premiums paid during months when the taxpayer and the spouse are not eligible under an employer's medical plan. Premiums not deductible as a deduction for AGI are treated as a medical expense on Schedule A (line 1). Deductible insurance premiums include Medicare premiums withheld from the monthly checks of taxpayers receiving social security income, premiums paid to supplement Medicare coverage, prepaid insurance plans, and payments to health maintenance organizations (HMOs) or other group providers. A deduction is also available for long-term care insurance premiums.

Certain types of medical insurance are nondeductible. They include the medical portion of auto insurance, premiums paid through cafeteria plans at work, life insurance, loss of earnings coverage, coverage for loss of limb or sight, premiums that guarantee a specific daily or weekly payment regardless of any hospitalization requirements, and any premiums paid by an employer.

EXAMPLE 2

The Neals paid $11,772 in insurance premiums during the year. The premiums consist of $9,972 for family medical coverage, $1,200 for life insurance, and $600 for disability. Only the $9,972 may be included as a medical deduction.

Other Medical Expenses

General Items

Taxpayers can deduct only payments made directly to medical providers, such as doctors, dentists, nurses, hospitals, or clinics. Deductible payments to other providers include those made to authorized Christian Science practitioners, chiropractors, osteopaths, podiatrists, and therapists. Deductible forms of medical care include laboratory work, medical procedures, X-rays, and MRIs.

Some treatments designed to stop smoking also qualify as a medical expense deduction. This includes participation in a stop-smoking program. It also includes the purchase of drugs requiring a physician's prescription to alleviate the effects of nicotine withdrawal.

Cosmetic surgury is deductible only when it is necessary for medical reasons, such as correction of a birth defect or repair of damage from injury or disease. Taxpayers include these medical costs and other medical expenses on Schedule A (line 1). They cannot deduct cosmetic surgery for vanity reasons.

Special Medical Expenses

Aside from the preceding items, other health-related expenses may qualify for the medical deduction, depending on the level of care needed. Nursing and convalescent care, in-home care, special schools, equipment and home remodeling, and transportation and travel costs are reasonable medical deductions.

Nursing Home Care

Depending on the condition of a nursing home resident and the types of services offered by the home, the entire amount paid to the facility may be deductible. When the main purpose of the stay relates to a medical condition, the taxpayer deducts all expenses, even the cost of food and lodging. Some conditions that qualify for 100% medical treatment include Alzheimer's disease, paralysis, alcoholism, drug recovery, and physical injury or handicap. If the main reason for living in the home relates to personal care or family convenience, the taxpayer deducts only the specific medical expenses. However, expenditures for qualified long-term care are deductible when such services are required by a chronically ill person.

School for the Handicapped

Amounts paid to send a mentally or physically handicapped spouse or disabled dependent to a special school or facility constitute medical costs. The school's main focus must be to help students compensate or overcome problems in order to function better.

Employee Physicals

Many employees involved with hazardous materials or dangerous jobs get annual physicals. When the employer requires physicals, the costs are deducted as miscellaneous employee business expenses (see Chapter 6). Employees getting physicals on their own deduct their out-of-pocket costs as a medical expense.

Transportation Expenses

Taxpayers may use either the standard mileage rate or actual expenses to compute deductible expenses they incur in traveling to receive medical care. For 2006, the standard mileage rate for medical expenses is $.18 per mile plus the costs of tolls and parking. While individuals may deduct their actual expenses, the standard mileage rate is easier to use. When choosing to use the actual expense method, taxpayers may deduct only out-of-pocket expenses. Taxpayers must keep a log showing the mileage and expenses, as well as receipts for all items paid. Under the special provision allowing a taxpayer to deduct the expenses of others, parents may deduct a child's expenses. For instance, parents can deduct the mileage for driving their child from Los Angeles to San Diego to consult a specialist for the child's illness.

Travel Expenses

When a patient and/or the taxpayer must travel overnight for medical treatments, a travel expense deduction is available. The Code limits lodging to $50 per night for each person.

Capital Expenditures

Home improvements and special equipment installed in a home may be deducted when prescribed by a medical provider as part of a specific treatment. Three common improvements are swimming pools, air conditioners, and elevators. When the improvement increases the value of the home by more than the cost of the improvement, no medical deduction results. The reasoning is that the taxpayer will be repaid when the home is later sold for more money.

When the cost exceeds the increase in value of the home, the excess is taken as a medical expense. One exception occurs when the improvements make it possible for a physically handicapped individual to live independently. Here, deductible expenses include constructing entrance and exit ramps, widening hallways and doorways for wheelchair use, installing support bars and railings, and adjusting outlets and fixtures. In this special case, the IRS treats the costs of the improvements as adding no value to the home for tax purposes.

EXAMPLE 3

Under a doctor's prescription for muscle problems, the Neals installed a spa costing $7,000. It increased the fair market value (FMV) of the house by $4,000. The medical expense equals to $3,000.

EXAMPLE 4

Robin Turk is confined to a wheelchair. In order to live alone, Turk pays $10,000 to have ramps, bars and railings installed in her home. Although these features might add as much as $2,000 to the value of her home, the IRS treats their added value as $0. This allows Turk to deduct the full $10,000 as a medical expense deduction. She adds this to her other unreimbursed medical expenses. She then reduces the total by 7.5% of her AGI.

Other Medical Expenditures

Other commonly deductible medical expenses include eyeglasses, dentures, braces, crutches, canes, wheelchairs, and guide dogs. Common nondeductible medical items include health club memberships, massages, burial and funeral expenses, and illegal drugs or operations.

Reimbursements

To record the medical deduction, taxpayers (1) add all the costs of qualified medical items reportable on Schedule A, (2) subtract the funds received from insurance and other sources, and (3) enter the difference on Schedule A (line 1).

EXAMPLE 5

The Neals' total medical expenses are $50,000. Their insurance company reimbursed them $38,000 for their medical costs. The Neals enter the $12,000 ($50,000 – $38,000) difference on Schedule A (line 1). They reduce this amount by 7.5% of AGI to compute the net medical expense deduction, $1,219 (line 4).

Two situations occur that make medical reimbursements taxable. First, when an employer-paid insurance policy provides reimbursements greater than the medical expenses actually paid, the excess is taxable. When the employee pays the premium, the excess is not taxable. Second, when the taxpayer takes a medical deduction and receives a reimbursement in the following year, all or part of that reimbursement may constitute taxable income (based on the tax benefit rule described in Chapter 3). This rule requires that taxpayers report the reimbursement in gross income only when they benefited from deducting medical expenses in an earlier year.

EXAMPLE 6

Terri Greene pays $5,000 of medical expenses in 20x1. Although this amount exceeds 7.5% of her AGI, Greene's standard deduction is higher than her total itemized deductions. Early in 20x2, Greene is reimbursed $2,000 by her insurance company for medical costs she paid in 20x1. Greene does not include any of the $2,000 in gross income in 20x2. Because Greene's income taxes were not lowered by the $5,000 of medical costs in 20x1, she did not receive a tax benefit from the amounts reimbursed.

TAXES PAID, SCHEDULE A (LINE 9)

The tax law limits the types of taxes that are deductible. Generally, only income taxes and property taxes qualify as itemized deductions, and these must be levied by an agency other than the federal government. Qualifying taxes must meet two conditions before a deduction is available. First, the taxpayer must actually pay the taxes. Second, the taxes paid must be those of the taxpayer. Amounts paid for someone else's taxes cannot be deducted.

About 35% of the total itemized deductions claimed by taxpayers is for taxes, making it the second largest itemized deduction.

DEDUCTIBLE TAXES

Tax Category	Description of Deductible Taxes
Income taxes	State and local income taxes
	Foreign income taxes (if not used as a tax credit)
	Employee contributions to a state unemployment fund
Real estate taxes	State, local, and foreign real estate taxes
	Tenant's share of real estate taxes paid by a cooperative housing corporation
Personal property taxes	State and local personal property taxes (if based on value)

State and Local Income Taxes, Schedule A (Line 5)

Three primary sources of deductible state and local income taxes include (1) W-2 withholdings, (2) estimated taxes paid in the current tax year, and (3) additional taxes paid for the current or previous years. The interest and penalties included in those bills are not treated as taxes. Refunds of prior year's state or local income taxes do not reduce the taxes paid. When the refund stems from taxes deducted in a prior tax year, the amount is reported on Form 1040 as "Taxable refunds, etc." in accordance with the "tax benefit rule" (Chapter 3).

EXAMPLE 7

In 2006, the Neals paid various taxes:

State income tax withheld during 2006	$1,420
Estimated state income tax paid during 2006	400
2005 state income tax paid with 2005 return when filed in 2006	175
Additional tax assessment on 2004 state income tax paid in 2006	55
Total deduction for state income taxes in 2006	$2,050

EXAMPLE 8

During 20x1, Jason White's employer withheld $3,600 for state income taxes from his wages. White's itemized deductions in 20x1 exceeded his standard deduction by $8,000. In April of 20x2, White files his state tax return. Two months later he receives a $700 refund from the state. Since White's tax liability was lowered in 20x1 when he deducted the $3,600 as an itemized deduction, he reports the $700 in gross income in 20x2. The tax benefit rule (Chapter 3) taxes White on the *lesser of* (i) the $700 refund, or (ii) the $8,000 excess of his 20x1 itemized deductions over his standard deduction amount.

Real Estate Taxes, Schedule A (Line 6)

The tax laws allow individuals to deduct from AGI ad valorum taxes they pay to state and local governments. **Ad valorum taxes** are taxes imposed on the value of the property. Local governments levy real estate taxes on the owners of real property based on the property's value. Thus, individuals can deduct state and local real estate taxes as an itemized deduction. They also can deduct real estate taxes paid to foreign governments.

When real estate is sold during the year, the seller is responsible for the real estate taxes up until the day of the sale. The buyer's responsibility starts on the day of the sale. Real estate taxes are normally levied once a year. The tax bill is sent to the property owner. As a rule, the tax laws allow taxpayers to deduct expenses that they both pay and are responsible for. When real estate is sold during the year, the party who pays the real estate tax bill may not be the one responsible for all of the taxes being paid. In these situations, only the portion of the taxes that the owner is responsible for could be deducted. To ensure no deductions are lost, at the time real estate is sold, sellers need to remit to the buyers their share of real estate taxes for the year. Standard language to this effect is found in most sales contracts. If the real estate taxes are not apportioned between the seller and the buyer at the closing, the tax laws require that the seller's share real estate costs that the buyer pays be added to the seller's amount realized from the sale. The buyer then adds this amount to the cost of buying the property. The parties can then each deduct their respective share of the real estate taxes for the year.

EXAMPLE 9

On May 11, 20x1, Jill Corley sells her home to Peggy and Tom Ryan for $200,000. Real estate taxes on the home are expected to be $3,000 for 20x1. At the closing, Corley remits to the Ryans $1,068 ($3,000 × 130/365). This amount is her share of the real estate taxes for the 130 days she owned the home during 20x1. In turn, Corley deducts this amount on Schedule A in 20x1. At the end of the year, the local government sends the Ryans the tax bill for 20x1. Although they will pay the entire amount due, the Ryans' out-of-pocket costs will be the amount paid minus the $1,068 they received from Corley at the closing. This net amount is the Ryans' share of the real estate taxes. They deduct this amount on Schedule A in 20x1.

EXAMPLE 10

Same as in Example 9, except that the taxes were not apportioned at the closing. Corley's $1,068 share of the real estate taxes that she will never pay increases her amount realized from the sale from $200,000 to $201,068. Likewise, the amount the Ryans paid for Corley's share of the taxes increases their basis in the home to $201,068. Both parties will then deduct their respective shares of the 20x1 real estate taxes.

Condominium and cooperative housing owners may deduct their shares of real estate taxes paid on these properties. When necessary, the association must identify the actual pass-through of property taxes to provide for a tax deduction. All other assessments from housing associations do not qualify as taxes. "Special assessments" added to the property tax bill for local improvements like streets, sidewalks, and sewers do not qualify as deductible taxes. Instead, these amounts are added to the basis of the property.

Personal Property Taxes, Schedule A (Line 7)

State or local personal property taxes are deductible only if:

1. The tax base used is the value of the personal property,
2. The tax is imposed on an annual basis, and
3. The tax is imposed on personal property.

Real estate is not the only type of property subject to property taxes. Some states levy taxes on personal property. For tax purposes, "personal property" is all property that is not real estate. This means that all property that is neither land nor buildings is called personal property. Personal property should not be confused with the property that individuals own and use in their personal lives. This type of property is personal-use property. Other uses of property include business and investment-use.

Individuals and businesses can own personal property. Individuals can own personal property that they use in their personal lives or hold for investment. This would include clothing, home furnishings, artwork, and stock. Examples of personal property businesses might own include trucks, office furniture, and machinery.

Personal property can be tangible or intangible. Tangible property has physical characteristics. Intangible property does not. Examples of tangible personal property include automobiles, books, clothing, and equipment. Examples of intangible property include patents, copyrights, goodwill, trademarks, etc. The tax laws also include as intangible property stocks, bonds, mutual funds, and money market accounts. Almost all states that impose a tax on intangible property impose a tax on these latter intangibles. If the amount is tax depends on the property's value, the tax is deductible.

States that impose a tax on tangible personal property generally tax property that taxpayers register with the state (e.g. motor vehicles, boats, and aircraft). This allows the tax to be included as part of the annual registration fee charged to owners. In states where the annual registration fee is based on the property's value, individuals can deduct that portion of the fee as an itemized deduction. Any added fees not based on the property's value cannot be deducted.

EXAMPLE 11

In 2006, the Neals paid the DMV $300 for the annual cost to register their car. The $300 fee includes $50 to renew Steven's driver's license. The remainder of the fee is based on the value of the car. They deduct only the $250 as personal property tax on Schedule A.

NONDEDUCTIBLE TAXES

Federal income taxes
Social security and Medicare taxes
Federal or state estate, gift, or inheritance taxes
State and local sales taxes
State and local license fees (driver's, marriage, fishing)
Use and excise taxes (gasoline, cigarette, alcohol)
All taxes paid on behalf of others
Penalties and interest included in tax bills

INTEREST PAID, SCHEDULE A (LINE 14)

Most personal interest is not deductible. However, home mortgage interest, points, and investment interest can qualify as itemized deductions. In contrast, interest on student loans may qualify as a deduction for AGI.

Overall, interest is the largest itemized deduction. About 40% of the total itemized deductions claimed by taxpayers is for interest.

Interest on Qualified Personal Residence, Schedule A (Line 10)

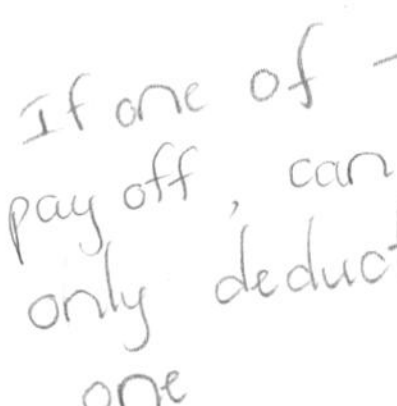

If one of
pay off, can
only deduct
one

Qualified personal residences include the taxpayer's principal residence and one more personal residence. A vacation home or a home in another city qualifies as a second residence. Houses, condominiums, and mobile homes all count as personal residences. Sometimes boats and motor homes qualify as personal residences. To take the mortgage interest deduction, the one paying the interest must also own the home.

A person who owns three or more residences can use the mortgage interest deduction on only two of them. Taxpayers must identify each year which residence to designate as the second home. When allowing others to use a home or when renting it out, the residence will qualify as a second residence if the taxpayer uses the home for more than the *greater of* (i) 14 days or (ii) 10% of the total days rented.

EXAMPLE 12

The Neals make house payments of $300 per month. They pay a total of $3,600 for the year: $1,100 principal and $2,500 interest expense. They deduct $2,500 on Schedule A.

EXAMPLE 13

The Garcias live most of the year in Dallas, Texas. They vacation in Park City, Utah and Phoenix, Arizona. They own homes in all three locations and owe mortgages on all three properties. In the current year, the Garcias paid interest expense on the mortgages on the Dallas, Park City, and Phoenix homes of $6,000, $18,500, and $10,000, respectively. When filing their income tax return, the Garcias can deduct the $6,000 interest paid on the loan used to finance their principal residence (the Dallas home). They also can deduct the $18,500 paid on their mortgage to finance the purchase of their Park City home. The $10,000 is nondeductible personal interest.

Acquisition Indebtedness

One type of qualifying home interest is **acquisition indebtedness.** This includes money borrowed to buy, build, or extensively remodel the taxpayer's principal or second home. Only the interest on total acquisition debt up to $1,000,000 ($500,000 for married filing separately) can be deducted. However, no interest deduction limits exist on debt incurred before October 13, 1987. Still, a sizable loan on the main home may limit the interest deduction on a second home acquired after this date.

Special rules limit the deduction when refinancing the original debt. If the new loan has a balance higher than the old loan, some nondeductible interest may result. Only the amount of interest on the portion of the new debt that replaces the old debt qualifies for the acquisition indebtedness deduction. However, any portion of the additional debt used to remodel the home extensively also qualifies as acquisition debt. The excess also may qualify as home equity indebtedness.

EXAMPLE 14

Jenny and Benny Tremlin own a home in Evanston, Illinois. They paid $1 million for the home two years ago. Their current mortgage on the home is $860,000. The current value of their home is $1.5 million. In the current year the Tremlins refinanced their mortgage. Their new mortgage is for $1.2 million. The Tremlins did not use any of the loan proceeds to improve their home. Thus, only the interest paid on $860,000 is deductible as acquisition indebtedness. Some of the interest paid on the rest of the debt may qualify as home equity debt (see discussion to follow). Any interest that is neither acquisition nor home equity debt is nondeductible personal interest.

EXAMPLE 15

Same as in Example 14, except that the Tremlins used $120,000 of the loan proceeds to remodel their kitchen. The Tremlins can deduct interest on $980,000 ($860,000 + $120,000) of the $1.2 million mortgage as acquisition indebtedness. Interest on some of the $220,000 excess debt may be deductible as home equity debt.

EXAMPLE 16

Same as in Example 15, except that in addition to using $120,000 to improve their home, the Tremlins also used $200,000 of the loan proceeds to pay cash for second residence. The Tremlins can deduct interest on $1 million of the $1.2 million mortgage as acquisition indebtedness. Interest on some of the $200,000 excess debt may be deductible as home equity debt.

Home Equity Indebtedness

Within limits, taxpayers may deduct interest on any loan secured by their homes. These include home equity loans and bill consolidation loans. Such debt, plus the acquisition debt, cannot exceed the fair market value (FMV) of the home. Total home equity debt cannot exceed $100,000 ($50,000 if married filing separately). Home equity debt allows homeowners to borrow up to $100,000 on their homes without any restrictions on how the money is spent.

EXAMPLE 17

Continuing with Example 16, $200,000 of the $1.2 million mortgage that did not count as acquisition debt qualifies as home equity debt. However, the Code limits the Tremlins' deduction to interest on $100,000 of such debt. Thus, they will be allowed to deduct interest related to $1.1 million of their debt as home mortgage interest on Schedule A. Once the Tremlins' loan balance falls below $1.1 million, their interest deduction will not be limited.

EXAMPLE 18

Back on June 5, 1995, the Neals bought a home for $60,000 with a $40,000 acquisition debt. By February 10, 2006, the loan had a balance of $18,000. The Neals took out a second mortgage of $20,000 and used the money to buy a car and take a trip. Since this money was not used to remodel the home, it falls under the definition of home equity debt.

On August 15, 2006, the Neals decided to add a pool and a patio, which cost $15,000. The builder financed the work. The property secures the builder's loan, along with the other loans. This loan qualifies as acquisition debt. Total interest on these house payments is $2,500 ($1,700 acquisition debt; $800, home equity debt). They deduct this amount on Schedule A.

Points, Schedule A (Line 12)

Also called "loan origination fees" or "loan fees," **points** are a type of prepaid interest. In exchange for paying points (interest) up front, the borrower gets a lower interest rate over the term of the loan. One point equals 1% of the loan amount. The more points paid, the lower the interest rate. Taxpayers may deduct points as interest. However, not all loan costs qualify as deductible points. Charges for loan services provided by the lender are not deductible. To be deductible, the points must meet these conditions:

1. Paying points on borrowed money is an established business practice in the area.
2. The amount of the payment does not exceed the amount usually charged in the area.
3. Funds to pay the points must come from the borrower's own money, not from the lender's funds.

As a rule, cash basis taxpayers must deduct prepaid expenses over the periods to which they apply. Since points are the same as prepaying interest, they usually must be deducted (amortized) evenly over the life of the loan. However, when the proceeds of the loan are used to buy or improve the taxpayer's principal residence, cash basis taxpayers can deduct points in the year paid. This special rule only applies to cash basis taxpayers who take out loans to buy or improve their principal residences. It does not extend to vacation homes or second homes or to refinancing of loans. It also does not apply to accrual basis taxpayers.

A special situation arises when the taxpayer pays points on a loan but then pay off the loan early. This occurs when the property is sold or when the loan is refinanced. If the property is sold, any unamortized (not yet deducted) points are deducted in the year of the sale. If the loan is refinanced, then the unamortized points plus any new points paid with the refinancing are deducted over the life of the new loan. However, if a part of the proceeds from refinancing a principal residence are used to improve the residence, cash basis taxpayers can deduct a portion of the points in the year paid. The rest are deducted evenly over the life of the loan.

EXAMPLE 19

In 20x1, Van Carrey took out a mortgage to buy his principal home. In 20x6, Carrey refinanced his mortgage with a 30-year, $150,000 loan. To get a lower interest rate, he paid three points ($150,000 x 3% = $4,500). Two points ($3,000) were for prepaid interest. One point ($1,500) was charged for services provided by the lender. The payment of points is an established practice in the area. The 2% charged is not more than the amount typically charged for points. Carrey's first payment on the new loan was due May 1. He made eight payments on the loan in 20x6. He uses the cash basis.

Carrey used the proceeds from the new mortgage to repay his existing mortgage. Although the new loan was for his main home, it was not use to buy or improve that home. Thus, he cannot deduct all of the points in 20x6. He deducts the $3,000 evenly over the life of the loan. The $1,000 for the other one point cannot be deducted. In 20x6, his deduction is $133 [($3,000/180 months) × 8 payments].

Investment Interest Expense, Schedule A (Line 13)

Investment interest includes any interest paid to buy or hold on to investment property. It also includes the amortization of points paid to get a loan to buy investments of real estate. Investment property includes stocks, bonds, vacant land, gemstones, and artwork. The IRS defines some investments as "passive" investments. The IRS does not treat interest expense on a passive investment as investment interest. The investor deducts this interest elsewhere on the tax return. For instance, interest expense on rental property (a passive investment) belongs on Schedule E, not on Schedule A. Interest expense on passive investments is discussed in Chapter 9.

The investment interest limitation limits the deduction of investment interest to the amount of the taxpayer's net investment income. Any investment interest not deducted because of this limit may be carried over and used in future years. When carried to the next year, it acts just like that year's investment interest and faces the same limits.

Investment income includes interest, nonqualified dividends, and some royalties. It may also include qualified dividends and the gain from the sale of investments. If the taxpayer chooses to tax qualified dividends and net capital gains at the lower tax rates, then these amounts cannot count as investment income. However, if the taxpayer elects to pay the normal tax rates on qualified dividends and net capital gains, then these amounts count as investment income. This second option may allow the taxpayer to take a higher amount of investment interest as a deduction in the current year.

EXAMPLE 20

Joe Pippen borrows $30,000 to purchase taxable investments. He pays $2,800 of interest on the loan during the year. Pippen is in the 31% tax bracket. During the year his investments produce $1,600 in taxable interest, $600 in qualified dividends, $240 in nonqualified dividends, and $1,600 in net capital gains. The $1,840 of taxable interest and nonqualified dividends count as investment income. However, $2,200 of qualified dividends and net capital gains only count as investment income if Pippen elects to tax these amounts at his normal (31%) tax rate.

Thus, Pippen's options regarding the investment interest are as follows. First, he can choose to tax the $2,200 of qualified dividends and net capital gains at the lower 15% tax rate. This will result in his investment interest expense being limited to his $1,840 of investment income. He would carry over the $960 excess ($2,800 - $1,840) to next tax year. His second option is to elect tax $960 of the qualified dividends and net capital gains at the 31% tax rate. If he does this, then his investment income will increase to $2,800 ($1,840 + $960). This will allow him to deduct the entire $2,800 of investment interest in the current year. He will then be allowed to tax the remaining $1,240 of qualified dividends and net capital gains ($1,840 - $960) at the lower 15% tax rate.

For the purpose of the investment interest deduction limitation, **net investment income** is the excess of the taxpayer's investment income over the amount of investment expenses actually deducted on Schedule A as miscellaneous deductions. These expenses include safe deposit boxes, investment publications, and costs of trust managers. Taxpayers file Form 4952 to compute the net interest reportable on Schedule A (line 13).

Many investors acquire municipal bonds as an investment because the bonds earn tax-free interest. Taxpayers may not deduct the interest paid on funds borrowed to buy or hold on to these bonds. The IRS does not allow tax deductions on expenses related to nontaxable income.

EXAMPLE 21

Included in the Neals' AGI of $143,750 is $2,000 of investment income. They paid investment interest of $4,000 and investment-related expenses of $3,009 (miscellaneous deduction, line 22). The Neals may deduct investment interest of $1,866 computed as follows:

Investment income		$2,000
Investment expenses	$3,009	
Less 2% of AGI*	(2,875)	
Less investment expenses actually deducted		(134)
Net investment income		$1,866

The Neals carry the $2,134 ($4,000 – $1,866) not deducted in 2006 forward to 2007.

* Only the investment expenses in excess of 2% of AGI are deductible on Schedule A.

GIFTS TO CHARITY, SCHEDULE A (LINE 18)

Gifts by Cash or Check, Schedule A (Line 15)

Deductible gifts must be made to qualified charitable organizations. To deduct gifts to foreign countries for disaster relief and other causes, taxpayers must make the donations to qualified U.S. nonprofit organizations.

Gifts may be made by cash, check, or credit card. As a rule, gift donations are deducted in the year that they are made, regardless of whether the taxpayer uses the cash or accrual method. Taxpayers must support each separate gift of $250 or more by getting a written receipt from the charity. The receipt must show the amount of money received and identify any noncash items donated to the charity. The taxpayer must get the receipts by the filing deadline for the tax return. If the charity gave the taxpayer any gifts or services in return for the donation, the receipt must identify these items. If the value of these goods and services is more than $75, the charity must provide a "good faith" estimate of their value. The statement from the charity must also spell out the net amount of the deduction. The amount of the deduction must be reduced by the value of what the taxpayer received in return for their donation.

EXAMPLE 22

The Neals paid $400 a plate for a YMCA benefit and made a cash donation of $3,000 at the banquet. The YMCA's cost for the dinner was $35 per person. The Neals could have bought the same two meals at a bistro for $75. The charitable contribution deduction is $3,725, the difference between the FMV of the dinner and the total donations ($3,000 + $800 meals – $75 FMV). The Neals do not take the YMCA's cost into account. This deduction limit holds true even if they do not go to the banquet.

Gifts given to individuals are not deductible. Taxpayers may deduct only donations to religious, educational and other qualified non-profit organizations. Handouts to people on the street may be generous, but they are not deductible.

EXAMPLE 23

The Neals have a widowed neighbor to whom they gave $200 each month over a four-month period for groceries. The Neals' gifts to the widow do not qualify as a deductible charitable contribution.

Donations to a College or University with the Right to Buy Athletic Tickets

A special rule applies to certain donations to a college or university. When the taxpayer's donation provides the right to buy athletic tickets, 80% of the gift is considered the charitable contribution. The other 20% is the value of the right to buy the tickets. The taxpayer may not deduct as a charitable contribution the value of this right or the purchase price of the tickets paid to the school.

EXAMPLE 24

Jack Reese donates $1,000 to his alma mater. His gift allows him to buy season tickets to the university's football and basketball games. The Code treats $800 of the gift ($1,000 x 80%) as a charitable contribution. The rest ($200) is treated as a nondeductible payment for the right to purchase athletic tickets.

Charitable contributions account for about 14% of the total itemized deductions claimed by taxpayers.

Noncash Gifts, Schedule A (Line 16)

Among other items, taxpayers may deduct car expenses and donations of property. For car expenses, taxpayers may use either the standard mileage rate of $.14 per mile or actual expenses. Limits on deductions of property contributed to a charity follow the same rules that apply to cash contributions. The type of property contributed, the recipient, and the property's use determine the amount of the deduction. Property contributions fall into two categories: (1) ordinary income property (includes short-term capital gain property) and (2) capital gain property held over 12 months. Contributions in both categories may include real estate, tangible personal property, or intangible personal property.

Generally, the deduction for noncash gifts is equal to the FMV of the property at the time of donation. This holds true when the FMV is less than the taxpayer's basis (investment) in the property. However, when the FMV is greater than the basis, the amount of the deduction depends on whether the item takes the form of (1) ordinary income property or long-term capital gain property and (2) how the charity uses the property. When the deduction exceeds $500, the donor shows the details of the donation on Form 8283. For any noncash donation, a letter from the qualifying organization must specify how the organization uses the property.

The Katrina Emergency Tax Relief Act of 2005 allows taxpayers who use their automobile for charitable purposes related to Hurricane Katrina to deduct a (higher) mileage rate equal to 70% of the standard business mileage rate, rounded to the next highest cent. Thus, special mileage rate for 2006 is $.32 per mile ($.445 × 70%, rounded up). The higher mileage rate remains in effect through 2006.

Tangible personal property consists of most property that a taxpayer owns except assets used for trade or business and real estate. The usual items contributed under this category include clothing, toys, furniture, appliances, and books. Normally, the FMV of these items is less than the taxpayer's basis. The FMV of household goods and clothing is their thrift shop or garage sale value. "Blue books" are the common source of values for most types of vehicles.

The intangible assets most commonly donated include stocks, bonds, and mutual funds. For the most part, these assets are widely traded and their FMV is easy to determine.

Taxpayers who donate vehicles to charities can only deduct what the charity obtains from selling it. The charity, under threat of penalties, must report the sales price to both the donor and the IRS.

Ordinary Income Property

Ordinary income property is property that, if sold, would generate income taxed at the regular (ordinary) tax rates. It includes such items as investments held for one year or less, many manuscripts or works of art created by the taxpayer, and business inventory. When the taxpayers donate ordinary income property, tax law limits the value of the contribution to the taxpayer's basis (investment) in the property.

EXAMPLE 25

Stephen Neal built a bookcase and donated it to the local public elementary school. The bookcase was appraised at $800. He spent $125 on materials. The Neals deduct only the $125 cost of materials as this would be ordinary income property if they had sold it. They receive no deduction for the value of Stephen's time in constructing the bookcase.

Capital Gain Property

Capital gain property consists of certain appreciated assets held for more than one year that, if sold, would produce capital gain. This category includes stocks, bonds, and real estate. It also includes most investments and an individual's personal belongings. Usually, FMV at the date of the donation determines the value of the gift. Taxpayers can get written appraisals or stock market quotes to establish the value. Taxpayers who have decided to make donations to qualifying organizations have a tax incentive when the FMV of the item exceeds the taxpayer's basis. The donor avoids reporting the increased value as income. In addition to avoiding paying taxes on the appreciated value of the asset, the donor benefits from the higher FMV of the contribution.

EXAMPLE 26

The Neals contributed a few shares of IBM stock to their church. They bought the stock for $200 several years ago. On the date of the donation, the stock had a FMV of $350. The Neals' noncash charitable contribution equals the FMV of $350. They do not report the $150 of appreciation as income.

Reduced Deduction. The Code allows taxpayers to deduct only their basis in appreciated tangible personal property when such property is not used by the charity directly for its tax exempt purpose. This rule only applies to gifts of appreciated tangible personal property. Thus, the reduced deduction does not apply to gifts of intangible property or to gifts of real estate.

EXAMPLE 27

Terrance Rayburn, an art collector, donates a painting worth $25,000 to the local hospital. Rayburn paid $3,000 for the painting years ago. Since the hospital cannot use the painting in relation to its exempt purpose (treating patients), Rayburn's charitable deduction is limited to $3,000.

EXAMPLE 28

Same as in Example 27, except that Rayburn donates the painting to a local art museum. Rayburn can deduct the full $25,000 FMV of the painting.

EXAMPLE 29

Same as in Example 27, except that Rayburn purchased the painting nine months earlier. Since the painting was not held for more than one year at the time it was donated, it is ordinary income property. The Code limits the deduction of such property to Rayburn's $3,000 basis.

EXAMPLE 30

Same as in Example 27, except that the property donated is stock in a corporation. Stock is an intangible asset and Rayburn held it for more than one year prior to donating it. Thus, the Code allows him to deduct the $25,000 FMV of the stock.

EXAMPLE 31

Same as in Example 27, except that the property donated is land held as an investment. Since land is real property that Rayburn held it for more than one year, he can deduct the $25,000 FMV of the land.

EXAMPLE 32

Same as in Example 27, except that Rayburn paid $25,000 for the painting and at the time it was donated, it was worth $3,000. Since the painting declined in value since Rayburn bought it, it is not capital gain (appreciated) property. The general rule for such gifts allows Rayburn to deduct the ($3,000) FMV of the property.

Nondeductible Gifts

A taxpayer should verify an organization's status before making a gifts. The IRS publishes a list of accepted charities. Many fund-raising groups try to look like qualified charities, but are not. Donations to the lobbying or political action groups of qualified organizations may not be deductible. Other contributions that cannot be deducted include dues to clubs or lodges and tuition at private or religious schools. The cost of raffle tickets is also not deductible.

Limitations

The IRS limits a taxpayer's total charitable contribution deduction each year to 50%, 30%, or 20% of a taxpayer's AGI. The percentage limitation that applies depends on the type of contribution being made and the nature of the charity. The deduction of contributions of cash and property to most organizations may never exceed 50% of AGI. The deduction for appreciated capital gain property contributed to any qualified organization can never exceed 30% of AGI. The 30% limit also applies to donations of cash and ordinary income property to certain private nonoperating foundations. Appreciated capital gain property includes any capital asset held for more than one year that would result in capital gain if sold at its FMV. Avoidance of the 30% of AGI limit occurs if the taxpayer reports the donation of the appreciated capital gain property at the taxpayer's basis. Then the limitation increases to 50% of AGI. When taxpayers contribute capital gain property, instead of cash, to certain private foundations not operating for the benefit of the public at large, the contribution is limited to 20% of AGI.

These limitations sometimes reduce or eliminate a taxpayer's net contribution. Taxpayers carry forward the unused contributions for up to five years. When carried forward, the contribution limits of 50%, 30%, and 20% apply to the specific contributions. For example, an unused contribution with a 30% limitation in 20x1 retains the same 30% limitation when carried to 20x2. If the taxpayer does not itemize, charitable contributions generated in that year are not carried forward.

EXAMPLE 33

In 20x1, Jackie Cho donates stock worth $35,000 to the local university. Cho paid $25,000 for the stock three years ago. In 20x1, Cho's AGI is $60,000. If Cho reports a $35,000 FMV donation for the stock, she will only be able to deduct $18,000 in 20x1 ($60,000 x 30%). She carries over the $17,000 excess to 20x2-20x6. When preparing her tax returns for 20x2-20x6, the same 30% AGI limit will apply to the $17,000 deduction.

EXAMPLE 34

Same as in Example 33, except that Cho elects to report her donation using her $25,000 basis in the stock and apply the 50% AGI limit. Cho will be able to deduct the full $25,000 on Schedule A in 20x1. Since she elected to reduce the amount of her deduction, the $10,000 difference between FMV and her basis in the stock will never be deducted. This is the "price" Cho paid to be able to use the higher 50% AGI limit.

EXAMPLE 35

In the current year, the Neals donated land worth $80,000 to their church. They bought the land years ago for $20,000. The Neals' total contribution of capital gain property includes the $80,000 for the land and $350 for the IBM stock (Example 26). Since they have chosen to deduct the FMV of the appreciated property, the 30% AGI limit applies. Thus, of the $80,350 FMV, the Neals deduct $43,125 in the current year ($143,750 AGI x 30%). They carry forward the $37,225 excess ($80,350 - $43,125) for five years. The Neals' total charitable contribution equals $46,975 ($43,125 + $3,725 to the YMCA from Example 22 + $125 for bookcases from Example 25). Since this total amount does not exceed 50% of their AGI, the Neals deduct $46,975 as an itemized deduction on Schedule A.

In Example 35, the Neals chose to deduct the higher FMV for the donations of the capital gain property and apply the 30% AGI limit. Assuming that their AGI will be large enough in the next five years to absorb the $37,225 carryover, this option will result in the largest tax deduction. Their other option would have been to reduce their deduction to $20,200 ($20,000 basis for the land + $200 for the stock) and apply the 50% AGI limit. However, their deduction would have been lower had they used this option. A third option would have been to have the Neals sell the properties and then donate the net proceeds. If they had done this, they would owe capital gains tax (at a 15% rate) on the $60,150 gain ($80,000 - $20,000 = $60,000 from the land; $350 - $200 = $150 from the stock). After paying the $9,023 tax on capital gains ($60,150 x 15%), they would gift their net proceeds of $71,327 ($80,350 - $9,023) to their church. This would have resulted in charitable donations for the current year of $75,177 ($71,327 + $3,725 + $125). They would have been allowed to deduct $71,875 ($143,750 x 50%) in the current year. They would carry over $3,302 ($75,177 - $71,875) for up to five years. However, their total charitable deduction would be lower by the $9,023 of taxes they would pay to the IRS on the capital gains.

CASUALTY AND THEFT LOSSES, SCHEDULE A (LINE 19)

Individuals are allowed to deduct losses they incur when their personal belongings are stolen or damaged in a casualty. They measure each casualty loss as the *lesser of*: (i) the difference between the FMV before and after the casualty or (ii) the basis of the property. They then must reduce this amount by:

apply to each item, not total

1. Insurance and other proceeds received, and
2. $100 per event (not per item)

see Ex. 26

Taxpayers then total the net loss from each casualty event occurring during the year. From this total they subtract 10% of AGI. Only the remaining amount is deductible.

These provisions make losses from personal casualties hard to deduct. Personal casualty deductions rarely take place without a major uninsured disaster. Lesser casualties generally result in losses below the 10% of AGI threshold and result in no tax benefits. Taxpayers report casualty losses on Form 4684 and bring the net losses over to Schedule A (line 19). If more than one casualty takes place during the year, the law requires a separate Form 4684 for each event.

EXAMPLE 36

Mr. Neal wrecked a personal automobile that originally cost $30,000. This was the Neals only casualty for the year. The vehicle had a FMV of $25,855 before the accident. The estimated FMV after the accident was $1,000. The Neals collected $16,355 of insurance proceeds. Their AGI of $143,750 reduces the casualty loss deduction to zero.

FMV before casualty loss	$25,855	
FMV after casualty loss	(1,000)	
Net casualty loss, change in FMV		$24,855
Basis of the auto		$30,000
Lesser of change in FMV or basis		$24,855
Less insurance proceeds		(16,355)
Less $100 reduction		(100)
Less 10% of AGI		(14,375)
Net casualty loss deduction, not less than $0		$ 0

Generally, taxpayers do not report in gross income reimbursements they receive for temporary living expenses. Such reimbursements are nontaxable to the extent that they compensate a taxpayer for a temporary increase in living expenses. Reimbursements in excess of actual costs are taxable, as are reimbursements that cover normal expenses. While often associated with casualties, these reimbursements do not affect the casualty loss deduction.

EXAMPLE 37

A storm damages the Neals' home. While repairing the home, the Neals live in another house which costs $3,500 per month. The Neals' normal living expenses before the storm were $2,500 per month, which they continue to pay. The insurance company reimburses them at the rate of $4,000 per month. The Neals include $500 per month in gross income for the reimbursement they receive in excess of the temporary living expenses.

Casualty Events

The IRS defines a **casualty** as a sudden, unexpected, or unusual event. Events creating casualty losses include accidents, fires, storms, earthquakes, floods, hurricanes, thefts, and other disasters. Taxpayers should report the loss to a government authority, such as police, to get a written report for their files. Taxpayers having insurance coverage must report the damage and loss of property to the insurance company. Any reimbursements must be deducted to yield the loss for tax purposes. Small Business Administration (SBA) loans and any other loans are not counted as reimbursements when computing the net casualty loss. When a taxpayer has insurance coverage but declines to report the incident in order to avoid raising insurance premiums, no deduction results for the insurance benefits given up.

Events Not Considered Casualties

Many irritating events, although expensive and inconvenient, do not qualify as casualties. Some examples include long-term termite or moth damage, plant disease, property value reduction due to a landslide on a nearby lot, or loss of a diamond ring dropped down a drain.

Proof

The mere loss of an item does not create a casualty. The taxpayer must prove that a theft, accident, or disaster took place. The taxpayer must also establish the amount of the casualty loss. "Before" and "after" pictures (photographs or videocassettes) can help prove the extent of the damage. Objective appraisals of the asset both before and after the event provide evidence of the loss suffered. The IRS generally accepts the cost of repairing the asset as the amount of the loss. However, the cost of repairs cannot be used if the repairs restore the property to a better condition and a higher value than it had before the loss. No deductions are allowed for items deliberately destroyed or damaged by willful neglect. Deductions are allowed only for damage to the taxpayer's own property. Therefore, if a driver hits and destroys the neighbor's fence, the cost of repairing the neighbor's fence would not qualify as a casualty loss on the driver's income tax return.

Year of Deduction

The general rule allows a casualty loss deduction only in the year the casualty occurs. A theft loss is deducted in the year the taxpayer discovers the theft. When the President of the United States designates a disaster area, the taxpayer can elect to deduct the loss in the year of the disaster or in the previous tax year. This special rule makes it possible for taxpayers to get disaster-based tax refunds sooner. Unless the casualty occurs in a federally declared disaster area, a taxpayer should attach complete documentation to the tax return. The documentation must include the costs of the items and the details of the events surrounding the loss. In a disaster area, records generally suffer complete destruction from fire, flood, earthquake, or storms. Because of these conditions, the IRS makes special allowances for reconstructed or alternate information.

LIMITATIONS ON ITEMIZED DEDUCTIONS

The Code imposes an overall limit on itemized deductions to collect more taxes from higher-income taxpayers. For 2006, itemized deductions can be lowered by 2% of the difference between AGI and $150,500 ($75,250 married filing separately). The reduction cannot exceed 53¹/₃% of the deductions subject to the limitation. These include all taxes, mortgage interest and points, charitable contributions, and most miscellaneous deductions (except gambling losses). The deductions not subject to reduction are medical expenses; investment interest; and casualty, theft, and gambling losses.

EXAMPLE 38

In 2006 Art McBurney and his wife file a joint tax return. They report AGI of $183,950. The McBurneys' itemized deductions include: $14,000 of medical expenses, $12,300 of taxes, $12,500 of mortgage interest, $2,800 of investment interest, $26,200 of charitable contributions, $9,500 of casualty losses, and $6,800 of miscellaneous deductions. Their total itemized deductions are as follows:

Medical expenses [$14,000 – (7.5% × $183,950)]	$ 204
Taxes	12,300
Interest expense ($12,500 mortgage + $2,800 investment)	15,300
Charitable contributions	26,200
Casualty losses [$9,500 – $100 – (10% × $183,950)]	0
Miscellaneous deductions [$6,800 – (2% × $183,950)]	3,121
Deductible expenses before overall limitation	$57,125

Itemized deductions subject to limitation are as follows:

Taxes	$12,300	
Mortgage interest	15,300	
Charitable contributions	26,200	
Miscellaneous deductions	3,121	
Total	$56,921	
Reduce otherwise allowable itemized deductions by the *lesser of* (i) $30,358 (53¹/₃% × $56,921) or (ii) $669 [2% × ($183,950 – $150,500)]		(669)
Total itemized deductions		$56,456

This limit on total itemized deductions for high-income taxpayers was enacted as part of the Tax Reform Act of 1986. Currently, less than 5% of all taxpayers are subject to this limit. The original tax law reduced itemized deductions by the *lesser of* (i) 3% of AGI in excess of a certain amount, or (ii) 80% of deductions subject to the limitation. The Economic Growth and Tax Relief Reconciliation Act of 2001 repealed this limit. The repeal is being phased in over four years. In 2006 and 2007, the limit is reduced by one-third. Thus for these years, itemized deductions will be reduced by the *lesser of* (i) 2% (two-thirds of 3%) of excess AGI or (ii) 53 1/3% of deductions subject to the limit (two-thirds of 80%). In 2008 and 2009, the limit will be reduced by another one-third. In those years itemized deductions will be reduced by the *lesser of* (i) 1% (one-third) of excess AGI or (ii) 26 2/3% of deductions subject to the limit (one-third of 80%). When the repeal is fully in effect for tax years beginning after 2009, taxpayers will no longer be required to reduce the amount of their itemized deductions. However, all changes made by the 2001 Tax Act, including the one to repeal of the limit on itemized deductions, are set to expire after 2010. If that happens, then starting in 2011, the tax law will revert back to the original limitation using the 3% and 80% amounts.

Name ______________________________

Section _______________ Date ___________

QUESTIONS AND PROBLEMS

1. **Medical Expense Deduction.** Roger Brown and his wife Jenny maintain a home in which they live with their disabled daughter, Brenda, age 24. AGI on the Brown's joint return is $24,000. Unreimbursed amounts paid for medical and dental expenses during the year follow.

	Brenda	*The Browns*
R. J. Stone, M.D.	$260	$ 250
G. O. Wright, D.D.S.	220	200
Hearing aid		525
Premium on hospital insurance		240
Eyeglasses		130
Toothpaste	20	35
Prescription drugs	275	125
Total	$775	$1,505

Compute the Brown's Schedule A, Medical and Dental Expenses.

2. **Medical Expense Deduction.** Mei Ling, a single taxpayer, has paid the expenses listed during the year. Her AGI is $17,900.

a. In the space after each item, indicate whether or not the item is deductible as a medical expense. If the item is deductible, also enter the amount (without regard to the 7.5% of AGI limitation). Assume that these amounts have already been reduced by insurance reimbursement, when applicable.

Item	*Deductible?*	*Deductible Amount*
1. Premium on health insurance, $386	________	________
2. Premium on life insurance, $275	________	________
3. Premium on automobile accident insurance, $610	________	________
4. Acne cream, $30	________	________
5. Prescription medication, $300	________	________
6. Over-the-counter vitamins, $60	________	________
7. Cosmetics, $150	________	________
8. Dr. Wall, dentist, $120	________	________
9. Dues to health spa, $325	________	________
10. X-ray examination, $60	________	________
11. City Hospital, room and services, $375	________	________
12. Eyeglasses, $125	________	________
13. Cemetery plot, $600	________	________
14. Miles driven for medical—1,000	________	________

Item	*Deductible?*	*Deductible Amount*
15. Illegal drugs, $135	N	0
16. Vacation recommended by doctor to improve general health, $875	N	0
17. Dr. Root, minor surgery, $350	Y	350
18. Used wheelchair, $275	Y	
19. Dr. Spencer for false teeth, $480, and fittings, $100	Y	580

b. Compute Ling's Medical and Dental Expenses deduction on Schedule A.

3. **Medical Reimbursements.** A taxpayer receives reimbursement for a medical expense of $455 in 20x2. What is the proper tax treatment of the $455 if

a. The reimbursed expense was paid in 20x2.

b. The reimbursed expense was paid in 20x1. The taxpayer took the standard deduction in 20x1.

c. Some of the reimbursed expense was paid in 20x0. In 20x0, the taxpayer's total itemized deductions exceeded the standard deduction by $2,000. Medical expenses in excess of 7.5% AGI were $840.

d. Same as in Part c. except that medical expenses in excess of 7.5% AGI were $350.

e. The total reimbursement includes $75 in excess of the taxpayer's current year's medical expenses? (The premium on the policy was paid by the taxpayer.)

f. The total reimbursement includes $75 in excess of the taxpayer's current year's medical expenses? (The employer paid the total cost of the medical insurance plan, and the cost of the medical premiums were not included in the taxpayer's gross income.)

4. **Physical Exams.** If an employee pays for a periodic medical checkup required by an employer, can the amount paid be deducted, and if so, is there any limitation? Explain.

5. **Medical Deduction.** Jack Sparks suffers from arthritis. His doctor has recommended that he install a hot tub at his home to help relieve the pain. Sparks pays $7,500 to have a hot tub installed. The hot tub is expected to increase the value of his home by $3,000. What amount, if any, can Sparks deduct as a medical expense on his tax return?

6. **State and Local Income Taxes.** In April, 2006, Jose Sanchez filed his 2005 federal and state income tax returns. He paid $800 with his federal return and $450 when he filed his state income tax return. During 2006, Sanchez's employer withheld $6,600 and $3,100, respectively for federal and state income taxes. Sanchez files as single.

   a. What amount can Sanchez deduct as an itemized deduction on his 2006 tax return?

   b. When Sanchez files his 2006 tax returns early in 2007, he receives a $90 refund from the federal government and $120 back from the state. Discuss the tax consequences to Sanchez of receiving refunds totaling $210. Sanchez's other itemized deductions in 2006 total $3,000.

   c. Same as in Part b. except that Sanchez's other itemized deductions in 2006 total $1,000.

7. **Estimated State and Local Income Taxes.** Trina Ivy is self-employed. During 2005 and 2006, she makes quarterly estimated tax payments to the state, as shown below. When she files her 2005 tax return in April, 2006, she receives a $300 refund from the state. When she files her 2006 tax return in April, 2007, she owes $650 to the state. Compute Ivy's 2006 state and local income tax deduction on Schedule A.

	Date Paid	*Amount Paid*
1st installment	April 15, 2005	$220
2nd installment	June 15, 2005	220
3rd installment	September 15, 2005	250
4th installment	January 15, 2006	250
1st installment	April 15, 2006	$300
2nd installment	June 15, 2006	300
3rd installment	September 15, 2006	275
4th installment	January 15, 2007	250

8. **Property Tax Allocation.** On March 14, 2005, Rudy Valquez sold a ten-acre piece of property to Eric Volkan for $40,000. In the closing of the transaction, nothing was specified about the payment of property taxes for the year 2005. Volkan paid the entire 2005 property tax bill on January 31, 2006, in the amount of $800. Based on this data, answer the following:

   a. How much of the paid property taxes can Volkan deduct on his tax return?

   b. In which year may Volkan take the property tax deduction on Schedule A for the amount of taxes determined in Part a.? Explain.

   c. What is the amount of paid property taxes, if any, that Volkan may not take as an itemized deduction. Explain how, if at all, Volkan and Valquez should account for this portion of the taxes.

   d. What could Valquez and Volkan have done to avoid the described complications in handling the deductibility of property taxes?

9. **Personal Property Taxes.** Jan Adams lives in a state that imposes a property tax on the value on motor vehicles. Tina Reed lives in a state that imposes a flat $55 renewal fee for license tags. In 2006, Adams pays the state $430 to renew her license tags for 2006. Included in this amount is a $25 license plate fee. The rest is an ad valorem tax. Discuss the tax consequences to each of these taxpayers on their federal income tax returns.

10. Home Mortgage Interest. The Hughes own three homes. Their principal residence is located in Pittsburg. They also own condos in Las Vegas and Miami. The amount of acquisition indebtedness and interest paid on each property is shown below.

Location of Home	*Acquisition Indebtedness*	*Interest Paid*
Pittsburg	$140,000	$ 8,330
Las Vegas	440,000	21,555
Miami	400,000	23,443

a. Compute the Hughes's home mortgage interest deduction.

b. How would your answer to Part a. change if the Pittsburg home were fully paid for, and the Hugheses only had mortgages on the two vacation homes?

11. Home Mortgage Interest. June and Johnny Stephen own a home in Boston. They paid $780,000 for the home three years ago. Their current balance on their mortgage is $660,000. At the time that their home was worth $900,000, they refinanced their mortgage. Their new mortgage is for $800,000. In addition to the home in Boston, the Stephens also own a vacation home in Florida. They paid $350,000 for the home several years ago, and the current mortgage on the second home is $295,000.

a. Discuss how much interest the Stephens are allowed to deduct if the excess proceeds from the refinancing are used to buy or improve their principal residence.

b. Same as in Part a. except that the excess proceeds from the loan are used to buy or improve their Florida home.

c. Same as in Part a. except that the excess proceeds from the loan are used to buy June and Johnny new cars.

12. **Points.** During 2006, Yaeko Lee borrowed money on two different occasions from the local savings bank. She took out the first loan on March 1, 2006, to purchase land for a place to graze horses and livestock as an investment activity. Lee paid $33,000 for the land, making a down payment of $6,000 and borrowing $27,000 for 10 years at 9% interest. To obtain the loan, she was required to pay two points, amounting to $540 (2% × $27,000). In August, 2006, Lee bought a new personal residence. Her mortgage was $48,000 at 8% for 20 years. Lee paid the lender one point, $480 (1% × $48,000).

    a. Determine the amount of points Lee may use as a 2006 interest deduction in connection with the two loans.

    b. What is the tax treatment of any amount paid as points (if any), to the extent not deducted in 2006?

13. **Points.** Years ago, Brad and Angie Devon took out a 30-year mortgage on their vacation home. When they originally took out the loan, they paid the lender $24,000 in points. On September 1 of the current year, the Devons refinanced their $650,000 balance of the mortgage with another 30-year mortgage. To get a lower interest rate, the Devons paid the lender points (prepaid interest) totaling $13,000. At the time of the refinancing, the Devons had unamortized points from the first loan of $18,000. How much can the Devons deduct as points on their tax return for the current year?

14. **Investment Interest.** In 2004 Ginnie and Dave Edlin borrowed money to purchase stocks and taxable corporate bonds. During 2006, the Edlins paid $11,900 of interest in conjunction with this loan. Their investment income for 2006 consists of $5,000 of qualified dividend income, $2,400 of interest income, and $3,300 of long-term capital gain. How much of the $11,900 can the Edlins deduct on their 2006 Schedule A? Be sure to discuss all options available to the Edlins.

15. Interest Deduction. Indicate the correct treatment for each listed item by placing an *X* in the most appropriate column.

Description	*Deductible*	*Nondeductible*
a. Al took out a $20,000 home equity loan to buy an airplane. Al paid interest of $1,750.	________	________
b. Betty paid $300 in credit card interest, including $30 in late fees.	________	________
c. Charles borrowed $50,000 to buy City of Cucamonga bonds. The interest he paid was $3,000. His net investment interest income was $2,500.	________	________
d. David constructed a new home for $175,000. He borrowed $157,500 as a construction loan. The interest on the new mortgage was $8,500.	________	________
e. Eddie paid $80 in interest on a state tax deficiency.	________	________
f. Fred borrowed $125 from his friend to buy this semester's textbooks. Fred paid interest of $25.	________	________
g. Gabe borrowed $60,000 to buy common stock of ASF, Inc. Gabe paid $4,000 interest for this loan. ASF, Inc. paid him $5,000 in dividends.	________	________

16. Interest Deduction. George and Mary Greenfield had an AGI of $98,500 in 2006 (includes $620 of taxable interest income). They incurred the following interest expenses during the year:

Credit card interest	$ 79
Automobile loan interest (older car)	337
Mortgage interest on personal residence	13,500
Investment interest expense on broker's margin account to carry corporate stocks	543
Investment interest expense on broker's margin account to carry tax-exempt bonds	381
Mortgage interest on vacation home	13,080
Points paid on vacation home refinancing (3% × $190,000)	5,700

The original cost of the Greenfields' personal residence was $160,000. It now has a FMV of $166,000. There have been no capital improvements. The balance of the mortgage was $140,000 on January 1, 2006, and $139,000 on December 31, 2006. The vacation home was originally purchased in 1989. On May 1, 2006, the Greenfields took out a ten-year mortgage of $190,000 on the vacation home. They used the proceeds to buy a new car, take a vacation, and consolidate other loans. On December 31, 2006, the mortgage balance was $187,000. Based on the preceding information, determine how much interest the Greenfields may deduct in 2006 on Schedule A.

17. Charitable Contribution Deduction. Place an *X* in the proper column to indicate whether each of the following gifts or other expenditures is deductible as a contribution, deductible but not as a contribution, or not deductible.

Item	*Deductible Contribution*	*Deductible Noncontribution*	*Not Deductible*
a. Cash to American Red Cross	________	________	________
b. Pledge to church	________	________	________
c. Auto expense of church employee	________	________	________
d. Cash to Girl Scouts of America	________	________	________
e. Inherited land to American Legion	________	________	________
f. Cash to political party	________	________	________
g. Cash to public library	________	________	________
h. Clothing to Salvation Army	________	________	________
i. Common stock to St. Mary's	________	________	________
j. Cash to Brigham Young University	________	________	________
k. U.S. Bond to Mayo Clinic	________	________	________
l. Reading at Braille Institute (10 hours @ $7, minimum wage in state)	________	________	________
m. Auto expense for volunteer work with Cancer Society	________	________	________

18. Charitable Contribution—Benefit Event. A professional football team plays a game for the benefit of the Heart Association each year. The admission charge is $32 per ticket, the usual admission price for a professional football game. One-half of the purchase price goes directly to the Heart Association. Denise Clark purchases four tickets at a total cost of $128. Clark itemizes deductions.

a. How much can Clark deduct per ticket as a charitable contribution on her income tax return? Explain.

b. How would your answer to Part a. differ if Clark had no intention of going to the football game and in fact did not go, leaving the tickets unused? Explain.

c. Would your answer be different if $32 were paid for each ticket, while the usual admission charge were $20 per ticket? Explain.

19. Charitable Contribution Deduction. John Dilly, a single man, has an AGI of $60,000. He makes the following contributions:

Item	*FMV*	*Cost*
Check to Temple Beth El		$4,000
Used clothing to Children's Hospital	$100	380
Cash to University of Fullerton		1,200
Check to Mayor Fred's election campaign		300
Used camping equipment to the Boy Scouts of America	300	1,200
Cash to homeless father for his children's clothing		100

Using the listed information, compute Dilly's Gifts to Charity deducted on Schedule A.

20. Charitable Contribution—Property.

a. Can a contribution of a book, an antique, a wild animal, used furniture, or a work of art currently on loan to a museum be deducted? If so, how is such a contribution reported?

b. If qualified contributions exceed the amount that can be deducted in the current year, is the excess deduction lost? Explain.

21. Charitable Contribution—Appreciated Property. A taxpayer contributed land worth $190,000 to the City General Hospital in 2006. The land has been held for five years and had a basis of $72,000. The taxpayer had AGI of $389,200 for 2006.

a. What amount can the taxpayer deduct as a charitable gift in 2006?

b. How would your answer change the property were artwork, rather than land?

22. **Charitable Contribution—Appreciated Property.** An individual with AGI of $49,000 transfers common stock with a market value of $15,000 to an educational institution to be sold and used for scholarships. The stock's basis is $3,575. It was purchased six years ago.

a. What amount may be claimed as an itemized deduction resulting from this contribution?

b. How would your answer to Part a. change if the stock had been purchased 6 months ago?

23. **Charitable Contributions.** Jan Bortz occasionally donates her services as an attorney to a qualified charitable organization (unrelated to Hurricane Katrina relief). During 2006, Bortz spent 45 hours working for the charity. Her normal billing rate id $250 an hour. Bortz drove 115 miles going to and from the offices for the charitable. She also spent $160 for supplies necessary in conjunction with providing her services.

a. Compute Bortz's charitable deduction for 2006.

b. How would your answer to Part a. change if the charitable work was associated with charitable purposes related to Hurricane Katrina?

24. Casualty Loss. On May 10, 2006, Roy and Jane Wilde's home was damaged by a severe storm. The home had been purchased in 1980 for $73,000, excluding the cost of the land. The building's FMV just before the storm was $97,000, and its FMV after the storm was estimated at $79,000. The Wildes collected $15,000 in insurance proceeds, and their 2006 AGI is $22,000. This was their only casualty loss during the year.

a. Determine the amount that the Wildes can report as a casualty loss on Schedule A if they itemize their deductions for 2006.

b. The Wildes lived in a motel while their home was being repaired. The cost of living at the motel was $2,000 each month. Their normal living expenses are $900 per month, but only $500 of these expenses continued during the repair period. They were reimbursed at the rate of $1,900 per month for the three months they lived in the motel. How much of the reimbursement, if any, must they include in gross income?

25. Personal Casualty Loss. Ralph and Jane Tavel left for vacation on December 18, 2006. When they returned home on January 4, 2007, they found their home had been burglarized. Taken from their home were a high definition TV worth $4,000 and artwork worth $22,500. The Tavels had purchased the TV in March 2006 for $5,600. They had purchased the artwork for $8,400 in 2003. Unfortunately, the Tavels allowed their homeowners' insurance to lapse last year. The Tavel's AGI in 2006 and 2007 is $83,000 and $92,000, respectively.

a. In which year can the Tavels claim a casualty loss deduction?

b. Compute the Tavels' casualty loss deduction.

c. How would your answer to Part b. change if the Tavels had insured the artwork and received $7,500 from the insurance company for their loss?

26. Casualty Loss Deduction. Kevin and Jane Steel file a joint return each year. During 2006 their house was burglarized, and the following items were taken. Their AGI for 2006 is $20,000.

Item	*Cost*	*FMV before Theft*
Television set	$ 595	$ 375
Microwave oven	575	400
VCR	850	700
Jewelry	2,200	2,500

The Steels collected $500 from the insurance company. Prepare a worksheet showing the amount of the net casualty loss.

27. Itemized Deductions. Can each of the following payments be deducted from AGI (as an itemized deduction on Schedule A), assuming the amount is within any limitation applicable? Check "Yes" or "No" in the appropriate column. If deductible, indicate the number of the line on Schedule A where the amount would appear.

Item	*Yes*	*No*	*Line Number*
a. Payment to a convalescent home for a person physically incapable of self-care:			
(1) Meals	___	___	___
(2) Lodging	___	___	___
(3) Nursing care	___	___	___
b. Interest paid on a note to purchase and carry municipal bonds	___	___	___
c. Supplementary medical insurance premiums under Medicare	___	___	___
d. Interest on a credit card	___	___	___
e. Interest on a gambling debt	___	___	___
f. Real estate taxes passed on to tenants in the form of a rent increase	___	___	___
g. Interest paid on delinquent income tax	___	___	___
h. Interest paid on a loan to purchase bonds of the City of Wilmington	___	___	___
i. Finance charges paid on revolving credit	___	___	___
j. Interest paid on a life insurance policy loan (The loan was used to buy a new convertible car.)	___	___	___

28. Limitation on Itemized Deductions. Brian Pido (SSN 476-93-3477) files his tax return as a single taxpayer. Pido's AGI for 2006 is $172,552, including $15,000 of taxable interest. Pido has the following itemized deductions for 2006.

Amount paid to the state with 2005 tax return	$ 425
Charitable contributions	5,000
Investment interest expense	12,000
Unreimbursed employee business expenses (from Form 2106)	2,749
Mortgage interest	11,880
Real estate taxes	6,898
State and local income taxes withheld from wages	3,583
Unreimbursed medical	3,200

a. Compute Pido's total itemized deductions for 2006.

b. Prepare Pido's Schedule A on the page that follows.

29. Limitation on Itemized Deductions. Misty and Randy Moore (SSN 937-46-8266) file a joint tax return. Their AGI for 2006 is $184,583, including $2,600 of taxable interest income. They report the following itemized deductions for 2006.

Amount paid to the state with 2005 tax return	$ 888
Charitable contributions	13,540
Investment interest expense	1,800
Unreimbursed employee business expenses (from Form 2106)	749
Mortgage interest	17,559
Real estate taxes	4,582
State and local income taxes withheld from wages	6,682
Unreimbursed medical	15,800

a. Compute the Moores' total itemized deductions for 2006.

b. Prepare the Moores' Schedule A on the page that follows.

(Use for Problem 28.)

SCHEDULES A&B (Form 1040)
Department of the Treasury Internal Revenue Service (99)

Schedule A—Itemized Deductions

(Schedule B is on back)

▶ Attach to Form 1040. ▶ See Instructions for Schedules A&B (Form 1040).

OMB No. 1545-0074
2006
Attachment Sequence No. 07

Name(s) shown on Form 1040 | Your social security number

Medical and Dental Expenses		Caution. Do not include expenses reimbursed or paid by others.		
	1	Medical and dental expenses (see page A-2)	1	
	2	Enter amount from Form 1040, line 38 [2]		
	3	Multiply line 2 by 7.5% (.075)	3	
	4	Subtract line 3 from line 1. If line 3 is more than line 1, enter -0-		4
Taxes You Paid (See page A-2.)	5	State and local income taxes	5	
	6	Real estate taxes (see page A-5)	6	
	7	Personal property taxes	7	
	8	Other taxes. List type and amount ▶	8	
	9	Add lines 5 through 8		9
Interest You Paid (See page A-5.)	10	Home mortgage interest and points reported to you on Form 1098	10	
	11	Home mortgage interest not reported to you on Form 1098. If paid to the person from whom you bought the home, see page A-6 and show that person's name, identifying no., and address ▶	11	
Note. Personal interest is not deductible.	12	Points not reported to you on Form 1098. See page A-6 for special rules	12	
	13	Investment interest. Attach Form 4952 if required. (See page A-6.)	13	
	14	Add lines 10 through 13		14
Gifts to Charity If you made a gift and got a benefit for it, see page A-7.	15	Gifts by cash or check. If you made any gift of $250 or more, see page A-7	15	
	16	Other than by cash or check. If any gift of $250 or more, see page A-7. You **must** attach Form 8283 if over $500	16	
	17	Carryover from prior year	17	
	18	Add lines 15 through 17		18
Casualty and Theft Losses	19	Casualty or theft loss(es). Attach Form 4684. (See page A-8.)		19
Job Expenses and Certain Miscellaneous Deductions (See page A-8.)	20	Unreimbursed employee expenses—job travel, union dues, job education, etc. Attach Form 2106 or 2106-EZ if required. (See page A-8.) ▶	20	
	21	Tax preparation fees	21	
	22	Other expenses—investment, safe deposit box, etc. List type and amount ▶	22	
	23	Add lines 20 through 22	23	
	24	Enter amount from Form 1040, line 38 [24]		
	25	Multiply line 24 by 2% (.02)	25	
	26	Subtract line 25 from line 23. If line 25 is more than line 23, enter -0-		26
Other Miscellaneous Deductions	27	Other—from list on page A-9. List type and amount ▶		27
Total Itemized Deductions	28	Is Form 1040, line 38, over $150,500 (over $75,250 if married filing separately)? ☐ **No.** Your deduction is not limited. Add the amounts in the far right column for lines 4 through 27. Also, enter this amount on Form 1040, line 40. ☐ **Yes.** Your deduction may be limited. See page A-9 for the amount to enter. ▶		28
	29	If you elect to itemize deductions even though they are less than your standard deduction, check here ▶ ☐		

For Paperwork Reduction Act Notice, see Form 1040 instructions. Cat. No. 11330X **Schedule A (Form 1040) 2006**

(Use for Problem 29.)

SCHEDULES A&B (Form 1040)

Department of the Treasury Internal Revenue Service (99)

Schedule A—Itemized Deductions

(Schedule B is on back)

▶ Attach to Form 1040. ▶ See Instructions for Schedules A&B (Form 1040).

OMB No. 1545-0074

2006

Attachment Sequence No. 07

Name(s) shown on Form 1040 | Your social security number

Medical and Dental Expenses		**Caution.** Do not include expenses reimbursed or paid by others.		
	1	Medical and dental expenses (see page A-2)	1	
	2	Enter amount from Form 1040, line 38 [2]		
	3	Multiply line 2 by 7.5% (.075)	3	
	4	Subtract line 3 from line 1. If line 3 is more than line 1, enter -0-		4
Taxes You Paid (See page A-2.)	5	State and local income taxes	5	
	6	Real estate taxes (see page A-5)	6	
	7	Personal property taxes	7	
	8	Other taxes. List type and amount ▶	8	
	9	Add lines 5 through 8		9
Interest You Paid (See page A-5.)	10	Home mortgage interest and points reported to you on Form 1098	10	
Note. Personal interest is not deductible.	11	Home mortgage interest not reported to you on Form 1098. If paid to the person from whom you bought the home, see page A-6 and show that person's name, identifying no., and address ▶	11	
	12	Points not reported to you on Form 1098. See page A-6 for special rules	12	
	13	Investment interest. Attach Form 4952 if required. (See page A-6.)	13	
	14	Add lines 10 through 13		14
Gifts to Charity If you made a gift and got a benefit for it, see page A-7.	15	Gifts by cash or check. If you made any gift of $250 or more, see page A-7	15	
	16	Other than by cash or check. If any gift of $250 or more, see page A-7. You **must** attach Form 8283 if over $500	16	
	17	Carryover from prior year	17	
	18	Add lines 15 through 17		18
Casualty and Theft Losses	19	Casualty or theft loss(es). Attach Form 4684. (See page A-8.)		19
Job Expenses and Certain Miscellaneous Deductions (See page A-8.)	20	Unreimbursed employee expenses—job travel, union dues, job education, etc. Attach Form 2106 or 2106-EZ if required. (See page A-8.) ▶	20	
	21	Tax preparation fees	21	
	22	Other expenses—investment, safe deposit box, etc. List type and amount ▶	22	
	23	Add lines 20 through 22	23	
	24	Enter amount from Form 1040, line 38 [24]		
	25	Multiply line 24 by 2% (.02)	25	
	26	Subtract line 25 from line 23. If line 25 is more than line 23, enter -0-		26
Other Miscellaneous Deductions	27	Other—from list on page A-9. List type and amount ▶		27
Total Itemized Deductions	28	Is Form 1040, line 38, over $150,500 (over $75,250 if married filing separately)? ☐ **No.** Your deduction is not limited. Add the amounts in the far right column for lines 4 through 27. Also, enter this amount on Form 1040, line 40. ☐ **Yes.** Your deduction may be limited. See page A-9 for the amount to enter. ▶		28
	29	If you elect to itemize deductions even though they are less than your standard deduction, check here ▶ ☐		

For Paperwork Reduction Act Notice, see Form 1040 instructions. Cat. No. 11330X **Schedule A (Form 1040) 2006**

30. Internet Problem: Researching Instructions to Form 4684. If a taxpayer experiences a loss from a deposit in a credit union that became financially insolvent, what options are available for recognizing this loss on the tax return?

Go to the IRS Web site. Locate the Instructions for Form 4684 and find the solution to the above question.

See Appendix A for instructions on use of the IRS Web site.

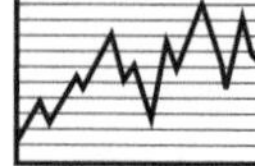

31. Business Entity Problem: This problem is designed for those using the "business entity" approach. The solution may require information from Chapters 14 and 15.

A corporation has taxable income before consideration of charitable contributions of $350,000.

a. If the corporation donates $50,000 to a recognized charity, what are the tax implications to the company?

b. By what date must the corporation make its donation?

c. If the above company is an S corporation, what are the tax implications of the charitable contribution to the company?

d. If the above company was a partnership, what are the tax implications of the charitable contribution to the company?

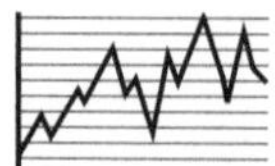

32. Business Entity Problem: This problem is designed for those using the "business entity" approach. The solution may require information from Chapters 14 and 15.

The Blasto Company lost its entire office building in a fire. The adjusted basis of the building was $800,000. Insurance proceeds were only $740,000. The company's taxable income before consideration of any casualty loss was $2,350,000. What amount, if any, may the company deduct as a casualty loss?

COMPREHENSIVE PROBLEMS

33. Marcus and Debra Cross (SSN 397-73-8399) own three homes. Information regarding the amount of acquisition indebtedness, as well as interest and taxes paid on each home during the year is as follows:

	Acquisition Indebtedness	*Interest Paid*	*Taxes Paid*
Principal residence	$240,000	$18,330	$2,400
Vacation home #1	300,000	18,583	2,800
Vacation home #2	350,000	19,044	3,400

During 2006, the Crosses made cash gifts totaling $12,000 to various qualified public charities. The Crosses gifted 150 shares of stock to their church during 2006. They purchased 100 shares of the stock for $10 a share in 2004. The other 50 shares were purchased earlier in 2006 for $18 a share. At the time the shares were donated to the church, their fair market value was $24 a share. The Crosses' only other itemized deductions for 2006 were $4,240 that their employers withheld from their paychecks for state income taxes. The Crosses' AGI for 2006 is $208,640.

Prepare the Crosses' Schedule A on the following page.

34. Maurice Prior (SSN 839-44-9222) files separately from his spouse. Below is a summary of expenditures that Maurice has made. In addition, Prior's employer withheld $3,967 and $13,550 in state and federal income taxes in 2006. His employer also withheld $6,511 in social security and Medicare taxes. Prior's AGI for 2006 is $140,942.

Prior made the following quarterly estimated payments taxes for 2005 and 2006.

Date Paid	*Amount Paid to the State*	*Amount Paid to the IRS*
April 15, 2005	$700	$3,500
June 15, 2005	700	3,500
September 15, 2005	800	3,500
January 15, 2006	800	3,500
April 15, 2006	$1,200	$5,000
June 15, 2006	1,200	5,000
September 15, 2006	1,200	5,000
January 15, 2007	1,200	5,000

Use for Problem 33.

SCHEDULES A&B (Form 1040)

Department of the Treasury Internal Revenue Service (99)

Schedule A—Itemized Deductions

(Schedule B is on back)

▶ Attach to Form 1040. ▶ See Instructions for Schedules A&B (Form 1040).

OMB No. 1545-0074

2006

Attachment Sequence No. 07

Name(s) shown on Form 1040

Your social security number

Medical and Dental Expenses		**Caution.** Do not include expenses reimbursed or paid by others.		
	1	Medical and dental expenses (see page A-2)	1	
	2	Enter amount from Form 1040, line 38 [2]		
	3	Multiply line 2 by 7.5% (.075)	3	
	4	Subtract line 3 from line 1. If line 3 is more than line 1, enter -0-		4
Taxes You Paid (See page A-2.)	5	State and local income taxes	5	
	6	Real estate taxes (see page A-5)	6	
	7	Personal property taxes	7	
	8	Other taxes. List type and amount ▶	8	
	9	Add lines 5 through 8		9
Interest You Paid (See page A-5.)	10	Home mortgage interest and points reported to you on Form 1098	10	
	11	Home mortgage interest not reported to you on Form 1098. If paid to the person from whom you bought the home, see page A-6 and show that person's name, identifying no., and address ▶	11	
Note. Personal interest is not deductible.	12	Points not reported to you on Form 1098. See page A-6 for special rules	12	
	13	Investment interest. Attach Form 4952 if required. (See page A-6.)	13	
	14	Add lines 10 through 13		14
Gifts to Charity If you made a gift and got a benefit for it, see page A-7.	15	Gifts by cash or check. If you made any gift of $250 or more, see page A-7	15	
	16	Other than by cash or check. If any gift of $250 or more, see page A-7. You **must** attach Form 8283 if over $500	16	
	17	Carryover from prior year	17	
	18	Add lines 15 through 17		18
Casualty and Theft Losses	19	Casualty or theft loss(es). Attach Form 4684. (See page A-8.)		19
Job Expenses and Certain Miscellaneous Deductions (See page A-8.)	20	Unreimbursed employee expenses—job travel, union dues, job education, etc. Attach Form 2106 or 2106-EZ if required. (See page A-8.) ▶	20	
	21	Tax preparation fees	21	
	22	Other expenses—investment, safe deposit box, etc. List type and amount ▶	22	
	23	Add lines 20 through 22	23	
	24	Enter amount from Form 1040, line 38 [24]		
	25	Multiply line 24 by 2% (.02)	25	
	26	Subtract line 25 from line 23. If line 25 is more than line 23, enter -0-		26
Other Miscellaneous Deductions	27	Other—from list on page A-9. List type and amount ▶		27
Total Itemized Deductions	28	Is Form 1040, line 38, over $150,500 (over $75,250 if married filing separately)? ☐ **No.** Your deduction is not limited. Add the amounts in the far right column for lines 4 through 27. Also, enter this amount on Form 1040, line 40. ☐ **Yes.** Your deduction may be limited. See page A-9 for the amount to enter. ▶		28
	29	If you elect to itemize deductions even though they are less than your standard deduction, check here ▶ ☐		

For Paperwork Reduction Act Notice, see Form 1040 instructions. Cat. No. 11330X **Schedule A (Form 1040) 2006**

Other taxes Prior paid during 2006 include $3,290 in real estate taxes; $296 for ad valorem taxes on his boat; $800 for a special assessment for a new sidewalk; and $32 in federal excise taxes on his telephone usage.

Prior paid home mortgage interest totaling $16,940 during 2006, and he gave cash totaling $1,500 to his church.

Prepare Prior's Schedule A on the following page.

35. John Saad (SSN 432-61-7809) and his wife Mary file a joint return. Their 2006 AGI is $162,000, including dividends and interest income of $5,000. The Saads assembled the following list of expenses:

Medical expenses	$14,300
Jacuzzi for John's aching back	2,500
Real estate taxes	4,400
Assessment for street repairs	1,200
State and local income taxes	4,800
Federal income tax	22,300
Sales taxes	785
Mortgage interest	5,200
Credit card interest	945
Investment interest	3,700
Charitable contributions (cash)	6,400
Uninsured damage to auto from accident	3,300

Prepare the Saads' Schedule A on the page that follows.

(Use for Problem 34.)

SCHEDULES A&B (Form 1040)

Department of the Treasury Internal Revenue Service (99)

Schedule A—Itemized Deductions

(Schedule B is on back)

▶ Attach to Form 1040. ▶ See Instructions for Schedules A&B (Form 1040).

OMB No. 1545-0074

2006

Attachment Sequence No. 07

Name(s) shown on Form 1040 | Your social security number

Medical and Dental Expenses		**Caution.** Do not include expenses reimbursed or paid by others.		
	1	Medical and dental expenses (see page A-2)	1	
	2	Enter amount from Form 1040, line 38 [2]		
	3	Multiply line 2 by 7.5% (.075)	3	
	4	Subtract line 3 from line 1. If line 3 is more than line 1, enter -0-		4
Taxes You Paid (See page A-2.)	5	State and local income taxes	5	
	6	Real estate taxes (see page A-5)	6	
	7	Personal property taxes	7	
	8	Other taxes. List type and amount ▶	8	
	9	Add lines 5 through 8		9
Interest You Paid (See page A-5.)	10	Home mortgage interest and points reported to you on Form 1098	10	
	11	Home mortgage interest not reported to you on Form 1098. If paid to the person from whom you bought the home, see page A-6 and show that person's name, identifying no., and address ▶	11	
Note. Personal interest is not deductible.	12	Points not reported to you on Form 1098. See page A-6 for special rules	12	
	13	Investment interest. Attach Form 4952 if required. (See page A-6.)	13	
	14	Add lines 10 through 13		14
Gifts to Charity	15	Gifts by cash or check. If you made any gift of $250 or more, see page A-7	15	
If you made a gift and got a benefit for it, see page A-7.	16	Other than by cash or check. If any gift of $250 or more, see page A-7. You **must** attach Form 8283 if over $500	16	
	17	Carryover from prior year	17	
	18	Add lines 15 through 17		18
Casualty and Theft Losses	19	Casualty or theft loss(es). Attach Form 4684. (See page A-8.)		19
Job Expenses and Certain Miscellaneous Deductions	20	Unreimbursed employee expenses—job travel, union dues, job education, etc. Attach Form 2106 or 2106-EZ if required. (See page A-8.) ▶	20	
	21	Tax preparation fees	21	
(See page A-8.)	22	Other expenses—investment, safe deposit box, etc. List type and amount ▶	22	
	23	Add lines 20 through 22	23	
	24	Enter amount from Form 1040, line 38 [24]		
	25	Multiply line 24 by 2% (.02)	25	
	26	Subtract line 25 from line 23. If line 25 is more than line 23, enter -0-		26
Other Miscellaneous Deductions	27	Other—from list on page A-9. List type and amount ▶		27
Total Itemized Deductions	28	Is Form 1040, line 38, over $150,500 (over $75,250 if married filing separately)? ☐ **No.** Your deduction is not limited. Add the amounts in the far right column for lines 4 through 27. Also, enter this amount on Form 1040, line 40. ☐ **Yes.** Your deduction may be limited. See page A-9 for the amount to enter. ▶		28
	29	If you elect to itemize deductions even though they are less than your standard deduction, check here ▶ ☐		

For Paperwork Reduction Act Notice, see Form 1040 instructions. Cat. No. 11330X **Schedule A (Form 1040) 2006**

(Use for Problem 35.)

SCHEDULES A&B (Form 1040)
Department of the Treasury Internal Revenue Service (99)

Schedule A—Itemized Deductions

(Schedule B is on back)

▶ Attach to Form 1040. ▶ See Instructions for Schedules A&B (Form 1040).

OMB No. 1545-0074
2006
Attachment Sequence No. **07**

Name(s) shown on Form 1040 | Your social security number

Medical and Dental Expenses		**Caution.** Do not include expenses reimbursed or paid by others.				
	1	Medical and dental expenses (see page A-2)	1			
	2	Enter amount from Form 1040, line 38 [2]				
	3	Multiply line 2 by 7.5% (.075)	3			
	4	Subtract line 3 from line 1. If line 3 is more than line 1, enter -0-			4	
Taxes You Paid (See page A-2.)	5	State and local income taxes	5			
	6	Real estate taxes (see page A-5)	6			
	7	Personal property taxes	7			
	8	Other taxes. List type and amount ▶	8			
	9	Add lines 5 through 8			9	
Interest You Paid (See page A-5.)	10	Home mortgage interest and points reported to you on Form 1098	10			
	11	Home mortgage interest not reported to you on Form 1098. If paid to the person from whom you bought the home, see page A-6 and show that person's name, identifying no., and address ▶	11			
Note. Personal interest is not deductible.	12	Points not reported to you on Form 1098. See page A-6 for special rules	12			
	13	Investment interest. Attach Form 4952 if required. (See page A-6.)	13			
	14	Add lines 10 through 13			14	
Gifts to Charity If you made a gift and got a benefit for it, see page A-7.	15	Gifts by cash or check. If you made any gift of $250 or more, see page A-7	15			
	16	Other than by cash or check. If any gift of $250 or more, see page A-7. You **must** attach Form 8283 if over $500	16			
	17	Carryover from prior year	17			
	18	Add lines 15 through 17			18	
Casualty and Theft Losses	19	Casualty or theft loss(es). Attach Form 4684. (See page A-8.)			19	
Job Expenses and Certain Miscellaneous Deductions (See page A-8.)	20	Unreimbursed employee expenses—job travel, union dues, job education, etc. Attach Form 2106 or 2106-EZ if required. (See page A-8.) ▶	20			
	21	Tax preparation fees	21			
	22	Other expenses—investment, safe deposit box, etc. List type and amount ▶	22			
	23	Add lines 20 through 22	23			
	24	Enter amount from Form 1040, line 38 [24]				
	25	Multiply line 24 by 2% (.02)	25			
	26	Subtract line 25 from line 23. If line 25 is more than line 23, enter -0-			26	
Other Miscellaneous Deductions	27	Other—from list on page A-9. List type and amount ▶			27	
Total Itemized Deductions	28	Is Form 1040, line 38, over $150,500 (over $75,250 if married filing separately)? ☐ **No.** Your deduction is not limited. Add the amounts in the far right column for lines 4 through 27. Also, enter this amount on Form 1040, line 40. ☐ **Yes.** Your deduction may be limited. See page A-9 for the amount to enter. ▶			28	
	29	If you elect to itemize deductions even though they are less than your standard deduction, check here ▶ ☐				

For Paperwork Reduction Act Notice, see Form 1040 instructions. Cat. No. 11330X **Schedule A (Form 1040) 2006**

6

Other Itemized Deductions

CHAPTER CONTENTS

CHAPTER OVERVIEW

Chapter 5 examined itemized deductions that are somewhat personal in nature: medical expenses, taxes, interest, charitable contributions, and casualty and theft losses. This chapter focuses on the remaining itemized deductions: job-related expenses and miscellaneous deductions. It illustrates the flow of data from Form 2106, Employee Business Expenses, to Schedule A and then to Form 1040.

JOB EXPENSES AND MOST OTHER MISCELLANEOUS DEDUCTIONS

Schedule A allows for two types of miscellaneous deductions. One type is subject to a 2% AGI floor. The other is not. "Job Expenses and Most Other Miscellaneous Deductions" provides for job-related expenses of employees and other itemized deductions not reported elsewhere. Taxpayers must reduce the total of these other expenses by 2% of the AGI before taking a deduction. Taxpayers report the net amount of these expenses on Schedule A (line 26).

While limiting most miscellaneous deductions to this 2% floor, the IRS allows some deductions in full. These are called "Other Miscellaneous Deductions" on Schedule A (line 27). This book covers these deductions later in the chapter.

While most employees report the total amount of their job-related expenses on Schedule A, they use Form 2106 to compute their total expenses. A notable exception is the "statutory employee."

Statutory employees include full-time employees in the following occupations: outside salesperson, life insurance sales agent, certain agent-driver/commission-driver, and home-based piece-goods worker with income reported on a W-2. The tax law treats statutory employees as self-employed taxpayers. These workers deduct all work-related expenses on Schedule C. However, self-employment taxes do not apply since the employer and the employee must each pay the FICA taxes through the tax withholding system. The employer alerts the IRS of this situation by checking the "Statutory Employee" box on the W-2. If the employer neglects to mark this box, the special treatment still applies when the taxpayer qualifies in all other respects.

EMPLOYEE BUSINESS EXPENSES, FORM 2106

Employees incurring job-related expenses may or may not be reimbursed by their employers. They deduct any unreimbursed expenses from AGI as miscellaneous itemized deductions by completing Form 2106. Treatment of reimbursed expenses depends on whether the reimbursement comes from an "accountable" or "nonaccountable" reimbursement plan.

Accountable Reimbursement Plans

Employees receiving reimbursement under an accountable plan do not report them in gross income. Likewise, employers do not report them on the employee's Form W-2. On the expense side, employees do not deduct reimbursed expenses on their tax returns. However, when the expenses exceed the reimbursements, the employee reports all expenses and reimbursements on Form 2106 in order to deduct the excess on Schedule A.

Reimbursements from an accountable plan are those that meet each of the following requirements:

1. To be reimbursed, employees must account for (substantiate) their expenses to the employer.
2. Employees must return any reimbursement in excess of the substantiated expenses covered under the plan.

Employee business expense records must include six elements:

1. Amount
2. Date
3. Place
4. Business purpose
5. Business relationship
6. Identity of individuals

To satisfy the substantiation requirement, employees must keep good records. The IRS will accept date books, logs, and trip sheets to verify travel and mileage. To support other expenses, the employee must keep receipts and paid bills, canceled checks, expense reports, etc. The IRS usually does not require a receipt for expenses less than $75. However, any reimbursement for lodging requires a receipt. If the taxpayer loses any records, the IRS may accept written statements made by witnesses.

Nonaccountable Reimbursement Plans

If an employer's reimbursement program does not require employees to substantiate their expenses or allows them to keep excess reimbursements, the arrangement is not an accountable plan. Under these plans, employers report reimbursements as wages on the employee's Form W-2. Thus, employees include them as gross income on their tax return. Employees then deduct all expenses using Form 2106 and Schedule A. Even though these plans are "nonaccountable," taxpayers must still substantiate their expense claims.

Reimbursements under a nonaccountable plan are subject to income and FICA taxes. After paying these taxes, the employee is left with less reimbursement than expense. Also, some or all of the expense may be disallowed as a result of the 2% AGI rule. Accountable plans avoid all of this.

EXAMPLE 1

Sark Industries pays its sales staff a $1,000 a month to cover their travel expenses. Sark does not require that its workers to submit any receipts for their expenses. Jimmy Randen is one of Sark's salesmen. Randen's annual salary is $60,000. During the year, Randen receives $12,000 in travel allowances from Sark. According to his receipts, his deductible travel expenses total $15,420. Because Sark runs a nonaccountable reimbursement plan, it must add the travel allowances as taxable wages on its employees' W-2s. Thus, Randen's taxable wages reported on Form W-2 will be $72,000 ($60,000 + $12,000). Randen can deduct the entire $15,420 on Schedule A as a miscellaneous itemized deduction (the type subject to the 2% of AGI floor). If Randen does not itemize, he will be taxed on the $12,000 with no offsetting deduction for his travel expense.

EXAMPLE 2

Same as in Example 1 except that Sark requires that its employees submit receipts to support their travel expenses and requires that any excess amounts be returned. Since Sark now runs an accountable reimbursement plan, Randen's taxable wages will show up on his W-2 as $60,000. He will report the $15,240 in actual expenses and the $12,000 reimbursement on Form 2106. He will then be allowed to deduct the $3,240 excess as a miscellaneous itemized deduction on Schedule A. Even if Randen does not itemize, or if his total miscellaneous itemized deductions do not exceed 2% of AGI, he will avoid being taxed on the $12,000 reimbursement he received during the year.

UNREIMBURSED EMPLOYEE BUSINESS EXPENSES REPORTED ON FORM 2106

- Vehicle(s) used for business
- Parking fees, tolls, and local transportation
- Travel while away from home, including lodging, airfare, car rental, etc.
- Other business expenses not included elsewhere on Form 2106
- Meals and entertainment

Vehicle Expenses

Most taxpayers can choose to use either the standard mileage rate or actual expenses when using a vehicle for business purposes. Under both methods, the taxpayer keeps track of three types of information on vehicle usage:

- Date the vehicle was first used for work
- Total miles driven during the year
- Total work-related miles driven

Taxpayers provide this information for each vehicle driven for business. The IRS also requires employees to respond to four specific questions on Form 2106:

1. Is another vehicle available for use?
2. Does the employer provide for personal use of the vehicle?
3. Does the taxpayer have evidence to support the deduction?
4. Is the evidence written?

Responding "No" to the third or fourth question may trigger an audit. If there is an audit, lack of evidence can result in the loss of the deductions.

Employee Transportation

Employees may deduct the cost of getting from one job location to another in the course of their employment. Normally, commuting costs are not deductible. These costs include getting to and from work as well as parking while at work. However, when a taxpayer has two jobs, the cost of getting from one job to the other is deductible. When taxpayers go home before going to the second job, they base their deduction on the distance between the two jobs. To claim a deduction, employees must keep detailed records of their business mileage.

EXAMPLE 3

Dena Tyra works for two different employers. Each morning, Tyra drive 25 miles to her first job. After work, she then drives 15 miles to her second job. At the end of the day, she drives 22 miles home. The 25 miles Tyra drives to her first job and the 22 miles she drives home from her second job are nondeductible commuting miles. The 15 miles she drives between the two jobs counts as deductible business miles. As an employee, Tyra deducts her deductible employee transportation as a miscellaneous itemized deduction (subject to the 2% AGI rule). She can use either the standard mileage rate or the actual mileage method to compute her deduction.

EXAMPLE 4

Same as in Example 3 except that Tyra drives home between the two jobs to change clothes. The tax laws require that Tyra base her deduction on the mileage between the two jobs. Therefore, the Trya's deduction does not change.

Standard Mileage Rate

For 2006, the standard mileage rate is $.445 per mile for each business mile driven. The taxpayer must prove the business miles driven for all vehicles by keeping detailed records. When an employer reimburses an employee for business miles at a rate in excess of this amount, the employee reports the excess in gross income. To take advantage of the standard mileage rate, the taxpayer cannot have used an accelerated depreciation method in prior years. (see Chapter 8.) Those using the standard rate may also deduct parking and toll fees.

EXAMPLE 5

Winn Yoshi uses her personal car to make deliveries for her employer. During 2006, Yoshi drove 7,200 miles, of which 1,820 were work-related. Yoshi deducts $810 (1,820 x $.445) as vehicle expenses. She reports this amount on Form 2106, which supports her employee business expense deduction on Schedule A (as a miscellaneous itemized deduction).

EXAMPLE 6

Same as in Example 5 except that Yoshi's employer reimburses her $.40 a mile for the 1,820 of business miles she drove during the year. Yoshi can deduct as an employee business expense the excess of the $810 over the $728 (1,820 x $.40) that she was reimbursed during the year.

The standard mileage method requires taxpayers to reduce the adjusted basis of the vehicle using the following recovery rates for the total business miles driven each year. Taxpayers use the rate that applies to each year of business use.

Year	*Rate Per Mile*
2005–2006	$.17
2003–2004	$.16
2001–2002	$.15
2000	$.14

Therefore, taxpayers compute the depreciation built into the standard mileage rates to adjust the vehicle's basis before a sale or exchange. The adjusted basis of the vehicle affects the gain or loss when sold or exchanged (see Chapter 10).

Actual Expenses

When the actual expenses exceed the standard rate, taxpayers can deduct the actual costs of operating the vehicle(s). When using the actual method, taxpayers must keep records of their car expenses. They also must keep a record of their total miles and total business miles driven during the year. The deductible amount equals the total car expenses times the percentage of business use during the year.

Taxpayers compute depreciation using the regular depreciation methods. These methods include MACRS, which allows employees to take more depreciation in the earlier years of the vehicle's life. The "luxury automobile" rules restrict the total annual depreciation on vehicles. The listed property rules require using straight-line depreciation when the business use does not exceed 50%. The depreciation rules are the focus of Chapter 8.

ITEMS INCLUDED IN DEDUCTIBLE VEHICLE EXPENSES

- Depreciation
- Lease and rental payments
- Gasoline, oil, and lubrications
- Insurance, license, and auto club fees
- Maintenance, repairs, and parts
- Personal property taxes
- Garage rent

Leasing

When leasing a car, employees may elect to use the standard mileage rate, or they may elect to deduct the entire business portion of the monthly lease payments, including the personal property tax and sales tax portions of the payment. When using the actual expense method, employees enter these amounts on Form 2106 as "Vehicle rentals" (line 24a). For more expensive cars, the IRS limits the benefit of deducting business lease payments. It requires taxpayers to report an additional amount in gross income that effectively reduces the lease expense reported on Form 2106. This additional lease income brings the expense deduction for leasing an automobile closer to the automobile expenses allowed to vehicle owners. The IRS publishes the specific tables for this "lease income" in Publication 463 (see Chapter 8).

Parking Fees, Tolls, and Transportation That Do Not Involve Overnight Travel

In addition to car expenses, employees can claim deductible parking and other transportation expenses regardless of whether the standard rate or the actual expense method of reporting is used. Employees using transportation in the course of business or work can deduct the costs of local transportation expenses. Deductible transportation expenses include the costs of parking (away from work), tolls, cab fares, buses, trains, airfares, and shuttles.

EXAMPLE 7

Harvey Bergmann uses his personal car for his work as an employee at Hargrove Enterprises. In 2006, Bergmann drove 8,300 business-related miles and 21,430 total miles. For 2006, Bergmann's expenses for the car are as follows. In addition to these amounts, Bergmann paid $253 in business-related parking and tolls during the year.

Depreciation	$1,875
Gas	2,670
Insurance	1,540
License tags	75
Repairs and maintenance	850
	$7,010

Under the actual mileage method, Bergmann deducts $2,968 [($7,010 x 8,300/21,430) + $253]. Under the standard mileage method, his deduction would be $3,947 [(8,300 x $.445) + $253]. Under both methods, the business parking and tolls are deducted in addition to the other car-related expenses. Based on these calculations, Bergmann would be better off using the standard mileage method to deduct his car expenses. He can use this method as long as he has not used an accelerated depreciation method in a prior year with respect to this car.

Travel Expenses

Employee travel expenses include amounts paid or charged when an employee is temporarily away from home overnight for work-related reasons. "Temporary" absences from home are those not exceeding one year. Generally, travel expenses are not deductible when the absence exceeds one year. The IRS defines "home" as an employee's workplace, regardless of where the employee lives. Travel expenses include all transportation costs, plus lodging and the incidental costs incurred while away from home. Employees can deduct meals purchased while traveling (subject to the same 50% limitation as other meals and entertainment). A spouse's travel expenses are deducted only when the spouse actually works during the bulk of the trip and the spouse works for the same employer.

EXAMPLE 8

Kathy Knott's travel expenses included airfare $120, hotel $75, car rental $35, meals $150, and a bathing suit $25. Knott's total travel expenses amount to $230 ($120 + $75 + $35). Knott includes the $150 cost of meals with her other meals and entertainment, but only 50% can be deducted. The bathing suit does not qualify as a travel expense.

Per Diem Option

The IRS allows employers to reimburse their employees using a flat daily amount that covers the costs of meals, lodging, and incidentals. This flat daily amount is called a **per diem**. When the per diem approach is used, the employer must use it with respect to that employee for all travel during the year. The IRS announces per diem rates for various cities or counties. The per diem rates can change every few months. These rates can be found in IRS Publication 1546, which is available from the IRS website at www.irs.gov. Separate rates apply to lodging and for meals and incidentals. Since the per diem rates include the value of meals, employees using Form 2106 must split the daily rate between travel (line 3) and meals and entertainment (line 5). Only 50% of the meal allowance is deductible.

When the employer's per diem allowance is less than or equal to the allowable federal rate, nothing is reported on the employee's W-2. This is true even if the employee's actual expenses are less than the allowance received. Not only is the excess is not taxable, but the employee does not have to return the excess. However, when the employer's per diem allowance exceeds the federal rate, the employer reports the excess as compensation to the employee on Form W-2.

When the reimbursement is less than or equal to the federal rate and the actual expenses do not exceed the reimbursement, employees do not report the reimbursement or the expenses on their tax returns. If the actual expenses exceed the reimbursement, employees may deduct the excess on Schedule A by filling out Form 2106 and reporting all expenses and reimbursements. In this situation, employees must be able to prove the amounts of their expenses.

Employees who are not reimbursed for business-related meals may take a deduction on Form 2106 for the federal per diem for meals instead of deducting their actual meal costs. Of course, this amount must be reduced by 50% as with all meals and entertainment. Employees cannot deduct the per diem rate for lodging. Only the actual cost of lodging is deductible. Use of the per diem meal allowance as a measure of the meal expense also applies to self-employed individuals.

EXAMPLE 9

Brad Mayo's employer sends him on a business trip to New York City. Mayo is gone for 3 days, and is reimbursed for his airfare, transportation to and from the airport and hotel, and a per diem for meals and lodging. At the time of his travels, the per diem rate for New York City is $332 ($64 for meals and $268 for lodging). Mayo's actual costs for meals and lodging for his trip were $820. Although the amount of the reimbursement ($332 x 3 = $996) exceeds Mayo's actual expenses, he is not required to return the excess to his employer. Furthermore, he is not taxed on the excess.

EXAMPLE 10

Same as in Example 9 except that Mayo's actual costs of meals and lodging were $1,154. He reports both the expenses and reimbursement on Form 2106. He deducts the excess (after subtracting out 50% of the meals) as an employee business expense on Schedule A (as a miscellaneous itemized deduction subject to the 2% AGI rule).

Business and Pleasure

Employees who combine business and pleasure on the same trip face limits on the deduction. There are different limits for trips within the United States and foreign travel. When traveling in the United States on a trip primarily for business (more than 50% work-related activity), employees deduct 100% of the travel expenses to and from the destination. Once at their destination, they deduct only the work-related expenses (lodging, meals, and local transportation for work days only). On 50% or less work-related trips, employees deduct only the work-related expenses. They do not deduct any airfare or other traveling costs getting to and from their destination.

When counting business and personal days, travel days count as business days. Also, weekends and holidays count as business days if a business day precedes and follows the weekend or holiday. If this condition is not met, the weekend or holiday counts as personal time (unless business is conducted on that day).

EXAMPLE 11

Andy Blake attends a three-day seminar in Boston. After the seminar he stays five additional days in Boston to visit friends from college. Blake spent $450 on airfare, $250 a night for lodging, and $100 a day for meals. Because Blake's trip was not primarily for business, the cost of his airfare is not deductible. He can, however, deduct the hotel and 50% of the cost of his meals for the three days he spent conducting business.

On trips involving travel outside the United States, the employee must separate the business and personal portions of the trip. The employee divides the business and personal costs based on the time devoted to each activity. For instance, trips composed of 40% personal activities permit the employee to deduct only 60% of the total travel expenses. However, if the trip is primarily personal, no travel expenses to and from destination are deductible. Any of the following three conditions eliminates the need to allocate travel expenses to and from destination: (1) The employee has no control over arranging the trip and there is no element of vacation; (2) The employee travels away from home for less than eight days; and (3) The personal portion of the trip is less than 25%. Business days include days devoted to travel when the travel days immediately precede or follow a business day.

EXAMPLE 12

Edward Santiago attends a trade show in Paris that begins on Tuesday and ends on Friday, with no meetings on Wednesday or Thursday. Santiago travels to the trade show on Monday and returns home on Saturday. The trip lasts less than eight days. Therefore, the trip qualifies as a deductible business trip, and all qualified travel expenses to and from destination are deductible. The rest of the expenses must be allocated between business and personal. The business expenses (but only 50% of the meals and entertainment) would be deducted.

EXAMPLE 13

Toddra Milton is sent by her employer to a training seminar in London. She is gone for a total of 10 days. To avoid jet lag, she flies to London on Saturday. The seminar takes place Monday through Friday, and she stays an extra 3 days in London to sightsee. Milton's business days include her travel day (Saturday) and the following day (Sunday) since it is a weekend day that precedes a business day (Monday). The five days of training also count as business days, as would the travel day home. Thus, of the 10 days Milton is gone, 8 count as business days. Since none of the three exceptions apply, she must allocate her travel costs between business and personal days. Eight percent (8/10) of her travel costs are deductible; 20% are nondeductible personal expenses. If Milton's employer reimburses her for her trip, she subtracts the amount of the reimbursement from the deductible portion of her travel costs.

Special rules apply for travel outside of North America. The IRS defines North America as the United States and its possessions, the Trust Territories, Canada, and Mexico. For an employee to deduct expenses for traveling to conventions outside the North American area, the meeting must meet the following two qualifications:

1. The convention must be directly related to the employee's job.
2. It must be as reasonable to hold the meeting outside North America as it would be to hold it in North America.

Meals and Entertainment Expenses

Taxpayers may deduct 50% of all qualified meals and entertainment expenses. Two categories of meals and entertainment exist: (1) those incurred while conducting business with clients and associates and (2) those incurred while traveling. In the first instance, only costs either directly related to or associated with business can be deducted. **Directly related to** means that the meal or entertainment takes place during a business discussion. **Associated with** means that the event takes place immediately before or after a business meeting.

Taxpayers can deduct the costs of qualified meals and entertainment. No deduction is allowed for lavish costs. For meals to be deductible, the taxpayer must be present at the event. Paying for a professional dinner meeting and not attending it does not qualify the expense for a deduction. This rule does not apply to other forms of entertainment (e.g., tickets to the theater or sporting events). Here, the taxpayer does not need to be present to take the deduction. However, only the business portion of meals and entertainment is deductible.

EXAMPLE 14

Janet Johan spent $250 on meals and entertainment while away from home overnight on a business trip. Of that, Johan spent $100 on meals for family members. Johan reports $150 ($250 – $100) as a business meals and entertainment expense. After applying the 50% limitation, Johan deducts $75 for meals on Form 2106.

EXAMPLE 15

Marty Fisher pays $200 for four tickets to a Yankees game. Fisher gives the tickets to a client. He does not attend the event. Fisher's entertainment expense deduction equals $100 ($200 x 50%).

Employees often receive supper money when required to work overtime. Supper money is not reimbursement or gross income. However, when paid as a disguised form of compensation, the supper money becomes taxable.

The IRS does not allow a deduction for the practice of taking turns paying for meals or entertainment. Also, the Code does not permit deductions for dues paid to various clubs and societies. The entities whose dues are not deductible include business, social, athletic, luncheon, and sporting clubs, as well as airline and hotel clubs. However, taxpayers may deduct some of the country club usage as a valid meal or entertainment expense. In addition, dues paid to professional, civic, and public service organizations (e.g., Lions, Kiwanis, Rotary) are deductible.

EXAMPLE 16

Ralph Platt keeps receipts for his employee business expenses. The totals consist of $150 for meals and entertainment, $522 for car expenses, $35 of transportation costs, and $230 for travel. None of these amounts were reimbursed by his employer. The employee business deduction on Form 2106 consists of the following amounts:

Total meals and entertainment	$150	
Less 50% limit	(75)	
Deductible meals and entertainment		$ 75
Travel		230
Transportation		35
Car expenses		522
Total employee business expenses		$862

Other Business Expenses Not Included Elsewhere on Form 2106

A number of other work-related expenses can be deducted by employees as miscellaneous itemized deductions subject to the 2% AGI rule. These expenses are reported on Form 2106 along with unreimbursed employee travel, transportation, meals and entertainment. A brief discussion of these other expenses follows.

Union Dues

Employees can pay deductible union dues and initiation fees either directly or through payroll deductions. If the payroll deduction includes specific retirement or savings plan contributions paid to the union by the employee, they are not included in the deductible union dues.

Licenses and Insurance

Employees deduct malpractice and other professional insurance. Nursing licenses, hair stylist licenses, health department certifications, and any other professional licenses are also deductible.

Uniforms and Safety Equipment

Employees deduct the costs of special protective clothing and devices required for safety purposes. Hard hats, gloves, goggles, back supports, and steel-toed shoes not provided by the employer all qualify. Employees may also deduct the costs of uniforms specifically designed for the job or industry when the employer requires clothing not suitable for everyday wear. Uniforms suitable for street wear cannot be deducted.

Employee Physicals

Some employers require personnel to take annual physicals. The employee deducts the cost as a miscellaneous business expense, not as a medical expense. Only the costs not covered by insurance (the employee's out-of-pocket costs) are deductible.

EXAMPLE 17

John Spadia's employer required that he take an annual physical as a condition of his employment. In the current year, $550 of the cost of his physical was not covered by insurance. Spadia deducts this amount as an employee business expenses on Schedule A. This amount will be included along with his other miscellaneous itemized deductions subject to the 2% AGI rule.

Equipment, Telephones, and Computers

For an employee to deduct the cost of capital equipment, the employer must have a written policy requiring the items as standard job tools. All other employees of the same company doing the same or similar work must have the same equipment requirements. Employees must depreciate capital equipment with a useful life in excess of one year. Employees do not deduct the costs of capital assets directly on Form 2106. They use Form 4562, Depreciation and Amortization, to report the costs of employees' telephone, computer, or other equipment.

EXAMPLE 18

Joseph Amir buys a home computer for the convenience of working at home at night. Amir prefers not to stay late at the office. Amir may not deduct depreciation on the computer. The IRS considers the purchase of the computer as simply for the employee's convenience.

Other equipment falling in this category includes cellular telephones, tools, fax machines, and the like. After determining the depreciation deduction on Form 4562, the taxpayer carries the total allowable depreciation to Form 2106 as an other business expense. Depriciation of property is discussed in Chapter 8.

Supplies

Employees may deduct office supplies, organizers and other low-cost business supplies. This category also includes watches, calculators, and briefcases, depending on the job requirements. Each industry has its own version of supplies. For instance, construction workers include disposable masks and small tools.

Education

An employee's education must meet one of two conditions in order to qualify as an employee business expense:

1. The employer, the law, or the employee's profession must require the education, or
2. The education must maintain or improve the employee's present skills for the employee's present job.

Generally, taxpayers must be employed or self-employed to claim a deduction for education expenses. However, even after meeting one of the above conditions, two situations will cause the deduction to be disallowed. This first is when the employee uses the courses to meet the minimum requirements of a present job. The second is when the courses lead to a degree that qualifies the employee for a *new* trade or business.

EXAMPLE 19

Brian Seth, a junior accountant with an associate's degree in accounting, works for a CPA firm as a tax preparer. Seth attended Grover State College and earned a bachelor's degree in accounting. Although Seth continued doing the same work for his current employer, with a bachelor's degree he now qualifies for a new line of work as an accountant. Therefore, Seth may not deduct the education expenses.

EXAMPLE 20

Scarlett Hartman works as a tax accountant for a CPA firm. Hartman holds a Bachelor's of Science degree in accounting. She is currently taking night classes towards a Master's in Taxation degree. Hartman has already met the minimum educational requirements of her current position. Furthermore, the degree she is pursuing will not enable her to enter a new profession. Instead, the courses Hartman is taking will help her improve her current skills as a tax accountant. Thus, her educational costs are deductible as an employee business expense.

Expenses eligible for the education deduction include tuition, books, supplies, lab fees, transportation costs, and costs of travel to seminars. Instructors and students may not deduct expenses incurred for travel as a form of education (e.g., a trip to France to study the culture).

Unless the taxpayer is self-employed or an employee, education expenses are nondeductible personal expenses. People who use a "temporary leave of absence" to pursue their education on a full-time basis are treated as maintaining their employee or business status. This holds true even if they take another job after completing their courses.

Job or Employment Search

Taxpayers may deduct the costs of looking for work in a comparable position or in the same line of employment. Neither first-time job seekers nor someone returning to the work force after a long absence can deduct their job hunting costs. The job search deduction includes the cost of career counseling when used to find employment in the same trade or business. Even if the search is unsuccessful, qualified job search expenses fulfill the requirements for the miscellaneous deduction. Deductible costs include, travel, postage, office supplies, printing, employment agency fees, and job counseling.

EXAMPLE 21

Josh Tremble is currently employed as a sales person. During the year he spends $3,500 for qualified job search expenses in his pursuit of a new sales position. His efforts are not successful. Tremble can deduct the $3,500 as an employee business expense.

EXAMPLE 22

Several years ago, Dana Sealy was employed as a consultant. Sealy left the workforce six years ago when she was pregnant with her first child. Now that her children are in school, Sealy would like to return to work. During the year she spends $350 in qualified job hunting expenses. Since Sealy is not currently working and has not recently worked as a consultant, she cannot deduct these costs.

Office in Home

Under very limited circumstances, employees may qualify to take a deduction for working at home. The employee must use a specific portion of the residence exclusively and on a regular basis for work. The employee must maintain an office area as either the principal place of work or the place where the employee regularly meets with clients. In addition, the employee must work at home for the convenience of the employer. The office-in-home deduction would apply if an employee worked for a company that did not have an office in the employee's town but needed a representative in that area. (See Chapter 7 for more on this topic.)

EXAMPLE 23

Kimberly Kim teaches school 25 hours a week at Public School 51. Kim spends another 35 hours a week in the office at home grading tests, writing assignments, and developing lesson plans. While her work at home is essential and time-consuming, Kim cannot deduct the cost of the office at home. Working at home is simply more convenient for her.

People using their home office to carry out investment activities do not qualify for a home office deduction.

Information for Figure 6-1: Filled-In Form 2106

Art McBurney is a district manager for the Drake Corporation. McBurney took a five-day business trip for his employer in November. Drake has an accountable reimbursement plan. However, it does not reimburse all expenses. It reimbursed McBurney only for his business miles (see below) and for a business meal with a client **($190)** and for air travel **($210).** McBurney was expected to pay his own meals **($140)** and lodging **($250)** and other transportation (taxi) expenses **($12)**. In addition to this trip, McBurney drove his personal automobile for business a total of **22,746** miles of the **34,060** miles driven during the year. His commuting miles were **2,500.** He began using his car for business on **January 2, 2005.** Employer reimbursement of **$9,098** (at $.40 per mile) were received for mileage. Reimbursements from his employer of **$9,498** ($9,098 + $210 + $190) were not included on McBurney's Form W-2. Parking fees and tolls paid for business totaled **$445.**

McBurney elects to claim the standard mileage deduction rather than the actual vehicle expenses. Since the reimbursement was paid under an accountable arrangement, only McBurney's excess employee expenses of $1,801 are deductible as a miscellaneous itemized deduction subject to the 2% AGI rule.

FIGURE 6-1 Filled-In form 2106, Page 1

Form **2106** | **Employee Business Expenses** | OMB No. 1545-0074

Department of the Treasury Internal Revenue Service (99)

► See separate instructions.

► Attach to Form 1040 or Form 1040NR.

2006 Attachment Sequence No. **54**

Your name	Occupation in which you incurred expenses	Social security number
Art McBurney	Management	727 22 7134

Part I **Employee Business Expenses and Reimbursements**

Step 1 Enter Your Expenses		**Column A** Other Than Meals and Entertainment	**Column B** Meals and Entertainment
1 Vehicle expense from line 22 or line 29. (Rural mail carriers: See instructions.)	1	10,122 00	
2 Parking fees, tolls, and transportation, including train, bus, etc., that **did not** involve overnight travel or commuting to and from work	2	457 00	
3 Travel expense while away from home overnight, including lodging, airplane, car rental, etc. **Do not** include meals and entertainment	3	460 00	
4 Business expenses not included on lines 1 through 3. **Do not** include meals and entertainment	4		
5 Meals and entertainment expenses (see instructions)	5		330 00
6 **Total expenses.** In Column A, add lines 1 through 4 and enter the result. In Column B, enter the amount from line 5	6	11,039 00	330 00

Note: *If you were not reimbursed for any expenses in Step 1, skip line 7 and enter the amount from line 6 on line 8.*

Step 2 Enter Reimbursements Received From Your Employer for Expenses Listed in Step 1

		Column A	Column B
7 Enter reimbursements received from your employer that were **not** reported to you in box 1 of Form W-2. Include any reimbursements reported under code "L" in box 12 of your Form W-2 (see instructions)	7	9,308 00	190 00

Step 3 Figure Expenses To Deduct on Schedule A (Form 1040)

		Column A	Column B
8 Subtract line 7 from line 6. If zero or less, enter -0-. However, if line 7 is greater than line 6 in Column A, report the excess as income on Form 1040, line 7 (or on Form 1040NR, line 8)	8	1,731 00	140 00
Note: *If* ***both columns*** *of line 8 are zero, you cannot deduct employee business expenses. Stop here and attach Form 2106 to your return.*			
9 In Column A, enter the amount from line 8. In Column B, multiply line 8 by 50% (.50). (Employees subject to Department of Transportation (DOT) hours of service limits: Multiply meal expenses incurred while away from home on business by 75% (.75) instead of 50%. For details, see instructions.)	9	1,731 00	70 00

10 Add the amounts on line 9 of both columns and enter the total here. **Also, enter the total on Schedule A (Form 1040), line 20** (or on Schedule A (Form 1040NR), line 9). (Reservists, qualified performing artists, fee-basis state or local government officials, and individuals with disabilities: See the instructions for special rules on where to enter the total.) ►	10	1,801 00

For Paperwork Reduction Act Notice, see instructions. Cat. No. 11700N Form **2106** (2006)

Other Information

2: Parking fees, tolls, and transportation, **$457** ($445 + $12)

3: Travel expense, **$460** ($210 + $250)

5: Meals and entertainment, **$330** ($190 + $140)

FIGURE 6-1 Filled-In form 2106, Page 2

Form 2106 (2006) Page 2

Part II Vehicle Expenses

Section A—General Information (You must complete this section if you are claiming vehicle expenses.)		**(a)** Vehicle 1	**(b)** Vehicle 2
11 Enter the date the vehicle was placed in service	11	01 / 02 / 05	/ /
12 Total miles the vehicle was driven during 2006	12	34,060 miles	miles
13 Business miles included on line 12	13	22,746 miles	miles
14 Percent of business use. Divide line 13 by line 12	14	68.78 %	%
15 Average daily roundtrip commuting distance	15	10 miles	miles
16 Commuting miles included on line 12	16	2,500 miles	miles
17 Other miles. Add lines 13 and 16 and subtract the total from line 12	17	8,814 miles	miles

18 Do you (or your spouse) have another vehicle available for personal use? ☒ Yes ☐ No

19 Was your vehicle available for personal use during off-duty hours? ☒ Yes ☐ No

20 Do you have evidence to support your deduction? ☒ Yes ☐ No

21 If "Yes," is the evidence written? ☒ Yes ☐ No

Section B—Standard Mileage Rate (See the instructions for Part II to find out whether to complete this section or Section C.)

22 Multiply line 13 by 44.5¢ (.445)	22	10,122 00

Section C—Actual Expenses		**(a)** Vehicle 1	**(b)** Vehicle 2
23 Gasoline, oil, repairs, vehicle insurance, etc.	23		
24a Vehicle rentals	24a		
b Inclusion amount (see instructions)	24b		
c Subtract line 24b from line 24a	24c		
25 Value of employer-provided vehicle (applies only if 100% of annual lease value was included on Form W-2—see instructions)	25		
26 Add lines 23, 24c, and 25	26		
27 Multiply line 26 by the percentage on line 14	27		
28 Depreciation (see instructions)	28		
29 Add lines 27 and 28. Enter total here and on line 1	29		

Section D—Depreciation of Vehicles (Use this section only if you owned the vehicle and are completing Section C for the vehicle.)

		(a) Vehicle 1	**(b)** Vehicle 2
30 Enter cost or other basis (see instructions)	30		
31 Enter section 179 deduction (see instructions)	31		
32 Multiply line 30 by line 14 (see instructions if you claimed the section 179 deduction or special allowance)	32		
33 Enter depreciation method and percentage (see instructions)	33		
34 Multiply line 32 by the percentage on line 33 (see instructions)	34		
35 Add lines 31 and 34	35		
36 Enter the applicable limit explained in the line 36 instructions	36		
37 Multiply line 36 by the percentage on line 14	37		
38 Enter the **smaller** of line 35 or line 37. If you skipped lines 36 and 37, enter the amount from line 35. Also enter this amount on line 28 above	38		

Form 2106 (2006)

MISCELLANEOUS DEDUCTIONS REPORTED ON SCHEDULE A (LINES 21 AND 22)

Schedule A also provides a place to deduct a variety of other allowable expenses. These expenses are added to employee business expenses. The taxpayer then reduces total miscellaneous deductions by 2% of AGI. The three primary categories of other nonbusiness expense include the following:

1. Costs paid to produce or collect taxable income
2. Costs to manage or protect income-producing (investment) property
3. Amounts spent to determine, contest, pay, or claim a refund of any tax

Taxpayers can deduct only expenses relating to the income they generate on the property they own. Also, taxpayers deduct the expenses related to producing interest, dividend, and other investment income. When added to other allowable expenses, small totals in each miscellaneous expense category might produce enough of a deduction to overcome the 2% AGI floor.

In recent years, many areas of the United States have experienced disasters. As a result, many taxpayers have learned about documentation rules relating to casualty losses. Ensuring the deductibility of losses requires objective verification of the assets' costs. Taxpayers incur appraisal and other evaluation expenses. They deduct these costs as miscellaneous expenses on Schedule A, not as a part of the casualty loss.

Taxpayers often employ competent tax professionals to respond to IRS, state, or local tax agency inquiries or to represent them in audits. Tax professionals also deal with refund claims and contested tax bills. Taxpayers combine all costs associated with tax representation and tax advice under other miscellaneous deductions. Other deductible tax preparation fees include the costs of electronic filing, certified postage for tax return mailing, and tax software.

EXAMPLE 24

Leroy Lerner buys Quicken for $50 for personal bookkeeping. Though paying a tax professional to prepare the tax return, Lerner buys Turbo Tax for $50 to do tax projections during the year. Lerner also subscribes to *Money Magazine,* the *Wall Street Journal,* and *Value Line* for a total of $400. The deductible investment expenses total $500, before the 2% AGI limitation.

Recall that casualty losses are reduced by 10% AGI. Thus, allowing appraisal costs to count as miscellaneous deductions may make it more likely that taxpayers can deduct these amounts.

Hobby Losses

When an activity has elements of both personal pleasure and profit, the question often arises as to whether the taxpayer had a profit motive. The presence of a profit motive affects the amount of expenses taxpayers deduct as well as where on the tax return they deduct them. Taxpayers who enter into an activity expecting to make a profit can deduct all expenses from the activity as a deduction for AGI. In contrast, expenses from an activity in which the taxpayer did not have a profit motive (a hobby) can be deducted as a miscellaneous itemized deduction (subject to the 2% AGI rule) to the extent of income from the activity.

Of the expenses related to the hobby activity, taxpayers would deduct expenses like home mortgage interest, property taxes, and casualty losses, even if the hobby activity did not exist. Other expenses, like supplies, utilities, insurance, and depreciation, are deductible only because of tax laws that allow taxpayers to deduct them against hobby income. The hobby loss rules limit the taxpayer's deduction for these otherwise nondeductible expenses to the gross income from the hobby activity minus the expenses deductible elsewhere on the return. Any disallowed expenses are lost and cannot be carried over to future years.

EXAMPLE 25

Rob Gray paints pictures as a hobby. Gray does his painting in a separate studio located in his home. During the year, Gray sold some paintings for $2,300. His expenses totaled $3,025 and consisted of $400 for real estate taxes on the studio, $1,125 for utilities, and $1,500 for painting supplies.

Gross income		$2,300
Less expenses deductible whether or not the activity is a hobby (real estate taxes)		(400)
Maximum "other expenses" allowed		$1,900
"Other expenses" related to the hobby:		
Utilities	$1,125	
Painting supplies	1,500	
Total "other expenses"	$2,625	
Deductible "other expenses"		(1,900)
Net hobby income or loss		$ 0

Gray reports the gross income from the hobby ($2,300) as "Other Income" on Form 1040. On Schedule A, Gray deducts $400 as real estate taxes and the remaining $1,900 of "other expenses" as a miscellaneous itemized deduction. Gray adds the $1,900 to his other miscellaneous deductions, and reduces the total by 2% of AGI. Gray cannot deduct the $725 of painting supplies and utilities that exceed $1,900 ($2,625 – $1,900 = $725).

EXAMPLE 26

Assume the same facts as in Example 25 except that Gray's activity has a profit motive. In this case, Gray reports $2,300 as income and deducts the entire $3,025 of expenses on Schedule C. Gray carries the net loss of $725 to Form 1040, page 1 to offset other income items. Schedue C is the focus of Chapter 7.

Unlike hobby losses, losses from a profit activity can be used to offset other income. The drawback of having an activity treated as a hobby should help explain why taxpayers make every effort to treat an activity as a business. The fact that a taxpayer enjoys an activity does not prevent it from being profitable. The burden of proving whether an activity is engaged in for profit generally rests with the taxpayer. However, the burden of proof shifts to the IRS for an activity that shows a profit in any three of five consecutive years (two of seven for activities involving horses). When this happens, it is assumed that a profit motive exists, and the IRS must prove that the activity is a hobby.

Taxpayers involved in an activity for less than three years may elect to postpone any challenge from the IRS until after the first five years. This gives taxpayers the opportunity to show a profit in three of those years and shift the burden of proof to the IRS. However, filing such an election may alert the IRS to a possible hobby activity. Factors the IRS considers in deciding whether an activity is a business or a hobby include the following:

1. The taxpayer's expertise in the area
2. Whether the taxpayer keeps separate books and records for the activity
3. Whether the activity showed profits in some years and losses in others
4. The amount of occasional profits the taxpayer earned from the activity
5. The relative amount of pleasure the taxpayer derives from the activity
6. The extent to which the taxpayer depends on the activity for financial support
7. The time and effort the taxpayer devotes to the activity
8. The taxpayer's past success with other activities
9. The taxpayer's expectation that the property used in the activity will rise in value

When the taxpayer uses the standard deduction, all hobby loss deductions are lost. Thus, all of the gross income from the hobby is taxed. Likewise, when the taxpayer's miscellaneous deductions do not exceed 2% of AGI, those hobby-related costs do not offset hobby income.

EXAMPLES OF OTHER EXPENSES (LINE 22)

- Safe deposit box fees
- Investment advice and fees paid to financial planner
- Subscriptions to financial newspapers, newsletters, magazines, etc.
- Investment fees
- Costs associated with attending investment seminars and conventions
- Collection fees
- Legal, accounting, and related software
- Bank/trustee costs for investment or retirement plans
- Depreciation on computer used for investment (subject to limitations)
- Appraisal fees for casualty loss or charitable contributions
- Trustee's commission to administer a revocable trust

OTHER MISCELLANEOUS DEDUCTIONS, SCHEDULE A (LINE 27)

Taxpayers report the following expenses as "Other Miscellaneous Deductions" on Schedule A (line 27). These deductions are not reduced by 2% of AGI:

- Gambling losses to the extent of gambling income
- Casualty losses from investment property (from Chapter 5)
- Federal estate taxes on income in respect of a decedent
- Repayment under claim of right doctrine
- Certain unrecovered investments in pension plans (as discussed in Chapter 3)
- Impairment-related work expenses of disabled persons

Gambling Losses

Taxpayers report gross gambling winnings on Form 1040, page 1, as "Other income." They may deduct their gambling losses up to the amount of their reported winnings as an itemized deduction. Thus, taxpayers who do not itemize lose the gambling deduction, but are still taxed on their gambling winnings.

EXAMPLE 27

In several trips to Las Vegas, Phillip Newman lost $8,000 playing blackjack and poker. However, on the state lottery, Newman won $4,500. Newman reports the $4,500 lottery winnings as "Other income" on Form 1040. Of the gambling losses, Newman reports only $4,500 on Schedule A (line 27). Newman cannot deduct the other $3,500 of gambling losses. Newman cannot take advantage of any deduction for the gambling loss unless his total itemized deductions exceed the standard deductions amount.

Impairment-Related Work Expenses

An impairment is a physical or mental disability when it limits a taxpayer's employment. Impairments include those limiting vision, hearing, or movement. When impaired taxpayers purchase special tools or devices to make it possible to work, they deduct the costs directly on Schedule A (line 27). They are not required to depreciate these special purchases. Deductible expenses include modifications to computers, special listening devices, and reading devices.

Nondeductible Expenses

Over the years, some taxpayers have become accustomed to taking deductions for certain expenses that are not deductible. A list of a few of these nondeductible expenses follows:

- Adoption costs (may qualify for a tax credit)
- Funeral costs, including the lot
- Political contributions and campaign costs
- Parking tickets and fines, even if related to business
- Hobby losses in excess of income
- Personal living expenses, like rent, insurance, utilities and banking fees
- Illegal bribes and kickbacks
- Life insurance premiums and premiums for personal disability insurance

Information for Figure 6-2: Filled-In Schedule A (Form 1040)

Gary and Nancy Redlin have **$91,517** of AGI. They use the following substantiated information to determine their itemized deductions on Schedule A.

1: Unreimbursed medical and dental expenses		**$7,466**
5: State of Wisconsin income taxes		**1,730**
6: Real estate taxes		**2,858**
7: Personal (ad valorem) property taxes		**96**
10: Home mortgage interest		**1,426**
15: Gifts by cash or check		**1,287**
16: Noncash gifts, (used clothing ($160) and use of personal automobile (150 miles × $.14 = $21))		**181**
17: Charitable contribution carryover from a prior year		**200**
19: Casualty and theft losses:		
Property damage sustained in an auto accident (*lesser of* (i) change in FMV or (ii) adjusted basis)	$5,734	
Less insurance proceeds	(2,000)	
Less: $100 floor per casualty	(100)	
Less: 10% AGI ($91,517 x 10%)	(9,152)	**0**
20: Unreimbursed employee expenses (source: Form 2106)		**1,850**
21: Income tax preparation fees (for 2005 tax return)		**400**
22: Other expenses, including safe deposit box rental **($50)** and Subscriptions to investment magazines **($273)**		**323**

FIGURE 6-2 Filled-In Schedule A (Form 1040)

SCHEDULES A&B (Form 1040)
Department of the Treasury Internal Revenue Service (99)

Schedule A—Itemized Deductions
(Schedule B is on back)
▶ Attach to Form 1040. ▶ See Instructions for Schedules A&B (Form 1040).

OMB No. 1545-0074
2006
Attachment Sequence No. **07**

Name(s) shown on Form 1040: Gary B. and Nancy L. Redlin
Your social security number: 272 11 8345

Section	Line	Description		Amount		Total
Medical and Dental Expenses		**Caution.** Do not include expenses reimbursed or paid by others.				
	1	Medical and dental expenses (see page A-2)	1	7,466 00		
	2	Enter amount from Form 1040, line 38 [2] 91,517 00				
	3	Multiply line 2 by 7.5% (.075)	3	6,864 00		
	4	Subtract line 3 from line 1. If line 3 is more than line 1, enter -0-			4	602 00
Taxes You Paid (See page A-2.)	5	State and local income taxes	5	1,730 00		
	6	Real estate taxes (see page A-5)	6	2,858 00		
	7	Personal property taxes	7	96 00		
	8	Other taxes. List type and amount ▶	8			
	9	Add lines 5 through 8			9	4,684 00
Interest You Paid (See page A-5.)	10	Home mortgage interest and points reported to you on Form 1098	10	1,426 00		
	11	Home mortgage interest not reported to you on Form 1098. If paid to the person from whom you bought the home, see page A-6 and show that person's name, identifying no., and address ▶	11			
Note. Personal interest is not deductible.	12	Points not reported to you on Form 1098. See page A-6 for special rules	12			
	13	Investment interest. Attach Form 4952 if required. (See page A-6.)	13			
	14	Add lines 10 through 13			14	1,426 00
Gifts to Charity If you made a gift and got a benefit for it, see page A-7.	15	Gifts by cash or check. If you made any gift of $250 or more, see page A-7	15	1,287 00		
	16	Other than by cash or check. If any gift of $250 or more, see page A-7. You **must** attach Form 8283 if over $500	16	181 00		
	17	Carryover from prior year	17	200 00		
	18	Add lines 15 through 17			18	1,668 00
Casualty and Theft Losses	19	Casualty or theft loss(es). Attach Form 4684. (See page A-8.)			19	0
Job Expenses and Certain Miscellaneous Deductions (See page A-8.)	20	Unreimbursed employee expenses—job travel, union dues, job education, etc. Attach Form 2106 or 2106-EZ if required. (See page A-8.) ▶	20	1,850 00		
	21	Tax preparation fees	21	400 00		
	22	Other expenses—investment, safe deposit box, etc. List type and amount ▶ Safe Deposit 50 Subscriptions 273	22	323 00		
	23	Add lines 20 through 22	23	2,573 00		
	24	Enter amount from Form 1040, line 38 [24] 91,517 00				
	25	Multiply line 24 by 2% (.02)	25	1,830 00		
	26	Subtract line 25 from line 23. If line 25 is more than line 23, enter -0-			26	743 00
Other Miscellaneous Deductions	27	Other—from list on page A-9. List type and amount ▶			27	
Total Itemized Deductions	28	Is Form 1040, line 38, over $150,500 (over $75,250 if married filing separately)? ☒ **No.** Your deduction is not limited. Add the amounts in the far right column for lines 4 through 27. Also, enter this amount on Form 1040, line 40. ☐ **Yes.** Your deduction may be limited. See page A-9 for the amount to enter. ▶			28	9,123 00
	29	If you elect to itemize deductions even though they are less than your standard deduction, check here ▶ ☐				

For Paperwork Reduction Act Notice, see Form 1040 instructions. Cat. No. 11330X **Schedule A (Form 1040) 2006**

FORM 1040 ILLUSTRATED

Taxpayers who choose to itemize deductions must use Form 1040. They determine AGI on page 1 of this two-page form. On page 2, they compute their taxable income, tax liability, and refund or tax due using the following basic format:

	AGI
–	Itemized or standard deduction
–	Exemptions
=	Taxable income
×	Taxable income rate (or Tax Table)
=	Tax liability before:
+	Additions to tax
–	Credit to tax (including tax payments)
=	Final tax due (refund)

Information for Figure 6-3: Filled-In Form 1040, Pages 1 and 2

Gary and Nancy Redlin elect to itemize deductions and file a joint return using the following amount. Neither is a participant in an employer's pension program.

Other Information

7: Wages, **$87,000** (Gary, $55,000; Nancy, $32,000) (source: Form W-2)
8a: Taxable interest, **$1,913** (source: Form 1099-INT)
10: Taxable refund, **$342** (source: 2004 state income tax return)
13: Short-term capital gain, **$250** (source: Schedule D)
17: Net rent from apartments, **$5,212** (source: Schedule E)
21: **Door prize**, **$800** (source: Form 1099-MISC)
32: IRA deduction, **$4,000** (neither Gary nor Nancy is an active participant)
40: Itemized deductions, **$13,190** (source: Schedule A)
48: Child care credit, **$1,200** (source: Form 2441)
53: Child tax credit, **$2,000** (2 children × $1,000)
64: Federal income tax withheld, **$7,200** (Gary, $5,200; Nancy, $2,000) (source: Form W-2)
71: Credit for federal telephone excise tax paid, **$60** (standard amount when four or more exemptions are claimed)

FIGURE 6-3 Filled-In Form 1040, Page 1

Form **1040** Department of the Treasury—Internal Revenue Service
U.S. Individual Income Tax Return 2006 (99) IRS Use Only—Do not write or staple in this space.

Label (See instructions on page 16.) **Use the IRS label.** Otherwise, please print or type. LABEL HERE

For the year Jan. 1–Dec. 31, 2006, or other tax year beginning , 2006, ending , 20 | OMB No. 1545-0074

Your first name and initial	Last name	Your social security number
Gary R.	Redlin	272 11 8245
If a joint return, spouse's first name and initial	Last name	Spouse's social security number
Nancy L.	Redlin	369 41 3822
Home address (number and street). If you have a P.O. box, see page 16.	Apt. no.	▲ You **must** enter your SSN(s) above. ▲
1438 East Second Street		
City, town or post office, state, and ZIP code. If you have a foreign address, see page 16.		Checking a box below will not change your tax or refund.
Verona, WI 53593-9088		

Presidential Election Campaign ▶ Check here if you, or your spouse if filing jointly, want $3 to go to this fund (see page 16) ▶ ☒ You ☒ Spouse

Filing Status

Check only one box.

1 ☐ Single
2 ☒ Married filing jointly (even if only one had income)
3 ☐ Married filing separately. Enter spouse's SSN above and full name here. ▶
4 ☐ Head of household (with qualifying person). (See page 17.) If the qualifying person is a child but not your dependent, enter this child's name here. ▶
5 ☐ Qualifying widow(er) with dependent child (see page 17)

Exemptions

6a ☒ **Yourself.** If someone can claim you as a dependent, **do not** check box 6a
b ☒ **Spouse**

Boxes checked on 6a and 6b: 2

c **Dependents:**

(1) First name Last name	(2) Dependent's social security number	(3) Dependent's relationship to you	(4) ✓ if qualifying child for child tax credit (see page 19)
Mary R. Relin	453 26 8190	daughter	☒
Douglas J. Redlin	453 26 8189	son	☒
Mildred A. Redlin	168 29 4501	mother	☐
			☐

If more than four dependents, see page 19.

No. of children on 6c who:
- lived with you: 3
- did not live with you due to divorce or separation (see page 20)

Dependents on 6c not entered above

d Total number of exemptions claimed — Add numbers on lines above ▶ 5

Income

Attach Form(s) W-2 here. Also attach Forms W-2G and 1099-R if tax was withheld.

If you did not get a W-2, see page 22.

Enclose, but do not attach, any payment. Also, please use **Form 1040-V.**

7	Wages, salaries, tips, etc. Attach Form(s) W-2		7	87,000 00
8a	**Taxable** interest. Attach Schedule B if required		8a	1,913 00
b	**Tax-exempt** interest. **Do not** include on line 8a	8b		
9a	Ordinary dividends. Attach Schedule B if required		9a	
b	Qualified dividends (see page 23)	9b		
10	Taxable refunds, credits, or offsets of state and local income taxes (see page 23)		10	342 00
11	Alimony received		11	
12	Business income or (loss). Attach Schedule C or C-EZ		12	
13	Capital gain or (loss). Attach Schedule D if required. If not required, check here ▶ ☐		13	250 00
14	Other gains or (losses). Attach Form 4797		14	
15a	IRA distributions 15a	b Taxable amount (see page 25)	15b	
16a	Pensions and annuities 16a	b Taxable amount (see page 25)	16b	
17	Rental real estate, royalties, partnerships, S corporations, trusts, etc. Attach Schedule E		17	5,212 00
18	Farm income or (loss). Attach Schedule F		18	
19	Unemployment compensation		19	
20a	Social security benefits 20a	b Taxable amount (see page 27)	20b	
21	Other income. List type and amount (see page 29) Door Prize		21	800 00
22	Add the amounts in the far right column for lines 7 through 21. This is your **total income** ▶		22	95,517 00

Adjusted Gross Income

23	Archer MSA deduction. Attach Form 8853	23			
24	Certain business expenses of reservists, performing artists, and fee-basis government officials. Attach Form 2106 or 2106-EZ	24			
25	Health savings account deduction. Attach Form 8889	25			
26	Moving expenses. Attach Form 3903	26			
27	One-half of self-employment tax. Attach Schedule SE	27			
28	Self-employed SEP, SIMPLE, and qualified plans	28			
29	Self-employed health insurance deduction (see page 30)	29			
30	Penalty on early withdrawal of savings	30			
31a	Alimony paid b Recipient's SSN ▶	31a			
32	IRA deduction (see page 31)	32	4,000 00		
33	Student loan interest deduction (see page 33)	33			
34	Jury duty pay you gave to your employer	34			
35	Domestic production activities deduction. Attach Form 8903	35			
36	Add lines 23 through 31a and 32 through 35			36	4,000 00
37	Subtract line 36 from line 22. This is your **adjusted gross income** ▶			37	91,517 00

For Disclosure, Privacy Act, and Paperwork Reduction Act Notice, see page 78. Cat. No. 11320B Form **1040** (2006)

FIGURE 6-3 Filled-In Form 1040, Page 2

Form 1040 (2006) Page **2**

Tax and Credits

Line	Description	Sub-line	Sub-amount	Line	Amount
38	Amount from line 37 (adjusted gross income)			38	91,517 00
39a	Check if: ☐ **You** were born before January 2, 1942, ☐ Blind. ☐ **Spouse** was born before January 2, 1942, ☐ Blind. **Total boxes checked ▶ 39a** ☐				
b	If your spouse itemizes on a separate return or you were a dual-status alien, see page 35 and check here ▶**39b** ☐				
40	**Itemized deductions** (from Schedule A) **or** your **standard deduction** (see left margin)			40	13,190 00
41	Subtract line 40 from line 38			41	78,327 00
42	If line 38 is over $112,875, or you provided housing to a person displaced by Hurricane Katrina, see page 37. Otherwise, multiply $3,300 by the total number of exemptions claimed on line 6d			42	16,500 00
43	**Taxable income.** Subtract line 42 from line 41. If line 42 is more than line 41, enter -0-			43	61,827 00
44	**Tax** (see page 37). Check if any tax is from: **a** ☐ Form(s) 8814 **b** ☐ Form 4972			44	8,571 00
45	**Alternative minimum tax** (see page 39). Attach Form 6251			45	
46	Add lines 44 and 45 ▶			46	8,571 00
47	Foreign tax credit. Attach Form 1116 if required	47			
48	Credit for child and dependent care expenses. Attach Form 2441	48	1,200 00		
49	Credit for the elderly or the disabled. Attach Schedule R	49			
50	Education credits. Attach Form 8863	50			
51	Retirement savings contributions credit. Attach Form 8880	51			
52	Residential energy credits. Attach Form 5695	52			
53	Child tax credit (see page XX). Attach Form 8901 if required	53	2,000 00		
54	Credits from: **a** ☐ Form 8396 **b** ☐ Form 8839 **c** ☐ Form 8859	54			
55	Other credits: **a** ☐ Form 3800 **b** ☐ Form 8801 **c** ☐ Form____	55			
56	Add lines 47 through 55. These are your **total credits**			56	3,200 00
57	Subtract line 56 from line 46. If line 56 is more than line 46, enter -0- ▶			57	5,371 00

Standard Deduction for—
- People who checked any box on line 39a or 39b **or** who can be claimed as a dependent, see page 36.
- All others:

Single or Married filing separately, $5,150

Married filing jointly or Qualifying widow(er), $10,300

Head of household, $7,550

Other Taxes

Line	Description	Line	Amount
58	Self-employment tax. Attach Schedule SE	58	
59	Social security and Medicare tax on tip income not reported to employer. Attach Form 4137	59	
60	Additional tax on IRAs, other qualified retirement plans, etc. Attach Form 5329 if required	60	
61	Advance earned income credit payments from Form(s) W-2, box 9	61	
62	Household employment taxes. Attach Schedule H	62	
63	Add lines 57 through 62. This is your **total tax** ▶	63	5,371 00

Payments

If you have a qualifying child, attach Schedule EIC.

Line	Description	Sub-line	Sub-amount	Line	Amount
64	Federal income tax withheld from Forms W-2 and 1099	64	7,200 00		
65	2006 estimated tax payments and amount applied from 2005 return	65			
66a	**Earned income credit (EIC)**	66a			
b	Nontaxable combat pay election ▶ 66b				
67	Excess social security and tier 1 RRTA tax withheld (see page 59)	67			
68	Additional child tax credit. Attach Form 8812	68			
69	Amount paid with request for extension to file (see page 59)	69			
70	Payments from: **a** ☐ Form 2439 **b** ☐ Form 4136 **c** ☐ Form 8885	70			
71	Credit for federal telephone excise tax paid. Attach Form 8913 if required	71	60 00		
72	Add lines 64, 65, 66a, and 67 through 71. These are your **total payments** ▶			72	7,260 00

Refund

Direct deposit? See page 59 and fill in 74b, 74c, and 74d, or Form 8888.

Line	Description	Line	Amount
73	If line 72 is more than line 63, subtract line 63 from line 72. This is the amount you **overpaid**	73	1,889 00
74a	Amount of line 73 you want **refunded to you.** If Form 8888 is attached, check here ▶ ☐	74a	1,889 00
▶ b	Routing number ▶ **c** Type: ☐ Checking ☐ Savings		
▶ d	Account number		
75	Amount of line 73 you want **applied to your 2007 estimated tax** ▶ 75		

Amount You Owe

Line	Description	Line	Amount
76	**Amount you owe.** Subtract line 72 from line 63. For details on how to pay, see page 60 ▶	76	
77	Estimated tax penalty (see page 60) 77		

Third Party Designee

Do you want to allow another person to discuss this return with the IRS (see page 61)? ☐ **Yes.** Complete the following. ☐ **No**

Designee's name ▶ Phone no. ▶ ( ) Personal identification number (PIN) ▶

Sign Here

Joint return? See page 17. Keep a copy for your records.

Under penalties of perjury, I declare that I have examined this return and accompanying schedules and statements, and to the best of my knowledge and belief, they are true, correct, and complete. Declaration of preparer (other than taxpayer) is based on all information of which preparer has any knowledge.

Your signature	Date	Your occupation	Daytime phone number
Gary R. Redlin	4/12/07	Manager	( )
Spouse's signature. If a joint return, **both** must sign.	Date	Spouse's occupation	
Nancy L. Redlin	4/12/07	Nurse	

Paid Preparer's Use Only

Preparer's signature ▶ Date Check if self-employed ☐ Preparer's SSN or PTIN

Firm's name (or yours if self-employed), address, and ZIP code ▶ EIN Phone no. ( )

Form **1040** (2006)

Printed on recycled paper

Name ______________________________

Section ______________ Date ____________

QUESTIONS AND PROBLEMS

1. **Miscellaneous Deductions.** Identify the following as **(A)** deductible for AGI, **(B)** deductible from AGI, or **(C)** not deductible. Ignore any AGI limitations that may apply in determining the deductibility of certain types of expenses.

Item	*Answer*
a. State inheritance taxes	________
b. Commuting costs	________
c. Safe deposit box rental (used to store securities)	B
d. CPA examination testing fee	C
e. IRS penalty for late filing	A
f. Fee to accountant to prepare the personal property tax return on rental property	C
g. Loss on bookstore operations (Schedule C is used)	________
h. Auto registration for business vehicle	________

2. **Miscellaneous Deductions.** Identify the following as **(A)** deductible for AGI, **(B)** deductible from AGI, or **(C)** not deductible. Ignore any AGI limitations that may apply in determining the deductibility of certain types of expenses.

	Answer
a. Purchase of uniforms suitable for street wear	________
b. Insurance on personal residence	________
c. Union dues paid by a steelworker	________
d. Unreimbursed employee business travel expense	________
e. Mortgage interest on apartment building	________
f. Storm damage to trees in front yard of home, after insurance	________
g. Loss on sale of personal automobile	________
h. Repairs to friend's car for damage caused when taxpayer's car hit friend's car	________

3. **Miscellaneous Deductions.** Identify the following as **(A)** deductible for AGI, **(B)** deductible from AGI, or **(C)** not deductible. Ignore any AGI limitations that may apply in determining the deductibility of certain types of expenses.

		Answer
a.	Loss on sale of stock (from Schedule D)	________
b.	Interest on loan to pay for family vacation	________
c.	Unreimbursed salesperson's entertainment expenses	________
d.	Depreciation on apartment building	________
e.	Charitable contributions to a university	________
f.	Proprietor's cost for continuing education seminar	________
g.	Storm damage to farmer's rental property	________

4. **Substantiation.** Describe the six elements that are required to properly substantiate an employee's business expense records.

5. **Accountable vs. Nonaccountable Reimbursement Plans.** Angel Martin works as a delivery person for a local restaurant. His job requires that he use his own personal car to deliver food to customers' homes. During 2006, Martin drives 4,305 business miles. His employer pays him $10 for each delivery he makes and reimburses him $.35 a mile for each business mile.

   a. Discuss the tax consequences of the $1,506.75 (4,305 x $.35) reimbursement Martin receives if his employer has an accountable reimbursement plan.

   b Discuss the tax consequences of the $1,506.75 reimbursement Martin receives if his employer has a nonaccountable reimbursement plan.

   c. What are the characteristics of an accountable reimbursement plan and what distinguishes it from a nonaccountable plan?

6. **Vehicle Expenses.** Shaun Estes uses his personal car for work. Estes is employed as a messenger. In 2006, he drove 12,400 business-related miles and 18,340 total miles. His employer reimburses him $.30 a mile for his documented business miles under an accountable reimbursement plan. Estes's car expenses for the year were as follows. In addition, Estes paid $398 in business-related parking.

Depreciation	$2,498
Gas	2,347
Insurance	1,840
License tags	120
Repairs and maintenance	122
	$6,927

a. Compute the amount of Estes's car expense deduction using the standard mileage method.

b. Compute the amount of his car expense deduction using the actual method.

c. Based on your answers to Parts a. and b., under what conditions should Estes use the standard mileage method?

d. Based on your answers to Parts a. and b., under what conditions should he use the actual method?

7. **Vehicle Expenses.** Gina Plank uses her personal car for work as an employee. In 2006, Plank drove 2,235 business-related miles and 15,544 total miles. For 2006, Plank's expenses for the car are as follows.

Depreciation	$4,800
Gas	1,579
Insurance	1,112
License tags	60
Repairs and maintenance	533
	$8,084

Plank uses an accelerated depreciation method to compute her depreciation expense deduction. Last year was the first year Plank used her car for business. Her employer reimburses her $.40 a mile for each documented business mile under an accountable reimbursement plan. Last year Plank used the standard mileage deduction to compute her car expense deduction.

a. Discuss the alternatives Plank has for computing her car expense deduction. What amount should Plank deduct for car expenses for 2006?

b. Discuss where Plank reports the reimbursement and car expense on her tax return.

8. **Transportation Expense.** Ricardo Montella works two jobs each day, Monday through Friday. He works eight hours at his first job and three hours at his second job. He drives the following miles each day:

Home to first job	20 miles
First job to second job	12 miles
Second job to home	30 miles

a. If Montella follows this routine for 250 days during 2006, how many miles qualify for the mileage deduction?

3,000

b. Compute Montella's mileage deduction using the standard mileage method.

3000 x $.445

9. Travel Expense. Joshua Jones went on a business trip lasting ten days. He spent six days on business (includes travel time). He spent four days playing golf and visiting with a friend. He incurred the following unreimbursed expenses:

Lodging	$1,250
Meals	500
Entertainment of clients	130
Airfare	1,500

a. If the trip was within the United States, how much can Jones deduct?

$ 2,465

b. If the trip was outside the United States, how much can Jones deduct?

$ 1,865

10. Travel Expenses. Katie Barnes works as an employee. She attends a week long convention related to her employment. Her employer, however, does not reimburse her for any of her expenses. After the convention, Barnes takes a vacation in the area and stays an additional week. Barnes is gone a total of 14 days, seven of which are spent conducing business. Her travel costs are as follows.

Airfare	$650
Transportation to and from the airport	180
Hotel ($200 a night for 13 nights -- 6 business, 7 personal)	2,600
Meals ($40 a day for 14 days – 7 business, 7 personal)	560

a. Compute Barnes's travel expense deduction assuming the convention was located in the United States.

b. Compute her travel expense deduction assuming the convention was located outside of the United States.

c. How, if at all, would you answers to Part a. change if Barnes stayed one less personal day?

d. How, if at all, would you answers to Part b. change if she stayed one less personal day?

11. Meals and Entertainment. Courtney Fitch is employed as a sales person. During the year, Fitch pays $250 for tickets to a concert that she gives to a customer. Fitch does not attend the concert with the client. She also picks up the $210 tab for a dinner for one of her customers. She was in the restaurant at the time the customer was dining, but did not dine with customer. Fitch was not reimbursed for either of these amounts. Compute the amount of Fitch's meals and entertainment deduction and discuss where she reports this amount on her tax return.

12. Education Expenses. For each situation described in Parts a. through d., state whether the expenses paid qualify as deductible educational expenses. If the expenses qualify as deductions, state whether the expenses are deductible for (adjustments to income) or from AGI (itemized deductions).

a. Accounting courses taken by an accountant, who works for a CPA firm to meet the state's continuing professional education (CPE) requirement. (Total CPE expenses were $525.)

b. Tuition and books totalling $3,500 for a CPA enrolled in law school.

c. Tuition and books totalling $2,700 for a high school teacher enrolled in graduate school to meet the state law requirements in order to renew her teaching certificate.

d. A company executive's expenditure of $8,000 on tuition, books, and transportation to attend an executive program to improve his business management, employee relations, and marketing skills.

13. **Job Search Expenses.** During the year, Kris Patel spends $1,700 on qualified job search expenses in his pursuit of a job as a manager.

    a. Can Patel can deduct the $1,700 if he is currently employed as a manager and as a result of his efforts, he finds a new managerial position. Where would he report his deduction?

    b. Same as in Part a. except that his efforts are unsuccessful.

    c. Can Patel can deduct the $1,700 if he is not currently employed as a manager, but as a result of his efforts, he finds a managerial position. Where would he report his deduction?

    d. Same as in Part d. except that his efforts are unsuccessful.

14. **Hobby Criteria.**

    a. What are the criteria for determining whether an activity is a legitimate business or a hobby?

    b. If a doctor operates on the side a farm that is used to graze cattle, will the showing of a profit automatically keep the IRS from considering the activity a hobby? Explain.

15. **Hobby Losses.** Russell Long is retired from his regular work and now spends his time painting landscapes in a studio set up in his home. The studio occupies 12% of the living space in his home. During 2006 Long sold some of his paintings for the first time. Long is not certain whether he is required to file a tax return and, if so, whether he will be required to pay any taxes on his painting as a business. The revenue from sales of paintings in 2006 was $2,300. Long's expenses were as follows: property taxes on his home, $3,600; interest on a loan for painting supplies, $140; painting supplies, $1,750; electricity for the home, $2,400; and heat for the home, $2,900.

    a. How much can Long deduct of the above expenses if his painting activity is treated as a business? Show calculations.

    b. How much can Long deduct of the above expenses if his painting activity is treated as a hobby? Show calculations.

    c. Explain what Long might do in the way of tax planning to further support a claim that his painting is a business activity.

16. **Employee Business Expenses.** Wendy Rogers, a single taxpayer, is a plumber employed by a company in the city where she lives. She attends the monthly dinner meeting of the local union. During the year, she paid $120 of meeting expenses and drove 240 miles (20 miles each month) to attend the meetings. Rogers paid union dues of $110 and a plumbing license fee of $35.

    a. Compute Rogers's itemized deductions for the work-related expenses.

    b. Explain how to use the employee business expenses as itemized deductions.

17. Gambling Losses. During the year, Mark Downing won $1,400 from football bets. He lost $750 from basketball wagering. Downing also lost $1,150 at the track.

a. How do these gambling activities affect Downing's gross income and his deductible expenses?

b. Where would the appropriate income and expenses be entered on Downing's income tax returns?

18. Form 2106. Nancy Lopez (SSN 234–56–7891) works for Professional Services, Inc. (PSI). During the year, she incurs the following employment-related expenses:

Travel expenses (not including meals, entertainment, and auto expenses)	$3,750
Parking	180
Toll charges	30
Meals (while away overnight)	1,500
Entertainment of clients	426
Miscellaneous	135

Lopez's employer provides a business expense allowance of $750 per month to cover all expenses. Lopez does not account to PSI for her expenses, but she keeps detailed records of her business expenses and mileage. During the year she drove 25,200 miles, and 16,620 of these miles were business related. The miles do not include Lopez's 10-mile round-trip commuting distance when she is not traveling. Her total commuting miles for the year are 2,200. Lopez uses the standard mileage rate to determine the tax deduction for the use of her automobile, which she acquired on November 10, 2005. Using this data, prepare Form 2106 for Lopez.

19. Tax Planning.

a. Under what circumstances should a taxpayer plan to control the timing of payments that are deductible as itemized deductions?

b. Identify some specific ways in which the current tax law allows for tax planning with regard to itemized deductions.

(Use for Problem 18.)

Form **2106** Department of the Treasury Internal Revenue Service (99)

Employee Business Expenses

▶ See separate instructions.

▶ Attach to Form 1040 or Form 1040NR.

OMB No. 1545-0074 2006 Attachment Sequence No. 54

Your name	Occupation in which you incurred expenses	Social security number

Part I Employee Business Expenses and Reimbursements

Step 1 Enter Your Expenses		**Column A** Other Than Meals and Entertainment	**Column B** Meals and Entertainment
1 Vehicle expense from line 22 or line 29. (Rural mail carriers: See instructions.)	1		
2 Parking fees, tolls, and transportation, including train, bus, etc., that **did not** involve overnight travel or commuting to and from work	2		
3 Travel expense while away from home overnight, including lodging, airplane, car rental, etc. **Do not** include meals and entertainment	3		
4 Business expenses not included on lines 1 through 3. **Do not** include meals and entertainment.	4		
5 Meals and entertainment expenses (see instructions)	5		
6 **Total expenses.** In Column A, add lines 1 through 4 and enter the result. In Column B, enter the amount from line 5	6		

Note: *If you were not reimbursed for any expenses in Step 1, skip line 7 and enter the amount from line 6 on line 8.*

Step 2 Enter Reimbursements Received From Your Employer for Expenses Listed in Step 1

7 Enter reimbursements received from your employer that were **not** reported to you in box 1 of Form W-2. Include any reimbursements reported under code "L" in box 12 of your Form W-2 (see instructions)	7		

Step 3 Figure Expenses To Deduct on Schedule A (Form 1040)

8 Subtract line 7 from line 6. If zero or less, enter -0-. However, if line 7 is greater than line 6 in Column A, report the excess as income on Form 1040, line 7 (or on Form 1040NR, line 8)	8		
Note: *If* ***both columns*** *of line 8 are zero, you cannot deduct employee business expenses. Stop here and attach Form 2106 to your return.*			
9 In Column A, enter the amount from line 8. In Column B, multiply line 8 by 50% (.50). (Employees subject to Department of Transportation (DOT) hours of service limits: Multiply meal expenses incurred while away from home on business by 75% (.75) instead of 50%. For details, see instructions.)	9		

10 Add the amounts on line 9 of both columns and enter the total here. **Also, enter the total on Schedule A (Form 1040), line 20** (or on Schedule A (Form 1040NR), line 9). (Reservists, qualified performing artists, fee-basis state or local government officials, and individuals with disabilities: See the instructions for special rules on where to enter the total.) ▶	10	

For Paperwork Reduction Act Notice, see instructions. Cat. No. 11700N Form **2106** (2006)

(Use for Problem 18.)

Form 2106 (2006) Page **2**

Part II Vehicle Expenses

Section A—General Information (You must complete this section if you are claiming vehicle expenses.)		**(a)** Vehicle 1	**(b)** Vehicle 2
11 Enter the date the vehicle was placed in service	11	/ /	/ /
12 Total miles the vehicle was driven during 2006	12	miles	miles
13 Business miles included on line 12	13	miles	miles
14 Percent of business use. Divide line 13 by line 12	14	%	%
15 Average daily roundtrip commuting distance	15	miles	miles
16 Commuting miles included on line 12	16	miles	miles
17 Other miles. Add lines 13 and 16 and subtract the total from line 12	17	miles	miles

18 Do you (or your spouse) have another vehicle available for personal use? ☐ Yes ☐ No

19 Was your vehicle available for personal use during off-duty hours? ☐ Yes ☐ No

20 Do you have evidence to support your deduction? ☐ Yes ☐ No

21 If "Yes," is the evidence written? ☐ Yes ☐ No

Section B—Standard Mileage Rate (See the instructions for Part II to find out whether to complete this section or Section C.)

22 Multiply line 13 by 44.5¢ (.445)	22	

Section C—Actual Expenses		**(a)** Vehicle 1		**(b)** Vehicle 2	
23 Gasoline, oil, repairs, vehicle insurance, etc.	23				
24a Vehicle rentals	24a				
b Inclusion amount (see instructions)	24b				
c Subtract line 24b from line 24a	24c				
25 Value of employer-provided vehicle (applies only if 100% of annual lease value was included on Form W-2—see instructions)	25				
26 Add lines 23, 24c, and 25	26				
27 Multiply line 26 by the percentage on line 14	27				
28 Depreciation (see instructions)	28				
29 Add lines 27 and 28. Enter total here and on line 1	29				

Section D—Depreciation of Vehicles (Use this section only if you owned the vehicle and are completing Section C for the vehicle.)

		(a) Vehicle 1		**(b)** Vehicle 2	
30 Enter cost or other basis (see instructions)	30				
31 Enter section 179 deduction (see instructions)	31				
32 Multiply line 30 by line 14 (see instructions if you claimed the section 179 deduction or special allowance)	32				
33 Enter depreciation method and percentage (see instructions)	33				
34 Multiply line 32 by the percentage on line 33 (see instructions)	34				
35 Add lines 31 and 34	35				
36 Enter the applicable limit explained in the line 36 instructions	36				
37 Multiply line 36 by the percentage on line 14	37				
38 Enter the **smaller** of line 35 or line 37. If you skipped lines 36 and 37, enter the amount from line 35. Also enter this amount on line 28 above	38				

Form **2106** (2006)

20. Internet Problem: Researching Publication 463.

The Alpha-Beta Company rents a 12-seat luxury skybox at a football stadium for the entire season. The season consists of eight home games. Alpha-Beta uses the skybox exclusively for entertaining clients. The cost of renting the skybox for the season is $20,000. In contrast, nonluxury box seats sell for $50 for each game.

How much can Alpha-Beta deduct for its luxury skybox?

Go to the IRS Web site. Locate Publication 463, and find an answer to the above question involving luxury skyboxes. Print out a copy of the page where you found your answer. Underline or highlight the pertinent information.

See Appendix A for instructions on use of the IRS Web site.

21. Business Entity Problem: This problem is designed for those using the "business entity" approach. The solution may require information from Chapters 14 and 15.

For each statement, check true or false.	*True*	*False*
a. Self-employed taxpayers use Form 2106 to report their deductible travel expenses.	______	______
b. A self-employed taxpayer may claim the federal per diem for meals instead of deducting the actual meal costs.	______	______.
c. Employers that reimburse their employees using an "accountable reimbursement plan" are able to deduct the entire cost of meal reimbursements paid to their employees.	______	______
d. When a self-employed taxpayer incurs deductible education expenses, the expenses are deductible as a miscellaneous itemized deduction subject to the 2% rule.	______	______
e. When a taxpayer owns stock in an S corporation that breeds and races horses, the pass-through losses from the corporation may be treated as hobby losses if the corporation has never shown a profit in its ten years of operation.	______	______

COMPREHENSIVE PROBLEMS

22. **Miscellaneous Deductions.** Mr. and Mrs. Virgil Pierre had an AGI of $47,400. They incurred the following expenses:

Mr. Pierre:

Employee business expenses:	
Employee mileage deduction	$569
Meals while away from home overnight	90
Hotels	185
Miscellaneous travel expenses	18
Total travel expenses	$862
Travel expenses reimbursed by employer (including all meals) under a qualified plan	(486)
Net travel expenses paid out of pocket	$376
Other business expenses:	
Subscriptions to professional journals	$115
Unreimbursed meals and entertainment	256
Other expenses:	
Tax return preparation fee	175
Gambling losses (gambling winnings were $65)	120

Mrs. Pierre:

Safe deposit box rent (stock stored)	$ 45
Investment publications	120
Nurse's uniform cost and upkeep	340
Professional liability insurance	85

Using the preceding information, fill in the following lines, which summarize Schedule A (Job Expenses and Most Other Miscellaneous Deductions):

Job Expenses and Most Other Miscellaneous Deductions:

1. Unreimbursed employee expenses __________
2. Tax preparation fees __________
3. Other expenses subject to the 2% rule __________
4. Total expenses __________
5. Less 2% of AGI __________
6. Deductible expenses __________

Other Miscellaneous Deductions:

7. Miscellaneous expenses not subject to the 2% rule __________

23. Schedule A. Charlie P. (SSN 367-83-9403) and Maggie S. (SSN 361-73-4098) Church file a joint income tax return with an AGI of $74,105. They reside in Evanston, IL. Mr. Church, a chemist, worked for Drake Corporation for the first six months of the year. He was employed by Potter Company for the last six months of the year. Mrs. Church worked part-time as a nurse at City Hospital.

The Churchs's expenses follow. They have canceled checks or receipts for each item.

Mortgage interest on home	$4,200
Contributions to church (with receipts)	900
Hunting license	90
Marriage license	16
Cash to street person begging for money	50
Contribution to American Red Cross (with receipts)	30
Paid to United Way (no canceled check or receipt)	310
Property tax on residence	2,450
R. K. Snell, physician (unreimbursed by insurance)	980
E. I. Newman, dentist (unreimbursed by insurance)	290
G. R. Gross, veterinarian (unreimbursed by insurance)	125
Medical insurance premiums	556
Safe deposit box rental (storing securities)	22
Paid to Evanston Drug for over-the-counter medications	160
State income taxes withheld	2,890

Complete the Schedule A on page 6-41 for Charlie and Maggie Church.

24. Schedule A. Roberto (SSN 123-45-6789) and Lena Gomez, both engineers, file a joint return reporting AGI of $175,130, including $163,500 in wages and $11,630 in dividend income. Their Schedule A shows the following itemized deductions:

Medical expenses	$12,000
State income taxes	2,500
Property taxes	3,000
Mortgage interest	8,000
Investment interest	2,000
Charitable contributions (with receipts)	4,000

a. Prepare the Gomez's Schedule A on page 6-42.

b. Assuming they are entitled to three exemptions, determine the Gomez's taxable income.

c. Look up the Gomez's marginal tax rate and determine the effect that the reduction in itemized deduction (due to excess AGI) has on their net income tax liability.

(Use for Problem 23.)

SCHEDULES A&B (Form 1040)

Department of the Treasury
Internal Revenue Service (99)

Schedule A—Itemized Deductions

(Schedule B is on back)

▶ Attach to Form 1040. ▶ See Instructions for Schedules A&B (Form 1040).

OMB No. 1545-0074
2006
Attachment Sequence No. **07**

Name(s) shown on Form 1040 | Your social security number

Section	Line	Description	Box	Amount	Total Line	Total
Medical and Dental Expenses		**Caution.** Do not include expenses reimbursed or paid by others.				
	1	Medical and dental expenses (see page A-2)	1			
	2	Enter amount from Form 1040, line 38 [2]				
	3	Multiply line 2 by 7.5% (.075).	3			
	4	Subtract line 3 from line 1. If line 3 is more than line 1, enter -0-			4	
Taxes You Paid (See page A-2.)	5	State and local income taxes	5			
	6	Real estate taxes (see page A-5)	6			
	7	Personal property taxes	7			
	8	Other taxes. List type and amount ▶	8			
	9	Add lines 5 through 8			9	
Interest You Paid (See page A-5.)	10	Home mortgage interest and points reported to you on Form 1098	10			
	11	Home mortgage interest not reported to you on Form 1098. If paid to the person from whom you bought the home, see page A-6 and show that person's name, identifying no., and address ▶	11			
Note. Personal interest is not deductible.	12	Points not reported to you on Form 1098. See page A-6 for special rules	12			
	13	Investment interest. Attach Form 4952 if required. (See page A-6.)	13			
	14	Add lines 10 through 13			14	
Gifts to Charity	15	Gifts by cash or check. If you made any gift of $250 or more, see page A-7	15			
If you made a gift and got a benefit for it, see page A-7.	16	Other than by cash or check. If any gift of $250 or more, see page A-7. You **must** attach Form 8283 if over $500	16			
	17	Carryover from prior year	17			
	18	Add lines 15 through 17			18	
Casualty and Theft Losses	19	Casualty or theft loss(es). Attach Form 4684. (See page A-8.)			19	
Job Expenses and Certain Miscellaneous Deductions (See page A-8.)	20	Unreimbursed employee expenses—job travel, union dues, job education, etc. Attach Form 2106 or 2106-EZ if required. (See page A-8.) ▶	20			
	21	Tax preparation fees	21			
	22	Other expenses—investment, safe deposit box, etc. List type and amount ▶	22			
	23	Add lines 20 through 22	23			
	24	Enter amount from Form 1040, line 38 [24]				
	25	Multiply line 24 by 2% (.02)	25			
	26	Subtract line 25 from line 23. If line 25 is more than line 23, enter -0-			26	
Other Miscellaneous Deductions	27	Other—from list on page A-9. List type and amount ▶			27	
Total Itemized Deductions	28	Is Form 1040, line 38, over $150,500 (over $75,250 if married filing separately)? ☐ **No.** Your deduction is not limited. Add the amounts in the far right column for lines 4 through 27. Also, enter this amount on Form 1040, line 40. ☐ **Yes.** Your deduction may be limited. See page A-9 for the amount to enter. ▶			28	
	29	If you elect to itemize deductions even though they are less than your standard deduction, check here ▶ ☐				

For Paperwork Reduction Act Notice, see Form 1040 instructions. Cat. No. 11330X **Schedule A (Form 1040) 2006**

(Use for Problem 24.)

SCHEDULES A&B (Form 1040)

Department of the Treasury Internal Revenue Service (99)

Schedule A—Itemized Deductions

(Schedule B is on back)

▶ Attach to Form 1040. ▶ See Instructions for Schedules A&B (Form 1040).

OMB No. 1545-0074

2006

Attachment Sequence No. 07

Name(s) shown on Form 1040 | Your social security number

Medical and Dental Expenses		**Caution.** Do not include expenses reimbursed or paid by others.		
	1	Medical and dental expenses (see page A-2)	1	
	2	Enter amount from Form 1040, line 38 [2]		
	3	Multiply line 2 by 7.5% (.075)	3	
	4	Subtract line 3 from line 1. If line 3 is more than line 1, enter -0-		4
Taxes You Paid (See page A-2.)	5	State and local income taxes	5	
	6	Real estate taxes (see page A-5)	6	
	7	Personal property taxes	7	
	8	Other taxes. List type and amount ▶	8	
	9	Add lines 5 through 8		9
Interest You Paid (See page A-5.)	10	Home mortgage interest and points reported to you on Form 1098	10	
	11	Home mortgage interest not reported to you on Form 1098. If paid to the person from whom you bought the home, see page A-6 and show that person's name, identifying no., and address ▶	11	
Note. Personal interest is not deductible.	12	Points not reported to you on Form 1098. See page A-6 for special rules	12	
	13	Investment interest. Attach Form 4952 if required. (See page A-6.)	13	
	14	Add lines 10 through 13		14
Gifts to Charity	15	Gifts by cash or check. If you made any gift of $250 or more, see page A-7	15	
If you made a gift and got a benefit for it, see page A-7.	16	Other than by cash or check. If any gift of $250 or more, see page A-7. You **must** attach Form 8283 if over $500	16	
	17	Carryover from prior year	17	
	18	Add lines 15 through 17		18
Casualty and Theft Losses	19	Casualty or theft loss(es). Attach Form 4684. (See page A-8.)		19
Job Expenses and Certain Miscellaneous Deductions (See page A-8.)	20	Unreimbursed employee expenses—job travel, union dues, job education, etc. Attach Form 2106 or 2106-EZ if required. (See page A-8.) ▶	20	
	21	Tax preparation fees	21	
	22	Other expenses—investment, safe deposit box, etc. List type and amount ▶	22	
	23	Add lines 20 through 22	23	
	24	Enter amount from Form 1040, line 38 [24]		
	25	Multiply line 24 by 2% (.02)	25	
	26	Subtract line 25 from line 23. If line 25 is more than line 23, enter -0-		26
Other Miscellaneous Deductions	27	Other—from list on page A-9. List type and amount ▶		27
Total Itemized Deductions	28	Is Form 1040, line 38, over $150,500 (over $75,250 if married filing separately)? ☐ **No.** Your deduction is not limited. Add the amounts in the far right column for lines 4 through 27. Also, enter this amount on Form 1040, line 40. ☐ **Yes.** Your deduction may be limited. See page A-9 for the amount to enter. ▶		28
	29	If you elect to itemize deductions even though they are less than your standard deduction, check here ▶ ☐		

For Paperwork Reduction Act Notice, see Form 1040 instructions. Cat. No. 11330X **Schedule A (Form 1040) 2006**

CUMULATIVE PROBLEM (CHAPTERS 1–6)

Frank A. (SSN 811-26-3717) and Sandra K. (SSN 820-47-9231) Anderson (ages 48 and 51, respectively) reside at 2121 Century Avenue, Middleton, CA 92657, with their three children whom they fully support: Martha A. (age 9), Charles R. (age 11), and Carol T. (age 14). The children's social security numbers are Martha 998-21-5246, Charles 998-21-5247, and Carol 998-21-1827.

The Andersons file a joint return, and neither elects to have money go to the presidential election campaign fund. Frank is employed by Maintaineers, Inc., as a customer representative. Sandra is employed by Mission Instruments as a computer operator. Details of their salaries and withholdings, are as follows:

	Gross Wages	*State Income Tax Withheld*	*Federal Income Tax Withheld*	*Social Security Tax Withheld*	*Medicare Insurance Tax Withheld*
Frank	$52,500	$3,623	$2,100	$3,255	$761
Sandra	24,000	1,656	980	1,488	348

In addition to his salary, Frank received a business travel expense reimbursement of $6,600 from Maintaineers, Inc., which was not included on his Form W-2. By agreement with his employer, none of the allowance was for meals and entertainment expenses. Frank must make an adequate accounting of his expenses to his employer and return any excess reimbursements. His daily business journal disclosed that from January 2 (the date of purchase) through December 31, he drove his own automobile 29,151 miles, of which 16,735 were business related. Frank's average roundtrip commuting distance is six miles, and his commuting miles total 1,440 for the year. Since Frank dislikes keeping records, he uses the standard mileage rate to determine his automobile tax deduction. His substantiated paid business expenses are as follows:

Travel expenses	$2,168*
Parking fees	210
Meals and entertainment	560
Miscellaneous expenses	91

*Excludes meals, entertainment, and auto expenses

Sandra belongs to a car pool and drives to work every fourth week. In addition, her car is used on vacations.

In August, Sandra received $400 of interest when she cashed in a CD from State Bank. The Middleton Farmers Bank credited $300 of interest to the Andersons' joint savings account during the year. The Andersons itemized deductions in 2005 and overpaid their state income tax by $142, all of which provided a tax benefit. They received a refund of this amount in March, 2006. Since they both work outside the home, they are unable to be there when their children return from school. This year the Andersons paid a neighbor, Gloria Dryden (SSN 992-31-4270), $4,100 to care for their children in her home after school hours and during the summer vacation period while the Andersons were at work. Gloria Dryden's address is 2132 Century Avenue, Middleton, CA 92657.

During January, Sandra received unemployment compensation of $1,000, covering two months between jobs. Frank is covered by a qualified pension plan at work; Sandra is not. The Andersons are interested in contributing to their respective traditional IRAs the maximum that they can deduct on their 2006 tax return. Both contributions take place before April 15, 2007.

Cancelled checks, receipts, and paid bills support the following expenditures:

Orlo T. Miller, M.D. (not covered by insurance)	$ 818
Qualified Stop Smoking program for Sandra	175
Alex B. Kramer, D.V.M. (treatment of Fritz, the Andersons' dog)	168
Life insurance premiums on Frank with Sandra as beneficiary	1,200
Kathryn R. Smith, dentist (not covered by insurance)	459
Weight loss program for Frank (cosmetic purposes)	180
Martin R. Anderson, optometrist (not covered by insurance)	50
Maternity clothes for Sandra	450
Eyeglasses for Martha (not covered by insurance)	175
Driver's license renewal for Sandra	32
Fishing license for Frank	12
Interest on personal loan for vacation	275
Interest on home mortgage of principal residence	1,272
Real estate taxes	2,851
Trash pickup fees	120
Home repairs and improvements	620
Homeowner's insurance	500
General sales taxes	572
State gasoline taxes	98
Contribution to First Unity Church of California (with receipts)	986
Value of Frank's time volunteered to Girl Scouts	300
Political contributions	50
Bingo and lottery tickets	260
Rental for safe deposit box to store investment items	27
Legal fees paid on personal injury case	875

In addition, the Andersons paid $280 to Homer P. Gill (SSN 726-20-3334) of 5732 Monona Drive, Madison, CA 92657, to prepare their 2005 tax return.

Carol earned $360 from baby-sitting on weekends. Her parents also paid $500 for summer computer camp for her to get ready for the fall semester.

When Frank's father died on Christmas day, Frank immediately inherited the father's savings account (on which he also had signed, as an emergency measure). The account contained $20,000.

Part of Frank's compensation package included group-term life insurance equal to 75% of his annual salary. The cost to the company for the premium was $240.

Sandra's best friend, Nancy, had moved to Sweden. Nancy's daughter, Inga, came to stay with the Andersons for the school year. Inga had a part-time job after school and earned $3,500 to use for spending money and touring. The Andersons provided all of her support.

Required: Assume you are Homer P. Gill. Prepare the Andersons' joint income tax return using Form 1040, Schedule A, Form 2106, and Form 2441. All parties sign and date the income tax return on April 1, 2007. The Andersons will take the standard credit allowed to them for federal telephone excise tax paid.

(Use for Cumulative Problem.)

Form **1040** Department of the Treasury—Internal Revenue Service **U.S. Individual Income Tax Return 2006** (99) IRS Use Only—Do not write or staple in this space.

For the year Jan. 1–Dec. 31, 2006, or other tax year beginning , 2006, ending , 20 OMB No. 1545-0074

Label (See instructions on page 16.) **Use the IRS label.** Otherwise, please print or type.

LABEL HERE

Your first name and initial	Last name	Your social security number
If a joint return, spouse's first name and initial	Last name	Spouse's social security number
Home address (number and street). If you have a P.O. box, see page 16.	Apt. no.	▲ You **must** enter your SSN(s) above. ▲
City, town or post office, state, and ZIP code. If you have a foreign address, see page 16.		Checking a box below will not change your tax or refund.

Presidential Election Campaign ▶ Check here if you, or your spouse if filing jointly, want $3 to go to this fund (see page 16) ▶ ☐ **You** ☐ **Spouse**

Filing Status

Check only one box.

1 ☐ Single
2 ☐ Married filing jointly (even if only one had income)
3 ☐ Married filing separately. Enter spouse's SSN above and full name here. ▶
4 ☐ Head of household (with qualifying person). (See page 17.) If the qualifying person is a child but not your dependent, enter this child's name here. ▶
5 ☐ Qualifying widow(er) with dependent child (see page 17)

Exemptions

6a ☐ **Yourself.** If someone can claim you as a dependent, **do not** check box 6a
b ☐ **Spouse**
c **Dependents:**

If more than four dependents, see page 19.

(1) First name Last name	(2) Dependent's social security number	(3) Dependent's relationship to you	(4) ✓ if qualifying child for child tax credit (see page 19)
			☐
			☐
			☐
			☐

d Total number of exemptions claimed

Boxes checked on 6a and 6b ____
No. of children on 6c who:
• lived with you ____
• did not live with you due to divorce or separation (see page 20) ____
Dependents on 6c not entered above ____
Add numbers on lines above ▶ ☐

Income

Attach Form(s) W-2 here. Also attach Forms W-2G and 1099-R if tax was withheld.

If you did not get a W-2, see page 22.

Enclose, but do not attach, any payment. Also, please use **Form 1040-V.**

7	Wages, salaries, tips, etc. Attach Form(s) W-2		7	
8a	**Taxable** interest. Attach Schedule B if required		8a	
b	**Tax-exempt** interest. **Do not** include on line 8a	8b		
9a	Ordinary dividends. Attach Schedule B if required		9a	
b	Qualified dividends (see page 23)	9b		
10	Taxable refunds, credits, or offsets of state and local income taxes (see page 23)		10	
11	Alimony received		11	
12	Business income or (loss). Attach Schedule C or C-EZ		12	
13	Capital gain or (loss). Attach Schedule D if required. If not required, check here ▶ ☐		13	
14	Other gains or (losses). Attach Form 4797		14	
15a	IRA distributions 15a	b Taxable amount (see page 25)	15b	
16a	Pensions and annuities 16a	b Taxable amount (see page 25)	16b	
17	Rental real estate, royalties, partnerships, S corporations, trusts, etc. Attach Schedule E		17	
18	Farm income or (loss). Attach Schedule F		18	
19	Unemployment compensation		19	
20a	Social security benefits 20a	b Taxable amount (see page 27)	20b	
21	Other income. List type and amount (see page 29)		21	
22	Add the amounts in the far right column for lines 7 through 21. This is your **total income** ▶		22	

Adjusted Gross Income

23	Archer MSA deduction. Attach Form 8853	23		
24	Certain business expenses of reservists, performing artists, and fee-basis government officials. Attach Form 2106 or 2106-EZ	24		
25	Health savings account deduction. Attach Form 8889	25		
26	Moving expenses. Attach Form 3903	26		
27	One-half of self-employment tax. Attach Schedule SE	27		
28	Self-employed SEP, SIMPLE, and qualified plans	28		
29	Self-employed health insurance deduction (see page 30)	29		
30	Penalty on early withdrawal of savings	30		
31a	Alimony paid b Recipient's SSN ▶	31a		
32	IRA deduction (see page 31)	32		
33	Student loan interest deduction (see page 33)	33		
34	Jury duty pay you gave to your employer	34		
35	Domestic production activities deduction. Attach Form 8903	35		
36	Add lines 23 through 31a and 32 through 35		36	
37	Subtract line 36 from line 22. This is your **adjusted gross income** ▶		37	

For Disclosure, Privacy Act, and Paperwork Reduction Act Notice, see page 78. Cat. No. 11320B Form **1040** (2006)

(Use for Cumulative Problem.)

Form 1040 (2006) Page 2

Tax and Credits

	38	Amount from line 37 (adjusted gross income)		38
	39a	Check if: ☐ **You** were born before January 2, 1942, ☐ Blind. ☐ **Spouse** was born before January 2, 1942, ☐ Blind. Total boxes checked ▶ 39a		
Standard Deduction for—	b	If your spouse itemizes on a separate return or you were a dual-status alien, see page 35 and check here ▶39b ☐		
• People who checked any box on line 39a or 39b **or** who can be claimed as a dependent, see page 36.	40	**Itemized deductions** (from Schedule A) **or** your **standard deduction** (see left margin)		40
• All others:	41	Subtract line 40 from line 38		41
Single or Married filing separately, $5,150	42	If line 38 is over $112,875, or you provided housing to a person displaced by Hurricane Katrina, see page 37. Otherwise, multiply $3,300 by the total number of exemptions claimed on line 6d		42
Married filing jointly or Qualifying widow(er), $10,300	43	**Taxable income.** Subtract line 42 from line 41. If line 42 is more than line 41, enter -0-		43
Head of household, $7,550	44	**Tax** (see page 37). Check if any tax is from: **a** ☐ Form(s) 8814 **b** ☐ Form 4972		44
	45	**Alternative minimum tax** (see page 39). Attach Form 6251		45
	46	Add lines 44 and 45 ▶		46
	47	Foreign tax credit. Attach Form 1116 if required	47	
	48	Credit for child and dependent care expenses. Attach Form 2441	48	
	49	Credit for the elderly or the disabled. Attach Schedule R	49	
	50	Education credits. Attach Form 8863	50	
	51	Retirement savings contributions credit. Attach Form 8880	51	
	52	Residential energy credits. Attach Form 5695	52	
	53	Child tax credit (see page XX). Attach Form 8901 if required	53	
	54	Credits from: **a** ☐ Form 8396 **b** ☐ Form 8839 **c** ☐ Form 8859	54	
	55	Other credits: **a** ☐ Form 3800 **b** ☐ Form 8801 **c** ☐ Form ____	55	
	56	Add lines 47 through 55. These are your **total credits**		56
	57	Subtract line 56 from line 46. If line 56 is more than line 46, enter -0- ▶		57

Other Taxes

58	Self-employment tax. Attach Schedule SE	58
59	Social security and Medicare tax on tip income not reported to employer. Attach Form 4137	59
60	Additional tax on IRAs, other qualified retirement plans, etc. Attach Form 5329 if required	60
61	Advance earned income credit payments from Form(s) W-2, box 9	61
62	Household employment taxes. Attach Schedule H	62
63	Add lines 57 through 62. This is your **total tax** ▶	63

Payments

	64	Federal income tax withheld from Forms W-2 and 1099	64	
	65	2006 estimated tax payments and amount applied from 2005 return	65	
If you have a qualifying child, attach Schedule EIC.	66a	**Earned income credit (EIC)**	66a	
	b	Nontaxable combat pay election ▶ 66b		
	67	Excess social security and tier 1 RRTA tax withheld (see page 59)	67	
	68	Additional child tax credit. Attach Form 8812	68	
	69	Amount paid with request for extension to file (see page 59)	69	
	70	Payments from: **a** ☐ Form 2439 **b** ☐ Form 4136 **c** ☐ Form 8885	70	
	71	Credit for federal telephone excise tax paid. Attach Form 8913 if required	71	
	72	Add lines 64, 65, 66a, and 67 through 71. These are your **total payments** ▶		72

Refund

	73	If line 72 is more than line 63, subtract line 63 from line 72. This is the amount you **overpaid**	73
Direct deposit? See page 59 and fill in 74b, 74c, and 74d, or Form 8888.	74a	Amount of line 73 you want **refunded to you.** If Form 8888 is attached, check here ▶ ☐	74a
▶	b	Routing number ▶ **c** Type: ☐ Checking ☐ Savings	
▶	d	Account number	
	75	Amount of line 73 you want **applied to your 2007 estimated tax** ▶ 75	

Amount You Owe

76	**Amount you owe.** Subtract line 72 from line 63. For details on how to pay, see page 60 ▶	76
77	Estimated tax penalty (see page 60) 77	

Third Party Designee

Do you want to allow another person to discuss this return with the IRS (see page 61)? ☐ **Yes.** Complete the following. ☐ **No**

Designee's name ▶ Phone no. ▶ ( ) Personal identification number (PIN) ▶

Sign Here

Joint return? See page 17. Keep a copy for your records.

Under penalties of perjury, I declare that I have examined this return and accompanying schedules and statements, and to the best of my knowledge and belief, they are true, correct, and complete. Declaration of preparer (other than taxpayer) is based on all information of which preparer has any knowledge.

Your signature	Date	Your occupation	Daytime phone number ( )
Spouse's signature. If a joint return, **both** must sign.	Date	Spouse's occupation	

Paid Preparer's Use Only

Preparer's signature	Date	Check if self-employed ☐	Preparer's SSN or PTIN
Firm's name (or yours if self-employed), address, and ZIP code		EIN	
		Phone no.	( )

Form **1040** (2006)

Printed on recycled paper

(Use for Cumulative Problem.)

SCHEDULES A&B (Form 1040)
Department of the Treasury Internal Revenue Service (99)

Schedule A—Itemized Deductions

(Schedule B is on back)

▶ Attach to Form 1040. ▶ See Instructions for Schedules A&B (Form 1040).

OMB No. 1545-0074
2006
Attachment Sequence No. **07**

Name(s) shown on Form 1040 | **Your social security number**

Medical and Dental Expenses		**Caution.** Do not include expenses reimbursed or paid by others.				
	1	Medical and dental expenses (see page A-2)	1			
	2	Enter amount from Form 1040, line 38 [2]				
	3	Multiply line 2 by 7.5% (.075)	3			
	4	Subtract line 3 from line 1. If line 3 is more than line 1, enter -0-			4	
Taxes You Paid (See page A-2.)	5	State and local income taxes	5			
	6	Real estate taxes (see page A-5)	6			
	7	Personal property taxes	7			
	8	Other taxes. List type and amount ▶	8			
	9	Add lines 5 through 8			9	
Interest You Paid (See page A-5.)	10	Home mortgage interest and points reported to you on Form 1098	10			
Note. Personal interest is not deductible.	11	Home mortgage interest not reported to you on Form 1098. If paid to the person from whom you bought the home, see page A-6 and show that person's name, identifying no., and address ▶	11			
	12	Points not reported to you on Form 1098. See page A-6 for special rules	12			
	13	Investment interest. Attach Form 4952 if required. (See page A-6.)	13			
	14	Add lines 10 through 13			14	
Gifts to Charity If you made a gift and got a benefit for it, see page A-7.	15	Gifts by cash or check. If you made any gift of $250 or more, see page A-7	15			
	16	Other than by cash or check. If any gift of $250 or more, see page A-7. You **must** attach Form 8283 if over $500	16			
	17	Carryover from prior year	17			
	18	Add lines 15 through 17			18	
Casualty and Theft Losses	19	Casualty or theft loss(es). Attach Form 4684. (See page A-8.)			19	
Job Expenses and Certain Miscellaneous Deductions (See page A-8.)	20	Unreimbursed employee expenses—job travel, union dues, job education, etc. Attach Form 2106 or 2106-EZ if required. (See page A-8.) ▶	20			
	21	Tax preparation fees	21			
	22	Other expenses—investment, safe deposit box, etc. List type and amount ▶	22			
	23	Add lines 20 through 22	23			
	24	Enter amount from Form 1040, line 38 [24]				
	25	Multiply line 24 by 2% (.02)	25			
	26	Subtract line 25 from line 23. If line 25 is more than line 23, enter -0-			26	
Other Miscellaneous Deductions	27	Other—from list on page A-9. List type and amount ▶			27	
Total Itemized Deductions	28	Is Form 1040, line 38, over $150,500 (over $75,250 if married filing separately)? ☐ **No.** Your deduction is not limited. Add the amounts in the far right column for lines 4 through 27. Also, enter this amount on Form 1040, line 40. ☐ **Yes.** Your deduction may be limited. See page A-9 for the amount to enter. ▶			28	
	29	If you elect to itemize deductions even though they are less than your standard deduction, check here ▶ ☐				

For Paperwork Reduction Act Notice, see Form 1040 instructions. Cat. No. 11330X **Schedule A (Form 1040) 2006**

(Use for Cumulative Problem.)

Form **2106** | **Employee Business Expenses** | OMB No. 1545-0074

▶ See separate instructions. | **2006**

Department of the Treasury Internal Revenue Service (99) | ▶ Attach to Form 1040 or Form 1040NR. | Attachment Sequence No. **54**

Your name	Occupation in which you incurred expenses	Social security number

Part I **Employee Business Expenses and Reimbursements**

Step 1 Enter Your Expenses		**Column A** Other Than Meals and Entertainment	**Column B** Meals and Entertainment
1 Vehicle expense from line 22 or line 29. (Rural mail carriers: See instructions.)	1		
2 Parking fees, tolls, and transportation, including train, bus, etc., that **did not** involve overnight travel or commuting to and from work	2		
3 Travel expense while away from home overnight, including lodging, airplane, car rental, etc. **Do not** include meals and entertainment	3		
4 Business expenses not included on lines 1 through 3. **Do not** include meals and entertainment	4		
5 Meals and entertainment expenses (see instructions)	5		
6 **Total expenses.** In Column A, add lines 1 through 4 and enter the result. In Column B, enter the amount from line 5	6		

Note: *If you were not reimbursed for any expenses in Step 1, skip line 7 and enter the amount from line 6 on line 8.*

Step 2 Enter Reimbursements Received From Your Employer for Expenses Listed in Step 1

		Column A	Column B
7 Enter reimbursements received from your employer that were **not** reported to you in box 1 of Form W-2. Include any reimbursements reported under code "L" in box 12 of your Form W-2 (see instructions)	7		

Step 3 Figure Expenses To Deduct on Schedule A (Form 1040)

		Column A	Column B
8 Subtract line 7 from line 6. If zero or less, enter -0-. However, if line 7 is greater than line 6 in Column A, report the excess as income on Form 1040, line 7 (or on Form 1040NR, line 8)	8		
Note: *If **both columns** of line 8 are zero, you cannot deduct employee business expenses. Stop here and attach Form 2106 to your return.*			
9 In Column A, enter the amount from line 8. In Column B, multiply line 8 by 50% (.50). (Employees subject to Department of Transportation (DOT) hours of service limits: Multiply meal expenses incurred while away from home on business by 75% (.75) instead of 50%. For details, see instructions.)	9		
10 Add the amounts on line 9 of both columns and enter the total here. **Also, enter the total on Schedule A (Form 1040), line 20** (or on Schedule A (Form 1040NR), line 9). (Reservists, qualified performing artists, fee-basis state or local government officials, and individuals with disabilities: See the instructions for special rules on where to enter the total.) ▶	10		

For Paperwork Reduction Act Notice, see instructions. Cat. No. 11700N Form **2106** (2006)

(Use for Cumulative Problem.)

Form 2106 (2006) Page **2**

Part II Vehicle Expenses

Section A—General Information (You must complete this section if you are claiming vehicle expenses.)		**(a)** Vehicle 1	**(b)** Vehicle 2
11 Enter the date the vehicle was placed in service	11	/ /	/ /
12 Total miles the vehicle was driven during 2006	12	miles	miles
13 Business miles included on line 12	13	miles	miles
14 Percent of business use. Divide line 13 by line 12	14	%	%
15 Average daily roundtrip commuting distance	15	miles	miles
16 Commuting miles included on line 12	16	miles	miles
17 Other miles. Add lines 13 and 16 and subtract the total from line 12	17	miles	miles

18 Do you (or your spouse) have another vehicle available for personal use? ☐ Yes ☐ No

19 Was your vehicle available for personal use during off-duty hours? ☐ Yes ☐ No

20 Do you have evidence to support your deduction? ☐ Yes ☐ No

21 If "Yes," is the evidence written? ☐ Yes ☐ No

Section B—Standard Mileage Rate (See the instructions for Part II to find out whether to complete this section or Section C.)

22 Multiply line 13 by 44.5¢ (.445) . . . **22**

Section C—Actual Expenses		**(a)** Vehicle 1	**(b)** Vehicle 2
23 Gasoline, oil, repairs, vehicle insurance, etc.	23		
24a Vehicle rentals	24a		
b Inclusion amount (see instructions)	24b		
c Subtract line 24b from line 24a	24c		
25 Value of employer-provided vehicle (applies only if 100% of annual lease value was included on Form W-2—see instructions)	25		
26 Add lines 23, 24c, and 25	26		
27 Multiply line 26 by the percentage on line 14	27		
28 Depreciation (see instructions)	28		
29 Add lines 27 and 28. Enter total here and on line 1	29		

Section D—Depreciation of Vehicles (Use this section only if you owned the vehicle and are completing Section C for the vehicle.)

		(a) Vehicle 1	**(b)** Vehicle 2
30 Enter cost or other basis (see instructions)	30		
31 Enter section 179 deduction (see instructions)	31		
32 Multiply line 30 by line 14 (see instructions if you claimed the section 179 deduction or special allowance)	32		
33 Enter depreciation method and percentage (see instructions)	33		
34 Multiply line 32 by the percentage on line 33 (see instructions)	34		
35 Add lines 31 and 34	35		
36 Enter the applicable limit explained in the line 36 instructions	36		
37 Multiply line 36 by the percentage on line 14	37		
38 Enter the **smaller** of line 35 or line 37. If you skipped lines 36 and 37, enter the amount from line 35. Also enter this amount on line 28 above	38		

Form **2106** (2006)

(Use for Cumulative Problem.)

Form **2441**

Department of the Treasury Internal Revenue Service (99)

Child and Dependent Care Expenses

▶ Attach to Form 1040 or Form 1040NR.

▶ See separate instructions.

OMB No. 1545-0074

2006

Attachment Sequence No. 21

Name(s) shown on Form 1040 | Your social security number

Before you begin: You need to understand the following terms. See **Definitions** on page 1 of the instructions.

- **Dependent Care Benefits**
- **Qualifying Person(s)**
- **Qualified Expenses**

Part I Persons or Organizations Who Provided the Care—You **must** complete this part. (If you need more space, use the bottom of page 2.)

1 (a) Care provider's name	(b) Address (number, street, apt. no., city, state, and ZIP code)	(c) Identifying number (SSN or EIN)	(d) Amount paid (see instructions)

Did you receive **dependent care benefits?**
- **No** ▶ Complete only Part II below.
- **Yes** ▶ Complete Part III on the back next.

Caution. If the care was provided in your home, you may owe employment taxes. See the instructions for Form 1040, line 62, or Form 1040NR, line 57.

Part II Credit for Child and Dependent Care Expenses

2 Information about your **qualifying person(s).** If you have more than two qualifying persons, see the instructions.

(a) Qualifying person's name — First	Last	(b) Qualifying person's social security number	(c) **Qualified expenses** you incurred and paid in 2006 for the person listed in column (a)

3 Add the amounts in column (c) of line 2. **Do not** enter more than $3,000 for one qualifying person or $6,000 for two or more persons. If you completed Part III, enter the amount from line 33 . . . . . **3**

4 Enter your **earned income.** See instructions **4**

5 If married filing jointly, enter your spouse's earned income (if your spouse was a student or was disabled, see the instructions); **all others,** enter the amount from line 4 . . . **5**

6 Enter the **smallest** of line 3, 4, or 5 . . . . . **6**

7 Enter the amount from Form 1040, line 38, or Form 1040NR, line 36 . . . . . **7**

8 Enter on line 8 the decimal amount shown below that applies to the amount on line 7

If line 7 is: Over	But not over	Decimal amount is	If line 7 is: Over	But not over	Decimal amount is
$0—	15,000	.35	$29,000—	31,000	.27
15,000—	17,000	.34	31,000—	33,000	.26
17,000—	19,000	.33	33,000—	35,000	.25
19,000—	21,000	.32	35,000—	37,000	.24
21,000—	23,000	.31	37,000—	39,000	.23
23,000—	25,000	.30	39,000—	41,000	.22
25,000—	27,000	.29	41,000—	43,000	.21
27,000—	29,000	.28	43,000—	No limit	.20

8 X .

9 Multiply line 6 by the decimal amount on line 8. If you paid 2005 expenses in 2006, see the instructions **9**

10 Enter the amount from Form 1040, line 46, minus any amount on Form 1040, line 47, or Form 1040NR, line 43, minus any amount on Form 1040NR, line 44 . . . . . **10**

11 **Credit for child and dependent care expenses.** Enter the **smaller** of line 9 or line 10 here and on Form 1040, line 48, or Form 1040NR, line 45 . . . . . **11**

For Paperwork Reduction Act Notice, see page 4 of the instructions. Cat. No. 11862M Form **2441** (2006)

Self-Employment

CHAPTER CONTENTS

CHAPTER OVERVIEW

Chapters 1 through 6 presented the basic structure for reporting income and deductions. This chapter focuses on the tax reporting for self-employed taxpayers. It shows how they compute their self-employment net income and self-employment taxes. This chapter also covers retirement plans available to self-employed persons.

Sole proprietors report income and expenses on Schedule C (Form 1040), Profit or Loss From Business. They then compute the self-employment tax on their profits on Schedule SE (Form 1040), Self-Employment Tax. After they complete Schedules C and SE they can compute the amount they can contribute (and deduct for AGI) to their retirement plans.

To understand the reporting process for self-employed taxpayers, it is important to realize that tax and financial accounting rules may differ. Thus, net income shown on Schedule C may not be the same as the net income reflected on the "books" of the business. For example, self-employed taxpayers who sell business property do not report the gain or loss on Schedule C. Instead, they report it on Form 4797, Sales of Business Property. However, for financial accounting purposes, they include the gain or loss in computing "book" net income. With the exception of the section on self-employment tax and retirement plans for self-employed taxpayers, the scope of this chapter is limited to income and expense items reported on Schedule C.

ACCOUNTING METHODS

All businesses must keep records to support the calculation of taxable income. Most taxpayers use either the cash or accrual method of accounting, but other methods may apply. Some taxpayers use one method for tax purposes and another for their financial statements. Taxpayers using the cash method to report income must use it to deduct expenses. Likewise, those who deduct expenses using the accrual method must use the accrual method to report income.

Taxpayers may use the accrual method to compute business profits and the cash method for their nonbusiness items. Those with more than one business may use different accounting methods for each separate and distinct business. Most businesses with gross receipts in excess of $5 million must use the accrual method.

Cash Method

Under the cash method, taxpayers report income when they actually or constructively receive it. Taxpayers constructively receive income when it is credited to their accounts or made available to them without restrictions. Taxpayers who receive income other than cash report as income the fair market value (FMV) of the property or services received.

EXAMPLE 1

On December 31, 20x1, Ben Carson receives a check for $200 in payment of fees earned. Carson constructively receives the $200 in 20x1, even if the check cannot be cashed until January 2, 20x2. Thus, Carson reports the $200 as income in 20x1.

EXAMPLE 2

On December 30, 20x1, Jane Dillow receives a check for $500 as payment for services rendered. The customer informs Dillow that the check will bounce if cashed before January 2, 20x2. Because the funds are not available until 20x2 Dillow has not constructively received the $500 in 20x1. Dillow reports the $500 as income in 20x2.

EXAMPLE 3

Scott Edwards receives ten shares of stock in exchange for services rendered. The market value of a share of stock is $28. Edwards reports income of $280 ($28 × 10 shares).

Under the cash method, taxpayers deduct expenses when they pay the cash, but only if the expenses relate to the current or a previous tax year. Taxpayers usually deduct prepaid amounts in the year the prepaid item is used in their businesses. Thus, cash basis taxpayers who prepay rent, insurance, etc., must wait until it is used in their businesses before they deduct it.

EXAMPLE 4

On September 23, 20x1, Laura Fuller pays $36,000 for two years' insurance coverage that begins on October 1, 20x1. Although Fuller is a cash basis taxpayer, she cannot deduct the $36,000 payment in 20x1. Instead she deducts $4,500 ($36,000/24 × 3) in 20x1. Fuller will deduct $18,000 ($36,000/24 × 12) in 20x2 and the rest ($36,000/24 × 9 = $13,500) in 20x3.

Businesses that sell services rather than merchandise often use the cash method of accounting. For example, lawyers who use the cash method will keep logs of fees charged to clients but record the fees as income only when they receive the cash. Likewise, they record expenses for rent, supplies, and other items when they pay the cash.

Accrual Method

Under the accrual method, income includes amounts earned or accrued but not received. Expenses include liabilities incurred but not paid. The accrual method acts on the right to receive the revenue rather than the actual receipt of cash. It acts on the use of the asset or service rather than the actual cash payment.

EXAMPLE 5

On January 3, 20x2, an employer pays salaries that employees earned for the week ended December 31, 20x1. Under the accrual method, the employer reports the salaries as an expense in 20x1. Under the cash method, the employer reports the expense in 20x2.

Taxpayers account for prepaid expenses the same way under both the cash and accrual methods. That is, they deduct only the amounts properly allocable to a given year and carry forward the rest to the next year. In Example 4, the amount deducted each year would be the same had Fuller used the accrual method of accounting.

The tax law generally requires taxpayers using the accrual method to recognize prepaid income in the year they receive it. However, when the taxpayer sells goods or performs services that extend beyond the current tax year, most prepaid income can be spread over the current year and the next tax year. Also, some accrual-method taxpayers do not have to accrue service revenue that experience indicates will not be collectible. These taxpayers include those who perform qualified services (like health, law, consulting) and those whose businesses had average annual gross receipts of $5 million or less for the last three years.

EXAMPLE 6

James Clark is in the business of selling and repairing televisions. On April 1, 20x1, Clark receives $1,200 from one of his customers for a 2-year warranty contract. Clark can report $450 ($1,200 × 9/24) on his 20x1 tax return and the rest ($1,200 × 15/24 = $750) on his 20x2 tax return. Clark must report the entire $1,200 on his 20x1 and 20x2 tax returns, even though some of the services extend into 20x3.

The exception for postponing prepaid income does not extend to prepaid interest. It also does not extend to prepaid warranty income received by third parties and to some prepaid rent. Taxpayers who receive these types of prepaid items report the full amounts in income in the year they receive it.

EXAMPLE 7

Same as in Example 6, except that Clark offers the warranty contract as a third-party provider. Here, Clark reports the entire $1,200 in gross income in 20x1.

REPORTING PROFIT OR LOSS BY INDIVIDUALS, PARTNERSHIPS, AND CORPORATIONS

Partnerships and corporations are entities separate from their owners and must file separate returns. A self-employed taxpayer who owns a business reports net profit or (loss) on Form 1040. Schedule C (Form 1040), Profit or Loss From Business, summarizes the revenues and expenses of sole proprietors.

Only self-employment income and related expenses are reported on Schedule C. Income that is not self-employment income is not reported on Schedule C. Instead, it is reported on some other form or schedule. For example, fees earned from an occasional lecture are not self-employment income. These fees are reported as "Other income" on Form 1040, page 1.

EXAMPLES OF SELF-EMPLOYMENT INCOME

- Consulting fees
- Director's fees
- Earnings of a registered nurse or licensed practicing nurse employed directly by the patient
- Fees charged by a child-care provider, unless services are provided in the parent's home
- Earnings of a newspaper vendor over age 17
- Fees earned by a clergy member or a Christian Science practitioner
- General partner's distributive share of partnership ordinary income and loss
- Guaranteed payments to partners
- Fees earned by a professional executor
- Commissions earned by a real estate agent
- Royalties received by an author

EXAMPLES OF INCOME OTHER THAN SELF-EMPLOYMENT INCOME

- Dividends, unless a dealer in securities
- Earnings of a corporate employee, even if a 100% shareholder of the corporation
- Fees earned from an occasional lecture
- Gains and losses on the sale of property
- Interest
- Limited partner's distributive share of partnership ordinary income or loss
- Real estate rentals, unless a real estate dealer
- Payment to a registered nurse or licensed nurse hired by an agency, doctor, or hospital
- S corporation shareholder's prorata share of the corporation's ordinary income or loss
- Wages and tips received for services performed as an employee
- Wages of a newspaper carrier under age 18

To be deductible, expenses from a business must be *ordinary and necessary* for its operation. Also, the expenses must be *reasonable* in amount. An expense is ordinary if it is customary or usual in the taxpayer's line of business. An expense is necessary if it helps the taxpayer's business. As a rule, revenues need not exceed expenses in any given year. However, in the case of a hobby activity, a taxpayer cannot deduct expenses in excess of revenues. (Hobby losses were covered in Chapter 6.) For the most part, the same rules for reporting revenues and expenses apply to all businesses. For example, all self-employed taxpayers must elect an accounting method regardless of whether they operate a farm or a professional practice.

DEDUCTIBLE BUSINESS EXPENSES

- Accounting and bookkeeping fees
- Advertising
- Bad debts
- Bank service charges
- Commissions and fees
- Contract labor costs
- Cost of goods sold
- Depletion and depreciation
- Education
- Employee achievement awards
- Employee benefit programs
- Employees' pension and profit-sharing plans
- Employment agency fees
- Gifts
- Insurance, license fees, and taxes
- Interest on business loans
- Legal and professional services
- Maintenance and repairs
- Meals and entertainment
- Office supplies and expense
- Rent
- Salaries and wages
- Professional dues and subscriptions
- Tax planning and tax preparation fees
- Telephone and utilities
- Transportation, including car and truck expenses
- Travel away from home

REPORTING NET PROFIT (OR LOSS) BY SOLE PROPRIETORSHIPS

Any net profit derived from a business or a profession operated as a sole proprietorship is taxable. A net loss is deducted in arriving at adjusted gross income. In computing the amount of net profit (or loss), sole proprietors subtract from business income the cost of goods sold and all ordinary, necessary, and reasonable business expenses. The costs of capital expenditures, such as trucks, office machinery, and buildings, are deducted over several years through annual depreciation deductions (covered in Chapter 8).

Sole proprietorships report net profit on either Schedule C-EZ, Net Profit From Business, or Schedule C, Profit or Loss From Business. Only certain businesses can file Schedule C-EZ. Therefore, this chapter focuses on Schedule C.

REQUIREMENTS FOR USING SCHEDULE C-EZ

- Cash method of accounting is used
- Only one business operated as a sole proprietor
- No employees during the year
- No inventory at any time during the year
- Business expenses of $5,000 or less
- No net loss from the business
- No unallowed prior year passive activity loss from the business
- No deduction for business use of the home
- Not required to file Form 4562, Depreciation and Amortization, for the business

STRUCTURE OF SCHEDULE C

Schedule C, Profit or Loss From Business, is a two-page schedule that reports the net profit or (loss) from a business operated as a sole proprietorship. A sole proprietor must pay self-employment tax on Schedule C profits. When a married couple files a joint return and each spouse owns a business, each spouse must file a Schedule C. If only one spouse owns a business, only the proprietor's name appears on Schedule C. If a proprietor owns more than one business, a separate Schedule C must be filed for each business.

Schedule C (Figure 7-1) supports the amount shown on Form 1040, page 1 (line 12). Page 1 (Schedule C) focuses on the calculation of net profit (or loss). It also requests general information about the business. Page 2 provides the supporting data for cost of goods sold and other expenses shown on page 1.

Information for Figure 7-1: Filled-In Schedule C (Form 1040)

Figure 7-1 illustrates Schedule C for George L. Monroe, owner of George L. Monroe, Consulting. The principal business code for consulting is 541600 (found in instructions to Schedule C). Monroe uses the cash method and materially participates in the operation of his consulting business. Because Monroe is required to withhold and pay payroll taxes on behalf of his employees, he applied for and received from the IRS an Employer ID number. Monroe reports this number on Schedule C (line D).

ITEM-BY-ITEM REPORTING ON SCHEDULE C

This section comments on each line item shown on Schedule C. The amounts reported relate to Monroe's filled-in Schedule C from Figure 7-1.

Schedule C, Part I: Income

Gross Receipts or Sales, $156,921 (Line 1)

Monroe operates a consulting practice (line A) and uses the cash method of accounting to report income and expenses (line F). Thus, Monroe's gross sales include amounts actually or constructively received during the year.

Returns and Allowances, $0 (Line 2)

Taxpayers subtract returns and allowances from gross receipts or sales to arrive at net receipts or sales (line 3). Since Monroe operates a service business, he had no returns or allowances. Thus, net receipts or sales of $156,921 equals gross receipts or sales.

Cost of Goods Sold, $0 (Line 4)

Taxpayers deduct the cost of goods sold from net receipts or sales to arrive at gross profit (line 5). Taxpayers calculate cost of goods sold on Schedule C, Part III (covered later in the chapter). Since Monroe's business does not involve selling products, he does not complete Part III. Monroe's gross profit of $156,921 equals net receipts or sales.

Gross Income, $156,921 (Line 7)

Gross income equals other income (line 6) plus gross profit (line 5). Other income includes Federal and state gasoline or fuel tax credits or refunds. It also includes interest income earned by the business.

FIGURE 7-1 Filled-In Schedule C, Form 1040, Page 1

SCHEDULE C (Form 1040)
Department of the Treasury Internal Revenue Service (99)

Profit or Loss From Business
(Sole Proprietorship)

▶ Partnerships, joint ventures, etc., must file Form 1065 or 1065-B.
▶ Attach to Form 1040, 1040NR, or 1041. ▶ See Instructions for Schedule C (Form 1040).

OMB No. 1545-0074
2006
Attachment Sequence No. 09

Name of proprietor: George L. Monroe
Social security number (SSN): 139 24 6880

A Principal business or profession, including product or service (see page C-2 of the instructions): Management Consultant
B Enter code from pages C-8, 9, & 10 ▶ 541600

C Business name. If no separate business name, leave blank. George L. Monroe, Consulting
D Employer ID number (EIN), if any: 39-6420797

E Business address (including suite or room no.) ▶ 1712 Market Street
City, town or post office, state, and ZIP code: Cincinnati, OH 45227-3193

F Accounting method: (1) ☒ Cash (2) ☐ Accrual (3) ☐ Other (specify) ▶
G Did you "materially participate" in the operation of this business during 2006? If "No," see page C-2 for limit on losses ☒ Yes ☐ No
H If you started or acquired this business during 2006, check here ▶ ☐

Part I Income

		Line	Amount
1	Gross receipts or sales. **Caution.** If this income was reported to you on Form W-2 and the "Statutory employee" box on that form was checked, see page C-3 and check here ▶ ☐	1	156,921 00
2	Returns and allowances	2	
3	Subtract line 2 from line 1	3	156,921 00
4	Cost of goods sold (from line 42 on page 2)	4	
5	**Gross profit.** Subtract line 4 from line 3	5	156,921 00
6	Other income, including federal and state gasoline or fuel tax credit or refund (see page C-3)	6	
7	**Gross income.** Add lines 5 and 6 ▶	7	156,921 00

Part II Expenses. Enter expenses for business use of your home **only** on line 30.

		Line	Amount			Line	Amount
8	Advertising	8	492 00	18	Office expense	18	1,640 00
9	Car and truck expenses (see page C-4)	9	2,940 00	19	Pension and profit-sharing plans	19	
10	Commissions and fees	10		20	Rent or lease (see page C-5):		
11	Contract labor (see page C-4)	11		a	Vehicles, machinery, and equipment	20a	1,200 00
12	Depletion	12		b	Other business property	20b	
13	Depreciation and section 179 expense deduction (not included in Part III) (see page C-4)	13	1,619 00	21	Repairs and maintenance	21	1,389 00
14	Employee benefit programs (other than on line 19)	14		22	Supplies (not included in Part III)	22	1,642 00
15	Insurance (other than health)	15	742 00	23	Taxes and licenses	23	7,210 00
16	Interest:			24	Travel, meals, and entertainment:		
a	Mortgage (paid to banks, etc.)	16a		a	Travel	24a	842 00
b	Other	16b		b	Deductible meals and entertainment (see page C-5)	24b	215 00
17	Legal and professional services	17	310 00	25	Utilities	25	3,600 00
				26	Wages (less employment credits)	26	40,616 00
				27	Other expenses (from line 48 on page 2)	27	780 00

		Line	Amount
28	**Total expenses** before expenses for business use of home. Add lines 8 through 27 in columns ▶	28	65,237 00
29	Tentative profit (loss). Subtract line 28 from line 7	29	91,684 00
30	Expenses for business use of your home. Attach **Form 8829**	30	1,084 00
31	**Net profit or (loss).** Subtract line 30 from line 29. • If a profit, enter on **Form 1040, line 12,** and **also** on **Schedule SE, line 2** or **Form 1040NR, line 13** (statutory employees, see page C-6). Estates and trusts, enter on Form 1041, line 3. • If a loss, you **must** go to line 32.	31	90,600 00

32 If you have a loss, check the box that describes your investment in this activity (see page C-6).
• If you checked 32a, enter the loss on **Form 1040, line 12,** and **also** on **Schedule SE, line 2** or **Form 1040NR, line 13** (statutory employees, see page C-6). Estates and trusts, enter on Form 1041, line 3.
• If you checked 32b, you **must** attach **Form 6198.** Your loss may be limited.

32a ☐ All investment is at risk.
32b ☐ Some investment is not at risk.

For Paperwork Reduction Act Notice, see page C-7 of the instructions. Cat. No. 11334P **Schedule C (Form 1040) 2006**

FIGURE 7-1 Filled-In Schedule C, Form 1040, Page 2

Schedule C (Form 1040) 2006 — Page **2**

Part III **Cost of Goods Sold** (see page C-7)

33 Method(s) used to value closing inventory: **a** ☐ Cost **b** ☐ Lower of cost or market **c** ☐ Other (attach explanation)

34 Was there any change in determining quantities, costs, or valuations between opening and closing inventory? If "Yes," attach explanation . . . ☐ **Yes** ☐ **No**

35	Inventory at beginning of year. If different from last year's closing inventory, attach explanation	35	
36	Purchases less cost of items withdrawn for personal use	36	
37	Cost of labor. Do not include any amounts paid to yourself	37	
38	Materials and supplies	38	
39	Other costs	39	
40	Add lines 35 through 39	40	
41	Inventory at end of year	41	
42	**Cost of goods sold.** Subtract line 41 from line 40. Enter the result here and on page 1, line 4	42	

Part IV **Information on Your Vehicle.** Complete this part **only** if you are claiming car or truck expenses on line 9 and are not required to file Form 4562 for this business. See the instructions for line 13 on page C-4 to find out if you must file Form 4562.

43 When did you place your vehicle in service for business purposes? (month, day, year) ▶ ____/____/____

44 Of the total number of miles you drove your vehicle during 2006, enter the number of miles you used your vehicle for:

a Business ________ **b** Commuting (see instructions) ________ **c** Other ________

45 Do you (or your spouse) have another vehicle available for personal use? . . . ☐ **Yes** ☐ **No**

46 Was your vehicle available for personal use during off-duty hours? . . . ☐ **Yes** ☐ **No**

47a Do you have evidence to support your deduction? . . . ☐ **Yes** ☐ **No**

b If "Yes," is the evidence written? . . . ☐ **Yes** ☐ **No**

Part V **Other Expenses.** List below business expenses not included on lines 8–26 or line 30.

Education expenses		780 00
48 **Total other expenses.** Enter here and on page 1, line 27	48	780 00

Printed on recycled paper

Schedule C (Form 1040) 2006

Schedule C, Part II: Expenses

Sole proprietors generally can deduct all ordinary, necessary, and reasonable expenses of operating a business. Schedule C, Part II lists 19 separate expenses that sole proprietors can deduct.

Advertising, $492 (Line 8)

Taxpayers generally can deduct advertising expenses related to their businesses. They cannot, however, deduct advertising for purposes of influencing legislation.

Car and Truck Expenses, $2,940 (Line 9)

Chapter 6 covered the deduction of transportation costs for employees. Employees use either the actual method or the standard mileage method ($.445 cents per mile for 2006), plus business parking and tolls to compute their deductible transportation costs. Employees provide support for their deduction on Form 2106. Self-employed taxpayers compute their transportation deduction using the same two methods. However, self-employed taxpayers support their transportation deduction on Schedule C, page 2, Part IV (or on Form 4562, Depreciation and Amortization, page 2). Monroe uses the standard mileage method in 2006. Monroe drove a total of 6,607 miles during the year. His car and truck expense deduction equals $2,940 [(6,607 × $.445)]. Because Monroe completes Form 4562 to support his depreciation deduction, he does not complete Schedule C, Part IV.

DEDUCTIBLE CAR AND TRUCK EXPENSES

- Garage rent, parking, and tolls
- Gasoline, oil, and lubrication
- Insurance, licenses, and auto club dues
- Lease payments
- Maintenance and repairs
- Property taxes
- Tires and batteries
- Washing and polishing

EXAMPLE 8

In 2006, Terry Madden drove 6,000 business miles and 20,000 total miles. In 2005, Madden used the actual method to deduct expenses related to the business use of his car. Madden's 2006 expenses for the car include the following:

Business parking and tolls	$ 100
Depreciation	3,000
Gas	1,000
Insurance	450
License tags	50
Oil change	20
Total	$4,620

Under the actual method, Madden deducts $1,456 [($4,520 × 6,000/20,000) + $100 business parking and tolls]. Since Madden used the actual method in 2005, the IRS requires its use in 2006. Had Madden been able to use the standard mileage method, the deduction would have been $2,770 [(6,000 × $.445) + $100].

Commissions and Fees, $0 (Line 10)

Taxpayers can deduct commissions and fees paid for business purposes.

Contract Labor, $0 (Line 11)

Taxpayers deduct amounts paid for contract labor on Schedule C (line 11). Contract labor includes amounts paid to workers who are independent contractors. They do not include on this line any wages paid to employees. Wages paid to employees are reported on Schedule C (line 26).

Depletion, $0 (Line 12)

Taxpayers who own and operate a business with a natural resource, such as an oil well, a coal mine or a gold mine, may claim a depletion deduction. **Depletion** is the process that allows taxpayers to deduct the cost of natural resources as units from the resource are sold (under the accrual method) or sold and payment is received (under the cash method). The two methods for computing the depletion deduction are the cost method and the percentage depletion method. Each year the taxpayer may use whichever method produces the greatest deduction.

The *cost method* allows taxpayers to deduct the costs of natural resources as the resource units are recovered and sold. The cost of the natural resource is divided by the number of units expected to be recovered. This provides depletion per unit. This per unit cost is multiplied by the number of units sold during the year.

Under the *percentage depletion method,* taxpayers multiply a set percentage by the "gross income" generated by the resource during the year. The government specifies the percentages used, which range from 5% for sand and gravel to 22% for lead, zinc, tin, and sulfur. A 15% rate applies to copper, gold, silver, iron, oil, and gas. The percentage depletion method has a distinct advantage over cost depletion in that the taxpayer can continue to take the percentage depletion deduction even after the entire cost invested in the natural resource has been fully recovered through annual depletion deductions.

Depreciation and Section 179 Expense Deduction, $1,619 (Line 13)

Monroe completes and attaches Form 4562, Depreciation and Amortization, to support the depreciation and section 179 expense deduction. Also on Form 4562, Monroe will provide information to support his car and truck expenses reported on Schedule C. Depreciation expense is the focus of Chapter 8.

Employee Benefit Programs, $0 (Line 14)

Employers generally can deduct the costs of benefits they provide for their employees. For example, employers can deduct life insurance premiums paid for policies on employees' lives, but only for policies that do not list the employer as the beneficiary. Employers also can deduct the cost of medical insurance paid for employees. Other examples include adoption expenses, child care, parking, transportation, and athletic facilities.

Insurance, $742 (Line 15)

Taxpayers can deduct insurance premiums on business property, including real estate, furniture, machinery, and equipment. Employers deduct premiums paid for medical and life insurance for employees as employee benefits (line 14). As mentioned earlier in the chapter, cash method taxpayers cannot deduct advance payments for premiums on policies that cover more than one tax year. They can deduct only the portions that apply during the year.

Interest, $0 (Lines 16a and 16b)

Business interest includes interest on mortgages (line 16a) and other business loans (line 16b). If the taxpayer borrows money and uses the loan proceeds partly for nonbusiness purposes, then only the interest related to the business-use portion of the borrowed funds can be deducted.

EXAMPLE 9

Jay Jackson borrows funds secured by business property. Jackson uses 25% of the funds to buy a car for personal use. He uses the rest in his business. Jackson deducts 75% of the interest on Schedule C. The personal interest cannot be deducted.

Legal and Professional Services, $310 (Line 17)

Taxpayers can deduct legal and professional fees, including the portion of tax preparation fees that relate to preparation of Schedule C. They cannot deduct legal fees incurred to acquire business property. Instead, these amounts are added to the amount the taxpayer pays for the property.

Office Expense, $1,640 (Line 18)

Office expense includes postage, stationery, and other general expenses of operating a business office.

Pension and Profit-Sharing Plans, $0 (Line 19)

Sole proprietors deduct on Schedule C amounts they contribute to their employees' qualified pension and profit-sharing plans. Under a qualified plan, the employer must offer the plan to all eligible full-time employees. Two common qualified plans are defined contribution and defined benefit plans.

A **defined benefit plan** focuses on the annual benefits at retirement. Employers must contribute annually to the plan so that the promised benefits will be available at retirement. The benefit formula used in computing the annual contribution considers employees' compensation levels and years of service. This calculation usually requires professional assistance.

In contrast, a **defined contribution plan** focuses on annual contributions. The amount contributed is usually a percentage of the employee's compensation. Unlike a defined benefit plan, this type of plan promises no predetermined benefits. Instead, annual contributions are made to individual employee accounts and employees receive whatever benefits the accumulated contributions (plus any earnings) provide.

A **simplified employee pension (SEP) plan** is a defined contribution plan employers can establish for their employees. In 2006, the maximum contribution an employer can make to an employee's SEP is the *lesser of* (i) $44,000 or (ii) 25% of the employee's compensation. For SEP plans established after 1986, only employers (not employees) can make contributions to an employee's SEP plan.

An alternative to a SEP is a 401(k) plan. The main advantage to a 401(k) plan over a SEP is that employees can make pre-tax contributions to their 401(k) plans and reduce their taxable salaries. In 2006, employees can contribute up to $15,000 to a 401(k) plan. Employees age 50 and older can contribute up to $20,000 in 2006. Employers may match employees' contributions, but are not required to do so. A common practice for employers is to match 50% of the employee's contributions, up to 6% of the employee's wages. Employers deduct only their matching contributions on Schedule C (line 19).

For tax years beginning in 2006, employers can offer Roth 401(k) plans to their employees. Employees' contributions to a Roth 401(k) are made with after-tax funds. This means that the wages contributed to a Roth 401(k) are reported in their taxable wages on their Form W-2s. Only the employee can contribute to a Roth 401(k). Employer contributions are not allowed. Although contributions to Roth 401(k) plans are made with post-tax dollars, all amounts in a Roth 401(k) plan grow tax-free. Thus, when qualified distributions are eventually made from a Roth 401(k), both employee contributions and the accumulated earnings are exempt from tax. Roth 401(k) plans are subject to the same contribution limits that apply to 401(k) plans, including catch up provisions for participants age 50 or older. The $15,000 limit ($20,000 for age 50 and older) applies to all 401(k) contributions made during 2006.

EXAMPLE 10

Robbie Rentry is 42 years old. He participates in a 401(k) plan maintained by his employer. His employer offers both a standard 401(k) and a Roth 401(k). In 2006, Rentry designates that $12,000 of his pre-tax wages be designated to his 401(k). This allows him to designate up to another $3,000 as an after-tax contribution to his Roth 401(k). His taxable wages will be reduced by the $12,000 that he contributes to his 401(k).

EXAMPLE 11

Same as in Example 10, except that Rentry's age is 51. He can contribute up to $8,000 ($20,000 maximum contribution - $12,000) of his after-tax wages to his Roth 401(k).

Employers that have 100 or fewer employees who earned $5,000 or more in the prior year can adopt a **savings incentive match plan for employees (SIMPLE).** Employers can set up SIMPLE plans using either IRAs or 401(k)s. Employees who earned at least $5,000 in any two prior years and expect to earn at least $5,000 in the current year would be allowed to contribute up to $10,000 of their salaries to the plan for 2006. (Employees age 50 and older can contribute up to $12,500). Employers generally are required to make matching contributions up to 3% of the employee's compensation. Only the employer's contribution is deductible on Schedule C.

Calculating the annual contribution to a defined benefit plan often requires professional assistance from an actuary. The additional administrative costs may keep employers from setting up defined benefit plans. SEP, SIMPLE and 401(k) plans are much easier and less costly to administer. SIMPLE plans offer the advantage of allowing employees the option of whether they want to participate in the plan. However, employer matching is required for all employees who elect to participate. Employer matching is elective for 401(k) plans.

Rent or Lease, $1,200 (Line 20a) and $0 (Line 20b)

Rent or lease expense is the amount paid for the use of property not owned by the taxpayer. If the taxpayer will receive title to the property at the end of the lease, then the amount paid is not rent expense. The payments are instead added to the taxpayer's cost in the property.

Taxpayers can deduct rent on property used in their trade or business. Those that pay rent in advance only deduct the amount that applies to the tax year to which they made the rent payment. They deduct the rest in the year or years to which the rent applies.

EXAMPLE 12

Katie Norton leases property for three years beginning June 1, 20x1. On June 1, 20x1, Norton pays $12,000 for 12 months' rent, but can deduct only $7,000 in 20x1 ($12,000/12 × 7) using either the cash or the accrual method. On June 1, 20x2, she pays $12,000 for another 12 months' rent. In 20x2, Norton will deduct the remaining $5,000 paid in 20x1, and $7,000 of the $12,000 paid on June 1, 20x2.

Taxpayers who lease a car deduct the costs related to the business-use portion of the lease. Taxpayers must spread any advance lease payments over the entire lease period. Payments made to buy a car are not deductible as rent, even if they are described as lease payments. Chapter 8 describes the rules for leased cars in greater detail.

Repairs and Maintenance, $1,389 (Line 21)

Taxpayers can deduct the costs of keeping business property in its normal operating condition. Deductible costs include labor, supplies, and other related types of expenses. Repair expenses must be distinguished from capital expenditures. Taxpayers capitalize any costs that either add to the value or usefulness of the property or significantly extend its useful life. Repairs and maintenance allocable to the cost of goods sold should be deducted on Schedule C under Part III in calculating cost of goods sold, and not in Part II.

Supplies, $1,642 (Line 22)

Taxpayers can deduct the cost of supplies that they normally use within one year. The cost of supplies not expected to be used within one year are deducted in the year the supplies are used.

Taxes and Licenses, $7,210 (Line 23)

Sole proprietors can deduct property taxes paid on business property. They also can deduct their share of social security and Medicare taxes paid for employees plus amounts paid for state and federal unemployment taxes. Deductible licenses include business licenses required by state and local governments for operating a trade or business.

Travel, $842 (Line 24a), Deductible Meals and Entertainment, $215 (Line 24b)

Chapter 6 presented the rules employees use for deducting travel, meals, and entertainment. For the most part, the same rules govern the amount sole proprietors can deduct. Amounts owners pay for business-related travel, meals and entertainment on behalf of themselves or their employees are deductible on Schedule C. When an owner reimburses an employee, the treatment depends on whether an "accountable" or "nonaccountable" plan is in place. An accountable plan requires the employee to, (1) adequately report the expenses to the employer, and (2) return any excess reimbursements to the employer. Owners with an accountable plan deduct the reimbursements under "Travel, meals, and entertainment," but can deduct only 50% of the meals and entertainment.

When a nonaccountable plan exists (one that does not meet both criteria for an accountable plan), the reimbursement is treated as "Wages" and is deductible as such on Schedule C. Employees are taxed on these additional wages and can deduct their expenses (but only 50% of meals and entertainment) as miscellaneous deductions subject to the 2% AGI rule.

EXAMPLE 13

Gene Keys is self-employed. He reimbursed an employee $10,000 for travel expenses and $2,000 for meals and entertainment under an accountable plan. Keys deducts $10,000 as travel on Schedule C (line 24a) and $1,000 (50% × $2,000) as deductible meals and entertainment (line 24b).

EXAMPLE 14

Assume the same facts as in Example 13 except that Keys has a nonaccountable plan. Keys deducts all $12,000 as wages on Schedule C (line 26). The employee is taxed on the $12,000, and can deduct $11,000 (only 50% of meals and entertainment) as miscellaneous deductions subject to the 2% AGI rule.

DEDUCTIBLE TRAVEL EXPENSES

- Air, rail, and bus transportation, including transportation to and from the airport and the hotel, from one customer to another, or from one place of business to another
- Baggage charges
- Dry cleaning and laundry
- Lodging
- Meals and entertainment (subject to limitations)
- Car expenses, including car rental
- Telephone and fax costs
- Tips related to travel

As described in Chapter 6, some employers use the "per diem" approach to reimburse employees for the costs of meals and lodging. Employers deduct the reimbursement under "Travel, meals, and entertainment," but deduct only 50% of the per diem meal allowance. The rules regarding the use of per diems in lieu of actual expenses for meals and entertainment also apply to sole proprietors. However, the per diem for lodging can only be used for purposes of reimbursing employees. When the owner of the business is away from home overnight on business, the owner must deduct the actual costs for lodging.

The federal per diem rates vary from city to city. These rates can be found in IRS publication 1542.

When a person's travels combine business and pleasure, only the business portion of the trip can be deducted. The rules described for employees in Chapter 6 also apply to sole proprietors. Thus, when taking a business trip in the U.S., the costs of traveling to and from the destination are only allowed if the trip is primarily (more than 50%) for business. When the trip involves travel outside of the U.S. the costs of traveling to and from the destination must be prorated unless one of the three exceptions described in Chapter 6 applies. For all travels, the business portion of all other expenses is deductible.

EXAMPLE 15

Mandy Simms is self-employed. During 2006, Simms takes a business trip to Boston. She is gone a total of six days (five nights), four of which were spent conducting business. Her travel costs include $600 for airfare, $220 for transportation to and from the airport, $150 a night for lodging, and $60 a day for meals. At the time of her trip, the per diem for Boston is $270, which includes $67 for meals and incidentals.

Because her trip is primarily for business (4/6 > 50%), Simms can deduct the $820 she spent for traveling to and from the destination ($600 + $220). The $67 daily per diem rate for meals exceeds her actual costs for meals. Thus, she is allowed to deduct $134 ($67 x 4 days x 50%) for business meals. She also can deduct $450 for lodging ($150 x 3 nights). Although the nightly per diem for lodging ($203) exceeds her actual daily lodging costs ($150), sole proprietors cannot use the per diem rates for lodging. They must deduct their actual lodging costs.

EXAMPLE 16

Jerry Lucas is self-employed. During 2006, Lucas sends his employee on a business trip to Boston. The employee is gone four days (three nights), all of which were spent conducting business. The employee's travel costs include $600 for airfare, $220 for transportation to and from the airport, $150 a night for lodging, and $60 a day for meals. At the time of the trip, the per diem for Boston is $270, which includes $67 for meals and incidentals.

Lucas reimburses the employee $1,697 under an accountable reimbursement plan. This amount includes $820 for traveling to and from the destination ($600 + $220), $609 for lodging ($203 x 3), and $268 ($67 x 4) for meals. The employee is not taxed on the $1,697 reimbursement. On his Schedule C, Lucas deducts $1,429 ($820 + $609) for travel (line 24a) and $134 ($268 x 50%) for meals (line 24b).

EXAMPLE 17

Same as Example 16 except that Lucas advances the employee $1,500 before the trip to Boston and does not require the employee to turn in receipts for amounts spent on the trip. Lucas now has made a reimbursement from a nonaccountable plan. He adds the $1,500 to the employee's taxable wages on Form W-2. He then deducts the $1,500 as wage expense on Schedule C (line 26). It is up to the employee to report his deductible travel expenses on Form 2106. These amounts will then be deducted as miscellaneous itemized deductions (subject to the 2% AGI rule) on the employee's Schedule A.

Utilities, $3,600 (Line 25)

Utilities include the costs for heat, power, water, and telephone. Taxpayers can deduct the costs for utilities to the extent the costs are not incurred for personal use. They can deduct the cost of operating a cellular phone, but only for the time it is used for conducting business. Taxpayers deduct utilities for an office located in their home on Form 8829, Business Use of the Home (covered later in the chapter).

Wages, $40,616 (Line 26)

Employers deduct amounts paid as wages to employees. They also deduct amounts paid to them as bonuses, vacation pay, taxable employee achievement awards, and reimbursements under nonaccountable plans. The amount reported on Schedule C *excludes any wages included* in cost of goods sold. It also does not include any withdrawals the owner makes from the business.

Other Expenses, $780 (Line 27)

Other expenses are amounts not deductible elsewhere on Schedule C. Sole proprietors deducting other expenses list the type and amount of each expense on Schedule C, page 2, Part V. Four common other expenses sole proprietors incur are education expenses, business gifts, dues and subscriptions, and bad debts.

Self-employed taxpayers can deduct on Schedule C professional dues and subscriptions related to their line of business. They also can deduct the ordinary and necessary costs incurred to educate and train employees in operating the business. Deductible education expenses include tuition, books, transportation, meals (subject to the 50% rule), and lodging. In addition, sole proprietors can deduct amounts spent on their own education as long as it does not (1) prepare them to meet the minimum education requirements of their present profession or (2) qualify them for a new trade or business. Assuming neither of these situations apply, to deduct these costs, sole proprietors must show that the education (1) maintains or improves the skills required in their business or (2) is required by law to keep their status in the profession. The rules for deducting education expenses for self-employed taxpayers are essentially the same as those presented in Chapter 6 for employees. Monroe deducts $780 for educational courses taken in 2006.

EXAMPLE 18

Elwood Raines is a self-employed tax accountant. Raines holds a Bachelor's of Science degree in accounting. He is currently taking night classes in pursuit of his law degree. During 2006, his education costs include $2,500 for tuition, $620 for books and $220 for transportation. Since getting a law degree will allow him to enter a new profession (the practice of law), the costs of his education are not deductible on Schedule C. The facts that the content of the courses will enable him to be a better tax accountant are irrelevant if the courses are part of a program of study that will enable him to enter into a new (different) profession.

EXAMPLE 19

Same as in Example 18 except that the classes Raines is taking are in pursuit of a Master's of Taxation degree. Since completion of this degree prepares Raines to be a tax accountant (which he already is), the education is not preparing him to enter into a new profession. Instead, the courses help him improve his skills at his existing profession. Thus, Raines can deduct $3,340 ($2,500 + $620 + $200) as an other expense on Schedule C (line 27).

Sole proprietors can deduct the costs of business gifts to customers and clients. The maximum deduction cannot exceed $25 for business gifts given to any one individual during the tax year. Gifts not subject to the $25 limit include:

1. A widely distributed item costing $4 or less on which the donor's company name is permanently imprinted. Examples include pens and key chains.
2. Signs, display racks, and other promotional material used on the recipient's business premises.
3. Incidental costs, such as engraving, packaging, insuring, and mailing.

Employees can deduct the costs of business gifts to clients and customers using these same rules. They can deduct the cost of gifts they make to people who work for them. They cannot deduct the cost of gifts to people they work for. Employees deduct these costs as miscellaneous itemized deductions subject to the 2% rule.

Any item that can be considered either a gift or entertainment generally is considered entertainment. A taxpayer who gives a business client tickets to an event but does not attend the event with the client can treat the tickets either as a gift or as entertainment. However, if the taxpayer goes with the client to the event, the tickets must be treated as entertainment. Employers may also deduct property valued at up to $400 given to employees for their length of service or safety achievement.

EXAMPLE 20

Tamara Banker is self-employed. During the current year she pays $35 for a ticket to a sporting event. She gives the ticket to a client. She does not attend the event with her client. Banker can choose between treating the $35 as either a business gift or as entertainment. If she includes the $35 as entertainment, she will deduct $17.50 ($35 x 50%). Banker would be better off deducting $25 (maximum deduction for business gifts) as a business gift on Schedule C (line 27).

EXAMPLE 21

Same as in Example 20 except that the ticket costs $75. Since the deduction for business gifts is limited to $25, Banker would be better off taking the cost of the tickets as entertainment expense. She will deduct $37.50 ($75 x 50%) on Schedule C (line 24b).

EXAMPLE 22

Same as in Example 20 except that Banker attends the event with her client. Banker must treat the cost of the ticket as entertainment expense. Thus, she will be able to deduct 50% of the costs of the tickets for her client and herself.

Taxpayers deduct bad debts that result from business operations. Bad debts may result from credit sales to customers. They also may result from loans to suppliers, clients, employees, or distributors. Sole proprietors deduct bad debts when a receivable, or a portion of a receivable, becomes uncollectible (known as the direct write-off method). The tax law does not permit the use of the "reserve" method, which is an acceptable financial accounting practice. For a bad debt to be deductible, a true creditor-debtor relationship must exist between the taxpayer (creditor) and the debtor. Also, the taxpayer must incur an actual loss of money or have previously reported the amount owed in gross income. Thus, a cash basis taxpayer who renders services cannot take a bad debt deduction when a customer's receivable becomes uncollectible because no income was ever reported.

To deduct a business bad debt, the taxpayer must show a dominant business reason for making the loan or sale. Only the uncollectible portion of a receivable qualifies as a business bad debt. A business bad debt is deductible in the year it becomes partially or completely worthless. Should the IRS challenge the bad debt deduction, the taxpayer must prove that the debt is worthless and will remain worthless. Doing so may involve going to court, which taxpayers can avoid by showing that the court would rule that the receivable was uncollectible. This usually occurs in the case of a bankrupt debtor.

EXAMPLE 23

Mike Tucker is self-employed. During 20x1, Tucker loans his friend $5,000 so that his friend can start his own business. In 20x3, the friend files for bankruptcy and Tucker is told that he should expect to receive $.15 on the dollar. Since the purpose of the loan was not related to Tucker's business, he will be able to take a nonbusiness bad debt deduction in the year in which he receives a final settlement from the bankruptcy court. A nonbusiness bad debt is treated as a short-term capital loss (see Chapter 10).

EXAMPLE 24

Same as in Example 23 except that Tucker's loan is to his business supplier. The reason for the loan is to keep the supplier in business and prevent delivery of Tucker's inventory from being delayed. Because the purpose of the loan is related to Tucker's business, Tucker can begin taking a bad debt deduction inn 20x3 when the debt becomes partially worthless. He deducts $4,250 ($5,000 – ($5,000 x $.15)) as an other expense on Schedule C (line 27).

EXAMPLE 25

Continuing with Example 24, assume that in 20x4, the bankruptcy proceedings are finalized and Tucker receives $300 for his $5,000 loan. Tucker's total bad debt deduction is $4,700 ($5,000 - $300). Since Tucker deducted $4,250 in 20x3, he deducts $450 ($4,700 - $4,250) as an other expense on his 20x4 Schedule C (line 27).

EXAMPLE 26

Same as Example 25 except that Tucker receives $1,000 (instead of $300) from the bankruptcy court. Tucker's total bad debt deduction is now $4,000 ($5,000 - $1,000). Because Tucker deducted $4,250 in 20x3, the tax benefit rule (Chapter 3) requires that he include $250 as other income on his 20x4 Schedule C (line 6).

Total Expenses, $65,237 (Line 28)

Monroe subtracts total expenses from gross income (line 7) to arrive at tentative profit (loss) of $91,684 (line 29).

Business Use of the Home

Chapter 6 presented the rules for the home office deduction for employees. Sole proprietors who use part of their home as a place of business can deduct expenses for part of the home. Although the rules for employees and sole proprietors overlap in several ways, sole proprietors must complete Form 8829, Expenses for Business Use of Your Home, to support the home office deduction.

Sole proprietors may deduct expenses related to an office located in the home only if they use that part of the home regularly and exclusively as either (1) the principal place of business or (2) a place to meet or deal with patients, clients, or customers in the normal course of business. However, sole proprietors can deduct expenses for using part of the home as a day-care facility or as a place to store inventory even if they sometimes use that part of the home for personal purposes.

To claim a home office deduction, the taxpayer usually must be able to demonstrate that, relative to the work done outside the office, the work done in the office is more important to the business. However, this rule does not apply to those who use their home office exclusively and regularly for administrative or management activities and have no other location to perform these duties. For example, a self-employed plumber who spends several hours each week scheduling appointments, preparing bills, etc. qualifies for the home office deduction, provided that the office is used regularly and exclusively for business purposes.

EXAMPLE 27

Stan Smith, a self-employed writer, uses an office located in his home exclusively and regularly to write. Smith conducts most of his interviews outside of the office. He also spends many hours doing research at the library. Although doing research and conducting interviews are important to the business, the most important part is writing. Since Smith does his writing at the office located in his home, he qualifies for the home office deduction.

EXAMPLE 28

Samuel Robinson is a self-employed physical therapist who is works at three different hospitals. Robinson uses one room in his two bedroom apartment exclusively as a home office. He uses the office to schedule and confirm appointments. He also uses it prepare and file medical insurance claims for his patients. None of the hospitals provide him with an office to perform these tasks. Although the most important aspect to his job is treating patients (which is done at the hospitals), he must perform these administrative tasks in order to make a living. Since his home office is used regularly and exclusively to perform these tasks and there is no other place for him to do this, he qualifies for the home office deduction.

EXAMPLE 29

Same as in Example 28, except that one of the hospitals provides its contractors with an office to perform their administrative tasks. Robinson, however, prefers to do these tasks in the comfort of his own home. Because he has been given another place to perform his administrative duties, he cannot take the home office deduction.

To allocate expenses to the home office, taxpayers divide the square feet of the room used as the home office by the total square feet of the home. Taxpayers who provide child care and use part of their home exclusively as a child care facility also use this method to allocate a portion of their expenses of the home to the child care business. However, for areas of the home used to provide child care, but not on an exclusive basis, the deductible costs must be reduced by the ratio of hours the area is used for day care to the total hours in the year. Total hours in 2006 were 8,760 (24 hours × 365 days).

EXAMPLE 30

Betty Glover provides child care in her home. The area of the home used in her child care business is 40% of the total area of the home. For 50 weeks, Glover provides child care services 10 hours a day, 5 days a week, for a total of 2,500 hours (10 × 5 × 50). Glover can deduct 11.42% (40% × 2,500/8,760) of the expenses of her home against the income she earns providing child care.

Information for Figure 7-2: Filled-In Form 8829

George Monroe (from Figure 7-1) has been operating his consulting business out of his home since 2001. The business portion of the home is 240 square feet. The total square footage of the home is 2,400.

Other Information

8: Tentative profit from Schedule C, line 29, **$91,684.00**
10b: Mortgage interest, **$4,300.00**
11b: Real estate taxes, **$1,500.00**
17b: Insurance, **$280.00**
18b: Repairs and maintenance, **$950.00**
19b: Utilities, **$1,810.00**
35: Smaller of the home's adjusted basis ($90,000.00) or its FMV ($128,000.00), **$90,000.00**
36: Value of land included on line 35, **$12,000.00**
39: Depreciation percentage, **2.564%** (1/39 years) [explained in Chapter 8]

In Figure 7-2, the income from the business activity exceeded both the business expenses reported on Schedule C, Part II, and the expenses related to the office in the home. With the exception of the business portion of home mortgage interest, real estate taxes, and casualty losses, home office expenses cannot create a loss on Schedule C. Specifically, taxpayers cannot deduct these other types of home office expenses to the extent they exceed the net income derived from the business. **Net income derived from the business** equals tentative profit shown on Schedule C (line 29) minus the home office expenses for home mortgage interest, real estate taxes, and casualty losses. Any disallowed expenses carry over to the next year.

FIGURE 7-2 Filled-In Form 8829

Form **8829** — Department of the Treasury, Internal Revenue Service (99)

Expenses for Business Use of Your Home

▶ File only with Schedule C (Form 1040). Use a separate Form 8829 for each home you used for business during the year.

▶ See separate instructions.

OMB No. 1545-0074 — 2006 — Attachment Sequence No. 66

Name(s) of proprietor(s): George L. Monroe — Your social security number: 139:24:6880

Part I Part of Your Home Used for Business

Line	Description				Amount
1	Area used regularly and exclusively for business, regularly for daycare, or for storage of inventory or product samples (see instructions)			1	240
2	Total area of home			2	2,400
3	Divide line 1 by line 2. Enter the result as a percentage			3	10 %
	• **For daycare facilities not used exclusively for business, also complete lines 4–6.** • **All others, skip lines 4–6 and enter the amount from line 3 on line 7.**				
4	Multiply days used for daycare during year by hours used per day	4	hr.		
5	Total hours available for use during the year (365 days × 24 hours) (see instructions)	5	8,760 hr.		
6	Divide line 4 by line 5. Enter the result as a decimal amount	6	.		
7	Business percentage. For daycare facilities not used exclusively for business, multiply line 6 by line 3 (enter the result as a percentage). All others, enter the amount from line 3 ▶			7	10 %

Part II Figure Your Allowable Deduction

Line	Description		(a) Direct expenses	(b) Indirect expenses		Amount
8	Enter the amount from Schedule C, line 29, **plus** any net gain or (loss) derived from the business use of your home and shown on Schedule D or Form 4797. If more than one place of business, see instructions				8	91,684 00
	See instructions for columns (a) and (b) before completing lines 9–20.					
9	Casualty losses (see instructions)	9				
10	Deductible mortgage interest (see instructions)	10		4,300 00		
11	Real estate taxes (see instructions)	11		1,500 00		
12	Add lines 9, 10, and 11	12		5,800 00		
13	Multiply line 12, column (b) by line 7		13	580 00		
14	Add line 12, column (a) and line 13				14	580 00
15	Subtract line 14 from line 8. If zero or less, enter -0-				15	91,104 00
16	Excess mortgage interest (see instructions)	16				
17	Insurance	17		280 00		
18	Repairs and maintenance	18		950 00		
19	Utilities	19		1,810 00		
20	Other expenses (see instructions)	20				
21	Add lines 16 through 20	21		3,040 00		
22	Multiply line 21, column (b) by line 7		22	304 00		
23	Carryover of operating expenses from 2005 Form 8829, line 41		23			
24	Add line 21 in column (a), line 22, and line 23				24	304 00
25	Allowable operating expenses. Enter the **smaller** of line 15 or line 24				25	304 00
26	Limit on excess casualty losses and depreciation. Subtract line 25 from line 15				26	90,800 00
27	Excess casualty losses (see instructions)		27			
28	Depreciation of your home from Part III below		28	200 00		
29	Carryover of excess casualty losses and depreciation from 2005 Form 8829, line 42		29			
30	Add lines 27 through 29				30	200 00
31	Allowable excess casualty losses and depreciation. Enter the **smaller** of line 26 or line 30				31	200 00
32	Add lines 14, 25, and 31				32	1,084 00
33	Casualty loss portion, if any, from lines 14 and 31. Carry amount to **Form 4684,** Section B				33	
34	Allowable expenses for business use of your home. Subtract line 33 from line 32. Enter here and on Schedule C, line 30. If your home was used for more than one business, see instructions ▶				34	1,084 00

Part III Depreciation of Your Home

35	Enter the **smaller** of your home's adjusted basis or its fair market value (see instructions)	35	90,000 00
36	Value of land included on line 35	36	12,000 00
37	Basis of building. Subtract line 36 from line 35	37	78,000 00
38	Business basis of building. Multiply line 37 by line 7	38	7,800 00
39	Depreciation percentage (see instructions)	39	2.564 %
40	Depreciation allowable (see instructions). Multiply line 38 by line 39. Enter here and on line 28 above	40	200 00

Part IV Carryover of Unallowed Expenses to 2007

41	Operating expenses. Subtract line 25 from line 24. If less than zero, enter -0-	41	
42	Excess casualty losses and depreciation. Subtract line 31 from line 30. If less than zero, enter -0-	42	

For Paperwork Reduction Act Notice, see page 4 of separate instructions. Cat. No. 13232M Form **8829** (2006)

EXAMPLE 31

Neil Morgan conducts a business in his home. The business portion equals 20% of the total square footage of the home. Expenses of operating the home include utilities, $3,500; real estate taxes, $5,000; mortgage interest, $6,000; insurance, $800; general home repairs, $2,000; and depreciation, $4,500. Tentative profit from the business is $3,300. Morgan computes net income derived from the business as follows.

Tentative profit	$3,300
Less business portion of mortgage interest and real estate taxes [20% × ($6,000 + $5,000)]	(2,200)
Net income derived from the business	$1,100

After the business portion of interest and taxes are deducted, taxpayers deduct the other home office expenses (to the extent of net income derived from the business) in the following order:

1. The business portion of expenses (other than depreciation) incurred in operating the business in the home. These expenses include repairs, maintenance, insurance, and utilities.
2. The depreciation on the business portion of the home.

Any home office expenses in excess of net income derived from the business carry over to the next year.

EXAMPLE 32

Continuing with Example 31, Morgan computes the rest of the home office deduction and the expenses carried over to the next year as follows.

Business use of other home office expenses:	
Utilities, insurance, repairs (20% × $6,300)	$1,260
Depreciation on the home office (20% × $4,500)	900
Total other home office expenses	$2,160
Deductible expenses limited to net income derived from the business	(1,100)
Home office expenses not deductible in the current year, to be carried forward to next year	$1,060

The $1,100 of deductible home office expenses comes from the home office portion of expenses for utilities, insurance, and repairs. The $1,060 of expenses carried over consists of $160 ($1,260 – $1,100) of utilities, insurance, and repairs, and $900 of depreciation.

Schedule C, Part III: Cost of Goods Sold

Inventory is a major part of manufacturing, wholesale, and retail businesses. For sole proprietors, the calculation of cost of goods sold (line 4) is done on Schedule C, Part III. Cost of goods sold equals beginning inventory plus the cost of net purchases, labor, materials, and other costs for the year minus ending inventory. Cost of goods sold should include only expenses directly related to getting or producing the goods sold.

For merchants, beginning inventory consists of products held for sale. For manufacturers, beginning inventory is the sum of raw materials, work in process, and finished goods. Beginning inventory of one year should be the same as ending inventory of the prior year.

For merchants, purchases include all goods bought for sale during the year. For manufacturers, purchases of raw materials include all materials bought during the year to be used in making the finished products. Any freight paid is added to the costs of purchases. The cost of goods returned reduce total purchases. Cash discounts either can be credited to separate discount accounts (as other income) or deducted from total purchases. The method for handling cash discounts must be used consistently from year to year. Figure 7-4 shows a filled-in Schedule C for a taxpayer in the retail business.

Information for Figure 7-4: Filled-In Schedule C (Form 1040)

Harold R. Wilson is the owner of Wilson's Hardware Store. He operates the business as a sole proprietorship. Figure 7-3 shows Wilson's income statement. He completes Schedule C (Figure 7-4) using the information from the income statement. His business code is 444130. Wilson materially participates in the business. He uses the accrual method of accounting and the cost method to value inventory.

Net income from Wilson's income statement is $60,496. Schedule C, however, shows a net profit of $61,131. Part of the $635 difference ($61,131 – $60,496) relates to the $460 of charitable contributions. Although the business paid this amount, the tax laws require charitable contributions of a sole proprietor to be deducted as an itemized deduction on Schedule A. The remaining $175 difference relates to reducing meals and entertainment by 50% on Schedule C.

SELF-EMPLOYMENT TAX FOR SELF-EMPLOYED INDIVIDUALS

For the government to generate enough funds to pay social security and Medicare benefits, taxpayers who work must pay social security and Medicare taxes (FICA). Employees pay FICA through withholdings from their wages. Their employers match the amounts withheld and send the entire sum to the government. Employers deduct as a payroll tax expense amounts paid to match employees' FICA contributions.

FICA consists of two parts: (1) social security or OASDI (Old-Age, Survivors, and Disability Insurance) and (2) Medicare or HI (Health Insurance). The OASDI tax rate is 6.2% (12.4% after employer matching). The HI rate is 1.45% (2.9% after employer matching). For 2006, the first $94,200 of a taxpayer's earnings is subject to OASDI. All earnings are subject to HI.

The self-employment tax is similar to FICA withheld from employees' wages. However, instead of having the tax withheld from their wages, self-employed taxpayers pay the tax with their (quarterly) estimated payments. They make up any balance due when they file their tax return. Because there is no employer to match their contributions, self-employed taxpayers must pay both halves of FICA (12.4% for OASDI and 2.9% for HI). They can, however, deduct one-half of the self-employment tax from their gross income. This amount represents the employer's share of the tax. However, the deduction is taken on Form 1040, page 1, not on Schedule C.

Employees' FICA withholding is based on their gross earnings, Self-employed taxpayers pay self-employment tax on their *net earnings from self-employment.* Net earnings from self-employment equals self-employment net profit multiplied by .9235. This calculation provides a substitute for what is normally an employer's deduction for one-half of the OASDI

FIGURE 7-3 Income Statement for Wilson's Hardware Store

WILSON'S HARDWARE STORE
Income Statement
For Year Ended December 31, 2006

Operating revenue:			
Sales		$284,280	
Less sales returns and allowances		(2,751)	
Net sales			$281,529
Cost of merchandise sold:			
Merchandise inventory, beginning of period		$131,216	
Purchases	$180,716		
Less purchases discount	(3,614)		
Net purchases	$177,102		
Less merchandise withdrawn for personal use	(400)	176,702	
Merchandise available for sale		$307,918	
Less merchandise inventory end of period		(167,546)	
Cost of merchandise sold			(140,372)
Gross profit on sales			$141,157
Operating expenses:			
Advertising expense		$ 5,437	
Charitable contributions		460	
Depreciation expense		1,133	
Entertainment expense		350	
Insurance expense		2,250	
Legal and professional services		6,693	
Miscellaneous expense		15	
Payroll taxes		8,845	
Personal property taxes		960	
Rent expense		10,200	
Repairs to store equipment		2,125	
Supplies expense		3,400	
Telephone expense		1,258	
Travel		184	
Truck rental expense		2,498	
Utilities expense		3,908	
Wage expense		31,297	
Total operating expenses			(81,013)
Operating income			$ 60,144
Other income:			
Interest income			584
			$ 60,728
Other expenses:			
Interest expense			(232)
Net income			$ 60,496

FIGURE 7-4 Filled-In Schedule C, Form 1040, Page 1

SCHEDULE C (Form 1040) Department of the Treasury Internal Revenue Service (99)

Profit or Loss From Business
(Sole Proprietorship)

▶ Partnerships, joint ventures, etc., must file Form 1065 or 1065-B.
▶ Attach to Form 1040, 1040NR, or 1041. ▶ See Instructions for Schedule C (Form 1040).

OMB No. 1545-0074 **2006** Attachment Sequence No. **09**

Name of proprietor: Harold R. Wilson — Social security number (SSN): 272:11 8855

A Principal business or profession, including product or service (see page C-2 of the instructions): Retail Hardware — **B** Enter code from pages C-8, 9, & 10 ▶ 441130

C Business name. If no separate business name, leave blank.: Wilson's Hardware Store — **D** Employer ID number (EIN), if any: 91:0624431

E Business address (including suite or room no.) ▶ 27 Main Street
City, town or post office, state, and ZIP code: Madison, WI 53593-3644

F Accounting method: (1) ☐ Cash (2) ☒ Accrual (3) ☐ Other (specify) ▶

G Did you "materially participate" in the operation of this business during 2006? If "No," see page C-2 for limit on losses ☒ Yes ☐ No

H If you started or acquired this business during 2006, check here ▶ ☐

Part I Income

		Line	Amount
1	Gross receipts or sales. **Caution.** If this income was reported to you on Form W-2 and the "Statutory employee" box on that form was checked, see page C-3 and check here ▶ ☐	1	284,280 00
2	Returns and allowances	2	2,751 00
3	Subtract line 2 from line 1	3	281,529 00
4	Cost of goods sold (from line 42 on page 2)	4	140,372 00
5	**Gross profit.** Subtract line 4 from line 3	5	141,157 00
6	Other income, including federal and state gasoline or fuel tax credit or refund (see page C-3)	6	584 00
7	**Gross income.** Add lines 5 and 6 ▶	7	141,741 00

Part II Expenses. Enter expenses for business use of your home **only** on line 30.

8	Advertising	8	5,437 00	18	Office expense	18	
9	Car and truck expenses (see page C-4)	9		19	Pension and profit-sharing plans	19	
				20	Rent or lease (see page C-5):		
10	Commissions and fees	10		a	Vehicles, machinery, and equipment	20a	2,498 00
11	Contract labor (see page C-4)	11		b	Other business property	20b	10,200 00
12	Depletion	12		21	Repairs and maintenance	21	2,125 00
13	Depreciation and section 179 expense deduction (not included in Part III) (see page C-4)	13	1,133 00	22	Supplies (not included in Part III)	22	3,400 00
				23	Taxes and licenses	23	9,805 00
				24	Travel, meals, and entertainment:		
				a	Travel	24a	184 00
14	Employee benefit programs (other than on line 19)	14		b	Deductible meals and entertainment (see page C-5)	24b	175 00
15	Insurance (other than health)	15	2,250 00	25	Utilities	25	5,166 00
16	Interest:			26	Wages (less employment credits)	26	31,297 00
a	Mortgage (paid to banks, etc.)	16a		27	Other expenses (from line 48 on page 2)	27	15 00
b	Other	16b	232 00				
17	Legal and professional services	17	6,693 00				

		Line	Amount
28	**Total expenses** before expenses for business use of home. Add lines 8 through 27 in columns ▶	28	80,610 00
29	Tentative profit (loss). Subtract line 28 from line 7	29	61,131 00
30	Expenses for business use of your home. Attach **Form 8829**	30	
31	**Net profit or (loss).** Subtract line 30 from line 29. • If a profit, enter on **Form 1040, line 12,** and **also** on **Schedule SE, line 2** or **Form 1040NR, line 13** (statutory employees, see page C-6). Estates and trusts, enter on Form 1041, line 3. • If a loss, you **must** go to line 32.	31	61,131 00

32 If you have a loss, check the box that describes your investment in this activity (see page C-6).
• If you checked 32a, enter the loss on **Form 1040, line 12,** and **also** on **Schedule SE, line 2** or **Form 1040NR, line 13** (statutory employees, see page C-6). Estates and trusts, enter on Form 1041, line 3.
• If you checked 32b, you **must** attach **Form 6198.** Your loss may be limited.

32a ☐ All investment is at risk.
32b ☐ Some investment is not at risk.

For Paperwork Reduction Act Notice, see page C-7 of the instructions. Cat. No. 11334P **Schedule C (Form 1040) 2006**

FIGURE 7-4 Filled-In Schedule C, Form 1040, Page 2

Schedule C (Form 1040) 2006 Page **2**

Part III **Cost of Goods Sold** (see page C-7)

33 Method(s) used to value closing inventory: **a** ☒ Cost **b** ☐ Lower of cost or market **c** ☐ Other (attach explanation)

34 Was there any change in determining quantities, costs, or valuations between opening and closing inventory? If "Yes," attach explanation . . . ☐ **Yes** ☒ **No**

35 Inventory at beginning of year. If different from last year's closing inventory, attach explanation	35	131,216	00
36 Purchases less cost of items withdrawn for personal use	36	176,702	00
37 Cost of labor. Do not include any amounts paid to yourself	37		
38 Materials and supplies	38		
39 Other costs	39		
40 Add lines 35 through 39	40	307,918	00
41 Inventory at end of year	41	167,546	00
42 **Cost of goods sold.** Subtract line 41 from line 40. Enter the result here and on page 1, line 4	42	140,372	00

Part IV **Information on Your Vehicle.** Complete this part **only** if you are claiming car or truck expenses on line 9 and are not required to file Form 4562 for this business. See the instructions for line 13 on page C-4 to find out if you must file Form 4562.

43 When did you place your vehicle in service for business purposes? (month, day, year) ▶ ____/____/____

44 Of the total number of miles you drove your vehicle during 2006, enter the number of miles you used your vehicle for:

a Business ________ **b** Commuting (see instructions) ________ **c** Other ________

45 Do you (or your spouse) have another vehicle available for personal use? . . . ☐ **Yes** ☐ **No**

46 Was your vehicle available for personal use during off-duty hours? . . . ☐ **Yes** ☐ **No**

47a Do you have evidence to support your deduction? . . . ☐ **Yes** ☐ **No**

b If "Yes," is the evidence written? . . . ☐ **Yes** ☐ **No**

Part V **Other Expenses.** List below business expenses not included on lines 8–26 or line 30.

Miscellaneous expenses		15	00
48 **Total other expenses.** Enter here and on page 1, line 27	48	15	00

Printed on recycled paper **Schedule C (Form 1040) 2006**

and HI taxes (100% – 7.65% = 92.35%). Conceptually, this procedure reduces the net profit figure by approximately one-half of the FICA taxes.

Taxpayers pay self-employment tax only on self-employment net profit. Taxpayers reporting net losses from self-employment do not pay self-employment tax. Computing self-employment net profit involves adding the following:

1. Net profit (or loss) an individual derives from any trade or business reported on Schedule C (line 31) or net profit reported on Schedule C-EZ (line 3).
2. Net profit (or loss) an individual derives from farming reported on Schedule F.
3. The individual's guaranteed payments or distributive share of the ordinary net income (or loss) from a partnership. (Most advanced tax textbooks cover this topic.)

EXAMPLE 33

Jessica Whitten owns two businesses. Whitten uses a separate Schedule C to report the net profit (or loss) from each business. Net profit from the first business is $45,000, net profit from the second business is $5,000. Whitten's self-employment net profit is $50,000.

EXAMPLE 34

Assume the same facts as in Example 33, except that Whitten reports a net loss of $5,000 from the second business. Whitten's self-employment net profit is $40,000.

EXAMPLE 35

Assume the same facts as in Example 34, except that Whitten is married and her spouse owns the second business. Jessica's self-employment net profit is $45,000. Because her spouse reports a net loss, he has no self-employment net profit. Only Jessica pays self-employment tax on her $45,000 of net earnings from self-employment.

Once self-employment net profit has been computed, net earnings from self-employment equals 92.35% of self-employment net profit.

EXAMPLE 36

Todd Avery reports $10,000 of self-employment net profit. Avery's net earnings from self-employment equals $9,235 ($10,000 × .9235). His self-employment tax is $1,413 ($9,235 × 15.3%). He deducts one-half of this amount ($707) on Form 1040, page 1.

Only taxpayers with more than $400 of net earnings from self-employment owe self-employment tax. For self-employed taxpayers who are also employees, their wages subject to social security tax reduce the maximum earnings subject to OASDI.

EXAMPLE 37

Same facts as in Example 36, except that in addition to the $10,000 of self-employment net profit, Avery has FICA withheld on $87,600 of wages earned as an employee in 2006. The first $94,200 of earnings is subject to OASDI. Through withholding on wages, Avery has paid OASDI on $87,600. All $9,235 of net earnings from self-employment is subject to HI, but only $6,600 ($94,200 – $87,600) is subject to OASDI. Avery's self-employment tax equals $1,086 [($6,600 × 12.4%) + ($9,235 × 2.9%)]. Avery deducts one-half of this amount ($543) for AGI on Form 1040, page 1.

Short Schedule SE

Taxpayers compute self-employment tax on Schedule SE. Self-employed taxpayers who do not have wages subject to FICA use the short schedule (Section A) to compute their self-employment tax. Taxpayers whose net earnings from self-employment plus their wages and tips subject to social security tax do not exceed $94,200 also use the short schedule. Taxpayers using the short schedule report their self-employment net profit (lines 1, 2, and 3). They compute their net earnings from self-employment (line 4) by multiplying self-employment net profit (line 3) by 92.35%. They compute self-employment tax (line 5) by multiplying the first $94,00 of net earnings from self-employment by 15.3% and the rest by 2.9%. Taxpayers then enter one-half of this amount on Schedule SE (line 6) and then deduct it for AGI on Form 1040, page 1. Figure 7-5 shows Schedule SE, Section A, for Harold R. Wilson (from Figure 7-4).

Information for Figure 7-5: Filled-In Schedule SE (Section A)

Show only the name of person with self-employment income.

Other Information

2: Net profit from Schedule C, line 31, **$61,131.00**

Long Schedule SE

Taxpayers whose net earnings from self-employment plus their wages and tips subject to social security tax exceed $94,200 cannot use the Short Schedule SE. They instead must use Section B—Long Schedule SE. As in Section A, taxpayers first compute their self-employment net profit (lines 1 through 3) and their net earnings from self-employment (lines 4 through 6). They then report the amount of their wages for the year subject to social security withholding (line 8). If this amount exceeds $94,200, the taxpayer is not subject to the 12.4% OASDI. If the amount does not exceed $94,200 then the taxpayer multiplies 12.4% by the *lesser of* the difference (line 9) or net earnings from self-employment (line 6). The taxpayer adds this amount to 2.9% of net earnings from self-employment to compute the self-employment tax (line 12). The taxpayer then enters one-half of the self-employment tax on line 13 and again on Form 1040, page 1.

Information for Figure 7-6: Filled-In Schedule SE (Section B)

This filled-in Schedule SE is prepared for **Todd Avery** in Example 37.

Other Information

2: Net profit from Schedule C, line 31, **$10,000.00**

8a: Total social security wages, **$87,600.00** (Source: box 3 on Form W-2)

FIGURE 7-5 Filled-In Schedule SE (Section A)

SCHEDULE SE (Form 1040)

Department of the Treasury Internal Revenue Service (99)

Self-Employment Tax

▶ Attach to Form 1040. ▶ See Instructions for Schedule SE (Form 1040).

OMB No. 1545-0074

2006

Attachment Sequence No. 17

Name of person with **self-employment** income (as shown on Form 1040): Harold R. Wilson

Social security number of person with **self-employment** income ▶ 272 11 8855

Who Must File Schedule SE

You must file Schedule SE if:

- You had net earnings from self-employment from **other than** church employee income (line 4 of Short Schedule SE or line 4c of Long Schedule SE) of $400 or more, **or**
- You had church employee income of $108.28 or more. Income from services you performed as a minister or a member of a religious order **is not** church employee income (see page SE-1).

Note. Even if you had a loss or a small amount of income from self-employment, it may be to your benefit to file Schedule SE and use either "optional method" in Part II of Long Schedule SE (see page SE-3).

Exception. If your only self-employment income was from earnings as a minister, member of a religious order, or Christian Science practitioner **and** you filed Form 4361 and received IRS approval not to be taxed on those earnings, **do not** file Schedule SE. Instead, write "Exempt–Form 4361" on Form 1040, line 58.

May I Use Short Schedule SE or Must I Use Long Schedule SE?

Note. Use this flowchart **only if** you must file Schedule SE. If unsure, see Who Must File Schedule SE, above.

Did you receive wages or tips in 2006?

No ▶ Are you a minister, member of a religious order, or Christian Science practitioner who received IRS approval **not** to be taxed on earnings from these sources, **but** you owe self-employment tax on other earnings? — Yes ▶ You must use Long Schedule SE on page 2

No ▶ Are you using one of the optional methods to figure your net earnings (see page SE-3)? — Yes ▶ You must use Long Schedule SE on page 2

No ▶ Did you receive church employee income reported on Form W-2 of $108.28 or more? — Yes ▶ You must use Long Schedule SE on page 2

No ▶ You may use Short Schedule SE below

Yes ▶ Was the total of your wages and tips subject to social security or railroad retirement tax **plus** your net earnings from self-employment more than $94,200? — Yes ▶ You must use Long Schedule SE on page 2

No ▶ Did you receive tips subject to social security or Medicare tax that you **did not** report to your employer? — Yes ▶ You must use Long Schedule SE on page 2; No

Section A—Short Schedule SE. Caution. Read above to see if you can use Short Schedule SE.

		Line	Amount
1	Net farm profit or (loss) from Schedule F, line 36, and farm partnerships, Schedule K-1 (Form 1065), box 14, code A	1	
2	Net profit or (loss) from Schedule C, line 31; Schedule C-EZ, line 3; Schedule K-1 (Form 1065), box 14, code A (other than farming); and Schedule K-1 (Form 1065-B), box 9, code J1. Ministers and members of religious orders, see page SE-1 for amounts to report on this line. See page SE-2 for other income to report	2	61,131 00
3	Combine lines 1 and 2	3	61,131 00
4	**Net earnings from self-employment.** Multiply line 3 by 92.35% (.9235). If less than $400, **do not** file this schedule; you do not owe self-employment tax ▶	4	56,454 00
5	**Self-employment tax.** If the amount on line 4 is: • $94,200 or less, multiply line 4 by 15.3% (.153). Enter the result here and on **Form 1040, line 58.** • More than $94,200, multiply line 4 by 2.9% (.029). Then, add $11,680.80 to the result. Enter the total here and on **Form 1040, line 58.**	5	8,637 00
6	**Deduction for one-half of self-employment tax.** Multiply line 5 by 50% (.5). Enter the result here and on **Form 1040, line 27** — 6: 4,319 00		

For Paperwork Reduction Act Notice, see Form 1040 instructions. Cat. No. 11358Z **Schedule SE (Form 1040) 2006**

FIGURE 7-6 Filled-In Schedule SE (Section B)

Schedule SE (Form 1040) 2006 | Attachment Sequence No. **17** | Page **2**

Name of person with **self-employment** income (as shown on Form 1040)	Social security number of person with **self-employment** income ▶
Todd Avery	692 43 1922

Section B—Long Schedule SE

Part I **Self-Employment Tax**

Note. If your only income subject to self-employment tax is **church employee income,** skip lines 1 through 4b. Enter -0- on line 4c and go to line 5a. Income from services you performed as a minister or a member of a religious order **is not** church employee income. See page SE-1.

A If you are a minister, member of a religious order, or Christian Science practitioner **and** you filed Form 4361, but you had $400 or more of **other** net earnings from self-employment, check here and continue with Part I . . . . ▶ ☐

1	Net farm profit or (loss) from Schedule F, line 36, and farm partnerships, Schedule K-1 (Form 1065), box 14, code A. **Note.** Skip this line if you use the farm optional method (see page SE-4)			1		
2	Net profit or (loss) from Schedule C, line 31; Schedule C-EZ, line 3; Schedule K-1 (Form 1065), box 14, code A (other than farming); and Schedule K-1 (Form 1065-B), box 9, code J1. Ministers and members of religious orders, see page SE-1 for amounts to report on this line. See page SE-2 for other income to report. **Note.** Skip this line if you use the nonfarm optional method (see page SE-4)			2	10,000	00
3	Combine lines 1 and 2			3	10,000	00
4a	If line 3 is more than zero, multiply line 3 by 92.35% (.9235). Otherwise, enter amount from line 3			4a	9,235	00
b	If you elect one or both of the optional methods, enter the total of lines 15 and 17 here . . .			4b		
c	Combine lines 4a and 4b. If less than $400, **stop**; you do not owe self-employment tax. **Exception.** If less than $400 and you had **church employee income,** enter -0- and continue . . . . . ▶			4c	9,235	00
5a	Enter your **church employee income** from Form W-2. See page SE-1 for definition of church employee income	5a				
b	Multiply line 5a by 92.35% (.9235). If less than $100, enter -0-			5b		
6	**Net earnings from self-employment.** Add lines 4c and 5b			6	9,235	00
7	Maximum amount of combined wages and self-employment earnings subject to social security tax or the 6.2% portion of the 7.65% railroad retirement (tier 1) tax for 2006			7	94,200	00
8a	Total social security wages and tips (total of boxes 3 and 7 on Form(s) W-2) and railroad retirement (tier 1) compensation. If $94,200 or more, skip lines 8b through 10, and go to line 11	8a	87,600 00			
b	Unreported tips subject to social security tax (from Form 4137, line 9)	8b				
c	Add lines 8a and 8b			8c	87,600	00
9	Subtract line 8c from line 7. If zero or less, enter -0- here and on line 10 and go to line 11 . ▶			9	6,600	00
10	Multiply the **smaller** of line 6 or line 9 by 12.4% (.124)			10	818	00
11	Multiply line 6 by 2.9% (.029)			11	268	00
12	**Self-employment tax.** Add lines 10 and 11. Enter here and on **Form 1040, line 58**			12	1,086	00
13	**Deduction for one-half of self-employment tax.** Multiply line 12 by 50% (.5). Enter the result here and on **Form 1040, line 27**	13	543 00			

Part II **Optional Methods To Figure Net Earnings** (see page SE-3)

Farm Optional Method. You may use this method **only** if **(a)** your gross farm income[1] was not more than $2,400, **or (b)** your net farm profits[2] were less than $1,733.

14	Maximum income for optional methods	14	1,600	00
15	Enter the **smaller** of: two-thirds (⅔) of gross farm income[1] (not less than zero) **or** $1,600. Also include this amount on line 4b above	15		

Nonfarm Optional Method. You may use this method **only** if **(a)** your net nonfarm profits[3] were less than $1,733 and also less than 72.189% of your gross nonfarm income,[4] **and (b)** you had net earnings from self-employment of at least $400 in 2 of the prior 3 years.

Caution. You may use this method no more than five times.

16	Subtract line 15 from line 14	16		
17	Enter the **smaller** of: two-thirds (⅔) of gross nonfarm income[4] (not less than zero) **or** the amount on line 16. Also include this amount on line 4b above	17		

[1] From Sch. F, line 11, and Sch. K-1 (Form 1065), box 14, code B.

[2] From Sch. F, line 36, and Sch. K-1 (Form 1065), box 14, code A.

[3] From Sch. C, line 31; Sch. C-EZ, line 3; Sch. K-1 (Form 1065), box 14, code A; and Sch. K-1 (Form 1065-B), box 9, code J1.

[4] From Sch. C, line 7; Sch. C-EZ, line 1; Sch. K-1 (Form 1065), box 14, code C; and Sch. K-1 (Form 1065-B), box 9, code J2.

Schedule SE (Form 1040) 2006

RETIREMENT PLANS FOR SELF-EMPLOYED INDIVIDUALS

Sole proprietors can establish retirement plans for themselves and deduct the contributions from their gross income on Form 1040, page 1. Thus, any contributions sole proprietors make to their own retirement plans do not reduce their Schedule C net profits, but will reduce their AGI. Sole proprietors who set up retirement plans for themselves also may have to provide retirement plans for eligible employees. They deduct any contributions they make to their employees' retirement plans on Schedule C (line 19).

Self-employed taxpayers have several retirement plan options. They can set up defined benefit and defined contribution plans. When set up for self-employed taxpayers, these plans are commonly referred to as Keoghs. They can also set up SEP, 401(k), and SIMPLE plans. Whichever retirement plan they choose, they must also make it available to all eligible employees.

The same contribution limits that apply to employees apply to sole proprietors. For defined contribution plans, the maximum contribution is the *lesser of* (i) $44,000 or (ii) 25% of the participant's compensation. Those 50 and older can contribute an additional $5,000 in 2006. **Compensation** for a self-employed taxpayer equals self-employment net profit minus both the deduction for one-half of the self-employment tax and the contribution made to the retirement plan.

In computing their maximum allowable contribution, self-employed taxpayers first complete Schedule C to determine net profit. They then compute their self-employment tax on Schedule SE and deduct one-half of the SE tax from their net profit. Self-employed taxpayers may contribute up to 20% of the remaining amount to a defined contribution plan. This percentage is less than the 25% maximum contribution limit that is allowed for employees because net profit must be reduced by the amount of the contribution to determine compensation. Example 38 shows how the 20% is determined.

Keogh Plans

EXAMPLE 38

Lloyd Mills, a self-employed taxpayer, has Schedule C net profit of $60,000. Mills's Keogh plan requires a 25% contribution each year. Net earnings from self-employment are $55,410 ($60,000 × 92.35%). Self-employment tax is $8,478 ($55,410 × 15.3%). Mills deducts one-half of this amount, or $4,239 (½ × $8,478) on Form 1040, page 1. Mills contributes $11,152 to his Keogh. He deducts this amount for AGI on Form 1040, page 1.

Using the required percentage of 25% of his compensation, Mills sets up a formula to solve for the required contribution (C):

25% × (Schedule C net profit – ½ of SE tax – C) = C

For Mills, this equation is:

25% × ($60,000 – $4,239 – C) = C

which reduces to:

25% × ($55,761 – C) = C

which reduces to:

$13,940 = 125% × C

solving for C:

$11,152 = C

As shown in Example 38, 20% of the Schedule C net profit minus one-half of the self-employment tax [20% × ($60,000 – $4,239) = $11,152] is the same as 25% of the Schedule C net profit minus one-half of the self-employment tax and the contribution [25% × ($60,000 – $4,239 – $11,152) = $11,152]. Another way to compute the 20% is to divide the required percentage by the sum of 100% and the required percentage (25%/125% = 20%). This short cut is used in Example 39.

EXAMPLE 39

Assume the same facts as in Example 38, except that the plan requires a 10% contribution. Using the short cut approach, Mills computes his deductible contribution as follows.

10%/110% = .0909 × $55,761 = $5,069

The maximum Keogh plan contribution can be made only if the plan specifies 25% as the percentage. If the required percentage is less than 25%, then either the formula from Example 38 or the short cut approach from Example 39 determines the maximum contribution.

KEOGH REQUIREMENTS FOR 2006

1. The plan must be established before the end of the tax year.
2. The plan must be in writing and employees must be provided a summary description including the rules on discrimination and vesting.
3. The plan should be intended as a permanent plan.
4. The plan must have a designated trustee.
5. The contribution must be made by the due date of the tax return (including extensions).

Taxpayers can make contributions to qualified retirement plans until the due date of the tax return (including extensions). The big benefit of a Keogh plan is the ability to deduct the contributions each year plus postpone paying taxes on the accrued earnings until the funds are withdrawn. For this reason, the sooner the taxpayer contributes to the plan, the sooner the contributions begin earning tax-deferred (postponed) income.

For example, on January 2, 20x1, a self-employed taxpayer makes a $30,000 contribution to a Keogh plan. During 20x1, $2,000 of earnings accrue on the $30,000. The income tax on that $2,000 is postponed until retirement. Had the taxpayer held the $30,000 in a taxable investment account and waited until December 31, 20x1, to make the Keogh contribution, the $2,000 earned by the taxable investment during 20x1 would be taxable in 20x1.

Simplified Employee Pension (SEP) Plans

Another retirement plan option for sole proprietors is the SEP plan. A SEP is a defined contribution plan, so the maximum contribution self-employed taxpayers can make to a SEP is the *lesser of* (i) $44,000 or (ii) 25% of the participant's compensation. This is the same as the *lesser of* (i) $44,000 or (ii) 20% of self-employment net profit after it is reduced by one-half of the self-employment tax. Participants age 50 and older can contribute an extra $5,000 in 2006. As with a Keogh, self-employed taxpayers may contribute to a SEP until the due date of the return, including extensions. However, unlike a Keogh, a SEP does not need to be set up before the end of the tax year. Self-employed taxpayers have until the due date of their tax returns (including extensions) to set up a SEP plan. SEP plans have another advantage—they have no annual reporting requirements. Keoghs have annual reporting requirements, even if the taxpayer is the only participant. (These requirements are beyond the scope of this textbook).

EXAMPLE 40

Vince Shaw is self-employed and has a SEP. During 2006, he reports Schedule C net profits of $49,520. His self-employment tax on this amount is $6,997 ($49,520 x 92.35% x 15.3%). He computes his maximum SEP contribution as follows.

25%/125% = 20% x ($49,520 - $3,499 one-half SE tax) = $9,204

EXAMPLE 41

Kulbur Singh (age 45) is self-employed and has a SEP. During 2006, she reports Schedule C net profits of $355,405. Her self-employment tax on this amount is $21,199 [($94,200 x 12.4%) + ($355,405 x 92.35% x 2.9%)]. One-half of this amount is $10,600 ($21,199 x 50%). Although the formula shows a maximum contribution of $68,961 (20% x ($355,405 - $10,600), her contribution is limited to $44,000 in 2006.

EXAMPLE 42

Same as in Example 41 except that Singh's age is 55. Singh can contribute up to $49,000 to her SEP in 2006 ($44,000 + $5,000 for being age 50 or older).

The choice of a retirement plan will depend on the extent of compliance requirements, administrative and other costs contribution limits, and flexibility. Sole proprietors considering setting up retirement plans should carefully review the requirements and limitations of each type of plan and determine the type of plan best suited to their needs. Since most plans require that all eligible employees be allowed to participate, proprietors with employees may want to consider the potential costs of matching contributions when deciding on a retirement plan for themselves.

SEP REQUIREMENTS FOR 2006

1. Each employee has an individual account.
2. Contributions must be made for all full-time employees who are at least age 21, have worked for the employer for three of the last five years, and have received at least $450 of wages during 2006.
3. The employer must contribute the same percentage of compensation for each employee.
4. Employees must be able to withdraw the employer's contributions without restriction.

Savings Incentive Match Plan for Employees (SIMPLE)

Sole proprietors can set up a SIMPLE plan for themselves and their employees. The maximum that sole proprietors can contribute in 2006 to their SIMPLE plan is $10,000 or 100% of their compensation, whichever is less. (Sole proprietors age 50 and older can contribute up to $12,500). An advantage to having a SIMPLE plan is that it is not subject to the non-discrimination and top-heavy rules associated with other retirement plans. A disadvantage is that employer matching is required with a SIMPLE plan. Neither of these are issues for sole proprietors with no employees. Due to the $10,000 ($12,500) limit, sole proprietors with no employees may want to consider a SEP plan, which has a higher contribution limit.

SIMPLE REQUIREMENTS FOR 2006

1. There must be 100 or fewer employees in the previous year.
2. The SIMPLE plan is the only retirement plan offered.
3. All employees who had at least $5,000 of compensation in the previous year and expect to have at least $5,000 of compensation in the current year must be allowed to participate.

Name ______________________________

Section ______________ Date ___________

QUESTIONS AND PROBLEMS

1. Cash vs. Accrual Method. Ramon S. Torres is an attorney. Torres wants to know how reporting each of the following items would differ if he used the cash method versus the accrual method. In the space provided with each item, enter the correct amount to be included on Schedule C assuming the cash method is used. Then enter the correct amount assuming the use of the accrual method. If there is no amount to be reported, enter a zero.

			Cash Method	*Accrual Method*
a.	Cash received from last year's fees	$ 7,200	$______	$______
b.	Cash received from current year's fees	49,000	______	______
c.	Fees billed for current year for which cash has not been received	10,200	______	______
d.	Cash received for computer with book value of $200	200	______	______
e.	Cash received from bank loan	2,500	______	______
f.	Cash received from client to repay loan made last year	500	______	______
g.	Cash received for retainer from client for whom work is to be done next year	3,800	______	______

2. Cash vs. Accrual Method. Lis Schultz is a CPA. Schultz wants to know how reporting each of the following items would differ if she uses the cash method versus the accrual method. In the space provided with each item, enter the correct amount to include on Schedule C assuming the cash method is used. Then enter the correct amount assuming the use of the accrual method. If there is no amount to be reported, enter a zero.

			Cash Method	*Accrual Method*
a.	Repaid loan at bank: Principal	$1,000	$______	$______
	Interest	60	______	______
b.	Paid contribution pledged to church	1,000	______	______
c.	Paid for supplies used last year	150	______	______
d.	Paid for supplies used during current year	850	______	______
e.	Paid for professional journals	200	______	______
f.	Supplies not used during current year and not paid for	40	______	______
g.	Paid for new computer	1,564	______	______

3. **Cash vs. Accrual Method.** Andrew Taylor is a dentist. Taylor wants to know how reporting each of the following items would differ if he uses the cash method versus the accrual method. In the space provided with each item, enter the correct amount to include on Schedule C assuming the cash method is used. Then enter the correct amount assuming the use of the accrual method. If there is no amount to be reported, enter a zero.

		Cash Method	*Accrual Method*
a. Salary paid to receptionist	$12,500	$______	$______
b. Paid for long-distance phone charges made during last year	4	______	______
c. Written-off client billing for fees; work performed in current year	150	______	______
d. Written-off client billing for fees; work performed last year	135	______	______
e. Paid annual subscription to magazines for office	50	______	______
f. Paid life insurance premium on the owner's life	516	______	______

4. **Prepaid Income.** Scott Williams operates a fitness center as a sole proprietorship. On May 1, 2006, Williams sells a 24-month membership for $1,200.

   a. How much of the $1,200 must Williams report on his 2006-2008 tax returns if he uses the accrual method of accounting?

   b. How would your answer to Part a. change if Williams uses the cash method?

5. **Prepaid Income.** Cliff Downs is a sole proprietor. He uses the accrual method of accounting for his business. Downs fixes major appliances, but does not sell them. He also sells warranty contracts. On April 1, 2006, Downs collects $480 for a 36-month warranty contract. How much of the $480 must he include in gross income in 2006-2009?

6. **Prepaid Expenses.** On August 1, 2006, a sole proprietor pays $24,000 for two years' rent.

   a. How much of the $24,000 can be deducted in 2006 if the cash method is used?

   b. How much of the $24,000 can be deducted in 2006 if the accrual method is used?

7. **Prepaid Expenses.** A sole proprietor who operates a warehouse purchases insurance for his building and equipment in three-year increments to get a good insurance premium rate. The insurance policy in force was acquired on October 1, 2004, for $4,800 and will be in effect until September 30, 2007. The premium on this policy was paid on July 1, 2004.

   a. What amount of insurance premium can the taxpayer include as an expense on Schedule C for 2006, assuming the taxpayer uses the cash method of accounting?

   b. What amount of insurance premium is deductible in 2006 if the taxpayer uses the accrual method?

8. **Self-Employment Income.** Indicate with Y (yes) or N (no) if the following items are net earnings from self-employment:

		Item
______	a.	Net rentals from an apartment building
______	b.	Net income from an accounting practice
______	c.	Interest income on a loan to a friend
______	d.	Limited partner's share of partnership ordinary income
______	e.	Net income for services as a minister
______	f.	Dividends from domestic corporations

9. **Self-Employment Income.** Indicate with Y (yes) or N (no) if the following items are net earnings from self-employment:

		Item
______	a.	Gross rent received on an office building
______	b.	Net profit from a doctor's practice
______	c.	Prize for winning an essay contest
______	d.	Salary for a secretary
______	e.	Net gain on the sale of property
______	f.	Director's fees

10. Self-Employment Income. Indicate whether each statement is T (true) or F (false):

_____ a. Interest on accounts receivable received in a trade or business is treated as self-employment income.

_____ b. Babysitters who provide child care in the parents' homes must treat their earnings as self-employment income.

_____ c. Registered nurses who are hired directly by patients to provide private nursing services are treated as self-employed individuals.

_____ d. Licensed real estate agents working out of a real estate agency are generally treated as employees of the real estate agency.

_____ e. Amway, Avon, Shaklee, and Tupperware distributors are treated as self-employed individuals.

_____ f. All executors of estates are treated as self-employed.

11. Car and Truck Expense. Keith Bernard is self-employed. During 2006, he drove his car a total of 9,569 miles for work. He drove a total of 22,405 miles during the year. His car expenses for the year were as follows.

Business parking and tolls	$ 360
Depreciation	1,475
Gas	2,557
Insurance	940
License tags	50
Repairs and maintenance	52
	$ 5,434

a. Compute Bernard's car expense deduction using the standard mileage method.

b. Compute Bernard's car expense deduction using the actual method.

12. Pension Plans. Three common pension plans employers can provide to their employees are SEP, 401(k) and SIMPLE plans. For each of the following statements, identify the plan or plans having the described characteristics.

_____ a. This plan allows employees under age 50 to contribute up to $10,000 of their wages to their plan in 2006.

_____ b. This plan allows only employers to make contributions to employees' plans.

_____ c. Employers are required to make matching contributions to this plan.

_____ d. The maximum contribution to this plan is the lesser of $44,000 or 25% of the employee's compensation.

_____ e. Employees can contribute pre-tax earnings to this plan.

13. Travel Expense. Andre Grafton is self-employed. During 2006, he attends a three-day seminar. Grafton is out of town for 5 days and 4 nights. He spends the two extra days visiting friends and sightseeing. His travel costs are as follows.

Airfare	$ 850
Transportation to and from the airport	150
Hotel ($170 a night for 4 nights -- 2 for business)	680
Meals ($42 a day for 5 days – 3 for business)	210
	$1,890

a. Compute Grafton's travel expense deduction assuming the seminar was held in Dallas, Texas.

b. Compute his travel expense deduction assuming the seminar was held in Frankfort, Germany.

14. Accountable vs. Nonaccountable Plans. Robin Clark owns a business that she operates as a sole proprietorship. Clark's business has two full-time employees. The business reimburses each employee at the rate of $250 per month for meals and entertainment ($6,000 per year) without any specific accounting. Assuming that the employees incur meal expenses of $2,000 and entertainment expenses of $4,900 during 2006, answer the following questions about the way the $6,000 should be reported on Clark's 2006 tax return.

a. How much and where on Schedule C should Clark deduct the reimbursements?

b. How would your answer to Part a. differ if Clark required her employees to make an adequate accounting of their meals and entertainment expenses and also required them to return any excess reimbursement?

15. **Education Expense.** Wendy Malcolm is a self-employed CPA. She holds both a bachelor's and a master's degree in accounting. Each year she takes two graduate courses at the local university to satisfy her continuing education requirements, as required by state law to keep her CPA license. Her coursework will not lead to her getting another degree. During 2006, Malcolm spent $2,400 for tuition and $600 for books. She also drove her personal car 580 miles getting to and from her classes. What amount, if any is Malcolm able to deduct as an education expense on Schedule C?

16. **Business Gifts.** Dabny Pinnacle operates his business as a sole proprietorship. During the year, he sends holiday gifts to 20 of his clients. Each gift cost $55. What amount can Pinnacle deduct as business gifts on Schedule C?

17. **Business Gifts and Entertainment.** Stu Mayor is self-employed. During the year, paid $60 for a concert ticket. He gave the ticket to a client.

    a. What amount can Mayor deduct on Schedule C if he did not attend the event with the client?

    b. What amount can Mayor deduct if he were to attend the event with his client?

18. **Bad Debt Expense.** Mickey Cullum is self-employed. In 2004, Cullum loaned a business associate $10,000 so that the associate could stay in business. Cullum's business would suffer if his associate went out of business. In 2006, the business associate filed for bankruptcy and Cullum was told that he might not receive more than $1,000 of the loaned amount back. In 2007, Cullum receives $800 from the bankruptcy court. Discuss the tax consequences of the loan to Cullum, including the amount and year in which he can take a deduction for a bad debt.

19. Schedule C Expenses. Robert Applewood works as a cost accountant for the Craft Manufacturing Company. He also moonlights at night and on weekends preparing tax returns for a regular set of clients. He does not have a regular office in his home, so he does not take a deduction for a home office. However, he does prepare a Schedule C to reflect the income from his tax practice. He has asked you to review his Schedule C to determine whether he is properly reporting the operating expenses of his business in relation to other aspects of his tax return. He has included the following expenses on Schedule C:

Supplies and postage	$ 72
Professional dues paid to AICPA tax division	120
Professional dues to the Institute of Management Accountants (IMA)	175
Meals ($80) and entertainment ($120) for tax clients	200
Automobile expenses for tax clients (148 miles @ $.445)	66
Contribution to State Accounting Society's Political Action Committee	100
CPE course fees to meet the annual requirements to be a member of AICPA and the state society	600
Cost of new printer for use with tax clients (shown under repairs and maintenance)	650
Long-distance telephone charges related to tax clients	44
Interest paid on bank loan used to buy computer for tax and personal use (used for tax clients 60% of the time during the tax year)	400

Of these expenses, indicate what amounts, if any, can not be deducted on Schedule C, and explain why in each case.

20. Home Office Expense. Rita Porter operates a child care service in her home. The rooms used for this purpose constitute 30% of the total living space of the home. Expenses of operating the home during the year included electricity, $480; water, $340; heating, $3,600; property taxes, $4,000; and home repairs, $800. The depreciation on the rooms and related equipment used for child care was $1,800. What is the total amount of expenses that Porter can deduct for using her own home to provide the child care services if she uses these rooms 2,000 hours in 2006 for her child care business?

21. Form 8829. Elaine Gerber conducts a business in her home. Tentative profit from Schedule C (line 29) was $9,600. Complete Form 8829 on the following page.

(Use for Problem 21.)

Form **8829** — **Expenses for Business Use of Your Home**

▶ File only with Schedule C (Form 1040). Use a separate Form 8829 for each home you used for business during the year.

▶ See separate instructions.

Department of the Treasury Internal Revenue Service (99)

OMB No. 1545-0074 | 2006 | Attachment Sequence No. 66

Name(s) of proprietor(s): Elaine Gerber — Your social security number: 243:56:7182

Part I — Part of Your Home Used for Business

1	Area used regularly and exclusively for business, regularly for daycare, or for storage of inventory or product samples (see instructions)			1	240
2	Total area of home			2	3,000
3	Divide line 1 by line 2. Enter the result as a percentage			3	%
	• **For daycare facilities not used exclusively for business, also complete lines 4–6.**				
	• **All others, skip lines 4–6 and enter the amount from line 3 on line 7.**				
4	Multiply days used for daycare during year by hours used per day	4	hr.		
5	Total hours available for use during the year (365 days × 24 hours) (see instructions)	5	8,760 hr.		
6	Divide line 4 by line 5. Enter the result as a decimal amount	6	.		
7	Business percentage. For daycare facilities not used exclusively for business, multiply line 6 by line 3 (enter the result as a percentage). All others, enter the amount from line 3 ▶			7	%

Part II — Figure Your Allowable Deduction

			(a) Direct expenses	(b) Indirect expenses		
8	Enter the amount from Schedule C, line 29, **plus** any net gain or (loss) derived from the business use of your home and shown on Schedule D or Form 4797. If more than one place of business, see instructions				8	
	See instructions for columns (a) and (b) before completing lines 9–20.					
9	Casualty losses (see instructions)	9				
10	Deductible mortgage interest (see instructions)	10		1,800 00		
11	Real estate taxes (see instructions)	11		1,500 00		
12	Add lines 9, 10, and 11	12				
13	Multiply line 12, column (b) by line 7		13			
14	Add line 12, column (a) and line 13				14	
15	Subtract line 14 from line 8. If zero or less, enter -0-				15	
16	Excess mortgage interest (see instructions)	16				
17	Insurance	17		500 00		
18	Repairs and maintenance	18				
19	Utilities	19		750 00		
20	Other expenses (see instructions)	20				
21	Add lines 16 through 20	21				
22	Multiply line 21, column (b) by line 7		22			
23	Carryover of operating expenses from 2005 Form 8829, line 41		23			
24	Add line 21 in column (a), line 22, and line 23				24	
25	Allowable operating expenses. Enter the **smaller** of line 15 or line 24				25	
26	Limit on excess casualty losses and depreciation. Subtract line 25 from line 15				26	
27	Excess casualty losses (see instructions)		27			
28	Depreciation of your home from Part III below		28			
29	Carryover of excess casualty losses and depreciation from 2005 Form 8829, line 42		29			
30	Add lines 27 through 29				30	
31	Allowable excess casualty losses and depreciation. Enter the **smaller** of line 26 or line 30				31	
32	Add lines 14, 25, and 31				32	
33	Casualty loss portion, if any, from lines 14 and 31. Carry amount to **Form 4684,** Section B				33	
34	Allowable expenses for business use of your home. Subtract line 33 from line 32. Enter here and on Schedule C, line 30. If your home was used for more than one business, see instructions ▶				34	

Part III — Depreciation of Your Home

35	Enter the **smaller** of your home's adjusted basis or its fair market value (see instructions)	35	60,000 00
36	Value of land included on line 35	36	10,000 00
37	Basis of building. Subtract line 36 from line 35	37	
38	Business basis of building. Multiply line 37 by line 7	38	
39	Depreciation percentage (see instructions)	39	2.564 %
40	Depreciation allowable (see instructions). Multiply line 38 by line 39. Enter here and on line 28 above	40	

Part IV — Carryover of Unallowed Expenses to 2007

41	Operating expenses. Subtract line 25 from line 24. If less than zero, enter -0-	41	
42	Excess casualty losses and depreciation. Subtract line 31 from line 30. If less than zero, enter -0-	42	

For Paperwork Reduction Act Notice, see page 4 of separate instructions. Cat. No. 13232M Form **8829** (2006)

22. Schedule C, Part III, Cost of Goods Sold. Roger Harkin operates a novelty shop as a sole proprietor. You have been asked to compute the Cost of Goods Sold section of Schedule C for his 2006 income tax return since he is unfamiliar with detailed accounting concepts. You have been given the following information from his records to help meet his request:

Sales revenue	$200,000
Purchases	80,000
Cash operating expenses	40,000
Depreciation expense	15,000
Beginning inventory	60,000
Ending inventory	54,000
Bad debts written off	3,200

Using the appropriate information from Harkin's books, prepare the Cost of Goods Sold section of Schedule C for 2006. Harkin uses the cost method to value inventory.

Schedule C (Form 1040) 2006 Page **2**

Part III **Cost of Goods Sold** (see page C-7)

33 Method(s) used to value closing inventory: **a** ☐ Cost **b** ☐ Lower of cost or market **c** ☐ Other (attach explanation)

34 Was there any change in determining quantities, costs, or valuations between opening and closing inventory? If "Yes," attach explanation . . . ☐ **Yes** ☐ **No**

35	Inventory at beginning of year. If different from last year's closing inventory, attach explanation . .	**35**	
36	Purchases less cost of items withdrawn for personal use . . .	**36**	
37	Cost of labor. Do not include any amounts paid to yourself . . .	**37**	
38	Materials and supplies . . .	**38**	
39	Other costs . . .	**39**	
40	Add lines 35 through 39 . . .	**40**	
41	Inventory at end of year . . .	**41**	
42	**Cost of goods sold.** Subtract line 41 from line 40. Enter the result here and on page 1, line 4 . .	**42**	

23. Self-Employment Tax. Determine the self-employment tax that would be paid for 2006 by each of the following taxpayers. If there is no self-employment tax, explain why.

Taxpayer A: Age, 42; net business profit, $39,000; dividend income, $300; wages subject to social security, $5,000; gross rental income, $6,000; net rental income, $1,500

Taxpayer B: Age, 71; net business profit, $29,000; dividend income, $500; wages subject to social security, $52,200

Taxpayer C: Age, 35; net business profit, $70,000; dividend income, $200

Taxpayer D: Age, 27; net business profit, $15,000; dividend income, $100; wages subject to social security, $90,200

Taxpayer E: Age, 56; net business profit, $3,000; dividend income, $450; net rental income, ($500)

Taxpayer F: Age, 64; net business profit, $420; dividend income, $50; wages subject to social security, $400

24. Self-Employment Tax. Rosemary R. James is employed as an attorney and also operates a consulting business on the side. If her net profit reported on Schedule C was $425, how much self-employment tax would James pay?

25. Self-Employment Tax. Dennis Connor has Schedule C net profit of $10,000. Compute Connor's self-employment tax if his salary as a CPA was $106,000.

26. Self-Employment Tax. Theodore Williams reports net profit on Schedule C of $130,000. How much self-employment tax would he pay if his salary as an accountant were $51,700?

27. Retirement Plans.

a. Assume that Louise Bell (SSN 304-16-1059) earned $14,000 from self-employment in 2006 and wants to make the maximum contribution to a SEP. Prepare Schedule SE on the next page to determine the amount of self-employment tax that Bell owes on her self-employment income.

b. What is the maximum Bell can contribute to a SEP plan that would be fully deducted from gross income on her 2006 income tax return? Where on the tax return is the deduction claimed?

c. If Bell wants to contribute to a SEP plan, by what date must she make a contribution for 2006?

(Use for Problem 27.)

SCHEDULE SE (Form 1040)

Department of the Treasury Internal Revenue Service (99)

Self-Employment Tax

▶ Attach to Form 1040. ▶ See Instructions for Schedule SE (Form 1040).

OMB No. 1545-0074

2006

Attachment Sequence No. **17**

Name of person with **self-employment** income (as shown on Form 1040)	Social security number of person with **self-employment** income ▶	

Who Must File Schedule SE

You must file Schedule SE if:

- You had net earnings from self-employment from **other than** church employee income (line 4 of Short Schedule SE or line 4c of Long Schedule SE) of $400 or more, **or**
- You had church employee income of $108.28 or more. Income from services you performed as a minister or a member of a religious order **is not** church employee income (see page SE-1).

Note. Even if you had a loss or a small amount of income from self-employment, it may be to your benefit to file Schedule SE and use either "optional method" in Part II of Long Schedule SE (see page SE-3).

Exception. If your only self-employment income was from earnings as a minister, member of a religious order, or Christian Science practitioner **and** you filed Form 4361 and received IRS approval not to be taxed on those earnings, **do not** file Schedule SE. Instead, write "Exempt–Form 4361" on Form 1040, line 58.

May I Use Short Schedule SE or Must I Use Long Schedule SE?

Note. Use this flowchart **only if** you must file Schedule SE. If unsure, see Who Must File Schedule SE, above.

Did you receive wages or tips in 2006?

No ▼

Are you a minister, member of a religious order, or Christian Science practitioner who received IRS approval **not** to be taxed on earnings from these sources, **but** you owe self-employment tax on other earnings? — Yes ▶ You must use Long Schedule SE on page 2

No ▼

Are you using one of the optional methods to figure your net earnings (see page SE-3)? — Yes ▶ You must use Long Schedule SE on page 2

No ▼

Did you receive church employee income reported on Form W-2 of $108.28 or more? — Yes ▶ You must use Long Schedule SE on page 2

No ▼

You may use Short Schedule SE below

Yes ▼

Was the total of your wages and tips subject to social security or railroad retirement tax **plus** your net earnings from self-employment more than $94,200? — Yes ▶ You must use Long Schedule SE on page 2

No ▼

Did you receive tips subject to social security or Medicare tax that you **did not** report to your employer? — Yes ▶ You must use Long Schedule SE on page 2; No ◀ (go to the question on church employee income / optional methods path)

You must use Long Schedule SE on page 2

Section A—Short Schedule SE. Caution. Read above to see if you can use Short Schedule SE.

1	Net farm profit or (loss) from Schedule F, line 36, and farm partnerships, Schedule K-1 (Form 1065), box 14, code A	1	
2	Net profit or (loss) from Schedule C, line 31; Schedule C-EZ, line 3; Schedule K-1 (Form 1065), box 14, code A (other than farming); and Schedule K-1 (Form 1065-B), box 9, code J1. Ministers and members of religious orders, see page SE-1 for amounts to report on this line. See page SE-2 for other income to report	2	
3	Combine lines 1 and 2	3	
4	**Net earnings from self-employment.** Multiply line 3 by 92.35% (.9235). If less than $400, **do not** file this schedule; you do not owe self-employment tax . . . . ▶	4	
5	**Self-employment tax.** If the amount on line 4 is: • $94,200 or less, multiply line 4 by 15.3% (.153). Enter the result here and on **Form 1040, line 58.** • More than $94,200, multiply line 4 by 2.9% (.029). Then, add $11,680.80 to the result. Enter the total here and on **Form 1040, line 58.** . . .	5	
6	**Deduction for one-half of self-employment tax.** Multiply line 5 by 50% (.5). Enter the result here and on **Form 1040, line 27** . . . | 6 |		

28. Retirement Plans. Diana Smith, (self-employed) operates a consulting practice. She has no employees. For the 2006 tax year, Smith's gross consulting revenue was $140,000, and her operating expenses, not including retirement plan contributions, totaled $30,000. In addition to her consulting income, Smith also received $5,000 of earned income in 2006 for writing a chapter in a book about management consulting. During 2006 Smith established a defined contribution (Keogh) plan. The plan stipulates a fixed percentage of 10% of compensation as the amount of the required annual contribution.

a. What is the amount of self-employment tax that Smith must pay in 2006 on the basis of her self-employment income?

b. What is the required dollar contribution that Smith must make to her plan for 2006?

c. By what date must the Keogh be established in order for Smith to take a deduction for the contributions on her 2006 tax return?

d. By what date must the contributions be paid into the Keogh plan in order for Smith to take a deduction on her 2006 tax return?

29. Internet Problem: Researching Publication 560.

Normally a 10% penalty is assessed when employees and self-employed taxpayers take distributions from a retirement plan before reaching age 59½. However, exceptions do exist.

What are the various circumstances under which individuals can take early distributions from the various retirement plans for small business discussed in Chapter 7 and not have to pay the 10% penalty?

Go to the IRS Web site. Locate the Instructions for Form 5329, and find the answer to the above question regarding exceptions to the 10% penalty. Print out a copy of the page where you found your answer. Underline or highlight the pertinent information.

See Appendix A for instructions on use of the IRS Web site.

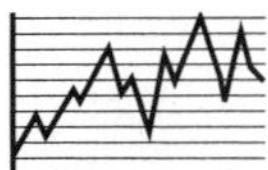

30. Business Entity Problem: This problem is designed for those using the "business entity" approach. The solution may require information from Chapters 14 and 15.

Tom Jones is a general partner in a partnership that reports ordinary income of $80,000 for the current year. His distributive share of partnership ordinary income is $40,000. During the year his guaranteed payments were $30,000 and he withdrew $25,000 from the partnership.

a. What amount would be subject to social security and Medicare taxes? Explain.

b. Is the partnership responsible for withholding income taxes and FICA taxes on the partner's earnings? Explain how these taxes are paid to the government.

c. How would your answers to Parts a. and b. change if the business was operated as an S Corporation?

COMPREHENSIVE PROBLEMS

31. Rob Dunkin operates a consulting business out of his home. During 2006, his business generates income of $51,488 and he has the following expenses: advertising, $150; car expense, $290; depreciation expense, $1,630; office expense, $695; and supplies, $450. Dunkin uses one of the rooms in his house regularly and exclusively as a home office. The size of the room used as an office is 224 square feet. The total square footage of his home is 2,800 square feet. The expenses of operating the home during the year included gas and electric, $3,300; water, $200; insurance, $250; home mortgage interest, $8,500; and real estate taxes, $3,205. The depreciable basis in the home is $110,840.

a. Finish completing Schedule C and Form 8829 for Dunkin (parts of these forms have been completed for you). Then complete Dunkin's Schedule SE.

b. Based on your answers to Part a., what is the maximum amount Dunkin can contribute to a SEP plan for 2006?

c. How long does Dunkin have to set up a SEP and make his SEP contribution for 2006?

d. If Dunkin has no other sources of gross income in 2006 and his only other deduction for AGI is $3,600 that he pays during the year for health insurance. Complete Form 1040 (page 1). Assume that he makes the maximum contribution to his SEP for 2006. Dunkin files as single with no dependents.

(Use for Problem 31.)

Form **1040** Department of the Treasury—Internal Revenue Service
U.S. Individual Income Tax Return **2006** (99) IRS Use Only—Do not write or staple in this space.

For the year Jan. 1–Dec. 31, 2006, or other tax year beginning , 2006, ending , 20 — OMB No. 1545-0074

Label (See instructions on page 16.) **Use the IRS label.** Otherwise, please print or type. — LABEL HERE

- Your first name and initial | Last name | **Your social security number**
- If a joint return, spouse's first name and initial | Last name | **Spouse's social security number**
- Home address (number and street). If you have a P.O. box, see page 16. | Apt. no. | ▲ You **must** enter your SSN(s) above. ▲
- City, town or post office, state, and ZIP code. If you have a foreign address, see page 16.

Presidential Election Campaign ▶ Check here if you, or your spouse if filing jointly, want $3 to go to this fund (see page 16) ▶ Checking a box below will not change your tax or refund. ☐ **You** ☐ **Spouse**

Filing Status

Check only one box.

1 ☐ Single
2 ☐ Married filing jointly (even if only one had income)
3 ☐ Married filing separately. Enter spouse's SSN above and full name here. ▶
4 ☐ Head of household (with qualifying person). (See page 17.) If the qualifying person is a child but not your dependent, enter this child's name here. ▶
5 ☐ Qualifying widow(er) with dependent child (see page 17)

Exemptions

6a ☐ **Yourself.** If someone can claim you as a dependent, **do not** check box 6a
b ☐ **Spouse**
c **Dependents:**

(1) First name Last name	(2) Dependent's social security number	(3) Dependent's relationship to you	(4) ✓ if qualifying child for child tax credit (see page 19)
			☐
			☐
			☐
			☐

If more than four dependents, see page 19.

d Total number of exemptions claimed

Boxes checked on 6a and 6b ____
No. of children on 6c who:
• lived with you ____
• did not live with you due to divorce or separation (see page 20) ____
Dependents on 6c not entered above ____
Add numbers on lines above ▶ ☐

Income

Attach Form(s) W-2 here. Also attach Forms W-2G and 1099-R if tax was withheld.

If you did not get a W-2, see page 22.

Enclose, but do not attach, any payment. Also, please use **Form 1040-V.**

7	Wages, salaries, tips, etc. Attach Form(s) W-2		7
8a	**Taxable** interest. Attach Schedule B if required		8a
b	**Tax-exempt** interest. **Do not** include on line 8a	8b	
9a	Ordinary dividends. Attach Schedule B if required		9a
b	Qualified dividends (see page 23)	9b	
10	Taxable refunds, credits, or offsets of state and local income taxes (see page 23)		10
11	Alimony received		11
12	Business income or (loss). Attach Schedule C or C-EZ		12
13	Capital gain or (loss). Attach Schedule D if required. If not required, check here ▶ ☐		13
14	Other gains or (losses). Attach Form 4797		14
15a	IRA distributions 15a	b Taxable amount (see page 25)	15b
16a	Pensions and annuities 16a	b Taxable amount (see page 25)	16b
17	Rental real estate, royalties, partnerships, S corporations, trusts, etc. Attach Schedule E		17
18	Farm income or (loss). Attach Schedule F		18
19	Unemployment compensation		19
20a	Social security benefits 20a	b Taxable amount (see page 27)	20b
21	Other income. List type and amount (see page 29)		21
22	Add the amounts in the far right column for lines 7 through 21. This is your **total income** ▶		22

Adjusted Gross Income

23	Archer MSA deduction. Attach Form 8853	23	
24	Certain business expenses of reservists, performing artists, and fee-basis government officials. Attach Form 2106 or 2106-EZ	24	
25	Health savings account deduction. Attach Form 8889	25	
26	Moving expenses. Attach Form 3903	26	
27	One-half of self-employment tax. Attach Schedule SE	27	
28	Self-employed SEP, SIMPLE, and qualified plans	28	
29	Self-employed health insurance deduction (see page 30)	29	
30	Penalty on early withdrawal of savings	30	
31a	Alimony paid **b** Recipient's SSN ▶	31a	
32	IRA deduction (see page 31)	32	
33	Student loan interest deduction (see page 33)	33	
34	Jury duty pay you gave to your employer	34	
35	Domestic production activities deduction. Attach Form 8903	35	
36	Add lines 23 through 31a and 32 through 35		36
37	Subtract line 36 from line 22. This is your **adjusted gross income** ▶		37

For Disclosure, Privacy Act, and Paperwork Reduction Act Notice, see page 78. Cat. No. 11320B Form **1040** (2006)

(Use for Problem 31.)

SCHEDULE C (Form 1040)
Department of the Treasury Internal Revenue Service (99)

Profit or Loss From Business
(Sole Proprietorship)

▶ Partnerships, joint ventures, etc., must file Form 1065 or 1065-B.
▶ Attach to Form 1040, 1040NR, or 1041. ▶ See Instructions for Schedule C (Form 1040).

OMB No. 1545-0074
2006
Attachment Sequence No. 09

Name of proprietor: Robert Dunkin
Social security number (SSN): 392 48 6844

A Principal business or profession, including product or service (see page C-2 of the instructions): Consulting
B Enter code from pages C-8, 9, & 10 ▶ 999999
C Business name. If no separate business name, leave blank.
D Employer ID number (EIN), if any
E Business address (including suite or room no.) ▶ 293 E. Main Street
City, town or post office, state, and ZIP code: Lafayette, LA 70503
F Accounting method: (1) ☒ Cash (2) ☐ Accrual (3) ☐ Other (specify) ▶
G Did you "materially participate" in the operation of this business during 2006? If "No," see page C-2 for limit on losses ☐ Yes ☐ No
H If you started or acquired this business during 2006, check here ▶ ☐

Part I Income

1	Gross receipts or sales. **Caution.** If this income was reported to you on Form W-2 and the "Statutory employee" box on that form was checked, see page C-3 and check here ▶ ☐	1	
2	Returns and allowances	2	
3	Subtract line 2 from line 1	3	
4	Cost of goods sold (from line 42 on page 2)	4	
5	**Gross profit.** Subtract line 4 from line 3	5	
6	Other income, including federal and state gasoline or fuel tax credit or refund (see page C-3)	6	
7	**Gross income.** Add lines 5 and 6 ▶	7	

Part II Expenses. Enter expenses for business use of your home **only** on line 30.

8	Advertising	8		18	Office expense	18	
9	Car and truck expenses (see page C-4)	9		19	Pension and profit-sharing plans	19	
10	Commissions and fees	10		20	Rent or lease (see page C-5):		
11	Contract labor (see page C-4)	11		a	Vehicles, machinery, and equipment	20a	
12	Depletion	12		b	Other business property	20b	
13	Depreciation and section 179 expense deduction (not included in Part III) (see page C-4)	13		21	Repairs and maintenance	21	
14	Employee benefit programs (other than on line 19)	14		22	Supplies (not included in Part III)	22	
15	Insurance (other than health)	15		23	Taxes and licenses	23	
16	Interest:			24	Travel, meals, and entertainment:		
a	Mortgage (paid to banks, etc.)	16a		a	Travel	24a	
b	Other	16b		b	Deductible meals and entertainment (see page C-5)	24b	
17	Legal and professional services	17		25	Utilities	25	
				26	Wages (less employment credits)	26	
				27	Other expenses (from line 48 on page 2)	27	

28	**Total expenses** before expenses for business use of home. Add lines 8 through 27 in columns ▶	28	
29	Tentative profit (loss). Subtract line 28 from line 7	29	
30	Expenses for business use of your home. Attach **Form 8829**	30	
31	**Net profit or (loss).** Subtract line 30 from line 29. • If a profit, enter on **Form 1040, line 12,** and **also** on **Schedule SE, line 2** or **Form 1040NR, line 13** (statutory employees, see page C-6). Estates and trusts, enter on Form 1041, line 3. • If a loss, you **must** go to line 32.	31	

32 If you have a loss, check the box that describes your investment in this activity (see page C-6).
• If you checked 32a, enter the loss on **Form 1040, line 12,** and **also** on **Schedule SE, line 2** or **Form 1040NR, line 13** (statutory employees, see page C-6). Estates and trusts, enter on Form 1041, line 3.
• If you checked 32b, you **must** attach **Form 6198.** Your loss may be limited.

32a ☐ All investment is at risk.
32b ☐ Some investment is not at risk.

For Paperwork Reduction Act Notice, see page C-7 of the instructions. Cat. No. 11334P **Schedule C (Form 1040) 2006**

(Use for Problem 31.)

SCHEDULE SE (Form 1040)

Department of the Treasury Internal Revenue Service (99)

Self-Employment Tax

▶ Attach to Form 1040. ▶ See Instructions for Schedule SE (Form 1040).

OMB No. 1545-0074

2006

Attachment Sequence No. 17

Name of person with **self-employment** income (as shown on Form 1040) | Social security number of person with **self-employment** income ▶

Who Must File Schedule SE

You must file Schedule SE if:

- You had net earnings from self-employment from **other than** church employee income (line 4 of Short Schedule SE or line 4c of Long Schedule SE) of $400 or more, **or**
- You had church employee income of $108.28 or more. Income from services you performed as a minister or a member of a religious order **is not** church employee income (see page SE-1).

Note. Even if you had a loss or a small amount of income from self-employment, it may be to your benefit to file Schedule SE and use either "optional method" in Part II of Long Schedule SE (see page SE-3).

Exception. If your only self-employment income was from earnings as a minister, member of a religious order, or Christian Science practitioner **and** you filed Form 4361 and received IRS approval not to be taxed on those earnings, **do not** file Schedule SE. Instead, write "Exempt–Form 4361" on Form 1040, line 58.

May I Use Short Schedule SE or Must I Use Long Schedule SE?

Note. Use this flowchart **only if** you must file Schedule SE. If unsure, see Who Must File Schedule SE, above.

Did you receive wages or tips in 2006?

No → Are you a minister, member of a religious order, or Christian Science practitioner who received IRS approval **not** to be taxed on earnings from these sources, **but** you owe self-employment tax on other earnings? — Yes → You must use Long Schedule SE on page 2

No → Are you using one of the optional methods to figure your net earnings (see page SE-3)? — Yes → You must use Long Schedule SE on page 2

No → Did you receive church employee income reported on Form W-2 of $108.28 or more? — Yes → You must use Long Schedule SE on page 2

No → **You may use Short Schedule SE below**

Yes → Was the total of your wages and tips subject to social security or railroad retirement tax **plus** your net earnings from self-employment more than $94,200? — Yes → **You must use Long Schedule SE on page 2**

No → Did you receive tips subject to social security or Medicare tax that you **did not** report to your employer? — Yes → You must use Long Schedule SE on page 2; No → (to the minister question)

Section A—Short Schedule SE. Caution. Read above to see if you can use Short Schedule SE.

1	Net farm profit or (loss) from Schedule F, line 36, and farm partnerships, Schedule K-1 (Form 1065), box 14, code A	1	
2	Net profit or (loss) from Schedule C, line 31; Schedule C-EZ, line 3; Schedule K-1 (Form 1065), box 14, code A (other than farming); and Schedule K-1 (Form 1065-B), box 9, code J1. Ministers and members of religious orders, see page SE-1 for amounts to report on this line. See page SE-2 for other income to report	2	
3	Combine lines 1 and 2	3	
4	**Net earnings from self-employment.** Multiply line 3 by 92.35% (.9235). If less than $400, **do not** file this schedule; you do not owe self-employment tax ▶	4	
5	**Self-employment tax.** If the amount on line 4 is: • $94,200 or less, multiply line 4 by 15.3% (.153). Enter the result here and on **Form 1040, line 58.** • More than $94,200, multiply line 4 by 2.9% (.029). Then, add $11,680.80 to the result. Enter the total here and on **Form 1040, line 58.**	5	
6	**Deduction for one-half of self-employment tax.** Multiply line 5 by 50% (.5). Enter the result here and on **Form 1040, line 27** . . . 6		

For Paperwork Reduction Act Notice, see Form 1040 instructions. Cat. No. 11358Z **Schedule SE (Form 1040) 2006**

(Use for Problem 31.)

Form **8829** | **Expenses for Business Use of Your Home** | OMB No. 1545-0074

▶ File only with Schedule C (Form 1040). Use a separate Form 8829 for each home you used for business during the year.

▶ See separate instructions.

Department of the Treasury Internal Revenue Service (99) | **2006** Attachment Sequence No. 66

Name(s) of proprietor(s) | Your social security number

Part I — Part of Your Home Used for Business

Line	Description			Box	Amount
1	Area used regularly and exclusively for business, regularly for daycare, or for storage of inventory or product samples (see instructions)			1	
2	Total area of home			2	
3	Divide line 1 by line 2. Enter the result as a percentage			3	%
	• **For daycare facilities not used exclusively for business, also complete lines 4–6.**				
	• **All others, skip lines 4–6 and enter the amount from line 3 on line 7.**				
4	Multiply days used for daycare during year by hours used per day	4	hr.		
5	Total hours available for use during the year (365 days × 24 hours) (see instructions)	5	8,760 hr.		
6	Divide line 4 by line 5. Enter the result as a decimal amount	6	.		
7	Business percentage. For daycare facilities not used exclusively for business, multiply line 6 by line 3 (enter the result as a percentage). All others, enter the amount from line 3 ▶			7	%

Part II — Figure Your Allowable Deduction

			(a) Direct expenses	(b) Indirect expenses		
8	Enter the amount from Schedule C, line 29, **plus** any net gain or (loss) derived from the business use of your home and shown on Schedule D or Form 4797. If more than one place of business, see instructions				8	
	See instructions for columns (a) and (b) before completing lines 9–20.					
9	Casualty losses (see instructions)	9				
10	Deductible mortgage interest (see instructions)	10				
11	Real estate taxes (see instructions)	11				
12	Add lines 9, 10, and 11	12				
13	Multiply line 12, column (b) by line 7		13			
14	Add line 12, column (a) and line 13				14	
15	Subtract line 14 from line 8. If zero or less, enter -0-				15	
16	Excess mortgage interest (see instructions)	16				
17	Insurance	17				
18	Repairs and maintenance	18				
19	Utilities	19				
20	Other expenses (see instructions)	20				
21	Add lines 16 through 20	21				
22	Multiply line 21, column (b) by line 7		22			
23	Carryover of operating expenses from 2005 Form 8829, line 41		23			
24	Add line 21 in column (a), line 22, and line 23				24	
25	Allowable operating expenses. Enter the **smaller** of line 15 or line 24				25	
26	Limit on excess casualty losses and depreciation. Subtract line 25 from line 15				26	
27	Excess casualty losses (see instructions)		27			
28	Depreciation of your home from Part III below		28			
29	Carryover of excess casualty losses and depreciation from 2005 Form 8829, line 42		29			
30	Add lines 27 through 29				30	
31	Allowable excess casualty losses and depreciation. Enter the **smaller** of line 26 or line 30				31	
32	Add lines 14, 25, and 31				32	
33	Casualty loss portion, if any, from lines 14 and 31. Carry amount to **Form 4684,** Section B				33	
34	Allowable expenses for business use of your home. Subtract line 33 from line 32. Enter here and on Schedule C, line 30. If your home was used for more than one business, see instructions ▶				34	

Part III — Depreciation of Your Home

35	Enter the **smaller** of your home's adjusted basis or its fair market value (see instructions)	35	130,840 00
36	Value of land included on line 35	36	20,000 00
37	Basis of building. Subtract line 36 from line 35	37	110,840 00
38	Business basis of building. Multiply line 37 by line 7	38	
39	Depreciation percentage (see instructions)	39	2.564 %
40	Depreciation allowable (see instructions). Multiply line 38 by line 39. Enter here and on line 28 above	40	

Part IV — Carryover of Unallowed Expenses to 2007

41	Operating expenses. Subtract line 25 from line 24. If less than zero, enter -0-	41	
42	Excess casualty losses and depreciation. Subtract line 31 from line 30. If less than zero, enter -0-	42	

For Paperwork Reduction Act Notice, see page 4 of separate instructions. Cat. No. 13232M Form **8829** (2006)

32. Marie A. Lopez (SSN 318-01-6921) lives at 190 Glenn Drive, Grand Rapids, Michigan 49527-2005. Lopez (age 45 and single) claims her aunt, Selda Ray (SSN 282-61-4011), as a dependent. Ray lives with Lopez. Lopez owns and operates the Reliable Drug Company at 1816 First Street in Grand Rapids, Michigan 49503-1902, in which she actively participates the entire year. Her EIN is 38-9654321. Employer quarterly payroll tax returns were filed as required, and Lopez values inventory at cost. The income statement for 2006 is reproduced on the next page. Lopez reports on the accrual method, but uses the "direct write-off" method to compute bad debt expense. Her business code is 446110. She does not deduct expenses for an office in her home.

An examination of Lopez's business records reveals that the depreciable property includes furniture and fixtures, a heavy-duty delivery truck, and store equipment. The depreciation expense shown on the 2006 income statement meets the income tax requirements for depreciation for using the mentioned assets during 2006. Lopez rounds calculations to the nearest dollar. Miscellaneous expenses include the following:

Reimbursement to Lopez for actual expenses of a purchasing trip ($256 for airfare and lodging, $70 for meals)	$326
Contributions to Red Cross and United Way	350
Chamber of Commerce dues	125
Personal electric bill for August	80
Total miscellaneous expenses	$881

Other income for Lopez included a salary of $100 each month for her services as a member of a working committee of the Drug Association. Her Form W-2 from the association showed gross wages of $1,200 and federal income tax withheld of $296. Lopez also earned $320 in interest. Lopez made federal estimated tax payments totaling $6,300 during 2006. This amount is reported on Form 1040 (line 65).

Prepare Form 1040, and Schedules C and SE for Lopez using the forms provided on the pages that follow. Lopez claims the standard credit for federal telephone excise tax paid.

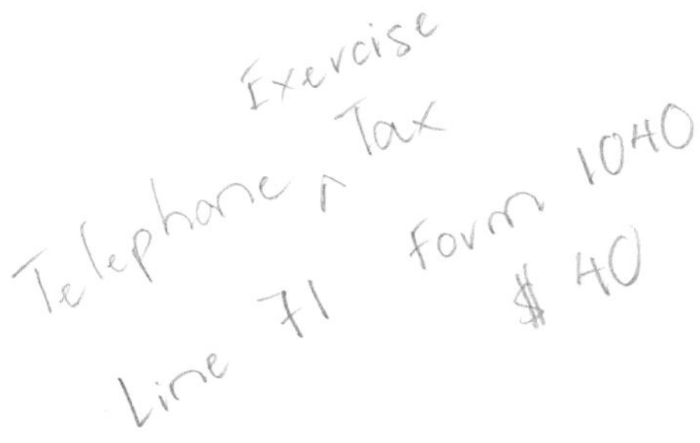

Exercise
Telephone Tax
Line 71 Form 1040
$ 40

RELIABLE DRUG COMPANY
Income Statement for Year Ended December 31, 2006

Operating revenue:		
Sales		$324,200
Less sales returns and allowances		(3,390)
Net sales		$320,810
Cost of merchandise sold:		
Merchandise inventory, beginning (FIFO)	$ 68,920	
Purchases	$198,240	
Less purchases returns and allowances	(8,100)	
Net purchases	$190,140	
Merchandise available for sale	$259,060	
Less merchandise inventory, ending (FIFO)	(69,185)	
Cost of merchandise sold		(189,875)
Gross profit on sales		$130,935
Operating expenses:		
Advertising expense	$ 6,541	
Bad debt expense (direct write off method)	850	
Car and truck expense	7,967[1]	
Depreciation expense	3,396	
Insurance expense (other than health)	644	
Miscellaneous expense	881	
Payroll taxes	3,471	
Rent expense (other business property)	12,000	
Telephone and utilities expense	2,395	
Wages expense	62,500	
Total operating expenses		(100,645)
Net income		$ 30,290

[1]Lopez drove her personal automobile for 17,093 business miles during the year. Total miles for the year were 32,815. There were 1,300 commuting miles. This is Lopez's only car. She has kept a written log documenting her business miles. Lopez first used the car in her business on May 4, 2005.

(Use for Problem 32.)

Form **1040** Department of the Treasury—Internal Revenue Service
U.S. Individual Income Tax Return 2006 (99) IRS Use Only—Do not write or staple in this space.

For the year Jan. 1–Dec. 31, 2006, or other tax year beginning , 2006, ending , 20 OMB No. 1545-0074

Label (See instructions on page 16.) **Use the IRS label.** Otherwise, please print or type.

LABEL HERE

Your first name and initial	Last name	**Your social security number**
If a joint return, spouse's first name and initial	Last name	**Spouse's social security number**
Home address (number and street). If you have a P.O. box, see page 16.	Apt. no.	▲ You **must** enter your SSN(s) above. ▲
City, town or post office, state, and ZIP code. If you have a foreign address, see page 16.		Checking a box below will not change your tax or refund.

Presidential Election Campaign ▶ Check here if you, or your spouse if filing jointly, want $3 to go to this fund (see page 16) ▶ ☐ **You** ☐ **Spouse**

Filing Status

Check only one box.

1 ☐ Single
2 ☐ Married filing jointly (even if only one had income)
3 ☐ Married filing separately. Enter spouse's SSN above and full name here. ▶
4 ☐ Head of household (with qualifying person). (See page 17.) If the qualifying person is a child but not your dependent, enter this child's name here. ▶
5 ☐ Qualifying widow(er) with dependent child (see page 17)

Exemptions

6a ☐ **Yourself.** If someone can claim you as a dependent, **do not** check box 6a
b ☐ **Spouse**

Boxes checked on 6a and 6b ____
No. of children on 6c who:
• lived with you ____
• did not live with you due to divorce or separation (see page 20) ____
Dependents on 6c not entered above ____
Add numbers on lines above ▶ ☐

c **Dependents:**

If more than four dependents, see page 19.

(1) First name Last name	(2) Dependent's social security number	(3) Dependent's relationship to you	(4) ✓ if qualifying child for child tax credit (see page 19)
			☐
			☐
			☐
			☐

d Total number of exemptions claimed

Income

Attach Form(s) W-2 here. Also attach Forms W-2G and 1099-R if tax was withheld.

If you did not get a W-2, see page 22.

Enclose, but do not attach, any payment. Also, please use **Form 1040-V.**

7	Wages, salaries, tips, etc. Attach Form(s) W-2		7
8a	**Taxable** interest. Attach Schedule B if required		8a
b	**Tax-exempt** interest. **Do not** include on line 8a	8b	
9a	Ordinary dividends. Attach Schedule B if required		9a
b	Qualified dividends (see page 23)	9b	
10	Taxable refunds, credits, or offsets of state and local income taxes (see page 23)		10
11	Alimony received		11
12	Business income or (loss). Attach Schedule C or C-EZ		12
13	Capital gain or (loss). Attach Schedule D if required. If not required, check here ▶ ☐		13
14	Other gains or (losses). Attach Form 4797		14
15a	IRA distributions	15a	b Taxable amount (see page 25) 15b
16a	Pensions and annuities	16a	b Taxable amount (see page 25) 16b
17	Rental real estate, royalties, partnerships, S corporations, trusts, etc. Attach Schedule E		17
18	Farm income or (loss). Attach Schedule F		18
19	Unemployment compensation		19
20a	Social security benefits	20a	b Taxable amount (see page 27) 20b
21	Other income. List type and amount (see page 29)		21
22	Add the amounts in the far right column for lines 7 through 21. This is your **total income** ▶		22

Adjusted Gross Income

23	Archer MSA deduction. Attach Form 8853	23	
24	Certain business expenses of reservists, performing artists, and fee-basis government officials. Attach Form 2106 or 2106-EZ	24	
25	Health savings account deduction. Attach Form 8889	25	
26	Moving expenses. Attach Form 3903	26	
27	One-half of self-employment tax. Attach Schedule SE	27	
28	Self-employed SEP, SIMPLE, and qualified plans	28	
29	Self-employed health insurance deduction (see page 30)	29	
30	Penalty on early withdrawal of savings	30	
31a	Alimony paid b Recipient's SSN ▶	31a	
32	IRA deduction (see page 31)	32	
33	Student loan interest deduction (see page 33)	33	
34	Jury duty pay you gave to your employer	34	
35	Domestic production activities deduction. Attach Form 8903	35	
36	Add lines 23 through 31a and 32 through 35		36
37	Subtract line 36 from line 22. This is your **adjusted gross income** ▶		37

For Disclosure, Privacy Act, and Paperwork Reduction Act Notice, see page 78. Cat. No. 11320B Form **1040** (2006)

(Use for Problem 32.)

Form 1040 (2006) Page 2

Tax and Credits

Standard Deduction for—
- People who checked any box on line 39a or 39b **or** who can be claimed as a dependent, see page 36.
- All others:

Single or Married filing separately, $5,150

Married filing jointly or Qualifying widow(er), $10,300

Head of household, $7,550

38	Amount from line 37 (adjusted gross income)		38
39a	Check if: ☐ **You** were born before January 2, 1942, ☐ Blind. ☐ **Spouse** was born before January 2, 1942, ☐ Blind. **Total boxes checked** ▶ **39a**		
b	If your spouse itemizes on a separate return or you were a dual-status alien, see page 35 and check here ▶**39b** ☐		
40	**Itemized deductions** (from Schedule A) **or** your **standard deduction** (see left margin)		40
41	Subtract line 40 from line 38		41
42	If line 38 is over $112,875, or you provided housing to a person displaced by Hurricane Katrina, see page 37. Otherwise, multiply $3,300 by the total number of exemptions claimed on line 6d		42
43	**Taxable income.** Subtract line 42 from line 41. If line 42 is more than line 41, enter -0-		43
44	**Tax** (see page 37). Check if any tax is from: **a** ☐ Form(s) 8814 **b** ☐ Form 4972		44
45	**Alternative minimum tax** (see page 39). Attach Form 6251		45
46	Add lines 44 and 45 ▶		46
47	Foreign tax credit. Attach Form 1116 if required	47	
48	Credit for child and dependent care expenses. Attach Form 2441	48	
49	Credit for the elderly or the disabled. Attach Schedule R	49	
50	Education credits. Attach Form 8863	50	
51	Retirement savings contributions credit. Attach Form 8880	51	
52	Residential energy credits. Attach Form 5695	52	
53	Child tax credit (see page XX). Attach Form 8901 if required	53	
54	Credits from: **a** ☐ Form 8396 **b** ☐ Form 8839 **c** ☐ Form 8859	54	
55	Other credits: **a** ☐ Form 3800 **b** ☐ Form 8801 **c** ☐ Form ____	55	
56	Add lines 47 through 55. These are your **total credits**		56
57	Subtract line 56 from line 46. If line 56 is more than line 46, enter -0- ▶		57

Other Taxes

58	Self-employment tax. Attach Schedule SE	58
59	Social security and Medicare tax on tip income not reported to employer. Attach Form 4137	59
60	Additional tax on IRAs, other qualified retirement plans, etc. Attach Form 5329 if required	60
61	Advance earned income credit payments from Form(s) W-2, box 9	61
62	Household employment taxes. Attach Schedule H	62
63	Add lines 57 through 62. This is your **total tax** ▶	63

Payments

If you have a qualifying child, attach Schedule EIC.

64	Federal income tax withheld from Forms W-2 and 1099	64	
65	2006 estimated tax payments and amount applied from 2005 return	65	
66a	**Earned income credit (EIC)**	66a	
b	Nontaxable combat pay election ▶ **66b**		
67	Excess social security and tier 1 RRTA tax withheld (see page 59)	67	
68	Additional child tax credit. Attach Form 8812	68	
69	Amount paid with request for extension to file (see page 59)	69	
70	Payments from: **a** ☐ Form 2439 **b** ☐ Form 4136 **c** ☐ Form 8885	70	
71	Credit for federal telephone excise tax paid. Attach Form 8913 if required	71	
72	Add lines 64, 65, 66a, and 67 through 71. These are your **total payments** ▶		72

Refund

Direct deposit? See page 59 and fill in 74b, 74c, and 74d, or Form 8888.

73	If line 72 is more than line 63, subtract line 63 from line 72. This is the amount you **overpaid**		73
74a	Amount of line 73 you want **refunded to you.** If Form 8888 is attached, check here ▶ ☐		74a
▶ b	Routing number ▶ **c** Type: ☐ Checking ☐ Savings		
▶ d	Account number		
75	Amount of line 73 you want **applied to your 2007 estimated tax** ▶	75	

Amount You Owe

76	**Amount you owe.** Subtract line 72 from line 63. For details on how to pay, see page 60 ▶		76
77	Estimated tax penalty (see page 60)	77	

Third Party Designee

Do you want to allow another person to discuss this return with the IRS (see page 61)? ☐ **Yes.** Complete the following. ☐ **No**

Designee's name ▶ Phone no. ▶ ( ) Personal identification number (PIN) ▶

Sign Here

Joint return? See page 17. Keep a copy for your records.

Under penalties of perjury, I declare that I have examined this return and accompanying schedules and statements, and to the best of my knowledge and belief, they are true, correct, and complete. Declaration of preparer (other than taxpayer) is based on all information of which preparer has any knowledge.

Your signature	Date	Your occupation	Daytime phone number ( )
Spouse's signature. If a joint return, **both** must sign.	Date	Spouse's occupation	

Paid Preparer's Use Only

Preparer's signature	Date	Check if self-employed ☐	Preparer's SSN or PTIN
Firm's name (or yours if self-employed), address, and ZIP code		EIN	
		Phone no.	( )

Form **1040** (2006)

Printed on recycled paper

(Use for Problem 32.)

SCHEDULE C (Form 1040)

Department of the Treasury
Internal Revenue Service (99)

Profit or Loss From Business

(Sole Proprietorship)

▶ Partnerships, joint ventures, etc., must file Form 1065 or 1065-B.

▶ Attach to Form 1040, 1040NR, or 1041. ▶ See Instructions for Schedule C (Form 1040).

OMB No. 1545-0074

2006

Attachment Sequence No. **09**

Name of proprietor | Social security number (SSN)

A Principal business or profession, including product or service (see page C-2 of the instructions) | **B Enter code from pages C-8, 9, & 10** ▶

C Business name. If no separate business name, leave blank. | **D Employer ID number (EIN), if any**

E Business address (including suite or room no.) ▶
City, town or post office, state, and ZIP code

F Accounting method: (1) ☐ Cash (2) ☐ Accrual (3) ☐ Other (specify) ▶

G Did you "materially participate" in the operation of this business during 2006? If "No," see page C-2 for limit on losses ☐ **Yes** ☐ **No**

H If you started or acquired this business during 2006, check here . . . ▶ ☐

Part I Income

1	Gross receipts or sales. **Caution.** If this income was reported to you on Form W-2 and the "Statutory employee" box on that form was checked, see page C-3 and check here . . . ▶ ☐	1	
2	Returns and allowances	2	
3	Subtract line 2 from line 1	3	
4	Cost of goods sold (from line 42 on page 2)	4	
5	**Gross profit.** Subtract line 4 from line 3	5	
6	Other income, including federal and state gasoline or fuel tax credit or refund (see page C-3)	6	
7	**Gross income.** Add lines 5 and 6 . . . ▶	7	

Part II Expenses. Enter expenses for business use of your home only on line 30.

8	Advertising	8		18	Office expense	18	
9	Car and truck expenses (see page C-4)	9		19	Pension and profit-sharing plans	19	
10	Commissions and fees	10		20	Rent or lease (see page C-5):		
11	Contract labor (see page C-4)	11		a	Vehicles, machinery, and equipment	20a	
12	Depletion	12		b	Other business property	20b	
13	Depreciation and section 179 expense deduction (not included in Part III) (see page C-4)	13		21	Repairs and maintenance	21	
				22	Supplies (not included in Part III)	22	
				23	Taxes and licenses	23	
				24	Travel, meals, and entertainment:		
				a	Travel	24a	
14	Employee benefit programs (other than on line 19)	14		b	Deductible meals and entertainment (see page C-5)	24b	
15	Insurance (other than health)	15		25	Utilities	25	
16	Interest:			26	Wages (less employment credits)	26	
a	Mortgage (paid to banks, etc.)	16a		27	Other expenses (from line 48 on page 2)	27	
b	Other	16b					
17	Legal and professional services	17					

28	**Total expenses** before expenses for business use of home. Add lines 8 through 27 in columns . ▶	28	
29	Tentative profit (loss). Subtract line 28 from line 7	29	
30	Expenses for business use of your home. Attach **Form 8829**	30	
31	**Net profit or (loss).** Subtract line 30 from line 29. • If a profit, enter on **Form 1040, line 12,** and **also** on **Schedule SE, line 2** or **Form 1040NR, line 13** (statutory employees, see page C-6). Estates and trusts, enter on Form 1041, line 3. • If a loss, you **must** go to line 32.	31	
32	If you have a loss, check the box that describes your investment in this activity (see page C-6). • If you checked 32a, enter the loss on **Form 1040, line 12,** and **also** on **Schedule SE, line 2** or **Form 1040NR, line 13** (statutory employees, see page C-6). Estates and trusts, enter on Form 1041, line 3. • If you checked 32b, you **must** attach **Form 6198.** Your loss may be limited.	32a ☐ All investment is at risk. 32b ☐ Some investment is not at risk.	

For Paperwork Reduction Act Notice, see page C-7 of the instructions. Cat. No. 11334P **Schedule C (Form 1040) 2006**

(Use for Problem 32.)

Schedule C (Form 1040) 2006 Page 2

Part III **Cost of Goods Sold** (see page C-7)

33 Method(s) used to value closing inventory: a ☐ Cost b ☐ Lower of cost or market c ☐ Other (attach explanation)

34 Was there any change in determining quantities, costs, or valuations between opening and closing inventory? If "Yes," attach explanation ☐ Yes ☐ No

35 Inventory at beginning of year. If different from last year's closing inventory, attach explanation	35	
36 Purchases less cost of items withdrawn for personal use	36	
37 Cost of labor. Do not include any amounts paid to yourself	37	
38 Materials and supplies	38	
39 Other costs	39	
40 Add lines 35 through 39	40	
41 Inventory at end of year	41	
42 **Cost of goods sold.** Subtract line 41 from line 40. Enter the result here and on page 1, line 4	42	

Part IV **Information on Your Vehicle.** Complete this part **only** if you are claiming car or truck expenses on line 9 and are not required to file Form 4562 for this business. See the instructions for line 13 on page C-4 to find out if you must file Form 4562.

43 When did you place your vehicle in service for business purposes? (month, day, year) ▶ ____/____/____

44 Of the total number of miles you drove your vehicle during 2006, enter the number of miles you used your vehicle for:

a Business ____________ b Commuting (see instructions) ____________ c Other ____________

45 Do you (or your spouse) have another vehicle available for personal use? ☐ Yes ☐ No

46 Was your vehicle available for personal use during off-duty hours? ☐ Yes ☐ No

47a Do you have evidence to support your deduction? ☐ Yes ☐ No

b If "Yes," is the evidence written? ☐ Yes ☐ No

Part V **Other Expenses.** List below business expenses not included on lines 8–26 or line 30.

48 **Total other expenses.** Enter here and on page 1, line 27	48	

Printed on recycled paper Schedule C (Form 1040) 2006

(Use for Problem 32.)

SCHEDULE SE (Form 1040)
Department of the Treasury Internal Revenue Service (99)

Self-Employment Tax

▶ Attach to Form 1040. ▶ See Instructions for Schedule SE (Form 1040).

OMB No. 1545-0074
2006
Attachment Sequence No. **17**

Name of person with **self-employment** income (as shown on Form 1040) | Social security number of person with **self-employment** income ▶

Who Must File Schedule SE

You must file Schedule SE if:

- You had net earnings from self-employment from **other than** church employee income (line 4 of Short Schedule SE or line 4c of Long Schedule SE) of $400 or more, **or**
- You had church employee income of $108.28 or more. Income from services you performed as a minister or a member of a religious order **is not** church employee income (see page SE-1).

Note. Even if you had a loss or a small amount of income from self-employment, it may be to your benefit to file Schedule SE and use either "optional method" in Part II of Long Schedule SE (see page SE-3).

Exception. If your only self-employment income was from earnings as a minister, member of a religious order, or Christian Science practitioner **and** you filed Form 4361 and received IRS approval not to be taxed on those earnings, **do not** file Schedule SE. Instead, write "Exempt–Form 4361" on Form 1040, line 58.

May I Use Short Schedule SE or Must I Use Long Schedule SE?

Note. Use this flowchart **only if** you must file Schedule SE. If unsure, see Who Must File Schedule SE, above.

Did you receive wages or tips in 2006?

No ▼

Are you a minister, member of a religious order, or Christian Science practitioner who received IRS approval **not** to be taxed on earnings from these sources, **but** you owe self-employment tax on other earnings? — Yes ▶ You must use Long Schedule SE on page 2

No ▼

Are you using one of the optional methods to figure your net earnings (see page SE-3)? — Yes ▶ You must use Long Schedule SE on page 2

No ▼

Did you receive church employee income reported on Form W-2 of $108.28 or more? — Yes ▶ You must use Long Schedule SE on page 2

No ▼

You may use Short Schedule SE below

Yes ▼

Was the total of your wages and tips subject to social security or railroad retirement tax **plus** your net earnings from self-employment more than $94,200? — Yes ▶ You must use Long Schedule SE on page 2

No ▼

Did you receive tips subject to social security or Medicare tax that you **did not** report to your employer? — Yes ▶ You must use Long Schedule SE on page 2; No ◀ (go to the minister question above)

You must use Long Schedule SE on page 2

Section A—Short Schedule SE. Caution. Read above to see if you can use Short Schedule SE.

1	Net farm profit or (loss) from Schedule F, line 36, and farm partnerships, Schedule K-1 (Form 1065), box 14, code A . . .	1	
2	Net profit or (loss) from Schedule C, line 31; Schedule C-EZ, line 3; Schedule K-1 (Form 1065), box 14, code A (other than farming); and Schedule K-1 (Form 1065-B), box 9, code J1. Ministers and members of religious orders, see page SE-1 for amounts to report on this line. See page SE-2 for other income to report . . .	2	
3	Combine lines 1 and 2 . . .	3	
4	**Net earnings from self-employment.** Multiply line 3 by 92.35% (.9235). If less than $400, **do not** file this schedule; you do not owe self-employment tax . . . ▶	4	
5	**Self-employment tax.** If the amount on line 4 is: • $94,200 or less, multiply line 4 by 15.3% (.153). Enter the result here and on **Form 1040, line 58.** • More than $94,200, multiply line 4 by 2.9% (.029). Then, add $11,680.80 to the result. Enter the total here and on **Form 1040, line 58.** . . .	5	
6	**Deduction for one-half of self-employment tax.** Multiply line 5 by 50% (.5). Enter the result here and on **Form 1040, line 27** . . . | 6 |		

For Paperwork Reduction Act Notice, see Form 1040 instructions. Cat. No. 11358Z **Schedule SE (Form 1040) 2006**

TAX ETHICS CASE*

33. The date is April 14, and Helen Baldwin, CPA tax practitioner, sits at her desk, pondering the tax return before her. Helen has spent plenty of time pondering during the past year since moving from her home in a large eastern city to set up her new tax practice in a small western town. Clients in this small town have not exactly beaten a path to Helen's door to take advantage of her services. Building a client base has proven much more difficult than she had anticipated.

The return in front of Helen was completed on behalf of her newest client, Billy Joe Carter, who owns Honest Bill's Used Car Lot. He is a cousin of half of the members of the town council and is very influential in the local business community. Establishing a client relationship with Billy is the break that Helen has been looking for. In fact, Billy has made it clear that if Helen can complete and file his return before the April 15 deadline, Helen will receive his tax return business, as well as that of his family, for years to come.

Of concern to Helen, however, are several items on Billy's return. Billy insists that he is entitled to a business deduction for his new four-wheel-drive truck, since he uses it 100% of the time for business errands (such as traveling to car auctions, picking up parts, etc.). Helen thinks she has seen Billy driving the truck a number of times on what appeared to be personal trips. Also, Billy insists that the expenses associated with several trips to Las Vegas are deductible since the trips were "primarily of a business nature." Billy also claims several other large deductions without offering what Helen would consider to be "substantial documentation." As if anticipating Helen's skepticism, Billy said, "I don't know how things were in the big city where you came from, but around here people believe that a person's word is worth something. You'll just have to trust good old 'Honest Bill' this year, and next year I'll try to keep some better records."

a. What are the ethical issues in this case?

b. Who and what are the stakeholders who will be affected directly or indirectly by an inappropriate decision on Helen's part?

c. What are Helen's options in this situation

d. What do you recommend that Helen do?

*Case adapted from ethics cases prepared for publication by the American Accounting Association..

The rules in effect when the asset is placed in service continue to apply during the entire time the taxpayer owns the property. For example, to compute the 2006 depreciation expense for a building placed in service in 2001, the taxpayer uses the rules that applied to property placed in service in 2001.

Taxpayers need to understand how to depreciate property correctly. Depreciation expense reduces a property's "adjusted basis," even if the taxpayer fails to deduct it on the tax return. Thus, the adjusted basis must be reduced by the *greater of* depreciation "allowed or allowable." This refers to depreciation that is deducted or that which the taxpayer is entitled to deduct. A taxpayer can claim overlooked depreciation expense by deducting it on an amended return. An amended return must be filed within three years of the due date of the original return on which the expense was not claimed. After three years, overlooked depreciation cannot be claimed, but it still reduces the taxpayer's basis in the property.

Taxpayers can place in service property acquired by purchase, exchange, gift, or inheritance. This chapter focuses on business property acquired by purchase. It also focuses on the rules that apply to the depreciation of property placed in service after 1986, since property placed in service before 1987 is fully depreciated. Those interested in learning more about ACRS should refer to IRS Publication 534. The depreciation rules for tangible personal property are presented first, followed by the rules for real property.

DEPRECIATION OF TANGIBLE PERSONAL PROPERTY

"Bonus" First-Year Depreciation

To encourage purchases of new property after the events of September 11, 2001, Congress enacted a "bonus" depreciation in the first year for purchases of new personal property used for business or investment acquired after September 10, 2001, and placed in service by December 31, 2004. Taxpayers were required to deduct the bonus depreciation for all eligible purchases unless they made an election not to take it. After deducting the bonus depreciation from the cost of the property, taxpayers depreciated the remaining cost using the MACRS rules discussed in the next section. For property placed in service on or before May 5, 2003, the bonus percentage was 30%. After that date, it increased to 50%. Although bonus depreciation is not allowed for property placed in service after December 31, 2004, to be able to continue depreciating property on which bonus depreciation was taken, it is important to understand how bonus depreciation affected the basis in such property.

EXAMPLE 1

On August 1, 2004, Victor Myers paid $20,000 for new personal property to be used in his business. Myers deducted $10,000 ($20,000 × 50%) of bonus depreciation in 2004, and used MACRS to depreciate the remaining $10,000 ($20,000 – $10,000) starting in 2004.

EXAMPLE 2

Same as in Example 1, except that Myers purchased the property in 2006. Since property placed in service after December 31, 2004 is not eligible for the bonus depreciation, Myers depreciates the $20,000 using MACRS starting in 2006.

> A provision in the Gulf Opportunity Zone Act of 2005 allows businesses (including sole proprietorships) affected by Hurricanes Katrina, Rita and Wilma to take a 50% bonus first year depreciation on qualifying property placed in service in the Gulf Opportunity Zone (Go Zone) between the date of the hurricane and December 31, 2007.

Modified Accelerated Cost Recovery System (MACRS)

To calculate depreciation expense using MACRS, taxpayers multiply the MACRS basis of the property by a percentage taken from an IRS-provided table. Under MACRS, personal property is assigned a life of 3, 5, 7, 10, or 15 years, regardless of its actual useful life. MACRS assigns the more common properties a 5-year or 7-year life. The 5-year-life class includes automobiles, office equipment, and cellular phones. Office equipment includes copiers, fax machines, computers, printers, and the like. The 7-year-life class includes furniture and fixtures, machinery, and equipment other than office equipment.

MACRS uses the 200% declining balance method to recover the costs of 3-, 5-, 7-, and 10-year property. The 150% declining balance method is used to recover the cost of 15-year property. However, MACRS switches to the straight-line method when straight-line yields a greater deduction.

MACRS ignores salvage value. Instead, taxpayers multiply the percentage from the table by the property's MACRS basis to compute their MACRS deduction. Computing MACRS basis begins with computing the unadjusted basis in the property. The unadjusted basis equals the total cost of preparing the property for use at its operating location. This amount includes the purchase price, sales tax, plus any delivery and installation costs. Any Section 179 expense or bonus depreciation taken in the first year is subtracted from the unadjusted basis to compute the taxpayer's MACRS basis. The unadjusted basis of nonbusiness property that a taxpayer converts to business use equals the *lesser of* (i) the fair market value of the property on the conversion date or (ii) the taxpayer's adjusted basis in the property on the conversion date. Special rules also apply for determining the unadjusted basis of property acquired by exchange, gift, or inheritance. These rules are discussed in Chapter 10.

FIGURE 8-2 Cost Recovery Periods for Property under MACRS

Recovery Class	Rate and Method	Special Rules for Each Asset Class
3-year	200% D.B.*	Includes tractor units for over-the-road use and race horses over 2 years old
5-year	200% D.B.	Includes automobiles, light trucks, computers, printers, copiers, typewriters, fax machines, cellular phones, and residential rental furnishings
7-year	200% D.B.	Includes office furniture and fixtures, railroad tracks, and property not assigned to another class (machinery and equipment)
10-year	200% D.B.	Includes vessels, barges, tugs, similar water transportation equipment, and single-purpose agricultural and horticultural structures
15-year	150% D.B.	Includes shrubbery, fences, roads, and bridges

*D.B. stands for declining balance

Averaging Conventions

Two averaging conventions determine the date when taxpayers can begin depreciating personal property. These two conventions are the half-year convention and the mid-quarter convention. The half-year convention applies when at least 60% of the MACRS depreciable basis of personal property for the year is placed in service during the first nine months of the year. The mid-quarter convention applies when more than 40% of all personal property is placed in service during the last three months of the year.

Half-Year Convention

When at least 60% of all personal property is placed in service during the first three quarters of the year, all personal property placed in service during the year is depreciated using the half-year convention. When using the half-year convention, the actual date on which personal property is placed in service is ignored. Instead, the **half-year convention** assumes that taxpayers place personal property in service halfway through the tax year. The half-year convention also assumes that taxpayers dispose of (e.g., sell) such property halfway through the tax year. Thus, under the half-year convention, taxpayers get one-half year's depreciation in the first and last years, regardless of how long the taxpayer actually owned the property in those years. Figure 8-3 shows the MACRS percentages for 3-, 5-, 7-, and 10-year classes under the half-year convention. To compute MACRS on property depreciated under the half-year convention, taxpayers multiply these percentages by the MACRS basis of the property.

FIGURE 8-3 MACRS Table for 3-, 5-, 7-, and 10-Year Classes Using the Half-Year Convention (from Appendix A in IRS Publication 946)

	Recovery Period			
Year	**3-Year**	**5-Year**	**7-Year**	**10-Year**
1	33.33%	20.00%	14.29%	10.00%
2	44.45	32.00	24.49	18.00
3	14.81*	19.20	17.49	14.40
4	7.41	11.52*	12.49	11.52
5		11.52	8.93*	9.22
6		5.76	8.92	7.37
7			8.93	6.55*
8			4.46	6.55
9				6.56
10				6.55
11				3.28

*Switching to straight-line results in the maximum depreciation deduction

The Year 1 percentages from Figure 8-3 reflect a half year's depreciation. Using the 200% declining balance method, taxpayers should deduct 40% of the cost of 5-year property in the first year (1/5 × 200%). However, because the half-year convention assumes taxpayers place property in service halfway through the year, the MACRS percentage for Year 1 is one-half of the full-year percentage, or 20% for 5-year property. Starting in Year 2, the percentages shown in Figure 8-3 reflect a full year of depreciation under the 200% declining balance method. An asterisk shows the switch to the straight-line method when straight-line yields a greater deduction. Figure 8-3 also shows that the rest of the first year's depreciation is deducted in the year after the recovery period ends. This is the sixth year for 5-year property and the eighth year for 7-year property.

EXAMPLE 3

On March 2, 2004, a taxpayer placed in service new 5-year property costing $10,000. After deducting $5,000 ($10,000 × 50%) of bonus depreciation, the remaining $5,000 MACRS basis ($10,000 – $5,000) is depreciated using the 5-year column in Figure 8-3. Total depreciation deductions using the half-year convention are shown below. Note that in 2004, the taxpayer deducted depreciation totalling $6,000 ($5,000 + $1,000). At the end of 2006, the taxpayer's adjusted basis in the property is $1,440 ($10,000 – $6,000 – $1,600 – $960).

Year	Depreciation	
2004	$5,000	($10,000 × 50%) bonus depreciation
2004	1,000	($5,000 × 20%) MACRS depreciation
2005	1,600	($5,000 × 32%) MACRS depreciation
2006	960	($5,000 × 19.2%) MACRS depreciation
2007	576	($5,000 × 11.52%) MACRS depreciation
2008	576	($5,000 × 11.52%) MACRS depreciation
2009	288	($5,000 × 5.76%) MACRS depreciation
	$10,000	

Except in the last year of the recovery period, when taxpayers dispose of property under the half-year convention, they multiply the MACRS percentage from the table by one-half. In the last year of the recovery period (for example, year 6 for 5-year property), taxpayers use the full MACRS percentage even if they dispose of the property in that year.

EXAMPLE 4

On April 10, 2005, Kate Roberts placed in service 5-year property costing $10,000. In 2009, Roberts sells the property. Under the half-year convention, the annual depreciation for the property is shown below.

Year	MACRS	
2005	$2,000*	($10,000 × 20%)
2006	3,200	($10,000 × 32%)
2007	1,920	($10,000 × 19.2%)
2008	1,152	($10,000 × 11.52%)
2009	576	($10,000 × 11.52% × ½)
	$8,848	

*No bonus depreciation was taken in 2005 since the property was purchased after 2004.

It does not matter when in 2009 Roberts actually sells the property. The half-year convention assumes that she sells the property on June 30, 2009, halfway through the tax year.

Mid-Quarter Convention

During the first few years after the half-year convention was enacted, many taxpayers took advantage of it by purchasing assets near the end of the year and taking a half-year's depreciation in the first year. To counter this strategy, the government now imposes a mid-quarter convention. Taxpayers who purchase over 40% of their depreciable personal property (equipment, furniture, etc.) during the last quarter of the year must use the mid-quarter convention to depreciate all personal property placed in service during that year.

Like the half-year convention, the mid-quarter convention ignores the actual date personal property is placed in service. Instead, the **mid-quarter convention** assumes that taxpayers placed the personal property in service in the middle of the quarter. Thus, taxpayers who place personal property in service between January 1 and March 31 are assumed to place it in service on February 15. This means that, in the first year, they can depreciate the property from February 15 until December 31 (10.5 months). Figure 8-4 shows the four mid-quarter tables for 3-, 5-, and 7-year classes.

The Year 1 percentages in Figure 8-4 reflect the portion of the year in which the property is assumed to be placed in service. For property placed in service in the first quarter, depreciation on the property begins on February 15. For 5-year property, the first-year percentage equals 35% (1/5 × 200% × 10.5/12). For 7-year property placed in service in the fourth quarter (deemed placed in service on November 15), the first-year percentage equals 3.57% (1/7 × 200% × 1.5/12). Starting in Year 2, the percentages reflect a full year of depreciation under the 200% declining balance method, switching to straight-line at the most opportune time.

The mid-quarter convention also assumes that taxpayers dispose of property halfway through the quarter. Thus, all personal property sold during October, November, and December is deemed to have been sold on November 15, regardless of the quarter in which the property was purchased. Likewise, all personal property sold during April, May, and June is deemed sold on May 15. Except in the last year of the recovery period, in the year taxpayers dispose of personal property depreciated using the mid-quarter convention, the percentage from the table must be reduced to reflect the portion of the year the property was assumed to be in service. This would be from January 1 until the middle of the quarter in which the property is sold.

FIGURE 8-4 MACRS Table for 3-, 5-, and 7-Year Classes Using the Mid-Quarter Convention (from Appendix A in IRS Publication 946)

Property Placed in Service				**Years**				
1st quarter	**1**	**2**	**3**	**4**	**5**	**6**	**7**	**8**
3-year	58.33%	27.78%	12.35%	1.54%				
5-year	35.00	26.00	15.60	11.01	11.01%	1.38%		
7-year	25.00	21.43	15.31	10.93	8.75	8.74	8.75%	1.09%
2nd quarter								
3-year	41.67	38.89	14.14	5.30				
5-year	25.00	30.00	18.00	11.37	11.37	4.26		
7-year	17.85	23.47	16.76	11.97	8.87	8.87	8.87	3.34
3rd quarter								
3-year	25.00	50.00	16.67	8.33				
5-year	15.00	34.00	20.40	12.24	11.30	7.06		
7-year	10.71	25.51	18.22	13.02	9.30	8.85	8.86	5.53
4th quarter								
3-year	8.33	61.11	20.37	10.19				
5-year	5.00	38.00	22.80	13.68	10.94	9.58		
7-year	3.57	27.55	19.68	14.06	10.04	8.73	8.73	7.64

EXAMPLE 5

In March 2002, George Rodgers placed in service 5-year property that cost $14,286. He deducted 30% bonus depreciation in 2002. This left him with an MACRS basis in the property of $10,000 ($14,286 – $4,286 bonus depreciation). Rodgers sold the property in June 2006. Under the mid-quarter convention, depreciation for the property is as follows.

Year	MACRS	
2002	$3,500	($10,000 × 35%)
2003	2,600	($10,000 × 26%)
2004	1,560	($10,000 × 15.6%)
2005	1,101	($10,000 × 11.01%)
2006	413	($10,000 × 11.01% × 4.5/12)
	$9,174	

The MACRS first-quarter percentages apply since Rodgers placed the property in service during the first quarter. Although Rodgers actually sold the property in June, the property is deemed sold halfway through the second quarter (May 15). Rodgers multiplies the Year 5 MACRS percentage by 4.5/12 to reflect the property's depreciation from January 1 through May 15. Notice that Rodgers uses the 5-year percentages for the 1st quarter for all years that he depreciates the property.

Each year taxpayers must determine whether the half-year or mid-quarter convention applies to personal property placed in service that year. If the mid-quarter convention applies, then taxpayers may need to use four different tables to compute depreciation on personal property placed in service that year. (Under the half-year convention, taxpayers use one table to depreciate all personal property placed in service during the year.) The mid-quarter convention applies when the taxpayer placed in service in the fourth quarter more than 40% of the total depreciable personal property placed in service that year. Otherwise, the half-year convention applies.

It is important to note that real property placed in service during the year is not used when determining whether more than 40% of all personal property placed in service during the year is done so in the fourth quarter. The relevant percentage is fourth quarter depreciable personal property purchases divided by total depreciable personal property purchases during the year. Also, only the cost of personal property after Section 179 and bonus depreciation have been subtracted out is used in this calculation.

EXAMPLE 6

On June 21, 2006, Jean Nelson placed in service 7-year property that costs $20,000. On October 10, 2006, she placed in service 5-year property that costs $15,000. These are the only properties placed in service in 2006. Since Nelson placed in service 42.9% ($15,000/$35,000) of the personal property in the fourth quarter, the mid-quarter convention applies to all personal property placed in service in 2006. Depreciation on the 7-year property equals $3,570 ($20,000 × 17.85%); on the 5-year property it equals $750 ($15,000 × 5%).

EXAMPLE 7

Assume the same facts as in Example 6, except that Nelson placed the 5-year property in service on September 30, 2006. Since 40% or less of the personal property placed in service in 2006 was placed in service in the fourth quarter, the half-year convention applies to both properties. Depreciation on the 7-year property would be $2,858 ($20,000 × 14.29%). Depreciation on the 5-year property would be $3,000 ($15,000 × 20%).

Election Choices

Taxpayers who do not wish to use the regular MACRS (accelerated) method can elect to use either the alternate MACRS method or the Alternative Depreciation System (ADS).

Alternate MACRS

Alternate MACRS uses the straight-line method instead of the accelerated method. Straight-line depreciation spreads the cost evenly over the recovery period. When the taxpayer elects the straight-line method, the recovery periods and averaging conventions continue to apply.

EXAMPLE 8

On June 5, 2005, a taxpayer places in service 5-year property costing $10,000. The half year convention applies to all personal property placed in service that year. The taxpayer sells the property on January 14, 2007. A comparison of regular MACRS and alternative MACRS follows.

Year	Regular MACRS		Alternative MACRS	
2005	$10,000 x 20%	$2,000	$10,000 x 1/5 x ½	$1,000
2006	$10,000 x 32%	3,200	$10,000 x 1/5	2,000
2007	$10,000 x 19.2% x ½	960	$10,000 x 1/5 x ½	1,000
		$6,160		$4,000

EXAMPLE 9

Same as in Example 8 except that the mid-quarter convention applies to all personal property placed in service during 2005.

Year	Regular MACRS		Alternative MACRS	
2005	$10,000 x 25%	$2,500	$10,000 x 1/5 x 7.5/12	$1,250
2006	$10,000 x 30%	3,000	$10,000 x 1/5	2,000
2007	$10,000 x 18% x 1.5/12	225	$10,000 x 1/5 x 1.5/12	250
		$5,725		$3,500

Under the mid-quarter convention, the taxpayer begins depreciating the property in the middle of the quarter in which it is placed in service. In this case, that would be on May 15 (the middle of the second quarter). Thus, in the first year, depreciation is allowed for 7.5 months (built into the MACRS tables). This property was sold in the first quarter. Thus, depreciation in that year was allowed until the middle of the first quarter (February 15, or 1.5 months (not built into the MACRS tables).

The election to use the straight-line method can be made annually for each class of property. For example, a taxpayer who elects the straight-line method in 2006 for 5-year property must use the straight-line method to depreciate all 5-year property placed in service in 2006. However, the taxpayer can use the regular (accelerated) MACRS for 7-year property purchased in 2006. This is called an election on a **class-by-class basis.** A taxpayer who uses the straight-line method to depreciate 5-year property placed in service in 2006 does not have to use it to depreciate 5-year property placed in service in 2007.

EXAMPLE 10

Jones Company placed in service the following properties during 20x1.

Equipment (7-year personal property)
Furniture (7-year personal property)
Delivery van (5-year personal property)
Warehouse (commercial real property)
Office building (commercial real property)

If Jones wants to use alternative MACRS to depreciate the equipment, it must use that method to depreciate all 7-year property placed in service during 20x1. This would require that the furniture placed in service during 20x1 be depreciated using alternative MACRS. Jones's decision to use alternative MACRS to depreciate the 7-year property placed in service during 20x1 does not affect the depreciation method it uses to depreciate the 5-year property or the real properties placed in service during 20x1. Also, its decision to use alternative MACRS to depreciate the 7-year property placed in service during in 20x1 does not affect the depreciation method it uses to depreciate 7-year property placed in service in 20x2 or any future tax year.

Alternative Depreciation System (ADS)

The **Alternative Depreciation System (ADS)** differs from MACRS in that most properties have longer recovery periods. For most property, the taxpayer can choose between the straight-line method and the 150% declining balance method. The half-year and mid-quarter conventions apply to personal property depreciated under the ADS method. Separate tables are available for this method. The IRS provides these tables in Publication 946. The following comparison shows the recovery periods under MACRS and ADS.

	MACRS	*ADS*
Office furniture, fixtures, and equipment	7 years	10 years
Automobiles, light general purpose trucks, computers, and printers	5 years	5 years
Copiers, calculators, and typewriters	5 years	6 years
Heavy general purpose trucks	5 years	6 years

Personal property with no designated class life has a recovery period of 12 years under ADS. The taxpayer makes the election to use ADS annually on a class-by-class basis. Once a taxpayer elects to depreciate specific property using ADS, that election for that property cannot be revoked.

Example 11 illustrates the four different options available for depreciating personal property. ADS must be used to depreciate property used less than 50 percent for business. It also is used to compute a corporation's "earnings and profits."

EXAMPLE 11

In 2006, Natalie Brown places in service a desk. To recover the cost of the desk and all other 7-year property placed in service during 2006, Brown can choose from the following methods:

MACRS:
- 200% declining balance over 7 years (regular MACRS)
- Straight-line over 7 years (alternate MACRS)

ADS:
- Straight-line over 10 years
- 150% declining balance over 10 years

No matter which method Brown selects, the percentage of all personal property placed in service in the fourth quarter will determine whether the half-year or mid-quarter convention applies. Also, the method Brown selects will apply to all 7-year property placed in service in 2006. Regardless of which depreciation method Brown selects, she must continue to depreciate the desk (plus all other 7-year property placed in service in 2006) using this method in all future years.

In determining the depreciation deduction for a given tax year, it is often assumed that the taxpayer should take the maximum deduction allowed at the earliest possible time. However, this may not always be the best policy. For example, a taxpayer currently in a low tax bracket may expect to be in a higher tax bracket in future years. This taxpayer will benefit most by delaying the large depreciation deductions until the higher tax bracket years. This can be accomplished by electing alternative MACRS or ADS to depreciate property.

Section 179 Expense Election

Taxpayers that qualify can elect to take an up-front deduction in the year certain personal property is placed in service. For 2006, taxpayers can expense up to $108,000 of Section 179 property placed in service during 2006. The Code defines **Section 179 property** as *tangible personal property purchased* by the taxpayer and *used in a trade or business.* Thus, real property and property acquired by means other than a purchase are not Section 179 property. Likewise, depreciable personal property used for investment is not Section 179 property. However, used property that the taxpayer purchases for use in the taxpayer's business is eligible for Section 179 expensing.

The amount of Section 179 property that taxpayers can expense in the first year is reduced dollar for dollar when more than $430,000 of Section 179 property is placed in service during 2006. For example, taxpayers who place in service $469,000 of Section 179 property during 2006 would be allowed to expense up to $69,000 [$105,000 – ($469,000 – $430,000)] of the Section 179 property in that year. Taxpayers compute the maximum Section 179 expense they can take each year on Form 4562, Part I (lines 1 to 5).

A provision in the Gulf Opportunity Zone Act of 2005 allows businesses (including sole proprietorships) affected by Hurricanes Katrina, Rita and Wilma to elect to expense an additional $100,000 under Section 179 (up to $208,000, in 2006). In addition, the amount eligible to be expensed under Section 179 is not reduced until the taxpayer's total Section 179 property placed in service during 2006 exceeds $1,030,000 ($600,000 more than under the normal rules). Real property normally cannot be expensed under Section 179. However, this special provision allows certain types of residential realty placed in service before December 31, 2008 to be expensed in the first year under Code Section 179.

Taxpayers can elect Section 179 expense only in the year they place the property in service. Once taxpayers determine the amount of Section 179 expense they wish to elect, they allocate it among one or more of the Section 179 properties. Taxpayers must identify on the tax return the property (or properties) they elect to expense under Section 179. Taxpayers make this election on Form 4562, Part I (line 6). After selecting the property (or properties) to expense under Section 179, they can recover the rest of the unadjusted basis of the property (or properties) using regular MACRS, alternate MACRS, or ADS.

For Section 179 property placed in service between 2003 and 2007, taxpayers can make or revoke a Section 179 election on an amended return. An amended return must be filed within three years of the due date of the original tax return (including extensions). See Chapter 12 for more details on how to file an amended return.

EXAMPLE 12

On February 10, 2006, Lowe Enterprises placed in service personal property that costs $517,000, which includes $80,000 of equipment (7-year property). The half-year convention applies to personal property placed in service in 2006. Lowe elects to expense part of the equipment under Section 179. Since Lowe placed in service more than $430,000 of Section 179 property, it can elect to expense up to $21,000 under Section 179 [$108,000 – ($517,000 – $430,000)]. Lowe can then deduct regular MACRS on the remaining $59,000 ($80,000 – $21,000). In 2006, total depreciation on the equipment equals $29,431 [$21,000 Section 179 expense + $8,431 MACRS ($59,000 × 14.29%)].

Section 179 expense cannot exceed a taxpayer's taxable income from any trade or business after regular depreciation has been taken. Taxpayers can carry over to the next tax year any Section 179 expense disallowed because of the taxable income limit. However, this carryover is subject to the Section 179 limit that applies to the next year(s). For purposes of MACRS, taxpayers must reduce the basis in the property by the total amount they *elect* to expense under Section 179.

EXAMPLE 13

Assume the same facts as in Example 12, except that Lowe's taxable income from the business (after regular depreciation) is $5,000. Although Lowe can elect up to $21,000 of Section 179 expense, only $5,000 can be deducted in 2006. The $16,000 of disallowed expense can be carried over to 2007 and later years.

For purposes of computing MACRS on the equipment, Lowe reduces its basis by the amount it elects to expense under Section 179, even though part of the expense must be postponed. If Lowe does not do this, over the next eight years Lowe will deduct $21,000 under Section 179 ($5,000 in 2006 and $16,000 in a future year) and $75,000 ($80,000 – $5,000) as MACRS depreciation. The total deductions of $96,000 would exceed the $80,000 cost of the equipment.

Figure 8-5 illustrates how Lowe from Example 13 elects Section 179 for $21,000 of the equipment.

FIGURE 8-5 Filled-In Form 4562, Part I

Form **4562** | **Depreciation and Amortization** | OMB No. 1545-0172

Department of the Treasury
Internal Revenue Service

(Including Information on Listed Property)

► See separate instructions. ► Attach to your tax return.

2006 Attachment Sequence No. **67**

Name(s) shown on return	Business or activity to which this form relates	Identifying number
Lowe Enterprises		71-6928490

Part I Election To Expense Certain Property Under Section 179
Note: *If you have any listed property, complete Part V before you complete Part I.*

1	Maximum amount. See the instructions for a higher limit for certain businesses	1	$108,000
2	Total cost of section 179 property placed in service (see instructions)	2	517,000
3	Threshold cost of section 179 property before reduction in limitation	3	$430,000
4	Reduction in limitation. Subtract line 3 from line 2. If zero or less, enter -0-	4	87,000
5	Dollar limitation for tax year. Subtract line 4 from line 1. If zero or less, enter -0-. If married filing separately, see instructions	5	21,000

	(a) Description of property	(b) Cost (business use only)	(c) Elected cost
6	Equipment	80,000	21,000
7	Listed property. Enter the amount from line 29	7	

8	Total elected cost of section 179 property. Add amounts in column (c), lines 6 and 7	8	21,000
9	Tentative deduction. Enter the **smaller** of line 5 or line 8	9	21,000
10	Carryover of disallowed deduction from line 13 of your 2005 Form 4562	10	
11	Business income limitation. Enter the smaller of business income (not less than zero) or line 5 (see instructions)	11	5,000
12	Section 179 expense deduction. Add lines 9 and 10, but do not enter more than line 11	12	5,000
13	Carryover of disallowed deduction to 2007. Add lines 9 and 10, less line 12 ►	13	16,000

Note: *Do not use Part II or Part III below for listed property. Instead, use Part V.*

In determining whether the half-year or mid-quarter convention applies to personal property placed in service during the year, the 40% test is applied after Section 179 expensing.

Listed Property Limitations

Special rules apply to property *suitable for personal use.* Such property, referred to as **listed property,** commonly includes automobiles, cellular phones, computers, and printers. Listed property that the taxpayer does not use more than 50% of the time for business does not qualify for regular (accelerated) MACRS or Section 179 first-year expense. Instead, such property must be depreciated under ADS using the straight-line method. The half-year and mid-quarter provisions apply to listed property.

PROPERTY SUITABLE FOR PERSONAL USE

Property used for transportation

- Passenger automobiles and motorcycles
- Trucks, buses, boats, and airplanes

Property used for entertainment, recreation, or amusement

- Cameras and VCRs
- Communication and stereo equipment

Computers and related equipment (but not if used only at the taxpayer's regular business establishment, including a qualified home office)

Cellular telephones

For property used for transportation (like passenger automobiles), the 50% test should be based on *miles used for business* in relation to total miles used. For other types of listed property, taxpayers should use the appropriate *units of time* (hours) to allocate between business use and other use. Although any investment use of the property is not considered in meeting the more-than-50% test, taxpayers can depreciate the portion of the property's cost that involves investment use. Whichever depreciation method (regular MACRS or ADS) is chosen, that method is used to depreciate both the business and the investment use portions of the property.

Part V of Form 4562 is where taxpayers report the depreciation of listed property. In Part V, taxpayers confirm that they have written evidence to support the business or investment use of the property. They then separate the listed property used more than 50% of the time for business from property not used more than 50% of the time for business. Only property used more than 50% for business can be expensed under Section 179 and depreciated using regular (accelerated) MACRS.

EXAMPLE 14

On August 9, 2006, Tom Richards placed in service a computer that costs $4,000. This is the only property Richards placed in service in 2006, so the half-year convention applies. Richards uses the computer 60% of the time for business, 15% of the time for investment purposes, and 25% of the time for personal use. Since the business use of the computer exceeds 50%, MACRS can be taken on the 75% combined business and investment use ($4,000 × 75% = $3,000 business/investment basis). MACRS for 2006 equals $600 ($3,000 × 20%). MACRS on the business use alone is $1,440 ($1,800 × 60/75).

Since business use exceeds 50%, Richards could elect to expense $2,400 ($4,000 × 60%) under Section 179 and use MACRS to depreciate the $600 ($4,000 × 15%) investment basis.

EXAMPLE 15

Assume the same facts as in Example 14, except that Richards uses the computer 40% for business, 15% for investment purposes, and 45% for personal use. Because business use does not exceed 50%, Section 179 cannot be elected and regular (accelerated) MACRS cannot be used. Richards must use ADS and the half-year convention to depreciate the 55% combined business/investment basis.

Figure 8-6 shows where Richards from Example 15 reports the depreciation on his computer. Richards has written evidence to support his 40% business use and 15% investment use. He enters the information on line 27 because his business use alone does not exceed 50%. The $220 depreciation deduction on line 27(h) reflects the straight-line methods and half-year convention ($2,200 × ⅕ × ½).

FIGURE 8-6 Filled-In Form 4562, Part V

Form 4562 (2006) Page **2**

Part V **Listed Property** (Include automobiles, certain other vehicles, cellular telephones, certain computers, and property used for entertainment, recreation, or amusement.)

Note: *For any vehicle for which you are using the standard mileage rate or deducting lease expense, complete **only** 24a, 24b, columns (a) through (c) of Section A, all of Section B, and Section C if applicable.*

Section A—Depreciation and Other Information (Caution: *See the instructions for limits for passenger automobiles.*)

24a Do you have evidence to support the business/investment use claimed? ☒ **Yes** ☐ **No** **24b** If "Yes," is the evidence written? ☒ **Yes** ☐ **No**

(a) Type of property (list vehicles first)	(b) Date placed in service	(c) Business/ investment use percentage	(d) Cost or other basis	(e) Basis for depreciation (business/investment use only)	(f) Recovery period	(g) Method/ Convention	(h) Depreciation deduction	(i) Elected section 179 cost
25 Special allowance for qualified New York Liberty or Gulf Opportunity Zone property placed in service during the tax year and used more than 50% in a qualified business use (see instructions) **25**								
26 Property used more than 50% in a qualified business use:								
		%						
		%						
		%						
27 Property used 50% or less in a qualified business use:								
Computer	8-9-06	55 %	4,000	2,200	5 yr	S/L –	220	
		%				S/L –		
		%				S/L –		
28 Add amounts in column (h), lines 25 through 27. Enter here and on line 21, page 1. . **28**							220	
29 Add amounts in column (i), line 26. Enter here and on line 7, page 1. . . . . **29**								

Sole proprietors deduct depreciation expense on their business property on Schedule C, which reduces their net profits from the business. Depreciation expense taken on rental property is reported on Schedule E and reduces the taxpayer's rental net income. Depreciation expense on other types of investment property is taken as a deduction on Schedule A as a miscellaneous itemized deduction (subject to the 2% AGI rule)

If the business usage of listed property drops below 50% in a future year and the taxpayer has used Section 179, bonus depreciation or regular (accelerated) MACRS to depreciate the property, the taxpayer must permanently switch to the straight-line method (ADS). Also, the taxpayer must recompute what depreciation would have been in all prior years for that property using only ADS to depreciate the listed property. The difference between accumulated depreciation taken on the property (including any bonus depreciation and Section 179 expense) and what accumulated depreciation would have been using ADS must be included in the taxpayer's income in the year business usage drops below 50%. "Recapture" is the term used to describe the inclusion of the excess amount in gross income.

EXAMPLE 16

Fred Newman paid $3,000 for a computer on April 3, 2005. He uses the computer 60% for business and 40% for personal use during both 2005 and 2006. Newman used regular (accelerated) MACRS and the half-year convention to depreciate the computer. On his 2005 and 2006 tax returns, Newman deducted $360 ($3,000 × 60% × 20%) and $576 ($3,000 × 60% × 32%), respectively. In 2007, Newman's business usage drops to 45%. Beginning in 2007, Newman must permanently switch to the straight-line method. His 2007 depreciation expense deduction is $270 ($3,000 × 45% × ⅕). In addition, Newman must compute what his depreciation expense would have been in 2005 and 2006 using ADS. His depreciation would have been $180 ($3,000 × 60% × ⅕ × ½) in 2005 and $360 ($3,000 × 60% × ⅕) in 2006. Newman must include in 2007 income the $396 difference between the amounts deducted in 2005 and 2006 and the amounts that would have been deducted had he used ADS from the beginning.

	MACRS deduction	ADS deduction	Recapture Amount
2005	$360	$180	$180
2006	576	360	216
	$936	$540	$396

Taxpayers must be able to substantiate the amount, time, place, and business purpose of transportation expenses. For automobiles and other vehicles, they must establish both the business/ investment miles and total miles the vehicle was driven during the year. They do this by keeping adequate records or by producing evidence that supports statements they prepare. Mileage records created at or around the time the vehicle was used for business/investment have a higher degree of credibility than records prepared at a later date. The Tax Court has disallowed unsubstantiated transportation expenses primarily because the mileage summary did not contain odometer readings entered at the time the vehicle was used. Instead, the business miles had been computed from figures in a computer atlas database.

Luxury Automobile Limits

The tax laws limit the depreciation of automobiles used for business, even those used 100% for business. These limits apply to all types of depreciation, including Section 179 expenses and bonus depreciation. Figure 8-7 shows the depreciation limits for the years 2002 to 2006. Due to the bonus depreciation allowed from September 11, 2001 until December 31, 2004, the first year limits for these years are much higher than the first year limits for 2005 and 2006.

FIGURE 8-7 Luxury Automobile Depreciation Limits for the Years 2002–2006

	Automobiles Placed in Service During				
Year	**2002**	**2003**	**2004**	**2005**	**2006**
1*	$7,660	$7,660/$10,710	$10,610	$2,960	$2,960
2	4,900	4,900	4,800	4,700	4,800
3	2,950	2,950	2,850	2,850	2,850
4 and on	1,775	1,775	1,675	1,675	1,775

*The $10,710/$10,610 limit applied to new automobiles purchased after May 5, 2003, when the 50% bonus was used. The $7,660 limit applied to new automobiles after September 10, 2001, when the 30% bonus was used. For 2002 and 2003, the limit was $3,060 for automobiles placed in service before September 11, 2001; for any used automobile; and for any automobile used 50% or less for business. For 2004, the limit for used automobiles and automobiles used 50% or less for business was $2,960.

Figure 8-8 shows that if there were no limits, simply by using regular MACRS, a taxpayer could deduct the entire cost of a $25,000 automobile in the first six years of use (assuming 100% business use). However, the luxury automobile limits allow only $15,935 in the first six years. In Year 7, taxpayers can continue to deduct $1,775 each year a deduction of the remaining cost is recovered.

FIGURE 8-8 2006 Depreciation Limitations for a $25,000 Luxury Automobile

Year	Depreciation Using Potential MACRS Deduction		Luxury Automobile Limitation
2006	$ 5,000	($25,000 × 20%)	$ 2,960
2007	8,000	($25,000 × 32%)	4,800
2008	4,800	($25,000 × 19.2%)	2,850
2009	2,880	($25,000 × 11.52%)	1,775
2010	2,880	($25,000 × 11.52%)	1,775
2011	1,440	($25,000 × 5.76%)	1,775
	$25,000		$15,935
2012			1,775
2013			1,775
2014			1,775
2015			1,775
2016			1,775
2017			190
			$25,000

The limits in Figure 8-7 apply only to passenger automobiles. A passenger automobile is any four-wheeled vehicle made primarily for use on public streets, roads, and highways and whose unloaded gross vehicle weight is 6,000 pounds or less. Slightly higher limits apply to light trucks and vans (including minivans and sports utility vehicles (SUVs)). Ambulances, hearses, taxis, and limousines are not subject to the luxury automobile rules. Neither are trucks and vans placed in service after July 6, 2003, that have been specially modified so that they are not likely to be used for personal use.

When the luxury automobile rules were first enacted, the rules applied to "passenger automobiles" that did not weigh over 6,000 pounds. Since then, many sport-utility vehicles (SUVs) now weigh over 6,000 pounds and taxpayers could avoid the luxury automobile limits by purchasing these heavier SUVs and using them in their businesses. This allowed them to expense the SUV's cost (up to $108,000 in 2006) under Section 179 (assuming 100% business use).

Congress addressed this issue by enacting tax rules that now limit the amount of Section 179 expense allowed on SUVs weighing between 6,000 and 14,000 pounds to a maximum of $25,000 (based on 100% business use). Amounts not expensed under Section 179 are depreciated using the MACRS rules discussed in this chapter. The new limits apply to SUVs placed in service after October 22, 2004. Under this tax rule, only SUVs weighing more than 14,000 pounds are exempt from the $25,000 Section 179 limit. SUVs placed in service on or before this date are subject to the same luxury automobile rules as trucks and vans (thus SUVs weighing over 6,000 pounds would be exempt from these rules).

The amounts in Figure 8-7 show the limits imposed for automobiles used 100% of the time for business. Taxpayers must reduce these amounts for automobiles used less than 100% for business. For luxury automobiles used partially for business, taxpayers must combine the rules for listed property with those for luxury automobiles.

EXAMPLE 17

On August 2, 2004, Paula Hendricks placed in service a new car that cost $40,000. The half-year convention applied to personal property Hendricks placed in service in 2004. Hendricks uses the car 70% of the time for business. Since Hendricks's business use exceeds 50%, both bonus depreciation and regular MACRS were taken on the car. She uses the 2004 column from Figure 8-7 to compute her luxury automobile limits. In 2004, Hendricks deducted $7,427 [the *lesser of* (i) $16,800 (($40,000 × 70% business use × 50% bonus) + ($20,000 × 70% × 20% MACRS)) or (ii) $7,427 ($10,610 × 70%)]. In 2006 (year 3), she deducts $1,995 [the *lesser of* (i) ($20,000 × 70% × 19.2% MACRS) or (ii) ($2,850 × 70%)].

EXAMPLE 18

On July 15, 2005, Anne Jones placed in service a car that cost $30,000. The half-year convention applies to 5-year property Jones placed in service in 2005. Jones uses the car 80% of the time for business. Jones uses the 2005 column from Figure 8-7 to compute her first-year luxury automobile limit. Jones is limited to $2,368 ($2,960 × 80%) of depreciation in 2005, since it is less than $4,800 ($30,000 × 80% × 20% MACRS).

EXAMPLE 19

On November 5, 2006, Frank Yaeger places in service a car costing $45,000. Yaeger uses the car 100% for business and chooses to use ADS to depreciate the car. The half-year convention applies to all personal property placed in service during 2006. Yaeger computes his first year ADS depreciation on the car to be $4,500 ($45,000 x 1/5 x ½). However, this amount exceeds the $2,960 first year limit for automobiles placed in service during 2006 (Figure 8-7). Accordingly, his deduction in 2006 is limited to $2,960. In 2007, ADS depreciation equals $9,000 ($45,000 x 1/5). Again, this amount exceeds the $4,800 year 2 limit for automobiles placed in service during 2006. Thus, Yaeger's deduction in 2007 depreciation deduction will be limited to $4,800.

Leased Automobiles

Taxpayers leasing automobiles can either use the standard mileage rate ($.445 in 2006) or deduct the business portion of their lease payments. To prevent taxpayers from getting around the luxury automobile limits by leasing (rather than buying) expensive cars, the government reduces the amount taxpayers can deduct for their lease payments. They do this by reducing the taxpayer's car expense deduction by an "inclusion amount." The inclusion amount is based on the fair market value (FMV) of the car. Taxpayers multiply the inclusion amount from the IRS table by the business use percentage. In the first and last years of the lease, the amount is further reduced to reflect the portion of the year the car was leased.

The IRS publishes inclusion amounts for leased cars in Publication 463. Figure 8-9 shows the portion of the table for cars with a FMV between $35,000 and $40,000 that were first leased during 2006. Inclusion amounts for trucks, vans, and electric cars are slightly lower. These amounts, along with inclusion amounts for car values not listed in Figure 8-9, can be found in IRS Publication 463, Appendix A.

FIGURE 8-9 Inclusion Amounts for Cars First Leased in 2006

Fair Market Value		Tax Year of Lease				
Over	Not Over	1st	2nd	3rd	4th	5th and later
$35,000	$36,000	$ 135	$295	$439	$523	$604
36,000	37,000	142	309	460	549	633
37,000	38,000	148	324	481	575	662
38,000	39,000	155	338	502	601	691
39,000	40,000	161	353	523	626	721

EXAMPLE 20

On September 1, 2006, Janet Lane began leasing a car for $400 a month. Lane leased the car for 122 days during 2006 (September 1 to December 31). The FMV of the car was $37,200 and Lane's business usage is 70%. In 2006, Lane's lease deduction initially equals 70% of her lease payments, or $1,120 ($400 × 4 × 70%). From Figure 8-9, the inclusion amount for 2006 (1st year of the lease) is $148. Lane reduces her 2006 lease deduction by $35 ($148 × 70% × 122/365) and deducts $1,085 ($1,120 – $35) on Schedule C (line 20a). In 2007, Lane's lease deduction is $3,133 [$3,360 for her lease payments ($400 × 12 × 70%) – $227 ($324 inclusion amount × 70%)].

EXAMPLE 21

On March 2, 2006, Michelle Wilson entered into a 36-month lease. The FMV of the car she leased is $39,430. Wilson drives the car 75% for business each year. To compute her inclusion amount in 2006, Wilson multiplies the $161 first year inclusion amount from Figure 8-9 by 75% and then by 305/365 (the portion of 2006 that she leased the car). For 2007 and 2008, she multiplies the $353 and $523 inclusion amounts by 75% to compute the amount she includes in gross income in those years. In 2009 (the last year of the lease), Wilson multiplies the $626 fourth year inclusion amount by both 75% and 60/365 (the portion of the fourth year that she leased the car during 2009).

DEPRECIATION OF REAL PROPERTY

MACRS

Under MACRS, taxpayers depreciate real property using the straight-line method. The recovery period for real property under MACRS depends on whether the property is residential or nonresidential real property. Taxpayers recover the cost of residential rental property over 27.5 years. Real property is residential realty if the building is used as a place where people live. Examples of residential realty include apartment buildings and rental vacation homes. The recovery period for nonresidential (commercial and industrial) real estate, such as office buildings, manufacturing plants, and warehouses, is 31.5 years if placed in service before May 13, 1993. For nonresidential property placed in service after May 12, 1993, the recovery period is 39 years. Although land is real property, it is not depreciated.

The **mid-month convention** applies to real property depreciated under MACRS. The mid-month convention assumes taxpayers place real property in service in the middle of the month they actually place it in service. The mid-month convention also assumes that taxpayers dispose of real property in the middle of a month.

EXAMPLE 22

On March 1, 1993, Vicky Mathews placed in service residential real property that cost $100,000. Mathews sells the property on December 5, 2006. Mathews's annual cost recovery for the property follows.

Year	MACRS	
1993	$ 2,879	($100,000 × 1/27.5 × 9.5/12)
1994–2005	43,636	($100,000 × 1/27.5 × 12 years)
2006	3,485	($100,000 × 1/27.5 × 11.5/12)
	$50,000	

EXAMPLE 23

Assume the same facts as in Example 22, except that on March 1, 1993, Mathews placed in service nonresidential real property.

Year	MACRS	
1993	$ 2,513	($100,000 × 1/31.5 × 9.5/12)
1994–2005	38,095	($100,000 × 1/31.5 × 12 years)
2006	3,042	($100,000 × 1/31.5 × 11.5/12)
	$43,650	

EXAMPLE 24

Assume the same facts as in Example 22, except that Mathews placed the nonresidential real property in service on July 1, 1993.

Year	MACRS	
1993	$ 1,175	($100,000 × 1/39 × 5.5/12)
1994–2005	30,769	($100,000 × 1/39 × 12 years)
2006	2,457	($100,000 × 1/39 × 11.5/12)
	$34,401	

EXAMPLE 25

Chuck Waters operates a business out of his home. During 2006 Waters begins using one room in his home exclusive as an office where he regularly meets with clients. Although the rest of the home is where Waters lives, the room where Waters conducts his business is used solely for work. Thus, the home office is nonresidential realty. Under MACRS, the home office is depreciated over 39 years using the straight-line method.

Optional Recovery Periods

Instead of using MACRS recovery periods of 27.5 (for residential realty) and 31.5 or 39 years (for nonresidential realty), taxpayers can elect under the Alternative Depreciation System (ADS) to depreciate both residential and nonresidential real realty over 40 years. Those who elect ADS continue to use the straight-line method and the mid-month convention. Taxpayers can elect to use the 40-year recovery period on a **property-by-property** basis. This allows them to depreciate one piece of real property over 40 years and another over the regular MACRS recovery period.

EXAMPLE 26

During the year, a taxpayer places in service an office building and a warehouse. The taxpayer can elect to use MACRS to depreciate one of the buildings and ADS to depreciate the other. Regardless of which depreciate method is used to depreciate the buildings, the mid-month convention applies to both the first and last years.

Depreciation of a Business in the Home

Persons who use part of their home for business purposes can depreciate the business portion of the home. Chapter 7 discussed the rules regarding deductions for the business use of the home. To compute the depreciation deduction, taxpayers first compute the percentage of the total square footage of the home used for business. If the rooms are all of approximately equal size, they can divide the number of rooms used for business by the total number of rooms in the home. The business-use percentage of the home is used to compute depreciation on the home.

The depreciable basis for the home is the *lesser of* (i) the home's adjusted basis or (ii) its fair market value (FMV) at the time the home office was placed in service. In determining the depreciable basis, the cost of the land must be removed from the adjusted basis. Likewise, the value of the land cannot be included when computing the FMV of the residence. Taxpayers report the allowable depreciation deduction for a business in the home for a sole proprietor on Form 8829, Expenses for Business Use of Your Home, Part III. Figure 8-10 shows the calculation of the depreciation deduction.

The value of the land often is shown separately from the value of the building on a professional real estate appraisal. The value of the land is often reported apart from the building on the taxpayer's real estate tax bill.

Information for Figure 8-10: Filled-In Form 8829

In 1994 Darryl Collins bought a home for $320,000 (includes $80,000 for the land). On March 1, 1998, when the FMV of the home was $340,000 (includes $80,000 for the land), Collins began using one room exclusively as a business office. The square footage of the office is 200; the total square footage of the home is 4,000. Since Collins uses the business portion of the home as an office, it meets the definition of nonresidential real property. Thus, a depreciation percentage of 2.564% (straight-line over 39 years applies to nonresidential realty placed in service after May 12, 1993).

FIGURE 8-10 Filled-In Form 8829

Form **8829**

Department of the Treasury
Internal Revenue Service (99)

Expenses for Business Use of Your Home

▶ **File only with Schedule C (Form 1040). Use a separate Form 8829 for each home you used for business during the year.**

▶ **See separate instructions.**

OMB No. 1545-0074

2006

Attachment Sequence No. **66**

Name(s) of proprietor(s): Darryl Collins

Your social security number: 531 64 9923

Part I Part of Your Home Used for Business

1	Area used regularly and exclusively for business, regularly for daycare, or for storage of inventory or product samples (see instructions)	1	200
2	Total area of home	2	4,000
3	Divide line 1 by line 2. Enter the result as a percentage	3	5 %
	• **For daycare facilities not used exclusively for business, also complete lines 4–6.**		
	• **All others, skip lines 4–6 and enter the amount from line 3 on line 7.**		
4	Multiply days used for daycare during year by hours used per day	4	hr.
5	Total hours available for use during the year (365 days × 24 hours) (see instructions)	5	8,760 hr.
6	Divide line 4 by line 5. Enter the result as a decimal amount	6	.
7	Business percentage. For daycare facilities not used exclusively for business, multiply line 6 by line 3 (enter the result as a percentage). All others, enter the amount from line 3 ▶	7	5 %

Part II Figure Your Allowable Deduction

			(a) Direct expenses	(b) Indirect expenses		
8	Enter the amount from Schedule C, line 29, **plus** any net gain or (loss) derived from the business use of your home and shown on Schedule D or Form 4797. If more than one place of business, see instructions				8	
	See instructions for columns (a) and (b) before completing lines 9–20.					
9	Casualty losses (see instructions)	9				
10	Deductible mortgage interest (see instructions)	10				
11	Real estate taxes (see instructions)	11				
12	Add lines 9, 10, and 11	12				
13	Multiply line 12, column (b) by line 7	13				
14	Add line 12, column (a) and line 13				14	
15	Subtract line 14 from line 8. If zero or less, enter -0-				15	
16	Excess mortgage interest (see instructions)	16				
17	Insurance	17				
18	Repairs and maintenance	18				
19	Utilities	19				
20	Other expenses (see instructions)	20				
21	Add lines 16 through 20	21				
22	Multiply line 21, column (b) by line 7	22				
23	Carryover of operating expenses from 2005 Form 8829, line 41	23				
24	Add line 21 in column (a), line 22, and line 23				24	
25	Allowable operating expenses. Enter the **smaller** of line 15 or line 24				25	
26	Limit on excess casualty losses and depreciation. Subtract line 25 from line 15				26	
27	Excess casualty losses (see instructions)	27				
28	Depreciation of your home from Part III below	28		308 00		
29	Carryover of excess casualty losses and depreciation from 2005 Form 8829, line 42	29				
30	Add lines 27 through 29				30	
31	Allowable excess casualty losses and depreciation. Enter the **smaller** of line 26 or line 30				31	
32	Add lines 14, 25, and 31				32	
33	Casualty loss portion, if any, from lines 14 and 31. Carry amount to **Form 4684,** Section B				33	
34	Allowable expenses for business use of your home. Subtract line 33 from line 32. Enter here and on Schedule C, line 30. If your home was used for more than one business, see instructions ▶				34	

Part III Depreciation of Your Home

35	Enter the **smaller** of your home's adjusted basis or its fair market value (see instructions)	35	320,000 00
36	Value of land included on line 35	36	80,000 00
37	Basis of building. Subtract line 36 from line 35	37	240,000 00
38	Business basis of building. Multiply line 37 by line 7	38	12,000 00
39	Depreciation percentage (see instructions)	39	2.564 %
40	Depreciation allowable (see instructions). Multiply line 38 by line 39. Enter here and on line 28 above	40	308 00

Part IV Carryover of Unallowed Expenses to 2007

41	Operating expenses. Subtract line 25 from line 24. If less than zero, enter -0-	41	
42	Excess casualty losses and depreciation. Subtract line 31 from line 30. If less than zero, enter -0-	42	

For Paperwork Reduction Act Notice, see page 4 of separate instructions. Cat. No. 13232M Form **8829** (2006)

Printed on recycled paper

Chapter 7 discussed the order in which taxpayers deduct home office expenses:

1. All non–home office expenses from Schedule C. This amount includes depreciation on personal and real property (other than the home office).
2. The portion of mortgage interest, real estate taxes, and casualty losses taken on Form 8829 that relates to the home office.
3. The portion of operating expenses that relates to the business use of the home. These amounts include repairs, maintenance, utilities, and insurance.
4. The business portion of depreciation on the home.

Expenses listed in items 3 and 4 cannot create or increase a business loss. Any expenses disallowed because they create or increase a business loss do not reduce business income on Schedule C. The disallowed expenses may be carried forward and included on Form 8829 in the following year. Form 8829, Part IV, computes the expenses carried over to 2007. Form 8829 (line 23) reports the disallowed operating expenses (insurance, utilities, etc.) from 2005. Form 8829 (line 29) reports the disallowed depreciation from 2005.

EXAMPLE 27

In 2006 John MacDonald reports $1,600 as tentative profit on Schedule C. He uses 10% of his home exclusively as an office. Expenses for the 10% business portion of the home include mortgage interest and real estate taxes of $420, operating expenses (insurance, maintenance, and utilities) of $1,000, and depreciation of $650. MacDonald's deduction on Form 8829 for the business use of his home follows:

Tentative profit (line 8)	$1,600
Less interest and taxes (line 14)	(420)
Net income derived from the business	$1,180
Less operating expenses (line 25)	(1,000)
Limit on depreciation (line 26)	$ 180
Depreciation	(650)
Depreciation expense not deductible in 2006 (show on line 42 and carry forward to 2007)	($ 470)

All the business expenses except $470 of the depreciation expense offset 2006 income. Since MacDonald cannot deduct $470 of depreciation expense in 2006, he reduces the basis of the home office by the $180 deducted in 2006. The basis in the home will be reduced for the rest of the $470 of depreciation expense in the year MacDonald deducts it.

Information for Figure 8-12: Filled-In Form 4562

Figure 7-3 in Chapter 7, the income statement from Wilson's Hardware Store gave an amount of $1,133 for depreciation expense. Figure 8-11 shows how to compute Wilson's depreciation expense. The half-year convention applies to the 5-year property placed in service in 2005. Wilson has written evidence to support the business use of the computer.

FIGURE 8-11 Calculation of Depreciation for Wilson's Hardware Store

Property	Date Acquired	Basis for Depreciation	Recovery Period	% or Method	Depreciation in 2006
Computer (80% business)	8-01-05	$ 480[1]	5	200% DB	$ 154[2]
Paint mixer	3-01-06	1,546	7	200% DB	221[3]
Tool cabinet	3-14-06	1,400	7	200% DB	200[4]
Small tools	7-16-06	441	7	200% DB	63[5]
Wet/dry vac	11-03-06	357	7	200% DB	51[6]
Table saw	1-15-00	516	12*	ADS/SL	43
Jointer/planer	6-29-00	420	12*	ADS/SL	35
Storage shed	2-06-99	14,274	39	SL	366
Total cost recovery					$1,133

*Since no designated class life applies to the equipment, the recovery period is 12 years.
[1] $600 cost × 80% = $480
[2] $480 × 32%
[3] $1,546 × 14.29%
[4] $1,400 × 14.29%
[5] $441 × 14.29%
[6] $357 × 14.29%

Because computers are listed property, the depreciation deduction is first recorded in Part V, and then is entered on Part IV (line 21). See Figure 8-12.

Other Information

26(c): Business/investment use percentage, **80%**
26(d): Cost or other basis, **$600**
26(e): Basis for depreciation, **$480** ($600 × 80%)
26(h): Depreciation deduction, **$154** ($480 × 32%)
16: Other depreciation, **$78** (ADS property, $516/12 + $420/12)
17: MACRS on pre-2006 assets, **$366** (storage shed, $14,274/39)
19c(c): Basis for depreciation, **$3,744** ($1,546 + $1,400 + $441 + $357)
19c(e): Convention, **HY** (half-year, since $357 ÷ $3,744 = 9.5%, which is ≤ 40%)
19c(g): Depreciation deduction, **$535** ($3,744 × 14.29%)

FIGURE 8-12 Filled-In Form 4562, Page 1

Form **4562** — Department of the Treasury, Internal Revenue Service

Depreciation and Amortization
(Including Information on Listed Property)

▶ See separate instructions. ▶ Attach to your tax return.

OMB No. 1545-0172 — **2006** — Attachment Sequence No. **67**

Name(s) shown on return	Business or activity to which this form relates	Identifying number
Harold R. Wilson	Wilson's Hardware Store	272-11-8855

Part I — Election To Expense Certain Property Under Section 179
Note: *If you have any listed property, complete Part V before you complete Part I.*

1	Maximum amount. See the instructions for a higher limit for certain businesses	1	$108,000
2	Total cost of section 179 property placed in service (see instructions)	2	
3	Threshold cost of section 179 property before reduction in limitation	3	$430,000
4	Reduction in limitation. Subtract line 3 from line 2. If zero or less, enter -0-	4	
5	Dollar limitation for tax year. Subtract line 4 from line 1. If zero or less, enter -0-. If married filing separately, see instructions	5	

	(a) Description of property	(b) Cost (business use only)	(c) Elected cost
6			
7	Listed property. Enter the amount from line 29	7	

8	Total elected cost of section 179 property. Add amounts in column (c), lines 6 and 7	8	
9	Tentative deduction. Enter the **smaller** of line 5 or line 8	9	
10	Carryover of disallowed deduction from line 13 of your 2005 Form 4562	10	
11	Business income limitation. Enter the smaller of business income (not less than zero) or line 5 (see instructions)	11	
12	Section 179 expense deduction. Add lines 9 and 10, but do not enter more than line 11	12	
13	Carryover of disallowed deduction to 2007. Add lines 9 and 10, less line 12 ▶	13	

Note: *Do not use Part II or Part III below for listed property. Instead, use Part V.*

Part II — Special Depreciation Allowance and Other Depreciation (Do not include listed property.) (See instructions.)

14	Special allowance for qualified New York Liberty or Gulf Opportunity Zone property (other than listed property) placed in service during the tax year (see instructions)	14	
15	Property subject to section 168(f)(1) election	15	
16	Other depreciation (including ACRS)	16	78

Part III — MACRS Depreciation (Do not include listed property.) (See instructions.)

Section A

17	MACRS deductions for assets placed in service in tax years beginning before 2006	17	366
18	If you are electing to group any assets placed in service during the tax year into one or more general asset accounts, check here ▶ ☐		

Section B—Assets Placed in Service During 2006 Tax Year Using the General Depreciation System

(a) Classification of property	(b) Month and year placed in service	(c) Basis for depreciation (business/investment use only—see instructions)	(d) Recovery period	(e) Convention	(f) Method	(g) Depreciation deduction
19a 3-year property						
b 5-year property						
c 7-year property		3,744	7 yr.	HY	DDB	535
d 10-year property						
e 15-year property						
f 20-year property						
g 25-year property			25 yrs.		S/L	
h Residential rental property			27.5 yrs.	MM	S/L	
			27.5 yrs.	MM	S/L	
i Nonresidential real property			39 yrs.	MM	S/L	
				MM	S/L	

Section C—Assets Placed in Service During 2006 Tax Year Using the Alternative Depreciation System

(a) Classification of property	(b) Month and year placed in service	(c) Basis for depreciation	(d) Recovery period	(e) Convention	(f) Method	(g) Depreciation deduction
20a Class life					S/L	
b 12-year			12 yrs.		S/L	
c 40-year			40 yrs.	MM	S/L	

Part IV — Summary (see instructions)

21	Listed property. Enter amount from line 28	21	154
22	**Total.** Add amounts from line 12, lines 14 through 17, lines 19 and 20 in column (g), and line 21. Enter here and on the appropriate lines of your return. Partnerships and S corporations—see instr.	22	1,133
23	For assets shown above and placed in service during the current year, enter the portion of the basis attributable to section 263A costs	23	

For Paperwork Reduction Act Notice, see separate instructions. Cat. No. 12906N Form **4562** (2006)

FIGURE 8-12 Filled-In Form 4562, Page 2

Form 4562 (2006) Page **2**

Part V **Listed Property** (Include automobiles, certain other vehicles, cellular telephones, certain computers, and property used for entertainment, recreation, or amusement.)

Note: *For any vehicle for which you are using the standard mileage rate or deducting lease expense, complete **only** 24a, 24b, columns (a) through (c) of Section A, all of Section B, and Section C if applicable.*

Section A—Depreciation and Other Information (Caution: *See the instructions for limits for passenger automobiles.***)**

24a Do you have evidence to support the business/investment use claimed? ☒ **Yes** ☐ **No** **24b** If "Yes," is the evidence written? ☒ **Yes** ☐ **No**

(a) Type of property (list vehicles first)	(b) Date placed in service	(c) Business/ investment use percentage	(d) Cost or other basis	(e) Basis for depreciation (business/investment use only)	(f) Recovery period	(g) Method/ Convention	(h) Depreciation deduction	(i) Elected section 179 cost
25 Special allowance for qualified New York Liberty or Gulf Opportunity Zone property placed in service during the tax year and used more than 50% in a qualified business use (see instructions) **25**								
26 Property used more than 50% in a qualified business use:								
Computer	8-01-05	80 %	600	480	5yrs	DDB/HY	154	
		%						
		%						
27 Property used 50% or less in a qualified business use:								
		%				S/L –		
		%				S/L –		
		%				S/L –		
28 Add amounts in column (h), lines 25 through 27. Enter here and on line 21, page 1 . . **28**							154	
29 Add amounts in column (i), line 26. Enter here and on line 7, page 1 . . . . **29**								

Section B—Information on Use of Vehicles

Complete this section for vehicles used by a sole proprietor, partner, or other "more than 5% owner," or related person.
If you provided vehicles to your employees, first answer the questions in Section C to see if you meet an exception to completing this section for those vehicles.

	(a) Vehicle 1		(b) Vehicle 2		(c) Vehicle 3		(d) Vehicle 4		(e) Vehicle 5		(f) Vehicle 6	
30 Total business/investment miles driven during the year (**do not** include commuting miles)												
31 Total commuting miles driven during the year												
32 Total other personal (noncommuting) miles driven												
33 Total miles driven during the year. Add lines 30 through 32												
	Yes	**No**	**Yes**	**No**	**Yes**	**No**	**Yes**	**No**	**Yes**	**No**	**Yes**	**No**
34 Was the vehicle available for personal use during off-duty hours?												
35 Was the vehicle used primarily by a more than 5% owner or related person?												
36 Is another vehicle available for personal use?												

Section C—Questions for Employers Who Provide Vehicles for Use by Their Employees

Answer these questions to determine if you meet an exception to completing Section B for vehicles used by employees who **are not** more than 5% owners or related persons (see instructions).

	Yes	No
37 Do you maintain a written policy statement that prohibits all personal use of vehicles, including commuting, by your employees?		
38 Do you maintain a written policy statement that prohibits personal use of vehicles, except commuting, by your employees? See the instructions for vehicles used by corporate officers, directors, or 1% or more owners		
39 Do you treat all use of vehicles by employees as personal use?		
40 Do you provide more than five vehicles to your employees, obtain information from your employees about the use of the vehicles, and retain the information received?		
41 Do you meet the requirements concerning qualified automobile demonstration use? (See instructions.)		

Note: *If your answer to 37, 38, 39, 40, or 41 is "Yes," do not complete Section B for the covered vehicles.*

Part VI **Amortization**

(a) Description of costs	(b) Date amortization begins	(c) Amortizable amount	(d) Code section	(e) Amortization period or percentage	(f) Amortization for this year
42 Amortization of costs that begins during your 2006 tax year (see instructions):					
43 Amortization of costs that began before your 2006 tax year				**43**	
44 **Total.** Add amounts in column (f). See the instructions for where to report				**44**	

Printed on recycled paper

Form **4562** (2006)

AMORTIZATION OF INTANGIBLE PROPERTY

Depreciation applies to the cost recovery of tangible personal and real property. Amortization applies to the cost recovery of intangible personal property. Amortization recovers certain costs through annual deductions over a fixed period of time (similar to the straight-line method). Section 197 intangible personal property acquired after August 10, 1993 in the purchase of a business must be amortized over 15 years using the straight-line method, starting with the month of acquisition. Certain intangibles acquired separately, like patents and copyrights, are amortized the *lesser of* (i) 15 years or (ii) their remaining useful lives. Computer software not acquired in the purchase of a business is amortized over three years beginning in the month the software is placed in service. Leasehold improvements acquired between September 11, 2001, and December 31, 2006, are amortized over five years. Taxpayers report the amortization of intangible property on Part VI of Form 4562, Depreciation and Amortization.

ITEMS INCLUDED AS SECTION 197 INTANGIBLE PERSONAL PROPERTY

- Business books and records, operating systems, or any other information base
- Covenant not to compete entered into in connection with the acquisition of a business
- Customer-based intangibles, including customer lists
- Franchise (other than a sports franchise), trademark, or trade name
- Goodwill
- Patent, copyright, formula, process design, or similar item
- Supplier-based intangibles

The amortization of intangibles applies only to purchased intangibles. It does not apply to self-created intangibles, like self-created goodwill, or self-created copyrights. Although self-created goodwill provides value to the business, there is no cost basis to amortize.

EXAMPLE 28

Kantarian Corporation pays $75,000 to a departing executive in exchange for his promise not to compete with the corporation for a period of three years. The covenant not to compete is not a Section 197 intangible because it was not entered into in connection with the acquisition of a trade or business. Thus, Kantarian will write-off (expense) the $75,000 over the next three years.

EXAMPLE 29

On June 1, 2006, Blake Industries acquires all of the assets of Fontaine, Inc. Of the $10 million purchase price, $2 million is allocated to goodwill. Since goodwill is a Section 197 intangible, the $2 million cost basis for the goodwill must be amortized using the straight-line method over 15 years beginning on June 1, 2006. If Blake uses a calendar year-end, it can deduct $77,778 ($2,000,000/180 months x 7 months) on its 2006 tax return. From 2007-2020 it will deduct $133,333 ($2,000,000/180 x 12 months). In 2021, Blake will deduct the last of the goodwill ($2,000,000/180 months x 5 months = $55,556).

EXAMPLE 30

On February 1, 2006, Amicable Company purchases the leasehold interest in a two-story building from another corporation. Amicable pays $60,000 for the company's 10-year lease, on which 6 years (72 months) remain. Amicable deducts $9,167 ($60,000/72 × 11 months) in 2006. From 2007-2011, it will deduct $10,000 ($60,000/72 × 12). It will deduct the final $833 ($60,000/72 × 1 month) in 2012.

Name ______________________

Section ______________ Date ____________

QUESTIONS AND PROBLEMS

1. **MACRS Recovery Periods.** For each of the following types of properties, state the IRS-specified useful life, depreciation method, and averaging convention(s) that are used to depreciate the property under MACRS.

	Useful Life in Years	*Depreciation Method*	*Averaging Convention*
Automobiles	______	______	______
Light trucks	______	______	______
Computers	______	______	______
Furniture and fixtures	______	______	______
Machinery and equipment	______	______	______
Commercial buildings	______	______	______
Residential buildings	______	______	______

2. **Mid-Quarter vs. Half-Year Convention.** Quentin Miller, a calendar-year taxpayer, acquired the following four new machines in 2006 on the dates indicated.

February 1	$25,000
April 1	35,000
October 1	30,000
December 1	40,000

a. Compute Miller's total depreciation deduction for 2006 that would be reported on Schedule C, using MACRS with the appropriate averaging convention.

b. Compute the total depreciation for 2006 had the $30,000 machine been acquired on September 30. Comment on the significance of the difference between this amount and the answer to Part a.

3. **Mid-Quarter vs. Half-Year Convention.** Florence Cargill placed in service the following properties during 2006.

Type of Property	*Cost*	*Date Placed in Service*
Machine	$ 65,000	March 3, 2006
Equipment	55,000	June 8, 2006
Office building	200,000	October 4, 2006
Furniture	24,000	December 15, 2006

a. Which averaging convention applies to the property placed in service during 2006?

b. Compute MACRS depreciation on each of the properties for 2006 and 2007, assuming that Cargill does not elect Section 179 expensing.

4. **MACRS, Year of Sale.** Bradford Company sold the following properties in 2006. Compute the allowable depreciation deduction for 2006 for each property.

Property	*Date Acquired*	*MACRS Basis*	*Depreciation Method*	*Averaging Convention*	*Date of Sale*
Computer	7-1-03	$ 4,200*	DDB	HY	3-5-06
Automobile	4-1-04	12,000*	DDB	HY	9-1-06
Furniture	7-10-01	24,000	DDB	MQ	7-1-06

*After subtracting bonus depreciation from the original cost

5. **ADS and MACRS.** Peter Baker uses the following properties in his business.

Equipment:	Acquired in April, 2001 at a cost of $72,000
Furniture:	Acquired in March, 2003 at a cost of $60,000
Computer:	Acquired in July, 2004 at a cost of $10,000

   a. Compute the 2006 depreciation deduction. In 2001 Baker elected the ADS straight-line method with a ten-year life for the equipment. He used regular (accelerated) MACRS for the furniture and the computer. He did not elect Section 179 for any of the properties. In 2003, he took the 30% bonus depreciation on the furniture, thereby reducing its MACRS basis to $42,000. In 2004, the computer qualified for the 50% bonus depreciation, thereby reducing its MACRS basis to $5,000. The half-year convention applies to all three properties.

   b. Same as in Part a., except that the mid-quarter convention applied to all personal property placed in service in 2003.

   c. Same as in Part a., except that Baker purchased each of these properties new in 2006. Compute depreciation for each of these properties for 2006 using the maximum depreciation allowed for each property without electing Section 179 expense.

6. **Section 179.** Sands Corporation purchases one asset in 2006—machinery costing $463,000. The machine was placed in service on June 2, 2006. Sands wants to elect the maximum Section 179 possible, even if some must be carried over to 2007. Sands's 2006 taxable income before Section 179 is $67,000.

   a. Compute the maximum Section 179 Sands can elect in 2006 and the Section 179 carryover to 2007.

   b. Compute the maximum total depreciation on the machine for 2006.

7. **Section 179.** In May 2006, Roddick Enterprises placed in service 7-year property costing $120,000 and 5-year property costing $120,000. These are the only two properties Roddick placed in service during the year. Roddick's taxable income before deducting depreciation expense is $330,000.

   a. Compute Roddick's total depreciation expense deduction assuming he elects to take the maximum Section 179 expense on the 5-year property and uses MACRS.

   b. Compute Roddick's total depreciation expense deduction assuming he elects to take the maximum Section 179 expense on the 7-year property and uses MACRS.

   c. Which choice results in the largest total depreciation deduction? Comment on your answers to Parts a. and b.

8. **MACRS, Section 179.** The Redwood Company, a calendar-year corporation, acquired the following new properties during 2006.

Item	*Cost*	*Date Acquired*
Automobile	$ 18,500	July 2, 2006
Copier	14,200	March 1, 2006
Furniture	42,000	June 1, 2006
Equipment	128,000	June 30, 2006
Warehouse	110,250	July 9, 2006

   a. Compute the maximum depreciation deduction that Redwood can take on each of these properties assuming no Section 179 is elected.

b. Assume that Redwood elects to take the maximum allowed Section 179 expense on the equipment acquired on June 30, 2006. The company uses regular (accelerated) MACRS for the remainder of the cost. Redwood's taxable income before Section 179 expense is $250,000. Compute the maximum total depreciation deduction for the equipment for 2006 and 2007.

c. Same as in Part b. except that Redwood elects to take the maximum allowed Section 179 expense first on the copier, then the furniture, and finally the equipment.

9. **Listed Property, Section 179.** Dewey Terrell is a self-employed personal financial adviser. In March 2006, Terrell purchased a computer for $2,800. During 2006 he used the computer 60% of the time in providing financial advice to clients, 15% of the time for his own investments, and 25% of the time for personal use.

a. What is the maximum amount of depreciation Terrell is entitled to take in 2006 for the computer, assuming he does not elect Section 179?

b. How much total depreciation is Terrell entitled to take in 2006 for the computer assuming he elects to take the maximum Section 179 deduction?

c. Where on his tax return does Terrell deduct this depreciation expense?

10. **Listed Property.** During 2006, Tim Simon (self-employed) pays $14,500 for an automobile that he uses 45% of the time for business, 25% of the time for investment purposes, and 30% of the time for personal use. The half-year convention applies to the automobile. How much depreciation is Simon entitled to deduct in 2006?

11. **Luxury Automobiles.** Charlotte Milone helps install computer systems for a variety of clients. Since Milone often drives considerable distances to work in client offices, she decides to buy a new automobile to use in her work. She purchased the car on March 1, 2005, for $30,000 and uses it 80% of the time for business purposes. Prepare a schedule for Milone that shows the maximum depreciation she will be entitled to take in each of the years 2005 through 2010, assuming that she uses the automobile 80% of the time for business each year.

12. **Luxury Automobiles.** On September 13, 2006, Dolly Martin places in service a new automobile costing $25,000. This is Martin's only acquisition during 2006. She uses the automobile 90% of the time for business. What is the maximum total depreciation Martin can deduct in 2006?

13. **Leased Automobiles.** On March 1, 2006, Casey Stukel enters into a 36-month lease for a car valued at $36,400. Her monthly lease payment is $470, and she uses the car 75% for business. What amount will Stukel deduct in 2006 and 2007?

14. **Leased Automobiles.** Bart Rentz operates his business as a sole proprietorship. On October 1, 2006, Rentz enters into a 24-month lease on a car valued at $39,900. His monthly payments are $800. Rentz uses the car 85% for business each year. Compute Rentz's lease deduction and inclusion amounts for 2006-2008.

15. MACRS and Averaging Conventions. Jan Stephenson purchased the following new properties during 2006.

Description	*Date Placed in Service*	*Cost*
Computer	March 9, 2006	$ 3,000
Machinery	July 17, 2006	35,000
Office building	September 6, 2006	270,000
Equipment	December 27, 2006	42,000

Compute Stephenson's depreciation for each of these properties for 2006 and 2007 using the maximum depreciation allowed without taking Section 179.

16. MACRS and Averaging Conventions. Howard Fields (SSN 748-29-4631) operates the H. B. Fields Company as a sole proprietorship. Fields acquires the following new properties in 2006. The automobile is used 100% for business. Fields has written evidence of the business use, which was 19,280 miles in 2006. Fields has another vehicle he uses for personal use. He does not elect Section 179.

Date of Acquisition	*Item*	*Cost*
January 30	Automobile	$18,000
March 10	Garage for auto	39,000
November 6	Machine	1,246
December 1	Office desk	910

a. Compute Fields's depreciation deduction reported on Schedule C for 2006, using regular (accelerated) MACRS.

b. Complete Form 4562, Depreciation and Amortization, on the pages that follow to report the depreciation deduction reported on Schedule C as computed in Part a.

17. MACRS, Real Property. In January 2006, a taxpayer purchased an office building for $320,000 and an apartment building for $400,000. These amounts include only the buildings, not the land. Compute the 2006 depreciation expense for each building.

(Use for Problem 16.)

Form **4562**
Department of the Treasury
Internal Revenue Service

Depreciation and Amortization
(Including Information on Listed Property)

▶ See separate instructions. ▶ Attach to your tax return.

OMB No. 1545-0172
2006
Attachment Sequence No. 67

Name(s) shown on return	Business or activity to which this form relates	Identifying number

Part I Election To Expense Certain Property Under Section 179
Note: *If you have any listed property, complete Part V before you complete Part I.*

1	Maximum amount. See the instructions for a higher limit for certain businesses	1	$108,000
2	Total cost of section 179 property placed in service (see instructions)	2	
3	Threshold cost of section 179 property before reduction in limitation	3	$430,000
4	Reduction in limitation. Subtract line 3 from line 2. If zero or less, enter -0-	4	
5	Dollar limitation for tax year. Subtract line 4 from line 1. If zero or less, enter -0-. If married filing separately, see instructions	5	

	(a) Description of property	(b) Cost (business use only)	(c) Elected cost
6			

7	Listed property. Enter the amount from line 29	7	
8	Total elected cost of section 179 property. Add amounts in column (c), lines 6 and 7	8	
9	Tentative deduction. Enter the **smaller** of line 5 or line 8	9	
10	Carryover of disallowed deduction from line 13 of your 2005 Form 4562	10	
11	Business income limitation. Enter the smaller of business income (not less than zero) or line 5 (see instructions)	11	
12	Section 179 expense deduction. Add lines 9 and 10, but do not enter more than line 11	12	
13	Carryover of disallowed deduction to 2007. Add lines 9 and 10, less line 12 ▶	13	

Note: *Do not use Part II or Part III below for listed property. Instead, use Part V.*

Part II Special Depreciation Allowance and Other Depreciation (Do not include listed property.) (See instructions.)

14	Special allowance for qualified New York Liberty or Gulf Opportunity Zone property (other than listed property) placed in service during the tax year (see instructions)	14	
15	Property subject to section 168(f)(1) election	15	
16	Other depreciation (including ACRS)	16	

Part III MACRS Depreciation (Do not include listed property.) (See instructions.)

Section A

17	MACRS deductions for assets placed in service in tax years beginning before 2006	17	
18	If you are electing to group any assets placed in service during the tax year into one or more general asset accounts, check here ▶ ☐		

Section B—Assets Placed in Service During 2006 Tax Year Using the General Depreciation System

(a) Classification of property	(b) Month and year placed in service	(c) Basis for depreciation (business/investment use only—see instructions)	(d) Recovery period	(e) Convention	(f) Method	(g) Depreciation deduction
19a 3-year property						
b 5-year property						
c 7-year property						
d 10-year property						
e 15-year property						
f 20-year property						
g 25-year property			25 yrs.		S/L	
h Residential rental property			27.5 yrs.	MM	S/L	
			27.5 yrs.	MM	S/L	
i Nonresidential real property			39 yrs.	MM	S/L	
				MM	S/L	

Section C—Assets Placed in Service During 2006 Tax Year Using the Alternative Depreciation System

20a Class life					S/L	
b 12-year			12 yrs.		S/L	
c 40-year			40 yrs.	MM	S/L	

Part IV Summary (see instructions)

21	Listed property. Enter amount from line 28	21	
22	**Total.** Add amounts from line 12, lines 14 through 17, lines 19 and 20 in column (g), and line 21. Enter here and on the appropriate lines of your return. Partnerships and S corporations—see instr.	22	
23	For assets shown above and placed in service during the current year, enter the portion of the basis attributable to section 263A costs	23	

For Paperwork Reduction Act Notice, see separate instructions. Cat. No. 12906N Form **4562** (2006)

(Use for Problem 16.)

Form 4562 (2006) Page **2**

Part V **Listed Property** (Include automobiles, certain other vehicles, cellular telephones, certain computers, and property used for entertainment, recreation, or amusement.)

Note: *For any vehicle for which you are using the standard mileage rate or deducting lease expense, complete* **only** *24a, 24b, columns (a) through (c) of Section A, all of Section B, and Section C if applicable.*

Section A—Depreciation and Other Information (Caution: *See the instructions for limits for passenger automobiles.***)**

24a Do you have evidence to support the business/investment use claimed? ☐ **Yes** ☐ **No** **24b** If "Yes," is the evidence written? ☐ **Yes** ☐ **No**

(a) Type of property (list vehicles first)	(b) Date placed in service	(c) Business/ investment use percentage	(d) Cost or other basis	(e) Basis for depreciation (business/investment use only)	(f) Recovery period	(g) Method/ Convention	(h) Depreciation deduction	(i) Elected section 179 cost
25 Special allowance for qualified New York Liberty or Gulf Opportunity Zone property placed in service during the tax year and used more than 50% in a qualified business use (see instructions) **25**								
26 Property used more than 50% in a qualified business use:								
		%						
		%						
		%						
27 Property used 50% or less in a qualified business use:								
		%				S/L –		
		%				S/L –		
		%				S/L –		
28 Add amounts in column (h), lines 25 through 27. Enter here and on line 21, page 1. . **28**								
29 Add amounts in column (i), line 26. Enter here and on line 7, page 1. . . . . **29**								

Section B—Information on Use of Vehicles

Complete this section for vehicles used by a sole proprietor, partner, or other "more than 5% owner," or related person.
If you provided vehicles to your employees, first answer the questions in Section C to see if you meet an exception to completing this section for those vehicles.

	(a) Vehicle 1		(b) Vehicle 2		(c) Vehicle 3		(d) Vehicle 4		(e) Vehicle 5		(f) Vehicle 6	
30 Total business/investment miles driven during the year (**do not** include commuting miles)												
31 Total commuting miles driven during the year												
32 Total other personal (noncommuting) miles driven												
33 Total miles driven during the year. Add lines 30 through 32												
	Yes	**No**	**Yes**	**No**	**Yes**	**No**	**Yes**	**No**	**Yes**	**No**	**Yes**	**No**
34 Was the vehicle available for personal use during off-duty hours?												
35 Was the vehicle used primarily by a more than 5% owner or related person?												
36 Is another vehicle available for personal use?												

Section C—Questions for Employers Who Provide Vehicles for Use by Their Employees

Answer these questions to determine if you meet an exception to completing Section B for vehicles used by employees who **are not** more than 5% owners or related persons (see instructions).

	Yes	**No**
37 Do you maintain a written policy statement that prohibits all personal use of vehicles, including commuting, by your employees?		
38 Do you maintain a written policy statement that prohibits personal use of vehicles, except commuting, by your employees? See the instructions for vehicles used by corporate officers, directors, or 1% or more owners		
39 Do you treat all use of vehicles by employees as personal use?		
40 Do you provide more than five vehicles to your employees, obtain information from your employees about the use of the vehicles, and retain the information received?		
41 Do you meet the requirements concerning qualified automobile demonstration use? (See instructions.)		
Note: *If your answer to 37, 38, 39, 40, or 41 is "Yes," do not complete Section B for the covered vehicles.*		

Part VI **Amortization**

(a) Description of costs	(b) Date amortization begins	(c) Amortizable amount	(d) Code section	(e) Amortization period or percentage	(f) Amortization for this year
42 Amortization of costs that begins during your 2006 tax year (see instructions):					
43 Amortization of costs that began before your 2006 tax year.				**43**	
44 **Total.** Add amounts in column (f). See the instructions for where to report.				**44**	

Printed on recycled paper Form **4562** (2006)

18. **MACRS, Real Property.** In 1991, a taxpayer purchased an office building for $250,000. On August 2, 2006, the taxpayer sold the office building. Compute MACRS on the building for 2006.

19. **MACRS and ADS, Real Property.** Drew Lankin operates a business as a sole proprietorship. On January 3, 2006, Lankin placed in service a warehouse costing $650,000. On November 25, 2006, he placed in service an apartment complex costing $990,000.

   a. Compute Lankin's depreciation expense on each building assuming he uses MACRS to depreciate the warehouse and elects to use ADS to depreciate the apartment building.

   b. Compute Lankin's depreciation expense on each building assuming he elects to depreciate the warehouse using ADS and uses MACRS to depreciate the apartment building.

   c. Compute Lankin's depreciation expense on each building assuming he uses MACRS to depreciate both buildings.

   d. Compute Lankin's depreciation expense on each building assuming he elects to use ADS to depreciate both buildings.

20. **MACRS and ADS, Real Property.** On April 29, 1999, Conley, Inc. placed in service an office building warehouse costing $450,000. Conley depreciates the office building under ADS. It sold the building on January 4, 2006. Compute Conley's depreciation expense on the building for 1999-2006.

21. **MACRS, Realty.** What depreciation method and useful life are used to depreciate a home office placed in service in 2006?

22. Amortization of Intangibles. For each of the following intangibles, which ones can be amortized, what method should be used to amortize them, and how quickly can they be amortized?

a. A customer list purchased as part of a business acquired during the year

b. A copyright purchased from an author

c. Self-created goodwill

d. A trademark purchased as part of a business acquired during the year; the trademark has a 10-year remaining life

e. A patent created internally by an employee

23. Internet Problem: Researching Publication 463.

On August 29, 2004, Renee Woodby entered into a 36-month lease for a car valued at $40,220. Woodby's monthly lease payment is $590. She uses the car 65% for business.

a. What affect does this lease arrangement have on the amount Woodby must include in gross income in 2006?

b. How much of the lease payment can be deducted?

c. How is this information presented on the tax return?

Go to the IRS Web site. Locate Publication 463 and find the appropriate page in Appendix A to answer the above question regarding Woodby's inclusion amount. Print out a copy of the page where you found your answer. Underline or highlight the pertinent information.

See Appendix A for instructions on use of the IRS Web site.

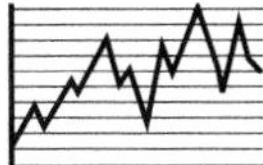

24. Business Entity Problem: This problem is designed for those using the "business entity" approach. The solution may require information from Chapters 14 and 15.

MSO Corporation owns a residential apartment building that it depreciates over 27.5 years. The building originally cost $550,000.

a. How much depreciation expense can the company claim on its tax return in the fifth year of ownership?

b. Earnings and profits serves as the source of taxable dividends. By what amount does depreciation reduce the corporation's earnings and profits in the fifth year of ownership?

COMPREHENSIVE PROBLEM

25. Patrick A. and Danielle R. Beckman file a joint return for 2006. The Beckmans rent a three-bedroom apartment located at 529 W. Maywood #4, Aurora, IL 60505. They provide over half of the support for Danielle's mother, Ellen Tyler (SSN 384-58-7338), who qualifies as their dependent. Ellen lives in a nursing home in Peoria, Illinois. The Beckmans claim their 20-year-old daughter, Susan (SSN 487-58-3957) as a dependent. Susan lives with the Beckmans while attending college full-time.

Danielle (SSN 394-59-3948) works full-time as an employee for an advertising firm. In 2006, Danielle earned wages of $34,000, from which her employer withheld $4,800 in federal income taxes and $1,020 in state income taxes.

Patrick (SSN 549-82-2497) began operating a carpet cleaning service in 2004. The business code for Schedule C is 812990. The guest bedroom doubles as Patrick's office. Patrick uses the office periodically to schedule appointments and keep track of his business records. Patrick uses the cash method, and during 2006 he earned $18,000 from his business. He paid $2,928 for cleaning chemicals and supplies. He also paid $300 for advertising and $50 for office expenses.

On November 10, 2004, Patrick purchased carpet cleaning equipment for $24,000. This was the only acquisition of depreciable property Patrick made during 2004. Patrick did not elect Section 179, but took the 50% bonus depreciation on the equipment. He deducts regular (accelerated) MACRS on the remaining $12,000 basis [$24,000 – ($24,000 × 50% bonus depreciation)].

On June 8, 2005, Patrick purchased a computer for $800 and a printer for $200. During 2005 and 2006, Patrick used the computer and printer 60% for business and 40% for personal use. This was Patrick's only acquisition during 2005. Patrick has written evidence to support the 60% business use. He uses regular MACRS to depreciate these assets.

Patrick uses his van to get to and from customers' homes. During the year Patrick drove his van 2,342 miles for business and keeps a written log as evidence of these miles. Total miles for the year on the van were 10,540. Danielle has her own car that she uses to get to and from work. Patrick bought the van on March 5, 2004. He used the standard mileage method in 2004 and 2005. Patrick incurred no business-related parking or tolls in 2006.

Prepare the Beckmans' Form 1040 and accompanying Schedules C and SE, and Form 4562. Be sure to complete lines 26 and 30–36 on Form 4562 for Patrick's business automobile. The Beckmans claim the standard credit for telephone excise tax paid.

(Use for Problem 25.)

Form **1040** Department of the Treasury—Internal Revenue Service **U.S. Individual Income Tax Return** **2006** (99) IRS Use Only—Do not write or staple in this space.

For the year Jan. 1–Dec. 31, 2006, or other tax year beginning , 2006, ending , 20 OMB No. 1545-0074

Label (See instructions on page 16.) **Use the IRS label.** Otherwise, please print or type.

LABEL HERE

Your first name and initial	Last name	Your social security number
If a joint return, spouse's first name and initial	Last name	Spouse's social security number
Home address (number and street). If you have a P.O. box, see page 16.	Apt. no.	▲ You **must** enter your SSN(s) above. ▲
City, town or post office, state, and ZIP code. If you have a foreign address, see page 16.		Checking a box below will not change your tax or refund.

Presidential Election Campaign ▶ Check here if you, or your spouse if filing jointly, want $3 to go to this fund (see page 16) ▶ ☐ You ☐ Spouse

Filing Status

Check only one box.

1 ☐ Single
2 ☐ Married filing jointly (even if only one had income)
3 ☐ Married filing separately. Enter spouse's SSN above and full name here. ▶
4 ☐ Head of household (with qualifying person). (See page 17.) If the qualifying person is a child but not your dependent, enter this child's name here. ▶
5 ☐ Qualifying widow(er) with dependent child (see page 17)

Exemptions

6a ☐ **Yourself.** If someone can claim you as a dependent, **do not** check box 6a

b ☐ **Spouse**

Boxes checked on 6a and 6b ____

c **Dependents:**

(1) First name Last name	(2) Dependent's social security number	(3) Dependent's relationship to you	(4) ✓ if qualifying child for child tax credit (see page 19)
			☐
			☐
			☐
			☐

No. of children on 6c who:
- lived with you ____
- did not live with you due to divorce or separation (see page 20) ____

Dependents on 6c not entered above ____

If more than four dependents, see page 19.

d Total number of exemptions claimed . . . Add numbers on lines above ▶

Income

Attach Form(s) W-2 here. Also attach Forms W-2G and 1099-R if tax was withheld.

If you did not get a W-2, see page 22.

Enclose, but do not attach, any payment. Also, please use **Form 1040-V.**

7	Wages, salaries, tips, etc. Attach Form(s) W-2		7
8a	**Taxable** interest. Attach Schedule B if required		8a
b	**Tax-exempt** interest. **Do not** include on line 8a	8b	
9a	Ordinary dividends. Attach Schedule B if required		9a
b	Qualified dividends (see page 23)	9b	
10	Taxable refunds, credits, or offsets of state and local income taxes (see page 23)		10
11	Alimony received		11
12	Business income or (loss). Attach Schedule C or C-EZ		12
13	Capital gain or (loss). Attach Schedule D if required. If not required, check here ▶ ☐		13
14	Other gains or (losses). Attach Form 4797		14
15a	IRA distributions 15a	b Taxable amount (see page 25)	15b
16a	Pensions and annuities 16a	b Taxable amount (see page 25)	16b
17	Rental real estate, royalties, partnerships, S corporations, trusts, etc. Attach Schedule E		17
18	Farm income or (loss). Attach Schedule F		18
19	Unemployment compensation		19
20a	Social security benefits 20a	b Taxable amount (see page 27)	20b
21	Other income. List type and amount (see page 29)		21
22	Add the amounts in the far right column for lines 7 through 21. This is your **total income** ▶		22

Adjusted Gross Income

23	Archer MSA deduction. Attach Form 8853	23	
24	Certain business expenses of reservists, performing artists, and fee-basis government officials. Attach Form 2106 or 2106-EZ	24	
25	Health savings account deduction. Attach Form 8889	25	
26	Moving expenses. Attach Form 3903	26	
27	One-half of self-employment tax. Attach Schedule SE	27	
28	Self-employed SEP, SIMPLE, and qualified plans	28	
29	Self-employed health insurance deduction (see page 30)	29	
30	Penalty on early withdrawal of savings	30	
31a	Alimony paid b Recipient's SSN ▶	31a	
32	IRA deduction (see page 31)	32	
33	Student loan interest deduction (see page 33)	33	
34	Jury duty pay you gave to your employer	34	
35	Domestic production activities deduction. Attach Form 8903	35	
36	Add lines 23 through 31a and 32 through 35		36
37	Subtract line 36 from line 22. This is your **adjusted gross income** ▶		37

For Disclosure, Privacy Act, and Paperwork Reduction Act Notice, see page 78. Cat. No. 11320B Form **1040** (2006)

(Use for Problem 25.)

Form 1040 (2006) Page 2

Tax and Credits

38 Amount from line 37 (adjusted gross income) . . . 38

39a Check if: ☐ **You** were born before January 2, 1942, ☐ Blind. ☐ **Spouse** was born before January 2, 1942, ☐ Blind. } **Total boxes checked** ▶ 39a

b If your spouse itemizes on a separate return or you were a dual-status alien, see page 35 and check here ▶39b ☐

40 **Itemized deductions** (from Schedule A) **or** your **standard deduction** (see left margin) . . 40

41 Subtract line 40 from line 38 . . . 41

42 If line 38 is over $112,875, or you provided housing to a person displaced by Hurricane Katrina, see page 37. Otherwise, multiply $3,300 by the total number of exemptions claimed on line 6d 42

43 **Taxable income.** Subtract line 42 from line 41. If line 42 is more than line 41, enter -0- . 43

44 **Tax** (see page 37). Check if any tax is from: **a** ☐ Form(s) 8814 **b** ☐ Form 4972 . . . 44

45 **Alternative minimum tax** (see page 39). Attach Form 6251 . . . 45

46 Add lines 44 and 45 . . . ▶ 46

47 Foreign tax credit. Attach Form 1116 if required . . . 47

48 Credit for child and dependent care expenses. Attach Form 2441 48

49 Credit for the elderly or the disabled. Attach Schedule R . 49

50 Education credits. Attach Form 8863 . . . 50

51 Retirement savings contributions credit. Attach Form 8880. 51

52 Residential energy credits. Attach Form 5695 . . . 52

53 Child tax credit (see page XX). Attach Form 8901 if required 53

54 Credits from: **a** ☐ Form 8396 **b** ☐ Form 8839 **c** ☐ Form 8859 54

55 Other credits: **a** ☐ Form 3800 **b** ☐ Form 8801 **c** ☐ Form____ 55

56 Add lines 47 through 55. These are your **total credits** . . . 56

57 Subtract line 56 from line 46. If line 56 is more than line 46, enter -0- . . . ▶ 57

Standard Deduction for—

- People who checked any box on line 39a or 39b **or** who can be claimed as a dependent, see page 36.
- All others:

Single or Married filing separately, $5,150

Married filing jointly or Qualifying widow(er), $10,300

Head of household, $7,550

Other Taxes

58 Self-employment tax. Attach Schedule SE . . . 58

59 Social security and Medicare tax on tip income not reported to employer. Attach Form 4137 . . 59

60 Additional tax on IRAs, other qualified retirement plans, etc. Attach Form 5329 if required . . 60

61 Advance earned income credit payments from Form(s) W-2, box 9 . . . 61

62 Household employment taxes. Attach Schedule H . . . 62

63 Add lines 57 through 62. This is your **total tax** . . . ▶ 63

Payments

64 Federal income tax withheld from Forms W-2 and 1099 . . 64

65 2006 estimated tax payments and amount applied from 2005 return 65

66a **Earned income credit (EIC)** . . . 66a

b Nontaxable combat pay election ▶ 66b

67 Excess social security and tier 1 RRTA tax withheld (see page 59) 67

68 Additional child tax credit. Attach Form 8812 . . . 68

69 Amount paid with request for extension to file (see page 59) 69

70 Payments from: **a** ☐ Form 2439 **b** ☐ Form 4136 **c** ☐ Form 8885 . 70

71 Credit for federal telephone excise tax paid. Attach Form 8913 if required 71

72 Add lines 64, 65, 66a, and 67 through 71. These are your **total payments** . . . ▶ 72

If you have a qualifying child, attach Schedule EIC.

Refund

73 If line 72 is more than line 63, subtract line 63 from line 72. This is the amount you **overpaid** 73

74a Amount of line 73 you want **refunded to you.** If Form 8888 is attached, check here ▶ ☐ 74a

▶ b Routing number ▶ c Type: ☐ Checking ☐ Savings

▶ d Account number

75 Amount of line 73 you want **applied to your 2007 estimated tax** ▶ 75

Direct deposit? See page 59 and fill in 74b, 74c, and 74d, or Form 8888.

Amount You Owe

76 **Amount you owe.** Subtract line 72 from line 63. For details on how to pay, see page 60 ▶ 76

77 Estimated tax penalty (see page 60) . . . 77

Third Party Designee

Do you want to allow another person to discuss this return with the IRS (see page 61)? ☐ **Yes.** Complete the following. ☐ **No**

Designee's name ▶ Phone no. ▶ ( ) Personal identification number (PIN) ▶

Sign Here

Joint return? See page 17. Keep a copy for your records.

Under penalties of perjury, I declare that I have examined this return and accompanying schedules and statements, and to the best of my knowledge and belief, they are true, correct, and complete. Declaration of preparer (other than taxpayer) is based on all information of which preparer has any knowledge.

Your signature | Date | Your occupation | Daytime phone number ( )

Spouse's signature. If a joint return, **both** must sign. | Date | Spouse's occupation

Paid Preparer's Use Only

Preparer's signature ▶ | Date | Check if self-employed ☐ | Preparer's SSN or PTIN

Firm's name (or yours if self-employed), address, and ZIP code ▶ | EIN | Phone no. ( )

Form **1040** (2006)

Printed on recycled paper

(Use for Problem 25.)

SCHEDULE C (Form 1040)
Department of the Treasury Internal Revenue Service (99)

Profit or Loss From Business
(Sole Proprietorship)

▶ Partnerships, joint ventures, etc., must file Form 1065 or 1065-B.
▶ Attach to Form 1040, 1040NR, or 1041. ▶ See Instructions for Schedule C (Form 1040).

OMB No. 1545-0074
2006
Attachment Sequence No. **09**

Name of proprietor | Social security number (SSN)

A Principal business or profession, including product or service (see page C-2 of the instructions) | **B Enter code from pages C-8, 9, & 10** ▶

C Business name. If no separate business name, leave blank. | **D Employer ID number (EIN), if any**

E Business address (including suite or room no.) ▶
City, town or post office, state, and ZIP code

F Accounting method: (1) ☐ Cash (2) ☐ Accrual (3) ☐ Other (specify) ▶
G Did you "materially participate" in the operation of this business during 2006? If "No," see page C-2 for limit on losses ☐ Yes ☐ No
H If you started or acquired this business during 2006, check here ▶ ☐

Part I Income

1	Gross receipts or sales. **Caution.** If this income was reported to you on Form W-2 and the "Statutory employee" box on that form was checked, see page C-3 and check here ▶ ☐	1	
2	Returns and allowances	2	
3	Subtract line 2 from line 1	3	
4	Cost of goods sold (from line 42 on page 2)	4	
5	**Gross profit.** Subtract line 4 from line 3	5	
6	Other income, including federal and state gasoline or fuel tax credit or refund (see page C-3)	6	
7	**Gross income.** Add lines 5 and 6 ▶	7	

Part II Expenses. Enter expenses for business use of your home **only** on line 30.

8	Advertising	8		18	Office expense	18	
9	Car and truck expenses (see page C-4)	9		19	Pension and profit-sharing plans	19	
10	Commissions and fees	10		20	Rent or lease (see page C-5):		
11	Contract labor (see page C-4)	11		a	Vehicles, machinery, and equipment	20a	
12	Depletion	12		b	Other business property	20b	
13	Depreciation and section 179 expense deduction (not included in Part III) (see page C-4)	13		21	Repairs and maintenance	21	
				22	Supplies (not included in Part III)	22	
				23	Taxes and licenses	23	
				24	Travel, meals, and entertainment:		
				a	Travel	24a	
14	Employee benefit programs (other than on line 19)	14		b	Deductible meals and entertainment (see page C-5)	24b	
15	Insurance (other than health)	15		25	Utilities	25	
16	Interest:			26	Wages (less employment credits)	26	
a	Mortgage (paid to banks, etc.)	16a		27	Other expenses (from line 48 on page 2)	27	
b	Other	16b					
17	Legal and professional services	17					

28	**Total expenses** before expenses for business use of home. Add lines 8 through 27 in columns ▶	28	
29	Tentative profit (loss). Subtract line 28 from line 7	29	
30	Expenses for business use of your home. Attach **Form 8829**	30	
31	**Net profit or (loss).** Subtract line 30 from line 29. • If a profit, enter on **Form 1040, line 12,** and **also** on **Schedule SE, line 2** or **Form 1040NR, line 13** (statutory employees, see page C-6). Estates and trusts, enter on Form 1041, line 3. • If a loss, you **must** go to line 32.	31	
32	If you have a loss, check the box that describes your investment in this activity (see page C-6). • If you checked 32a, enter the loss on **Form 1040, line 12,** and **also** on **Schedule SE, line 2** or **Form 1040NR, line 13** (statutory employees, see page C-6). Estates and trusts, enter on Form 1041, line 3. • If you checked 32b, you **must** attach **Form 6198.** Your loss may be limited.	32a ☐ All investment is at risk. 32b ☐ Some investment is not at risk.	

For Paperwork Reduction Act Notice, see page C-7 of the instructions. Cat. No. 11334P **Schedule C (Form 1040) 2006**

(Use for Problem 25.)

Schedule C (Form 1040) 2006 Page 2

Part III **Cost of Goods Sold** (see page C-7)

33 Method(s) used to value closing inventory: **a** ☐ Cost **b** ☐ Lower of cost or market **c** ☐ Other (attach explanation)

34 Was there any change in determining quantities, costs, or valuations between opening and closing inventory? If "Yes," attach explanation . . . ☐ **Yes** ☐ **No**

35	Inventory at beginning of year. If different from last year's closing inventory, attach explanation	**35**	
36	Purchases less cost of items withdrawn for personal use	**36**	
37	Cost of labor. Do not include any amounts paid to yourself	**37**	
38	Materials and supplies	**38**	
39	Other costs	**39**	
40	Add lines 35 through 39	**40**	
41	Inventory at end of year	**41**	
42	**Cost of goods sold.** Subtract line 41 from line 40. Enter the result here and on page 1, line 4	**42**	

Part IV **Information on Your Vehicle.** Complete this part **only** if you are claiming car or truck expenses on line 9 and are not required to file Form 4562 for this business. See the instructions for line 13 on page C-4 to find out if you must file Form 4562.

43 When did you place your vehicle in service for business purposes? (month, day, year) ▶ ____/____/____

44 Of the total number of miles you drove your vehicle during 2006, enter the number of miles you used your vehicle for:

a Business ____________ **b** Commuting (see instructions) ____________ **c** Other ____________

45 Do you (or your spouse) have another vehicle available for personal use? . . . ☐ **Yes** ☐ **No**

46 Was your vehicle available for personal use during off-duty hours? . . . ☐ **Yes** ☐ **No**

47a Do you have evidence to support your deduction? . . . ☐ **Yes** ☐ **No**

b If "Yes," is the evidence written? . . . ☐ **Yes** ☐ **No**

Part V **Other Expenses.** List below business expenses not included on lines 8–26 or line 30.

48 **Total other expenses.** Enter here and on page 1, line 27	**48**	

Printed on recycled paper

Schedule C (Form 1040) 2006

(Use for Problem 25.)

SCHEDULE SE (Form 1040)

Department of the Treasury
Internal Revenue Service (99)

Self-Employment Tax

▶ Attach to Form 1040. ▶ See Instructions for Schedule SE (Form 1040).

OMB No. 1545-0074

2006

Attachment Sequence No. **17**

Name of person with **self-employment** income (as shown on Form 1040) | Social security number of person with **self-employment** income ▶

Who Must File Schedule SE

You must file Schedule SE if:

- You had net earnings from self-employment from **other than** church employee income (line 4 of Short Schedule SE or line 4c of Long Schedule SE) of $400 or more, **or**
- You had church employee income of $108.28 or more. Income from services you performed as a minister or a member of a religious order **is not** church employee income (see page SE-1).

Note. Even if you had a loss or a small amount of income from self-employment, it may be to your benefit to file Schedule SE and use either "optional method" in Part II of Long Schedule SE (see page SE-3).

Exception. If your only self-employment income was from earnings as a minister, member of a religious order, or Christian Science practitioner **and** you filed Form 4361 and received IRS approval not to be taxed on those earnings, **do not** file Schedule SE. Instead, write "Exempt–Form 4361" on Form 1040, line 58.

May I Use Short Schedule SE or Must I Use Long Schedule SE?

Note. Use this flowchart **only if** you must file Schedule SE. If unsure, see Who Must File Schedule SE, above.

Did you receive wages or tips in 2006?

No → Are you a minister, member of a religious order, or Christian Science practitioner who received IRS approval **not** to be taxed on earnings from these sources, **but** you owe self-employment tax on other earnings?
- Yes → You must use Long Schedule SE on page 2
- No → Are you using one of the optional methods to figure your net earnings (see page SE-3)?
  - Yes → You must use Long Schedule SE on page 2
  - No → Did you receive church employee income reported on Form W-2 of $108.28 or more?
    - Yes → You must use Long Schedule SE on page 2
    - No → **You may use Short Schedule SE below**

Yes → Was the total of your wages and tips subject to social security or railroad retirement tax **plus** your net earnings from self-employment more than $94,200?
- Yes → You must use Long Schedule SE on page 2
- No → Did you receive tips subject to social security or Medicare tax that you **did not** report to your employer?
  - Yes → **You must use Long Schedule SE on page 2**
  - No → Are you a minister, member of a religious order, or Christian Science practitioner ... (continue with the question above)

Section A—Short Schedule SE. Caution. Read above to see if you can use Short Schedule SE.

1	Net farm profit or (loss) from Schedule F, line 36, and farm partnerships, Schedule K-1 (Form 1065), box 14, code A . . .	1	
2	Net profit or (loss) from Schedule C, line 31; Schedule C-EZ, line 3; Schedule K-1 (Form 1065), box 14, code A (other than farming); and Schedule K-1 (Form 1065-B), box 9, code J1. Ministers and members of religious orders, see page SE-1 for amounts to report on this line. See page SE-2 for other income to report . . .	2	
3	Combine lines 1 and 2 . . .	3	
4	**Net earnings from self-employment.** Multiply line 3 by 92.35% (.9235). If less than $400, **do not** file this schedule; you do not owe self-employment tax . . . ▶	4	
5	**Self-employment tax.** If the amount on line 4 is: • $94,200 or less, multiply line 4 by 15.3% (.153). Enter the result here and on **Form 1040, line 58.** • More than $94,200, multiply line 4 by 2.9% (.029). Then, add $11,680.80 to the result. Enter the total here and on **Form 1040, line 58.**	5	
6	**Deduction for one-half of self-employment tax.** Multiply line 5 by 50% (.5). Enter the result here and on **Form 1040, line 27** . . . 6		

(Use for Problem 25.)

Form **4562** Department of the Treasury Internal Revenue Service

Depreciation and Amortization
(Including Information on Listed Property)

▶ See separate instructions. ▶ Attach to your tax return.

OMB No. 1545-0172 **2006** Attachment Sequence No. **67**

Name(s) shown on return	Business or activity to which this form relates	Identifying number

Part I **Election To Expense Certain Property Under Section 179**
Note: *If you have any listed property, complete Part V before you complete Part I.*

1	Maximum amount. See the instructions for a higher limit for certain businesses	1	$108,000
2	Total cost of section 179 property placed in service (see instructions)	2	
3	Threshold cost of section 179 property before reduction in limitation	3	$430,000
4	Reduction in limitation. Subtract line 3 from line 2. If zero or less, enter -0-	4	
5	Dollar limitation for tax year. Subtract line 4 from line 1. If zero or less, enter -0-. If married filing separately, see instructions	5	

	(a) Description of property	(b) Cost (business use only)	(c) Elected cost
6			

7	Listed property. Enter the amount from line 29	7	
8	Total elected cost of section 179 property. Add amounts in column (c), lines 6 and 7	8	
9	Tentative deduction. Enter the **smaller** of line 5 or line 8	9	
10	Carryover of disallowed deduction from line 13 of your 2005 Form 4562	10	
11	Business income limitation. Enter the smaller of business income (not less than zero) or line 5 (see instructions)	11	
12	Section 179 expense deduction. Add lines 9 and 10, but do not enter more than line 11	12	
13	Carryover of disallowed deduction to 2007. Add lines 9 and 10, less line 12 ▶	13	

Note: *Do not use Part II or Part III below for listed property. Instead, use Part V.*

Part II **Special Depreciation Allowance and Other Depreciation (Do not** include listed property.) (See instructions.)

14	Special allowance for qualified New York Liberty or Gulf Opportunity Zone property (other than listed property) placed in service during the tax year (see instructions)	14	
15	Property subject to section 168(f)(1) election	15	
16	Other depreciation (including ACRS)	16	

Part III **MACRS Depreciation (Do not** include listed property.) (See instructions.)

Section A

17	MACRS deductions for assets placed in service in tax years beginning before 2006	17	
18	If you are electing to group any assets placed in service during the tax year into one or more general asset accounts, check here ▶ ☐		

Section B—Assets Placed in Service During 2006 Tax Year Using the General Depreciation System

(a) Classification of property	(b) Month and year placed in service	(c) Basis for depreciation (business/investment use only—see instructions)	(d) Recovery period	(e) Convention	(f) Method	(g) Depreciation deduction
19a 3-year property						
b 5-year property						
c 7-year property						
d 10-year property						
e 15-year property						
f 20-year property						
g 25-year property			25 yrs.		S/L	
h Residential rental property			27.5 yrs.	MM	S/L	
			27.5 yrs.	MM	S/L	
i Nonresidential real property			39 yrs.	MM	S/L	
				MM	S/L	

Section C—Assets Placed in Service During 2006 Tax Year Using the Alternative Depreciation System

20a Class life					S/L	
b 12-year			12 yrs.		S/L	
c 40-year			40 yrs.	MM	S/L	

Part IV **Summary** (see instructions)

21	Listed property. Enter amount from line 28	21	
22	**Total.** Add amounts from line 12, lines 14 through 17, lines 19 and 20 in column (g), and line 21. Enter here and on the appropriate lines of your return. Partnerships and S corporations—see instr.	22	
23	For assets shown above and placed in service during the current year, enter the portion of the basis attributable to section 263A costs	23	

For Paperwork Reduction Act Notice, see separate instructions. Cat. No. 12906N Form **4562** (2006)

(Use for Problem 25.)

Form 4562 (2006) Page 2

Part V Listed Property (Include automobiles, certain other vehicles, cellular telephones, certain computers, and property used for entertainment, recreation, or amusement.)

Note: *For any vehicle for which you are using the standard mileage rate or deducting lease expense, complete **only** 24a, 24b, columns (a) through (c) of Section A, all of Section B, and Section C if applicable.*

Section A—Depreciation and Other Information (Caution: *See the instructions for limits for passenger automobiles.*)

24a Do you have evidence to support the business/investment use claimed? ☐ Yes ☐ No 24b If "Yes," is the evidence written? ☐ Yes ☐ No

(a) Type of property (list vehicles first)	(b) Date placed in service	(c) Business/investment use percentage	(d) Cost or other basis	(e) Basis for depreciation (business/investment use only)	(f) Recovery period	(g) Method/Convention	(h) Depreciation deduction	(i) Elected section 179 cost
25 Special allowance for qualified New York Liberty or Gulf Opportunity Zone property placed in service during the tax year and used more than 50% in a qualified business use (see instructions) **25**								
26 Property used more than 50% in a qualified business use:								
		%						
		%						
		%						
27 Property used 50% or less in a qualified business use:								
		%				S/L –		
		%				S/L –		
		%				S/L –		
28 Add amounts in column (h), lines 25 through 27. Enter here and on line 21, page 1. . **28**								
29 Add amounts in column (i), line 26. Enter here and on line 7, page 1. . . . . **29**								

Section B—Information on Use of Vehicles

Complete this section for vehicles used by a sole proprietor, partner, or other "more than 5% owner," or related person.
If you provided vehicles to your employees, first answer the questions in Section C to see if you meet an exception to completing this section for those vehicles.

	(a) Vehicle 1		(b) Vehicle 2		(c) Vehicle 3		(d) Vehicle 4		(e) Vehicle 5		(f) Vehicle 6	
30 Total business/investment miles driven during the year (**do not** include commuting miles)												
31 Total commuting miles driven during the year												
32 Total other personal (noncommuting) miles driven												
33 Total miles driven during the year. Add lines 30 through 32												
	Yes	No	Yes	No	Yes	No	Yes	No	Yes	No	Yes	No
34 Was the vehicle available for personal use during off-duty hours?												
35 Was the vehicle used primarily by a more than 5% owner or related person?												
36 Is another vehicle available for personal use?												

Section C—Questions for Employers Who Provide Vehicles for Use by Their Employees

Answer these questions to determine if you meet an exception to completing Section B for vehicles used by employees who **are not** more than 5% owners or related persons (see instructions).

	Yes	No
37 Do you maintain a written policy statement that prohibits all personal use of vehicles, including commuting, by your employees?		
38 Do you maintain a written policy statement that prohibits personal use of vehicles, except commuting, by your employees? See the instructions for vehicles used by corporate officers, directors, or 1% or more owners		
39 Do you treat all use of vehicles by employees as personal use?		
40 Do you provide more than five vehicles to your employees, obtain information from your employees about the use of the vehicles, and retain the information received?		
41 Do you meet the requirements concerning qualified automobile demonstration use? (See instructions.)		

Note: *If your answer to 37, 38, 39, 40, or 41 is "Yes," do not complete Section B for the covered vehicles.*

Part VI Amortization

(a) Description of costs	(b) Date amortization begins	(c) Amortizable amount	(d) Code section	(e) Amortization period or percentage	(f) Amortization for this year
42 Amortization of costs that begins during your 2006 tax year (see instructions):					
43 Amortization of costs that began before your 2006 tax year.				**43**	
44 **Total.** Add amounts in column (f). See the instructions for where to report.				**44**	

Printed on recycled paper

Form **4562** (2006)

Rental Activities

CHAPTER CONTENTS

CHAPTER OVERVIEW

In addition to earning income from their jobs, many individuals earn income from property they own. For instance, taxpayers who own stocks often earn dividend income. Likewise, those who own bonds earn interest income. Taxpayers also can earn income by renting their property. Chapters 3 and 4 described the tax consequences of interest and dividend income. This chapter focuses on the income and expenses from rental activities. Taxpayers report rental income and expenses on their tax returns. However, in cases where rental expenses exceed rental income, the vacation home rules, at-risk rules, or passive loss rules may limit the losses taxpayers can deduct on their tax returns. The chapter begins with a discussion of rental income and expenses. The focus then shifts to the areas of the tax law that may limit deductions for losses from rental activities.

RENTAL INCOME AND EXPENSES

Although taxpayers can rent both personal and real property, this chapter focuses on the tax aspects of owning residential rental property. **Residential rental property** is rental property where at least 80% of the income comes from the rental of dwelling units. In general, a **dwelling unit** is property that provides the basic living accommodations—kitchen, sleeping, and toilet facilities. Dwelling units include houses, apartments, condominiums, and mobile homes because they are residential property. They do not include hotels, motels, and similar establishments.

Rental Income

Rental income includes the payments taxpayers receive for allowing others to *use or occupy* their property. Usually rent payments are received in cash. However, when a tenant performs services in exchange for the use of the taxpayer's property, rental income includes the value of those services. Rental income includes payments a tenant makes to cancel a lease. It also includes the value of improvements a tenant makes to the taxpayer's property in lieu of rent.

EXAMPLE 1

Jay Haas rents property to a tenant for $500 a month. In November the tenant installs a ceiling fan valued at $100. Haas then reduces the tenant's December rent by $100. Haas's rental income equals $6,000 ($500 × 11 months + $400 for December + $100 improvement substituted for rent). Haas then capitalizes and depreciates the ceiling fan.

Cash basis taxpayers report rental income the year they receive it, even when it applies to a prior or future tax year. Accrual basis taxpayers usually report rental income in the year it is due to them, but must report rent received in advance in the year they receive it. Therefore, if on December 26, 20x1, the taxpayer receives $600 from a tenant for January 20x2 rent, the $600 would be reported as rental income in 20x1 under both the cash and accrual methods. A security deposit is considered rent received in advance when the deposit represents the tenant's final rent payment. It is not considered rent received in advance if the taxpayer intends to return the deposit at the end of the lease. However, should the tenant forfeit any part of the deposit in a future year (for example, to cover late charges), the forfeited amount is rental income to the taxpayer in the year forfeited.

EXAMPLE 2

Connie Esmond enters into a 5-year lease to rent property she owns. On July 1, 20x1, Esmond receives $6,000 for the first year's rent and $6,000 of rent in advance for the final year of the lease. Esmond also receives a $1,000 security deposit that she intends to return to the tenant at the end of the lease. Esmond's 20x1 rental income equals $12,000, regardless of whether she uses the cash or accrual method of accounting.

Rental Expenses

Taxpayers can deduct against rental income all ordinary expenses related to the rental property. Examples of common rental expenses include advertising, cleaning, maintenance, utilities, real estate taxes, mortgage interest, insurance premiums, management fees, and necessary travel and transportation. Other rental expenses include repairs and depreciation. Accrual basis taxpayers take deductions in the year that services are received or assets are used. Cash basis taxpayers generally deduct rental expenses in the year the expenses are paid. However, prepaid expenses are spread over the periods benefited.

Repairs

Repairs and maintenance keep the rental property in good operating condition. Taxpayers can deduct the costs to repair rental property as a rental expense. Examples of repairs to rental property include painting the property (inside and out), fixing gutters or leaks, and replacing broken windows. Repairs are minor costs and should not be confused with improvements, which add value to the rental property or prolong its useful life. Improvements to rental property include such items as adding a bathroom, paving a driveway, installing new cabinets, or replacing the roof. Improvements increase the taxpayer's investment (basis) in the rental property. Taxpayers recover the cost of improvements through the depreciation methods described in Chapter 8.

EXAMPLE 3

Jake Dugan spends $15,000 to replace the roof and $3,000 to repaint the exterior of an apartment building he owns. Dugan can deduct the $3,000 spent on repairs from rental income in the current year. Dugan adds the $15,000 of improvements to his cost basis in the apartment building and depreciates this amount using the depreciation rules from Chapter 8.

Depreciation

Taxpayers depreciate furniture, appliances, and carpeting used in rental property over five years under MACRS (nine years if ADS is elected). Section 179 expense cannot be taken on rental property. However, bonus depreciation was allowed on new furnishings placed in service between September 11, 2001 and December 31, 2004. Taxpayers depreciate residential realty placed in service after 1986 using the straight-line method over 27.5 years (MACRS) or 40 years (ADS). They do not depreciate the land.

EXAMPLE 4

On April 5, 2006, Maria and Jay Sharpe purchase a furnished beach house that they intend to use as rental property. This is the only depreciable property placed in service during the year. The Sharpes can depreciate the cost of the home (minus the land) over 27.5 years (MACRS) or 40 years (ADS) beginning on April 15, 2006 under the mid-month convention. They depreciate the furnishings over five years (MACRS) or nine years (ADS) using the half-year convention.

A provision in the Gulf Opportunity Zone Act of 2005 allows businesses (including sole proprietorships) affected by Hurricanes Katrina, Rita and Wilma to take a 50% bonus first year depreciation on qualifying property placed in service in the Gulf Opportunity Zone (Go Zone). Qualifying property includes certain residential realty and its furnishings. The time frame for making these purchases is between the date of the hurricane and December 31, 2007 for personal property. They have until December 31, 2008 for qualifying residential realty.

Special Rules When Only Part of the Property Is Rented

The rules previously described assume that the rental property is used exclusively by or available for use by rent-paying tenants. Sometimes an individual rents only part of the property, as is the case when an owner of a duplex rents one unit and lives in the other. In such instances, the taxpayer must allocate expenses between rental and personal use. The taxpayer then deducts the rental portion of each expense against rental income and can deduct the personal portion of the mortgage interest and real estate taxes as itemized deductions.

Some expenses are easy to split between rental and personal use. For example, taxpayers can fully deduct the cost of repairs performed on rental units but cannot deduct the cost to repair their own personal units. Other expenses, like real estate taxes and depreciation, are harder to divide between rental and personal use. For these expenses, taxpayers can use any reasonable method to divide expenses between rental and personal use. The number of rooms or the relative square footage are two widely used methods for allocating these types of expenses.

EXAMPLE 5

Marvin Greene rents one room in his home. The area of the rented room is 140 square feet. The area of the entire home is 1,400 square feet. Greene deducts against rental income 10% (140/1,400) of the expenses related to the home during the year. Thus, if Greene's real estate taxes are $2,000, he can deduct $200 against rental income and the rest ($1,800) as an itemized deduction.

Converting a Personal Residence to Rental Use

When individual taxpayers convert their personal residence to rental property, they must divide the expenses for the year of the conversion between the two uses. Rental use begins when the property is offered for rent. Taxpayers deduct the rental portion of these expenses against rental income. They can deduct the personal portion of the interest and taxes as itemized deductions.

EXAMPLE 6

In September, Sylvia Black moved out of her home. Black listed her home for rent on October 1, and on November 1, she entered into a 2-year lease. Black can deduct 25% (October–December) of the annual expenses (real estates taxes, insurance, depreciation) against the rental income she receives during the year. She also can deduct any other expenses (interest, utilities, etc.) allocated to the last three months of the year. Black can deduct the personal portion (the other 75%) of the interest and taxes as itemized deductions.

RENTAL OF VACATION HOMES

The previous section dealt with situations where the rental income was derived from rental property used solely by the tenant. Special rules apply when taxpayers rent out vacation homes for part of the year and personally use the property during other parts of the year. The tax treatment of this type of rental activity depends on the number of rental and personal days during the year.

Property Rented Less Than 15 Days

When individual taxpayers rent their vacation home or principal residence for less than 15 days during the year, they do not report the rental income and do not deduct any rental expenses. However, home mortgage interest (but only for a principal residence or second residence), real estate taxes, and casualty losses may be deducted as itemized deductions.

EXAMPLE 7

Darren Benton rents his vacation home for 12 days during the year and personally uses it for 80 days. Benton collects rents of $1,200 and incurs the following expenses.

Home mortgage interest	$ 6,000
Real estate taxes	1,800
Utilities	400
Depreciation	2,000
Total expenses	$10,200

Since Benton rents the property for less than 15 days, he does not report the $1,200 of rental income. Benton can deduct as itemized deductions the $6,000 of home mortgage interest as his second residence and the $1,800 of real estate taxes.

Congress has failed on several occasions to get rid of the loophole in the tax law that allows taxpayers to rent out their residences for up to two weeks each year and not report the rental income to the IRS. This loophole made the headlines during the 1984 summer Olympics, when Los Angeles–area residents rented out their mansions for over $10,000 a day. Although the most they could rent their homes for was for 14 days, at more than $10,000 a day, they could generate over $140,000 in tax-free income.

Property Rented More Than 14 Days

Individual taxpayers who rent their vacation homes or principal residence for more than 14 days during the year report the rental income on their personal tax returns. They allocate the expenses related to the property between rental and personal use and deduct the rental portion of the expenses against their rental income. The Code states that taxpayers allocate expenses other than interest, taxes, and casualty losses on the basis of the days the property is used during the year. To compute the rental portion of expenses like utilities, repairs, and depreciation, taxpayers multiply the expense by the ratio of the number of days rented at fair rental value to the number of days used during the year.

$$\text{Percent allocated to rental activity} = \frac{\text{Number of days rented at fair rental value during the year}}{\text{Number of days used during the year}}$$

The Code does not address how to allocate interest, taxes, and casualty losses between rental and personal use. In Publication 527, the IRS suggests that taxpayers use the same method used to allocate other expenses. The courts, however, have allowed interest and taxes to be allocated based on the days rented to the number of days in the year. For purposes of this chapter, the same ratio (days rented/days used) is used to allocate all expenses to rental use.

EXAMPLE 8

Dan Walsh rents out his vacation home for 120 days during the year. He personally uses it for 80 days. Walsh collects rents of $12,000 and incurs the following expenses.

Home mortgage interest	$ 8,000
Real estate taxes	2,500
Utilities	800
Depreciation	3,000
Total expenses	$14,300

Walsh allocates 60% of the expenses (120 rental days/200 total days used during the year) to rental use. Walsh deducts $8,580 ($14,300 × 60%) as rental expense. He can deduct the rest of the home mortgage interest of $3,200 ($8,000 × 40%) and real estate taxes of $1,000 ($2,500 × 40%) as itemized deductions.

Before taxpayers can allocate expenses between rental and personal use, they first must determine what days count as rental days and what days count as personal days. Personal use includes days when the taxpayer donates use of the property to a charitable organization. Personal use also includes days when the property is used by:

1. The owner, unless the owner is working full time to repair or maintain the property.
2. A member of an owner's family, unless the family member pays a fair rental price *and* the family member uses the property as a principal residence. Family members include siblings (brothers and sisters), ancestors (parents, grandparents, etc.), and lineal descendants (children, grandchildren, etc.).
3. Anyone who has a reciprocal agreement that allows the owner to use some other dwelling unit.
4. Anyone who pays less than fair rental to use the property.

A rental day is any day the taxpayer rents the property for a fair rental price (however, see 2. above for special rules for family members). Days that the property is offered for rental but is not actually rented do not count as days rented at fair rental value.

EXAMPLE 9

The June and Ray Linden own a vacation home that they personally use 24 days during the year. The rest of the year the home was used by the following occupants. The property was vacant during the rest of the year. Fair rental value is $125 a night.

Occupant	**Number of Days**
June's parents, who pay no rent	32
Friends of the Lindens, who paid rent of $2,000	40
Ray's brother, who paid rent of $875	7
Unrelated persons, who paid rent of $7,500	60

The 60 days the home was used by unrelated persons counts as rental days, since they paid fair rental value for use of the home. Although Ray's brother paid fair rental for his use of the home, his seven days count as personal days since he does not use the home as his principal residence. The parents did not pay fair rental, nor did they use the home as their principal residence. Thus, their 32 days of use are personal days. The 40 days that the home is used by the Lindens' friends count as personal days since they did not pay fair rental price to use the home. The Lindens' total personal days equal 103 (24 + 32 + 40 + 7). The total number of days the property was used during the year was 163 (103 + 60 rental days).

EXAMPLE 10

Same as in Example 9 except that five of the days the Linden spent at the vacation home were spent making repairs to the property. These five days no longer count as personal days. Thus, the Lindens' personal days would be reduced to 98 (103 – 5) of the 163 total days the home was used during the year.

WHAT IS A FAIR RENTAL PRICE?

A fair rental price is the amount of rent that an *unrelated person* would be willing to pay to use the property. If the rent charged is substantially less than the rents received on *similar* properties, it might not be considered a fair rental price. The following questions can be used to determine whether two properties are *similar:*

- Are the properties used for the same purpose?
- Are the properties about the same size?
- Are the properties in about the same condition?
- Do the properties have similar furnishings?
- Are the properties in similar locations?

Generally, answering "No" to any of these questions means that the two properties are not similar.

EXAMPLE 11

Jane Sherman owns a house that she rents to her son. The son pays a fair rental price to use the home as his principal residence. The son's use of the home is not considered personal use by Sherman since the son is using the home as his principal residence and paying fair rental.

EXAMPLE 12

Bruce Reynolds rents his vacation home for 200 days during the year. On 40 of the 200 days, Reynolds's sister paid fair rental to use the house. The other 160 days also were rented at fair rental. Reynolds treats the days his sister rents the house as personal days, since she does not use the house as her principal residence. Thus, Reynolds's rental days equal 160. Reynolds allocates 80% (160 rental days/200 days used) of the expenses related to the house to rental use. He deducts these amounts against rental income.

Expenses Limited for Certain Vacation Homes

When the property is considered a "residence," rental expenses are deductible only to the extent of rental income. Disallowed expenses carry over to offset rental income in future tax years. A vacation home qualifies as a **residence** if the number of personal days exceeds the *greater of* (i) 14 days or (ii) 10% of the days the property is rented at fair rental. Thus, if the taxpayer's personal days exceed *both* (i) 14 days and (ii) 10% of the number of days rented at fair rental, then the property is considered a residence. When the property is treated as a residence, the personal portion of the interest can be deducted as an itemized deduction if the property is chosen as the taxpayer's second residence. When the property does not qualify as a residence, the personal portion of the interest cannot be deducted.

EXAMPLE 13

From June 1 through October 31 (153 days), Denise Miller rents her cabin (used as a vacation home) and receives fair rental. Miller uses the cabin five days during the year. Miller's parents stayed at the cabin for 12 days in May. In deciding whether the cabin qualifies as a residence, personal days include days the parents used the cabin (12 days). Thus, the total number of personal days equals 17 (5 + 12).

Miller treats the cabin as a residence since her 17 personal days exceed the *greater of* (i) 14 days or (ii) 15.3 days (10% of the 153 days rented at fair rental). Thus, Miller can deduct the rental portion of the expenses on the cabin only to the extent of rental income. She carries over any excess rental expense to the next year. In allocating expenses between rental and personal use, Miller allocates 90% (153 rental days/170 days used) of the expenses to the rental activity.

When renting out a vacation home, the owner's personal use of the property will determine whether the vacation home rules apply. The vacation home rules cannot take effect until the owner's personal days exceed 14. Thus, to avoid having the vacation home rules limit the deduction for rental expenses, owners might consider limiting their personal usage of the home to two weeks a year.

If the rental property qualifies as a residence and the taxpayer's rental expenses exceed rental income, the taxpayer deducts the expenses in the following order:

1. Home mortgage interest, real estate taxes, casualty and theft losses, and rent expenses not directly related to the rental property (management fees, advertising, etc.)
2. All other rental expenses other than depreciation on the rental property
3. Depreciation of the rental property

EXAMPLE 14

Jan Lehman rents her vacation home at fair rental to an unrelated party for 35 days during the year. Lehman personally uses the home for 15 days. The property is not used during any other time. During the year, Lehman collects $6,000 in rents and has the following expenses:

Home mortgage interest	$ 6,000
Real estate taxes	1,500
Utilities	300
Depreciation	3,000
Total expenses	$10,800

Lehman allocates 70% (35 rental days/50 total days used) of the expenses to the rental use. The rental portion of the expenses related to the home equals $7,560 ($10,800 × 70%). Because Lehman's personal use (15 days) exceeds the *greater of* (i) 14 days or (ii) 10% of the days rented at fair rental (35 × 10% = 3.5), the vacation home qualifies as a residence. Thus, Lehman's rental expenses cannot exceed rental income. Lehman deducts the rental expenses in the following order:

Rental income	$6,000
Less rental portion of interest and taxes ($7,500 × 70%)	(5,250)
Rental income left to cover rent expenses other than interest and taxes	$ 750
Less rent expenses other than depreciation ($300 × 70%)	(210)
Rental income left to cover depreciation expense	$ 540
Less depreciation ($3,000 × 70% = $2,100)	(540)
Net rental income	$ 0

Because the vacation home qualifies as a residence, Lehman can deduct only $540 of the $2,100 of depreciation allocated to rental use. Lehman carries over the disallowed depreciation of $1,560 ($2,100 – $540) to the next year. She adds this amount to next year's depreciation expense. If next year, Lehman's personal days exceed the *greater of* (i) 14 days, or (ii) 10% of the days rented at fair rental, then her rental expenses (including depreciation carried over from the current year) may be limited as well.

REPORTING RENTAL ACTIVITIES ON SCHEDULE E

Taxpayers use Schedule E (Form 1040), Supplemental Income and Loss, to report income and expenses from rental activities. In Part I (line 1), taxpayers describe the rental realty and provide its location. In Part I (line 2), taxpayers answer a question that determines whether the property qualifies as a residence. Taxpayers also report in Part I rental income (line 3) and expenses (lines 5 through 20) in computing their overall income or loss from the rental activity (line 22). For taxpayers who answer "Yes" to the question in Part I (line 2), total expenses (line 21) cannot exceed rental income (line 3). For taxpayers who answer "No" to this question, the vacation home rules do not apply and there is no limit on the total expenses. However, the expenses may be limited under either the *at-risk* or *passive loss* rules (discussed later in the chapter).

Information for Figure 9-1: Filled-In Schedule E

During 2006, Kurt F. and Heather M. Reding received rents of **$38,168** from an eight-unit apartment complex. The Redings paid $375,000 for the apartment building in 1996, which includes $100,000 for the land. They depreciate the building using MACRS (straight-line over 27.5 years). Expenses related to the building include **$250** advertising, **$2,500** cleaning and maintenance, **$1,227** insurance, **$300** legal fees, **$14,329** mortgage interest, **$3,262** supplies, **$4,290** real estate taxes, and **$1,800** utilities.

The Redings also own a condominium in Naples, Florida, that they used for 30 days in 2006. The Redings rented the condo for 90 days and received fair rentals totaling **$12,000.** None of the tenants were members of the Redings' family. The Redings paid $220,000 for the condo in 1995 and depreciate it using MACRS (straight-line over 27.5 years). The expenses related to the condo include $9,200 home mortgage interest, $3,400 real estate taxes, $1,000 utilities, $300 insurance, and $100 cleaning and maintenance.

Other Information

1A: Description: 8-unit apartment building, 505 West Street, Verona, WI

1B: Description: Condominium, 1500 Vanderbelt Beach Road, Naples, FL

2A: **No.** Personal use did not exceed the *greater of* (i) 14 days or (ii) 10% of the days rented at fair rental.

2B: **Yes.** The Redings's 30 days of personal use exceeds the *greater of* (i) 14 days or (ii) 9 days (10% of the 90 days rented at fair rental). Therefore, total rental expenses cannot exceed rental income.

7B: Cleaning and maintenance, **$75.00** (90 rental days/120 total days used × $100)

9B: Insurance, **$225.00** (90/120 × $300)

12B: Mortgage interest, **$6,900.00** (90/120 × $9,200)

16B: Taxes, **$2,550.00** (90/120 × $3,400)

17B: Utilities, **$750.00** (90/120 × $1,000)

20A: Depreciation expense, **$10,000.00** ($275,000/27.5)

20B: Depreciation expense, **$1,500.00** ($220,000/27.5 × 90/120 = $6,000; however, total rental expenses cannot exceed rental income of $12,000. Expenses other than depreciation total $10,500 [line 19B]; therefore depreciation is limited to $1,500).

FIGURE 9-1 Filled-In Schedule E, Page 1

SCHEDULE E (Form 1040)
Department of the Treasury Internal Revenue Service (99)

Supplemental Income and Loss

(From rental real estate, royalties, partnerships, S corporations, estates, trusts, REMICs, etc.)

▶ Attach to Form 1040, 1040NR, or Form 1041. ▶ See Instructions for Schedule E (Form 1040).

OMB No. 1545-0074
2006
Attachment Sequence No. **13**

Name(s) shown on return: Kurt F. and Heather M. Reding
Your social security number: 885-46-5566

Part I **Income or Loss From Rental Real Estate and Royalties** **Note.** If you are in the business of renting personal property, use **Schedule C** or **C-EZ** (see page E-3). Report farm rental income or loss from **Form 4835** on page 2, line 40.

1	List the type and location of each **rental real estate property:**
A	8-unit apartment building 505 West Street, Vernoa, WI
B	Condominim 1500 Vanderbelt Beach Road, Naples, FL
C	

2 For each rental real estate property listed on line 1, did you or your family use it during the tax year for personal purposes for more than the greater of:
- 14 days **or**
- 10% of the total days rented at fair rental value?

(See page E-3.)

	Yes	No
A		X
B	X	
C		

	Line	Properties A	Properties B	Properties C	Line	Totals (Add columns A, B, and C.)
Income:						
3 Rents received	3	38,168 00	12,000 00		3	50,168 00
4 Royalties received	4				4	
Expenses:						
5 Advertising	5	250 00				
6 Auto and travel (see page E-4)	6					
7 Cleaning and maintenance	7	2,500 00	75 00			
8 Commissions	8					
9 Insurance	9	1,227 00	225 00			
10 Legal and other professional fees	10	300 00				
11 Management fees	11					
12 Mortgage interest paid to banks, etc. (see page E-4)	12	14,329 00	6,900 00		12	21,229 00
13 Other interest	13					
14 Repairs	14					
15 Supplies	15	3,262 00				
16 Taxes	16	4,290 00	2,550 00			
17 Utilities	17	1,800 00	750 00			
18 Other (list) ▶	18					
19 Add lines 5 through 18	19	27,958 00	10,500 00		19	38,458 00
20 Depreciation expense or depletion (see page E-4)	20	10,000 00	1,500 00		20	11,500 00
21 Total expenses. Add lines 19 and 20	21	37,958 00	12,000 00			
22 Income or (loss) from rental real estate or royalty properties. Subtract line 21 from line 3 (rents) or line 4 (royalties). If the result is a (loss), see page E-5 to find out if you must file **Form 6198**	22	210 00	0			
23 Deductible rental real estate loss. **Caution.** Your rental real estate loss on line 22 may be limited. See page E-5 to find out if you must file **Form 8582.** Real estate professionals must complete line 43 on page 2	23	( )	( )	( )		

24 **Income.** Add positive amounts shown on line 22. **Do not** include any losses	24	210 00
25 **Losses.** Add royalty losses from line 22 and rental real estate losses from line 23. Enter total losses here	25	( )
26 **Total rental real estate and royalty income or (loss).** Combine lines 24 and 25. Enter the result here. If Parts II, III, IV, and line 40 on page 2 do not apply to you, also enter this amount on Form 1040, line 17, or Form 1040NR, line 18. Otherwise, include this amount in the total on line 41 on page 2	26	210 00

For Paperwork Reduction Act Notice, see page E-7 of the instructions. Cat. No. 11344L **Schedule E (Form 1040) 2006**

LOSS LIMITATIONS

When rental expenses exceed rental income and the rental property is considered a "residence," the vacation home rules limit the amount of rental expenses taxpayers can deduct against rental income. For rental property not subject to the vacation home limitation rules, two other sets of rules may affect the taxpayer's ability to deduct losses arising from rental activities: the at-risk rules and the passive activity loss rules. These rules not only affect rental activities but can affect losses arising from any trade, business, or income-producing activity. Because this chapter focuses on rental activities, the discussion will focus on these activities.

AT-RISK RULES

The at-risk rules limit a taxpayer's loss to the amount the taxpayer could actually lose from the activity. This is known as the amount the taxpayer is "at-risk." The at-risk rules apply to any activity carried on as a trade or business (reported on Schedule C) or for the production of income (reported on Schedule E).

Amounts at Risk

A taxpayer's risk in any activity equals the following:

1. The money and adjusted basis (cost + improvements – accumulated depreciation) of any property contributed to the activity, **plus**
2. Amounts borrowed for use in the activity if the taxpayer either is personally liable for the loan or pledges personal assets as security for the loan.

Disallowed Losses

Taxpayers determine the amount of their deductible loss on Form 6198, At-Risk Limitations. They file this form with their tax return if they have a loss from an at-risk activity and some of their investment in the activity is not at risk. A net loss limited because of the at-risk rules is treated as a deduction for the activity in the next year. When taxpayers sell or dispose of property used in an activity where the at-risk rules apply, they include any gain or loss from the disposal in computing the activity's overall profit or loss for the year.

PASSIVE ACTIVITY LOSSES

After applying the at-risk rules, taxpayers must consider the passive activity loss rules. Losses generated by activities of a passive nature can only offset income and gains generated from passive activities. Taxpayers carry over excess losses to offset passive income in future tax years. When the taxpayer disposes of the entire interest in a passive activity, any suspended losses left on that activity are fully deductible in that year.

Passive Activity Income Defined

The passive activity rules classify all income and losses into one of three categories: active, portfolio, or passive. **Active income** consists of wages, salaries, and income from material participation in a trade or business. **Portfolio income** comes from investments that generate dividends and interest. Portfolio income also includes gains from the sale of securities (stocks and bonds). **Passive income** generally comes from (1) a trade or business in which the taxpayer does not materially participate, (2) rental activities, and (3) limited partnerships. Any of these activities may produce losses. Losses from portfolio investments are treated as capital losses. However, losses not classified as portfolio are either active or passive. The distinction is important, as taxpayers can offset losses from active activities against both portfolio and passive income. They can only offset losses from passive activities against income from other passive activities.

Material participation in a trade or business produces active income and losses. **Material participation** occurs when the taxpayer is involved in the operations of the activity on a regular, continuous, and substantial basis. Except for real estate rental activities (which must meet a stricter test, discussed later), the material participation requirement can be met if the taxpayer participates in the activity for more than 500 hours during the year. (Participation by the owner's spouse is considered participation by the owner.) Another way to meet this requirement is for the taxpayer to participate in the activity for more than 100 hours during the year and for the taxpayer's participation to be at least as much as the participation of any other individual, including employees. IRS Publication 925 describes other ways to meet the material participation requirement.

The tax laws usually treat all rental activities as passive activities. However, exceptions do exist. One exception applies to taxpayers involved in the business of renting real property. This situation is described in the next section. Other exceptions include rental activities where: (1) the average rental period is less than eight days (e.g., a video rental store); (2) the average rental period is less than 31 days and significant personal services are provided (e.g., motels and hotels); and (3) the rental activity is incidental to the taxpayer's business. If one of these three exceptions applies, taxpayers need only meet the material participation requirements to avoid the passive loss rules. This will allow them to treat the income and losses from these rental activities as active income and losses.

EXAMPLE 15

Ginny Ness and Barry Tambler jointly operate a business together that does not involve rental realty. Both Ness and Tambler work for the business. Ness also works part-time as an employee for a consulting firm. During the year she spends 425 hours working for the business, and 600 hours as an employee. Tambler, on the other hand, is not employed elsewhere and spends at least 40 hours a week working for the business. Because his hours exceed 500, Tambler materially participates in the business. Ness does not participate more than 500 hours, and although her hours exceed 100, the hours she works do not equal Tambler's hours. Thus, unless one of the other ways for meeting the material participation requirement applies to Ness, she would be subject to the passive activity loss rules with respect to this activity.

EXAMPLE 16

Same as in Example 15 except that Ness averages over 10 hours a week working for the business. Since her hours exceed 500 hours, she materially participates in the activity. Thus, the passive activity loss rules would not apply.

LOSSES FROM RENTAL REAL ESTATE

Real Estate Trade or Business

Real estate rental activities usually are treated as "passive," even if the taxpayer meets one of the seven tests described in IRS Publication 925. However, a real estate rental activity may qualify as an active trade or business if the taxpayer satisfies both of the following conditions:

1. More than 50% of the personal services rendered during the year are performed in a trade or business involving real estate, **and**
2. At a minimum, the taxpayer performs more than 750 hours of personal service in the real property trade or business.

If the taxpayer meets both conditions, then the income or loss from the real estate rental activity is not considered passive, and all rental expenses are deductible, even if they exceed rental income. A married couple passes the two tests only if one spouse separately satisfies both tests. In other words, couples cannot pool their time and efforts in meeting the material participation test for real estate rental activities. If these conditions are not met, then the real estate rental activity is considered a passive activity. Accordingly, expenses related to the taxpayer's passive activities are deductible only to the extent that the taxpayer's passive activities generate passive income.

EXAMPLE 17

Same as in Example 16 except that Ness and Tambler's business involves rental realty. Tambler performs more than 750 hours of personal services in businesses involving real property. In addition, this work is more than 50% of his total hours of personal services rendered during the year. Thus, Tambler materially participates in the rental realty business. Ness's hours, on the other hand, do not exceed 750. Thus, she is not a material participant in the business. Accordingly, the passive activity loss rules apply to her losses from the rental activity.

EXAMPLE 18

A husband and wife each work 400 hours in a rental realty business. Although as a couple they work at least 750 hours in the rental realty business, the tax laws require that at least one spouse meet the two requirements for material participation. Thus, the rental activity is a passive activity to the couple.

The taxpayer has the burden of providing proof that any personal service tests have been met. To do this, taxpayers should keep a weekly log of their hours spent on the activity as evidence of their participation.

$25,000 Special Deduction for Active Participants

Taxpayers who are not in a "real estate trade or business" and have losses from rental real estate activities may deduct up to $25,000 of rental real estate losses from active and portfolio income. The deduction limit is $12,500 for married taxpayers filing separately and living apart at all times during the year. No special deduction is allowed for married taxpayers filing separately if the couple lived together at any time during the year. To qualify for this special deduction, the taxpayer must meet both of the following requirements:

1. The taxpayer actively participates in the rental real estate activity, **and**
2. The taxpayer owns at least 10% of the value of all interests in the activity throughout the entire year.

Active participation and material participation are two different concepts. **Active participation** requires less involvement than material participation. Active participation does not require regular, continuous, and substantial involvement. However, it does require that the taxpayer participate in management decisions in a significant and real sense. Examples of this level of involvement include approving new tenants, deciding on rental terms, approving improvements or repairs, or arranging for others to provide services such as repairs.

EXAMPLE 19

Going back to Example 17, although Ness's hours do not constitute material participation, they do indicate active participation in the rental realty business. Since Ness's owns at least 10% of the business, she qualifies for the $25,000 special deduction. Thus, in years in which the activity produces a net loss, Ness may be able to deduct up to $25,000 of her share of the loss against her active and portfolio income.

Phase-Out of the $25,000 Deduction

The $25,000 annual deduction is reduced by 50% of the taxpayer's modified AGI in excess of $100,000 ($50,000 for married taxpayers who file separately). Thus, the deduction is completely phased out when modified AGI reaches $150,000 ($75,000 for married taxpayers filing separately). Modified AGI is computed the same as AGI except that it does not include the following:

1. Taxable social security and railroad retirement payments
2. Deductible contributions to individual retirement accounts (IRAs) and self-employed retirement plans
3. The deduction for one-half of self-employment taxes
4. The interest exclusion for Series EE and I savings bonds
5. Passive losses in excess of passive income

EXAMPLE 20

Rachel Phillips, a single taxpayer, earned $110,000 from her job, $15,000 of passive income from a non–real estate activity, and $20,000 of interest income. Phillips also incurred a $50,000 loss from a rental real estate activity in which she actively participates. Phillips made a $5,000 deductible IRA contribution in 2006. Under the general rule, passive losses usually can offset only passive income. Therefore, Phillips can use $15,000 of her $50,000 rental real estate loss to offset the $15,000 of the income from the non–real estate passive activity. Because Phillips is actively involved in the rental real estate activities, she may be able to deduct more than $15,000 of her loss. Phillips computes the additional deduction and passive loss carryover as follows.

Modified AGI (does not include the $5,000 IRA deduction or the $35,000 of passive losses in excess of passive income):

Wages	$110,000	
Interest income	20,000	
Passive income	15,000	
Passive losses allowed under the general rule	(15,000)	
Modified AGI		$130,000
Less AGI threshold for the phase-out		(100,000)
Amount subject to phase-out		$ 30,000
		× 50%
Amount of deduction lost due to phase-out		$ 15,000
Passive loss from rental real estate in excess of passive income ($50,000 – $15,000)		$ 35,000
Additional passive loss deduction for active participation in rental real estate ($25,000 initial deduction – $15,000 lost due to phase-out)		(10,000)
Passive loss carried forward to 2007		$ 25,000

Phillips will deduct a total of $25,000 of passive activity losses ($15,000 under the general rule and $10,000 special deduction) against passive activity income of $15,000.

SUSPENDED LOSSES

Passive activity losses not deducted in the current tax year carry forward to the next year. Passive losses that are carried forward must be allocated among the various activities that produced the loss.

Multiple Activities

When multiple passive activities exist, taxpayers must determine the suspended loss for each separate activity through an allocation process. The following formula is used.

$$\text{Total } \textbf{disallowed} \text{ loss} \times \frac{\text{Loss from separate activity}}{\text{Sum of } \textbf{all} \text{ losses}}$$

EXAMPLE 21

Dick White reports the following income and losses from his four passive activities for 2006.

Activity A	($40,000)
Activity B	30,000
Activity C	(32,000)
Activity D	(8,000)
Net passive loss	($50,000)

White allocates his net passive loss of $50,000 to activities A, C, and D (the activities producing a total of $80,000 of losses) as follows:

Activity A ($50,000 × $40,000/$80,000)	($25,000)
Activity C ($50,000 × $32,000/$80,000)	(20,000)
Activity D ($50,000 × $8,000/$80,000)	(5,000)
Total suspended losses	($50,000)

These suspended losses carry forward indefinitely as deductions associated with the activity to which each relates. Thus, the $25,000 passive loss carryover associated with Activity A is added to/netted against any passive income (loss) generated by Activity A in 2007. This net amount becomes White's passive income (loss) from Activity A for 2007. The same process is applied to Activities C and D.

DISPOSING OF A PASSIVE ACTIVITY

When taxpayers dispose of a passive activity, any suspended losses relating to that activity are deductible in full. To qualify for this treatment, taxpayers must dispose of their entire interest in the activity in a fully taxable transaction. Also, the new property owner cannot be the taxpayer's sibling (sister or brother), ancestor (parent, grandparent, etc.), or descendent (child, grandchild, etc.). Special rules apply when taxpayers dispose of a passive activity by way of gift or inheritance. These rules are beyond the scope of this book.

The gain or loss from the sale of a passive activity receives special treatment. If a loss results, the loss is either an ordinary loss or capital loss depending on the circumstances. The loss is not treated as a passive loss, so it is not limited to passive income. Chapter 11 explains the difference between ordinary and capital losses in greater detail.

EXAMPLE 22

Continuing with Example 21, if White sells Activity A in 2007, any part of the $25,000 passive loss carryover from 2006 that is not utilized in 2007 to offset passive income and gains is deducted against White's active and portfolio income.

REPORTING PASSIVE ACTIVITY LOSSES

Taxpayers with income or loss from passive activities complete Form 8582, Passive Activity Loss Limitations, to compute the amount of passive loss allowed from such activities. Taxpayers then report the passive loss allowed on the appropriate tax form or schedule. For example, taxpayers report the passive loss allowed from rental activities on Schedule E.

Form 8582

Regardless of the number or complexity of passive activities, taxpayers file only one Form 8582, Passive Activity Loss Limitations. Taxpayers prepare Form 8582 to determine whether the passive loss rules disallow any of the losses shown on those forms.

Form 8582 consists of three parts. In Part I, taxpayers report net income (line 1a), net loss (line 1b), and prior year carry forwards (line 1c) from rental real estate activities with active participation. They also report in Part I net income (line 3a), net loss (line 3b), and prior year carry forwards (line 3c) from all other passive activities. Taxpayers then combine these amounts (line 4). If net income results, taxpayers enter the net amount on the appropriate form/schedule to which the activity relates (for example, Schedule E for rental real estate). If a net loss results, then taxpayers proceed to Part II to see whether they can utilize any of the $25,000 special allowance for active participation in rental real estate activities.

In Part II, taxpayers determine the amount of net loss available for the $25,000 special allowance (line 5). They then compute their modified adjusted gross income and determine the amount of phase-out, if any, that applies (lines 6–8). In Part IV, taxpayers compute the passive income and loss reported on that year's tax return. Deductible passive losses (line 16) equal the total passive income (from lines 1a and 3a) plus the special allowance amount from Part II (line 10).

Information for Figure 9-2: Filled-In Form 8582

Derrick Smart earned $120,000 from his job, $15,000 of interest income, $10,000 from a passive activity (non–real estate), and a $20,000 loss from a rental real estate activity in which he actively participates (see accompanying Schedule E). Smart has no other income and no passive loss carryovers from prior years. Form 8582 shows that Smart has deductible passive losses of $17,500. He deducts this amount on Schedule E (line 23). Smart's passive loss carryover to 2007 is $2,500 ($20,000 – $17,500).

Other Information

1b: Activities with net loss (rental real estate activities with active participation), **$20,000.00**

3a: Activities with net income (all other passive activities), **$10,000.00**

7: Modified adjusted gross income, **$135,000.00** [$120,000 + $15,000 + $10,000 (non–real estate passive net income) – $10,000 (rental real estate passive loss to the extent of passive net income)]

FIGURE 9-2 Filled-In Form 8582

Form **8582** — Department of the Treasury, Internal Revenue Service (99)

Passive Activity Loss Limitations

▶ See separate instructions.
▶ Attach to Form 1040 or Form 1041.

OMB No. 1545-1008 — 2006 — Attachment Sequence No. 88

Name(s) shown on return: Derrick Smart — Identifying number: 421-68-5546

Part I 2006 Passive Activity Loss

Caution: *Complete Worksheets 1, 2, and 3 on page 2 before completing Part I.*

Rental Real Estate Activities With Active Participation (For the definition of active participation see **Special Allowance for Rental Real Estate Activities** on page 3 of the instructions.)

Line	Description	Box	Amount	Line	Amount
1a	Activities with net income (enter the amount from Worksheet 1, column (a))	1a			
b	Activities with net loss (enter the amount from Worksheet 1, column (b))	1b	(20,000 00)		
c	Prior years unallowed losses (enter the amount from Worksheet 1, column (c))	1c	( )		
d	Combine lines 1a, 1b, and 1c			1d	(20,000 00)

Commercial Revitalization Deductions From Rental Real Estate Activities

Line	Description	Box	Amount	Line	Amount
2a	Commercial revitalization deductions from Worksheet 2, column (a)	2a	( )		
b	Prior year unallowed commercial revitalization deductions from Worksheet 2, column (b)	2b	( )		
c	Add lines 2a and 2b			2c	( )

All Other Passive Activities

Line	Description	Box	Amount	Line	Amount
3a	Activities with net income (enter the amount from Worksheet 3, column (a))	3a	10,000 00		
b	Activities with net loss (enter the amount from Worksheet 3, column (b))	3b	( )		
c	Prior years unallowed losses (enter the amount from Worksheet 3, column (c))	3c	( )		
d	Combine lines 3a, 3b, and 3c			3d	10,000 00

4 Combine lines 1d, 2c, and 3d. If the result is net income or zero, all losses are allowed, including any prior year unallowed losses entered on line 1c, 2b, or 3c. **Do not** complete Form 8582. Report the losses on the forms and schedules normally used — **4** (10,000 00)

If line 4 is a loss and:
- Line 1d is a loss, go to Part II.
- Line 2c is a loss (and line 1d is zero or more), skip Part II and go to Part III.
- Line 3d is a loss (and lines 1d and 2c are zero or more), skip Parts II and III and go to line 15.

Caution: *If your filing status is married filing separately and you lived with your spouse at any time during the year,* **do not** *complete Part II or Part III. Instead, go to line 15.*

Part II Special Allowance for Rental Real Estate Activities With Active Participation

Note: *Enter all numbers in Part II as positive amounts. See page 8 of the instructions for an example.*

Line	Description	Box	Amount	Line	Amount
5	Enter the **smaller** of the loss on line 1d or the loss on line 4			5	10,000 00
6	Enter $150,000. If married filing separately, see page 8	6	150,000 00		
7	Enter modified adjusted gross income, but not less than zero (see page 8)	7	135,000 00		
	Note: *If line 7 is greater than or equal to line 6, skip lines 8 and 9, enter -0- on line 10. Otherwise, go to line 8.*				
8	Subtract line 7 from line 6	8	15,000 00		
9	Multiply line 8 by 50% (.5). **Do not** enter more than $25,000. If married filing separately, see page 8			9	7,500 00
10	Enter the **smaller** of line 5 or line 9. If line 2c is a loss, go to Part III. Otherwise, go to line 15.			10	7,500 00

Part III Special Allowance for Commercial Revitalization Deductions From Rental Real Estate Activities

Note: *Enter all numbers in Part III as positive amounts. See the example for Part II on page 8 of the instructions.*

11	Enter $25,000 reduced by the amount, if any, on line 10. If married filing separately, see instructions	11	
12	Enter the loss from line 4	12	
13	Reduce line 12 by the amount on line 10	13	
14	Enter the **smallest** of line 2c (treated as a positive amount), line 11, or line 13	14	

Part IV Total Losses Allowed

15	Add the income, if any, on lines 1a and 3a and enter the total	15	10,000 00
16	**Total losses allowed from all passive activities for 2006.** Add lines 10, 14, and 15. See pages 10 and 11 of the instructions to find out how to report the losses on your tax return	16	17,500 00

For Paperwork Reduction Act Notice, see page 12 of the instructions. Cat. No. 63704F Form **8582** (2006)

FIGURE 9-2 Schedule E to Accompany Filled-In Form 8582

SCHEDULE E (Form 1040)
Department of the Treasury Internal Revenue Service (99)

Supplemental Income and Loss
(From rental real estate, royalties, partnerships, S corporations, estates, trusts, REMICs, etc.)
► Attach to Form 1040, 1040NR, or Form 1041. ► See Instructions for Schedule E (Form 1040).

OMB No. 1545-0074
2006
Attachment Sequence No. 13

Name(s) shown on return: Derrick Smart
Your social security number: 421 68 5546

Part I Income or Loss From Rental Real Estate and Royalties **Note.** If you are in the business of renting personal property, use **Schedule C** or **C-EZ** (see page E-3). Report farm rental income or loss from **Form 4835** on page 2, line 40.

1 List the type and location of each **rental real estate property:**
A Condominium, 1802 Eighth Street #207 Danville, IL 60529
B
C

2 For each rental real estate property listed on line 1, did you or your family use it during the tax year for personal purposes for more than the greater of:
• 14 days **or**
• 10% of the total days rented at fair rental value?
(See page E-3.)

	Yes	No
A		X
B		
C		

Income:	Line	Properties A	B	C	Totals (Add columns A, B, and C.)
3 Rents received	3	7,800 00			3 7,800 00
4 Royalties received	4				4
Expenses:					
5 Advertising	5				
6 Auto and travel (see page E-4).	6				
7 Cleaning and maintenance	7	1,600 00			
8 Commissions	8				
9 Insurance	9	140 00			
10 Legal and other professional fees	10				
11 Management fees	11				
12 Mortgage interest paid to banks, etc. (see page E-4)	12	11,700 00			12 11,700 00
13 Other interest	13				
14 Repairs	14	3,100 00			
15 Supplies	15				
16 Taxes	16	2,950 00			
17 Utilities	17	1,620 00			
18 Other (list) ► Condo Association Fees	18	1,880 00			
19 Add lines 5 through 18	19	22,990 00			19 22,990 00
20 Depreciation expense or depletion (see page E-4)	20	4,810 00			20 4,810 00
21 Total expenses. Add lines 19 and 20	21	27,800 00			
22 Income or (loss) from rental real estate or royalty properties. Subtract line 21 from line 3 (rents) or line 4 (royalties). If the result is a (loss), see page E-5 to find out if you must file **Form 6198**	22	(20,000 00)			
23 Deductible rental real estate loss. **Caution.** Your rental real estate loss on line 22 may be limited. See page E-5 to find out if you must file **Form 8582.** Real estate professionals must complete line 43 on page 2	23	(17,500 00)	( )	( )	

24 **Income.** Add positive amounts shown on line 22. **Do not** include any losses 24

25 **Losses.** Add royalty losses from line 22 and rental real estate losses from line 23. Enter total losses here . . . 25 (17,500 00)

26 **Total rental real estate and royalty income or (loss).** Combine lines 24 and 25. Enter the result here. If Parts II, III, IV, and line 40 on page 2 do not apply to you, also enter this amount on Form 1040, line 17, or Form 1040NR, line 18. Otherwise, include this amount in the total on line 41 on page 2 . . . 26 (17,500 00)

For Paperwork Reduction Act Notice, see page E-7 of the instructions. Cat. No. 11344L **Schedule E (Form 1040) 2006**

Name ______________________________

Section ______________ Date ___________

QUESTIONS AND PROBLEMS

1. **Rental Income.** State the amount of rental income that must be reported on Schedule E for 2006 by each of the following taxpayers.

Taxpayer	*Description*	*Amount*
A	On November 30, 2006, the taxpayer receives $1,000 as a security deposit, $1,000 for the December rent, and an advance payment of $5,000 for an additional five months' of rent.	$ 6,000
B	The taxpayer normally receives rent of $300 per month on the first of each month. In 2006, the tenant made $600 of improvements in lieu of two months' rent.	$ 3,600
C	Rent of $1,200 is received when the taxpayer rents a personal residence to friends for 12 days during the Mardi Gras festivities.	$ 0

2. **Rental Expenses.** State the maximum amount of rental expenses attributable to the property that can be claimed by each of the following taxpayers.

Taxpayer	*Description*	*Amount*
A	A dwelling unit is rented to a friend for $100 per month for two months and to an unrelated party for $275 per month for three months. Fair rental value is $275 per month.	$ 1,025
B	A personal residence rented for 12 days during 2006 for a total of $300.	$ 0

3. **Net Rental Income.** Derek Quinn owns a two-family home. He rents out the first floor and resides on the second floor. Each floor is of equal size. He incurred the following expenses attributable to the building for the year.

	Expenses For		
	Entire Building	*First Floor*	*Second Floor*
Depreciation	$4,000		
Real estate taxes	2,000		
Mortgage interest	1,600		
Utilities	1,200		
Repairs		$500	
Painting			$400

a. What portion of the expenses can Quinn deduct on Schedule E of Form 1040?

b. What portion of the expenses can Quinn take as itemized deductions on Schedule A of Form 1040?

4. **Net Rental Income.** Sandee Scott, a cash basis taxpayer, owns a house with two identical apartments. Scott resides in one apartment and rents out the other. The tenant made timely monthly rental payments of $500 for the months of January through November 2006. Rents for December 2006 and January 2007 were paid by the tenant on January 5, 2007. Scott incurred the following expenses relating to the building in 2006.

Utilities	$3,600
Depreciation of building	3,000
Maintenance and repairs (rental apartment)	400
Insurance on building	600

What amount should Scott report as net rental income for 2006?

5. **Vacation Homes.** The Danielle Haywood owns a vacation home that she personally uses 13 days during the year. The rest of the year the home was used by the following occupants. Fair rental value is $100 a night.

Occupant	*Number of Days*
Haywood's sorority sister, who paid no rent	5
Haywood's brother, who paid fair rental	21
Couple who won a charity auction	7
Unrelated persons, who paid rent of $5,000	50

Haywood's expenses related to the vacation home were as follows:

Mortgage interest	$ 6,700
Real estate taxes	3,300
Utilities and repairs	2,540
Depreciation	6,650
	$19,190

a. Compute the number of personal vs. total days the property was used during the year.

b. Compute Haywood's net rental income and any expenses that she must carryover to 2007.

6. **Vacation Homes.** Henry Schuller owns a fishing cabin in Wisconsin. Schuller offered the cabin for rent from June 1 through September 30, except for 16 days in August when his family used it. Schuller was unable to rent the cabin for two weeks (14 days) during the remaining rental period. At all other times, the cabin was rented.

   a. Will Schuller's cabin be treated as a residence? Explain.

   b. For purposes of allocating expenses, how many days of rental use and personal use does Schuller have?

7. **Vacation Homes.**

   a. What is the tax advantage to having a vacation home treated as a residence?

   b. What is the disadvantage to having a vacation home considered a residence?

8. **Vacation Homes.** During the year, Barry Barone (SSN 839-62-1444) rents his vacation home for 90 days and spends 60 days there. The vacation home is a townhome located at 610 Oak St. in Boulder, Colorado. Gross rental income from the property totals $6,000. Barone's expenses for the property are shown below.

Mortgage interest	$3,000
Real estate taxes	1,500
Utilities	800
Maintenance	900
Depreciation	4,000

Complete Barone's Schedule E on the next page.

(Use for Problem 8.)

SCHEDULE E (Form 1040)

Department of the Treasury Internal Revenue Service (99)

Supplemental Income and Loss

(From rental real estate, royalties, partnerships, S corporations, estates, trusts, REMICs, etc.)

▶ Attach to Form 1040, 1040NR, or Form 1041. ▶ See Instructions for Schedule E (Form 1040).

OMB No. 1545-0074

2006

Attachment Sequence No. **13**

Name(s) shown on return | **Your social security number**

Part I **Income or Loss From Rental Real Estate and Royalties** **Note.** If you are in the business of renting personal property, use **Schedule C** or **C-EZ** (see page E-3). Report farm rental income or loss from **Form 4835** on page 2, line 40.

1	List the type and location of each **rental real estate property:**	2 For each rental real estate property listed on line 1, did you or your family use it during the tax year for personal purposes for more than the greater of: • 14 days **or** • 10% of the total days rented at fair rental value? (See page E-3.)		**Yes**	**No**
A			A		
B			B		
C			C		

Income:		Properties A	Properties B	Properties C		Totals (Add columns A, B, and C.)
3 Rents received	3				3	
4 Royalties received	4				4	
Expenses:						
5 Advertising	5					
6 Auto and travel (see page E-4)	6					
7 Cleaning and maintenance	7					
8 Commissions	8					
9 Insurance	9					
10 Legal and other professional fees	10					
11 Management fees	11					
12 Mortgage interest paid to banks, etc. (see page E-4)	12				12	
13 Other interest	13					
14 Repairs	14					
15 Supplies	15					
16 Taxes	16					
17 Utilities	17					
18 Other (list) ▶	18					
19 Add lines 5 through 18	19				19	
20 Depreciation expense or depletion (see page E-4)	20				20	
21 Total expenses. Add lines 19 and 20	21					
22 Income or (loss) from rental real estate or royalty properties. Subtract line 21 from line 3 (rents) or line 4 (royalties). If the result is a (loss), see page E-5 to find out if you must file **Form 6198**	22					
23 Deductible rental real estate loss. **Caution.** Your rental real estate loss on line 22 may be limited. See page E-5 to find out if you must file **Form 8582.** Real estate professionals must complete line 43 on page 2	23	( )	( )	( )		
24 **Income.** Add positive amounts shown on line 22. **Do not** include any losses					24	
25 **Losses.** Add royalty losses from line 22 and rental real estate losses from line 23. Enter total losses here					25	( )
26 **Total rental real estate and royalty income or (loss).** Combine lines 24 and 25. Enter the result here. If Parts II, III, IV, and line 40 on page 2 do not apply to you, also enter this amount on Form 1040, line 17, or Form 1040NR, line 18. Otherwise, include this amount in the total on line 41 on page 2					26	

For Paperwork Reduction Act Notice, see page E-7 of the instructions. Cat. No. 11344L **Schedule E (Form 1040) 2006**

9. At-risk.

a. What is the significance of the at-risk rules?

b. What activities are subject to the at-risk loss limitations?

10. Passive Activities.

a. What types of trade or business activities are considered passive activities?

b. Distinguish between material participation and active participation in rental activities. Explain the significance of this difference.

c. Historically, dividend income and interest income have been treated as passive income. How are these categories of income treated in relation to the passive loss limitations?

11. Material vs. Active Participation. For each of the following independent situations, discuss whether (**A**) the taxpayer materially participates in the activity or (**B**) the activity is a passive activity. In activities involving rental real estate, discuss whether the special deduction for activity participation would apply.

a. The taxpayer works 900 hours in a nonrental real estate activity and 1,000 hours as an employee (not involved in real property).

b. The taxpayer works 650 hours in a rental real estate activity and 500 hours as an employee (not involved in real property).

c. The taxpayer works in an activity (not involving real property) 150 hours during the year. The taxpayer is retired, so this is the only activity he works for during the year.

d. A couple both participate in an activity (not involving real property). The husband works 300 hours; the wife works 250 hours. Both spouses work full-time for firms that have nothing to do with rental real estate.

e. A couple both participate in a rental real estate activity. The husband works 400 hours; the wife works 500 hours. Both spouses also work full-time as employees for companies that have nothing to do with rental real estate.

f. Same as in Part e. except that the wife's hours are 800 instead of 500.

12. Passive Activities. A taxpayer owned four passive activities. Net income (loss) for each activity is shown below.

Passive Activity	*Gross Income*	*Deductions*	*Net Income (or Loss)*
A	$12,000	$ 8,000	$ 4,000
B	20,000	32,000	(12,000)
C	3,000	6,000	(3,000)
D	14,000	12,000	2,000

a. What is the amount of passive loss that can offset passive income in the current year?

b. What is the amount of passive loss that can be carried forward for each activity?

13. Passive Activities. Gary Bartlett owns three passive activities. Net income (loss) for each activity is shown below.

Passive Activity	*Net Income (or Loss)*
1	$ 26,000
2	(13,500)
3	(18,000)

a. Compute the amount of passive loss that can offset passive income in the current year.

b. Determine the amount of passive loss that can be carried forward to each activity.

14. Rental Real Estate. Mark and Martha Matthews report $130,000 of AGI before considering a $22,000 loss from rental real estate activities in which they actively participate. The Matthewses own more than 10% of the activity. What amount of the loss can the Matthewses deduct on their joint return?

15. Rental Real Estate. Bobby Southworth actively participates in three different rental real estate activities. His ownership in each activity exceeds 10%. Southworth's income and losses from these activities are shown below.

Activity	*Income (or Loss)*
X	($10,000)
Y	(30,000)
Z	9,000

Southworth has AGI of $80,000 before consideration of the rental real estate activities. Calculate his loss allowed and any suspended losses.

a. Loss allowed ____________________

b. Suspended loss ____________________

16. Passive Activities. Bob Jefferson owns three passive activities, none of which involve rental real estate. As of January 1, 2006, the suspended losses on these activities included the following:

Activity	*Suspended Losses*
X	($20,000)
Y	(30,000)
Z	0

In 2006 his passive activities generated the following income and losses during the year:

Activity	*Income (or Loss)*
X	$ 10,000
Y	(10,000)
Z	20,000

How will Jefferson report the results of his activities for 2006?

17. Rental Real Estate, Active Participation. In 2002, Tyler Tomey (548-55-9234) paid $135,000 for a condominium that he used as rental property. Also in 2002, he spent $18,500 furnishing the condo. During 2006, Tomey received $15,000 in rental income and paid the following expenses:

Association dues	$ 2,800
Insurance	350
Mortgage interest	7,460
Real estate taxes	1,400
Repairs	760
Utilities	360

The property is located at 5505 West End Road, #5, Farmington, IN 46883. Tomey actively participates in the rental of the condominium. His AGI before considering the above income and expenses is $121,400. He depreciates the condominium and its furnishings using MACRS. The half-year converntion applies to the furnishings. Prepare Schedule E and Form 8582 for Tomey using the forms provided on the following pages.

(Use for Problem 17.)

SCHEDULE E (Form 1040)

Department of the Treasury
Internal Revenue Service (99)

Supplemental Income and Loss

(From rental real estate, royalties, partnerships, S corporations, estates, trusts, REMICs, etc.)

▶ Attach to Form 1040, 1040NR, or Form 1041. ▶ See Instructions for Schedule E (Form 1040).

OMB No. 1545-0074

2006

Attachment Sequence No. 13

Name(s) shown on return | Your social security number

Part I Income or Loss From Rental Real Estate and Royalties **Note.** If you are in the business of renting personal property, use **Schedule C** or **C-EZ** (see page E-3). Report farm rental income or loss from **Form 4835** on page 2, line 40.

1	List the type and location of each **rental real estate property:**	2 For each rental real estate property listed on line 1, did you or your family use it during the tax year for personal purposes for more than the greater of: • 14 days **or** • 10% of the total days rented at fair rental value? (See page E-3.)		Yes	No
A			A		
B			B		
C			C		

Income:		Properties A	Properties B	Properties C	Totals (Add columns A, B, and C.)	
3 Rents received	3				3	
4 Royalties received	4				4	
Expenses:						
5 Advertising	5					
6 Auto and travel (see page E-4).	6					
7 Cleaning and maintenance	7					
8 Commissions	8					
9 Insurance	9					
10 Legal and other professional fees	10					
11 Management fees	11					
12 Mortgage interest paid to banks, etc. (see page E-4)	12				12	
13 Other interest	13					
14 Repairs	14					
15 Supplies	15					
16 Taxes	16					
17 Utilities	17					
18 Other (list) ▶	18					
19 Add lines 5 through 18	19				19	
20 Depreciation expense or depletion (see page E-4)	20				20	
21 Total expenses. Add lines 19 and 20	21					
22 Income or (loss) from rental real estate or royalty properties. Subtract line 21 from line 3 (rents) or line 4 (royalties). If the result is a (loss), see page E-5 to find out if you must file **Form 6198**	22					
23 Deductible rental real estate loss. **Caution.** Your rental real estate loss on line 22 may be limited. See page E-5 to find out if you must file **Form 8582.** Real estate professionals must complete line 43 on page 2	23	( )	( )	( )		
24 **Income.** Add positive amounts shown on line 22. **Do not** include any losses					24	
25 **Losses.** Add royalty losses from line 22 and rental real estate losses from line 23. Enter total losses here					25	( )
26 **Total rental real estate and royalty income or (loss).** Combine lines 24 and 25. Enter the result here. If Parts II, III, IV, and line 40 on page 2 do not apply to you, also enter this amount on Form 1040, line 17, or Form 1040NR, line 18. Otherwise, include this amount in the total on line 41 on page 2					26	

For Paperwork Reduction Act Notice, see page E-7 of the instructions. Cat. No. 11344L **Schedule E (Form 1040) 2006**

(Use for Problem 17.)

Form **8582**

Department of the Treasury
Internal Revenue Service (99)

Passive Activity Loss Limitations

▶ See separate instructions.
▶ Attach to Form 1040 or Form 1041.

OMB No. 1545-1008

2006

Attachment Sequence No. **88**

Name(s) shown on return | **Identifying number**

Part I **2006 Passive Activity Loss**

Caution: *Complete Worksheets 1, 2, and 3 on page 2 before completing Part I.*

Rental Real Estate Activities With Active Participation (For the definition of active participation see **Special Allowance for Rental Real Estate Activities** on page 3 of the instructions.)

1a Activities with net income (enter the amount from Worksheet 1, column (a))	1a		
b Activities with net loss (enter the amount from Worksheet 1, column (b))	1b	( )	
c Prior years unallowed losses (enter the amount from Worksheet 1, column (c))	1c	( )	
d Combine lines 1a, 1b, and 1c			1d

Commercial Revitalization Deductions From Rental Real Estate Activities

2a Commercial revitalization deductions from Worksheet 2, column (a)	2a	( )	
b Prior year unallowed commercial revitalization deductions from Worksheet 2, column (b)	2b	( )	
c Add lines 2a and 2b			2c ( )

All Other Passive Activities

3a Activities with net income (enter the amount from Worksheet 3, column (a))	3a		
b Activities with net loss (enter the amount from Worksheet 3, column (b))	3b	( )	
c Prior years unallowed losses (enter the amount from Worksheet 3, column (c))	3c	( )	
d Combine lines 3a, 3b, and 3c			3d

4 Combine lines 1d, 2c, and 3d. If the result is net income or zero, all losses are allowed, including any prior year unallowed losses entered on line 1c, 2b, or 3c. **Do not** complete Form 8582. Report the losses on the forms and schedules normally used . . . **4**

If line 4 is a loss and:
- Line 1d is a loss, go to Part II.
- Line 2c is a loss (and line 1d is zero or more), skip Part II and go to Part III.
- Line 3d is a loss (and lines 1d and 2c are zero or more), skip Parts II and III and go to line 15.

Caution: *If your filing status is married filing separately and you lived with your spouse at any time during the year,* **do not** *complete Part II or Part III. Instead, go to line 15.*

Part II **Special Allowance for Rental Real Estate Activities With Active Participation**

Note: *Enter all numbers in Part II as positive amounts. See page 8 of the instructions for an example.*

5 Enter the **smaller** of the loss on line 1d or the loss on line 4			5
6 Enter $150,000. If married filing separately, see page 8	6		
7 Enter modified adjusted gross income, but not less than zero (see page 8)	7		
Note: *If line 7 is greater than or equal to line 6, skip lines 8 and 9, enter -0- on line 10. Otherwise, go to line 8.*			
8 Subtract line 7 from line 6	8		
9 Multiply line 8 by 50% (.5). **Do not** enter more than $25,000. If married filing separately, see page 8			9
10 Enter the **smaller** of line 5 or line 9			10

If line 2c is a loss, go to Part III. Otherwise, go to line 15.

Part III **Special Allowance for Commercial Revitalization Deductions From Rental Real Estate Activities**

Note: *Enter all numbers in Part III as positive amounts. See the example for Part II on page 8 of the instructions.*

11 Enter $25,000 reduced by the amount, if any, on line 10. If married filing separately, see instructions	11
12 Enter the loss from line 4	12
13 Reduce line 12 by the amount on line 10	13
14 Enter the **smallest** of line 2c (treated as a positive amount), line 11, or line 13	14

Part IV **Total Losses Allowed**

15 Add the income, if any, on lines 1a and 3a and enter the total	15
16 **Total losses allowed from all passive activities for 2006.** Add lines 10, 14, and 15. See pages 10 and 11 of the instructions to find out how to report the losses on your tax return	16

For Paperwork Reduction Act Notice, see page 12 of the instructions. Cat. No. 63704F Form **8582** (2006)

18. Rental Real Estate, Active Participation. In 1990, Jeremy L. Schultz (SSN 678-88-5244) paid $90,000 for a townhouse purchased as an investment. The townhouse is located at 812 E. Locust, Springfield, MO. During 2006, Schultz received $9,600 in rental income from the tenants and paid the following expenses:

Association dues	$ 400
Insurance	130
Mortgage interest	6,200
Real estate taxes	1,100
Repairs	320
Utilities	440

Schultz actively participates in the rental of the townhome. His AGI before considering the income and expenses from the rental property is $140,000. He depreciates the townhouse using MACRS (straight-line over 27.5 years). Prepare Schedule E and Form 8582 using the forms provided on the following pages.

19. Internet Problem: Researching Publication 925.

The chapter discussed two ways to meet the material participation test: (1) participate in the activity for more than 500 hours during the year, and (2) participate in the activity for more than 100 hours during the year and have that participation be at least as much as the participation by all other individuals, including employees. There are several other ways in which to meet the material participation test.

Go to the IRS Web site. Locate Publication 925 and find the appropriate page that lists all the various ways to meet the material participation test. Print out a copy of the page where you found your answer. Underline or highlight the pertinent information.

See Appendix A for instructions on use of the IRS Web site.

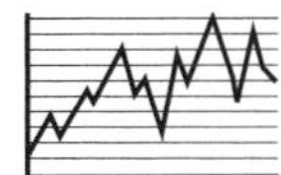

20. Business Entity Problem: This problem is designed for those using the "business entity" approach. The solution may require information from Chapters 14 and 15.

The Hampton-Lewis Partnership owns an apartment building. Gross income from the apartments was $200,000. Total deductions were $260,000. The two partners share profits and losses equally.

a. How will the partnership report the resulting $60,000 loss?

b. If Hampton-Lewis was an S corporation (with two shareholders who each own 50% of the stock), how would the loss be reported?

c. If Hampton-Lewis was a regular C corporation (with two shareholders who each own 50% of the stock), how would the loss be reported?

(Use for Problem 18.)

SCHEDULE E (Form 1040)

Department of the Treasury Internal Revenue Service (99)

Supplemental Income and Loss

(From rental real estate, royalties, partnerships, S corporations, estates, trusts, REMICs, etc.)

▶ Attach to Form 1040, 1040NR, or Form 1041. ▶ See Instructions for Schedule E (Form 1040).

OMB No. 1545-0074

2006

Attachment Sequence No. 13

Name(s) shown on return | Your social security number

Part I Income or Loss From Rental Real Estate and Royalties **Note.** If you are in the business of renting personal property, use **Schedule C** or **C-EZ** (see page E-3). Report farm rental income or loss from **Form 4835** on page 2, line 40.

1	List the type and location of each **rental real estate property:**	2 For each rental real estate property listed on line 1, did you or your family use it during the tax year for personal purposes for more than the greater of: • 14 days **or** • 10% of the total days rented at fair rental value? (See page E-3.)		Yes	No
A			A		
B			B		
C			C		

		Properties A	Properties B	Properties C		Totals (Add columns A, B, and C.)
Income:						
3 Rents received	3				3	
4 Royalties received	4				4	
Expenses:						
5 Advertising	5					
6 Auto and travel (see page E-4).	6					
7 Cleaning and maintenance	7					
8 Commissions	8					
9 Insurance	9					
10 Legal and other professional fees	10					
11 Management fees	11					
12 Mortgage interest paid to banks, etc. (see page E-4)	12				12	
13 Other interest	13					
14 Repairs	14					
15 Supplies	15					
16 Taxes	16					
17 Utilities	17					
18 Other (list) ▶	18					
19 Add lines 5 through 18	19				19	
20 Depreciation expense or depletion (see page E-4)	20				20	
21 Total expenses. Add lines 19 and 20	21					
22 Income or (loss) from rental real estate or royalty properties. Subtract line 21 from line 3 (rents) or line 4 (royalties). If the result is a (loss), see page E-5 to find out if you must file **Form 6198**	22					
23 Deductible rental real estate loss. **Caution.** Your rental real estate loss on line 22 may be limited. See page E-5 to find out if you must file **Form 8582.** Real estate professionals must complete line 43 on page 2	23	( )	( )	( )		
24 **Income.** Add positive amounts shown on line 22. **Do not** include any losses					24	
25 **Losses.** Add royalty losses from line 22 and rental real estate losses from line 23. Enter total losses here					25	( )
26 **Total rental real estate and royalty income or (loss).** Combine lines 24 and 25. Enter the result here. If Parts II, III, IV, and line 40 on page 2 do not apply to you, also enter this amount on Form 1040, line 17, or Form 1040NR, line 18. Otherwise, include this amount in the total on line 41 on page 2					26	

For Paperwork Reduction Act Notice, see page E-7 of the instructions. Cat. No. 11344L **Schedule E (Form 1040) 2006**

(Use for Problem 18.)

Form **8582**

Department of the Treasury
Internal Revenue Service (99)

Passive Activity Loss Limitations

▶ See separate instructions.
▶ Attach to Form 1040 or Form 1041.

OMB No. 1545-1008
2006
Attachment Sequence No. 88

Name(s) shown on return | Identifying number

Part I **2006 Passive Activity Loss**
Caution: *Complete Worksheets 1, 2, and 3 on page 2 before completing Part I.*

Rental Real Estate Activities With Active Participation (For the definition of active participation see **Special Allowance for Rental Real Estate Activities** on page 3 of the instructions.)

1a Activities with net income (enter the amount from Worksheet 1, column (a))	1a		
b Activities with net loss (enter the amount from Worksheet 1, column (b))	1b	( )	
c Prior years unallowed losses (enter the amount from Worksheet 1, column (c))	1c	( )	
d Combine lines 1a, 1b, and 1c			1d

Commercial Revitalization Deductions From Rental Real Estate Activities

2a Commercial revitalization deductions from Worksheet 2, column (a)	2a	( )	
b Prior year unallowed commercial revitalization deductions from Worksheet 2, column (b)	2b	( )	
c Add lines 2a and 2b			2c ( )

All Other Passive Activities

3a Activities with net income (enter the amount from Worksheet 3, column (a))	3a		
b Activities with net loss (enter the amount from Worksheet 3, column (b))	3b	( )	
c Prior years unallowed losses (enter the amount from Worksheet 3, column (c))	3c	( )	
d Combine lines 3a, 3b, and 3c			3d

4 Combine lines 1d, 2c, and 3d. If the result is net income or zero, all losses are allowed, including any prior year unallowed losses entered on line 1c, 2b, or 3c. **Do not** complete Form 8582. Report the losses on the forms and schedules normally used . . . **4**

If line 4 is a loss and:
- Line 1d is a loss, go to Part II.
- Line 2c is a loss (and line 1d is zero or more), skip Part II and go to Part III.
- Line 3d is a loss (and lines 1d and 2c are zero or more), skip Parts II and III and go to line 15.

Caution: *If your filing status is married filing separately and you lived with your spouse at any time during the year, **do not** complete Part II or Part III. Instead, go to line 15.*

Part II **Special Allowance for Rental Real Estate Activities With Active Participation**
Note: *Enter all numbers in Part II as positive amounts. See page 8 of the instructions for an example.*

5 Enter the **smaller** of the loss on line 1d or the loss on line 4			5
6 Enter $150,000. If married filing separately, see page 8	6		
7 Enter modified adjusted gross income, but not less than zero (see page 8)	7		
Note: *If line 7 is greater than or equal to line 6, skip lines 8 and 9, enter -0- on line 10. Otherwise, go to line 8.*			
8 Subtract line 7 from line 6	8		
9 Multiply line 8 by 50% (.5). **Do not** enter more than $25,000. If married filing separately, see page 8			9
10 Enter the **smaller** of line 5 or line 9			10

If line 2c is a loss, go to Part III. Otherwise, go to line 15.

Part III **Special Allowance for Commercial Revitalization Deductions From Rental Real Estate Activities**
Note: *Enter all numbers in Part III as positive amounts. See the example for Part II on page 8 of the instructions.*

11 Enter $25,000 reduced by the amount, if any, on line 10. If married filing separately, see instructions	11
12 Enter the loss from line 4	12
13 Reduce line 12 by the amount on line 10	13
14 Enter the **smallest** of line 2c (treated as a positive amount), line 11, or line 13	14

Part IV **Total Losses Allowed**

15 Add the income, if any, on lines 1a and 3a and enter the total	15
16 **Total losses allowed from all passive activities for 2006.** Add lines 10, 14, and 15. See pages 10 and 11 of the instructions to find out how to report the losses on your tax return	16

For Paperwork Reduction Act Notice, see page 12 of the instructions. Cat. No. 63704F Form **8582** (2006)

COMPREHENSIVE PROBLEM

21. On January 2, 1995, Janis R. Jetson (SSN 344-46-5768), a cash basis taxpayer, purchased a two-unit apartment building at 1626 Flat Street, Detroit, Michigan 48270-8224. The costs of the land and building were $10,000 and $41,250, respectively. Jetson depreciates the building using the straight-line method over 27.5 years. Both apartments are the same size, with one on the ground floor and the other upstairs. Jetson has lived in the upstairs apartment since she acquired the building. The tenant in the ground-floor apartment at the time the building was purchased has continued to rent from Jetson. The tenant pays $350 a month in rent. On June 30 the tenant moved out. The apartment was vacant until August 1, even though Jetson advertised and attempted to rent it. On August 1, a new tenant moved in, paying rent of $400 per month. Rent is due on the first day of the month. Information on the apartment follows:

Revenue	
Rent from the first tenant (6 months @ $350)	$2,100
Rent from the second tenant (5 months @ $400)	2,000
Total revenue	$4,100
Expenses	
Entire house:	
Real estate taxes	$1,700
Janitor and yard work	160
Electricity and water	440
Repairs	300
Heat (gas)	800
Interest on mortgage	1,100
Insurance	376
Expenses other than depreciation	$4,876
Ground-floor apartment:	
Advertising	100
Painting and papering	420
Repairs	70
	$ 590
Upstairs apartment:	
Repairs	$ 90
Cleaning and maintenance	480
	$ 570

In addition to the rental property, Jetson works as an administrative assistant and earned $17,600 in wages. From this amount, $1,080 of federal income tax was withheld. Jetson also earned $147 in interest from Bank of America. Jetson is single and has no dependents. She does not want to contribute $3 to the presidential campaign fund.

Prepare Form 1040 and Schedule E, Supplemental Income and Loss, on the pages that follow. She claims the standard credit for federal telephone excise tax paid.

(Use for Problem 21).

Form **1040** Department of the Treasury—Internal Revenue Service
U.S. Individual Income Tax Return 2006 (99) IRS Use Only—Do not write or staple in this space.

For the year Jan. 1–Dec. 31, 2006, or other tax year beginning , 2006, ending , 20 OMB No. 1545-0074

Label (See instructions on page 16.) **Use the IRS label.** Otherwise, please print or type. LABEL HERE

Your first name and initial	Last name	**Your social security number**
If a joint return, spouse's first name and initial	Last name	**Spouse's social security number**
Home address (number and street). If you have a P.O. box, see page 16.	Apt. no.	▲ You **must** enter your SSN(s) above. ▲
City, town or post office, state, and ZIP code. If you have a foreign address, see page 16.		Checking a box below will not change your tax or refund.

Presidential Election Campaign ▶ Check here if you, or your spouse if filing jointly, want $3 to go to this fund (see page 16) ▶ ☐ **You** ☐ **Spouse**

Filing Status

Check only one box.

1 ☐ Single
2 ☐ Married filing jointly (even if only one had income)
3 ☐ Married filing separately. Enter spouse's SSN above and full name here. ▶
4 ☐ Head of household (with qualifying person). (See page 17.) If the qualifying person is a child but not your dependent, enter this child's name here. ▶
5 ☐ Qualifying widow(er) with dependent child (see page 17)

Exemptions

6a ☐ **Yourself.** If someone can claim you as a dependent, **do not** check box 6a
b ☐ **Spouse**

Boxes checked on 6a and 6b ____

c **Dependents:**

(1) First name Last name	(2) Dependent's social security number	(3) Dependent's relationship to you	(4) ✓ if qualifying child for child tax credit (see page 19)
			☐
			☐
			☐
			☐

If more than four dependents, see page 19.

No. of children on 6c who:
- **lived with you** ____
- **did not live with you due to divorce or separation (see page 20)** ____

Dependents on 6c not entered above ____

d Total number of exemptions claimed

Add numbers on lines above ▶ ☐

Income

Attach Form(s) W-2 here. Also attach Forms W-2G and 1099-R if tax was withheld.

If you did not get a W-2, see page 22.

Enclose, but do not attach, any payment. Also, please use **Form 1040-V.**

7	Wages, salaries, tips, etc. Attach Form(s) W-2	7	
8a	**Taxable** interest. Attach Schedule B if required	8a	
b	**Tax-exempt** interest. **Do not** include on line 8a — 8b		
9a	Ordinary dividends. Attach Schedule B if required	9a	
b	Qualified dividends (see page 23) — 9b		
10	Taxable refunds, credits, or offsets of state and local income taxes (see page 23)	10	
11	Alimony received	11	
12	Business income or (loss). Attach Schedule C or C-EZ	12	
13	Capital gain or (loss). Attach Schedule D if required. If not required, check here ▶ ☐	13	
14	Other gains or (losses). Attach Form 4797	14	
15a	IRA distributions — 15a — b Taxable amount (see page 25)	15b	
16a	Pensions and annuities — 16a — b Taxable amount (see page 25)	16b	
17	Rental real estate, royalties, partnerships, S corporations, trusts, etc. Attach Schedule E	17	
18	Farm income or (loss). Attach Schedule F	18	
19	Unemployment compensation	19	
20a	Social security benefits — 20a — b Taxable amount (see page 27)	20b	
21	Other income. List type and amount (see page 29)	21	
22	Add the amounts in the far right column for lines 7 through 21. This is your **total income** ▶	22	

Adjusted Gross Income

23	Archer MSA deduction. Attach Form 8853	23	
24	Certain business expenses of reservists, performing artists, and fee-basis government officials. Attach Form 2106 or 2106-EZ	24	
25	Health savings account deduction. Attach Form 8889	25	
26	Moving expenses. Attach Form 3903	26	
27	One-half of self-employment tax. Attach Schedule SE	27	
28	Self-employed SEP, SIMPLE, and qualified plans	28	
29	Self-employed health insurance deduction (see page 30)	29	
30	Penalty on early withdrawal of savings	30	
31a	Alimony paid **b** Recipient's SSN ▶	31a	
32	IRA deduction (see page 31)	32	
33	Student loan interest deduction (see page 33)	33	
34	Jury duty pay you gave to your employer	34	
35	Domestic production activities deduction. Attach Form 8903	35	
36	Add lines 23 through 31a and 32 through 35	36	
37	Subtract line 36 from line 22. This is your **adjusted gross income** ▶	37	

For Disclosure, Privacy Act, and Paperwork Reduction Act Notice, see page 78. Cat. No. 11320B Form **1040** (2006)

(Use for Problem 21).

Form 1040 (2006) Page **2**

Tax and Credits	38	Amount from line 37 (adjusted gross income)	38
	39a	Check if: ☐ **You** were born before January 2, 1942, ☐ Blind. ☐ **Spouse** was born before January 2, 1942, ☐ Blind. **Total boxes checked** ▶ 39a	
Standard Deduction for— • People who checked any box on line 39a or 39b **or** who can be claimed as a dependent, see page 36. • All others: Single or Married filing separately, $5,150 Married filing jointly or Qualifying widow(er), $10,300 Head of household, $7,550	b	If your spouse itemizes on a separate return or you were a dual-status alien, see page 35 and check here ▶39b ☐	
	40	**Itemized deductions** (from Schedule A) **or** your **standard deduction** (see left margin)	40
	41	Subtract line 40 from line 38	41
	42	If line 38 is over $112,875, or you provided housing to a person displaced by Hurricane Katrina, see page 37. Otherwise, multiply $3,300 by the total number of exemptions claimed on line 6d	42
	43	**Taxable income.** Subtract line 42 from line 41. If line 42 is more than line 41, enter -0-	43
	44	**Tax** (see page 37). Check if any tax is from: **a** ☐ Form(s) 8814 **b** ☐ Form 4972	44
	45	**Alternative minimum tax** (see page 39). Attach Form 6251	45
	46	Add lines 44 and 45 ▶	46
	47	Foreign tax credit. Attach Form 1116 if required — 47	
	48	Credit for child and dependent care expenses. Attach Form 2441 — 48	
	49	Credit for the elderly or the disabled. Attach Schedule R — 49	
	50	Education credits. Attach Form 8863 — 50	
	51	Retirement savings contributions credit. Attach Form 8880 — 51	
	52	Residential energy credits. Attach Form 5695 — 52	
	53	Child tax credit (see page XX). Attach Form 8901 if required — 53	
	54	Credits from: **a** ☐ Form 8396 **b** ☐ Form 8839 **c** ☐ Form 8859 — 54	
	55	Other credits: **a** ☐ Form 3800 **b** ☐ Form 8801 **c** ☐ Form_____ — 55	
	56	Add lines 47 through 55. These are your **total credits**	56
	57	Subtract line 56 from line 46. If line 56 is more than line 46, enter -0- ▶	57
Other Taxes	58	Self-employment tax. Attach Schedule SE	58
	59	Social security and Medicare tax on tip income not reported to employer. Attach Form 4137	59
	60	Additional tax on IRAs, other qualified retirement plans, etc. Attach Form 5329 if required	60
	61	Advance earned income credit payments from Form(s) W-2, box 9	61
	62	Household employment taxes. Attach Schedule H	62
	63	Add lines 57 through 62. This is your **total tax** ▶	63
Payments	64	Federal income tax withheld from Forms W-2 and 1099 — 64	
	65	2006 estimated tax payments and amount applied from 2005 return — 65	
If you have a qualifying child, attach Schedule EIC.	66a	**Earned income credit (EIC)** — 66a	
	b	Nontaxable combat pay election ▶ 66b	
	67	Excess social security and tier 1 RRTA tax withheld (see page 59) — 67	
	68	Additional child tax credit. Attach Form 8812 — 68	
	69	Amount paid with request for extension to file (see page 59) — 69	
	70	Payments from: **a** ☐ Form 2439 **b** ☐ Form 4136 **c** ☐ Form 8885 — 70	
	71	Credit for federal telephone excise tax paid. Attach Form 8913 if required — 71	
	72	Add lines 64, 65, 66a, and 67 through 71. These are your **total payments** ▶	72
Refund	73	If line 72 is more than line 63, subtract line 63 from line 72. This is the amount you **overpaid**	73
Direct deposit? See page 59 and fill in 74b, 74c, and 74d, or Form 8888.	74a	Amount of line 73 you want **refunded to you.** If Form 8888 is attached, check here ▶ ☐	74a
	▶ b	Routing number ▶ **c** Type: ☐ Checking ☐ Savings	
	▶ d	Account number	
	75	Amount of line 73 you want **applied to your 2007 estimated tax** ▶ 75	
Amount You Owe	76	**Amount you owe.** Subtract line 72 from line 63. For details on how to pay, see page 60 ▶	76
	77	Estimated tax penalty (see page 60) — 77	

Third Party Designee — Do you want to allow another person to discuss this return with the IRS (see page 61)? ☐ **Yes.** Complete the following. ☐ **No**

Designee's name ▶ Phone no. ▶ ( ) Personal identification number (PIN) ▶

Sign Here — Under penalties of perjury, I declare that I have examined this return and accompanying schedules and statements, and to the best of my knowledge and belief, they are true, correct, and complete. Declaration of preparer (other than taxpayer) is based on all information of which preparer has any knowledge.

Joint return? See page 17. Keep a copy for your records.

Your signature	Date	Your occupation	Daytime phone number ( )
Spouse's signature. If a joint return, **both** must sign.	Date	Spouse's occupation	

Paid Preparer's Use Only

Preparer's signature ▶	Date	Check if self-employed ☐	Preparer's SSN or PTIN
Firm's name (or yours if self-employed), address, and ZIP code ▶		EIN	
		Phone no.	( )

Form **1040** (2006)

(Use for Problem 21).

SCHEDULE E (Form 1040)

Department of the Treasury Internal Revenue Service (99)

Supplemental Income and Loss

(From rental real estate, royalties, partnerships, S corporations, estates, trusts, REMICs, etc.)

▶ Attach to Form 1040, 1040NR, or Form 1041. ▶ See Instructions for Schedule E (Form 1040).

OMB No. 1545-0074

2006

Attachment Sequence No. 13

Name(s) shown on return | Your social security number

Part I **Income or Loss From Rental Real Estate and Royalties** **Note.** If you are in the business of renting personal property, use **Schedule C** or **C-EZ** (see page E-3). Report farm rental income or loss from **Form 4835** on page 2, line 40.

1	List the type and location of each **rental real estate property:**	2 For each rental real estate property listed on line 1, did you or your family use it during the tax year for personal purposes for more than the greater of: • 14 days **or** • 10% of the total days rented at fair rental value? (See page E-3.)		Yes	No
A			A		
B			B		
C			C		

Income:		Properties A	Properties B	Properties C		Totals (Add columns A, B, and C.)
3 Rents received	3				3	
4 Royalties received	4				4	
Expenses:						
5 Advertising	5					
6 Auto and travel (see page E-4)	6					
7 Cleaning and maintenance	7					
8 Commissions	8					
9 Insurance	9					
10 Legal and other professional fees	10					
11 Management fees	11					
12 Mortgage interest paid to banks, etc. (see page E-4)	12				12	
13 Other interest	13					
14 Repairs	14					
15 Supplies	15					
16 Taxes	16					
17 Utilities	17					
18 Other (list) ▶	18					
19 Add lines 5 through 18	19				19	
20 Depreciation expense or depletion (see page E-4)	20				20	
21 Total expenses. Add lines 19 and 20	21					
22 Income or (loss) from rental real estate or royalty properties. Subtract line 21 from line 3 (rents) or line 4 (royalties). If the result is a (loss), see page E-5 to find out if you must file **Form 6198**	22					
23 Deductible rental real estate loss. **Caution.** Your rental real estate loss on line 22 may be limited. See page E-5 to find out if you must file **Form 8582.** Real estate professionals must complete line 43 on page 2	23	( )	( )	( )		
24 **Income.** Add positive amounts shown on line 22. **Do not** include any losses					24	
25 **Losses.** Add royalty losses from line 22 and rental real estate losses from line 23. Enter total losses here					25	( )
26 **Total rental real estate and royalty income or (loss).** Combine lines 24 and 25. Enter the result here. If Parts II, III, IV, and line 40 on page 2 do not apply to you, also enter this amount on Form 1040, line 17, or Form 1040NR, line 18. Otherwise, include this amount in the total on line 41 on page 2					26	

For Paperwork Reduction Act Notice, see page E-7 of the instructions. Cat. No. 11344L **Schedule E (Form 1040) 2006**

10

Property: Basis and Nontaxable Exchanges

CHAPTER CONTENTS

CHAPTER OVERVIEW

When taxpayers sell or otherwise dispose of property, a gain or loss usually results. This chapter explains how taxpayers compute those gains and losses. It also explains which gains and losses taxpayers report on the tax return. The chapter begins by presenting the formula used to compute realized gains and losses when disposing of property. Realized gains and losses reflect the taxpayer's economic gain or loss from the transaction. They are the difference between the amount realized from the transaction and the taxpayer's adjusted basis in the property. When the amount realized exceeds the adjusted basis, a realized gain results. A realized loss occurs when the amount realized is less than the adjusted basis. The rules for computing amount realized and adjusted basis are presented in the chapter.

Although disposing of property results in a realized gain or loss, not all realized gains and losses are reported on the tax return. As a rule, taxpayers are taxed on all realized gains but can deduct only realized losses that result from the disposal of investment or business property. One exception to this rule involves property destroyed in a casualty or a theft. Although the general rule does not allow taxpayers to deduct losses from the disposal of personal-use property, Chapter 5 presented the rules for the (itemized) deduction for nonbusiness casualty or theft losses. Other exceptions are described later in the chapter.

REALIZED GAIN OR LOSS

Realized gains or losses occur when taxpayers sell, exchange, or otherwise dispose of property. They also occur when the government takes the taxpayer's property in a condemnation. When the amount realized from the transaction exceeds the adjusted basis in the property given up, the difference is a **realized gain.** When the adjusted basis exceeds the amount realized, the difference is a **realized loss.** Stated another way,

Realized gain (loss) = Amount realized – Adjusted basis

Amount Realized

The **amount realized** equals the sales price minus selling expenses. Selling expenses include commissions, legal fees, and other costs related to the sale. The sales price is the sum of the fair market value (FMV) of the property (which includes cash) and services received in return for the property given up. It also includes any debt of the taxpayer that the buyer assumes or pays off. (When the buyer assumes the taxpayer's debt, it is similar to the buyer giving the taxpayer cash that the taxpayer uses to pay off the debt.)

EXAMPLE 1

Howard Trier sells stock for $12,000 cash plus a car valued at $5,000. Trier's amount realized is $17,000 ($12,000 + $5,000).

EXAMPLE 2

Martha Simms exchanges land for a building that has a FMV of $90,000. The land is subject to a $50,000 mortgage, which the other party assumes. Simms's amount realized is $140,000 ($90,000 + $50,000).

Adjusted Basis

When disposing of property, the tax laws allow taxpayers to recover their investment in property tax free. **Basis** is the term used to describe the taxpayer's investment in property. Taxpayers realize a gain when the amount realized exceeds their basis in the property. If the entire basis is not recovered, taxpayers realize a loss for the unrecovered amount.

Between the time taxpayers acquire property and the time they dispose of it, events may occur that require taxpayers to adjust their basis in property. **Adjusted basis** is the term for the taxpayer's investment in property after making those adjustments. Adjusted basis can be stated as follows:

Adjusted basis = Initial basis in property + Capital additions − Capital recoveries

The initial basis of purchased property usually is its cost. However, taxpayers can acquire property in other ways, such as through gift or inheritance. The initial basis of a property depends on how the taxpayer acquired it. The rules for computing initial basis are presented later in the chapter.

Capital Additions

Capital additions include costs incurred in transferring or defending title to the property. Examples of such costs include commissions and legal fees. Capital additions also include the cost of improvements that increase the property's value, lengthen its useful life, or convert it to a different use. Improvements have a useful life that exceeds one year. Maintenance and repairs are not improvements since they are routine and recurring costs.

EXAMPLES OF IMPROVEMENTS

- Installing a new furnace
- Putting up a fence
- Paving a driveway
- Rebuilding a car engine
- Landscaping
- Building a recreation room in an unfinished basement
- Paying special assessments for sidewalks, roads, etc.
- Adding a room onto a house

EXAMPLE 3

In 1995, Leroy Rigley paid $125,000 for property that he uses as a vacation home. Over the years, Rigley has paid $35,000 to remodel the kitchen, $5,000 to install a wooden fence around the property, and $3,000 to reshingle the roof. He also has paid $13,800 to keep the property in good condition. Rigley's adjusted basis in the home is $168,000 ($125,000 + $35,000 + $5,000 + $3,000). The vacation home is a personal belonging. Thus, amounts spent on repairs and maintenance are nondeductible personal expenses. If Rigley were to sell the home, his realized gain or loss would be the difference between the amount realized from the sale and his $168,000 adjusted basis in the home.

Capital Recoveries

Capital recoveries are a return of the taxpayer's investment in property. They occur when taxpayers receive money or take tax deductions in connection with the property. Any time taxpayers recover part of their investment in property prior to disposing of it, they must reduce their basis in the property accordingly. When property is damaged in a casualty, taxpayers reduce their basis in the property by the amount of proceeds they receive from the insurance company. The basis then increases by amounts spent to restore the property. The same basis reduction rule applies to amounts taxpayers receive from the government for the right to use part of their property (known as an easement). The amounts taxpayers receive from the insurance company or from the government represent a return of their initial investment in the property. After receiving these amounts, the taxpayer has less invested in the property. Thus, the taxpayer's basis (investment) in the property must be reduced accordingly.

EXAMPLE 4

In 1990 Ralph Cuthbert paid $120,000 for land. In the current year, Cuthbert receives $20,000 from the government in exchange for the right to use part of the land. Cuthbert must reduce his basis in the land by $20,000. Although Cuthbert initially paid $120,000 for the land, after receiving $20,000 from the government, his net investment is $100,000. Cuthbert's adjusted basis in the land equals $100,000 ($120,000 initial basis – $20,000 capital recovery).

Taxpayers also reduce the basis in property by amounts deducted on the tax return in connection with the property. This includes amounts deducted for casualty or theft losses. It also includes amounts deducted for Section 179 and depreciation expense.

EXAMPLE 5

Jennie Grange is a sole proprietor. During 2006, Grange placed in service equipment costing $24,000. She elected to expense the entire amount under Section 179. Grange's adjusted basis in the equipment is $0. Thus, the entire amount realized on the sale of the equipment will result in realized gain.

EXAMPLE 6

In 1993 Lisa Lee paid $62,000 for a building. Lee spent $10,000 in 1999 for a new roof. In 2006 a fire damaged the building. The insurance company paid Lee $20,000 for the loss. Lee claimed a $10,000 casualty loss deduction on her 2006 tax return for the unreimbursed portion of the loss. In 2006 Lee spent $29,000 to rebuild the part of the building destroyed in the fire. Over the years, Lee has deducted $22,000 for depreciation on the building. Lee computes the adjusted basis in the building as follows.

Initial basis in the building		$62,000
Plus capital additions		
Improvements	$10,000	
Restoration costs	29,000	39,000
Less capital recoveries		
Depreciation	$22,000	
Insurance proceeds	20,000	
Casualty loss	10,000	(52,000)
Adjusted basis in the building		$49,000

INITIAL BASIS

When computing their adjusted basis in property, taxpayers start with the initial basis. The initial basis of purchased property is its cost. However, taxpayers can acquire property through other means, such as through gifts, inheritances, and divorce settlements.

Property Acquired by Purchase

The initial basis of purchased property is its cost (what the taxpayer gives up to buy the property). It includes amounts taxpayers borrow to buy the property. It also includes any costs incurred to acquire clear title or make the property ready for use. Examples of such costs include the following:

1. Sales or excise taxes paid on the purchase
2. Title insurance and survey costs
3. Expenses paid to deliver, install, and test the property
4. Recording, legal, and accounting fees

EXAMPLE 7

Burt Compall buys real estate, paying \$50,000 cash and assuming the seller's \$75,000 mortgage on the property. Compall's initial basis is \$125,000 (\$50,000 + \$75,000).

EXAMPLE 8

Kelly Hall purchases a machine for \$10,000. Hall pays \$600 in sales tax and \$400 for delivery and installation. Hall's initial basis in the machine equals \$11,000 (\$10,000 + \$600 + \$400).

When the taxpayer performs services in exchange for property, the initial basis in the property is the value of the services the taxpayer includes in income.

EXAMPLE 9

Al Barkin received ten shares of stock in exchange for services he rendered. The market value of the shares is \$300. Barkin is taxed on \$300 for his services. His initial basis in the shares is \$300.

Bargain Purchases

Sometimes companies sell goods or other property to their employees for less than FMV. Often the employee reports the difference between the FMV and the purchase price as income on the tax return. In such cases, the employee's initial basis ends up the same as the FMV of the property since the initial basis includes amounts taxed as income. If the employee does not have to report any income from the bargain purchase (as in a qualified employee discount), then the employee's initial basis equals the amount paid for the property.

EXAMPLE 10

Frank Morgan pays $60 for property from a company where he is an employee. The FMV of the property is $100. Morgan reports the $40 difference between FMV and the purchase price on his tax return. Morgan's initial basis in the property equals $100 ($60 purchase price + $40 reported in income).

Basket Purchases

Sometimes a single purchase price buys more than one property. As we learned in Chapter 8, different depreciation rules can apply to different properties. Also, taxpayers may sell the properties at various times in the future. For these reasons, the purchase price must be allocated among the properties acquired. Taxpayers allocate the purchase price among the properties on the basis of their relative FMVs. The amount allocated to one property equals the purchase price times the ratio of the FMV of that property to the total FMV of all properties.

$$\text{Initial basis} = \text{Purchase price} \times \frac{\text{FMV of the property}}{\text{FMV of all properties}}$$

EXAMPLE 11

George Casteil pays $90,000 for land and a building. At the time of the purchase, the FMV of the land and building are $80,000 and $40,000, respectively. Casteil's basis in the land equals $60,000 [$90,000 × ($80,000/$120,000)]. The basis in the building equals $30,000 [$90,000 × ($40,000/$120,000)].

Property Received from a Spouse

When a taxpayer receives property from a spouse, the spouse's adjusted basis in the property carries over to the taxpayer. No tax consequences occur when property is transferred between spouses (or ex-spouses when the transfer is part of a divorce settlement).

EXAMPLE 12

Drew and April Pantoni divorced in 2006. As part of the divorce agreement, Drew transferred to April title to his mountain cabin. Drew paid $80,000 for the cabin six years prior to his marriage to April. Over the years, he spent $23,500 on improvements to the cabin. At the time of the transfer, the cabin was worth $240,000. April's basis in the home equals Drew's adjusted basis in the home $103,500 ($80,000 + $23,500). If she were to sell the home for its current fair market value, her realized and recognized gain would equal $136,500 ($240,000 - $103,500).

Inherited Property

When a person dies, an executor is assigned to handle the decedent's property (known as the estate). Before distributing the estate to the decedent's heirs, the executor first computes the estate tax due. Estate tax is computed on the total FMV of the decedent's estate. Estate tax is due only when the value of the estate exceeds a certain amount.

In computing the estate tax, the executor usually values the estate on the date of the decedent's death (DOD). However, under certain conditions, the executor can elect to value the estate six months later (known as the alternative valuation date, or AVD). When the executor values the estate on the AVD, the heir's initial basis in the property is its FMV on the AVD or on the date it is distributed to the heir, whichever occurs first.

EXAMPLE 13

Rhonda Valdez inherited land from her grandfather, who died on April 5, 2006. On that day, the land was valued at $45,000. On October 5, 2006, its value was $42,000. The land was distributed to Valdez on March 2, 2007. Valdez's basis in the land is $45,000 using the DOD to value the grandfather's estate. If the AVD is used, Valdez's basis is $42,000 (since the AVD occurs before the date of distribution).

EXAMPLE 14

Assume the same facts as in Example 13, except that the land was distributed to Valdez on August 22, 2006, when its value was $43,000. Using DOD to value the grandfather's estate, Valdez's basis in the land is still $45,000. If the AVD is used, Valdez's basis is $43,000 (since the distribution date occurs first).

Gifted Property

Two sets of rules apply to property received as a gift. One set applies when, at the time of the gift, the FMV of the property exceeds the donor's adjusted basis in the property. Another set applies when the donor's adjusted basis exceeds the FMV of the property.

FMV Less Than Donor's Basis

If at the time of the gift the FMV of the property is less than the donor's (adjusted) basis, then the donee's basis in the property is not known until the donee (the person receiving the gifted property) disposes of the property. If the donee realizes a gain (the amount realized exceeds the donor's basis), then the donee's basis equals the donor's basis. If the donee realizes a loss (the amount realized is less than the FMV of the property at the time of the gift), then the donee's basis equals the FMV at the time of the gift. When the amount realized falls between the donor's basis and the FMV at the time of the gift, there is no gain or loss and the donee's basis equals the amount realized.

EXAMPLE 15

Joan Kemp receives stock as a gift. At the time of the gift, the stock was worth $15,000. The donor paid $20,000 for the stock. Kemp sells the stock for $23,000. Since Kemp sells the stock for a gain (more than the donor's $20,000 basis), Kemp's basis in the stock is $20,000. Kemp realizes a $3,000 gain ($23,000 – $20,000).

EXAMPLE 16

Same facts as in Example 15, except that Kemp sells the stock for $13,000. Kemp sells the stock for a loss (less than the $15,000 FMV). Thus, her basis in the stock is $15,000, and she realizes a $2,000 loss ($13,000 – $15,000).

EXAMPLE 17

Same facts as in Example 15, except that Kemp sells the stock for $17,000. Here, Kemp realizes neither a gain nor a loss. Her basis in the stock equals $17,000.

When the gifted property is depreciable property to the donee, the donee uses the donor's basis to compute depreciation on the property. This rule applies regardless of which basis (donor's basis or FMV at the time of the gift) the donee uses to compute the realized gain or loss at the time of the sale.

FMV Exceeds Donor's Basis

If at the time of the gift the FMV of the property exceeds the donor's basis, the donee takes over the donor's basis. If the donor paid gift tax on the transfer, then the donee adds a portion of the gift tax to the basis. The portion of the gift tax added to the donee's basis depends on when the gift was made. For gifts made prior to 1977, 100% of the gift tax is added to the donee's basis. For gifts made after 1976, only a fraction of the gift tax is added to the donee's basis. This fraction equals the ratio of the amount the property appreciated in value while owned by the donor (FMV at the time of the gift – donor's basis) to its FMV at the time of the gift. In both cases, the donee's basis cannot exceed the FMV of the property at the time of the gift.

EXAMPLE 18

In 1993 Sue Miller received property from her uncle worth $75,000. The uncle paid $15,000 in gift tax on the transfer. The uncle's adjusted basis in the property was $30,000. Since the FMV exceeds the uncle's basis, Miller takes her uncle's $30,000 basis. While her uncle owned the property, it went up in value by $45,000 ($75,000 – $30,000). Therefore, Miller adds 60% ($45,000/$75,000) of the gift tax to her basis. Miller's initial basis in the gifted property equals $39,000 [$30,000 + (60% × $15,000)].

EXAMPLE 19

Assume the same facts as in Example 18, except that the gift occurred in 1973. Miller still takes her uncle's basis in the property but adds 100% of the gift tax to arrive at her initial basis in the property. Miller's initial basis equals $45,000 ($30,000 + $15,000).

DONEE'S INITIAL BASIS IN GIFTED PROPERTY

When FMV < donor's basis and the donee disposes of the property for

- a gain: donee's basis = donor's basis
- a loss: donee's basis = FMV at time of gift
- no gain or loss: donee's basis = amount realized

When FMV > donor's basis,

Donee's basis = Donor's basis + Percentage of the gift tax

Percentage for pre-1977 gifts: 100%

Percentage for post-1976 gifts: $\frac{\text{FMV at time of gift} - \text{Donor's basis}}{\text{FMV at time of gift}}$

Property Converted to Business or Rental Use

Instead of buying new property to use in a business or rental activity, taxpayers can convert their personal belongings to such use. For example, taxpayers can convert their principal residences to rental property, or they can start using their personal automobiles or computers in their businesses. As with gifted property, two sets of rules apply to the basis of converted property. The first set applies if the FMV of the property at the time of conversion exceeds the taxpayer's adjusted basis. Another set applies if the adjusted basis exceeds the FMV.

FMV Exceeds Adjusted Basis (Appreciated Property)

When taxpayers convert appreciated property, they use the general rule to compute the adjusted basis: Initial basis + Capital additions – Capital recoveries. If the converted property is depreciable property, taxpayers use the adjusted basis at the time of conversion to compute depreciation expense.

EXAMPLE 20

On June 4, 20x6, Donna Wise converted her home into rental property. Wise paid $93,630 for the home in 20x0. Over the years she has made improvements to the home totaling $25,300. Thus, her adjusted basis in the home is $118,930 ($93,630 + $25,300). On June 4, 20x6, the home is worth $155,300. Wise's adjusted basis in the rental property is $118,930 (the *lesser of* (i) the $118,930 adjusted basis, or (ii) $155,300 FMV at the time of the conversion). She uses this amount to compute her annual depreciation expense. Using the mid-month convention, Wise's depreciation expense for 20x6 equals $2,703 ($118,930/27.5 x 7.5/12). For each subsequent full year that she uses the home as rental property, her depreciation expense will equal $4,325 ($118,930/27.5).

FMV Less Than Adjusted Basis

When taxpayers convert property that has declined in value, the adjusted basis of the property is determined when they dispose of it. To compute realized gains, taxpayers use the general rule for computing adjusted basis: Initial basis + Capital additions – Capital recoveries. To compute realized losses, they use: FMV at conversion + Postconversion capital additions – Postconversion capital recoveries. If the converted property is depreciable property, taxpayers use the FMV of property at the time of the conversion to compute depreciation.

ADJUSTED BASIS IN CONVERTED PROPERTY

When at conversion FMV > adjusted basis,

- Adjusted basis = Initial basis + Capital additions – Capital recoveries
- Depreciable basis = Adjusted basis

When at conversion FMV < adjusted basis,

- Adjusted basis for gains = Initial basis + Capital additions – Capital recoveries
- Adjusted basis for losses = FMV at conversion + Postconversion capital additions – Postconversion capital recoveries
- Depreciable basis = FMV at conversion

EXAMPLE 21

On January 1, 2000, Emily Connors converted her home to rental property. At the time of the conversion, the FMV of the home was $50,000. Connors paid $56,000 for the home and made $4,000 of capital improvements prior to 2000. After converting the property, Connors deducted $6,000 for depreciation and made $3,000 in capital improvements. Connors sells the property in 2006 for $59,000. Since at the time of conversion the $50,000 FMV was less than $60,000 the adjusted basis ($56,000 + $4,000 preconversion improvements), Connors computes an adjusted basis for gain and an adjusted basis for loss.

Initial basis		$56,000
Plus capital additions	$4,000	
	3,000	7,000
Less capital recoveries		(6,000)
Adjusted basis for gain		$57,000
FMV at conversion		$50,000
Plus postconversion capital additions		3,000
Less postconversion capital recoveries		(6,000)
Adjusted basis for loss		$47,000

Because the amount realized exceeds the adjusted basis for gain, Connors sells the property for a gain. Using an adjusted basis of $57,000, Connors realizes a $2,000 gain ($59,000 – $57,000). Had Connors sold the property for a loss (an amount realized less than $47,000), her adjusted basis would have been $47,000. Had the amount realized been between $47,000 and $57,000, Connors would have realized no gain or loss, and her adjusted basis would have equaled the amount realized.

Special Rules for Stock Ownership

When taxpayers buy stock, their basis in the shares equals the purchase price plus commissions or transfer fees paid. If taxpayers acquire stock through other means (gift, inheritance, etc.), the rules presented in this chapter for computing adjusted basis apply.

Identification of Shares

Taxpayers can acquire identical shares of stock in the same company at various times for different amounts. When taxpayers sell stock in that company, they should identify which shares they are selling at the time of the sale. If no identification is made, the taxpayer must use the first-in, first-out method.

EXAMPLE 22

In 20x0 Hugh Steadman paid $10,000 for 1,000 shares of common stock in ABC corporation. In 20x2 he paid $12,500 for another 1,000 shares. During the current year, Steadman sells 1,000 of his shares in ABC for $11,000. If he does not specify which 1,000 were sold, the tax laws require him to use the $10,000 basis in the earliest shares he purchased. This would result in a $1,000 realized gain ($11,000 amount realized - $10,000 adjusted basis). However, if Steadman were to specify with his stock broker that he wants to sell the 1,000 shares that he purchased in 20x2, he would have a realized loss of $1,500 ($11,000 - $12,500).

To identify shares sold, taxpayers should deliver the stock certificates to the broker or agent. If a broker or agent holds the stock certificates, then taxpayers should instruct the broker in writing which shares they wish to sell. Taxpayers should then request written confirmation from the broker to document that the instructions were followed.

Stock Splits

Taxpayers owning stock may later acquire additional shares either through a stock split or a stock dividend. In a stock split, the corporation distributes to its shareholders a ratable portion of additional shares. This results in more shares outstanding without affecting the ownership percentages. With a stock split, taxpayers prorate the adjusted basis in the original shares to all shares held. No income is realized on a stock split.

EXAMPLE 23

Several years ago, Rex Davenport paid $14,000 for 1,000 shares of stock in ABCO ($14 a share). During the current year, ABCO declared a two-for-one stock split. Each shareholder received two shares of stock for every one share they returned to the company. The shareholders of ABCO are not taxed on the split. After the split, Davenport owns 2,000 shares of ABCO stock. His adjusted basis in those shares is his original $14,000 adjusted basis in the stock. Thus, Davenport's basis is each share of stock has been reduced to $7 ($14,000/2,000).

Stock Dividends

Shareholders receive a stock dividend when the corporation pays them a dividend with shares of stock instead of cash. If shareholders have the option to receive either a stock or a cash dividend, then the cash or FMV of the stock (whichever they choose) must be included as income on the tax return. If they choose to receive a stock dividend, then the FMV of the stock becomes their basis in the newly acquired shares.

When the corporation pays shareholders a stock dividend without giving them the option of a cash dividend, it is a nontaxable stock dividend. As with stock splits, taxpayers must allocate some basis from the original shares to the shares acquired in a nontaxable stock dividend. When the stock dividend is of the same class, the taxpayer prorates the original basis among the total number of shares. An example of a *same class of stock* dividend would be a common stock shareholder receiving a common stock dividend. When the stock dividend is not of the same class, the taxpayer allocates the basis in the original shares using the relative FMV of the total shares. Taxpayers use the same formula to allocate the purchase price among properties acquired in a basket purchase. An example of a stock dividend *not of the same class* would be a common stock shareholder's receiving a preferred stock dividend.

EXAMPLE 24

Pat Brown paid $1,100 for 50 shares of common stock. This year Brown received five shares of common stock as a nontaxable stock dividend. Brown's basis in 55 shares of common stock is $1,100, or $20 a share.

Return-of-Capital

Corporations pay dividends from earnings and profits (E&P). E&P is roughly the same as retained earnings on the corporate balance sheet. When a corporation with no E&P distributes property (including cash) to its shareholders, the distribution is treated as a return of the shareholder's investment. The amount distributed is not taxable, but as with other capital recoveries, the shareholder reduces the basis in the stock by the amount distributed. If the amount distributed exceeds the shareholder's basis in the stock, then the shareholder realizes a gain for the excess amount.

Corporations report their distributions to shareholders on Form 1099-DIV. On this form, the corporation reports the taxable dividends paid to the shareholder during the year (distributions from the corporation's E&P), as well as distributions made to the shareholder during the year that represent a return of the shareholder's investment. Shareholders report the taxable dividends on Schedule B and reduce their basis (investment) in the stock by the nontaxable distributions.

RECOGNIZED GAINS AND LOSSES

Recognized gains and losses are realized gains and losses taxpayers report on their tax returns. Not all realized gains and losses result in taxable gains and losses. As a general rule, taxpayers recognize all realized gains but recognize losses only from the disposal of business or investment property. Chapter 5 described an exception to this rule that allows taxpayers to deduct casualty or theft losses on personal-use property. This chapter covers the following six additional exceptions to the general rule.

- Losses involving wash sales
- Losses from sales between related parties
- Gains from qualified small business stock
- Gains and losses from like-kind exchanges
- Most gains from the sale of a principal residence
- Certain gains from involuntary conversions

WASH SALES

Because securities (stocks and bonds) are an investment, the taxpayer usually recognizes any realized loss on the sale of securities. However, no loss is allowed when the taxpayer repurchases "substantially identical" securities within 30 days before or after the sale. The term used to describe these sales and repurchases is **wash sales.**

Substantially identical securities are securities *in the same company* that have similar features. For stocks, substantially identical would be the same class of stock with the same voting rights. For bonds, substantially identical would be bonds with similar interest rates and maturity dates. If the taxpayer repurchases only a fraction of the securities within the 61-day period surrounding the sale, then only that fraction of the loss is denied.

EXAMPLE 25

On January 5, 2006, Tom Mathy sold 1,000 shares of common stock in Omega Co. for $5,000. Mathy's purchases of Omega common stock follow:

1,000 shares on June 6, 2004	$8,000
600 shares on November 6, 2005	4,500
250 shares on December 17, 2005	2,000
350 shares on January 10, 2006	3,000

Assuming Mathy does not identify which shares were sold, he is assumed to sell the 1,000 shares purchased on June 6, 2004. The sale results in a $3,000 realized loss ($5,000 – $8,000), which normally would be recognized for tax purposes. However, since Mathy repurchased 600 (250 + 350) of the 1,000 shares between December 6, 2005, and February 4, 2006 (61 days surrounding January 5, 2006), 60% (600/1,000) of the loss is disallowed ($3,000 × 60% = $1,800). Mathy recognizes a $1,200 loss ($3,000 – $1,800) for the 40% of the shares sold and not repurchased.

Any disallowed loss due to a wash sale is merely postponed and will be allowed when the taxpayer later sells the (repurchased) shares. To postpone the loss, the taxpayer adds the disallowed loss to the basis of the repurchased shares.

EXAMPLE 26

In Example 25, Mathy allocates the $1,800 disallowed loss among the 600 shares that caused the wash sale ($1,800/600 = $3 a share). The basis in the 250 shares purchased on December 17, 2005, equals $2,750 [$2,000 + ($3 × 250)]. The basis in the 350 shares purchased on January 10, 2006, equals $4,050 [$3,000 + ($3 × 350)]. The basis in the 600 shares purchased on November 6, 2005, is their $4,500 cost since the shares were not involved in the wash sale.

SALES BETWEEN RELATED PARTIES

The sale of investment or business property for less than its adjusted basis usually results in a recognized loss. However, taxpayers cannot recognize losses when they sell business or investment property to a related party. For tax purposes, individuals and their family members are related parties. **Family members** include spouses, siblings (brothers and sisters), descendants (children, grandchildren, etc.), and ancestors (parents, grandparents, etc.). Unlike wash sales, the disallowed loss does not increase the (related) buyer's basis in the property. Instead, the buyer can use the disallowed loss to offset any realized gain when the property is later sold. The buyer cannot use the disallowed loss to create or increase a loss.

EXAMPLE 27

Pete sold stock to his son, Stan, for $10,000. Pete bought the stock several years ago for $16,000. Although stock is investment property, Pete cannot recognize the $6,000 realized loss ($10,000 – $16,000) since he sold the stock to a related party. Stan's basis in the stock is $10,000, the amount he paid for it.

If Stan later sells the stock for $12,000, Stan uses Pete's disallowed loss to offset his $2,000 realized gain ($12,000 – $10,000). Since the disallowed loss can only reduce realized gains and cannot create a loss, Stan can use only $2,000 of the disallowed loss. The rest of the disallowed loss will never be used.

EXAMPLE 28

Assume the same facts as in Example 27, except that Stan sells the stock for $9,000. Stan realizes a $1,000 loss ($9,000 – $10,000). Since a disallowed loss cannot create or increase a loss, Stan cannot use any of Pete's disallowed loss. Stan recognizes the $1,000 loss from the sale, and Pete's entire $6,000 disallowed loss is gone.

Besides individuals and their family members, related parties also involve individuals and corporations when an individual owns more than 50% of the voting stock in the corporation. Stock owned by family members counts as stock owned by the individual. This indirect ownership of stock is known as **constructive ownership.**

EXAMPLE 29

Henry owns 30% of Alpha Corporation. The following people own the rest of the stock:

Henry's aunt	35%
Henry's brother	25%
Henry's father	10%

Henry owns 30% of Alpha outright. He constructively owns the 35% owned by his brother (25%) and father (10%). Henry's actual plus constructive ownership exceeds 50%.

EXAMPLE 30

Continuing on with Example 29, in current year, Henry sells land held as an investment to Alpha Corporation for its current FMV of $75,000. Henry paid $112,000 for the land. Since Henry's actual and constructive ownership in Alpha exceeds 50%, he cannot deduct the $37,000 loss he realizes on the sale ($75,000 amount realized - $112,000 basis). Alpha's basis in the land is the $75,000 it paid for the land.

EXAMPLE 31

Continuing on with Example 30, in a future tax year Alpha sells the land for $102,000. Its realized gain is $27,000 ($102,000 - $75,000). Alpha can use Henry's $37,000 disallowed loss to reduce its recognized gain to $0.

QUALIFIED SMALL BUSINESS STOCK

Individuals can exclude 50% of the gain realized on the sale of Section 1202 qualified small business stock, provided the stock is held for more than five years. To qualify for the 50% exclusion, the stock purchased must have been part of the corporation's original issuance of stock. Only certain corporations are able to issue qualified small business stock. These restrictions are beyond the scope of this discussion.

EXAMPLE 32

On September 6, 1996, Philip Markel acquires $100,000 of Section 1202 qualified small business stock from Alpha Corporation. On November 19, 2006, Markel sells the stock for $230,000. Markel's realized gain from the sale is $130,000 ($230,000 – $100,000). However, since he held the stock for more than five years, Markel recognizes 50% of the gain, or $65,000.

The ability to exclude 50% of the gain on the sale of Section 1202 qualified small business stock provides taxpayers with a great incentive to buy stock in a new corporation that qualifies under Section 1202. Shareholders can continue to exclude 50% of the gains until the total excluded gains on the sale of Section 1202 stock equals the greater of $10 million or 10 times the shareholder's aggregate adjusted basis in the Section 1202 stock disposed of during the year.

TAX-DEFERRED EXCHANGES

Taxpayers usually must recognize any gain realized on the exchange of property. However, certain exchanges do not result in taxable gain (or deductible loss). Instead, these realized gains and losses are postponed (deferred) to a future tax year. Like-kind exchanges are one example of a tax-deferred exchange.

LIKE-KIND EXCHANGES

Instead of selling property for cash, taxpayers can exchange property they own for other property. When this occurs, a realized gain or loss results from the difference between the FMV of the property received and the adjusted basis of the property given up. Under the general rule, taxpayers recognize all gains from such exchanges but recognize losses only from exchanges that involve business or investment property. One exception to the general rule exists when the exchange involves like-kind property. In a like-kind exchange, taxpayers generally do not recognize gains or losses. Instead, realized gains and losses are postponed. To postpone the gains and losses until such time that the property is disposed of in a non-like-kind exchange, taxpayers adjust the basis of the property they receive in the like-kind exchange. This new basis is also used to depreciate depreciable property.

Basis of the new property = FMV of the new property + Postponed losses – Postponed gains

EXAMPLE 33

Joan Wright exchanges property with an adjusted basis of $100,000 for like-kind property valued at $60,000. Wright realizes a $40,000 loss ($60,000 – $100,000) but does not recognize the loss on her tax return. Wright's basis in the new property equals $100,000 ($60,000 FMV of new property + $40,000 postponed loss). If the new property is depreciable property, the basis in the property for purposes of depreciation is $100,000.

Like-Kind Property

The rules just described apply only to exchanges involving like-kind property. To qualify as like-kind property, four conditions must be met.

1. A direct exchange must occur. Certain exchanges involving three parties can qualify as a direct exchange. Also, a direct exchange can occur if the property to be received is identified within 45 days and received within 180 days after the taxpayer transfers the property.
2. Both the property traded and the property received must be business or investment property.
3. Real property must be exchanged for other real property. Personal property must be exchanged for similar personal property.
4. The property exchanged cannot be inventory, foreign real property, securities (stocks and bonds), or partnership interests.

The like-kind rules are not elective. When all four conditions are met, taxpayers must postpone any realized gain or loss resulting from the like-kind exchange.

The like-kind exchange rules are mandatory. If the taxpayer exchanges like-kind property that results in a loss, the loss must be postponed. To deduct the loss, the taxpayer needs to fail at least one of the four requirements. For example, the taxpayer could fail to meet the requirements for a direct exchange.

Like-Kind Exchanges of Business or Investment Personal Property

To qualify as a like-kind exchange, taxpayers must exchange personal property held for business or investment for similar personal property to be held for business or investment. Similar personal property is that which is *nearly identical.* The following are five examples of like-kind personal property.

- Office furniture, fixtures, and office equipment are all like-kind
- All automobiles are like-kind
- Computers, printers, and peripheral equipment are like-kind
- All light general-purpose trucks are like-kind
- All heavy general-purpose trucks are nearly identical, but different from light general-purpose trucks

EXAMPLE 34

A corporation exchanges an automobile for a light general purposes truck. Although both assets are vehicles, they are not nearly identical. Thus, the like-kind exchange rules would not apply to this exchange. The corporation would recognize gain or loss for the difference between the FMV of the property it receives and the adjusted basis of the property it gives up in the exchange.

EXAMPLE 35

A sole proprietor exchanges a computer and cash for a new computer and printer. The like-kind exchange rules apply to this exchange, as computers, printers, and peripheral equipment are all nearly identical.

Like-Kind Exchanges of Business or Investment Real Property

The like-kind exchange rules are more lenient for exchanges of real property. To qualify as a like-kind exchange, real property used for business or investment must be exchanged for any other real property to be used for business or investment. Thus, unimproved land held for investment can be exchanged for a warehouse used in the taxpayer's business. Likewise, an office building used in the taxpayer's business can be exchanged for an apartment building to be held as an investment.

EXAMPLE 36

An individual exchanges his vacation home for land he plans to hold as an investment. The like-kind exchange rules do not apply to this exchange. Although both the property given up and the property received are real property, the vacation home is a personal belonging. For the like-kind exchange rules to apply, real property held for business or investment must be exchanged for other real property held for business or investment

Boot

Not all like-kind exchanges involve properties of equal value. When exchanging properties of unequal value, the one receiving property of lesser value will require more property from the other party. The non-like-kind property thrown in to even up the deal is known as **boot.** Often boot involves cash, but it can involve other property. Boot occurs when one party takes over the other party's debt. The party who assumes the debt is treated as giving boot. The party relieved of debt is treated as receiving boot. When both parties assume each other's debt, only the net (excess) liability counts as boot. The amount of gain or loss recognized on like-kind exchanges involving boot depends on whether the taxpayer gave or received boot.

EXAMPLE 37

Elaine Dorn exchanges land valued at $100,000 for Bill Lane's building valued at $80,000. Both properties qualify as like-kind. To even up the deal, Lane agrees to assume Dorn's $20,000 liability on the land. Dorn's release from debt is similar to her receiving $20,000 cash and using it to pay off the debt. Thus, Dorn receives $20,000 boot; Lane gives $20,000 boot.

EXAMPLE 38

Sam Hackman exchanges land valued at $80,000 for Diane Glover's building valued at $100,000. Both properties qualify as like-kind. Hackman owes $40,000 on the land; Glover owes $60,000 on the building. Both parties agree to assume each other's debt.

In this exchange, each party receives property worth $140,000. Hackman receives a building worth $100,000 and is relieved of $40,000 of debt. Glover receives land valued at $80,000 and is relieved of $60,000 of debt. Because the parties assume each other's debt, only the net liability of $20,000 ($60,000 – $40,000) is treated as boot. Hackman takes on more debt than he is relieved of; therefore, Hackman gives $20,000 of boot. Glover is relieved of more debt than she assumed; therefore, Glover receives $20,000 of boot.

Receipt of Boot

Receiving boot has no affect on realized losses from the like-kind exchange. Those losses are postponed and increase the taxpayer's basis in the like-kind property received. However, taxpayers recognize gains to the extent of the FMV of the boot received.

EXAMPLE 39

Ken Hart exchanges a machine with an adjusted basis of $47,000 for a machine valued at $45,000 and $5,000 cash. Hart's realized gain equals $3,000 ($50,000 amount realized – $47,000 adjusted basis). Hart receives boot of $5,000; therefore, he recognizes the entire $3,000 gain. Hart's basis in the new machine is its FMV of $45,000 since there is no postponed gain.

EXAMPLE 40

Assume the same facts as in Example 39, except that Hart's adjusted basis in the old machine is $42,000. Hart realizes an $8,000 gain ($50,000 – $42,000). Hart recognizes the gain to the extent of the boot received. Therefore, Hart reports a $5,000 gain on his tax return and postpones the rest. Hart reduces the basis in the new machine by the postponed gain ($45,000 FMV – $3,000 postponed gain = $42,000 basis in the new machine).

EXAMPLE 41

Assume the same facts as in Example 39, except that Hart's adjusted basis in the old machine is $52,000. Hart realizes a $2,000 loss ($50,000 – $52,000). Since the receipt of boot has no affect on his realized losses, Hart postpones the entire loss by increasing the basis in the new machine to $47,000 ($45,000 FMV + $2,000 postponed loss).

Boot Given

When boot is received in a like-kind exchange, any realized gain is recognized to the extent of the boot received. Realized losses are never recognized when boot is received. When the taxpayer gives boot in a like-kind exchange, no gain or loss is recognized as long as the FMV of the boot equals the taxpayer's basis in the boot. This occurs when the taxpayer gives cash or assumes the other party's debt. When the FMV of the boot is different from the taxpayer's basis in the boot given, the taxpayer is treated as having sold the boot to the other party and the taxpayer has a realized gain or loss for the difference between the FMV and basis. Under the general rule, the taxpayer will recognize a gain to the extent that the FMV of the boot exceeds its basis. However, the taxpayer will recognize a loss if the FMV is less than the basis in the boot only if the boot was business or investment property.

Exchanges between Related Parties

Related parties can use the like-kind exchange rules. However, if either (related) party disposes of the like-kind property within two years after the exchange, any postponed gain or loss must be recognized in the disposal year. The basis of the like-kind property is increased by the recognized gain or reduced by the recognized loss.

SALE OF A PRINCIPAL RESIDENCE

Since taxpayers own and use a principal residence for personal purposes, usually they would recognize the gain from the sale of a principal residence but would not recognize a loss. However, the tax law allows taxpayers to exclude up to $250,000 of the gain. Married couples who file a joint tax return can exclude up to $500,000. To qualify for the exclusion, taxpayers must use the home as their principal residence for two of the previous five years. Partial exclusions are available to taxpayers who fail to meet the two-out-of-five-year requirement because of change in employment location, health, or other specified reasons.

Since taxpayers can exclude up to $250,000 of gain ($500,000 if MFJ) from the sale of their principal residence, very few taxpayers will report gain when selling their home. However, taxpayers still will want to keep track of their basis in their home to show that the gain from the sale does not exceed the exclusion amount. This includes keeping a copy of the closing statement and receipts for all capital improvements made to the home. Keeping good records is also important in casualty loss situations. In addition, when some or all of the home is converted to income-producing property, basis becomes important in determining depreciation deductions.

EXAMPLE 42

On September 11, 2006, the Duncans sell their principal residence for $200,000. Selling expenses are $10,000. The Duncans paid $50,000 for the home. The Duncans do not recognize any of the $140,000 ($200,000 – $10,000 – $50,000) gain.

EXAMPLE 43

On July 11, 2006, Dale Lincoln (a single taxpayer) sells his principal residence for $450,000. Selling expenses are $25,000. Lincoln paid $115,000 for the home in 1982. In 1988 he paid $15,000 to finish the basement. In 1990, he paid $5,000 for landscaping. Of the $290,000 realized gain, Lincoln recognizes $40,000.

Sales price	$450,000
Less selling expenses	(25,000)
Amount realized	$425,000
Less adjusted basis ($115,000 + $15,000 + $5,000)	(135,000)
Realized gain	$290,000
Less $250,000 exclusion for single taxpayers	(250,000)
Recognized gain	$ 40,000

INVOLUNTARY CONVERSIONS

Taxpayers realize a gain or loss on property involved in an involuntary conversion. The most common involuntary conversions are casualties, thefts, and condemnations.

Condemnation Gains and Losses

When the government takes the taxpayer's real property (known as a condemnation), the taxpayer often receives cash in exchange for the condemned property. Occasionally the taxpayer will receive property other than cash. Taxpayers realize a gain when the amount received from the government exceeds the adjusted basis in the condemned property. They realize a loss when the amount received is less than the adjusted basis of the property. Under the general rule, taxpayers pay tax on all recognized gains resulting from condemnations but deduct losses only on condemned business or investment property. There is no deduction for condemnation losses on personal-use property, even though it is an involuntary event.

Casualty or Theft Gains and Losses

Taxpayers realize a casualty or theft loss when the amount of the loss exceeds the amount reimbursed by insurance. The amount of the loss for *personal-use property* and for *partially destroyed business or investment property* equals the *lesser of* (i) the property's adjusted basis or (ii) its decline in FMV. Decline in FMV is measured as the difference between the FMV before and after the casualty or theft. The amount of the loss for *completely destroyed (includes stolen) business or investment property* equals the adjusted basis in the property, even if the decline in FMV is less. When the insurance proceeds exceed the amount of the loss, the taxpayer does not realize a casualty or theft loss. Instead, the taxpayer realizes a casualty or theft gain when the insurance proceeds exceed the adjusted basis in the property.

EXAMPLE 44

In March, Scott Talbot's business auto was damaged in an accident. In June, Talbot's business computer was stolen. Information about the properties is shown below.

	FMV Before	FMV After	Adjusted Basis	Insurance Proceeds
Auto	$22,000	$8,000	$15,000	$16,000
Computer	3,000	0	1,000	2,900

The business auto was partially destroyed; therefore, Talbot computes his casualty loss using the *lesser of* (i) the decline in value ($22,000 – $8,000 = $14,000) or (ii) the adjusted basis ($15,000). However, because the insurance proceeds ($16,000) exceed the amount of the loss ($14,000), Talbot does not incur a casualty loss on the auto. Instead, Talbot realizes a $1,000 casualty gain ($16,000 insurance proceeds – $15,000 adjusted basis).

The business computer was completely destroyed; therefore, Talbot measures the loss using the adjusted basis ($1,000). Talbot does not realize a theft loss on the computer since the insurance proceeds ($2,900) exceed the amount of the loss. Talbot realizes a $1,900 business theft gain on the computer ($2,900 insurance proceeds – $1,000 adjusted basis).

Generally, taxpayers recognize both gains and losses from casualty or theft events. Chapter 5 discussed the special rules for calculating an itemized deduction for casualty or theft losses on personal-use property. It should be noted that casualty and theft losses are the only deductible losses that an individual may claim on personal-use property.

Election to Postpone Realized Gains

Under the general rule, taxpayers recognize gains from property involved in an involuntary conversion. However, taxpayers can postpone these gains if they invest the *entire* proceeds in qualified replacement property within a specified period of time. This provision is elective if the taxpayer receives cash for the converted property. If the election is made, taxpayers recognize a gain (up to the amount of realized gain) for amounts not reinvested.

EXAMPLE 45

The local government condemns Tracy Kraig's property. The government pays Kraig $200,000 for the property. The property has an adjusted basis of $170,000. Kraig can avoid recognizing the $30,000 realized gain ($200,000 – $170,000) if she reinvests at least $200,000 in qualified replacement property within the required time period. Assuming Kraig buys qualified replacement property costing $190,000, she recognizes $10,000 of the gain ($200,000 – $190,000) and could elect to postpone the rest ($30,000 – $10,000 = $20,000).

When the election is made to postpone gains, taxpayers reduce the basis in the new property by the amount of postponed gain. In Example 45, if Kraig made the election, her basis in the qualified replacement property would equal $170,000 ($190,000 cost – $20,000 postponed gain).

Qualified Replacement Property

Qualified replacement property for property involved in an involuntary conversion normally is property related in service or use. Thus, taxpayers usually must replace an office building with another office building. Likewise, they must replace equipment with similar functioning equipment. Two exceptions to this rule follow.

The first exception applies to taxpayers who lease out property involved in an involuntary conversion. Qualified replacement property for these taxpayers involves investing in other rental property. The rental property need not be of the same type. Thus, taxpayers who lease out an office building can replace it with an apartment building or any other rental real estate that they lease out.

The second exception allows taxpayers to replace condemned business or investment realty with any other business or investment realty. Taxpayers can replace a condemned office building with land to be held for investment. Alternatively, they could replace it with an apartment building, a warehouse, or any other business or investment realty.

Replacement Period

Taxpayers who want to postpone the gain from an involuntary conversion must replace the converted property within a specified period. The replacement period begins on the date the property was damaged, destroyed, condemned, or stolen. However, for condemned property, the period starts when the government officially threatens to condemn the property. Taxpayers then have until two years after the close of the tax year (December 31 for calendar year taxpayers) in which they realize any part of the gain to replace converted property. They have one additional year to replace condemned business or investment realty.

EXAMPLE 46

On October 19, 2005, Jim Rollins's business property was completely destroyed in a fire. At the time of the fire, the property was worth $40,000. Rollins paid $80,000 for the property in 1992, and its adjusted basis at the time of the fire was $30,000. In 2006 the insurance company paid Rollins $40,000. Rollins's business casualty gain equals $10,000 ($40,000 – $30,000 adjusted basis). If Rollins wants to postpone the entire gain, he must reinvest at least $40,000 in qualified replacement property between October 19, 2005, and December 31, 2008 (two years after 2006, the year in which Rollins receives the proceeds and realizes the gain).

EXAMPLE 47

Assume the same facts as in Example 46, except that Rollins's business property was condemned and in 2006 the government paid Rollins $40,000 for the property. Rollins's realized gain equals $10,000 ($40,000 proceeds – $30,000 adjusted basis). To avoid recognition of any gain, Rollins has from October 19, 2005 (or the official date of threat, if earlier) until December 31, 2009 (three years after 2006) to buy qualified replacement property costing at least $40,000.

Taxpayers with business or investment property located in the Hurricane Katrina disaster area that was involuntarily converted due to Hurricane Katrina on or after August 25, 2005, have five years to buy qualified replacement property as long as substantially all of the replacement property is used in the Hurricane Katrina disaster area.

Name ______________________________

Section ______________ Date ___________

QUESTIONS AND PROBLEMS

1. **Amount Realized, Realized Gain or Loss.** Jane Barnett sells land that has a $60,000 mortgage. In return for the land, Barnett receives cash of $40,000 and stock with a FMV of $30,000. The buyer also assumes the mortgage. Barnett's adjusted basis in the land is $80,000.

   a. What is Barnett's amount realized?

   b. What is Barnett's realized gain or loss?

   c. How would these amounts change if the buyer had not assumed the mortgage but instead had paid Barnett an additional $60,000 to pay off the mortgage before the transfer of the land took place?

2. **Adjusted Basis, Realized Gain or Loss.** In 2006, Alexis Drayer sells for $200,000 rental property that she purchased in 2002 for $160,000. In 2003, Drayer spent $12,000 on landscaping the $2,200 for lawn care. Over the years, Drayer has deducted a total of $18,440 for depreciation on the property. Compute Drayer's recognized gain or loss on the sale.

3. **Basket Purchase.** Leo Small purchased an apartment building. Small paid $300,000 in cash, assumed a $200,000 mortgage, and paid the following:

Brokerage commission	$35,000
Attorney's fee to acquire title	2,000

   What is Small's basis for depreciation on this building if the FMV of the land and building are $100,000 and $400,000, respectively?

4. **Bargain Purchase.** George O'Brien, president of Sugarman Corporation, was given the opportunity to buy 1,000 shares of the corporation's stock for $120 per share. The par value of the stock was $100. O'Brien took advantage of this offer and purchased 100 shares of stock at a time when the stock was selling for $150 per share. O'Brien includes as income the difference between the FMV of the stock and his cost. The company also gave O'Brien an additional 100 shares of stock as a bonus when the stock was selling for $160 per share.

   a. What amount of income must O'Brien recognize as a result of these stock acquisitions?

   b. What is O'Brien's per-share basis in the stock he acquired?

5. **Property Received in a Divorce.** Hal and Wendy are divorced. Under the terms of the divorce agreement, Hal transferred 100 shares of Big Rig stock (cost $30,000, market value $45,000) to Wendy in satisfaction of Wendy's property rights. If Wendy sells the stock for $50,000, what is her recognized gain?

6. **Inherited Property.** Sharon Bedford inherited 10 shares of Alpha Corporation stock when her aunt died. Her aunt paid $10,000 for the stock, but it was worth only $7,000 at the date of her death. No estate tax return was required. Bedford sold the stock this year for $8,000. What is Bedford's recognized gain or loss from the sale?

7. **Inherited Property.** Terry Taylor purchased 5,000 shares of Ferrero Corporation stock in 1980 for $60,000. Terry died on August 1, 2005, leaving the stock to his daughter, Tina. Tina received the stock on November 1, 2005. The FMV of the stock for various dates follows:

August 1, 2005	$80,000
November 1, 2005	78,000
February 1, 2006	77,000

   a. Tina sold the stock for $75,000 on March 10, 2006. What is Tina's recognized gain or loss from the sale if the executor uses date of death (DOD) to value the estate?

   b. Same as in Part a. except that the executor uses the alternative valuation date (AVD).

c. Assume instead that Tina received the stock on March 1, 2006, when the FMV of the stock was $79,000. What is Tina's recognized gain or loss if the executor uses DOD to value the estate?

d. Same as in Part c. except that the executor uses the AVD to value the estate.

8. **Gifted Property.** Max Fisher purchased 100 shares of XQM stock in 1998 for $10,000. In 2002 Fisher gave the stock to his daughter, Linda, when the FMV of the stock was $8,000. No gift tax was paid.

   a. What is Linda's basis in the stock if she sells it in the current year for $11,000?

   b. What is Linda's basis in the stock if she sells it in the current year for $9,000?

   c. What is Linda's recognized gain or loss if she sells the stock in the current year for $7,000?

9. **Gifted Property.** In 1975, Sam Smythe gave his son, Al, land worth $80,000. Sam paid $60,000 for the land in 1970. He paid $12,000 in gift tax on the transfer. What is Al's basis in the land?

10. **Gifted Property.** In 2006, Bruce Fogg gave Shirley Hayes a house worth $100,000. Fogg's adjusted basis in the house was $80,000. He paid $8,000 in gift tax on the transfer. What is Hayes's initial basis in the house?

11. Gifted Property. Years ago, Darren Franklin gave stock worth $12,000 to his son. Franklin paid $9,000 for the stock back in 1954. He paid $5,000 of gift tax on the transfer. In 2006, the son sold the stock for $42,000.

a. Compute the son's recognized gain or loss assuming that the gift took place in 1970.

b. Same as in Part a. except that the gift took place in 1985.

12. Converted Property. In 1999, Parker Lewis converted his personal residence to rental property. The FMV of the home at the time of conversion was $85,000, Lewis paid $90,000 for the home ten years ago.

a. If Parker sells the property for $100,000 after taking depreciation deductions of $10,000, what is his recognized gain or loss?

b. If Parker sells the property for $70,000 after taking depreciation deductions of $10,000, what is his recognized gain or loss?

c. If Parker sells the property for $78,000 after taking depreciation deductions of $10,000, what is his recognized gain or loss?

13. Sale of Stock. Ima O. Witch had the following purchases of common stock of Halloween Tricks, Inc.

1980	400 shares at $10 per share
1983	100 shares at $20 per share
1986	300 shares at $30 per share
1988	200 shares at $40 per share

a. In 2006 Witch sold 500 shares at $35 per share. Assuming that Witch kept incomplete records and did not identify which blocks of stock were sold, compute Witch's recognized gain or loss on the sale.

b. If Witch's objective is to minimize taxes and she could adequately identify which stock she was selling, which stock should she sell, and what is the recognized gain or loss that would result?

14. Stock Splits. Diane Watkins owned 100 shares of common stock in the Delta Corporation when it had a two-for-one-stock split. The original 100 shares cost $50 each, for a total cost of $5,000. After the split, Watkins had 200 shares that were valued at $30 each, for a total value of $6,000. As a result of the stock split, what is Watkins's basis in each share of stock, and how much income must she recognize?

15. Stock Dividends. In 1995, Debra Hopkins paid $1,200 for 100 shares of UPI common stock. In the current year, UPI offers Hopkins the choice between a $50 cash dividend or 8 additional shares of common stock valued at $9 a share. Hopkins opts for the stock dividend.

a. What is Hopkins's basis in each of the 108 shares she now owns?

b. How would your answer to Part a. change if Hopkins did not have the option of a cash dividend?

16. Wash Sales.

a. An individual taxpayer, not a dealer or trader in securities, completed the following transactions in Micro Products Company common stock:

September 15, 2006, purchased 100 shares at a cost of $4,800
December 10, 2006, sold the above shares for $3,200
January 4, 2007, purchased 60 shares at a cost of $1,800

(1) What is the total taxable capital gain or deductible capital loss from the sale on December 10?

(2) What is the basis of the stock purchased on January 4?

b. Assume that the sales price of the 100 shares sold on December 10 was $5,300; all other facts stated in Part a. remain the same.

(1) What is the total capital gain or deductible capital loss from the sale on December 10?

(2) What is the basis of the stock purchased on January 4?

c. Assume that the sales price of the shares sold on December 10 was $3,200 and that the original 100 shares of stock had been inherited by the taxpayer from the taxpayer's father on September 15, 2006, when they were valued at $2,500. The stock had been purchased by the taxpayer's father two months earlier for $2,000. No estate tax return was filed.

(1) What is the total capital gain or deductible loss from the sale on December 10?

(2) What is the basis of the stock purchased on January 4?

17. **Sale to a Related Party.** Fred sold common stock, which cost him $12,000, to his sister, Sara, for $9,000. Three years later Sara sold the stock for $14,000 to an unrelated party.

a. What was Fred's recognized loss when he sold the stock to Sara?

b. What is Sara's basis in the stock she purchased from Fred?

c. What is Sara's recognized gain or loss when she sells the stock?

d. If Sara had sold the stock for $11,000, what would be her recognized gain or loss?

e. If Sara had sold the stock for $7,000, what would be her recognized gain or loss?

18. **Qualified Small Business Stock.** Van Jenson pays $30,000 for Section 1202 qualified small business stock on February 6, 1998. In October 2006, Jenson sells the stock for $80,000. Compute Jenson's realized and recognized gain on the sale of the stock.

19. Like-Kind Exchange. Which of the following transactions qualify as like-kind exchanges?

a. Grocery store for rental house
b. Apartment building for parking lot
c. GM common stock for land to be held for investment
d. 100 shares of Ford common stock for 100 shares of Chrysler common stock
e. Duplex apartment (investment property) for personal residence

20. Like-Kind Exchange. Which of the following transactions qualify as like-kind exchanges?

a. Old computer for new computer (both used in business)
b. Inventory traded for computer (used in business)
c. Old personal auto for new business auto
d. Office furniture for office equipment (both used in business)
e. Automobile for machinery (both used in business)

21. Like-Kind Exchange. Dottie Packard exchanges real estate held for investment for other real estate to be held for investment. The following facts relate to the exchange.

Adjusted basis of old property	$ 75,000
FMV of new property	100,000
Cash received by Packard	10,000
Mortgage on old property assumed by other party	30,000

a. What is the amount of Packard's realized and recognized gain?

b. What is Packard's basis in the new property?

22. Like-Kind Exchange. For each of the following nontaxable exchanges, compute the realized gain or loss, the recognized gain or loss, and the basis of the new property acquired.

	Basis of Old Asset	*FMV of New Asset*	*Cash Received or Paid*
Exchange a:	$ 8,000	$ 5,000	$ 0
Exchange b:	6,000	10,000	5,000 paid
Exchange c:	6,000	10,000	2,000 paid
Exchange d:	10,000	7,000	2,000 received
Exchange e:	10,000	7,000	5,000 received
Exchange f:	10,000	11,000	2,000 received

23. **Like-Kind Exchange.** Jim Bates wanted Jack McKean's farm as a site for an amusement park and offered him $200,000 for the farm. McKean did not want to sell his farm, which had a basis of $50,000. Bates is now considering acquiring another farm for $180,000 and then offering this farm plus $20,000 in cash to McKean in exchange for McKean's farm. If McKean accepts this offer, what tax consequences does he face?

24. **Sale of a Principal Residence.** Adam Hodges, who is single, sold his principal residence for $440,000. He paid $28,000 in selling expenses. Hodges paid $107,000 for the house 17 years ago. Over the years Hodges made capital improvements to the house totaling $42,000. Compute Hodges's recognized gain on the sale of his home.

25. **Involuntary Conversion.** The Wholesale Dress Shop was destroyed by fire in January. The adjusted basis of the store was $150,000. In March, the insurance company paid $140,000 to cover the loss. Shortly thereafter a new shop was purchased for $200,000.

    a. What, if any, is the recognized gain or loss?

    b. What is the basis of the new dress shop?

26. **Involuntary Conversion.** Duffy & Co.'s warehouse, which had an adjusted basis of $1,100,000, was destroyed by fire. Duffy received insurance in the amount of $2,000,000. Duffy immediately invested $1,800,000 in a new warehouse and elected to postpone as much of the gain as possible.

    a. What is the amount of gain recognized for income tax purposes?

    b. What is the basis of the new warehouse?

27. Involuntary Conversion. On February 17, 2005, Kari Baker was notified by the state that the land she owned as an investment was needed for a state park and that the land would be condemned. The state took possession of the land on January 15, 2006, and Baker received her condemnation award on January 20, 2006.

a. If Baker elects to postpone recognition of her gain, by what date must she purchase replacement property?

b. What type of property could Baker purchase and still postpone recognition of her gain?

28. Internet Problem: Researching Publication 550.

Beta Corporation is a C Corporation whose total gross assets have never exceeded $35 million. Donald Adams purchased stock from Beta Corporation in March 1995 as part of Beta's initial issuance. Adams is interested in selling his stock in Beta Corporation and wants to know whether Beta Corporation meets the requirements of a qualified small business corporation under Section 1202.

Go to the IRS Web site. Locate Publication 550 and find the appropriate page that discusses the requirements for a qualified small business corporation under Section 1202. Print out a copy of the page where you found your answer. Underline or highlight the pertinent information. Comment on whether you can answer Adams's question with the information that has been provided.

See Appendix A for instructions on use of the IRS Web site.

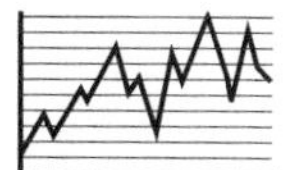

29. Business Entity Problem: This problem is designed for those using the "business entity" approach. The solution may require information from Chapters 14 and 15.

Judy Davis converts her sole proprietorship into a regular C corporation. The basis of the assets she transfers into the corporation is $225,000. The fair market value is $265,000. In return for these assets, Davis received all of the corporation's stock—50,000 shares.

a. What is the basis of these assets to the corporation?

b. What is Davis's basis in stock she receives?

CUMULATIVE PROBLEM (CHAPTERS 8-10)

On September 29, 2006, Tripper Udah sold rental property for $230,000. Five percent of the purchase price was allocated to the furnishings. Udah originally purchased the home (a condominium) as his principal residence back in 1990. He paid $160,000 for the home and spent $35,000 on its furnishings. From 1990-1999, Udah made improvements to the home totaling $34,000. On March 4, 2000, he converted the home to rental property. The fair market value (FMV) of the home itself at the time of the conversion was $182,000. The FMV of the furnishings were $5,000. Udah used MACRS to depreciate both the realty and its furnishings. This was the only depreciable property Udah placed in service during 2000. Compute Udah's recognized gain or loss on the sale of the home and on the sale of its furnishings.

11

Property: Capital Gains and Losses, and Depreciation Recapture

CHAPTER CONTENTS

CHAPTER OVERVIEW

Chapter 10 covered the calculation of realized gains and losses from the sale, exchange, or other disposal of property. It also covered which realized gains and losses taxpayers recognize for tax purposes. This chapter examines the nature of those gains and losses. Recognized gains may be capital gains or ordinary income. Recognized losses may be treated as capital losses or ordinary deductions. The distinction is important because capital gains and losses are treated differently than ordinary gains and losses. This chapter explains which gains and losses are capital and which are ordinary. It also shows where taxpayers report gains and losses on the tax return.

CAPITAL GAINS AND LOSSES

The tax laws treat capital gains and losses differently from ordinary gains and losses. Individual taxpayers are limited on the amount of capital losses they can deduct each year, whereas reduced tax rates can apply to capital gains. There are several ways gains and losses can be classified as capital gains and losses. The most common way is through the sale or exchange of a capital asset.

Capital Assets Defined

All property that taxpayers own is a capital asset unless it falls into one of the following five categories:

1. Inventory held primarily for sale to customers. This includes property that will become part of inventory, such as materials and work-in-process.
2. Business receivables, including accounts and notes receivable.
3. Depreciable property and land used in a trade or business.
4. Copyrights; literary, musical, or artistic compositions; letters; memorandums; etc., created by the taxpayer, or letters and memorandums prepared or produced for the taxpayer. (However, effective for sales starting after May 17, 2006 and until December 31, 2010, the composer of a musical composition or copyright may elect to treat their works as capital assets).
5. U.S. government publications purchased for less than the normal sales price.

A closer look at the five categories reveals that the first three involve business property. Thus, except for items described in the last two categories, capital assets can be defined as the taxpayer's personal belongings and investment property. Common examples of capital assets include the taxpayer's clothing, residence, and automobile (personal-use property). Other examples include stock, bonds, and land held for speculation (investment property).

Using the rules from Chapter 10, taxpayers compute the realized gains and losses that result from the sale or exchange of capital assets. Next, they determine which realized gains and losses they recognize for tax purposes. (Recall from Chapter 10 that not all realized gains and losses are recognized on the tax return.) Taxpayers then classify the recognized gains and losses as short-term or long-term capital gains and losses.

Short-term capital gains and losses result from the sale or exchange of capital assets held for one year or less. **Long-term capital gains and losses** result if the capital asset was held for more than one year. In determining whether property has been held for more than one year, the date taxpayers acquire property does not count, but the disposal date does.

EXAMPLE 1

On June 3, 20x1, Joel Thomas buys 100 shares of common stock. Thomas's holding period begins on June 4, 20x1. On June 4, 20x2, Thomas will have held the shares for more than one year. If Thomas sells the shares after June 3, 20x2, he will recognize a long-term capital gain or loss. This, of course, assumes that neither the wash sale rules nor the related party rules from Chapter 10 prevent Thomas from recognizing a loss on the sale.

Holding Periods for Property

Not all holding periods begin the day after the taxpayer physically acquires property. Special rules apply to inherited property and to property with a carryover basis.

Inherited Property

When taxpayers dispose of inherited property, a long-term gain or loss results, regardless of the actual holding period. Thus, if the property inherited is a capital asset, any recognized gain or loss upon its sale or exchange results in a long-term capital gain or loss.

EXAMPLE 2

Mariah Fairchild inherited stock from her deceased aunt. Fairchild's basis in the stock is its $10,000 fair market value (FMV) on the date of her aunt's death. Fairchild took possession of the property on October 5, 20x4 and sold it for $12,400 on October 10, 20x4. Although Fairchild's actual ownership in the property did not exceed one year, she recognizes a $2,400 long-term capital gain ($12,400–$10,000) on the sale of the inherited stock.

Carryover Basis Property

When property has a carryover basis, the holding period also carries over. A carryover basis and holding period can occur one of three ways.

1. The taxpayer uses the previous owner's basis to compute the basis in property. This occurs with transfers of property between spouses and gifted property where the taxpayer uses the donor's basis. In these cases, the previous owner's holding period carries over to the taxpayer.
2. The taxpayer allocates part of the basis in existing property to the basis of newly acquired property. This happens with nontaxable stock dividends and stock splits. When this occurs, the holding period of the original property carries over to the new property.
3. The taxpayer adjusts the basis in property to reflect a postponed gain or loss from previously owned property. This can occur with like-kind exchanges, involuntary conversions, and wash sales. In these cases, the holding period of the old property becomes the holding period of the new property.

EXAMPLE 3

On July 11, 2006, Tara Reynolds gave her nephew, Chris Adams, stock worth $6,000. Reynolds paid $7,000 for the stock on May 9, 1982. Adams sells the stock on December 21, 2006, for $7,500.

Recall from Chapter 10 that when the FMV of gifted property is less than the donor's basis, the donee's basis is determined when the donee disposes of the property. The donee uses the donor's basis to compute gains, and the FMV of the property at the time of the gift to compute losses. Because Adams sells the stock for a gain (more than the donor's basis), his basis in the stock is the donor's basis. Using his aunt's basis, Adams realizes a $500 gain ($7,500 – $7,000). Since Adams uses the donor's basis as his basis in the stock, his holding period begins on May 10, 1982 (the day after the day his aunt bought the stock). Therefore, Adams recognizes a $500 long-term capital gain.

EXAMPLE 4

On May 7, 20x7, Norm Major received land as part of a divorce settlement. Major holds the land as an investment. He sells the land for $72,500 on December 4, 20x7. The FMV of the land on May 7, 20x7 was $70,000. Major's wife paid $30,000 for the land in 20x0. His holding period dates back to 20x0 – the date on which his spouse bought the land. His wife's basis carries over and becomes his basis in the land (see Chapter 10). Thus, Major recognizes a $42,500 long-term capital gain ($72,500 - $30,000).

EXAMPLE 5

On March 10, 2006, Doug Simpson exchanges land for a building in a like-kind exchange. Simpson purchased the land on August 18, 1991. Simpson is treated as having owned the building acquired in the like-kind exchange since August 18, 1991.

Netting Capital Gains and Losses

The netting process begins by separating short-term gains and losses from long-term capital gains and losses. The netting process continues by offsetting these gains and losses within each of these two groups. The result is a *net short-term capital gain or loss* and a *net long-term capital gain or loss.*

EXAMPLE 6

Janice Altman sold the following capital assets during the year.

Description	Gain (Loss)	Group
Stock held 6 months	$5,000	short-term
Stock held 8 months	(7,000)	short-term
Stock held 3 years	(14,000)	long-term
Stock held 6 years	21,000	long-term

The first step in the netting process involves separating the gains and losses into two groups (see the column **Group** above). Altman then begins netting within each group.

Short-Term	Long-Term
$5,000	($14,000)
(7,000)	21,000
($2,000)	$ 7,000

The netting process produces a $2,000 net short-term capital loss and a $7,000 net long-term capital gain.

When a net gain results in both groups, the netting process is complete. Likewise, the netting process is complete when both groups show a net loss. Otherwise, netting losses against gains between the two groups occurs. Examples 7, 8 and 9 demonstrate netting between groups.

EXAMPLE 7

Continuing with Example 6, Altman offsets the $2,000 net short-term loss against the $7,000 net long-term gain. This leaves Altman with a $5,000 overall net long-term capital gain.

Short-Term	Long-Term
$5,000	($14,000)
(7,000)	21,000
($2,000)	$7,000
→	(2,000)
	$ 5,000

EXAMPLE 8

Jim Brooks sold four capital assets during the year. After separating the gains and losses into two groups, Brooks nets the gains and losses within each group. This netting within groups produces a $2,000 net short-term loss and a $3,000 net long-term loss. Since both groups result in a loss, the netting process is complete.

Short-Term	Long-Term
$6,000	$1,000
(8,000)	(4,000)
($2,000)	$ (3,000)

EXAMPLE 9

Lynda Tymes sold five capital assets during the year. After separating the gains and losses into two groups, Tymes nets the gains and losses within each group. This netting within groups produces a $5,000 net short-term capital gain, and a $1,000 net long-term capital loss. Tymes uses the $1,000 net long-term capital loss to offset the net short-term gain. Tymes has a $4,000 overall net short-term capital gain.

Short-Term	Long-Term
($13,000)	$3,000
7,000	(4,000)
11,000	
$5,000	($1,000)
(1,000)	←
$ 4,000	

Once the netting process is complete, individual taxpayers with a *net capital gain* pay a reduced tax rate on the net capital gain. **Net capital gain** equals the excess of net long-term capital gain over net short-term capital loss. If there is both a net long-term capital gain and a net short-term capital gain, then net capital gain equals the net long-term capital gain. Taxpayers with a net capital gain or qualified dividends compute their tax liability by subtracting out these amounts from taxable income and computing tax on the remaining amount. They then add to this amount the tax on the net capital gain and qualified dividends. The tax rate on net capital gain and qualified dividends is 5% for taxpayers whose taxable income both with and without these items falls in the 10% or 15% tax brackets. For taxpayers whose taxable income both with and without these items falls in the 25% and higher tax brackets, the tax rate on net capital gain and qualified dividends is 15%.

EXAMPLE 10

The taxable income for Janice Altman from Examples 6 and 7 is $95,000 for 2006. Altman's filing status is single and she has no qualified dividends included in taxable income. Altman computes her 2006 tax liability as follows.

Tax on $90,000 ($95,000 – $5,000 net capital gain)	$19,539
Plus $5,000 × 15%	750
Tax liability on $95,000	$20,239

EXAMPLE 11

Same as in Example 10, except that Altman's taxable income is $25,000.

Tax on $20,000 ($25,000 – $5,000)	$2,626
Plus $5,000 × 5% (Altman is in the 15% bracket)	250
Tax liability on $25,000	$2,876

For taxpayers whose taxable income with the net capital gain and qualified dividends falls in the 25% or higher tax bracket, but whose taxable income without these items drops down to the 10% or 15% tax bracket, only part of the net capital gain will be taxed at 5%. The rest is taxed at 15%. Example 12 shows how this calculation is made.

EXAMPLE 12

Same as in Example 10, except that Altman's taxable income is $32,000. This falls in the 25% tax bracket (the cutoff is $30,650 – see inside front cover of the book). However, when you take out the qualified dividends ($0) and net capital gain ($5,000), taxable income drops to $27,000, which is in the 15% tax bracket. Thus, only $3,650 of her net capital gain ($30,650 - $27,000) is taxed at the lowest 5% tax rate. The rest is taxed at 15%.

Tax on $27,000 (using the tax table for Single taxpayers)	$3,676
Plus $3,650 x 5% ($30,650 - $27,000)	183
Plus $1,350 x 15% ($32,000 - $30,650)	203
Tax liability on $32,000 taxable income	$4,062

Net capital gains from the sale of collectibles and Section 1202 qualified small business stock are taxed at a higher 28% rate for taxpayers in the 28% or higher tax brackets. Collectibles include any work of art, rugs, antiques and gemstones, plus the taxpayer's stamp and coin collections. Those interested in learning more about how the sale of these assets fits into the netting process should refer to the Instructions to Schedule D (Form 1040), Capital Gains and Losses.

Net Capital Losses

When capital losses exceed capital gains, the excess is a net capital loss. Each year, individual taxpayers can use up to $3,000 of net capital losses to offset ordinary income. Ordinary income includes wages, interest, dividends, and net profit from a business. Any net capital loss in excess of $3,000 can be carried forward indefinitely. Should the netting process produce both a net short-term and a net long-term capital loss, taxpayers first use up their net short-term capital loss, and then net long-term capital loss. Any unused short-term capital loss is carried over to the next year to offset next year's short-term capital gains. Any unused long-term capital loss is carried over to the next year to offset next year's long-term capital gains.

EXAMPLE 13

In 2006, Meg Fortin sold three capital assets that produced a $4,000 short-term gain, a $13,000 short-term capital loss, and a $2,000 long-term capital loss.

Short-Term	Long-Term
$4,000	($2,000)
(13,000)	
($9,000)	($2,000)

Fortin's capital losses exceed capital gains by $11,000. Fortin uses $3,000 of the net short-term capital loss to offset ordinary income on her 2006 tax return. Fortin carries over to 2007 a $6,000 short-term capital loss ($9,000 – $3,000) and a $2,000 long-term capital loss.

EXAMPLE 14

Mary Hill sells three capital assets in 2006 that produce a $5,000 short-term gain, a $1,000 long-term gain, and a $4,000 long-term capital loss. Hill has a $6,000 short-term capital loss carryover and a $2,000 long-term capital loss carryover from 2005. She nets these amounts against her 2006 capital gains and losses as shown below.

	Short-Term	Long-Term
carryover	($6,000)	($2,000)
	5,000	1,000
		(4,000)
	($1,000)	($5,000)

Hill uses the $1,000 net short-term capital loss and $2,000 of the net long-term capital loss to offset ordinary income on her 2006 tax return. She carries over to 2007 a $3,000 long-term capital loss ($5,000 – $2,000).

EXAMPLE 15

Continuing with Example 14, Hill sells two capital assets n 2007. Those assets produce a $14,000 long-term capital gain and a $2,000 short-term capital loss. Hill's netting process in 2007 is as follows.

	Short-Term	Long-Term
carryover		($ 3,000)
	($2,000)	14,000
	($2,000)	$11,000
	→	(2,000)
		$ 9,000

Hill uses the $3,000 long-term capital loss to offset long-term capital gain generated in 2007. She then offsets the net short-term capital loss against the net long-term capital gain. This results in a $9,000 net capital gain that will be taxed at no more than 15%.

Schedule D

Individual taxpayers report capital gains and losses on Schedule D (Form 1040), Capital Gains and Losses. They report short-term capital gains and losses in Part I. Taxpayers report long-term capital gains and losses in Part II. All gains and losses are reported in column (f).

In Part III, taxpayers combine the net short-term capital gain or loss (line 7) and the net long-term capital gain or loss (line 15). If combining these amounts results in an overall net loss, the taxpayer enters up to $3,000 of the net loss ($1,500 if married filing separately) on Schedule D (line 21) and transfers this amount to Form 1040. When an overall net gain results, the taxpayer completes lines 17–20, which may involve completing a worksheet to pay a reduced the tax rate on net capital gain. Even if the taxpayer does not report a net capital gain, when the taxpayer reports qualified dividends on Form 1040 (line 9b), line 22 of Schedule D is answered **Yes.** The taxpayer then completes the **Qualified Dividends and Capital Gains Tax Worksheet** located in the Instructions to Form 1040 to pay a 5%/15% tax rate on the qualified dividends. This worksheet is shown on page 11-11.

Information for Figure 11-1: Filled-In Schedule D and Schedule D Tax Worksheet

On November 20, 2006, Curt R. Stevens (single, age 40) sold 100 shares of Comco Corporation common stock for $2,975. Stevens paid a $20 commission on the sale. Stevens purchased the stock on June 27, 2006, for $750.

On September 3, 2006, Stevens sold 100 shares of Wilcox Industries preferred stock for $6,000. Stevens paid a $120 commission on the sale. Stevens received the stock as a gift from his father on May 8, 1994. The FMV of the stock on May 8, 1994, was $9,000. His father paid $3,192 for the stock on February 7, 1981. The father did not pay gift tax on the transfer.

In 2005, Stevens's capital losses exceeded his capital gains by $4,000. Stevens used $3,000 of the excess of the net capital loss to offset ordinary income and carried over to 2006 a $1,000 short-term capital loss.

FIGURE 11-1 Filled-In Schedule D, Page 1

SCHEDULE D (Form 1040)
Department of the Treasury Internal Revenue Service (99)

Capital Gains and Losses

▶ Attach to Form 1040 or Form 1040NR. ▶ See Instructions for Schedule D (Form 1040).
▶ Use Schedule D-1 to list additional transactions for lines 1 and 8.

OMB No. 1545-0074
2006
Attachment Sequence No. 12

Name(s) shown on Form 1040: Curtis R. Stevens
Your social security number: 992 84 5922

Part I Short-Term Capital Gains and Losses—Assets Held One Year or Less

(a) Description of property (Example: 100 sh. XYZ Co.)	(b) Date acquired (Mo., day, yr.)	(c) Date sold (Mo., day, yr.)	(d) Sales price (see page D-6 of the instructions)	(e) Cost or other basis (see page D-7 of the instructions)	(f) Gain or (loss) Subtract (e) from (d)
1 100 shares Comco Corp.	6/27/06	11/20/06	2,955 00	750 00	2,205 00
2 Enter your short-term totals, if any, from Schedule D-1, line 2 2					
3 **Total short-term sales price amounts.** Add lines 1 and 2 in column (d) 3			2,955 00		

4 Short-term gain from Form 6252 and short-term gain or (loss) from Forms 4684, 6781, and 8824	4	
5 Net short-term gain or (loss) from partnerships, S corporations, estates, and trusts from Schedule(s) K-1	5	
6 Short-term capital loss carryover. Enter the amount, if any, from line 10 of your **Capital Loss Carryover Worksheet** on page D-7 of the instructions	6	(1,000 00)
7 **Net short-term capital gain or (loss).** Combine lines 1 through 6 in column (f)	7	1,205 00

Part II Long-Term Capital Gains and Losses—Assets Held More Than One Year

(a) Description of property (Example: 100 sh. XYZ Co.)	(b) Date acquired (Mo., day, yr.)	(c) Date sold (Mo., day, yr.)	(d) Sales price (see page D-6 of the instructions)	(e) Cost or other basis (see page D-7 of the instructions)	(f) Gain or (loss) Subtract (e) from (d)
8 100 Shares Wilcox Industries	2/7/81	9/3/06	5,880 00	3,192 00	2,688 00
9 Enter your long-term totals, if any, from Schedule D-1, line 9 9					
10 **Total long-term sales price amounts.** Add lines 8 and 9 in column (d) 10			5,880 00		

11 Gain from Form 4797, Part I; long-term gain from Forms 2439 and 6252; and long-term gain or (loss) from Forms 4684, 6781, and 8824	11	
12 Net long-term gain or (loss) from partnerships, S corporations, estates, and trusts from Schedule(s) K-1	12	
13 Capital gain distributions. See page D-1 of the instructions	13	
14 Long-term capital loss carryover. Enter the amount, if any, from line 15 of your **Capital Loss Carryover Worksheet** on page D-7 of the instructions	14	( )
15 **Net long-term capital gain or (loss).** Combine lines 8 through 14 in column (f). Then go to Part III on the back	15	2,688 00

For Paperwork Reduction Act Notice, see Form 1040 instructions. Cat. No. 11338H **Schedule D (Form 1040) 2006**

FIGURE 11-1 Filled-In Schedule D, Page 2

Schedule D (Form 1040) 2006 — Page 2

Part III Summary

16	Combine lines 7 and 15 and enter the result. If line 16 is a loss, skip lines 17 through 20, and go to line 21. If a gain, enter the gain on Form 1040, line 13, or Form 1040NR, line 14. Then go to line 17 below	16	3,893 00
17	Are lines 15 and 16 **both** gains? ☒ **Yes.** Go to line 18. ☐ **No.** Skip lines 18 through 21, and go to line 22.		
18	Enter the amount, if any, from line 7 of the **28% Rate Gain Worksheet** on page D-8 of the instructions ▶	18	0
19	Enter the amount, if any, from line 18 of the **Unrecaptured Section 1250 Gain Worksheet** on page D-9 of the instructions ▶	19	0
20	Are lines 18 and 19 **both** zero or blank? ☒ **Yes.** Complete Form 1040 through line 43, or Form 1040NR through line 40. Then complete the **Qualified Dividends and Capital Gain Tax Worksheet** on page 38 of the Instructions for Form 1040 (or in the Instructions for Form 1040NR). **Do not** complete lines 21 and 22 below. ☐ **No.** Complete Form 1040 through line 43, or Form 1040NR through line 40. Then complete the **Schedule D Tax Worksheet** on page D-10 of the instructions. **Do not** complete lines 21 and 22 below.		
21	If line 16 is a loss, enter here and on Form 1040, line 13, or Form 1040NR, line 14, the **smaller** of: • The loss on line 16 or • ($3,000), or if married filing separately, ($1,500) **Note.** When figuring which amount is smaller, treat both amounts as positive numbers.	21	( )
22	Do you have qualified dividends on Form 1040, line 9b, or Form 1040NR, line 10b? ☐ **Yes.** Complete Form 1040 through line 43, or Form 1040NR through line 40. Then complete the **Qualified Dividends and Capital Gain Tax Worksheet** on page 38 of the Instructions for Form 1040 (or in the Instructions for Form 1040NR). ☐ **No.** Complete the rest of Form 1040 or Form 1040NR.		

Schedule D (Form 1040) 2006

Other Information

1(d): Sales price, **$2,955.00** ($2,975 – $20 selling expenses)

6: Short-term capital loss carryover, **$1,000.00**

8(b): Date acquired, **2/7/81** (donor's holding period carries over since donor's basis is used)

8(d): Sales price, **$5,880.00** ($6,000 – $120)

8(e): Cost or other basis, **$3,192.00** (donor's basis carries over since donor's basis < FMV at the time of the gift)

18: Stevens has no amount taxed at 28%

19: Stevens has no unrecaptured Section 1250 gain

20: Stevens answers **Yes** to this question. He transfers the $3,893 total capital gain from Schedule D (line 16) to Form 1040 (line 13). He then calculates his tax by completing the **Schedule D Tax Worksheet** to pay a reduced tax rate on his $2,688 net capital gain. Using the worksheet on the next page, and the additional information provided, Stevens computes his tax. He then transfers this amount to Form 1040, line 44.

FIGURE 11-1 Filled-In Schedule D Tax Worksheet

Schedule D Tax Worksheet

Keep for Your Records

Complete this worksheet only if line 18 or line 19 of Schedule D is more than zero. Otherwise, complete the Qualified Dividends and Capital Gain Tax Worksheet on page 38 of the Instructions for Form 1040 (or in the Instructions for Form 1040NR) to figure your tax.

Exception: Do not use the Qualified Dividends and Capital Gain Tax Worksheet **or** this worksheet to figure your tax if:

- Line 15 or line 16 of Schedule D is zero or less **and** you have no qualified dividends on Form 1040, line 9b (or Form 1040NR, line 10b); **or**
- Form 1040, line 43 (or Form 1040NR, line 40) is zero or less.

Instead, see the instructions for Form 1040, line 44 (or Form 1040NR, line 41).

1. Enter your taxable income from Form 1040, line 43 (or Form 1040NR, line 40) . . . **1.** 72,350
2. Enter your qualified dividends from Form 1040, line 9b (or Form 1040NR, line 10b) . . . **2.** 500
3. Enter the amount from Form 4952, line 4g **3.** ______
4. Enter the amount from Form 4952, line 4e* **4.** ______
5. Subtract line 4 from line 3. If zero or less, enter -0- . . . **5.** 0
6. Subtract line 5 from line 2. If zero or less, enter -0- . . . **6.** 500
7. Enter the **smaller** of line 15 or line 16 of Schedule D . . . **7.** 2,688
8. Enter the **smaller** of line 3 or line 4 . . . **8.** 0
9. Subtract line 8 from line 7. If zero or less, enter -0- . . . **9.** 2,688
10. Add lines 6 and 9 . . . **10.** 3,188
11. Add lines 18 and 19 of Schedule D . . . **11.** 0
12. Enter the **smaller** of line 9 or line 11 . . . **12.** 0
13. Subtract line 12 from line 10 . . . **13.** 3,188
14. Subtract line 13 from line 1. If zero or less, enter -0- . . . **14.** 69,162
15. Enter the **smaller** of:
    - The amount on line 1 **or**
    - $30,650 if single or married filing separately; $61,300 if married filing jointly or qualifying widow(er); or $41,050 if head of household } . . . **15.** 30,650
16. Enter the **smaller** of line 14 or line 15 . . . **16.** 30,650
17. Subtract line 10 from line 1. If zero or less, enter -0- . . . **17.** 69,162
18. Enter the **larger** of line 16 or line 17 . . . ▶ **18.** 69,162
    If lines 15 and 16 are the same, skip lines 19 and 20 and go to line 21. Otherwise, go to line 19.
19. Subtract line 16 from line 15 . . . ▶ **19.** 0
20. Multiply line 19 by 5% (.05) . . . **20.** 0
    If lines 1 and 15 are the same, skip lines 21 through 33 and go to line 34. Otherwise, go to line 21.
21. Enter the **smaller** of line 1 or line 13 . . . **21.** 3,188
22. Enter the amount from line 19 (if line 19 is blank, enter -0-) . . . **22.** 0
23. Subtract line 22 from line 21. If zero or less, enter -0- . . . ▶ **23.** 3,188
24. Multiply line 23 by 15% (.15) . . . **24.** 478
    If Schedule D, line 19, is zero or blank, skip lines 25 through 30 and go to line 31. Otherwise, go to line 25.
25. Enter the **smaller** of line 9 above or Schedule D, line 19 . . . **25.** ______
26. Add lines 10 and 18 . . . **26.** ______
27. Enter the amount from line 1 above . . . **27.** ______
28. Subtract line 27 from line 26. If zero or less, enter -0- . . . **28.** ______
29. Subtract line 28 from line 25. If zero or less, enter -0- . . . ▶ **29.** ______
30. Multiply line 29 by 25% (.25) . . . **30.** ______
    If Schedule D, line 18, is zero or blank, skip lines 31 through 33 and go to line 34. Otherwise, go to line 31.
31. Add lines 18, 19, 23, and 29 . . . **31.** ______
32. Subtract line 31 from line 1 . . . **32.** ______
33. Multiply line 32 by 28% (.28) . . . **33.** ______
34. Figure the tax on the amount on **line 18**. Use the Tax Table or Tax Computation Worksheet, whichever applies . . . **34.** 13,851
35. Add lines 20, 24, 30, 33, and 34 . . . **35.** 14,329
36. Figure the tax on the amount on **line 1.** Use the Tax Table or Tax Computation Worksheet, whichever applies . . . **36.** 14,651
37. **Tax on all taxable income (including capital gains and qualified dividends).** Enter the **smaller** of line 35 or line 36. Also include this amount on Form 1040, line 44 (or Form 1040NR, line 41) . . . **37.** 14,329

*If applicable, enter instead the smaller amount you entered on the dotted line next to line 4e of Form 4952.

Additional Information for Schedule D Tax Worksheet

1:	Taxable income (Form 1040, line 43)	$72,350
2:	Qualified dividends (Form 1040, line 9b)	500

Steven's total tax liability from the Schedule D Tax Worksheet (Figure 11-1) can also be calculated using the approach shown earlier in the chapter.

Tax on $69,162* (using the tax table for Single taxpayers)	$13,851
Plus $3,188 x 15% (Stevens is in the 25% tax bracket)	478
Tax liability on $72,350 taxable income	$14,329

* ($72,350 - $2,688 net capital gain - $500 qualified dividends)

Special Rules

Special rules apply to losses from worthless securities and from the sale of Section 1244 stock. Special rules also apply to gains from sales between certain related parties and from sales of subdivided real estate.

Worthless Securities

In the year securities become worthless, the taxpayer is treated as having sold the securities for $0 on the last day of the tax year. For most taxpayers, securities are capital assets. Hence, worthless securities produce a capital loss. A long-term capital loss results if, on the last day of the tax year, the taxpayer held the securities for more than one year.

EXAMPLE 16

On April 3, 20x1, Randy Harmon pays $10,000 for stock. On January 23, 20x2, the stock is declared worthless. Harmon is deemed to have sold the stock for $0 on December 31, 20x2. Since the period from April 4, 20x1 (the day after the purchase) until December 31, 20x2 (the "sales date") exceeds one year, Harmon recognizes a $10,000 long-term capital loss. He reports the loss in Part II on Schedule D (line 8) and identifies the loss as coming from a worthless security by writing "worthless" in the columns for date sold and sales price.

Section 1244 Stock

For most people, stock is an investment. A loss on the sale of an investment normally produces a capital loss. However, each year individuals can deduct as ordinary losses up to $50,000 ($100,000 on a joint return) of the loss on the sale, exchange, or worthlessness of *qualified small business stock* (Section 1244 stock). Annual losses in excess of $50,000 ($100,000 on a joint return) are capital losses. Although both common and preferred stock qualify as Section 1244 stock, only the original owner of the stock qualifies for the ordinary loss treatment. To qualify as Section 1244 stock, the corporation issuing the stock must meet certain requirements. Two main requirements are:

1. The corporation's contributed capital plus paid-in-surplus cannot exceed $1,000,000 at the time the stock is issued.
2. The corporation must be primarily an operating company rather than an investment company.

EXAMPLE 17

Page Walters, a single taxpayer, sells Section 1244 stock for $17,000. Walters purchased the stock several years ago for $80,000. Walters's realized loss equals $63,000 ($17,000 – $80,000). Walters recognizes a $50,000 ordinary loss and a $13,000 long-term capital loss. She enters the long-term capital loss into the netting process and uses the ordinary loss to offset ordinary income such as wages and dividends. If Walters has no other capital gains or losses, only $3,000 of the $13,000 long-term capital loss can be used to offset ordinary income in the current year. Had the stock not qualified as Section 1244 stock, Walters would have recognized a $63,000 long-term capital loss.

Each year taxpayers are allowed up to $50,000 ($100,000 for MFJ) of ordinary losses from the sale of Section 1244 stock. Taxpayers whose Section 1244 stock has declined in value more than $50,000 ($100,000 MFJ) from when they bought it should plan on selling their stock over more than one tax year to take advantage of the $50,000 ($100,000) of ordinary losses allowed each year.

Gains from Sales between Certain Related Parties

When individuals sell capital assets to a corporation, they should recognize capital gains or losses. However, for individuals who own (directly or constructively) more than 50% of the value of the corporation's outstanding stock, capital gain treatment does not apply if the property is depreciable property to the corporation. Instead, the individual recognizes ordinary income. The same rule applies to individuals who sell capital assets to a partnership in which they own (directly or constructively) more than a 50% interest. If the property is depreciable property to the partnership, then capital gain treatment does not apply, and the individual recognizes ordinary income. Note that this rule applies only to gains between certain related parties. See Chapter 10 for rules disallowing losses between related parties, as well as the rules governing constructive ownership.

EXAMPLE 18

Aaron Scott sells property to a corporation for a $10,000 gain. Scott owns 60% of the stock in the corporation. The property is a capital asset to Scott, but will be a depreciable asset in the hands of the corporation. Scott recognizes $10,000 of ordinary income.

EXAMPLE 19

Same as in Example 18, except that Scott owns 50% of the stock in the corporation. Because he does not own *more than* a 50% interest in the corporation's stock, Scott recognizes a $10,000 capital gain on the sale of the property to the corporation.

EXAMPLE 20

Same as in Example 19, except that the property is land, and therefore is not depreciable property in the hands of the corporation. Scott recognizes a $10,000 capital gain on the sale of the land.

Subdivided Property

Although a capital gain or loss usually results when investors sell parcels of land, special rules apply to *gains* on the sale of subdivided property. To receive capital gain treatment, taxpayers must first meet the following four conditions.

1. The taxpayer cannot be a real estate dealer.
2. The taxpayer cannot be a corporation.
3. The taxpayer cannot make substantial improvements to the lots sold. Filling, draining, clearing, and leveling activities normally are not considered substantial improvements.
4. The taxpayer must hold the lots for at least five years before selling them. Inherited property has no minimum holding requirement.

Taxpayers who meet these four conditions recognize capital gain on the sale of all lots sold until the tax year in which they sell the sixth lot. Starting with the tax year in which the sixth lot is sold, they recognize ordinary income for up to 5% of the sales price. Gain not taxed as ordinary income is taxed as long-term capital gain. Any selling expenses are first absorbed by the ordinary income.

EXAMPLE 21

Eric Marmoll bought a tract of land in 20x0. Marmoll, who is not a real estate dealer, subdivides the land in 20x6 and sells four lots for $12,000 each. There were no selling expenses. The adjusted basis of each lot is $9,000. Marmoll recognizes a $3,000 long-term capital gain on the sale of each lot ($12,000 – $9,000).

EXAMPLE 22

Continuing with Example 21, in 20x7, in Marmoll sells two more lots for $12,000 each. There were no selling expenses. The adjusted basis of each lot is $9,000. Marmoll recognizes a $3,000 gain on the sale of each lot. Because Marmoll sells the sixth lot in 20x7, he recognizes $600 ($12,000 × 5%) of ordinary income and $2,400 ($3,000 – $600) of long-term capital gain for each lot sold in 20x7. Marmoll will recognize up to 5% of the sales price as ordinary income on lots sold in future years.

EXAMPLE 23

Assume the same facts as in Example 22, except that Marmoll incurred $500 of selling expenses for each lot. The selling expenses reduce the recognized gain for each lot to $2,500 ($3,000 – $500). The selling expenses are first absorbed by the ordinary income. Thus, for each lot sold Marmoll recognizes $100 ($600 – $500 selling expenses) of ordinary income and $2,400 ($2,500 – $100) of long-term capital gain. Had the selling expenses exceeded $600, the entire recognized gain would have been long-term capital gain.

Other Ways of Producing Capital Gains and Losses

Besides the sale or exchange of capital assets, other activities can produce capital gains and losses. These activities include nonbusiness bad debts, net casualty or theft gains on personal-use property, and disposing of business property.

Nonbusiness Bad Debts

Chapter 7 described the rules for deducting business bad debts. A nonbusiness bad debt is a bona fide debt that does not qualify as a business bad debt. A nonbusiness bad debt is reported as a short-term capital loss, regardless of how long the debt was held. This differs from business bad debts, which sole proprietors deduct on Schedule C. Also, unlike a business bad debt, which taxpayers can start deducting in the year the debt becomes partially worthless, taxpayers cannot deduct a nonbusiness bad debt until it becomes completely worthless.

In the year taxpayers claim a nonbusiness bad debt, they enter the name of the debtor and the words *statement attached* on Schedule D, Part I [line 1(a)]. They then report the amount of the loss on line 1(f). Finally, they attach to the tax return a statement describing the following:

1. The amount of the debt and the date it was due,
2. Their business or family relationship with the debtor,
3. Their efforts to collect the debt, and
4. Their reason for concluding the debt was worthless.

EXAMPLE 24

Pam McMillan lent a friend $10,000 in 20x1. A bona fide debtor-creditor relationship existed between McMillan and her friend. In 20x3 the friend filed for bankruptcy, and McMillan was told to expect $.60 on the dollar for her loan. The friend completed bankruptcy proceedings in 20x4, and McMillan received $4,500. McMillan recognizes a $5,500 ($10,000 – $4,500) short-term capital loss in 20x4, the year in which the loan became completely worthless.

Net Personal Casualty or Theft Gains

Chapters 5 and 10 discussed the calculation of casualty or theft gains and losses on personal-use property. A casualty or theft gain occurs when the insurance proceeds exceed the taxpayer's adjusted basis in the property. A casualty or theft loss occurs when the amount of the loss exceeds the insurance reimbursement. For *personal-use property,* the amount of the loss is measured as the *lesser of* the property's adjusted basis or its decline in value.

Sometimes the taxpayer incurs just one personal casualty or theft during the year. When this happens, the taxpayer determines the gain or loss from each property damaged or destroyed in the casualty or theft. The taxpayer then nets the gains and losses to compute a *net personal casualty or theft gain or loss.* If the result is a net gain, then all personal casualty or theft gains and losses are treated as capital gains and losses. If the result is a net loss, then the taxpayer reduces the loss by $100 and by 10% of AGI. Any remaining loss is deducted as an itemized deduction (Chapter 5).

EXAMPLE 25

Martha Voit's home was burglarized. A family heirloom and a TV were stolen. Information about the items reveals the following:

	FMV Before	FMV After	Adjusted Basis	Insurance Proceeds
TV	$ 500	$0	$ 700	$ 0
Heirloom	3,000	0	1,000	2,900

Since Voit did not insure the TV, the theft of the TV produces a $500 casualty or theft loss (the *lesser of* its (i) $700 adjusted basis or (ii) the $500 decline in value). Voit insured the heirloom, which results in a $1,900 casualty or theft gain ($2,900 insurance proceeds – $1,000 adjusted basis). Voit's net casualty or theft gain equals $1,400 ($1,900 – $500). Assuming Voit held both the TV and the heirloom long-term, she treats the $1,400 as a long-term capital gain in the netting process.

When several personal casualties and thefts occur during the year, the taxpayer first computes a net personal casualty or theft gain or loss for each casualty or theft. If a single casualty or theft results in a net personal casualty or theft loss, the taxpayer reduces the loss by $100 (Chapter 5). A net personal casualty gain is not reduced by $100. The taxpayer then nets the gains and losses from the various personal casualties and thefts. If the result is an overall net gain, all personal casualty or theft gains and losses for the year are treated as capital gains and losses.

Taxpayers compute their net personal casualty or theft gain or loss on Form 4684 (Section A), Casualties and Thefts. If a net loss results, the taxpayer attaches Form 4684 to the tax return to support the itemized deduction for the amount that exceeds 10% of AGI. If the result is a net gain, the taxpayer transfers the personal casualty or theft gains and losses to the appropriate short-term/long-term parts on Schedule D.

BUSINESS GAINS AND LOSSES

Disposing of real and depreciable business property can produce a long-term capital gain, even though the definition of a capital asset specifically excludes business property. To understand how and when this can happen, it is necessary to examine the tax laws regarding the disposal of real and depreciable business property.

By definition, real and depreciable business property are not capital assets. However, under certain conditions, disposing of real and depreciable business property held for over one year can produce a long-term capital gain. (The disposal of real and depreciable business property held one year or less always produces ordinary income or loss). Real and depreciable business property held long-term is known as **Section 1231 property.** The sale, exchange, or condemnation of Section 1231 property produces a Section 1231 gain or loss. If Section 1231 gains for the year exceed Section 1231 losses, the net Section 1231 gain may be treated as long-term capital gain. If Section 1231 losses exceed Section 1231 gains, the net Section 1231 loss is treated as an ordinary loss.

EXAMPLE 26

For the year, Jerry Novak reports a $12,000 Section 1231 gain and a $5,000 Section 1231 loss. Novak's net Section 1231 gain equals $7,000 ($12,000 – $5,000). Novak enters this amount as long-term capital gain in the netting process.

EXAMPLE 27

For the year, Nancy Morris reports a $10,000 Section 1231 gain and a $23,000 Section 1231 loss. Morris's net Section 1231 loss equals $13,000 ($10,000 – $23,000). Morris deducts this amount as an ordinary loss.

Business Casualty or Theft Gains and Losses

Chapter 10 presented the rules for computing business casualty or theft gains and losses. At the end of the year, taxpayers sum all casualty or theft gains and losses from Section 1231 property (business property held long-term). When gains exceed losses, the excess is a *net business casualty or theft gain.* A net business casualty or theft gain is treated as a Section 1231 gain. When losses exceed gains, the difference is a *net business casualty or theft loss.* A net business casualty or theft loss is treated as an ordinary loss. Casualty or theft gains and losses from business property held short-term produce ordinary income and losses.

EXAMPLE 28

For the year, Leslie Burton recognizes a $10,000 business casualty gain and a $4,000 business casualty loss from properties held long-term. Burton also recognizes a $2,000 Section 1231 loss. Burton treats the $6,000 net business casualty or theft gain ($10,000 – $4,000) as a Section 1231 gain. Burton's net Section 1231 gain equals $4,000 ($6,000 – $2,000). Burton includes the $4,000 as a long-term capital gain in the netting process.

EXAMPLE 29

In the current year, Mary Clark has a $6,000 business casualty gain, a $13,000 business casualty loss, and a $5,000 Section 1231 gain. Clark's net business casualty or theft loss equals $7,000 ($6,000 – $13,000). Clark deducts the $7,000 as an ordinary loss. Clark treats the $5,000 net Section 1231 gain as a long-term capital gain.

Section 1231 provides taxpayers with the best of both situations: long-term capital gains for net Section 1231 gains and ordinary losses for net Section 1231 losses. For this reason, Congress did not want taxpayers taking unfair advantage of the Section 1231 rules. Over the years, Congress identified two situations where taxpayers might take advantage of the rules for Section 1231 property. The first situation involves the sale or exchange of depreciable property for a gain. The second situation involves unrecaptured Section 1231 losses.

Depreciation Recapture

Depreciation expense is a deduction that reduces ordinary income. The tax benefits a taxpayer receives from deducting depreciation expense are equal to the amount of the deduction times the taxpayer's marginal tax rate. (The marginal tax rate is that tax imposed on the next dollar of taxable income. It corresponds to the taxpayer's "tax bracket.") When individual taxpayers sell property that generates long-term capital gain, such gain may be taxed at a rate that is lower than the taxpayer's marginal tax rate. Currently the tax laws tax net capital gain at a maximum 15% rate (5% for taxpayers in the 10% and 15% tax brackets).

Because net Section 1231 gain becomes long-term capital gain, depreciating property as quickly as possible increases the chance of recognizing long-term capital gain when the property is sold. This results in larger depreciation deductions (where the tax benefits are computed using the taxpayer's marginal tax rate) and possibly greater long-term capital gains (where net capital gain is taxed at a lower tax rate). Example 30 illustrates this point.

EXAMPLE 30

In March 2005, Henry Wallace paid $20,000 for a machine that he used in his business. Wallace elected to expense the entire machine under Section 179, therefore his adjusted basis in the machine is $0 at the end of 2005. On October 12, 2006, Wallace sold the machine for $12,000, resulting in a $12,000 Section 1231 gain. If Wallace had no other Section 1231 or capital gains and losses in 2006, the entire $12,000 becomes long-term capital gain, which is taxed at no more than 15%.

Assume instead that Wallace had not elected Section 179, but chose to depreciate the machine using regular (accelerated) MACRS. He would have deducted $2,858 in 2005 ($20,000 × 14.29%) and $2,449 in 2006 ($20,000 × 24.49% × ½). His adjusted basis in the machine at the time of the sale would have been $14,693 ($20,000 – $2,858 – $2,449) and he would have recognized a $2,693 Section 1231 loss on the sale ($12,000 – $14,693). Again assuming no other Section 1231 gains or losses, Wallace would deduct the $2,693 as an ordinary loss.

In both scenarios, Wallace's overall deduction equals $8,000. In the first case, Wallace deducts $20,000 for depreciation expense but reports a $12,000 gain on the sale. In the second case, he deducts $5,307 for depreciation expense plus another $2,693 for the loss on the sale, for a total of $8,000.

Now assume that Wallace's marginal tax rate in both years is 28%. In the first case, Wallace receives a $5,600 tax benefit from the depreciation expense ($20,000 × 28%) but pays tax of $1,800 ($12,000 × 15%) on the gain from the sale. The net tax benefit equals $3,800 ($5,600 – $1,800). In the second case, everything is taxed at the marginal tax rate, so Wallace's tax benefit is only $2,240 ($8,000 × 28%). By electing Section 179, Wallace ends up saving $1,560 in taxes ($3,800 – $2,240).

As you see from Example 30, an incentive existed for taxpayers to use the fastest depreciation method possible. To limit this opportunity, Congress introduced the concept of **depreciation recapture.** Depreciation recapture requires taxpayers to tax gains as ordinary income to the extent of "excessive depreciation." Under the Section 1245 depreciation recapture rules, gains on the disposal of depreciable personal property are taxed as ordinary income to the extent of the *lesser of* (i) the gain, or (ii) all depreciation taken. Gain not taxed as ordinary income is Section 1231 gain. [Note that depreciation recapture only affects gains on the disposal of depreciable Section 1231 property. Losses on the disposal of Section 1231 property are always treated as Section 1231 losses.]

For personal property, all depreciation taken (including Section 179 expense and bonus depreciation) is subject to depreciation recapture. Even when the taxpayer uses the straight-line method to depreciate personal property, the entire amount of straight-line depreciation is subject to recapture.

EXAMPLE 31

Tony Bonnell bought a business machine on January 3, 2004, for $20,000. Bonnell sold the machine on April 25, 2006, for $21,000. In 2004, 2005, and 2006, Bonnell deducted depreciation totaling $9,505. Bonnell's adjusted basis in the machine equals $10,495 ($20,000 – $9,505). Bonnell recognizes a $10,505 gain ($21,000 – $10,495), of which $9,505 is ordinary income and $1,000 is Section 1231 gain.

Depreciation recapture only applies to real property when an accelerated depreciation method is used to depreciate the realty. Since the only depreciation method for realty under MACRS is the straight-line method, there is no depreciation recapture on the sale of real property placed in service after 1986.

Recapture of Section 1231 Losses

The tax treatment of Section 1231 gains and losses gives taxpayers the opportunity to treat net Section 1231 gains as long-term capital gains and net Section 1231 losses as ordinary losses. To keep taxpayers from bunching all Section 1231 gains in one year to get long-term capital gain treatment, and then bunching Section 1231 losses in the next year to deduct them as ordinary losses, Congress introduced Section 1231 recapture.

Before net Section 1231 gain can become long-term capital gain, taxpayers must look back over the past five years and compute the amount of unrecaptured Section 1231 losses. Unrecaptured Section 1231 losses act like depreciation recapture. That is, net Section 1231 gain is taxed as ordinary income to the extent of unrecaptured Section 1231 losses. **Unrecaptured Section 1231 losses** equal Section 1231 losses from the past five years that have not been used to offset Section 1231 gains.

EXAMPLE 32

In 20x6, Jose Mandella has Section 1231 gains of $30,000 and Section 1231 losses of $12,000. Mandella also has unrecaptured Section 1231 losses from 20x1-20x5 of $7,000. Mandella's net Section 1231 gains for 20x6 equals $18,000 ($30,000 – $12,000). He reports $7,000 of this gain as ordinary income and the rest, $11,000 ($18,000 – $7,000), as long-term capital gain. Since all unrecaptured Section 1231 losses from 20x1-20x5 have been "recaptured" by turning Section 1231 gains in 20x6 into ordinary income, there are no unrecaptured Section 1231 losses from 20x2-20x6 to apply against net Section 1231 gains in 20x7.

Unrecaptured Section 1250 Gain

When business real property placed in service after 1986 is sold at a gain, individual taxpayers treat the gain as Section 1231 gain. When Section 1231 gains exceed Section 1231 losses for the year (a net Section 1231 gain), such gain may be treated as long-term capital gain. However, the tax law requires that any unrecaptured Section 1250 gain be taxed at the higher 25% for taxpayers in the 25% or higher tax brackets.

Unrecaptured Section 1250 gain equals the *lesser of* (i) the gain or (ii) the depreciation taken on the property. Unrecaptured Section 1250 gain applies only to real property sold at a gain. It does not apply to realty sold at a loss. It also applies only to individual taxpayers, not corporations.

EXAMPLE 33

Jane Everett sold residential realty during 2006 for $400,000. Everett paid $520,000 for the building in 1996. Depreciation taken on the building from 1996–2006 totaled $193,818. Thus, Everett's basis in the building is $326,182 ($520,000 – $193,818). Her recognized gain is $73,818 ($400,000 – $326,182). Everett's unrecaptured Section 1250 gain equals $73,818 (*lesser of* (i) the gain, $73,818, or (ii) depreciation taken, $193,818).

EXAMPLE 34

Same as in Example 33, except that Everett sold the property for $600,000. Unrecaptured Section 1250 gain equals $193,818 [*lesser of* (i) the $273,818 gain ($600,000 – $326,182) or (ii) $193,818 depreciation taken]. When Everett goes to transfer net Section 1231 gain to long-term capital gain in the netting process, she will report the first $193,818 of the net gain as 25% long-term gain and the rest as 15% long-term gain.

Taxpayers with unrecaptured Section 1250 gain report this gain in the netting process between the short-term and long-term columns. When unrecaptured Section 1250 gain exists, netting of gains and losses is done as follows.

1. If the amount in the 15% long-term column is a net loss, it is used first to offset any 25% long-term gain, followed by any short-term gain. If there is no net 15% long-term loss, proceed to Step 2.
2. Use any net short-term capital loss to offset any 25% long-term gain, and then any net 15% long-term gain. The netting process is complete when only all gains or all losses remain.

EXAMPLE 35

Brook and Jerry Daniels sold several assets during 2006. Their taxable income is $142,125, which does not include any qualified dividends. The netting within the groups resulted in a $2,000 net short-term loss; a $6,000 25% long-term gain; and a $7,000 net 15% long-term gain. The netting process within and between groups is as follows.

	Long-Term	
Short-Term	**25%**	**15%**
$ 6,000	$6,000	$18,000
(8,000)		(11,000)
($2,000) →	(2,000)	$7,000
	$4,000	

Since there is no net 15% long-term loss, the Daniels begin the netting process between groups by offsetting the $2,000 net short-term loss against the net 25% long-term gain (Step 2). This results in a $4,000 25% long-term gain and a $7,000 net 15% long-term gain. The Daniels compute their tax liability as follows.

Tax on $131,125 ($142,125 – $11,000 net capital gain)	$26,119
Plus $4,000 × 25% (the Daniels are in the 28% bracket)	1,000
Plus $7,000 × 15%	1,050
Tax liability on $142,125	$28,169

EXAMPLE 36

Kelli Rogers sold several capital assets during 2006. These assets produced a $9,000 net short-term loss; a $4,000 25% long-term gain; and a $13,000 net 15% long-term gain. Rogers files as head of household and her 2006 taxable income is $64,230 (no qualified dividends). The netting process between groups is as follows.

	Long-Term	
Short-Term	**25%**	**15%**
$6,000	$4,000	$14,000
(15,000)		(1,000)
($9,000)		$13,000
→	(4,000) →	(5,000)
	$ 0	$ 8,000

Rogers skips Step 1 and uses the $9,000 net short-term loss to offset first the 25% long-term gain and then the net 15% long-term gain. Rogers is left with $8,000 net 15% long-term gain. Her tax liability is computed as follows.

Tax on $56,230 ($64,230 – $8,000)	$ 9,414
Plus $8,000 × 15% (Rogers is in the 25% bracket)	1,200
Tax liability on $64,230	$10,614

EXAMPLE 37

Jim and Erin Stegall sold several assets during 2006. These assets produced a $6,000 net short-term loss; a $15,000 25% long-term gain; and a $2,000 net 15% long-term loss. The Stegalls file a joint return for 2006 and report taxable income of $129,230 (including $2,200 of qualified dividends). The netting process between groups is as follows.

	Long-Term	
Short-Term	**25%**	**15%**
($13,000)	$15,000	($3,000)
7,000		1,000
($ 6,000)	(2,000) ←	($2,000)
	$13,000	
→	(6,000)	
	$ 7,000	

The Stegalls offset the net 15% long-term loss against the 25% gain (Step 1). They then use the short-term loss to offset more of the 25% gain (Step 2). The Stegalls are left with a $7,000 net 25% long-term capital gain. They compute their tax liability as follows.

Tax on $120,030 ($129,230 – $7,000 net gain – $2,200 qualified dividends)	$23,123
Plus $7,000 × 25% (the Stegalls are in the 25% bracket)	1,750
Plus $2,200 × 15%	330
Tax liability on $129,230	$25,203

A special rule applies to corporations. When corporations sell depreciable real property, they are not entitled to treat the entire gain as Section 1231 gain. Instead, the *lesser of* (i) 20% of depreciation taken or (2) the recognized gain is taxed as ordinary income. Any remaining gain is treated as Section 1231 gain. For example, a building is purchased for $100,000 and over the years, $20,000 of MACRS is deducted, resulting in an $80,000 adjusted basis. If the property is sold for $120,000, then $4,000 the *lesser of* (i) 20% × $20,000 or (ii) $40,000 gain is taxed as ordinary income. The rest ($40,000 – $4,000 = $36,000) is taxed as Section 1231 gain.

REPORTING BUSINESS GAINS AND LOSSES ON THE TAX RETURN

In the end, all of an individual taxpayer's recognized gains and losses appear on Form 1040. Similarly, all of a C corporation's recognized gains and losses appear on Form 1120. However, only gains and losses that appear on Schedule D, Capital Gains and Losses, receive capital gain and loss treatment. Taxpayers report the gain and loss on the sale, exchange, or condemnation of business property on Form 4797, Sales of Business Property. They report the gains and losses resulting from casualties and thefts of business property on Form 4684 (Section B), Casualties and Thefts. (Taxpayers also use Form 4684 [Section B] to report casualty or theft gains and losses from investment property. However, the scope of this chapter is limited to business casualties or thefts. Those interested in casualty or theft gains and losses on investment property should refer to IRS Publication 547.) Net gains and losses from Form 4684 (Section B) flow through to Form 4797. Therefore, taxpayers should begin by completing Form 4684.

Form 4684 (Section B), Casualties and Thefts

Taxpayers compute business casualty or theft gains and losses on Form 4684 (Section B), Casualties and Thefts. Taxpayers with more than one business casualty or theft during the year complete a separate Form 4684, Part I, for each casualty or theft. In Part II, taxpayers separate gains and losses involving Section 1231 property from gains and losses involving business property held short-term. They transfer a net business casualty or theft gain to Form 4797, Part I (line 3), and treat it as a gain from the sale of Section 1231 property. They transfer a net business casualty or theft loss to Form 4797, Part II (line 14), and deduct it as an ordinary loss. A net casualty or theft gain or loss from business property held short-term is also transferred to Form 4797, Part II (line 14), and deducted as an ordinary gain or loss.

Information for Figure 11-2: Filled-In Form 4684 (Section B)

On October 15, 2006, Jonathan Miller's laptop computer and laser printer were stolen from his office. Miller purchased both properties on December 4, 2004. Before the theft, the FMV of the computer and printer were $1,500 and $1,800, respectively. The insurance company reimbursed Miller $1,500 for the computer (adjusted basis, $2,200) and $2,150 for the printer (adjusted basis, $2,000).

Other Information

29: **$2,200.00** is entered since the property was completely destroyed. See **Note:** below line 26. Miller transfers the $550 net business casualty or theft loss to Form 4797 (line 14).

FIGURE 11-2 Filled-In Form 4684 (Section B), Casualties and Thefts

Form 4684 (2006) Attachment Sequence No. **26** Page **2**

Name(s) shown on tax return. Do not enter name and identifying number if shown on other side. Jonathan L. Miller

Identifying number 668-58-9977

SECTION B—Business and Income-Producing Property

Part I Casualty or Theft Gain or Loss (Use a separate Part I for each casualty or theft.)

22 Description of properties (show type, location, and date acquired for each property). Use a separate line for each property lost or damaged from the same casualty or theft.

Property **A** Laptop Computer, acquired December 4, 2004

Property **B** Laser Printer, acquired December 4, 2004

Property **C**

Property **D**

			Properties A	B	C	D
23	Cost or adjusted basis of each property	23	2,200 00	2,000 00		
24	Insurance or other reimbursement (whether or not you filed a claim). See the instructions for line 3. **Note:** *If line 23 is **more** than line 24, skip line 25*	24	1,500 00	2,150 00		
25	Gain from casualty or theft. If line 24 is **more** than line 23, enter the difference here and on line 32 or line 37, column (c), except as provided in the instructions for line 36. Also, skip lines 26 through 30 for that column. See the instructions for line 4 if line 24 includes insurance or other reimbursement you did not claim, or you received payment for your loss in a later tax year.	25		150 00		
26	Fair market value **before** casualty or theft	26	1,500 00			
27	Fair market value **after** casualty or theft	27	0 00			
28	Subtract line 27 from line 26	28	1,500 00			
29	Enter the **smaller** of line 23 or line 28. **Note:** *If the property was totally destroyed by casualty or lost from theft, enter on line 29 the amount from line 23.*	29	2,200 00			
30	Subtract line 24 from line 29. If zero or less, enter -0-	30	700 00			

31 Casualty or theft loss. Add the amounts on line 30. Enter the total here and on line 32 **or** line 37 (see instructions). **31** (700 00)

Part II Summary of Gains and Losses (from separate Parts I)

Line	(a) Identify casualty or theft		(b) Losses from casualties or thefts: (i) Trade, business, rental or royalty property	(b) (ii) Income-producing and employee property	(c) Gains from casualties or thefts includible in income
	Casualty or Theft of Property Held One Year or Less				
32			( )	( )	
			( )	( )	
33	Totals. Add the amounts on line 32	33	( )	( )	
34	Combine line 33, columns (b)(i) and (c). Enter the net gain or (loss) here and on Form 4797, line 14. If Form 4797 is not otherwise required, see instructions	34			
35	Enter the amount from line 33, column (b)(ii) here. Individuals, enter the amount from income-producing property on Schedule A (Form 1040), line 27, and enter the amount from property used as an employee on Schedule A (Form 1040), line 22. Estates and trusts, partnerships, and S corporations, see instructions	35			
	Casualty or Theft of Property Held More Than One Year				
36	Casualty or theft gains from Form 4797, line 32	36			
37			(700 00)	( )	150 00
			( )	( )	
38	Total losses. Add amounts on line 37, columns (b)(i) and (b)(ii)	38	(700 00)	( )	
39	Total gains. Add lines 36 and 37, column (c)	39			150 00
40	Add amounts on line 38, columns (b)(i) and (b)(ii)	40			700 00
41	If the loss on line 40 is **more** than the gain on line 39:				
a	Combine line 38, column (b)(i) and line 39, and enter the net gain or (loss) here. Partnerships (except electing large partnerships) and S corporations, see the note below. All others, enter this amount on Form 4797, line 14. If Form 4797 is not otherwise required, see instructions	41a			(550 00)
b	Enter the amount from line 38, column (b)(ii) here. Individuals, enter the amount from income-producing property on Schedule A (Form 1040), line 27, and enter the amount from property used as an employee on Schedule A (Form 1040), line 22. Estates and trusts, enter on the "Other deductions" line of your tax return. Partnerships (except electing large partnerships) and S corporations, see the note below. Electing large partnerships, enter on Form 1065-B, Part II, line 11.	41b			
42	If the loss on line 40 is **less** than or **equal** to the gain on line 39, combine lines 39 and 40 and enter here. Partnerships (except electing large partnerships), see the note below. All others, enter this amount on Form 4797, line 3	42			

Note: *Partnerships, enter the amount from line 41a, 41b, or line 42 on Form 1065, Schedule K, line 11. S corporations, enter the amount from line 41a or 41b on Form 1120S, Schedule K, line 10.*

Printed on recycled paper Form **4684** (2006)

Form 4797

Taxpayers use Form 4797, Sales of Business Property, to report gains and losses from the sale, exchange, or condemnation of business property. Form 4797 consists of three parts. Part I summarizes Section 1231 gains and losses. Part II summarizes ordinary gains and losses. Part III separates the gain from the sale or exchange of property subject to depreciation recapture between ordinary income and Section 1231 gain.

Part I

In Part I, taxpayers report gains and losses from Section 1231 property not subject to depreciation recapture. Also included in Part I are net business casualty gains from Form 4684 and Section 1231 gains from the sale of depreciable property from Form 4797, Part III. After entering all Section 1231 gains and losses in Part I, taxpayers compute their net Section 1231 gain or loss (line 7). They transfer a net Section 1231 loss to Part II (line 11) so that it can be treated as an ordinary loss. A net Section 1231 gain is first reduced by the nonrecaptured net Section 1231 losses from the past five years (line 8), and the rest is reported as a long-term capital gain on Schedule D (line 11). Taxpayers report the recaptured gain as ordinary income in Part II (line 12).

Part II

Taxpayers report gains and losses from the sale, exchange, or condemnation of business property held one year or less in Part II (line 10). Taxpayers also report in Part II (line 14) net business casualty or theft losses and casualty or theft gains and losses from business property held short-term. Net Section 1231 losses and recaptured Section 1231 gains from Part I also appear in Part II. After netting the ordinary gains and losses (line 17), the taxpayer transfers the net amount to Form 1040 (line 14).

Part III

This chapter introduced the concept of depreciation recapture. The recapture where gain is taxed as ordinary income to the extent of the *accumulated depreciation* taken is referred to as **Section 1245 recapture.** Section 1245 applies to tangible personal property sold for a gain. Taxpayers report property subject to Section 1245 depreciation recapture on Form 4797, Part III (line 25).

In Part III, total gains from the disposition of property subject to recapture are separated between amounts recaptured as ordinary income (line 31) and Section 1231 gain (line 32). Taxpayers report the ordinary income on Part II (line 13) and the Section 1231 gain on Part I (line 6).

Information for Figure 11-3: Filled-In Form 4797

On July 3, 2002, Teresa F. Lohman placed in service equipment costing $36,000. On May 10, 2006, she sold the equipment for $15,000. Depreciation taken on the equipment was $26,361. On January 3, 2006, Lohman sold land used in her business for $22,800. Commissions paid on the sale were $1,000. Lohman bought the land on February 6, 1978, for $14,000.

In 2006 the government notified Lohman that land she held for investment was to be condemned. Lohman paid $33,200 for the land on March 5, 1983. She received $30,200 from the government for the land on May 2, 2006. Lohman has $2,500 of unrecaptured Section 1231 losses from the past five years.

FIGURE 11-3 Filled-In Form 4797, Page 1

Form **4797** — **Sales of Business Property** (Also Involuntary Conversions and Recapture Amounts Under Sections 179 and 280F(b)(2)) ▶Attach to your tax return. ▶See separate instructions.

Department of the Treasury Internal Revenue Service (99)

OMB No. 1545-0184 — 2006 — Attachment Sequence No. 27

Name(s) shown on return: Teresa F. Lohman — Identifying number: 271-57-2696

1 Enter the gross proceeds from sales or exchanges reported to you for 2006 on Form(s) 1099-B or 1099-S (or substitute statement) that you are including on line 2, 10, or 20 (see instructions). . . . 1 | 53,000

Part I Sales or Exchanges of Property Used in a Trade or Business and Involuntary Conversions From Other Than Casualty or Theft—Most Property Held More Than 1 Year (see instructions)

	(a) Description of property	(b) Date acquired (mo., day, yr.)	(c) Date sold (mo., day, yr.)	(d) Gross sales price	(e) Depreciation allowed or allowable since acquisition	(f) Cost or other basis, plus improvements and expense of sale	(g) Gain or (loss) Subtract (f) from the sum of (d) and (e)
2	Land	2/6/78	1/3/06	22,800		15,000	7,800
	Land (involuntary conversion)	3/5/83	5/2/06	30,200		33,200	(3,000)

3	Gain, if any, from Form 4684, line 42	3	
4	Section 1231 gain from installment sales from Form 6252, line 26 or 37	4	
5	Section 1231 gain or (loss) from like-kind exchanges from Form 8824	5	
6	Gain, if any, from line 32, from other than casualty or theft	6	0
7	Combine lines 2 through 6. Enter the gain or (loss) here and on the appropriate line as follows:	7	4,800

Partnerships (except electing large partnerships) and S corporations. Report the gain or (loss) following the instructions for Form 1065, Schedule K, line 10, or Form 1120S, Schedule K, line 9. Skip lines 8, 9, 11, and 12 below.

Individuals, partners, S corporation shareholders, and all others. If line 7 is zero or a loss, enter the amount from line 7 on line 11 below and skip lines 8 and 9. If line 7 is a gain and you did not have any prior year section 1231 losses, or they were recaptured in an earlier year, enter the gain from line 7 as a long-term capital gain on the Schedule D filed with your return and skip lines 8, 9, 11, and 12 below.

8	Nonrecaptured net section 1231 losses from prior years (see instructions)	8	2,500
9	Subtract line 8 from line 7. If zero or less, enter -0-. If line 9 is zero, enter the gain from line 7 on line 12 below. If line 9 is more than zero, enter the amount from line 8 on line 12 below and enter the gain from line 9 as a long-term capital gain on the Schedule D filed with your return (see instructions).	9	2,300

Part II Ordinary Gains and Losses (see instructions)

10 Ordinary gains and losses not included on lines 11 through 16 (include property held 1 year or less):

11	Loss, if any, from line 7	11	( )
12	Gain, if any, from line 7 or amount from line 8, if applicable	12	2,500
13	Gain, if any, from line 31	13	5,361
14	Net gain or (loss) from Form 4684, lines 34 and 41a	14	
15	Ordinary gain from installment sales from Form 6252, line 25 or 36	15	
16	Ordinary gain or (loss) from like-kind exchanges from Form 8824	16	
17	Combine lines 10 through 16	17	7,861
18	For all except individual returns, enter the amount from line 17 on the appropriate line of your return and skip lines a and b below. For individual returns, complete lines a and b below:		
a	If the loss on line 11 includes a loss from Form 4684, line 38, column (b)(ii), enter that part of the loss here. Enter the part of the loss from income-producing property on Schedule A (Form 1040), line 27, and the part of the loss from property used as an employee on Schedule A (Form 1040), line 22. Identify as from "Form 4797, line 18a." See instructions	18a	
b	Redetermine the gain or (loss) on line 17 excluding the loss, if any, on line 18a. Enter here and on Form 1040, line 14	18b	7,861

For Paperwork Reduction Act Notice, see separate instructions. Cat. No. 13086I Form **4797** (2006)

Other Information

1: Gross proceeds from the sale or exchange of real estate reported on Forms 1099-S and included on lines 2, 10, and 20, **$53,000** ($22,800 + $30,200)

2(f): Cost or other basis plus improvements and expenses of sale, **$15,000** ($14,000 + $1,000)

8: Nonrecaptured net section 1231 losses from prior years, **$2,500**

Lohman transfers the $2,300 net Section 1231 gain to Schedule D (line 11). She transfers the $7,861 ordinary gain to Form 1040 (line 14).

FIGURE 11-3 Filled-In Form 4797, Page 2

Form 4797 (2006) Page 2

Part III Gain From Disposition of Property Under Sections 1245, 1250, 1252, 1254, and 1255 (see instructions)

19 (a) Description of section 1245, 1250, 1252, 1254, or 1255 property:	(b) Date acquired (mo., day, yr.)	(c) Date sold (mo., day, yr.)
A Equipment	7/3/02	5/10/06
B		
C		
D		

These columns relate to the properties on lines 19A through 19D. ▶		Property A	Property B	Property C	Property D
20 Gross sales price (**Note:** *See line 1 before completing.*)	20	15,000			
21 Cost or other basis plus expense of sale	21	36,000			
22 Depreciation (or depletion) allowed or allowable	22	26,361			
23 Adjusted basis. Subtract line 22 from line 21	23	9,639			
24 Total gain. Subtract line 23 from line 20	24	5,361			
25 **If section 1245 property:**					
a Depreciation allowed or allowable from line 22	25a	26,361			
b Enter the **smaller** of line 24 or 25a	25b	5,361			
26 **If section 1250 property:** If straight line depreciation was used, enter -0- on line 26g, except for a corporation subject to section 291.					
a Additional depreciation after 1975 (see instructions)	26a				
b Applicable percentage multiplied by the **smaller** of line 24 or line 26a (see instructions)	26b				
c Subtract line 26a from line 24. If residential rental property **or** line 24 is not more than line 26a, skip lines 26d and 26e	26c				
d Additional depreciation after 1969 and before 1976	26d				
e Enter the **smaller** of line 26c or 26d	26e				
f Section 291 amount (corporations only)	26f				
g Add lines 26b, 26e, and 26f	26g				
27 **If section 1252 property:** Skip this section if you did not dispose of farmland or if this form is being completed for a partnership (other than an electing large partnership).					
a Soil, water, and land clearing expenses	27a				
b Line 27a multiplied by applicable percentage (see instructions)	27b				
c Enter the **smaller** of line 24 or 27b	27c				
28 **If section 1254 property:**					
a Intangible drilling and development costs, expenditures for development of mines and other natural deposits, and mining exploration costs (see instructions)	28a				
b Enter the **smaller** of line 24 or 28a	28b				
29 **If section 1255 property:**					
a Applicable percentage of payments excluded from income under section 126 (see instructions)	29a				
b Enter the **smaller** of line 24 or 29a (see instructions)	29b				

Summary of Part III Gains. Complete property columns A through D through line 29b before going to line 30.

30 Total gains for all properties. Add property columns A through D, line 24	30	5,361
31 Add property columns A through D, lines 25b, 26g, 27c, 28b, and 29b. Enter here and on line 13	31	5,361
32 Subtract line 31 from line 30. Enter the portion from casualty or theft on Form 4684, line 36. Enter the portion from other than casualty or theft on Form 4797, line 6	32	0

Part IV Recapture Amounts Under Sections 179 and 280F(b)(2) When Business Use Drops to 50% or Less (see instructions)

		(a) Section 179	(b) Section 280F(b)(2)
33 Section 179 expense deduction or depreciation allowable in prior years	33		
34 Recomputed depreciation (see instructions)	34		
35 Recapture amount. Subtract line 34 from line 33. See the instructions for where to report	35		

Printed on recycled paper Form **4797** (2006)

Other Information

25a: Depreciation allowed or allowable, **$26,361**

INSTALLMENT SALES

When property is sold, the seller may collect the sales price in full at the time of sale. Alternatively, the sales price may be collected over a number of months or years. If the full sales price is collected in the year of sale, recognized gain or loss is reported in that year. When collections extend beyond the year of sale, any gain (but not loss) may be recognized on the installment method. The installment method allows taxpayers to report the gain (and pay the related taxes) as they collect payments on the installment obligation. To use the installment sales method, at least one payment must be received in the tax year following the year of the sale. Taxpayers, however, may elect not to use the installment method. They make this election by reporting the entire gain in the year of sale. The election must be made before the due date of the return (including extensions) for the year of the sale.

The installment sales method is intended for casual sales of personal and real property by nondealers. It cannot be used by most dealers. A dealer is someone who regularly sells personal or real property in the ordinary course of a trade or business. The installment method cannot be used to report gain from the sale of publicly traded stock or securities.

Computing Installment Gain

The amount of gain that must be reported in a given tax year is computed as follows:

Gain recognized = payments received × (gross profit ÷ contract price)

Payments Received

As payments on the sales price are collected, a portion of the profit is reported (recognized). Payments include cash and property the seller receives. Payments do not include notes or other obligations received from the buyer.

Gross Profit

Gross profit equals the amount realized less the adjusted basis of the property. Gross profit is the amount of gain that would be recognized in the year of sale if the installment method were not used. The amount realized includes cash and other property received. It also includes notes received from the buyer or mortgages the buyer assumes. It does not include any interest to be received from the transaction.

EXAMPLE 38

In 2006, Ellen Brown sells land held for investment and receives $18,000. Brown paid $11,200 for the land and over the years made $1,400 worth of improvements. The gross profit is determined as follows.

Amount realized		$18,000
Less adjusted basis		
Cost	$11,200	
Improvements	1,400	(12,600)
Gross profit		$ 5,400

Contract Price

The contract price is the amount realized less mortgages the buyer assumes. It is usually the sum of the principal payments, excluding interest, that the seller expects to receive. In Example 38, Brown's gross profit ratio equals 30% [$5,400 (gross profit) ÷ $18,000 (contract price)].

Taxpayers compute the current year's recognized gain by multiplying the amounts received on the principal during the year by the gross profit ratio. Keep in mind that payments on notes normally include interest as well as principal. Interest received by the seller is ordinary income reported on Schedule B.

EXAMPLE 39

Assume the same facts as in Example 38, except that the purchaser gives Brown a $4,000 down payment plus an interest-bearing note for the rest ($14,000). From this note, $12,000 of principal is due in 2006, and $2,000 is due in 2007. If the notes are paid when due, Brown reports the gain as follows.

2006	($4,000 + $12,000) × 30%	$4,800
2007	$2,000 × 30%	600
Total		$5,400

A special rule applies to the sale of nondepreciable property to a related party. If nondepreciable property is sold to a related party (descendant, ancestor, sibling, or spouse) in an installment sale AND the related party sells the property within two years of the sale, the rest of the installment gain is taxable to the seller in the year that the related party sells the property. Thus, the subsequent sale by a related party accelerates the gain reported by the original seller.

EXAMPLE 40

On March 1, 20x1, Lucy Phillips sells land to her sister for $220,000. She accepts $20,000 down and a note that calls for four annual payments of $50,000, plus interest. The first installment is due on March 1, 20x2. Phillips paid $165,000 for the land several years ago. She realizes gross profit of $55,000 on the sale.

Amount realized	$220,000
Less adjusted basis	(165,000)
Gross profit	$ 55,000

Philips's gross profit ratio equals 25% ($55,000 gross profit ÷ $220,000 contract price). She will report the $55,000 gain from the sale as follows.

Year		**Amount**
20x1	$20,000 x 25%	$ 5,000
20x2	$50,000 x 25%	12,500
20x3	$50,000 x 25%	12,500
20x4	$50,000 x 25%	12,500
20x5	$50,000 x 25%	12,500
Total		$55,000

EXAMPLE 41

Same as in Example 40 except that on January 25, 20x3 the sister sells the land. Because the sister sold the land within two years, Philips reports the $55,000 gain from the sale as follows.

Year		**Amount**
20x1	$20,000 x 25%	$ 5,000
20x2	$50,000 x 25%	12,500
20x3	rest of the gain	37,500
Total		$55,000

EXAMPLE 42

Same as in Example 41 except that the sister sells the land on July 25, 20x3. Since the sale occurred after more than two years, the timing of the gain reported by Philips is the same as in Example 40.

Depreciation Recapture

If property sold as an installment sale is subject to depreciation recapture, the recapture must be recognized as ordinary income in the year of the sale, regardless of the payments received during the year. The gain reported in the first year as a recapture of depreciation reduces gross profit used in computing the gross profit ratio. Likewise, it reduces the amount of each installment gain to be included in income as capital gain or Section 1231 gain.

EXAMPLE 43

Mark Jamar sells depreciable personal property for $180,000, accepting five equal installments of $36,000 plus interest. Jamar realizes gross profit of $120,000 on the sale.

Amount realized		$180,000
Less adjusted basis		
Cost	$90,000	
Accumulated depreciation	(30,000)	(60,000)
Gross profit		$120,000

Gain on the sale of personal property is recaptured as ordinary income to the extent of depreciation taken on the property. Thus, Jamar recognizes the $30,000 of accumulated depreciation as ordinary income in the year of the sale. In addition, a portion of each year's receipts is recognized as section 1231 gain. The portion of gain recognized each year is computed by reducing Jamar's gross profit by $30,000 and recalculating the gross profit ratio.

Income Recognized in Year 1

Ordinary income (depreciation recapture)	$ 30,000
Recomputing the gross profit ratio:	
($120,000 – $30,000) ÷ $180,000 = 50% gross profit ratio	
Section 1231 gain reportable in Year 1 (50% × $36,000)	18,000
Total gain recognized in Year 1	$ 48,000

Income Recognized in Years 2–5

Section 1231 gain (50% × $36,000 = $18,000 × 4 years)	72,000
Total gain recognized in the five years	$120,000

Name ______________________________

Section ______________ Date ___________

QUESTIONS AND PROBLEMS

1. **Capital Assets.** Are the following properties capital assets? (Indicate your answer by writing *yes* or *no* in the column at the right.)

Item	*Answer*
a. House occupied as a residence by the owner	________
b. Delivery truck used in a contractor's business	________
c. Corporate stocks owned by a doctor	________
d. Valuable jewelry held for sale by Jones Jewelers	________
e. Land held for speculation by an accountant	________
f. Automobile used for personal purposes by the owner	________
g. Business suits worn only to work	________
h. House used strictly as a summer residence	________
i. Musical copyright owned by the composer	________

2. **Capital Gains and Losses.**

   a. Distinguish between long-term capital gain and short-term capital gain for capital assets acquired January 10, 2005.

   b. If an individual has gains and losses from the sale of stocks and other investments, what schedule is used to supplement Form 1040 in reporting this gain or loss?

3. **Holding Period.** State the time when the holding period begins on capital assets acquired by the following methods:

   a. Capital asset acquired by gift, if sold at a gain

   b. Capital asset acquired by gift, if sold at a loss (FMV < donor's basis at time of the gift)

   c. Inherited property

4. **Capital Gains and Losses.** For each of the following cases, determine whether the gain should be classified in the netting process as short-term capital gain, long-term capital gain taxed at 15%, or long-term capital gain taxed at 5%. Assume that in each case the taxpayer files as single.

   a. On February 3, 2006, stock held for four years is sold for a $3,000 gain. The taxpayer has taxable income of $25,000 in 2006.

b. On March 13, 2006, stock held for eight months is sold for a $3,000 gain. The taxpayer has taxable income of $25,000 in 2006.

c. On June 2, 2006, stock held for four years is sold for a $2,000 gain. The taxpayer has taxable income of $20,000 in 2006.

d. On August 5, 2006, stock held for four years is sold for a $4,000 gain. The taxpayer has taxable income of $80,000 in 2006.

e. On October 30, 2006, stock held four months is sold for a $4,000 gain. The taxpayer has taxable income of $80,000 in 2006.

5. **Netting Capital Gains and Losses.** In each of the following cases, use the netting process between groups to determine the taxpayer's net capital gain and determine the tax rate to be paid on such gain.

   a. A $2,000 loss on the sale of a capital asset held six months; a $9,000 gain on the sale of a capital asset held for three years. The taxpayer is in the 25% tax bracket.

   b. Same as Part a., except that the taxpayer is in the 15% bracket.

   c. A $6,000 gain on the sale of a capital asset held nine months; a $5,000 gain on the sale of a capital asset held four years. The taxpayer is in the 28% tax bracket.

   d. Same as Part c., except that the taxpayer is in the 10% bracket.

6. **Capital Gains Tax.** During 2006, Brady Cartwright (single) sells two capital assets. The first results in a $4,000 short-term capital gain. The second results in a $9,500 long-term capital gain. Cartwright's AGI without taking these two gains into consideration is $71,034 (no qualified dividends). Cartwright deducts the standard deduction and one personal exemption for 2006. Compute Cartwright's 2006 income tax liability.

7. **Capital Gains Tax.** During 2006, Angie Rosette sells two capital assets. The first results in a $4,000 short-term capital loss. The second results in a $7,500 long-term capital gain. Rosette's AGI without taking these gains and losses into consideration is $43,735 (no qualified dividends). She files as head of household and deducts the standard deduction. She claims three personal and dependency exemptions in 2006. Compute Rosette's 2006 income tax liability.

8. **Capital Gains Tax.** During 2006, Lauren Taylor sells two capital assets. The first results in a $9,000 short-term capital gain. The second results in a $2,600 long-term capital loss. Taylor's AGI without taking these gains and losses into consideration is $124,944 (no qualified dividends). She files as a surviving spouse and deducts the standard deduction. She claims two personal and dependency exemptions in 2006. Compute Taylor's 2006 income tax liability.

9. **Capital Gains Tax.** In March of 2006, Shirley Thompson sold stock of the Wingate Corporation for $15,000. She had acquired the stock three years earlier at a cost of $11,600. Exclusive of this gain she expects to have a taxable income of $34,000 (after deductions and exemptions) for the year. Thompson files a joint return with her husband, who has no income. The Thompsons have no qualified dividends. In December 2006 Thompson contemplated selling stock of the Roberts Printing Company, which she acquired on January 15, 2005, for $18,000. It has since declined in value to $13,000.

   a. Compute Thompson's total tax liability for 2006, assuming that she did not sell the Roberts stock in 2006.

   b. Compute Thompson's total tax liability for 2006, assuming that she did sell the Roberts stock for $13,000 in 2006. What amount of tax savings would result from the sale?

10. Capital Losses. What capital loss deduction can be claimed in 2006 for each of the following individual taxpayers? Also, what is the capital loss carryover to 2007 by type of loss? If none, insert *None.*

Gains and Losses	*A*	*B*	*C*	*D*	*E*
Short-term capital gains	$ 900	$ 800	$ 0	$ 400	$3,200
Short-term capital losses	(6,200)	(1,200)	(400)	(2,400)	(8,600)
Long-term capital gains	800	2,200	800	1,600	1,400
Long-term capital losses	(600)	(800)	(1,150)	(4,200)	(2,600)
Capital loss deduction in 2006	$______	$______	$______	$______	$______
Short-term loss carryover to 2007	$______	$______	$______	$______	$______
Long-term loss carryover to 2007	$______	$______	$______	$______	$______

11. Stock Sales. A taxpayer sold 100 shares of stock on August 13, 2006, for $7,500 cash. Before this sale, the taxpayer owned shares in the company as evidenced by the following certificates:

Certificate Number	*Date Acquired*	*Number of Shares*	*Cost*
CR642	4-11-77	300	$15,000
DO111	9-10-82	100	9,000
EA002	8-13-84	100	6,000

Which certificate should be delivered to the broker to cover the stock sold, and what are the tax consequences of this selection?

12. Worthless Securities. On July 17, 2005, Bonnie Martin paid $15,000 for 4,500 shares of stock in ABC corporation. On December 29, 2005, the stock was trading for $.03 a share. On January 6, 2006 Martin's stock broker let her know that the stock was worthless. Discuss the tax consequences of the ABC stock on Martin's 2005 and 2006 tax return.

13. Section 1244 Stock.

a. Roger Razaki sells 1,000 shares of his Section 1244 stock ("small business corporation" stock) at a loss of $200,000. If Roger and his wife file a joint return, how will this loss be treated on the tax return?

b. If Roger were single, how would he treat the loss on his tax return?

c. How might Roger have better planned for the sale of his Section 1244 stock?

14. Subdivided Realty. Juan Alvarez, a farmer, subdivided an unimproved tract of land that he acquired 20 years ago. In 2006, he sold four lots for $10,000 each. The basis of each lot is $2,000, and the selling expenses are $400 per lot.

a. What is the gain or loss on these transactions, and how will these transactions be taxed?

b. Assuming that Alvarez sells five more lots in 2007 at the same price with selling expenses of $400 per lot, what will be the gain or loss, and how will these transactions be taxed?

15. Subdivided Realty. Benji Baba, a real estate dealer, purchased two lots for $12,000 each in May 2003. On August 30, 2005, Baba sold the tracts of land for $20,000 each. Compute the gain and describe how it will be treated on the tax return.

16. Bad Debts. Rita loaned her brother, Richard, $7,500 on February 14, 2005. The loan represents a bona fide loan. Richard filed for bankruptcy in 2006, and Rita learned that she could expect to receive only $.70 on the dollar on the personal loan that she had made to him. On May 17, 2007, Rita received a final settlement of $4,000.

a. How much loss can Rita deduct in 2006?

b. How much loss can Rita deduct in 2007?

c. How will this loss be treated on Rita's tax return?

17. Section 1231 and Capital Gains and Losses. Use the following information to answer Parts a. through c.

	Period Property Was Held	*Amount of Gain or Loss*
Nonbusiness bad debt	Three years	($2,600)
Sale of equipment used in business	Two months	(1,500)
Sale of equipment used in business	Two years	(3,000)
Sale of corporate stock	Five years	2,500
Sale of land used in business	Four years	5,000

a. What, if any, is the amount of net short-term capital loss?

b. What, if any, is the amount of net Section 1231 gain or (loss)?

c. What, if any, is the ordinary loss deduction?

18. Sale of Business Property. Carlotta Sanchez purchased computer equipment for her business in 2004 for $50,000. In 2006 she sold the computers for $30,000. Depreciation information follows:

Regular (accelerated) MACRS deduction claimed	$30,800
Straight-line depreciation would have been	$20,000

What is Sanchez's gain or loss on the sale of the computers, and how will it be treated?

19. Unrecaptured Section 1250 Gain. Victor Soto purchased a warehouse in 1996 for $1,000,000. Soto sold the warehouse in July of 2006 for $1,200,000. Soto claimed $309,524 of depreciation during the period when he owned the building. How will this transaction be reported on the tax return? How will the gain on this transaction be taxed?

20. Unrecaptured Section 1250 Gain. On November 10, 2006, Beverly Peterman sold residential realty for $300,000. Peterman purchased the realty on August 5, 1998, for $275,000. She depreciated the property over 27.5 years using the straight-line method. Compute Peterman's unrecaptured Section 1250 (amount taxed at 25%).

21. Sale of Business Property. In 2006 Virginia Banks, SSN 364-25-8153, had the following transactions involving property used in her manufacturing business.

a. Machinery purchased for $50,000 on August 6, 2003 was sold on April 6, 2006 for $22,000. Total depreciation taken on the machine was $31,258.

b. Land used in Banks's business was sold for $23,000 on June 6, 2006. The land was purchased for $16,000 on May 3, 1989.

c. A small tool shed was destroyed by fire during 2006. The loss was not covered by insurance. The shed had been used for several years and had an adjusted basis of $2,500 at the time of the fire. The loss was initially reported on Form 4684. (Enter loss on Form 4797 [line 14]).

d. A warehouse purchased for $50,000 on August 10, 1997, was condemned by the city in order to acquire the land upon which it stood for a new highway. Banks was paid $45,000 for the building on May 1, 2006. Depreciation totaled $10,897.

e. Banks received $36,000 for the condemned land. The land had a basis of $30,000.

Banks will not reinvest any of the proceeds from the condemned land or building in qualified replacement property and wants to report the gain on her 2006 return. Banks's unrecaptured net Section 1231 losses the previous five years are $3,500. Prepare Form 4797, Sales of Business Property, using the blank forms provided.

22. Installment Sales. Yvonne Saburo, a consulting engineer and cash basis taxpayer, decided to close her office and go back to college and study business. One of her business assets was an automobile that she had purchased in 2005 for $12,000. She still owed $5,000 on the car when she sold it for $10,600 on January 10, 2006. The buyer agreed to assume the $5,000 note. Further, the buyer agreed to pay $1,600 as a down payment and pay $2,000 (plus 12% interest) on January 10, 2007, and $2,000 (plus 12% interest on the remaining balance) on January 10, 2008. Under the MACRS rules, Saburo took $2,400 of depreciation on the automobile. Assume that Saburo has no other liabilities.

a. What is the realized gain to Saburo on the sale of the automobile?

b. If the realized gain is reported on the installment basis, how much and what type of gain will Saburo report as income in 2006, 2007, and 2008?

c. How much interest income will Saburo report in 2007 and 2008?

(Use for Problem 21.)

Form **4797**

Department of the Treasury
Internal Revenue Service (99)

Sales of Business Property

(Also Involuntary Conversions and Recapture Amounts Under Sections 179 and 280F(b)(2))

▶Attach to your tax return. ▶See separate instructions.

OMB No. 1545-0184

2006

Attachment Sequence No. **27**

Name(s) shown on return | **Identifying number**

1 Enter the gross proceeds from sales or exchanges reported to you for 2006 on Form(s) 1099-B or 1099-S (or substitute statement) that you are including on line 2, 10, or 20 (see instructions) 1

Part I Sales or Exchanges of Property Used in a Trade or Business and Involuntary Conversions From Other Than Casualty or Theft—Most Property Held More Than 1 Year (see instructions)

	(a) Description of property	(b) Date acquired (mo., day, yr.)	(c) Date sold (mo., day, yr.)	(d) Gross sales price	(e) Depreciation allowed or allowable since acquisition	(f) Cost or other basis, plus improvements and expense of sale	(g) Gain or (loss) Subtract (f) from the sum of (d) and (e)
2							

3 Gain, if any, from Form 4684, line 42 3

4 Section 1231 gain from installment sales from Form 6252, line 26 or 37 4

5 Section 1231 gain or (loss) from like-kind exchanges from Form 8824 5

6 Gain, if any, from line 32, from other than casualty or theft 6

7 Combine lines 2 through 6. Enter the gain or (loss) here and on the appropriate line as follows: 7

Partnerships (except electing large partnerships) and S corporations. Report the gain or (loss) following the instructions for Form 1065, Schedule K, line 10, or Form 1120S, Schedule K, line 9. Skip lines 8, 9, 11, and 12 below.

Individuals, partners, S corporation shareholders, and all others. If line 7 is zero or a loss, enter the amount from line 7 on line 11 below and skip lines 8 and 9. If line 7 is a gain and you did not have any prior year section 1231 losses, or they were recaptured in an earlier year, enter the gain from line 7 as a long-term capital gain on the Schedule D filed with your return and skip lines 8, 9, 11, and 12 below.

8 Nonrecaptured net section 1231 losses from prior years (see instructions) 8

9 Subtract line 8 from line 7. If zero or less, enter -0-. If line 9 is zero, enter the gain from line 7 on line 12 below. If line 9 is more than zero, enter the amount from line 8 on line 12 below and enter the gain from line 9 as a long-term capital gain on the Schedule D filed with your return (see instructions) 9

Part II Ordinary Gains and Losses (see instructions)

10 Ordinary gains and losses not included on lines 11 through 16 (include property held 1 year or less):

11 Loss, if any, from line 7 . . . . 11 ( )

12 Gain, if any, from line 7 or amount from line 8, if applicable 12

13 Gain, if any, from line 31 13

14 Net gain or (loss) from Form 4684, lines 34 and 41a 14

15 Ordinary gain from installment sales from Form 6252, line 25 or 36 15

16 Ordinary gain or (loss) from like-kind exchanges from Form 8824 16

17 Combine lines 10 through 16 17

18 For all except individual returns, enter the amount from line 17 on the appropriate line of your return and skip lines a and b below. For individual returns, complete lines a and b below:

a If the loss on line 11 includes a loss from Form 4684, line 38, column (b)(ii), enter that part of the loss here. Enter the part of the loss from income-producing property on Schedule A (Form 1040), line 27, and the part of the loss from property used as an employee on Schedule A (Form 1040), line 22. Identify as from "Form 4797, line 18a." See instructions 18a

b Redetermine the gain or (loss) on line 17 excluding the loss, if any, on line 18a. Enter here and on Form 1040, line 14 . . . . 18b

For Paperwork Reduction Act Notice, see separate instructions. Cat. No. 13086I Form **4797** (2006)

(Use for Problem 21.)

Form 4797 (2006) Page **2**

Part III **Gain From Disposition of Property Under Sections 1245, 1250, 1252, 1254, and 1255** (see instructions)

19	**(a)** Description of section 1245, 1250, 1252, 1254, or 1255 property:	**(b)** Date acquired (mo., day, yr.)	**(c)** Date sold (mo., day, yr.)
A			
B			
C			
D			

	These columns relate to the properties on lines 19A through 19D. ▶		Property A	Property B	Property C	Property D
20	Gross sales price (**Note:** *See line 1 before completing.*)	20				
21	Cost or other basis plus expense of sale	21				
22	Depreciation (or depletion) allowed or allowable	22				
23	Adjusted basis. Subtract line 22 from line 21	23				
24	Total gain. Subtract line 23 from line 20	24				
25	**If section 1245 property:**					
a	Depreciation allowed or allowable from line 22	25a				
b	Enter the **smaller** of line 24 or 25a	25b				
26	**If section 1250 property:** If straight line depreciation was used, enter -0- on line 26g, except for a corporation subject to section 291.					
a	Additional depreciation after 1975 (see instructions)	26a				
b	Applicable percentage multiplied by the **smaller** of line 24 or line 26a (see instructions)	26b				
c	Subtract line 26a from line 24. If residential rental property **or** line 24 is not more than line 26a, skip lines 26d and 26e	26c				
d	Additional depreciation after 1969 and before 1976	26d				
e	Enter the **smaller** of line 26c or 26d	26e				
f	Section 291 amount (corporations only)	26f				
g	Add lines 26b, 26e, and 26f	26g				
27	**If section 1252 property:** Skip this section if you did not dispose of farmland or if this form is being completed for a partnership (other than an electing large partnership).					
a	Soil, water, and land clearing expenses	27a				
b	Line 27a multiplied by applicable percentage (see instructions)	27b				
c	Enter the **smaller** of line 24 or 27b	27c				
28	**If section 1254 property:**					
a	Intangible drilling and development costs, expenditures for development of mines and other natural deposits, and mining exploration costs (see instructions)	28a				
b	Enter the **smaller** of line 24 or 28a	28b				
29	**If section 1255 property:**					
a	Applicable percentage of payments excluded from income under section 126 (see instructions)	29a				
b	Enter the **smaller** of line 24 or 29a (see instructions)	29b				

Summary of Part III Gains. Complete property columns A through D through line 29b before going to line 30.

30	Total gains for all properties. Add property columns A through D, line 24	30	
31	Add property columns A through D, lines 25b, 26g, 27c, 28b, and 29b. Enter here and on line 13	31	
32	Subtract line 31 from line 30. Enter the portion from casualty or theft on Form 4684, line 36. Enter the portion from other than casualty or theft on Form 4797, line 6	32	

Part IV **Recapture Amounts Under Sections 179 and 280F(b)(2) When Business Use Drops to 50% or Less** (see instructions)

			(a) Section 179	(b) Section 280F(b)(2)
33	Section 179 expense deduction or depreciation allowable in prior years	33		
34	Recomputed depreciation (see instructions)	34		
35	Recapture amount. Subtract line 34 from line 33. See the instructions for where to report	35		

Printed on recycled paper Form **4797** (2006)

23. Installment Sales. Virginia Mann sold depreciable personal property for $70,000 on August 4, 2006. The buyer agreed to pay $10,000 at the time of sale and $20,000 on August 4 in each of the next three years. In addition, interest at the current market rate will be paid on the remaining installment balance. Mann bought the property several years ago for $43,000. Its adjusted basis at the time of the sale was $25,000. Depreciation totalling $18,000 was taken on the property.

a. Compute the total gain from the sale.

b. How much gain and what type of gain must be reported in the year of sale?

c. How much gain and what type of gain must be reported in each of the next three years?

24. Internet Problem: Researching Publication 537.

During 2006, Leo Hunt, a cash basis taxpayer, sold land at a gain to an unrelated party. Hunt received part of the proceeds in 2006 and will receive the rest of the proceeds in 2007 and 2008. Hunt is fairly sure he would like to elect out of the installment sales method and has asked for advice on how to accomplish this. He also wants to know if he elects out of the installment method whether he can later change his mind and use the installment method to report the gain on the sale.

Go to the IRS Web site. Locate Publication 537. Print out a copy of the page where the answer to Hunt's questions can be found. Underline or highlight the pertinent information. Prepare a brief discussion of the answer to Hunt's questions.

See Appendix A for instructions on use of the IRS Web site.

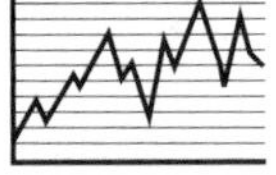

25. Business Entity Problem: This problem is designed for those using the "business entity" approach. The solution may require information from Chapters 14 and 15.

Kazoo Corporation purchased a commercial building 10 years ago for $390,000. The building was sold in the current year for $450,000. Straight-line depreciation over the period of ownership was $100,000.

a. How much of the gain from the sale of the building is ordinary income?

b. How will the remaining gain be treated?

COMPREHENSIVE PROBLEM

26. Michael L. (SSN 374-47-7774) and Joyce A. (SSN 642-81-9982) Sea, married taxpayers filing a joint return, sold the following securities in 2006:

No. of Shares	*Company*	*Date Acquired*	*Cost or Other Basis*	*Date Sold*	*Sales Price*
20	Red Corporation	7-1-94	$1,661	12–6-06	$2,311
50	Lee Corporation	9-15-94	5,820	11-14-06	4,320
60	Alf Corporation	6-10-06	850	10-15-06	715
100	RST Corporation	5-10-83	4,600	8-5-06	2,430
—	$1,000 par value bond, TF Company	5-5-06	800	10-15-06	900

A short-term capital loss of $260 and a long-term capital loss of $2,500 were carried over from 2005. In addition, the Seas report total wages of $41,920. From this amount $1,190 was withheld for federal income taxes. This represents the Seas's only other item of income during 2006.

Prepare the 2006 tax return for Mr. and Mrs. Sea using the forms on the pages that follow. The Seas live at 1319 Mayfair Drive, Champaign, IL 61821. They claim one dependent, their 13-year-old son, Tad (SSN 629-43-7881). The Seas both elect to have $3 go to the presidential election campaign fund. They also want to claim the standard credit for federal telephone excise tax paid.

(Use for Problem 26.)

Form **1040** Department of the Treasury—Internal Revenue Service
U.S. Individual Income Tax Return **2006** (99) IRS Use Only—Do not write or staple in this space.

For the year Jan. 1–Dec. 31, 2006, or other tax year beginning , 2006, ending , 20 OMB No. 1545-0074

Label (See instructions on page 16.) **Use the IRS label.** Otherwise, please print or type.

LABEL HERE

Your first name and initial | Last name | **Your social security number**

If a joint return, spouse's first name and initial | Last name | **Spouse's social security number**

Home address (number and street). If you have a P.O. box, see page 16. | Apt. no. | ▲ You **must** enter your SSN(s) above. ▲

City, town or post office, state, and ZIP code. If you have a foreign address, see page 16. | Checking a box below will not change your tax or refund.

Presidential Election Campaign ▶ Check here if you, or your spouse if filing jointly, want $3 to go to this fund (see page 16) ▶ ☐ **You** ☐ **Spouse**

Filing Status

Check only one box.

1 ☐ Single
2 ☐ Married filing jointly (even if only one had income)
3 ☐ Married filing separately. Enter spouse's SSN above and full name here. ▶
4 ☐ Head of household (with qualifying person). (See page 17.) If the qualifying person is a child but not your dependent, enter this child's name here. ▶
5 ☐ Qualifying widow(er) with dependent child (see page 17)

Exemptions

6a ☐ **Yourself.** If someone can claim you as a dependent, **do not** check box 6a . . . . } **Boxes checked on 6a and 6b** ____
b ☐ **Spouse** . . . . } **No. of children on 6c who:**

c **Dependents:**

(1) First name Last name	(2) Dependent's social security number	(3) Dependent's relationship to you	(4) ✓ if qualifying child for child tax credit (see page 19)
			☐
			☐
			☐
			☐

If more than four dependents, see page 19.

• **lived with you** ____
• **did not live with you due to divorce or separation (see page 20)** ____
Dependents on 6c not entered above ____
Add numbers on lines above ▶ ☐

d Total number of exemptions claimed . . . .

Income

Attach Form(s) W-2 here. Also attach Forms W-2G and 1099-R if tax was withheld.

If you did not get a W-2, see page 22.

Enclose, but do not attach, any payment. Also, please use **Form 1040-V.**

7	Wages, salaries, tips, etc. Attach Form(s) W-2		7	
8a	**Taxable** interest. Attach Schedule B if required		8a	
b	**Tax-exempt** interest. **Do not** include on line 8a	8b		
9a	Ordinary dividends. Attach Schedule B if required		9a	
b	Qualified dividends (see page 23)	9b		
10	Taxable refunds, credits, or offsets of state and local income taxes (see page 23)		10	
11	Alimony received		11	
12	Business income or (loss). Attach Schedule C or C-EZ		12	
13	Capital gain or (loss). Attach Schedule D if required. If not required, check here ▶ ☐		13	
14	Other gains or (losses). Attach Form 4797		14	
15a	IRA distributions 15a	b Taxable amount (see page 25)	15b	
16a	Pensions and annuities 16a	b Taxable amount (see page 25)	16b	
17	Rental real estate, royalties, partnerships, S corporations, trusts, etc. Attach Schedule E		17	
18	Farm income or (loss). Attach Schedule F		18	
19	Unemployment compensation		19	
20a	Social security benefits 20a	b Taxable amount (see page 27)	20b	
21	Other income. List type and amount (see page 29)		21	
22	Add the amounts in the far right column for lines 7 through 21. This is your **total income** ▶		22	

Adjusted Gross Income

Line	Description	Line	Amount	Line	Amount
23	Archer MSA deduction. Attach Form 8853	23			
24	Certain business expenses of reservists, performing artists, and fee-basis government officials. Attach Form 2106 or 2106-EZ	24			
25	Health savings account deduction. Attach Form 8889	25			
26	Moving expenses. Attach Form 3903	26			
27	One-half of self-employment tax. Attach Schedule SE	27			
28	Self-employed SEP, SIMPLE, and qualified plans	28			
29	Self-employed health insurance deduction (see page 30)	29			
30	Penalty on early withdrawal of savings	30			
31a	Alimony paid b Recipient's SSN ▶	31a			
32	IRA deduction (see page 31)	32			
33	Student loan interest deduction (see page 33)	33			
34	Jury duty pay you gave to your employer	34			
35	Domestic production activities deduction. Attach Form 8903	35			
36	Add lines 23 through 31a and 32 through 35			36	
37	Subtract line 36 from line 22. This is your **adjusted gross income** ▶			37	

For Disclosure, Privacy Act, and Paperwork Reduction Act Notice, see page 78. Cat. No. 11320B Form **1040** (2006)

(Use for Problem 26.)

Form 1040 (2006) Page **2**

Tax and Credits

38	Amount from line 37 (adjusted gross income)	38	
39a	Check if: ☐ **You** were born before January 2, 1942, ☐ Blind. ☐ **Spouse** was born before January 2, 1942, ☐ Blind. } **Total boxes checked ▶ 39a**		
b	If your spouse itemizes on a separate return or you were a dual-status alien, see page 35 and check here ▶39b ☐		
40	**Itemized deductions** (from Schedule A) **or** your **standard deduction** (see left margin)	40	
41	Subtract line 40 from line 38	41	
42	If line 38 is over $112,875, or you provided housing to a person displaced by Hurricane Katrina, see page 37. Otherwise, multiply $3,300 by the total number of exemptions claimed on line 6d	42	
43	**Taxable income.** Subtract line 42 from line 41. If line 42 is more than line 41, enter -0-	43	
44	**Tax** (see page 37). Check if any tax is from: **a** ☐ Form(s) 8814 **b** ☐ Form 4972	44	
45	**Alternative minimum tax** (see page 39). Attach Form 6251	45	
46	Add lines 44 and 45 ▶	46	
47	Foreign tax credit. Attach Form 1116 if required	47	
48	Credit for child and dependent care expenses. Attach Form 2441	48	
49	Credit for the elderly or the disabled. Attach Schedule R	49	
50	Education credits. Attach Form 8863	50	
51	Retirement savings contributions credit. Attach Form 8880	51	
52	Residential energy credits. Attach Form 5695	52	
53	Child tax credit (see page XX). Attach Form 8901 if required	53	
54	Credits from: **a** ☐ Form 8396 **b** ☐ Form 8839 **c** ☐ Form 8859	54	
55	Other credits: **a** ☐ Form 3800 **b** ☐ Form 8801 **c** ☐ Form____	55	
56	Add lines 47 through 55. These are your **total credits**	56	
57	Subtract line 56 from line 46. If line 56 is more than line 46, enter -0- ▶	57	

Standard Deduction for—

- People who checked any box on line 39a or 39b **or** who can be claimed as a dependent, see page 36.
- All others:

Single or Married filing separately, $5,150

Married filing jointly or Qualifying widow(er), $10,300

Head of household, $7,550

Other Taxes

58	Self-employment tax. Attach Schedule SE	58	
59	Social security and Medicare tax on tip income not reported to employer. Attach Form 4137	59	
60	Additional tax on IRAs, other qualified retirement plans, etc. Attach Form 5329 if required	60	
61	Advance earned income credit payments from Form(s) W-2, box 9	61	
62	Household employment taxes. Attach Schedule H	62	
63	Add lines 57 through 62. This is your **total tax** ▶	63	

Payments

If you have a qualifying child, attach Schedule EIC.

64	Federal income tax withheld from Forms W-2 and 1099	64	
65	2006 estimated tax payments and amount applied from 2005 return	65	
66a	**Earned income credit (EIC)**	66a	
b	Nontaxable combat pay election ▶ 66b		
67	Excess social security and tier 1 RRTA tax withheld (see page 59)	67	
68	Additional child tax credit. Attach Form 8812	68	
69	Amount paid with request for extension to file (see page 59)	69	
70	Payments from: **a** ☐ Form 2439 **b** ☐ Form 4136 **c** ☐ Form 8885	70	
71	Credit for federal telephone excise tax paid. Attach Form 8913 if required	71	
72	Add lines 64, 65, 66a, and 67 through 71. These are your **total payments** ▶	72	

Refund

Direct deposit? See page 59 and fill in 74b, 74c, and 74d, or Form 8888.

73	If line 72 is more than line 63, subtract line 63 from line 72. This is the amount you **overpaid**	73	
74a	Amount of line 73 you want **refunded to you.** If Form 8888 is attached, check here ▶ ☐	74a	
▶ b	Routing number ▶ **c** Type: ☐ Checking ☐ Savings		
▶ d	Account number		
75	Amount of line 73 you want **applied to your 2007 estimated tax** ▶ 75		

Amount You Owe

76	**Amount you owe.** Subtract line 72 from line 63. For details on how to pay, see page 60 ▶	76	
77	Estimated tax penalty (see page 60) 77		

Third Party Designee

Do you want to allow another person to discuss this return with the IRS (see page 61)? ☐ **Yes.** Complete the following. ☐ **No**

Designee's name ▶ Phone no. ▶ (   ) Personal identification number (PIN) ▶

Sign Here

Joint return? See page 17. Keep a copy for your records.

Under penalties of perjury, I declare that I have examined this return and accompanying schedules and statements, and to the best of my knowledge and belief, they are true, correct, and complete. Declaration of preparer (other than taxpayer) is based on all information of which preparer has any knowledge.

Your signature	Date	Your occupation	Daytime phone number ( )
Spouse's signature. If a joint return, **both** must sign.	Date	Spouse's occupation	

Paid Preparer's Use Only

Preparer's signature ▶	Date	Check if self-employed ☐	Preparer's SSN or PTIN
Firm's name (or yours if self-employed), address, and ZIP code ▶		EIN	
		Phone no.	( )

Form **1040** (2006)

Printed on recycled paper

(Use for Problem 26.)

SCHEDULE D (Form 1040)

Department of the Treasury Internal Revenue Service (99)

Capital Gains and Losses

► Attach to Form 1040 or Form 1040NR. ► See Instructions for Schedule D (Form 1040).

► Use Schedule D-1 to list additional transactions for lines 1 and 8.

OMB No. 1545-0074

2006

Attachment Sequence No. 12

Name(s) shown on Form 1040 | Your social security number

Part I Short-Term Capital Gains and Losses—Assets Held One Year or Less

	(a) Description of property (Example: 100 sh. XYZ Co.)	(b) Date acquired (Mo., day, yr.)	(c) Date sold (Mo., day, yr.)	(d) Sales price (see page D-6 of the instructions)	(e) Cost or other basis (see page D-7 of the instructions)	(f) Gain or (loss) Subtract (e) from (d)
1						

2	Enter your short-term totals, if any, from Schedule D-1, line 2	2	
3	**Total short-term sales price amounts.** Add lines 1 and 2 in column (d)	3	
4	Short-term gain from Form 6252 and short-term gain or (loss) from Forms 4684, 6781, and 8824	4	
5	Net short-term gain or (loss) from partnerships, S corporations, estates, and trusts from Schedule(s) K-1	5	
6	Short-term capital loss carryover. Enter the amount, if any, from line 10 of your **Capital Loss Carryover Worksheet** on page D-7 of the instructions	6	( )
7	**Net short-term capital gain or (loss).** Combine lines 1 through 6 in column (f)	7	

Part II Long-Term Capital Gains and Losses—Assets Held More Than One Year

	(a) Description of property (Example: 100 sh. XYZ Co.)	(b) Date acquired (Mo., day, yr.)	(c) Date sold (Mo., day, yr.)	(d) Sales price (see page D-6 of the instructions)	(e) Cost or other basis (see page D-7 of the instructions)	(f) Gain or (loss) Subtract (e) from (d)
8						

9	Enter your long-term totals, if any, from Schedule D-1, line 9	9	
10	**Total long-term sales price amounts.** Add lines 8 and 9 in column (d)	10	
11	Gain from Form 4797, Part I; long-term gain from Forms 2439 and 6252; and long-term gain or (loss) from Forms 4684, 6781, and 8824	11	
12	Net long-term gain or (loss) from partnerships, S corporations, estates, and trusts from Schedule(s) K-1	12	
13	Capital gain distributions. See page D-1 of the instructions	13	
14	Long-term capital loss carryover. Enter the amount, if any, from line 15 of your **Capital Loss Carryover Worksheet** on page D-7 of the instructions	14	( )
15	**Net long-term capital gain or (loss).** Combine lines 8 through 14 in column (f). Then go to Part III on the back	15	

For Paperwork Reduction Act Notice, see Form 1040 instructions. Cat. No. 11338H **Schedule D (Form 1040) 2006**

(Use for Problem 26.)

Schedule D (Form 1040) 2006 Page **2**

Part III **Summary**

16	Combine lines 7 and 15 and enter the result. If line 16 is a loss, skip lines 17 through 20, and go to line 21. If a gain, enter the gain on Form 1040, line 13, or Form 1040NR, line 14. Then go to line 17 below . . .	**16**		
17	Are lines 15 and 16 **both** gains? ☐ **Yes.** Go to line 18. ☐ **No.** Skip lines 18 through 21, and go to line 22.			
18	Enter the amount, if any, from line 7 of the **28% Rate Gain Worksheet** on page D-8 of the instructions . . . ▶	**18**		
19	Enter the amount, if any, from line 18 of the **Unrecaptured Section 1250 Gain Worksheet** on page D-9 of the instructions . . . ▶	**19**		
20	Are lines 18 and 19 **both** zero or blank? ☐ **Yes.** Complete Form 1040 through line 43, or Form 1040NR through line 40. Then complete the **Qualified Dividends and Capital Gain Tax Worksheet** on page 38 of the Instructions for Form 1040 (or in the Instructions for Form 1040NR). **Do not** complete lines 21 and 22 below. ☐ **No.** Complete Form 1040 through line 43, or Form 1040NR through line 40. Then complete the **Schedule D Tax Worksheet** on page D-10 of the instructions. **Do not** complete lines 21 and 22 below.			
21	If line 16 is a loss, enter here and on Form 1040, line 13, or Form 1040NR, line 14, the **smaller** of: • The loss on line 16 or • ($3,000), or if married filing separately, ($1,500) } . . . **Note.** When figuring which amount is smaller, treat both amounts as positive numbers.	**21**	(	)
22	Do you have qualified dividends on Form 1040, line 9b, or Form 1040NR, line 10b? ☐ **Yes.** Complete Form 1040 through line 43, or Form 1040NR through line 40. Then complete the **Qualified Dividends and Capital Gain Tax Worksheet** on page 38 of the Instructions for Form 1040 (or in the Instructions for Form 1040NR). ☐ **No.** Complete the rest of Form 1040 or Form 1040NR.			

Schedule D (Form 1040) 2006

12

NOL, AMT, and Business Tax Credits

CHAPTER CONTENTS

CHAPTER OVERVIEW

This chapter describes the tax rules for net operating losses and the alternative minimum tax. It also discusses the various business credits available to business owners and lessors of real property. Consideration is also given to both the audit and the appeals processes, as well as filing an amended tax return. Taxpayer rights and tax preparer responsibilities are described in the chapter.

NET OPERATING LOSS (NOL)

A special rule applies when individual business owners and C corporations report a loss in one year and profits in other years. It would be unfair if business profits were always taxed, but no tax relief was available when the business suffered a loss. The net operating loss (NOL) provisions allow business losses to offset income from other tax years. An NOL generated in 2006 offsets taxable income of the two previous years (2004, 2005) and then is carried forward to offset income in the next 20 years (2007-2026).

A 5-year carryback period applies to NOLs due to losses that stem from destruction caused by hurricanes Katrina, Rita, or Wilma. This special rule applies only to losses paid or incurred after August 27, 2005 and before January 1, 2008. Alternatively, taxpayers could forego the carryback of the NOL and carry forward the NOL 20 years.

Calculating NOL

For individuals, an NOL is not the same as negative taxable income on Form 1040. In fact, it is not computed anywhere on the tax return for the year in which it occurs. Instead, the NOL is computed on Form 1045, Schedule A (not shown). Filed separately from Form 1040, Form 1045 is the application for a refund of prior year income taxes. In computing the NOL, individuals make the following adjustments to negative taxable income.

1. The deduction for personal and dependency exemptions is added back.
2. Nonbusiness capital losses can offset only nonbusiness capital gains. Nonbusiness capital gains and losses arise from transactions involving nonbusiness property (for example, investment property). Thus, any nonbusiness net capital loss is added back.
3. The NOL of a preceding or a succeeding year is added back.
4. Nonbusiness deductions in excess of nonbusiness income are added back. Nonbusiness deductions include all itemized deductions except casualty and theft losses. For individuals who do not itemize deductions, their standard deduction is a nonbusiness deduction. Nonbusiness income comes from sources other than the taxpayer's business. Examples include interest, dividends, and net gains from the sale of nonbusiness property. Salaries, net gains from the sale of business property, and rental income are treated as business income.

EXAMPLE 1

Chris and Dana Bosky are married and file a joint tax return. Chris operates a business that generated $120,000 of gross revenues and $150,000 of operating expenses during 2006. The Boskys show a negative taxable income of $28,800.

Salary		$15,000
Business loss ($120,000 – $150,000)		(30,000)
Net business capital gains		3,000
Net nonbusiness capital gains		4,000
Interest income		1,500
AGI		($ 6,500)
Less itemized deductions:		
Mortgage interest and real estate taxes	$9,500	
Casualty loss	6,200	(15,700)
Less personal exemptions		(6,600)
Taxable income (loss)		($28,800)

Using this information, the Bosky's $18,200 NOL for 2006 is computed:

Taxable loss			($28,800)
Add back:			
Personal exemptions		$6,600	
Net nonbusiness deductions	$9,500		
Nonbusiness income ($4,000 + $1,500)	(5,500)	4,000	10,600
NOL for 2006			($18,200)

NOL Deduction

Once determined, an NOL generated in 2006 is carried back two years, then carried forward 20 years. Alternatively, taxpayers can elect to forgo the carryback and carry forward an NOL 20 years. When carried over to another year, an individual taxpayer treats an NOL deduction as a *deduction for AGI.* An NOL carried forward is entered as a negative amount on the "Other income" line of Form 1040, page 1.

In Example 1, the Boskys could have applied the NOL to their 2004 taxable income and recomputed their 2004 tax liability. The difference between the Bosky's original tax liability and the recomputed tax liability would be refunded to them. Alternatively, the Boskys could elect to forgo the carryback and use the $18,200 as a deduction for AGI when filing their 2007 tax return.

Taxpayers elect to forego the carryback period by attaching a statement to the tax return that produced the NOL. Once made, the election to forego the carryback of an NOL is final. When a 2006 tax return showing an NOL is filed without such a statement, the IRS assumes the taxpayer is carrying back the NOL to the 2004 tax year.

ALTERNATIVE MINIMUM TAX (AMT)

The tax law contains many exclusions, deductions, and other tax breaks that allow taxpayers to reduce their tax liabilities. Some individuals with high incomes used these tax benefits so much that they paid little or no income tax. As a result, Congress enacted an alternative minimum tax (AMT). The AMT works with the regular income tax to ensure that taxpayers with high total incomes pay some amount of income tax.

The AMT operates as a completely separate tax system. If subject to the AMT, the taxpayer will pay the AMT plus the regular income tax. Below is the basic format for computing the AMT.

	Regular taxable income
±	Tax preferences and positive adjustments
–	Negative adjustments
–	Allowed net operating losses
=	Alternative minimum taxable income (AMTI)
–	Allowable exemption
=	Amount subject to tax (AMT Base)
×	AMT tax rate
=	Tentative minimum tax
–	Regular income tax
=	AMT (if positive)

Preferences and Adjustments

Alternative minimum taxable income (AMTI) is regular taxable income modified by preferences and adjustments. Preferences and adjustments allow taxpayers to receive large exclusions and deductions in computing regular taxable income. The AMT computation reduces the benefits of these tax incentives by limiting the exclusions or the amounts currently deductible. The amounts disallowed for AMT are added back to the regular taxable income in computing AMTI.

Preference items are always added back to regular taxable income in computing AMTI. Thus, preferences increase income subject to the AMT. Adjustments, on the other hand, can be positive or negative. Adjustments generally arise from timing differences. **Timing differences** occur when a deduction is allowed for regular income tax in a year before it is allowed for the AMT. Thus, adjustments tend to be positive in the first years to which they apply (the deduction for regular tax is greater than the deduction for AMT) and become negative in later years when they reverse (the deduction for regular tax is less than the deduction for AMT). When adjustments are negative, they reduce the amount subject to the AMT.

For the most part, the adjustments and preferences used in computing the AMT fall into four categories: (1) preferences and adjustments related to the recovery of costs, (2) income recognition adjustments, (3) tax shelter losses, and (4) tax-exempt or excluded items.

Recovery of Costs

The adjustments and preferences in this category involve costs that are capital in nature. The regular income tax system allows taxpayers to immediately expense (Section 179) and/or use an accelerated method (200% declining balance) to recover the costs of tangible personal property. AMT also allows Section 179 expensing, but can require slower recovery methods or longer recovery periods. Two of the more common cost recovery adjustments are:

1. **Cost recovery on real property.** Real property placed in service between 1987 and 1998 must be recovered using straight-line depreciation over 40 years for AMT. MACRS depreciates real property over 27.5, 31.5, or 39 years using the straight-line method. The difference in the two methods is the AMT adjustment. There is no AMT depreciation adjustment for realty placed in service after 1998.
2. **Cost recovery on personal property.** AMT uses the 150% declining balance (DB) method over the longer alternative depreciation system (ADS) lives. For computing regular taxable income, both the 200% DB and straight-line methods are allowed. The difference in the cost recovery between the methods used for computing regular tax and computing AMT is an adjustment for AMT. However, there is no AMT adjustment required for personal property on which bonus depreciation was taken. (See Chapter 8 for a discussion of bonus depreciation).

EXAMPLE 2

In 1990, Nadia and Tim Orlean paid $430,000 for a ski villa in Aspen, Colorado. The Orleans use the villa solely as rental property. They depreciate the villa using the straight-line method over 27.5 years (MACRS, see Chapter 8). Each year they deduct $15,636 ($430,000/27.5) of depreciation against their rental income in computing the taxable income. For purposes of computing AMT, depreciation allowed is $10,750 ($430,000/40). Thus during the years that MACRS is deducted in computing the Orleans' taxable income, they must add back to taxable income the $4,886 excess ($15,636 - $10,750) to compute AMTI. After the property is fully depreciated under MACRS, the Orleans can continue to take depreciation deductions when computing AMTI.

EXAMPLE 3

Same as in Example 2 except that the Orleans bought the villa in 2000. For real property placed n service after 1998, there is no difference in the depreciation rules for regular income tax and AMT. Thus, no AMT adjustment is needed.

EXAMPLE 4

A taxpayer owns business property that cost $30,000. The half-year convention applies to the property. The recovery period is five years for regular income tax purposes and eight years for AMT. The cost recovery for regular income tax (200% DB over 5 years) is $6,000 in year 1 ($30,000 × 20%). The AMT cost recovery (150% DB over 8 years) is $2,813 ($30,000 × ⅛ × 150% × ½). The $3,187 difference ($6,000 – $2,813) is added back to taxable income in computing AMTI.

Passive Losses

Neither the regular tax nor the AMT system allows for passive losses in excess of passive income to be deducted in the year they occur. Such losses carry forward and offset passive income in future years. Any losses carried forward are deducted in full when the taxpayer disposes of the entire interest in the activity. While the loss recognition for both tax calculations is deferred, the amount of the loss to be deferred will generally differ. The difference occurs because the loss for AMT purposes is determined using all required AMT tax adjustments rather than the regular income tax deductions.

For example, MACRS depreciates residential realty over 27.5 years using the straight-line method. For AMT, this property is depreciated over 40 years. Because this difference affects the amount of passive loss carryover for regular tax versus AMT, it will affect the amount of the recognized gain when the property is sold as well as the passive loss deduction allowed.

Tax-Exempt and Excluded Income

Three other items of income may result in adjustments for AMT. First, AMTI includes interest from private activity bonds (a type of municipal bond). Interest from all municipal bonds is not taxable in computing regular taxable income. Thus, any interest from private activity bonds is added to taxable income in computing AMTI. Second, when exercising an incentive stock option, the excess of the FMV of the stock over the exercise price is income for purposes of computing AMT. Since exercising an incentive stock option does not affect regular taxable income, the excess amount is added to taxable income in computing AMTI. Third, 7% of the excluded gain on the sale of Section 1202 small business stock is a preference item. This amount is added to taxable income to compute AMTI (Recall from Chapter 9 that only 50% of the realized gain on the sale of Section 1202 stock is taxed.)

EXAMPLE 5

Julie Pethridge owns private activity bonds issued by the state of Utah. During the current year, the bonds pay interest totaling $2,850. All interest from state and local government bonds (municipal bonds) is excluded from gross income under the regular income tax system (see Chapter 3). However, interest from private activity bonds is not an exclusion under the AMT system. Thus, in computing AMTI, Pethridge must add back the $2,850 to taxable income.

EXAMPLE 6

Rick Dreyfus paid $60 a share for 1,000 shares of stock under an incentive stock option program at work. At the time, the stock was selling for $85 a share. The excess of the fair market value of the stock over the amount he paid for the stock is excluded from Dreyfus's gross income under the regular income tax system. However, no such exclusion is allowed for purposes of computing AMT. Thus, Dreyfus must add back to taxable income the $25,000 excess (($85 - $60) x 1,000 shares) to taxable income when computing AMTI.

EXAMPLE 7

During 2006 Lucas Brown realized a $30,000 gain on the sale of Section 1202 stock. Under the regular income tax system, 50% of this gain is excluded from gross income. Thus, his recognized gain is $15,000. In computing his AMTI, Brown must add back to taxable income 7% of the excluded gain, or $4,200 ($15,000 x 7%).

The tax law allows taxpayers to earn tax-free interest income when they invest in state and local government bonds (municipal bonds) under the assumption that municipalities would use the bond proceeds for various government purposes. However, sometimes municipalities issue bonds and then loan the proceeds to private parties, or alternatively, they raise funds to construct facilities to be used for private purposes. Bonds of this nature are referred to as private activity bonds. For private activity bonds issued after May 15, 1997, the tax law still allows the interest earned on such bonds to be tax-free from regular income taxes, but requires taxpayers to report the interest as a preference item for purposes of computing AMT.

AMT Itemized Deductions

The AMTI calculation disallows certain itemized deductions used to compute the regular taxable income. Taxpayers adjust regular taxable income for the following itemized deductions:

1. Taxes
2. Miscellaneous deductions subject to the 2% AGI limit
3. Medical expenses
4. Interest

The 2% reduction in itemized deductions required for taxpayers with AGI in excess of $150,500 ($75,250 for couples filing separately) does not apply in computing the itemized deductions for the AMT.

Taxes and Miscellaneous Deductions

All state and local income or property taxes deducted on Schedule A must be added back in computing AMTI. Any state income tax refunds included in regular taxable income are not included in AMTI, and therefore must be subtracted from taxable income in computing AMTI. Also, any miscellaneous itemized deductions in excess of the 2% AGI limit deduction on Schedule A are added back when computing AMTI.

EXAMPLE 8

On his 2006 tax return, Kyle Davis's itemized deductions exceeded the standard deduction amount. Included in his itemized deductions were $4,500 of real estate taxes and $2,350 for state and local income taxes. Also included was $240 of miscellaneous itemized deductions in excess of 2% AGI. In computing AMTI, Davis must add back to taxable income the $7,090 he deducted for taxes and miscellaneous deductions on Schedule A ($4,500 + $2,350 + $240).

Medical Expenses

Only medical expenses that exceed 10% of AGI may be deducted for purposes of computing AMTI. In computing regular taxable income, medical expenses in excess of 7.5% of AGI are deductible. The taxpayer recomputes the medical expense deduction using a 10% AGI "floor." The taxpayer then adds back to regular taxable income the difference between the medical expense deduction in excess of 7.5% AGI and the recomputed medical expense deduction using 10% AGI.

EXAMPLE 9

Tom Rosen's AGI is $120,000 and he has $10,000 of unreimbursed medical expenses. When computing his itemized deductions, Rosen deducts $1,000 of medical expenses ($10,000 – (7.5% × $120,000)). When computing AMTI, he only can deduct medical expenses in excess of $12,000 (10% × $120,000). Since no medical expense deduction would be allowed in computing AMTI, Rosen must add back $1,000 to taxable income when computing AMTI.

Interest

The AMT mortgage interest on personal residences is limited to interest on acquisition indebtedness. Interest on equity loans qualifies only if the loan proceeds were used to acquire or substantially improve the residence. Thus, the interest on equity loans whose proceeds are used for personal items is not *qualified housing interest* under the AMT system.

Investment interest is deductible for both regular tax and the AMT to the extent of net investment income. However, the interest deduction may vary because the net investment income may not be the same for both regular tax and AMT.

EXAMPLE 10

On their 2006 tax return, Trey and Rita Smith deducted $9,600 of home equity interest on Schedule A. They used the proceeds from the $100,000 home equity loan to remodel their kitchen and master bath. The interest on the first $100,000 of home equity loans is deductible under the regular income tax system. Because the proceeds from the loan were used to buy or improve their principal residence, the deduction is also allowed for purposes of computing AMT. Thus, no adjustment to taxable income is necessary in computing AMTI.

EXAMPLE 11

Same as in Example 10 except that the Smiths used the proceeds to pay off their credit card debt, buy a new car, and take a vacation. The interest is no longer deductible for purposes of computing AMT. Thus, in computing AMTI, the Smiths must add back the $9,600 to their taxable income.

AMT Exemption

No personal and dependency exemptions or standard deduction is used to compute AMTI. Instead, a special AMT exemption is intended to keep most lower- and middle-income taxpayers from being subject to the AMT. The exemption varies by taxpayer filing status, but begins being phased out once AMTI reaches certain levels. The phase-out is 25% of the amount of AMTI above a specified level. Figure 12-1 shows the exemption amounts, the phase-out levels for 2006 and the calculation for the AMT exemption for each filing status.

FIGURE 12-1 AMT Exemption

	Exemption	Phase-Out Starts (AMTI)	Phase-Out Calculation
Married filing jointly	$62,550	$150,000	25% × (AMTI – $150,000)
Unmarried	42,500	112,500	25% × (AMTI – $112,500)
Married filing separately	31,275	75,000	25% × (AMTI – $75,000)

EXAMPLE 12

Jess Milton files a separate tax return from his wife. During 2006, Milton's AMTI is $94,550. He computes his AMT exemption as follows.

Initial AMT exemption		$31,275
AMTI	$94,550	
AMTI threshold for MFS	(75,000)	
Excess	$19,550	
Phase-out percentage	× 25%	(4,888)
AMT exemption		$26,387

EXAMPLE 13

Rocky and Randi Ray file a joint tax return. Their 2006 AMTI is $173,503. The Rays compute their AMT exemption as follows.

Initial AMT exemption		$62, 550
AMTI	$173,503	
AMTI threshold for MFJ	(150,000)	
Excess	$ 23,503	
Phase-out percentage	× 25%	(5,876)
AMT exemption		$56,674

AMT Rates and Credits

Tax Rate

A two-tiered rate schedule is used to compute the AMT. The tax rate on the first $175,000 of AMTI in excess of the allowable exemption is 26%. A 28% rate applies to the excess. The AMT rates do not apply to net capital gain and qualified dividends taxed at 5%/15%.

Minimum Tax Credit

The portion of the AMT caused by adjustment and preference timing differences creates a minimum tax credit in future years when the regular tax exceeds the taxpayer's tentative minimum tax. This credit can reduce the regular tax liability only in future years and may be carried forward until used. Its purpose is to help avoid double taxing of those adjustments resulting from timing differences. Those interested in learning more about the minimum tax credit should refer to the instructions to Form 8801.

Calculating AMT

EXAMPLE 14

Jeffrey Q. Lang (single, age 47) calculates his regular tax liability for 2006 as follows.

Salary			$95,000
Rental income		$ 6,000	
Rental expenses:			
Depreciation—real property	$2,400		
Depreciation—personal property	600		
Interest expense	5,000		
Property taxes	800		
Other expenses	200	(9,000)	
Net rental loss (active participation)			(3,000)
Short-term capital gain on the sale of stock			5,000
Adjusted gross income			$97,000
Less itemized deductions:			
Charitable contributions		$20,600	
Home mortgage interest		14,400	
Equity loan interest (proceeds used to buy a yacht)		7,450	
Real estate taxes		4,400	(46,850)
Less personal exemption			(3,300)
Taxable income			$46,850
Regular tax liability (using the 2006 Tax Table)			$ 8,276

Lang used accelerated MACRS to compute depreciation. Had he depreciated the property using the AMT depreciation rules, he would have deducted $2,200 for the real property and $450 for the personal property. During 2006 Lang received $41,500 in tax-exempt interest from private activity bonds. He also paid $40,000 for $50,000 of stock through an incentive stock option plan set up by his employer. Using this information, Lang's AMT is $10,363, computed as follows.

Regular taxable income		$ 46,850
Add: (1) Excess depreciation		
Real property ($2,400 – $2,200)	$ 200	
Personal property ($600 – $450)	150	350
(2) Disallowed itemized deductions:		
Equity loan interest	$ 7,450	
Property taxes	4,400	11,850
(3) Personal exemption		3,300
(4) Tax-exempt interest (private activity bonds)		41,500
(5) Stock option bargain ($50,000 – $40,000)		10,000
AMTI		$113,850
Less AMT exemption	$42,500	
($113,850 – $112,500) × .25	(338)	(42,162)
AMT base		$ 71,688
AMT rate		× 26%
Tentative minimum tax		$ 18,639
Less regular income tax		(8,276)
AMT		$ 10,363

Information for Figure 12-2: Filled-In Form 6251

The information for Form 6251, Alternative Minimum Tax—Individuals, comes from Example 14, Jeffrey Q. Lang. Lang's AMT appears on his Form 1040 (line 45) as part of his 2006 tax liability.

Other Information

1: Amount from Form 1040, line 41, **$50,150.00** ($97,000 AGI– $46,850 itemized deductions).
17: Post-1986 depreciation, difference between regular tax and AMT, **$350.00** ($200 + $150)
29: Exemption amount, **$42,162.00** [$42,500 – (.25 × ($113,850 – $112, 500))]
34: Tax from Form 1040, line 44, **$8,276.00**

Generally, taxpayers who invest in depreciable property will have AMT adjustments because of the differences between the depreciation methods used to compute regular tax and AMT. These differences can be reduced by electing the alternative depreciation system (ADS). Taxpayers must carefully plan the mix of their investments and the methods and patterns of asset disposals to mitigate the effect of the AMT. Planning must be done for extended periods, not just for one year at a time.

BUSINESS TAX CREDITS

Several tax credits are available to businesses. Chapter 2 described the personal tax credits available to individual taxpayers. This chapter describes the more common tax credits available to businesses, which includes sole proprietorships, corporations and partnerships.

General Business Credit

After all other nonrefundable credits have been offset against the income tax liability, taxpayers may claim the general business credit (another nonrefundable credit). This credit is equal to the sum of several separately computed tax credits. While some credits are beyond the scope of this text, the remaining sections examine the following business credits:

1. Investment credit (including the business energy credit and the credit for rehabilitation expenditures)—Form 3468
2. Work opportunity credit—Form 5884
3. Low-income housing credit—Form 8586
4. Disabled access credit—Form 8826
5. FICA credit for employee tips—Form 8846
6. Empowerment zone and renewal community employment credit—Form 8844
7. Welfare-to-work credit—Form 8861
8. Employer-provided child care credit—Form 8882
9. Small employer pension plan startup credit—Form 8881
10. New markets credit-Form 8874
11. Alternative motor vehicles credit-Form 8910

FIGURE 12-2 Filled-In Form 6251

Form **6251** | **Alternative Minimum Tax—Individuals** | OMB No. 1545-0074

▶ See separate instructions. | **2006**

Department of the Treasury Internal Revenue Service (99) | ▶ Attach to Form 1040 or Form 1040NR. | Attachment Sequence No. **32**

Name(s) shown on Form 1040: Jeffrey Q. Lang | Your social security number: 367 41 3101

Part I Alternative Minimum Taxable Income (See instructions for how to complete each line.)

1	If filing Schedule A (Form 1040), enter the amount from Form 1040, line 41 (minus any amount on Form 8914, line 6), and go to line 2. Otherwise, enter the amount from Form 1040, line 38 (minus any amount on Form 8914, line 6), and go to line 7. (If less than zero, enter as a negative amount.)	1	50,150 00
2	Medical and dental. Enter the **smaller** of Schedule A (Form 1040), line 4, **or** 2½ % of Form 1040, line 38	2	
3	Taxes from Schedule A (Form 1040), line 9	3	4,400 00
4	Enter the home mortgage interest adjustment, if any, from line 6 of the worksheet on page 2 of the instructions	4	7,450 00
5	Miscellaneous deductions from Schedule A (Form 1040), line 26	5	
6	If Form 1040, line 38, is over $150,500 (over $75,250 if married filing separately), enter the amount from line 11 of the **Itemized Deductions Worksheet** on page A-6 of the Instructions for Schedule A (Form 1040)	6	( )
7	Tax refund from Form 1040, line 10 or line 21	7	( )
8	Investment interest expense (difference between regular tax and AMT)	8	
9	Depletion (difference between regular tax and AMT)	9	
10	Net operating loss deduction from Form 1040, line 21. Enter as a positive amount	10	
11	Interest from specified private activity bonds exempt from the regular tax	11	41,500 00
12	Qualified small business stock (7% of gain excluded under section 1202)	12	
13	Exercise of incentive stock options (excess of AMT income over regular tax income)	13	10,000 00
14	Estates and trusts (amount from Schedule K-1 (Form 1041), box 12, code A)	14	
15	Electing large partnerships (amount from Schedule K-1 (Form 1065-B), box 6)	15	
16	Disposition of property (difference between AMT and regular tax gain or loss)	16	
17	Depreciation on assets placed in service after 1986 (difference between regular tax and AMT)	17	350 00
18	Passive activities (difference between AMT and regular tax income or loss)	18	
19	Loss limitations (difference between AMT and regular tax income or loss)	19	
20	Circulation costs (difference between regular tax and AMT)	20	
21	Long-term contracts (difference between AMT and regular tax income)	21	
22	Mining costs (difference between regular tax and AMT)	22	
23	Research and experimental costs (difference between regular tax and AMT)	23	
24	Income from certain installment sales before January 1, 1987	24	( )
25	Intangible drilling costs preference	25	
26	Other adjustments, including income-based related adjustments	26	
27	Alternative tax net operating loss deduction	27	( )
28	**Alternative minimum taxable income.** Combine lines 1 through 27. (If married filing separately and line 28 is more than $200,100, see page 7 of the instructions.)	28	113,850 00

Part II Alternative Minimum Tax

29	Exemption. (If this form is for a child under age 18, see page 7 of the instructions.) **IF your filing status is . . .** / **AND line 28 is not over . . .** / **THEN enter on line 29 . . .** Single or head of household — $112,500 — $42,500 Married filing jointly or qualifying widow(er) — 150,000 — 62,550 Married filing separately — 75,000 — 31,275 If line 28 is **over** the amount shown above for your filing status, see page 7 of the instructions.	29	42,162 00
30	Subtract line 29 from line 28. If more than zero **or** you are filing Form 2555 or 2555-EZ, go to line 31. If zero or less and you are not filing Form 2555 or 2555-EZ, enter -0- on lines 33 and 35 and skip the rest of Part II	30	71,688 00
31	• If you are filing Form 2555 or 2555-EZ, see page 8 of the instructions for the amount to enter. • If you reported capital gain distributions directly on Form 1040, line 13; you reported qualified dividends on Form 1040, line 9b; **or** you had a gain on both lines 15 and 16 of Schedule D (Form 1040) (as refigured for the AMT, if necessary), complete Part III on the back and enter the amount from line 55 here. • **All others:** If line 30 is $175,000 or less ($87,500 or less if married filing separately), multiply line 30 by 26% (.26). Otherwise, multiply line 30 by 28% (.28) and subtract $3,500 ($1,750 if married filing separately) from the result.	31	18,639 00
32	Alternative minimum tax foreign tax credit (see page 7 of the instructions)	32	
33	Tentative minimum tax. Subtract line 32 from line 31	33	18,639 00
34	Tax from Form 1040, line 44 (minus any tax from Form 4972 and any foreign tax credit from Form 1040, line 47). If you used Schedule J to figure your tax, the amount for line 44 of Form 1040 must be refigured without using Schedule J (see page 9 of the instructions)	34	8,276 00
35	**Alternative minimum tax.** Subtract line 34 from line 33. If zero or less, enter -0-. Enter here and on Form 1040, line 45	35	10,363 00

For Paperwork Reduction Act Notice, see page 9 of the instructions. Cat. No. 13600G Form **6251** (2006)

Any part of the general business credit not used in the current tax year carries back to the previous tax year. Any unused credit then carries forward and combines with business credits generated in that year. The unused credit is carried forward until it is used up or the 20-year carry forward period expires. In each carry forward year, the oldest credit is used first, but only after the current year's credit is used. This minimizes the possible expiration of any unused general business credit.

Investment Credit

The investment credit consists of two separate credits: the business energy investment credit and the credit for substantial rehabilitation expenditures. The amount of these two credits are claimed on Form 3468, Investment Credit, and are included as part of the taxpayer's general business credit.

Business Energy Investment Credit

A 10% tax credit is available for qualified investment in *solar* and *geothermal* energy property. Any energy credit taken reduces the basis of the energy property by 50% of the credit. Taxpayers may either construct or purchase the energy property. However, the taxpayer must be the original user of the property. The credit is not available for public utility property.

Credit for Substantial Rehabilitation Expenditures

The purpose of the credit for rehabilitation expenditures is to encourage businesses to stay in economically distressed areas and to preserve historical structures. The credit equals a percentage of the costs incurred in substantially rehabilitating qualified buildings and certified historic structures. Only the costs to substantially rehabilitate a building qualify for the credit. A building is substantially rehabilitated when the rehabilitation costs during a 24-month period exceed the *greater of* (i) the building's adjusted basis before the rehabilitation, or (ii) $5,000. The percentage used in computing the credit is as follows:

Type of Property Credit	*Credit*
Certified historical structures (both nonresidential and residential)	20%
Nonresidential and residential buildings originally placed in service before 1936	10%

When taxpayers make capital expenditures to property, they normally increase their basis in the property by such costs. However, taxpayers must reduce their basis by the amount of the rehabilitation credit. This keeps them from taking depreciation deductions on the portion of the cost of the building that is taken as a tax credit.

EXAMPLE 15

Barry Tamblyn pays $50,000 for a certified historical structure. Tamblyn spends $60,000 to restore the structure. The $60,000 qualifies for the rehabilitation credit since it exceeds $50,000 (the *greater of* (i) the $50,000 adjusted basis in the building before the rehabilitation, or (ii) $5,000). Tamblyn's credit for rehabilitation expenditures equals $12,000 ($60,000 × 20%). His basis in the building increases by $48,000 ($60,000 – $12,000) to $98,000 ($50,000 + $48,000). Tamblyn uses MACRS or ADS to depreciate the $98,000 basis in the building (see Chapter 8).

Taxpayers who dispose of the property within five years of taking the credit for rehabilitation expenditures must recapture 20% of the credit taken for each year shy of five years. Any recaptured amount is added to the adjusted basis of the building.

EXAMPLE 16

Same as in Example 15 except that after two years Tamblyn disposes of the rehabilitated property. Tamblyn must recapture 60% of the credit, or $7,200 ($12,000 x 60%). The amount of the recapture is 20% for each of the three years Tamblyn is shy of holding the property for five years. Before computing the gain or loss on the sale, Tamblyn increases his basis in the property by the $7,200 of the credit that is recaptured.

The Gulf Opportunity Act of 2005 increased the rehabilitation credit for expenditures paid or incurred in the substantial rehabilitation of buildings located in the Gulf Opportunity Zone (an area specified by the federal government). For certified historical structures, the tax credit is increased to 26% (up from 20%). For all other buildings, the credit increases to 13% (up from 10%). This increase in credit is available for expenditures paid or incurred after August 27, 2005 and before January 1, 2009.

Work Opportunity Credit

Employers who hire certain individuals may qualify for the work opportunity credit. To qualify for this credit, the individuals must be from one of the following targeted groups.

1. Qualified Aid to Families with Dependent Children (AFDC) recipients
2. Qualified veterans
3. Qualified ex-felons
4. High-risk youths (age 18 to 24 when hired) who live in an empowerment zone or enterprise community (as specified by the federal government)
5. Vocational rehabilitation referrals
6. Qualified summer youth employees
7. Qualified food stamp recipients
8. Qualified SSI (social security) recipients
9. Hurricane Katrina employees

A provision in the Katrina Emergency Tax Relief Act of 2005 added "Hurricane Katrina employees" to the list of eligible persons for whom the work opportunity credit could be taken. A **Hurricane Katrina employee** is a person who on August 28, 2005 had a principal place of abode in the core disaster area (as specified by the federal government), who was displaced from such abode by the hurricane, and who is hired between August 28, 2005 and December 31, 2005. It also includes any person who on August 28, 2005 had a principal place of abode in the core disaster area and who is hired between August 28, 2005 and August 27, 2007 to work at a business located within the core disaster area. This provision rewards employers with tax breaks for hiring persons who lived in core disaster areas at the time of the hurricane. If the employer's business is located outside the core disaster area, the wages of qualified employees hired by the end of 2005 qualify for the work opportunity credit. For employers whose businesses are located in the core disaster area, the wages of any qualified employee hired before August 28, 2007 qualify for the work opportunity credit.

The credit equals 40% of up to $6,000 of qualified first-year wages for each qualified employee. The percentage drops to 25% for employees who work at least 120 hours, but less than 400 hours during their first year. No credit is allowed for wages of employees who have worked less than 120 hours during their first year. If the employee's first 12 months of employment spans over two of the employer's tax years, the employer can take the credit over two tax years. Employers who claim this credit must reduce their wage expense deduction by the amount of the credit claimed.

EXAMPLE 17

On April 10, 2005, Joe Oliver hired two qualified employees to help him out in his shop. Both employees worked more than 400 hours for Oliver during their first year. Each employee was paid $9,000 of wages in their first year. Of this amount $5,500 was paid in 2005 and $3,500 in 2006.

Oliver is entitled to a work opportunity credit for 40% of the employees' first-year wages. Oliver's work opportunity credit for 2005 equals $4,400 [40% × ($5,500 × 2)]. Only the first $6,000 of qualified first-year wages are used in computing the work opportunity credit. Therefore in 2006 his work opportunity credit is $400 [40% × ($500 × 2)].

A qualified summer youth employee is a 16- or 17-year old that the employer hires to work between May 1 and September 15. The youth must live in an empowerment zone or enterprise community for his or her wages to qualify for the work opportunity credit. The youth need only work 90 days during the May 1 to September 15 period, and only the first $3,000 of wages qualify for the credit.

For the first 8 of 9 types of workers in the list of targeted groups, the work opportunity credit applies only to their first year wages if they were hired before January 1, 2006. Congress has allowed this tax credit to lapse several times in the past, but has always retroactively reinstated it into the tax law. It is anticipated that this will happen again. However, that had not happened at the time this book went to press. Even if Congress fails to reinstate the work opportunity credit, it remains applicable to 2006 tax returns since first year wages paid to workers hired in 2005 may continue into the 2006 tax year. Also, first year wages paid to Hurricane Katrina employees hired up until August 27, 2007 for businesses located in the core disaster area remain eligible for the credit.

Low-Income Housing Credit

The low-income rental housing credit is available to certain owners of residential rental property who provide low-income housing. The credit may be taken each year for a period of 10 years. The IRS sets the credit rate monthly to reflect changes in the applicable federal rate (AFR). Once determined, however, the rate remains constant for that property. The credit equals the basis of the building multiplied by the credit rate. The credit has a number of special requirements and interrelationships with other federal programs. The project must continue to meet requirements for 15 years, or recapture of a portion of the credit may occur. The credit can be claimed on Form 8586, Low-Income Housing Credit.

Disabled Access Credit

This nonrefundable credit is an incentive to small businesses to make themselves more accessible to disabled persons. The credit is claimed on Form 8826, Disabled Access Credit. The credit equals 50% of the eligible expenditures for the year that exceed $250 but do not exceed $10,250. Thus, the maximum credit available is $5,000 [50% × ($10,250 – $250)]. A business qualifies for the credit if it satisfies one of the following criteria in the previous tax year:

1. The business did not have gross receipts in excess of $1 million, or
2. The business did not employ more than 30 full-time employees.

Expenditures eligible for the credit include those that lead to the removal of architectural, communication, physical, or transportation barriers on buildings placed in service before November 1990. Qualifying barriers prevent a business from being accessible to, or usable by, disabled persons. Amounts paid for qualified interpreters or readers to effect the communication of materials to hearing- and visually-impaired individuals also qualify. The depreciable basis of the property is increased by the amount of the improvements and reduced by the amount of credit.

EXAMPLE 18

In the current tax year, Harvey Enterprises pays to install ramps to the entrance of its building to allow disabled persons easier access to its building. Last year Harvey reported gross receipts of $1.2 million and employed 30 full-time workers. Harvey qualifies for the disabled access credit because it did not employ more than 30 full-time workers in the previous tax year. In order to qualify for the disabled access credit, a business must only satisfy one of the two criteria listed above.

EXAMPLE 19

In the current tax year, April Industries pays to make improvements to its office building to make it more assessable to disabled persons. Last year April reported gross receipts of $900,000 and had 35 full-time employees. April qualifies for the disabled access credit because its gross receipts did not exceed $1 million.

EXAMPLE 20

Jenny Bandos owns a small business that she reports on Schedule C. During the year Bandos pays $8,500 to make her office building more accessible to disabled persons. The building was placed in service in 1987. Bandos's disabled access credit equals $4,125 [50% × ($8,500 – $250)]. Bandos completes Form 8826 to claim this credit. Bandos's basis in the building increases by $4,375 ($8,500 – $4,125). She can use the straight-line method to depreciate the $4,375 over 39 (MACRS) or 40 years (ADS) (see Chapter 8).

FICA Tax Credit

Food and beverage establishments are allowed a tax credit for the employer's FICA tax contribution on qualifying employee cash tips. These are tips the employee reports to the employer that are in excess of the amount required to satisfy the federal minimum wage requirements. No wage deduction can be taken on any amount used in computing the credit calculation.

Empowerment Zone and Renewal Community Employment Credit

An employer whose business is located in a designated empowerment zone may receive a 20% tax credit on the first $15,000 of wages paid to each qualified employee. Only wages paid during the calendar year that ends within the employer's tax year qualify for the annual credit. The $15,000 limit is reduced by any wages used in computing the work opportunity credit for a qualified employee. Qualified employees are individuals who live within the empowerment zone and who work primarily within the zone in the employer's trade or business. The amount of the credit claimed reduces the employer's wage expense deduction.

EXAMPLE 21

Tony Silver's business is located in a designated empowerment zone. Silver uses a calendar tax year. During 2006 Silver hired two people who live in the empowerment zone. Neither person belongs to a work opportunity credit–targeted group. During 2006 one employee was paid wages of $12,000. The other was paid wages of $13,000. Silver's 2006 empowerment zone employment credit equals $5,000 [($12,000 + $13,000) × 20%].

EXAMPLE 22

Same as Example 21, except that the wages paid to the second employee during 2006 were $17,000 (instead of $13,000). Silver's 2006 empowerment zone employment credit equals $5,400 [($12,000 + $15,000) × 20%].

An employer whose business is located in a designated renewal community zone may receive a 15% tax credit on the first $10,000 of wages paid to workers that both live and work in the renewal community zone. Like with the empowerment zone portion of this credit, only wages paid during the calendar year that ends within the employer's tax year count in computing the credit.

EXAMPLE 23

A business uses a fiscal year that ends on January 31. For the tax year that runs from February 1, 20x1 to January 31, 20x2, only wages paid or incurred during the 20x1 calendar year can be used in computing the tax credit during that fiscal year. Qualified wages paid during January 20x2 will be included in the calculation of the business's tax credit for the fiscal year that ends on January 31, 20x3.

EXAMPLE 24

During 2006, a calendar year taxpayer paid $20,000 of qualified wages to George Madison and $11,000 of qualified wages to Maria Gold. Madison worked for the taxpayer's business located in an empowerment zone, where he also lives. Gold worked for the taxpayer's business located in a renewal community where she lives. The taxpayer's tax credit for the year equals $4,500. This includes a $3,000 tax credit for the wages paid to Madison ($15,000 x 20%) and a $1,500 tax credit for wages paid to Gold ($10,000 x 15%). As a result of claiming this credit, the taxpayer must reduce its 2006 deduction for wages by $4,500.

Empowerment zones and renewal communities are specific areas within the U.S. that the federal government has identified as being in need of revitalization. Employers that hire individuals who both live and work in either an empowerment zone or a renewal community are entitled to tax credits for a portion of the wages paid to those workers. Employers can determine whether their business or their employees' residences are located in an empowerment zone or renewal community by using the RC/EZ/EC address locator at http://egis.hud.gov/egis/.

Welfare-to-Work Credit

The welfare-to-work credit is designed to encourage employers to hire and continue to employ persons on welfare. The credit equals 35% of qualified first-year wages plus 50% of qualified second year wages. The maximum wages that can be used in computing the credit in each year is $10,000. Thus, the maximum credit for each employee is $8,500 ($3,500 in the first year plus $5,000 in the second year). When the employee's first two years of employment span over three of the employer's tax years, the employer can take the credit over three tax years.

EXAMPLE 25

On July 29, 2005, Devry, Inc. hired Dana Brant, a qualified long-term family assistance recipient. First year wages paid to Brant were $9,800 of which $3,000 was paid during 2005. The rest were paid during 2006. Second year wages paid to Brant were $10,250, of which $4,500 was paid in 2006. The rest was paid in 2007. Devry's welfare-to-work credit reported on its 2005 through 2007 tax returns as shown below.

2005 Welfare-to-Work Credit

$3,000 qualified first-year wages × 35%	$1,050

2006 Welfare-to-Work Credit

$6,800 qualified first-year wages × 35%	$2,380
$4,500 qualified second-year wages × 50%	2,250
	$4,630

2007 Welfare-to-Work Credit

$5,500 qualified second-year wages × 50%	$2,750

Qualified wages are wages paid to long-term family assistance recipients. Such recipients include members of a family who have been receiving family assistance for at least 18 months prior to being hired. It also includes wages paid to recipients within two years after welfare payments stop because of the length of time the family has been receiving welfare payments. In order to include an employee's wages in computing the welfare-to-work credit, the employee must have worked for an employer for at least 180 days or have completed 400 hours of service. Employers who take the welfare-to-work credit for a worker cannot claim the work opportunity credit for the same worker.

EXAMPLE 26

On January 1, 2005, Bob Sanford hired one employee who qualified for the welfare-to-work credit. Qualified wages for this employee were $7,000 in 2005 and $12,000 in 2006. Sanford's 2005 welfare-to-work credit is $2,450 ($7,000 × 35%). His credit for 2006 is $5,000 ($10,000 maximum wages for the second year × 50%).

Only first and second year wages paid to qualified workers hired before January 1, 2006 qualify for the welfare-to-work credit. Congress has allowed this tax credit to lapse several times in the past, but has always retroactively reinstated it into the tax law. It is anticipated that this will happen once again. However, that had not happened at the time this book went to press. Even if Congress fails to reinstate the welfare-to-work credit, first and second year wages paid to workers hired in 2005 may continue into the 2006 and 2007 tax years.

Employer-Provided Child Care Credit

Employers can take a tax credit for providing child care to their employees. The amount of the credit is the sum of (i) 25% of qualified child care expenses plus (ii) 10% of qualified child care resources or referral expenses. The maximum credit allowed each year is $150,000.

Qualified child care expenses include amounts paid to acquire or construct property used as part of a qualified child care facility. It also includes costs incurred to operate a qualified child care facility and amounts paid to a qualified child care facility that provides child care services to employees. **Qualified child care resource and referral expenses** are amounts paid under a contract to provide child care resource and referral services to an employee. However, these services cannot discriminate in favor of highly-paid employees.

EXAMPLE 27

In 2004, Stanley Emory started a qualified child care program for his employees. During 2006, he pays $7,000 in qualified child care expenses and $1,000 in qualified child care resource and referral expenses. Emory's employer-provided child care credit for 2006 is $1,850 ([$7,000 × 25%] + [$1,000 × 10%]). He includes this amount as part of the General Business Credit when he files his 2006 tax return.

Small Employer Pension Plan Startup Credit

Certain employers can take a tax credit equal to 50% of qualified startup costs when they establish a new defined benefit plan, defined contribution plan (including a 401(k) plan), SIMPLE plan, or SEP plan for their employees. The new pension plan must cover at least one employee who is not a highly compensated employee. The tax credit is limited to $500 in each of the first three years the pension plan is offered. **Qualified startup costs** include amounts paid to establish or administer the new plan, as well as amounts paid to educate employees about retirement planning. Only employers who employed no more than 100 employees earning at least $5,000 in the prior year can claim to this credit. Furthermore, the credit is available only to employers who have not maintained a qualified plan during any of the previous three tax years.

New Markets Credit

Taxpayers that invest in a qualified community development entity may be entitled to a new markets credit. This credit is part of the general business credit. A **qualified community development entity (qualified CDE)** is a domestic corporation or partnership whose primary mission is serving, or providing investment capital for, low-income communities or low-income persons. A qualified CDE must be certified as such by the federal government. During its first six years, a qualified CDE must use at least 85% of the cash it raises to make qualified low-income community investments. After the sixth year, it need only use 75% of its cash towards low-income community investments.

An equity investment in a qualified CDE is an investment in the stock of a qualified CDE (in the case of a corporation) or an investment in a capital interest of a qualified CDE (in the case of a partnership). Cash must be used to pay for the investment. However, taxpayers can borrow to get the cash needed to buy the CDE investment. The new markets credit equals a percentage times the amount invested in a qualified CDE. The percentage is 5% for the first three years. It increases to 6% for the next four years. Amounts claimed as a credit reduce the taxpayer's basis in the investment.

If at any time during the 7-year period in which the new markets credit is available, (1) the investment ceases to be a qualified CDE, (2) the taxpayer's investment is redeemed by the qualified CDE, or (3) the CDE fails to make qualified low-income community investments, the recapture rules apply. This would result in the taxpayer's taxes being increased for an amount equal by which the taxpayer's general business credit would have been reduced had there been no new markets credit.

EXAMPLE 28

On October 5, 2006, Creekside Corporation paid $200,000 for a qualified equity investment in a CDE. Creekside uses the calendar year. It is entitled to a new markets credit equal to $10,000 (5% × $200,000) for 2006 and will be entitled to another $10,000 credit on its 2007 and 2008 tax returns. The company will be entitled to a $12,000 (6% × $200,000) credit on its 2009–2012 tax returns. Creekside reduces its $200,000 initial basis in the CDE by the amounts is claims for the new markets credit.

Alternative Motor Vehicles Credit

This tax credit was introduced in Chapter 2. This credit can be taken by individuals as a personal tax credit. It is also available to businesses as part of the general business credit. The rules for calculating the amount of the credit that were discussed in Chapter 2 also apply to businesses that purchase and place into service hybrid vehicles.

TAX PENALTIES

When taxpayers fail to file a tax return or fail to pay the proper amount of tax, a penalty applies. Other actions may also invoke a penalty. Tax penalties are generally based on the amount of tax due on the tax return (tax liability – credits and prepayments = tax due). Having a "reasonable cause" for not complying with the law may save the taxpayer from a penalty.

April 15th is the tax filing deadline for individual taxpayers. It is the deadline for both filing their income tax return as well as for paying any taxes owed. Taxpayers that file their tax returns on time but do not pay all the taxes they owe by April 15 will pay a late payment penalty. The **late payment penalty** is equal to one-half of 1% of the taxes owed for each month, or part of a month, that the tax remains unpaid. The maximum late payment penalty is 25% of the taxes owed. For persons, who file their tax returns by the due date, the one-half of 1% rate is reduced to one-quarter of 1% for any month in which an installment agreement is in effect.

Persons who owe taxes and do not file a tax return by the deadline (including extensions) will be charged a **late-filing penalty**. This penalty is 5% of the taxes owed for each month, or part of a month, that the tax return is late. The maximum late filing penalty is 25% of the taxes owed.

Type of Penalty	*Amount of Penalty*
Failure to file	5% of the amount due for each month or fraction of month that the return is late (maximum penalty = 25%)
Failure to pay	.5% of the amount due for each month or fraction of month that the payment is late (maximum penalty = 25%)
Accuracy-related (negligence, substantial understatement of income tax, or substantial valuation misstatement)	20% of the tax due
Fraud	75% of the tax due (accuracy-related penalties will not be applied)
Frivolous return filing	$500
Preparer penalties	From $5 to $500 for each wrongful act
Improper disclosure of information acquired from a taxpayer by a tax preparer	$1,000 and/or one year in prison

Reasonable Cause

Taxpayers may avoid a penalty if failure to comply was due to reasonable cause. The IRS lists the following circumstances as reasonable causes for failing to comply with the tax laws. Other reasonable causes may exist. The IRS judges each case on its merits.

1. Death or serious illness
2. Unavoidable absence
3. Destruction of certain facilities or records
4. Timely mailing
5. Wrong filing place
6. Reliance on competent tax advisor
7. Unobtainable records
8. IRS office visit in which an IRS employee was unable to be seen for reasons beyond the taxpayer's control
9. Erroneous IRS information

INFORMATION RETURNS

Information returns play an important part in the IRS computerized taxpayer compliance program. Persons and organizations making specific types of payments must report them to the IRS and the taxpayer. Taxpayers must then report these amounts on their income tax returns. This reporting process makes it possible for the IRS to determine whether taxpayers have reported the appropriate amounts on their tax returns. The taxpayer's identification number (SSN for individuals; EIN for businesses), shown on both the information return and the income tax return, is the basis for comparing reported data. Unlike Forms W-2 and W-2G that are filed with the taxpayer's tax return, taxpayers do not attach information returns to the tax return. They should, however, retain copies of the information returns for their records.

Most organizations or persons required to file information returns use magnetic media to transmit the data to the IRS. However, some payers still report this data in paper form. They must use a separate transmittal Form 1096, Annual Summary and Transmittal of U.S. Information Returns, for each different type of information return.

IRS Comparisons

The IRS routinely examines the amounts reported on information returns filed by the payers of interest, dividends, and other types of payments. It compares these amounts to those reported by taxpayers on their income tax returns. Taxpayers should report all amounts received on their returns as separate items. For example, the taxpayer may receive two Form 1099-DIVs from ABC Company. One is for a $300 dividend on stock held personally by the taxpayer. The other is for a $176 dividend on stock held by a trustee for a dividend reinvestment plan. The taxpayer should enter both amounts separately on Schedule B. If only one Form 1099-DIV is received for the $476 total, then only one amount should be reported on Schedule B. When taxpayers detect an error on an information return, they should ask the payer to correct the mistake and issue them a corrected information return.

AVOIDING DEFICIENCY NOTICES

The computer may detect a difference between the amounts reported on the information returns and the amounts reported by the taxpayer. It may then generate a deficiency notice that will require an explanation by the taxpayer. The differences may be easily explained by the taxpayer with no penalty assessed. However, much time and effort can be saved if the taxpayer carefully reports the amounts as shown on the information returns.

Penalty for Failure to File Information Returns

The penalty for failure to furnish a required return or statement to a taxpayer in a timely manner is $50 for each statement not furnished. The maximum penalty for any calendar year is $100,000.

A penalty also applies for filing late, incorrect, or incomplete information returns with the IRS. The following penalty structure applies.

1. Any reporting failure corrected within 30 days after the due date—$15 per return, with a yearly maximum of $75,000 ($25,000 for small businesses)
2. Any reporting failure corrected after the 30-day period up to August 1—$30 per return, with a yearly maximum of $150,000 ($50,000 for small businesses)
3. Any reporting failure corrected after August 1—$50 per return, with a yearly maximum of $250,000 ($100,000 for small businesses)

These penalties also apply to companies that fail to file by means of magnetic media when required to do so. However, the penalty applies only on the number of returns in excess of 250. "**Small businesses**" are those having average annual gross receipts of less than $5 million for the last three years.

The IRS imposes a penalty of $50 for each failure to provide certain specified information, such as taxpayer identification numbers. The maximum penalty is $100,000 a year.

No penalty applies if it can be shown that the reporting failure was due to reasonable cause and not to willful neglect. Also, a penalty waiver is available when only a small number of returns contain incomplete or incorrect information. To apply, correction of the errors must take place by August 1. In addition, the waiver limits the benefits to the *greater of*:

1. Ten returns, or
2. One-half of 1% of the total number of information returns required to be filed.

COMMON INFORMATION RETURNS

Form 1098, Mortgage Interest Statement
Form 1099-B, Proceeds from Broker and Barter Exchange Transactions
Form 1099-DIV, Dividends and Distributions
Form 1099-INT, Interest Income
Form 1099-G, Certain Government Payments
Form 1099-MISC, Miscellaneous Income
Form 1099-R, Distributions from Pensions, Annuities, Retirement or Profit-Sharing Plans, IRAs, Insurance Contracts, Etc.
Form 1099-S, Proceeds from Real Estate Transactions
Form 5498, Individual Retirement Arrangement Information
Form 8027, Employer's Annual Information Return of Tip Income and Allocated Tips

THE AUDIT PROCESS

When returns reach the IRS service centers, a computer makes an initial check for mathematical or clerical errors. The IRS corrects these mathematical errors and sends a notice of the correction to the taxpayer. It either requests payment for additional tax or encloses a refund for an overpayment. The types of errors include:

1. An error in arithmetic shown on the return
2. Incorrect use of any IRS table, if such use is apparent from the existence of other information on the return
3. Inconsistent entries on the return
4. Omission of information necessary to backup an amount shown on the return
5. Entry of a deduction or credit item that exceeds a statutory limit based on information appearing on the return

Returns most in need of examination are identified by computer, using mathematical formulas developed by the IRS to single out returns that are likely to have errors. The system focuses on those returns that stand the best chance of producing enough additional tax revenue to justify the audit. Examples of factors that could affect a return's selection for audit include:

1. Large amounts of gross income
2. Self-employed taxpayers with high incomes and large deductions
3. Cash businesses (e.g., restaurants, businesses that provide services)
4. Excessive itemized deductions in relation to income level
5. Claims for large refunds
6. Disagreement between reported income and information returns (e.g., Form 1099, Form W-2)
7. A large increase in exemptions
8. A major decrease in rental income
9. Informant information
10. Prior tax deficiencies

Returns containing minor items that need clarification go to the audit division at the Regional Service Center for correction by *correspondence.* Such returns may contain questionable charitable contributions or medical expenses, as an example.

Returns having the greatest audit possibility are sent to the district audit division to be examined. Within the district audit division, there are two types of audits. One is the *office audit* which usually takes place in an IRS office and is limited in scope. A short discussion may be all that is needed to clear up any questions. The other is the *field audit* which normally takes place on the taxpayer's premises. This is typically a much more extensive audit involving a number of major issues.

Facing budget constraints, the IRS audits less than 1% of the tax returns.

Burden of Proof

Historically, the burden of proof for most tax disputes has rested with the taxpayer. During the mid-1980s, the IRS came under scrutiny for the way taxpayers were being treated during the audit process. Congress responded by enacting tax laws that shift the burden of proof to the IRS in court proceedings over factual issues when:

1. The taxpayer has provided the IRS with relevant, credible evidence,
2. The taxpayer has complied with the IRS's substantiation and record-keeping requirements, and
3. The taxpayer has maintained proper records and cooperates with any reasonable IRS request for witnesses, information, documents, meetings, and interviews.

To illustrate these rules, take a situation where the taxpayer uses the standard business mileage method to deduct automobile expenses on Schedule C. As discussed in Chapter 7, the tax laws require that the taxpayer maintain contemporaneous records to support the number of business miles driven during the year. Thus, if the taxpayer provides the IRS with the mileage log used to record the number of business miles driven during the tax year in question, the burden of proving that the deduction is not valid rests with the IRS.

In addition to the situations Congress recently added, the IRS has the burden of proof whenever it (1) uses statistics to reconstruct the taxpayer's income, (2) assesses the taxpayer with a penalty or other addition to tax, or (3) accuses the taxpayer of fraud with intent to evade taxes. The IRS also has the burden or proof in any case that involves hobby losses (Chapter 6) or the accumulated earnings tax (Chapter 14).

THE APPEAL PROCESS

After the audit, the taxpayer will receive a report of the findings, along with a *30-day-letter* describing the taxpayer's appeal rights. A taxpayer who does not agree with the findings of an audit may appeal. The taxpayer has a right to request a meeting with the examining officer to work out their differences. This request should be made within 15 days from the date of the letter. Taxpayers not wanting to meet with the examining officer should either start the formal appeal process or make arrangements to pay the tax within 30 days.

An *Appeals Office* headed by a Regional Director of Appeals is established in each of the seven Internal Revenue Service regions. Each office has the authority to fully settle cases. When the amount involved does not exceed $2,500, the taxpayer will be granted an Appeals

Office conference merely by requesting it. However, when the amount exceeds $2,500, an Appeals Office conference is available only to taxpayers who file a written protest stating the facts upon which the appeal is based.

If the taxpayer and the Appeals Office cannot agree on the issues in dispute, the taxpayer receives a *90-day deficiency notice.* This must be mailed to the taxpayer within three years of the date that the income tax return was filed. The taxpayer may petition for a judicial review with one of three trial courts. The taxpayer may file a petition with the Tax Court within 90 days after the deficiency notice is mailed. The taxpayer may also file a petition with the district court or U.S. Court of Claims to have the case heard. After 90 days have lapsed, the taxpayer's only avenues for a judicial review are with the district court or U.S. Court of Claims.

Either the taxpayer or the IRS can petition the Circuit Court of Appeals to review the trial court's decision. Final disposition of the case may be taken to the United States Supreme Court. The Supreme Court will hear only those cases it chooses to review. All of these steps may take years. However, final assessment of the tax due from a taxpayer may not be made until the case is closed. The IRS Commissioner then has 60 days from the final decision to make an assessment of the tax.

TAXPAYER RIGHTS

Taxpayers have the right to plan their business and personal affairs so they will pay the least amount of tax due under the law. They also have the right to be treated fairly, professionally, promptly, and courteously by the IRS. The law entitles taxpayers to information and IRS assistance in complying with the tax laws. The IRS provides a wide variety of informational material, educational programs, and tax assistance programs to aid people in understanding and complying with the tax laws. IRS Publication 910, *Guide to Free Tax Services,* is a catalog of free IRS services and publications.

Taxpayers who need a copy of a prior year tax return may receive it by completing Form 4506, Request for Copy of Tax Form. This form is sent to the IRS along with a small fee. If only certain information is needed, such as reported income from a prior year, the taxpayer may get this information for free. To receive this information, the taxpayer should write, visit, or call an IRS office.

Special assistance programs are available to people who cannot resolve their tax problems through normal channels. Help is also available to those whose tax problems cause significant hardship (that is, the inability to provide necessities).

People who have a complaint about the IRS may write to the district director or the service center director for their area. Additional information on taxpayer rights may be found in IRS Publication 1, *Your Rights as a Taxpayer.*

TAX PREPARERS' RESPONSIBLITIES

Currently, over one-half of all individuals have someone else prepare their tax returns. The tax laws consider anyone receiving pay in exchange for preparing an income tax return as an **income tax return preparer.** In the tax law, there are standards that must be adhered to by all income tax return preparers. Penalties that may be assessed for failing to adhere to these standards include the following.

1. A $50 penalty each time the tax preparer fails to sign the tax return as a paid preparer. The maximum annual penalty is $25,000.
2. A $50 penalty each time the tax preparer fails to provide the taxpayer with a copy of his or her tax return. The maximum annual penalty is $25,000.
3. A $50 penalty each time the tax preparer fails to keep a copy of the taxpayer's tax return. The maximum annual penalty is $25,000.
4. A $250 penalty for any tax return in which the tax preparer allows a position to be taken that is either frivolous or does not have a realistic possibility of being sustained on its merits. A position has a realistic possibility of being sustained if it has at least a one-in-three chance of prevailing in court, should the IRS challenge it.
5. A $1,000 penalty for any tax return where the tax preparer intentionally disregards the rules and regulations, or willfully understates the taxpayer's tax liability.

Neither the tax law nor the IRS have minimum education or experience requirements to prepare another person's tax return. However, only professional tax preparers can represent taxpayers before the IRS. **Professional tax preparers** prepare tax returns, provide tax planning and give tax advice to their clients. They include attorneys, certified public accountants (CPAs) and enrolled agents. Attorneys and CPAs who prepare tax returns have met certain educational standards, passed a standardized exam, and met specific experience requirements that allow them to be licensed to practice in their respective professions. Enrolled agents, while neither CPAs nor attorneys, have passed an IRS exam and have been granted the authority to represent taxpayers before the IRS. Other paid preparers can receive compensation for their services, but are not allowed to communicate with the IRS on behalf of their clients.

The IRS imposes additional standards for professional tax preparers. Failure to adhere to these standards may result in penalties being assessed, including disbarment from practicing before the IRS. Those interested in learning more about the additional standards for professional tax preparers should refer to IRS Circular 230, which can be obtained from the IRS website. (See the back inside cover of the book for instructions on how to access the IRS website.)

AMENDED RETURNS

Form 1040X, Amended U.S. Individual Income Tax Return, is available to amend an individual income tax return. Taxpayers may file an amended return up until three years after the date the original return was due or filed, whichever was later. Use of Form 1040X is not mandatory, but the IRS prefers its use over a regular Form 1040 or Form 1040A marked "Revised." The design of Form 1040X expedites processing by the IRS. Thus, use of Form 1040X could speed up a claim for a refund. Taxpayers use Form 1040X only after having filed their original returns.

Information for Figure 12-3: Filled-In Form 1040X, Pages 1 and 2

Steven and Sarah Martin failed to claim a **$300** contribution made during 2005 to the General Hospital, Peoria, Illinois, a qualifying charity. Accordingly, they amend their Form 1040 for 2005 and claim a refund by filing a Form 1040X on **June 15, 2007.** The following 2005 information is used.

Other Information

1: Adjusted gross income, **$49,094**
2A: Itemized deductions, **$11,200**
4: Exemptions, **$9,600** ($3,200 exemption for 2005 × 3)
6: Tax, **$3,511** (corrected tax, **$3,466,** from 2005 Tax Table)
9: Other taxes, **$4,177** (self-employment tax on net profits from Sarah's business)
11: Federal income withheld, **$856**
12: Estimated payments, **$9,500**
19: Overpayment, reported on original return, **$2,668** [$10,356 payments ($856 withheld + $9,500 estimated payments) minus $7,688 total tax ($3,511 regular tax + $4,177 self-employment tax)]

FIGURE 12-3 Filled-In Form 1040X, Page 1

Form **1040X** (Rev. November 2006)

Department of the Treasury—Internal Revenue Service

Amended U.S. Individual Income Tax Return

► See separate instructions.

OMB No. 1545-0074

This return is for calendar year ► 2005 **, or fiscal year ended ►**

Please print or type			
Your first name and initial: Steven M.	Last name: Martin		Your social security number: 471 91 0417
If a joint return, spouse's first name and initial: Sarah J.	Last name: Martin		Spouse's social security number: 916 38 2124
Home address (no. and street) or P.O. box if mail is not delivered to your home: 2886 Linwood Ct.		Apt. no.	Phone number: (309)721-0846
City, town or post office, state, and ZIP code. If you have a foreign address, see page 2 of the instructions. Peoria, IL 61064-5417			

A If the address shown above is different from that shown on your last return filed with the IRS, would you like us to change it in our records? . . . ► ☐ **Yes** ☐ **No**

B Filing status. Be sure to complete this line. **Note.** You cannot change from joint to separate returns after the due date.

On original return ► ☐ Single ☒ Married filing jointly ☐ Married filing separately ☐ Head of household ☐ Qualifying widow(er)

On this return ► ☐ Single ☒ Married filing jointly ☐ Married filing separately ☐ Head of household* ☐ Qualifying widow(er)

* If the qualifying person is a child but not your dependent, see page 2 of the instructions.

Use Part II on the back to explain any changes	Line	A. Original amount or as previously adjusted (see page 3)	B. Net change—amount of increase or (decrease)—explain in Part II	C. Correct amount
Income and Deductions (see instructions)				
1 Adjusted gross income (see page 3)	1	49,094		49,094
2 Itemized deductions or standard deduction (see page 3)	2	11,200	300	11,500
3 Subtract line 2 from line 1	3	37,894		37,594
4 Exemptions. If changing, fill in Parts I and II on the back (see page 3)	4	9,600		9,600
5 Taxable income. Subtract line 4 from line 3	5	28,294		27,994
Tax Liability				
6 Tax (see page 4). Method used in col. C Tax Table	6	3,511		3,466
7 Credits (see page 4)	7	0		0
8 Subtract line 7 from line 6. Enter the result but not less than zero	8	3,511		3,466
9 Other taxes (see page 4)	9	4,177		4,177
10 Total tax. Add lines 8 and 9	10	7,688		7,643
Payments				
11 Federal income tax withheld and excess social security and tier 1 RRTA tax withheld. If changing, see page 4	11	856		856
12 Estimated tax payments, including amount applied from prior year's return	12	9,500		9,500
13 Earned income credit (EIC)	13			
14 Additional child tax credit from Form 8812	14			
15 Credits from Form 2439, Form 4136, or Form 8885	15			
16 Amount paid with request for extension of time to file (see page 4)	16			
17 Amount of tax paid with original return plus additional tax paid after it was filed	17			
18 Total payments. Add lines 11 through 17 in column C	18			10,356
Refund or Amount You Owe				
19 Overpayment, if any, as shown on original return or as previously adjusted by the IRS	19			2,668
20 Subtract line 19 from line 18 (see page 5)	20			7,688
21 **Amount you owe.** If line 10, column C, is more than line 20, enter the difference and see page 5	21			
22 If line 10, column C, is less than line 20, enter the difference	22			45
23 Amount of line 22 you want **refunded to you**	23			45
24 Amount of line 22 you want **applied to your** estimated tax	24			

Sign Here

Joint return? See page 2. Keep a copy for your records.

Under penalties of perjury, I declare that I have filed an original return and that I have examined this amended return, including accompanying schedules and statements, and to the best of my knowledge and belief, this amended return is true, correct, and complete. Declaration of preparer (other than taxpayer) is based on all information of which the preparer has any knowledge.

► *Steven M. Martin* 6/15/07 ► *Sarah J. Martin* 6/15/07

Your signature Date Spouse's signature. If a joint return, **both** must sign. Date

Paid Preparer's Use Only

Preparer's signature ►	Date	Check if self-employed ☐	Preparer's SSN or PTIN
Firm's name (or yours if self-employed), address, and ZIP code ►		EIN	
		Phone no. ( )	

For Paperwork Reduction Act Notice, see page 6 of instructions. Cat. No. 11360L Form **1040X** (Rev. 11-2006)

FIGURE 12-3 Filled-In Form 1040X, Page 2

Form 1040X (Rev. 11-2006) Page **2**

Part I Exemptions. See Form 1040 or 1040A instructions.

Complete this part **only** if you are:
- Increasing or decreasing the number of exemptions claimed on line 6d of the return you are amending, or
- Increasing or decreasing the exemption amount for housing individuals displaced by Hurricane Katrina.

		Line	A. Original number of exemptions reported or as previously adjusted	B. Net change	C. Correct number of exemptions
25	Yourself and spouse **Caution.** If someone can claim you as a dependent, you cannot claim an exemption for yourself.	25			
26	Your dependent children who lived with you	26			
27	Your dependent children who did not live with you due to divorce or separation	27			
28	Other dependents	28			
29	Total number of exemptions. Add lines 25 through 28	29			
30	Multiply the number of exemptions claimed on line 29 by the amount listed below for the tax year you are amending. Enter the result here and on line 4.	30			
31	If you are claiming an exemption amount for housing individuals displaced by Hurricane Katrina, enter the amount from Form 8914, line 2 for 2005 or line 6 for 2006 (see instructions for line 4)	31			
32	Add lines 30 and 31. Enter the result here and on line 4	32			

Tax year	Exemption amount	But see the instructions for line 4 on page 3 if the amount on line 1 is over:
2006	$3,300	$112,875
2005	3,200	109,475
2004	3,100	107,025
2003	3,050	104,625

33 Dependents (children and other) not claimed on original (or adjusted) return:

(a) First name	Last name	(b) Dependent's social security number	(c) Dependent's relationship to you	(d) ✓ if qualifying child for child tax credit (see page 5)
				☐
				☐
				☐
				☐
				☐
				☐

No. of children on 33 who:
- lived with you ▶ ☐
- **did not** live with you due to divorce or separation (see page 5) ▶ ☐

Dependents on 33 not entered above ▶ ☐

Part II Explanation of Changes

Enter the line number from the front of the form for each item you are changing and give the reason for each change. Attach only the supporting forms and schedules for the items changed. If you do not attach the required information, your Form 1040X may be returned. Be sure to include your name and social security number on any attachments.

If the change relates to a net operating loss carryback or a general business credit carryback, attach the schedule or form that shows the year in which the loss or credit occurred. See page 2 of the instructions. Also, check here ▶ ☐

Line 2: Contribution of $300 paid to
General Hospital, Peoria, Illinois,
on July 15, 2005 was omitted
in error on line 15,
Schedule A, Form 1040.

Part III Presidential Election Campaign Fund. Checking below will not increase your tax or reduce your refund.

If you did not previously want $3 to go to the fund but now want to, check here ▶ ☐

If a joint return and your spouse did not previously want $3 to go to the fund but now wants to, check here ▶ ☐

Form **1040X** (Rev. 11-2006)

Printed on recycled paper

Name ______________________________

Section ______________ Date __________

QUESTIONS AND PROBLEMS

1. **Net Operating Loss (NOL).**

   a. What is meant by an NOL?

   b. Can an individual who does not operate a business have an NOL? Explain.

   c. For what taxable years may an NOL created in 2006 be used as a deduction for AGI?

2. **Net Operating Loss.**

   a. What types of adjustments must be made in order to convert negative taxable income into an NOL?

   b. Jamie Wang (single) reports on his 2006 tax return negative taxable income of \$36,450. Included in this amount is business income of \$70,000 and business deductions of \$98,000. Wang took the standard deduction and claimed one personal exemption. What is the amount of Wang's 2006 NOL, assuming that no other adjustments are necessary?

   c. What would be the amount of the NOL if, in Part b., Wang's gross income included net nonbusiness long-term capital gains of \$6,000 and business income of \$64,000?

3. **Net Operating Loss (NOL).** Chris Robin, a single lawyer, has opened his own law office. The following summarizes Robin's 2006 net loss. Compute his NOL.

Business income	$54,500	
Nonbusiness income (dividends and interest)	2,300	
Long-term capital gain (nonbusiness income)	1,800	
Total income		$58,600
Business deductions	$58,800	
Ordinary nonbusiness deductions (includes a $400 theft loss)	5,670	
Personal and dependency exemption	3,300	
Total deductions		(67,770)
Net loss as computed by Robin		($ 9,170)

4. **AMT.** Explain in general the computation of the alternative minimum tax and how the computation differs from the regular tax computation.

5. **AMT.**

a. How must depreciation expense for real and personal property be determined in computing the alternative minimum tax (AMT)?

b. Explain the *types* of adjustments that must be made to regular taxable income in order to compute the AMT income.

6. **Alternative Minimum Tax.** The Davies paid $295,000 for a condominium in Florida. The condo is used solely as rental property. They depreciate the villa using the straight-line method over 27.5 years.

   a. Compute the Davies's AMT adjustment for 2006 if the condo was purchased in 1994.

   b. Compute their AMT adjustment for 2006 if they purchased the condo in 2004.

7. **AMT.** James M. (SSN 346-57-4657) and Tammy S. (SSN 465-46-3647) Livingston prepared a joint income tax return for 2006 and claimed four total exemptions. Their regular taxable income and tax liability were computed as follows:

Salaries	$40,000
Schedule C net profit	52,000
Nonqualified dividend income	4,700
Interest income	2,350
Adjusted gross income	$99,050
Itemized deductions	(18,000)
	$81,050
Personal exemptions	(13,200)
Taxable income	$67,850
Tax liability	$10,084

   The Livingstons received $15,000 of tax-exempt interest from private activity bonds. In computing taxable income, the Livingstons took $7,000 depreciation on Schedule C, using the MACRS 200% declining balance method on property with a five-year class life. AMT allows $5,500 of depreciation for the same property. Itemized deductions include charitable contributions of $9,000, state and local property taxes of $4,712, casualty losses of $775 (after 10% AGI floor), and state income taxes of $3,513.

   a. Compute the Livingstons' AMT.

   b. Complete Form 6251 for the Livingstons using the form on the following page.

(Use for Problem 7).

Form **6251**

Department of the Treasury
Internal Revenue Service (99)

Alternative Minimum Tax—Individuals

▶ See separate instructions.

▶ Attach to Form 1040 or Form 1040NR.

OMB No. 1545-0074

2006

Attachment Sequence No. **32**

Name(s) shown on Form 1040 | **Your social security number**

Part I **Alternative Minimum Taxable Income** (See instructions for how to complete each line.)

1	If filing Schedule A (Form 1040), enter the amount from Form 1040, line 41 (minus any amount on Form 8914, line 6), and go to line 2. Otherwise, enter the amount from Form 1040, line 38 (minus any amount on Form 8914, line 6), and go to line 7. (If less than zero, enter as a negative amount.)	1	
2	Medical and dental. Enter the **smaller** of Schedule A (Form 1040), line 4, **or** 2½% of Form 1040, line 38	2	
3	Taxes from Schedule A (Form 1040), line 9	3	
4	Enter the home mortgage interest adjustment, if any, from line 6 of the worksheet on page 2 of the instructions	4	
5	Miscellaneous deductions from Schedule A (Form 1040), line 26	5	
6	If Form 1040, line 38, is over $150,500 (over $75,250 if married filing separately), enter the amount from line 11 of the **Itemized Deductions Worksheet** on page A-6 of the Instructions for Schedule A (Form 1040)	6	( )
7	Tax refund from Form 1040, line 10 or line 21	7	( )
8	Investment interest expense (difference between regular tax and AMT)	8	
9	Depletion (difference between regular tax and AMT)	9	
10	Net operating loss deduction from Form 1040, line 21. Enter as a positive amount	10	
11	Interest from specified private activity bonds exempt from the regular tax	11	
12	Qualified small business stock (7% of gain excluded under section 1202)	12	
13	Exercise of incentive stock options (excess of AMT income over regular tax income)	13	
14	Estates and trusts (amount from Schedule K-1 (Form 1041), box 12, code A)	14	
15	Electing large partnerships (amount from Schedule K-1 (Form 1065-B), box 6)	15	
16	Disposition of property (difference between AMT and regular tax gain or loss)	16	
17	Depreciation on assets placed in service after 1986 (difference between regular tax and AMT)	17	
18	Passive activities (difference between AMT and regular tax income or loss)	18	
19	Loss limitations (difference between AMT and regular tax income or loss)	19	
20	Circulation costs (difference between regular tax and AMT)	20	
21	Long-term contracts (difference between AMT and regular tax income)	21	
22	Mining costs (difference between regular tax and AMT)	22	
23	Research and experimental costs (difference between regular tax and AMT)	23	
24	Income from certain installment sales before January 1, 1987	24	( )
25	Intangible drilling costs preference	25	
26	Other adjustments, including income-based related adjustments	26	
27	Alternative tax net operating loss deduction	27	( )
28	**Alternative minimum taxable income.** Combine lines 1 through 27. (If married filing separately and line 28 is more than $200,100, see page 7 of the instructions.)	28	

Part II **Alternative Minimum Tax**

29 Exemption. (If this form is for a child under age 18, see page 7 of the instructions.)

IF your filing status is . . .	**AND line 28 is not over . . .**	**THEN enter on line 29 . . .**
Single or head of household	$112,500	$42,500
Married filing jointly or qualifying widow(er)	150,000	62,550
Married filing separately	75,000	31,275

If line 28 is **over** the amount shown above for your filing status, see page 7 of the instructions. — **29**

30	Subtract line 29 from line 28. If more than zero **or** you are filing Form 2555 or 2555-EZ, go to line 31. If zero or less and you are not filing Form 2555 or 2555-EZ, enter -0- on lines 33 and 35 and skip the rest of Part II	30	
31	• If you are filing Form 2555 or 2555-EZ, see page 8 of the instructions for the amount to enter. • If you reported capital gain distributions directly on Form 1040, line 13; you reported qualified dividends on Form 1040, line 9b; **or** you had a gain on both lines 15 and 16 of Schedule D (Form 1040) (as refigured for the AMT, if necessary), complete Part III on the back and enter the amount from line 55 here. • **All others:** If line 30 is $175,000 or less ($87,500 or less if married filing separately), multiply line 30 by 26% (.26). Otherwise, multiply line 30 by 28% (.28) and subtract $3,500 ($1,750 if married filing separately) from the result.	31	
32	Alternative minimum tax foreign tax credit (see page 7 of the instructions)	32	
33	Tentative minimum tax. Subtract line 32 from line 31	33	
34	Tax from Form 1040, line 44 (minus any tax from Form 4972 and any foreign tax credit from Form 1040, line 47). If you used Schedule J to figure your tax, the amount for line 44 of Form 1040 must be refigured without using Schedule J (see page 9 of the instructions)	34	
35	**Alternative minimum tax.** Subtract line 34 from line 33. If zero or less, enter -0-. Enter here and on Form 1040, line 45	35	

For Paperwork Reduction Act Notice, see page 9 of the instructions. Cat. No. 13600G Form **6251** (2006)

8. **General Business Tax Credit.**

   a. Which credits discussed in the text are combined into the general business credit?

   b. What option is available to taxpayers who are unable to deduct all of the general business credit from their tax liability in the current year?

   c. When the general business credit is carried to other tax years, in what year order are the carryover credits used? If general business credits from more than one year are carried over, in what order are they used?

9. **Rehabilitation Credit.** Harriet Glanville purchased an office building that had originally been placed in service in 1932. Glanville paid $100,000 for the building and spent an additional $150,000 to rehabilitate it. The building was placed in service in May, 2006.

   a. Compute Glanville's credit for rehabilitation expenditures.

   b. Compute Glanville's basis in the building for depreciation purposes if she elects to take the rehabilitation credit.

   c. How would your answers to Parts a. and b. differ if the building were a certified historical structure located in the Gulf Opportunity Zone?

10. Work Opportunity Credit. During 2005, RST, Inc., hired three people (Albertson, Baines, and Cantella), all of whom qualified RST for the work opportunity credit. During 2005, RST, paid first-year wages as follows: Albertson, $4,000; Baines, $2,000; and Cantella, $1,800.

a. Compute RST's work opportunity credit for 2005.

b. Compute RST's work opportunity credit for 2006 if it paid first year wages during 2006 as follows: Albertson, $3,000; Baines, $3,500; and Cantella, $4,500.

c. Assuming that RST paid a total of $180,000 in wages to its employees in 2006, compute RST's wage expense deduction if the work opportunity credit is taken.

11. Disabled Access Credit.

a. Can a company with $5,000,000 in gross receipts qualify for the disabled access credit? Explain.

b. Can a company with 40 full-time employees qualify for the disabled access credit? Explain.

c. What is the maximum disabled access credit?

12. **Empowerment Zone Employment Credit.** Ambly Inc. is located in a qualified empowerment zone. During 2006, Ambly hired two people who live in the empowerment zone. These two employees were paid $3,500 and $2,000, respectively. Neither worker was from one of the eight groups targeted for purposes of the work opportunity credit. Compute Ambly's 2006 empowerment zone employment credit.

13. **Empowerment Zone and Renewal Communities Employment Credit.** During 2006, Tango, Incorporated (a calendar year taxpayer) paid $13,000 of qualified wages to Reba Sutherland. Sutherland works at Tango's factory located in the empowerment zone where she also lives. Also during 2006, Tango pays $11,000 of qualified wages to Marc Simmons. Simmons works at Tango's warehouse located in a renewal community where he lives. Compute Tango's tax credit for 2006.

14. **Welfare-to-Work Credit.** Back in 2005, Teresa Somner hired two employees who qualified for the welfare-to-work credit. Qualified first-year wages paid during 2006 for these two employees totalled $7,500. Qualified second-year wages paid during 2006 totalled $20,000. Compute Somner's 2006 welfare-to-work credit.

15. **Employer-Provided Child Care Credit.** In 2006, Sarah Peterson started a qualified child care program for her employees. During 2006, Peterson paid $8,000 in qualified child care expenditures and $12,000 in qualified child care resource and referral expenses. Compute Peterson's employer-provided child care credit for 2006.

16. **Small Employer Pension Plan Startup Credit.** Certain employers are entitled to a tax credit for costs associated with establishing a new pension plan for their employees.

a. Which employers qualify for this credit?

b. Are there restrictions on the types of pension plans that are eligible for this credit?

c. How is the credit computed? For how many years can the credit be taken?

17. **New Markets Credit.**

a. What types of investments are eligible for the new markets credit?

b. How is the new markets credit computed and to which years is it available?

18. **New Markets Credit.** On January 1, 2006 a taxpayer paid $350,000 for a qualified equity investment in a CDE.

a. Calculate the taxpayer's new markets credit for 2006-2009.

b. Discuss what happens if on February 10, 2010, the taxpayer's investment no longer qualifies as a CDE.

19. Audits and Penalties. Insert the answer to each of the following questions in the space provided.

a. What is the monthly penalty for failure to file a tax return? __________

b. What is the monthly penalty for late payment of taxes? __________

c. What is the penalty for filing a frivolous return? __________

d. What is the penalty for each information statement that is filed late? __________

e. What is the penalty assessed on a tax preparer for failing to provide a copy of the tax return to the taxpayer? __________

f. Within the district audit division, there are two types of audits. One is the field audit. What is the other? __________

g. After receiving a *30-day letter,* how long does the taxpayer have to request a conference with the examining officer? __________

h. After a tax return is filed, how many years does the IRS have to issue a *90-day deficiency?* __________

20. Form 1040X. Eight months after filing their Form 1040 for 2006 with the IRS Center in Memphis, Tennessee, Jack L. (SSN 347-47-5784) and Judith K. (SSN 457-58-4758) Keith, 1618 Redford Lane, Kingsport, Tennessee 37664-3322, discovered several items that had been omitted from their original return. These items are as follows.

- A contribution of 20 shares of stock in the ABC Corporation to the Building Fund of the Second Church on January 7, 2006, that had not been claimed. Mrs. Keith purchased the stock for $600 on August 6, 2000. Its FMV on January 7, 2006 was $950.
- Qualified dividends received during 2006 that had not been reported:

Wye Corporation (owned by Mr. Keith)	$46
ABC Corporation (owned by Mrs. Keith)	
Dividend had been declared on December 22, 2005, to shareholders of record January 2, 2006. Paid February 1, 2006	52

Information available from the 2006 Form 1040 that had been filed by Mr. and Mrs. Keith is shown below.

Married filing jointly, claiming two personal and one dependency exemptions	
Total income and AGI (no dividends or capital gains)	$71,000
Itemized deductions	14,370
Taxable income	46,730
Total tax liability	6,254
Federal income tax withheld	6,600
Amount refunded from original return	346

The Keiths have not been advised that their 2006 income tax return is under audit. Prepare an Amended U.S. Individual Income Tax Return, Form 1040X, for Mr. and Mrs. Keith, using the form on the following pages. The amended return was filed November 6, 2007.

(Use for Problem 20).

Form **1040X** (Rev. November 2006)

Department of the Treasury—Internal Revenue Service

Amended U.S. Individual Income Tax Return

▶ See separate instructions.

OMB No. 1545-0074

This return is for calendar year ▶ , or fiscal year ended ▶

Please print or type

Your first name and initial	Last name		Your social security number
If a joint return, spouse's first name and initial	Last name		Spouse's social security number
Home address (no. and street) or P.O. box if mail is not delivered to your home		Apt. no.	Phone number ( )
City, town or post office, state, and ZIP code. If you have a foreign address, see page 2 of the instructions.			

A If the address shown above is different from that shown on your last return filed with the IRS, would you like us to change it in our records? . . . ▶ ☐ **Yes** ☐ **No**

B Filing status. Be sure to complete this line. **Note.** You cannot change from joint to separate returns after the due date.

On original return ▶ ☐ Single ☐ Married filing jointly ☐ Married filing separately ☐ Head of household ☐ Qualifying widow(er)

On this return ▶ ☐ Single ☐ Married filing jointly ☐ Married filing separately ☐ Head of household* ☐ Qualifying widow(er)

* If the qualifying person is a child but not your dependent, see page 2 of the instructions.

Use Part II on the back to explain any changes		A. Original amount or as previously adjusted (see page 3)	B. Net change—amount of increase or (decrease)—explain in Part II	C. Correct amount
Income and Deductions (see instructions)				
1 Adjusted gross income (see page 3)	1			
2 Itemized deductions or standard deduction (see page 3)	2			
3 Subtract line 2 from line 1	3			
4 Exemptions. If changing, fill in Parts I and II on the back (see page 3)	4			
5 Taxable income. Subtract line 4 from line 3	5			
Tax Liability				
6 Tax (see page 4). Method used in col. C	6			
7 Credits (see page 4)	7			
8 Subtract line 7 from line 6. Enter the result but not less than zero	8			
9 Other taxes (see page 4)	9			
10 Total tax. Add lines 8 and 9	10			
Payments				
11 Federal income tax withheld and excess social security and tier 1 RRTA tax withheld. If changing, see page 4	11			
12 Estimated tax payments, including amount applied from prior year's return	12			
13 Earned income credit (EIC)	13			
14 Additional child tax credit from Form 8812	14			
15 Credits from Form 2439, Form 4136, or Form 8885	15			
16 Amount paid with request for extension of time to file (see page 4)				16
17 Amount of tax paid with original return plus additional tax paid after it was filed				17
18 Total payments. Add lines 11 through 17 in column C				18

Refund or Amount You Owe

19 Overpayment, if any, as shown on original return or as previously adjusted by the IRS	19
20 Subtract line 19 from line 18 (see page 5)	20
21 **Amount you owe.** If line 10, column C, is more than line 20, enter the difference and see page 5	21
22 If line 10, column C, is less than line 20, enter the difference	22
23 Amount of line 22 you want **refunded to you**	23
24 Amount of line 22 you want **applied to your** **estimated tax** 24	

Sign Here

Joint return? See page 2. Keep a copy for your records.

Under penalties of perjury, I declare that I have filed an original return and that I have examined this amended return, including accompanying schedules and statements, and to the best of my knowledge and belief, this amended return is true, correct, and complete. Declaration of preparer (other than taxpayer) is based on all information of which the preparer has any knowledge.

▶ Your signature Date ▶ Spouse's signature. If a joint return, **both** must sign. Date

Paid Preparer's Use Only

Preparer's signature ▶	Date	Check if self-employed ☐	Preparer's SSN or PTIN
Firm's name (or yours if self-employed), address, and ZIP code ▶		EIN	
		Phone no. ( )	

For Paperwork Reduction Act Notice, see page 6 of instructions. Cat. No. 11360L Form **1040X** (Rev. 11-2006)

(Use for Problem 20).

Form 1040X (Rev. 11-2006) Page **2**

Part I **Exemptions.** See Form 1040 or 1040A instructions.

Complete this part **only** if you are:

- Increasing or decreasing the number of exemptions claimed on line 6d of the return you are amending, or
- Increasing or decreasing the exemption amount for housing individuals displaced by Hurricane Katrina.

			A. Original number of exemptions reported or as previously adjusted	B. Net change	C. Correct number of exemptions
25	Yourself and spouse . . . . **Caution.** If someone can claim you as a dependent, you cannot claim an exemption for yourself.	25			
26	Your dependent children who lived with you	26			
27	Your dependent children who did not live with you due to divorce or separation	27			
28	Other dependents	28			
29	Total number of exemptions. Add lines 25 through 28	29			
30	Multiply the number of exemptions claimed on line 29 by the amount listed below for the tax year you are amending. Enter the result here and on line 4.	30			
31	If you are claiming an exemption amount for housing individuals displaced by Hurricane Katrina, enter the amount from Form 8914, line 2 for 2005 or line 6 for 2006 (see instructions for line 4)	31			
32	Add lines 30 and 31. Enter the result here and on line 4	32			

Tax year	Exemption amount	But see the instructions for line 4 on page 3 if the amount on line 1 is over:
2006	$3,300	$112,875
2005	3,200	109,475
2004	3,100	107,025
2003	3,050	104,625

33 Dependents (children and other) not claimed on original (or adjusted) return:

(a) First name	Last name	(b) Dependent's social security number	(c) Dependent's relationship to you	(d) ✓ if qualifying child for child tax credit (see page 5)
				☐
				☐
				☐
				☐
				☐
				☐

No. of children on 33 who:
- lived with you . . ▶ ☐
- **did not** live with you due to divorce or separation (see page 5) . . ▶ ☐

Dependents on 33 not entered above ▶ ☐

Part II **Explanation of Changes**

Enter the line number from the front of the form for each item you are changing and give the reason for each change. Attach only the supporting forms and schedules for the items changed. If you do not attach the required information, your Form 1040X may be returned. Be sure to include your name and social security number on any attachments.

If the change relates to a net operating loss carryback or a general business credit carryback, attach the schedule or form that shows the year in which the loss or credit occurred. See page 2 of the instructions. Also, check here. . . . . . . ▶ ☐

Part III **Presidential Election Campaign Fund.** Checking below will not increase your tax or reduce your refund.

If you did not previously want $3 to go to the fund but now want to, check here . . . . ▶ ☐
If a joint return and your spouse did not previously want $3 to go to the fund but now wants to, check here . . . . . ▶ ☐

Form **1040X** (Rev. 11-2006)

Printed on recycled paper

21. Internet Problem: Researching Instructions to Form 8882

The employer-provided child care credit allows a tax credit for 25% of qualified child care expenses, which includes amounts paid to a qualified child care facility that provides child care services to employees.

Go to the IRS Web site and locate the Instructions to Form 8882, Employer-Provided Child Care Credit. Find the information in the instructions that describes what constitutes a qualified child care facility. Print out that page from the instructions.

See Appendix A for instructions on use of the IRS Web site.

22. Business Entity Problem: This problem is designed for those using the "business entity" approach. The solution may require information from Chapters 14 and 15.

a. Budget Corporation has a net operating loss (NOL) of $150,000 in 2006. What may the corporation do with this loss?

b. If the business was operated as a partnership, how would the loss be treated?

c. If Budget was an S corporation, how would the loss be treated?

COMPREHENSIVE PROBLEM

23. Ted R. Langley (SSN 556-89-8227) lives at 118 Oxford Ave., Oak Park, IL 60725. In 2006, he has the following income and deductions.

Income:

Salary	$105,000
Tax-exempt interest from private activity bonds	20,000
Interest from Bank of America	10,600

Deductions:

Cash contributions to the American Red Cross	$ 2,000
Home mortgage interest	11,520
Real estate taxes	3,850
State income taxes withheld	3,000
State income taxes paid when filing 2005 taxes	160

In addition to the above, Langley had federal income taxes withheld of $23,908 during the year. He also paid $25,000 for $37,000 of stock through an incentive stock option plan at work. Langley is divorced and claims his 15-year-old daughter, Teresa Langley (SSN 882-94-6648), as a dependent. Teresa lived with her father 10 months during the year.

Based on this information, prepare Langley's 2006 tax return, including Form 6251 to compute his AMT. Langley does not want to contribute $3 to the Presidential Campaign Fund. He does not have a foreign bank account nor did he receive a distribution from a foreign trust. Langley claims the standard credit for federal telephone excise tax paid. He signs his return on April 15, 2007.

(Use for Problem 23).

Form **1040** Department of the Treasury—Internal Revenue Service **U.S. Individual Income Tax Return 2006** (99) IRS Use Only—Do not write or staple in this space.

For the year Jan. 1–Dec. 31, 2006, or other tax year beginning , 2006, ending , 20 OMB No. 1545-0074

Label (See instructions on page 16.) **Use the IRS label.** Otherwise, please print or type.

LABEL HERE

Your first name and initial | Last name | **Your social security number**

If a joint return, spouse's first name and initial | Last name | **Spouse's social security number**

Home address (number and street). If you have a P.O. box, see page 16. | Apt. no. | ▲ You **must** enter your SSN(s) above. ▲

City, town or post office, state, and ZIP code. If you have a foreign address, see page 16. | Checking a box below will not change your tax or refund.

Presidential Election Campaign ▶ Check here if you, or your spouse if filing jointly, want $3 to go to this fund (see page 16) ▶ ☐ **You** ☐ **Spouse**

Filing Status

Check only one box.

1 ☐ Single
2 ☐ Married filing jointly (even if only one had income)
3 ☐ Married filing separately. Enter spouse's SSN above and full name here. ▶
4 ☐ Head of household (with qualifying person). (See page 17.) If the qualifying person is a child but not your dependent, enter this child's name here. ▶
5 ☐ Qualifying widow(er) with dependent child (see page 17)

Exemptions

6a ☐ **Yourself.** If someone can claim you as a dependent, **do not** check box 6a
b ☐ **Spouse**

Boxes checked on 6a and 6b ____

c **Dependents:**

(1) First name Last name	(2) Dependent's social security number	(3) Dependent's relationship to you	(4) ✓ if qualifying child for child tax credit (see page 19)
			☐
			☐
			☐
			☐

If more than four dependents, see page 19.

No. of children on 6c who:
- lived with you ____
- did not live with you due to divorce or separation (see page 20) ____

Dependents on 6c not entered above ____

d Total number of exemptions claimed

Add numbers on lines above ▶ ☐

Income

Attach Form(s) W-2 here. Also attach Forms W-2G and 1099-R if tax was withheld.

If you did not get a W-2, see page 22.

Enclose, but do not attach, any payment. Also, please use **Form 1040-V.**

7	Wages, salaries, tips, etc. Attach Form(s) W-2		7	
8a	**Taxable** interest. Attach Schedule B if required		8a	
b	**Tax-exempt** interest. **Do not** include on line 8a	8b		
9a	Ordinary dividends. Attach Schedule B if required		9a	
b	Qualified dividends (see page 23)	9b		
10	Taxable refunds, credits, or offsets of state and local income taxes (see page 23)		10	
11	Alimony received		11	
12	Business income or (loss). Attach Schedule C or C-EZ		12	
13	Capital gain or (loss). Attach Schedule D if required. If not required, check here ▶ ☐		13	
14	Other gains or (losses). Attach Form 4797		14	
15a	IRA distributions 15a	b Taxable amount (see page 25)	15b	
16a	Pensions and annuities 16a	b Taxable amount (see page 25)	16b	
17	Rental real estate, royalties, partnerships, S corporations, trusts, etc. Attach Schedule E		17	
18	Farm income or (loss). Attach Schedule F		18	
19	Unemployment compensation		19	
20a	Social security benefits 20a	b Taxable amount (see page 27)	20b	
21	Other income. List type and amount (see page 29)		21	
22	Add the amounts in the far right column for lines 7 through 21. This is your **total income** ▶		22	

Adjusted Gross Income

23	Archer MSA deduction. Attach Form 8853	23		
24	Certain business expenses of reservists, performing artists, and fee-basis government officials. Attach Form 2106 or 2106-EZ	24		
25	Health savings account deduction. Attach Form 8889	25		
26	Moving expenses. Attach Form 3903	26		
27	One-half of self-employment tax. Attach Schedule SE	27		
28	Self-employed SEP, SIMPLE, and qualified plans	28		
29	Self-employed health insurance deduction (see page 30)	29		
30	Penalty on early withdrawal of savings	30		
31a	Alimony paid b Recipient's SSN ▶	31a		
32	IRA deduction (see page 31)	32		
33	Student loan interest deduction (see page 33)	33		
34	Jury duty pay you gave to your employer	34		
35	Domestic production activities deduction. Attach Form 8903	35		
36	Add lines 23 through 31a and 32 through 35		36	
37	Subtract line 36 from line 22. This is your **adjusted gross income** ▶		37	

For Disclosure, Privacy Act, and Paperwork Reduction Act Notice, see page 78. Cat. No. 11320B Form **1040** (2006)

(Use for Problem 23).

Form 1040 (2006) Page **2**

Tax and Credits

Standard Deduction for—
- People who checked any box on line 39a or 39b **or** who can be claimed as a dependent, see page 36.
- All others:

Single or Married filing separately, $5,150

Married filing jointly or Qualifying widow(er), $10,300

Head of household, $7,550

38	Amount from line 37 (adjusted gross income)	38	
39a	Check if: ☐ **You** were born before January 2, 1942, ☐ Blind. ☐ **Spouse** was born before January 2, 1942, ☐ Blind. **Total boxes checked ▶ 39a**		
b	If your spouse itemizes on a separate return or you were a dual-status alien, see page 35 and check here ▶39b ☐		
40	**Itemized deductions** (from Schedule A) **or** your **standard deduction** (see left margin)	40	
41	Subtract line 40 from line 38	41	
42	If line 38 is over $112,875, or you provided housing to a person displaced by Hurricane Katrina, see page 37. Otherwise, multiply $3,300 by the total number of exemptions claimed on line 6d	42	
43	**Taxable income.** Subtract line 42 from line 41. If line 42 is more than line 41, enter -0-	43	
44	**Tax** (see page 37). Check if any tax is from: **a** ☐ Form(s) 8814 **b** ☐ Form 4972	44	
45	**Alternative minimum tax** (see page 39). Attach Form 6251	45	
46	Add lines 44 and 45 ▶	46	
47	Foreign tax credit. Attach Form 1116 if required	47	
48	Credit for child and dependent care expenses. Attach Form 2441	48	
49	Credit for the elderly or the disabled. Attach Schedule R	49	
50	Education credits. Attach Form 8863	50	
51	Retirement savings contributions credit. Attach Form 8880	51	
52	Residential energy credits. Attach Form 5695	52	
53	Child tax credit (see page XX). Attach Form 8901 if required	53	
54	Credits from: **a** ☐ Form 8396 **b** ☐ Form 8839 **c** ☐ Form 8859	54	
55	Other credits: **a** ☐ Form 3800 **b** ☐ Form 8801 **c** ☐ Form_____	55	
56	Add lines 47 through 55. These are your **total credits**	56	
57	Subtract line 56 from line 46. If line 56 is more than line 46, enter -0- ▶	57	

Other Taxes

58	Self-employment tax. Attach Schedule SE	58	
59	Social security and Medicare tax on tip income not reported to employer. Attach Form 4137	59	
60	Additional tax on IRAs, other qualified retirement plans, etc. Attach Form 5329 if required	60	
61	Advance earned income credit payments from Form(s) W-2, box 9	61	
62	Household employment taxes. Attach Schedule H	62	
63	Add lines 57 through 62. This is your **total tax** ▶	63	

Payments

If you have a qualifying child, attach Schedule EIC.

64	Federal income tax withheld from Forms W-2 and 1099	64	
65	2006 estimated tax payments and amount applied from 2005 return	65	
66a	**Earned income credit (EIC)**	66a	
b	Nontaxable combat pay election ▶ 66b		
67	Excess social security and tier 1 RRTA tax withheld (see page 59)	67	
68	Additional child tax credit. Attach Form 8812	68	
69	Amount paid with request for extension to file (see page 59)	69	
70	Payments from: **a** ☐ Form 2439 **b** ☐ Form 4136 **c** ☐ Form 8885	70	
71	Credit for federal telephone excise tax paid. Attach Form 8913 if required	71	
72	Add lines 64, 65, 66a, and 67 through 71. These are your **total payments** ▶	72	

Refund

Direct deposit? See page 59 and fill in 74b, 74c, and 74d, or Form 8888.

73	If line 72 is more than line 63, subtract line 63 from line 72. This is the amount you **overpaid**	73	
74a	Amount of line 73 you want **refunded to you.** If Form 8888 is attached, check here ▶ ☐	74a	
▶ b	Routing number ▶ **c** Type: ☐ Checking ☐ Savings		
▶ d	Account number		
75	Amount of line 73 you want **applied to your 2007 estimated tax** ▶	75	

Amount You Owe

76	**Amount you owe.** Subtract line 72 from line 63. For details on how to pay, see page 60 ▶	76	
77	Estimated tax penalty (see page 60)	77	

Third Party Designee

Do you want to allow another person to discuss this return with the IRS (see page 61)? ☐ **Yes.** Complete the following. ☐ **No**

Designee's name ▶ Phone no. ▶ ( ) Personal identification number (PIN) ▶

Sign Here

Joint return? See page 17. Keep a copy for your records.

Under penalties of perjury, I declare that I have examined this return and accompanying schedules and statements, and to the best of my knowledge and belief, they are true, correct, and complete. Declaration of preparer (other than taxpayer) is based on all information of which preparer has any knowledge.

Your signature	Date	Your occupation	Daytime phone number ( )
Spouse's signature. If a joint return, **both** must sign.	Date	Spouse's occupation	

Paid Preparer's Use Only

Preparer's signature	Date	Check if self-employed ☐	Preparer's SSN or PTIN
Firm's name (or yours if self-employed), address, and ZIP code		EIN	
		Phone no.	( )

Form **1040** (2006)

Printed on recycled paper

(Use for Problem 23).

SCHEDULES A&B (Form 1040) Department of the Treasury Internal Revenue Service (99)

Schedule A—Itemized Deductions

(Schedule B is on back)

▶ Attach to Form 1040. ▶ See Instructions for Schedules A&B (Form 1040).

OMB No. 1545-0074 **2006** Attachment Sequence No. **07**

Name(s) shown on Form 1040 | Your social security number

Medical and Dental Expenses		**Caution.** Do not include expenses reimbursed or paid by others.		
	1	Medical and dental expenses (see page A-2)	1	
	2	Enter amount from Form 1040, line 38 [2]		
	3	Multiply line 2 by 7.5% (.075)	3	
	4	Subtract line 3 from line 1. If line 3 is more than line 1, enter -0-		4
Taxes You Paid (See page A-2.)	5	State and local income taxes	5	
	6	Real estate taxes (see page A-5)	6	
	7	Personal property taxes	7	
	8	Other taxes. List type and amount ▶	8	
	9	Add lines 5 through 8		9
Interest You Paid (See page A-5.)	10	Home mortgage interest and points reported to you on Form 1098	10	
	11	Home mortgage interest not reported to you on Form 1098. If paid to the person from whom you bought the home, see page A-6 and show that person's name, identifying no., and address ▶	11	
Note. Personal interest is not deductible.	12	Points not reported to you on Form 1098. See page A-6 for special rules	12	
	13	Investment interest. Attach Form 4952 if required. (See page A-6.)	13	
	14	Add lines 10 through 13		14
Gifts to Charity If you made a gift and got a benefit for it, see page A-7.	15	Gifts by cash or check. If you made any gift of $250 or more, see page A-7	15	
	16	Other than by cash or check. If any gift of $250 or more, see page A-7. You **must** attach Form 8283 if over $500	16	
	17	Carryover from prior year	17	
	18	Add lines 15 through 17		18
Casualty and Theft Losses	19	Casualty or theft loss(es). Attach Form 4684. (See page A-8.)		19
Job Expenses and Certain Miscellaneous Deductions (See page A-8.)	20	Unreimbursed employee expenses—job travel, union dues, job education, etc. Attach Form 2106 or 2106-EZ if required. (See page A-8.) ▶	20	
	21	Tax preparation fees	21	
	22	Other expenses—investment, safe deposit box, etc. List type and amount ▶	22	
	23	Add lines 20 through 22	23	
	24	Enter amount from Form 1040, line 38 [24]		
	25	Multiply line 24 by 2% (.02)	25	
	26	Subtract line 25 from line 23. If line 25 is more than line 23, enter -0-		26
Other Miscellaneous Deductions	27	Other—from list on page A-9. List type and amount ▶		27
Total Itemized Deductions	28	Is Form 1040, line 38, over $150,500 (over $75,250 if married filing separately)? ☐ **No.** Your deduction is not limited. Add the amounts in the far right column for lines 4 through 27. Also, enter this amount on Form 1040, line 40. ☐ **Yes.** Your deduction may be limited. See page A-9 for the amount to enter. ▶		28
	29	If you elect to itemize deductions even though they are less than your standard deduction, check here ▶ ☐		

For Paperwork Reduction Act Notice, see Form 1040 instructions. Cat. No. 11330X **Schedule A (Form 1040) 2006**

(Use for Problem 23).

Schedules A&B (Form 1040) 2006 — OMB No. 1545-0074 — Page **2**

Name(s) shown on Form 1040. Do not enter name and social security number if shown on other side. | **Your social security number**

Schedule B—Interest and Ordinary Dividends

Attachment Sequence No. **08**

Part I Interest

(See page B-1 and the instructions for Form 1040, line 8a.)

Note. If you received a Form 1099-INT, Form 1099-OID, or substitute statement from a brokerage firm, list the firm's name as the payer and enter the total interest shown on that form.

			Amount
1	List name of payer. If any interest is from a seller-financed mortgage and the buyer used the property as a personal residence, see page B-1 and list this interest first. Also, show that buyer's social security number and address ▶	1	
2	Add the amounts on line 1	2	
3	Excludable interest on series EE and I U.S. savings bonds issued after 1989. Attach Form 8815	3	
4	Subtract line 3 from line 2. Enter the result here and on Form 1040, line 8a ▶	4	

Note. If line 4 is over $1,500, you must complete Part III.

Part II Ordinary Dividends

(See page B-1 and the instructions for Form 1040, line 9a.)

Note. If you received a Form 1099-DIV or substitute statement from a brokerage firm, list the firm's name as the payer and enter the ordinary dividends shown on that form.

			Amount
5	List name of payer ▶	5	
6	Add the amounts on line 5. Enter the total here and on Form 1040, line 9a . ▶	6	

Note. If line 6 is over $1,500, you must complete Part III.

Part III Foreign Accounts and Trusts

(See page B-2.)

You must complete this part if you **(a)** had over $1,500 of taxable interest or ordinary dividends; or **(b)** had a foreign account; or **(c)** received a distribution from, or were a grantor of, or a transferor to, a foreign trust.

		Yes	No
7a	At any time during 2006, did you have an interest in or a signature or other authority over a financial account in a foreign country, such as a bank account, securities account, or other financial account? See page B-2 for exceptions and filing requirements for Form TD F 90-22.1.	☐	☐
b	If "Yes," enter the name of the foreign country ▶		
8	During 2006, did you receive a distribution from, or were you the grantor of, or transferor to, a foreign trust? If "Yes," you may have to file Form 3520. See page B-2	☐	☐

For Paperwork Reduction Act Notice, see Form 1040 instructions. — **Schedule B (Form 1040) 2006**

Printed on recycled paper

(Use for Problem 23).

Form **6251**
Department of the Treasury
Internal Revenue Service (99)

Alternative Minimum Tax—Individuals

► See separate instructions.

► Attach to Form 1040 or Form 1040NR.

OMB No. 1545-0074

2006

Attachment Sequence No. **32**

Name(s) shown on Form 1040 | Your social security number

Part I Alternative Minimum Taxable Income (See instructions for how to complete each line.)

1	If filing Schedule A (Form 1040), enter the amount from Form 1040, line 41 (minus any amount on Form 8914, line 6), and go to line 2. Otherwise, enter the amount from Form 1040, line 38 (minus any amount on Form 8914, line 6), and go to line 7. (If less than zero, enter as a negative amount.)	1	
2	Medical and dental. Enter the **smaller** of Schedule A (Form 1040), line 4, **or** 2½ % of Form 1040, line 38	2	
3	Taxes from Schedule A (Form 1040), line 9	3	
4	Enter the home mortgage interest adjustment, if any, from line 6 of the worksheet on page 2 of the instructions	4	
5	Miscellaneous deductions from Schedule A (Form 1040), line 26	5	
6	If Form 1040, line 38, is over $150,500 (over $75,250 if married filing separately), enter the amount from line 11 of the **Itemized Deductions Worksheet** on page A-6 of the Instructions for Schedule A (Form 1040)	6	( )
7	Tax refund from Form 1040, line 10 or line 21	7	( )
8	Investment interest expense (difference between regular tax and AMT)	8	
9	Depletion (difference between regular tax and AMT)	9	
10	Net operating loss deduction from Form 1040, line 21. Enter as a positive amount	10	
11	Interest from specified private activity bonds exempt from the regular tax	11	
12	Qualified small business stock (7% of gain excluded under section 1202)	12	
13	Exercise of incentive stock options (excess of AMT income over regular tax income)	13	
14	Estates and trusts (amount from Schedule K-1 (Form 1041), box 12, code A)	14	
15	Electing large partnerships (amount from Schedule K-1 (Form 1065-B), box 6)	15	
16	Disposition of property (difference between AMT and regular tax gain or loss)	16	
17	Depreciation on assets placed in service after 1986 (difference between regular tax and AMT)	17	
18	Passive activities (difference between AMT and regular tax income or loss)	18	
19	Loss limitations (difference between AMT and regular tax income or loss)	19	
20	Circulation costs (difference between regular tax and AMT)	20	
21	Long-term contracts (difference between AMT and regular tax income)	21	
22	Mining costs (difference between regular tax and AMT)	22	
23	Research and experimental costs (difference between regular tax and AMT)	23	
24	Income from certain installment sales before January 1, 1987	24	( )
25	Intangible drilling costs preference	25	
26	Other adjustments, including income-based related adjustments	26	
27	Alternative tax net operating loss deduction	27	( )
28	**Alternative minimum taxable income.** Combine lines 1 through 27. (If married filing separately and line 28 is more than $200,100, see page 7 of the instructions.)	28	

Part II Alternative Minimum Tax

29 Exemption. (If this form is for a child under age 18, see page 7 of the instructions.)

IF your filing status is . . .	**AND line 28 is not over . . .**	**THEN enter on line 29 . . .**
Single or head of household	$112,500	$42,500
Married filing jointly or qualifying widow(er)	150,000	62,550
Married filing separately	75,000	31,275

If line 28 is **over** the amount shown above for your filing status, see page 7 of the instructions. — **29**

30	Subtract line 29 from line 28. If more than zero **or** you are filing Form 2555 or 2555-EZ, go to line 31. If zero or less and you are not filing Form 2555 or 2555-EZ, enter -0- on lines 33 and 35 and skip the rest of Part II	30	
31	• If you are filing Form 2555 or 2555-EZ, see page 8 of the instructions for the amount to enter. • If you reported capital gain distributions directly on Form 1040, line 13; you reported qualified dividends on Form 1040, line 9b; **or** you had a gain on both lines 15 and 16 of Schedule D (Form 1040) (as refigured for the AMT, if necessary), complete Part III on the back and enter the amount from line 55 here. • **All others:** If line 30 is $175,000 or less ($87,500 or less if married filing separately), multiply line 30 by 26% (.26). Otherwise, multiply line 30 by 28% (.28) and subtract $3,500 ($1,750 if married filing separately) from the result.	31	
32	Alternative minimum tax foreign tax credit (see page 7 of the instructions)	32	
33	Tentative minimum tax. Subtract line 32 from line 31	33	
34	Tax from Form 1040, line 44 (minus any tax from Form 4972 and any foreign tax credit from Form 1040, line 47). If you used Schedule J to figure your tax, the amount for line 44 of Form 1040 must be refigured without using Schedule J (see page 9 of the instructions)	34	
35	**Alternative minimum tax.** Subtract line 34 from line 33. If zero or less, enter -0-. Enter here and on Form 1040, line 45	35	

For Paperwork Reduction Act Notice, see page 9 of the instructions. Cat. No. 13600G Form **6251** (2006)

CUMULATIVE PROBLEM (CHAPTERS 8-12)

In February 2002, a Jon Haines paid $110,000 for a certified historical structure. During the next 14 months, Haines spent $150,000 to rehabilitate the building. The building was placed in service as Haines's office building on May 4, 2003. Haines took the rehabilitation credit in that year and used MACRS to depreciate the remaining basis in the building. On July 19, 2006, he sold the building for $280,000. Selling costs related to the sale were $20,000. Compute the realized and recognized gain on the sale of the building. Be sure to discuss the nature of the gain and how it is treated in the netting process.

CUMULATIVE PROBLEM (CHAPTERS 1–12)

This problem is suitable for manual preparation or computer software application.

Using the following information, prepare a joint federal income tax return for Jerry and Janet Apps.

Jerry R. (SSN 367-83-9403) and Janet K. (SSN 361-73-4098) Apps, married, under age 65, file a joint return. They reside at 410 E. Vernon Avenue, Carlock, Illinois 61725-1287. Both elect to have $3 go to the presidential campaign fund. The Apps claim the standard credit for federal telephone excise tax paid.

Their household includes David A. Apps, their 12-year-old son (SSN 965-26-4381), and Edwin R. Apps (SSN 157-43-2587), Jerry's 70-year-old father. Janet and Jerry provide over half of the support of both David and Edwin. David has no income of his own; Edwin received $4,500 in nontaxable social security benefits during the year.

Jerry, who works as a carpenter for Evergreen Enterprises, received the following information on his Form W-2. Jerry does not participate in an employer-sponsored pension plan.

Gross wages	$42,000
Social security and Medicare tax withheld	3,213
Federal income tax withheld	2,160
State income tax withheld	950

Janet owns and operates J&J Networking, a Dolmore distributorship. The principal business code is 454390. Janet has no employer ID number. She is a cash basis taxpayer but uses the accrual basis in her business. She uses the cost method for valuing the inventory. No changes have been made in the inventory system. Janet operated her business for all 12 months and had an office in her home. She materially participated in the business throughout the year.

Information relating to Janet's business operation is shown below.

Gross receipts	$30,200
Returns and allowances	200
Beginning inventory	700
Purchases	22,625
Ending inventory	825

Expenses:

Advertising	$ 100	Office expense	$ 80
Bank service charges	24	Supplies	50
Car expenses (see below)		Travel	400
Commissions	1,200	Meals and entertainment	180
Depreciation on equipment placed in service in 2003	625	Business seminars	264
		Other business taxes	560
Dues and publications	220	Miscellaneous expenses	35
Insurance (business)	150	Postage expense	260

Janet uses her personal car in her business. She keeps good records of her business mileage and uses the standard mileage method. The car was first used in the business on May 1, 2004. During 2006 Janet drove 7,631 miles, of which 1,516 were for business. The rest were personal miles. Information relating to the home is shown below.

Total area of home	1,800 square feet
Area used for business	180 square feet
FMV of home, for purposes of Form 8829, line 35	$150,000
Adjusted basis of home, for purposes of Form 8829, line 35	115,000
Value of land, Form 8829, line 36	20,000
Year the home office was first placed in service	1991
Mortgage interest	$6,250
Real estate taxes	2,400
Homeowner's insurance	680
Utilities	3,200

The Appses own a four-unit apartment building, which they actively manage. The Appses paid $125,000 for the building in 1994 and depreciate it using MACRS over 27.5 years. The building is located at 19 Sunset Road in Carlock. All units were rented for the entire year. Information on the apartments is shown below.

Revenue from rents	$33,600
Expenses:	
Real estate taxes	$ 4,800
Utilities	1,780
Insurance	1,550
Cleaning and maintenance	5,200
Legal and professional fees	125
Mortgage interest	7,200
Repairs	827
Supplies	325

The Appses had other income consisting of the following. Neither Jerry nor Janet had any interest in a foreign trust or bank account.

Interest from Champion Savings	$750
Interest on bonds from the State of Illinois	930
Qualified dividends from General Morris Corporation	120
Qualified dividends from Eagle Corporation	150
Qualified dividends from Roper Corporation	70

The Appses have a $4,950 long-term capital loss carryover from 2005. They also sold the following securities during 2006.

Number of Shares	*Company*	*Date Acquired*	*Cost*	*Date Sold*	*Sales Price*
100	Roper Corp.	5-1-00	$5,000	6-12-06	$7,500
50	Fastco Corp.	2-14-06	3,250	7-20-06	2,950
200	Eagle Corp.	3-16-99	6,200	8-10-06	8,100
100	South Corp.	3-14-05	1,500	1-24-06	6,500

The Appses made the following payments during the year:

Medical expenses (unreimbursed):

	Jerry	*Janet*	*David*	*Edwin*	*Total*
Prescription medicines	$ 50	$ 200	$ 25	$ 100	$ 375
Doctor bills	60	500	30	200	790
Dentist bills	150	40	200	0	390
Hospital bills	0	1,800	0	2,100	3,900
Transportation	8	72	24	16	120
Eyeglasses	0	0	125	0	125
Over-the-counter medicine	0	50	30	70	150

Taxes:

Sales tax	$1,200
Balance due on 2005 state income tax return	625
Balance due on 2005 federal income tax return	725
Estimated federal income tax payments	1,000
Real estate taxes	2,400

Interest:

Mortgage interest	$6,250
Credit card interest	975

Contributions:

Church	$1,200
United Way	100
Presidential election campaign	50

In addition to these cash contributions, the Appses donated five shares of S&W common stock to their church on July 30. The stock had been purchased on December 15, 2004, for $200. The fair market value of the stock on July 30 was $400. Other payments the Appses made in 2006 are as follows.

Rental of safe deposit box for securities	$ 24
2005 tax preparation fee (personal return)	300
Union dues for Jerry	1,200
Automobile license	50
IRA for Jerry	1,800
IRA for Janet	500

(Use for Cumulative Problem).

Form **1040** Department of the Treasury—Internal Revenue Service **U.S. Individual Income Tax Return 2006** (99) IRS Use Only—Do not write or staple in this space.

Label (See instructions on page 16.) **Use the IRS label.** Otherwise, please print or type. LABEL HERE

For the year Jan. 1–Dec. 31, 2006, or other tax year beginning , 2006, ending , 20 — OMB No. 1545-0074

Your first name and initial	Last name	**Your social security number**
If a joint return, spouse's first name and initial	Last name	**Spouse's social security number**
Home address (number and street). If you have a P.O. box, see page 16.	Apt. no.	▲ You **must** enter your SSN(s) above. ▲
City, town or post office, state, and ZIP code. If you have a foreign address, see page 16.		Checking a box below will not change your tax or refund.

Presidential Election Campaign ▶ Check here if you, or your spouse if filing jointly, want $3 to go to this fund (see page 16) ▶ ☐ **You** ☐ **Spouse**

Filing Status

Check only one box.

1 ☐ Single
2 ☐ Married filing jointly (even if only one had income)
3 ☐ Married filing separately. Enter spouse's SSN above and full name here. ▶
4 ☐ Head of household (with qualifying person). (See page 17.) If the qualifying person is a child but not your dependent, enter this child's name here. ▶
5 ☐ Qualifying widow(er) with dependent child (see page 17)

Exemptions

6a ☐ **Yourself.** If someone can claim you as a dependent, **do not** check box 6a — **Boxes checked on 6a and 6b** ____
b ☐ **Spouse** — **No. of children on 6c who:**
c **Dependents:**

(1) First name Last name	(2) Dependent's social security number	(3) Dependent's relationship to you	(4) ✓ if qualifying child for child tax credit (see page 19)
			☐
			☐
			☐
			☐

• **lived with you** ____
• **did not live with you due to divorce or separation (see page 20)** ____
Dependents on 6c not entered above ____

If more than four dependents, see page 19.

d Total number of exemptions claimed — **Add numbers on lines above ▶**

Income

Attach Form(s) W-2 here. Also attach Forms W-2G and 1099-R if tax was withheld.

If you did not get a W-2, see page 22.

Enclose, but do not attach, any payment. Also, please use **Form 1040-V.**

7	Wages, salaries, tips, etc. Attach Form(s) W-2		7	
8a	**Taxable** interest. Attach Schedule B if required		8a	
b	**Tax-exempt** interest. **Do not** include on line 8a	8b		
9a	Ordinary dividends. Attach Schedule B if required		9a	
b	Qualified dividends (see page 23)	9b		
10	Taxable refunds, credits, or offsets of state and local income taxes (see page 23)		10	
11	Alimony received		11	
12	Business income or (loss). Attach Schedule C or C-EZ		12	
13	Capital gain or (loss). Attach Schedule D if required. If not required, check here ▶ ☐		13	
14	Other gains or (losses). Attach Form 4797		14	
15a	IRA distributions 15a	b Taxable amount (see page 25)	15b	
16a	Pensions and annuities 16a	b Taxable amount (see page 25)	16b	
17	Rental real estate, royalties, partnerships, S corporations, trusts, etc. Attach Schedule E		17	
18	Farm income or (loss). Attach Schedule F		18	
19	Unemployment compensation		19	
20a	Social security benefits 20a	b Taxable amount (see page 27)	20b	
21	Other income. List type and amount (see page 29)		21	
22	Add the amounts in the far right column for lines 7 through 21. This is your **total income** ▶		22	

Adjusted Gross Income

23	Archer MSA deduction. Attach Form 8853	23		
24	Certain business expenses of reservists, performing artists, and fee-basis government officials. Attach Form 2106 or 2106-EZ	24		
25	Health savings account deduction. Attach Form 8889	25		
26	Moving expenses. Attach Form 3903	26		
27	One-half of self-employment tax. Attach Schedule SE	27		
28	Self-employed SEP, SIMPLE, and qualified plans	28		
29	Self-employed health insurance deduction (see page 30)	29		
30	Penalty on early withdrawal of savings	30		
31a	Alimony paid **b** Recipient's SSN ▶	31a		
32	IRA deduction (see page 31)	32		
33	Student loan interest deduction (see page 33)	33		
34	Jury duty pay you gave to your employer	34		
35	Domestic production activities deduction. Attach Form 8903	35		
36	Add lines 23 through 31a and 32 through 35		36	
37	Subtract line 36 from line 22. This is your **adjusted gross income** ▶		37	

For Disclosure, Privacy Act, and Paperwork Reduction Act Notice, see page 78. Cat. No. 11320B Form **1040** (2006)

(Use for Cumulative Problem).

Form 1040 (2006) Page **2**

Tax and Credits

38	Amount from line 37 (adjusted gross income)	38	
39a	Check if: ☐ **You** were born before January 2, 1942, ☐ Blind. ☐ **Spouse** was born before January 2, 1942, ☐ Blind. **Total boxes checked** ▶ 39a ☐		
b	If your spouse itemizes on a separate return or you were a dual-status alien, see page 35 and check here ▶39b ☐		
40	**Itemized deductions** (from Schedule A) **or** your **standard deduction** (see left margin)	40	
41	Subtract line 40 from line 38	41	
42	If line 38 is over $112,875, or you provided housing to a person displaced by Hurricane Katrina, see page 37. Otherwise, multiply $3,300 by the total number of exemptions claimed on line 6d	42	
43	**Taxable income.** Subtract line 42 from line 41. If line 42 is more than line 41, enter -0-	43	
44	**Tax** (see page 37). Check if any tax is from: **a** ☐ Form(s) 8814 **b** ☐ Form 4972	44	
45	**Alternative minimum tax** (see page 39). Attach Form 6251	45	
46	Add lines 44 and 45 ▶	46	
47	Foreign tax credit. Attach Form 1116 if required	47	
48	Credit for child and dependent care expenses. Attach Form 2441	48	
49	Credit for the elderly or the disabled. Attach Schedule R	49	
50	Education credits. Attach Form 8863	50	
51	Retirement savings contributions credit. Attach Form 8880	51	
52	Residential energy credits. Attach Form 5695	52	
53	Child tax credit (see page XX). Attach Form 8901 if required	53	
54	Credits from: **a** ☐ Form 8396 **b** ☐ Form 8839 **c** ☐ Form 8859	54	
55	Other credits: **a** ☐ Form 3800 **b** ☐ Form 8801 **c** ☐ Form______	55	
56	Add lines 47 through 55. These are your **total credits**	56	
57	Subtract line 56 from line 46. If line 56 is more than line 46, enter -0- ▶	57	

Standard Deduction for—

- People who checked any box on line 39a or 39b **or** who can be claimed as a dependent, see page 36.
- All others:

Single or Married filing separately, $5,150

Married filing jointly or Qualifying widow(er), $10,300

Head of household, $7,550

Other Taxes

58	Self-employment tax. Attach Schedule SE	58	
59	Social security and Medicare tax on tip income not reported to employer. Attach Form 4137	59	
60	Additional tax on IRAs, other qualified retirement plans, etc. Attach Form 5329 if required	60	
61	Advance earned income credit payments from Form(s) W-2, box 9	61	
62	Household employment taxes. Attach Schedule H	62	
63	Add lines 57 through 62. This is your **total tax** ▶	63	

Payments

64	Federal income tax withheld from Forms W-2 and 1099	64	
65	2006 estimated tax payments and amount applied from 2005 return	65	
66a	**Earned income credit (EIC)**	66a	
b	Nontaxable combat pay election ▶ 66b		
67	Excess social security and tier 1 RRTA tax withheld (see page 59)	67	
68	Additional child tax credit. Attach Form 8812	68	
69	Amount paid with request for extension to file (see page 59)	69	
70	Payments from: **a** ☐ Form 2439 **b** ☐ Form 4136 **c** ☐ Form 8885	70	
71	Credit for federal telephone excise tax paid. Attach Form 8913 if required	71	
72	Add lines 64, 65, 66a, and 67 through 71. These are your **total payments** ▶	72	

If you have a qualifying child, attach Schedule EIC.

Refund

Direct deposit? See page 59 and fill in 74b, 74c, and 74d, or Form 8888.

73	If line 72 is more than line 63, subtract line 63 from line 72. This is the amount you **overpaid**	73	
74a	Amount of line 73 you want **refunded to you.** If Form 8888 is attached, check here ▶ ☐	74a	
▶ b	Routing number ▶ **c** Type: ☐ Checking ☐ Savings		
▶ d	Account number		
75	Amount of line 73 you want **applied to your 2007 estimated tax** ▶ 75		

Amount You Owe

76	**Amount you owe.** Subtract line 72 from line 63. For details on how to pay, see page 60 ▶	76	
77	Estimated tax penalty (see page 60) 77		

Third Party Designee

Do you want to allow another person to discuss this return with the IRS (see page 61)? ☐ **Yes.** Complete the following. ☐ **No**

Designee's name ▶ Phone no. ▶ ( ) Personal identification number (PIN) ▶

Sign Here

Joint return? See page 17. Keep a copy for your records.

Under penalties of perjury, I declare that I have examined this return and accompanying schedules and statements, and to the best of my knowledge and belief, they are true, correct, and complete. Declaration of preparer (other than taxpayer) is based on all information of which preparer has any knowledge.

Your signature	Date	Your occupation	Daytime phone number ( )
Spouse's signature. If a joint return, **both** must sign.	Date	Spouse's occupation	

Paid Preparer's Use Only

Preparer's signature	Date	Check if self-employed ☐	Preparer's SSN or PTIN
Firm's name (or yours if self-employed), address, and ZIP code		EIN	
		Phone no.	( )

Form **1040** (2006)

Printed on recycled paper

(Use for Cumulative Problem).

SCHEDULES A&B (Form 1040)

Department of the Treasury Internal Revenue Service (99)

Schedule A—Itemized Deductions

(Schedule B is on back)

▶ Attach to Form 1040. ▶ See Instructions for Schedules A&B (Form 1040).

OMB No. 1545-0074

2006

Attachment Sequence No. 07

Name(s) shown on Form 1040 | Your social security number

Medical and Dental Expenses		**Caution.** Do not include expenses reimbursed or paid by others.				
	1	Medical and dental expenses (see page A-2)	1			
	2	Enter amount from Form 1040, line 38 [2]				
	3	Multiply line 2 by 7.5% (.075)	3			
	4	Subtract line 3 from line 1. If line 3 is more than line 1, enter -0-			4	
Taxes You Paid (See page A-2.)	5	State and local income taxes	5			
	6	Real estate taxes (see page A-5)	6			
	7	Personal property taxes	7			
	8	Other taxes. List type and amount ▶	8			
	9	Add lines 5 through 8			9	
Interest You Paid (See page A-5.)	10	Home mortgage interest and points reported to you on Form 1098	10			
	11	Home mortgage interest not reported to you on Form 1098. If paid to the person from whom you bought the home, see page A-6 and show that person's name, identifying no., and address ▶	11			
Note. Personal interest is not deductible.	12	Points not reported to you on Form 1098. See page A-6 for special rules	12			
	13	Investment interest. Attach Form 4952 if required. (See page A-6.)	13			
	14	Add lines 10 through 13			14	
Gifts to Charity If you made a gift and got a benefit for it, see page A-7.	15	Gifts by cash or check. If you made any gift of $250 or more, see page A-7	15			
	16	Other than by cash or check. If any gift of $250 or more, see page A-7. You **must** attach Form 8283 if over $500	16			
	17	Carryover from prior year	17			
	18	Add lines 15 through 17			18	
Casualty and Theft Losses	19	Casualty or theft loss(es). Attach Form 4684. (See page A-8.)			19	
Job Expenses and Certain Miscellaneous Deductions (See page A-8.)	20	Unreimbursed employee expenses—job travel, union dues, job education, etc. Attach Form 2106 or 2106-EZ if required. (See page A-8.) ▶	20			
	21	Tax preparation fees	21			
	22	Other expenses—investment, safe deposit box, etc. List type and amount ▶	22			
	23	Add lines 20 through 22	23			
	24	Enter amount from Form 1040, line 38 [24]				
	25	Multiply line 24 by 2% (.02)	25			
	26	Subtract line 25 from line 23. If line 25 is more than line 23, enter -0-			26	
Other Miscellaneous Deductions	27	Other—from list on page A-9. List type and amount ▶			27	
Total Itemized Deductions	28	Is Form 1040, line 38, over $150,500 (over $75,250 if married filing separately)? ☐ **No.** Your deduction is not limited. Add the amounts in the far right column for lines 4 through 27. Also, enter this amount on Form 1040, line 40. ☐ **Yes.** Your deduction may be limited. See page A-9 for the amount to enter. ▶			28	
	29	If you elect to itemize deductions even though they are less than your standard deduction, check here ▶ ☐				

For Paperwork Reduction Act Notice, see Form 1040 instructions. Cat. No. 11330X **Schedule A (Form 1040) 2006**

(Use for Cumulative Problem).

Schedules A&B (Form 1040) 2006 — OMB No. 1545-0074 — Page 2

Name(s) shown on Form 1040. Do not enter name and social security number if shown on other side. — Your social security number

Schedule B—Interest and Ordinary Dividends

Attachment Sequence No. 08

Part I Interest

(See page B-1 and the instructions for Form 1040, line 8a.)

Note. If you received a Form 1099-INT, Form 1099-OID, or substitute statement from a brokerage firm, list the firm's name as the payer and enter the total interest shown on that form.

			Amount
1	List name of payer. If any interest is from a seller-financed mortgage and the buyer used the property as a personal residence, see page B-1 and list this interest first. Also, show that buyer's social security number and address ▶	1	
2	Add the amounts on line 1	2	
3	Excludable interest on series EE and I U.S. savings bonds issued after 1989. Attach Form 8815	3	
4	Subtract line 3 from line 2. Enter the result here and on Form 1040, line 8a ▶	4	

Note. If line 4 is over $1,500, you must complete Part III.

Part II Ordinary Dividends

(See page B-1 and the instructions for Form 1040, line 9a.)

Note. If you received a Form 1099-DIV or substitute statement from a brokerage firm, list the firm's name as the payer and enter the ordinary dividends shown on that form.

			Amount
5	List name of payer ▶	5	
6	Add the amounts on line 5. Enter the total here and on Form 1040, line 9a . ▶	6	

Note. If line 6 is over $1,500, you must complete Part III.

Part III Foreign Accounts and Trusts

(See page B-2.)

You must complete this part if you **(a)** had over $1,500 of taxable interest or ordinary dividends; or **(b)** had a foreign account; or **(c)** received a distribution from, or were a grantor of, or a transferor to, a foreign trust.

		Yes	No
7a	At any time during 2006, did you have an interest in or a signature or other authority over a financial account in a foreign country, such as a bank account, securities account, or other financial account? See page B-2 for exceptions and filing requirements for Form TD F 90-22.1	☐	☐
b	If "Yes," enter the name of the foreign country ▶		
8	During 2006, did you receive a distribution from, or were you the grantor of, or transferor to, a foreign trust? If "Yes," you may have to file Form 3520. See page B-2	☐	☐

For Paperwork Reduction Act Notice, see Form 1040 instructions. — **Schedule B (Form 1040) 2006**

(Use for Cumulative Problem).

SCHEDULE C (Form 1040)
Department of the Treasury Internal Revenue Service (99)

Profit or Loss From Business
(Sole Proprietorship)

▶ Partnerships, joint ventures, etc., must file Form 1065 or 1065-B.
▶ Attach to Form 1040, 1040NR, or 1041. ▶ See Instructions for Schedule C (Form 1040).

OMB No. 1545-0074
2006
Attachment Sequence No. 09

Name of proprietor | Social security number (SSN)

A Principal business or profession, including product or service (see page C-2 of the instructions) | **B** Enter code from pages C-8, 9, & 10 ▶

C Business name. If no separate business name, leave blank. | **D** Employer ID number (EIN), if any

E Business address (including suite or room no.) ▶
City, town or post office, state, and ZIP code

F Accounting method: **(1)** ☐ Cash **(2)** ☐ Accrual **(3)** ☐ Other (specify) ▶

G Did you "materially participate" in the operation of this business during 2006? If "No," see page C-2 for limit on losses ☐ Yes ☐ No

H If you started or acquired this business during 2006, check here . . . ▶ ☐

Part I Income

1	Gross receipts or sales. **Caution.** If this income was reported to you on Form W-2 and the "Statutory employee" box on that form was checked, see page C-3 and check here . . . ▶ ☐	1	
2	Returns and allowances . . .	2	
3	Subtract line 2 from line 1 . . .	3	
4	Cost of goods sold (from line 42 on page 2) . . .	4	
5	**Gross profit.** Subtract line 4 from line 3 . . .	5	
6	Other income, including federal and state gasoline or fuel tax credit or refund (see page C-3) . . .	6	
7	**Gross income.** Add lines 5 and 6 . . . ▶	7	

Part II Expenses. Enter expenses for business use of your home **only** on line 30.

8	Advertising . . .	8		18	Office expense . . .	18	
9	Car and truck expenses (see page C-4) . . .	9		19	Pension and profit-sharing plans	19	
10	Commissions and fees . .	10		20	Rent or lease (see page C-5):		
11	Contract labor (see page C-4)	11		a	Vehicles, machinery, and equipment .	20a	
12	Depletion . . .	12		b	Other business property . . .	20b	
13	Depreciation and section 179 expense deduction (not included in Part III) (see page C-4) . . .	13		21	Repairs and maintenance . .	21	
				22	Supplies (not included in Part III) .	22	
				23	Taxes and licenses . . .	23	
				24	Travel, meals, and entertainment:		
				a	Travel . . .	24a	
14	Employee benefit programs (other than on line 19) . .	14		b	Deductible meals and entertainment (see page C-5)	24b	
15	Insurance (other than health) .	15		25	Utilities . . .	25	
16	Interest:			26	Wages (less employment credits) .	26	
a	Mortgage (paid to banks, etc.) .	16a		27	Other expenses (from line 48 on page 2) . . .	27	
b	Other . . .	16b					
17	Legal and professional services . . .	17					

28	**Total expenses** before expenses for business use of home. Add lines 8 through 27 in columns . ▶	28	
29	Tentative profit (loss). Subtract line 28 from line 7 . . .	29	
30	Expenses for business use of your home. Attach **Form 8829** . . .	30	
31	**Net profit or (loss).** Subtract line 30 from line 29. • If a profit, enter on **Form 1040, line 12,** and **also** on **Schedule SE, line 2** or **Form 1040NR, line 13** (statutory employees, see page C-6). Estates and trusts, enter on Form 1041, line 3. • If a loss, you **must** go to line 32.	31	

32 If you have a loss, check the box that describes your investment in this activity (see page C-6).
• If you checked 32a, enter the loss on **Form 1040, line 12,** and **also** on **Schedule SE, line 2** or **Form 1040NR, line 13** (statutory employees, see page C-6). Estates and trusts, enter on Form 1041, line 3.
• If you checked 32b, you **must** attach **Form 6198.** Your loss may be limited.

32a ☐ All investment is at risk.
32b ☐ Some investment is not at risk.

For Paperwork Reduction Act Notice, see page C-7 of the instructions. Cat. No. 11334P **Schedule C (Form 1040) 2006**

(Use for Cumulative Problem).

Schedule C (Form 1040) 2006 Page **2**

Part III **Cost of Goods Sold** (see page C-7)

33 Method(s) used to value closing inventory: **a** ☐ Cost **b** ☐ Lower of cost or market **c** ☐ Other (attach explanation)

34 Was there any change in determining quantities, costs, or valuations between opening and closing inventory? If "Yes," attach explanation . . . ☐ **Yes** ☐ **No**

35	Inventory at beginning of year. If different from last year's closing inventory, attach explanation	35	
36	Purchases less cost of items withdrawn for personal use	36	
37	Cost of labor. Do not include any amounts paid to yourself	37	
38	Materials and supplies	38	
39	Other costs	39	
40	Add lines 35 through 39	40	
41	Inventory at end of year	41	
42	**Cost of goods sold.** Subtract line 41 from line 40. Enter the result here and on page 1, line 4	42	

Part IV **Information on Your Vehicle.** Complete this part **only** if you are claiming car or truck expenses on line 9 and are not required to file Form 4562 for this business. See the instructions for line 13 on page C-4 to find out if you must file Form 4562.

43 When did you place your vehicle in service for business purposes? (month, day, year) ▶ ______/______/______

44 Of the total number of miles you drove your vehicle during 2006, enter the number of miles you used your vehicle for:

a Business ______________ **b** Commuting (see instructions) ______________ **c** Other ______________

45 Do you (or your spouse) have another vehicle available for personal use? . . . ☐ **Yes** ☐ **No**

46 Was your vehicle available for personal use during off-duty hours? . . . ☐ **Yes** ☐ **No**

47a Do you have evidence to support your deduction? . . . ☐ **Yes** ☐ **No**

b If "Yes," is the evidence written? . . . ☐ **Yes** ☐ **No**

Part V **Other Expenses.** List below business expenses not included on lines 8–26 or line 30.

48 Total other expenses. Enter here and on page 1, line 27	48	

Printed on recycled paper

Schedule C (Form 1040) 2006

(Use for Cumulative Problem).

SCHEDULE D (Form 1040)

Department of the Treasury Internal Revenue Service (99)

Capital Gains and Losses

▶ Attach to Form 1040 or Form 1040NR. ▶ See Instructions for Schedule D (Form 1040).

▶ Use Schedule D-1 to list additional transactions for lines 1 and 8.

OMB No. 1545-0074

2006

Attachment Sequence No. 12

Name(s) shown on Form 1040 | Your social security number

Part I **Short-Term Capital Gains and Losses—Assets Held One Year or Less**

	(a) Description of property (Example: 100 sh. XYZ Co.)	(b) Date acquired (Mo., day, yr.)	(c) Date sold (Mo., day, yr.)	(d) Sales price (see page D-6 of the instructions)	(e) Cost or other basis (see page D-7 of the instructions)	(f) Gain or (loss) Subtract (e) from (d)
1						

2	Enter your short-term totals, if any, from Schedule D-1, line 2	2	
3	**Total short-term sales price amounts.** Add lines 1 and 2 in column (d)	3	
4	Short-term gain from Form 6252 and short-term gain or (loss) from Forms 4684, 6781, and 8824	4	
5	Net short-term gain or (loss) from partnerships, S corporations, estates, and trusts from Schedule(s) K-1	5	
6	Short-term capital loss carryover. Enter the amount, if any, from line 10 of your **Capital Loss Carryover Worksheet** on page D-7 of the instructions	6	( )
7	**Net short-term capital gain or (loss).** Combine lines 1 through 6 in column (f)	7	

Part II **Long-Term Capital Gains and Losses—Assets Held More Than One Year**

	(a) Description of property (Example: 100 sh. XYZ Co.)	(b) Date acquired (Mo., day, yr.)	(c) Date sold (Mo., day, yr.)	(d) Sales price (see page D-6 of the instructions)	(e) Cost or other basis (see page D-7 of the instructions)	(f) Gain or (loss) Subtract (e) from (d)
8						

9	Enter your long-term totals, if any, from Schedule D-1, line 9	9	
10	**Total long-term sales price amounts.** Add lines 8 and 9 in column (d)	10	
11	Gain from Form 4797, Part I; long-term gain from Forms 2439 and 6252; and long-term gain or (loss) from Forms 4684, 6781, and 8824	11	
12	Net long-term gain or (loss) from partnerships, S corporations, estates, and trusts from Schedule(s) K-1	12	
13	Capital gain distributions. See page D-1 of the instructions	13	
14	Long-term capital loss carryover. Enter the amount, if any, from line 15 of your **Capital Loss Carryover Worksheet** on page D-7 of the instructions	14	( )
15	**Net long-term capital gain or (loss).** Combine lines 8 through 14 in column (f). Then go to Part III on the back	15	

For Paperwork Reduction Act Notice, see Form 1040 instructions. Cat. No. 11338H **Schedule D (Form 1040) 2006**

(Use for Cumulative Problem).

Schedule D (Form 1040) 2006 Page **2**

Part III **Summary**

16	Combine lines 7 and 15 and enter the result. If line 16 is a loss, skip lines 17 through 20, and go to line 21. If a gain, enter the gain on Form 1040, line 13, or Form 1040NR, line 14. Then go to line 17 below	**16**	
17	Are lines 15 and 16 **both** gains? ☐ **Yes.** Go to line 18. ☐ **No.** Skip lines 18 through 21, and go to line 22.		
18	Enter the amount, if any, from line 7 of the **28% Rate Gain Worksheet** on page D-8 of the instructions . . . . ▶	**18**	
19	Enter the amount, if any, from line 18 of the **Unrecaptured Section 1250 Gain Worksheet** on page D-9 of the instructions . . . . ▶	**19**	
20	Are lines 18 and 19 **both** zero or blank? ☐ **Yes.** Complete Form 1040 through line 43, or Form 1040NR through line 40. Then complete the **Qualified Dividends and Capital Gain Tax Worksheet** on page 38 of the Instructions for Form 1040 (or in the Instructions for Form 1040NR). **Do not** complete lines 21 and 22 below. ☐ **No.** Complete Form 1040 through line 43, or Form 1040NR through line 40. Then complete the **Schedule D Tax Worksheet** on page D-10 of the instructions. **Do not** complete lines 21 and 22 below.		
21	If line 16 is a loss, enter here and on Form 1040, line 13, or Form 1040NR, line 14, the **smaller** of: • The loss on line 16 or • ($3,000), or if married filing separately, ($1,500) } . . . . **Note.** When figuring which amount is smaller, treat both amounts as positive numbers.	**21**	( )
22	Do you have qualified dividends on Form 1040, line 9b, or Form 1040NR, line 10b?* ☐ **Yes.** Complete Form 1040 through line 43, or Form 1040NR through line 40. Then complete the **Qualified Dividends and Capital Gain Tax Worksheet** on page 38 of the Instructions for Form 1040 (or in the Instructions for Form 1040NR). ☐ **No.** Complete the rest of Form 1040 or Form 1040NR.		

Schedule D (Form 1040) 2006

*Note: Compute tax using the method shown in the chapter or on the Qualified Dividends and Capital Gain Tax Worksheet on page 12-66.

(Use for Cumulative Problem).

SCHEDULE E (Form 1040)

Department of the Treasury Internal Revenue Service (99)

Supplemental Income and Loss

(From rental real estate, royalties, partnerships, S corporations, estates, trusts, REMICs, etc.)

▶ Attach to Form 1040, 1040NR, or Form 1041. ▶ See Instructions for Schedule E (Form 1040).

OMB No. 1545-0074

2006

Attachment Sequence No. **13**

Name(s) shown on return | Your social security number

Part I **Income or Loss From Rental Real Estate and Royalties** **Note.** If you are in the business of renting personal property, use **Schedule C** or **C-EZ** (see page E-3). Report farm rental income or loss from **Form 4835** on page 2, line 40.

	1 List the type and location of each **rental real estate property:**	2 For each rental real estate property listed on line 1, did you or your family use it during the tax year for personal purposes for more than the greater of: • 14 days **or** • 10% of the total days rented at fair rental value? (See page E-3.)		Yes	No
A			A		
B			B		
C			C		

Income:		Properties A	Properties B	Properties C		Totals (Add columns A, B, and C.)
3 Rents received	3				3	
4 Royalties received	4				4	
Expenses:						
5 Advertising	5					
6 Auto and travel (see page E-4).	6					
7 Cleaning and maintenance	7					
8 Commissions	8					
9 Insurance	9					
10 Legal and other professional fees	10					
11 Management fees	11					
12 Mortgage interest paid to banks, etc. (see page E-4)	12				12	
13 Other interest	13					
14 Repairs	14					
15 Supplies	15					
16 Taxes	16					
17 Utilities	17					
18 Other (list) ▶	18					
19 Add lines 5 through 18	19				19	
20 Depreciation expense or depletion (see page E-4)	20				20	
21 Total expenses. Add lines 19 and 20	21					
22 Income or (loss) from rental real estate or royalty properties. Subtract line 21 from line 3 (rents) or line 4 (royalties). If the result is a (loss), see page E-5 to find out if you must file **Form 6198**	22					
23 Deductible rental real estate loss. **Caution.** Your rental real estate loss on line 22 may be limited. See page E-5 to find out if you must file **Form 8582.** Real estate professionals must complete line 43 on page 2	23	( )	( )	( )		

24 **Income.** Add positive amounts shown on line 22. **Do not** include any losses	24	
25 **Losses.** Add royalty losses from line 22 and rental real estate losses from line 23. Enter total losses here	25	( )
26 **Total rental real estate and royalty income or (loss).** Combine lines 24 and 25. Enter the result here. If Parts II, III, IV, and line 40 on page 2 do not apply to you, also enter this amount on Form 1040, line 17, or Form 1040NR, line 18. Otherwise, include this amount in the total on line 41 on page 2	26	

For Paperwork Reduction Act Notice, see page E-7 of the instructions. Cat. No. 11344L **Schedule E (Form 1040) 2006**

(Use for Cumulative Problem).

SCHEDULE SE (Form 1040)
Department of the Treasury
Internal Revenue Service (99)

Self-Employment Tax

► Attach to Form 1040. ► See Instructions for Schedule SE (Form 1040).

OMB No. 1545-0074
2006
Attachment Sequence No. 17

Name of person with **self-employment** income (as shown on Form 1040) | Social security number of person with **self-employment** income ►

Who Must File Schedule SE

You must file Schedule SE if:

- You had net earnings from self-employment from **other than** church employee income (line 4 of Short Schedule SE or line 4c of Long Schedule SE) of $400 or more, **or**
- You had church employee income of $108.28 or more. Income from services you performed as a minister or a member of a religious order **is not** church employee income (see page SE-1).

Note. Even if you had a loss or a small amount of income from self-employment, it may be to your benefit to file Schedule SE and use either "optional method" in Part II of Long Schedule SE (see page SE-3).

Exception. If your only self-employment income was from earnings as a minister, member of a religious order, or Christian Science practitioner **and** you filed Form 4361 and received IRS approval not to be taxed on those earnings, **do not** file Schedule SE. Instead, write "Exempt–Form 4361" on Form 1040, line 58.

May I Use Short Schedule SE or Must I Use Long Schedule SE?

Note. Use this flowchart **only if** you must file Schedule SE. If unsure, see Who Must File Schedule SE, above.

Did you receive wages or tips in 2006?

No → Are you a minister, member of a religious order, or Christian Science practitioner who received IRS approval **not** to be taxed on earnings from these sources, **but** you owe self-employment tax on other earnings? Yes → You must use Long Schedule SE on page 2

No → Are you using one of the optional methods to figure your net earnings (see page SE-3)? Yes → You must use Long Schedule SE on page 2

No → Did you receive church employee income reported on Form W-2 of $108.28 or more? Yes → You must use Long Schedule SE on page 2

No → You may use Short Schedule SE below

Yes → Was the total of your wages and tips subject to social security or railroad retirement tax **plus** your net earnings from self-employment more than $94,200? Yes → You must use Long Schedule SE on page 2

No → Did you receive tips subject to social security or Medicare tax that you **did not** report to your employer? Yes → You must use Long Schedule SE on page 2

Section A—Short Schedule SE. Caution. Read above to see if you can use Short Schedule SE.

1	Net farm profit or (loss) from Schedule F, line 36, and farm partnerships, Schedule K-1 (Form 1065), box 14, code A	1	
2	Net profit or (loss) from Schedule C, line 31; Schedule C-EZ, line 3; Schedule K-1 (Form 1065), box 14, code A (other than farming); and Schedule K-1 (Form 1065-B), box 9, code J1. Ministers and members of religious orders, see page SE-1 for amounts to report on this line. See page SE-2 for other income to report	2	
3	Combine lines 1 and 2	3	
4	**Net earnings from self-employment.** Multiply line 3 by 92.35% (.9235). If less than $400, **do not** file this schedule; you do not owe self-employment tax . . . . . ►	4	
5	**Self-employment tax.** If the amount on line 4 is: • $94,200 or less, multiply line 4 by 15.3% (.153). Enter the result here and on **Form 1040, line 58.** • More than $94,200, multiply line 4 by 2.9% (.029). Then, add $11,680.80 to the result. Enter the total here and on **Form 1040, line 58.**	5	
6	**Deduction for one-half of self-employment tax.** Multiply line 5 by 50% (.5). Enter the result here and on **Form 1040, line 27** . . . 6		

For Paperwork Reduction Act Notice, see Form 1040 instructions. Cat. No. 11358Z **Schedule SE (Form 1040) 2006**

(Use for Cumulative Problem).

Form **4562** Department of the Treasury Internal Revenue Service

Depreciation and Amortization
(Including Information on Listed Property)
▶ See separate instructions. ▶ Attach to your tax return.

OMB No. 1545-0172
2006
Attachment Sequence No. **67**

Name(s) shown on return	Business or activity to which this form relates	Identifying number

Part I Election To Expense Certain Property Under Section 179
Note: *If you have any listed property, complete Part V before you complete Part I.*

1	Maximum amount. See the instructions for a higher limit for certain businesses	1	$108,000
2	Total cost of section 179 property placed in service (see instructions)	2	
3	Threshold cost of section 179 property before reduction in limitation	3	$430,000
4	Reduction in limitation. Subtract line 3 from line 2. If zero or less, enter -0-	4	
5	Dollar limitation for tax year. Subtract line 4 from line 1. If zero or less, enter -0-. If married filing separately, see instructions	5	

6	(a) Description of property	(b) Cost (business use only)	(c) Elected cost

7	Listed property. Enter the amount from line 29	7	
8	Total elected cost of section 179 property. Add amounts in column (c), lines 6 and 7	8	
9	Tentative deduction. Enter the **smaller** of line 5 or line 8	9	
10	Carryover of disallowed deduction from line 13 of your 2005 Form 4562	10	
11	Business income limitation. Enter the smaller of business income (not less than zero) or line 5 (see instructions)	11	
12	Section 179 expense deduction. Add lines 9 and 10, but do not enter more than line 11	12	
13	Carryover of disallowed deduction to 2007. Add lines 9 and 10, less line 12 ▶	13	

Note: *Do not use Part II or Part III below for listed property. Instead, use Part V.*

Part II Special Depreciation Allowance and Other Depreciation (Do not include listed property.) (See instructions.)

14	Special allowance for qualified New York Liberty or Gulf Opportunity Zone property (other than listed property) placed in service during the tax year (see instructions)	14	
15	Property subject to section 168(f)(1) election	15	
16	Other depreciation (including ACRS)	16	

Part III MACRS Depreciation (Do not include listed property.) (See instructions.)

Section A

17	MACRS deductions for assets placed in service in tax years beginning before 2006	17	
18	If you are electing to group any assets placed in service during the tax year into one or more general asset accounts, check here ▶ ☐		

Section B—Assets Placed in Service During 2006 Tax Year Using the General Depreciation System

(a) Classification of property	(b) Month and year placed in service	(c) Basis for depreciation (business/investment use only—see instructions)	(d) Recovery period	(e) Convention	(f) Method	(g) Depreciation deduction
19a 3-year property						
b 5-year property						
c 7-year property						
d 10-year property						
e 15-year property						
f 20-year property						
g 25-year property			25 yrs.		S/L	
h Residential rental property			27.5 yrs.	MM	S/L	
			27.5 yrs.	MM	S/L	
i Nonresidential real property			39 yrs.	MM	S/L	
				MM	S/L	

Section C—Assets Placed in Service During 2006 Tax Year Using the Alternative Depreciation System

20a Class life					S/L	
b 12-year			12 yrs.		S/L	
c 40-year			40 yrs.	MM	S/L	

Part IV Summary (see instructions)

21	Listed property. Enter amount from line 28	21	
22	**Total.** Add amounts from line 12, lines 14 through 17, lines 19 and 20 in column (g), and line 21. Enter here and on the appropriate lines of your return. Partnerships and S corporations—see instr.	22	
23	For assets shown above and placed in service during the current year, enter the portion of the basis attributable to section 263A costs	23	

For Paperwork Reduction Act Notice, see separate instructions. Cat. No. 12906N Form **4562** (2006)

(Use for Cumulative Problem).

Form 4562 (2006) Page **2**

Part V **Listed Property** (Include automobiles, certain other vehicles, cellular telephones, certain computers, and property used for entertainment, recreation, or amusement.)

Note: *For any vehicle for which you are using the standard mileage rate or deducting lease expense, complete* ***only*** *24a, 24b, columns (a) through (c) of Section A, all of Section B, and Section C if applicable.*

Section A—Depreciation and Other Information (Caution: *See the instructions for limits for passenger automobiles.***)**

24a Do you have evidence to support the business/investment use claimed? ☐ Yes ☐ No **24b** If "Yes," is the evidence written? ☐ Yes ☐ No

(a) Type of property (list vehicles first)	(b) Date placed in service	(c) Business/ investment use percentage	(d) Cost or other basis	(e) Basis for depreciation (business/investment use only)	(f) Recovery period	(g) Method/ Convention	(h) Depreciation deduction	(i) Elected section 179 cost
25 Special allowance for qualified New York Liberty or Gulf Opportunity Zone property placed in service during the tax year and used more than 50% in a qualified business use (see instructions) **25**								
26 Property used more than 50% in a qualified business use:								
		%						
		%						
		%						
27 Property used 50% or less in a qualified business use:								
		%				S/L –		
		%				S/L –		
		%				S/L –		
28 Add amounts in column (h), lines 25 through 27. Enter here and on line 21, page 1. . **28**								
29 Add amounts in column (i), line 26. Enter here and on line 7, page 1. . . . . **29**								

Section B—Information on Use of Vehicles

Complete this section for vehicles used by a sole proprietor, partner, or other "more than 5% owner," or related person.
If you provided vehicles to your employees, first answer the questions in Section C to see if you meet an exception to completing this section for those vehicles.

	(a) Vehicle 1		(b) Vehicle 2		(c) Vehicle 3		(d) Vehicle 4		(e) Vehicle 5		(f) Vehicle 6	
30 Total business/investment miles driven during the year (**do not** include commuting miles)												
31 Total commuting miles driven during the year												
32 Total other personal (noncommuting) miles driven												
33 Total miles driven during the year. Add lines 30 through 32												
	Yes	No	Yes	No	Yes	No	Yes	No	Yes	No	Yes	No
34 Was the vehicle available for personal use during off-duty hours?												
35 Was the vehicle used primarily by a more than 5% owner or related person?												
36 Is another vehicle available for personal use?												

Section C—Questions for Employers Who Provide Vehicles for Use by Their Employees

Answer these questions to determine if you meet an exception to completing Section B for vehicles used by employees who **are not** more than 5% owners or related persons (see instructions).

	Yes	No
37 Do you maintain a written policy statement that prohibits all personal use of vehicles, including commuting, by your employees?		
38 Do you maintain a written policy statement that prohibits personal use of vehicles, except commuting, by your employees? See the instructions for vehicles used by corporate officers, directors, or 1% or more owners		
39 Do you treat all use of vehicles by employees as personal use?		
40 Do you provide more than five vehicles to your employees, obtain information from your employees about the use of the vehicles, and retain the information received?		
41 Do you meet the requirements concerning qualified automobile demonstration use? (See instructions.)		
Note: *If your answer to 37, 38, 39, 40, or 41 is "Yes," do not complete Section B for the covered vehicles.*		

Part VI **Amortization**

(a) Description of costs	(b) Date amortization begins	(c) Amortizable amount	(d) Code section	(e) Amortization period or percentage	(f) Amortization for this year
42 Amortization of costs that begins during your 2006 tax year (see instructions):					
43 Amortization of costs that began before your 2006 tax year.				**43**	
44 **Total.** Add amounts in column (f). See the instructions for where to report.				**44**	

Printed on recycled paper Form **4562** (2006)

(Use for Cumulative Problem).

Form **8829** — Department of the Treasury, Internal Revenue Service (99)

Expenses for Business Use of Your Home

► File only with Schedule C (Form 1040). Use a separate Form 8829 for each home you used for business during the year.

► See separate instructions.

OMB No. 1545-0074 — **2006** — Attachment Sequence No. **66**

Name(s) of proprietor(s) | Your social security number

Part I Part of Your Home Used for Business

Line	Description			No.	Amount
1	Area used regularly and exclusively for business, regularly for daycare, or for storage of inventory or product samples (see instructions)			1	
2	Total area of home			2	
3	Divide line 1 by line 2. Enter the result as a percentage			3	%
	• **For daycare facilities not used exclusively for business, also complete lines 4–6.**				
	• **All others, skip lines 4–6 and enter the amount from line 3 on line 7.**				
4	Multiply days used for daycare during year by hours used per day	4	hr.		
5	Total hours available for use during the year (365 days × 24 hours) (see instructions)	5	8,760 hr.		
6	Divide line 4 by line 5. Enter the result as a decimal amount	6	.		
7	Business percentage. For daycare facilities not used exclusively for business, multiply line 6 by line 3 (enter the result as a percentage). All others, enter the amount from line 3 ►			7	%

Part II Figure Your Allowable Deduction

			(a) Direct expenses		(b) Indirect expenses		
8	Enter the amount from Schedule C, line 29, **plus** any net gain or (loss) derived from the business use of your home and shown on Schedule D or Form 4797. If more than one place of business, see instructions					8	
	See instructions for columns (a) and (b) before completing lines 9–20.						
9	Casualty losses (see instructions)	9					
10	Deductible mortgage interest (see instructions)	10					
11	Real estate taxes (see instructions)	11					
12	Add lines 9, 10, and 11	12					
13	Multiply line 12, column (b) by line 7			13			
14	Add line 12, column (a) and line 13					14	
15	Subtract line 14 from line 8. If zero or less, enter -0-					15	
16	Excess mortgage interest (see instructions)	16					
17	Insurance	17					
18	Repairs and maintenance	18					
19	Utilities	19					
20	Other expenses (see instructions)	20					
21	Add lines 16 through 20	21					
22	Multiply line 21, column (b) by line 7			22			
23	Carryover of operating expenses from 2005 Form 8829, line 41			23			
24	Add line 21 in column (a), line 22, and line 23					24	
25	Allowable operating expenses. Enter the **smaller** of line 15 or line 24					25	
26	Limit on excess casualty losses and depreciation. Subtract line 25 from line 15					26	
27	Excess casualty losses (see instructions)			27			
28	Depreciation of your home from Part III below			28			
29	Carryover of excess casualty losses and depreciation from 2005 Form 8829, line 42			29			
30	Add lines 27 through 29					30	
31	Allowable excess casualty losses and depreciation. Enter the **smaller** of line 26 or line 30					31	
32	Add lines 14, 25, and 31					32	
33	Casualty loss portion, if any, from lines 14 and 31. Carry amount to **Form 4684,** Section B					33	
34	Allowable expenses for business use of your home. Subtract line 33 from line 32. Enter here and on Schedule C, line 30. If your home was used for more than one business, see instructions ►					34	

Part III Depreciation of Your Home

35	Enter the **smaller** of your home's adjusted basis or its fair market value (see instructions)	35	
36	Value of land included on line 35	36	
37	Basis of building. Subtract line 36 from line 35	37	
38	Business basis of building. Multiply line 37 by line 7	38	
39	Depreciation percentage (see instructions)	39	%
40	Depreciation allowable (see instructions). Multiply line 38 by line 39. Enter here and on line 28 above	40	

Part IV Carryover of Unallowed Expenses to 2007

41	Operating expenses. Subtract line 25 from line 24. If less than zero, enter -0-	41	
42	Excess casualty losses and depreciation. Subtract line 31 from line 30. If less than zero, enter -0-	42	

For Paperwork Reduction Act Notice, see page 4 of separate instructions. Cat. No. 13232M Form **8829** (2006)

Printed on recycled paper

(Use for Cumulative Problem).

Qualified Dividends and Capital Gain Tax Worksheet—Line 44 *Keep for Your Records*

Before you begin:
√ See the instructions for line 44 that begin on page 36 to see if you can use this worksheet to figure your tax.
√ If you do not have to file Schedule D and you received capital gain distributions, be sure you checked the box on line 13 of Form 1040.

1. Enter the amount from Form 1040, line 43 . . . . 1. ______
2. Enter the amount from Form 1040, line 9b . . . . . . 2. ______
3. Are you filing Schedule D?
   - ☐ **Yes.** Enter the **smaller** of line 15 or 16 of Schedule D. If either line 15 or line 16 is a loss, enter -0-
   - ☐ **No.** Enter the amount from Form 1040, line 13

   3. ______
4. Add lines 2 and 3 . . . . 4. ______
5. If you are claiming investment interest expense on Form 4952, enter the amount from line 4g of that form. Otherwise, enter -0- . . . . 5. ______
6. Subtract line 5 from line 4. If zero or less, enter -0- . . . . 6. ______
7. Subtract line 6 from line 1. If zero or less, enter -0- . . . . 7. ______
8. Enter the **smaller** of:
   - The amount on line 1, or
   - $30,650 if single or married filing separately, $61,300 if married filing jointly or qualifying widow(er), $41,050 if head of household.

   . . . . 8. ______
9. Is the amount on line 7 equal to or more than the amount on line 8?
   - ☐ **Yes.** Skip lines 9 through 11; go to line 12 and check the ''No'' box.
   - ☐ **No.** Enter the amount from line 7 . . . . 9. ______
10. Subtract line 9 from line 8 . . . . 10. ______
11. Multiply line 10 by 5% (.05) . . . . 11. ______
12. Are the amounts on lines 6 and 10 the same?
    - ☐ **Yes.** Skip lines 12 through 15; go to line 16.
    - ☐ **No.** Enter the **smaller** of line 1 or line 6 . . . . 12. ______
13. Enter the amount from line 10 (if line 10 is blank, enter -0-) . . . . 13. ______
14. Subtract line 13 from line 12 . . . . 14. ______
15. Multiply line 14 by 15% (.15) . . . . 15. ______
16. Figure the tax on the amount on line 7. Use the Tax Table or Tax Computation Worksheet, whichever applies . . . . 16. ______
17. Add lines 11, 15, and 16 . . . . 17. ______
18. Figure the tax on the amount on line 1. Use the Tax Table or Tax Computation Worksheet, whichever applies . . . . 18. ______
19. **Tax on all taxable income.** Enter the **smaller** of line 17 or line 18. Also include this amount on Form 1040, line 44 . . . . 19. ______

13

Withholding, Payroll, and Estimated Taxes

CHAPTER CONTENTS

CHAPTER OVERVIEW

On January 1, 1943, the income of most wage earners became subject to pay-as-you-go withholding. Under this system, the government collects tax revenue by having the payer withhold taxes before distributing the income. This gives the government a steady cash flow and reduces tax collection problems. Withholding also lessens the cash burdens of taxpayers when they file their tax returns. This chapter provides background information about the tax withholding process.

Large depositors of payroll taxes, withheld income taxes, estimated income taxes, and various excise taxes must use the Treasury's electronic funds transfer (EFT) system to make their deposits. Since the rules do not affect small and medium-size depositors (those who deposit less than $200,000 a year), this chapter does not discuss the mechanics of the EFT system but instead focuses on the existing paper system.

ELECTRONIC DEPOSIT OF PAYROLL AND OTHER TAXES

The Treasury has developed an Electronic Funds Transfer (EFT) System for depositing the following:

- Payroll taxes
- Various excise taxes
- Withheld income taxes
- Corporate income and estimated taxes

Businesses with deposits in the previous year in excess of $200,000 must start making EFT deposits on January 1 of the next year. For example, businesses with more than $200,000 of deposits in 2005 must start making EFT deposits on January 1, 2007. Likewise, businesses with more than $200,000 of deposits in 2006 must start making EFT deposits on January 1, 2008.

WITHHOLDING SYSTEM

Under the pay-as-you-go system, *employers* withhold taxes from *employees*' wages that approximate their tax liabilities. Employers deposit these withholdings with a specified depository. To credit withholdings to the proper taxpayer accounts, each employee must have an identification number.

Identification Numbers

The IRS uses computer programs to process withholding data and taxpayer returns. Taxpayer identification numbers (TINs) provide the key to unlock related data. Individual taxpayers use their SSN (social security number) as their TIN. By law, employers request, receive, and enter a taxpayer's TIN on tax withholding and reporting forms.

Individuals

Individuals who need a SSN apply for one by filing Form SS-5, Application for a Social Security Card. Individuals can get Form SS-5 from any social security office or from the IRS website. All U.S. citizens, including infants, should obtain a SSN. This allows them to be claimed as a dependent on another's tax return. Also, taxpayers who claim the child tax credit must provide a SSN for each eligible child.

Businesses

Employers use an employer identification number (EIN) on payroll tax reporting forms, tax returns, and other government reports. Employers apply for an EIN by filing Form SS-4, Application for Employer Identification Number. Employers can get Form SS-4 from the IRS.

Withholding from Income

Withholding is based primarily on the employee's gross income from employment. This includes wages, salaries, fees, tips, bonuses, and commissions. From gross pay, an employer withholds income and payroll taxes (social security and Medicare taxes).

Withholding Allowance Certificate

Form W-4, Employee's Withholding Allowance Certificate, is the focal point of the income tax withholding system. The amount of income tax withheld from an employee's gross pay depends on the employee's filing status and the number of withholding allowances claimed on Form W-4. The more allowances claimed, the less tax withheld.

Employees receive withholding allowances for the personal and dependency exemptions they expect to claim in the current tax year. They also receive withholding allowances for anticipated deductions.

Employers request a Form W-4 from each employee. If an employee fails to furnish Form W-4, the employer withholds the maximum amount of taxes allowed for single taxpayers. Thus, married employees must complete Form W-4 to take advantage of the lower withholding rates.

Form W-4 has four sections. Each of these sections is described in the text that follows.

1. Personal Allowances Worksheet
2. Employee's Withholding Allowance Certificate
3. Deductions and Adjustments Worksheet
4. Two-Earner/Two-Job Worksheet

Personal Withholding Allowances

On the Personal Allowances Worksheet, employees enter whole numbers for personal withholding allowances (lines A through G). Single employees with more than one job, but no dependents, claim only one withholding allowance. They should claim this allowance with the employer that pays them the highest wage. At the other job(s), they should claim zero withholding allowances. Figure 13-1 describes the calculation of the withholding allowance on the Personal Allowances Worksheet for 2006.

An employee with more than one job or may want to request that an additional amount be withheld from each paycheck if combined wages exceed $35,000. This helps ensure that the employee will not be underwithheld for the year. Likewise, if the employee is married and both spouses work, each spouse may want to have additional amounts withheld from their respective paychecks when their combined wages exceed $25,000. Alternatively, they could ask their respective employers to withhold taxes at the single rate. They do this by marking an "X" in the box on the Form W-4 (line 3), "Married, but withhold at higher Single rate."

FIGURE 13-1 Personal Allowances Worksheet

A. One exemption allowance for the employee, as long as the employee does not qualify as a dependent on another person's return.
B. One additional exemption allowance for employees who are:
    1. Single and have only one job;
    2. Married, have one job, and their spouse does not work; or
    3. Married and their spouse's wages plus their second job wages do not exceed $1,000.
C. One exemption for the employee's spouse. However, the IRS recommends that married employees who have more than one job, or have spouses who work, claim a zero spousal allowance. This may avoid being underwithheld for the year.
D. One exemption for each person (other than the employee's spouse) who qualifies as the employee's dependent.
E. One exemption if the employee files as head of household.
F. One exemption if the employee plans to claim the child or dependent care credit for at least $1,500 of expenses.
G. Additional exemptions for employees who plan to claim the child tax credit.
    - For single employees, two exemptions are allowed for each eligible child if total income is expected to be less than $55,000. If total income between $55,000 and $84,000 is expected, one exemption is allowed for each eligible child, plus one additional exemption is allowed when there are more than three eligible children.
    - For married employees, two exemptions are allowed for each eligible child if total income is expected to be less than $82,000. If total income between $82,000 and $119,000 is expected, one exemption is allowed for each eligible child, plus one additional exemption is allowed when there are more than three eligible children.

Married couples with dependents can choose how to divide their withholding allowances among their employers. If the husband claims withholding allowances for a particular child on his Form W-4, the wife should not claim an allowance for that same child.

Employee's Withholding Allowance Certificate

After completing the other three parts of Form W-4, employees complete and sign Form W-4. They then clip the bottom portion of Form W-4 and give the Employee's Withholding Allowance Certificate to their employer. They keep the top portion for their records.

Deductions and Adjustments Allowances

The Deduction and Adjustments Worksheet helps employees compute additional allowances based on their expected itemized deductions and other adjustments to income. The employee estimates itemized deductions for the current year. To the extent the itemized deductions exceed the standard deduction, the excess is added to other adjustments the employee might have. The other adjustments include (1) IRA deductions, (2) moving expenses, (3) alimony paid, (4) penalties on early withdrawals of savings, (5) student loan interest, and (6) deductions for self-employed individuals. The total of excess itemized deductions and adjustments equals the employee's estimate of reductions for the year (line 5).

Next, the employee estimates the amount of nonwage income for the current year. Nonwage income includes (1) interest, (2) dividends, (3) taxable payments from retirement plans, (4) income or losses from passive activities, and (5) capital gains and losses. The nonwage income (line 6) is subtracted from the excess income reductions (line 5), resulting in the net reductions (line 7). A positive net reduction is divided by $3,300. This number (use whole numbers and round down any fraction) represents additional withholding allowances that the employee claims. A negative net reduction results in no additional allowances.

Use of the additional allowance helps bring withholdings more into line with the employee's actual tax liability. The employee adds the personal withholding allowances (page 1, line H) to the additional withholding allowances. Employees who do not use the Two-Earner/Two-Job Worksheet enter the total on page 1 of Form W-4 (line 5). Employees who use the Two-Earner/Two-Job Worksheet enter this total on the Two-Earner/Two Job Worksheet (line 1).

Additional Withholding for Two-Earner/Two-Job Employees

Employees who are married and whose spouses also work use the Two-Earner/Two-Job Worksheet (page 2) when combined earnings exceed $25,000. The same rule applies to unmarried employees with more than one job and combined earnings in excess of $35,000. The goal of this worksheet is to compute additional amounts employees should have withheld. The extra withholding helps employees avoid being underwithheld for the year.

Information for Figure 13-2: Filled-In Form W-4

Jerry J. Page starts a new job in January, 2006. Jerry must complete Form W-4 for his new employer. He expects to file a joint tax return for 2006 with his wife Belle. For 2006 Jerry expects to earn $46,000; Belle expects to earn $33,000. The Pages provide all the support for their two children, who have no income. Both are eligible children for purposes of the child tax credit. They decide that Jerry will claim all withholding allowances. The Pages estimate that they will pay or receive the following amounts during 2006.

Deductible IRA payment for Belle	$4,000
Deductible IRA payment for Jerry	4,000
Child and dependent care expenses	2,300
Interest income on corporate bonds	500
Dividend income	250
Home mortgage interest	8,460
Property taxes	2,750
State income taxes	2,300
Charitable contributions	540

Personal Allowances Worksheet, page 1

Other Information

C: The Pages choose to enter -0- because both spouses work
F: Enter **1** because the Pages expect to have at least $1,500 of child care expenses
G: Enter **4.** The Pages expect their total income to be less than $82,000, so they enter two exemptions for each eligible child.

Deductions and Adjustments Worksheet, page 2

Other Information

1: Estimate of itemized deductions, **$14,050** ($8,460 + $2,750 + $2,300 + $540)
4: Estimate of adjustments to income, **$8,000** ($4,000 + $4,000 IRA deductions)
6: Nonwage income, **$750** ($500 + $250)
8: $11,000 ÷ $3,300 = **3** when the fraction is dropped

Two-Earner/Two-Job Worksheet, page 2

Other Information

1: Number from line 10 of the Deduction and Adjustments Worksheet, **11**
2: Table 1 number that applies to $46,000 and $33,000, **6**

Changing Withholding Allowances

Employees are not required to file a new Form W-4 with their employer each year. However, the employee should make sure that the form on file indicates the proper number of allowances for the year. While the IRS does not assess penalties for being overwithheld, it does assess a penalty for being underwithheld. Therefore, when an employee's withholding allowances decrease, a new Form W-4 should be filed within ten days of the changing event (such as divorce). When an employee's withholding allowances increase, the employee can file a new Form W-4 or leave the old Form W-4 in effect. When a continuing employee files an updated Form W-4, the employer places it in effect at the beginning of the next payroll period or 30 days after an employer receives the new Form W-4, whichever is later.

The death of a spouse or dependent in the current year does not change an employee's withholding allowances. However, an employee should file a new Form W-4 by December 1 to ensure that it becomes effective at the start of the next tax year. For the two years after a spouse's death, surviving spouses who has a dependents son or daughter living with them can use the married filing jointly tax rates and standard deduction (Chapter 1). However, the surviving spouse cannot claim a withholding allowance for the deceased spouse. A surviving spouse should take these facts into consideration when completing Form W-4.

Exemption from Withholding

Certain employees can claim exemption from federal income tax withholding on Form W-4. However, social security and Medicare taxes must still be withheld. The provision to claim exemption from withholding of federal income taxes helps people who work short periods or earn small amounts. Without this provision, employers would withhold taxes from employees with no tax liability. If an employer does withhold taxes, the employee would need to file a tax return just to get back the amounts withheld.

To claim exemption from withholding in 2006, an employee must have had no federal income tax liability in 2005. Also, the employee must not expect to owe any federal income taxes for 2006. Also, dependents with income in excess of $850 that includes more than $300 of unearned income cannot claim an exemption from withholding.

FIGURE 13-2 Filled-In Form W-4, Employee's Withholding Allowance Certificate, Page 1

Form W-4 (2006)

Purpose. Complete Form W-4 so that your employer can withhold the correct federal income tax from your pay. Because your tax situation may change, you may want to refigure your withholding each year.

Exemption from withholding. If you are exempt, complete only lines 1, 2, 3, 4, and 7 and sign the form to validate it. Your exemption for 2006 expires February 16, 2007. See Pub. 505, Tax Withholding and Estimated Tax.

Note. You cannot claim exemption from withholding if (a) your income exceeds $850 and includes more than $300 of unearned income (for example, interest and dividends) and (b) another person can claim you as a dependent on their tax return.

Basic instructions. If you are not exempt, complete the **Personal Allowances Worksheet** below. The worksheets on page 2 adjust your withholding allowances based on itemized deductions, certain credits, adjustments to income, or two-earner/two-job situations. Complete all worksheets that apply. However, you may claim fewer (or zero) allowances.

Head of household. Generally, you may claim head of household filing status on your tax return only if you are unmarried and pay more than 50% of the costs of keeping up a home for yourself and your dependent(s) or other qualifying individuals. See line **E** below.

Tax credits. You can take projected tax credits into account in figuring your allowable number of withholding allowances. Credits for child or dependent care expenses and the child tax credit may be claimed using the **Personal Allowances Worksheet** below. See Pub. 919, How Do I Adjust My Tax Withholding, for information on converting your other credits into withholding allowances.

Nonwage income. If you have a large amount of nonwage income, such as interest or dividends, consider making estimated tax payments using Form 1040-ES, Estimated Tax for Individuals. Otherwise, you may owe additional tax.

Two earners/two jobs. If you have a working spouse or more than one job, figure the total number of allowances you are entitled to claim on all jobs using worksheets from only one Form W-4. Your withholding usually will be most accurate when all allowances are claimed on the Form W-4 for the highest paying job and zero allowances are claimed on the others.

Nonresident alien. If you are a nonresident alien, see the Instructions for Form 8233 before completing this Form W-4.

Check your withholding. After your Form W-4 takes effect, use Pub. 919 to see how the dollar amount you are having withheld compares to your projected total tax for 2006. See Pub. 919, especially if your earnings exceed $130,000 (Single) or $180,000 (Married).

Recent name change? If your name on line 1 differs from that shown on your social security card, call 1-800-772-1213 to initiate a name change and obtain a social security card showing your correct name.

Personal Allowances Worksheet (Keep for your records.)

- **A** Enter "1" for **yourself** if no one else can claim you as a dependent . . . . . **A** 1
- **B** Enter "1" if: • You are single and have only one job; or • You are married, have only one job, and your spouse does not work; or • Your wages from a second job or your spouse's wages (or the total of both) are $1,000 or less. . . **B** ____
- **C** Enter "1" for your **spouse.** But, you may choose to enter "-0-" if you are married and have either a working spouse or more than one job. (Entering "-0-" may help you avoid having too little tax withheld.) . . . . **C** 0
- **D** Enter number of **dependents** (other than your spouse or yourself) you will claim on your tax return . . . **D** 2
- **E** Enter "1" if you will file as **head of household** on your tax return (see conditions under **Head of household** above) . **E** ____
- **F** Enter "1" if you have at least $1,500 of **child or dependent care expenses** for which you plan to claim a credit . . **F** 1
  (**Note.** Do **not** include child support payments. See **Pub. 503,** Child and Dependent Care Expenses, for details.)
- **G** **Child Tax Credit** (including additional child tax credit):
  - If your total income will be less than $55,000 ($82,000 if married), enter "2" for each eligible child.
  - If your total income will be between $55,000 and $84,000 ($82,000 and $119,000 if married), enter "1" for each eligible child plus "1" **additional** if you have four or more eligible children. **G** 4
- **H** Add lines A through G and enter total here. (**Note.** This may be different from the number of exemptions you claim on your tax return.) ▶ **H** 8

For accuracy, complete all worksheets that apply.
- If you plan to **itemize or claim adjustments to income** and want to reduce your withholding, see the **Deductions and Adjustments Worksheet** on page 2.
- If you have **more than one job** or are **married and you and your spouse both work** and the combined earnings from all jobs exceed $35,000 ($25,000 if married) see the **Two-Earner/Two-Job Worksheet** on page 2 to avoid having too little tax withheld.
- If **neither** of the above situations applies, **stop here** and enter the number from line H on line 5 of Form W-4 below.

Cut here and give Form W-4 to your employer. Keep the top part for your records.

Form **W-4** — Department of the Treasury, Internal Revenue Service

Employee's Withholding Allowance Certificate

▶ **Whether you are entitled to claim a certain number of allowances or exemption from withholding is subject to review by the IRS. Your employer may be required to send a copy of this form to the IRS.**

OMB No. 1545-0074 — **2006**

1 Type or print your first name and middle initial.	Last name	2 Your social security number
Jerry J.	Page	432 : 16 : 8410

Home address (number and street or rural route)	3 ☐ Single ☒ Married ☐ Married, but withhold at higher Single rate.
1222 West Main Street	Note. If married, but legally separated, or spouse is a nonresident alien, check the "Single" box.
City or town, state, and ZIP code	4 **If your last name differs from that shown on your social security card, check here. You must call 1-800-772-1213 for a new card.** ▶ ☐
San Diego, CA 91344-8135	

- **5** Total number of allowances you are claiming (from line **H** above **or** from the applicable worksheet on page 2) **5** 5
- **6** Additional amount, if any, you want withheld from each paycheck . . . . . **6** $ 0
- **7** I claim exemption from withholding for 2006, and I certify that I meet **both** of the following conditions for exemption.
  - Last year I had a right to a refund of **all** federal income tax withheld because I had **no** tax liability **and**
  - This year I expect a refund of **all** federal income tax withheld because I expect to have **no** tax liability.

  If you meet both conditions, write "Exempt" here . . . . . ▶ **7**

Under penalties of perjury, I declare that I have examined this certificate and to the best of my knowledge and belief, it is true, correct, and complete.

Employee's signature (Form is not valid unless you sign it.) ▶ *Jerry J. Page* **Date** ▶ January 15, 2006

8 Employer's name and address (Employer: Complete lines 8 and 10 only if sending to the IRS.)	9 Office code (optional)	10 Employer identification number (EIN)

For Privacy Act and Paperwork Reduction Act Notice, see page 2. Cat. No. 10220Q Form **W-4** (2006)

FIGURE 13-2: Filled-In Form W-4, Employee's Withholding Allowance Certificate, Page 2

Form W-4 (2006) Page **2**

Deductions and Adjustments Worksheet

Note. Use this worksheet *only* if you plan to itemize deductions, claim certain credits, or claim adjustments to income on your 2006 tax return.

1	Enter an estimate of your 2006 itemized deductions. These include qualifying home mortgage interest, charitable contributions, state and local taxes, medical expenses in excess of 7.5% of your income, and miscellaneous deductions. (For 2006, you may have to reduce your itemized deductions if your income is over $150,500 ($75,250 if married filing separately). See *Worksheet 3* in Pub. 919 for details.) . . .	1	$ 14,050
2	Enter: { $10,300 if married filing jointly or qualifying widow(er); $ 7,550 if head of household; $ 5,150 if single or married filing separately }	2	$ 10,300
3	**Subtract** line 2 from line 1. If line 2 is greater than line 1, enter "-0-"	3	$ 3,750
4	Enter an estimate of your 2006 adjustments to income, including alimony, deductible IRA contributions, and student loan interest	4	$ 8,000
5	**Add** lines 3 and 4 and enter the total. (Include any amount for credits from *Worksheet 7* in Pub. 919) .	5	$ 11,750
6	Enter an estimate of your 2006 nonwage income (such as dividends or interest)	6	$ 750
7	**Subtract** line 6 from line 5. Enter the result, but not less than "-0-"	7	$ 11,000
8	**Divide** the amount on line 7 by $3,300 and enter the result here. Drop any fraction	8	3
9	Enter the number from the **Personal Allowances Worksheet,** line H, page 1	9	8
10	**Add** lines 8 and 9 and enter the total here. If you plan to use the **Two-Earner/Two-Job Worksheet,** also enter this total on line 1 below. Otherwise, **stop here** and enter this total on Form W-4, line 5, page 1 .	10	11

Two-Earner/Two-Job Worksheet (See *Two earners/two jobs* on page 1.)

Note. Use this worksheet *only* if the instructions under line H on page 1 direct you here.

1	Enter the number from line H, page 1 (or from line 10 above if you used the **Deductions and Adjustments Worksheet**)	1	11
2	Find the number in **Table 1** below that applies to the **LOWEST** paying job and enter it here	2	6
3	If line 1 is **more than or equal to** line 2, subtract line 2 from line 1. Enter the result here (if zero, enter "-0-") and on Form W-4, line 5, page 1. **Do not** use the rest of this worksheet	3	5

Note. If line 1 is *less than* line 2, enter "-0-" on Form W-4, line 5, page 1. Complete lines 4–9 below to calculate the additional withholding amount necessary to avoid a year-end tax bill.

4	Enter the number from line 2 of this worksheet . . . . 4 ______		
5	Enter the number from line 1 of this worksheet . . . . 5 ______		
6	**Subtract** line 5 from line 4	6	
7	Find the amount in **Table 2** below that applies to the **HIGHEST** paying job and enter it here	7	$
8	**Multiply** line 7 by line 6 and enter the result here. This is the additional annual withholding needed . .	8	$
9	Divide line 8 by the number of pay periods remaining in 2006. For example, divide by 26 if you are paid every two weeks and you complete this form in December 2005. Enter the result here and on Form W-4, line 6, page 1. This is the additional amount to be withheld from each paycheck	9	$

Table 1: Two-Earner/Two-Job Worksheet

Married Filing Jointly

If wages from **HIGHEST** paying job are—	AND, wages from **LOWEST** paying job are—	Enter on line 2 above
$0 - $42,000	$0 - $4,500	0
	4,501 - 9,000	1
	9,001 - 18,000	2
	18,001 and over	3
$42,001 and over	$0 - $4,500	0
	4,501 - 9,000	1
	9,001 - 18,000	2
	18,001 - 22,000	3
	22,001 - 26,000	4
	26,001 - 32,000	5

If wages from **HIGHEST** paying job are—	AND, wages from **LOWEST** paying job are—	Enter on line 2 above
$42,001 and over	32,001 - 38,000	6
	38,001 - 46,000	7
	46,001 - 55,000	8
	55,001 - 60,000	9
	60,001 - 65,000	10
	65,001 - 75,000	11
	75,001 - 95,000	12
	95,001 - 105,000	13
	105,001 - 120,000	14
	120,001 and over	15

All Others

If wages from **LOWEST** paying job are—	Enter on line 2 above
$0 - $6,000	0
6,001 - 12,000	1
12,001 - 19,000	2
19,001 - 26,000	3
26,001 - 35,000	4
35,001 - 50,000	5
50,001 - 65,000	6
65,001 - 80,000	7
80,001 - 90,000	8
90,001 - 120,000	9
120,001 and over	10

Table 2: Two-Earner/Two-Job Worksheet

Married Filing Jointly

If wages from **HIGHEST** paying job are—	Enter on line 7 above
$0 - $60,000	$500
60,001 - 115,000	830
115,001 - 165,000	920
165,001 - 290,000	1,090
290,001 and over	1,160

All Others

If wages from **HIGHEST** paying job are—	Enter on line 7 above
$0 - $30,000	$500
30,001 - 75,000	830
75,001 - 145,000	920
145,001 - 330,000	1,090
330,001 and over	1,160

Privacy Act and Paperwork Reduction Act Notice. We ask for the information on this form to carry out the Internal Revenue laws of the United States. The Internal Revenue Code requires this information under sections 3402(f)(2)(A) and 6109 and their regulations. Failure to provide a properly completed form will result in your being treated as a single person who claims no withholding allowances; providing fraudulent information may also subject you to penalties. Routine uses of this information include giving it to the Department of Justice for civil and criminal litigation, to cities, states, and the District of Columbia for use in administering their tax laws, and using it in the National Directory of New Hires. We may also disclose this information to other countries under a tax treaty, to federal and state agencies to enforce federal nontax criminal laws, or to federal law enforcement and intelligence agencies to combat terrorism.

You are not required to provide the information requested on a form that is subject to the Paperwork Reduction Act unless the form displays a valid OMB control number. Books or records relating to a form or its instructions must be retained as long as their contents may become material in the administration of any Internal Revenue law. Generally, tax returns and return information are confidential, as required by Code section 6103.

The average time and expenses required to complete and file this form will vary depending on individual circumstances. For estimated averages, see the instructions for your income tax return.

If you have suggestions for making this form simpler, we would be happy to hear from you. See the instructions for your income tax return.

Printed on recycled paper

The exemption from withholding for a given year expires on February 15 of the next year. Employees who wish to continue a withholding exemption for the next year must file a new Form W-4 by February 15. They must revoke the exemption within 10 days of an event that causes them to no longer qualify as exempt.

EXAMPLE 1

Jamie Landis's parents claim her as a dependent. She has never filed a tax return. Landis is in the process of filling out her first W-4 for her job. Landis expects her total income for the year to be about $1,500. She has no other sources of taxable income. Thus, her standard deduction will reduce her taxable income to $0. Landis can claim exemption from withholding for the current year. She can do this because (1) she has no unearned income, (2) she had no federal income tax liability in the previous year, and (3) she does not expect to owe taxes in the current year.

EXAMPLE 2

Same as in Example 1 except that Landis will earn about $500 of taxable interest from bonds given to her by her parents. Because Landis's income exceeds $850 and more than $300 of that amount comes from unearned sources, Landis cannot claim exemption from withholding. Any amounts her employer withholds in excess of her tax liability can be refunded to her when she files her tax return for the current tax year.

FICA TAXES

FICA provides for an old age, survivors, and disability insurance (OASDI) tax. FICA also provides for a health insurance (HI) tax. On Form W-2, the IRS calls the OASDI portion the **social security tax.** It calls the HI portion the **Medicare tax.** The government assesses an equal amount of FICA taxes on employers and employees. Each employer withholds the employee's share of FICA from the employee's wages, then matches that amount using the employer's funds, and deposits both shares (employer and employee) with a specified depository.

Social Security and Medicare Taxes

The social security or OASDI tax rate equals 6.2%. For 2006, employers apply the rate to each employee's wages up to $94,200. This includes employees who have reached the maximum wage base with another employer. However, an employee's total OASDI tax for 2006 cannot exceed $5,840.40 (6.2% × $94,200). Thus, an employee who works for two or more employers may qualify to get a refund. This refund is claimed in the "Payments" section of Form 1040, page 2. The Medicare or HI tax rate equals 1.45%. The HI rate applies to employees' total wages. This includes employees who work for another employer.

Special FICA Situations

Not all wages nor are all employees subject to FICA withholding. Moreover, certain types of income receive special FICA withholding treatment.

Family Employees of a Business

Taxpayers do not withhold FICA on wages paid to their children under the age of 18 who work for them in their businesses. This rule applies only when the parent's business is operated as a sole proprietorship. Once the child turns 18, the child's wages are subject to FICA withholding. Wages paid to a spouse who works for the taxpayer's business are subject to FICA withholding.

Household Employees

Household employees can include maids, babysitters, private nurses, gardeners, and nannies. These employees are subject to FICA withholding if they are paid $1,500 or more during 2006. This rule does not apply to individuals who are under age 18 at any time during the calendar year. It also does not apply to wages paid to a spouse, the taxpayer's child under age 21, and in most instances, a parent. Employers of household workers report both their share and their employee's share of the social security and Medicare taxes they withheld on their Form 1040. Schedule H documents the amount reported in the "Other Taxes" section of Form 1040, page 2.

Employee Fringe Benefits

Nontaxable fringe benefits are not subject to FICA taxes. However, taxable fringe benefits may be subject to FICA withholding. For example, personal use of a company car and group term life insurance purchased for the employee in excess of the excludable amount are subject to FICA withholding.

Penalty for Failure to Collect or Deposit Taxes

The IRS can assess a 100% penalty against employers who fail to collect or deposit FICA taxes. The 100% penalty does not apply to direct taxes (federal unemployment tax or employer's share of FICA taxes). The IRS can assess the penalty against (1) employers who willfully try to avoid withholding income and payroll taxes by classifying employees as independent contractors and (2) employees responsible for an employer's tax withholdings. However, the employee must have the authority to decide which creditors receive payment when a shortage of funds exists.

REPORTING TO EMPLOYEES AND THE GOVERNMENT

In January, employers prepare a Form W-2, Wage and Tax Statement, for each employee. Thus, in January 2007, employers prepare a 2006 Form W-2 for each employee. Form W-2 shows an employee's gross wages, wages subject to OASDI withholding and wages subject to HI withholding. Form W-2 also shows the income taxes withheld as well as amounts withheld for OASDI and HI. Form W-2 can show an employee's pension plan contributions, state income taxes withheld, and other items. When filing their tax return, an employee attaches one copy of Form W-2 (Copy B) to the tax return.

Distribution of Forms W-2

Employers prepare six copies of Form W-2 for each employee. They send Copy A, along with Form W-3, Transmittal of Wage and Tax Statements, to the Social Security Administration before March 1. If applicable, they file Copy 1 with the proper state or local government agency. Employers send Copies B, C, and 2 to each employee before February 1. The employer keeps Copy D.

When employment ends before the close of a calendar year, employers still send former employees their copies of Form W-2 before February 1 of the next year. Former employees can request a Form W-2 before this date. When requested, employers must give former employees their Form W-2 by the later of 30 days after the request or 30 days after the last wage payment.

Form W-2

A machine usually reads Copy A of Form W-2. Therefore, if possible, the forms should be typed and without erasures, whiteouts, or strikeovers. The employer should make all dollar entries without dollar signs or commas, but with decimal points (00000.00). The rest of this section describes the information contained on Form W-2. Not all boxes are covered since many are self-explanatory. For a full description of all boxes on Form W-2, see the *Instructions for Form W-2* provided by the IRS.

Control Number (Box a)

Employers can assign control numbers of up to seven digits to identify individual Forms W-2. Employers should include this number on any correspondence with the Social Security Administration regarding an individual Form W-2.

Void

Employers mark this box when a form contains an incorrect entry. The employer cannot simply discard a Form W-2 containing a mistake. The government printing office prints two Forms W-2 on a single sheet of paper. Copy A, sent to the Social Security Administration, cannot be cut or separated. Therefore, Forms W-2 with errors also get sent to the Social Security Administration.

Box 12

Employers complete this box to report up to four items of information. For each item, a code and the dollar amount are listed. Examples of items reported in this box include:

1. Taxable amounts for providing the employee with more than $50,000 of group life insurance (Code C)
2. Elective deferrals to a section 401(k) plan (Code D)
3. Elective deferrals under a salary reduction SEP (Code F)
4. Nontaxable sick pay (Code J)
5. Reimbursements received from a nonaccountable plan (Code L)
6. Excludable moving expense reimbursements (Code P)
7. Employee salary reduction contributions to a SIMPLE plan not part of a 401(k) plan (Code S)
8. Amounts received under an adoption assistance program (Code T)

Statutory Employee, Retirement Plan, Third-Party Sick Pay (Box 13)

Employers place an *X* in the proper square (box 13) to identify the employee or Form W-2 situation.

Statutory Employee. Employers withhold FICA taxes, but not federal income taxes, from **statutory employee** wages. Statutory employees include certain employees from one of four occupation groups. Group 1 includes drivers who are agents of the employer or those who deliver laundry, dry-cleaning, and food products (other than milk) to customers and who are paid on commission. Group 2 includes full-time life insurance salespersons. Group 3 includes workers who work at home using materials provided by and returned to the employer. Group 4 includes traveling or city salespersons who take orders on behalf of the employer. To qualify as statutory employees, group members must meet the three tests shown below.

1. Work under a service contract that states or implies that they will provide most of the services,
2. Work in a continuing (ongoing) employment relationship, and
3. Have little or no investment in the equipment or property used to perform the contracted services (other than transportation facilities).

Retirement Plan. This square identifies active participants in the employer's retirement plan. Recall from Chapter 4 that limits may apply to the deduction for IRA contributions for taxpayers who are active participants in an employer's retirement plan. Employers do not mark this square for contributions to nonqualified pension plans or Section 457 plans. Section 457 covers the deferred compensation plans of state and local governments.

Third-Party Sick Pay. This square is checked only if the payer is a third-party sick pay provider filing Form W-2 for an insured's employee.

Other (Box 14)

Employers use this box to provide any other information they feel is necessary to their employees. Each amount is labeled by its type. Items that may be listed include union dues, health insurance premiums deducted, nontaxable income, voluntary after-tax contributions to retirement plans, and educational assistance payments.

WHEN EMPLOYEES SHOULD RECEIVE A W-2

1. When they had income tax or FICA taxes withheld from wages
2. When they would have had income taxes withheld from wages had they not claimed more than one withholding allowance exemption or had not claimed exemption from withholding

---

Information for Figure 13-3: Filled-In Form W-2

Harriet R. Shawver works for Anderson, Berger, and Green (ABG). From Shawver's $43,500 of wages, ABG withheld $7,356 for federal; $2,039 for state; $2,697 for social security (OASDI); and $630.75 for Medicare (HI) taxes.

Form W-3

Employers send to the Social Security Administration Copy A, Form W-2, for all employees along with Form W-3, Transmittal of Income and Tax Statements. These forms must reach the employer's regional Social Security Administration Data Operations Center by March 1. When completing Form W-3, employers type all data entries, omitting dollar signs and commas but using decimal points and zeros to show cents (00000.00). The amounts on Form W-3 represent the totals from all the amounts on all Copies A of Forms W-2 attached (except Forms W-2 that were voided). The actual person who completes Form W-3 signs it, certifying the correctness and completeness of it and of the accompanying Forms W-2.

This section describes the data contained on Form W-3. However, it does not cover every box since most boxes contain clear descriptive headings. The instructions for Form W-3 describe the data needs of all boxes.

FIGURE 13-3 Filled-In Form W-2, Wage and Tax Statement

a Control number 22222	Void ☐	For Official Use Only ▶ OMB No. 1545-0008

	1 Wages, tips, other compensation	2 Federal income tax withheld
b Employer identification number (EIN) 92-0446587	43500.00	7356.00
c Employer's name, address, and ZIP code Anderson, Berger, and Green 2700 South Park Avenue Milwaukee, WI 53202-2645	3 Social security wages 43500.00	4 Social security tax withheld 2697.00
	5 Medicare wages and tips 43500.00	6 Medicare tax withheld 630.75
	7 Social security tips	8 Allocated tips
d Employee's social security number 364-74-6560	9 Advance EIC payment	10 Dependent care benefits
e Employee's first name and initial Harriet R. — Last name Shawver — Suff.	11 Nonqualified plans	12a See instructions for box 12
2123 Fairmount Drive Milwaukee, WI 53209-3685	13 Statutory employee ☐ Retirement plan ☐ Third-party sick pay ☐	12b
	14 Other	12c
f Employee's address and ZIP code		12d

15 State	Employer's state ID number	16 State wages, tips, etc.	17 State income tax	18 Local wages, tips, etc.	19 Local income tax	20 Locality name
WI	104693	43500.00	2039.00			

Form **W-2** **Wage and Tax Statement** **2006**

Department of the Treasury—Internal Revenue Service

For Privacy Act and Paperwork Reduction Act Notice, see back of Copy D.

Copy A For Social Security Administration — Send this entire page with Form W-3 to the Social Security Administration; photocopies are **not** acceptable.

Cat. No. 10134D

Do Not Cut, Fold, or Staple Forms on This Page — Do Not Cut, Fold, or Staple Forms on This Page

Control Number (Box a)

As with Form W-2, employers can assign a *control* number of up to seven digits or leave the box blank.

Kind of Payer (Box b)

Employers check one of the following six groups:

1. *941.* Check this square when filing Form 941 and no other group applies.
2. *Military.* Check this square when sending Forms W-2 for members of the armed forces.
3. *943.* Check this square when filing Forms 943 for agricultural employees. Employers of agricultural and nonagricultural workers send a separate Form W-3.
4. *CT-1.* Check this square when sending Forms W-2 for employees under the Railroad Retirement Tax Act (RRTA).
5. *Hshld. emp.* Check this square when sending Forms W-2 for household workers. Employers of household workers and nonhousehold workers send a separate Form W-3 with each group of Forms W-2.
6. *Medicare gov't. emp.* Check this box for government and local agency employees subject to the 1.45% Medicare (HI) tax.
7. *Third-party sick pay.* Check this box if the payer is a third-party sick pay provider filing Form W-2 for an insured's employee.

Total Number of Forms W-2 (Box c)

Employers enter the number of individual Forms W-2 they are sending with Form W-3. However, they exclude voided forms from the count.

Establishment Number (Box d)

Employers enter a four-digit number to identify separate establishments of their business. For each establishment, employers file a separate Form W-3 with related Forms W-2. They file a separate Form W-3 even though each establishment has the same EIN.

Employer's State I.D. Number (Box 15)

A state in which an employer does business may assign a state I.D. number. Employers that report in two states enter one state's I.D. number in each box.

Information for Figure 13-4: Filled-In Form W-3

Martinez Enterprises, Inc., sends two Forms W-2 (Copy A) to the Social Security Administration with Form W-3. The wages for the two employees total $87,560. For both employees, social security (OASDI) and Medicare (HI) wages were the same as overall wages. Federal income tax withheld for the two employees was $13,518.40. Social security and Medicare taxes withheld were $5,428.72 and $1,269.62, respectively. Since Florida does not have a state income tax, lines 15–19 are blank.

FIGURE 13-4 Filled-In Form W-3, Transmittal of Wage and Tax Statements

DO NOT STAPLE

33333 a Control number 01	For Official Use Only ► OMB No. 1545-0008	
b Kind of Payer: 941 [X] Military [ ] 943 [ ] 944 [ ] CT-1 [ ] Hshld. emp. [ ] Medicare govt. emp. [ ] Third-party sick pay [ ]	1 Wages, tips, other compensation 87560.00	2 Federal income tax withheld 13518.40
	3 Social security wages 87560.00	4 Social security tax withheld 5428.72
c Total number of Forms W-2 2 / d Establishment number	5 Medicare wages and tips 87560.00	6 Medicare tax withheld 1269.62
e Employer identification number (EIN) 91-0118224	7 Social security tips	8 Allocated tips
f Employer's name Martinez Enterprises, Inc. 64 Bay Road Miami, FL 33139-5670	9 Advance EIC payments	10 Dependent care benefits
	11 Nonqualified plans	12 Deferred compensation
	13 For third-party sick pay use only	
g Employer's address and ZIP code	14 Income tax withheld by payer of third-party sick pay	
h Other EIN used this year		
15 State Employer's state ID number	16 State wages, tips, etc.	17 State income tax
	18 Local wages, tips, etc.	19 Local income tax
Contact person Edward L. Martinez	Telephone number (305) 555-3544	For Official Use Only
Email address	Fax number ( )	

Under penalties of perjury, I declare that I have examined this return and accompanying documents, and, to the best of my knowledge and belief, they are true, correct, and complete.

Signature ► *Edward L. Martinez* Title ► President Date ► 1/29/2007

UNEMPLOYMENT TAXES

In conjunction with state unemployment systems, the Federal Unemployment Tax Act (FUTA) furnishes payments to workers who have lost their jobs. The funds for the unemployment compensation come solely from employers. Employers make no withholdings from employees for this tax. Most employers pay taxes into both the state and the federal systems.

Rate and Base

Employers pay a maximum unemployment tax of 6.2% on the first $7,000 of each employee's taxable wages in the calendar year. For computing FUTA taxes, employees do not include the following:

1. Children under age 21 who work for their parents
2. Spouses working for the other spouse
3. Parents working for their children
4. Statutory employees who work at home
5. Domestic workers (nannies, gardeners, housekeepers, etc.) who earn less than $1,000 each quarter in both the current and preceding calendar years

Employers generally reduce the FUTA tax rate by the *lesser of* 5.4% or the rate paid to their state unemployment tax fund. Thus, after the reduction for the state, the net FUTA rate may be as low as 0.8% (6.2% – 5.4%). Employers who pay a proper state unemployment rate but do not pay the state tax on time reduce their state credit by 10%.

Without an extension of the FUTA filing date, employers must file their FUTA returns by January 31 of the next year. Depending on the situation, employers use either Form 940 or Form 940EZ, Employer's Annual Federal Unemployment (FUTA) Tax Return. Both forms have the same name. If employers make tax deposits on a timely basis, they may file the Form 940 or 940EZ by February 10.

EXAMPLE 3

Wild Card has two employees, Susan and Mike Thompson. During 2006 Susan and Mike earned taxable gross wages of $10,000 and $5,000, respectively. The Thompsons live and work in a state with a 5.4% unemployment tax. Wild Card pays the state unemployment tax by January 31, 2007. For 2006 Wild Card pays $96 of FUTA tax ($56 for Susan and $40 for Mike).

	Susan	**Mike**
Gross wages	$10,000	$ 5,000
Lesser of $7,000 or gross wages	$ 7,000	$ 5,000
Times net FUTA rate (6.2% – 5.4%)	× 0.8%	× 0.8%
FUTA tax	$ 56	$ 40

Depositing FUTA Taxes

Employers deposit FUTA taxes with an authorized depository when their debt exceeds $500. The FUTA tax is due on the last day of the month that follows the end of a quarter. When an employer's FUTA debt for any quarter does not exceed $500, the deposit due carries over to the next quarter. Employers with a fourth-quarter FUTA tax of $500 or less can either pay the tax when they file their FUTA return or make a deposit. If the fourth-quarter FUTA tax exceeds $500, they deposit the tax with an authorized depository by January 31. Making a timely deposit extends the due date for filing the FUTA return until February 10. When a deposit date falls on a Saturday, Sunday, or banking holiday, the deposit is timely if made by the next business banking day.

FUTA TAX DEPOSIT DUE DATES

Quarter Ending	Due Date
March 31	April 30
June 30	July 31
September 30	October 31
December 31	January 31

EXAMPLE 4

After reduction by the state unemployment credit, the Bucket Company's quarterly FUTA taxes for 2007 are: first, $235; second, $250; third, $245; and fourth, $200. No deposits are needed for the first and second quarters since the cumulative debt does not exceed $500 until the third quarter. Bucket must deposit $730 ($235 + $250 + $245) by October 31, 2007. For the fourth quarter, Bucket can either deposit the tax by January 31, 2008, or include the payment when filing its FUTA return. If Bucket makes timely deposits of its 2007 FUTA taxes, the due date for its FUTA tax return is extended to February 11, 2008 (February 10, 2008 falls on a Sunday).

WITHHOLDING ON PENSIONS, ANNUITIES, AND DEFERRED INCOME

Withholding of income taxes also applies to the taxable part of distributions from pensions, profit-sharing plans, individual retirement accounts, annuities, and deferred compensation plans. Unless recipients of pension and annuity payments ask for no withholding, payers must withhold taxes. Recipients can request nonwithholding for any reason. They do so by filing Form W-4P, Withholding Certificate for Pension or Annuity Payments, with their pension or annuity payer.

By filing a Form W-4P with the payer of an annuity or pension, payees may request withholding on the basis of their marital status and withholding allowances. They make this request by entering the proper number of withholding allowances on Form W-4P. Payees can request that the payer withhold an additional amount. The format of Form W-4P is similar to that of Form W-4.

EMPLOYER'S QUARTERLY REPORT

Most employers who withhold income taxes or who owe FICA taxes, file a quarterly Form 941, Employer's Quarterly Federal Tax Return. Seasonal employers who do not pay wages in a quarter do not file a Form 941 for that quarter. On every Form 941 that seasonal employers file, they place an *X* in the seasonal employer box (line 17).

All depositors complete both pages of Form 941. Semiweekly depositors also complete Schedule B (Form 941), Report of Tax Liability for Semiweekly Depositors, and attach it to Form 941.

Filing the Quarterly Report

Employers must file Form 941 by the last day of the month that follows the close of a calendar quarter. For example, for the quarter ending September 30, 20x1, employers must file a Form 941 by October 31, 20x1. Employers who deposit all taxes before the due dates get an additional ten days to file Form 941. Thus, if the employer deposits its taxes by the required due dates, Form 941 for the quarter ending December 31, 20x1, would be due by February 10, 20x2. Employers cannot use a Form 941 to report taxes from more than one calendar quarter. Instead, each quarter must be reported separately.

EXAMPLE 5

Betz, Inc., which uses the calendar year, withholds employment taxes from its employees' wages. It then matches the employees' FICA taxes and deposits them on time during all of 2006. These actions allow Betz until May 10, 2006 to file its first quarter Form 941 (the normal due date is April 30). It has until August 10 to file form 941 for the second quarter, and until November 10, 2006 to file the third quarter Form 941. The due date for Betz's Form 941 for the fourth quarter is February 13, 2007 (February 10, 2007 falls on a Saturday).

EXAMPLE 6

Same as in Example 5 except that Betz fails to deposit its employment taxes on time. The due dates for filing Form 941 are the last day of the month that follows the close of the calendar quarter. This would be April 30, July 31, October 31 and January 31. If any of these days falls on a weekend or holiday, the return would be due the next business day.

Adjusting for Overwithholding or Underwithholding

Employers who find an error in withheld income taxes for an earlier quarter of the same year correct it on Form 941 for the quarter in which the error is discovered. Employers correct FICA tax reporting errors in the same manner. For every correction (adjustment), employers attach a statement explaining and identifying the earlier return with the error(s). Employers who withhold *less* than the correct amount of tax from wages deduct the amounts underwithheld from future wages. When employers withhold *more* than the correct amount, they can repay the excess to the proper employees in any quarter of the same year. Employers keep the employee's dated and signed receipts for the repayment. Also, these employers include excess withholdings not repaid in the withholding quarter on their quarterly Form 941.

Final Returns

A special rule applies when an employer goes out of business. The employer marks an "X" in the box on line 16 and then enters the final date wages were paid in the space provided. Employers who temporarily cease to pay wages continue to file Form 941. They simply check the box on line 4 and complete the rest of Form 941.

Information for Figure 13-5: Filled-In Form 941

Martinez Enterprises, Inc., (from Figure 13-4) reports combined wages for withholding and employment taxes of $22,396 for the first quarter ($6,172.61 in January, $6,714.90 in February, and $9,508.49 in March). Martinez withheld $3,369.49 in federal income taxes from its two employees ($928.31 in January, $1,010.41 in February, and $1,430.77 in March).

Other Information

15: Month 1 liability, **$1,872.71** [($6,172.61 × .124) + ($6,172.61 × .029) + $928.31]
Month 2 liability, **$2,037.79** [($6,714.90 × .124) + ($6,714.90 × .029) + $1,010.41]
Month 3 liability, **$2,885.57** [($9,508.49 × .124) + ($9,508.49 × .029) + $1,430.77]
Total: **$6,796.07** ($1,872.71 + $2,037.79 + $2,885.57)

FEDERAL TAX DEPOSIT SYSTEM

Employers use the federal tax deposit system to transfer payroll taxes to the government. They usually deposit these taxes with a specified depository servicing the employer's area. Under certain conditions, employers send some tax payments directly to the IRS.

Federal Tax Deposit Coupon Book

The IRS issues Form 8109, Federal Tax Deposit Coupon Book, to employers. Each coupon book contains 24 deposit coupons. The sixth and seventh coupons contain an identification number that automatically triggers a coupon reorder request. Thus, depositors do not need to reorder a supply of deposit coupons. For each tax deposit, employers prepare a deposit coupon. They enter the numerical data, omitting dollar signs, leading zeros, commas, and decimal points. Commas and decimal points already appear in the form's entry area. Employers depositing dollars and no cents write zeros in the boxes for cents. At the top right of each deposit coupon, a list of tax period ovals appears. Employers darken one to show the quarter that a deposit covers. To the left of these ovals a list of payment ovals appears with form numbers. Employers darken one to identify the deposit type.

Information for Figure 13-6: Filled-In Form 8109

Martinez Enterprises, Inc. (from Figure 13-5) is a calendar year corporation. Martinez makes a deposit of $6,796.07 with Form 941 (FICA taxes and withheld income taxes) for the first quarter on filled-in Form 8109. The IRS preprints Martinez's EIN and address on its forms.

Other Information

TAX YEAR MONTH, enter **12** (for December 31 year end)

FIGURE 13-5 Filled-In Form 941, Employer's Quarterly Federal Tax Return, Page 1

Form **941 for 2006: Employer's QUARTERLY Federal Tax Return** 990106

(Rev. January 2006) Department of the Treasury — Internal Revenue Service OMB No. 1545-0029

(EIN) Employer identification number 9 1 – 0 1 1 8 2 2 4

Name *(not your trade name)* Edward L. Martinez

Trade name *(if any)* Martinez Enterprises, Inc.

Address 64 Bay Road
Number Street Suite or room number
Miami FL 33139
City State ZIP code

Report for this Quarter ... (Check one.)

- [X] **1:** January, February, March
- [ ] **2:** April, May, June
- [ ] **3:** July, August, September
- [ ] **4:** October, November, December

Read the separate instructions before you fill out this form. Please type or print within the boxes.

Part 1: Answer these questions for this quarter.

1	**Number of employees who received wages, tips, or other compensation for the pay period including:** ***Mar. 12*** **(Quarter 1),** ***June 12*** **(Quarter 2),** ***Sept. 12*** **(Quarter 3),** ***Dec. 12*** **(Quarter 4)**			**1**	2
2	**Wages, tips, and other compensation**			**2**	22,396.00
3	**Total income tax withheld from wages, tips, and other compensation**			**3**	3,369.49
4	**If no wages, tips, and other compensation are subject to social security or Medicare tax**				☐ Check and go to line 6.
5	**Taxable social security and Medicare wages and tips:**	*Column 1*	*Column 2*		
5a	**Taxable social security wages**	22,396.00 × .124 =	2,777.10		
5b	**Taxable social security tips**	. × .124 =	.		
5c	**Taxable Medicare wages & tips**	22,396.00 × .029 =	649.48		
5d	**Total social security and Medicare taxes** (*Column 2,* lines 5a + 5b + 5c = line 5d)			**5d**	3,426.58
6	**Total taxes before adjustments** (lines 3 + 5d = line 6)			**6**	6,796.07
7	**TAX ADJUSTMENTS** (Read the instructions for line 7 before completing lines 7a through 7h.):				
7a	**Current quarter's fractions of cents**		.		
7b	**Current quarter's sick pay**		.		
7c	**Current quarter's adjustments for tips and group-term life insurance**		.		
7d	**Current year's income tax withholding** (attach Form 941c)		.		
7e	**Prior quarters' social security and Medicare taxes** (attach Form 941c)		.		
7f	**Special additions to federal income tax** (attach Form 941c)		.		
7g	**Special additions to social security and Medicare** (attach Form 941c)		.		
7h	**TOTAL ADJUSTMENTS** (Combine all amounts: lines 7a through 7g.)			**7h**	0.
8	**Total taxes after adjustments** (Combine lines 6 and 7h.)			**8**	6,796.07
9	**Advance earned income credit (EIC) payments made to employees**			**9**	.
10	**Total taxes after adjustment for advance EIC** (line 8 – line 9 = line 10)			**10**	6,796.07
11	**Total deposits for this quarter, including overpayment applied from a prior quarter**			**11**	6,796.07
12	**Balance due** (If line 10 is more than line 11, write the difference here.) Make checks payable to *United States Treasury.*			**12**	0.
13	**Overpayment** (If line 11 is more than line 10, write the difference here.)		.		Check one ☐ Apply to next return. ☐ Send a refund.

▶ You **MUST** fill out both pages of this form and **SIGN** it.

Next ➔

For Privacy Act and Paperwork Reduction Act Notice, see the back of the Payment Voucher. Cat. No. 17001Z Form **941** (Rev. 1-2006)

FIGURE 13-5 Filled-In Form 941, Employer's Quarterly Federal Tax Return, Page 2

Name *(not your trade name)* Edward L. Martinez

Employer identification number (EIN) 91-0118224

Part 2: Tell us about your deposit schedule and tax liability for this quarter.

If you are unsure about whether you are a monthly schedule depositor or a semiweekly schedule depositor, see *Pub. 15 (Circular E)*, section 11.

14 [F] [L] **Write the state abbreviation for the state where you made your deposits** OR **write "MU" if you made your deposits in *multiple* states.**

15 **Check one:** ☐ **Line 10 is less than $2,500.** Go to Part 3.

☒ **You were a monthly schedule depositor for the entire quarter. Fill out your tax liability for each month.** Then go to Part 3.

Tax liability: Month 1	1,872.71
Month 2	2,037.79
Month 3	2,885.57
Total liability for quarter	6,796.07

Total must equal line 10.

☐ **You were a semiweekly schedule depositor for any part of this quarter.** Fill out *Schedule B (Form 941): Report of Tax Liability for Semiweekly Schedule Depositors*, and attach it to this form.

Part 3: Tell us about your business. If a question does NOT apply to your business, leave it blank.

16 **If your business has closed or you stopped paying wages** . . . . ☐ Check here, and

enter the final date you paid wages __/__/__.

17 **If you are a seasonal employer and you do not have to file a return for every quarter of the year** . . ☐ Check here.

Part 4: May we speak with your third-party designee?

Do you want to allow an employee, a paid tax preparer, or another person to discuss this return with the IRS? See the instructions for details.

☐ Yes. Designee's name

Phone ( ) – Personal Identification Number (PIN) ☐☐☐☐☐

☐ No.

Part 5: Sign here. You MUST fill out both sides of this form and **SIGN it.**

Under penalties of perjury, I declare that I have examined this return, including accompanying schedules and statements, and to the best of my knowledge and belief, it is true, correct, and complete.

✗ Sign your name here *Edward L. Martinez*

Print name and title Edward L. Martinez, President

Date 4/26/06 Phone (305) 555-3544

Part 6: For PAID preparers only *(optional)*

Paid Preparer's Signature

Firm's name

Address EIN

ZIP code

Date / / Phone ( ) – SSN/PTIN

☐ Check if you are self-employed.

Page **2** Form **941** (Rev. 1-2006)

FIGURE 13-6 Filled-In Form 8109, Federal Tax Deposit Coupon

AMOUNT OF DEPOSIT (Do NOT type, please print.)

DOLLARS | CENTS

6,796.07

TAX YEAR MONTH → 1 2

EMPLOYER IDENTIFICATION NUMBER → 9 1 0 1 1 8 2 2 4

BANK NAME/ DATE STAMP

Name Martinez Enterprises, Inc.

Address 64 Bay Road

City Miami

State FL ZIP 33139-5670

Telephone number (305) 555-3544

IRS USE ONLY

Darken only one TYPE OF TAX		and	Darken only one TAX PERIOD
● 941	○ 945		● 1st Quarter
○ 990-C	○ 1120		○ 2nd Quarter
○ 943	○ 990-T		○ 3rd Quarter
○ 720	○ 990-PF		○ 4th Quarter
○ CT-1	○ 1042		
○ 940			35

FOR BANK USE IN MICR ENCODING

FORM 8109 TAX DEPOSIT TYPES BY FORM NUMBER

Form 720—Excise Tax

Form 940—Federal Unemployment Tax (FUTA)

Form 941—Income Tax and Social Security and Medicare Taxes Withheld

Form 943—Agricultural Withheld Income, Social Security and Medicare Taxes

Form 990C—Farmers' Cooperative Association Income Tax

Form 990PF—Excise Tax on Private Foundation Net Investment Income

Form 990T—Exempt Organization Business Income Tax

Form 1042—Withholding on Foreign Persons

Form 1120—Corporate Income Tax

Form CT-1—Railroad Retirement Taxes

Form 945—Withholding Income Tax from Pensions, Annuities, IRAs, Gambling, Indian Gaming and Backup Withholding

Deposit Frequency

Employers make deposits using either a monthly or semiweekly deposit schedule. The schedule used depends on the total taxes the employer reported in the lookback period.

Lookback Period

Each employer's lookback period is the 12-month period ending on June 30 of the prior year. For 2007, the lookback period ended on June 30, 2006. The employment taxes reported on the four Forms 941, Employer's Quarterly Federal Tax Report, filed during the lookback period are used to determine the employer's deposit schedule. If an employer did not exist during the lookback period, the IRS treats the employer as having zero tax accumulations.

EMPLOYMENT TAXES: WHAT'S INCLUDED?

1. Income and FICA taxes withheld from employees
2. Employer's share of FICA taxes
3. Taxes withheld from pensions, annuities, and some deferred income
4. Taxes withheld under the backup withholding rules

Monthly Depositors

When total employment tax accumulations for an employer's lookback period are $50,000 or less, the employer deposits employment taxes monthly. Monthly depositors deposit each month's employment taxes by the 15th day of the next month.

EXAMPLE 7

For the 12-month period ending June 30, 2006, Kirkwall Enterprises reported total taxes on Form 941 totaling $47,000. Since this amount does not exceed $50,000, Kirkwall deposits its monthly employment taxes on the 15th day of the following month. Thus, its payroll taxes for the month of January would be deposited on February 15. Its taxes for February would be due by March 15. If Kirkwall makes timely deposits of its employment taxes, it will be allowed to extend the deadline for filing Form 941 by 10 days.

Semiweekly Depositors

When total employment tax accumulations for an employer's lookback period exceed $50,000, the employer makes semiweekly deposits. Semiweekly depositors deposit employment tax on Wednesday or Friday. Wednesday deposits include tax accumulations for payrolls paid on the previous Wednesday, Thursday, and Friday. Friday deposits include tax accumulations for payrolls paid on the previous Saturday, Sunday, Monday, and Tuesday.

SEMIWEEKLY DEPOSITORS

Deposit Day	Deposit for Payrolls Paid
	Prior days
Wednesday	Wednesday
	Thursday
	Friday
Friday	Saturday
	Sunday
	Monday
	Tuesday

EXAMPLE 8

Continuing with Example 7, for the 12-month period ending on June 30, 2007, Kirkwall's taxes reported on Form 941 total $53,000. Since this amount exceeds $50,000, Kirkwall will be required to make semiweekly deposits. On Wednesdays of each week, it will deposit the taxes related to the payrolls paid on Wednesday, Thursday or Friday of the previous week. Then on Fridays, it will deposit that taxes related to the payrolls paid on the prior Monday through Wednesday.

Semiweekly depositors make two deposits when the end of a calendar quarter does not fall on the employer's payday. They make one deposit for the last day(s) in the quarter just ended. They make another deposit for the starting day(s) in the new quarter. Employers must prepare a separate Form 8109, Federal Tax Deposit Coupon, for each deposit and make the deposits by the next regular deposit date.

EXAMPLE 9

Elite Corporation is a semiweekly depositor. Elite pays its employees every Friday. One of its payroll periods ends on June 24. The next payroll period ends on July 1 and the one after that ends on July 8. Elite normally deposits its payroll taxes on the Wednesday following its Friday payday. During the current year, the second quarter ends on Thursday, June 30. Thus, the end of the quarter does not coincide with the end of its payroll period. The taxes for the payroll period ending on Friday, June 24 would be deposited on Wednesday, June 29. They then must deposits the payroll taxes related to the period June 25 through June 30. They do this on the normal deposit date for Thursday payroll periods – the following Wednesday (July 6). They deposit the taxes for the short payroll period of July 1 on the following Wednesday (July 6).

EXAMPLE 10

Assume the same facts as in Example 9, except that Elete pays its employees once a month on the last day of each month. Although Elete is a semiweekly depositor, it makes only one deposit for the month of June. Since June 30, 2006, falls on Thursday, Elete makes the deposit the next Wednesday, July 6, 2006.

One-Day Rule

Whenever an employer's employment taxes reach $100,000 during a deposit period, the one-day rule applies. This rule requires the employer to deposit employment taxes by the close of the next business day. This rule applies whether the employer is a monthly or a semiweekly depositor. Furthermore, once this event occurs for monthly depositors, they switch to being semiweekly depositors for the rest of the current calendar year and for the next year. After that, the lookback period will determine whether the employer qualifies as a monthly or semiweekly depositor.

Semiweekly depositors determine whether they fall under the one-day rule by examining their employment tax accumulations since the last deposit date. They use Wednesday–Friday or Saturday–Tuesday for their examination period. On the day their accumulations reach $100,000, they meet the test for the one-day rule. Monthly depositors can determine if they fall under the one-day rule by examining their accumulations in the current month. They fall under the one-day rule on the day their accumulations reach $100,000. Once the employer deposits the employment taxes, the counting of accumulations starts over again at zero.

EXAMPLE 11

Cambry Company, a monthly depositor, has four payroll periods during the month. The first payroll period accumulates $40,000 of employment taxes. The second has $50,000 of employment taxes, for an accumulation of $90,000 ($40,000 + $50,000). The third payroll period involves $30,000 of payroll taxes. As of the end of the third payroll period, Cambry has accumulated employment taxes of $120,000 ($90,000 + $30,000). Cambry must deposit the $120,000 the next business day. From this day forward, Cambry becomes a semiweekly depositor, and will remain a semiweekly depositor for the rest of the current year and all of next year. Cambry's fourth payroll period for the month ends on a Saturday. As a semiweekly depositor, Cambry deposits its employment taxes by the following Friday.

Weekends and Holidays

When a deposit date falls on a Saturday, Sunday, or other depository holiday, the deposit is timely if made by the next business banking day.

EXAMPLE 12

RSV deposits employment taxes monthly. For March 2007, RSV accumulates $10,000 of employment taxes. RSV normally would deposit these taxes by April 15, 2007. However, April 15, 2007, falls on a Sunday. Thus, RSV must deposit the taxes by Monday, April 16, 2007, the next banking day.

Safe Harbor/De Minimis Rule

An employer satisfies its deposit requirement if the undeposited amount (shortfall) does not exceed the larger of $100 or 2% of a required deposit. **Shortfall** means the required deposit amount less the amount deposited before the end of a deposit date. To use this rule, employers must deposit unplanned shortfalls before the end of their make-up date.

The shortfall make-up date for monthly depositors falls on the due date of the quarterly Form 941 for the period in which the shortfall occurs. The employer sends the shortfall attached to the Form 941 or deposits it by the due date.

A different shortfall make-up date applies to semiweekly and one-day depositors. For these employers, the shortfall must be deposited by the first Wednesday or Friday (whichever is earlier) that falls after the 14th of the month following the month of the shortfall. However, if the quarterly due date of a Form 941 falls before the shortfall make-up date, the shortfall deposit must take place by the earlier Form 941 due date.

EXAMPLE 13

Romano Company, a semiweekly depositor, has a shortfall for September 2006. Romano's make-up period ends on the first Wednesday or Friday after October 14. Since October 14, 2006, falls on a Saturday, the first Wednesday or Friday after that date would be Wednesday, October 18, 2006.

EXAMPLE 14

Assume the same facts as in Example 13, except that Romano's shortfall occurs on October 10, 2006. Normally, Romano would be required to deposit the shortfall by Wednesday, November 15. However, Romano's third-quarter Form 941 is due on October 31. Thus, Romano must deposit the shortfall by October 31, 2006.

$2,500 Rule

A special deposit rule applies when the tax accumulations for a quarter do not reach $2,500. No deposits are necessary, and the employer may send the taxes with Form 941.

EXAMPLE 15

A corporation's tax accumulations for the third quarter of 2006 total $2,460. Since the total accumulations are less than $2,500, the corporation can send it the $2,460 when it files its third quarter Form 941. The due date for this return is November 30, 2006.

A flowchart of the employment tax deposit rules appears in Figure 13-7. It shows how the rules separate employment tax depositors by frequency of deposits.

ESTIMATED TAXES

Wage earners pay taxes on their wages through the payroll withholding system. Taxpayers with income from sources other than wages (self-employment profits, interest, dividends, etc.) estimate their taxes and make quarterly payments directly to the IRS. For 2007, quarterly tax payment due dates fall on April 16, 2007; June 15, 2007; September 17, 2007; and January 15, 2008.

To help taxpayers prepare a tax estimate, the IRS provides Form 1040-ES, Estimated Tax for Individuals. The Form 1040-ES package includes four taxpayer-identifying payment vouchers, a tax worksheet, and a schedule of payments.

Who Makes Estimated Payments?

In 2007, when individual taxpayers' *estimated unpaid tax* for the year equals or exceeds $1,000, they usually must make estimated tax payments. Unpaid taxes include income tax and self-employment taxes. Employees do not make estimated payments in 2007 unless their tax withholdings and credits for 2006 fall below the *lesser of* (i) 90% of the tax on their 2007 tax return or (ii) 100% of the tax on their 2006 tax return (110% for taxpayers whose 2006 AGI exceeded $150,000).

EXAMPLE 16

Tracy Shiver's AGI for 2006 was $62,500; her federal tax liability for 2006 was $5,530. Shiver expects her 2007 tax liability to be closer to $8,000. Shiver does not need to make estimated payments in 2007 unless her employer withholds less than $5,530 from her pay during the year. This amount is the *lesser of* (i) $7,200 ($8,000 x 90%), or (ii) $5,530 (100% of her 2006 tax liability).

FIGURE 13-7 A Summary of the Employment Tax Deposit Rules

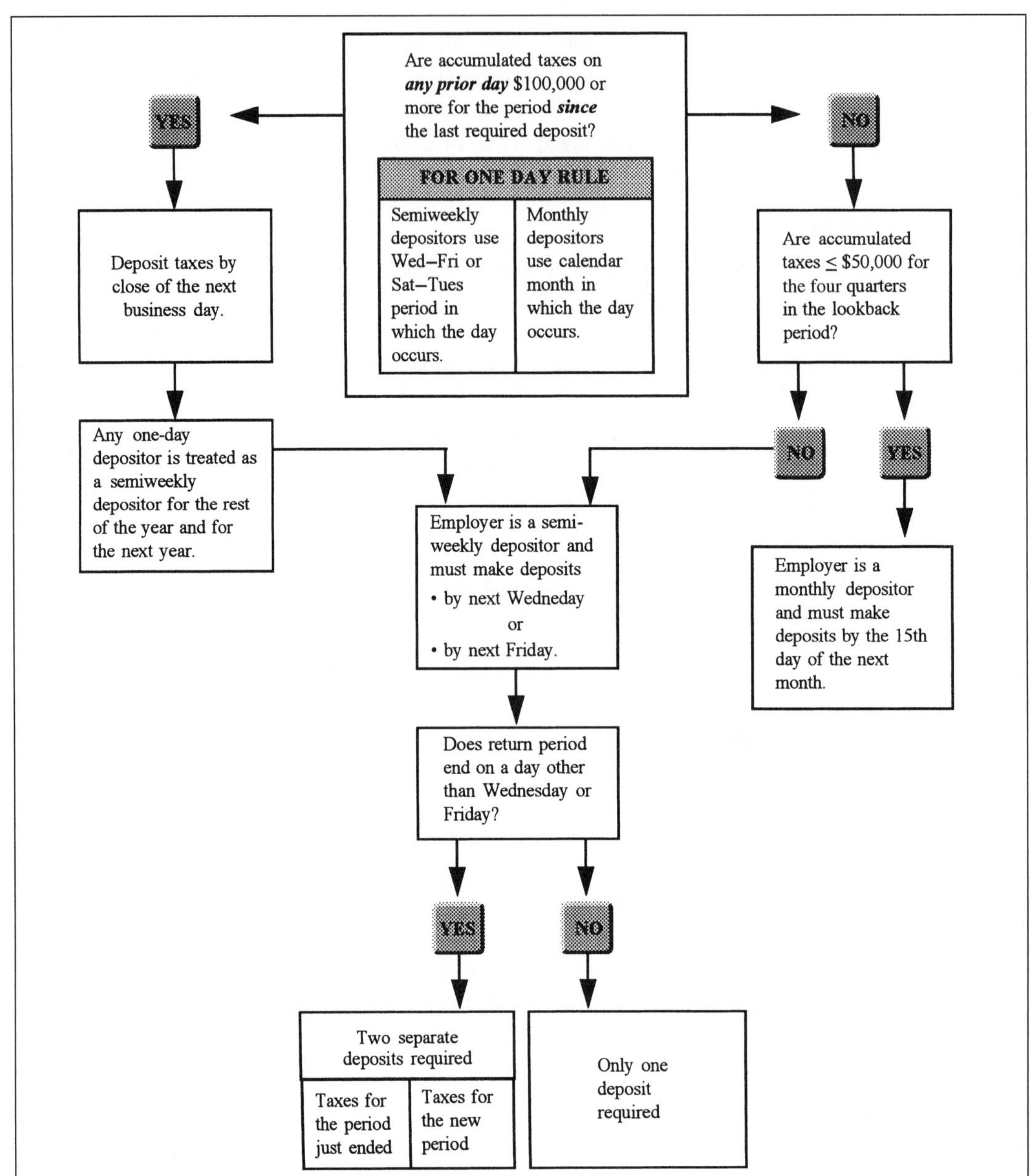

EXAMPLE 17

Kelly Chin's AGI for 2006 was $162,500; her federal tax liability for 2006 was $15,553. Chin expects her 2007 tax liability to be $18,000. Chin will not need to make estimated payments in 2007 unless her employer withholds less than $16,200 from her pay during the year. This amount is the *lesser of* (i) $16,200 ($18,000 x 90%), or (ii) $17,108 (110% of her 2006 tax liability).

EXAMPLE 18

Same as in Example 17 except that Chin expect her 2007 tax liability to be $24,000. She will not need to make estimated payments in 2007 unless her employer withholds less than $17,108 from her pay during the year. This amount is the *lesser of* (i) $21,600 ($24,000 x 90%), or (ii) $17,108 (110% of her 2006 tax liability).

Estimated Tax Worksheet

The IRS provides a worksheet to help taxpayers calculate their estimated tax. The difference between their total estimated tax, net of estimated credits and their employer's withholdings, represents the *estimated unpaid tax.* Taxpayers can make an immediate payment of the balance or pay it in four equal installments.

PERSONS WHO USUALLY MAKE QUARTERLY TAX PAYMENTS

1. Self-employed persons with business or professional income
2. Persons with large dividend, interest, rent, royalty, pension, and capital gain income
3. Wage earners whose income is not subject to withholding
4. Wage earners whose tax credits and withholdings fall short of their tax liability

Information for Figure 13-8: Filled-In Estimated Tax Worksheet

Audrey C. McGrath, single, age 25, with good vision and no dependents, prepares an estimated tax worksheet, shown in Figure 13-8. McGrath estimates her 2007 AGI at $22,873 and withholdings at $632. Her AGI estimate is based on the following:

Salary	$11,600
Net rentals from apartment building	9,600
Net income from business	1,800
Total income	$23,000
Less 50% of self-employment tax	(127)
AGI	$22,873

McGrath does not expect to itemize deductions in 2007. Her 2006 income taxes were $1,950.

FIGURE 13-8 Filled-In Estimated Tax Worksheet

1	AGI Expected in 2006		22,873
2	Larger of:		
	Estimated itemized deductions	0	
	Standard deduction (in 2007) for filing class	5,350	5,350
3	Subtract line 2 from line 1		17,523
4	Personal and dependency exemptions (in 2007)		3,400
5	Subtract line 4 from line 3		14,123
6	Tax on amount on line 5 (using the 2007 rates)*		1,728
7	Tax on Accumulation Distributions of Trusts	0	
	Tax on Lump-Sum Distributions	0	0
8	Add lines 6 and 7		1,728
9	Less: Credits		0
10	Subtract line 9 from line 8		1,728
11	Self-employment tax ($1,800 × 92.35% × 15.3%)		254
12	Other taxes (early distribution and AMT tax)		0
13a	Add lines 10 through 12		1,982
13b	Earned Income Credit and fuel credit		0
13c	Subtract line 13b from line 13a. TOTAL 2007 ESTIMATED TAX		1,982
14a	90% of 2007 ESTIMATED TAX	1,784	
14b	100% of tax on 2006 tax return	1,950	
14c	Enter the smaller of line 14a or 14b REQUIRED ANNUAL PAYMENT TO AVOID A PENALTY		1,784
15	Income taxes withheld and estimated to be withheld during 2007.		632
16	Subtract line 15 from 14c		1,152
17	Enter ¼ of line 16 ($1,152 ÷ 4), rounded up to nearest whole dollar		288

* The 2007 tax rates for single taxpayers are 10% on the first $7,800 of taxable income, and 15% on taxable income in excess of $7,800, but not more than $31,850.

Joint Estimated Tax Payments

A husband and wife can make joint estimated tax payments. Making a joint payment or separate payments does not commit the couple to filing a joint Form 1040. When a husband and wife make joint payments but file separate income tax returns, they can divide the estimate as they choose. One of them could use all the payments as a credit. A couple separated under a decree of divorce or separate maintenance cannot make joint estimated tax payments.

EXAMPLE 19

Britney and Caleb Stonewell make joint estimated payments during 2006 that total $25,000. The Stonewells decide to file separate tax returns for 2006. They are free to split up the $25,000 amongst themselves. Thus, if Britney's tax withholdings are large enough to cover her tax liability, Caleb can use the entire $25,000 as a refundable tax credit against his 2006 tax liability. However, if it turns out that Britney's withholdings are less than her tax liability by $4,000, the couple can choose to apply $4,000 of their joint estimated payments against Britney's tax liability. The remaining $21,000 would then be taken on Caleb's separate tax return.

Payment of Estimated Tax

Taxpayers who make estimated tax payments mail their payment vouchers to the IRS Service Center for their district. The annual preprinted Form 1040-ES package contains four dated payment vouchers and mailing envelopes. A taxpayer who files an estimated tax voucher for the first time will receive a preprinted Form 1040-ES package.

For calendar year taxpayers, the vouchers and payments are due April 15, June 15, and September 15 of the current year, and January 15 of the next year. If the due date falls on a weekend or a holiday, the voucher and payment are due the next business day.

Prior-Year Overpayments

If a taxpayer's Form 1040 tax return for the year results in overpayment of taxes, the taxpayer can choose to receive a refund. The taxpayer can also choose to apply the overpayment to any estimated tax due the next year. The taxpayer can use the overpayment either to reduce each subsequent installment until the overpayment is used up or to reduce each installment equally.

EXAMPLE 20

Betty Nystrum overpaid her 2006 taxes by $700. The overpayment was not refunded to her. Nystrum's 2007 tax payments and estimated withholding data are as follows.

Estimated tax for 2007	$14,200
Less estimated income tax withholding during the year	(12,600)
Estimated unpaid tax	$ 1,600

Nystrum's quarterly installment payments equal $400 ($1,600 ÷ 4). Nystrum does not have to pay the first installment because the amount falls below last year's overpayment of $700. When the second installment comes due on June 15, 2007, Nystrum pays $100 (second quarterly installment of $400 less the remaining $300 from her last year's overpayment). The payment due dates and installment amounts for Nystrum are as follows.

April 16, 2007	$ 0
June 15, 2007	100
September 17, 2007	400
January 15, 2008	400

Nystrum could make an election to apply the overpayment evenly against each installment rather than in full against the first and succeeding installments. If she makes this election, Nystrum divides last year's overpayment by the number of installments ($700 ÷ 4) and applies this amount to each installment. Nystrum would pay four installments of $225 each ($400 – $175).

Underpayment of Estimated Tax

No underpayment penalty will be assessed when the amount of tax due after withholding is less than $1,000. Taxpayers who expect to owe more than $1,000 after withholdings should make timely estimated tax payments. One way to avoid the underpayment penalty in 2006 is to make four equal payments that total 90% of 2006 tax liability. A second way to avoid the penalty was to make four equal payments that total 100% of 2005 tax liability (110% for taxpayers whose 2005 AGI exceeded $150,000 [$75,000 for married filing separately]). A third way to avoid the underpayment penalty was to make estimated payments based on 90% of 2006 annualized tax liability. The calculations required in annualizing taxable income and tax liability are rather involved and beyond the scope of this textbook. Those interested in learning more about the annualized method making estimated payments should look at IRS Publication 505.

Sometimes taxpayers need to make estimated payments, but also have wages subject to withholding. In calculating the amount of each estimated payment, wages are treated as occurring evenly throughout the year. Thus, taxpayers who work only part of the year and have $2,000 withheld from their wages will be treated as having had $500 withheld each quarter.

EXAMPLE 21

On October 1, Wesley Kim estimates that his tax liability for the current tax year will be $15,000. In the prior tax year, Kim's AGI was $160,000 and his tax liability was $22,000. Thus, to avoid underpayment penalties, Kim needs to have prepaid $13,500 during the year. This amount is the *lesser of* (i) 90% of his current year tax liability ($15,000 x 90% = $13,500), or (ii) 110% of his prior year's tax liability ($22,000 x 110% = $24,200). Kim's employer has been withholding $1,000 a month. Thus, he is on target to have a total of $12,000 withheld for the year. If Kim does nothing, he will be subject to an underpayment penalty for the $1,500 deficiency. If Kim decides to make an estimated payment for the fourth quarter to make up the $1,500 deficit, he will still be subject to penalties for not having paid enough during the first three quarters. However, if Kim files a new W-4 with his employer and has an additional $1,500 withheld through the end of the year, he will avoid any underpayment penalties. His employer will have withheld a total of $13,500 during the year, which will be treated as having been paid evenly throughout the year.

Determining the Penalty Amount

Taxpayers determine their penalty amount on Form 2210, Underpayment of Estimated Tax by Individuals. Taxpayers enter their penalty on Form 1040 (line 77). Then they add it to any other amounts due the government. Taxpayers may choose not to file Form 2210 and instead have the IRS calculate the penalty and bill them.

The IRS adjusts the underpayment penalty rate quarterly. The rate equals the short-term federal interest rate plus three percentage points. Although the penalty looks like an interest expense, taxpayers cannot deduct it.

Name ____________________

Section ____________ Date ____________

QUESTIONS AND PROBLEMS

1. **Withholding Allowances.**

   a. How do employees claim withholding allowances?

   b. If employees do not give their employer a filled-in Form W-4, Employee's Withholding Allowance Certificate, what withholding action must the employer take?

   c. If a taxpayer holds more than one job, can the taxpayer claim withholding allowances with more than one employer?

2. **Withholding Rules.** What tax withholding action, if any, must a taxpayer take for each of the following situations?

   a. Withholding allowances decrease.

   b. Withholding allowances increase.

   c. A qualifying dependent dies on July 23 of the current year.

3. **Withholding Rules.**

   a. An employee files a Form W-4 on June 10, 2007, claiming to be exempt from withholding. For what period does the exempt status apply?

   b. Does an exemption from withholding that an employee claims on Form W-4 apply to both FICA taxes and federal income taxes?

4. **Withholding Allowances.** On the basis of the information given, how many withholding allowances can be claimed for 2006 by each of the following taxpayers? Identify the type of each withholding allowance claimed.

Taxpayer A	A single taxpayer, age 12, is claimed as a dependent on his parents' return. The taxpayer will earn $800 in wages during the year and receive $50 in dividend income.
Taxpayer B	A single taxpayer, age 20, is not claimed as a dependent on another return. The taxpayer will have earned income of $18,500 and interest income of $150. The taxpayer uses the standard deduction and has no adjustments to income.
Taxpayer C	A married couple files jointly. The couple claim four dependent children (ages 3 to 16). The taxpayer has two jobs, and the spouse has one job. The taxpayer's total wages are $69,500, and the spouse's wages are $20,500. Dividend income equals $400. No adjustments to income exist. Child care expenses are $1,200, and expected itemized deductions are $17,000.
Taxpayer D	A single taxpayer has one dependent (age 9) and files as head of household. The taxpayer will earn $44,600 from one job. Expected interest income is $200. The taxpayer claims $2,000 as adjustments to income. Child care expenses equal $3,200, and expected itemized deductions are $6,800.

Taxpayer	*Number of Withholding Allowances*	*Type of Withholding Allowances*
A	________	________
B	________	________
C	________	________
D	________	________

5. **Form W-4.** Married taxpayers, Ethel P. (SSN 448-47-4747) and Irving J. (SSN 739-33-8990) Mead, file a joint return. They reside at 1001 West Wind Plaza, Fox Lake, Wisconsin 53933-4611. Both are 42 years of age. They have one dependent child, Mary Jean, age 14 (SSN 668-32-1184).

On November 15, 2006, the Meads became aware that their income tax for 2006 will be underpaid. Ethel decides to file a new Form W-4, Employee's Withholding Allowance Certificate, to change the number of withholding allowances to ensure more appropriate withholding in the future. Ethel will not claim an allowance for Irving but will claim Mary Jean. The Meads' estimated income and deductions is as follows.

Wages:	Ethel:	Henry Maintenance Company	$38,000
		Arnold Corporation	12,000
		Total gross wages—Ethel	$50,000
	Irving:	Readers' Specialty Store	8,500
		Total gross wages	$58,500
Dividend income—Ethel			1,316
Interest income—Irving			1,034
Total			$60,850

The Meads estimate that their itemized deductions will be $13,850. In addition, they anticipate the following "deductions for AGI" and "other payments."

IRA contributions	$4,000
Fees for Mary Jean's school textbooks	216
Contributions to political party	320
Total	$4,536

Complete the 2006 Form W-4 that Ethel files with her employer, Henry Maintenance Company. Ethel signs and dates the form on November 18, 2006. Also prepare the necessary Form W-4 worksheets to determine the number of withholding allowances. Use the form and worksheet provided on the following pages.

6. **Form W-2.**

   a. By what date must an employer file Copy A of an employee's Form W-2 with the Social Security Administration?

   b. By what date must an employer give an employee Copies B and C of the employee's Form W-2?

7. **Form W-2.** Examine a Form W-2, Wage and Tax Statement.

   a. Explain the special meaning of *Statutory employee* in box 13.

   b. Explain the special meaning of the Void box at the top of the Form W-2.

8. **Form W-2.** Speedy Department Store (EIN is 04-0450523) is located at 2706 Bluff Drive, Boston, Massachusetts 02101-3214. Prepare the original 2006 Form W-2, Wage and Tax Statement, for Susan W. Jenkins, a married employee with no dependents. Use the blank Form W-2 provided on page 13-36. The following data was taken from Speedy's payroll records:

   Susan W. Jenkins, 214 Northrup Street, Boston, Massachusetts 02112-1415, SSN 331-06-4821.

Total wages paid (before payroll deductions)	$45,000.00
Social security tax withheld	Calculate
Medicare tax withheld	Calculate
Federal income tax withheld	6,552.00
State income tax withheld	1,125.75
Form W-2 control number	0623
Employer's state I.D. number	25703

(Use for Problem 5.)

Form W-4 (2006)

Purpose. Complete Form W-4 so that your employer can withhold the correct federal income tax from your pay. Because your tax situation may change, you may want to refigure your withholding each year.

Exemption from withholding. If you are exempt, complete only lines 1, 2, 3, 4, and 7 and sign the form to validate it. Your exemption for 2006 expires February 16, 2007. See Pub. 505, Tax Withholding and Estimated Tax.

Note. You cannot claim exemption from withholding if (a) your income exceeds $850 and includes more than $300 of unearned income (for example, interest and dividends) and (b) another person can claim you as a dependent on their tax return.

Basic instructions. If you are not exempt, complete the **Personal Allowances Worksheet** below. The worksheets on page 2 adjust your withholding allowances based on itemized deductions, certain credits, adjustments to income, or two-earner/two-job situations. Complete all worksheets that apply. However, you may claim fewer (or zero) allowances.

Head of household. Generally, you may claim head of household filing status on your tax return only if you are unmarried and pay more than 50% of the costs of keeping up a home for yourself and your dependent(s) or other qualifying individuals. See line **E** below.

Tax credits. You can take projected tax credits into account in figuring your allowable number of withholding allowances. Credits for child or dependent care expenses and the child tax credit may be claimed using the **Personal Allowances Worksheet** below. See Pub. 919, How Do I Adjust My Tax Withholding, for information on converting your other credits into withholding allowances.

Nonwage income. If you have a large amount of nonwage income, such as interest or dividends, consider making estimated tax payments using Form 1040-ES, Estimated Tax for Individuals. Otherwise, you may owe additional tax.

Two earners/two jobs. If you have a working spouse or more than one job, figure the total number of allowances you are entitled to claim on all jobs using worksheets from only one Form W-4. Your withholding usually will be most accurate when all allowances are claimed on the Form W-4 for the highest paying job and zero allowances are claimed on the others.

Nonresident alien. If you are a nonresident alien, see the Instructions for Form 8233 before completing this Form W-4.

Check your withholding. After your Form W-4 takes effect, use Pub. 919 to see how the dollar amount you are having withheld compares to your projected total tax for 2006. See Pub. 919, especially if your earnings exceed $130,000 (Single) or $180,000 (Married).

Recent name change? If your name on line 1 differs from that shown on your social security card, call 1-800-772-1213 to initiate a name change and obtain a social security card showing your correct name.

Personal Allowances Worksheet (Keep for your records.)

A Enter "1" for **yourself** if no one else can claim you as a dependent . . . . A ______

B Enter "1" if:
- You are single and have only one job; or
- You are married, have only one job, and your spouse does not work; or
- Your wages from a second job or your spouse's wages (or the total of both) are $1,000 or less.

. . B ______

C Enter "1" for your **spouse.** But, you may choose to enter "-0-" if you are married and have either a working spouse or more than one job. (Entering "-0-" may help you avoid having too little tax withheld.) . . . . C ______

D Enter number of **dependents** (other than your spouse or yourself) you will claim on your tax return . . . . . . D ______

E Enter "1" if you will file as **head of household** on your tax return (see conditions under **Head of household** above) . E ______

F Enter "1" if you have at least $1,500 of **child or dependent care expenses** for which you plan to claim a credit . . F ______
(**Note.** Do **not** include child support payments. See **Pub. 503,** Child and Dependent Care Expenses, for details.)

G **Child Tax Credit** (including additional child tax credit):
- If your total income will be less than $55,000 ($82,000 if married), enter "2" for each eligible child.
- If your total income will be between $55,000 and $84,000 ($82,000 and $119,000 if married), enter "1" for each eligible child plus "1" **additional** if you have four or more eligible children. G ______

H Add lines A through G and enter total here. (**Note.** This may be different from the number of exemptions you claim on your tax return.) ▶ H ______

For accuracy, complete all worksheets that apply.
- If you plan to **itemize or claim adjustments to income** and want to reduce your withholding, see the **Deductions and Adjustments Worksheet** on page 2.
- If you have **more than one job** or are **married and you and your spouse both work** and the combined earnings from all jobs exceed $35,000 ($25,000 if married) see the **Two-Earner/Two-Job Worksheet** on page 2 to avoid having too little tax withheld.
- If **neither** of the above situations applies, **stop here** and enter the number from line H on line 5 of Form W-4 below.

Cut here and give Form W-4 to your employer. Keep the top part for your records.

Form **W-4** | **Employee's Withholding Allowance Certificate** | OMB No. 1545-0074

Department of the Treasury
Internal Revenue Service

▶ **Whether you are entitled to claim a certain number of allowances or exemption from withholding is subject to review by the IRS. Your employer may be required to send a copy of this form to the IRS.**

2006

1 Type or print your first name and middle initial.	Last name	2 Your social security number
Home address (number and street or rural route)		3 ☐ Single ☐ Married ☐ Married, but withhold at higher Single rate. **Note.** If married, but legally separated, or spouse is a nonresident alien, check the "Single" box.
City or town, state, and ZIP code		4 **If your last name differs from that shown on your social security card, check here. You must call 1-800-772-1213 for a new card.** ▶ ☐

5 Total number of allowances you are claiming (from line **H** above **or** from the applicable worksheet on page 2) | 5 |

6 Additional amount, if any, you want withheld from each paycheck . . . . | 6 | $

7 I claim exemption from withholding for 2006, and I certify that I meet **both** of the following conditions for exemption.
- Last year I had a right to a refund of **all** federal income tax withheld because I had **no** tax liability **and**
- This year I expect a refund of **all** federal income tax withheld because I expect to have **no** tax liability.

If you meet both conditions, write "Exempt" here . . . . ▶ | 7 |

Under penalties of perjury, I declare that I have examined this certificate and to the best of my knowledge and belief, it is true, correct, and complete.

Employee's signature
(Form is not valid unless you sign it.) ▶ **Date** ▶

8 Employer's name and address (Employer: Complete lines 8 and 10 only if sending to the IRS.)	9 Office code (optional)	10 Employer identification number (EIN)

For Privacy Act and Paperwork Reduction Act Notice, see page 2. Cat. No. 10220Q Form **W-4** (2006)

(Use for Problem 5.)

Form W-4 (2006) Page **2**

Deductions and Adjustments Worksheet

Note. Use this worksheet *only* if you plan to itemize deductions, claim certain credits, or claim adjustments to income on your 2006 tax return.

1	Enter an estimate of your 2006 itemized deductions. These include qualifying home mortgage interest, charitable contributions, state and local taxes, medical expenses in excess of 7.5% of your income, and miscellaneous deductions. (For 2006, you may have to reduce your itemized deductions if your income is over $150,500 ($75,250 if married filing separately). See *Worksheet 3* in Pub. 919 for details.) . . .	1	$
2	Enter: { $10,300 if married filing jointly or qualifying widow(er); $ 7,550 if head of household; $ 5,150 if single or married filing separately }	2	$
3	**Subtract** line 2 from line 1. If line 2 is greater than line 1, enter "-0-"	3	$
4	Enter an estimate of your 2006 adjustments to income, including alimony, deductible IRA contributions, and student loan interest	4	$
5	**Add** lines 3 and 4 and enter the total. (Include any amount for credits from *Worksheet 7* in Pub. 919) .	5	$
6	Enter an estimate of your 2006 nonwage income (such as dividends or interest)	6	$
7	**Subtract** line 6 from line 5. Enter the result, but not less than "-0-"	7	$
8	**Divide** the amount on line 7 by $3,300 and enter the result here. Drop any fraction	8	
9	Enter the number from the **Personal Allowances Worksheet,** line H, page 1	9	
10	**Add** lines 8 and 9 and enter the total here. If you plan to use the **Two-Earner/Two-Job Worksheet,** also enter this total on line 1 below. Otherwise, **stop here** and enter this total on Form W-4, line 5, page 1 .	10	

Two-Earner/Two-Job Worksheet (See *Two earners/two jobs* on page 1.)

Note. Use this worksheet *only* if the instructions under line H on page 1 direct you here.

1	Enter the number from line H, page 1 (or from line 10 above if you used the **Deductions and Adjustments Worksheet**)	1	
2	Find the number in **Table 1** below that applies to the **LOWEST** paying job and enter it here	2	
3	If line 1 is **more than or equal to** line 2, subtract line 2 from line 1. Enter the result here (if zero, enter "-0-") and on Form W-4, line 5, page 1. **Do not** use the rest of this worksheet	3	

Note. If line 1 is *less than* line 2, enter "-0-" on Form W-4, line 5, page 1. Complete lines 4–9 below to calculate the additional withholding amount necessary to avoid a year-end tax bill.

4	Enter the number from line 2 of this worksheet . . . . 4 ______		
5	Enter the number from line 1 of this worksheet . . . . 5 ______		
6	**Subtract** line 5 from line 4	6	
7	Find the amount in **Table 2** below that applies to the **HIGHEST** paying job and enter it here	7	$
8	**Multiply** line 7 by line 6 and enter the result here. This is the additional annual withholding needed . .	8	$
9	Divide line 8 by the number of pay periods remaining in 2006. For example, divide by 26 if you are paid every two weeks and you complete this form in December 2005. Enter the result here and on Form W-4, line 6, page 1. This is the additional amount to be withheld from each paycheck	9	$

Table 1: Two-Earner/Two-Job Worksheet

Married Filing Jointly						All Others	
If wages from **HIGHEST** paying job are—	AND, wages from **LOWEST** paying job are—	Enter on line 2 above	If wages from **HIGHEST** paying job are—	AND, wages from **LOWEST** paying job are—	Enter on line 2 above	If wages from **LOWEST** paying job are—	Enter on line 2 above
$0 - $42,000	$0 - $4,500	0	$42,001 and over	32,001 - 38,000	6	$0 - $6,000	0
	4,501 - 9,000	1		38,001 - 46,000	7	6,001 - 12,000	1
	9,001 - 18,000	2		46,001 - 55,000	8	12,001 - 19,000	2
	18,001 and over	3		55,001 - 60,000	9	19,001 - 26,000	3
				60,001 - 65,000	10	26,001 - 35,000	4
$42,001 and over	$0 - $4,500	0		65,001 - 75,000	11	35,001 - 50,000	5
	4,501 - 9,000	1		75,001 - 95,000	12	50,001 - 65,000	6
	9,001 - 18,000	2		95,001 - 105,000	13	65,001 - 80,000	7
	18,001 - 22,000	3		105,001 - 120,000	14	80,001 - 90,000	8
	22,001 - 26,000	4		120,001 and over	15	90,001 - 120,000	9
	26,001 - 32,000	5				120,001 and over	10

Table 2: Two-Earner/Two-Job Worksheet

Married Filing Jointly		All Others	
If wages from **HIGHEST** paying job are—	Enter on line 7 above	If wages from **HIGHEST** paying job are—	Enter on line 7 above
$0 - $60,000	$500	$0 - $30,000	$500
60,001 - 115,000	830	30,001 - 75,000	830
115,001 - 165,000	920	75,001 - 145,000	920
165,001 - 290,000	1,090	145,001 - 330,000	1,090
290,001 and over	1,160	330,001 and over	1,160

Privacy Act and Paperwork Reduction Act Notice. We ask for the information on this form to carry out the Internal Revenue laws of the United States. The Internal Revenue Code requires this information under sections 3402(f)(2)(A) and 6109 and their regulations. Failure to provide a properly completed form will result in your being treated as a single person who claims no withholding allowances; providing fraudulent information may also subject you to penalties. Routine uses of this information include giving it to the Department of Justice for civil and criminal litigation, to cities, states, and the District of Columbia for use in administering their tax laws, and using it in the National Directory of New Hires. We may also disclose this information to other countries under a tax treaty, to federal and state agencies to enforce federal nontax criminal laws, or to federal law enforcement and intelligence agencies to combat terrorism.

You are not required to provide the information requested on a form that is subject to the Paperwork Reduction Act unless the form displays a valid OMB control number. Books or records relating to a form or its instructions must be retained as long as their contents may become material in the administration of any Internal Revenue law. Generally, tax returns and return information are confidential, as required by Code section 6103.

The average time and expenses required to complete and file this form will vary depending on individual circumstances. For estimated averages, see the instructions for your income tax return.

If you have suggestions for making this form simpler, we would be happy to hear from you. See the instructions for your income tax return.

Printed on recycled paper

(Use for Problem 8.)

a Control number	22222	Void ☐	For Official Use Only ▶ OMB No. 1545-0008	
b Employer identification number (EIN)			1 Wages, tips, other compensation	2 Federal income tax withheld
c Employer's name, address, and ZIP code			3 Social security wages	4 Social security tax withheld
			5 Medicare wages and tips	6 Medicare tax withheld
			7 Social security tips	8 Allocated tips
d Employee's social security number			9 Advance EIC payment	10 Dependent care benefits
e Employee's first name and initial	Last name	Suff.	11 Nonqualified plans	12a See instructions for box 12
			13 Statutory employee ☐ Retirement plan ☐ Third-party sick pay ☐	12b
			14 Other	12c
f Employee's address and ZIP code				12d

15 State	Employer's state ID number	16 State wages, tips, etc.	17 State income tax	18 Local wages, tips, etc.	19 Local income tax	20 Locality name

Form **W-2** Wage and Tax Statement **2006**

Department of the Treasury—Internal Revenue Service

For Privacy Act and Paperwork Reduction Act Notice, see back of Copy D.

Copy A For Social Security Administration — Send this entire page with Form W-3 to the Social Security Administration; photocopies are **not** acceptable.

Cat. No. 10134D

Do Not Cut, Fold, or Staple Forms on This Page — Do Not Cut, Fold, or Staple Forms on This Page

9. **Withholding Rules.** Must a taxpayer who receives taxable annuity, pension, or deferred income payments have federal income taxes withheld from the payments? Explain.

10. **Form W-3.**

   a. What documents does an employer transmit with Form W-3 when filing with the Social Security Administration?

   b. By what date must an employer file these documents?

11. Form W-3. The Golden Door Company (EIN 39–0630726), 1906 North Avenue, Cheyenne, Wyoming 82001-1222, withheld income and social security taxes from each of its 28 employees during 2006. Golden's telephone number is (619) 438–2444. In 2007 it prepared and sent to each employee a separate Form W-2. All wages paid to employees total $225,250. Total federal income taxes withheld from employees were $36,250. Total social security and Medicare wages equaled $209,850. No employee's wages exceeded $94,200 during 2006. Compute the company's total employment tax liability for 2006, and prepare its Form W-3, Transmittal of Income and Tax Statements. Use blank Form W-3 and control number 01 to prepare the form as of January 21, 2007. If no entry applies to the box, leave it blank. Have Marsha A. Golden, president of Golden, sign the form.

DO NOT STAPLE

33333 | a Control number | For Official Use Only ▶ OMB No. 1545-0008

b Kind of Payer ▶ 941 ☐ Military ☐ 943 ☐ 944 ☐ CT-1 ☐ Hshld. emp. ☐ Medicare govt. emp. ☐ Third-party sick pay ☐

c Total number of Forms W-2 / d Establishment number	1 Wages, tips, other compensation	2 Federal income tax withheld
	3 Social security wages	4 Social security tax withheld
	5 Medicare wages and tips	6 Medicare tax withheld
e Employer identification number (EIN)	7 Social security tips	8 Allocated tips
f Employer's name	9 Advance EIC payments	10 Dependent care benefits
	11 Nonqualified plans	12 Deferred compensation
	13 For third-party sick pay use only	
g Employer's address and ZIP code	14 Income tax withheld by payer of third-party sick pay	
h Other EIN used this year		
15 State / Employer's state ID number	16 State wages, tips, etc.	17 State income tax
	18 Local wages, tips, etc.	19 Local income tax
Contact person	Telephone number ( )	For Official Use Only
Email address	Fax number ( )	

Under penalties of perjury, I declare that I have examined this return and accompanying documents, and, to the best of my knowledge and belief, they are true, correct, and complete.

12. FUTA Withholdings.

a. Should employers withhold FUTA taxes from employees? Explain.

b. When must an employer deposit FUTA taxes?

c. What is the FUTA tax rate? What is the effective FUTA tax rate for most taxpayers who are subject to it?

13. Form 941. During the third quarter of 2006, the Fillmore Restaurant (EIN 93-0530660) at 244 North Second Street, Fillmore, New York 14735-0022, withheld income and social security taxes from its five employees. It withheld income taxes of $3,117 from employees' wages and tips of $15,570. In addition, Fillmore withheld $912.95 of social security taxes on $14,725 of social security wages, and $52.39 of social security taxes on $845 of social security tips. It also withheld $225.77 of Medicare taxes on $15,570 of Medicare wages. During the quarter, Fillmore deposited income and employment taxes as follows: August 15, $1,739.50; September 15, $1,962.84; October 15, $1,796.87. Each deposit was accompanied by a federal tax deposit coupon. Data for quarterly wages and reported tips of employees is as follows:

Name	*Total Wages*	*Social Security Wages*	*Taxable Tips Reported*
Barker, J. R.	$ 7,025	$ 7,025	$315
Duwe, H. K.	3,000	3,000	180
Miller, M. M.	2,000	2,000	120
Pressman, R. M.	1,200	1,200	125
Smathers, H. H.	1,500	1,500	105
	$14,725	$14,725	$845

Prepare Form 941, Employer's Quarterly Federal Tax Return, for the Fillmore Restaurant, using the blank form provided on the pages that follow. Fillmore filed Form 941 and M. L. Wright, owner, signed it on October 25, 2006.

(Use for Problem 13.)

Form **941 for 2006: Employer's QUARTERLY Federal Tax Return** 990106

(Rev. January 2006) Department of the Treasury — Internal Revenue Service OMB No. 1545-0029

(EIN) Employer identification number ☐☐ – ☐☐☐☐☐☐☐

Name *(not your trade name)*

Trade name *(if any)*

Address Number Street Suite or room number

City State ZIP code

Report for this Quarter ... (Check one.)

☐ **1:** January, February, March

☐ **2:** April, May, June

☐ **3:** July, August, September

☐ **4:** October, November, December

Read the separate instructions before you fill out this form. Please type or print within the boxes.

Part 1: Answer these questions for this quarter.

1 **Number of employees who received wages, tips, or other compensation for the pay period including:** ***Mar. 12*** **(Quarter 1),** ***June 12*** **(Quarter 2),** ***Sept. 12*** **(Quarter 3),** ***Dec. 12*** **(Quarter 4)** . . . 1

2 **Wages, tips, and other compensation** . . . 2

3 **Total income tax withheld from wages, tips, and other compensation** . . . 3

4 **If no wages, tips, and other compensation are subject to social security or Medicare tax** . . ☐ Check and go to line 6.

5 **Taxable social security and Medicare wages and tips:**

	Column 1		Column 2
5a Taxable social security wages	.	× .124 =	.
5b Taxable social security tips	.	× .124 =	.
5c Taxable Medicare wages & tips	.	× .029 =	.

5d **Total social security and Medicare taxes** (*Column 2,* lines 5a + 5b + 5c = line 5d) . . 5d

6 **Total taxes before adjustments** (lines 3 + 5d = line 6) . . . 6

7 **TAX ADJUSTMENTS** (Read the instructions for line 7 before completing lines 7a through 7h.):

7a **Current quarter's fractions of cents** . . .

7b **Current quarter's sick pay** . . .

7c **Current quarter's adjustments for tips and group-term life insurance**

7d **Current year's income tax withholding** (attach Form 941c) . . .

7e **Prior quarters' social security and Medicare taxes** (attach Form 941c)

7f **Special additions to federal income tax** (attach Form 941c) . . .

7g **Special additions to social security and Medicare** (attach Form 941c)

7h **TOTAL ADJUSTMENTS** (Combine all amounts: lines 7a through 7g.) . . . 7h

8 **Total taxes after adjustments** (Combine lines 6 and 7h.) . . . 8

9 **Advance earned income credit (EIC) payments made to employees** . . . 9

10 **Total taxes after adjustment for advance EIC** (line 8 – line 9 = line 10) . . . 10

11 **Total deposits for this quarter, including overpayment applied from a prior quarter** . . . 11

12 **Balance due** (If line 10 is more than line 11, write the difference here.) . . . 12
Make checks payable to *United States Treasury.*

13 **Overpayment** (If line 11 is more than line 10, write the difference here.) Check one ☐ Apply to next return. ☐ Send a refund.

▶ You **MUST** fill out both pages of this form and **SIGN** it.

Next ➔

For Privacy Act and Paperwork Reduction Act Notice, see the back of the Payment Voucher. Cat. No. 17001Z Form **941** (Rev. 1-2006)

17. Deposit Dates. For each of the following situations, determine the employer's required deposit date.

a. A monthly depositor whose payroll period ends on Friday, October 28.

b. A semiweekly depositor whose payroll period ends on Wednesday, April 12.

c. A semiweekly depositor whose payroll period ends on Friday, December 28.

d. A monthly depositor whose payroll period ends on Tuesday, May 15.

18. Estimated Taxes. Indicate whether or not the following individuals are required to pay an estimated tax for 2007. (Check either the "Yes" or the "No" column.)

	Yes	*No*
a. Single taxpayer with income derived solely from wages subject to withholding expected to equal $6,000. Estimated unpaid tax expected to total $250.	_____	_____
b. Married couple with husband's income derived solely from wages subject to withholding expected to equal $10,500. Spouse does not receive wages. Estimated unpaid tax expected to total $400.	_____	_____
c. Qualifying widower with income derived from wages subject to withholding expected to equal $12,500; income from other sources not subject to withholding expected to total $5,000. Estimated unpaid tax expected to total $1,200.	_____	_____
d. Married couple with husband's income derived solely from wages subject to withholding expected to equal $11,000; spouse expects to receive dividend income totaling $3,000. Estimated unpaid tax expected to total $1,550.	_____	_____

19. Estimated Taxes. Prepare the Estimated Tax Worksheet, reproduced below, for George B. Lewis, 2111 North Second Street, Madison, Wisconsin 53705-4001. Lewis, an unmarried taxpayer, claims one personal exemption and no dependency exemptions. He elects to pay the minimum amount of estimated tax required. The data for the worksheet is as follows.

AGI (includes estimated salary, $18,650; estimated self-employment net profit, $14,000) before deduction for ½ SE tax	$32,650
Estimated itemized deductions	8,000
Estimated income tax withheld	2,216
Credit for overpayment on the 2006 tax return, elected as a credit on the 2007 estimated tax and subtracted evenly from each quarterly payment	250
Income taxes for 2006 as determined by the income tax return	4,200

1	AGI Expected in 2007		______
2	Larger of:		
	Estimated itemized deductions	______	
	Standard deduction (in 2007) for filing class	5,350	______
3	Subtract line 2 from line 1		______
4	Personal and dependency exemptions (in 2007)		3,400
5	Subtract line 4 from line 3		______
6	Tax on amount on line 5*		______
7	Tax on accumulation distributions of trusts	______	
	Tax on lump-sum distributions	______	
8	Add lines 6 and 7		______
9	Less credits		______
10	Subtract line 9 from line 8		______
11	Self-employment tax	______	
12	Other taxes (AMT tax)	______	______
13a	Add lines 10 through 12		______
13b	Earned income credit and fuel credit		______
13c	Subtract line 13b from line 13a TOTAL 2007 ESTIMATED TAX		______
14a	90% of 2007 ESTIMATED TAX	______	
14b	100% of tax on 2006 tax return	______	
14c	Enter the smaller of line 14a or 14b REQUIRED ANNUAL PAYMENT TO AVOID A PENALTY		______
15	Income taxes withheld and estimated to be withheld during 2007		______
16	Subtract line 15 from 14c		______
17	Enter ¼ of line 16, rounded to nearest whole dollar		______

*The 2007 tax rates for single taxpayers are 10% on the first $7,800 of taxable income, and 15% on taxable income in excess of $7,800 but not more than $31,850.

20. Estimated Taxes. What steps can an unmarried taxpayer with AGI in 2006 of $75,000 take to avoid a penalty for underpayment of estimated taxes in 2007?

21. Estimated Taxes. What steps can a married couple with AGI of $200,000 in 2006 take to avoid the penalty for underpayment of estimated taxes in 2007?

22. Internet Problem: Researching Publication 926.

Brad and Carol Thomas made an agreement with a neighbor's child to care for their lawn. The neighbor's son, Tad, takes care of the lawns of others in the neighborhood. Tad provides all of his own machinery, tools and necessary supplies. During 2006 the Thomases pay Tad $2,000 for various lawn care services. Since this amount exceeds $1,500, they are worried that they might be required to report Tad as a household employee and be required to withhold employment taxes.

Go to the IRS Web site. Locate Publication 926, *Household Employer's Tax Guide* and use it to answer the Thomas's question. Print out a copy of the page where you find the answer. Underline or highlight the pertinent information. Comment on what you believe to be the answer to the Thomas's question.

See Appendix A for instructions on how to access the IRS Web site.

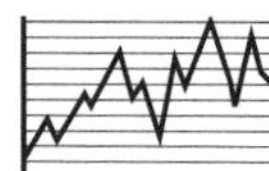

23. Business Entity Problem: This problem is designed for those using the "business entity" approach. The solution may require information from Chapters 14 and 15.

a. Sunset Corporation had taxable income of $300,000 last year. To avoid underpayment penalties for the current year, what amount of estimated taxes must the company deposit during the year?

b. If the corporation had taxable income of $3,000,000 last year, what amount of estimated taxes must be deposited in the current year to avoid an underpayment penalty?

14

C Corporations

CHAPTER CONTENTS

CHAPTER OVERVIEW

The sole proprietorship is the most common form of business ownership. Chapter 7 focuses on the taxation of income arising from proprietorship operations. However, partnerships and corporations are also popular ownership structures that are available to carry out business activities. Business owners must weigh the advantages and disadvantages of each when choosing the best entity from which to conduct their business operations. The impact of income taxation on each of these business entities plays a major role in this important choice.

A business organized as a corporation is a separate taxable entity. The corporation exists outside of its owners (shareholders), and it must pay a tax on its income. Such companies are called C corporations. The name comes from the location of the governing Code provisions (Subchapter C). However, Congress created another tax entity, called an S corporation, which has features of both corporations and partnerships. The tax aspects of C corporations is the focus of this chapter. S corporations and partnerships are the focus of Chapter 15.

THE NATURE OF C CORPORATIONS

Usually, a business organized as a corporation qualifies as a separate tax entity and pays tax on corporate taxable income. However, determining whether an organization is a corporation for federal tax purposes does not depend strictly on whether the entity is legally a corporation under state law. Rather, the decision is based on the number of tax-defined corporate traits the entity possesses. The law generally taxes a business as a corporation if it has these traits:

1. Business associates
2. A purpose to carry on a business and divide the profits
3. Continuity of life
4. Centralized management
5. Limited liability
6. Free transferability of ownership interests

The first two traits help distinguish a corporation from an estate or trust. Since partnerships and corporations have these first two traits in common, the IRS and the courts focus on the last four to distinguish the entities. To help avoid disputes in this area, the tax laws now allow businesses to choose which type of entity they wish to be taxed as. This choice is commonly known as the check-the-box rules. Thus, when businesses are now formed, they can choose their tax status without regard to its corporate or noncorporate traits. Corporations that pay tax on their taxable income are commonly called "C corporations" or "regular corporations." These corporations are the focus of this chapter. S corporations are a special type of corporation. They are discussed in Chapter 15.

Forming a Corporation

Investors setting up a corporation transfer either cash, property, or services to the corporation in exchange for the corporation's stock. Those purchasing stock have an investment (basis) in the stock equal to the cash paid. However, when investors form a corporation by tranferring property to the corporation solely in exchange for its stock, it is generally treated as a type of nontaxable exchange (Chapter 10). No gain or loss is recognized, and the basis of the stock is usually the basis of the property transferred. Also, the basis of the property acquired by the corporation is normally the same as that of the transferor. An exception applies if personal-use property is transferred to the corporation. Here, the basis of the investment (stock received) and the property transferred is equal to the *lesser of* (i) the taxpayer's basis in the property, or (ii) the property's FMV at the time of the transfer.

When people perform services in exchange for the corporation's stock, they recognize income equal to the FMV of the stock received. This amount also becomes the basis of their investment (stock) in the company.

EXAMPLE 1

Cara Bernardi and several business associates decide to set up a corporation. Bernardi transfers the assets of her proprietorship to the new corporation in exchange for 100,000 shares of stock. Bernardi's basis in the assets transferred is $250,000. Her basis in the stock received is $250,000 ($2.50 per share). The basis of the assets to the corporation is also $250,000.

EXAMPLE 2

Victoria Wise performs services in exchange for 1,000 shares of stock in a corporation. At the time the services were performed, the stock was worth $15 a share. Wise includes the $15,000 ($15 x 1,000) in gross income. This becomes her basis in the shares of stock.

CORPORATE TAXABLE INCOME

For the most part, corporations compute their taxable income as individuals compute their business profit or loss (Chapter 7). However, gains and loss from disposing of property are included in the calculation of a corporation's taxable income. (Recall that these items were not part of the individual's calculation of profits on Schedule C, but were part of the calculation of AGI). Most of the rules governing income and business deductions apply to both individuals and corporations. One major difference between corporations and individuals concerns the treatment of nonbusiness deductions. Whereas individuals deduct personal expenditures as itemized deductions, corporations have no personal expenses. Thus, corporations do not use the concept of adjusted gross income (AGI) because they have no deductions from AGI (no standard deduction or itemized deductions) and no personal or dependency exemptions. Furthermore, corporations have different limits on capital losses and charitable contributions. They also get a deduction based on the dividends they collect that individuals do not receive. These differences are covered in more detail later in this chapter.

Accounting Methods

A corporation must select an accounting method for determining its taxable income. Most corporations use the accrual method of accounting. With the **accrual method,** corporations report income when it is earned even though they may not have received it in cash. Also, they deduct expenses when they are incurred though they may remain unpaid at the end of the tax year.

Besides the accrual method, the other accounting options available to certain corporations are the cash and hybrid methods. With the **cash method,** income is taxable when received, and expenses are deductible when paid. The **hybrid method** combines cash and accrual methods. Here, the corporation uses the accrual method for computing gross profit from the sale of inventory and the cash method for other income and deductions.

The kinds of corporations permitted to use the cash method are limited. Farming and personal service corporations may use the cash method. All other corporations must have average gross receipts for the last three years of no more than $5 million. Even for these corporations, the law requires use of the accrual method for computing the gross profit from the sale of inventory.

Accounting Periods

Corporations normally use a 12-month year to report their taxable income. Unlike partnerships and S corporations, a C corporation may choose to use a calendar year or a fiscal year. A fiscal year can be any 12-month period that ends on the last day of a month other than December. For example, a corporation may use a tax year of July 1 to June 30 as its fiscal tax year.

Another fiscal year option that corporations may choose is a 52-53 week year. Corporations select this tax year when they want their tax year to end on the same day of the week each year. The day may be either the last one occurring in the last month of their tax year or the one occurring closest to their normal year end.

EXAMPLE 3

Carolina Corporation closes its tax year on the last Friday in December each year. In 20x0, the last Friday in December falls on December 29. In 20x1, it falls on December 28, and in 20x2, it falls on December 26. Thus, Carolina's 52-53 week tax year for 20x1 runs from December 30, 20x0 to December 28, 20x1. Its tax year for 20x2 runs from December 29, 20x2 until December 26, 20x3.

Corporations can have a tax year shorter than 12 months in three situations. The first is in the year in which the corporation is formed. The second generally occurs in the last year of the corporation's operations. The third is when a corporation changes its tax year. In the latter case, the corporation files a short-period return that covers the period between the close of its last year and the start of its new year. All taxpayers must get permission from the IRS to change their accounting period. For corporations, this is done by filing Form 1128, Application to Adopt, Change, or Retain a Tax Year.

EXAMPLE 4

A newly formed corporation selects a September 30 year end. The corporation begins operations on May 16, 20x1. For the fiscal year ending September 31, 20x1, the corporation files a short period return for the period May 16, 20x1 – September 30, 20x1. Its fiscal year ending on September 30, 20x2 includes the activities of the corporation from October 1, 20x1 until September 30, 20x2.

EXAMPLE 5

On July 1, 20x3, a corporation that has a calendar year end decides that it wants to change to a fiscal year that ends on October 31. This fiscal year end more closely reflects the end of the corporation's annual business cycle. The corporation files Form 1128 and is granted permission from the IRS to change its tax year effective October 31, 20x3. This requires the corporation to file a tax return for the short period that runs from January 1, 20x3 – October 31, 20x3. Its next tax return will be for the fiscal year November 1, 20x3 – October 31, 20x4.

Corporate Taxable Income Formula

Corporations compute their taxable income as gross income less business expenses. However, some specific deductions require special computations and therefore cannot be grouped with other business expenses. These include (1) charitable contribution deduction (CC), (2) dividends received deduction (DRD), (3) the domestic production activities deduction (DPA), (4) net operating loss (NOL) carrybacks, and (5) short-term capital loss (STCL) carrybacks. The formula for computing corporate taxable income is:

	Gross income
–	Deductions (except CC, DRD, DPA, NOL carryback, STCL carryback)
=	Taxable income for figuring CC
–	Charitable contribution (CC) deduction
=	Taxable income for figuring DRD
–	Dividends received deduction (DRD)
=	Taxable income before carrybacks and DPA deduction
–	DPA deduction
–	NOL carryback
–	(STCL) carryback
=	Taxable income

Income Items

Typically, the same Code provisions determine the tax status of income items for individual taxpayers (Chapters 3 and 4) and corporations. However, in some cases additional provisions apply.

Gross Profit from Sales

Net sales less cost of goods sold equals **gross profit from sales.** Gross sales less returns and allowances equals **net sales.** Corporations can deduct *sales discounts* directly from sales or treat them as a business expense. Corporate inventories usually make a material contribution to income. These inventories can include raw materials, supplies, work in process, and finished goods. Corporations that produce goods for sale include all production costs in inventories. These costs include direct materials, direct labor, and direct and indirect overhead. The term for this process is **full costing.**

To compute **cost of goods sold,** a corporation adds beginning inventories, labor, and overhead. Then, it subtracts ending inventories. An example follows:

Globe Manufacturing Company Cost of Goods Sold Computations:

Beginning inventories	$100,956
Add: Purchases	207,858
Labor	74,807
Other costs	30,529
Total inventory available for sale	$414,150
Less ending inventories	(90,283)
Cost of goods sold	$323,867

Capital Gains and Losses

Corporations report the sale of capital assets on Schedule D (Form 1120). Unlike individuals, corporations receive no special tax rate treatment of capital gains. They must include the full amount of capital gains in their regular taxable income. However, corporations must record capital gains separately from other income because capital losses can be deducted only from capital gains. Any capital losses in excess of capital gains for the year are carried back three years or forward five years. They may offset capital gains only in the carryover years. The corporation treats all carryovers as short-term capital losses. The corporation first uses capital losses arising in the carryover year. It then uses the carryover capital losses. If it has carry over losses from more than one year, the losses are used on a first-created-first-used basis. If it does not use the losses within the carryover period, the corporation loses the tax benefit of the losses.

EXAMPLE 6

McCann, Inc. has the following capital gains and losses during the 20x3.

Short-term capital gain	$ 18,000
Short-term capital loss	(14,000)
Long-term capital gain	13,000
Long-term capital loss	(22,000)

The netting process used in Chapter 11 applies to all types of taxpayers. Thus, McCann begins this process by offsetting short-term capital losses against short-term capital gains. It then offset long-term capital losses against long-term capital gains. This results in a $4,000 net short-term gain and a $9,000 net long-term loss. McCann uses $4,000 of the net long-term capital loss to offset its net short-term capital gain.

Short-Term	Long-Term
$18,000	$ 13,000
(14,000)	(22,000)
$ 4,000	($ 9,000)
(4,000) ←	┘
$ 0	

McCann must carry back $5,000 of its capital losses ($9,000 - $4,000 used in 20x3) to 20x0 (its third preceding tax year). These losses will be treated as short-term capital losses when the netting process for that year is redone. Any losses not used in 20x0 are carried forward to 20x1 and then 20x2. If McCann cannot use up all of the capital losses in those carryback years, it carries forward any remaining amount as a short-term capital loss to 20x4-20x8 (for a total of five carry forward years).

EXAMPLE 7

Continuing with Example 6, assume that McCann, Inc. had the following capital gains and losses during the 20x0.

Short-Term	Long-Term
$12,000	$ 7,000
(3,000)	(5,000)
$ 9,000	$ 2,000

When the $5,000 excess capital loss from 20x3 is carried back to 20x0 as a short-term capital loss, the netting process from 20x0 is as follows.

	Short-Term	Long-Term
Carryback from 20x3	($ 5,000)	
	12,000	$ 7,000
	(3,000)	(5,000)
	$ 4,000	$ 2,000

When McCann adds the $5,000 short-term capital loss to the netting process, its taxable income is reduced by $5,000 ($11,000 overall net gain reported originally vs. $6,000 overall net gain as recomputed). McCann files for a refund of the taxes paid on the $5,000 of capital gain by filing Form 1139, Corporation Application for Tentative Refund. If McCann's marginal tax rate in 20x0 was 35%, then the IRS will refund McCann $1,750 ($5,000 x 35%), which represents the overpaid taxes for that year.

Business Deductions

Many corporate deductions are the same as those taken by sole proprietors (Chapter 7). However, within any one deduction group, differences can exist.

Compensation

Corporations deduct payments for personal services as compensation when they pass three tests: (1) the payments represent an ordinary and necessary expense of the business, (2) the payments represent a reasonable amount for services received, and (3) the corporation pays or accrues them in the current tax year under its accounting method. In addition, for publicly held corporations, a special rule limits the deduction for corporate salaries paid to the Chief Executive Officer (CEO) and the other four most highly paid officers. Generally, the rule limits the compensation deduction for each of these officers to not more than $1 million. However, all compensation paid to an officer is taxable, even though some of it is not deductible.

The deduction on the tax return for salaries and wages equals paid or accrued compensation less any job tax credits taken on the tax return. These include the work opportunity, welfare-to-work and the empowerment zone and renewal communities tax credits (see Chapter 12).

Corporations having gross income of at least $500,000 must list out compensation paid to their officers on Form 1120, Schedule E, Compensation of Officers. This schedule includes each officer's name, SSN, percent of time devoted to business, and stock ownership percentage. Under the heading *Amount of compensation,* a corporation includes each officer's salary, commission, and bonus. This information allows the IRS to test the reasonableness of an officer's compensation. While a definite rule for determining reasonable compensation does not exist, some guidelines do exist. The main guideline relates to other organizations with like conditions. This guideline focuses on what other organizations pay for like services. Other guidelines include local living costs, officer's ability, and degree of responsibility. The completion of the corporate tax return (Form 1120) is discussed later in the chapter.

EXAMPLE 8

Easton Corporation pays its CEO $1.5 million in 2006. Easton cannot justify why the $1 million limit should not be imposed. Although Easton can pay its CEO $1.5 million, it can only deduct $1 million on its 2006 tax return. The CEO must include the $1.5 of compensation he received in gross income when filing his personal income tax return.

Bad Debts

Most taxpayers, including corporations, can use only the direct write-off method for bad debts. An exception exists for certain financial institutions. These organizations use the reserve method of accounting (used in financial reporting).

EXAMPLE 9

In August of 20x5, an accrual basis, calendar year corporation sold merchandise on account for $1,000. The corporation included the sale in 20x5 gross income. On June 15, 20x6, the accounts receivable becomes worthless. Since the corporation recognized the profit from the sale in 20x5, it takes a bad debt deduction for $1,000 in 20x6. It is important to note that the corporation must be able to specifically identify which accounts receivable became worthless before it can take a bad debt deduction. This is known as the "direct write-off method."

Organizational and Start-Up Costs

The Code allows corporations to elect to deduct up to $5,000 of organizational expenditures for the tax year in which business operations begin. The $5,000 amount is reduced by $1 for each dollar of total organizational costs that exceed $50,000. Thus, no current deduction is allowed to corporations that incur over $55,000 in organizational costs. At the taxpayer's election, any costs not currently expensed may be written off (amortized) over a 180-month period using the straight-line method. The amortization begins starting in the month in which the corporation begins operations. If no election is made, the organizational costs are capitalized to an asset account and used in the calculation of realized gain or loss when the corporation goes out of business.

The expenses qualifying as **organizational costs** include any costs related to the creation of the corporation that are chargeable to a capital account. They must be incurred within the first year of the corporation's operations. These costs include (1) legal expenses for setting up the corporation, (2) state costs of incorporation, (3) necessary accounting services, (4) expenses of temporary directors, and (5) costs of organizational meetings. Organizational expenditures do not include the costs of issuing or selling stocks or other securities or costs associated with transferring assets to the corporation. These latter costs simply reduce the amount of paid-in capital.

EXAMPLE 10

Branis Corporation incurs $53,500 of organizational costs. Branis uses a calendar year end and began its operations on November 1, 2006. Since the organizational costs exceed $50,000, Branis can elect to expense only $1,500 ($5,000 – $3,500) in 2006. It can then elect to amortize the remaining $52,000 ($53,500 – $1,500) over 180 months beginning on November 1, 2006.

Start-up costs are costs that normally would be currently deductible if they were incurred during the operations of an existing business. They often include expenditures incurred to investigate entering into or acquiring a new active trade or business. The deduction for start-up costs is similar to that of organizational costs. The Code allows businesses to elect to deduct up to $5,000 of start-up expenditures. However, the $5,000 is reduced by the amount by which the start-up expenditures exceed $50,000. The rest may be amortized evenly over 180 months beginning with the month in which the business begins. The rules that apply to start-up costs are available to all types of businesses, including sole proprietorships, C corporations, partnerships and S corporations.

EXAMPLE 11

Addison, Inc. uses a calendar year end. During 2006 it incurred $65,000 of start-up costs while looking into buying a new business. Addison acquired the business on November 22, 2006. Since the start-up costs exceed $55,000, all start-up costs must be capitalized. Addison can amortize this amount over 180 months beginning in November 2006. It deducts $722 ($65,000/180 × 2 months) in 2006 and will deduct $4,333 ($65,000/180 × 12 months) each year from 2007–2020. In 2021, Addison will deduct the final $3,611 ($65,000/180 × 10 months) of amortization expense.

Passive Losses

The passive loss limitations (Chapter 9) do not apply to most corporations. Thus, corporations can use passive losses to reduce active or portfolio income. However, closely-held corporations (over 50% owned by five or fewer individuals) and personal service corporations (PSCs) are subject to the passive loss limitations.

Special Deductions

The deductions for corporations, for the most part, are treated the same as business deductions for other business entities. Nevertheless, some special deductions for corporations receive distinctive treatment. In reviewing the formula for computing taxable income, these special deductions are listed separately. The discussion that follows describes each of these special deductions.

Charitable Contributions

Like individuals, corporations can take a deduction for contributions to charitable organizations. However, the corporate deduction cannot exceed 10% of the corporation's taxable income before certain items. These items include any deductions for charitable contributions, dividend received deductions, the domestic production activities deduction, NOL carrybacks, and capital loss carrybacks (see taxable income formula presented earlier in the chapter).

EXAMPLE 12

During 20x1, a corporation makes cash contributions of $20,000 to various charitable organizations. The corporation has taxable income of $180,000 before deducting any charitable contributions (CCs), dividends received deduction (DRD), the domestic production activities deduction (DPA) or any capital or net operating loss (NOL) carrybacks. The amount of the corporation's charitable deduction for the current year equals $18,000.

Taxable income (before deducting CC deduction)	$180,000
	× 10%
Maximum charitable contribution deduction	$ 18,000
Cash contributions made during 20x1	$ 20,000
Less corporate limitation	(18,000)
Charitable contribution carryover to 20x2	$ 2,000

The $2,000 excess contribution carries over for five years. However, total charitable deductions in those carryover years must also fall under the 10% taxable income limitation.

Sometimes, a corporation donates appreciated property to a public charity. The corporation figures the amount of the contribution in the same manner as individuals. Thus, when a corporation donates ordinary income property to a charity, it normally would be allowed to deduct its adjusted basis in the property. However, a special rule applies when a corporation donates its appreciated inventory items to public charities that use the inventory *solely* for the care of the ill or needy, or when the inventory is used to care for infants. In these cases, the corporation can deduct the inventory's adjusted basis plus one-half of its appreciation (excess of fair market value (FMV) over adjusted basis). However, the deduction cannot exceed twice the adjusted basis in the inventory. A similar rule applies to contributions of ordinary income property to colleges, universities, or scientific tax-exempt organizations for use in research.

EXAMPLE 13

J.K. Ramis, Inc. sells children's clothing. During the year it contributes clothing worth $3,000 to a charity. The charity will use the clothing for the care of infants, which is consistent with its intended purpose. Ramis's basis in the inventory is $800. Ramis initially computes its deduction as its $800 basis in the clothing plus $1,100 (($3,000 – $800) x ½). However, since this amount ($800 + $1,100 = $1,900) exceeds twice its basis in the inventory ($800 × 2 = $1,600), its charitable deduction is limited to $1,600.

EXAMPLE 14

Same as in Example 13 except that Ramis's basis in the clothing is $1,800. Ramis initially computes its deduction as $1,400 ($800 adjusted basis + (½ x ($3,000 - $1,800)). Since this amount does not exceed $1,600 (twice the adjusted basis in the inventory), Ramis's charitable contribution deduction is $1,400.

Ordinarily, a corporation deducts a contribution in the year it transfers property or cash to a charity. A corporation using the accrual method of accounting, however, can choose to deduct a contribution in the year it makes the accrual. To take the deduction in the accrual year, the corporation must pay the contribution within 2½ months after its year ends.

Dividends Received Deduction

Corporations get a deduction for a certain amount of the dividends they receive. The deduction lessens or avoids triple taxation of the gains of corporations. Triple taxation occurs when a corporation distributes its after-tax profits to corporate shareholders. These corporate shareholders normally would pay taxes on the dividends before they distribute their profits to their shareholders (who also pay taxes on the dividends they receive). The amount of the dividends received deduction (DRD) depends on the corporation's percentage of stock ownership in the dividend-paying corporation.

Percentage Owned	*DRD Percentage*
Less than 20%	70%
From 20% to less than 80%	80%
From 80% to 100%	100%

EXAMPLE 15

Delta Corporation owns 60% of the total value and outstanding shares of Epsilon Corporation. Epsilon makes a dividend distribution to Delta of $100,000. Delta includes the $100,000 of dividends in income and takes a $80,000 DRD ($100,000 × 80%). Thus, the net amount of dividends taxed to Delta is $20,000 ($100,000 – $80,000).

The DRD may be limited to an amount less than the standard percentage of the dividends received. The Code requires corporations whose ownership is less than 80% to also apply the standard percentages to taxable income (after deducting charitable contributions but before any capital or net operating loss carrybacks or the domestic production activities -- see the taxable income formula). The corporation's DRD is the *lesser of* (i) the standard percentage times dividends received, or (ii) the standard percentage times taxable income. However, if deducting a DRD based on the dividends received causes an NOL for the year, then this amount is the deduction. Thus, in this case, the DRD will not be based on the net income limitation.

EXAMPLE 16

Same as in Example 15 except that Delta's net income after the charitable contribution deduction and before any loss carrybacks is $90,000. If Delta were to deduct a DRD based on dividends received ($100,000 x 80%), the result would not be an NOL for the year ($90,000 - $80,000 = $10,000 taxable income). Thus, Delta computes its DRD as the *lesser of* (i) $80,000 (80% of $100,000 dividends received), or (ii) $72,000 (80% x $90,000 taxable income. Delta's DRD is $72,000.

EXAMPLE 17

Same as in Example 15 except that Delta's net income after the charitable contribution deduction and before any loss carrybacks is $70,000. Now when Delta deducts an $80,000 DRD based on dividends received, it results in an NOL ($70,000 - $80,000 = $10,000 NOL). Thus, the DRD limitation does not apply and Delta can use $80,000 as its DRD (80% x $100,000 dividends received).

COMPUTING THE DIVIDENDS RECEIVED DEDUCTION

Step 1 Multiply the standard percentage based on ownership times the dividends received.

Step 2 Multiply the standard percentage by the corporation's taxable income after deducting charitable contributions but before any loss carrybacks or the DPA deduction.

Step 3 Subtract the result from step 2 from the corporation's taxable income used in step 2. If a loss results, then use the amount from step 2 as the corporation's DRD. If a positive amount results, then use the *lesser of* step 1 or 2 as the DRD.

Net Operating Loss (NOL)

When a corporation's deductions exceed its income, the corporation may suffer a net loss for the year. A corporation need make only one adjustment to its taxable income in determining its NOL for the current year. It must add back any NOL carryovers from prior years. Like individuals, corporations carry their NOLs back 2 years and forward 20 (back 3, forward 15 for tax years starting before August 6, 1997). They have the option of not carrying back and just carrying forward the NOL. The carryover provisions reduce the hardship of the 12-month accounting period for those businesses with longer business cycles. It also allows corporations to offset profitable years with unprofitable ones.

In computing taxable income for the current year, a corporation deducts any NOL or capital loss *carry forwards* from gross income. Since these deductions are known at the time of the taxable income computation, they are not treated as special deductions. NOL and capital loss carrybacks are, however, considered special deductions because these deductions are not known at the time the corporation computes current taxable income. This is because carrybacks do not occur until the future. Consequently, corporations file amended returns for prior years when using NOL or capital loss carrybacks.

EXAMPLE 18

Cougar Corporation has the following income and deductions in 2006:

Gross sales	$600,000
Long-term capital gains	25,000
Dividend income (18% ownership in the stock)	40,000
Interest income	10,000
Cost of goods sold	400,000
Domestic production activities (DPA) deduction	18,000
Other business expenses	60,000
Charitable contributions	22,000
Short-term capital loss carry forward	15,000

Cougar computes its 2006 taxable income as follows. It carries forward a $2,000 charitable contribution to 2007 ($22,000 - $20,000).

Gross income [1]	$660,000
Less deductions [2]	(460,000)
Taxable income for computing CC deduction	$200,000
Less charitable contribution deduction [3]	(20,000)
Less DPA deduction	(18,000)
Taxable income for figuring DRD	$162,000
Less DRD [4]	(28,000)
Taxable income	$134,000

[1] $600,000 + ($25,000 capital gains - $15,000 capital losses) + $40,000 + $10,000
[2] $400,000 + $60,000
[3] $200,000 × 10%
[4] *lesser of* (i) $40,000 dividends received × 70% or (ii) 70% x $162,000

EXAMPLE 19

Continuing with Example 18, assume that in 2008 Cougar suffers a NOL of $80,000 which it carries back to 2006. Its 2006 taxable income is lowered to $46,000. Cougar recomputes its tax liability using $46,000 of taxable income and asks the IRS for a refund of the difference between that amount and the amount of taxes it owed based on $134,000 of taxable income.

Taxable income before carrybacks	$134,000
Less: NOL carryback	(80,000)
Recomputed taxable income for 2006	$ 46,000

CORPORATE TAX RETURNS AND TAX RATES

Every C corporation must file a tax return, regardless of the amount of its taxable income or loss. Once the corporation computes its taxable income, it applies the appropriate corporate tax rate. Both individual and corporate tax rates are **progressive** (the rates increase as taxable income increases). However, the corporate tax brackets are not indexed for inflation; the individual tax brackets are indexed each year. The next sections describe the corporate tax return and its tax rates.

Corporate Tax Return

Most C corporations use Form 1120, U.S. Corporation Income Tax Return, to report their taxable income (loss). Under certain conditions, they file Form 1120-A, U.S. Corporation Short-Form Income Tax Return. While Form 1120 has four pages, simplified Form 1120-A has two. Form 1120-A is for small corporations with gross receipts, total income, and total assets all under $500,000.

Due Date

The due date for most corporate returns falls on the 15th of the third month after the corporation's year ends. This date also applies to foreign corporations with a U.S. place of business. Other foreign corporations file their returns by the 15th day of the sixth month. When a due date falls on a Saturday, Sunday, or holiday, the due date becomes the next business day.

A corporation that cannot file its tax return by the due date can request an automatic six-month extension to file its return by filing Form 7004 by the due date of its tax return (see Chapter 1). As with all extensions, filing this form only extends the due date for filing the tax return. It does not extend the payment of taxed owed. Taxpayers that do not pay the taxes they owe by the original due date of their tax return are subject to interest and penalties.

EXAMPLE 20

Amel, Inc. (a calendar year corporation) normally must file its tax return by March 15. If Amel is unable to file its return by that date, it can file Form 7004 with the IRS by that date. It will then have until September 15 to file its tax return. It must, however, pay any taxes it owes when it files the extension. Any unpaid taxes would be subject to interest and penalty. Should September 15 fall on a Saturday, the deadline for filing a timely return with an extension would be the following business day.

EXAMPLE 21

Same as in Example 20 except that Amel uses a fiscal year that ends on March 31. Amel's due date for filing its tax return is June 15. This is 2½ months after the end of Amel's March 31 fiscal year end. If Amel files a timely extension, its tax return deadline would be extended to December 15. If either of these deadlines falls on a weekend or holiday, the deadline would be the next business day.

Corporate Tax Rates

Like the rate structure for individual taxpayers, the one for corporations is progressive. At higher income levels, benefits from the low rates phase out. Once the phase-out stops, the rates stay flat (same rate for all taxable income). Other than professional service corporations (described later), all regular C corporations compute their tax using the same rate structure, as follows:

Taxable Income	*Corporate Tax Rate*
\$0–\$50,000	15%
\$50,001–\$75,000	25
\$75,001–\$100,000	34
\$100,001–\$335,000	39
\$335,001–\$10,000,000	34
\$10,000,001–\$15,000,000	35
\$15,000,001–\$18,333,333	38
Over \$18,333,333	35

Rate Structure and Tax Calculation

The tax rate structure contains two phase-out ranges and two phase-out rates. Before and after the first phase-out, the marginal tax rate equals 34%. The marginal tax rate before and after the second phase-out equals 35%. For corporations with taxable income below \$75,000, Congress set the rates low (15% and 25%) to stimulate growth. The Code phases out the benefits of the low rates by a 5% additional tax on taxable income between \$100,000 and \$335,000 (39% rather than 34%). When taxable income reaches \$335,000, the government has recovered all low-rate benefits. The amount of these benefits equals \$11,750 {[(34% – 15%) × \$50,000] + [(34% – 25%) × \$25,000]} or [(\$335,000 – \$100,000) × 5%]. The tax rate is then a flat 34% for incomes up to \$10 million.

EXAMPLE 22

XYZ corporation, a calendar year corporation, has taxable income of $900,000. The computations for XYZ's income tax of $306,000 follow. Notice that XYZ's tax equals a flat rate of 34% (34% × $900,000 = $306,000).

	Income Tax
15% × $50,000	$ 7,500
25% × $25,000	6,250
34% × $25,000	8,500
39% × $235,000	91,650
34% × $565,000	192,100
Tax liability	$306,000

A similar phase-out takes place for corporations whose taxable income exceeds $15,000,000. This phase-out eliminates the 1% lower tax benefit (35% – 34%) on incomes below $10 million ($10,000,000 × 1% = $100,000 benefit). Between $15,000,000 and $18,333,333, the Code increases the 35% rate by 3 percentage points. This rate increase produces additional revenues of $100,000 (3% × $3,333,333 = $99,999.99, rounded to $100,000). For taxable incomes in excess of $18,333,333, corporations have a flat rate of 35%.

Personal Service Corporations

Personal service corporations (PSC) are corporations whose shareholders and employees provide professional services for a fee. Doctors, dentists, lawyers, architects, accountants, and others organize as PSCs. Such corporations provide the owners with several tax and nontax benefits. However, these corporations have some tax restrictions. PSCs generally may only use a calendar year as their tax year. This limits any benefits of income deferral. If they use other than a calendar year, the PSCs must make sure that the amount of salaries paid to shareholder-employees in the deferral period is consistent with the salaries paid in the nondeferral periods. Another limitation on PSCs is the tax rate they use for computing tax liability. PSCs have a flat tax rate of 35% on all taxable income. The purpose of this high tax rate on all income is to encourage the PSC to pay out its net earnings to its shareholder-employees as salaries. These salaries are then taxed at the individual tax rates.

Information for Figure 14-2: Filled-In Form 1120

Globe Manufacturing Company (EIN 86-0694770), located at 2468 E. Van Buren, Phoenix, AZ 85019-2468, began business on January 3, 2000. Globe has always been on the accrual method of accounting and uses the cost method for valuing inventory of electronic components which it manufactures. Globe made estimated payments of $4,000 during the year and paid out $16,446 in cash dividends.

The income and expense information for preparing Globe Manufacturing Company's Form 1120 comes from the 2006 Income Statement in Figure 14-1. The filled-in Form 1120 for Globe Manufacturing Company appears in Figure 14-2. The balance sheet information appears on Schedule L and is not provided elsewhere.

FIGURE 14-1 Income Statement For Globe Manufacturing Company

Globe Manufacturing Company
Income Statement
For Year Ended December 31, 2006

Revenue:		
Net sales (after subtracting $3,197 of goods returned)		$528,072
Interest income ($1,650 from municipal bonds)		2,559
Dividend income ($1,750 domestic, $235 foreign)		1,985
(Globe owns 55% of each corporation's stock)		
Gross rent		500
Total revenues		$533,116
Less Expenses:		
Advertising	$ 17,500	
Bad debts written off during the year	1,960	
Charitable contributions	5,200	
Cost of goods sold (COGS) other than depreciation	293,338	
Depreciation ($30,529 related to COGS)	36,744	
Insurance expense	2,270	
Interest expense	2,580	
Maintenance	3,140	
Officers' salaries	80,000	
Other employee salaries	52,047	
Office supplies	163	
Taxes and licenses	8,200	
Utilities expense	1,087	(504,229)
Net income before federal income taxes		$ 28,887
Less income tax		(4,333)
Net income per books		$24,554

Other Information

Form 1120 Schedule A, Page 1

D: Total assets, **$428,944** (source: Schedule L, line 15(d))

1a: Gross receipts or sales, **$531,269** ($528,072 net sales + $3,197 returns)

1b: Less returns and allowances, **$3,197**

5: Interest, **$909** ($2,559 total interest - $1,650 tax-exempt interest)

19: Charitable contributions, **$3,244** [10% x ($207,599 total income reported on line 11 minus $175,162 (total deductions other than the charitable contribution deduction on line 19 and the domestic production activities deduction on line 25)]

20: Depreciation not claimed on Schedule A (COGS), **$6,215** ($36,744 - $30,529)

25: Domestic production activities deduction, **$4,284** (*lesser of* (i) 3% x $142,800 qualified production activity income (calculated by the company) or (ii) 50% of $30,529 W-2 wages from manufacturing activities (provided by the company)). See Chapter 4 for the discussion of this deduction.

26: Other deductions, **$3,520** ($2,270 + $163 + $1,087)

Form 1120, Page 2 - Schedule A

1: Inventory at beginning of year, **$100,956** (from Schedule L, line 3(b))
2: Purchases, **$207,858** (source: provided by company)
3: Cost of labor, **$74,807** (source: provided by company)
5: Other costs, **$30,529** (given: depreciation associated with COGS)
7: Inventory at end of year, **$90,283** (from Schedule L, line 3(d))

Form 1120, Page 2 - Schedule C

2a: Dividends from 20%-or-more-owned domestic corporations, **$1,750**
13a: Other dividends from foreign corporations, **$235**

Form 1120, Page 3 - Schedule J

2: Income tax, **$3,526** (15% tax rate x $23,509 taxable income)

Form 1120 Schedule K, Page 3

3-7:Mark **No**

Form 1120, Page 4 - Schedule M-1

5b: Charitable contributions recorded on the books not deducted on the return, **$1,956** ($5,200 - $3,244)
7: Tax-exempt interest recorded on books this year not included on this return, **$1,650**
8b: Domestic production activities deduction deducted on this return not charged against book income, **$4,284**

Form 1120 Schedules M-1 and M-2

Corporations with total assets that exceed $250,000 must complete Schedules L, M-1 and M-2. The changes to retained earnings during the year are explained in Schedule M-2 on Form 1120, page 4. Also on Form 1120, page 4 net income (loss) per books is reconciled with the amount reported on Form 1120, line 28. This amount equals taxable income before any net operating loss (NOL) or and dividends received deduction (DRD). For Globe Manufacturing in Figure 14-2, differences between book net income and taxable income (before NOL and DRD) included:

- The deduction for federal income taxes (deducted on the income statement, but not deductible in computing taxable income)
- Charitable contributions limited on the tax return by 10% of taxable income
- Tax-exempt interest (included on the income statement, but not taxable)
- Domestic production activities deduction (deductible on the tax return, but not a deduction reported on the income statement).

However, other differences may exist. For example, differences between net income and taxable income that may be reported on Schedule M-1 may result from:

- Differences in methods used to compute depreciation expense,
- Amounts spent on travel, meals and entertainment that are not deductible on the tax return (for example, 50% of meals and entertainment),
- Differences in methods used to compute bad debt expense,
- Charitable contributions carried over from a prior tax year that are deducted on the tax return in the current year.

FIGURE 14-2 Filled-In Form 1120, Page 1

Form **1120** Department of the Treasury Internal Revenue Service (77)

U.S. Corporation Income Tax Return

For calendar year 2006 or tax year beginning ...., 2006, ending ...., 20 ....

► See separate instructions.

OMB No. 1545-0123

2006

A Check if:	Use IRS label. Otherwise, print or type.		
1 Consolidated return (attach Form 851) ☐	Name: Globe Manufacturing Company	B Employer identification number: 86 : 0694770
2 Personal holding co. (attach Sch. PH) ☐	Number, street, and room or suite no. If a P.O. box, see instructions. 2468 E. Van Buren	C Date incorporated: January 3, 2000
3 Personal service corp. (see instructions) ☐	City or town, state, and ZIP code: Phoenix, AZ 85019-2468	D Total assets (see instructions): $ 428,944
4 Schedule M-3 required (attach Sch. M-3) ☐		

E Check if: (1) ☐ Initial return (2) ☐ Final return (3) ☐ Name change (4) ☐ Address change

Income	1a	Gross receipts or sales 531,269 b Less returns and allowances 3,197 c Bal ►	1c	528,072
	2	Cost of goods sold (Schedule A, line 8)	2	323,867
	3	Gross profit. Subtract line 2 from line 1c	3	204,205
	4	Dividends (Schedule C, line 19)	4	1,985
	5	Interest	5	909
	6	Gross rents	6	500
	7	Gross royalties	7	
	8	Capital gain net income (attach Schedule D (Form 1120))	8	
	9	Net gain or (loss) from Form 4797, Part II, line 17 (attach Form 4797)	9	
	10	Other income (see instructions—attach schedule)	10	
	11	**Total income.** Add lines 3 through 10 ►	11	207,599
Deductions (See instructions for limitations on deductions.)	12	Compensation of officers (Schedule E, line 4)	12	80,000
	13	Salaries and wages (less employment credits)	13	52,047
	14	Repairs and maintenance	14	3,140
	15	Bad debts	15	1,960
	16	Rents	16	
	17	Taxes and licenses	17	8,200
	18	Interest	18	2,580
	19	Charitable contributions	19	3,244
	20	Depreciation from Form 4562 not claimed on Schedule A or elsewhere on return (attach Form 4562)	20	6,215
	21	Depletion	21	
	22	Advertising	22	17,500
	23	Pension, profit-sharing, etc., plans	23	
	24	Employee benefit programs	24	
	25	Domestic production activities deduction (attach Form 8903)	25	4,284
	26	Other deductions (attach schedule)	26	3,520
	27	**Total deductions.** Add lines 12 through 26 ►	27	182,690
	28	Taxable income before net operating loss deduction and special deductions. Subtract line 27 from line 11	28	24,909
	29	**Less:** a Net operating loss deduction (see instructions) 29a		
		b Special deductions (Schedule C, line 20) 29b 1,400	29c	1,400
Tax and Payments	30	**Taxable income.** Subtract line 29c from line 28 (see instructions)	30	23,509
	31	**Total tax** (Schedule J, line 10)	31	3,526
	32a	2005 overpayment credited to 2006 32a		
	b	2006 estimated tax payments 32b 4,000		
	c	2006 refund applied for on Form 4466 32c ( ) d Bal ► 32d 4,000		
	e	Tax deposited with Form 7004 32e		
	f	Credits: (1) Form 2439 ____ (2) Form 4136 ____ 32f		
	g	Credit for federal telephone excise tax paid (attach Form 8913) 32g	32h	4,000
	33	Estimated tax penalty (see instructions). Check if Form 2220 is attached ► ☐	33	
	34	**Amount owed.** If line 32h is smaller than the total of lines 31 and 33, enter amount owed	34	
	35	**Overpayment.** If line 32h is larger than the total of lines 31 and 33, enter amount overpaid	35	474
	36	Enter amount from line 35 you want: **Credited to 2007 estimated tax** ► Refunded ►	36	474

Sign Here

Under penalties of perjury, I declare that I have examined this return, including accompanying schedules and statements, and to the best of my knowledge and belief, it is true, correct, and complete. Declaration of preparer (other than taxpayer) is based on all information of which preparer has any knowledge.

Perry Mason — Signature of officer | 3/12/07 — Date | President — Title

May the IRS discuss this return with the preparer shown below (see instructions)? ☐ Yes ☐ No

Paid Preparer's Use Only

Preparer's signature: *Paul Drake*	Date: 3/12/07	Check if self-employed ☐	Preparer's SSN or PTIN
Firm's name (or yours if self-employed), address, and ZIP code: Tragg, Berger & Co. 2413 Thomas Rd., Phoenix, AZ		EIN 64 : 0824578	Phone no. ( )

For Privacy Act and Paperwork Reduction Act Notice, see separate instructions. Cat. No. 11450Q Form **1120** (2006)

FIGURE 14-2 Filled-In Form 1120, Page 2

Form 1120 (2006) Page 2

Schedule A **Cost of Goods Sold** (see instructions)

Line	Description		Amount
1	Inventory at beginning of year	1	100,956
2	Purchases	2	207,858
3	Cost of labor	3	74,807
4	Additional section 263A costs (attach schedule)	4	
5	Other costs (attach schedule)	5	30,529
6	**Total.** Add lines 1 through 5	6	414,150
7	Inventory at end of year	7	90,283
8	**Cost of goods sold.** Subtract line 7 from line 6. Enter here and on page 1, line 2	8	323,867

9a Check all methods used for valuing closing inventory:

(i) ☒ Cost

(ii) ☐ Lower of cost or market

(iii) ☐ Other (Specify method used and attach explanation.) ▶

b Check if there was a writedown of subnormal goods ▶ ☐

c Check if the LIFO inventory method was adopted this tax year for any goods (if checked, attach Form 970) ▶ ☐

d If the LIFO inventory method was used for this tax year, enter percentage (or amounts) of closing inventory computed under LIFO | 9d |

e If property is produced or acquired for resale, do the rules of section 263A apply to the corporation? ☐ Yes ☒ No

f Was there any change in determining quantities, cost, or valuations between opening and closing inventory? If "Yes," attach explanation ☐ Yes ☒ No

Schedule C **Dividends and Special Deductions** (see instructions)

		(a) Dividends received	(b) %	(c) Special deductions (a) × (b)
1	Dividends from less-than-20%-owned domestic corporations (other than debt-financed stock)		70	
2	Dividends from 20%-or-more-owned domestic corporations (other than debt-financed stock)	1,750	80	1,400
3	Dividends on debt-financed stock of domestic and foreign corporations		see instructions	
4	Dividends on certain preferred stock of less-than-20%-owned public utilities		42	
5	Dividends on certain preferred stock of 20%-or-more-owned public utilities		48	
6	Dividends from less-than-20%-owned foreign corporations and certain FSCs		70	
7	Dividends from 20%-or-more-owned foreign corporations and certain FSCs		80	
8	Dividends from wholly owned foreign subsidiaries		100	
9	**Total.** Add lines 1 through 8. See instructions for limitation			1,400
10	Dividends from domestic corporations received by a small business investment company operating under the Small Business Investment Act of 1958		100	
11	Dividends from affiliated group members		100	
12	Dividends from certain FSCs		100	
13	Dividends from foreign corporations not included on lines 3, 6, 7, 8, 11, or 12	235		
14	Income from controlled foreign corporations under subpart F (attach Form(s) 5471)			
15	Foreign dividend gross-up			
16	IC-DISC and former DISC dividends not included on lines 1, 2, or 3			
17	Other dividends			
18	Deduction for dividends paid on certain preferred stock of public utilities			
19	**Total dividends.** Add lines 1 through 17. Enter here and on page 1, line 4 ▶	1,985		
20	**Total special deductions.** Add lines 9, 10, 11, 12, and 18. Enter here and on page 1, line 29b ▶			1,400

Schedule E **Compensation of Officers** (see instructions for page 1, line 12)

Note: *Complete Schedule E only if total receipts (line 1a plus lines 4 through 10 on page 1) are $500,000 or more.*

	(a) Name of officer	(b) Social security number	(c) Percent of time devoted to business	Percent of corporation stock owned (d) Common	(e) Preferred	(f) Amount of compensation
1			%	%	%	
			%	%	%	
			%	%	%	
			%	%	%	
			%	%	%	

2	Total compensation of officers	
3	Compensation of officers claimed on Schedule A and elsewhere on return	
4	Subtract line 3 from line 2. Enter the result here and on page 1, line 12	

Form **1120** (2006)

FIGURE 14-2 Filled-In Form 1120, Page 23

Form 1120 (2006) Page 3

Schedule J **Tax Computation** (see instructions)

1	Check if the corporation is a member of a controlled group (attach Schedule O (Form 1120)) ▶ ☐			
2	Income tax. Check if a qualified personal service corporation (see instructions) ▶ ☐		2	3,526
3	Alternative minimum tax (attach Form 4626)		3	
4	Add lines 2 and 3		4	3,526
5a	Foreign tax credit (attach Form 1118)	5a		
b	Qualified electric vehicle credit (attach Form 8834)	5b		
c	General business credit. Check applicable box(es): ☐ Form 3800 ☐ Form 6478 ☐ Form 8835, Section B ☐ Form 8844	5c		
d	Credit for prior year minimum tax (attach Form 8827)	5d		
e	Bond credits from: ☐ Form 8860 ☐ Form 8912	5e		
6	**Total credits.** Add lines 5a through 5e		6	0
7	Subtract line 6 from line 4		7	3,526
8	Personal holding company tax (attach Schedule PH (Form 1120))		8	
9	Other taxes. Check if from: ☐ Form 4255 ☐ Form 8611 ☐ Form 8697 ☐ Form 8866 ☐ Form 8902 ☐ Other (attach schedule)		9	
10	**Total tax.** Add lines 7 through 9. Enter here and on page 1, line 31		10	3,526

Schedule K **Other Information** (see instructions)

		Yes	No
1	Check accounting method: a ☐ Cash b ☒ Accrual c ☐ Other (specify) ▶		
2	See the instructions and enter the:		
a	Business activity code no. ▶ 3670		
b	Business activity ▶ Manufacturing		
c	Product or service ▶ Electronic components		
3	At the end of the tax year, did the corporation own, directly or indirectly, 50% or more of the voting stock of a domestic corporation? (For rules of attribution, see section 267(c).)		X
	If "Yes," attach a schedule showing: **(a)** name and employer identification number (EIN), **(b)** percentage owned, and **(c)** taxable income or (loss) before NOL and special deductions of such corporation for the tax year ending with or within your tax year.		
4	Is the corporation a subsidiary in an affiliated group or a parent-subsidiary controlled group?		X
	If "Yes," enter name and EIN of the parent corporation ▶		
5	At the end of the tax year, did any individual, partnership, corporation, estate, or trust own, directly or indirectly, 50% or more of the corporation's voting stock? (For rules of attribution, see section 267(c).)		X
	If "Yes," attach a schedule showing name and identifying number. (Do not include any information already entered in **4** above.) Enter percentage owned ▶		
6	During this tax year, did the corporation pay dividends (other than stock dividends and distributions in exchange for stock) in excess of the corporation's current and accumulated earnings and profits? (See sections 301 and 316.)		X
	If "Yes," file **Form 5452,** Corporate Report of Nondividend Distributions.		
	If this is a consolidated return, answer here for the parent corporation and on **Form 851,** Affiliations Schedule, for each subsidiary.		
7	At any time during the tax year, did one foreign person own, directly or indirectly, at least 25% of **(a)** the total voting power of all classes of stock of the corporation entitled to vote or **(b)** the total value of all classes of stock of the corporation?		X
	If "Yes," enter: **(a)** Percentage owned ▶ and **(b)** Owner's country ▶		
c	The corporation may have to file **Form 5472,** Information Return of a 25% Foreign-Owned U.S. Corporation or a Foreign Corporation Engaged in a U.S. Trade or Business. Enter number of Forms 5472 attached ▶		
8	Check this box if the corporation issued publicly offered debt instruments with original issue discount ▶ ☐		
	If checked, the corporation may have to file **Form 8281,** Information Return for Publicly Offered Original Issue Discount Instruments.		
9	Enter the amount of tax-exempt interest received or accrued during the tax year ▶ $		
10	Enter the number of shareholders at the end of the tax year (if 100 or fewer) ▶		
11	If the corporation has an NOL for the tax year and is electing to forego the carryback period, check here ▶ ☐		
	If the corporation is filing a consolidated return, the statement required by Temporary Regulations section 1.1502-21T(b)(3) must be attached or the election will not be valid.		
12	Enter the available NOL carryover from prior tax years (Do not reduce it by any deduction on line 29a.) ▶ $		
13	Are the corporation's total receipts (line 1a plus lines 4 through 10 on page 1) for the tax year **and** its total assets at the end of the tax year less than $250,000?		X
	If "Yes," the corporation is not required to complete Schedules L, M-1, and M-2 on page 4. Instead, enter the total amount of cash distributions and the book value of property distributions (other than cash) made during the tax year. ▶ $		

Note: If the corporation, at any time during the tax year, had assets or operated a business in a foreign country or U.S. possession, it may be required to attach **Schedule N (Form 1120),** *Foreign Operations of U.S. Corporations, to this return. See Schedule N for details.*

Form **1120** (2006)

FIGURE 14-2 Filled-In Form 1120, Page 2

Form 1120 (2006) Page **4**

Schedule L Balance Sheets per Books

Assets	Beginning of tax year (a)	(b)	End of tax year (c)	(d)
1 Cash		12,572		48,678
2a Trade notes and accounts receivable	51,524		60,719	
b Less allowance for bad debts	(4,589)	46,935	(4,589)	56,130
3 Inventories		100,956		90,283
4 U.S. government obligations		3,000		3,000
5 Tax-exempt securities (see instructions)		949		4,678
6 Other current assets (attach schedule)				
7 Loans to shareholders				
8 Mortgage and real estate loans				
9 Other investments (attach schedule)		18,100		30,000
10a Buildings and other depreciable assets	200,001		220,500	
b Less accumulated depreciation	(16,401)	183,600	(53,175)	167,325
11a Depletable assets				
b Less accumulated depletion	( )		( )	
12 Land (net of any amortization)		3,650		28,850
13a Intangible assets (amortizable only)				
b Less accumulated amortization	( )		( )	
14 Other assets (attach schedule)				
15 Total assets		369,762		428,944
Liabilities and Shareholders' Equity				
16 Accounts payable		14,184		16,452
17 Mortgages, notes, bonds payable in less than 1 year		2,000		
18 Other current liabilities (attach schedule)		10,640		1,840
19 Loans from shareholders				
20 Mortgages, notes, bonds payable in 1 year or more		100,000		100,000
21 Other liabilities (attach schedule)		8,230		12,836
22 Capital stock: a Preferred stock	45,000		45,000	
b Common stock	125,000	170,000	180,000	225,000
23 Additional paid-in capital		20,000		20,000
24 Retained earnings—Appropriated (attach schedule)				
25 Retained earnings—Unappropriated		44,708		52,816
26 Adjustments to shareholders' equity (attach schedule)				
27 Less cost of treasury stock		( )		( )
28 Total liabilities and shareholders' equity		369,762		428,944

Schedule M-1 Reconciliation of Income (Loss) per Books With Income per Return

Note: Schedule M-3 required instead of Schedule M-1 if total assets are $10 million or more—see instructions

1 Net income (loss) per books	24,554	7 Income recorded on books this year not included on this return (itemize): Tax-exempt interest $ 1,650	1,650
2 Federal income tax per books	4,333		
3 Excess of capital losses over capital gains			
4 Income subject to tax not recorded on books this year (itemize):		8 Deductions on this return not charged against book income this year (itemize):	
5 Expenses recorded on books this year not deducted on this return (itemize):		a Depreciation $	
a Depreciation $		b Charitable contributions $	
b Charitable contributions $ 1,956		Domestic production activities, $4,284	4,284
c Travel and entertainment $	1,956	9 Add lines 7 and 8	5,934
6 Add lines 1 through 5	30,843	10 Income (page 1, line 28)—line 6 less line 9	24,909

Schedule M-2 Analysis of Unappropriated Retained Earnings per Books (Line 25, Schedule L)

1 Balance at beginning of year	44,708	5 Distributions: a Cash	16,446
2 Net income (loss) per books	24,554	b Stock	
3 Other increases (itemize):		c Property	
		6 Other decreases (itemize):	
		7 Add lines 5 and 6	16,446
4 Add lines 1, 2, and 3	69,262	8 Balance at end of year (line 4 less line 7)	52,816

Form **1120** (2006)

Printed on recycled paper

The amount to which book income (loss) is reconciled is taxable income before the dividends received deduction or net operating loss deduction. These deductions are subtracted last in arriving at taxable income.

CREDITS, SPECIAL TAXES AND PREPAYMENTS

Tax Credits

Like individuals, corporations may offset their tax liabilities with available tax credits. Most of the credits available to corporations are also available to other businesses (see Chapter 12). However, corporations cannot use the personal tax credits available to individuals, such as the earned income credit, the child tax credit, or the child and dependent care credit.

Special Taxes

Besides the regular income tax, corporations may be subject to the accumulated earnings tax, the personal holding company tax, and the alternative minimum tax (AMT). The first two taxes are penalty taxes on undistributed earnings. The AMT, on the other hand, is an alternative method of computing taxable income and income taxes. Careful tax planning can eliminate the need to pay these additional taxes. Discussion of these taxes is beyond the scope of this book.

Estimated Tax Payments

The IRS has a pay-as-you-go system for corporations. Under this plan, all corporations with an expected tax liability of $500 or more must make estimated tax payments. A corporation computes its estimated payments on Form 1120-W (Worksheet), Corporation Estimated Tax. These payments are due in equal quarterly installments by the following dates:

Date	*Percentage of Estimated Tax Due*
15th day of the fourth month	25%
15th day of the sixth month	25%
15th day of the ninth month	25%
15th day of the twelfth month	25%

For calendar year corporations, the payment dates are normally April 15, June 15, September 15, and December 15. If one of the above dates falls on a weekend or a holiday, the due date becomes the next business day.

The expectation of a $500 tax liability, however, may not materialize until late in the tax year. When this occurs, the law requires proportional payments of the estimated tax over the remaining payment dates. The full amount of any unpaid tax becomes due 2½ months after the end of the tax year (due date of tax return without extensions). Note that corporations must include the effect of the alternative minimum tax (AMT) in their quarterly payments. This complexity may force corporations subject to the AMT to overpay their quarterly taxes to avoid underpayment penalties.

Federal Tax Deposit System

The IRS requires that corporations make estimated tax payments to specified depositories. Form 8109, Federal Tax Deposit Coupon, must accompany the payment. (This form was discussed in Chapter 13). This deposit system applies to estimated tax payments and to actual income tax return payments.

Penalty for Underpayment of Estimated Tax: Small Corporations

Failure to pay the minimum amount due at each installment date causes an underpayment penalty. The IRS considers the estimated tax underpaid if payments total less than 100% of the amount due at each payment date. The 100% test applies to the actual tax liability of small corporations for the year prorated over the required payment dates.

Avoiding the Underpayment Penalty

Small corporations may avoid the penalty for underpayment of estimated taxes by making payments equal to the *lesser of* (i) 100% of the tax shown on the current year's return or (ii) 100% of the tax for the preceding year. Corporations use Form 2220, Underpayment of Estimated Tax by Corporations, to determine if an underpayment of taxes occurred. This form also provides for the calculation of any underpayment penalties.

Estimated Payment Requirements: Large Corporations

Large corporations must make estimated tax payments of 100% of the current year's tax liability. Large corporations cannot avoid the penalty for underpayment of taxes by making estimated tax payments that equal or exceed last year's tax liability. A large corporation has a taxable income of $1 million or more for any of its three immediately preceding tax years. A controlled group of corporations divides the $1 million amount equally among its members unless all such members consent to an unequal allocation of such amount.

CORPORATE DISTRIBUTIONS

Shareholders receiving corporate distributions may have taxable dividends, tax-free returns of capital, or capital gain. A given distribution may be subject to all three treatments. Determination of the general nature of a distribution takes place at the corporate level. However, the final taxability of a distribution may depend on shareholder circumstances. Most corporate distributions result in taxable income to the recipient shareholders. However, distributions from corporations in the process of terminating or downsizing operations under a qualified corporate liquidation may receive more favorable tax treatment. Also, some so-called dividends are not true dividends (stock dividends).

Taxable Dividends

Unless affected parties provide contrary evidence, corporate distributions receive ordinary dividend treatment. Shareholders include in gross income the full amounts of any ordinary dividends received. When the distribution involves property, the property's FMV at the distribution date determines the amount of dividend received. Technically, dividends receive ordinary income treatment only if the company has earnings and profits to absorb the distribution. Distributions come first from the current year's earnings and profits (CE&P) and then from prior years' accumulated earnings and profits (AE&P). Shareholders treat distributions in excess of E&P as a tax-free recovery of their capital investment. After shareholders recover their capital, any additional distribution is capital gain.

EXAMPLE 23

PDQ, a calendar-year corporation, had E&P of $90,000 at the end of the current year. On December 31 of the current year, PDQ distributed $120,000 to its three shareholders Xandra, Yang, and Zack ($40,000 to each shareholder). It was the only distribution by PDQ in the current year. These shareholders purchased their shares at different times for different prices. Also, some prior year distributions represented a return of capital to the shareholders. Immediately before the current distribution, the shareholders had the following basis in their stock: Xandra—$0, Yang—$5,000, and Zack—$60,000. As a result of the distribution, each shareholder recognizes an ordinary dividend of $30,000. The schedules below show that Xandra and Yang also have a capital gain of $10,000 and $5,000, respectively. After the distribution, Xandra and Yang each have a zero stock basis. The basis of Zack's stock after the distribution is $50,000 ($60,000 – $10,000 return of capital).

	Xandra	Yang	Zack
Distribution	$ 40,000	$ 40,000	$ 40,000
From E&P (dividend income)	(30,000)	(30,000)	(30,000)
Excess distribution	$ 10,000	$ 10,000	$ 10,000
Return of capital	(0)	(5,000)	(10,000)
Capital gain	$ 10,000	$ 5,000	$ -0-

Earnings and Profits

The Code does not contain a definition of earnings and profits (E&P). Consequently, many people compare E&P with retained earnings. While similarities exist, numerous differences make them very unlike, which causes much confusion. Corporate directors may think they can distribute cash or other property tax free when the corporation has zero retained earnings. However, this would be wrong.

If the corporation has E&P, some portion of the distribution will be a dividend. Basically, transactions that increase a corporation's ability to pay a dividend increase E&P. Transactions that decrease a corporation's ability to pay a dividend decrease E&P. Consider the following examples. When a corporation receives tax-exempt interest, the interest is not taxed. However, E&P is increased by the interest received because the interest can serve as a source for dividend distributions. In contrast, the deduction for charitable contributions is limited to 10% of income. When the actual contribution exceeds this limitation, E&P is decreased by the full contribution. The company has reduced its ability to pay a dividend by the full amount contributed to the charity. Also, while there is no definition of E&P, the law may require the use of certain accounting methods in some situations. For example, there are various acceptable methods by which to calculate depreciation expense for the tax return. However, a special Alternative Depreciation System (see Chapter 8) is required to calculate depreciation expense for E&P purposes.

Distributions of Property

Corporate distributions may involve either cash or property. For property, FMV determines the amount of the distribution. C corporations must recognize a gain on any appreciated property it distributes. E&P increases as a result of the gain. E&P decreases by the FMV of the property distributed. C corporations do not recognize a loss when the FMV of the property distributed is less than its basis. The basis of the property received by shareholders is FMV.

EXAMPLE 24

In the current year, CQ, a calendar-year corporation, distributes appreciated land to its sole shareholder. For the current year, its CE&P, before the distribution, is $100,000. It has no beginning AE&P. CQ's basis in the land at the distribution date was $10,000. The land's FMV at this date was $50,000. CQ must recognize a gain of $40,000 ($50,000 FMV - $10,000 adjusted basis) on the distribution.

EXAMPLE 25

At the end of the year, TLC distributes land (FMV of $10,000) with an adjusted basis of $4,000 to its only shareholder. TLC has no CE&P for the year and no AE&P. This distribution causes TLC to report gain of $6,000 ($10,000 – $4,000). This causes TLC's E&P to increase by $6,000. The shareholder receives a distribution equal to the FMV of the land. However, only $6,000 of the value is a dividend (amount of CE&P). The remaining portion of the distribution ($4,000) is a return of capital or capital gain, depending on the shareholder's basis in the stock. TLC's E&P is reduced to zero after the distribution.

Name ____________________

Section ____________ Date __________

QUESTIONS AND PROBLEMS

1. **Corporate Tax Status.** How do the tax laws determine whether a business should be taxed as a C corporation?

2. **Forming a Corporation.** Betty Sanchez forms a corporation by transferring land worth \$100,000 for 100% of the stock in the corporation. Sanchez paid \$30,000 for the land several years ago.

   a. How much gain or loss do Sanchez and the corporation recognize on the transfer?

   b. What is Sanchez's basis in her shares of stock in the corporation?

   c. What is the corporation's basis in the land?

3. **Forming a Corporation.** Daniel Diaz forms a corporation by transferring land worth \$20,000 in exchange for 100% of the stock in the corporation. Diaz paid \$30,000 for the land several years ago.

   a. How much gain or loss do Diaz and the corporation recognize on the transfer?

b. What is Diaz's basis in his shares of stock in the corporation?

c. What is the corporation's basis in the land?

4. **Forming a Corporation.** Herb Howard and Todd O'Brien form a corporation. Howard contributes $25,000 cash in exchange for 1,000 shares of stock. O'Brien performs services worth $25,000 in exchange for 1,000 shares of stock.

   a. How much gain or loss do Howard, O'Brien and the corporation recognize on the transfer?

   b. What is Howard's basis in his shares of stock in the corporation?

   c. What is O'Brien's basis in his shares of stock in the corporation?

5. **Corporation Taxable Income.**

   a. What is the difference in the tax treatment of corporate taxable income and business profits reported on Schedule C of a sole proprietor?

   b. Explain why corporations do not compute AGI.

6. **Accounting Periods.** What is a short year return? When would a corporation file one?

7. **Accounting Periods.**

   a. What is the difference between a calendar year and a fiscal year?

   b. What is a 52-53 week tax year? Why might a corporation want to use a 52-53 week tax year?

   c. If a corporation wants to change its tax year from October 31 to July 31 during the current year, what must it do?

8. **Corporate Capital Gains and Losses.**

   a. How does the tax treatment of net capital gain differ between individual and corporate taxpayers?

   b. How does the tax treatment of net capital losses differ between individual and corporate taxpayers?

9. **C Corporation Taxable Income.**

a. For the current year, the Wish Corporation had ordinary income from operations of $80,000, a net long-term capital gain of $17,000, and a net short-term capital loss of $7,000. What is its taxable income for the year?

b. For the current year, the BB Corporation had net income from operations of $65,000 and a net long-term capital loss of $9,000. It also had a net short-term capital gain of $7,000. What is its taxable income for the year?

c. For the current year, before considering capital loss carryovers, the Stitchell Corporation had a net long-term capital loss of $8,000 and a net short-term capital loss of $3,000. Its net capital loss carryover from last year was $2,000. How much is Stitchell's capital loss carryover to the next tax year, and what is its nature (long-term or short-term)?

10. **Corporate Taxable Income.** A corporation pays it Chief Executive Office (CEO) $2 million during the year. Discuss the tax implications of the CEO's salary both to the corporation and the CEO.

11. **Bad Debts.** A corporation properly uses the reserve method to deduct bad debts on the financial statements (as it is the only method allowed under Generally Accepted Accounting Principles). Does an accrual basis corporation use this method to deduct bad debts the corporate income tax return? Explain.

12. **Bad Debts.** Corporation ARM uses the accrual method of reporting for income taxes. It is a retail hardware store. On average, 1% of its gross sales on account ($500,000 for the current year) become uncollectable. During the year, ARM actually wrote off $4,700 of accounts receivable that were uncollectable. What is ARM's deduction for bad debts on its tax return?

13. **Organizational Costs.** At formation, a corporation incurs the following costs: legal services to obtain a corporate charter, $1,000; state incorporation fees, $700; and costs related to issuing common stock, $3,000. How quickly will the corporation be allowed to deduct these costs?

14. **Organizational Costs.** In the process of incorporating a business, a corporation incurs organizational costs. The corporation was incorporated on June 8, 2006. It officially began business on September 2, 2006. The officers of the corporation have asked that the corporation take the maximum deduction as allowed under the tax law.

    a. How much can the corporation deduct in 2006 if the total organizational costs are $45,000?

    b. How much can the corporation deduct in 2006 if the total organizational costs are $52,000?

    c. How much can the corporation deduct in 2006 if the total organizational costs are $75,000?

15. **Start-Up Costs.** A corporation incurs start-up costs prior to the beginning of its business operations. The corporation began business on March 1, 2006.

    a. How much can the corporation deduct in 2006 and 2007 if the total start up costs are $15,000?

b. How much can the corporation deduct in 2006 and 2007 if the total start up costs are $51,200?

c. How much can the corporation deduct in 2006 and 2007 if the total start up costs are $65,000?

16. Charitable Contributions. What is the charitable contribution limitation for a C corporation and how are excess charitable contributions treated?

17. Charitable Contributions. The following data relate to the Regal Corporation for the current year:

Gross income includable on the tax return	$115,000
Allowable business deductions, exclusive of contributions	90,000
Contributions to charitable organizations	2,750
Dividends received from domestic corporations (30% ownership and included in the gross income amount of $115,000)	2,000

a. What is the amount of the contributions deduction for the current year?

b. What is the amount of taxable income for the current year?

c. What is the amount of the contributions deduction carryover to the next year, if any?

18. Charitable Contributions. A corporation manufactures winter coats. During the year it donated from its inventory coats worth $25,000. The coats will be used by the charity for the care of the ill and needy. The corporation's basis in the coats is $10,000. What amount can the corporation deduct as a charitable contribution?

19. Charitable Contributions. A corporation has taxable income of $107,000 after all deductions except the charitable contribution deduction, dividends received deduction, domestic production activities deduction and loss carry forwards. The corporation made a $30,000 charitable contribution for the year. Compute the charitable contribution deduction for the current year. Discuss what happens to any excess contribution that can not be deducted in the current year.

20. Charitable Contributions. An accrual basis corporation reports the following income and expenses for 2006. The corporation does not manufacture the merchandise that is sells, and therefore is not entitled to the domestic production activities deduction.

Gross sales and receipts	$700,000
Returns and allowances	12,000
Cost of goods sold	330,000
Interest received	20,000
Rent expense	55,000
Wage expense	140,000
Charitable contributions	12,000
Other operating expenses	75,000
Depreciation expense	15,000

a. Compute the corporation's taxable income for the 2006 tax year.

b. What is the amount of the corporation's charitable contribution carryover (if any)? To which tax years can the corporation carry over this excess?

21. **Dividends Received Deduction.** During the year, Treeline Industries receives a $50,000 dividend from a corporation in which Treeline owns 35% of the stock. Treeline's revenues (not including the dividends) and operating expenses for the year are $400,000 and $375,000, respectively. Other than the dividends received deduction, these are Treeline's only items of revenue and expense that Treeline reports in taxable income.

a. Compute Treeline's taxable income for the year.

b. How, if at all, would your answer to Part a. change if Treeline owned 10% of the stock in the corporation?

c. How, if at all, would your answer to Part a. change if Treeline's revenues were $370,000 (instead of $400,000), but it continued to own 35% of the corporation's stock?

22. **Dividends Received Deduction.** During the year, Express Corporation receives a $120,000 dividend from a corporation in which it owns 55% of the stock. Express's revenues (not including the dividends) and operating expenses for the year are $370,000 and $390,000, respectively. These are Express's only items of revenue and expense for the year.

a. Compute Express's taxable income for the year.

b. How, if at all, would your answer to Part a. change if Express owned 90% of the stock in the corporation?

23. **Filing Deadlines.** For each of the following corporations, determine the deadline for filing the corporate income tax return.

    a. The original due date for a corporation with a calendar year end.

    b. The extended due date for a calendar year corporation that files Form 7004 prior to the original filing deadline.

    c. The original due date for a corporation with a May 31 year end.

    d. The extended due date for corporation with a May 31 year end that files Form 7004 prior to the original filing deadline.

    e. The original due date for a corporation with an August 31 year end.

    f. The extended due date for a corporation with an October 31 year end that files Form 7004 prior to the original filing deadline.

24. **Tax Liability.** Compute the corporate income tax liability for each of the following corporations.

    a. A corporation with taxable income of $25,000.

    b. A corporation with taxable income of $125,000.

c. A corporation with taxable income of $250,000.

d. A corporation with taxable income of $1,500,000.

e. A corporation with taxable income of $3,750,000.

f. A corporation with taxable income of $33,750,000.

25. Tax Liability. Sanford Corporation had gross income from business operations of $150,000 for the current year. Allowable business expenses were $40,000. In addition, the company received dividends from domestic corporations (less than 20% owned) in the amount of $10,000. What is Sanford's tax liability for the year?

COMPREHENSIVE PROBLEMS

26. A corporation has the following income and deductions in 2006.

Gross sales	$830,000
Long-term capital gains	15,000
Dividend income (33% ownership in the stock)	60,000
Interest income	70,000
Cost of goods sold	444,000
Domestic production activities (DPA) deduction	8,100
Other business expenses	260,000
Charitable contributions	72,000
Long-term capital losses	35,000

a. Compute the corporation's taxable income and tax liability.

b. Determine whether the corporation has any carryovers to 2007.

27. Randolph Manufacturing Company, EIN (46-7299870) was organized on February 1, 1998. Randolph manufactures electronic components. Its business activity code is 3670. The offices of the company are located at 350 Mission Street, San Jose, CA 95107-43211. Randolph's financial statements for 2006 are reproduced on the pages that follow. During the year Randolph made estimated federal income tax payments totaling $15,800. If there is any overpayment of taxes on its 2006, the accounting department has requested that it be applied towards the 2007 estimated tax. Randolph paid a total of $46,600 of dividends to its shareholders during the year. The stock is Randolph is held by 17 different shareholders, none of whom own more than 10% of the stock in the company.

During the year Randolph sold two investments. The Orange County municipal bonds were purchased on July 6, 2003 and sold on November 16, 2006 for $3,215. Randolph's adjusted basis in the bonds was $3,740. Randolph sold 100 shares of National Acme common stock on March 14, 2006 for $26,300. It purchased the stock on May 9, 2000 for $18,200.

Randolph's qualified production activities income for 2006 (used in computing its 3% domestic production activities (DPA) deduction) is $75,440. If this amount is less than Randolph's taxable income before the DPA deduction, 3% of this amount should be taken as a deduction on Form 1120 (line 25). The bad debt expense reported on the income statement is based on the reserve method of accounting. Actual bad debts written off during the year were $7,950. The difference between these two amounts will need to be reported on Schedule M-1 when net income (loss) per books is reconciled with taxable income before NOL deduction and special deductions (Form 1120, line 28).

Complete Randolph's Form 1120 and Schedule D (Form 1120) for the calendar year ended December 31, 2006 using the blank forms provided at the end of this problem. You can assume that Form 4562 has been correctly filled out and that the $6,068 depreciation expense on the buildings that is reported on the income statement is also the tax depreciation that should be deducted on the tax return. Randolph uses lower of cost or market to value its inventories. There were no changes in determining quantities of inventory during the year. The rules of Section 263A do not apply to Randolph's inventory.

RANDOLPH MANUFACTURING COMPANY
Comparative Balance Sheets
Beginning and End of 2006

ASSETS	**As of January 1, 2006**	**As of December 31, 2006**
Cash	$ 40,320	$63,600
Notes receivable	40,400	32,680
Accounts receivable	245,790	217,270
Allowance for doubtful accounts	(9,400)	(8,580)
Inventories at the lower of cost or market:		
Raw materials	46,980	77,616
Finished goods	108,756	140,625
Investment in municipal bonds—Orange County, CA	27,900	24,160
Investment in common stock—National Acme Co.	45,000	49,005
Land	98,700	98,700
Buildings	182,432	206,379
Machinery and equipment	207,450	207,450
Accumulated depreciation	(89,988)	(128,045)
Total assets	$944,340	$980,860

LIABILITIES AND STOCKHOLDERS' EQUITY		
Bank loans	$ 67,500	$ 56,250
Accounts payable	187,646	164,882
Accrued expenses	11,054	12,894
Bonds payable	200,000	200,000
Preferred stock	160,000	160,000
Common stock	180,000	200,000
Paid-in surplus	54,000	83,000
Retained earnings (unappropriated)	84,140	103,834
Total liabilities and stockholders' equity	$944,340	$980,860

RANDOLPH MANUFACTURING COMPANY
Income Statement
For Year Ended December 31, 2006

Sales (after subtracting out $224,054 for returns)		$1,704,201
Less cost of goods sold (see COGS schedule below)		(1,351,371)
Gross profit on sales		$ 352,830
Operating expenses:		
Officers' salaries	$141,350	
Salaries and wage expense	29,583	
Repairs	2,214	
Property taxes	4,200	
Payroll taxes	11,398	
Depreciation of buildings	6,068	
Bad debts expense	7,130	
Advertising	29,033	
Travel expenses (includes $2,000 for meals)	20,180	
Other administration expenses	10,300	(261,456)
Net operating income		$ 91,374
Other income:		
Dividends from domestic corporations (15% ownership)	$ 3,600	
Interest income ($950 from municipal bonds)	3,033	
Gain on sale of National Acme stock	8,100	14,733
		$ 106,107
Other deductions:		
Loss on sale of Orange County bonds	$ 525	
Interest expense	11,588	
Contributions to qualified charities	11,000	
Legal fees	900	(24,013)
Net income before federal income taxes		$ 82,094
Less estimated federal income taxes		(15,800)
Net income		$ 66,294

COST OF GOODS SOLD SCHEDULE

Inventories at beginning of year	$ 155,736
Materials bought for manufacture	1,224,000
Salaries and wages	112,860
Other costs (utilities, depreciation of machinery)	77,016
Total goods available for sale	$1,569,612
Less inventories at end of year	(218,241)
Cost of goods sold	$1,351,371

(Use for Problem 27).

Form **1120** Department of the Treasury Internal Revenue Service (77)

U.S. Corporation Income Tax Return

For calendar year 2006 or tax year beginning ...., 2006, ending ...., 20 ....
► See separate instructions.

OMB No. 1545-0123 **2006**

A Check if:
1 Consolidated return (attach Form 851) ☐
2 Personal holding co. (attach Sch. PH) ☐
3 Personal service corp. (see instructions) ☐
4 Schedule M-3 required (attach Sch. M-3) ☐

Use IRS label. Otherwise, print or type.
Name
Number, street, and room or suite no. If a P.O. box, see instructions.
City or town, state, and ZIP code

B Employer identification number
C Date incorporated
D Total assets (see instructions) $

E Check if: (1) ☐ Initial return (2) ☐ Final return (3) ☐ Name change (4) ☐ Address change

Income

1a	Gross receipts or sales ______ b Less returns and allowances ______ c Bal ►	1c	
2	Cost of goods sold (Schedule A, line 8)	2	
3	Gross profit. Subtract line 2 from line 1c	3	
4	Dividends (Schedule C, line 19)	4	
5	Interest	5	
6	Gross rents	6	
7	Gross royalties	7	
8	Capital gain net income (attach Schedule D (Form 1120))	8	
9	Net gain or (loss) from Form 4797, Part II, line 17 (attach Form 4797)	9	
10	Other income (see instructions—attach schedule)	10	
11	**Total income.** Add lines 3 through 10 ►	11	

Deductions (See instructions for limitations on deductions.)

12	Compensation of officers (Schedule E, line 4)	12	
13	Salaries and wages (less employment credits)	13	
14	Repairs and maintenance	14	
15	Bad debts	15	
16	Rents	16	
17	Taxes and licenses	17	
18	Interest	18	
19	Charitable contributions	19	
20	Depreciation from Form 4562 not claimed on Schedule A or elsewhere on return (attach Form 4562)	20	
21	Depletion	21	
22	Advertising	22	
23	Pension, profit-sharing, etc., plans	23	
24	Employee benefit programs	24	
25	Domestic production activities deduction (attach Form 8903)	25	
26	Other deductions (attach schedule)	26	
27	**Total deductions.** Add lines 12 through 26 ►	27	
28	Taxable income before net operating loss deduction and special deductions. Subtract line 27 from line 11	28	
29	**Less:** a Net operating loss deduction (see instructions) 29a ______		
	b Special deductions (Schedule C, line 20) 29b ______	29c	

Tax and Payments

30	**Taxable income.** Subtract line 29c from line 28 (see instructions)	30	
31	**Total tax** (Schedule J, line 10)	31	
32a	2005 overpayment credited to 2006 32a ______		
b	2006 estimated tax payments 32b ______		
c	2006 refund applied for on Form 4466 32c ( ) d Bal ► 32d ______		
e	Tax deposited with Form 7004 32e ______		
f	Credits: (1) Form 2439 ______ (2) Form 4136 ______ 32f ______		
g	Credit for federal telephone excise tax paid (attach Form 8913) 32g ______	32h	
33	Estimated tax penalty (see instructions). Check if Form 2220 is attached ► ☐	33	
34	**Amount owed.** If line 32h is smaller than the total of lines 31 and 33, enter amount owed	34	
35	**Overpayment.** If line 32h is larger than the total of lines 31 and 33, enter amount overpaid	35	
36	Enter amount from line 35 you want: **Credited to 2007 estimated tax** ► ______ **Refunded** ►	36	

Sign Here

Under penalties of perjury, I declare that I have examined this return, including accompanying schedules and statements, and to the best of my knowledge and belief, it is true, correct, and complete. Declaration of preparer (other than taxpayer) is based on all information of which preparer has any knowledge.

► Signature of officer Date ► Title

May the IRS discuss this return with the preparer shown below (see instructions)? ☐ **Yes** ☐ **No**

Paid Preparer's Use Only

Preparer's signature ► Date Check if self-employed ☐ Preparer's SSN or PTIN

Firm's name (or yours if self-employed), address, and ZIP code ► EIN Phone no. ( )

For Privacy Act and Paperwork Reduction Act Notice, see separate instructions. Cat. No. 11450Q Form **1120** (2006)

(Use for Problem 27).

Form 1120 (2006) Page **2**

Schedule A **Cost of Goods Sold** (see instructions)

1	Inventory at beginning of year	1	
2	Purchases	2	
3	Cost of labor	3	
4	Additional section 263A costs (attach schedule)	4	
5	Other costs (attach schedule)	5	
6	**Total.** Add lines 1 through 5	6	
7	Inventory at end of year	7	
8	**Cost of goods sold.** Subtract line 7 from line 6. Enter here and on page 1, line 2	8	

9a Check all methods used for valuing closing inventory:

(i) ☐ Cost

(ii) ☐ Lower of cost or market

(iii) ☐ Other (Specify method used and attach explanation.) ▶

b Check if there was a writedown of subnormal goods ▶ ☐

c Check if the LIFO inventory method was adopted this tax year for any goods (if checked, attach Form 970) ▶ ☐

d If the LIFO inventory method was used for this tax year, enter percentage (or amounts) of closing inventory computed under LIFO | 9d |

e If property is produced or acquired for resale, do the rules of section 263A apply to the corporation? ☐ Yes ☐ No

f Was there any change in determining quantities, cost, or valuations between opening and closing inventory? If "Yes," attach explanation ☐ Yes ☐ No

Schedule C **Dividends and Special Deductions** (see instructions)

		(a) Dividends received	(b) %	(c) Special deductions (a) × (b)
1	Dividends from less-than-20%-owned domestic corporations (other than debt-financed stock)		70	
2	Dividends from 20%-or-more-owned domestic corporations (other than debt-financed stock)		80	
3	Dividends on debt-financed stock of domestic and foreign corporations		see instructions	
4	Dividends on certain preferred stock of less-than-20%-owned public utilities		42	
5	Dividends on certain preferred stock of 20%-or-more-owned public utilities		48	
6	Dividends from less-than-20%-owned foreign corporations and certain FSCs		70	
7	Dividends from 20%-or-more-owned foreign corporations and certain FSCs		80	
8	Dividends from wholly owned foreign subsidiaries		100	
9	**Total.** Add lines 1 through 8. See instructions for limitation			
10	Dividends from domestic corporations received by a small business investment company operating under the Small Business Investment Act of 1958		100	
11	Dividends from affiliated group members		100	
12	Dividends from certain FSCs		100	
13	Dividends from foreign corporations not included on lines 3, 6, 7, 8, 11, or 12			
14	Income from controlled foreign corporations under subpart F (attach Form(s) 5471)			
15	Foreign dividend gross-up			
16	IC-DISC and former DISC dividends not included on lines 1, 2, or 3			
17	Other dividends			
18	Deduction for dividends paid on certain preferred stock of public utilities			
19	**Total dividends.** Add lines 1 through 17. Enter here and on page 1, line 4 ▶			
20	**Total special deductions.** Add lines 9, 10, 11, 12, and 18. Enter here and on page 1, line 29b ▶			

Schedule E **Compensation of Officers** (see instructions for page 1, line 12)

Note: *Complete Schedule E only if total receipts (line 1a plus lines 4 through 10 on page 1) are $500,000 or more.*

	(a) Name of officer	(b) Social security number	(c) Percent of time devoted to business	Percent of corporation stock owned (d) Common	(e) Preferred	(f) Amount of compensation
1			%	%	%	
			%	%	%	
			%	%	%	
			%	%	%	
			%	%	%	

2	Total compensation of officers	
3	Compensation of officers claimed on Schedule A and elsewhere on return	
4	Subtract line 3 from line 2. Enter the result here and on page 1, line 12	

Form **1120** (2006)

(Use for Problem 27).

Form 1120 (2006) Page **3**

Schedule J **Tax Computation** (see instructions)

1	Check if the corporation is a member of a controlled group (attach Schedule O (Form 1120)) . . ▶ ☐				
2	Income tax. Check if a qualified personal service corporation (see instructions) . . . . ▶ ☐			2	
3	Alternative minimum tax (attach Form 4626)			3	
4	Add lines 2 and 3			4	
5a	Foreign tax credit (attach Form 1118)	5a			
b	Qualified electric vehicle credit (attach Form 8834)	5b			
c	General business credit. Check applicable box(es): ☐ Form 3800 ☐ Form 6478 ☐ Form 8835, Section B ☐ Form 8844	5c			
d	Credit for prior year minimum tax (attach Form 8827)	5d			
e	Bond credits from: ☐ Form 8860 ☐ Form 8912	5e			
6	**Total credits.** Add lines 5a through 5e			6	
7	Subtract line 6 from line 4			7	
8	Personal holding company tax (attach Schedule PH (Form 1120))			8	
9	Other taxes. Check if from: ☐ Form 4255 ☐ Form 8611 ☐ Form 8697 ☐ Form 8866 ☐ Form 8902 ☐ Other (attach schedule) . .			9	
10	**Total tax.** Add lines 7 through 9. Enter here and on page 1, line 31			10	

Schedule K **Other Information** (see instructions)

		Yes	No
1	Check accounting method: a ☐ Cash b ☐ Accrual c ☐ Other (specify) ▶		
2	See the instructions and enter the:		
a	Business activity code no. ▶		
b	Business activity ▶		
c	Product or service ▶		
3	At the end of the tax year, did the corporation own, directly or indirectly, 50% or more of the voting stock of a domestic corporation? (For rules of attribution, see section 267(c).)		
	If "Yes," attach a schedule showing: **(a)** name and employer identification number (EIN), **(b)** percentage owned, and **(c)** taxable income or (loss) before NOL and special deductions of such corporation for the tax year ending with or within your tax year.		
4	Is the corporation a subsidiary in an affiliated group or a parent-subsidiary controlled group?		
	If "Yes," enter name and EIN of the parent corporation ▶		
5	At the end of the tax year, did any individual, partnership, corporation, estate, or trust own, directly or indirectly, 50% or more of the corporation's voting stock? (For rules of attribution, see section 267(c).)		
	If "Yes," attach a schedule showing name and identifying number. (Do not include any information already entered in **4** above.) Enter percentage owned ▶		
6	During this tax year, did the corporation pay dividends (other than stock dividends and distributions in exchange for stock) in excess of the corporation's current and accumulated earnings and profits? (See sections 301 and 316.) . .		
	If "Yes," file **Form 5452,** Corporate Report of Nondividend Distributions.		
	If this is a consolidated return, answer here for the parent corporation and on **Form 851,** Affiliations Schedule, for each subsidiary.		

		Yes	No
7	At any time during the tax year, did one foreign person own, directly or indirectly, at least 25% of **(a)** the total voting power of all classes of stock of the corporation entitled to vote or **(b)** the total value of all classes of stock of the corporation?		
	If "Yes," enter: **(a)** Percentage owned ▶ .... and **(b)** Owner's country ▶		
c	The corporation may have to file **Form 5472,** Information Return of a 25% Foreign-Owned U.S. Corporation or a Foreign Corporation Engaged in a U.S. Trade or Business. Enter number of Forms 5472 attached ▶		
8	Check this box if the corporation issued publicly offered debt instruments with original issue discount . ▶ ☐		
	If checked, the corporation may have to file **Form 8281,** Information Return for Publicly Offered Original Issue Discount Instruments.		
9	Enter the amount of tax-exempt interest received or accrued during the tax year ▶ $		
10	Enter the number of shareholders at the end of the tax year (if 100 or fewer) ▶		
11	If the corporation has an NOL for the tax year and is electing to forego the carryback period, check here ▶ ☐		
	If the corporation is filing a consolidated return, the statement required by Temporary Regulations section 1.1502-21T(b)(3) must be attached or the election will not be valid.		
12	Enter the available NOL carryover from prior tax years (Do not reduce it by any deduction on line 29a.) ▶ $		
13	Are the corporation's total receipts (line 1a plus lines 4 through 10 on page 1) for the tax year **and** its total assets at the end of the tax year less than $250,000? . . .		
	If "Yes," the corporation is not required to complete Schedules L, M-1, and M-2 on page 4. Instead, enter the total amount of cash distributions and the book value of property distributions (other than cash) made during the tax year. ▶ $		

Note: If the corporation, at any time during the tax year, had assets or operated a business in a foreign country or U.S. possession, it may be required to attach **Schedule N (Form 1120),** *Foreign Operations of U.S. Corporations, to this return. See Schedule N for details.*

Form **1120** (2006)

(Use for Problem 27).

Form 1120 (2006) Page 4

Schedule L Balance Sheets per Books

Assets	Beginning of tax year (a)	(b)	End of tax year (c)	(d)
1 Cash				
2a Trade notes and accounts receivable				
b Less allowance for bad debts	( )		( )	
3 Inventories				
4 U.S. government obligations				
5 Tax-exempt securities (see instructions)				
6 Other current assets (attach schedule)				
7 Loans to shareholders				
8 Mortgage and real estate loans				
9 Other investments (attach schedule)				
10a Buildings and other depreciable assets				
b Less accumulated depreciation	( )		( )	
11a Depletable assets				
b Less accumulated depletion	( )		( )	
12 Land (net of any amortization)				
13a Intangible assets (amortizable only)				
b Less accumulated amortization	( )		( )	
14 Other assets (attach schedule)				
15 Total assets				
Liabilities and Shareholders' Equity				
16 Accounts payable				
17 Mortgages, notes, bonds payable in less than 1 year				
18 Other current liabilities (attach schedule)				
19 Loans from shareholders				
20 Mortgages, notes, bonds payable in 1 year or more				
21 Other liabilities (attach schedule)				
22 Capital stock: a Preferred stock				
b Common stock				
23 Additional paid-in capital				
24 Retained earnings—Appropriated (attach schedule)				
25 Retained earnings—Unappropriated				
26 Adjustments to shareholders' equity (attach schedule)				
27 Less cost of treasury stock		( )		( )
28 Total liabilities and shareholders' equity				

Schedule M-1 Reconciliation of Income (Loss) per Books With Income per Return

Note: Schedule M-3 required instead of Schedule M-1 if total assets are $10 million or more—see instructions

1 Net income (loss) per books		7 Income recorded on books this year not included on this return (itemize): Tax-exempt interest $	
2 Federal income tax per books			
3 Excess of capital losses over capital gains			
4 Income subject to tax not recorded on books this year (itemize):		8 Deductions on this return not charged against book income this year (itemize):	
5 Expenses recorded on books this year not deducted on this return (itemize):		a Depreciation $	
a Depreciation $		b Charitable contributions $	
b Charitable contributions $			
c Travel and entertainment $		9 Add lines 7 and 8	
6 Add lines 1 through 5		10 Income (page 1, line 28)—line 6 less line 9	

Schedule M-2 Analysis of Unappropriated Retained Earnings per Books (Line 25, Schedule L)

1 Balance at beginning of year		5 Distributions: a Cash	
2 Net income (loss) per books		b Stock	
3 Other increases (itemize):		c Property	
		6 Other decreases (itemize):	
		7 Add lines 5 and 6	
4 Add lines 1, 2, and 3		8 Balance at end of year (line 4 less line 7)	

Form **1120** (2006)

Printed on recycled paper

(Use for Problem 27).

SCHEDULE D (Form 1120)

Department of the Treasury
Internal Revenue Service

Capital Gains and Losses

▶ Attach to Form 1120, 1120-A, 1120-C, 1120-F, 1120-FSC, 1120-H, 1120-IC-DISC, 1120-L, 1120-ND, 1120-PC, 1120-POL, 1120-REIT, 1120-RIC, 1120-SF, or certain Forms 990-T.

▶ See separate instructions.

OMB No. 1545-0123

2006

Name | Employer identification number

Part I Short-Term Capital Gains and Losses—Assets Held One Year or Less

	(a) Description of property (Example: 100 shares of Z Co.)	(b) Date acquired (mo., day, yr.)	(c) Date sold (mo., day, yr.)	(d) Sales price (see instructions)	(e) Cost or other basis (see instructions)	(f) Gain or (loss) (Subtract (e) from (d))
1						

2	Short-term capital gain from installment sales from Form 6252, line 26 or 37	2	
3	Short-term gain or (loss) from like-kind exchanges from Form 8824	3	
4	Unused capital loss carryover (attach computation)	4	( )
5	Net short-term capital gain or (loss). Combine lines 1 through 4	5	

Part II Long-Term Capital Gains and Losses—Assets Held More Than One Year

6						

7	Enter gain from Form 4797, line 7 or 9	7	
8	Long-term capital gain from installment sales from Form 6252, line 26 or 37	8	
9	Long-term gain or (loss) from like-kind exchanges from Form 8824	9	
10	Capital gain distributions (see instructions)	10	
11	Net long-term capital gain or (loss). Combine lines 6 through 10	11	

Part III Summary of Parts I and II

12	Enter excess of net short-term capital gain (line 5) over net long-term capital loss (line 11)	12	
13	Net capital gain. Enter excess of net long-term capital gain (line 11) over net short-term capital loss (line 5)	13	
14	Add lines 12 and 13. Enter here and on Form 1120, page 1, line 8, or the proper line on other returns	14	

Note. *If losses exceed gains, see* ***Capital losses*** *in the instructions.*

For Privacy Act and Paperwork Reduction Act Notice, see the Instructions for Forms 1120 and 1120-A. Cat. No. 11460M **Schedule D (Form 1120) (2006)**

Printed on recycled paper

15

Partnerships and S Corporations

CHAPTER CONTENTS

CHAPTER OVERVIEW

Partnerships and S corporations are separate legal entities. However, neither entity is responsible for the income taxes on the business's profits. Instead, the results of all of the business's activities belong to the owners, who report their respective shares of the business activities on their own tax returns. This results in only one level of tax being levied on the entity's profits. Partnerships and S corporations file informational tax returns at the end of each tax year. These returns tell the IRS the total income, deduction, gain, loss and credit generated by the business during the year. These returns also tell the IRS and each owner the share of each item that is attributable to each of the owners. For this reason, partnerships and S corporations are often called flow-through entities.

Although partnerships and S corporations share some common traits, S corporations have some corporate traits as well. For one, like a (regular) C corporation, the owners of an S corporation are shareholders. In contrast, the owners of a partnership are partners. Also, shareholders of an S corporation have the same protection from the debts of the corporation as do shareholders in a C corporation.

This focus of this chapter is the tax aspects of flow-through entities. The chapter looks at the tax aspects both from the standpoint of the entity and its owners. It begins with a discussion of partnerships and concludes with a discussion of S corporations.

THE NATURE OF PARTNERSHIPS

A partnership is an association of two or more persons (or other entities) that conduct business with an intent to share profits or losses. A partnership does not include a joint undertaking merely to share expenses. Each person contributing property or services to the partnership receives an ownership interest. Each becomes a partner. Partners can be individuals, corporations, estates, partnerships, or trusts.

EXAMPLE 1

If Tom Jones and Bessy Smith dig a ditch merely to drain surface water from their properties, they do not create a partnership. If they actively carry on a business and divide the profits, however, they do create a partnership and become partners.

A partner's interest in a partnership can be a profits-only interest or a capital and profits interest. The difference between the two depends upon whether the partner will share in the partnership assets should the partnership go out of business. When a partner contributes property or services to the partnership in exchange for the right to receive assets from the partnership should the entity go out of business, the partner is said to have a **capital and profits interest** in the partnership. If, on the other hand, the partner renders services to the partnership in exchange solely for the right to share in future profits and losses of the partnership, the partner's interest is a **profits-only interest**.

Partnerships can be formed as either general or limited partnerships. In a general partnership, all of the partners are general partners. A general partner is fully liable for the debts and actions of the partnership. A limited partnership has limited partner(s) and at least one general partner. A **limited partner** is liable for the debts and actions of the partnership only to the extent of the partner's investment (basis) in the partnership plus any amounts owed to the limited partner from the partnership.

PARTNERSHIP TAX RETURNS

In a partnership, each of the partners, rather than the partnership, are responsible for the income taxes. All items of partnership income and loss pass through to the partners. These items appear on the partners' own tax returns. Partners must pay taxes on their respective shares of the partnership income regardless of whether or not they receive distributions from the partnership. However, a partnership can choose to be taxed as a corporation. This is done by having the business "check the box" to be taxed as a corporation on its first income tax return.

Every partnership doing business within the United States files the informational return Form 1065, U.S. Partnership Return of Income. The return reports the partnership's revenues and expenses. It also provides each partner's share of all partnership items. The return is due by the 15th day of the fourth month after the partnership's year end. For a calendar year partnership, the due date is April 15. A partnership may receive an automatic six-month extension for filing by submitting a Form 8736. This form must be filed by the due date for the original return. The Code imposes a penalty on the partnership (not the partners) for its failure to file a complete Form 1065 in a timely manner. For each month that the failure continues (not to exceed five months), the penalty equals $50 times the number of partners. Thus, the maximum penalty equals $250 times the number of partners.

Form 1065 consists of four pages. Page 1 provides general information about the partnership and the calculation of ordinary income. Page 2 has Schedules A and B. Schedule A computes the cost of goods sold and Schedule B requests other information about the partnership. Question 5 on Schedule B asks whether the partnership meets each of the following requirements:

1. The partnership's total receipts were less than $250,000.
2. The partnership's total assets at the end of the tax year were less than $600,000; **and**
3. Schedules K-1 are filed with the return and furnished to the partners on or before the due date (including extensions) for the partnership return.

If the partnership can answer "yes," to Question 5, the partnership is not required to complete Schedules L, M-1, and M-2 on page 4 or provide total assets on page 1. Partnerships not meeting the requirements of Question 5, must complete these schedules.

Schedule K is found on Page 3 of the partnership tax return. Here all items that must be separately stated are listed. Finally, Page 4 contains the book balance sheet (Schedule L), reconciliation of book and tax income (Schedule M-1) and an analysis of the partners' capital account (Schedule M-2). The information reported on these pages and schedules of Form 1065 are explained in more detail later in the chapter.

Year to Report Partnership Income

Partners are taxed on their shares of partnership items in the year in which the partnership's tax year ends. They include the results of all partnership activities on their own tax returns.

EXAMPLE 2

The partnership and partner, Amber Brown, have a calendar tax year. Brown reports her share of partnership items for the calendar year 20x1 on her individual 20x1 tax return. Now, suppose the partnership uses a fiscal year from February 1, 20x1, to January 31, 20x2. Brown still uses a calendar tax year. Brown includes the partnership income, most of which was earned in 20x1, on her 20x2 return. Thus, 11 months of income earned by the partnership in 20x1 is not taxed until 20x2. Brown has an 11-month tax deferral on this income.

Partnership Tax Year

To prevent partners from deferring partnership income into the next year (like Brown in Example 2), Congress passed rules limiting a partnership's choice of year ends. The partnership must select the same tax year as the majority partners. Majority partners own in total more than 50% of capital and profits. Because most individual partners use a calendar year, most partnerships also use the calendar year. However, if the majority partners have different tax years, the partnership must select the same tax year as all of its principal partners. A principal partner owns at least 5% of capital or profits. Partnerships unable to determine a tax year using these rules must adopt a tax year that results in the least aggregate deferral of income. The details of this rule are beyond the scope of this discussion.

EXAMPLE 3

Partners A and B contribute property to form AB partnership in exchange for a 70% and 30% interest in capital and profits, respectively. Partner A uses a June 30 year-end; Partner B uses the calendar year end. Since Partner A is a majority partner, AB's required tax year is a June 30 fiscal year.

EXAMPLE 4

ABC partnership is formed when partners A, B and C contribute property in exchange for a 40%, 30%, and 30% interest in capital and profits, respectively. Partner A uses a June 30 year-end. Partners B and C use a calendar year end. Since Partners B and C together own a majority interest in the partnership, ABC's required tax year is the calendar year.

EXAMPLE 5

Same as in Example 4 except that Partner C's year end is October 31. No group of partners owns a majority interest in the partnership. Also, the principal partners (A, B, and C) do not all have the same year end. Thus, ABC's required tax year must be determined using the least aggregate deferral method.

EXAMPLE 6

D and E each own 25% of DE partnership. The remaining 50% is owned by 20 other partners, each of whom have less than a 5% partnership interest. D and E both have a June 30 year end. The other 20 partners all use a calendar year end. Since no group of partners having the same year end own more than a 50% interest in capital and profits in DE, the partnership's required tax year is not determined by the majority interest rule. However, A and B are the only two principal partners in DE. Since all principal partners share the same year end, DE's required tax year is June 30.

Exceptions

Two exceptions apply to the required tax year rules. The first permits a partnership to select a tax year based on the natural business year of the entity. A natural business year is one in which at least 25% of gross receipts are received in the last two months of a 12-month period. This requirement must be met for three consecutive years *before* the partnership can apply for a natural business year. Thus, the natural business year exception may be adopted only by partnerships that have been in existence for at least three years.

The second exception allows partnerships to select a tax year that provides no more than a three-month deferral for its partners. For partners using a calendar tax year, the partnership could select a tax year ending the last day of September, October, or November. The partnership makes the election by filing Form 8716, Election To Have a Tax Year Other Than a Required Tax Year. This election requires partnerships to make tax deposits approximating the amount of tax deferral due to the difference in the partnership and the partners' tax years. Thus, these tax deposits eliminate any income deferral benefits. Treasury Regulations provide details regarding the computation of the required tax deposits.

EXAMPLE 7

Continuing with Example 6, DE's required tax year is June 30. The partnership can elect to use a March 31, April 30 or May 31 year end as long as it agrees to make tax deposits equal to the estimated taxes the partners would owe on the profits generated during these months.

Tax Year Change

A partnership wanting to change its tax year must obtain permission from the IRS. Partnerships make the request on Form 8716. A partnership receiving permission to change its tax year files a short-year tax return in the year of change. This return covers the period from its prior year end to its new year end.

EXAMPLE 8

A change from a fiscal year ending March 31 to the calendar year ending December 31 requires a short-year return. The short-year return covers the nine-month period of April 1 to December 31. If a partnership changes from a calendar year to a March 31 year end, it files a short-year return covering January 1 to March 31.

Changes in partnership membership or in the relative interests among the partners sometimes terminate the partnership. Normally, the following occurrences will not automatically terminate the partnership tax year: death of a partner, addition of a partner, or a shift of a partial interest in the firm among partners. However, if the cumulative effect of any events during a 12-month period causes at least a 50% change in ownership, the tax year closes. The tax year also closes when the partnership ceases to carry on any business. Thus, all of the partners must recognize their shares of income/loss items at the time of closing. The rules are slightly different for the partner. Here the partnership tax year closes with respect to a partner whose entire partnership interest terminates by death or some other event, but it will not close the tax year for the other partners.

Reporting Partnership Income and Deductions

A partnership is not a taxable entity. A partnership *passes through* income and expenses to each of its partners. This pass-through treatment is an application of the *conduit principle.* Many partnership income and expense items receive special tax treatment on the partners' own tax returns. For example, net capital gain is taxed differently to individual and corporate taxpayers. Also, different limitations on charitable contributions apply to these two types of taxpayers. Accordingly, the partnership must report these types of items separately on its tax return. This separate reporting enables the partners to determine their shares of these income and expense items which they must separately report on their own tax returns. Any items that do not require separate reporting are passed through to the partners as ordinary income or loss from partnership operations.

Partners are not employees of the partnership. Thus, there are no taxes withheld on their earnings. Instead, partners must make estimated payments large enough to cover both income and self-employment taxes on their shares of partnership income.

Separately Stated Items

As previously mentioned, certain items of income and deductions are separately stated on the partnership return because they can affect partners' own tax liabilities differently. The partnership return Form 1065, Schedule K, is where these separately stated items are listed. Each partner receives a Form 1065, Schedule K-1, which shows that partner's share of each separately stated item. The following sections present the most common separately stated items.

Income Items

Rental income, interest, dividends, royalties, and gains (losses) from the sale of capital assets or business properties (Section 1231 assets) are separately stated on Schedules K and K-1. In addition, Schedule D (Form 1065) lists any long-term or short-term capital gains (losses) of the partnership. The partnership files a Form 4797 to report any gains (losses) on business properties. Partners add each separately stated item on Schedule K-1 to other similar items they have personally. They report these items in total on their tax returns. Their shares of partnership capital gains (losses) appear on each partner's own Schedule D. Similarly, partners report gains (losses) from partnership business properties with other such personal business gains (losses) on their own Form 4797.

Even though state and local (municipal) bond interest is exempt from federal income taxes, it is a separately stated item. The interest may be subject to state income tax, depending on the partner's state of residence. Also, an individual partner must report this income on the Form 1040 for use in computing the taxable portion of social security benefits.

Deduction Items

Relatively few deductions are separately stated on Schedules K and K-1. The partnership deducts most expenses in the computation of ordinary income. The three most common separately stated deductions include Section 179 expense, deductions related to portfolio (investment) income, and charitable contributions. Section 179 provides a special option that allows the immediate expensing of assets purchased in the current year. The partnership decides whether or not to take the Section 179 deduction. The dollar amount and placed in service limits apply at both the partnership level and again at the partner level. The partners add their distributive shares of this deduction to the amounts they have from businesses in determining their own Section 179 deductions.

Individual taxpayers deduct investment interest expense to the extent of their net investment income. Net investment income equals investment income less deductible investment expenses. Individual taxpayers deduct investment expenses as an itemized deduction on Form 1040, Schedule A. Any partnership item affecting this computation must be separately stated.

Charitable contributions do not qualify as business expenses. Therefore, the partnership does not claim them as a deduction in computing ordinary income. Instead, the partnership lists the total amount of charitable contributions on Schedule K. Individual partners add their shares of each contribution to their personal contributions and list the totals as itemized deductions on Form 1040, Schedule A, of their tax returns.

Net Operating Losses (NOLs)

A net operating loss (NOL) generally equals the excess of allowable deductions over taxable gross income in any tax year. A NOL from a trade or business may be carried back to the two preceding tax years and then forward to the next 20 years. A partnership, however, does not carry over its losses to other partnership tax years. Instead, the partners report their shares of the partnership's losses on their own returns as deductions from gross income. The partnership allocates income and losses to partners only for that portion of the year that the partner is a member of the partnership. Partners cannot be allocated losses for the period before they joined the partnership.

Also, partners may deduct losses only to the extent of the bases of (investment in) their interests in the partnership. These losses reduce their bases in the partnership. However, partners do not reduce their bases below zero. Any disallowed losses remain available to the partners in future years when their bases increase so as to absorb some or all of the loss.

EXAMPLE 9

Janet Monroe has a 40% partnership interest with a basis of $16,000 at the beginning of 20x1. The partnership has an ordinary loss of $60,000 in 20x1. Monroe's share of the loss would be $24,000 ($60,000 × 40%). However, she deducts only $16,000 (equal to her investment) which reduces her basis in the partnership to zero. The $8,000 ($24,000 – $16,000) of the loss not deductible in 20x1 carries forward to offset a future positive partnership basis.

Foreign Taxes

Partnerships engaging in business activities outside the United States may pay taxes to foreign countries. Such taxes receive special treatment on the tax return of an individual and therefore are separately stated. Individual partners report their shares of these foreign taxes on their own tax returns, either as itemized deductions on Form 1040, Schedule A, or as a tax credit.

Credits

Since partnerships pay no income tax, they do not take any credits. The benefits of any credits pass through to the partners as separately stated items. The partnerships make any elections necessary to qualify for the credits. The partners claim the benefits on their own returns to the extent they meet the limitations on the credits.

EXAMPLES OF SEPARATELY STATED ITEMS

Rental income	Section 179 deductions
Interest income	Investment expenses
Dividend income	Credits and credit recaptures
Royalty income	Guaranteed payments*
Short-term capital gains (losses)	AMT adjustments and preferences
Long-term capital gains (losses)	Foreign taxes
Other investment income	Tax-exempt income
Section 1231 gains	Nondeductible expenses
Charitable contributions	Personal expenses paid for partners

*Deducted in total in computing ordinary income but separately stated for each partner

Partnership Ordinary Income

When completing the partnership tax return, all income and expense items must be divided between separately stated items and ordinary items. The items not requiring separate statement are combined on Form 1065, page 1 and result in the ordinary income or loss for the partnership. Ordinary income generally consists of the receipts from the partnership's principal business activity. Thus, the gross profits from the sales of products or services are ordinary income. Any other income that is ordinary when passed-through to the partners is ordinary income for this purpose. Items such as gains from the sale of business property held short-term, depreciation recapture and interest received on accounts receivables fall into this category.

From the resulting income, the partnership deducts operating expenses. The net result of subtracting operation expenses from nonseparately stated income is income from operations. The partnership reports this amount on its tax return as ordinary income from trade or business activities.

Calculating Ordinary Income

Gross receipts or gross sales	$xx	
Less returns and allowances	(xx)	$xx
Less cost of goods sold		(xx)
Gross profit		$xx
Ordinary income or (loss) from other partnerships and fiduciaries		xx
Net ordinary gain or (loss) from Form 4797		xx
Other income or (loss)		xx
Total income or (loss)		$xx
Less:		
Allowable operating expenses	$xx	
Guaranteed payments to partners	xx	(xx)
Ordinary income or (loss) from trade or business		$xx

Guaranteed Payments to Partners

Partnership agreements frequently provide that some or all partners receive payments as compensation. These payments recognize the varying skills and amounts of time partners devote to partnership business. Also, partners may receive a stated rate of interest on the amount of capital that each has invested in the partnership.

The partnership generally deducts these guaranteed payments in computing partnership ordinary income. To be deductible, the payments must be reasonable and determined without regard to partnership income. Although guaranteed salaries and interest payments to partners are deducted to arrive at ordinary income, they are part of the profit allocation process. Thus, partners report these items as income for the partnership year to which they relate.

EXAMPLE 10

Dave and Bob Blunk are partners in the law firm of Blunk and Blunk which ends its tax year on December 31. Dave's monthly salary for the calendar year 20x1 is $3,000. Dave's share of the partnership's 20x1 ordinary income (after deducting guaranteed payments to partners) is $40,000. Dave's 20x1, tax return will report income from the partnership of $76,000. This includes his guaranteed salary of $36,000 ($3,000 × 12) paid during the partnership year and his share of ordinary income ($40,000).

While partners may receive payments for providing services, they are not considered employees. Therefore, the guaranteed payments are not subject to withholding of social security or income taxes. They are considered earned income and subject to self-employment taxes. The partners must report the guaranteed payments they receive as gross income on Form 1040, Schedule E, Supplemental Income and Loss, as nonpassive income. The partnership also deducts salaries and wages paid to spouses or other members of a partner's family. They are considered wages paid to employees. The deductible amounts must be reasonable for the services rendered. Any unreasonable portion is considered a payment to the related partner.

Deductions Not Applicable to Partnerships

Partnerships do not include any nonbusiness deductions in the computation of ordinary income. There is no deduction for personal exemptions, the standard deduction, or personal expenses. These benefits apply solely to individuals. Personal expenses of a partner paid directly by the partnership are treated as withdrawals. They are not included in the calculation of partnership income. Withdrawals are generally treated as tax-free reductions in the partner's investment. Usually, partners only pay taxes on partnership income, not withdrawals.

Information for Figure 15-2: Filled-In Form 1065

Sarah Morton (SSN 294-65-8321) and Doug Baker (SSN 598-20-6104) are active partners in M&B Partnership (EIN 56-0464077). M&B is a general partnership that has been in existence since July 1, 2000. The offices of M&B are located at 524 Southside, Raleigh, NC 27610-4241. M&B uses the accrual method of reporting for its sporting goods business (business code 5941). It values its inventory using the lower of cost or market. Morton is the tax matters partner. She lives at 418 N. Elm Street, Raleigh, NC 27604-1470. Under their partnership agreement, each partner is paid guaranteed payments of $1,600 per month. They share the remaining profits and losses equally. Of these profits, $7,000 was distributed in cash to Morton. No distributions (other than his guaranteed payments) were made to Baker during the year.

The primary information for preparing Form 1065 comes from the 2006 Income Statement, Schedule of Cost of Goods Sold, and Schedule of Operating Expenses provided in Figure 15-1. The filled-in Form 1065 for M&B Partnership appears in Figure 15-2. Although total assets and total gross receipts are not large enough to require completion of Schedules L, M-1 and M-2, these schedules are completed in Figure 15-2 for illustration purposes.

FIGURE 15-1 M&B Partnership Financial Statements

Income Statement
For Year Ended December 31, 2006

Sales	$216,410
Less sales returns and allowances	(3,502)
Net sales	$212,908
Less cost of goods sold (see statement)	(106,754)
Gross profit on sales	$106,154
Operating expenses	(87,622)
Operating income (see statement)	$ 18,532
Interest income (trade or business, $145; investment $1,100; tax-exempt, $50)	1,295
Qualified dividend income	1,700
Interest expense	(253)
Charitable contributions	(426)
Net income	$ 20,848

Schedule of Cost of Goods Sold
For Year Ended December 31, 2006

Inventory at beginning of year	$ 34,969
Purchases	$105,867
Less: Purchases returns and allowances	(775)
Purchase discounts	(1,003)
Net purchases	$104,089
Merchandise available for sale	$139,058
Less inventory at end of year	(32,304)
Cost of goods sold	$106,754

Schedule of Operating Expenses
For Year Ended December 31, 2006

General and administrative expenses:		Selling expenses:	
Sarah Morton, salary	$19,200	Sales salaries	$20,000
Doug Baker, salary	19,200	Advertising	1,164
Payroll taxes	4,378	Depreciation	1,400
Rent	5,400	Store supplies	492
Automobile	999	Miscellaneous	242
Utilities	1,345	Total selling expenses	$23,298
Bad debts (direct write-off)	750		
Insurance	571	Total operating expenses	$87,622
Travel	673		
Office supplies	408		
Office	11,250		
Depreciation	150		
Total G&A expenses	$64,324		

Other Information

F: Total assets, **$78,340** (source: Schedule L, line 14, column d)
7: Other income, **$145** (trade or business interest)
9: Salaries and wages, **$31,250** (sales salaries $20,000 + office salaries $11,250)
10: Guaranteed payments to partners, **$38,400** ($19,200 + $19,200)
16a: Depreciation, **$1,550** ($1,400 + $150)
20: Other deductions, **$5,894** (advertising expense $1,164 + automobile expense $999 + utilities expense, $1,345 + insurance expense $571 + travel expense $673 + store supplies $492 + office supplies $408 + miscellaneous selling expense $242)

Other Information (Schedule K)

1: Ordinary business income (loss), **$18,424** (source: page 1, line 22)
4: Guaranteed payments to partners, **$38,400** ($19,200 + $19,200)
5: Interest income, **$1,100** (taxable portfolio interest income)
14a: Net earnings from self-employment, **$56,824** ($18,424 ordinary income + $38,400 guaranteed payments)
20a: Investment income **$2,800** ($1,100 interest income + $1,700 dividend income)

Other Information (Analysis of Net Income (Loss))

1: Net income (loss), **$59,198** ($18,424 + $38,400 + $1,100 + $1,700 – $426)

Other Information (Schedule M-2)

3: Net income (loss) per books, **$20,848** (source: Income Statement)

Schedule K Items

Those items of partnership income and expense not included in the ordinary income calculation are separately stated items. Since the partnership is not a taxpaying entity, its credits are also separately stated. The Schedule K provides a summary of these items as well as listing the partnership's ordinary income.

Income Items

The income items requiring separate statement are those that receive special treatment or have limitations at the partner level. The partners combine their share of the partnership income items with their personal income items and then apply the special treatment or limitations. The resulting amounts appear on the partner's return.

Deductions

Most expenses of a partnership are incurred for the production of ordinary income. Therefore, there are only a few separately stated deductions. The expense items that must be separately stated on Schedule K include:

1. Section 179 deduction
2. Deductions related to portfolio income
3. AMT adjustments and preferences
4. Nondeductible expenses
5. Charitable contributions

FIGURE 15-2 Filled-In Form 1065, Page 1

Form **1065** — Department of the Treasury, Internal Revenue Service

U.S. Return of Partnership Income

For calendar year 2006, or tax year beginning ...., 2006, ending ...., 20.....
▶ See separate instructions.

OMB No. 1545-0099 — **2006**

A Principal business activity: Retail	Name of partnership: M&B Partnership	D Employer identification number: 56 : 0464077
B Principal product or service: Sporting goods	Number, street, and room or suite no. If a P.O. box, see the instructions.: 524 Southside	E Date business started: 7-1-00
C Business code number: 5941	City or town, state, and ZIP code: Raleigh, NC 27610-4241	F Total assets (see the instructions): $78,340

Use the IRS label. Otherwise, print or type.

G Check applicable boxes: (1) ☐ Initial return (2) ☐ Final return (3) ☐ Name change (4) ☐ Address change (5) ☐ Amended return

H Check accounting method: (1) ☐ Cash (2) ☒ Accrual (3) ☐ Other (specify) ▶

I Number of Schedules K-1. Attach one for each person who was a partner at any time during the tax year ▶ 2

J Check if Schedule M-3 required (attach Schedule M-3) ☐

Caution. *Include **only** trade or business income and expenses on lines 1a through 22 below. See the instructions for more information.*

Income	1a	Gross receipts or sales	1a	216,410		
	b	Less returns and allowances	1b	3,502	1c	212,908
	2	Cost of goods sold (Schedule A, line 8)			2	106,754
	3	Gross profit. Subtract line 2 from line 1c			3	106,154
	4	Ordinary income (loss) from other partnerships, estates, and trusts *(attach statement)*			4	
	5	Net farm profit (loss) *(attach Schedule F (Form 1040))*			5	
	6	Net gain (loss) from Form 4797, Part II, line 17 (attach Form 4797)			6	
	7	Other income (loss) *(attach statement)*			7	145
	8	**Total income (loss).** Combine lines 3 through 7			8	106,299
Deductions (see the instructions for limitations)	9	Salaries and wages (other than to partners) (less employment credits)			9	31,250
	10	Guaranteed payments to partners			10	38,400
	11	Repairs and maintenance			11	
	12	Bad debts			12	750
	13	Rent			13	5,400
	14	Taxes and licenses			14	4,378
	15	Interest			15	253
	16a	Depreciation *(if required, attach Form 4562)*	16a	1,550		
	b	Less depreciation reported on Schedule A and elsewhere on return	16b		16c	1,550
	17	Depletion **(Do not deduct oil and gas depletion.)**			17	
	18	Retirement plans, etc.			18	
	19	Employee benefit programs			19	
	20	Other deductions *(attach statement)*			20	5,894
	21	**Total deductions.** Add the amounts shown in the far right column for lines 9 through 20			21	87,875
	22	**Ordinary business income (loss).** Subtract line 21 from line 8			22	18,424
	23	Credit for federal telephone excise tax paid (attach Form 8913)			23	

Sign Here

Under penalties of perjury, I declare that I have examined this return, including accompanying schedules and statements, and to the best of my knowledge and belief, it is true, correct, and complete. Declaration of preparer (other than general partner or limited liability company member) is based on all information of which preparer has any knowledge.

▶ *Sarah Morton* — Signature of general partner or limited liability company member manager

▶ 4-12-07 — Date

May the IRS discuss this return with the preparer shown below (see instructions)? ☐ Yes ☐ No

Paid Preparer's Use Only

Preparer's signature	Date	Check if self-employed ▶ ☐	Preparer's SSN or PTIN
Firm's name (or yours if self-employed), address, and ZIP code ▶		EIN ▶	
		Phone no. ( )	

For Privacy Act and Paperwork Reduction Act Notice, see separate instructions. Cat. No. 11390Z Form **1065** (2006)

FIGURE 15-2 Filled-In Form 1065, Page 2

Form 1065 (2006) Page **2**

Schedule A **Cost of Goods Sold** (see the instructions)

1	Inventory at beginning of year	1	34,969
2	Purchases less cost of items withdrawn for personal use	2	104,089
3	Cost of labor	3	
4	Additional section 263A costs *(attach statement)*	4	
5	Other costs *(attach statement)*	5	
6	**Total.** Add lines 1 through 5	6	139,058
7	Inventory at end of year	7	32,304
8	**Cost of goods sold.** Subtract line 7 from line 6. Enter here and on page 1, line 2	8	106,754

9a Check all methods used for valuing closing inventory:
- (i) ☐ Cost as described in Regulations section 1.471-3
- (ii) ☒ Lower of cost or market as described in Regulations section 1.471-4
- (iii) ☐ Other (specify method used and attach explanation) ▶

b Check this box if there was a writedown of "subnormal" goods as described in Regulations section 1.471-2(c) ▶ ☐

c Check this box if the LIFO inventory method was adopted this tax year for any goods *(if checked, attach Form 970)*. ▶ ☐

d Do the rules of section 263A (for property produced or acquired for resale) apply to the partnership? ☐ Yes ☒ No

e Was there any change in determining quantities, cost, or valuations between opening and closing inventory? ☐ Yes ☒ No
If "Yes," attach explanation.

Schedule B **Other Information**

		Yes	No
1	What type of entity is filing this return? Check the applicable box: a ☒ Domestic general partnership b ☐ Domestic limited partnership c ☐ Domestic limited liability company d ☐ Domestic limited liability partnership e ☐ Foreign partnership f ☐ Other ▶		
2	Are any partners in this partnership also partnerships?		X
3	During the partnership's tax year, did the partnership own any interest in another partnership or in any foreign entity that was disregarded as an entity separate from its owner under Regulations sections 301.7701-2 and 301.7701-3? If yes, see instructions for required attachment		X
4	Did the partnership file Form 8893, Election of Partnership Level Tax Treatment, or an election statement under section 6231(a)(1)(B)(ii) for partnership-level tax treatment, that is in effect for this tax year? See Form 8893 for more details		X
5	Does this partnership meet all three of the following requirements? a The partnership's total receipts for the tax year were less than $250,000; b The partnership's total assets at the end of the tax year were less than $600,000; and c Schedules K-1 are filed with the return and furnished to the partners on or before the due date (including extensions) for the partnership return. If "Yes," the partnership is not required to complete Schedules L, M-1, and M-2; Item F on page 1 of Form 1065; or Item N on Schedule K-1.	X	
6	Does this partnership have any foreign partners? If "Yes," the partnership may have to file Forms 8804, 8805 and 8813. See the instructions		X
7	Is this partnership a publicly traded partnership as defined in section 469(k)(2)?		X
8	Has this partnership filed, or is it required to file, a return under section 6111 to provide information on any reportable transaction?		X
9	At any time during calendar year 2006, did the partnership have an interest in or a signature or other authority over a financial account in a foreign country (such as a bank account, securities account, or other financial account)? See the instructions for exceptions and filing requirements for Form TD F 90-22.1. If "Yes," enter the name of the foreign country. ▶		X
10	During the tax year, did the partnership receive a distribution from, or was it the grantor of, or transferor to, a foreign trust? If "Yes," the partnership may have to file Form 3520. See the instructions		X
11	Was there a distribution of property or a transfer (for example, by sale or death) of a partnership interest during the tax year? If "Yes," you may elect to adjust the basis of the partnership's assets under section 754 by attaching the statement described under *Elections Made By the Partnership* in the instructions		X
12	Enter the number of Forms 8865, Return of U.S. Persons With Respect to Certain Foreign Partnerships, attached to this return ▶		

Designation of Tax Matters Partner (see the instructions)

Enter below the general partner designated as the tax matters partner (TMP) for the tax year of this return:

Name of designated TMP ▶ Sarah Morton Identifying number of TMP ▶ 294-65-8321

Address of designated TMP ▶ 418 N. Elm Street
Raleigh, NC 27604-1470

Form **1065** (2006)

FIGURE 15-2 Filled-In Form 1065, Page 3

Form 1065 (2006) Page 3

Schedule K — Partners' Distributive Share Items

					Total amount
Income (Loss)	1	Ordinary business income (loss) (page 1, line 22)		1	18,424
	2	Net rental real estate income (loss) *(attach Form 8825)*		2	
	3a	Other gross rental income (loss)	3a		
	b	Expenses from other rental activities *(attach statement)*	3b		
	c	Other net rental income (loss). Subtract line 3b from line 3a		3c	
	4	Guaranteed payments		4	38,400
	5	Interest income		5	1,100
	6	Dividends: a Ordinary dividends		6a	1,700
		b Qualified dividends	6b 1,700		
	7	Royalties		7	
	8	Net short-term capital gain (loss) *(attach Schedule D (Form 1065))*		8	
	9a	Net long-term capital gain (loss) *(attach Schedule D (Form 1065))*		9a	
	b	Collectibles (28%) gain (loss)	9b		
	c	Unrecaptured section 1250 gain *(attach statement)*	9c		
	10	Net section 1231 gain (loss) *(attach Form 4797)*		10	
	11	Other income (loss) *(see instructions)* Type ▶		11	
Deductions	12	Section 179 deduction *(attach Form 4562)*		12	
	13a	Contributions		13a	426
	b	Investment interest expense		13b	
	c	Section 59(e)(2) expenditures: (1) Type ▶	(2) Amount ▶	13c(2)	
	d	Other deductions *(see instructions)* Type ▶		13d	
Self-Employment	14a	Net earnings (loss) from self-employment		14a	56,824
	b	Gross farming or fishing income		14b	
	c	Gross nonfarm income		14c	
Credits & Credit Recapture	15a	Low-income housing credit (section 42(j)(5))		15a	
	b	Low-income housing credit (other)		15b	
	c	Qualified rehabilitation expenditures (rental real estate) *(attach Form 3468)*		15c	
	d	Other rental real estate credits *(see instructions)*	Type ▶	15d	
	e	Other rental credits *(see instructions)*	Type ▶	15e	
	f	Other credits *(see instructions)*	Type ▶	15f	
Foreign Transactions	16a	Name of country or U.S. possession ▶			
	b	Gross income from all sources		16b	
	c	Gross income sourced at partner level		16c	
		Foreign gross income sourced at partnership level			
	d	Passive ▶ e Listed categories *(attach statement)* ▶	f General limitation ▶	16f	
		Deductions allocated and apportioned at partner level			
	g	Interest expense ▶ h Other	▶	16h	
		Deductions allocated and apportioned at partnership level to foreign source income			
	i	Passive ▶ j Listed categories *(attach statement)* ▶	k General limitation ▶	16k	
	l	Total foreign taxes (check one): ▶ Paid ☐ Accrued ☐		16l	
	m	Reduction in taxes available for credit *(attach statement)*		16m	
	n	Other foreign tax information *(attach statement)*			
Alternative Minimum Tax (AMT) Items	17a	Post-1986 depreciation adjustment		17a	
	b	Adjusted gain or loss		17b	
	c	Depletion (other than oil and gas)		17c	
	d	Oil, gas, and geothermal properties—gross income		17d	
	e	Oil, gas, and geothermal properties—deductions		17e	
	f	Other AMT items *(attach statement)*		17f	
Other Information	18a	Tax-exempt interest income		18a	50
	b	Other tax-exempt income		18b	
	c	Nondeductible expenses		18c	
	19a	Distributions of cash and marketable securities		19a	7,000
	b	Distributions of other property		19b	
	20a	Investment income		20a	2,800
	b	Investment expenses		20b	
	c	Other items and amounts *(attach statement)*			

Form 1065 (2006)

FIGURE 15-2 Filled-In Form 1065, Page 4

Form 1065 (2006) Page **4**

Analysis of Net Income (Loss)

1 Net income (loss). Combine Schedule K, lines 1 through 11. From the result, subtract the sum of Schedule K, lines 12 through 13d, and 16l **1** 59,198

2 Analysis by partner type:	(i) Corporate	(ii) Individual (active)	(iii) Individual (passive)	(iv) Partnership	(v) Exempt organization	(vi) Nominee/Other
a General partners		59,198				
b Limited partners						

Note: Schedules L, M-1, and M-2 are not required if Question 5 of Schedule B is answered "Yes."

Schedule L Balance Sheets per Books

Assets	Beginning of tax year (a)	(b)	End of tax year (c)	(d)
1 Cash		4,816		17,347
2a Trade notes and accounts receivable	10,415		11,918	
b Less allowance for bad debts	600	9,815	720	11,198
3 Inventories		34,969		32,304
4 U.S. government obligations				
5 Tax-exempt securities				
6 Other current assets *(attach statement)*				
7 Mortgage and real estate loans				
8 Other investments *(attach statement)*		9,465		9,465
9a Buildings and other depreciable assets	11,900		11,900	
b Less accumulated depreciation	3,850	8,050	5,400	6,500
10a Depletable assets				
b Less accumulated depletion				
11 Land (net of any amortization)				
12a Intangible assets (amortizable only)				
b Less accumulated amortization				
13 Other assets *(attach statement)*		1,475		1,526
14 Total assets		68,590		78,340
Liabilities and Capital				
15 Accounts payable		7,639		8,623
16 Mortgages, notes, bonds payable in less than 1 year		5,000		
17 Other current liabilities *(attach statement)*		479		397
18 All nonrecourse loans				
19 Mortgages, notes, bonds payable in 1 year or more				
20 Other liabilities *(attach statement)*				
21 Partners' capital accounts		55,472		69,320
22 Total liabilities and capital		68,590		78,340

Schedule M-1 Reconciliation of Income (Loss) per Books With Income (Loss) per Return

1 Net income (loss) per books	20,848	6 Income recorded on books this year not included on Schedule K, lines 1 through 11 (itemize): a Tax-exempt interest $ 50	50
2 Income included on Schedule K, lines 1, 2, 3c, 5, 6a, 7, 8, 9a, 10, and 11, not recorded on books this year (itemize):		7 Deductions included on Schedule K, lines 1 through 13d, and 16l, not charged against book income this year (itemize): a Depreciation $	
3 Guaranteed payments (other than health insurance)	38,400		
4 Expenses recorded on books this year not included on Schedule K, lines 1 through 13d, and 16l (itemize): a Depreciation $ b Travel and entertainment $		8 Add lines 6 and 7	50
5 Add lines 1 through 4	59,248	9 Income (loss) (Analysis of Net Income (Loss), line 1). Subtract line 8 from line 5	59,198

Schedule M-2 Analysis of Partners' Capital Accounts

1 Balance at beginning of year	55,472	6 Distributions: a Cash	7,000
2 Capital contributed: a Cash		b Property	
b Property		7 Other decreases (itemize):	
3 Net income (loss) per books	20,848		
4 Other increases (itemize):		8 Add lines 6 and 7	7,000
5 Add lines 1 through 4	76,320	9 Balance at end of year. Subtract line 8 from line 5	69,320

Printed on recycled paper Form **1065** (2006)

As previously noted, charitable contributions are not deductible by the partnership in computing ordinary income. Rather, on Schedule K-1 the partnership tells each partner the amount of contributions subject to the 50%, 30%, and 20% limitations. Individual partners combine their shares with their personal contributions and claim these on Schedule A (Form 1040). Corporate partners combine their share of the partnership contributions with their own and apply the 10% taxable income limit (see Chapter 14).

Other Schedules

Schedule L

This schedule shows the balance sheet at the beginning and end of the tax year. Some items require support from supplementary schedules, such as for other assets and other liabilities. The amounts on Schedule L should agree with the books of the partnership, whether or not the accounts are kept in accordance with income tax law. Figure 15-2 shows the balance sheet for M&B Partnership.

Schedule M-1

Schedule M-1, Reconciliation of Income per Books With Income per Return, reconciles the financial net income with the income on Form 1065. Form 1065 income includes ordinary income from page 1 plus separately stated income and deductions reported on Schedule K. Income and expenses appearing on the books but not on the tax return are disclosed in Schedule M-1. Also, income and expenses appearing on Form 1065 but not in the financial income statement are reconciling Schedule M-1 entries. The ending total of Schedule M-1 ties to the amount in the "Analysis" section found at the top of page 4 (Form 1065).

Most Schedule M-1 reconciliations tend to be more complex than the one in Figure 15-2. This occurs especially when the partnership keeps its books on a financial basis rather than a tax basis. Other reconciling items occurring in real partnerships include: differences in book and tax depreciation, life insurance proceeds from death of a partner, travel and entertainment expenses, and deduction estimates such as bad debts or warranty expenses.

Schedule M-2

Schedule M-2, Analysis of Partners' Capital Accounts, reconciles the beginning capital accounts balance to the ending balance. The beginning and ending balances appear on the balance sheets in Schedule L (line 21). The amounts in Schedule M-2 should agree with the partnership's books. The partnership attaches a statement to the Form 1065 to explain any differences. Also, the amounts on Schedule M-2 should equal the total of all the amounts reported in Item N (Analysis of Partner's Capital Account) of the partners' individual Schedules K-1.

Schedule K-1 (Form 1065))

The partnership prepares a Schedule K-1, Partner's Share of Income, Credits, Deductions, Etc., for each partner. This schedule informs the partners of their respective share of the items on Schedule K. The line numbers on the Schedule K and K-1 are coordinated to make transferring the information easier. For example, guaranteed payments appear on both the Schedule K and K-1 on line 4. Figure 15-3 shows Schedule K-1 for one partner of M&B Partnership. Since Baker's Schedule K-1 would resemble Morton's, only Morton's K-1 is shown here.

Information for Figure 15-3: Filled-In Schedule K-1 (Form 1065)

Sarah Morton's proportionate share of the ordinary income and separately stated items is 50%. Thus, in addition to the guaranteed payments she received during the year, she is allocated 50% of all other partnership items.

Other Information (Schedule K)

M: Partner's share of recourse liabilities at the end of the year, **$4,510** (as a general partner, Morton is responsible for 50% of the partnership's $9,020 of total liabilities)

N: Beginning capital account balance, **$27,736** (source: last year's ending balance)
Capital contributed during the year, **$10,424** (50% x $20,848 book net income)

1: Ordinary business income (loss), **$9,212** ($18,424 x 50%)

4: Guaranteed payments to partners, **$19,200** ($1,600 x 12 months)

5: Interest income, **$550** ($1,100 x 50%)

6: Dividends (both ordinary and qualified, **$850** ($1,700 x 50%)

13: Charitable contributions, **$213** ($426 x 50%) – Contributions subject to the 50% AGI limit are designated Code "A" according to the Schedule K-1 instructions

14: Self-employment earnings, **$28,412** ($9,212 + $19,200)

18: Tax-exempt income, **$25** ($50 x 50%) -- Designated Code "A" in the instructions

19: Distributions, **$7,000** (provided) – Cash distributions are designated Code "A" according to the instructions

20: Investment income, **$1,400** ($2,800 x 50%) -- Coded "A" in the instructions

TRANSACTIONS BETWEEN PARTNERSHIPS AND PARTNERS

Factors Affecting Investment (Basis)

Initially, a partner's investment in a partnership is equal to cash plus the partner's basis (investment) in any business assets contributed to a partnership. If personal-use assets are contributed, the partner's investment is the *lesser of* (i) basis or (ii) FMV of the assets. The partnership's basis in the assets contributed is equal to the partner's investment in the partnership.

Basis Adjustments

Partners adjust their initial basis in the partnership by the following:

1. Their shares of ordinary income (loss)
2. Their shares of separately stated items
3. Additional capital contributions they make to the partnership
4. Distributions (withdrawals) they make from the partnership
5. Their shares of the partnership's liabilities

Ordinary income, separately stated income, and additional contributions increase the partner's basis in the partnership. Ordinary losses, separately stated deductions or losses, and distributions reduce the partner's basis. An additional factor affecting the partner's basis is partnership liabilities. Because partners are personally liable for their share of any debts, a partner's basis increases or decreases as partnership liabilities increase or decrease. This adjustment is based on the partner's interest in the partnership. Thus, a 10% partner increases her investment by 10% of the partnership liabilities.

FIGURE 15-3 Filled-In Schedule K-1 (Form 1065)

651106

☐ Final K-1 ☐ Amended K-1 OMB No. 1545-0099

Schedule K-1 (Form 1065) **2006**

Department of the Treasury
Internal Revenue Service

For calendar year 2006, or tax year beginning ______, 2006 ending ______, 20__

Partner's Share of Income, Deductions, Credits, etc. ► See back of form and separate instructions.

Part I Information About the Partnership

A Partnership's employer identification number
56-0464077

B Partnership's name, address, city, state, and ZIP code
M&B Parnership
524 Southside
Raleigh, NC 27610-4241

C IRS Center where partnership filed return
Memphis

D ☐ Check if this is a publicly traded partnership (PTP)
E ☐ Tax shelter registration number, if any ______
F ☐ Check if Form 8271 is attached

Part II Information About the Partner

G Partner's identifying number
294-65-8321

H Partner's name, address, city, state, and ZIP code
Sarah Morton
418 Elm Street
Raleigh, NC 27640-1470

I ☒ General partner or LLC member-manager ☐ Limited partner or other LLC member

J ☐ Domestic partner ☐ Foreign partner

K What type of entity is this partner? Individual

L Partner's share of profit, loss, and capital:

	Beginning	Ending
Profit	50 %	50 %
Loss	50 %	50 %
Capital	50 %	50 %

M Partner's share of liabilities at year end:

Nonrecourse	$ 0
Qualified nonrecourse financing	$
Recourse	$ 4,510

N Partner's capital account analysis:

Beginning capital account	$ 27,736
Capital contributed during the year	$ 10,424
Current year increase (decrease)	$
Withdrawals & distributions	$(7,000)
Ending capital account	$ 31,160

☐ Tax basis ☐ GAAP ☒ Section 704(b) book
☐ Other (explain)

Part III Partner's Share of Current Year Income, Deductions, Credits, and Other Items

1	Ordinary business income (loss)	9,212
2	Net rental real estate income (loss)	
3	Other net rental income (loss)	
4	Guaranteed payments	19,200
5	Interest income	550
6a	Ordinary dividends	850
6b	Qualified dividends	850
7	Royalties	
8	Net short-term capital gain (loss)	
9a	Net long-term capital gain (loss)	
9b	Collectibles (28%) gain (loss)	
9c	Unrecaptured section 1250 gain	
10	Net section 1231 gain (loss)	
11	Other income (loss)	
12	Section 179 deduction	
13	Other deductions	A Charitable Contributions, 213
14	Self-employment earnings (loss)	28,412
15	Credits	
16	Foreign transactions	
17	Alternative minimum tax (AMT) items	
18	Tax-exempt income and nondeductible expenses	A 25
19	Distributions	A 7,000
20	Other information	A Investment Income, 1,400

*See attached statement for additional information.

For IRS Use Only

For Privacy Act and Paperwork Reduction Act Notice, see Instructions for Form 1065. Cat. No. 11394R **Schedule K-1 (Form 1065) 2006**

EXAMPLE 11

Jim Peabody and Mary Jones are business partners sharing profits and losses 40% and 60%, respectively. Peabody's basis in the business is $20,000 and Jones's basis is $30,000. The business incurs $10,000 of liabilities. As a result, Peabody's basis increases to $24,000 [$20,000 + ($10,000 × 40%)]. Jones's basis increases to $36,000 [$30,000 + ($10,000 × 60%)].

Partnership Distributions

Distributions to partners are generally tax free to the partners. Partners pay taxes on income, not distributions. In a distribution, partners are simply withdrawing previously taxed income from the partnership. However, distributions (withdrawals) of money or property to the partners decrease their investments in the partnership, but not below zero. Their partnership bases decrease by the adjusted basis of the property distributed. The basis of the property received by the partners is the same as it was while in the hands of the partnership. Generally, no gain or loss is recognized by either party at the time of distribution. However, if a cash distribution exceeds the partner's basis in the partnership interest, the partner's basis is reduced to zero. The partner recognizes gain for any excess.

EXAMPLE 12

A partnership purchases stock in 20x1 for $5,000. In 20x3, the partnership distributes the stock (now worth $23,000) to the partners. A 50% partner with a partnership basis of $50,000 receives stock with a market value of $11,500. His basis in this stock is only $2,500 ($5,000 × 50%). In addition, his partnership basis is reduced to $47,500. No gain is recognized until the partner sells his stock. Upon sale, his basis in computing gain or loss will be $2,500.

LIMITED LIABILITY COMPANIES AND PARTNERSHIPS

Limited liability companies (LLCs) are a popular form of business ownership. All states have laws recognizing this form of business. LLCs provide the owners with the limited personal liability of a corporation but partnerships for tax purposes. The reason they can receive partnership tax treatment is that they tend to lack the corporate characteristics of continuity of life and free transferability of interests. Form 1065, Schedule B, now recognizes limited liability companies as one of the partnership forms along with general partnerships and limited partnerships. The major advantage of the LLC form of partnership over the general and limited partnerships is the limited liability. With a general partnership, all partners become personally liable for the debts of the partnership. Even with a limited partnership, at least one general partner is personally liable. For limited partners to retain their limited liability, they cannot participate in the management of the partnership. The LLC grants personal limited liability for **all** of its owners and still allows each owner to participate in the management of the business. Thus, the LLC combines the corporate legal benefits of limited liability with the partnership tax benefits of a single level of tax.

While an LLC is a formal corporation for state legal purposes, a limited liability partnership (LLP) is a partnership for state legal and income tax purposes. Therefore, LLPs may avoid state taxes placed on corporations, such as franchise taxes. Yet the most important difference between LLCs and LLPs is in the owners' liability. LLC owners have the corporate benefit of limited liability. LLP owners, on the other hand, are liable for commercial debt and for their own malpractice and torts. However, they are not liable for the malpractice or torts of their partners. For this reason, most of the national and regional CPA firms have reorganized as LLPs. Changing from a general partnership to a LLP is not a taxable event. It is considered a continuation of the same partnership in most cases. Nevertheless, an LLP must register with the state to place the liability limitation on public record. The benefits of limited liability with the tax treatment as partnerships make LLCs and LLPs very popular business forms for doing business today.

THE NATURE OF S CORPORATIONS

When a corporation elects S corporation status, the shareholders, rather than the corporation, are responsible for the income taxes. The shareholders include their pro rata shares of the corporate taxable income on their personal tax returns. This happens regardless of whether the corporation makes cash distributions to the shareholders. The corporation files an informational return similar to a partnership's return. Hence, the conduit concept of passing through income and deductions to the owners applies to S corporations and partnerships.

Even though an S corporation generally pays no income tax, it is in all other respects a corporation under state law and must act accordingly. This means that the owners can choose the S corporation form of organization for such nontax reasons as limited liability and still have the benefit of the conduit principle for taxing income. It should be noted that some states do not recognize S corporation status in filing a corporation tax return. In such states, the corporation must file a state corporation tax return and pay a state corporation tax. A state tax must be paid even if the corporation is not required to pay a federal corporation tax.

S CORPORATION STATUS

A corporation must qualify as a "small business corporation" before it can elect S corporation status. The term **small business corporation** may seem misleading because the law provides no limit on the "size" of the corporation. Rather, the law limits the types and number of shareholders and the types of corporations that qualify for S status.

Requirements

A corporation must have certain traits to have small business corporation status. First, it must be a domestic corporation. Second, it can only have one class of stock. Third, it cannot have more than 100 shareholders. Fourth, it can only have certain types of shareholders.

Domestic Corporation

An S corporation must be a U.S. or U.S. territory corporation. The term *corporation* includes a joint-stock company and an association that has the traits of a corporation. Certain U.S. corporations cannot elect S corporation status. These corporations include Domestic International Sales Corporations, financial institutions, insurance companies, and corporations using the Puerto Rico or possessions tax credit.

One Class of Stock

The corporation must have only one class of stock outstanding. One class of stock means that the outstanding shares of the corporation must have identical rights in the distribution of profits and in the liquidation of corporate assets. The articles of incorporation, state law, and binding agreements determine whether all outstanding shares have identical rights. The tax law allows differences in the voting rights within the one class of stock.

EXAMPLE 13

All of the outstanding shares of an S corporation give the owners the same rights to distribution and liquidation proceeds. However, some shares give the owner the right to vote on corporate matters, while others do not. Because all shares have the same rights to distribution and liquidation proceeds, the corporation will be considered to have only one class of stock, even though some shares are voting and others are nonvoting.

Number of Shareholders

An S corporation may have up to 100 shareholders. However, family members are treated as one shareholder in determining the number of shareholders of an S corporation. "Family" includes a common ancestor and all lineal descendants within six generations of a common ancestor as well as the spouses, or former spouses, of these individuals. Thus, the S corporation can actually have more than 100 shareholders when some of the shareholders are family members. All other shareholders are counted separately even if they own the stock jointly with someone else. Finally, when a trust holds stock in an S corporation primarily for voting power, each "non-family" beneficiary of the trust, not the trust itself, counts as a shareholder for the 100 limit.

EXAMPLE 14

Lou and Marge Gartner own stock in an S corporation. Lou's father, as well as the Gartners' six children and nine grandchildren also own stock in the S corporation. These 18 individuals are automatically treated as one shareholder for purposes of calculating the number of shareholders of the corporation. This is because they all have a common ancestor (Lou's father) and the family members are within six generations of one another.

EXAMPLE 15

Jan Winton and her son own stock in an S corporation as joint tenants. Both Jan and her son are treated as shareholders for purposes of determining whether a corporation has more than 100 shareholders.

EXAMPLE 16

John and Mary, a married couple, each own shares in an S corporation. The corporation has 100 shareholders, counting John and Mary as one shareholder under the "family" election. If John and Mary got divorced and each retained shares in the S corporation, the corporation would still have 100 shareholders. Suppose John died and his shares were put in a voting trust for his five children. Using the "family" election, the children would be treated as one shareholder, and the corporation would not lose its S corporation status.

Shareholder Type Limitation

Shareholders in an S corporation must be individuals (other than nonresident aliens), estates, and certain trusts. Partnerships and corporations cannot be shareholders. If they were allowed to be owners, the 100 shareholder limit could easily be avoided. The trusts that can be shareholders include (1) a trust owned by one individual, (2) voting trusts, and (3) a "qualified S corporation trust." A qualified S corporation trust owns stock in one or more S corporations and distributes all of its income to only one qualified individual.

S CORPORATION REQUIREMENTS

To be an S corporation, the entity must have the following traits:

1. Be a domestic corporation
2. Have only one class of stock outstanding
3. Have not more than 100 shareholders
4. Limit shareholders to individuals (other than nonresident aliens), estates, and certain trusts

---

Election

A corporation meeting the four requirements listed may make an S election with the consent of all its shareholders. The corporation makes the election by filing Form 2553, Election by a Small Business Corporation.

Timing of Election

To have the election apply to the corporation's current tax year, the corporation files Form 2553 during the prior tax year or within the first 2½ months of the current year. The corporation must meet the requirements for S status from the beginning of the current year. It must continue meeting the requirements in order to maintain its S election. An election made after the first 2½ months applies to the following tax year. An election becomes effective only at the beginning of the corporation's tax year.

Only existing corporations can make elections for S status. Thus, deciding when a corporation comes into existence is important. This is especially true when determining the 2½ month election period. The election period begins in the month the corporation comes into existence. A corporation exists when (1) it begins having business transactions, (2) it acquires assets, or (3) it has shareholders.

EXAMPLE 17

On March 1, 20x1, a calendar year S corporation files Form 2553 with the IRS to elect S corporation status. Because the election is filed before March 15, it normally would be effective retroactive to January 1, 20x1. An election filed after March 15 would not be effective until January 1, 20x2.

Shareholder Consent

All shareholders must consent to the S corporation election. This includes any former shareholders who owned stock in the year the election is effective but prior to the filing of Form 2553. If a former shareholder will not agree to the election (but all current shareholders will), then the election will become effective on the first day of the next tax year.

EXAMPLE 18

Karen Ryzek owned stock in X Corporation on January 1, 20x1. She sold the stock on February 10, 20x1. On March 1, 20x1, X Corporation shareholders elect to be an S corporation effective January 1, 20x1. In order for the election to be valid, Ryzek must consent to the election even though she's no longer a shareholder on March 1, 20x1. Ryzek's consent is necessary because she will report on her 20x1 income tax return her share of income from January 1, 20x1, to February 10, 20x1, while she owned stock in X Corporation.

A shareholder's consent is binding and may be withdrawn only by following prescribed procedures. Shareholders execute a consent by providing all of the required information on Form 2553. Shareholders may also consent by signing a separate consent statement, which should be attached to Form 2553. The separate consent should furnish the following information:

1. The name, address, and identification number of the corporation,
2. The name, address, and identification number of the shareholder,
3. The number of shares owned by the shareholder and the dates on which the stock was acquired, and
4. The day and month of the end of the shareholder's tax year.

Any consent not filed on time invalidates the corporation's election of S status. Each co-owner, tenant by entirety, tenant in common, and joint tenant must consent. This means that each family member must consent even though treated as one shareholder. The legal representative or guardian may consent for a minor shareholder. The executor or administrator of an estate makes the consent for the estate. The consent of a qualified trust holding stock must be made by each person who is treated as a shareholder. Extensions of time to file a consent may be granted under certain circumstances.

Termination

An S corporation election may be terminated either voluntarily or automatically. An automatic termination occurs when the corporation ceases to meet the S corporation requirements.

Voluntary Termination

An election of S corporation status can be terminated voluntarily. Shareholders holding more than 50% of the shares must consent to end the S status. The corporation then files a statement to this effect with the IRS office where it had previously filed its election. If a timely filed revocation specifies an effective date, the revocation will be effective on that date. From that date forward, the corporation reports as a regular corporation. Thus, even though an election to become an S corporation must be effective on the first day of a tax year, a termination may be effective before the end of the regular tax year. If no specific revocation date is given, a revocation made within the first 2½ months of the corporation's tax year is retroactive to the first day of the tax year. If made after the first 2½ months, the revocation is effective on the first day of the following tax year.

EXAMPLE 19

On March 15, 20x1, a calendar year S corporation files a statement with the IRS to revoke its S election. If the statement does not specify a future date on which the revocation is to take effect, the corporation's S status will be revoked retroactively to January 1, 20x1.

EXAMPLE 20

Same as in Example 19, except that the corporation files the statement to revoke its S election on March 16, 20x1. If the statement does not specify a future date on which the revocation is to take effect, the corporation's S status will be revoked effective January 1, 20x2.

To elect S status, the tax law requires that all affected shareholders consent to the election. To revoke an S election, only a majority of the corporation's shareholders must consent.

Automatic Termination

S corporation status automatically terminates upon the occurrence of one of the following events:

1. The corporation fails to meet any of the requirements for being an S corporation. These requirements include the number of shareholders, type of stock, being a domestic corporation, and no shareholders other than individuals, estates, and certain trusts.
2. The corporation has passive investment income in excess of 25% of its gross receipts for three consecutive years. This applies only if a corporation has accumulated earnings and profits (AE&P) carried over from when it was a regular C corporation. Thus, if the corporation was always an S, passive income cannot trigger termination.

The election terminates as of the date on which the disqualifying event occurs. As a result, the day before the terminating event is the last day for the S corporation, and the day of termination becomes the first day of C Corporation status. However, if the election terminates because of excessive passive income, termination is effective beginning with the next tax year.

EXAMPLE 21

An S corporation has been operating on a calendar year basis for the last few years with 100 shareholders. On July 21, 20x1, one of the shareholders dies, with his shares passing equally to his wife and brother on that date. The status as an S corporation automatically terminates on July 21, 20x1, because of the addition of the 101st shareholder. The S corporation must file a return for the period January 1, 20x1, through July 20, 20x1. On July 21, 20x1, the corporation becomes a C corporation for the remainder of the year ending December 31, 20x1. All income (loss) and separately stated items are prorated between the S corporation tax return and the C corporation tax return on a daily basis.

Reelection

Generally, if an election terminates (either voluntarily or automatically), the corporation may not reelect S status for five years. However, the IRS may allow an earlier election when violations of the S corporation requirements were minor. If the S corporation election was inadvertently terminated, the IRS may even waive termination when the corporation makes a timely correction of the violation.

S CORPORATION TAX RETURNS

An S corporation files an annual informational tax return, Form 1120S, U.S. Income Tax Return for an S Corporation. It is due on the 15th day of the third month after the end of the corporation's tax year. For a calendar year corporation, the return is due March 15. An S corporation receives an automatic six-month extension of time to file when it submits a Form 7004, Application for Automatic Extension of Time To File Corporation Income Tax Return. Form 7004 must be filed by the due date for the original return.

The character of all items of income, deductions, losses, and credits passes through from the corporation to the shareholders in a manner similar to partnerships. The shareholders receive a Schedule K-1 (Form 1120S), that reports their shares of the ordinary income and each separately stated item. The law requires companies to furnish this information to owners no later than the filing date for Form 1120S. The S corporation receives a penalty of $50 for each Schedule K-1 not provided to its shareholders in a timely manner.

Tax Year

Like partnerships, S corporations must have the same tax year as the shareholders owning more than 50% of the stock. This is generally a calendar year. Exceptions may apply to this general requirement, however.

One exception involves the natural business year. As described previously in the partnership discussion, in a natural business year 25% of gross receipts are received in the last two months of the fiscal year. Another tax year exception comes under Section 444, which allows an S corporation to elect a tax year that provides no more than a three-month deferral for its shareholders. This same election is available to partnerships. The tax year rules prevent shareholders from deferring S corporation income into a future tax year. The taxation of income could be deferred if rules permitted shareholders to select an S corporation tax year that ended after the shareholders' year ended. This is because S corporation income is included in the shareholder's tax return in the year in which the S corporation's tax year ends.

EXAMPLE 22

The shareholders of an S corporation have calendar tax years. If allowed, they would prefer the S corporation to have a January 31 year end. This means that the income earned from February 1, 20x1, to January 31, 20x2, would be taxable on the shareholders' 20x2 tax returns. This confers an 11-month deferral of income taxes. The tax law, however, requires S corporations have a calendar year end unless they can meet requirements for one of the exceptions to the tax year rule.

Reporting Income and Deductions

To file a Form 1120S, the S corporation must divide its tax items into two categories: (1) separately stated items and (2) ordinary items. The ordinary items not separately stated comprise ordinary income or loss. The separately stated items and ordinary income (loss) are collectively known as the pass-through items. These items pass to the shareholders who report them on their personal tax returns.

Separately Stated Items

Separately stated items are income, deductions, and credits that have the possibility of affecting shareholders' personal tax liabilities differently. The most common separately stated items for S corporations are the same as the items separately stated for partnerships. These items appear on Form 1120S, Schedule K, Shareholders' Prorata Share Items. Schedule K-1 provides each shareholder's portion of ordinary income and separately stated items. A copy of each shareholder's Schedule K-1 is attached to the S corporation's Form 1120S. A copy is also given to the shareholder. The shareholders include taxable items from their Schedules K-1 on their own tax returns.

EXAMPLES OF SEPARATELY STATED ITEMS

- Charitable contributions
- Tax-exempt income
- Nondeductible expenses
- Investment expenses
- Personal expenses paid for shareholder's benefit
- Tax preferences and adjustments the AMT
- Capital gains (losses)
- Investment income (interest, dividends)
- Section 179 expense deduction
- Section 1231 gains (losses)
- Foreign taxes
- Tax credits
- Net income (loss) from rental real estate related to activities

---

Ordinary Income or Loss

Ordinary income (loss) is generally the net result of the S corporation's trade or business activities. Its computation includes all items of income or deductions that are not separately stated. These tend to be the same items used in determining partnership ordinary income and sole proprietorship income. The resulting amount of ordinary income (loss) passes through to the shareholders along with the separately stated items on the Schedule K-1. The ordinary income (loss) appears on the shareholder's Form 1040, Schedule E.

In partnerships, limited liability companies, and sole proprietorships, FICA taxes apply to all ordinary income passing to the owners who pay the self-employment taxes. However, in S corporations, FICA taxes apply only to designated salaries, and the corporation is responsible for paying the taxes. No FICA taxes are paid on the remaining ordinary income which passes to the owners.

Deductions Not Allowed

Like partnerships, certain individual deductions are not available to S corporations, such as the standard deduction, personal itemized deductions, and personal exemptions. S corporations also cannot take certain deductions available to regular taxable C corporations. The most notable of these deductions is the dividends received deduction.

Allocation of Tax Items to Shareholders

A shareholder's portion of S corporation income, deductions, losses, and credits is determined on a per-share-per-day basis. The S corporation allocates an equal amount of each item to each share on a per-day basis for the corporation's tax year. The per-share-per-day amount is multiplied by the number of shares the shareholder owned each day of the year. The shareholders' personal tax returns include their allocated yearly totals for each of the S corporation tax items.

EXAMPLE 23

An S corporation is owned equally by Adam Smith, Tom Jones, and James Brown on November 1, 20x1, the first day of a new fiscal year. Brown sells his shares to Shirley Black on August 8, 20x2. The corporation's fiscal year ends on October 31, 20x2. Thus, Brown held the shares for 281 days (76.99% of the year), and Black owned the shares for 84 days (23.01% of the year). Brown is considered to own the shares from November 1, 20x1, through August 8, 20x2. The corporation earns $150,000 of ordinary taxable income and $90,000 of long-term capital gains during its fiscal year ending October 31, 20x2.

On the basis of these facts, the shareholders report on their calendar year 20x2 tax returns the following S corporation income:

	Ordinary Income	*Capital Gains*
Adam Smith	$ 50,000	$30,000
Tom Jones	50,000	30,000
James Brown (76.99%)	38,495	23,097
Shirley Black (23.01%)	11,505	6,903
Totals	$150,000	$90,000

Utilizing Losses

Partnerships and S corporations both operate under the conduit principle (income and separately stated items pass through to the owners). Because the conduit principle applies, one might think that the utilization of operating losses by S corporation shareholders would be similar to that of partners. Both S corporation shareholders and partners may deduct losses only to the extent of their ownership basis. The losses cannot reduce the basis below zero. However, losses available to partners and S shareholders differ because the computation of basis is not the same for the two entities. Partners' basis includes their proportionate share of all partnership liabilities. On the other hand, a liability increases an S corporation shareholder's basis only if a loan is made directly by the shareholder to the corporation. The S corporation's liabilities are not part of the S shareholder's basis because of the limited liability feature of the corporate status. Thus, a partner generally has a larger basis for utilizing operating losses than would an S shareholder.

EXAMPLE 24

Swift, an S corporation, has five shareholders, each owning 100 shares of stock. They each materially participate in Swift. Each shareholder has a stock basis of $25,000. For 20x1 Swift reports an operating loss of $75,000. Each shareholder's portion of the loss ($15,000) is deductible on the shareholder's individual tax return because it does not reduce any shareholder's basis below zero. After the $15,000 loss, each shareholder's basis in Swift is $10,000 ($25,000 – $15,000).

Remember that losses deductible by each S corporation shareholder cannot reduce the shareholder's basis in the S stock below zero. Further, they must meet the at-risk and passive loss requirements (Chapter 9). Disallowed losses carry forward and are deductible when the shareholder has sufficient basis to cover the losses.

EXAMPLE 25

Su Lin Chang owns a 30% interest in Inco, an S corporation. At the end of 20x1, she has a basis in Inco stock of $15,000 and a basis in loans made to Inco of $12,000. Inco reports an operating loss for 20x1 of $120,000, of which Chang's share is $36,000. She deducts $27,000 of the total loss ($15,000 stock basis + $12,000 loan basis) on her personal tax return. The remaining loss of $9,000 ($36,000 – $27,000) carries over to 20x2 and later years to be offset against future positive ownership basis.

When the lack of basis limits the deductibility of losses, an allocation is necessary. A pro rata share of the ordinary loss and each separately stated loss item appears on the shareholder's tax return. The pro rata percentage equals the shareholder's basis divided by the shareholder's portion of losses for the year. The portion of each item disallowed carries forward.

EXAMPLE 26

Jerry Garcia has a $20,000 basis in his 40% ownership in an S corporation. Garcia's K-1 indicates that his share of the corporation's ordinary loss is $24,000 and his share of capital losses is $8,000. Thus, his total prorata share of losses equal $32,000 ($24,000 + $8,000). Garcia can deduct $20,000 of losses (an amount equal to his basis). The specific ordinary loss deducted on Garcia's tax return is $15,000 ($20,000 × $24,000/$32,000). In computing his personal net capital gain (loss), Garcia includes $5,000 of capital loss ($20,000 × $8,000/$32,000). Garcia carries forward to future years a total loss of $12,000. The carryover loss consists of an ordinary loss deduction of $9,000 ($24,000 – $15,000) and a capital loss deduction of $3,000 ($8,000 – $5,000).

When an S corporation election terminates, any disallowed loss can be taken if the shareholders restore their stock basis sufficiently to cover their losses. The basis must be restored by a specific date. The mandatory date is the *later* of the following:

1. One year after the effective date of termination or the due date of the last S corporation tax return, whichever is later, or
2. 120 days after a determination that the corporation's election had terminated for a previous year

Form 1120S

Form 1120S, U.S. Income Tax Return for an S Corporation, is set up very much like the partnership return. As with the partnership return, Form 1120S consists of four pages. On page 1, the S corporation provides general information about itself and computes its ordinary income. On page 2 of Form 1120S, the corporation computes its cost of goods sold on Schedule A and provides other information about itself on Schedule B. Schedule K (which concludes on page 3) begins at the bottom of page 2. Like with the partnership tax return, this schedule reports all items that must be separately stated. Finally, page 4 contains Schedules L, M-1, and M-2. Schedule L lists the book balance sheet. Schedule M-1 reconciles book and tax income, and Schedule M-2 analyzes the accumulated adjustment account and other capital accounts. The information reported on these pages and schedules of Form 1120S are explained in more detail in the sections that follow.

As with partnerships, the calculation of ordinary income on page 1 includes all items income and expense that are taxed identically to all taxpayers. These items are not subject to any limitations that would be unique to one taxpayer. The calculation of ordinary income for S corporations is essentially the same as that for partnerships, with one important exception. In Chapter 14 you learned that partners could not be employees of the corporations. Thus, payments that resemble "salaries" paid to partners were called guaranteed payments. These amounts were deducted in the calculation of ordinary income. With respect to an S corporation, all shareholders working for the S corporation are considered employees, and payments to shareholders in exchange for services they perform are deducted as such. Thus, S corporations do not pay guaranteed payments to its owners.

Schedule K Items

Income and expense items not part of ordinary income plus all tax credits are separately stated on Schedule K, Shareholders' Pro Rata Share Items. The S corporation uses the amounts found on the Schedule K to make its per share per day allocations to its shareholders. These are reported to each shareholder on a separate Schedule K-1. The shareholders combine their Schedule K-1 items with their other income, expense, and credit items. The resulting amounts appear on the shareholders' own income tax returns.

Schedule L

Schedule L, Balance Sheets per Books, contains a beginning and ending balance sheet for the S corporation. The amounts shown should agree with the corporation's regular books or records. Thus, they typically are not reported on a tax basis. An S corporation is required to complete Schedule L only when its total assets or total receipts are at least $250,000.

Schedule M-1

The corporation completes Schedule M-1, Reconciliation of Income (Loss) per Books With Income (Loss) per Return, if total assets or total receipts at year-end are at least $250,000. To complete this schedule, the preparer needs information about the corporation's financial (book) income and expenses. As its title states, Schedule M-1 reconciles the corporation's book income with the tax return computed income (loss). The tax return income includes ordinary income (loss) plus the separately stated items found on Schedule K. Any items included in financial income but not on Form 1120S or vice versa are reconciling items on Schedule M-1. Thus, the schedule accounts for all differences between book income and the income on Form 1120S. The most common reconciling items on Schedule M-1 are: (1) depreciation, (2) travel and entertainment expenses, and (3) tax exempt items.

Schedule M-2

Schedule M-2, Analysis of Accumulated Adjustments Account, Other Adjustments Account, and Shareholders' Undistributed Taxable Income Previously Taxed, provides an analysis of certain equity accounts for the tax year. It shows the changes in the equity accounts for the income and deductions reported on Form 1120S. Column (a) provides the changes in the accumulated adjustments account (AAA) for the year. (AAA is described in greater detail later in the chapter). The ending balance becomes the beginning balance of Schedule M-2 (line 1), Column (a) for the next year. Column (b), Other Adjustments Account, is for an analysis of other items, such as tax-exempt income and related expenses, not included in computing AAA. Column (b) distinguishes this income from E&P carried over from a prior C status years. It allows this income to be a separate pool from which distributions may be made. The tax treatment for shareholders of distributions from this pool is the same as for distributions from AAA. Given this treatment, S corporations without E&P from prior C status years need not keep track of this type of income. Thus, they do not use Column (b).

Column (c) on Schedule M-2 lists the amount of undistributed taxable income previously included in shareholders' income tax returns. Only corporations electing S status before 1983 might use this column. Distributions of PTI are not taxable to the shareholders.

Information for Figure 15-5: Filled-In Form 1120S

Kendall Management Company, a cash basis service business, had been a regular C corporation prior to it S status election on January 15, 2003 (EIN 52-1739257 and business activity code number 7389). Originally formed on October 1, 1989, it is located at 731 Delhi Road, Atlanta, GA 30307.

Tax Consultants, Inc. prepares Kendall's Form 1120S. Virginia Kendall (SSN 421-63-8045), president and 30% shareholder, is the tax matters person. Her address is 4524 Peachtree Drive, Atlanta, GA 30307. She signs the tax return for the corporation on March 1, 2007.

The amounts reported on Schedule L come from Kendall's balance sheet that it keeps with its set of books and records. The balance sheet is prepared on a book (not tax) basis. Kendall's beginning balance in the AAA account is $25,800. During the year, Kendall distributed a total of $30,000 to its shareholders out of AAA. The remaining information for preparing Kendall's Form 1120S comes from the 2006 income statement found in Figure 15-4.

Other Information

E: Total assets, **$225,650** (source: Schedule L, line 15, column d)
18: Employee benefits program, **$7,500** (employee health insurance)
19: Other deductions, **$4,500** ($1,000 + $800 + $2,700)

Other Information (Schedule K)

5b: Qualified dividends, **$1,250** (source: Income Statement)
8a: Net long-term capital gain, **$10,480** (source: Schedule D (Form 1120S), line 13)
17a: Investment income, **$2,720** ($720 taxable interest + $2,000 dividend income)
18: Income/loss reconciliation, **$46,200** ($40,000 + $720 + $2,000 + $10,480 - $7,000)

Other Information (Schedule M-2)

1b: Beginning balance Other adjustments account, **$1,000** (last year's ending balance)
3a: Other additions to AAA, **$13,200** ($720 taxable interest + $2,000 ordinary dividends + $10,480 capital gain)
3b: Other additions to Other adjustments account, **$1,100** (tax-exempt interest)
5a: Other reductions, **$7,000** (charitable contributions)

FIGURE 15-4 Kendall Management Company Income Statement

Kendall Management Company Income Statement For Year Ended December 31, 2006	
Income:	
Receipts from services	$165,350
Interest income (portfolio, $720; tax-exempt, $1,100)	1,820
Dividend income (qualified dividends, $1,250)	2,000
Gain on sale of stock	10,480
Total income	$179,650
Expenses:	
Advertising	$ 7,500
Bad debts	400
Charitable contributions	7,000
Depreciation	1,700
Employee health insurance	7,500
Insurance expense	1,000
Maintenance and repairs	1,200
Officers' salaries	70,000
Other employee salaries	21,550
Office supplies	800
Payroll taxes	5,000
Retirement plan contributions	6,000
Utilities	2,700
Total expenses	$132,350
Net Income	$ 47,300

Information for Figure 15-6: Filled-In Form 1120S, Schedule D

Kendall Management sold 200 shares of Rogers Company stock on October 14. The stock was acquired on July 18, 2000 for $20,800. The sales price (after commissions) was $31,280.

Information for Figure 15-7: Filled-In Schedule K-1

Virginia Kendall is the corporation's president and owns 30% of the corporation's stock.

Other Information

C: IRS Center where corporation filed return, **Atlanta**
1: Ordinary income, **$12,000** (30% x $40,000)
4: Interest income, **$216** (30% x $720)
5a: Ordinary dividends, **$600** (30% x $2,000)
5b: Qualified dividends, **$375** (30% x $1,250)
8a: Net long-term capital gain, **$3,144** (30% x $10,480)
12: Charitable contributions, **$2,100** (30% x $7,000) – Designated with a code "A" in the Schedule K-1 instructions
16: Tax exempt interest, **$330** (30% x $1,100) – Designated with a code "A"
17: Investment income, **$816** (30% x ($720 + $2,000)) -- Designated with a code "A"

FIGURE 15-5 Filled-In Form 1120S, Page 1

Form **1120S** Department of the Treasury Internal Revenue Service (77)

U.S. Income Tax Return for an S Corporation

▶ Do not file this form unless the corporation has filed Form 2553 to elect to be an S corporation.
▶ See separate instructions.

OMB No. 1545-0130 **2006**

For calendar year 2006 or tax year beginning , 2006, ending , 20

A Effective date of S election: 1-15-03	Name: Kendall Management Company	C Employer identification number: 52-1739257
B Business activity code number (see instructions): 7389	Number, street, and room or suite no.: 731 Delhi Road	D Date incorporated: 10-1-89
	City or town, state, and ZIP code: Atlanta, GA 30307	E Total assets (see instructions): $ 225,650

Use IRS label. Otherwise, print or type.

F Check if: (1) ☐ Initial return (2) ☐ Final return (3) ☐ Name change (4) ☐ Address change (5) ☐ Amended return
G Enter the number of shareholders in the corporation at the end of the tax year ▶ 6
H Check if Schedule M-3 is required (attach Schedule M-3) ▶ ☐

Caution. *Include **only** trade or business income and expenses on lines 1a through 21. See the instructions for more information.*

Income	1a	Gross receipts or sales 165,350 b Less returns and allowances c Bal ▶	1c	165,350
	2	Cost of goods sold (Schedule A, line 8)	2	
	3	Gross profit. Subtract line 2 from line 1c	3	165,350
	4	Net gain (loss) from Form 4797, Part II, line 17 *(attach Form 4797)*	4	
	5	Other income (loss) *(see instructions—attach statement)*	5	
	6	**Total income (loss).** Add lines 3 through 5 ▶	6	165,350
Deductions (see instructions for limitations)	7	Compensation of officers	7	70,000
	8	Salaries and wages (less employment credits)	8	21,550
	9	Repairs and maintenance	9	1,200
	10	Bad debts	10	400
	11	Rents	11	
	12	Taxes and licenses	12	5,000
	13	Interest	13	
	14	Depreciation not claimed on Schedule A or elsewhere on return *(attach Form 4562)*	14	1,700
	15	Depletion **(Do not deduct oil and gas depletion.)**	15	
	16	Advertising	16	7,500
	17	Pension, profit-sharing, etc., plans	17	6,000
	18	Employee benefit programs	18	7,500
	19	Other deductions *(attach statement)*	19	4,500
	20	**Total deductions.** Add lines 7 through 19 ▶	20	125,350
	21	**Ordinary business income (loss).** Subtract line 20 from line 6	21	40,000
Tax and Payments	22a	Excess net passive income or LIFO recapture tax *(see instructions)* — 22a: 0		
	b	Tax from Schedule D (Form 1120S) — 22b: 0		
	c	Add lines 22a and 22b *(see instructions for additional taxes)*	22c	0
	23a	2006 estimated tax payments and 2005 overpayment credited to 2006 — 23a		
	b	Tax deposited with Form 7004 — 23b		
	c	Credit for federal tax paid on fuels *(attach Form 4136)* — 23c		
	d	Credit for federal telephone excise tax paid *(attach Form 8913)* — 23d		
	e	Add lines 23a through 23d	23e	0
	24	Estimated tax penalty *(see instructions).* Check if Form 2220 is attached ▶ ☐	24	
	25	**Amount owed.** If line 23e is smaller than the total of lines 22c and 24, enter amount owed	25	0
	26	**Overpayment.** If line 23e is larger than the total of lines 22c and 24, enter amount overpaid	26	
	27	Enter amount from line 26 **Credited to 2007 estimated tax** ▶ **Refunded** ▶	27	

Sign Here Under penalties of perjury, I declare that I have examined this return, including accompanying schedules and statements, and to the best of my knowledge and belief, it is true, correct, and complete. Declaration of preparer (other than taxpayer) is based on all information of which preparer has any knowledge.

Signature of officer: *Virginia Kendall* Date: 3/1/07 Title:

May the IRS discuss this return with the preparer shown below (see instructions)? ☐ Yes ☐ No

Paid Preparer's Use Only
Preparer's signature: *John Downs* Date: 2-28-07 Check if self-employed ☐ Preparer's SSN or PTIN
Firm's name (or yours if self-employed), address, and ZIP code: Tax Consultants, Inc 12 Peachtree St. Atlanta EIN 61-9077665 Phone no. ( )

For Privacy Act and Paperwork Reduction Act Notice, see separate instructions. Cat. No. 11510H Form **1120S** (2006)

FIGURE 15-5 Filled-In Form 1120S, Page 2

Form 1120S (2006) Page 2

Schedule A Cost of Goods Sold (see instructions)

1	Inventory at beginning of year	1	
2	Purchases	2	
3	Cost of labor	3	
4	Additional section 263A costs *(attach statement)*	4	
5	Other costs *(attach statement)*	5	
6	**Total.** Add lines 1 through 5	6	
7	Inventory at end of year	7	
8	**Cost of goods sold.** Subtract line 7 from line 6. Enter here and on page 1, line 2	8	

9a Check all methods used for valuing closing inventory: *(i)* ☐ Cost as described in Regulations section 1.471-3
(ii) ☐ Lower of cost or market as described in Regulations section 1.471-4
(iii) ☐ Other (Specify method used and attach explanation.) ▶

b Check if there was a writedown of subnormal goods as described in Regulations section 1.471-2(c) ▶ ☐

c Check if the LIFO inventory method was adopted this tax year for any goods (if checked, attach Form 970) ▶ ☐

d If the LIFO inventory method was used for this tax year, enter percentage (or amounts) of closing inventory computed under LIFO 9d

e If property is produced or acquired for resale, do the rules of section 263A apply to the corporation? ☐ Yes ☐ No

f Was there any change in determining quantities, cost, or valuations between opening and closing inventory? ☐ Yes ☐ No
If "Yes," attach explanation.

Schedule B Other Information (see instructions)

		Yes	No
1	Check accounting method: a ☒ Cash b ☐ Accrual c ☐ Other (specify) ▶		
2	See the instructions and enter the: a Business activity ▶ Management Services b Product or service ▶ consulting		
3	At the end of the tax year, did the corporation own, directly or indirectly, 50% or more of the voting stock of a domestic corporation? (For rules of attribution, see section 267(c).) If "Yes," attach a statement showing: **(a)** name and employer identification number (EIN), **(b)** percentage owned, and **(c)** if 100% owned, was a QSub election made?		X
4	Was the corporation a member of a controlled group subject to the provisions of section 1561?		X
5	Has this corporation filed, or is it required to file, a return under section 6111 to provide information on any reportable transaction?		X
6	Check this box if the corporation issued publicly offered debt instruments with original issue discount ▶ ☐ If checked, the corporation may have to file **Form 8281,** Information Return for Publicly Offered Original Issue Discount Instruments.		
7	If the corporation: **(a)** was a C corporation before it elected to be an S corporation **or** the corporation acquired an asset with a basis determined by reference to its basis (or the basis of any other property) in the hands of a C corporation **and (b)** has net unrealized built-in gain (defined in section 1374(d)(1)) in excess of the net recognized built-in gain from prior years, enter the net unrealized built-in gain reduced by net recognized built-in gain from prior years ▶ $		
8	Enter the accumulated earnings and profits of the corporation at the end of the tax year. $		
9	Are the corporation's total receipts *(see instructions)* for the tax year **and** its total assets at the end of the tax year less than $250,000? If "Yes," the corporation is not required to complete Schedules L and M-1.		X

Note: *If the corporation, at any time during the tax year, had assets or operated a business in a foreign country or U.S. possession, it may be required to attach* **Schedule N (Form 1120)**, *Foreign Operations of U.S. Corporations, to this return. See Schedule N for details.*

Schedule K Shareholders' Pro Rata Share Items

Income (Loss)

					Total amount
1	Ordinary business income (loss) (page 1, line 21)			1	40,000
2	Net rental real estate income (loss) *(attach Form 8825)*			2	
3a	Other gross rental income (loss)	3a			
b	Expenses from other rental activities *(attach statement)*	3b			
c	Other net rental income (loss). Subtract line 3b from line 3a			3c	
4	Interest income			4	720
5	Dividends: **a** Ordinary dividends			5a	2,000
	b Qualified dividends	5b	1,250		
6	Royalties			6	
7	Net short-term capital gain (loss) *(attach Schedule D (Form 1120S))*			7	
8a	Net long-term capital gain (loss) *(attach Schedule D (Form 1120S))*			8a	10,480
b	Collectibles (28%) gain (loss)	8b			
c	Unrecaptured section 1250 gain *(attach statement)*	8c			
9	Net section 1231 gain (loss) *(attach Form 4797)*			9	
10	Other income (loss) *(see instructions)* Type ▶			10	

Form **1120S** (2006)

FIGURE 15-5 Filled-In Form 1120S, Page 3

Form 1120S (2006) Page 3

	Shareholders' Pro Rata Share Items (continued)		Total amount
Deductions	11 Section 179 deduction *(attach Form 4562)*	11	
	12a Contributions	12a	7,000
	b Investment interest expense	12b	
	c Section 59(e)(2) expenditures (1) Type ▶ (2) Amount ▶	12c(2)	
	d Other deductions *(see instructions)* Type ▶	12d	
Credits	13a Low-income housing credit (section 42(j)(5))	13a	
	b Low-income housing credit (other)	13b	
	c Qualified rehabilitation expenditures (rental real estate) *(attach Form 3468)*	13c	
	d Other rental real estate credits *(see instructions)* Type ▶	13d	
	e Other rental credits (see instructions) Type ▶	13e	
	f Credit for alcohol used as fuel *(attach Form 6478)*	13f	
	g Other credits *(see instructions)* Type ▶	13g	
Foreign Transactions	14a Name of country or U.S. possession ▶		
	b Gross income from all sources	14b	
	c Gross income sourced at shareholder level	14c	
	Foreign gross income sourced at corporate level		
	d Passive	14d	
	e Listed categories *(attach statement)*	14e	
	f General limitation	14f	
	Deductions allocated and apportioned at shareholder level		
	g Interest expense	14g	
	h Other	14h	
	Deductions allocated and apportioned at corporate level to foreign source income		
	i Passive	14i	
	j Listed categories *(attach statement)*	14j	
	k General limitation	14k	
	Other information		
	l Total foreign taxes (check one): ▶ ☐ Paid ☐ Accrued	14l	
	m Reduction in taxes available for credit *(attach statement)*	14m	
	n Other foreign tax information *(attach statement)*		
Alternative Minimum Tax (AMT) Items	15a Post-1986 depreciation adjustment	15a	
	b Adjusted gain or loss	15b	
	c Depletion (other than oil and gas)	15c	
	d Oil, gas, and geothermal properties—gross income	15d	
	e Oil, gas, and geothermal properties—deductions	15e	
	f Other AMT items *(attach statement)*	15f	
Items Affecting Shareholder Basis	16a Tax-exempt interest income	16a	1,100
	b Other tax-exempt income	16b	
	c Nondeductible expenses	16c	
	d Property distributions	16d	
	e Repayment of loans from shareholders	16e	
Other Information	17a Investment income	17a	2,720
	b Investment expenses	17b	
	c Dividend distributions paid from accumulated earnings and profits	17c	
	d Other items and amounts *(attach statement)*		
Recon-ciliation	18 **Income/loss reconciliation.** Combine the amounts on lines 1 through 10 in the far right column. From the result, subtract the sum of the amounts on lines 11 through 12d and 14l	18	46,200

Form **1120S** (2006)

FIGURE 15-5 Filled-In Form 1120S, Page 4

Form 1120S (2006) Page **4**

Schedule L **Balance Sheets per Books**

	Assets	Beginning of tax year (a)	(b)	End of tax year (c)	(d)
1	Cash		14,000		18,000
2a	Trade notes and accounts receivable	18,000		21,600	
b	Less allowance for bad debts	( )	18,000	( )	21,600
3	Inventories				
4	U.S. government obligations				
5	Tax-exempt securities *(see instructions)*		25,650		33,000
6	Other current assets *(attach statement)*				
7	Loans to shareholders				
8	Mortgage and real estate loans				
9	Other investments *(attach statement)*		100,000		111,400
10a	Buildings and other depreciable assets	53,550		53,550	
b	Less accumulated depreciation	(10,200)	43,350	(11,900)	41,650
11a	Depletable assets				
b	Less accumulated depletion	( )		( )	
12	Land (net of any amortization)				
13a	Intangible assets (amortizable only)				
b	Less accumulated amortization	( )		( )	
14	Other assets *(attach statement)*				
15	Total assets		201,000		225,650
	Liabilities and Shareholders' Equity				
16	Accounts payable		6,400		10,150
17	Mortgages, notes, bonds payable in less than 1 year				
18	Other current liabilities *(attach statement)*				
19	Loans from shareholders				
20	Mortgages, notes, bonds payable in 1 year or more				20,900
21	Other liabilities *(attach statement)*				
22	Capital stock		40,000		40,000
23	Additional paid-in capital		100,000		100,000
24	Retained earnings		54,600		54,600
25	Adjustments to shareholders' equity *(attach statement)*				
26	Less cost of treasury stock		( )		( )
27	Total liabilities and shareholders' equity		201,000		225,650

Schedule M-1 **Reconciliation of Income (Loss) per Books With Income (Loss) per Return**
Note: Schedule M-3 required instead of Schedule M-1 if total assets are $10 million or more—see instructions

		Amount			Amount
1	Net income (loss) per books	47,300	5	Income recorded on books this year not included on Schedule K, lines 1 through 10 (itemize): a Tax-exempt interest $ 1,100	1,100
2	Income included on Schedule K, lines 1, 2, 3c, 4, 5a, 6, 7, 8a, 9, and 10, not recorded on books this year (itemize):		6	Deductions included on Schedule K, lines 1 through 12 and 14l, not charged against book income this year (itemize): a Depreciation $	
3	Expenses recorded on books this year not included on Schedule K, lines 1 through 12 and 14l (itemize): a Depreciation $ b Travel and entertainment $		7	Add lines 5 and 6	
4	Add lines 1 through 3	47,300	8	Income (loss) (Schedule K, line 18). Line 4 less line 7	46,200

Schedule M-2 **Analysis of Accumulated Adjustments Account, Other Adjustments Account, and Shareholders' Undistributed Taxable Income Previously Taxed** (see instructions)

		(a) Accumulated adjustments account	(b) Other adjustments account	(c) Shareholders' undistributed taxable income previously taxed
1	Balance at beginning of tax year	25,800	1,000	
2	Ordinary income from page 1, line 21	40,000		
3	Other additions	13,200	1,100	
4	Loss from page 1, line 21	( )		
5	Other reductions	(7,000)	( )	
6	Combine lines 1 through 5	72,000		
7	Distributions other than dividend distributions	30,000		
8	Balance at end of tax year. Subtract line 7 from line 6	42,000	2,100	

Printed on recycled paper Form **1120S** (2006)

FIGURE 15-6 Filled-In Schedule D (Form 1120S)

SCHEDULE D (Form 1120S)

Department of the Treasury
Internal Revenue Service

Capital Gains and Losses and Built-In Gains

► Attach to Form 1120S.
► See separate instructions.

OMB No. 1545-0130

2006

Name: Kendall Management Company

Employer identification number: 52 1739257

Part I Short-Term Capital Gains and Losses—Assets Held One Year or Less

	(a) Description of property (Example: 100 shares of Z Co.)	(b) Date acquired (mo., day, yr.)	(c) Date sold (mo., day, yr.)	(d) Sales price	(e) Cost or other basis (see instructions)	(f) Gain or (loss) (Subtract (e) from (d))
1						

2	Short-term capital gain from installment sales from Form 6252, line 26 or 37	2	
3	Short-term capital gain or (loss) from like-kind exchanges from Form 8824	3	
4	Combine lines 1 through 3 in column (f)	4	
5	Tax on short-term capital gain included on line 21 below	5	( )
6	**Net short-term capital gain or (loss).** Combine lines 4 and 5. Enter here and on Form 1120S, Schedule K, line 7 or 10	6	

Part II Long-Term Capital Gains and Losses—Assets Held More Than One Year

	(a) Description of property (Example: 100 shares of Z Co.)	(b) Date acquired (mo., day, yr.)	(c) Date sold (mo., day, yr.)	(d) Sales price	(e) Cost or other basis (see instructions)	(f) Gain or (loss) (Subtract (e) from (d))
7	200sh. Rogers Co.	7/18/00	10/14/06	31,280	20,800	10,480

8	Long-term capital gain from installment sales from Form 6252, line 26 or 37	8	
9	Long-term capital gain or (loss) from like-kind exchanges from Form 8824	9	
10	Capital gain distributions	10	
11	Combine lines 7 through 10 in column (f)	11	10,480
12	Tax on long-term capital gain included on line 21 below	12	( )
13	**Net long-term capital gain or (loss).** Combine lines 11 and 12. Enter here and on Form 1120S, Schedule K, line 8a or 10	13	10,480

Part III Built-In Gains Tax (See instructions **before** completing this part.)

14	Excess of recognized built-in gains over recognized built-in losses (attach computation schedule)	14	
15	Taxable income (attach computation schedule)	15	
16	Net recognized built-in gain. Enter the smallest of line 14, line 15, or line 7 of Schedule B	16	
17	Section 1374(b)(2) deduction	17	
18	Subtract line 17 from line 16. If zero or less, enter -0- here and on line 21	18	
19	Enter 35% of line 18	19	
20	Section 1374(b)(3) business credit and minimum tax credit carryforwards from C corporation years	20	
21	**Tax.** Subtract line 20 from line 19 (if zero or less, enter -0-). Enter here and on Form 1120S, page 1, line 22b	21	

For Privacy Act and Paperwork Reduction Act Notice, see the Instructions for Form 1120S. Cat. No. 11516V **Schedule D (Form 1120S) 2006**

Printed on recycled paper

FIGURE 15-7 Filled-In Schedule K-1 (Form 1120S)

671106

☐ Final K-1 ☐ Amended K-1 OMB No. 1545-0130

Schedule K-1 (Form 1120S) **2006**
Department of the Treasury
Internal Revenue Service

For calendar year 2006, or tax year beginning ______, 2006 ending ______, 20__

Shareholder's Share of Income, Deductions, Credits, etc. ► See back of form and separate instructions.

Part I Information About the Corporation

A Corporation's employer identification number
52-1739257

B Corporation's name, address, city, state, and ZIP code
Kendall Management Company
731 Delhi Road
Atlanta, GA 30307

C IRS Center where corporation filed return
Atlanta

D ☐ Tax shelter registration number, if any ______
E ☐ Check if Form 8271 is attached

Part II Information About the Shareholder

F Shareholder's identifying number
421-63-8045

G Shareholder's name, address, city, state and ZIP code
Virginia Kendall
4524 Peachtree Dr.
Atlanta, GA 30307

H Shareholder's percentage of stock ownership for tax year . . . . 30 %

For IRS Use Only

Part III Shareholder's Share of Current Year Income, Deductions, Credits, and Other Items

1	Ordinary business income (loss) 12,000	13	Credits
2	Net rental real estate income (loss)		
3	Other net rental income (loss)		
4	Interest income 216		
5a	Ordinary dividends 600		
5b	Qualified dividends 375	14	Foreign transactions
6	Royalties		
7	Net short-term capital gain (loss)		
8a	Net long-term capital gain (loss) 3,144		
8b	Collectibles (28%) gain (loss)		
8c	Unrecaptured section 1250 gain		
9	Net section 1231 gain (loss)		
10	Other income (loss)	15	Alternative minimum tax (AMT) items
11	Section 179 deduction	16	Items affecting shareholder basis
12	Other deductions	A	Tax exempt interest, 330
A	Charitable contr. 2,100		
		17	Other information
		A	Investment income 816

* See attached statement for additional information.

For Privacy Act and Paperwork Reduction Act Notice, see Instructions for Form 1120S. Cat. No. 11520D **Schedule K-1 (Form 1120S) 2006**

TRANSACTIONS BETWEEN S CORPORATIONS AND SHAREHOLDERS

Shareholders' Investment (Basis) in Stock

Shareholders compute their initial basis in S corporation stock using the same rules as for regular C corporation formation. If the requirements are met, their basis in the assets contributed to the corporation becomes the basis of their investment (stock) in the corporation. Thus, shareholders can avoid the taxation of gains or losses on forming an S corporation. Partners receive similar treatment when they transfer property to the partnership. When shareholders purchase their shares, their basis in the stock is its cost.

Shareholders adjust their initial basis in S corporation stock by the following:

1. Ordinary income (loss)
2. Separately stated items
3. Additional contributions to the S corporation
4. Distributions from the S corporation

Ordinary income, separately stated income, and additional contributions increase the shareholder's basis in the stock. Ordinary loss, separately stated deductions or losses, and distributions reduce the shareholder's basis. Corporate liabilities are generally not a factor affecting basis unless the shareholder personally loans money to the corporation.

EXAMPLE 27

Jody Ryan pays $7,500 for 100 shares of S corporation stock at the beginning of the corporation's 20x1 calendar tax year. Her share of income and separately stated items of the S corporation are ordinary income, $1,500; long-term capital gains, $300; and cash distributions received, $1,000. Ryan's basis in her stock on December 31, 20x1, is $8,300, calculated as follows:

Purchase cost of S shares	$7,500
Add:	
Share of ordinary income	1,500
Share of capital gains	300
Less distributions received	(1,000)
Ryan's basis at December 31, 20x1	$8,300

When S corporation shareholders sell stock, the taxable gain or loss cannot be determined until after the end of the corporation's tax year. The shareholders who sell shares must adjust their stock bases by their portion of the S corporation's income, deductions, and separately stated items. This information will not be known until after the S corporation's year end. The unknown effect at the time of sale can be lessened if the seller and the buyer agree to an adjustment of the selling price based on the year-end profit or loss results. As an alternative, the affected shareholders can agree to divide the tax year into two parts for accounting purposes. One part would be from the beginning of the year through the day of sale; the second part would be the remainder of the year. This agreement limits the income or loss of the selling shareholder to the corporation's results up to the date of sale. The stockholders who remain will share income or losses occurring after the date of sale. Even though the tax year is split into two parts for shareholder income (loss) computations, the corporation files only one return for the year.

Distributions to Shareholders

Distributions from S corporations formed after 1983 are generally tax free to the shareholder. The distributions reduce the shareholder's basis in the stock, but not below zero. If the distributions exceed the shareholder's stock basis, the excess is treated as a capital gain.

The S corporation keeps track of all its taxable income and losses in a special account called the **accumulated adjustments account,** or **AAA.** The account can have a positive or negative balance, depending on the income and losses it has sustained. Distributions to shareholders reduce the AAA balance. However, distributions themselves cannot reduce the balance below zero. The distributions from AAA can be thought of as disbursing income that has already been taxed on the shareholders' personal income tax returns. When an S election terminates, shareholders can still receive distributions tax free. The payments cannot exceed the balance of AAA and must be made within an acceptable period (about one year after termination).

EXAMPLE 28

JL corporation, formed on January 1, 20x1, elected S corporation status. Shareholders Jill Jaffy and Lisa Laker each invested $30,000, and each received 50% of the stock. JL's taxable income for 20x1 was $20,000, all ordinary income. The shareholders each received $12,000 in cash distributions during 20x1, a total distribution of $24,000.

In 20x1, Jaffy and Laker each report $10,000 of income on their individual income tax returns. The $12,000 distribution to each shareholder is tax free. The basis of the stock to each shareholder at the end of 20x1 is $28,000 ($30,000 + $10,000 – $12,000). The balance in the AAA account is zero ($20,000 income – $20,000 distribution). The distribution cannot reduce AAA below zero. Thus, $2,000 of each shareholder's distribution in 20x1 is treated as a tax-free return of capital.

Distributions from an S corporation that was previously a regular C corporation may be taxable. This occurs when an S corporation has earnings and profits (E&P) carried over from C corporation years. Distributions are first payments out of AAA and not taxable. They reduce the shareholder's basis in the stock. To the extent that the distributions exceed AAA, they are payments out of E&P and taxable as dividends. The shareholders do not reduce their stock basis for these taxable distributions. Any distributions in excess of AAA and E&P are not taxable as long as they do not exceed the shareholder's remaining basis in the stock. Such distributions, however, reduce the shareholder's basis in the stock.

EXAMPLE 29

GY Corporation was a regular corporation until 20x1, when an S election was made. GY carried over $5,000 of E&P from its C corporation years. In 20x1 GY has $16,000 of ordinary income. It distributes $30,000 to its sole shareholder, Gary Gemberling, who has a stock basis of $40,000. The first $16,000 of distributions comes out of AAA and is not taxable. Gemberling reduces his stock basis by $16,000. The next $5,000 comes from E&P and is a taxable dividend. No stock basis reduction results from the $5,000. The last $9,000 distributed is not taxable. Gemberling reduces his stock basis by the nontaxable distributions. His stock basis at the end of 20x1 is $15,000 ($40,000 – $16,000 – $9,000).

S corporations can elect to have distributions come from E&P first, thus bypassing AAA. The election requires the consent of all shareholders and is irrevocable. The reason S corporations make this election is to remove all prior C corporation E&P at a time when its shareholders can most afford the income. Further, corporations benefit from the election by removing the possibility of being subject to a special tax on excess passive investment income (details are beyond the scope of this book).

When an S corporation with E&P has excess passive investment income for three years in a row, it loses its S election. The ability to have distributions first come from E&P helps the corporation reduce E&P to zero.

Distributions of Property

Distributions to shareholders may be in cash or property. The FMV of property determines the amount of the distribution. This is the amount by which the AAA balance and the shareholder's stock basis are reduced. The shareholder's basis in the property is its FMV. If an S corporation distributes appreciated property to shareholders, the corporation recognizes gain. The amount of gain recognized is the same as if the property had been sold to the shareholders at the FMV. The gain then passes through to the shareholders. However, the S corporation does not recognize a loss when the FMV of the property distributed is less than its corporate basis. The shareholder's basis in the property is its FMV, and the stock basis is reduced by this amount. Since neither the corporation nor the shareholder recognizes the loss, S corporations should not distribute property that has declined in value.

EXAMPLE 30

Freda Moon receives a distribution of property from the Flint S Corporation. Moon is the sole shareholder, with a basis in her stock of $75,000. The property she receives has a FMV of $30,000. Flint's basis in the property is $50,000. Moon's basis in the property is $30,000, and she reduces her basis in her Flint stock to $45,000 ($75,000 – $30,000). Flint does not recognize the $20,000 loss ($50,000 – $30,000) and reduces its AAA by $30,000.

EXAMPLE 31

Same as in Example 30 except that the FMV of the property is $70,000 (instead of $30,000). Flint recognizes gain of $20,000 ($70,000 – $50,000) when it distributes appreciated property to its shareholder. Flint's AAA will increase by the recognized gain. Moon will report the $20,000 of gain on her tax return when it flows through to her on the Schedule K-1 she receives from Flint. This will increase her basis in the partnership interest by $20,000. The distribution of the property will then reduce her basis in Flint partnership by $70,000 (its FMV).

Name ______________________

Section ______________ Date ____________

QUESTIONS AND PROBLEMS

1. **Partnership Characteristics.** Answer the following questions in the spaces provided.

   a. What tax form do partnerships use? __________

   b. Do partnerships withhold income taxes on guaranteed salaries paid to partners? __________

   c. An LLC is what type of tax entity? __________

   d. A partnership return for a calendar year is due on or before what date? __________

   e. A partnership return for a fiscal year ending April 30 is due on or before what date? __________

2. **Partnership Tax Year.** ABCD partnership consists of four partners, A, B, C, and D. Each of the partners' year end along with their ownership percentage of capital and profits is shown below. Use this information to determine ABCD's required tax year.

Partner	*Year-End*	*Percentage*
A	June 30	47%
B	May 31	3%
C	May 31	3%
D	June 30	47%
		100%

3. **Partnership Tax Year.** EFGH partnership consists of four partners, E, F, G, and H. Each of the partners' year end along with their ownership percentage of capital and profits is shown below. Use this information to determine EFGH's required tax year.

Partner	*Year-End*	*Percentage*
E	June 30	48%
F	October 31	4%
G	December 31	24%
H	December 31	24%
		100%

4. **Partnership Activities.** Indicate how each of the following items is reported on the partnership tax return by placing a check mark in the appropriate column.

Item	*Ordinary Income*	*Separately Stated*
a. Rent received from rental property	________	________
b. Sale of partnership capital asset	________	________
c. Dividends received from U.S. corporation	________	________
d. Contribution to the Red Cross	________	________
e. Guaranteed payments to partners	________	________
f. Section 179 expense	________	________
g. Interest expense on a business loan	________	________
h. Fee for membership in local Chamber of Commerce	________	________
i. Interest income from a municipal bond	________	________
j. Property taxes on partnership assets	________	________

5. **Partnership Income.** Helen Royal is a member of a partnership that reports ordinary income of $68,000 for the current taxable year. Her distributive share of the partnership income is $34,000, of which she withdrew $18,000 during the year. Compute the amount she should report as income from the partnership in preparing her individual return for the year.

6. **Partnership Income.** Which of the following is a separately stated partnership item?

   a. Business bad debts

   b. Charitable contributions

   c. Tax-exempt interest

   d. Guaranteed payments

   e. Losses from the sale of a capital assets held short-term

   f. Depreciation recapture

   g. Interest income from business activities

7. **Partnership Charitable Contributions.** Leona Mendez and Luisa Torres operate a placement service as partners, sharing profits and losses equally. During the current calendar year, the partnership contributes $3,000 to the partners' alma mater, State University. The partnership treats this contribution as an expense in the annual income statement that reports net income of $47,500.

   a. Is the partnership entitled to treat the contribution to State University as a deduction from ordinary income in the partnership return?

   b. What is each partner's distributive share of the taxable income shown by the partnership return?

   c. May each partner claim a deduction on her individual return for the partnership contribution to State University? If so, how much?

8. **Guaranteed Payments.** What are guaranteed payments to partners and how are they treated by the partnership and the partner?

9. **Guaranteed Payments and Allocation of Partnership Income.** ABC partnership provides for "salaries" (guaranteed payments) of $70,000, $64,000, and $60,000 for partners A, B, and C, respectively. After the guaranteed payments are deducted, the partnership agreement calls for sharing of profits and losses as follows: A - 40%; B - 35%; and C - 25%.

   a. If partnership profits before the guaranteed payments are $120,000, what amount of income from the partnership should each partner report on his or her individual income tax return?

b. How would your answer to Part a. change if partnership profits before guaranteed payments were $220,000 (instead of $120,000)?

10. Partnership Income. Fred Pingle and Ken Franz are general partners in a business sharing profits and losses 60% and 40% respectively. The partnership uses a calendar year. Franz files his individual return on the basis of the calendar year. The partnership's ordinary income for the fiscal year ending December 31, 2006, is $140,000 (after deducting partners' guaranteed payments). For the calendar year 2006, each partner received a guaranteed payment of $8,000 per month. Compute the amount of partnership income Franz should report on his 2006 tax return. How much of this amount is subject to self-employment tax?

11. Form 1065. On January 3, 2006, Ellen Elvers (SSN 299-84-1945) and Jack Ford form Elvers and Ford general partnership (EIN 31-0960341). Elvers and Ford operate a business that sells various types of merchandise (business code 5963) at 1425 Tryon Street, Charlotte, North Carolina 28201. To form the partnership, Elvers contributes $24,000; Ford contributes $16,000. The agreement provides that Elvers will participate in the partnership on a full-time basis and Ford on a half-time basis. The agreement further provides that Elvers and Ford will receive guaranteed payments of $34,000 and $18,000, respectively. The remaining profits go 60% to Elvers and 40% to Ford.

Prepare the income tax return for the calendar year 2006, the first year of operations. Use the Form 1065 provided and prepare all schedules, including Form 4562, Schedule D (Form 1065), and Schedule K-1 for Ellen Elvers. Her address is 1609 Amberway, Charlotte, NC 28201. Elvers will sign the partnership return on April 10, 2007. Elvers is also the Tax Matters Partner. The partnership tax return will be filed with the IRS Center in Cincinnati, Ohio.

The trial balance that follows was prepared as of December 31 after all necessary adjustments. Merchandise inventory is the exception. Total purchases of inventory during the year were $162,700. The ending balance in inventory was $22,000. The accounts for the partners' "Drawings" represent withdrawals in addition to their respective guaranteed payments. Net income per books (Schedule M-1, line 1) is $23,990.

No changes in the manner of determining quantities, costs, or valuations between the opening and closing inventories occurs in the current year. (Valuation is at cost.) The partnership uses the accrual method of accounting. Worthless accounts totaling to $800 were written off directly to bad debt expense during the year.

The partnership calculates depreciation using MACRS. The equipment was the only personal property purchased during 2006. The partnership does not elect Section 179. Book depreciation is reported on the trial balance. Book depreciation is based on a different method than MACRS. Charitable contributions are subject to the 50% limitation. On October 3, 2006, 50 shares of common stock in ZMT Corporation were sold for $2,900. The stock was purchased for $1,700 on March 29, 2006.

ELVERS AND FORD
Trial Balance
December 31, 2006

Account	*Debit*	*Credit*
Cash	$ 11,017	
Accounts and notes receivable	17,550	
Equipment (purchased January 4, 2006)	28,000	
Accumulated depreciation-equipment		$ 5,000
Prepaid assets	900	
Notes payable (to banks)		5,000
Accounts payable		8,797
Other accrued liabilities		1,880
Ellen Elvers, Capital		15,000
Ellen Elvers, Drawing	2,000	
Jack Ford, Capital		25,000
Jack Ford, Drawing	3,200	
Sales		260,500
Sales returns and allowances	3,000	
Gain on sale of stock		1,200
Purchases	162,700	
Interest expense (business related)	300	
Partners' salaries	52,000	
Office and store salaries	14,300	
Rent expense	6,500	
Office expense	3,000	
Depreciation expense	5,000	
Property taxes on business property	383	
Payroll taxes	4,052	
Delivery expense	2,010	
Bad debt expense	800	
Store expenses	2,600	
Advertising expense	2,705	
Taxable interest income		200
Charitable contributions	560	
Total	$322,577	$322,577

(Use for Problem 11).

Form **1065** Department of the Treasury Internal Revenue Service

U.S. Return of Partnership Income

For calendar year 2006, or tax year beginning ...., 2006, ending ...., 20.....
▶ See separate instructions.

OMB No. 1545-0099

2006

A Principal business activity	Use the IRS label. Otherwise, print or type.	Name of partnership	D Employer identification number
B Principal product or service		Number, street, and room or suite no. If a P.O. box, see the instructions.	E Date business started
C Business code number		City or town, state, and ZIP code	F Total assets (see the instructions) $

G Check applicable boxes: (1) ☐ Initial return (2) ☐ Final return (3) ☐ Name change (4) ☐ Address change (5) ☐ Amended return
H Check accounting method: (1) ☐ Cash (2) ☐ Accrual (3) ☐ Other (specify) ▶
I Number of Schedules K-1. Attach one for each person who was a partner at any time during the tax year ▶
J Check if Schedule M-3 required (attach Schedule M-3) . . . ☐

Caution. *Include **only** trade or business income and expenses on lines 1a through 22 below. See the instructions for more information.*

Income	1a	Gross receipts or sales	1a			
	b	Less returns and allowances	1b		1c	
	2	Cost of goods sold (Schedule A, line 8)			2	
	3	Gross profit. Subtract line 2 from line 1c			3	
	4	Ordinary income (loss) from other partnerships, estates, and trusts *(attach statement)*			4	
	5	Net farm profit (loss) *(attach Schedule F (Form 1040))*			5	
	6	Net gain (loss) from Form 4797, Part II, line 17 (attach Form 4797)			6	
	7	Other income (loss) *(attach statement)*			7	
	8	**Total income (loss).** Combine lines 3 through 7			8	
Deductions (see the instructions for limitations)	9	Salaries and wages (other than to partners) (less employment credits)			9	
	10	Guaranteed payments to partners			10	
	11	Repairs and maintenance			11	
	12	Bad debts			12	
	13	Rent			13	
	14	Taxes and licenses			14	
	15	Interest			15	
	16a	Depreciation *(if required, attach Form 4562)*	16a			
	b	Less depreciation reported on Schedule A and elsewhere on return	16b		16c	
	17	Depletion **(Do not deduct oil and gas depletion.)**			17	
	18	Retirement plans, etc.			18	
	19	Employee benefit programs			19	
	20	Other deductions *(attach statement)*			20	
	21	**Total deductions.** Add the amounts shown in the far right column for lines 9 through 20			21	
	22	**Ordinary business income (loss).** Subtract line 21 from line 8			22	
	23	Credit for federal telephone excise tax paid (attach Form 8913)			23	

Sign Here

Under penalties of perjury, I declare that I have examined this return, including accompanying schedules and statements, and to the best of my knowledge and belief, it is true, correct, and complete. Declaration of preparer (other than general partner or limited liability company member) is based on all information of which preparer has any knowledge.

▶ Signature of general partner or limited liability company member manager ▶ Date

May the IRS discuss this return with the preparer shown below (see instructions)? ☐ Yes ☐ No

Paid Preparer's Use Only

Preparer's signature	Date	Check if self-employed ▶ ☐	Preparer's SSN or PTIN
Firm's name (or yours if self-employed), address, and ZIP code ▶		EIN ▶	
		Phone no. ( )	

For Privacy Act and Paperwork Reduction Act Notice, see separate instructions. Cat. No. 11390Z Form **1065** (2006)

(Use for Problem 11).

Form 1065 (2006) Page **2**

Schedule A **Cost of Goods Sold** (see the instructions)

1	Inventory at beginning of year	1	
2	Purchases less cost of items withdrawn for personal use	2	
3	Cost of labor	3	
4	Additional section 263A costs *(attach statement)*	4	
5	Other costs *(attach statement)*	5	
6	**Total.** Add lines 1 through 5	6	
7	Inventory at end of year	7	
8	**Cost of goods sold.** Subtract line 7 from line 6. Enter here and on page 1, line 2	8	

9a Check all methods used for valuing closing inventory:

(i) ☐ Cost as described in Regulations section 1.471-3

(ii) ☐ Lower of cost or market as described in Regulations section 1.471-4

(iii) ☐ Other (specify method used and attach explanation) ▶

b Check this box if there was a writedown of "subnormal" goods as described in Regulations section 1.471-2(c) ▶ ☐

c Check this box if the LIFO inventory method was adopted this tax year for any goods *(if checked, attach Form 970)*. ▶ ☐

d Do the rules of section 263A (for property produced or acquired for resale) apply to the partnership? ☐ **Yes** ☐ **No**

e Was there any change in determining quantities, cost, or valuations between opening and closing inventory? ☐ **Yes** ☐ **No**
If "Yes," attach explanation.

Schedule B **Other Information**

		Yes	No
1	What type of entity is filing this return? Check the applicable box: **a** ☐ Domestic general partnership **b** ☐ Domestic limited partnership **c** ☐ Domestic limited liability company **d** ☐ Domestic limited liability partnership **e** ☐ Foreign partnership **f** ☐ Other ▶		
2	Are any partners in this partnership also partnerships?		
3	During the partnership's tax year, did the partnership own any interest in another partnership or in any foreign entity that was disregarded as an entity separate from its owner under Regulations sections 301.7701-2 and 301.7701-3? If yes, see instructions for required attachment		
4	Did the partnership file Form 8893, Election of Partnership Level Tax Treatment, or an election statement under section 6231(a)(1)(B)(ii) for partnership-level tax treatment, that is in effect for this tax year? See Form 8893 for more details		
5	Does this partnership meet all three of the following requirements? **a** The partnership's total receipts for the tax year were less than $250,000; **b** The partnership's total assets at the end of the tax year were less than $600,000; and **c** Schedules K-1 are filed with the return and furnished to the partners on or before the due date (including extensions) for the partnership return. If "Yes," the partnership is not required to complete Schedules L, M-1, and M-2; Item F on page 1 of Form 1065; or Item N on Schedule K-1.		
6	Does this partnership have any foreign partners? If "Yes," the partnership may have to file Forms 8804, 8805 and 8813. See the instructions		
7	Is this partnership a publicly traded partnership as defined in section 469(k)(2)?		
8	Has this partnership filed, or is it required to file, a return under section 6111 to provide information on any reportable transaction?		
9	At any time during calendar year 2006, did the partnership have an interest in or a signature or other authority over a financial account in a foreign country (such as a bank account, securities account, or other financial account)? See the instructions for exceptions and filing requirements for Form TD F 90-22.1. If "Yes," enter the name of the foreign country. ▶		
10	During the tax year, did the partnership receive a distribution from, or was it the grantor of, or transferor to, a foreign trust? If "Yes," the partnership may have to file Form 3520. See the instructions		
11	Was there a distribution of property or a transfer (for example, by sale or death) of a partnership interest during the tax year? If "Yes," you may elect to adjust the basis of the partnership's assets under section 754 by attaching the statement described under *Elections Made By the Partnership* in the instructions		
12	Enter the number of Forms 8865, Return of U.S. Persons With Respect to Certain Foreign Partnerships, attached to this return ▶		

Designation of Tax Matters Partner (see the instructions)

Enter below the general partner designated as the tax matters partner (TMP) for the tax year of this return:

Name of designated TMP ▶ Identifying number of TMP ▶

Address of designated TMP ▶

Form **1065** (2006)

(Use for Problem 11).

Form 1065 (2006) Page 3

Schedule K — Partners' Distributive Share Items

				Total amount
Income (Loss)	1 Ordinary business income (loss) (page 1, line 22)		1	
	2 Net rental real estate income (loss) *(attach Form 8825)*		2	
	3a Other gross rental income (loss)	3a		
	b Expenses from other rental activities *(attach statement)*	3b		
	c Other net rental income (loss). Subtract line 3b from line 3a		3c	
	4 Guaranteed payments		4	
	5 Interest income		5	
	6 Dividends: a Ordinary dividends		6a	
	b Qualified dividends	6b		
	7 Royalties		7	
	8 Net short-term capital gain (loss) *(attach Schedule D (Form 1065))*		8	
	9a Net long-term capital gain (loss) *(attach Schedule D (Form 1065))*		9a	
	b Collectibles (28%) gain (loss)	9b		
	c Unrecaptured section 1250 gain *(attach statement)*	9c		
	10 Net section 1231 gain (loss) *(attach Form 4797)*		10	
	11 Other income (loss) *(see instructions)* Type ▶		11	
Deductions	12 Section 179 deduction *(attach Form 4562)*		12	
	13a Contributions		13a	
	b Investment interest expense		13b	
	c Section 59(e)(2) expenditures: **(1)** Type ▶ **(2)** Amount ▶		13c(2)	
	d Other deductions *(see instructions)* Type ▶		13d	
Self-Employment	14a Net earnings (loss) from self-employment		14a	
	b Gross farming or fishing income		14b	
	c Gross nonfarm income		14c	
Credits & Credit Recapture	15a Low-income housing credit (section 42(j)(5))		15a	
	b Low-income housing credit (other)		15b	
	c Qualified rehabilitation expenditures (rental real estate) *(attach Form 3468)*		15c	
	d Other rental real estate credits *(see instructions)* Type ▶		15d	
	e Other rental credits *(see instructions)* Type ▶		15e	
	f Other credits *(see instructions)* Type ▶		15f	
Foreign Transactions	16a Name of country or U.S. possession ▶			
	b Gross income from all sources		16b	
	c Gross income sourced at partner level		16c	
	Foreign gross income sourced at partnership level			
	d Passive ▶ e Listed categories *(attach statement)* ▶ f General limitation ▶		16f	
	Deductions allocated and apportioned at partner level			
	g Interest expense ▶ h Other ▶		16h	
	Deductions allocated and apportioned at partnership level to foreign source income			
	i Passive ▶ j Listed categories *(attach statement)* ▶ k General limitation ▶		16k	
	l Total foreign taxes (check one): ▶ Paid ☐ Accrued ☐		16l	
	m Reduction in taxes available for credit *(attach statement)*		16m	
	n Other foreign tax information *(attach statement)*			
Alternative Minimum Tax (AMT) Items	17a Post-1986 depreciation adjustment		17a	
	b Adjusted gain or loss		17b	
	c Depletion (other than oil and gas)		17c	
	d Oil, gas, and geothermal properties—gross income		17d	
	e Oil, gas, and geothermal properties—deductions		17e	
	f Other AMT items *(attach statement)*		17f	
Other Information	18a Tax-exempt interest income		18a	
	b Other tax-exempt income		18b	
	c Nondeductible expenses		18c	
	19a Distributions of cash and marketable securities		19a	
	b Distributions of other property		19b	
	20a Investment income		20a	
	b Investment expenses		20b	
	c Other items and amounts *(attach statement)*			

Form **1065** (2006)

(Use for Problem 11).

Form 1065 (2006) Page **4**

Analysis of Net Income (Loss)

1 Net income (loss). Combine Schedule K, lines 1 through 11. From the result, subtract the sum of Schedule K, lines 12 through 13d, and 16l					1	
2 Analysis by partner type:	**(i)** Corporate	**(ii)** Individual (active)	**(iii)** Individual (passive)	**(iv)** Partnership	**(v)** Exempt organization	**(vi)** Nominee/Other
a General partners						
b Limited partners						

Note: Schedules L, M-1, and M-2 are not required if Question 5 of Schedule B is answered "Yes."

Schedule L **Balance Sheets per Books**

Assets	Beginning of tax year (a)	(b)	End of tax year (c)	(d)
1 Cash				
2a Trade notes and accounts receivable				
b Less allowance for bad debts				
3 Inventories				
4 U.S. government obligations				
5 Tax-exempt securities				
6 Other current assets *(attach statement)*				
7 Mortgage and real estate loans				
8 Other investments *(attach statement)*				
9a Buildings and other depreciable assets				
b Less accumulated depreciation				
10a Depletable assets				
b Less accumulated depletion				
11 Land (net of any amortization)				
12a Intangible assets (amortizable only)				
b Less accumulated amortization				
13 Other assets *(attach statement)*				
14 Total assets				
Liabilities and Capital				
15 Accounts payable				
16 Mortgages, notes, bonds payable in less than 1 year				
17 Other current liabilities *(attach statement)*				
18 All nonrecourse loans				
19 Mortgages, notes, bonds payable in 1 year or more				
20 Other liabilities *(attach statement)*				
21 Partners' capital accounts				
22 Total liabilities and capital				

Schedule M-1 **Reconciliation of Income (Loss) per Books With Income (Loss) per Return**

1 Net income (loss) per books		**6** Income recorded on books this year not included on Schedule K, lines 1 through 11 (itemize): **a** Tax-exempt interest $	
2 Income included on Schedule K, lines 1, 2, 3c, 5, 6a, 7, 8, 9a, 10, and 11, not recorded on books this year (itemize):			
3 Guaranteed payments (other than health insurance)		**7** Deductions included on Schedule K, lines 1 through 13d, and 16l, not charged against book income this year (itemize): **a** Depreciation $	
4 Expenses recorded on books this year not included on Schedule K, lines 1 through 13d, and 16l (itemize): **a** Depreciation $ **b** Travel and entertainment $		**8** Add lines 6 and 7	
		9 Income (loss) (Analysis of Net Income (Loss), line 1). Subtract line 8 from line 5	
5 Add lines 1 through 4			

Schedule M-2 **Analysis of Partners' Capital Accounts**

1 Balance at beginning of year		**6** Distributions: **a** Cash	
2 Capital contributed: **a** Cash		**b** Property	
b Property		**7** Other decreases (itemize):	
3 Net income (loss) per books			
4 Other increases (itemize):		**8** Add lines 6 and 7	
5 Add lines 1 through 4		**9** Balance at end of year. Subtract line 8 from line 5	

Printed on recycled paper Form **1065** (2006)

(Use for Problem 11).

SCHEDULE D (Form 1065)

Department of the Treasury Internal Revenue Service

Capital Gains and Losses

► Attach to Form 1065.

OMB No. 1545-0099

2006

Name of partnership | Employer identification number

Part I Short-Term Capital Gains and Losses—Assets Held 1 Year or Less

(a) Description of property (e.g., 100 shares of "Z" Co.)	(b) Date acquired (month, day, year)	(c) Date sold (month, day, year)	(d) Sales price (see instructions)	(e) Cost or other basis (see instructions)	(f) Gain or (loss) Subtract (e) from (d)
1					

2 Short-term capital gain from installment sales from Form 6252, line 26 or 37	2	
3 Short-term capital gain (loss) from like-kind exchanges from Form 8824	3	
4 Partnership's share of net short-term capital gain (loss), including specially allocated short-term capital gains (losses), from other partnerships, estates, and trusts	4	
5 **Net short-term capital gain or (loss).** Combine lines 1 through 4 in column (f). Enter here and on Form 1065, Schedule K, line 8 or 11	5	

Part II Long-Term Capital Gains and Losses—Assets Held More Than 1 Year

(a) Description of property (e.g., 100 shares of "Z" Co.)	(b) Date acquired (month, day, year)	(c) Date sold (month, day, year)	(d) Sales price (see instructions)	(e) Cost or other basis (see instructions)	(f) Gain or (loss) Subtract (e) from (d)
6					

7 Long-term capital gain from installment sales from Form 6252, line 26 or 37	7	
8 Long-term capital gain (loss) from like-kind exchanges from Form 8824	8	
9 Partnership's share of net long-term capital gain (loss), including specially allocated long-term capital gains (losses), from other partnerships, estates, and trusts	9	
10 Capital gain distributions	10	
11 **Net long-term capital gain or (loss).** Combine lines 6 through 10 in column (f). Enter here and on Form 1065, Schedule K, line 9a or 11	11	

For Privacy Act and Paperwork Reduction Act Notice, see the Instructions for Form 1065. Cat. No. 11393G **Schedule D (Form 1065) 2006**

(Use for Problem 11).

Form **4562** — Department of the Treasury, Internal Revenue Service

Depreciation and Amortization
(Including Information on Listed Property)

▶ See separate instructions. ▶ Attach to your tax return.

OMB No. 1545-0172 — **2006** — Attachment Sequence No. **67**

Name(s) shown on return	Business or activity to which this form relates	Identifying number

Part I — Election To Expense Certain Property Under Section 179
Note: *If you have any listed property, complete Part V before you complete Part I.*

1	Maximum amount. See the instructions for a higher limit for certain businesses	1	$108,000
2	Total cost of section 179 property placed in service (see instructions)	2	
3	Threshold cost of section 179 property before reduction in limitation	3	$430,000
4	Reduction in limitation. Subtract line 3 from line 2. If zero or less, enter -0-	4	
5	Dollar limitation for tax year. Subtract line 4 from line 1. If zero or less, enter -0-. If married filing separately, see instructions	5	

6	(a) Description of property	(b) Cost (business use only)	(c) Elected cost

7	Listed property. Enter the amount from line 29	7	
8	Total elected cost of section 179 property. Add amounts in column (c), lines 6 and 7	8	
9	Tentative deduction. Enter the **smaller** of line 5 or line 8	9	
10	Carryover of disallowed deduction from line 13 of your 2005 Form 4562	10	
11	Business income limitation. Enter the smaller of business income (not less than zero) or line 5 (see instructions)	11	
12	Section 179 expense deduction. Add lines 9 and 10, but do not enter more than line 11	12	
13	Carryover of disallowed deduction to 2007. Add lines 9 and 10, less line 12 ▶	13	

Note: *Do not use Part II or Part III below for listed property. Instead, use Part V.*

Part II — Special Depreciation Allowance and Other Depreciation (Do not include listed property.) (See instructions.)

14	Special allowance for qualified New York Liberty or Gulf Opportunity Zone property (other than listed property) placed in service during the tax year (see instructions)	14	
15	Property subject to section 168(f)(1) election	15	
16	Other depreciation (including ACRS)	16	

Part III — MACRS Depreciation (Do not include listed property.) (See instructions.)

Section A

17	MACRS deductions for assets placed in service in tax years beginning before 2006	17	
18	If you are electing to group any assets placed in service during the tax year into one or more general asset accounts, check here ▶ ☐		

Section B—Assets Placed in Service During 2006 Tax Year Using the General Depreciation System

(a) Classification of property	(b) Month and year placed in service	(c) Basis for depreciation (business/investment use only—see instructions)	(d) Recovery period	(e) Convention	(f) Method	(g) Depreciation deduction
19a 3-year property						
b 5-year property						
c 7-year property						
d 10-year property						
e 15-year property						
f 20-year property						
g 25-year property			25 yrs.		S/L	
h Residential rental property			27.5 yrs.	MM	S/L	
			27.5 yrs.	MM	S/L	
i Nonresidential real property			39 yrs.	MM	S/L	
				MM	S/L	

Section C—Assets Placed in Service During 2006 Tax Year Using the Alternative Depreciation System

(a)	(b)	(c)	(d)	(e)	(f)	(g)
20a Class life					S/L	
b 12-year			12 yrs.		S/L	
c 40-year			40 yrs.	MM	S/L	

Part IV — Summary (see instructions)

21	Listed property. Enter amount from line 28	21	
22	**Total.** Add amounts from line 12, lines 14 through 17, lines 19 and 20 in column (g), and line 21. Enter here and on the appropriate lines of your return. Partnerships and S corporations—see instr.	22	
23	For assets shown above and placed in service during the current year, enter the portion of the basis attributable to section 263A costs	23	

For Paperwork Reduction Act Notice, see separate instructions. Cat. No. 12906N Form **4562** (2006)

(Use for Problem 11).

651106

☐ Final K-1 ☐ Amended K-1 OMB No. 1545-0099

Schedule K-1 (Form 1065) **2006**

Department of the Treasury
Internal Revenue Service

For calendar year 2006, or tax year beginning ________, 2006 ending ________, 20____

Partner's Share of Income, Deductions, Credits, etc.

► See back of form and separate instructions.

Part I Information About the Partnership

A Partnership's employer identification number

B Partnership's name, address, city, state, and ZIP code

C IRS Center where partnership filed return

D ☐ Check if this is a publicly traded partnership (PTP)

E ☐ Tax shelter registration number, if any ________

F ☐ Check if Form 8271 is attached

Part II Information About the Partner

G Partner's identifying number

H Partner's name, address, city, state, and ZIP code

I ☐ General partner or LLC member-manager ☐ Limited partner or other LLC member

J ☐ Domestic partner ☐ Foreign partner

K What type of entity is this partner? ________

L Partner's share of profit, loss, and capital:

	Beginning	Ending
Profit	%	%
Loss	%	%
Capital	%	%

M Partner's share of liabilities at year end:

Nonrecourse . . . . $________

Qualified nonrecourse financing . . $________

Recourse . . . . $________

N Partner's capital account analysis:

Beginning capital account . . . . $________

Capital contributed during the year . $________

Current year increase (decrease) . . $________

Withdrawals & distributions . . . $(________)

Ending capital account . . . . $________

☐ Tax basis ☐ GAAP ☐ Section 704(b) book

☐ Other (explain)

Part III Partner's Share of Current Year Income, Deductions, Credits, and Other Items

1	Ordinary business income (loss)	15	Credits
2	Net rental real estate income (loss)		
3	Other net rental income (loss)	16	Foreign transactions
4	Guaranteed payments		
5	Interest income		
6a	Ordinary dividends		
6b	Qualified dividends		
7	Royalties		
8	Net short-term capital gain (loss)		
9a	Net long-term capital gain (loss)	17	Alternative minimum tax (AMT) items
9b	Collectibles (28%) gain (loss)		
9c	Unrecaptured section 1250 gain		
10	Net section 1231 gain (loss)	18	Tax-exempt income and nondeductible expenses
11	Other income (loss)		
		19	Distributions
12	Section 179 deduction		
13	Other deductions	20	Other information
14	Self-employment earnings (loss)		

*See attached statement for additional information.

For IRS Use Only

For Privacy Act and Paperwork Reduction Act Notice, see Instructions for Form 1065. Cat. No. 11394R **Schedule K-1 (Form 1065) 2006**

12. **Comparison of Business Entities.** What is an S corporation and how is it similar to, yet different from a partnership? How is it similar to, yet different, from a C corporation?

13. **S Corporation Eligibility Requirements.** What corporations qualify as a small business corporation?

14. **S Corporation Eligibility Requirements.** When will a corporation be treated as having one class of stock?

15. **S Corporation Eligibility Requirements.** The stock of an S corporation is owned by 105 different persons. Among its shareholders are Bob, Bob's mother and Bob's two children, Bob's brother and Bob's niece. Based on these facts, how many shareholders does the corporation have for purposes of determining whether it can elect S status?

16. **S Corporation Characteristics.** Answer each of the following questions in relation to an S corporation.

    a. How many shareholders may an S corporation have?

    b. What is the period during which the shareholders of a corporation may elect S corporation status?

c. What events automatically terminate a corporation's S status?

d. When is the termination of S corporation status effective under voluntary termination versus under automatic termination?

17. Electing S Corporation Status.

a. Sherwin Corporation is a U.S. corporation owned by 12 shareholders. All of the stock outstanding is common stock. At a regular meeting of the shareholders, all shareholders except one agreed to have the corporation become an S corporation. Can Sherwin Corporation elect S corporation status? Explain.

b. What are the tax advantages of S corporation status over C corporation status?

c. What are the advantages of S corporation status over being a general partnership?

18. Sale of S Corporation Stock. Sally Jordan owned a 10% interest in an S corporation for several years. The basis of her stock on January 1, 2006, is $40,000. On April 30, 2006, Jordan sells her entire interest in the S corporation for $58,000. For the calendar year 2006, the S corporation estimated that its ordinary income would be $80,000. No distributions were made in 2006 prior to the sale of Jordan's stock.

a. On April 30, 2006, the date of sale, what is the expected gain Jordan will report on her 2006 tax return as the result of the sale of her stock?

b. At year end, the S corporation determines that its actual ordinary income for 2006 is $100,000. On the basis of this year-end knowledge, does this additional information affect Jordan's 2006 tax return? If so, how is the 2006 tax return affected, and if it is not affected, why not?

19. S Corporation NOL. The Viking Corporation, a calendar year corporation, formed and immediately elected to become an S corporation as of January 2, 2004. Terry Trammel has owned 40% of the stock since the corporation's inception, with an original investment of $27,000. In 2004 and 2005, Viking had NOLs of $45,000 and $30,000, respectively. During 2006, Viking reported taxable income of $60,000, all ordinary income. During 2006, Viking made cash distributions of $40,000.

a. How does Trammel report her share of the 2004 and 2005 NOLs?

b. How does Trammel report her share of the 2006 taxable income and cash distributions from Viking?

c. What is the basis of the stock owned by Trammel at December 31, 2006?

20. S Corporation Income. Siegal Management Corporation has operated as an S corporation for the years 2004, 2005, and 2006. The shareholders of the corporation are Tracy Sherman and Flora Shaw. They each own 200 shares of stock of the corporation, for which each paid $25,000 at the beginning of 2004. The corporation's ordinary income and cash distributions for the three years follow.

	2004	*2005*	*2006*
Ordinary income	$10,000	$11,000	$16,000
Cash distributions	6,000	11,000	24,000

a. How much do Sherman and Shaw report as income on their individual income tax returns for 2006?

b. What are Sherman's and Shaw's stock bases at the end of 2006?

21. S Corporation Losses. Melbourne Corporation is an S corporation with ten shareholders. Bill Fox owns 100 shares of stock, which represents a 15% interest in the corporation. His basis for those 100 shares is $12,000. He also has loaned the corporation $4,000 to support the purchase of a special machine. For the year 2006, the corporation reports an operating loss of $120,000. In addition, the corporation made charitable contributions for the year of $10,000.

a. Explain how Fox reports his share of the S corporation's operating loss and charitable contributions.

b. What is Fox's basis in his S corporation stock at the end of 2006?

c. Compute the amount and type of carryover losses to 2007 that Fox is entitled to, if any.

22. **Accumulated Adjustments Account.** What is an accumulated adjustments account and what purpose does it serve?

23. **Shareholder's Basis in S Corporation Stock.** An S corporation (with a $3,000 balance in its AAA and no E&P) distributes $10,000 to one of its shareholders. The shareholder's adjusted basis in his shares of stock was $6,000 prior to the distribution.

    a. How will the shareholder be taxed on the distribution?

    b. What is the shareholder's basis in the S stock after the distribution?

24. **Shareholder's Basis in S Corporation Stock.** An S corporation (with a $6,000 balance in its AAA and $8,000 of E&P) distributes $15,000 to one of its shareholders. The shareholder's adjusted basis in his shares of stock was $12,000 prior to the distribution.

    a. How will the shareholder be taxed on the distribution?

    b. What is the shareholder's basis in the S stock after the distribution?

25. **Form 1120S.** Prince Corporation (EIN 78-2152973), an S corporation, operates as a small variety store on the accrual basis. It is located at 1701 Governors Drive, College Station, TX 77843. The company was incorporated on January 2, 1999, and elected S corporation status on the same day. The business code is 5995. John R. Prince (SSN 201-03-5064) and his wife, Joyce B. Prince (SSN 265-72-8133) each own 35% of the corporation. Together they manage the store. The remaining stock is owned by John's father. John is President. Joyce is VP and Treasurer.

At the end of the calendar year 2006, the income statement accounts, balance sheet accounts, and other information taken from the records are as follows.

Inventory, January 1, 2006 (at cost)	$ 29,500
Inventory, December 31, 2006 (at cost)	32,400
Purchases (net)	133,800
Sales revenue	246,500
Sales returns and allowances	15,900
Taxable interest income	4,650
Tax exempt interest	6,000
Depreciation expense ("book" depreciation was $7,000)	5,200
Bad debts expense ("book" bad debt expense was $1,000)	1,500
Repairs and maintenance	3,300
Interest expense (business related)	2,700
Payroll taxes	7,800
Compensation of officers	30,000
Salaries and wages	24,500
Rental of equipment	700
Charitable contributions	1,600
Advertising	1,400
Distributions made during the year	24,000
Total assets, December 31, 2006	108,700

Based on this information, the Princes have asked you to prepare their 2006 Form 1120S. The return will be filed at the IRS Center in Ogden, Utah and will be signed by John Prince on April 10, 2007. You should prepare Schedules M-1 and M-2 on Form 1120S, but do not prepare Schedule L. On page 4, assume that the net income per books of Schedule M-1 (line 1) is $30,350 and the beginning balance of the AAA is $42,630 (Schedule M-2 (line 1a)). The beginning balance in the Other adjustments account (Schedule M-2 (line 1b)) is $19,400. Schedule K-1 should be prepared for Joyce's 35% share of the S corporation's items of income and deductions. John and Joyce live at 1074 Bright Leaf Square, College Station, TX 77841.

(Use for Problem 25).

Form **1120S** — Department of the Treasury, Internal Revenue Service (77)

U.S. Income Tax Return for an S Corporation

▶ **Do not file this form unless the corporation has filed Form 2553 to elect to be an S corporation.**

▶ **See separate instructions.**

OMB No. 1545-0130 — **2006**

For calendar year 2006 or tax year beginning , 2006, ending , 20

A Effective date of S election

B Business activity code number (see instructions)

Use IRS label. Otherwise, print or type.

Name

Number, street, and room or suite no. If a P.O. box, see instructions.

City or town, state, and ZIP code

C Employer identification number

D Date incorporated

E Total assets *(see instructions)* $

F Check if: (1) ☐ Initial return (2) ☐ Final return (3) ☐ Name change (4) ☐ Address change (5) ☐ Amended return

G Enter the number of shareholders in the corporation at the end of the tax year . . . ▶

H Check if Schedule M-3 is required *(attach Schedule M-3)* . . . ▶ ☐

Caution. *Include **only** trade or business income and expenses on lines 1a through 21. See the instructions for more information.*

Income	1a	Gross receipts or sales ___ b Less returns and allowances ___ c Bal ▶	1c	
	2	Cost of goods sold (Schedule A, line 8)	2	
	3	Gross profit. Subtract line 2 from line 1c	3	
	4	Net gain (loss) from Form 4797, Part II, line 17 *(attach Form 4797)*	4	
	5	Other income (loss) *(see instructions—attach statement)*	5	
	6	**Total income (loss).** Add lines 3 through 5 ▶	6	
Deductions (see instructions for limitations)	7	Compensation of officers	7	
	8	Salaries and wages (less employment credits)	8	
	9	Repairs and maintenance	9	
	10	Bad debts	10	
	11	Rents	11	
	12	Taxes and licenses	12	
	13	Interest	13	
	14	Depreciation not claimed on Schedule A or elsewhere on return *(attach Form 4562)*	14	
	15	Depletion **(Do not deduct oil and gas depletion.)**	15	
	16	Advertising	16	
	17	Pension, profit-sharing, etc., plans	17	
	18	Employee benefit programs	18	
	19	Other deductions *(attach statement)*	19	
	20	**Total deductions.** Add lines 7 through 19 ▶	20	
	21	**Ordinary business income (loss).** Subtract line 20 from line 6	21	
Tax and Payments	22a	Excess net passive income or LIFO recapture tax *(see instructions)*	22a	
	b	Tax from Schedule D (Form 1120S)	22b	
	c	Add lines 22a and 22b *(see instructions for additional taxes)*	22c	
	23a	2006 estimated tax payments and 2005 overpayment credited to 2006	23a	
	b	Tax deposited with Form 7004	23b	
	c	Credit for federal tax paid on fuels *(attach Form 4136)*	23c	
	d	Credit for federal telephone excise tax paid *(attach Form 8913)*	23d	
	e	Add lines 23a through 23d	23e	
	24	Estimated tax penalty *(see instructions)*. Check if Form 2220 is attached ▶ ☐	24	
	25	**Amount owed.** If line 23e is smaller than the total of lines 22c and 24, enter amount owed	25	
	26	**Overpayment.** If line 23e is larger than the total of lines 22c and 24, enter amount overpaid	26	
	27	Enter amount from line 26 **Credited to 2007 estimated tax** ▶ ___ **Refunded** ▶	27	

Sign Here

Under penalties of perjury, I declare that I have examined this return, including accompanying schedules and statements, and to the best of my knowledge and belief, it is true, correct, and complete. Declaration of preparer (other than taxpayer) is based on all information of which preparer has any knowledge.

▶ Signature of officer — Date ▶ Title

May the IRS discuss this return with the preparer shown below (see instructions)? ☐ **Yes** ☐ **No**

Paid Preparer's Use Only

Preparer's signature ▶ — Date — Check if self-employed ☐ — Preparer's SSN or PTIN

Firm's name (or yours if self-employed), address, and ZIP code ▶ — EIN — Phone no. ( )

For Privacy Act and Paperwork Reduction Act Notice, see separate instructions. Cat. No. 11510H Form **1120S** (2006)

(Use for Problem 25).

Form 1120S (2006) Page **2**

Schedule A **Cost of Goods Sold** (see instructions)

1	Inventory at beginning of year	1	
2	Purchases	2	
3	Cost of labor	3	
4	Additional section 263A costs *(attach statement)*	4	
5	Other costs *(attach statement)*	5	
6	**Total.** Add lines 1 through 5	6	
7	Inventory at end of year	7	
8	**Cost of goods sold.** Subtract line 7 from line 6. Enter here and on page 1, line 2	8	

9a Check all methods used for valuing closing inventory: *(i)* ☐ Cost as described in Regulations section 1.471-3
(ii) ☐ Lower of cost or market as described in Regulations section 1.471-4
(iii) ☐ Other (Specify method used and attach explanation.) ▶ ____

b Check if there was a writedown of subnormal goods as described in Regulations section 1.471-2(c) ▶ ☐

c Check if the LIFO inventory method was adopted this tax year for any goods (if checked, attach Form 970) ▶ ☐

d If the LIFO inventory method was used for this tax year, enter percentage (or amounts) of closing inventory computed under LIFO | 9d |

e If property is produced or acquired for resale, do the rules of section 263A apply to the corporation? ☐ Yes ☐ No

f Was there any change in determining quantities, cost, or valuations between opening and closing inventory? ☐ Yes ☐ No
If "Yes," attach explanation.

Schedule B **Other Information** (see instructions) — Yes / No

1 Check accounting method: **a** ☐ Cash **b** ☐ Accrual **c** ☐ Other (specify) ▶ ____

2 See the instructions and enter the:
a Business activity ▶ ____ **b** Product or service ▶ ____

3 At the end of the tax year, did the corporation own, directly or indirectly, 50% or more of the voting stock of a domestic corporation? (For rules of attribution, see section 267(c).) If "Yes," attach a statement showing: **(a)** name and employer identification number (EIN), **(b)** percentage owned, and **(c)** if 100% owned, was a QSub election made?

4 Was the corporation a member of a controlled group subject to the provisions of section 1561?

5 Has this corporation filed, or is it required to file, a return under section 6111 to provide information on any reportable transaction?

6 Check this box if the corporation issued publicly offered debt instruments with original issue discount ▶ ☐
If checked, the corporation may have to file **Form 8281,** Information Return for Publicly Offered Original Issue Discount Instruments.

7 If the corporation: **(a)** was a C corporation before it elected to be an S corporation **or** the corporation acquired an asset with a basis determined by reference to its basis (or the basis of any other property) in the hands of a C corporation **and (b)** has net unrealized built-in gain (defined in section 1374(d)(1)) in excess of the net recognized built-in gain from prior years, enter the net unrealized built-in gain reduced by net recognized built-in gain from prior years ▶ $ ____

8 Enter the accumulated earnings and profits of the corporation at the end of the tax year. $ ____

9 Are the corporation's total receipts *(see instructions)* for the tax year **and** its total assets at the end of the tax year less than $250,000? If "Yes," the corporation is not required to complete Schedules L and M-1.

Note: *If the corporation, at any time during the tax year, had assets or operated a business in a foreign country or U.S. possession, it may be required to attach* **Schedule N (Form 1120),** *Foreign Operations of U.S. Corporations, to this return. See Schedule N for details.*

Schedule K **Shareholders' Pro Rata Share Items**

					Total amount
Income (Loss)	1	Ordinary business income (loss) (page 1, line 21)		1	
	2	Net rental real estate income (loss) *(attach Form 8825)*		2	
	3a	Other gross rental income (loss)	3a		
	b	Expenses from other rental activities *(attach statement)*	3b		
	c	Other net rental income (loss). Subtract line 3b from line 3a		3c	
	4	Interest income		4	
	5	Dividends: **a** Ordinary dividends		5a	
		b Qualified dividends	5b		
	6	Royalties		6	
	7	Net short-term capital gain (loss) *(attach Schedule D (Form 1120S))*		7	
	8a	Net long-term capital gain (loss) *(attach Schedule D (Form 1120S))*		8a	
	b	Collectibles (28%) gain (loss)	8b		
	c	Unrecaptured section 1250 gain *(attach statement)*	8c		
	9	Net section 1231 gain (loss) *(attach Form 4797)*		9	
	10	Other income (loss) *(see instructions)* Type ▶		10	

Form **1120S** (2006)

(Use for Problem 25).

Form 1120S (2006) Page **3**

Section	Shareholders' Pro Rata Share Items (continued)	Line	Total amount
Deductions	11 Section 179 deduction *(attach Form 4562)*	11	
	12a Contributions	12a	
	b Investment interest expense	12b	
	c Section 59(e)(2) expenditures **(1)** Type ▶ **(2)** Amount ▶	12c(2)	
	d Other deductions *(see instructions)* Type ▶	12d	
Credits	13a Low-income housing credit (section 42(j)(5))	13a	
	b Low-income housing credit (other)	13b	
	c Qualified rehabilitation expenditures (rental real estate) *(attach Form 3468)*	13c	
	d Other rental real estate credits *(see instructions)* Type ▶	13d	
	e Other rental credits (see instructions) Type ▶	13e	
	f Credit for alcohol used as fuel *(attach Form 6478)*	13f	
	g Other credits *(see instructions)* Type ▶	13g	
Foreign Transactions	14a Name of country or U.S. possession ▶		
	b Gross income from all sources	14b	
	c Gross income sourced at shareholder level	14c	
	Foreign gross income sourced at corporate level		
	d Passive	14d	
	e Listed categories *(attach statement)*	14e	
	f General limitation	14f	
	Deductions allocated and apportioned at shareholder level		
	g Interest expense	14g	
	h Other	14h	
	Deductions allocated and apportioned at corporate level to foreign source income		
	i Passive	14i	
	j Listed categories *(attach statement)*	14j	
	k General limitation	14k	
	Other information		
	l Total foreign taxes (check one): ▶ ☐ Paid ☐ Accrued	14l	
	m Reduction in taxes available for credit *(attach statement)*	14m	
	n Other foreign tax information *(attach statement)*		
Alternative Minimum Tax (AMT) Items	15a Post-1986 depreciation adjustment	15a	
	b Adjusted gain or loss	15b	
	c Depletion (other than oil and gas)	15c	
	d Oil, gas, and geothermal properties—gross income	15d	
	e Oil, gas, and geothermal properties—deductions	15e	
	f Other AMT items *(attach statement)*	15f	
Items Affecting Shareholder Basis	16a Tax-exempt interest income	16a	
	b Other tax-exempt income	16b	
	c Nondeductible expenses	16c	
	d Property distributions	16d	
	e Repayment of loans from shareholders	16e	
Other Information	17a Investment income	17a	
	b Investment expenses	17b	
	c Dividend distributions paid from accumulated earnings and profits	17c	
	d Other items and amounts *(attach statement)*		
Recon-ciliation	18 **Income/loss reconciliation.** Combine the amounts on lines 1 through 10 in the far right column. From the result, subtract the sum of the amounts on lines 11 through 12d and 14l	18	

Form **1120S** (2006)

(Use for Problem 25).

Form 1120S (2006) Page **4**

Schedule L **Balance Sheets per Books**

Assets	Beginning of tax year (a)	(b)	End of tax year (c)	(d)
1 Cash				
2a Trade notes and accounts receivable				
b Less allowance for bad debts	( )		( )	
3 Inventories				
4 U.S. government obligations				
5 Tax-exempt securities *(see instructions)*				
6 Other current assets *(attach statement)*				
7 Loans to shareholders				
8 Mortgage and real estate loans				
9 Other investments *(attach statement)*				
10a Buildings and other depreciable assets				
b Less accumulated depreciation	( )		( )	
11a Depletable assets				
b Less accumulated depletion	( )		( )	
12 Land (net of any amortization)				
13a Intangible assets (amortizable only)				
b Less accumulated amortization	( )		( )	
14 Other assets *(attach statement)*				
15 Total assets				
Liabilities and Shareholders' Equity				
16 Accounts payable				
17 Mortgages, notes, bonds payable in less than 1 year				
18 Other current liabilities *(attach statement)*				
19 Loans from shareholders				
20 Mortgages, notes, bonds payable in 1 year or more				
21 Other liabilities *(attach statement)*				
22 Capital stock				
23 Additional paid-in capital				
24 Retained earnings				
25 Adjustments to shareholders' equity *(attach statement)*				
26 Less cost of treasury stock		( )		( )
27 Total liabilities and shareholders' equity				

Schedule M-1 **Reconciliation of Income (Loss) per Books With Income (Loss) per Return**
Note: Schedule M-3 required instead of Schedule M-1 if total assets are $10 million or more—see instructions

1 Net income (loss) per books		5 Income recorded on books this year not included on Schedule K, lines 1 through 10 (itemize): a Tax-exempt interest $	
2 Income included on Schedule K, lines 1, 2, 3c, 4, 5a, 6, 7, 8a, 9, and 10, not recorded on books this year (itemize):			
3 Expenses recorded on books this year not included on Schedule K, lines 1 through 12 and 14l (itemize): a Depreciation $ b Travel and entertainment $		6 Deductions included on Schedule K, lines 1 through 12 and 14l, not charged against book income this year (itemize): a Depreciation $	
		7 Add lines 5 and 6	
4 Add lines 1 through 3		8 Income (loss) (Schedule K, line 18). Line 4 less line 7	

Schedule M-2 **Analysis of Accumulated Adjustments Account, Other Adjustments Account, and Shareholders' Undistributed Taxable Income Previously Taxed** (see instructions)

	(a) Accumulated adjustments account	(b) Other adjustments account	(c) Shareholders' undistributed taxable income previously taxed
1 Balance at beginning of tax year			
2 Ordinary income from page 1, line 21			
3 Other additions			
4 Loss from page 1, line 21	( )		
5 Other reductions	( )	( )	
6 Combine lines 1 through 5			
7 Distributions other than dividend distributions			
8 Balance at end of tax year. Subtract line 7 from line 6			

Printed on recycled paper

Form **1120S** (2006)

(Use for Problem 25).

671106

☐ Final K-1 ☐ Amended K-1 OMB No. 1545-0130

Schedule K-1 (Form 1120S) **2006**
Department of the Treasury
Internal Revenue Service

For calendar year 2006, or tax year beginning ________, 2006 ending ________, 20__

Shareholder's Share of Income, Deductions, Credits, etc. ► **See back of form and separate instructions.**

Part I Information About the Corporation

A Corporation's employer identification number

B Corporation's name, address, city, state, and ZIP code

C IRS Center where corporation filed return

D ☐ Tax shelter registration number, if any ________

E ☐ Check if Form 8271 is attached

Part II Information About the Shareholder

F Shareholder's identifying number

G Shareholder's name, address, city, state and ZIP code

H Shareholder's percentage of stock ownership for tax year . . . . ________ %

For IRS Use Only

Part III Shareholder's Share of Current Year Income, Deductions, Credits, and Other Items

1	Ordinary business income (loss)	13	Credits
2	Net rental real estate income (loss)		
3	Other net rental income (loss)		
4	Interest income		
5a	Ordinary dividends		
5b	Qualified dividends	14	Foreign transactions
6	Royalties		
7	Net short-term capital gain (loss)		
8a	Net long-term capital gain (loss)		
8b	Collectibles (28%) gain (loss)		
8c	Unrecaptured section 1250 gain		
9	Net section 1231 gain (loss)		
10	Other income (loss)	15	Alternative minimum tax (AMT) items
11	Section 179 deduction	16	Items affecting shareholder basis
12	Other deductions		
		17	Other information

* See attached statement for additional information.

For Privacy Act and Paperwork Reduction Act Notice, see Instructions for Form 1120S. Cat. No. 11520D **Schedule K-1 (Form 1120S) 2006**

CUMULATIVE PROBLEM (CHAPTERS 14 AND 15)

Bebop, Inc. (a C corporation) distributes investment property to its shareholders. The property was acquired five years ago and has a basis of $50,000 and a market value of $80,000.

a. How will this distribution be treated for tax purposes at both the corporate and shareholder levels?

b. If Bebop, Inc. was an S corporation, how would you answer Part a. differ?

c. If the company was a partnership, how would the distribution be treated for tax purposes at the partnership and partner levels?

Tax Tables

2006 Tax Table

See the instructions for line 44 that begin on page 37 to see if you must use the Tax Table below to figure your tax.

Example. Mr. and Mrs. Brown are filing a joint return. Their taxable income on Form 1040, line 43, is $25,300. First, they find the $25,300–25,350 taxable income line. Next, they find the column for married filing jointly and read down the column. The amount shown where the taxable income line and filing status column meet is $3,044. This is the tax amount they should enter on Form 1040, line 44.

Sample Table

At least	But less than	Single	Married filing jointly *	Married filing sepa-rately	Head of a house-hold
		Your tax is—			
25,200	**25,250**	3,406	3,029	3,406	3,246
25,250	**25,300**	3,414	3,036	3,414	3,254
25,300	**25,350**	3,421	(3,044)	3,421	3,261
25,350	**25,400**	3,429	3,051	3,429	3,269

If line 43 (taxable income) is—		And you are—			
At least	But less than	Single	Married filing jointly *	Married filing sepa-rately	Head of a house-hold
		Your tax is—			
0	**5**	0	0	0	0
5	**15**	1	1	1	1
15	**25**	2	2	2	2
25	**50**	4	4	4	4
50	**75**	6	6	6	6
75	**100**	9	9	9	9
100	**125**	11	11	11	11
125	**150**	14	14	14	14
150	**175**	16	16	16	16
175	**200**	19	19	19	19
200	**225**	21	21	21	21
225	**250**	24	24	24	24
250	**275**	26	26	26	26
275	**300**	29	29	29	29
300	**325**	31	31	31	31
325	**350**	34	34	34	34
350	**375**	36	36	36	36
375	**400**	39	39	39	39
400	**425**	41	41	41	41
425	**450**	44	44	44	44
450	**475**	46	46	46	46
475	**500**	49	49	49	49
500	**525**	51	51	51	51
525	**550**	54	54	54	54
550	**575**	56	56	56	56
575	**600**	59	59	59	59
600	**625**	61	61	61	61
625	**650**	64	64	64	64
650	**675**	66	66	66	66
675	**700**	69	69	69	69
700	**725**	71	71	71	71
725	**750**	74	74	74	74
750	**775**	76	76	76	76
775	**800**	79	79	79	79
800	**825**	81	81	81	81
825	**850**	84	84	84	84
850	**875**	86	86	86	86
875	**900**	89	89	89	89
900	**925**	91	91	91	91
925	**950**	94	94	94	94
950	**975**	96	96	96	96
975	**1,000**	99	99	99	99
1,000					
1,000	**1,025**	101	101	101	101
1,025	**1,050**	104	104	104	104
1,050	**1,075**	106	106	106	106
1,075	**1,100**	109	109	109	109
1,100	**1,125**	111	111	111	111
1,125	**1,150**	114	114	114	114
1,150	**1,175**	116	116	116	116
1,175	**1,200**	119	119	119	119
1,200	**1,225**	121	121	121	121
1,225	**1,250**	124	124	124	124
1,250	**1,275**	126	126	126	126
1,275	**1,300**	129	129	129	129

If line 43 (taxable income) is—		And you are—			
At least	But less than	Single	Married filing jointly *	Married filing sepa-rately	Head of a house-hold
		Your tax is—			
1,300	**1,325**	131	131	131	131
1,325	**1,350**	134	134	134	134
1,350	**1,375**	136	136	136	136
1,375	**1,400**	139	139	139	139
1,400	**1,425**	141	141	141	141
1,425	**1,450**	144	144	144	144
1,450	**1,475**	146	146	146	146
1,475	**1,500**	149	149	149	149
1,500	**1,525**	151	151	151	151
1,525	**1,550**	154	154	154	154
1,550	**1,575**	156	156	156	156
1,575	**1,600**	159	159	159	159
1,600	**1,625**	161	161	161	161
1,625	**1,650**	164	164	164	164
1,650	**1,675**	166	166	166	166
1,675	**1,700**	169	169	169	169
1,700	**1,725**	171	171	171	171
1,725	**1,750**	174	174	174	174
1,750	**1,775**	176	176	176	176
1,775	**1,800**	179	179	179	179
1,800	**1,825**	181	181	181	181
1,825	**1,850**	184	184	184	184
1,850	**1,875**	186	186	186	186
1,875	**1,900**	189	189	189	189
1,900	**1,925**	191	191	191	191
1,925	**1,950**	194	194	194	194
1,950	**1,975**	196	196	196	196
1,975	**2,000**	199	199	199	199
2,000					
2,000	**2,025**	201	201	201	201
2,025	**2,050**	204	204	204	204
2,050	**2,075**	206	206	206	206
2,075	**2,100**	209	209	209	209
2,100	**2,125**	211	211	211	211
2,125	**2,150**	214	214	214	214
2,150	**2,175**	216	216	216	216
2,175	**2,200**	219	219	219	219
2,200	**2,225**	221	221	221	221
2,225	**2,250**	224	224	224	224
2,250	**2,275**	226	226	226	226
2,275	**2,300**	229	229	229	229
2,300	**2,325**	231	231	231	231
2,325	**2,350**	234	234	234	234
2,350	**2,375**	236	236	236	236
2,375	**2,400**	239	239	239	239
2,400	**2,425**	241	241	241	241
2,425	**2,450**	244	244	244	244
2,450	**2,475**	246	246	246	246
2,475	**2,500**	249	249	249	249
2,500	**2,525**	251	251	251	251
2,525	**2,550**	254	254	254	254
2,550	**2,575**	256	256	256	256
2,575	**2,600**	259	259	259	259
2,600	**2,625**	261	261	261	261
2,625	**2,650**	264	264	264	264
2,650	**2,675**	266	266	266	266
2,675	**2,700**	269	269	269	269

If line 43 (taxable income) is—		And you are—			
At least	But less than	Single	Married filing jointly *	Married filing sepa-rately	Head of a house-hold
		Your tax is—			
2,700	**2,725**	271	271	271	271
2,725	**2,750**	274	274	274	274
2,750	**2,775**	276	276	276	276
2,775	**2,800**	279	279	279	279
2,800	**2,825**	281	281	281	281
2,825	**2,850**	284	284	284	284
2,850	**2,875**	286	286	286	286
2,875	**2,900**	289	289	289	289
2,900	**2,925**	291	291	291	291
2,925	**2,950**	294	294	294	294
2,950	**2,975**	296	296	296	296
2,975	**3,000**	299	299	299	299
3,000					
3,000	**3,050**	303	303	303	303
3,050	**3,100**	308	308	308	308
3,100	**3,150**	313	313	313	313
3,150	**3,200**	318	318	318	318
3,200	**3,250**	323	323	323	323
3,250	**3,300**	328	328	328	328
3,300	**3,350**	333	333	333	333
3,350	**3,400**	338	338	338	338
3,400	**3,450**	343	343	343	343
3,450	**3,500**	348	348	348	348
3,500	**3,550**	353	353	353	353
3,550	**3,600**	358	358	358	358
3,600	**3,650**	363	363	363	363
3,650	**3,700**	368	368	368	368
3,700	**3,750**	373	373	373	373
3,750	**3,800**	378	378	378	378
3,800	**3,850**	383	383	383	383
3,850	**3,900**	388	388	388	388
3,900	**3,950**	393	393	393	393
3,950	**4,000**	398	398	398	398
4,000					
4,000	**4,050**	403	403	403	403
4,050	**4,100**	408	408	408	408
4,100	**4,150**	413	413	413	413
4,150	**4,200**	418	418	418	418
4,200	**4,250**	423	423	423	423
4,250	**4,300**	428	428	428	428
4,300	**4,350**	433	433	433	433
4,350	**4,400**	438	438	438	438
4,400	**4,450**	443	443	443	443
4,450	**4,500**	448	448	448	448
4,500	**4,550**	453	453	453	453
4,550	**4,600**	458	458	458	458
4,600	**4,650**	463	463	463	463
4,650	**4,700**	468	468	468	468
4,700	**4,750**	473	473	473	473
4,750	**4,800**	478	478	478	478
4,800	**4,850**	483	483	483	483
4,850	**4,900**	488	488	488	488
4,900	**4,950**	493	493	493	493
4,950	**5,000**	498	498	498	498

* This column must also be used by a qualifying widow(er)

(Continued on page 24)

2006 Tax Table—*Continued*

If line 43 (taxable income) is— At least	But less than	And you are— Single	Married filing jointly *	Married filing separately	Head of a household
		Your tax is—			
5,000					
5,000	**5,050**	503	503	503	503
5,050	**5,100**	508	508	508	508
5,100	**5,150**	513	513	513	513
5,150	**5,200**	518	518	518	518
5,200	**5,250**	523	523	523	523
5,250	**5,300**	528	528	528	528
5,300	**5,350**	533	533	533	533
5,350	**5,400**	538	538	538	538
5,400	**5,450**	543	543	543	543
5,450	**5,500**	548	548	548	548
5,500	**5,550**	553	553	553	553
5,550	**5,600**	558	558	558	558
5,600	**5,650**	563	563	563	563
5,650	**5,700**	568	568	568	568
5,700	**5,750**	573	573	573	573
5,750	**5,800**	578	578	578	578
5,800	**5,850**	583	583	583	583
5,850	**5,900**	588	588	588	588
5,900	**5,950**	593	593	593	593
5,950	**6,000**	598	598	598	598
6,000					
6,000	**6,050**	603	603	603	603
6,050	**6,100**	608	608	608	608
6,100	**6,150**	613	613	613	613
6,150	**6,200**	618	618	618	618
6,200	**6,250**	623	623	623	623
6,250	**6,300**	628	628	628	628
6,300	**6,350**	633	633	633	633
6,350	**6,400**	638	638	638	638
6,400	**6,450**	643	643	643	643
6,450	**6,500**	648	648	648	648
6,500	**6,550**	653	653	653	653
6,550	**6,600**	658	658	658	658
6,600	**6,650**	663	663	663	663
6,650	**6,700**	668	668	668	668
6,700	**6,750**	673	673	673	673
6,750	**6,800**	678	678	678	678
6,800	**6,850**	683	683	683	683
6,850	**6,900**	688	688	688	688
6,900	**6,950**	693	693	693	693
6,950	**7,000**	698	698	698	698
7,000					
7,000	**7,050**	703	703	703	703
7,050	**7,100**	708	708	708	708
7,100	**7,150**	713	713	713	713
7,150	**7,200**	718	718	718	718
7,200	**7,250**	723	723	723	723
7,250	**7,300**	728	728	728	728
7,300	**7,350**	733	733	733	733
7,350	**7,400**	738	738	738	738
7,400	**7,450**	743	743	743	743
7,450	**7,500**	748	748	748	748
7,500	**7,550**	753	753	753	753
7,550	**7,600**	759	758	759	758
7,600	**7,650**	766	763	766	763
7,650	**7,700**	774	768	774	768
7,700	**7,750**	781	773	781	773
7,750	**7,800**	789	778	789	778
7,800	**7,850**	796	783	796	783
7,850	**7,900**	804	788	804	788
7,900	**7,950**	811	793	811	793
7,950	**8,000**	819	798	819	798

If line 43 (taxable income) is— At least	But less than	And you are— Single	Married filing jointly *	Married filing separately	Head of a household
		Your tax is—			
8,000					
8,000	**8,050**	826	803	826	803
8,050	**8,100**	834	808	834	808
8,100	**8,150**	841	813	841	813
8,150	**8,200**	849	818	849	818
8,200	**8,250**	856	823	856	823
8,250	**8,300**	864	828	864	828
8,300	**8,350**	871	833	871	833
8,350	**8,400**	879	838	879	838
8,400	**8,450**	886	843	886	843
8,450	**8,500**	894	848	894	848
8,500	**8,550**	901	853	901	853
8,550	**8,600**	909	858	909	858
8,600	**8,650**	916	863	916	863
8,650	**8,700**	924	868	924	868
8,700	**8,750**	931	873	931	873
8,750	**8,800**	939	878	939	878
8,800	**8,850**	946	883	946	883
8,850	**8,900**	954	888	954	888
8,900	**8,950**	961	893	961	893
8,950	**9,000**	969	898	969	898
9,000					
9,000	**9,050**	976	903	976	903
9,050	**9,100**	984	908	984	908
9,100	**9,150**	991	913	991	913
9,150	**9,200**	999	918	999	918
9,200	**9,250**	1,006	923	1,006	923
9,250	**9,300**	1,014	928	1,014	928
9,300	**9,350**	1,021	933	1,021	933
9,350	**9,400**	1,029	938	1,029	938
9,400	**9,450**	1,036	943	1,036	943
9,450	**9,500**	1,044	948	1,044	948
9,500	**9,550**	1,051	953	1,051	953
9,550	**9,600**	1,059	958	1,059	958
9,600	**9,650**	1,066	963	1,066	963
9,650	**9,700**	1,074	968	1,074	968
9,700	**9,750**	1,081	973	1,081	973
9,750	**9,800**	1,089	978	1,089	978
9,800	**9,850**	1,096	983	1,096	983
9,850	**9,900**	1,104	988	1,104	988
9,900	**9,950**	1,111	993	1,111	993
9,950	**10,000**	1,119	998	1,119	998
10,000					
10,000	**10,050**	1,126	1,003	1,126	1,003
10,050	**10,100**	1,134	1,008	1,134	1,008
10,100	**10,150**	1,141	1,013	1,141	1,013
10,150	**10,200**	1,149	1,018	1,149	1,018
10,200	**10,250**	1,156	1,023	1,156	1,023
10,250	**10,300**	1,164	1,028	1,164	1,028
10,300	**10,350**	1,171	1,033	1,171	1,033
10,350	**10,400**	1,179	1,038	1,179	1,038
10,400	**10,450**	1,186	1,043	1,186	1,043
10,450	**10,500**	1,194	1,048	1,194	1,048
10,500	**10,550**	1,201	1,053	1,201	1,053
10,550	**10,600**	1,209	1,058	1,209	1,058
10,600	**10,650**	1,216	1,063	1,216	1,063
10,650	**10,700**	1,224	1,068	1,224	1,068
10,700	**10,750**	1,231	1,073	1,231	1,073
10,750	**10,800**	1,239	1,078	1,239	1,079
10,800	**10,850**	1,246	1,083	1,246	1,086
10,850	**10,900**	1,254	1,088	1,254	1,094
10,900	**10,950**	1,261	1,093	1,261	1,101
10,950	**11,000**	1,269	1,098	1,269	1,109

If line 43 (taxable income) is— At least	But less than	And you are— Single	Married filing jointly *	Married filing separately	Head of a household
		Your tax is—			
11,000					
11,000	**11,050**	1,276	1,103	1,276	1,116
11,050	**11,100**	1,284	1,108	1,284	1,124
11,100	**11,150**	1,291	1,113	1,291	1,131
11,150	**11,200**	1,299	1,118	1,299	1,139
11,200	**11,250**	1,306	1,123	1,306	1,146
11,250	**11,300**	1,314	1,128	1,314	1,154
11,300	**11,350**	1,321	1,133	1,321	1,161
11,350	**11,400**	1,329	1,138	1,329	1,169
11,400	**11,450**	1,336	1,143	1,336	1,176
11,450	**11,500**	1,344	1,148	1,344	1,184
11,500	**11,550**	1,351	1,153	1,351	1,191
11,550	**11,600**	1,359	1,158	1,359	1,199
11,600	**11,650**	1,366	1,163	1,366	1,206
11,650	**11,700**	1,374	1,168	1,374	1,214
11,700	**11,750**	1,381	1,173	1,381	1,221
11,750	**11,800**	1,389	1,178	1,389	1,229
11,800	**11,850**	1,396	1,183	1,396	1,236
11,850	**11,900**	1,404	1,188	1,404	1,244
11,900	**11,950**	1,411	1,193	1,411	1,251
11,950	**12,000**	1,419	1,198	1,419	1,259
12,000					
12,000	**12,050**	1,426	1,203	1,426	1,266
12,050	**12,100**	1,434	1,208	1,434	1,274
12,100	**12,150**	1,441	1,213	1,441	1,281
12,150	**12,200**	1,449	1,218	1,449	1,289
12,200	**12,250**	1,456	1,223	1,456	1,296
12,250	**12,300**	1,464	1,228	1,464	1,304
12,300	**12,350**	1,471	1,233	1,471	1,311
12,350	**12,400**	1,479	1,238	1,479	1,319
12,400	**12,450**	1,486	1,243	1,486	1,326
12,450	**12,500**	1,494	1,248	1,494	1,334
12,500	**12,550**	1,501	1,253	1,501	1,341
12,550	**12,600**	1,509	1,258	1,509	1,349
12,600	**12,650**	1,516	1,263	1,516	1,356
12,650	**12,700**	1,524	1,268	1,524	1,364
12,700	**12,750**	1,531	1,273	1,531	1,371
12,750	**12,800**	1,539	1,278	1,539	1,379
12,800	**12,850**	1,546	1,283	1,546	1,386
12,850	**12,900**	1,554	1,288	1,554	1,394
12,900	**12,950**	1,561	1,293	1,561	1,401
12,950	**13,000**	1,569	1,298	1,569	1,409
13,000					
13,000	**13,050**	1,576	1,303	1,576	1,416
13,050	**13,100**	1,584	1,308	1,584	1,424
13,100	**13,150**	1,591	1,313	1,591	1,431
13,150	**13,200**	1,599	1,318	1,599	1,439
13,200	**13,250**	1,606	1,323	1,606	1,446
13,250	**13,300**	1,614	1,328	1,614	1,454
13,300	**13,350**	1,621	1,333	1,621	1,461
13,350	**13,400**	1,629	1,338	1,629	1,469
13,400	**13,450**	1,636	1,343	1,636	1,476
13,450	**13,500**	1,644	1,348	1,644	1,484
13,500	**13,550**	1,651	1,353	1,651	1,491
13,550	**13,600**	1,659	1,358	1,659	1,499
13,600	**13,650**	1,666	1,363	1,666	1,506
13,650	**13,700**	1,674	1,368	1,674	1,514
13,700	**13,750**	1,681	1,373	1,681	1,521
13,750	**13,800**	1,689	1,378	1,689	1,529
13,800	**13,850**	1,696	1,383	1,696	1,536
13,850	**13,900**	1,704	1,388	1,704	1,544
13,900	**13,950**	1,711	1,393	1,711	1,551
13,950	**14,000**	1,719	1,398	1,719	1,559

* This column must also be used by a qualifying widow(er)

(Continued on page 25)

2006 Tax Table–*Continued*

If line 43 (taxable income) is—		And you are—			
At least	But less than	Single	Married filing jointly *	Married filing sepa-rately	Head of a house-hold
		Your tax is—			
14,000					
14,000	**14,050**	1,726	1,403	1,726	1,566
14,050	**14,100**	1,734	1,408	1,734	1,574
14,100	**14,150**	1,741	1,413	1,741	1,581
14,150	**14,200**	1,749	1,418	1,749	1,589
14,200	**14,250**	1,756	1,423	1,756	1,596
14,250	**14,300**	1,764	1,428	1,764	1,604
14,300	**14,350**	1,771	1,433	1,771	1,611
14,350	**14,400**	1,779	1,438	1,779	1,619
14,400	**14,450**	1,786	1,443	1,786	1,626
14,450	**14,500**	1,794	1,448	1,794	1,634
14,500	**14,550**	1,801	1,453	1,801	1,641
14,550	**14,600**	1,809	1,458	1,809	1,649
14,600	**14,650**	1,816	1,463	1,816	1,656
14,650	**14,700**	1,824	1,468	1,824	1,664
14,700	**14,750**	1,831	1,473	1,831	1,671
14,750	**14,800**	1,839	1,478	1,839	1,679
14,800	**14,850**	1,846	1,483	1,846	1,686
14,850	**14,900**	1,854	1,488	1,854	1,694
14,900	**14,950**	1,861	1,493	1,861	1,701
14,950	**15,000**	1,869	1,498	1,869	1,709
15,000					
15,000	**15,050**	1,876	1,503	1,876	1,716
15,050	**15,100**	1,884	1,508	1,884	1,724
15,100	**15,150**	1,891	1,514	1,891	1,731
15,150	**15,200**	1,899	1,521	1,899	1,739
15,200	**15,250**	1,906	1,529	1,906	1,746
15,250	**15,300**	1,914	1,536	1,914	1,754
15,300	**15,350**	1,921	1,544	1,921	1,761
15,350	**15,400**	1,929	1,551	1,929	1,769
15,400	**15,450**	1,936	1,559	1,936	1,776
15,450	**15,500**	1,944	1,566	1,944	1,784
15,500	**15,550**	1,951	1,574	1,951	1,791
15,550	**15,600**	1,959	1,581	1,959	1,799
15,600	**15,650**	1,966	1,589	1,966	1,806
15,650	**15,700**	1,974	1,596	1,974	1,814
15,700	**15,750**	1,981	1,604	1,981	1,821
15,750	**15,800**	1,989	1,611	1,989	1,829
15,800	**15,850**	1,996	1,619	1,996	1,836
15,850	**15,900**	2,004	1,626	2,004	1,844
15,900	**15,950**	2,011	1,634	2,011	1,851
15,950	**16,000**	2,019	1,641	2,019	1,859
16,000					
16,000	**16,050**	2,026	1,649	2,026	1,866
16,050	**16,100**	2,034	1,656	2,034	1,874
16,100	**16,150**	2,041	1,664	2,041	1,881
16,150	**16,200**	2,049	1,671	2,049	1,889
16,200	**16,250**	2,056	1,679	2,056	1,896
16,250	**16,300**	2,064	1,686	2,064	1,904
16,300	**16,350**	2,071	1,694	2,071	1,911
16,350	**16,400**	2,079	1,701	2,079	1,919
16,400	**16,450**	2,086	1,709	2,086	1,926
16,450	**16,500**	2,094	1,716	2,094	1,934
16,500	**16,550**	2,101	1,724	2,101	1,941
16,550	**16,600**	2,109	1,731	2,109	1,949
16,600	**16,650**	2,116	1,739	2,116	1,956
16,650	**16,700**	2,124	1,746	2,124	1,964
16,700	**16,750**	2,131	1,754	2,131	1,971
16,750	**16,800**	2,139	1,761	2,139	1,979
16,800	**16,850**	2,146	1,769	2,146	1,986
16,850	**16,900**	2,154	1,776	2,154	1,994
16,900	**16,950**	2,161	1,784	2,161	2,001
16,950	**17,000**	2,169	1,791	2,169	2,009
17,000					
17,000	**17,050**	2,176	1,799	2,176	2,016
17,050	**17,100**	2,184	1,806	2,184	2,024
17,100	**17,150**	2,191	1,814	2,191	2,031
17,150	**17,200**	2,199	1,821	2,199	2,039
17,200	**17,250**	2,206	1,829	2,206	2,046
17,250	**17,300**	2,214	1,836	2,214	2,054
17,300	**17,350**	2,221	1,844	2,221	2,061
17,350	**17,400**	2,229	1,851	2,229	2,069
17,400	**17,450**	2,236	1,859	2,236	2,076
17,450	**17,500**	2,244	1,866	2,244	2,084
17,500	**17,550**	2,251	1,874	2,251	2,091
17,550	**17,600**	2,259	1,881	2,259	2,099
17,600	**17,650**	2,266	1,889	2,266	2,106
17,650	**17,700**	2,274	1,896	2,274	2,114
17,700	**17,750**	2,281	1,904	2,281	2,121
17,750	**17,800**	2,289	1,911	2,289	2,129
17,800	**17,850**	2,296	1,919	2,296	2,136
17,850	**17,900**	2,304	1,926	2,304	2,144
17,900	**17,950**	2,311	1,934	2,311	2,151
17,950	**18,000**	2,319	1,941	2,319	2,159
18,000					
18,000	**18,050**	2,326	1,949	2,326	2,166
18,050	**18,100**	2,334	1,956	2,334	2,174
18,100	**18,150**	2,341	1,964	2,341	2,181
18,150	**18,200**	2,349	1,971	2,349	2,189
18,200	**18,250**	2,356	1,979	2,356	2,196
18,250	**18,300**	2,364	1,986	2,364	2,204
18,300	**18,350**	2,371	1,994	2,371	2,211
18,350	**18,400**	2,379	2,001	2,379	2,219
18,400	**18,450**	2,386	2,009	2,386	2,226
18,450	**18,500**	2,394	2,016	2,394	2,234
18,500	**18,550**	2,401	2,024	2,401	2,241
18,550	**18,600**	2,409	2,031	2,409	2,249
18,600	**18,650**	2,416	2,039	2,416	2,256
18,650	**18,700**	2,424	2,046	2,424	2,264
18,700	**18,750**	2,431	2,054	2,431	2,271
18,750	**18,800**	2,439	2,061	2,439	2,279
18,800	**18,850**	2,446	2,069	2,446	2,286
18,850	**18,900**	2,454	2,076	2,454	2,294
18,900	**18,950**	2,461	2,084	2,461	2,301
18,950	**19,000**	2,469	2,091	2,469	2,309
19,000					
19,000	**19,050**	2,476	2,099	2,476	2,316
19,050	**19,100**	2,484	2,106	2,484	2,324
19,100	**19,150**	2,491	2,114	2,491	2,331
19,150	**19,200**	2,499	2,121	2,499	2,339
19,200	**19,250**	2,506	2,129	2,506	2,346
19,250	**19,300**	2,514	2,136	2,514	2,354
19,300	**19,350**	2,521	2,144	2,521	2,361
19,350	**19,400**	2,529	2,151	2,529	2,369
19,400	**19,450**	2,536	2,159	2,536	2,376
19,450	**19,500**	2,544	2,166	2,544	2,384
19,500	**19,550**	2,551	2,174	2,551	2,391
19,550	**19,600**	2,559	2,181	2,559	2,399
19,600	**19,650**	2,566	2,189	2,566	2,406
19,650	**19,700**	2,574	2,196	2,574	2,414
19,700	**19,750**	2,581	2,204	2,581	2,421
19,750	**19,800**	2,589	2,211	2,589	2,429
19,800	**19,850**	2,596	2,219	2,596	2,436
19,850	**19,900**	2,604	2,226	2,604	2,444
19,900	**19,950**	2,611	2,234	2,611	2,451
19,950	**20,000**	2,619	2,241	2,619	2,459
20,000					
20,000	**20,050**	2,626	2,249	2,626	2,466
20,050	**20,100**	2,634	2,256	2,634	2,474
20,100	**20,150**	2,641	2,264	2,641	2,481
20,150	**20,200**	2,649	2,271	2,649	2,489
20,200	**20,250**	2,656	2,279	2,656	2,496
20,250	**20,300**	2,664	2,286	2,664	2,504
20,300	**20,350**	2,671	2,294	2,671	2,511
20,350	**20,400**	2,679	2,301	2,679	2,519
20,400	**20,450**	2,686	2,309	2,686	2,526
20,450	**20,500**	2,694	2,316	2,694	2,534
20,500	**20,550**	2,701	2,324	2,701	2,541
20,550	**20,600**	2,709	2,331	2,709	2,549
20,600	**20,650**	2,716	2,339	2,716	2,556
20,650	**20,700**	2,724	2,346	2,724	2,564
20,700	**20,750**	2,731	2,354	2,731	2,571
20,750	**20,800**	2,739	2,361	2,739	2,579
20,800	**20,850**	2,746	2,369	2,746	2,586
20,850	**20,900**	2,754	2,376	2,754	2,594
20,900	**20,950**	2,761	2,384	2,761	2,601
20,950	**21,000**	2,769	2,391	2,769	2,609
21,000					
21,000	**21,050**	2,776	2,399	2,776	2,616
21,050	**21,100**	2,784	2,406	2,784	2,624
21,100	**21,150**	2,791	2,414	2,791	2,631
21,150	**21,200**	2,799	2,421	2,799	2,639
21,200	**21,250**	2,806	2,429	2,806	2,646
21,250	**21,300**	2,814	2,436	2,814	2,654
21,300	**21,350**	2,821	2,444	2,821	2,661
21,350	**21,400**	2,829	2,451	2,829	2,669
21,400	**21,450**	2,836	2,459	2,836	2,676
21,450	**21,500**	2,844	2,466	2,844	2,684
21,500	**21,550**	2,851	2,474	2,851	2,691
21,550	**21,600**	2,859	2,481	2,859	2,699
21,600	**21,650**	2,866	2,489	2,866	2,706
21,650	**21,700**	2,874	2,496	2,874	2,714
21,700	**21,750**	2,881	2,504	2,881	2,721
21,750	**21,800**	2,889	2,511	2,889	2,729
21,800	**21,850**	2,896	2,519	2,896	2,736
21,850	**21,900**	2,904	2,526	2,904	2,744
21,900	**21,950**	2,911	2,534	2,911	2,751
21,950	**22,000**	2,919	2,541	2,919	2,759
22,000					
22,000	**22,050**	2,926	2,549	2,926	2,766
22,050	**22,100**	2,934	2,556	2,934	2,774
22,100	**22,150**	2,941	2,564	2,941	2,781
22,150	**22,200**	2,949	2,571	2,949	2,789
22,200	**22,250**	2,956	2,579	2,956	2,796
22,250	**22,300**	2,964	2,586	2,964	2,804
22,300	**22,350**	2,971	2,594	2,971	2,811
22,350	**22,400**	2,979	2,601	2,979	2,819
22,400	**22,450**	2,986	2,609	2,986	2,826
22,450	**22,500**	2,994	2,616	2,994	2,834
22,500	**22,550**	3,001	2,624	3,001	2,841
22,550	**22,600**	3,009	2,631	3,009	2,849
22,600	**22,650**	3,016	2,639	3,016	2,856
22,650	**22,700**	3,024	2,646	3,024	2,864
22,700	**22,750**	3,031	2,654	3,031	2,871
22,750	**22,800**	3,039	2,661	3,039	2,879
22,800	**22,850**	3,046	2,669	3,046	2,886
22,850	**22,900**	3,054	2,676	3,054	2,894
22,900	**22,950**	3,061	2,684	3,061	2,901
22,950	**23,000**	3,069	2,691	3,069	2,909

* This column must also be used by a qualifying widow(er)

(Continued on page 26)

2006 Tax Table—*Continued*

If line 43 (taxable income) is—		And you are—			
At least	But less than	Single	Married filing jointly *	Married filing sepa-rately	Head of a house-hold
		Your tax is—			
23,000					
23,000	**23,050**	3,076	2,699	3,076	2,916
23,050	**23,100**	3,084	2,706	3,084	2,924
23,100	**23,150**	3,091	2,714	3,091	2,931
23,150	**23,200**	3,099	2,721	3,099	2,939
23,200	**23,250**	3,106	2,729	3,106	2,946
23,250	**23,300**	3,114	2,736	3,114	2,954
23,300	**23,350**	3,121	2,744	3,121	2,961
23,350	**23,400**	3,129	2,751	3,129	2,969
23,400	**23,450**	3,136	2,759	3,136	2,976
23,450	**23,500**	3,144	2,766	3,144	2,984
23,500	**23,550**	3,151	2,774	3,151	2,991
23,550	**23,600**	3,159	2,781	3,159	2,999
23,600	**23,650**	3,166	2,789	3,166	3,006
23,650	**23,700**	3,174	2,796	3,174	3,014
23,700	**23,750**	3,181	2,804	3,181	3,021
23,750	**23,800**	3,189	2,811	3,189	3,029
23,800	**23,850**	3,196	2,819	3,196	3,036
23,850	**23,900**	3,204	2,826	3,204	3,044
23,900	**23,950**	3,211	2,834	3,211	3,051
23,950	**24,000**	3,219	2,841	3,219	3,059
24,000					
24,000	**24,050**	3,226	2,849	3,226	3,066
24,050	**24,100**	3,234	2,856	3,234	3,074
24,100	**24,150**	3,241	2,864	3,241	3,081
24,150	**24,200**	3,249	2,871	3,249	3,089
24,200	**24,250**	3,256	2,879	3,256	3,096
24,250	**24,300**	3,264	2,886	3,264	3,104
24,300	**24,350**	3,271	2,894	3,271	3,111
24,350	**24,400**	3,279	2,901	3,279	3,119
24,400	**24,450**	3,286	2,909	3,286	3,126
24,450	**24,500**	3,294	2,916	3,294	3,134
24,500	**24,550**	3,301	2,924	3,301	3,141
24,550	**24,600**	3,309	2,931	3,309	3,149
24,600	**24,650**	3,316	2,939	3,316	3,156
24,650	**24,700**	3,324	2,946	3,324	3,164
24,700	**24,750**	3,331	2,954	3,331	3,171
24,750	**24,800**	3,339	2,961	3,339	3,179
24,800	**24,850**	3,346	2,969	3,346	3,186
24,850	**24,900**	3,354	2,976	3,354	3,194
24,900	**24,950**	3,361	2,984	3,361	3,201
24,950	**25,000**	3,369	2,991	3,369	3,209
25,000					
25,000	**25,050**	3,376	2,999	3,376	3,216
25,050	**25,100**	3,384	3,006	3,384	3,224
25,100	**25,150**	3,391	3,014	3,391	3,231
25,150	**25,200**	3,399	3,021	3,399	3,239
25,200	**25,250**	3,406	3,029	3,406	3,246
25,250	**25,300**	3,414	3,036	3,414	3,254
25,300	**25,350**	3,421	3,044	3,421	3,261
25,350	**25,400**	3,429	3,051	3,429	3,269
25,400	**25,450**	3,436	3,059	3,436	3,276
25,450	**25,500**	3,444	3,066	3,444	3,284
25,500	**25,550**	3,451	3,074	3,451	3,291
25,550	**25,600**	3,459	3,081	3,459	3,299
25,600	**25,650**	3,466	3,089	3,466	3,306
25,650	**25,700**	3,474	3,096	3,474	3,314
25,700	**25,750**	3,481	3,104	3,481	3,321
25,750	**25,800**	3,489	3,111	3,489	3,329
25,800	**25,850**	3,496	3,119	3,496	3,336
25,850	**25,900**	3,504	3,126	3,504	3,344
25,900	**25,950**	3,511	3,134	3,511	3,351
25,950	**26,000**	3,519	3,141	3,519	3,359

If line 43 (taxable income) is—		And you are—			
At least	But less than	Single	Married filing jointly *	Married filing sepa-rately	Head of a house-hold
		Your tax is—			
26,000					
26,000	**26,050**	3,526	3,149	3,526	3,366
26,050	**26,100**	3,534	3,156	3,534	3,374
26,100	**26,150**	3,541	3,164	3,541	3,381
26,150	**26,200**	3,549	3,171	3,549	3,389
26,200	**26,250**	3,556	3,179	3,556	3,396
26,250	**26,300**	3,564	3,186	3,564	3,404
26,300	**26,350**	3,571	3,194	3,571	3,411
26,350	**26,400**	3,579	3,201	3,579	3,419
26,400	**26,450**	3,586	3,209	3,586	3,426
26,450	**26,500**	3,594	3,216	3,594	3,434
26,500	**26,550**	3,601	3,224	3,601	3,441
26,550	**26,600**	3,609	3,231	3,609	3,449
26,600	**26,650**	3,616	3,239	3,616	3,456
26,650	**26,700**	3,624	3,246	3,624	3,464
26,700	**26,750**	3,631	3,254	3,631	3,471
26,750	**26,800**	3,639	3,261	3,639	3,479
26,800	**26,850**	3,646	3,269	3,646	3,486
26,850	**26,900**	3,654	3,276	3,654	3,494
26,900	**26,950**	3,661	3,284	3,661	3,501
26,950	**27,000**	3,669	3,291	3,669	3,509
27,000					
27,000	**27,050**	3,676	3,299	3,676	3,516
27,050	**27,100**	3,684	3,306	3,684	3,524
27,100	**27,150**	3,691	3,314	3,691	3,531
27,150	**27,200**	3,699	3,321	3,699	3,539
27,200	**27,250**	3,706	3,329	3,706	3,546
27,250	**27,300**	3,714	3,336	3,714	3,554
27,300	**27,350**	3,721	3,344	3,721	3,561
27,350	**27,400**	3,729	3,351	3,729	3,569
27,400	**27,450**	3,736	3,359	3,736	3,576
27,450	**27,500**	3,744	3,366	3,744	3,584
27,500	**27,550**	3,751	3,374	3,751	3,591
27,550	**27,600**	3,759	3,381	3,759	3,599
27,600	**27,650**	3,766	3,389	3,766	3,606
27,650	**27,700**	3,774	3,396	3,774	3,614
27,700	**27,750**	3,781	3,404	3,781	3,621
27,750	**27,800**	3,789	3,411	3,789	3,629
27,800	**27,850**	3,796	3,419	3,796	3,636
27,850	**27,900**	3,804	3,426	3,804	3,644
27,900	**27,950**	3,811	3,434	3,811	3,651
27,950	**28,000**	3,819	3,441	3,819	3,659
28,000					
28,000	**28,050**	3,826	3,449	3,826	3,666
28,050	**28,100**	3,834	3,456	3,834	3,674
28,100	**28,150**	3,841	3,464	3,841	3,681
28,150	**28,200**	3,849	3,471	3,849	3,689
28,200	**28,250**	3,856	3,479	3,856	3,696
28,250	**28,300**	3,864	3,486	3,864	3,704
28,300	**28,350**	3,871	3,494	3,871	3,711
28,350	**28,400**	3,879	3,501	3,879	3,719
28,400	**28,450**	3,886	3,509	3,886	3,726
28,450	**28,500**	3,894	3,516	3,894	3,734
28,500	**28,550**	3,901	3,524	3,901	3,741
28,550	**28,600**	3,909	3,531	3,909	3,749
28,600	**28,650**	3,916	3,539	3,916	3,756
28,650	**28,700**	3,924	3,546	3,924	3,764
28,700	**28,750**	3,931	3,554	3,931	3,771
28,750	**28,800**	3,939	3,561	3,939	3,779
28,800	**28,850**	3,946	3,569	3,946	3,786
28,850	**28,900**	3,954	3,576	3,954	3,794
28,900	**28,950**	3,961	3,584	3,961	3,801
28,950	**29,000**	3,969	3,591	3,969	3,809

If line 43 (taxable income) is—		And you are—			
At least	But less than	Single	Married filing jointly *	Married filing sepa-rately	Head of a house-hold
		Your tax is—			
29,000					
29,000	**29,050**	3,976	3,599	3,976	3,816
29,050	**29,100**	3,984	3,606	3,984	3,824
29,100	**29,150**	3,991	3,614	3,991	3,831
29,150	**29,200**	3,999	3,621	3,999	3,839
29,200	**29,250**	4,006	3,629	4,006	3,846
29,250	**29,300**	4,014	3,636	4,014	3,854
29,300	**29,350**	4,021	3,644	4,021	3,861
29,350	**29,400**	4,029	3,651	4,029	3,869
29,400	**29,450**	4,036	3,659	4,036	3,876
29,450	**29,500**	4,044	3,666	4,044	3,884
29,500	**29,550**	4,051	3,674	4,051	3,891
29,550	**29,600**	4,059	3,681	4,059	3,899
29,600	**29,650**	4,066	3,689	4,066	3,906
29,650	**29,700**	4,074	3,696	4,074	3,914
29,700	**29,750**	4,081	3,704	4,081	3,921
29,750	**29,800**	4,089	3,711	4,089	3,929
29,800	**29,850**	4,096	3,719	4,096	3,936
29,850	**29,900**	4,104	3,726	4,104	3,944
29,900	**29,950**	4,111	3,734	4,111	3,951
29,950	**30,000**	4,119	3,741	4,119	3,959
30,000					
30,000	**30,050**	4,126	3,749	4,126	3,966
30,050	**30,100**	4,134	3,756	4,134	3,974
30,100	**30,150**	4,141	3,764	4,141	3,981
30,150	**30,200**	4,149	3,771	4,149	3,989
30,200	**30,250**	4,156	3,779	4,156	3,996
30,250	**30,300**	4,164	3,786	4,164	4,004
30,300	**30,350**	4,171	3,794	4,171	4,011
30,350	**30,400**	4,179	3,801	4,179	4,019
30,400	**30,450**	4,186	3,809	4,186	4,026
30,450	**30,500**	4,194	3,816	4,194	4,034
30,500	**30,550**	4,201	3,824	4,201	4,041
30,550	**30,600**	4,209	3,831	4,209	4,049
30,600	**30,650**	4,216	3,839	4,216	4,056
30,650	**30,700**	4,226	3,846	4,226	4,064
30,700	**30,750**	4,239	3,854	4,239	4,071
30,750	**30,800**	4,251	3,861	4,251	4,079
30,800	**30,850**	4,264	3,869	4,264	4,086
30,850	**30,900**	4,276	3,876	4,276	4,094
30,900	**30,950**	4,289	3,884	4,289	4,101
30,950	**31,000**	4,301	3,891	4,301	4,109
31,000					
31,000	**31,050**	4,314	3,899	4,314	4,116
31,050	**31,100**	4,326	3,906	4,326	4,124
31,100	**31,150**	4,339	3,914	4,339	4,131
31,150	**31,200**	4,351	3,921	4,351	4,139
31,200	**31,250**	4,364	3,929	4,364	4,146
31,250	**31,300**	4,376	3,936	4,376	4,154
31,300	**31,350**	4,389	3,944	4,389	4,161
31,350	**31,400**	4,401	3,951	4,401	4,169
31,400	**31,450**	4,414	3,959	4,414	4,176
31,450	**31,500**	4,426	3,966	4,426	4,184
31,500	**31,550**	4,439	3,974	4,439	4,191
31,550	**31,600**	4,451	3,981	4,451	4,199
31,600	**31,650**	4,464	3,989	4,464	4,206
31,650	**31,700**	4,476	3,996	4,476	4,214
31,700	**31,750**	4,489	4,004	4,489	4,221
31,750	**31,800**	4,501	4,011	4,501	4,229
31,800	**31,850**	4,514	4,019	4,514	4,236
31,850	**31,900**	4,526	4,026	4,526	4,244
31,900	**31,950**	4,539	4,034	4,539	4,251
31,950	**32,000**	4,551	4,041	4,551	4,259

* This column must also be used by a qualifying widow(er)

(Continued on page 27)

2006 Tax Table–*Continued*

If line 43 (taxable income) is—		And you are—			
At least	But less than	Single	Married filing jointly *	Married filing sepa-rately	Head of a house-hold
		Your tax is—			
32,000					
32,000	**32,050**	4,564	4,049	4,564	4,266
32,050	**32,100**	4,576	4,056	4,576	4,274
32,100	**32,150**	4,589	4,064	4,589	4,281
32,150	**32,200**	4,601	4,071	4,601	4,289
32,200	**32,250**	4,614	4,079	4,614	4,296
32,250	**32,300**	4,626	4,086	4,626	4,304
32,300	**32,350**	4,639	4,094	4,639	4,311
32,350	**32,400**	4,651	4,101	4,651	4,319
32,400	**32,450**	4,664	4,109	4,664	4,326
32,450	**32,500**	4,676	4,116	4,676	4,334
32,500	**32,550**	4,689	4,124	4,689	4,341
32,550	**32,600**	4,701	4,131	4,701	4,349
32,600	**32,650**	4,714	4,139	4,714	4,356
32,650	**32,700**	4,726	4,146	4,726	4,364
32,700	**32,750**	4,739	4,154	4,739	4,371
32,750	**32,800**	4,751	4,161	4,751	4,379
32,800	**32,850**	4,764	4,169	4,764	4,386
32,850	**32,900**	4,776	4,176	4,776	4,394
32,900	**32,950**	4,789	4,184	4,789	4,401
32,950	**33,000**	4,801	4,191	4,801	4,409
33,000					
33,000	**33,050**	4,814	4,199	4,814	4,416
33,050	**33,100**	4,826	4,206	4,826	4,424
33,100	**33,150**	4,839	4,214	4,839	4,431
33,150	**33,200**	4,851	4,221	4,851	4,439
33,200	**33,250**	4,864	4,229	4,864	4,446
33,250	**33,300**	4,876	4,236	4,876	4,454
33,300	**33,350**	4,889	4,244	4,889	4,461
33,350	**33,400**	4,901	4,251	4,901	4,469
33,400	**33,450**	4,914	4,259	4,914	4,476
33,450	**33,500**	4,926	4,266	4,926	4,484
33,500	**33,550**	4,939	4,274	4,939	4,491
33,550	**33,600**	4,951	4,281	4,951	4,499
33,600	**33,650**	4,964	4,289	4,964	4,506
33,650	**33,700**	4,976	4,296	4,976	4,514
33,700	**33,750**	4,989	4,304	4,989	4,521
33,750	**33,800**	5,001	4,311	5,001	4,529
33,800	**33,850**	5,014	4,319	5,014	4,536
33,850	**33,900**	5,026	4,326	5,026	4,544
33,900	**33,950**	5,039	4,334	5,039	4,551
33,950	**34,000**	5,051	4,341	5,051	4,559
34,000					
34,000	**34,050**	5,064	4,349	5,064	4,566
34,050	**34,100**	5,076	4,356	5,076	4,574
34,100	**34,150**	5,089	4,364	5,089	4,581
34,150	**34,200**	5,101	4,371	5,101	4,589
34,200	**34,250**	5,114	4,379	5,114	4,596
34,250	**34,300**	5,126	4,386	5,126	4,604
34,300	**34,350**	5,139	4,394	5,139	4,611
34,350	**34,400**	5,151	4,401	5,151	4,619
34,400	**34,450**	5,164	4,409	5,164	4,626
34,450	**34,500**	5,176	4,416	5,176	4,634
34,500	**34,550**	5,189	4,424	5,189	4,641
34,550	**34,600**	5,201	4,431	5,201	4,649
34,600	**34,650**	5,214	4,439	5,214	4,656
34,650	**34,700**	5,226	4,446	5,226	4,664
34,700	**34,750**	5,239	4,454	5,239	4,671
34,750	**34,800**	5,251	4,461	5,251	4,679
34,800	**34,850**	5,264	4,469	5,264	4,686
34,850	**34,900**	5,276	4,476	5,276	4,694
34,900	**34,950**	5,289	4,484	5,289	4,701
34,950	**35,000**	5,301	4,491	5,301	4,709

If line 43 (taxable income) is—		And you are—			
At least	But less than	Single	Married filing jointly *	Married filing sepa-rately	Head of a house-hold
		Your tax is—			
35,000					
35,000	**35,050**	5,314	4,499	5,314	4,716
35,050	**35,100**	5,326	4,506	5,326	4,724
35,100	**35,150**	5,339	4,514	5,339	4,731
35,150	**35,200**	5,351	4,521	5,351	4,739
35,200	**35,250**	5,364	4,529	5,364	4,746
35,250	**35,300**	5,376	4,536	5,376	4,754
35,300	**35,350**	5,389	4,544	5,389	4,761
35,350	**35,400**	5,401	4,551	5,401	4,769
35,400	**35,450**	5,414	4,559	5,414	4,776
35,450	**35,500**	5,426	4,566	5,426	4,784
35,500	**35,550**	5,439	4,574	5,439	4,791
35,550	**35,600**	5,451	4,581	5,451	4,799
35,600	**35,650**	5,464	4,589	5,464	4,806
35,650	**35,700**	5,476	4,596	5,476	4,814
35,700	**35,750**	5,489	4,604	5,489	4,821
35,750	**35,800**	5,501	4,611	5,501	4,829
35,800	**35,850**	5,514	4,619	5,514	4,836
35,850	**35,900**	5,526	4,626	5,526	4,844
35,900	**35,950**	5,539	4,634	5,539	4,851
35,950	**36,000**	5,551	4,641	5,551	4,859
36,000					
36,000	**36,050**	5,564	4,649	5,564	4,866
36,050	**36,100**	5,576	4,656	5,576	4,874
36,100	**36,150**	5,589	4,664	5,589	4,881
36,150	**36,200**	5,601	4,671	5,601	4,889
36,200	**36,250**	5,614	4,679	5,614	4,896
36,250	**36,300**	5,626	4,686	5,626	4,904
36,300	**36,350**	5,639	4,694	5,639	4,911
36,350	**36,400**	5,651	4,701	5,651	4,919
36,400	**36,450**	5,664	4,709	5,664	4,926
36,450	**36,500**	5,676	4,716	5,676	4,934
36,500	**36,550**	5,689	4,724	5,689	4,941
36,550	**36,600**	5,701	4,731	5,701	4,949
36,600	**36,650**	5,714	4,739	5,714	4,956
36,650	**36,700**	5,726	4,746	5,726	4,964
36,700	**36,750**	5,739	4,754	5,739	4,971
36,750	**36,800**	5,751	4,761	5,751	4,979
36,800	**36,850**	5,764	4,769	5,764	4,986
36,850	**36,900**	5,776	4,776	5,776	4,994
36,900	**36,950**	5,789	4,784	5,789	5,001
36,950	**37,000**	5,801	4,791	5,801	5,009
37,000					
37,000	**37,050**	5,814	4,799	5,814	5,016
37,050	**37,100**	5,826	4,806	5,826	5,024
37,100	**37,150**	5,839	4,814	5,839	5,031
37,150	**37,200**	5,851	4,821	5,851	5,039
37,200	**37,250**	5,864	4,829	5,864	5,046
37,250	**37,300**	5,876	4,836	5,876	5,054
37,300	**37,350**	5,889	4,844	5,889	5,061
37,350	**37,400**	5,901	4,851	5,901	5,069
37,400	**37,450**	5,914	4,859	5,914	5,076
37,450	**37,500**	5,926	4,866	5,926	5,084
37,500	**37,550**	5,939	4,874	5,939	5,091
37,550	**37,600**	5,951	4,881	5,951	5,099
37,600	**37,650**	5,964	4,889	5,964	5,106
37,650	**37,700**	5,976	4,896	5,976	5,114
37,700	**37,750**	5,989	4,904	5,989	5,121
37,750	**37,800**	6,001	4,911	6,001	5,129
37,800	**37,850**	6,014	4,919	6,014	5,136
37,850	**37,900**	6,026	4,926	6,026	5,144
37,900	**37,950**	6,039	4,934	6,039	5,151
37,950	**38,000**	6,051	4,941	6,051	5,159

If line 43 (taxable income) is—		And you are—			
At least	But less than	Single	Married filing jointly *	Married filing sepa-rately	Head of a house-hold
		Your tax is—			
38,000					
38,000	**38,050**	6,064	4,949	6,064	5,166
38,050	**38,100**	6,076	4,956	6,076	5,174
38,100	**38,150**	6,089	4,964	6,089	5,181
38,150	**38,200**	6,101	4,971	6,101	5,189
38,200	**38,250**	6,114	4,979	6,114	5,196
38,250	**38,300**	6,126	4,986	6,126	5,204
38,300	**38,350**	6,139	4,994	6,139	5,211
38,350	**38,400**	6,151	5,001	6,151	5,219
38,400	**38,450**	6,164	5,009	6,164	5,226
38,450	**38,500**	6,176	5,016	6,176	5,234
38,500	**38,550**	6,189	5,024	6,189	5,241
38,550	**38,600**	6,201	5,031	6,201	5,249
38,600	**38,650**	6,214	5,039	6,214	5,256
38,650	**38,700**	6,226	5,046	6,226	5,264
38,700	**38,750**	6,239	5,054	6,239	5,271
38,750	**38,800**	6,251	5,061	6,251	5,279
38,800	**38,850**	6,264	5,069	6,264	5,286
38,850	**38,900**	6,276	5,076	6,276	5,294
38,900	**38,950**	6,289	5,084	6,289	5,301
38,950	**39,000**	6,301	5,091	6,301	5,309
39,000					
39,000	**39,050**	6,314	5,099	6,314	5,316
39,050	**39,100**	6,326	5,106	6,326	5,324
39,100	**39,150**	6,339	5,114	6,339	5,331
39,150	**39,200**	6,351	5,121	6,351	5,339
39,200	**39,250**	6,364	5,129	6,364	5,346
39,250	**39,300**	6,376	5,136	6,376	5,354
39,300	**39,350**	6,389	5,144	6,389	5,361
39,350	**39,400**	6,401	5,151	6,401	5,369
39,400	**39,450**	6,414	5,159	6,414	5,376
39,450	**39,500**	6,426	5,166	6,426	5,384
39,500	**39,550**	6,439	5,174	6,439	5,391
39,550	**39,600**	6,451	5,181	6,451	5,399
39,600	**39,650**	6,464	5,189	6,464	5,406
39,650	**39,700**	6,476	5,196	6,476	5,414
39,700	**39,750**	6,489	5,204	6,489	5,421
39,750	**39,800**	6,501	5,211	6,501	5,429
39,800	**39,850**	6,514	5,219	6,514	5,436
39,850	**39,900**	6,526	5,226	6,526	5,444
39,900	**39,950**	6,539	5,234	6,539	5,451
39,950	**40,000**	6,551	5,241	6,551	5,459
40,000					
40,000	**40,050**	6,564	5,249	6,564	5,466
40,050	**40,100**	6,576	5,256	6,576	5,474
40,100	**40,150**	6,589	5,264	6,589	5,481
40,150	**40,200**	6,601	5,271	6,601	5,489
40,200	**40,250**	6,614	5,279	6,614	5,496
40,250	**40,300**	6,626	5,286	6,626	5,504
40,300	**40,350**	6,639	5,294	6,639	5,511
40,350	**40,400**	6,651	5,301	6,651	5,519
40,400	**40,450**	6,664	5,309	6,664	5,526
40,450	**40,500**	6,676	5,316	6,676	5,534
40,500	**40,550**	6,689	5,324	6,689	5,541
40,550	**40,600**	6,701	5,331	6,701	5,549
40,600	**40,650**	6,714	5,339	6,714	5,556
40,650	**40,700**	6,726	5,346	6,726	5,564
40,700	**40,750**	6,739	5,354	6,739	5,571
40,750	**40,800**	6,751	5,361	6,751	5,579
40,800	**40,850**	6,764	5,369	6,764	5,586
40,850	**40,900**	6,776	5,376	6,776	5,594
40,900	**40,950**	6,789	5,384	6,789	5,601
40,950	**41,000**	6,801	5,391	6,801	5,609

* This column must also be used by a qualifying widow(er)

(Continued on page 28)

2006 Tax Table–*Continued*

If line 43 (taxable income) is—		And you are—			
At least	But less than	Single	Married filing jointly *	Married filing separately	Head of a household
		Your tax is—			
41,000					
41,000	41,050	6,814	5,399	6,814	5,616
41,050	41,100	6,826	5,406	6,826	5,626
41,100	41,150	6,839	5,414	6,839	5,639
41,150	41,200	6,851	5,421	6,851	5,651
41,200	41,250	6,864	5,429	6,864	5,664
41,250	41,300	6,876	5,436	6,876	5,676
41,300	41,350	6,889	5,444	6,889	5,689
41,350	41,400	6,901	5,451	6,901	5,701
41,400	41,450	6,914	5,459	6,914	5,714
41,450	41,500	6,926	5,466	6,926	5,726
41,500	41,550	6,939	5,474	6,939	5,739
41,550	41,600	6,951	5,481	6,951	5,751
41,600	41,650	6,964	5,489	6,964	5,764
41,650	41,700	6,976	5,496	6,976	5,776
41,700	41,750	6,989	5,504	6,989	5,789
41,750	41,800	7,001	5,511	7,001	5,801
41,800	41,850	7,014	5,519	7,014	5,814
41,850	41,900	7,026	5,526	7,026	5,826
41,900	41,950	7,039	5,534	7,039	5,839
41,950	42,000	7,051	5,541	7,051	5,851
42,000					
42,000	42,050	7,064	5,549	7,064	5,864
42,050	42,100	7,076	5,556	7,076	5,876
42,100	42,150	7,089	5,564	7,089	5,889
42,150	42,200	7,101	5,571	7,101	5,901
42,200	42,250	7,114	5,579	7,114	5,914
42,250	42,300	7,126	5,586	7,126	5,926
42,300	42,350	7,139	5,594	7,139	5,939
42,350	42,400	7,151	5,601	7,151	5,951
42,400	42,450	7,164	5,609	7,164	5,964
42,450	42,500	7,176	5,616	7,176	5,976
42,500	42,550	7,189	5,624	7,189	5,989
42,550	42,600	7,201	5,631	7,201	6,001
42,600	42,650	7,214	5,639	7,214	6,014
42,650	42,700	7,226	5,646	7,226	6,026
42,700	42,750	7,239	5,654	7,239	6,039
42,750	42,800	7,251	5,661	7,251	6,051
42,800	42,850	7,264	5,669	7,264	6,064
42,850	42,900	7,276	5,676	7,276	6,076
42,900	42,950	7,289	5,684	7,289	6,089
42,950	43,000	7,301	5,691	7,301	6,101
43,000					
43,000	43,050	7,314	5,699	7,314	6,114
43,050	43,100	7,326	5,706	7,326	6,126
43,100	43,150	7,339	5,714	7,339	6,139
43,150	43,200	7,351	5,721	7,351	6,151
43,200	43,250	7,364	5,729	7,364	6,164
43,250	43,300	7,376	5,736	7,376	6,176
43,300	43,350	7,389	5,744	7,389	6,189
43,350	43,400	7,401	5,751	7,401	6,201
43,400	43,450	7,414	5,759	7,414	6,214
43,450	43,500	7,426	5,766	7,426	6,226
43,500	43,550	7,439	5,774	7,439	6,239
43,550	43,600	7,451	5,781	7,451	6,251
43,600	43,650	7,464	5,789	7,464	6,264
43,650	43,700	7,476	5,796	7,476	6,276
43,700	43,750	7,489	5,804	7,489	6,289
43,750	43,800	7,501	5,811	7,501	6,301
43,800	43,850	7,514	5,819	7,514	6,314
43,850	43,900	7,526	5,826	7,526	6,326
43,900	43,950	7,539	5,834	7,539	6,339
43,950	44,000	7,551	5,841	7,551	6,351

If line 43 (taxable income) is—		And you are—			
At least	But less than	Single	Married filing jointly *	Married filing separately	Head of a household
		Your tax is—			
44,000					
44,000	44,050	7,564	5,849	7,564	6,364
44,050	44,100	7,576	5,856	7,576	6,376
44,100	44,150	7,589	5,864	7,589	6,389
44,150	44,200	7,601	5,871	7,601	6,401
44,200	44,250	7,614	5,879	7,614	6,414
44,250	44,300	7,626	5,886	7,626	6,426
44,300	44,350	7,639	5,894	7,639	6,439
44,350	44,400	7,651	5,901	7,651	6,451
44,400	44,450	7,664	5,909	7,664	6,464
44,450	44,500	7,676	5,916	7,676	6,476
44,500	44,550	7,689	5,924	7,689	6,489
44,550	44,600	7,701	5,931	7,701	6,501
44,600	44,650	7,714	5,939	7,714	6,514
44,650	44,700	7,726	5,946	7,726	6,526
44,700	44,750	7,739	5,954	7,739	6,539
44,750	44,800	7,751	5,961	7,751	6,551
44,800	44,850	7,764	5,969	7,764	6,564
44,850	44,900	7,776	5,976	7,776	6,576
44,900	44,950	7,789	5,984	7,789	6,589
44,950	45,000	7,801	5,991	7,801	6,601
45,000					
45,000	45,050	7,814	5,999	7,814	6,614
45,050	45,100	7,826	6,006	7,826	6,626
45,100	45,150	7,839	6,014	7,839	6,639
45,150	45,200	7,851	6,021	7,851	6,651
45,200	45,250	7,864	6,029	7,864	6,664
45,250	45,300	7,876	6,036	7,876	6,676
45,300	45,350	7,889	6,044	7,889	6,689
45,350	45,400	7,901	6,051	7,901	6,701
45,400	45,450	7,914	6,059	7,914	6,714
45,450	45,500	7,926	6,066	7,926	6,726
45,500	45,550	7,939	6,074	7,939	6,739
45,550	45,600	7,951	6,081	7,951	6,751
45,600	45,650	7,964	6,089	7,964	6,764
45,650	45,700	7,976	6,096	7,976	6,776
45,700	45,750	7,989	6,104	7,989	6,789
45,750	45,800	8,001	6,111	8,001	6,801
45,800	45,850	8,014	6,119	8,014	6,814
45,850	45,900	8,026	6,126	8,026	6,826
45,900	45,950	8,039	6,134	8,039	6,839
45,950	46,000	8,051	6,141	8,051	6,851
46,000					
46,000	46,050	8,064	6,149	8,064	6,864
46,050	46,100	8,076	6,156	8,076	6,876
46,100	46,150	8,089	6,164	8,089	6,889
46,150	46,200	8,101	6,171	8,101	6,901
46,200	46,250	8,114	6,179	8,114	6,914
46,250	46,300	8,126	6,186	8,126	6,926
46,300	46,350	8,139	6,194	8,139	6,939
46,350	46,400	8,151	6,201	8,151	6,951
46,400	46,450	8,164	6,209	8,164	6,964
46,450	46,500	8,176	6,216	8,176	6,976
46,500	46,550	8,189	6,224	8,189	6,989
46,550	46,600	8,201	6,231	8,201	7,001
46,600	46,650	8,214	6,239	8,214	7,014
46,650	46,700	8,226	6,246	8,226	7,026
46,700	46,750	8,239	6,254	8,239	7,039
46,750	46,800	8,251	6,261	8,251	7,051
46,800	46,850	8,264	6,269	8,264	7,064
46,850	46,900	8,276	6,276	8,276	7,076
46,900	46,950	8,289	6,284	8,289	7,089
46,950	47,000	8,301	6,291	8,301	7,101

If line 43 (taxable income) is—		And you are—			
At least	But less than	Single	Married filing jointly *	Married filing separately	Head of a household
		Your tax is—			
47,000					
47,000	47,050	8,314	6,299	8,314	7,114
47,050	47,100	8,326	6,306	8,326	7,126
47,100	47,150	8,339	6,314	8,339	7,139
47,150	47,200	8,351	6,321	8,351	7,151
47,200	47,250	8,364	6,329	8,364	7,164
47,250	47,300	8,376	6,336	8,376	7,176
47,300	47,350	8,389	6,344	8,389	7,189
47,350	47,400	8,401	6,351	8,401	7,201
47,400	47,450	8,414	6,359	8,414	7,214
47,450	47,500	8,426	6,366	8,426	7,226
47,500	47,550	8,439	6,374	8,439	7,239
47,550	47,600	8,451	6,381	8,451	7,251
47,600	47,650	8,464	6,389	8,464	7,264
47,650	47,700	8,476	6,396	8,476	7,276
47,700	47,750	8,489	6,404	8,489	7,289
47,750	47,800	8,501	6,411	8,501	7,301
47,800	47,850	8,514	6,419	8,514	7,314
47,850	47,900	8,526	6,426	8,526	7,326
47,900	47,950	8,539	6,434	8,539	7,339
47,950	48,000	8,551	6,441	8,551	7,351
48,000					
48,000	48,050	8,564	6,449	8,564	7,364
48,050	48,100	8,576	6,456	8,576	7,376
48,100	48,150	8,589	6,464	8,589	7,389
48,150	48,200	8,601	6,471	8,601	7,401
48,200	48,250	8,614	6,479	8,614	7,414
48,250	48,300	8,626	6,486	8,626	7,426
48,300	48,350	8,639	6,494	8,639	7,439
48,350	48,400	8,651	6,501	8,651	7,451
48,400	48,450	8,664	6,509	8,664	7,464
48,450	48,500	8,676	6,516	8,676	7,476
48,500	48,550	8,689	6,524	8,689	7,489
48,550	48,600	8,701	6,531	8,701	7,501
48,600	48,650	8,714	6,539	8,714	7,514
48,650	48,700	8,726	6,546	8,726	7,526
48,700	48,750	8,739	6,554	8,739	7,539
48,750	48,800	8,751	6,561	8,751	7,551
48,800	48,850	8,764	6,569	8,764	7,564
48,850	48,900	8,776	6,576	8,776	7,576
48,900	48,950	8,789	6,584	8,789	7,589
48,950	49,000	8,801	6,591	8,801	7,601
49,000					
49,000	49,050	8,814	6,599	8,814	7,614
49,050	49,100	8,826	6,606	8,826	7,626
49,100	49,150	8,839	6,614	8,839	7,639
49,150	49,200	8,851	6,621	8,851	7,651
49,200	49,250	8,864	6,629	8,864	7,664
49,250	49,300	8,876	6,636	8,876	7,676
49,300	49,350	8,889	6,644	8,889	7,689
49,350	49,400	8,901	6,651	8,901	7,701
49,400	49,450	8,914	6,659	8,914	7,714
49,450	49,500	8,926	6,666	8,926	7,726
49,500	49,550	8,939	6,674	8,939	7,739
49,550	49,600	8,951	6,681	8,951	7,751
49,600	49,650	8,964	6,689	8,964	7,764
49,650	49,700	8,976	6,696	8,976	7,776
49,700	49,750	8,989	6,704	8,989	7,789
49,750	49,800	9,001	6,711	9,001	7,801
49,800	49,850	9,014	6,719	9,014	7,814
49,850	49,900	9,026	6,726	9,026	7,826
49,900	49,950	9,039	6,734	9,039	7,839
49,950	50,000	9,051	6,741	9,051	7,851

* This column must also be used by a qualifying widow(er)

(Continued on page 29)

2006 Tax Table–*Continued*

If line 43 (taxable income) is—		And you are—			
At least	But less than	Single	Married filing jointly *	Married filing sepa-rately	Head of a house-hold
		Your tax is—			
50,000					
50,000	**50,050**	9,064	6,749	9,064	7,864
50,050	**50,100**	9,076	6,756	9,076	7,876
50,100	**50,150**	9,089	6,764	9,089	7,889
50,150	**50,200**	9,101	6,771	9,101	7,901
50,200	**50,250**	9,114	6,779	9,114	7,914
50,250	**50,300**	9,126	6,786	9,126	7,926
50,300	**50,350**	9,139	6,794	9,139	7,939
50,350	**50,400**	9,151	6,801	9,151	7,951
50,400	**50,450**	9,164	6,809	9,164	7,964
50,450	**50,500**	9,176	6,816	9,176	7,976
50,500	**50,550**	9,189	6,824	9,189	7,989
50,550	**50,600**	9,201	6,831	9,201	8,001
50,600	**50,650**	9,214	6,839	9,214	8,014
50,650	**50,700**	9,226	6,846	9,226	8,026
50,700	**50,750**	9,239	6,854	9,239	8,039
50,750	**50,800**	9,251	6,861	9,251	8,051
50,800	**50,850**	9,264	6,869	9,264	8,064
50,850	**50,900**	9,276	6,876	9,276	8,076
50,900	**50,950**	9,289	6,884	9,289	8,089
50,950	**51,000**	9,301	6,891	9,301	8,101
51,000					
51,000	**51,050**	9,314	6,899	9,314	8,114
51,050	**51,100**	9,326	6,906	9,326	8,126
51,100	**51,150**	9,339	6,914	9,339	8,139
51,150	**51,200**	9,351	6,921	9,351	8,151
51,200	**51,250**	9,364	6,929	9,364	8,164
51,250	**51,300**	9,376	6,936	9,376	8,176
51,300	**51,350**	9,389	6,944	9,389	8,189
51,350	**51,400**	9,401	6,951	9,401	8,201
51,400	**51,450**	9,414	6,959	9,414	8,214
51,450	**51,500**	9,426	6,966	9,426	8,226
51,500	**51,550**	9,439	6,974	9,439	8,239
51,550	**51,600**	9,451	6,981	9,451	8,251
51,600	**51,650**	9,464	6,989	9,464	8,264
51,650	**51,700**	9,476	6,996	9,476	8,276
51,700	**51,750**	9,489	7,004	9,489	8,289
51,750	**51,800**	9,501	7,011	9,501	8,301
51,800	**51,850**	9,514	7,019	9,514	8,314
51,850	**51,900**	9,526	7,026	9,526	8,326
51,900	**51,950**	9,539	7,034	9,539	8,339
51,950	**52,000**	9,551	7,041	9,551	8,351
52,000					
52,000	**52,050**	9,564	7,049	9,564	8,364
52,050	**52,100**	9,576	7,056	9,576	8,376
52,100	**52,150**	9,589	7,064	9,589	8,389
52,150	**52,200**	9,601	7,071	9,601	8,401
52,200	**52,250**	9,614	7,079	9,614	8,414
52,250	**52,300**	9,626	7,086	9,626	8,426
52,300	**52,350**	9,639	7,094	9,639	8,439
52,350	**52,400**	9,651	7,101	9,651	8,451
52,400	**52,450**	9,664	7,109	9,664	8,464
52,450	**52,500**	9,676	7,116	9,676	8,476
52,500	**52,550**	9,689	7,124	9,689	8,489
52,550	**52,600**	9,701	7,131	9,701	8,501
52,600	**52,650**	9,714	7,139	9,714	8,514
52,650	**52,700**	9,726	7,146	9,726	8,526
52,700	**52,750**	9,739	7,154	9,739	8,539
52,750	**52,800**	9,751	7,161	9,751	8,551
52,800	**52,850**	9,764	7,169	9,764	8,564
52,850	**52,900**	9,776	7,176	9,776	8,576
52,900	**52,950**	9,789	7,184	9,789	8,589
52,950	**53,000**	9,801	7,191	9,801	8,601

If line 43 (taxable income) is—		And you are—			
At least	But less than	Single	Married filing jointly *	Married filing sepa-rately	Head of a house-hold
		Your tax is—			
53,000					
53,000	**53,050**	9,814	7,199	9,814	8,614
53,050	**53,100**	9,826	7,206	9,826	8,626
53,100	**53,150**	9,839	7,214	9,839	8,639
53,150	**53,200**	9,851	7,221	9,851	8,651
53,200	**53,250**	9,864	7,229	9,864	8,664
53,250	**53,300**	9,876	7,236	9,876	8,676
53,300	**53,350**	9,889	7,244	9,889	8,689
53,350	**53,400**	9,901	7,251	9,901	8,701
53,400	**53,450**	9,914	7,259	9,914	8,714
53,450	**53,500**	9,926	7,266	9,926	8,726
53,500	**53,550**	9,939	7,274	9,939	8,739
53,550	**53,600**	9,951	7,281	9,951	8,751
53,600	**53,650**	9,964	7,289	9,964	8,764
53,650	**53,700**	9,976	7,296	9,976	8,776
53,700	**53,750**	9,989	7,304	9,989	8,789
53,750	**53,800**	10,001	7,311	10,001	8,801
53,800	**53,850**	10,014	7,319	10,014	8,814
53,850	**53,900**	10,026	7,326	10,026	8,826
53,900	**53,950**	10,039	7,334	10,039	8,839
53,950	**54,000**	10,051	7,341	10,051	8,851
54,000					
54,000	**54,050**	10,064	7,349	10,064	8,864
54,050	**54,100**	10,076	7,356	10,076	8,876
54,100	**54,150**	10,089	7,364	10,089	8,889
54,150	**54,200**	10,101	7,371	10,101	8,901
54,200	**54,250**	10,114	7,379	10,114	8,914
54,250	**54,300**	10,126	7,386	10,126	8,926
54,300	**54,350**	10,139	7,394	10,139	8,939
54,350	**54,400**	10,151	7,401	10,151	8,951
54,400	**54,450**	10,164	7,409	10,164	8,964
54,450	**54,500**	10,176	7,416	10,176	8,976
54,500	**54,550**	10,189	7,424	10,189	8,989
54,550	**54,600**	10,201	7,431	10,201	9,001
54,600	**54,650**	10,214	7,439	10,214	9,014
54,650	**54,700**	10,226	7,446	10,226	9,026
54,700	**54,750**	10,239	7,454	10,239	9,039
54,750	**54,800**	10,251	7,461	10,251	9,051
54,800	**54,850**	10,264	7,469	10,264	9,064
54,850	**54,900**	10,276	7,476	10,276	9,076
54,900	**54,950**	10,289	7,484	10,289	9,089
54,950	**55,000**	10,301	7,491	10,301	9,101
55,000					
55,000	**55,050**	10,314	7,499	10,314	9,114
55,050	**55,100**	10,326	7,506	10,326	9,126
55,100	**55,150**	10,339	7,514	10,339	9,139
55,150	**55,200**	10,351	7,521	10,351	9,151
55,200	**55,250**	10,364	7,529	10,364	9,164
55,250	**55,300**	10,376	7,536	10,376	9,176
55,300	**55,350**	10,389	7,544	10,389	9,189
55,350	**55,400**	10,401	7,551	10,401	9,201
55,400	**55,450**	10,414	7,559	10,414	9,214
55,450	**55,500**	10,426	7,566	10,426	9,226
55,500	**55,550**	10,439	7,574	10,439	9,239
55,550	**55,600**	10,451	7,581	10,451	9,251
55,600	**55,650**	10,464	7,589	10,464	9,264
55,650	**55,700**	10,476	7,596	10,476	9,276
55,700	**55,750**	10,489	7,604	10,489	9,289
55,750	**55,800**	10,501	7,611	10,501	9,301
55,800	**55,850**	10,514	7,619	10,514	9,314
55,850	**55,900**	10,526	7,626	10,526	9,326
55,900	**55,950**	10,539	7,634	10,539	9,339
55,950	**56,000**	10,551	7,641	10,551	9,351

If line 43 (taxable income) is—		And you are—			
At least	But less than	Single	Married filing jointly *	Married filing sepa-rately	Head of a house-hold
		Your tax is—			
56,000					
56,000	**56,050**	10,564	7,649	10,564	9,364
56,050	**56,100**	10,576	7,656	10,576	9,376
56,100	**56,150**	10,589	7,664	10,589	9,389
56,150	**56,200**	10,601	7,671	10,601	9,401
56,200	**56,250**	10,614	7,679	10,614	9,414
56,250	**56,300**	10,626	7,686	10,626	9,426
56,300	**56,350**	10,639	7,694	10,639	9,439
56,350	**56,400**	10,651	7,701	10,651	9,451
56,400	**56,450**	10,664	7,709	10,664	9,464
56,450	**56,500**	10,676	7,716	10,676	9,476
56,500	**56,550**	10,689	7,724	10,689	9,489
56,550	**56,600**	10,701	7,731	10,701	9,501
56,600	**56,650**	10,714	7,739	10,714	9,514
56,650	**56,700**	10,726	7,746	10,726	9,526
56,700	**56,750**	10,739	7,754	10,739	9,539
56,750	**56,800**	10,751	7,761	10,751	9,551
56,800	**56,850**	10,764	7,769	10,764	9,564
56,850	**56,900**	10,776	7,776	10,776	9,576
56,900	**56,950**	10,789	7,784	10,789	9,589
56,950	**57,000**	10,801	7,791	10,801	9,601
57,000					
57,000	**57,050**	10,814	7,799	10,814	9,614
57,050	**57,100**	10,826	7,806	10,826	9,626
57,100	**57,150**	10,839	7,814	10,839	9,639
57,150	**57,200**	10,851	7,821	10,851	9,651
57,200	**57,250**	10,864	7,829	10,864	9,664
57,250	**57,300**	10,876	7,836	10,876	9,676
57,300	**57,350**	10,889	7,844	10,889	9,689
57,350	**57,400**	10,901	7,851	10,901	9,701
57,400	**57,450**	10,914	7,859	10,914	9,714
57,450	**57,500**	10,926	7,866	10,926	9,726
57,500	**57,550**	10,939	7,874	10,939	9,739
57,550	**57,600**	10,951	7,881	10,951	9,751
57,600	**57,650**	10,964	7,889	10,964	9,764
57,650	**57,700**	10,976	7,896	10,976	9,776
57,700	**57,750**	10,989	7,904	10,989	9,789
57,750	**57,800**	11,001	7,911	11,001	9,801
57,800	**57,850**	11,014	7,919	11,014	9,814
57,850	**57,900**	11,026	7,926	11,026	9,826
57,900	**57,950**	11,039	7,934	11,039	9,839
57,950	**58,000**	11,051	7,941	11,051	9,851
58,000					
58,000	**58,050**	11,064	7,949	11,064	9,864
58,050	**58,100**	11,076	7,956	11,076	9,876
58,100	**58,150**	11,089	7,964	11,089	9,889
58,150	**58,200**	11,101	7,971	11,101	9,901
58,200	**58,250**	11,114	7,979	11,114	9,914
58,250	**58,300**	11,126	7,986	11,126	9,926
58,300	**58,350**	11,139	7,994	11,139	9,939
58,350	**58,400**	11,151	8,001	11,151	9,951
58,400	**58,450**	11,164	8,009	11,164	9,964
58,450	**58,500**	11,176	8,016	11,176	9,976
58,500	**58,550**	11,189	8,024	11,189	9,989
58,550	**58,600**	11,201	8,031	11,201	10,001
58,600	**58,650**	11,214	8,039	11,214	10,014
58,650	**58,700**	11,226	8,046	11,226	10,026
58,700	**58,750**	11,239	8,054	11,239	10,039
58,750	**58,800**	11,251	8,061	11,251	10,051
58,800	**58,850**	11,264	8,069	11,264	10,064
58,850	**58,900**	11,276	8,076	11,276	10,076
58,900	**58,950**	11,289	8,084	11,289	10,089
58,950	**59,000**	11,301	8,091	11,301	10,101

* This column must also be used by a qualifying widow(er)

(Continued on page 30)

2006 Tax Table—*Continued*

If line 43 (taxable income) is—		And you are—			
At least	But less than	Single	Married filing jointly *	Married filing sepa-rately	Head of a house-hold
		Your tax is—			
59,000					
59,000	**59,050**	11,314	8,099	11,314	10,114
59,050	**59,100**	11,326	8,106	11,326	10,126
59,100	**59,150**	11,339	8,114	11,339	10,139
59,150	**59,200**	11,351	8,121	11,351	10,151
59,200	**59,250**	11,364	8,129	11,364	10,164
59,250	**59,300**	11,376	8,136	11,376	10,176
59,300	**59,350**	11,389	8,144	11,389	10,189
59,350	**59,400**	11,401	8,151	11,401	10,201
59,400	**59,450**	11,414	8,159	11,414	10,214
59,450	**59,500**	11,426	8,166	11,426	10,226
59,500	**59,550**	11,439	8,174	11,439	10,239
59,550	**59,600**	11,451	8,181	11,451	10,251
59,600	**59,650**	11,464	8,189	11,464	10,264
59,650	**59,700**	11,476	8,196	11,476	10,276
59,700	**59,750**	11,489	8,204	11,489	10,289
59,750	**59,800**	11,501	8,211	11,501	10,301
59,800	**59,850**	11,514	8,219	11,514	10,314
59,850	**59,900**	11,526	8,226	11,526	10,326
59,900	**59,950**	11,539	8,234	11,539	10,339
59,950	**60,000**	11,551	8,241	11,551	10,351
60,000					
60,000	**60,050**	11,564	8,249	11,564	10,364
60,050	**60,100**	11,576	8,256	11,576	10,376
60,100	**60,150**	11,589	8,264	11,589	10,389
60,150	**60,200**	11,601	8,271	11,601	10,401
60,200	**60,250**	11,614	8,279	11,614	10,414
60,250	**60,300**	11,626	8,286	11,626	10,426
60,300	**60,350**	11,639	8,294	11,639	10,439
60,350	**60,400**	11,651	8,301	11,651	10,451
60,400	**60,450**	11,664	8,309	11,664	10,464
60,450	**60,500**	11,676	8,316	11,676	10,476
60,500	**60,550**	11,689	8,324	11,689	10,489
60,550	**60,600**	11,701	8,331	11,701	10,501
60,600	**60,650**	11,714	8,339	11,714	10,514
60,650	**60,700**	11,726	8,346	11,726	10,526
60,700	**60,750**	11,739	8,354	11,739	10,539
60,750	**60,800**	11,751	8,361	11,751	10,551
60,800	**60,850**	11,764	8,369	11,764	10,564
60,850	**60,900**	11,776	8,376	11,776	10,576
60,900	**60,950**	11,789	8,384	11,789	10,589
60,950	**61,000**	11,801	8,391	11,801	10,601
61,000					
61,000	**61,050**	11,814	8,399	11,814	10,614
61,050	**61,100**	11,826	8,406	11,826	10,626
61,100	**61,150**	11,839	8,414	11,839	10,639
61,150	**61,200**	11,851	8,421	11,851	10,651
61,200	**61,250**	11,864	8,429	11,864	10,664
61,250	**61,300**	11,876	8,436	11,876	10,676
61,300	**61,350**	11,889	8,446	11,889	10,689
61,350	**61,400**	11,901	8,459	11,901	10,701
61,400	**61,450**	11,914	8,471	11,914	10,714
61,450	**61,500**	11,926	8,484	11,926	10,726
61,500	**61,550**	11,939	8,496	11,939	10,739
61,550	**61,600**	11,951	8,509	11,951	10,751
61,600	**61,650**	11,964	8,521	11,964	10,764
61,650	**61,700**	11,976	8,534	11,976	10,776
61,700	**61,750**	11,989	8,546	11,989	10,789
61,750	**61,800**	12,001	8,559	12,001	10,801
61,800	**61,850**	12,014	8,571	12,014	10,814
61,850	**61,900**	12,026	8,584	12,027	10,826
61,900	**61,950**	12,039	8,596	12,041	10,839
61,950	**62,000**	12,051	8,609	12,055	10,851

If line 43 (taxable income) is—		And you are—			
At least	But less than	Single	Married filing jointly *	Married filing sepa-rately	Head of a house-hold
		Your tax is—			
62,000					
62,000	**62,050**	12,064	8,621	12,069	10,864
62,050	**62,100**	12,076	8,634	12,083	10,876
62,100	**62,150**	12,089	8,646	12,097	10,889
62,150	**62,200**	12,101	8,659	12,111	10,901
62,200	**62,250**	12,114	8,671	12,125	10,914
62,250	**62,300**	12,126	8,684	12,139	10,926
62,300	**62,350**	12,139	8,696	12,153	10,939
62,350	**62,400**	12,151	8,709	12,167	10,951
62,400	**62,450**	12,164	8,721	12,181	10,964
62,450	**62,500**	12,176	8,734	12,195	10,976
62,500	**62,550**	12,189	8,746	12,209	10,989
62,550	**62,600**	12,201	8,759	12,223	11,001
62,600	**62,650**	12,214	8,771	12,237	11,014
62,650	**62,700**	12,226	8,784	12,251	11,026
62,700	**62,750**	12,239	8,796	12,265	11,039
62,750	**62,800**	12,251	8,809	12,279	11,051
62,800	**62,850**	12,264	8,821	12,293	11,064
62,850	**62,900**	12,276	8,834	12,307	11,076
62,900	**62,950**	12,289	8,846	12,321	11,089
62,950	**63,000**	12,301	8,859	12,335	11,101
63,000					
63,000	**63,050**	12,314	8,871	12,349	11,114
63,050	**63,100**	12,326	8,884	12,363	11,126
63,100	**63,150**	12,339	8,896	12,377	11,139
63,150	**63,200**	12,351	8,909	12,391	11,151
63,200	**63,250**	12,364	8,921	12,405	11,164
63,250	**63,300**	12,376	8,934	12,419	11,176
63,300	**63,350**	12,389	8,946	12,433	11,189
63,350	**63,400**	12,401	8,959	12,447	11,201
63,400	**63,450**	12,414	8,971	12,461	11,214
63,450	**63,500**	12,426	8,984	12,475	11,226
63,500	**63,550**	12,439	8,996	12,489	11,239
63,550	**63,600**	12,451	9,009	12,503	11,251
63,600	**63,650**	12,464	9,021	12,517	11,264
63,650	**63,700**	12,476	9,034	12,531	11,276
63,700	**63,750**	12,489	9,046	12,545	11,289
63,750	**63,800**	12,501	9,059	12,559	11,301
63,800	**63,850**	12,514	9,071	12,573	11,314
63,850	**63,900**	12,526	9,084	12,587	11,326
63,900	**63,950**	12,539	9,096	12,601	11,339
63,950	**64,000**	12,551	9,109	12,615	11,351
64,000					
64,000	**64,050**	12,564	9,121	12,629	11,364
64,050	**64,100**	12,576	9,134	12,643	11,376
64,100	**64,150**	12,589	9,146	12,657	11,389
64,150	**64,200**	12,601	9,159	12,671	11,401
64,200	**64,250**	12,614	9,171	12,685	11,414
64,250	**64,300**	12,626	9,184	12,699	11,426
64,300	**64,350**	12,639	9,196	12,713	11,439
64,350	**64,400**	12,651	9,209	12,727	11,451
64,400	**64,450**	12,664	9,221	12,741	11,464
64,450	**64,500**	12,676	9,234	12,755	11,476
64,500	**64,550**	12,689	9,246	12,769	11,489
64,550	**64,600**	12,701	9,259	12,783	11,501
64,600	**64,650**	12,714	9,271	12,797	11,514
64,650	**64,700**	12,726	9,284	12,811	11,526
64,700	**64,750**	12,739	9,296	12,825	11,539
64,750	**64,800**	12,751	9,309	12,839	11,551
64,800	**64,850**	12,764	9,321	12,853	11,564
64,850	**64,900**	12,776	9,334	12,867	11,576
64,900	**64,950**	12,789	9,346	12,881	11,589
64,950	**65,000**	12,801	9,359	12,895	11,601

If line 43 (taxable income) is—		And you are—			
At least	But less than	Single	Married filing jointly *	Married filing sepa-rately	Head of a house-hold
		Your tax is—			
65,000					
65,000	**65,050**	12,814	9,371	12,909	11,614
65,050	**65,100**	12,826	9,384	12,923	11,626
65,100	**65,150**	12,839	9,396	12,937	11,639
65,150	**65,200**	12,851	9,409	12,951	11,651
65,200	**65,250**	12,864	9,421	12,965	11,664
65,250	**65,300**	12,876	9,434	12,979	11,676
65,300	**65,350**	12,889	9,446	12,993	11,689
65,350	**65,400**	12,901	9,459	13,007	11,701
65,400	**65,450**	12,914	9,471	13,021	11,714
65,450	**65,500**	12,926	9,484	13,035	11,726
65,500	**65,550**	12,939	9,496	13,049	11,739
65,550	**65,600**	12,951	9,509	13,063	11,751
65,600	**65,650**	12,964	9,521	13,077	11,764
65,650	**65,700**	12,976	9,534	13,091	11,776
65,700	**65,750**	12,989	9,546	13,105	11,789
65,750	**65,800**	13,001	9,559	13,119	11,801
65,800	**65,850**	13,014	9,571	13,133	11,814
65,850	**65,900**	13,026	9,584	13,147	11,826
65,900	**65,950**	13,039	9,596	13,161	11,839
65,950	**66,000**	13,051	9,609	13,175	11,851
66,000					
66,000	**66,050**	13,064	9,621	13,189	11,864
66,050	**66,100**	13,076	9,634	13,203	11,876
66,100	**66,150**	13,089	9,646	13,217	11,889
66,150	**66,200**	13,101	9,659	13,231	11,901
66,200	**66,250**	13,114	9,671	13,245	11,914
66,250	**66,300**	13,126	9,684	13,259	11,926
66,300	**66,350**	13,139	9,696	13,273	11,939
66,350	**66,400**	13,151	9,709	13,287	11,951
66,400	**66,450**	13,164	9,721	13,301	11,964
66,450	**66,500**	13,176	9,734	13,315	11,976
66,500	**66,550**	13,189	9,746	13,329	11,989
66,550	**66,600**	13,201	9,759	13,343	12,001
66,600	**66,650**	13,214	9,771	13,357	12,014
66,650	**66,700**	13,226	9,784	13,371	12,026
66,700	**66,750**	13,239	9,796	13,385	12,039
66,750	**66,800**	13,251	9,809	13,399	12,051
66,800	**66,850**	13,264	9,821	13,413	12,064
66,850	**66,900**	13,276	9,834	13,427	12,076
66,900	**66,950**	13,289	9,846	13,441	12,089
66,950	**67,000**	13,301	9,859	13,455	12,101
67,000					
67,000	**67,050**	13,314	9,871	13,469	12,114
67,050	**67,100**	13,326	9,884	13,483	12,126
67,100	**67,150**	13,339	9,896	13,497	12,139
67,150	**67,200**	13,351	9,909	13,511	12,151
67,200	**67,250**	13,364	9,921	13,525	12,164
67,250	**67,300**	13,376	9,934	13,539	12,176
67,300	**67,350**	13,389	9,946	13,553	12,189
67,350	**67,400**	13,401	9,959	13,567	12,201
67,400	**67,450**	13,414	9,971	13,581	12,214
67,450	**67,500**	13,426	9,984	13,595	12,226
67,500	**67,550**	13,439	9,996	13,609	12,239
67,550	**67,600**	13,451	10,009	13,623	12,251
67,600	**67,650**	13,464	10,021	13,637	12,264
67,650	**67,700**	13,476	10,034	13,651	12,276
67,700	**67,750**	13,489	10,046	13,665	12,289
67,750	**67,800**	13,501	10,059	13,679	12,301
67,800	**67,850**	13,514	10,071	13,693	12,314
67,850	**67,900**	13,526	10,084	13,707	12,326
67,900	**67,950**	13,539	10,096	13,721	12,339
67,950	**68,000**	13,551	10,109	13,735	12,351

* This column must also be used by a qualifying widow(er)

(Continued on page 31)

2006 Tax Table–*Continued*

If line 43 (taxable income) is— At least	But less than	Single	Married filing jointly *	Married filing separately	Head of a household
		Your tax is—			
68,000					
68,000	**68,050**	13,564	10,121	13,749	12,364
68,050	**68,100**	13,576	10,134	13,763	12,376
68,100	**68,150**	13,589	10,146	13,777	12,389
68,150	**68,200**	13,601	10,159	13,791	12,401
68,200	**68,250**	13,614	10,171	13,805	12,414
68,250	**68,300**	13,626	10,184	13,819	12,426
68,300	**68,350**	13,639	10,196	13,833	12,439
68,350	**68,400**	13,651	10,209	13,847	12,451
68,400	**68,450**	13,664	10,221	13,861	12,464
68,450	**68,500**	13,676	10,234	13,875	12,476
68,500	**68,550**	13,689	10,246	13,889	12,489
68,550	**68,600**	13,701	10,259	13,903	12,501
68,600	**68,650**	13,714	10,271	13,917	12,514
68,650	**68,700**	13,726	10,284	13,931	12,526
68,700	**68,750**	13,739	10,296	13,945	12,539
68,750	**68,800**	13,751	10,309	13,959	12,551
68,800	**68,850**	13,764	10,321	13,973	12,564
68,850	**68,900**	13,776	10,334	13,987	12,576
68,900	**68,950**	13,789	10,346	14,001	12,589
68,950	**69,000**	13,801	10,359	14,015	12,601
69,000					
69,000	**69,050**	13,814	10,371	14,029	12,614
69,050	**69,100**	13,826	10,384	14,043	12,626
69,100	**69,150**	13,839	10,396	14,057	12,639
69,150	**69,200**	13,851	10,409	14,071	12,651
69,200	**69,250**	13,864	10,421	14,085	12,664
69,250	**69,300**	13,876	10,434	14,099	12,676
69,300	**69,350**	13,889	10,446	14,113	12,689
69,350	**69,400**	13,901	10,459	14,127	12,701
69,400	**69,450**	13,914	10,471	14,141	12,714
69,450	**69,500**	13,926	10,484	14,155	12,726
69,500	**69,550**	13,939	10,496	14,169	12,739
69,550	**69,600**	13,951	10,509	14,183	12,751
69,600	**69,650**	13,964	10,521	14,197	12,764
69,650	**69,700**	13,976	10,534	14,211	12,776
69,700	**69,750**	13,989	10,546	14,225	12,789
69,750	**69,800**	14,001	10,559	14,239	12,801
69,800	**69,850**	14,014	10,571	14,253	12,814
69,850	**69,900**	14,026	10,584	14,267	12,826
69,900	**69,950**	14,039	10,596	14,281	12,839
69,950	**70,000**	14,051	10,609	14,295	12,851
70,000					
70,000	**70,050**	14,064	10,621	14,309	12,864
70,050	**70,100**	14,076	10,634	14,323	12,876
70,100	**70,150**	14,089	10,646	14,337	12,889
70,150	**70,200**	14,101	10,659	14,351	12,901
70,200	**70,250**	14,114	10,671	14,365	12,914
70,250	**70,300**	14,126	10,684	14,379	12,926
70,300	**70,350**	14,139	10,696	14,393	12,939
70,350	**70,400**	14,151	10,709	14,407	12,951
70,400	**70,450**	14,164	10,721	14,421	12,964
70,450	**70,500**	14,176	10,734	14,435	12,976
70,500	**70,550**	14,189	10,746	14,449	12,989
70,550	**70,600**	14,201	10,759	14,463	13,001
70,600	**70,650**	14,214	10,771	14,477	13,014
70,650	**70,700**	14,226	10,784	14,491	13,026
70,700	**70,750**	14,239	10,796	14,505	13,039
70,750	**70,800**	14,251	10,809	14,519	13,051
70,800	**70,850**	14,264	10,821	14,533	13,064
70,850	**70,900**	14,276	10,834	14,547	13,076
70,900	**70,950**	14,289	10,846	14,561	13,089
70,950	**71,000**	14,301	10,859	14,575	13,101

If line 43 (taxable income) is— At least	But less than	Single	Married filing jointly *	Married filing separately	Head of a household
		Your tax is—			
71,000					
71,000	**71,050**	14,314	10,871	14,589	13,114
71,050	**71,100**	14,326	10,884	14,603	13,126
71,100	**71,150**	14,339	10,896	14,617	13,139
71,150	**71,200**	14,351	10,909	14,631	13,151
71,200	**71,250**	14,364	10,921	14,645	13,164
71,250	**71,300**	14,376	10,934	14,659	13,176
71,300	**71,350**	14,389	10,946	14,673	13,189
71,350	**71,400**	14,401	10,959	14,687	13,201
71,400	**71,450**	14,414	10,971	14,701	13,214
71,450	**71,500**	14,426	10,984	14,715	13,226
71,500	**71,550**	14,439	10,996	14,729	13,239
71,550	**71,600**	14,451	11,009	14,743	13,251
71,600	**71,650**	14,464	11,021	14,757	13,264
71,650	**71,700**	14,476	11,034	14,771	13,276
71,700	**71,750**	14,489	11,046	14,785	13,289
71,750	**71,800**	14,501	11,059	14,799	13,301
71,800	**71,850**	14,514	11,071	14,813	13,314
71,850	**71,900**	14,526	11,084	14,827	13,326
71,900	**71,950**	14,539	11,096	14,841	13,339
71,950	**72,000**	14,551	11,109	14,855	13,351
72,000					
72,000	**72,050**	14,564	11,121	14,869	13,364
72,050	**72,100**	14,576	11,134	14,883	13,376
72,100	**72,150**	14,589	11,146	14,897	13,389
72,150	**72,200**	14,601	11,159	14,911	13,401
72,200	**72,250**	14,614	11,171	14,925	13,414
72,250	**72,300**	14,626	11,184	14,939	13,426
72,300	**72,350**	14,639	11,196	14,953	13,439
72,350	**72,400**	14,651	11,209	14,967	13,451
72,400	**72,450**	14,664	11,221	14,981	13,464
72,450	**72,500**	14,676	11,234	14,995	13,476
72,500	**72,550**	14,689	11,246	15,009	13,489
72,550	**72,600**	14,701	11,259	15,023	13,501
72,600	**72,650**	14,714	11,271	15,037	13,514
72,650	**72,700**	14,726	11,284	15,051	13,526
72,700	**72,750**	14,739	11,296	15,065	13,539
72,750	**72,800**	14,751	11,309	15,079	13,551
72,800	**72,850**	14,764	11,321	15,093	13,564
72,850	**72,900**	14,776	11,334	15,107	13,576
72,900	**72,950**	14,789	11,346	15,121	13,589
72,950	**73,000**	14,801	11,359	15,135	13,601
73,000					
73,000	**73,050**	14,814	11,371	15,149	13,614
73,050	**73,100**	14,826	11,384	15,163	13,626
73,100	**73,150**	14,839	11,396	15,177	13,639
73,150	**73,200**	14,851	11,409	15,191	13,651
73,200	**73,250**	14,864	11,421	15,205	13,664
73,250	**73,300**	14,876	11,434	15,219	13,676
73,300	**73,350**	14,889	11,446	15,233	13,689
73,350	**73,400**	14,901	11,459	15,247	13,701
73,400	**73,450**	14,914	11,471	15,261	13,714
73,450	**73,500**	14,926	11,484	15,275	13,726
73,500	**73,550**	14,939	11,496	15,289	13,739
73,550	**73,600**	14,951	11,509	15,303	13,751
73,600	**73,650**	14,964	11,521	15,317	13,764
73,650	**73,700**	14,976	11,534	15,331	13,776
73,700	**73,750**	14,989	11,546	15,345	13,789
73,750	**73,800**	15,001	11,559	15,359	13,801
73,800	**73,850**	15,014	11,571	15,373	13,814
73,850	**73,900**	15,026	11,584	15,387	13,826
73,900	**73,950**	15,039	11,596	15,401	13,839
73,950	**74,000**	15,051	11,609	15,415	13,851

If line 43 (taxable income) is— At least	But less than	Single	Married filing jointly *	Married filing separately	Head of a household
		Your tax is—			
74,000					
74,000	**74,050**	15,064	11,621	15,429	13,864
74,050	**74,100**	15,076	11,634	15,443	13,876
74,100	**74,150**	15,089	11,646	15,457	13,889
74,150	**74,200**	15,101	11,659	15,471	13,901
74,200	**74,250**	15,115	11,671	15,485	13,914
74,250	**74,300**	15,129	11,684	15,499	13,926
74,300	**74,350**	15,143	11,696	15,513	13,939
74,350	**74,400**	15,157	11,709	15,527	13,951
74,400	**74,450**	15,171	11,721	15,541	13,964
74,450	**74,500**	15,185	11,734	15,555	13,976
74,500	**74,550**	15,199	11,746	15,569	13,989
74,550	**74,600**	15,213	11,759	15,583	14,001
74,600	**74,650**	15,227	11,771	15,597	14,014
74,650	**74,700**	15,241	11,784	15,611	14,026
74,700	**74,750**	15,255	11,796	15,625	14,039
74,750	**74,800**	15,269	11,809	15,639	14,051
74,800	**74,850**	15,283	11,821	15,653	14,064
74,850	**74,900**	15,297	11,834	15,667	14,076
74,900	**74,950**	15,311	11,846	15,681	14,089
74,950	**75,000**	15,325	11,859	15,695	14,101
75,000					
75,000	**75,050**	15,339	11,871	15,709	14,114
75,050	**75,100**	15,353	11,884	15,723	14,126
75,100	**75,150**	15,367	11,896	15,737	14,139
75,150	**75,200**	15,381	11,909	15,751	14,151
75,200	**75,250**	15,395	11,921	15,765	14,164
75,250	**75,300**	15,409	11,934	15,779	14,176
75,300	**75,350**	15,423	11,946	15,793	14,189
75,350	**75,400**	15,437	11,959	15,807	14,201
75,400	**75,450**	15,451	11,971	15,821	14,214
75,450	**75,500**	15,465	11,984	15,835	14,226
75,500	**75,550**	15,479	11,996	15,849	14,239
75,550	**75,600**	15,493	12,009	15,863	14,251
75,600	**75,650**	15,507	12,021	15,877	14,264
75,650	**75,700**	15,521	12,034	15,891	14,276
75,700	**75,750**	15,535	12,046	15,905	14,289
75,750	**75,800**	15,549	12,059	15,919	14,301
75,800	**75,850**	15,563	12,071	15,933	14,314
75,850	**75,900**	15,577	12,084	15,947	14,326
75,900	**75,950**	15,591	12,096	15,961	14,339
75,950	**76,000**	15,605	12,109	15,975	14,351
76,000					
76,000	**76,050**	15,619	12,121	15,989	14,364
76,050	**76,100**	15,633	12,134	16,003	14,376
76,100	**76,150**	15,647	12,146	16,017	14,389
76,150	**76,200**	15,661	12,159	16,031	14,401
76,200	**76,250**	15,675	12,171	16,045	14,414
76,250	**76,300**	15,689	12,184	16,059	14,426
76,300	**76,350**	15,703	12,196	16,073	14,439
76,350	**76,400**	15,717	12,209	16,087	14,451
76,400	**76,450**	15,731	12,221	16,101	14,464
76,450	**76,500**	15,745	12,234	16,115	14,476
76,500	**76,550**	15,759	12,246	16,129	14,489
76,550	**76,600**	15,773	12,259	16,143	14,501
76,600	**76,650**	15,787	12,271	16,157	14,514
76,650	**76,700**	15,801	12,284	16,171	14,526
76,700	**76,750**	15,815	12,296	16,185	14,539
76,750	**76,800**	15,829	12,309	16,199	14,551
76,800	**76,850**	15,843	12,321	16,213	14,564
76,850	**76,900**	15,857	12,334	16,227	14,576
76,900	**76,950**	15,871	12,346	16,241	14,589
76,950	**77,000**	15,885	12,359	16,255	14,601

* This column must also be used by a qualifying widow(er)

(Continued on page 32)

2006 Tax Table—*Continued*

If line 43 (taxable income) is—		And you are—			
At least	But less than	Single	Married filing jointly *	Married filing separately	Head of a household
		Your tax is—			
77,000					
77,000	**77,050**	15,899	12,371	16,269	14,614
77,050	**77,100**	15,913	12,384	16,283	14,626
77,100	**77,150**	15,927	12,396	16,297	14,639
77,150	**77,200**	15,941	12,409	16,311	14,651
77,200	**77,250**	15,955	12,421	16,325	14,664
77,250	**77,300**	15,969	12,434	16,339	14,676
77,300	**77,350**	15,983	12,446	16,353	14,689
77,350	**77,400**	15,997	12,459	16,367	14,701
77,400	**77,450**	16,011	12,471	16,381	14,714
77,450	**77,500**	16,025	12,484	16,395	14,726
77,500	**77,550**	16,039	12,496	16,409	14,739
77,550	**77,600**	16,053	12,509	16,423	14,751
77,600	**77,650**	16,067	12,521	16,437	14,764
77,650	**77,700**	16,081	12,534	16,451	14,776
77,700	**77,750**	16,095	12,546	16,465	14,789
77,750	**77,800**	16,109	12,559	16,479	14,801
77,800	**77,850**	16,123	12,571	16,493	14,814
77,850	**77,900**	16,137	12,584	16,507	14,826
77,900	**77,950**	16,151	12,596	16,521	14,839
77,950	**78,000**	16,165	12,609	16,535	14,851
78,000					
78,000	**78,050**	16,179	12,621	16,549	14,864
78,050	**78,100**	16,193	12,634	16,563	14,876
78,100	**78,150**	16,207	12,646	16,577	14,889
78,150	**78,200**	16,221	12,659	16,591	14,901
78,200	**78,250**	16,235	12,671	16,605	14,914
78,250	**78,300**	16,249	12,684	16,619	14,926
78,300	**78,350**	16,263	12,696	16,633	14,939
78,350	**78,400**	16,277	12,709	16,647	14,951
78,400	**78,450**	16,291	12,721	16,661	14,964
78,450	**78,500**	16,305	12,734	16,675	14,976
78,500	**78,550**	16,319	12,746	16,689	14,989
78,550	**78,600**	16,333	12,759	16,703	15,001
78,600	**78,650**	16,347	12,771	16,717	15,014
78,650	**78,700**	16,361	12,784	16,731	15,026
78,700	**78,750**	16,375	12,796	16,745	15,039
78,750	**78,800**	16,389	12,809	16,759	15,051
78,800	**78,850**	16,403	12,821	16,773	15,064
78,850	**78,900**	16,417	12,834	16,787	15,076
78,900	**78,950**	16,431	12,846	16,801	15,089
78,950	**79,000**	16,445	12,859	16,815	15,101
79,000					
79,000	**79,050**	16,459	12,871	16,829	15,114
79,050	**79,100**	16,473	12,884	16,843	15,126
79,100	**79,150**	16,487	12,896	16,857	15,139
79,150	**79,200**	16,501	12,909	16,871	15,151
79,200	**79,250**	16,515	12,921	16,885	15,164
79,250	**79,300**	16,529	12,934	16,899	15,176
79,300	**79,350**	16,543	12,946	16,913	15,189
79,350	**79,400**	16,557	12,959	16,927	15,201
79,400	**79,450**	16,571	12,971	16,941	15,214
79,450	**79,500**	16,585	12,984	16,955	15,226
79,500	**79,550**	16,599	12,996	16,969	15,239
79,550	**79,600**	16,613	13,009	16,983	15,251
79,600	**79,650**	16,627	13,021	16,997	15,264
79,650	**79,700**	16,641	13,034	17,011	15,276
79,700	**79,750**	16,655	13,046	17,025	15,289
79,750	**79,800**	16,669	13,059	17,039	15,301
79,800	**79,850**	16,683	13,071	17,053	15,314
79,850	**79,900**	16,697	13,084	17,067	15,326
79,900	**79,950**	16,711	13,096	17,081	15,339
79,950	**80,000**	16,725	13,109	17,095	15,351

If line 43 (taxable income) is—		And you are—			
At least	But less than	Single	Married filing jointly *	Married filing separately	Head of a household
		Your tax is—			
80,000					
80,000	**80,050**	16,739	13,121	17,109	15,364
80,050	**80,100**	16,753	13,134	17,123	15,376
80,100	**80,150**	16,767	13,146	17,137	15,389
80,150	**80,200**	16,781	13,159	17,151	15,401
80,200	**80,250**	16,795	13,171	17,165	15,414
80,250	**80,300**	16,809	13,184	17,179	15,426
80,300	**80,350**	16,823	13,196	17,193	15,439
80,350	**80,400**	16,837	13,209	17,207	15,451
80,400	**80,450**	16,851	13,221	17,221	15,464
80,450	**80,500**	16,865	13,234	17,235	15,476
80,500	**80,550**	16,879	13,246	17,249	15,489
80,550	**80,600**	16,893	13,259	17,263	15,501
80,600	**80,650**	16,907	13,271	17,277	15,514
80,650	**80,700**	16,921	13,284	17,291	15,526
80,700	**80,750**	16,935	13,296	17,305	15,539
80,750	**80,800**	16,949	13,309	17,319	15,551
80,800	**80,850**	16,963	13,321	17,333	15,564
80,850	**80,900**	16,977	13,334	17,347	15,576
80,900	**80,950**	16,991	13,346	17,361	15,589
80,950	**81,000**	17,005	13,359	17,375	15,601
81,000					
81,000	**81,050**	17,019	13,371	17,389	15,614
81,050	**81,100**	17,033	13,384	17,403	15,626
81,100	**81,150**	17,047	13,396	17,417	15,639
81,150	**81,200**	17,061	13,409	17,431	15,651
81,200	**81,250**	17,075	13,421	17,445	15,664
81,250	**81,300**	17,089	13,434	17,459	15,676
81,300	**81,350**	17,103	13,446	17,473	15,689
81,350	**81,400**	17,117	13,459	17,487	15,701
81,400	**81,450**	17,131	13,471	17,501	15,714
81,450	**81,500**	17,145	13,484	17,515	15,726
81,500	**81,550**	17,159	13,496	17,529	15,739
81,550	**81,600**	17,173	13,509	17,543	15,751
81,600	**81,650**	17,187	13,521	17,557	15,764
81,650	**81,700**	17,201	13,534	17,571	15,776
81,700	**81,750**	17,215	13,546	17,585	15,789
81,750	**81,800**	17,229	13,559	17,599	15,801
81,800	**81,850**	17,243	13,571	17,613	15,814
81,850	**81,900**	17,257	13,584	17,627	15,826
81,900	**81,950**	17,271	13,596	17,641	15,839
81,950	**82,000**	17,285	13,609	17,655	15,851
82,000					
82,000	**82,050**	17,299	13,621	17,669	15,864
82,050	**82,100**	17,313	13,634	17,683	15,876
82,100	**82,150**	17,327	13,646	17,697	15,889
82,150	**82,200**	17,341	13,659	17,711	15,901
82,200	**82,250**	17,355	13,671	17,725	15,914
82,250	**82,300**	17,369	13,684	17,739	15,926
82,300	**82,350**	17,383	13,696	17,753	15,939
82,350	**82,400**	17,397	13,709	17,767	15,951
82,400	**82,450**	17,411	13,721	17,781	15,964
82,450	**82,500**	17,425	13,734	17,795	15,976
82,500	**82,550**	17,439	13,746	17,809	15,989
82,550	**82,600**	17,453	13,759	17,823	16,001
82,600	**82,650**	17,467	13,771	17,837	16,014
82,650	**82,700**	17,481	13,784	17,851	16,026
82,700	**82,750**	17,495	13,796	17,865	16,039
82,750	**82,800**	17,509	13,809	17,879	16,051
82,800	**82,850**	17,523	13,821	17,893	16,064
82,850	**82,900**	17,537	13,834	17,907	16,076
82,900	**82,950**	17,551	13,846	17,921	16,089
82,950	**83,000**	17,565	13,859	17,935	16,101

2005 Tax Table—*Continued*

If line 43 (taxable income) is—		And you are—			
At least	But less than	Single	Married filing jointly *	Married filing separately	Head of a household
		Your tax is—			
83,000					
83,000	**83,050**	17,579	13,871	17,949	16,114
83,050	**83,100**	17,593	13,884	17,963	16,126
83,100	**83,150**	17,607	13,896	17,977	16,139
83,150	**83,200**	17,621	13,909	17,991	16,151
83,200	**83,250**	17,635	13,921	18,005	16,164
83,250	**83,300**	17,649	13,934	18,019	16,176
83,300	**83,350**	17,663	13,946	18,033	16,189
83,350	**83,400**	17,677	13,959	18,047	16,201
83,400	**83,450**	17,691	13,971	18,061	16,214
83,450	**83,500**	17,705	13,984	18,075	16,226
83,500	**83,550**	17,719	13,996	18,089	16,239
83,550	**83,600**	17,733	14,009	18,103	16,251
83,600	**83,650**	17,747	14,021	18,117	16,264
83,650	**83,700**	17,761	14,034	18,131	16,276
83,700	**83,750**	17,775	14,046	18,145	16,289
83,750	**83,800**	17,789	14,059	18,159	16,301
83,800	**83,850**	17,803	14,071	18,173	16,314
83,850	**83,900**	17,817	14,084	18,187	16,326
83,900	**83,950**	17,831	14,096	18,201	16,339
83,950	**84,000**	17,845	14,109	18,215	16,351
84,000					
84,000	**84,050**	17,859	14,121	18,229	16,364
84,050	**84,100**	17,873	14,134	18,243	16,376
84,100	**84,150**	17,887	14,146	18,257	16,389
84,150	**84,200**	17,901	14,159	18,271	16,401
84,200	**84,250**	17,915	14,171	18,285	16,414
84,250	**84,300**	17,929	14,184	18,299	16,426
84,300	**84,350**	17,943	14,196	18,313	16,439
84,350	**84,400**	17,957	14,209	18,327	16,451
84,400	**84,450**	17,971	14,221	18,341	16,464
84,450	**84,500**	17,985	14,234	18,355	16,476
84,500	**84,550**	17,999	14,246	18,369	16,489
84,550	**84,600**	18,013	14,259	18,383	16,501
84,600	**84,650**	18,027	14,271	18,397	16,514
84,650	**84,700**	18,041	14,284	18,411	16,526
84,700	**84,750**	18,055	14,296	18,425	16,539
84,750	**84,800**	18,069	14,309	18,439	16,551
84,800	**84,850**	18,083	14,321	18,453	16,564
84,850	**84,900**	18,097	14,334	18,467	16,576
84,900	**84,950**	18,111	14,346	18,481	16,589
84,950	**85,000**	18,125	14,359	18,495	16,601
85,000					
85,000	**85,050**	18,139	14,371	18,509	16,614
85,050	**85,100**	18,153	14,384	18,523	16,626
85,100	**85,150**	18,167	14,396	18,537	16,639
85,150	**85,200**	18,181	14,409	18,551	16,651
85,200	**85,250**	18,195	14,421	18,565	16,664
85,250	**85,300**	18,209	14,434	18,579	16,676
85,300	**85,350**	18,223	14,446	18,593	16,689
85,350	**85,400**	18,237	14,459	18,607	16,701
85,400	**85,450**	18,251	14,471	18,621	16,714
85,450	**85,500**	18,265	14,484	18,635	16,726
85,500	**85,550**	18,279	14,496	18,649	16,739
85,550	**85,600**	18,293	14,509	18,663	16,751
85,600	**85,650**	18,307	14,521	18,677	16,764
85,650	**85,700**	18,321	14,534	18,691	16,776
85,700	**85,750**	18,335	14,546	18,705	16,789
85,750	**85,800**	18,349	14,559	18,719	16,801
85,800	**85,850**	18,363	14,571	18,733	16,814
85,850	**85,900**	18,377	14,584	18,747	16,826
85,900	**85,950**	18,391	14,596	18,761	16,839
85,950	**86,000**	18,405	14,609	18,775	16,851

* This column must also be used by a qualifying widow(er)

(Continued on page 33)

2006 Tax Table–*Continued*

If line 43 (taxable income) is—		And you are—			
At least	But less than	Single	Married filing jointly *	Married filing separately	Head of a household
		Your tax is—			
86,000					
86,000	**86,050**	18,419	14,621	18,789	16,864
86,050	**86,100**	18,433	14,634	18,803	16,876
86,100	**86,150**	18,447	14,646	18,817	16,889
86,150	**86,200**	18,461	14,659	18,831	16,901
86,200	**86,250**	18,475	14,671	18,845	16,914
86,250	**86,300**	18,489	14,684	18,859	16,926
86,300	**86,350**	18,503	14,696	18,873	16,939
86,350	**86,400**	18,517	14,709	18,887	16,951
86,400	**86,450**	18,531	14,721	18,901	16,964
86,450	**86,500**	18,545	14,734	18,915	16,976
86,500	**86,550**	18,559	14,746	18,929	16,989
86,550	**86,600**	18,573	14,759	18,943	17,001
86,600	**86,650**	18,587	14,771	18,957	17,014
86,650	**86,700**	18,601	14,784	18,971	17,026
86,700	**86,750**	18,615	14,796	18,985	17,039
86,750	**86,800**	18,629	14,809	18,999	17,051
86,800	**86,850**	18,643	14,821	19,013	17,064
86,850	**86,900**	18,657	14,834	19,027	17,076
86,900	**86,950**	18,671	14,846	19,041	17,089
86,950	**87,000**	18,685	14,859	19,055	17,101
87,000					
87,000	**87,050**	18,699	14,871	19,069	17,114
87,050	**87,100**	18,713	14,884	19,083	17,126
87,100	**87,150**	18,727	14,896	19,097	17,139
87,150	**87,200**	18,741	14,909	19,111	17,151
87,200	**87,250**	18,755	14,921	19,125	17,164
87,250	**87,300**	18,769	14,934	19,139	17,176
87,300	**87,350**	18,783	14,946	19,153	17,189
87,350	**87,400**	18,797	14,959	19,167	17,201
87,400	**87,450**	18,811	14,971	19,181	17,214
87,450	**87,500**	18,825	14,984	19,195	17,226
87,500	**87,550**	18,839	14,996	19,209	17,239
87,550	**87,600**	18,853	15,009	19,223	17,251
87,600	**87,650**	18,867	15,021	19,237	17,264
87,650	**87,700**	18,881	15,034	19,251	17,276
87,700	**87,750**	18,895	15,046	19,265	17,289
87,750	**87,800**	18,909	15,059	19,279	17,301
87,800	**87,850**	18,923	15,071	19,293	17,314
87,850	**87,900**	18,937	15,084	19,307	17,326
87,900	**87,950**	18,951	15,096	19,321	17,339
87,950	**88,000**	18,965	15,109	19,335	17,351
88,000					
88,000	**88,050**	18,979	15,121	19,349	17,364
88,050	**88,100**	18,993	15,134	19,363	17,376
88,100	**88,150**	19,007	15,146	19,377	17,389
88,150	**88,200**	19,021	15,159	19,391	17,401
88,200	**88,250**	19,035	15,171	19,405	17,414
88,250	**88,300**	19,049	15,184	19,419	17,426
88,300	**88,350**	19,063	15,196	19,433	17,439
88,350	**88,400**	19,077	15,209	19,447	17,451
88,400	**88,450**	19,091	15,221	19,461	17,464
88,450	**88,500**	19,105	15,234	19,475	17,476
88,500	**88,550**	19,119	15,246	19,489	17,489
88,550	**88,600**	19,133	15,259	19,503	17,501
88,600	**88,650**	19,147	15,271	19,517	17,514
88,650	**88,700**	19,161	15,284	19,531	17,526
88,700	**88,750**	19,175	15,296	19,545	17,539
88,750	**88,800**	19,189	15,309	19,559	17,551
88,800	**88,850**	19,203	15,321	19,573	17,564
88,850	**88,900**	19,217	15,334	19,587	17,576
88,900	**88,950**	19,231	15,346	19,601	17,589
88,950	**89,000**	19,245	15,359	19,615	17,601
89,000					
89,000	**89,050**	19,259	15,371	19,629	17,614
89,050	**89,100**	19,273	15,384	19,643	17,626
89,100	**89,150**	19,287	15,396	19,657	17,639
89,150	**89,200**	19,301	15,409	19,671	17,651
89,200	**89,250**	19,315	15,421	19,685	17,664
89,250	**89,300**	19,329	15,434	19,699	17,676
89,300	**89,350**	19,343	15,446	19,713	17,689
89,350	**89,400**	19,357	15,459	19,727	17,701
89,400	**89,450**	19,371	15,471	19,741	17,714
89,450	**89,500**	19,385	15,484	19,755	17,726
89,500	**89,550**	19,399	15,496	19,769	17,739
89,550	**89,600**	19,413	15,509	19,783	17,751
89,600	**89,650**	19,427	15,521	19,797	17,764
89,650	**89,700**	19,441	15,534	19,811	17,776
89,700	**89,750**	19,455	15,546	19,825	17,789
89,750	**89,800**	19,469	15,559	19,839	17,801
89,800	**89,850**	19,483	15,571	19,853	17,814
89,850	**89,900**	19,497	15,584	19,867	17,826
89,900	**89,950**	19,511	15,596	19,881	17,839
89,950	**90,000**	19,525	15,609	19,895	17,851
90,000					
90,000	**90,050**	19,539	15,621	19,909	17,864
90,050	**90,100**	19,553	15,634	19,923	17,876
90,100	**90,150**	19,567	15,646	19,937	17,889
90,150	**90,200**	19,581	15,659	19,951	17,901
90,200	**90,250**	19,595	15,671	19,965	17,914
90,250	**90,300**	19,609	15,684	19,979	17,926
90,300	**90,350**	19,623	15,696	19,993	17,939
90,350	**90,400**	19,637	15,709	20,007	17,951
90,400	**90,450**	19,651	15,721	20,021	17,964
90,450	**90,500**	19,665	15,734	20,035	17,976
90,500	**90,550**	19,679	15,746	20,049	17,989
90,550	**90,600**	19,693	15,759	20,063	18,001
90,600	**90,650**	19,707	15,771	20,077	18,014
90,650	**90,700**	19,721	15,784	20,091	18,026
90,700	**90,750**	19,735	15,796	20,105	18,039
90,750	**90,800**	19,749	15,809	20,119	18,051
90,800	**90,850**	19,763	15,821	20,133	18,064
90,850	**90,900**	19,777	15,834	20,147	18,076
90,900	**90,950**	19,791	15,846	20,161	18,089
90,950	**91,000**	19,805	15,859	20,175	18,101
91,000					
91,000	**91,050**	19,819	15,871	20,189	18,114
91,050	**91,100**	19,833	15,884	20,203	18,126
91,100	**91,150**	19,847	15,896	20,217	18,139
91,150	**91,200**	19,861	15,909	20,231	18,151
91,200	**91,250**	19,875	15,921	20,245	18,164
91,250	**91,300**	19,889	15,934	20,259	18,176
91,300	**91,350**	19,903	15,946	20,273	18,189
91,350	**91,400**	19,917	15,959	20,287	18,201
91,400	**91,450**	19,931	15,971	20,301	18,214
91,450	**91,500**	19,945	15,984	20,315	18,226
91,500	**91,550**	19,959	15,996	20,329	18,239
91,550	**91,600**	19,973	16,009	20,343	18,251
91,600	**91,650**	19,987	16,021	20,357	18,264
91,650	**91,700**	20,001	16,034	20,371	18,276
91,700	**91,750**	20,015	16,046	20,385	18,289
91,750	**91,800**	20,029	16,059	20,399	18,301
91,800	**91,850**	20,043	16,071	20,413	18,314
91,850	**91,900**	20,057	16,084	20,427	18,326
91,900	**91,950**	20,071	16,096	20,441	18,339
91,950	**92,000**	20,085	16,109	20,455	18,351
92,000					
92,000	**92,050**	20,099	16,121	20,469	18,364
92,050	**92,100**	20,113	16,134	20,483	18,376
92,100	**92,150**	20,127	16,146	20,497	18,389
92,150	**92,200**	20,141	16,159	20,511	18,401
92,200	**92,250**	20,155	16,171	20,525	18,414
92,250	**92,300**	20,169	16,184	20,539	18,426
92,300	**92,350**	20,183	16,196	20,553	18,439
92,350	**92,400**	20,197	16,209	20,567	18,451
92,400	**92,450**	20,211	16,221	20,581	18,464
92,450	**92,500**	20,225	16,234	20,595	18,476
92,500	**92,550**	20,239	16,246	20,609	18,489
92,550	**92,600**	20,253	16,259	20,623	18,501
92,600	**92,650**	20,267	16,271	20,637	18,514
92,650	**92,700**	20,281	16,284	20,651	18,526
92,700	**92,750**	20,295	16,296	20,665	18,539
92,750	**92,800**	20,309	16,309	20,679	18,551
92,800	**92,850**	20,323	16,321	20,693	18,564
92,850	**92,900**	20,337	16,334	20,707	18,576
92,900	**92,950**	20,351	16,346	20,721	18,589
92,950	**93,000**	20,365	16,359	20,735	18,601
93,000					
93,000	**93,050**	20,379	16,371	20,749	18,614
93,050	**93,100**	20,393	16,384	20,763	18,626
93,100	**93,150**	20,407	16,396	20,777	18,639
93,150	**93,200**	20,421	16,409	20,791	18,651
93,200	**93,250**	20,435	16,421	20,805	18,664
93,250	**93,300**	20,449	16,434	20,819	18,676
93,300	**93,350**	20,463	16,446	20,833	18,689
93,350	**93,400**	20,477	16,459	20,847	18,701
93,400	**93,450**	20,491	16,471	20,861	18,714
93,450	**93,500**	20,505	16,484	20,875	18,726
93,500	**93,550**	20,519	16,496	20,889	18,739
93,550	**93,600**	20,533	16,509	20,903	18,751
93,600	**93,650**	20,547	16,521	20,917	18,764
93,650	**93,700**	20,561	16,534	20,931	18,776
93,700	**93,750**	20,575	16,546	20,945	18,789
93,750	**93,800**	20,589	16,559	20,959	18,801
93,800	**93,850**	20,603	16,571	20,973	18,814
93,850	**93,900**	20,617	16,584	20,987	18,826
93,900	**93,950**	20,631	16,596	21,001	18,839
93,950	**94,000**	20,645	16,609	21,015	18,851
94,000					
94,000	**94,050**	20,659	16,621	21,029	18,864
94,050	**94,100**	20,673	16,634	21,043	18,876
94,100	**94,150**	20,687	16,646	21,057	18,889
94,150	**94,200**	20,701	16,659	21,071	18,901
94,200	**94,250**	20,715	16,671	21,085	18,914
94,250	**94,300**	20,729	16,684	21,102	18,926
94,300	**94,350**	20,743	16,696	21,118	18,939
94,350	**94,400**	20,757	16,709	21,135	18,951
94,400	**94,450**	20,771	16,721	21,151	18,964
94,450	**94,500**	20,785	16,734	21,168	18,976
94,500	**94,550**	20,799	16,746	21,184	18,989
94,550	**94,600**	20,813	16,759	21,201	19,001
94,600	**94,650**	20,827	16,771	21,217	19,014
94,650	**94,700**	20,841	16,784	21,234	19,026
94,700	**94,750**	20,855	16,796	21,250	19,039
94,750	**94,800**	20,869	16,809	21,267	19,051
94,800	**94,850**	20,883	16,821	21,283	19,064
94,850	**94,900**	20,897	16,834	21,300	19,076
94,900	**94,950**	20,911	16,846	21,316	19,089
94,950	**95,000**	20,925	16,859	21,333	19,101

* This column must also be used by a qualifying widow(er)

(Continued on page 34)

2006 Tax Table–*Continued*

If line 43 (taxable income) is—		And you are—			
At least	But less than	Single	Married filing jointly *	Married filing separately	Head of a household
		Your tax is—			
95,000					
95,000	**95,050**	20,939	16,871	21,349	19,114
95,050	**95,100**	20,953	16,884	21,366	19,126
95,100	**95,150**	20,967	16,896	21,382	19,139
95,150	**95,200**	20,981	16,909	21,399	19,151
95,200	**95,250**	20,995	16,921	21,415	19,164
95,250	**95,300**	21,009	16,934	21,432	19,176
95,300	**95,350**	21,023	16,946	21,448	19,189
95,350	**95,400**	21,037	16,959	21,465	19,201
95,400	**95,450**	21,051	16,971	21,481	19,214
95,450	**95,500**	21,065	16,984	21,498	19,226
95,500	**95,550**	21,079	16,996	21,514	19,239
95,550	**95,600**	21,093	17,009	21,531	19,251
95,600	**95,650**	21,107	17,021	21,547	19,264
95,650	**95,700**	21,121	17,034	21,564	19,276
95,700	**95,750**	21,135	17,046	21,580	19,289
95,750	**95,800**	21,149	17,059	21,597	19,301
95,800	**95,850**	21,163	17,071	21,613	19,314
95,850	**95,900**	21,177	17,084	21,630	19,326
95,900	**95,950**	21,191	17,096	21,646	19,339
95,950	**96,000**	21,205	17,109	21,663	19,351
96,000					
96,000	**96,050**	21,219	17,121	21,679	19,364
96,050	**96,100**	21,233	17,134	21,696	19,376
96,100	**96,150**	21,247	17,146	21,712	19,389
96,150	**96,200**	21,261	17,159	21,729	19,401
96,200	**96,250**	21,275	17,171	21,745	19,414
96,250	**96,300**	21,289	17,184	21,762	19,426
96,300	**96,350**	21,303	17,196	21,778	19,439
96,350	**96,400**	21,317	17,209	21,795	19,451
96,400	**96,450**	21,331	17,221	21,811	19,464
96,450	**96,500**	21,345	17,234	21,828	19,476
96,500	**96,550**	21,359	17,246	21,844	19,489
96,550	**96,600**	21,373	17,259	21,861	19,501
96,600	**96,650**	21,387	17,271	21,877	19,514
96,650	**96,700**	21,401	17,284	21,894	19,526
96,700	**96,750**	21,415	17,296	21,910	19,539
96,750	**96,800**	21,429	17,309	21,927	19,551
96,800	**96,850**	21,443	17,321	21,943	19,564
96,850	**96,900**	21,457	17,334	21,960	19,576
96,900	**96,950**	21,471	17,346	21,976	19,589
96,950	**97,000**	21,485	17,359	21,993	19,601
97,000					
97,000	**97,050**	21,499	17,371	22,009	19,614
97,050	**97,100**	21,513	17,384	22,026	19,626
97,100	**97,150**	21,527	17,396	22,042	19,639
97,150	**97,200**	21,541	17,409	22,059	19,651
97,200	**97,250**	21,555	17,421	22,075	19,664
97,250	**97,300**	21,569	17,434	22,092	19,676
97,300	**97,350**	21,583	17,446	22,108	19,689
97,350	**97,400**	21,597	17,459	22,125	19,701
97,400	**97,450**	21,611	17,471	22,141	19,714
97,450	**97,500**	21,625	17,484	22,158	19,726
97,500	**97,550**	21,639	17,496	22,174	19,739
97,550	**97,600**	21,653	17,509	22,191	19,751
97,600	**97,650**	21,667	17,521	22,207	19,764
97,650	**97,700**	21,681	17,534	22,224	19,776
97,700	**97,750**	21,695	17,546	22,240	19,789
97,750	**97,800**	21,709	17,559	22,257	19,801
97,800	**97,850**	21,723	17,571	22,273	19,814
97,850	**97,900**	21,737	17,584	22,290	19,826
97,900	**97,950**	21,751	17,596	22,306	19,839
97,950	**98,000**	21,765	17,609	22,323	19,851
98,000					
98,000	**98,050**	21,779	17,621	22,339	19,864
98,050	**98,100**	21,793	17,634	22,356	19,876
98,100	**98,150**	21,807	17,646	22,372	19,889
98,150	**98,200**	21,821	17,659	22,389	19,901
98,200	**98,250**	21,835	17,671	22,405	19,914
98,250	**98,300**	21,849	17,684	22,422	19,926
98,300	**98,350**	21,863	17,696	22,438	19,939
98,350	**98,400**	21,877	17,709	22,455	19,951
98,400	**98,450**	21,891	17,721	22,471	19,964
98,450	**98,500**	21,905	17,734	22,488	19,976
98,500	**98,550**	21,919	17,746	22,504	19,989
98,550	**98,600**	21,933	17,759	22,521	20,001
98,600	**98,650**	21,947	17,771	22,537	20,014
98,650	**98,700**	21,961	17,784	22,554	20,026
98,700	**98,750**	21,975	17,796	22,570	20,039
98,750	**98,800**	21,989	17,809	22,587	20,051
98,800	**98,850**	22,003	17,821	22,603	20,064
98,850	**98,900**	22,017	17,834	22,620	20,076
98,900	**98,950**	22,031	17,846	22,636	20,089
98,950	**99,000**	22,045	17,859	22,653	20,101
99,000					
99,000	**99,050**	22,059	17,871	22,669	20,114
99,050	**99,100**	22,073	17,884	22,686	20,126
99,100	**99,150**	22,087	17,896	22,702	20,139
99,150	**99,200**	22,101	17,909	22,719	20,151
99,200	**99,250**	22,115	17,921	22,735	20,164
99,250	**99,300**	22,129	17,934	22,752	20,176
99,300	**99,350**	22,143	17,946	22,768	20,189
99,350	**99,400**	22,157	17,959	22,785	20,201
99,400	**99,450**	22,171	17,971	22,801	20,214
99,450	**99,500**	22,185	17,984	22,818	20,226
99,500	**99,550**	22,199	17,996	22,834	20,239
99,550	**99,600**	22,213	18,009	22,851	20,251
99,600	**99,650**	22,227	18,021	22,867	20,264
99,650	**99,700**	22,241	18,034	22,884	20,276
99,700	**99,750**	22,255	18,046	22,900	20,289
99,750	**99,800**	22,269	18,059	22,917	20,301
99,800	**99,850**	22,283	18,071	22,933	20,314
99,850	**99,900**	22,297	18,084	22,950	20,326
99,900	**99,950**	22,311	18,096	22,966	20,339
99,950	**100,000**	22,325	18,109	22,983	20,351

$100,000 or over — use the Tax Computation Worksheet on page 35

* This column must also be used by a qualifying widow(er)

Earned Income Credit Tables

2006 Earned Income Credit (EIC) Table

Caution. This is **not** a tax table.

1. To find your credit, read down the "At least - But less than" columns and find the line that includes the amount you were told to look up from your EIC Worksheet.

2. Then, go to the column that includes your filing status and the number of qualifying children you have. Enter the credit from that column on your EIC Worksheet.

Example. If your filing status is single, you have one qualifying child, and the amount you are looking up from your EIC Worksheet is $2,455, you would enter $842.

If the amount you are looking up from the worksheet is—		And your filing status is— Single, head of household, or qualifying widow(er) and you have—		
		No children	One child	Two children
At least	But less than	Your credit is—		
2,400	2,450	186	825	970
2,450	2,500	189	842	990

If the amount you are looking up from the worksheet is–		And your filing status is– Single, head of household, or qualifying widow(er) and you have–			Married filing jointly and you have–		
		No children	One child	Two children	No children	One child	Two children
At least	But less than	Your credit is–			Your credit is–		
$1	$50	$2	$9	$10	$2	$9	$10
50	100	6	26	30	6	26	30
100	150	10	43	50	10	43	50
150	200	13	60	70	13	60	70
200	250	17	77	90	17	77	90
250	300	21	94	110	21	94	110
300	350	25	111	130	25	111	130
350	400	29	128	150	29	128	150
400	450	33	145	170	33	145	170
450	500	36	162	190	36	162	190
500	550	40	179	210	40	179	210
550	600	44	196	230	44	196	230
600	650	48	213	250	48	213	250
650	700	52	230	270	52	230	270
700	750	55	247	290	55	247	290
750	800	59	264	310	59	264	310
800	850	63	281	330	63	281	330
850	900	67	298	350	67	298	350
900	950	71	315	370	71	315	370
950	1,000	75	332	390	75	332	390
1,000	1,050	78	349	410	78	349	410
1,050	1,100	82	366	430	82	366	430
1,100	1,150	86	383	450	86	383	450
1,150	1,200	90	400	470	90	400	470
1,200	1,250	94	417	490	94	417	490
1,250	1,300	98	434	510	98	434	510
1,300	1,350	101	451	530	101	451	530
1,350	1,400	105	468	550	105	468	550
1,400	1,450	109	485	570	109	485	570
1,450	1,500	113	502	590	113	502	590
1,500	1,550	117	519	610	117	519	610
1,550	1,600	120	536	630	120	536	630
1,600	1,650	124	553	650	124	553	650
1,650	1,700	128	570	670	128	570	670
1,700	1,750	132	587	690	132	587	690
1,750	1,800	136	604	710	136	604	710
1,800	1,850	140	621	730	140	621	730
1,850	1,900	143	638	750	143	638	750
1,900	1,950	147	655	770	147	655	770
1,950	2,000	151	672	790	151	672	790
2,000	2,050	155	689	810	155	689	810
2,050	2,100	159	706	830	159	706	830
2,100	2,150	163	723	850	163	723	850
2,150	2,200	166	740	870	166	740	870
2,200	2,250	170	757	890	170	757	890
2,250	2,300	174	774	910	174	774	910
2,300	2,350	178	791	930	178	791	930
2,350	2,400	182	808	950	182	808	950
2,400	2,450	186	825	970	186	825	970
2,450	2,500	189	842	990	189	842	990
2,500	2,550	193	859	1,010	193	859	1,010
2,550	2,600	197	876	1,030	197	876	1,030
2,600	2,650	201	893	1,050	201	893	1,050
2,650	2,700	205	910	1,070	205	910	1,070
2,700	2,750	208	927	1,090	208	927	1,090
2,750	2,800	212	944	1,110	212	944	1,110
2,800	2,850	216	961	1,130	216	961	1,130
2,850	2,900	220	978	1,150	220	978	1,150
2,900	2,950	224	995	1,170	224	995	1,170
2,950	3,000	228	1,012	1,190	228	1,012	1,190
3,000	3,050	231	1,029	1,210	231	1,029	1,210
3,050	3,100	235	1,046	1,230	235	1,046	1,230
3,100	3,150	239	1,063	1,250	239	1,063	1,250
3,150	3,200	243	1,080	1,270	243	1,080	1,270
3,200	3,250	247	1,097	1,290	247	1,097	1,290
3,250	3,300	251	1,114	1,310	251	1,114	1,310
3,300	3,350	254	1,131	1,330	254	1,131	1,330
3,350	3,400	258	1,148	1,350	258	1,148	1,350
3,400	3,450	262	1,165	1,370	262	1,165	1,370
3,450	3,500	266	1,182	1,390	266	1,182	1,390
3,500	3,550	270	1,199	1,410	270	1,199	1,410
3,550	3,600	273	1,216	1,430	273	1,216	1,430
3,600	3,650	277	1,233	1,450	277	1,233	1,450
3,650	3,700	281	1,250	1,470	281	1,250	1,470
3,700	3,750	285	1,267	1,490	285	1,267	1,490
3,750	3,800	289	1,284	1,510	289	1,284	1,510
3,800	3,850	293	1,301	1,530	293	1,301	1,530
3,850	3,900	296	1,318	1,550	296	1,318	1,550
3,900	3,950	300	1,335	1,570	300	1,335	1,570
3,950	4,000	304	1,352	1,590	304	1,352	1,590
4,000	4,050	308	1,369	1,610	308	1,369	1,610
4,050	4,100	312	1,386	1,630	312	1,386	1,630
4,100	4,150	316	1,403	1,650	316	1,403	1,650
4,150	4,200	319	1,420	1,670	319	1,420	1,670
4,200	4,250	323	1,437	1,690	323	1,437	1,690
4,250	4,300	327	1,454	1,710	327	1,454	1,710
4,300	4,350	331	1,471	1,730	331	1,471	1,730
4,350	4,400	335	1,488	1,750	335	1,488	1,750
4,400	4,450	339	1,505	1,770	339	1,505	1,770
4,450	4,500	342	1,522	1,790	342	1,522	1,790
4,500	4,550	346	1,539	1,810	346	1,539	1,810
4,550	4,600	350	1,556	1,830	350	1,556	1,830
4,600	4,650	354	1,573	1,850	354	1,573	1,850
4,650	4,700	358	1,590	1,870	358	1,590	1,870
4,700	4,750	361	1,607	1,890	361	1,607	1,890
4,750	4,800	365	1,624	1,910	365	1,624	1,910
4,800	4,850	369	1,641	1,930	369	1,641	1,930
4,850	4,900	373	1,658	1,950	373	1,658	1,950
4,900	4,950	377	1,675	1,970	377	1,675	1,970
4,950	5,000	381	1,692	1,990	381	1,692	1,990

(Continued on page 17)

2006 Earned Income Credit (EIC) Table—*Continued* (**Caution.** This is **not** a tax table.)

If the amount you are looking up from the worksheet is–		And your filing status is–					
		Single, head of household, or qualifying widow(er) and you have–			Married filing jointly and you have–		
		No children	One child	Two children	No children	One child	Two children
At least	But less than	Your credit is–			Your credit is–		
5,000	**5,050**	384	1,709	2,010	384	1,709	2,010
5,050	**5,100**	388	1,726	2,030	388	1,726	2,030
5,100	**5,150**	392	1,743	2,050	392	1,743	2,050
5,150	**5,200**	396	1,760	2,070	396	1,760	2,070
5,200	**5,250**	400	1,777	2,090	400	1,777	2,090
5,250	**5,300**	404	1,794	2,110	404	1,794	2,110
5,300	**5,350**	407	1,811	2,130	407	1,811	2,130
5,350	**5,400**	412	1,828	2,150	412	1,828	2,150
5,400	**5,450**	412	1,845	2,170	412	1,845	2,170
5,450	**5,500**	412	1,862	2,190	412	1,862	2,190
5,500	**5,550**	412	1,879	2,210	412	1,879	2,210
5,550	**5,600**	412	1,896	2,230	412	1,896	2,230
5,600	**5,650**	412	1,913	2,250	412	1,913	2,250
5,650	**5,700**	412	1,930	2,270	412	1,930	2,270
5,700	**5,750**	412	1,947	2,290	412	1,947	2,290
5,750	**5,800**	412	1,964	2,310	412	1,964	2,310
5,800	**5,850**	412	1,981	2,330	412	1,981	2,330
5,850	**5,900**	412	1,998	2,350	412	1,998	2,350
5,900	**5,950**	412	2,015	2,370	412	2,015	2,370
5,950	**6,000**	412	2,032	2,390	412	2,032	2,390
6,000	**6,050**	412	2,049	2,410	412	2,049	2,410
6,050	**6,100**	412	2,066	2,430	412	2,066	2,430
6,100	**6,150**	412	2,083	2,450	412	2,083	2,450
6,150	**6,200**	412	2,100	2,470	412	2,100	2,470
6,200	**6,250**	412	2,117	2,490	412	2,117	2,490
6,250	**6,300**	412	2,134	2,510	412	2,134	2,510
6,300	**6,350**	412	2,151	2,530	412	2,151	2,530
6,350	**6,400**	412	2,168	2,550	412	2,168	2,550
6,400	**6,450**	412	2,185	2,570	412	2,185	2,570
6,450	**6,500**	412	2,202	2,590	412	2,202	2,590
6,500	**6,550**	412	2,219	2,610	412	2,219	2,610
6,550	**6,600**	412	2,236	2,630	412	2,236	2,630
6,600	**6,650**	412	2,253	2,650	412	2,253	2,650
6,650	**6,700**	412	2,270	2,670	412	2,270	2,670
6,700	**6,750**	412	2,287	2,690	412	2,287	2,690
6,750	**6,800**	409	2,304	2,710	412	2,304	2,710
6,800	**6,850**	405	2,321	2,730	412	2,321	2,730
6,850	**6,900**	401	2,338	2,750	412	2,338	2,750
6,900	**6,950**	397	2,355	2,770	412	2,355	2,770
6,950	**7,000**	394	2,372	2,790	412	2,372	2,790
7,000	**7,050**	390	2,389	2,810	412	2,389	2,810
7,050	**7,100**	386	2,406	2,830	412	2,406	2,830
7,100	**7,150**	382	2,423	2,850	412	2,423	2,850
7,150	**7,200**	378	2,440	2,870	412	2,440	2,870
7,200	**7,250**	374	2,457	2,890	412	2,457	2,890
7,250	**7,300**	371	2,474	2,910	412	2,474	2,910
7,300	**7,350**	367	2,491	2,930	412	2,491	2,930
7,350	**7,400**	363	2,508	2,950	412	2,508	2,950
7,400	**7,450**	359	2,525	2,970	412	2,525	2,970
7,450	**7,500**	355	2,542	2,990	412	2,542	2,990
7,500	**7,550**	352	2,559	3,010	412	2,559	3,010
7,550	**7,600**	348	2,576	3,030	412	2,576	3,030
7,600	**7,650**	344	2,593	3,050	412	2,593	3,050
7,650	**7,700**	340	2,610	3,070	412	2,610	3,070
7,700	**7,750**	336	2,627	3,090	412	2,627	3,090
7,750	**7,800**	332	2,644	3,110	412	2,644	3,110
7,800	**7,850**	329	2,661	3,130	412	2,661	3,130
7,850	**7,900**	325	2,678	3,150	412	2,678	3,150
7,900	**7,950**	321	2,695	3,170	412	2,695	3,170
7,950	**8,000**	317	2,712	3,190	412	2,712	3,190

If the amount you are looking up from the worksheet is–		And your filing status is–					
		Single, head of household, or qualifying widow(er) and you have–			Married filing jointly and you have–		
		No children	One child	Two children	No children	One child	Two children
At least	But less than	Your credit is–			Your credit is–		
8,000	**8,050**	313	2,729	3,210	412	2,729	3,210
8,050	**8,100**	309	2,747	3,230	412	2,747	3,230
8,100	**8,150**	306	2,747	3,250	412	2,747	3,250
8,150	**8,200**	302	2,747	3,270	412	2,747	3,270
8,200	**8,250**	298	2,747	3,290	412	2,747	3,290
8,250	**8,300**	294	2,747	3,310	412	2,747	3,310
8,300	**8,350**	290	2,747	3,330	412	2,747	3,330
8,350	**8,400**	286	2,747	3,350	412	2,747	3,350
8,400	**8,450**	283	2,747	3,370	412	2,747	3,370
8,450	**8,500**	279	2,747	3,390	412	2,747	3,390
8,500	**8,550**	275	2,747	3,410	412	2,747	3,410
8,550	**8,600**	271	2,747	3,430	412	2,747	3,430
8,600	**8,650**	267	2,747	3,450	412	2,747	3,450
8,650	**8,700**	264	2,747	3,470	412	2,747	3,470
8,700	**8,750**	260	2,747	3,490	412	2,747	3,490
8,750	**8,800**	256	2,747	3,510	409	2,747	3,510
8,800	**8,850**	252	2,747	3,530	405	2,747	3,530
8,850	**8,900**	248	2,747	3,550	401	2,747	3,550
8,900	**8,950**	244	2,747	3,570	397	2,747	3,570
8,950	**9,000**	241	2,747	3,590	394	2,747	3,590
9,000	**9,050**	237	2,747	3,610	390	2,747	3,610
9,050	**9,100**	233	2,747	3,630	386	2,747	3,630
9,100	**9,150**	229	2,747	3,650	382	2,747	3,650
9,150	**9,200**	225	2,747	3,670	378	2,747	3,670
9,200	**9,250**	221	2,747	3,690	374	2,747	3,690
9,250	**9,300**	218	2,747	3,710	371	2,747	3,710
9,300	**9,350**	214	2,747	3,730	367	2,747	3,730
9,350	**9,400**	210	2,747	3,750	363	2,747	3,750
9,400	**9,450**	206	2,747	3,770	359	2,747	3,770
9,450	**9,500**	202	2,747	3,790	355	2,747	3,790
9,500	**9,550**	199	2,747	3,810	352	2,747	3,810
9,550	**9,600**	195	2,747	3,830	348	2,747	3,830
9,600	**9,650**	191	2,747	3,850	344	2,747	3,850
9,650	**9,700**	187	2,747	3,870	340	2,747	3,870
9,700	**9,750**	183	2,747	3,890	336	2,747	3,890
9,750	**9,800**	179	2,747	3,910	332	2,747	3,910
9,800	**9,850**	176	2,747	3,930	329	2,747	3,930
9,850	**9,900**	172	2,747	3,950	325	2,747	3,950
9,900	**9,950**	168	2,747	3,970	321	2,747	3,970
9,950	**10,000**	164	2,747	3,990	317	2,747	3,990
10,000	**10,050**	160	2,747	4,010	313	2,747	4,010
10,050	**10,100**	156	2,747	4,030	309	2,747	4,030
10,100	**10,150**	153	2,747	4,050	306	2,747	4,050
10,150	**10,200**	149	2,747	4,070	302	2,747	4,070
10,200	**10,250**	145	2,747	4,090	298	2,747	4,090
10,250	**10,300**	141	2,747	4,110	294	2,747	4,110
10,300	**10,350**	137	2,747	4,130	290	2,747	4,130
10,350	**10,400**	133	2,747	4,150	286	2,747	4,150
10,400	**10,450**	130	2,747	4,170	283	2,747	4,170
10,450	**10,500**	126	2,747	4,190	279	2,747	4,190
10,500	**10,550**	122	2,747	4,210	275	2,747	4,210
10,550	**10,600**	118	2,747	4,230	271	2,747	4,230
10,600	**10,650**	114	2,747	4,250	267	2,747	4,250
10,650	**10,700**	111	2,747	4,270	264	2,747	4,270
10,700	**10,750**	107	2,747	4,290	260	2,747	4,290
10,750	**10,800**	103	2,747	4,310	256	2,747	4,310
10,800	**10,850**	99	2,747	4,330	252	2,747	4,330
10,850	**10,900**	95	2,747	4,350	248	2,747	4,350
10,900	**10,950**	91	2,747	4,370	244	2,747	4,370
10,950	**11,000**	88	2,747	4,390	241	2,747	4,390

(Continued on page 18)

2006 Earned Income Credit (EIC) Table—*Continued*

(**Caution.** This is **not** a tax table.)

If the amount you are looking up from the worksheet is–		And your filing status is– Single, head of household, or qualifying widow(er) and you have–			Married filing jointly and you have–		
		No children	One child	Two children	No children	One child	Two children
At least	But less than	Your credit is–			Your credit is–		
11,000	**11,050**	84	2,747	4,410	237	2,747	4,410
11,050	**11,100**	80	2,747	4,430	233	2,747	4,430
11,100	**11,150**	76	2,747	4,450	229	2,747	4,450
11,150	**11,200**	72	2,747	4,470	225	2,747	4,470
11,200	**11,250**	68	2,747	4,490	221	2,747	4,490
11,250	**11,300**	65	2,747	4,510	218	2,747	4,510
11,300	**11,350**	61	2,747	4,536	214	2,747	4,536
11,350	**11,400**	57	2,747	4,536	210	2,747	4,536
11,400	**11,450**	53	2,747	4,536	206	2,747	4,536
11,450	**11,500**	49	2,747	4,536	202	2,747	4,536
11,500	**11,550**	46	2,747	4,536	199	2,747	4,536
11,550	**11,600**	42	2,747	4,536	195	2,747	4,536
11,600	**11,650**	38	2,747	4,536	191	2,747	4,536
11,650	**11,700**	34	2,747	4,536	187	2,747	4,536
11,700	**11,750**	30	2,747	4,536	183	2,747	4,536
11,750	**11,800**	26	2,747	4,536	179	2,747	4,536
11,800	**11,850**	23	2,747	4,536	176	2,747	4,536
11,850	**11,900**	19	2,747	4,536	172	2,747	4,536
11,900	**11,950**	15	2,747	4,536	168	2,747	4,536
11,950	**12,000**	11	2,747	4,536	164	2,747	4,536
12,000	**12,050**	7	2,747	4,536	160	2,747	4,536
12,050	**12,100**	3	2,747	4,536	156	2,747	4,536
12,100	**12,150**	*	2,747	4,536	153	2,747	4,536
12,150	**12,200**	0	2,747	4,536	149	2,747	4,536
12,200	**12,250**	0	2,747	4,536	145	2,747	4,536
12,250	**12,300**	0	2,747	4,536	141	2,747	4,536
12,300	**12,350**	0	2,747	4,536	137	2,747	4,536
12,350	**12,400**	0	2,747	4,536	133	2,747	4,536
12,400	**12,450**	0	2,747	4,536	130	2,747	4,536
12,450	**12,500**	0	2,747	4,536	126	2,747	4,536
12,500	**12,550**	0	2,747	4,536	122	2,747	4,536
12,550	**12,600**	0	2,747	4,536	118	2,747	4,536
12,600	**12,650**	0	2,747	4,536	114	2,747	4,536
12,650	**12,700**	0	2,747	4,536	111	2,747	4,536
12,700	**12,750**	0	2,747	4,536	107	2,747	4,536
12,750	**12,800**	0	2,747	4,536	103	2,747	4,536
12,800	**12,850**	0	2,747	4,536	99	2,747	4,536
12,850	**12,900**	0	2,747	4,536	95	2,747	4,536
12,900	**12,950**	0	2,747	4,536	91	2,747	4,536
12,950	**13,000**	0	2,747	4,536	88	2,747	4,536
13,000	**13,050**	0	2,747	4,536	84	2,747	4,536
13,050	**13,100**	0	2,747	4,536	80	2,747	4,536
13,100	**13,150**	0	2,747	4,536	76	2,747	4,536
13,150	**13,200**	0	2,747	4,536	72	2,747	4,536
13,200	**13,250**	0	2,747	4,536	68	2,747	4,536
13,250	**13,300**	0	2,747	4,536	65	2,747	4,536
13,300	**13,350**	0	2,747	4,536	61	2,747	4,536
13,350	**13,400**	0	2,747	4,536	57	2,747	4,536
13,400	**13,450**	0	2,747	4,536	53	2,747	4,536
13,450	**13,500**	0	2,747	4,536	49	2,747	4,536
13,500	**13,550**	0	2,747	4,536	46	2,747	4,536
13,550	**13,600**	0	2,747	4,536	42	2,747	4,536
13,600	**13,650**	0	2,747	4,536	38	2,747	4,536
13,650	**13,700**	0	2,747	4,536	34	2,747	4,536
13,700	**13,750**	0	2,747	4,536	30	2,747	4,536
13,750	**13,800**	0	2,747	4,536	26	2,747	4,536
13,800	**13,850**	0	2,747	4,536	23	2,747	4,536
13,850	**13,900**	0	2,747	4,536	19	2,747	4,536
13,900	**13,950**	0	2,747	4,536	15	2,747	4,536
13,950	**14,000**	0	2,747	4,536	11	2,747	4,536
14,000	**14,050**	0	2,747	4,536	7	2,747	4,536
14,050	**14,100**	0	2,747	4,536	3	2,747	4,536
14,100	**14,150**	0	2,747	4,536	*	2,747	4,536
14,150	**14,200**	0	2,747	4,536	0	2,747	4,536
14,200	**14,250**	0	2,747	4,536	0	2,747	4,536
14,250	**14,300**	0	2,747	4,536	0	2,747	4,536
14,300	**14,350**	0	2,747	4,536	0	2,747	4,536
14,350	**14,400**	0	2,747	4,536	0	2,747	4,536
14,400	**14,450**	0	2,747	4,536	0	2,747	4,536
14,450	**14,500**	0	2,747	4,536	0	2,747	4,536
14,500	**14,550**	0	2,747	4,536	0	2,747	4,536
14,550	**14,600**	0	2,747	4,536	0	2,747	4,536
14,600	**14,650**	0	2,747	4,536	0	2,747	4,536
14,650	**14,700**	0	2,747	4,536	0	2,747	4,536
14,700	**14,750**	0	2,747	4,536	0	2,747	4,536
14,750	**14,800**	0	2,747	4,536	0	2,747	4,536
14,800	**14,850**	0	2,747	4,536	0	2,747	4,536
14,850	**14,900**	0	2,737	4,522	0	2,747	4,536
14,900	**14,950**	0	2,729	4,512	0	2,747	4,536
14,950	**15,000**	0	2,721	4,501	0	2,747	4,536
15,000	**15,050**	0	2,713	4,491	0	2,747	4,536
15,050	**15,100**	0	2,705	4,480	0	2,747	4,536
15,100	**15,150**	0	2,697	4,470	0	2,747	4,536
15,150	**15,200**	0	2,689	4,459	0	2,747	4,536
15,200	**15,250**	0	2,681	4,449	0	2,747	4,536
15,250	**15,300**	0	2,673	4,438	0	2,747	4,536
15,300	**15,350**	0	2,665	4,428	0	2,747	4,536
15,350	**15,400**	0	2,657	4,417	0	2,747	4,536
15,400	**15,450**	0	2,649	4,406	0	2,747	4,536
15,450	**15,500**	0	2,641	4,396	0	2,747	4,536
15,500	**15,550**	0	2,633	4,385	0	2,747	4,536
15,550	**15,600**	0	2,625	4,375	0	2,747	4,536
15,600	**15,650**	0	2,617	4,364	0	2,747	4,536
15,650	**15,700**	0	2,609	4,354	0	2,747	4,536
15,700	**15,750**	0	2,601	4,343	0	2,747	4,536
15,750	**15,800**	0	2,593	4,333	0	2,747	4,536
15,800	**15,850**	0	2,585	4,322	0	2,747	4,536
15,850	**15,900**	0	2,577	4,312	0	2,747	4,536
15,900	**15,950**	0	2,569	4,301	0	2,747	4,536
15,950	**16,000**	0	2,561	4,291	0	2,747	4,536

(Continued on page 19)

*If the amount you are looking up from the worksheet is at least $12,100 ($14,100 if married filing jointly) but less than $12,120 ($14,120 if married filing jointly), your credit is $1. Otherwise, you cannot take the credit.

2006 Earned Income Credit (EIC) Table—*Continued* (**Caution.** This is **not** a tax table.)

If the amount you are looking up from the worksheet is—		And your filing status is— Single, head of household, or qualifying widow(er) and you have—			Married filing jointly and you have—		
		No children	One child	Two children	No children	One child	Two children
At least	But less than	Your credit is—			Your credit is—		
16,000	**16,050**	0	2,553	4,280	0	2,747	4,536
16,050	**16,100**	0	2,545	4,270	0	2,747	4,536
16,100	**16,150**	0	2,537	4,259	0	2,747	4,536
16,150	**16,200**	0	2,529	4,249	0	2,747	4,536
16,200	**16,250**	0	2,521	4,238	0	2,747	4,536
16,250	**16,300**	0	2,513	4,227	0	2,747	4,536
16,300	**16,350**	0	2,505	4,217	0	2,747	4,536
16,350	**16,400**	0	2,497	4,206	0	2,747	4,536
16,400	**16,450**	0	2,489	4,196	0	2,747	4,536
16,450	**16,500**	0	2,481	4,185	0	2,747	4,536
16,500	**16,550**	0	2,473	4,175	0	2,747	4,536
16,550	**16,600**	0	2,465	4,164	0	2,747	4,536
16,600	**16,650**	0	2,457	4,154	0	2,747	4,536
16,650	**16,700**	0	2,449	4,143	0	2,747	4,536
16,700	**16,750**	0	2,441	4,133	0	2,747	4,536
16,750	**16,800**	0	2,433	4,122	0	2,747	4,536
16,800	**16,850**	0	2,425	4,112	0	2,747	4,536
16,850	**16,900**	0	2,417	4,101	0	2,737	4,522
16,900	**16,950**	0	2,409	4,091	0	2,729	4,512
16,950	**17,000**	0	2,401	4,080	0	2,721	4,501
17,000	**17,050**	0	2,393	4,070	0	2,713	4,491
17,050	**17,100**	0	2,385	4,059	0	2,705	4,480
17,100	**17,150**	0	2,377	4,048	0	2,697	4,470
17,150	**17,200**	0	2,369	4,038	0	2,689	4,459
17,200	**17,250**	0	2,361	4,027	0	2,681	4,449
17,250	**17,300**	0	2,353	4,017	0	2,673	4,438
17,300	**17,350**	0	2,345	4,006	0	2,665	4,428
17,350	**17,400**	0	2,337	3,996	0	2,657	4,417
17,400	**17,450**	0	2,329	3,985	0	2,649	4,406
17,450	**17,500**	0	2,321	3,975	0	2,641	4,396
17,500	**17,550**	0	2,313	3,964	0	2,633	4,385
17,550	**17,600**	0	2,305	3,954	0	2,625	4,375
17,600	**17,650**	0	2,297	3,943	0	2,617	4,364
17,650	**17,700**	0	2,289	3,933	0	2,609	4,354
17,700	**17,750**	0	2,281	3,922	0	2,601	4,343
17,750	**17,800**	0	2,273	3,912	0	2,593	4,333
17,800	**17,850**	0	2,265	3,901	0	2,585	4,322
17,850	**17,900**	0	2,257	3,891	0	2,577	4,312
17,900	**17,950**	0	2,249	3,880	0	2,569	4,301
17,950	**18,000**	0	2,241	3,869	0	2,561	4,291
18,000	**18,050**	0	2,233	3,859	0	2,553	4,280
18,050	**18,100**	0	2,225	3,848	0	2,545	4,270
18,100	**18,150**	0	2,217	3,838	0	2,537	4,259
18,150	**18,200**	0	2,209	3,827	0	2,529	4,249
18,200	**18,250**	0	2,201	3,817	0	2,521	4,238
18,250	**18,300**	0	2,193	3,806	0	2,513	4,227
18,300	**18,350**	0	2,186	3,796	0	2,505	4,217
18,350	**18,400**	0	2,178	3,785	0	2,497	4,206
18,400	**18,450**	0	2,170	3,775	0	2,489	4,196
18,450	**18,500**	0	2,162	3,764	0	2,481	4,185
18,500	**18,550**	0	2,154	3,754	0	2,473	4,175
18,550	**18,600**	0	2,146	3,743	0	2,465	4,164
18,600	**18,650**	0	2,138	3,733	0	2,457	4,154
18,650	**18,700**	0	2,130	3,722	0	2,449	4,143
18,700	**18,750**	0	2,122	3,712	0	2,441	4,133
18,750	**18,800**	0	2,114	3,701	0	2,433	4,122
18,800	**18,850**	0	2,106	3,690	0	2,425	4,112
18,850	**18,900**	0	2,098	3,680	0	2,417	4,101
18,900	**18,950**	0	2,090	3,669	0	2,409	4,091
18,950	**19,000**	0	2,082	3,659	0	2,401	4,080
19,000	**19,050**	0	2,074	3,648	0	2,393	4,070
19,050	**19,100**	0	2,066	3,638	0	2,385	4,059
19,100	**19,150**	0	2,058	3,627	0	2,377	4,048
19,150	**19,200**	0	2,050	3,617	0	2,369	4,038
19,200	**19,250**	0	2,042	3,606	0	2,361	4,027
19,250	**19,300**	0	2,034	3,596	0	2,353	4,017
19,300	**19,350**	0	2,026	3,585	0	2,345	4,006
19,350	**19,400**	0	2,018	3,575	0	2,337	3,996
19,400	**19,450**	0	2,010	3,564	0	2,329	3,985
19,450	**19,500**	0	2,002	3,554	0	2,321	3,975
19,500	**19,550**	0	1,994	3,543	0	2,313	3,964
19,550	**19,600**	0	1,986	3,532	0	2,305	3,954
19,600	**19,650**	0	1,978	3,522	0	2,297	3,943
19,650	**19,700**	0	1,970	3,511	0	2,289	3,933
19,700	**19,750**	0	1,962	3,501	0	2,281	3,922
19,750	**19,800**	0	1,954	3,490	0	2,273	3,912
19,800	**19,850**	0	1,946	3,480	0	2,265	3,901
19,850	**19,900**	0	1,938	3,469	0	2,257	3,891
19,900	**19,950**	0	1,930	3,459	0	2,249	3,880
19,950	**20,000**	0	1,922	3,448	0	2,241	3,869
20,000	**20,050**	0	1,914	3,438	0	2,233	3,859
20,050	**20,100**	0	1,906	3,427	0	2,225	3,848
20,100	**20,150**	0	1,898	3,417	0	2,217	3,838
20,150	**20,200**	0	1,890	3,406	0	2,209	3,827
20,200	**20,250**	0	1,882	3,396	0	2,201	3,817
20,250	**20,300**	0	1,874	3,385	0	2,193	3,806
20,300	**20,350**	0	1,866	3,375	0	2,186	3,796
20,350	**20,400**	0	1,858	3,364	0	2,178	3,785
20,400	**20,450**	0	1,850	3,353	0	2,170	3,775
20,450	**20,500**	0	1,842	3,343	0	2,162	3,764
20,500	**20,550**	0	1,834	3,332	0	2,154	3,754
20,550	**20,600**	0	1,826	3,322	0	2,146	3,743
20,600	**20,650**	0	1,818	3,311	0	2,138	3,733
20,650	**20,700**	0	1,810	3,301	0	2,130	3,722
20,700	**20,750**	0	1,802	3,290	0	2,122	3,712
20,750	**20,800**	0	1,794	3,280	0	2,114	3,701
20,800	**20,850**	0	1,786	3,269	0	2,106	3,690
20,850	**20,900**	0	1,778	3,259	0	2,098	3,680
20,900	**20,950**	0	1,770	3,248	0	2,090	3,669
20,950	**21,000**	0	1,762	3,238	0	2,082	3,659
21,000	**21,050**	0	1,754	3,227	0	2,074	3,648
21,050	**21,100**	0	1,746	3,217	0	2,066	3,638
21,100	**21,150**	0	1,738	3,206	0	2,058	3,627
21,150	**21,200**	0	1,730	3,196	0	2,050	3,617
21,200	**21,250**	0	1,722	3,185	0	2,042	3,606
21,250	**21,300**	0	1,714	3,174	0	2,034	3,596
21,300	**21,350**	0	1,706	3,164	0	2,026	3,585
21,350	**21,400**	0	1,698	3,153	0	2,018	3,575
21,400	**21,450**	0	1,690	3,143	0	2,010	3,564
21,450	**21,500**	0	1,682	3,132	0	2,002	3,554
21,500	**21,550**	0	1,674	3,122	0	1,994	3,543
21,550	**21,600**	0	1,666	3,111	0	1,986	3,532
21,600	**21,650**	0	1,658	3,101	0	1,978	3,522
21,650	**21,700**	0	1,650	3,090	0	1,970	3,511
21,700	**21,750**	0	1,642	3,080	0	1,962	3,501
21,750	**21,800**	0	1,634	3,069	0	1,954	3,490
21,800	**21,850**	0	1,626	3,059	0	1,946	3,480
21,850	**21,900**	0	1,618	3,048	0	1,938	3,469
21,900	**21,950**	0	1,610	3,038	0	1,930	3,459
21,950	**22,000**	0	1,602	3,027	0	1,922	3,448

(Continued on page 20)

2006 Earned Income Credit (EIC) Table–*Continued* (**Caution.** This is **not** a tax table.)

If the amount you are looking up from the worksheet is–		And your filing status is–					
		Single, head of household, or qualifying widow(er) and you have–			Married filing jointly and you have–		
At least	But less than	No children	One child	Two children	No children	One child	Two children
		Your credit is–			Your credit is–		
22,000	22,050	0	1,594	3,017	0	1,914	3,438
22,050	22,100	0	1,586	3,006	0	1,906	3,427
22,100	22,150	0	1,578	2,995	0	1,898	3,417
22,150	22,200	0	1,570	2,985	0	1,890	3,406
22,200	22,250	0	1,562	2,974	0	1,882	3,396
22,250	22,300	0	1,554	2,964	0	1,874	3,385
22,300	22,350	0	1,546	2,953	0	1,866	3,375
22,350	22,400	0	1,538	2,943	0	1,858	3,364
22,400	22,450	0	1,530	2,932	0	1,850	3,353
22,450	22,500	0	1,522	2,922	0	1,842	3,343
22,500	22,550	0	1,514	2,911	0	1,834	3,332
22,550	22,600	0	1,506	2,901	0	1,826	3,322
22,600	22,650	0	1,498	2,890	0	1,818	3,311
22,650	22,700	0	1,490	2,880	0	1,810	3,301
22,700	22,750	0	1,482	2,869	0	1,802	3,290
22,750	22,800	0	1,474	2,859	0	1,794	3,280
22,800	22,850	0	1,466	2,848	0	1,786	3,269
22,850	22,900	0	1,458	2,838	0	1,778	3,259
22,900	22,950	0	1,450	2,827	0	1,770	3,248
22,950	23,000	0	1,442	2,816	0	1,762	3,238
23,000	23,050	0	1,434	2,806	0	1,754	3,227
23,050	23,100	0	1,426	2,795	0	1,746	3,217
23,100	23,150	0	1,418	2,785	0	1,738	3,206
23,150	23,200	0	1,410	2,774	0	1,730	3,196
23,200	23,250	0	1,402	2,764	0	1,722	3,185
23,250	23,300	0	1,394	2,753	0	1,714	3,174
23,300	23,350	0	1,387	2,743	0	1,706	3,164
23,350	23,400	0	1,379	2,732	0	1,698	3,153
23,400	23,450	0	1,371	2,722	0	1,690	3,143
23,450	23,500	0	1,363	2,711	0	1,682	3,132
23,500	23,550	0	1,355	2,701	0	1,674	3,122
23,550	23,600	0	1,347	2,690	0	1,666	3,111
23,600	23,650	0	1,339	2,680	0	1,658	3,101
23,650	23,700	0	1,331	2,669	0	1,650	3,090
23,700	23,750	0	1,323	2,659	0	1,642	3,080
23,750	23,800	0	1,315	2,648	0	1,634	3,069
23,800	23,850	0	1,307	2,637	0	1,626	3,059
23,850	23,900	0	1,299	2,627	0	1,618	3,048
23,900	23,950	0	1,291	2,616	0	1,610	3,038
23,950	24,000	0	1,283	2,606	0	1,602	3,027
24,000	24,050	0	1,275	2,595	0	1,594	3,017
24,050	24,100	0	1,267	2,585	0	1,586	3,006
24,100	24,150	0	1,259	2,574	0	1,578	2,995
24,150	24,200	0	1,251	2,564	0	1,570	2,985
24,200	24,250	0	1,243	2,553	0	1,562	2,974
24,250	24,300	0	1,235	2,543	0	1,554	2,964
24,300	24,350	0	1,227	2,532	0	1,546	2,953
24,350	24,400	0	1,219	2,522	0	1,538	2,943
24,400	24,450	0	1,211	2,511	0	1,530	2,932
24,450	24,500	0	1,203	2,501	0	1,522	2,922
24,500	24,550	0	1,195	2,490	0	1,514	2,911
24,550	24,600	0	1,187	2,479	0	1,506	2,901
24,600	24,650	0	1,179	2,469	0	1,498	2,890
24,650	24,700	0	1,171	2,458	0	1,490	2,880
24,700	24,750	0	1,163	2,448	0	1,482	2,869
24,750	24,800	0	1,155	2,437	0	1,474	2,859
24,800	24,850	0	1,147	2,427	0	1,466	2,848
24,850	24,900	0	1,139	2,416	0	1,458	2,838
24,900	24,950	0	1,131	2,406	0	1,450	2,827
24,950	25,000	0	1,123	2,395	0	1,442	2,816
25,000	25,050	0	1,115	2,385	0	1,434	2,806
25,050	25,100	0	1,107	2,374	0	1,426	2,795
25,100	25,150	0	1,099	2,364	0	1,418	2,785
25,150	25,200	0	1,091	2,353	0	1,410	2,774
25,200	25,250	0	1,083	2,343	0	1,402	2,764
25,250	25,300	0	1,075	2,332	0	1,394	2,753
25,300	25,350	0	1,067	2,322	0	1,387	2,743
25,350	25,400	0	1,059	2,311	0	1,379	2,732
25,400	25,450	0	1,051	2,300	0	1,371	2,722
25,450	25,500	0	1,043	2,290	0	1,363	2,711
25,500	25,550	0	1,035	2,279	0	1,355	2,701
25,550	25,600	0	1,027	2,269	0	1,347	2,690
25,600	25,650	0	1,019	2,258	0	1,339	2,680
25,650	25,700	0	1,011	2,248	0	1,331	2,669
25,700	25,750	0	1,003	2,237	0	1,323	2,659
25,750	25,800	0	995	2,227	0	1,315	2,648
25,800	25,850	0	987	2,216	0	1,307	2,637
25,850	25,900	0	979	2,206	0	1,299	2,627
25,900	25,950	0	971	2,195	0	1,291	2,616
25,950	26,000	0	963	2,185	0	1,283	2,606
26,000	26,050	0	955	2,174	0	1,275	2,595
26,050	26,100	0	947	2,164	0	1,267	2,585
26,100	26,150	0	939	2,153	0	1,259	2,574
26,150	26,200	0	931	2,143	0	1,251	2,564
26,200	26,250	0	923	2,132	0	1,243	2,553
26,250	26,300	0	915	2,121	0	1,235	2,543
26,300	26,350	0	907	2,111	0	1,227	2,532
26,350	26,400	0	899	2,100	0	1,219	2,522
26,400	26,450	0	891	2,090	0	1,211	2,511
26,450	26,500	0	883	2,079	0	1,203	2,501
26,500	26,550	0	875	2,069	0	1,195	2,490
26,550	26,600	0	867	2,058	0	1,187	2,479
26,600	26,650	0	859	2,048	0	1,179	2,469
26,650	26,700	0	851	2,037	0	1,171	2,458
26,700	26,750	0	843	2,027	0	1,163	2,448
26,750	26,800	0	835	2,016	0	1,155	2,437
26,800	26,850	0	827	2,006	0	1,147	2,427
26,850	26,900	0	819	1,995	0	1,139	2,416
26,900	26,950	0	811	1,985	0	1,131	2,406
26,950	27,000	0	803	1,974	0	1,123	2,395
27,000	27,050	0	795	1,964	0	1,115	2,385
27,050	27,100	0	787	1,953	0	1,107	2,374
27,100	27,150	0	779	1,942	0	1,099	2,364
27,150	27,200	0	771	1,932	0	1,091	2,353
27,200	27,250	0	763	1,921	0	1,083	2,343
27,250	27,300	0	755	1,911	0	1,075	2,332
27,300	27,350	0	747	1,900	0	1,067	2,322
27,350	27,400	0	739	1,890	0	1,059	2,311
27,400	27,450	0	731	1,879	0	1,051	2,300
27,450	27,500	0	723	1,869	0	1,043	2,290
27,500	27,550	0	715	1,858	0	1,035	2,279
27,550	27,600	0	707	1,848	0	1,027	2,269
27,600	27,650	0	699	1,837	0	1,019	2,258
27,650	27,700	0	691	1,827	0	1,011	2,248
27,700	27,750	0	683	1,816	0	1,003	2,237
27,750	27,800	0	675	1,806	0	995	2,227
27,800	27,850	0	667	1,795	0	987	2,216
27,850	27,900	0	659	1,785	0	979	2,206
27,900	27,950	0	651	1,774	0	971	2,195
27,950	28,000	0	643	1,763	0	963	2,185

(Continued on page 21)

2006 Earned Income Credit (EIC) Table–*Continued* (**Caution.** This is **not** a tax table.)

If the amount you are looking up from the worksheet is–		And your filing status is–					
		Single, head of household, or qualifying widow(er) and you have–			Married filing jointly and you have–		
		No children	One child	Two children	No children	One child	Two children
At least	But less than	Your credit is–			Your credit is–		
28,000	28,050	0	635	1,753	0	955	2,174
28,050	28,100	0	627	1,742	0	947	2,164
28,100	28,150	0	619	1,732	0	939	2,153
28,150	28,200	0	611	1,721	0	931	2,143
28,200	28,250	0	603	1,711	0	923	2,132
28,250	28,300	0	595	1,700	0	915	2,121
28,300	28,350	0	588	1,690	0	907	2,111
28,350	28,400	0	580	1,679	0	899	2,100
28,400	28,450	0	572	1,669	0	891	2,090
28,450	28,500	0	564	1,658	0	883	2,079
28,500	28,550	0	556	1,648	0	875	2,069
28,550	28,600	0	548	1,637	0	867	2,058
28,600	28,650	0	540	1,627	0	859	2,048
28,650	28,700	0	532	1,616	0	851	2,037
28,700	28,750	0	524	1,606	0	843	2,027
28,750	28,800	0	516	1,595	0	835	2,016
28,800	28,850	0	508	1,584	0	827	2,006
28,850	28,900	0	500	1,574	0	819	1,995
28,900	28,950	0	492	1,563	0	811	1,985
28,950	29,000	0	484	1,553	0	803	1,974
29,000	29,050	0	476	1,542	0	795	1,964
29,050	29,100	0	468	1,532	0	787	1,953
29,100	29,150	0	460	1,521	0	779	1,942
29,150	29,200	0	452	1,511	0	771	1,932
29,200	29,250	0	444	1,500	0	763	1,921
29,250	29,300	0	436	1,490	0	755	1,911
29,300	29,350	0	428	1,479	0	747	1,900
29,350	29,400	0	420	1,469	0	739	1,890
29,400	29,450	0	412	1,458	0	731	1,879
29,450	29,500	0	404	1,448	0	723	1,869
29,500	29,550	0	396	1,437	0	715	1,858
29,550	29,600	0	388	1,426	0	707	1,848
29,600	29,650	0	380	1,416	0	699	1,837
29,650	29,700	0	372	1,405	0	691	1,827
29,700	29,750	0	364	1,395	0	683	1,816
29,750	29,800	0	356	1,384	0	675	1,806
29,800	29,850	0	348	1,374	0	667	1,795
29,850	29,900	0	340	1,363	0	659	1,785
29,900	29,950	0	332	1,353	0	651	1,774
29,950	30,000	0	324	1,342	0	643	1,763
30,000	30,050	0	316	1,332	0	635	1,753
30,050	30,100	0	308	1,321	0	627	1,742
30,100	30,150	0	300	1,311	0	619	1,732
30,150	30,200	0	292	1,300	0	611	1,721
30,200	30,250	0	284	1,290	0	603	1,711
30,250	30,300	0	276	1,279	0	595	1,700
30,300	30,350	0	268	1,269	0	588	1,690
30,350	30,400	0	260	1,258	0	580	1,679
30,400	30,450	0	252	1,247	0	572	1,669
30,450	30,500	0	244	1,237	0	564	1,658
30,500	30,550	0	236	1,226	0	556	1,648
30,550	30,600	0	228	1,216	0	548	1,637
30,600	30,650	0	220	1,205	0	540	1,627
30,650	30,700	0	212	1,195	0	532	1,616
30,700	30,750	0	204	1,184	0	524	1,606
30,750	30,800	0	196	1,174	0	516	1,595
30,800	30,850	0	188	1,163	0	508	1,584
30,850	30,900	0	180	1,153	0	500	1,574
30,900	30,950	0	172	1,142	0	492	1,563
30,950	31,000	0	164	1,132	0	484	1,553
31,000	31,050	0	156	1,121	0	476	1,542
31,050	31,100	0	148	1,111	0	468	1,532
31,100	31,150	0	140	1,100	0	460	1,521
31,150	31,200	0	132	1,090	0	452	1,511
31,200	31,250	0	124	1,079	0	444	1,500
31,250	31,300	0	116	1,068	0	436	1,490
31,300	31,350	0	108	1,058	0	428	1,479
31,350	31,400	0	100	1,047	0	420	1,469
31,400	31,450	0	92	1,037	0	412	1,458
31,450	31,500	0	84	1,026	0	404	1,448
31,500	31,550	0	76	1,016	0	396	1,437
31,550	31,600	0	68	1,005	0	388	1,426
31,600	31,650	0	60	995	0	380	1,416
31,650	31,700	0	52	984	0	372	1,405
31,700	31,750	0	44	974	0	364	1,395
31,750	31,800	0	36	963	0	356	1,384
31,800	31,850	0	28	953	0	348	1,374
31,850	31,900	0	20	942	0	340	1,363
31,900	31,950	0	12	932	0	332	1,353
31,950	32,000	0	4	921	0	324	1,342
32,000	32,050	0	0	911	0	316	1,332
32,050	32,100	0	0	900	0	308	1,321
32,100	32,150	0	0	889	0	300	1,311
32,150	32,200	0	0	879	0	292	1,300
32,200	32,250	0	0	868	0	284	1,290
32,250	32,300	0	0	858	0	276	1,279
32,300	32,350	0	0	847	0	268	1,269
32,350	32,400	0	0	837	0	260	1,258
32,400	32,450	0	0	826	0	252	1,247
32,450	32,500	0	0	816	0	244	1,237
32,500	32,550	0	0	805	0	236	1,226
32,550	32,600	0	0	795	0	228	1,216
32,600	32,650	0	0	784	0	220	1,205
32,650	32,700	0	0	774	0	212	1,195
32,700	32,750	0	0	763	0	204	1,184
32,750	32,800	0	0	753	0	196	1,174
32,800	32,850	0	0	742	0	188	1,163
32,850	32,900	0	0	732	0	180	1,153
32,900	32,950	0	0	721	0	172	1,142
32,950	33,000	0	0	710	0	164	1,132
33,000	33,050	0	0	700	0	156	1,121
33,050	33,100	0	0	689	0	148	1,111
33,100	33,150	0	0	679	0	140	1,100
33,150	33,200	0	0	668	0	132	1,090
33,200	33,250	0	0	658	0	124	1,079
33,250	33,300	0	0	647	0	116	1,068
33,300	33,350	0	0	637	0	108	1,058
33,350	33,400	0	0	626	0	100	1,047
33,400	33,450	0	0	616	0	92	1,037
33,450	33,500	0	0	605	0	84	1,026
33,500	33,550	0	0	595	0	76	1,016
33,550	33,600	0	0	584	0	68	1,005
33,600	33,650	0	0	574	0	60	995
33,650	33,700	0	0	563	0	52	984
33,700	33,750	0	0	553	0	44	974
33,750	33,800	0	0	542	0	36	963
33,800	33,850	0	0	531	0	28	953
33,850	33,900	0	0	521	0	20	942
33,900	33,950	0	0	510	0	12	932
33,950	34,000	0	0	500	0	4	921

(Continued on page 22)

2006 Earned Income Credit (EIC) Table—*Continued* (**Caution.** This is **not** a tax table.)

If the amount you are looking up from the worksheet is–		And your filing status is–					
		Single, head of household, or qualifying widow(er) and you have–			Married filing jointly and you have–		
At least	But less than	No children	One child	Two children	No children	One child	Two children
		Your credit is–			Your credit is–		
34,000	**34,050**	0	0	489	0	0	911
34,050	**34,100**	0	0	479	0	0	900
34,100	**34,150**	0	0	468	0	0	889
34,150	**34,200**	0	0	458	0	0	879
34,200	**34,250**	0	0	447	0	0	868
34,250	**34,300**	0	0	437	0	0	858
34,300	**34,350**	0	0	426	0	0	847
34,350	**34,400**	0	0	416	0	0	837
34,400	**34,450**	0	0	405	0	0	826
34,450	**34,500**	0	0	395	0	0	816
34,500	**34,550**	0	0	384	0	0	805
34,550	**34,600**	0	0	373	0	0	795
34,600	**34,650**	0	0	363	0	0	784
34,650	**34,700**	0	0	352	0	0	774
34,700	**34,750**	0	0	342	0	0	763
34,750	**34,800**	0	0	331	0	0	753
34,800	**34,850**	0	0	321	0	0	742
34,850	**34,900**	0	0	310	0	0	732
34,900	**34,950**	0	0	300	0	0	721
34,950	**35,000**	0	0	289	0	0	710
35,000	**35,050**	0	0	279	0	0	700
35,050	**35,100**	0	0	268	0	0	689
35,100	**35,150**	0	0	258	0	0	679
35,150	**35,200**	0	0	247	0	0	668
35,200	**35,250**	0	0	237	0	0	658
35,250	**35,300**	0	0	226	0	0	647
35,300	**35,350**	0	0	216	0	0	637
35,350	**35,400**	0	0	205	0	0	626
35,400	**35,450**	0	0	194	0	0	616
35,450	**35,500**	0	0	184	0	0	605
35,500	**35,550**	0	0	173	0	0	595
35,550	**35,600**	0	0	163	0	0	584
35,600	**35,650**	0	0	152	0	0	574
35,650	**35,700**	0	0	142	0	0	563
35,700	**35,750**	0	0	131	0	0	553
35,750	**35,800**	0	0	121	0	0	542
35,800	**35,850**	0	0	110	0	0	531
35,850	**35,900**	0	0	100	0	0	521
35,900	**35,950**	0	0	89	0	0	510
35,950	**36,000**	0	0	79	0	0	500
36,000	**36,050**	0	0	68	0	0	489
36,050	**36,100**	0	0	58	0	0	479
36,100	**36,150**	0	0	47	0	0	468
36,150	**36,200**	0	0	37	0	0	458
36,200	**36,250**	0	0	26	0	0	447
36,250	**36,300**	0	0	15	0	0	437
36,300	**36,350**	0	0	**	0	0	426
36,350	**36,400**	0	0	0	0	0	416
36,400	**36,450**	0	0	0	0	0	405
36,450	**36,500**	0	0	0	0	0	395
36,500	**36,550**	0	0	0	0	0	384
36,550	**36,600**	0	0	0	0	0	373
36,600	**36,650**	0	0	0	0	0	363
36,650	**36,700**	0	0	0	0	0	352
36,700	**36,750**	0	0	0	0	0	342
36,750	**36,800**	0	0	0	0	0	331
36,800	**36,850**	0	0	0	0	0	321
36,850	**36,900**	0	0	0	0	0	310
36,900	**36,950**	0	0	0	0	0	300
36,950	**37,000**	0	0	0	0	0	289
37,000	**37,050**	0	0	0	0	0	279
37,050	**37,100**	0	0	0	0	0	268
37,100	**37,150**	0	0	0	0	0	258
37,150	**37,200**	0	0	0	0	0	247
37,200	**37,250**	0	0	0	0	0	237
37,250	**37,300**	0	0	0	0	0	226
37,300	**37,350**	0	0	0	0	0	216
37,350	**37,400**	0	0	0	0	0	205
37,400	**37,450**	0	0	0	0	0	194
37,450	**37,500**	0	0	0	0	0	184
37,500	**37,550**	0	0	0	0	0	173
37,550	**37,600**	0	0	0	0	0	163
37,600	**37,650**	0	0	0	0	0	152
37,650	**37,700**	0	0	0	0	0	142
37,700	**37,750**	0	0	0	0	0	131
37,750	**37,800**	0	0	0	0	0	121
37,800	**37,850**	0	0	0	0	0	110
37,850	**37,900**	0	0	0	0	0	100
37,900	**37,950**	0	0	0	0	0	89
37,950	**38,000**	0	0	0	0	0	79
38,000	**38,050**	0	0	0	0	0	68
38,050	**38,100**	0	0	0	0	0	58
38,100	**38,150**	0	0	0	0	0	47
38,150	**38,200**	0	0	0	0	0	37
38,200	**38,250**	0	0	0	0	0	26
38,250	**38,300**	0	0	0	0	0	15
38,300	**38,348**	0	0	0	0	0	5
38,348	**or more**	0	0	0	0	0	0

**If the amount you are looking up from the worksheet is at least $36,300 but less than $36,348, your credit is $5. Otherwise, you cannot take the credit.

Double click on the icon to the left for access to the EIC tables in Microsoft Excel (.xls) format

Appendix A
Accessing and Downloading IRS Tax Forms and Publications

In order to view IRS tax forms and publications, you must have Adobe (Acrobat Reader) installed on your computer. If you do not have Adobe Acrobat Reader on your computer, you can download a copy free from the Adobe web site:

http://www.adobe.com/products/acrobat/readstep2.html

- To access and download forms and publications, you must first go to the IRS website: www.irs.gov
- This will take you to the IRS web page, entitled **"Internal Revenue Service"** On this page you will see a number of different tabs across the page. Click on the far left tab "**Individuals.**" This will take you to the "**Tax Information for Individuals**" page. Click on the link for Forms and Publications on the left side of the screen. This will lead you to a page titled, **"Forms and Publications."**
    1. If you know the form number, the title, or keywords from the tax form or publication, enter the keywords in the box to the left of the SEARCH button and then click on the SEARCH button. This will bring up a list of the forms or publications that contain your keyword. Click on the link to the Form or Publication you are interested in viewing. Depending on your browser, either the material you selected will be opened in Acrobat Reader or you will receive additional instructions on how to open the material. If you are using either Internet Explorer or Netscape as your browser and are having difficulty opening the material, you can right click on the link and select the option that allows you to save the link to your computer. In Netscape, this option is called, "Save Link As. . . ." In Internet Explorer, this option is called, "Save Target As . . ." Once you have saved the .pdf file on your computer, you can then open it up directly in Acrobat Reader.
    2. To browse for a particular form, from the "Forms and Publications" page select the link for Form and Instruction number. As you scroll down the list of forms, click on the desired form to highlight (select) it. More than one form can be selected at a

time by holding the **Ctrl** button down when you click on additional forms. To view the selected forms, click on the **Review Selected Files** button. This will bring up a screen with a list of your selections. To select a particular form, click in the link. Depending on your browser, either the selected material will be opened in Acrobat Reader or you will receive additional instructions on how to open the material. See 1. above for instructions on how to save the file by right clicking on the link.

3. To browse for a particular publication, from the "Forms and Publications" page select the link for Publications number. As you scroll down the list of publications, click on the desired publication to highlight (select) it. More than one publication can be selected at a time by holding the **Ctrl** button down when you click on additional publications. To view the selected publications, click on the **Retrieve Selected Files** button. This will bring up a screen with a list of your selections. To select a particular publication, click in the link. Depending on your browser, either the selected material will be opened in Acrobat Reader or you will receive additional instructions on how to open the material. See 1. above for instructions on how to save the file by right clicking on the link.
4. **Fill-in Forms:** For each tax form and schedule, information can be typed in using the computer. This is not a computer software package, so the typist must still do the work and calculations. However, please note that not all information can be typed in when using Fill-in Forms. Some items will have to be added by hand on the final printout (for example, occupation, signature, date, etc.). Once the information has been entered on to the form, the form can be saved as a .pdf file and accessed at a later time. Use the instructions in 1. and 2. above to locate the form or schedule that you want to use.

Index

D

E

F

G

H

I

J

K

L

M

Q

R

T

U

V

W

Y